FEDERAL TAXATION
PRACTICE and PROCEDURE

Seventh Edition

Robert E. Meldman
Richard J. Sideman

CCH INCORPORATED
Chicago
A WoltersKluwer Company

Production: Christopher Zwirek

Cover Design: Don Torres

Index: Lynn Brown

ISBN 0-8080-1142-1

4025 W. Peterson Ave.
Chicago, IL 60646-6085
1 800 248 3248
http://tax.cchgroup.com

About the Authors

ROBERT E. MELDMAN, J.D., LL.M., is a shareholder in the law firm of Reinhart Boerner Van Deuren s.c. in Milwaukee, Wisconsin. His practice focuses on tax controversies and tax aspects of general business and international transactions. The author received his law degree from Marquette University and his Master of Laws in Taxation from New York University. Mr. Meldman currently serves as vice-chair of the IRS Taxpayer Advocacy Panel.

A fellow of the American College of Tax Counsel, Mr. Meldman is the author of *CCH Practical Tactics for Dealing with the IRS*, co-author of *A Practical Guide to U.S. Taxation of International Transactions*, and co-author of the previous six editions of *Federal Taxation—Practice and Procedure*. Mr. Meldman has also written numerous articles for professional journals and law reviews, and he is an editorial board member for the *Journal of Property Valuation and Taxation*.

Mr. Meldman served as adjunct professor at Marquette University Law School, adjunct professor at University of Queensland T.C. Beirne School of Law, Brisbane, Australia, adjunct professor at the University of Wisconsin—Milwaukee's Master of Taxation and Graduate International Business Program for over 30 years, and as an Executive in Residence at the Deloitte & Touche Center for Multistate Taxation at the University of Wisconsin—Milwaukee. He is a member of the American Bar Association, the International Bar Association, the Law Association for Asia and the Pacific, the State Bars of Wisconsin, Florida, and Colorado, and the Emeritus Panel of Federal Defenders Services program for the Eastern District of Wisconsin.

RICHARD J. SIDEMAN, LL.B., LL.M., is co-founder of the law firm Sideman & Bancroft LLP in San Francisco, California. Mr. Sideman's practice involves representation of taxpayers before the Examination Division, the Collection Division, and the Appeals Office of the IRS, as well as before the California Franchise Tax Board. He received his Bachelor of Laws from Harvard Law School and his Master of Laws in Taxation from New York University School of Law. Before co-founding his law firm, the author served as a trial attorney in the Tax Division of the Department of Justice and as Assistant United States Attorney in the Tax Division for the Northern District of California.

Mr. Sideman is a member of the Bars of the Unites States Tax Court, the United States Court of Federal Claims, the United States District Court for the Northern District of California, the United States Court of Appeals for the Ninth Circuit, and the United States Supreme Court. He is a frequent lecturer on tax practice and litigation at professional meetings and seminars. In addition to this book, he has published many articles for leading law and tax journals on a variety of tax issues.

Collectively, the authors' government representation, private practice, and teaching experience uniquely qualify them to offer a perfect balance of practical and technical discussion.

Acknowledgments

I would like to acknowledge the assistance of Shana M. Feuling, a summer associate at Reinhart Boerner Van Deuren s.c., who helped in the preparation of this seventh edition. Her persistence and dedication insured the timely publication. I also wish to acknowledge Carol A. Bannen, the Director of Information Resources at Reinhart Boerner Van Deuren s.c., for her aid in updating the citations.

—Robert E. Meldman

I wish to thank Steve Katz, Tracy Tierney and Lille Koske, my colleagues at Sideman & Bancroft, whose efforts and insights were critical to this endeavor.

—Richard J. Sideman

Preface

As a practitioner, it is extremely important to have an understanding of the organizational makeup of the Internal Revenue Service and the authority of its various employees. In this Edition, we continue to follow the implementation and interpretation of the Internal Revenue Service Restructuring and Reform Act of 1998. We have also updated the text to reflect changes to the Internal Revenue Manual and IRS forms. Significant case law developments are also noted. Finally, we have addressed modifications and further proposed modifications to Circular 230, relating to practice before the IRS, especially as it pertains to the IRS's new focus on tax shelter activities. [For the convenience of those using the text as a teaching tool, discussion questions are now included in the text.]

Robert E. Meldman

Richard J. Sideman

July 2004

TABLE OF CONTENTS

Chapter 4: Examination of Returns

Chapter 5: Large Case Audits

Chapter 9: Penalties and Interest

Chapter 10: Statute of Limitations on Assessment

Chapter 16: Private Rulings and Determination Letters

Chapter 17: International Tax Practice and Procedure

Chapter 18: Criminal Tax Procedure

Chapter 19: Indirect Methods of Proving Income

CHAPTER 1

ORGANIZATION OF THE INTERNAL REVENUE SERVICE

¶101 INTRODUCTION

All tax practitioners must possess an understanding of the organizational structure of the Internal Revenue Service (IRS). This should include an awareness of the responsibilities, power and authority granted to the various representatives of the IRS. The IRS is part of the Treasury Department. It is headed by the Commissioner of Internal Revenue, who serves under the direction of the Secretary of the Treasury. The Commissioner is appointed by the President for a five-year term.

¶102 THE RESTRUCTURED INTERNAL REVENUE SERVICE

In accordance with the IRS Restructuring and Reform Act of 1998 (the Act),[1] the IRS has modified its entire structure. In response to the Act, the IRS set out to make five fundamental changes:

1. Redefine its business practices;

2. Rebuild its organizational structure;

3. Establish management roles with clear responsibility;

4. Create a balanced set of performance measures; and

5. Implement new and revamped technology to support the changes mentioned above.

The IRS's restructuring primarily focuses on changes number two and three. The restructuring is designed to improve customer service, encourage voluntary compliance and streamline collection efforts.

The fundamental nature of the IRS's restructuring is reflected in the way its mission statement has changed. Its old mission statement provided as follows:

> The purpose of the Internal Revenue Service is to collect the proper amount of tax revenue at the least cost; serve the public by continually improving the quality of our products and services; and perform in a manner warranting the highest degree of public confidence in our integrity, efficiency, and fairness.[2]

The IRS's new mission is to:

> Provide America's taxpayers top quality service by helping them understand and meet their tax responsibilities and by applying the tax law with integrity and fairness to all.[3]

---

[1] P.L. 105-206.
[2] IRB 1998-01.

[3] See the IRS website (www.irs.gov/irs/article/0,,id=98141,00.html).

The IRS's new structure is vastly different from the old, pyramid-type organization. Under the old structure, the IRS was comprised of a National Office, four Regional Offices, 33 District Offices and 10 Service Centers. Each District Office and Service Center was charged with the responsibility of administering the entire tax law for every type of taxpayer within a defined geographic area (see Exhibit 1-1 at ¶151). The restructuring—while maintaining much of the National Office structure—eliminated Regional and District offices and in their place created operating divisions (see Exhibit 1-2 at ¶152).

National Office. Much of the National Office organization remains. The Commissioner and the Deputy Commissioner along with support functions such as Human Resources, Equal Employment Opportunity, Planning, etc., remain, as does Chief Counsel along with the Associate Chief Counsels. The various technical sections responsible for rulings and technical advice remain as before. The Chief Criminal Investigation and Chief Appeals as well as Chief Counsel now have direct line authority over the field personnel. The National Taxpayer Advocate remains in the National Office with supervisory authority over the local offices.

Each operating division is responsible for serving a group of similar taxpayers.

¶105 THE OPERATING DIVISIONS

The starting point to understanding the restructured IRS is the four major operating divisions.

The Wage and Investment Income Division (W & I). W & I covers individual taxpayers, including those who file jointly, who only receive wage and/or investment income. W & I is comprised of an estimated 88 million filers. Most of these taxpayers only deal with the IRS once a year when filing their income tax returns. Further, due to over-withholding, most of these taxpayers receive refunds. Compliance matters are focused on a limited range of issues such as dependency exemptions, credits, filing status and deductions.

Within the W & I group there are three operating units:

1. Communications Assistance, Research and Education (CARE)—this unit's primary role is education;

2. Customer Account Services (CAS)—this unit's role is to process returns submitted by taxpayers and validate that the proper taxes have been paid; and

3. Compliance—the role of this unit is to address the limited compliance and collection issues that may arise with respect to this group of taxpayers.

Most of the income earned by W & I taxpayers is reported by third parties (e.g., employers, banks, brokerage firms). Furthermore, almost all of the tax on this income is collected through third party withholding. Accordingly, this group is highly compliant. The bulk of these taxpayers (i.e., roughly 85 percent) earn under $50,000 per year, with 28 percent of them earning less than $10,000 per year. This group pays $46 billion directly to the IRS in addition to amounts withheld by third parties.

Small Business and Self-Employed Division (SB/SE). SB/SE is comprised of fully or partially self-employed individuals and small businesses. This division includes corporations and partnerships with assets less than or equal to $10 million. Further, estate and gift taxpayers, fiduciary returns and all individuals who file international returns are under the jurisdiction of this group. SB/SE includes approximately 45 million filers.

Taxpayers in the SB/SE are responsible for paying the IRS nearly $915 billion each year, which represents nearly 40 percent of the total revenue collected by the IRS. The typical SB/SE taxpayer interacts with the IRS four to 60 times per year. Tax obligations of these taxpayers include personal and corporate income taxes, employment taxes, excise taxes and tax withheld from employees. Because of the wide variety of complex tax issues involved, the probability of errors which results in collection and compliance problems is higher with respect to this group than the other divisions.

SB/SE is organized around three major operating units:

1. Taxpayer education and communication;

2. Customer account services; and

3. Compliance.

The mission of the third unit, Compliance, is to provide prompt, professional and helpful service to taxpayers. The goal is to increase overall compliance and the fairness of the compliance programs.

Large and Mid-Size Businesses Division (LMSB). LMSB includes businesses with assets over $10 million (i.e., about 210,000 filers). This group pays over $712 billion in taxes (i.e., income, employment, excise and withholding) each year. Collection issues are rare; however, many complex matters such as tax law interpretation, accounting and regulation issues are common. The largest taxpayers in this group deal with the IRS on a continuous basis.

The LMSB is aligned by industry groupings, as opposed to a geographical alignment. These groups are as follows:

1. Financial Services;

2. Natural Resources and Construction;

3. Heavy Manufacturing and Transportation;

4. Communications, Technology and Media; and

5. Retailers, Food and Pharmaceuticals.

Industry-aligned staffs focus on issues specific to that industry and have in-depth technical knowledge and expertise about the industry (see Exhibit 1-3 at ¶153).

Tax-Exempt Organizations and Governmental Entities Division (TE/GE). TE/GE includes pension plans, exempt organizations and the governmental entities. This group is comprised of about 24 million filers. These entities gener-

¶105

ally pay no income tax; however, this group pays over $220 billion in employment taxes and income tax withholding and controls about $7 trillion in assets.

¶114 INTERNAL REVENUE SERVICE OVERSIGHT BOARD

As part of the Act, Congress ordered the creation of an IRS Oversight Board. This Board recommends funding and staffing levels, training and career development requirements, taxpayer education, modernization needs and customer service issues. The Board is comprised of six members from private industry, a representative from the IRS employee's union, the IRS Commissioner and the Secretary of the Treasury or his designee.

¶115 CRIMINAL INVESTIGATION

Under the IRS's restructuring plan, Criminal Investigation (CI) reports directly to the IRS Commissioner and Deputy Commissioner. It operates as a nationwide unit with 35 Special Agents in Charge, reporting to six area directors. CI closely coordinates its activities with the operating divisions and is supported by specific attorneys within the Chief Counsel's office.

CI's mission is to serve the American public by investigating potential criminal violations of the Internal Revenue Code and related financial crimes. CI has been modernized in order to create the structures, systems and processes necessary to comply with its mission. The new CI focuses more on tax administration issues and less on nontax crimes (e.g., drug cases). It provides a streamlined investigative review process and a geographic alignment that is more consistent with the location of the various United States Attorney's Offices. Agents working for CI will obtain more training in basic tax law. Further, IRS counsel will be consulted throughout the investigative process.

¶117 THE OFFICE OF CHIEF COUNSEL

The Chief Counsel of the IRS is appointed by the President to provide legal services to the IRS through the Office of Chief Counsel. There are three major areas of the Office of Chief Counsel.

Technical. The Chief Counsel technical organization is located in the National Office and its role is to provide authoritative legal interpretations of the tax law. This responsibility involves issuing regulations, revenue rulings, private letter rulings, technical advice and advance pricing agreements.

Division Counsel. Within the Office of Chief Counsel there is an Operating Division Counsel for each operating division. This Operating Division Counsel provides legal advice and representation and participates in the plans and activities of the operating division management. Each Operating Division Counsel servesas a counterpart to the General Manager of each of the four operating divisions. The Operating Division Counsel and staff are physically located on site at each of the four operating division headquarters. Counsel's geographic co-location is important for maintaining a close working relationship with the General Manager of each operating division.[4]

The main focus of the Operating Division Counsel is to provide legal services to the operating divisions, to take part in planning the strategic use of litigation resources, and to assist the operating divisions in developing compliance approaches and new taxpayer service initiatives.

It is hoped that by physically locating the Operating Division Counsels at the operating division locations, taxpayers' needs will be more clearly understood, legal issues will be identified and resolved earlier, and better coordination and communication with the operating divisions will result. However, due to the close proximity of counsel with the operating divisions, it may be more difficult to retain impartiality, consistency and uniformity. To counter this possibility, the National Office Subject Matter Experts are organized by Internal Revenue Code section matter and report to the Chief Counsel, as opposed to the Operating Division Counsel. In addition, the Operating Division Counsel reports to the Chief Counsel rather than the Operating Division General Manager to ensure independence.

Field Counsel. Field Counsel provides litigation services and legal advice on locally managed cases. Field Counsel consists of attorney groups that report to an assigned Operating Division Counsel.

¶121 INTERNAL REVENUE SERVICE APPEALS OFFICE

The new Appeals Office is headquartered in Washington, D.C., but maintains the geographic location of current offices. The field staff has been realigned to closely mirror the new operating structure. Thus, within a particular office, Appeals Officers are designated to work on cases from a particular operating division. Three appeals operating units manage operations for each of the taxpayer segments. These units are as follows: (1) Appeals—LMSB, (2) Appeals—SB/SE, and (3) Appeals—W & I. Appeals for cases under the jurisdiction of TE/GE are handled by appeals officers within the SB/SE function. Appeals remains an independent channel for taxpayers who have a dispute over a recommended enforcement action.

¶122 NATIONAL TAXPAYER ADVOCATE

The National Taxpayer Advocate was designed to help taxpayers who have problems with the IRS that have not been resolved through the normal administrative process. The new National Taxpayer Advocate is organized around two major functions: (1) the casework function, and (2) the systemic analysis and the advocacy function. The purpose of the first function is resolving all individual taxpayer problems with theirs. The systemic analysis and advocacy function isresponsible for working with the operating divisions to identify systemic

---

[4] *IRS Watch* by David Blattner and Kristen Starling, and *Tax Practice and Procedure,* June/July 1999 edition, page 11.

problems, analyze root causes, implement solutions to mitigate such problems and proactively identify potential problems with new systems and procedures.

The National Taxpayer Advocate is physically located in geographic locations so as to allow contact with local taxpayers. A National Taxpayer Advocate within each operating division helps to identify systemic problems in the division.

As part of their ongoing effort to help taxpayers, the National Taxpayer Advocate established the Citizens Advocacy Panel (CAP) pilot program in 1998, which was expanded nationwide in 2002 and renamed the Taxpayer Advocacy Panel.

¶124 INTERNAL REVENUE SERVICE PERSONNEL

The IRS is creating new positions titled, "Tax Compliance Officer," "Tax Pre-filing Specialist" and "Tax Resolution Representative." The positions are being created with the assistance of the National Treasury Employee's Union, which represents approximately 98,000 IRS employees. A summary of the nature and duties of these positions follows.

Tax Compliance Officer (TCO). Approximately 1,200 positions will be created. These individuals will run examinations and investigations of the individual and business taxpayers. The Tax Compliance Officer should be an expert on tax law and tax related account matters. Most, if not all, of the former Tax Auditor/Examiners are now TCOs. These positions are in SB/SE.

Tax Pre-Filing Specialist. Approximately 500 positions will be created. These individuals provide tax and accounting advice during the pre-filing and filing process. They will also conduct surveys, studies and focus groups on agency activities. These positions are in SB/SE.

Tax Resolution Representative (TRR). Approximately 650 positions will be created. These individuals will resolve examination, collection and account issues. They will examine tax returns and provide tax and accounting help to taxpayers. Most of the former Taxpayer Service employees are now TRRs. These positions are in W & I.

¶128 COMMENTARY

While the position of District Director has been eliminated and districts are no more, there are still IRS employees in the offices that used to be District Offices. How do they fit into the new organization? These are the people most practitioners deal with on a daily basis and therefore it is important to understand where they fit into the new IRS (see Exhibit 1-4 at ¶154).

Most of the senior revenue agents have been reassigned to LMSB. They have been assigned to one of the five industry groupings and are in a group of other agents in the same grouping which is managed by a Team Manager. These revenue agents will complete cases presently assigned to them and new assignments will befrom within their assigned industry group. As LMSB is organized by industry rather than geographic area, new assignments may be outside of the former District boundaries. Depending on the concentration of a given industry in a geographic area, team managers may supervise agents from a number of former Districts. A number of team managers, within an industry grouping, will report to a Territory Manager who reports to an LMSB Director of Field Operations for that industry. Specialists in LMSB, such as engineers, computer audit specialists, international examiners and economists, are in groups within their specialty.

Employees who previously were assigned to Employee Plans (EP) or Exempt Organizations (EO) remain in EP or EO groups supervised by a group manager. The group managers report to an area manager who reports to either Director of Employee Plans or Director of Exempt Organizations.

The remainder of the local revenue agents and revenue officers are assigned to SB/SE. At the present time, revenue agents are supervised by revenue agent group managers, and are collectively referred to as the "examination function." Revenue officers are supervised by revenue officer group managers and are collectively referred to as the "collection function." These groups are supervised by Territory Managers. Territory Managers supervise a mix of functions based on geographic location. The Territory Managers report to Area Directors. The former Examination support units (Disclosure and Exam Support Branch which included Quality Measurement Staff and Processing) still exist, as does Collection Special Procedures Branch.

The bulk of W & I employees are at Service and Collection Centers; although at most former District Office sites there are W & I employees coordinating Taxpayer Education, Electronic Filing and similar activities.

With the elimination of District Directors, the delegation orders which delegated authority to the District Directors have been amended by replacing the District Directors with the various operating division directors: LMSB Directors Field Operations, SB/SE Area Directors, TE/GE Area Directors, and W & I Division Directors.[5]

---

[5] For this treatise, the use of the term "director" will be used to indicate the director of the appropriate operating division.

¶151 Exhibit 1-1

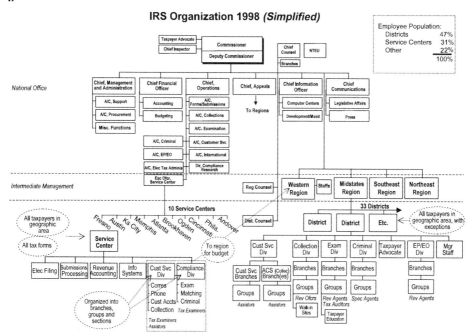

IRS Organization 1998 *(Simplified)*

¶152 Exhibit 1-2

IRS Organization

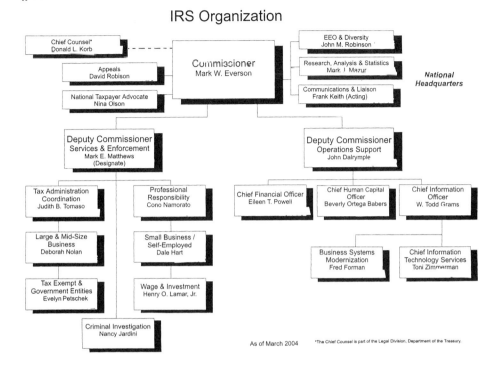

National Headquarters

As of March 2004   *The Chief Counsel is part of the Legal Division, Department of the Treasury.

¶153 Exhibit 1-3

Management Structure

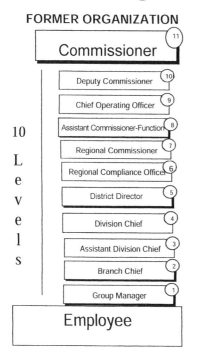

FORMER ORGANIZATION

Commissioner (11)

Deputy Commissioner (10)

Chief Operating Officer (9)

Assistant Commissioner-Function (8)

Regional Commissioner (7)

Regional Compliance Officer (6)

District Director (5)

Division Chief (4)

Assistant Division Chief (3)

Branch Chief (2)

Group Manager (1)

Employee

10 Levels

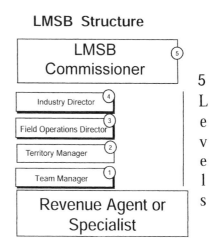

LMSB Structure

LMSB Commissioner (5)

Industry Director (4)

Field Operations Director (3)

Territory Manager (2)

Team Manager (1)

Revenue Agent or Specialist

5 Levels

¶154 Exhibit 1-4

Partial List of IRS Job Titles

OLD	RESTRUCTURED
National Office	*National Office*
Commissioner	Commissioner
Chief Counsel	Chief Counsel
Associate Chief Counsels (Technical)	Associate Chief Counsels (Technical)
	Division Counsels
Assistant Commissioner (Examination)	Eliminated
Assistant Commissioner (Collections)	Eliminated
	Commissioner SB/SE
	Commissioner LMSB
Assistant Commissioner (EP/EO)	Commissioner TE/GE
Chief Operations	Commissioner W&I
Assistant Commissioner (Criminal)	Chief Criminal Investigations (CI)
National Director of Appeals	Chief Appeals
Taxpayer Advocate	National Taxpayer Advocate
Regional Offices	*Area/Industry Offices*
Regional Commissioners	Eliminated
Assistant Regional Commissioner (Exam)	Eliminated
Assistant Regional Commissioner (Collections)	Eliminated
	LMSB Industry Directors
	SB/SE Area* Directors
Assistant Regional Commissioner (CI)	CI Area Directors
Regional Counsel	LMSB Industry Counsels
	SB/SE Area Counsels
	TE/GE Area Counsels
	CI Area Counsels
Regional Director of Appeals	LMSB Area Directors
	SB/SE Area Directors
Regional Problem Resolution Officer	National Advocate Area Director
Assistant Regional Commissioner (EP/EO)	EP Area Directors
	EO Area Directors
District Offices	*Field (Local) Offices*
District Director	Eliminated**
Chief Examination Division	Eliminated
Chief Collection Division	Eliminated
	LMSB Industry Territory Managers
	SB/SE Territory Managers
Chief Criminal Investigation	Special Agent in Charge
Chief Appeals	LMSB Team Managers
	SB/SE Team Managers
Chief Problem Resolution	National Advocate Local Manager
Examination Case Managers	LMSB Team Managers

District Offices	*Field (Local) Offices*
Examination Group Managers	SB/SE Group Managers
Collection Group Managers	SB/SE Group Managers
Revenue Agents	Revenue Agents
Revenue Officers	Revenue Officers
Tax Auditors	Tax Compliance Officers
Special Agents	Special Agents
Appeals Officers	Appeals Officers
Counsel Attorneys	Counsel Attorneys

* Areas differ geographically from prior Regions and differ geographically within the various functions.

** A manager in each office is designated "Senior Commissioner's Representative" and has responsibility for various internal administrative duties.

¶154

¶155 DISCUSSION QUESTIONS

1. The directory for the IRS at the Federal Building, 1234 West Main Street, Anywhereville, USA, contains the following listing:

Room 101—Appeals Officer

Room 102—Special Agent

Room 103—Revenue Agent SB/SE

Room 104—Team Member LMSB

Room 105—Local Taxpayer Advocate

Room 106—Tax Auditor/Tax Compliance Officer

Room 107—Reviewer

Room 108—Inspector

Room 109—Revenue Officer

Room 110—Customer Service Representative

Room 111—Chief Counsel

Room 112—Group Manager SB/SE

Room 113—Team Manager LMSB

Room 114—Territory Manager Financial Services LMSB

Situation A

Mary Mutual, a life insurance sales agent, receives a notice from the IRS that her return has been selected for audit. It asks her to bring her books and records for a conference at the Federal Building.

To which room should Mary Mutual go?

Situation B

Billy Bankrupt has received a bill for additional tax due in the amount of $5,000. At the moment Bankrupt cannot pay the entire amount, and he wishes to pay it off in installments.

To which room should Billy Bankrupt go?

Situation C

Ingrid Informer, who is employed as a nurse in Dr. Deceptive's office, is very upset at Deceptive because he cut her salary. She wishes to inform the IRS that Deceptive has been running a duplicate set of books and has been omitting a substantial portion of his gross receipts from his tax returns for the past five years. She has also read that as an informant she can receive a fee of up to 10% of the tax collected as the result of the information that she brings to the IRS.

To which office should she go?

Situation D

You recently accepted a job as tax manager for IBN Corporation. Your first day on the job you receive a letter from the IRS which is signed by "Harry Hawk, Group 6969." Later that day, while attending a luncheon seminar with other tax professionals, one of your colleagues tells you that Group 6969 is the "LMSB" group.

Which office is occupied by Harry Hawk?

Situation E

Friendly Fast Food LLC, owned and operated by Frank Friendly, is a small "family type" restaurant. On February 10, 2004, he received a notice that the restaurant's 2000, 2001 and 2002 tax returns are being examined by the IRS. He is notified that the IRS would like to begin the audit at the place of business on March 15, 2004. Frank would like to postpone the audit.

To whom would he address his request?

2. C-Ment Industries, Inc. is in the business of designing, manufacturing and selling concrete equipment vehicles. In 2004, C-Ment designed and manufactured a line of concrete pumping vehicles to transfer concrete from cement mixers to specific points within a construction site. The pumping equipment is mounted on a specially modified truck chassis.

Situation A

C-Ment wishes to ensure that the concrete pumping vehicles are not subject to excise tax under Internal Revenue Code Sec. 4051.

(1) With what *level* of the IRS will Wheeler have to deal?

(2) With which office?

Situation B

Assume that C-Ment goes ahead with the sales of the concrete pumping vehicles without seeking assurance as to the excise tax consequences from the IRS. Two years later its excise tax returns are reviewed at one of the IRS campuses.

(1) Who determines if the return should be audited?

(2) To what level of the IRS are C-Ment's returns sent if it is determined that it will be necessary to contact the corporation during the audit process?

Situation C

In discussing this case with the IRS representative, C-Ment has tried to convince the revenue agent that the concrete pumping vehicles are not subject to excise tax. Because the agent will not concede the issue, C-Ment now seeks to get a higher level of the IRS to advise the agent that "as a matter of law" the vehicles are not subject to excise tax under Code Sec. 4051.

(1) What *level* of the IRS, if any, would make such a determination?

(2) How would C-Ment go about requesting IRS participation?

Situation D

Assume that eventually the IRS determines that there is additional excise tax due as a result of C-Ment's improper accounting for the concrete pumping vehicles. C-Ment wishes to seek review of this determination within the IRS.

(1) With what level of the IRS must Wheeler deal for such formal review?

(2) What formalities must Wheeler follow?

Situation E

Assume that eventually the IRS determination is upheld throughout the formal review and that C-Ment is sent a bill for the tax due resulting from the deficiency.

(1) What level of the IRS sends the bill to C-Ment?

(2) Where can C-Ment make payment of the amount of the bill?

Situation F

Because of financial difficulties, C-Ment is not in a position to pay this bill in full.

(1) With what level or levels of the IRS will C-Ment deal in attempting to resolve the unpaid bill?

(2) If personal contact with C-Ment is required to resolve the problem, who will make the contact?

CHAPTER 2

PRACTICE BEFORE THE INTERNAL REVENUE SERVICE

¶201 INTRODUCTION

Taxpayers can have various dealings with the Internal Revenue Service (IRS): (1) a return may be selected for audit and the taxpayer invited to attend a conference with the examiner, (2) the collection function may request an interview to determine whether the taxpayer is in a financial position to pay a delinquency, or (3) the taxpayer may seek an advance determination as to the tax consequences of a proposed transaction. In each of these instances, a taxpayer can appear personally to deal with the IRS, or he or she can authorize another person to act as a representative. Such representation may constitute "practice before the Internal Revenue Service." Generally, the right to practice before the IRS is limited to attorneys, certified public accountants and "enrolled agents" who have passed an IRS examination.

Practice before the IRS encompasses any presentation of information to the IRS with respect to a taxpayer's rights, privileges or liabilities. It includes, but is not limited to, the preparation and filing of documents, communication with IRS personnel and the representation of a client at conferences, hearings or meetings.[1]

A federal statute allows two groups of professionals to represent others before the IRS without further qualification. Public Law 89-332[2] (the Act) provides that any attorney (defined as a member in good standing of the bar of the highest court of any state or the District of Columbia) can represent others before any agency of the federal government (except the Patent Office) upon filing a written declaration that he or she is qualified as an attorney and is authorized by his or her client. The Act further entitles any person duly qualified to practice as a certified public accountant in any state or the District of Columbia to represent others before the IRS, upon filing a declaration.[3] In addition, by Treasury Department rule, noncertified accountants and former IRS employees may practice as enrolled agents upon meeting the qualification requirements promulgated by the Treasury Department.[4] A limited right to practice also is extended to actuaries enrolled by the Joint Board for the Enrollment of Actuaries pursuant to Title 29 U.S.C. §1242.[5]

---

[1] Treasury Department Circular 230, §10.2(e). (These regulations are contained in Title 31, Part 10, Code of Federal Regulations, incorporated in Circular 230, Reg. §§10.0 to 10.101.)

[2] Act of November 8, 1965, 79 Stat. 1282 §1(a).

[3] P.L. 89-332, Act §1(b).

[4] Treasury Department Circular 230, §§10.3(c), 10.4.

[5] *Id.* at §10.3(d).

¶205 ATTORNEYS, CPAs AND ENROLLED AGENTS

The rules governing the right of attorneys, certified public accountants (CPAs) and enrolled agents to practice before the IRS are contained in a document published by the Treasury Department and commonly referred to as "Circular 230." Circular 230 was most recently amended in July, 2002, when the Treasury Department finalized the portion of Circular 230 regarding practice before the IRS in nonshelter matters. At that time, the Treasury Department indicated that they intended to re-propose amendments regarding the standards for practice in tax shelter cases. In 2004, the treasury withdrew the 2001 proposed amendments regarding the standards of practice for tax shelter cases and published new proposed amendments to Circular 230 concerning tax shelter matters. These proposed changes to Circular 230 have not yet been finalized.

Set forth below is the current text of relevant portions of Subpart A of Circular 230, Rules of Practice Before the IRS (31 C.F.R., Part 10, Subpart A, §§ 10.1-10.8).

PART 10—PRACTICE BEFORE THE INTERNAL REVENUE SERVICE

* * * * *

Subpart A—Rules Governing Authority to Practice

31 CFR §

§ 10.1. Director of practice. (a) *Establishment of office*. The Office of Director of Practice is established in the Office of the Secretary of the Treasury. The Director of Practice is appointed by the Secretary of the Treasury, or his or her designate.

(b) *Duties*. The Director of Practice acts on applications for enrollment to practice before the Internal Revenue Service; makes inquiries with respect to matters under his or her jurisdiction; institutes and provides for the conduct of disciplinary proceedings relating to attorneys, certified public accountants, enrolled agents, enrolled actuaries and appraisers; and performs other duties as are necessary or appropriate to carry out his or her functions under this part or as are prescribed by the Secretary of the Treasury, or his or her delegate.

(c) *Acting Director of Practice*. The Secretary of the Treasury, or his or herdelegate, will designate an officer or employee of the Treasury Department to act as Director of Practice in the absence of the Director or a vacancy in that office.

§ 10.2. Definitions. As used in this part, except where the text clearly provides otherwise:

(a) *Attorney* means any person who is a member in good standing of the bar of the highest court of any State, territory, or possession of the United States, including a Commonwealth, or the District of Columbia.

(b) *Certified Public Accountant* means any person who is duly qualified to practice as a certified public accountant in any State, territory, or possession of the United States, including a Commonwealth, or the District of Columbia.

(c) *Commissioner* refers to the Commissioner of Internal Revenue.

(d) *Practice before the Internal Revenue Service* comprehends all matters connected with a presentation to the Internal Revenue Service or any of its officers or employees relating to a taxpayer's rights, privileges, or liabilities under laws or regulations administered by the Internal Revenue Service. Such presentations include, but are not limited to, preparing and filing documents, corresponding and communicating with the Internal Revenue Service, and representing a client at conferences, hearings, and meetings.

(e) *Practitioner* means any individual described in paragraphs (a), (b), (c), or (d) of § 10.3.

(f) *A tax return* includes an amended tax return and a claim for refund.

(g) *Service* means the Internal Revenue Service.

§ 10.3. Who may practice. (a) *Attorneys.* Any attorney who is not currently under suspension or disbarment from practice before the Internal Revenue Service may practice before the Internal Revenue Service by filing with the Internal Revenue Service a written declaration that he or she is currently qualified as an attorney and is authorized to represent the party or parties on whose behalf he or she acts.

(b) *Certified public accountants.* Any certified public accountant who is not currently under suspension or disbarment from practice before the Internal Revenue Service may practice before the Internal Revenue Service by filing with the Internal Revenue Service a written declaration that he or she is currently qualified as a certified public accountant and is authorized to represent the party or parties on whose behalf he or she acts.

(c) *Enrolled agents.* Any individual enrolled as an agent pursuant to this part who is not currently under suspension or disbarment from practice before the Internal Revenue Service may practice before the Internal Revenue Service.

(d) *Enrolled actuaries.* (1) Any individual who is enrolled as an actuary by the Joint Board for the Enrollment of Actuaries pursuant to 29 U.S.C. 1242 who is not currently under suspension or disbarment from practice before the Internal Revenue Service may practice before the Internal Revenue Service by filing with the Internal Revenue Service a written declaration stating that he or she is currently qualified as an enrolled actuary and is authorized to represent the party or parties on whose behalf he or she acts.

(2) Practice as an enrolled actuary is limited to representation with respect to issues involving the following statutory provisions in title 26 of the United States Code: sections 401 (relating to qualification of employee plans), 403(a) (relating to whether an annuity plan meets the requirements of section 404(a)(2)), 404 (relating to deductibility of employer contributions), 405 (relating to qualification of bond purchase plans), 412 (relating to funding requirements for certain employee plans), 413 (relating to application of qualification requirements to collectively bargained plans and to plans maintained by more than one employer), 414 (relating to definitions and special rules with respect to the employee plan area), 419 (relating to treatment of funded welfare benefits), 419A (relating to qualified asset accounts), 420 (relating to transfers of excess pension assets to retiree health accounts), 4971 (relating to excise taxes payable as a result of an accumulated funding deficiency under section 412), 4972 (relating to tax on nondeductible contributions to qualified employer plans), 4976 (relating to taxes with respect to funded welfare benefit plans), 4980 (relating to tax on reversion of qualified plan assets to employer), 6057 (relating to annual registration of plans), 6058 (relating to information required in connection with certain plans of deferred compensation), 6059 (relating to periodic report of actuary), 6652(e) (relating to the failure to file annual registration and other notifications by pension plan), 6652(f) (relating to the failure to file information required in connection with certain plans of deferred compensa-

tion), 6692 (relating to the failure to file actuarial report), 7805(b) (relating to the extent to which an Internal Revenue Service ruling or determination letter coming under the statutory provisions listed here will be applied without retroactive effect); and 29 U.S.C. 1083 (relating to the waiver of funding for non-qualified plans).

(3) An individual who practices before the Internal Revenue Service pursuant to paragraph (d)(1) of this section is subject to the provisions of this part in the same manner as attorneys, certified public accountants and enrolled agents.

(e) *Others*. Any individual qualifying under paragraph (d) of § 10.5 or § 10.7 is eligible to practice before the Internal Revenue Service to the extent provided in those sections.

(f) *Government officers and employees, and others*. An individual, who is an officer or employee of the executive, legislative, or judicial branch of the United States Government; an officer or employee of the District of Columbia; a Member of Congress; or a Resident Commissioner may not practice before the Internal Revenue Service if such practice violates 18 U.S.C. 203 or 205.

(g) *State officers and employees*. No officer or employee of any State, or subdivision of any State, whose duties require him or her to pass upon, investigate, or deal with tax matters for such State or subdivision, may practice before the Internal Revenue Service, if such employment may disclose facts or information applicable to Federal tax matters.

§ 10.4. Eligibility for enrollment. (a) *Enrollment upon examination*. The Director of Practice may grant enrollment to an applicant who demonstrates special competence in tax matters by written examination administered by, or administered under the oversight of, the Director of Practice and who has not engaged in any conduct that would justify the censure, suspension, or disbarment of any practitioner under the provisions of this part.

(b) *Enrollment of former Internal Revenue Service employees*. The Director of Practice may grant enrollment to an appli-

cant who, by virtue of his or her past service and technical experience in the Internal Revenue Service, has qualified for such enrollment and who has not engaged in any conduct that would justify the censure, suspension, or disbarment of any practitioner under the provisions of this part, under the following circumstances—

(1) The former employee applies for enrollment to the Director of Practice on a form supplied by the Director of Practice and supplies the information requested on the form and such other information regarding the experience and training of the applicant as may be relevant.

(2) An appropriate office of the Internal Revenue Service, at the request of the Director of Practice, will provide the Director of Practice with a detailed report of the nature and rating of the applicant's work while employed by the Internal Revenue Service and a recommendation whether such employment qualifies the applicant technically or otherwise for the desired authorization.

(3) Enrollment based on an applicant's former employment with the Internal Revenue Service may be of unlimited scope or it may be limited to permit the presentation of matters only of the particular class or only before the particular unit or divisionof the Internal Revenue Service for which the applicant's former employment has qualified the applicant.

(4) Application for enrollment based on an applicant's former employment with the Internal Revenue Service must be made within 3 years from the date of separation from such employment.

(5) An applicant for enrollment who is requesting such enrollment based on his or her former employment with the Internal Revenue Service must have had a minimum of 5 years continuous employment with the Internal Revenue Service during which he or she must have been regularly engaged in applying and interpreting the provisions of the Internal Revenue Code and the regulations thereunder relating to income, estate, gift, employment, or excise taxes.

(6) For the purposes of paragraph (b)(5) of this section, an aggregate of 10 or more years of employment in posi-

tions involving the application and interpretation of the provisions of the Internal Revenue Code, at least 3 of which occurred within the 5 years preceding the date of application, is the equivalent of 5 years continuous employment.

(c) *Natural persons.* Enrollment to practice may be granted only to natural persons.

§10.5. Application for enrollment.

(a) *Form; address.* An applicant for enrollment must file an application on Form 23, Application for Enrollment to Practice Before the Internal Revenue Service, properly executed under oath or affirmation, with the Director of Practice. The address of the applicant entered on Form 23 will be the address under which a successful applicant is enrolled and is the address to which the Director of Practice will send correspondence concerning enrollment. An enrolled agent must send notification of any change to his or her enrollment address to the Director of Practice, Internal Revenue Service, 1111 Constitution Avenue, NW., Washington, DC 20224, or at such other address specified by the Director of Practice. This notification must include the enrolled agent's name, old address, new address, social security number or tax identification number, signature, and the date.

(b) *Fee.* The application for enrollment must be accompanied by a check or money order in the amount set forth on Form 23, payable to the Internal Revenue Service, which amount constitutes a fee charged to each applicant for enrollment. This fee will be retained by the United States whether or not the applicant is granted enrollment.

(c) *Additional information; examination.* The Director of Practice, as a condition to consideration of an application for enrollment, may require the applicant to file additional information and to submit to any written or oral examination under oath or otherwise. The Director of Practice will, on written request filed by an applicant, afford such applicant the opportunity to be heard with respect to his or her application for enrollment.

(d) *Temporary recognition.* On receipt of a properly executed application, the Director of Practice may grant the applicant temporary recognition to practice pending a determination as to whether enrollment to practice should be granted. Temporary recognition will be granted only in unusual circumstances and it will not be granted, in any circumstance, if the application is not regular on its face, if the information stated in the application, if true, is not sufficient to warrant enrollment to practice, or if there is any information before the Director of Practice indicating that the statements in the application are untrue or that the applicant would not otherwise qualify for enrollment. Issuance of temporary recognition does not constitute enrollment to practice or a finding of eligibility for enrollment, and the temporary recognition may be withdrawn at any time by the Director of Practice.

(e) *Appeal from denial of application.* The Director of Practice must inform the applicant as to the reason(s) for any denial of an application for enrollment. The applicant may, within 30 days after receipt of the notice of denial of enrollment, file a written appeal of the denial of enrollment with the Secretary of the Treasury or his or her delegate. A decision on the appeal will be rendered by the Secretary of the Treasury, or his or her delegate, as soon as practicable.

§10.6. Enrollment. (a) *Roster.* The
Director of Practice will maintain rosters of all individuals—

(1) Who have been granted active enrollment to practice before the Internal Revenue Service;

(2) Whose enrollment has been placed in inactive status for failure to meet the requirements for renewal of enrollment;

(3) Whose enrollment has been placed in inactive retirement status;

(4) Who have been censured, suspended, or disbarred from practice before the Internal Revenue Service;

(5) Whose offer of consent to resign from enrollment to practice before the Internal Revenue Service has been accepted by the Director of Practice under §10.61; and

(6) Whose application for enrollment has been denied.

(b) *Enrollment card.* The Director of Practice will issue an enrollment card to each individual whose application for enrollment to practice before the Internal Revenue Service is approved after July 26, 2002. Each enrollment card will be valid for the period stated on the enrollment card. An individual is not eligible to practice before the Internal Revenue Service if his or her enrollment card is not valid.

(c) *Term of enrollment.* Each individual enrolled to practice before the Internal Revenue Service will be accorded active enrollment status subject to his or her renewal of enrollment as provided in this part.

(d) *Renewal of enrollment.* To maintain active enrollment to practice before the Internal Revenue Service, each individual enrolled is required to have his or her enrollment renewed. Failure by an individual to receive notification from the Director of Practice of the renewal requirement will not be justification for the failure to satisfy this requirement.

(1) All individuals licensed to practice before the Internal Revenue Service who have a social security number or tax identification number that ends with the numbers 0, 1, 2, or 3, except for those individuals who received their initial enrollment after November 1, 2003, must apply for renewal between November 1, 2003, and January 31, 2004. The renewal will be effective April 1, 2004.

(2) All individuals licensed to practice before the Internal Revenue Service who have a social security number or tax identification number that ends with the numbers 4, 5, or 6, except for those individuals who received their initial enrollment after November 1, 2004, must apply for renewal between November 1, 2004, and January 31, 2005. The renewal will be effective April 1, 2005.

(3) All individuals licensed to practice before the Internal Revenue Service who have a social security number or tax identification number that ends with the numbers 7, 8, or 9, except for those individuals who received their initial enrollment after November 1, 2005, must apply for renewal between November 1, 2005,

and January 31, 2006. The renewal will be effective April 1, 2006.

(4) Thereafter, applications for renewal will be required between November 1 and January 31 of every subsequent third year as specified in paragraphs (d)(1),(2) or (3) of this section according to the last number of the individual's social security number or tax identification number. Those individuals who receive initial enrollment after November 1 and before April 2 of the applicable renewal period will not be required to renew their enrollment before thefirst full renewal period following the receipt of theirinitial enrollment.

(5) The Director of Practice will notify the individual of his or her renewal of enrollment and will issue the individual a card evidencing enrollment.

(6) A reasonable nonrefundable fee may be charged for each application for renewal of enrollment filed with the Director of Practice.Forms required for renewal may be obtained from the Director of Practice, Internal Revenue Service, Washington, DC 20224.

(7) Forms required for renewal may be obtained from the Director of Practice, Internal Revenue Service, 1111 Constitution Avenue, NW., Washington, DC 20224.

(e) *Condition for renewal: Continuing Professional Education.* In order to qualify for renewal of enrollment, an individual enrolled to practice before the Internal Revenue Service must certify, on the application for renewal form prescribed by the Director of Practice, that he or she has satisfied the following continuing professional education requirements.

(1) *For renewed enrollment effective March 31, 2004.*

(i) A minimum of 16 hours of continuing education credit must be completed during each calendar year in the enrollment term.

(2) *For renewed enrollment effective April 1, 2007.*

(i) A minimum of 72 hours of continuing education credit must be completed during each three year period described in paragraph (d)(4) of this section.

Each such three year period is known as an enrollment cycle.

(ii) A minimum of 16 hours of continuing education credit, including 2 hours of ethics or professional conduct, must be completed in each year of an enrollment cycle.

(iii) An individual who receives initial enrollment during an enrollment cycle must complete two (2) hours of qualifying continuing education credit for each month enrolled during the enrollment cycle. Enrollment for any part of a month is considered enrollment for the entire month.

(f) *Qualifying continuing education.*

(1) *General.* To qualify for continuing education credit, a course of learning must—

(i) Be a qualifying program designed to enhance professional knowledge in Federal taxation or Federal tax related matters, i.e., programs comprised of current subject matter in Federal taxation or Federal tax related matters, including accounting, tax preparation software and taxation or ethics; and

(ii) Be conducted by a qualifying sponsor.

(2) *Qualifying Programs.*

(i) *Formal programs.* A formal program qualifies ascontinuing education programs if it—:

(A) Requires attendance. Additionally, the program sponsor must provide each attendee with a certificate of attendance; and

(B) Requires that the program be conducted by a qualified instructor, discussion leader, or speaker, i.e., a person whose background, training, education and experience is appropriate for instructing or leading a discussion on the subject matter of the particular program; and

(C) Provides or requires a written outline, textbook, or suitable electronic educational materials.

(ii) *Correspondence or individual study programs (including taped programs).* Qualifying continuing education programs include correspondence or individual study programs that are conducted by qualifying sponsors and completed on an individual basis by the enrolled individual. The allowable credit hours for such programs will be measured on a basis comparable to the measurement of a seminar or course for credit in an accredited educational institution. Suchprograms qualify as continuing education programs if they—

(A) Require registration of the participants by the sponsor;

(B) Provide a means for measuring completion by the participants (e.g., written examination); including the issuance of a certificate of completion by the sponsor; and

(C) Provide a written outline, textbook, or suitable electronic educational materials.

(iii) *Serving as an instuctor, discussion leader or speaker.*

(A) One hour of continuing education credit will be awarded for each contact hour completed as an instructor, discussion leader or speaker at an educational program which meets the continuing education requirements of paragraph (f) of this section.

(B) Two hours of continuing education credit will be awarded for actual subject preparation time for each contact hour completed as an instructor, discussion leader, or speaker at such programs. It is the responsibility of the individual claiming such credit to maintain records to verify preparation time.

(C) The maximum credit for instruction and preparation may not exceed 50 percent of the continuing education requirement for an enrollment cycle.

(D) An instructor, discussion leader, or speaker who makes more than one presentation on the same subject matter during an enrollment cycle, will receive continuing education credit for only one such presentation for the enrollment cycle.

(iv) *Credit for published articles, books, etc.*

(A) Continuing education credit will be awarded for publications on Federal taxation or Federal tax related matters, including accounting, financial management, tax preparation software, and taxation, provided the content of such publications is current and designed for the enhancement of the professional knowledge of an individual enrolled to practice before the Internal Revenue Service.

(B) The credit allowed will be on the basis of one hour credit for each hour of preparation time for the material. It is the responsibility of the person claiming the credit to maintain records to verify preparation time.

(C) The maximum credit for publications may not exceed 25 percent of the continuing education requirement of any enrollment cycle.

(3) *Periodic examination.*

(i) Individuals may establish eligibility for renewal of enrollment for any enrollment cycle by—

(A) Achieving a passing score on each part of the Special EnrollmentExamination administered under this part during the three year period prior to renewal; and

(B) Completing a minimum of 16 hours of qualifying continuing education during the last year of an enrollment cycle.

(ii) Courses designed to help an applicant prepare for the examination specified in paragraph (a) of § 10.4 are considered basic in nature and are not qualifying continuing education.

(g) *Sponsors.*

(1) Sponsors are those responsible for presenting programs.

(2) To qualify as a sponsor, a program presenter must—

(i) Be an accredited educational institution;

(ii) Be recognized for continuing education purposes by the licensing body of any State, territory, or possession of the United States, including a Commonwealth, or the District of Columbia.

(iii) Be recognized by the Director of Practice as a professional organization or society whose programs include offering continuing professional education opportunities in subject matters within the scope of paragraph (f)(1)(i) of this section; or

(iv) File a sponsor agreement with the Director of Practice and obtain approval of the program as a qualified continuing education program.

(3) A qualifying sponsor must ensure the program complies with the following requirements—

(i) Programs must be developed by individual(s) qualified in the subject matter;

(ii) Program subject matter must be current;

(iii) Instructors, discussion leaders, and speakers must be qualified with respect to program content;

(iv) Programs must include some means for evaluation of technical content and presentation;

(v) Certificates of completion must be provided to the participants who successfully complete the program; and

(vi) Records must be maintained by the sponsor to verify the participants who attended and completed the program for a period of three years following completion of the program. In the case of continuous conferences, conventions, and the like, records must be maintained to verify completion of the program and attendance by each participant at each segment of the program.

(4) Professional organizations or societies wishing to be considered as qualified sponsors must request this status from the Director of Practice and furnish information in support of the request together with any further information deemed necessary by the Director of Practice.

(5) A professional organization or society recognized as a qualified sponsor by the Director of Practice will retain its status for one enrollment cycle. The Director of Practice will publish the names of such sponsors on a periodic basis.

(h) *Measurement of continuing education coursework.*

(1) All continuing education programs will be measured in terms of contact hours. The shortest recognized program will be one contact hour.

(2) A contact hour is 50 minutes of continuous participation in a program. Credit is granted only for a full contact

hour, i.e., 50 minutes or multiples thereof. For example, a program lasting more than 50 minutes but less than 100 minutes will count as one contact hour.

(3) Individual segments at continuous conferences, conventions and the like will be considered one total program. For example, two 90-minute segments (180 minutes) at a continuous conference will count as three contact hours.

(4) For university or college courses, each semester hour credit will equal 15 contact hours and a quarter hour credit will equal 10 contact hours.

(i) *Recordkeeping requirements.*

(1) Each individual applying for renewal mustretain for a period of three years following the date of renewal of enrollment the information required with regard to qualifying continuing professional education credit hours. Such information includes—

(i) The name of the sponsoring organization;

(ii) The location of the program;

(iii) The title of the program and description of its content;

(iv) Written outlines, course syllibi, textbook, and/or electronic materials provided or required for the course;

(v) The dates attended;

(vi) The credit hours claimed;

(vii) The name(s) of the instructor(s), discussion leader(s), or speaker(s), if appropriate; and

(viii) The certificate of completion and/or signed statement of the hours of attendance obtained from the sponsor.

(2) To receive continuing education credit for service completed as aninstructor,discussion leader, or speaker, the following information must be maintained for a period of three years following the date of renewal of enrollment—

(i) The name of the sponsoring organization;

(ii) The location of the program;

(iii) The title of the program and description of its content;

(iv) The dates of the program; and

(v) The credit hours claimed.

(3) To receive continuing education credit for publications, the following information must be maintained for a period of three years following the date of renewal of enrollment—

(i) The publisher;

(ii) The title of the publication;

(iii) A copy of the publication;

(iv) The date of publication; and

(v) Records that substantiate the hours worked on the publication.

(j) *Waivers.* (1) Waiver from the continuing education requirements for a given period may be granted by the Director of Practice for the following reasons—

(i) Health, which prevented compliance with the continuing education requirements;

(ii) Extended active military duty;

(iii) Absence from the United States for an extended period of time due to employment or other reasons, provided the individual does not practice before the Internal Revenue Service during such absence; and

(iv) Other compelling reasons, which will be considered on a case-by-case basis.

(2) A request for waiver must be accompanied by appropriate documentation. The individual is required to furnish any additional documentation or explanation deemed necessary by the Director of Practice. Examples of appropriate documentation could be a medical certificate or military orders.

(3) A request for waiver must be filed no later than the last day of the renewal application period.

(4) If a request for waiver is not approved, the individual will be placed in inactive status, so notified by the Director of Practice, and placed on a roster of inactive enrolled individuals.

(5) If a request for waiver is approved, the individual will be notified and issued a card evidencing renewal.

(6) Those who are granted waivers are required to file timely applications for renewal of enrollment.

(k) *Failure to comply.* (1) Compliance by an individual with the requirements of this part is determined by the Director of Practice. An individual who fails to meet the requirements of eligibility for renewal of enrollment will be notified by the Director of Practice at his or her enrollment address by first class mail. The notice will state the basis for the determination of noncompliance and will provide the individual an opportunity to furnish information in writing relating to the matter within 60 days of thedate of the notice. Such information will be considered by the Director of Practice in making a final determination as to eligibility for renewal of enrollment.

(2) The Director of Practice may require any individual, by notice sent by first class mail to his or her enrollment address, to provide copies of any records required to be maintained under this part. The Director of Practice may disallow any continuing professional education hours claimed if the individual fails to comply with this requirement.

(3) An individual who has not filed a timely application for renewal of enrollment, who has not made a timely response to the notice of noncompliance with the renewal requirements, or who has not satisfiedthe requirements of eligibility for renewal will be placed on a roster of inactive enrolled individuals. During this time, the individual will be ineligible to practice before the Internal Revenue Service.

(4) Individuals placed in inactive enrollment status and individuals ineligible to practice before the Internal Revenue Service may not state or imply that they are enrolled to practice before the Internal Revenue Service, or use the term enrolled agent, the designation "E. A.," or other form of reference to eligibility to practice before the Internal Revenue Service.

(5) An individual placed in an inactive status may be reinstated to an active enrollment status by filing an application for renewal of enrollment and providing evidence of the completion of all required continuing professional education hours for the enrollment cycle. Continuing education credit under this paragraph (k)(5) may not be used to satisfy the requirements of the enrollment cycle in which the individual has been placed back on the active roster.

(6) An individual placed in an inactive status must file an application for renewal of enrollment and satisfy the requirements for renewal as set forth in this section within three years of being placed in an inactive status. The name of such individual otherwise will be removed from the inactive enrollment roster and his or her enrollment will terminate. Eligibility for enrollment must then be reestablished by the individual as provided in this section.

(7) Inactive enrollment status is not available to an individual who is the subject of a disciplinary matter in the Office of Director of Practice.

(l) *Inactive retirement status.* An individual who no longer practices before the Internal Revenue Service may request being placed in an inactive status at any time and such individual will be placed in an inactive retirement status. The individual will be ineligible to practice before the Internal Revenue Service. Such individual must file a timely application for renewal of enrollment at each applicable renewal or enrollment period as provided in this section. An individual who is placed in an inactive retirement status may be reinstated to an active enrollment status by filing an application for renewal of enrollment and providing evidence of the completion of the required continuing professional education hours for the enrollment cycle. Inactive retirement status is not available to an individual who is subject of a disciplinary matter in the Office of Director of Practice.

(m) *Renewal while under suspension or disbarment.* An individual who isineligible to practice before the Internal Revenue Service by virtue of disciplinary action is required to be in conformance with the requirements for renewal of enrollment before his or her eligibility is restored.

(n) *Verification.* The Director of Practice may review the continuing education records of an enrolled individual and/or qualified sponsor in a manner deemed appropriate to determine compliance with the requirements and standards for renewal of enrollment as provided in paragraph (f) of this section.

(o) *Enrolled Actuaries.* The enrollment and the renewal of enrollment of actuaries authorized to practice under paragraph (d) of § 10.3 are governed by the regulations of the Joint Board for the Enrollment of Actuaries at 20 CFR 901.1 through 901.71. (Approved by the Office of Management and Budget under Control No. 1545-0946 and 1545-1726)

§10.7. Representing oneself; participating in rulemaking; limited practice; special appearances; and return preparation. (a) *Representing oneself.* Individuals may appear on their own behalf before the Internal Revenue Service provided they present satisfactory identification.

(b) *Participating in rulemaking.* Individuals may participate in rulemaking as provided by the Administrative Procedure Act. See 5 U.S.C. 553.

(c) *Limited practice.* (1) *In general.* Subject to the limitations in paragraph (c)(2) of this section, an individual who is not a practitioner may represent a taxpayer before the Internal Revenue Service in the circumstances described in this paragraph (c)(1), even if the taxpayer is not present, provided the individual presents satisfactory identification and proof of his or her authority to represent the taxpayer. The circumstances described in this paragraph (c)(1) are as follows:

(i) An individual may represent a member of his or her immediate family.

(ii) A regular full-time employee of an individual employer may represent the employer.

(iii) A general partner or a regular full-time employee of a partnership may represent the partnership.

(iv) A bona fide officer or a regular full-time employee of a corporation (including a parent, subsidiary, or other affiliated corporation), association, or organized group may represent the corporation, association, or organized group.

(v) A regular full-time employee of a trust, receivership, guardianship, or estate may represent the trust, receivership, guardianship, or estate.

(vi) An officer or a regular employee of a governmental unit, agency, or authority may represent the governmental unit, agency, or authority in the course of his or her official duties.

(vii) An individual may represent any individual or entity, who is outside the United States, before personnel of the Internal Revenue Service when such representation takes place outside the United States.

(viii) An individual who prepares and signs a taxpayer's tax return as the preparer, or who prepares a tax return but is not required (by the instructions to the tax return or regulations) to sign the tax return, may represent the taxpayer before revenue agents, customer service representatives or similar officers and employees of the Internal Revenue Service during an examination of the taxable year or period covered by that tax return, but, unless otherwise prescribed by regulation or notice, this right does not permit such individual to represent the taxpayer, regardless of the circumstances requiring representation, before appeals officers, revenue officers, Counsel or similar officers or employees of the Internal Revenue Service or the Department of Treasury.

(2) *Limitations.*

(i) An individual who is under suspension or disbarment from practice before the Internal Revenue Service may not engage in limited practice before the Internal Revenue Service under paragraph (c)(1) of this section.

(ii) The Director, after notice and opportunity for a conference, may deny eligibility to engage in limited practice before the Internal Revenue Service under paragraph (c)(1) of this section to any individual who has engaged in conduct that would justify censuring, suspending, or disbarring a practitioner from practice before the Internal Revenue Service.

(iii) An individual who represents a taxpayer under the authority of paragraph (c)(1) of this section is subject, to the extent of his or her authority, to such rules of general applicability regarding standards of conduct and other matters as the Director of Practice prescribes.

(d) *Special appearances.* The Director of Practice may, subject to suchconditions as he or she deems appropriate, authorize an individual who is not otherwise eligible to practice before the Internal Revenue Service to represent another person in a particular matter.

(e) *Preparing tax returns and furnishing information.* Any individual may prepare a tax return, appear as a witness for the taxpayer before the Internal RevenueService, or furnish information at the request of the Internal Revenue Service or any of its officers or employees.

(f) *Fiduciaries.* For purposes of this part, a fiduciary (i.e., a trustee, receiver, guardian, personal representative, administrator, or executor) is considered to be the taxpayer and not a representative of the taxpayer.

§ 10.8. Customhouse brokers. Nothing contained in the regulations in this part will affect or limit the right of a customhouse broker, licensed as such by the Commissioner of Customs in accordance with the regulations prescribed therefor, in any customs district in which he or she is so licensed, at a relevant local office of the Internal Revenue Service or before the National Office of the Internal Revenue Service, to act as a representative in respect to any matters relating specifically to the importation or exportation of merchandise under the customs or internal revenue laws, for any person for whom he or she has acted as a customhouse broker.

¶211 RECOGNITION REQUIREMENTS

Whenever a representative seeks to act for a taxpayer in dealing with the IRS, the representative must establish that he or she has been "duly authorized" by the taxpayer to so act. The Internal Revenue Manual guidelines[6] instruct agents that in dealing with representatives they should keep in mind that IRS personnel are prohibited from disclosing confidential tax information to unauthorized persons. They are also reminded that practice before the IRS is restricted to persons properly qualified under Circular 230. To assure that the representative has been properly authorized, the agent must seek evidence of recognition and authorization from the taxpayer[7] (see Exhibit 2-1 at ¶251, Recognition and Authorization Requirements for Persons Appearing Before the Service).

Generally, an individual may be authorized to inspect and receive tax information of a confidential nature, even though the representative does not seek to "act" on behalf of the taxpayer in any fashion beyond the receipt of such information. For example, if a representative merely wishes to know what adjustments a Revenue Agent is proposing without in any way protesting those adjustments, he or she can file a Form 8821, Tax Information Authorization (see Exhibit 2-2 at ¶252). This form authorizes *any* designated person to inspect or receive tax information of a confidential nature. A taxpayer may also authorize the IRS to discuss information about the processing of a particular return,

---

[6] IRM Handbook 4.10.1.6.10.

[7] See Exhibit 2-2 at ¶252, relating to limited authorization for return preparers authorizing the IRS to contact paid preparers relating to questions arising during the processing of a return. This limited authorization ends no later than the due date of the succeeding year's return.

including the status of a refund or a payment, with the individual listed on the "Third Party Designee" section on the Taxpayer's IRS Form 1040 (See Exhibit 2-3 ¶253; Code Sec. 6103(c)).

On the other hand, if the taxpayer's representative seeks to affirmatively "act" on behalf of the taxpayer, then further authorization of the representative is necessary. Because these acts constitute practice before the IRS, they can only be performed by a qualified person and only when evidence of authorization toperform such acts has been furnished to the IRS. The Power of Attorney, Form 2848 (see Exhibit 2-4 at ¶254), is generally used for such authorization. It must be filed if an individual wishes to represent the taxpayer before the IRS or to execute a waiver, consent or closing agreement on behalf of the taxpayer. In addition to giving the representative the right to receive confidential information, the Power of Attorney authorizes the representative to perform *any and all acts* with respect to the tax matters described in the Power of Attorney. This broad authority, however, does not include the power to receive refund checks or to sign tax returns.

Effective March 29, 2004, Form 2848, Power of Attorney and Declaration of Representative, will no longer be honored for any purpose other than for representation before the IRS. Form 2848, submitted by parties not eligible to practice under Circular 230 after March 29, will not be honored, and the third party will be advised to either submit Form 8821, or the taxpayer may grant an oral tax information authorization. If Form 2848 is not properly filled out, the form will be returned to the taxpayer, not the tax practitioner.

If the taxpayer wishes a representative to receive (but not cash or endorse) refund checks or to sign tax returns, these acts must be specifically authorized in the Power of Attorney.[8] If the signing of a tax return is authorized, the specific requirements of the regulations, Reg. §1.6012-1(a)(5), must be satisfied. In general, a representative is only permitted to sign a return if the taxpayer is unable to do so by reason of (1) disease or injury, or (2) continuous absence from the country for at least sixty days prior to the due date of the return. Specific permission to sign on behalf of a taxpayer also may be requested from the Director for other good cause.

Authorized representatives must sign and submit with their Power of Attorney a written declaration (Part II of Form 2848) stating that (1) they are not currently under suspension or disbarment from practice before the IRS or from practice of their profession, (2) they are aware of the regulations contained in Circular 230, (3) they are authorized to represent the taxpayer, and (4) they are one of the individuals recognized in Circular 230 as having the right to practice before the IRS. The eight classes of individuals having such right to practice before the IRS include attorneys, certified public accountants, enrolled agents, officers and full-time employers of the taxpayer, members of the taxpayer's immediate family, enrolled actuaries and unenrolled return preparers.

---

[8] Statement of Procedural Rules, §601.504(a)(5) and (6).

Although unenrolled return preparers have the right to practice before the IRS, the scope of their practice is limited by the provisions of Circular 230. In 2002, the modifications made by the final regulations to Circular 230 further restricted an unenrolled return preparer's right to practice before the IRS by providing that an unenrolled return preparer who prepared but is not required to sign the return is not permitted to represent the taxpayer before appeals officers, revenue officers, Counsel or similar officers or employees of the IRS or Treasury Department. The Office of the Taxpayer Advocate supports additional restrictions in order to ensure that tax practitioners are able to demonstrate a certain level of competency.[9]

The IRS will accept a Power of Attorney other than one on Form 2848, provided that such document includes all of the information required by the official form.[10] If such information is not included, the representative can cure the defect by executing a completed Form 2848 on behalf of the taxpayer and attaching it to the original power. Although the attached Form 2848 need not be signed by the taxpayer, the representative must sign the required declaration on the back of the form. A signed statement that the original power is valid under the laws of the governing jurisdiction also must be attached to the Form 2848. To be acceptable under these rules, an original power, not on Form 2848, must contemplate by its terms the authorization to handle federal tax matters. Broad language in an original power authorizing a representative to perform any and all acts would meet this requirement.

Either the original or a copy of the Power of Attorney will be accepted by the IRS. A copy of a power received by facsimile transmission (FAX) also is acceptable.[11]

A Power of Attorney is not required by a fiduciary involved in a tax matter. Instead, a fiduciary should file Form 56, Notice Concerning Fiduciary Relationship (see Exhibit 2-5 at ¶255).[12] Fiduciaries include trustees, executors, personal representatives, administrators, guardians and receivers. In addition to the Form 56, the IRS may require further verification of the fiduciary relationship.

An authorization to receive tax information or a Power of Attorney can cover a variety of taxes and a variety of tax years or periods. However, the taxpayer must clearly identify the types of taxes and the tax years or periods, as well as the tax form numbers of these taxes, on the authorization or power. A general reference to "all years," "all periods" or "all taxes" will not be accepted by the IRS.

---

[9] In its 2003 Annual Report, the Office of the Taxpayer Advocate restated a series of recommendations relating to an unenrolled preparer's right to practice before the IRS. These recommendations include requiring unenrolled preparers to register with the IRS, pass an examination, and receive certification from the IRS.

[10] Statement of Procedural Rules, §601.503(a) and (b). However, for purposes of processing into the Centralized Authorization File (CAF), a Form 2848 must be attached to the nonstandard form. The attached Form 2848 must be completed, but need not be signed by the taxpayer. §601.503(b)(2).

[11] Statement of Procedural Rules, §601.504(c)(4).

[12] Statement of Procedural Rules, §601.503(d).

The regulations specify that authorization of a person to receive confidential information must usually be written. However, under certain circumstances, an oral or implied consent for disclosure may be allowed. For example, where both the taxpayer and the representative are present at a conference, an agent may make disclosures concerning the taxpayer's return or income without receiving authorization from the taxpayer.

In most instances, the Power of Attorney will be executed by the named taxpayer. If a joint return was filed, and the representative is to act for both spouses, then both must sign the Power of Attorney. A Power of Attorney on behalf of a partnership must be executed by all partners, or if in the name of the partnership, by a duly authorized partner. If the partnership has been dissolved, the Power of Attorney must be executed by each former partner, or, for a deceased partner, by the legal representative of his or her estate. However, if state law gives surviving partners the right to wind up the affairs of the partnership upon the death of one partner, then the surviving partners can execute the Power of Attorney. A corporate Power of Attorney must be executed by an officer who has authority to bind the corporation. Where a corporation has been dissolved, the Power of Attorney must be executed by the liquidating trustee or the trustee under dissolution. If there is no such trustee, then it must be executed by the holders of the majority of the voting stock as of the date of dissolution.

Where the taxpayer is deceased, the Power of Attorney can be executed by the executor or administrator if one has been appointed by the court handling probate. The IRS may require submission of evidence of appointment. Normally, Form 56 (see Exhibit 2-5 at ¶255) is filed, along with a certified copy of the order of the court showing that the personal representative has been appointed. After an estate is closed, the Power of Attorney must usually be executed by the residuary legatee or a testamentary trustee.

The Internal Revenue Manual provides that after a Power of Attorney is received, any notice or other written communication given to a taxpayer in a matter before the IRS is also to be given to the taxpayer's recognized representative. If the taxpayer has designated more than one representative, the practice of the IRS is to give copies of notices to two of the representatives designated, and then only if the two have different mailing addresses.[13]

A qualified representative has the right to be present whenever his or her client is interviewed, interrogated or required to furnish information to the IRS. In most instances, this will mean that arrangements for direct examination or investigation of the taxpayer are conducted through the representative. Under certain circumstances, the IRS may bypass the taxpayer's representative, even though a valid Power of Attorney is on file.[14] Generally, the taxpayer will be contacted directly only when a representative has unreasonably delayed or hindered an examination by failing, after repeated requests, to furnish information for which there is no privilege. In such a situation, the examiner can report

---

[13] IRM Handbook 12(16)0, Section 550.   [14] Statement of Procedural Rules, § 601.506(b).

the situation to the Division Chief[15] and request permission to contact the taxpayer directly for such information. If such permission is granted, the case file will be documented to show how the examination was being delayed or hindered, and written notice of such permission will be given to the representative and to the taxpayer.[16]

Where permission to bypass the representative has been granted, it does not constitute suspension or disbarment of the representative. That representative may continue to represent the client upon making an appearance before the IRS for that purpose. The representative also will be afforded the courtesy of being advised regarding all future appointments with the taxpayer. Of course, in aggravated situations, the delay or hindrance of the examination may be referred to the Director of Practice for possible disciplinary proceedings.

When a Power of Attorney is received, the IRS assigns a central authorization file (CAF) number to each taxpayer representative.[17] The nine-digit CAF number identifies each representative and the scope of his or her authority. The automated CAF system expedites the mailing of refunds, notices and other correspondence by automatically directing them to authorized representatives.[18]

---

[15] IRM Handbook 12(16)0,621. This manual section has not been updated to reflect the new organizational titles; it is assumed approval at the level of territory manager will be required.

[16] The IRS has held that evidence received from a taxpayer after the representative was bypassed is still admissible evidence and need not be suppressed. See IRS Ltr. Rul. 8206011 (May 29, 1981).

[17] Statement of Procedural Rules, § 601.506(d).

[18] Announcement 82-147, IRB 1982-47, 54.

¶251 Exhibit 2-1

Recognition and Authorization Requirements for Persons Appearing Before the Service

This chart summarizes how these new forms may be used by different types of practitioners depending upon the capacity in which they appear.

Capacity of Person Appearing	Attorneys and CPAs	Enrolled Agents	Unenrolled Persons who are not Attorneys or CPAs		All Others
			Qualified for Limited Practice Under Sec. 10.7 or Cir. 230		
			Return Preparers	Others	
1. As an advocate who is to perform certain acts for taxpayer as prescribed in 26 CFR 601.504(a) (Constitutes "Practice" as defined in Cir. 230).	P/A and D Exception (2) may apply	P/A and D	P/A and D Exception (3) applies	P/A and D Exception (2) may apply	Ineligible
2. As a witness who may receive or inspect confidential tax information (Does not include "Practice" as defined in Cir. 230).	TIA Exception (1) or (2) may apply	TIA	TIA	TIA Exception (2) may apply	TIA
3. As a witness for taxpayer to present his books, records or returns to the examining officer (Does not include "Practice" as defined in Cir. 230).	No Requirements	No Requirements	No Requirements	No Requirements	No Requirements

Code for Requirements

P/A Must present or have a Power of Attorney on file.

TIA Must present or have a Tax Information Authorization or Power of Attorney on file if the taxpayer is not also present.

D Must present or have declaration on file.

Exceptions

(1) Any attorney who prepared the estate tax return and is attorney of record . . . but must have a declaration on file.

(2) A trustee, receiver or attorney may substitute a proper court certificate in lieu of a P/A or TIA.

(3) Unenrolled return preparers are limited to representation during the examination process.

¶252 Exhibit 2-2

Form **8821**		**Tax Information Authorization**	OMB No. 1545-1165

Form **8821**

(Rev. April 2004)
Department of the Treasury
Internal Revenue Service

Tax Information Authorization

▶ Do not use this form to request a copy or transcript of your tax return.
Instead, use Form 4506 or Form 4506-T.

OMB No. 1545-1165

For IRS Use Only

Received by:

Name _____

Telephone (____) _____

Function _____

Date ____/____/____

---

1   Taxpayer information. Taxpayer(s) must sign and date this form on line 7.

Taxpayer name(s) and address (type or print)

Social security number(s)

Employer identification number

Daytime telephone number

(   )

Plan number (if applicable)

---

2   Appointee. If you wish to name more than one appointee, attach a list to this form.

Name and address

CAF No. ....
Telephone No. ....
Fax No. ....
Check if new: Address ☐   Telephone No. ☐   Fax No. ☐

3 Tax matters. The appointee is authorized to inspect and/or receive confidential tax information in any office of the IRS for the tax matters listed on this line. Do not use Form 8821 to request copies of tax returns.

(a) Type of Tax (Income, Employment, Excise, etc.) or Civil Penalty	(b) Tax Form Number (1040, 941, 720, etc.)	(c) Year(s) or Period(s) (see the instructions for line 3)	(d) Specific Tax Matters (see instr.)

4 Specific use not recorded on Centralized Authorization File (CAF). If the tax information authorization is for a specific use not recorded on CAF, check this box. See the instructions on page 3. If you check this box, skip lines 5 and 6 . ▶ ☐

5 Disclosure of tax information (you **must** check a box on line 5a or 5b unless the box on line 4 is checked):

a If you want copies of tax information, notices, and other written communications sent to the appointee on an ongoing basis, check this box . . . . ▶ ☐

b If you do not want any copies of notices or communications sent to your appointee, check this box . . . . . . ▶ ☐

6 Retention/revocation of tax information authorizations. This tax information authorization automatically revokes all prior authorizations for the same tax matters you listed on line 3 above unless you checked the box on line 4. If you do not want to revoke a prior tax information authorization, you **must** attach a copy of any authorizations you want to remain in effect **and** check this box . . . . ▶ ☐

To revoke this tax information authorization, see the instructions on page 3.

7 Signature of taxpayer(s). If a tax matter applies to a joint return, **either** husband or wife must sign. If signed by a corporate officer, partner, guardian, executor, receiver, administrator, trustee, or party other than the taxpayer, I certify that I have the authority to execute this form with respect to the tax matters/periods on line 3 above.

▶ **IF NOT SIGNED AND DATED, THIS TAX INFORMATION AUTHORIZATION WILL BE RETURNED.**

Signature	Date	Signature	Date

Signature   Date

Signature   Date

Print Name   Title (if applicable)

☐ ☐ ☐ ☐ ☐   PIN number for electronic signature

Print Name   Title (if applicable)

☐ ☐ ☐ ☐ ☐   PIN number for electronic signature

For Privacy Act and Paperwork Reduction Act Notice, see page 4.   Cat. No. 11596P   Form **8821** (Rev. 4-2004)

General Instructions

Section references are to the Internal Revenue Code unless otherwise noted.

What's New

Authorization to file Form 8821 electronically. Your appointee may be able to file Form 8821 with the IRS electronically. PIN number boxes have been added to the taxpayer's signature section. Entering a PIN number will give your appointee authority to file Form 8821 electronically using the PIN number as the electronic signature. You can use any five digits other than all zeroes as a PIN number. You may use the same PIN number that you used on other filings with the IRS. See **Where To File** on page 3 if completing Form 8821 only for this purpose.

Purpose of Form

Form 8821 authorizes any individual, corporation, firm, organization, or partnership you designate to inspect and/or receive your confidential information in any office of the IRS for the type of tax and the years or periods you list on Form 8821. You may file your own tax information authorization without using Form 8821, but it must include all the information that is requested on Form 8821.

Form 8821 does not authorize your appointee to advocate your position with respect to the Federal tax laws; to execute waivers, consents, or closing agreements; or to otherwise represent you before the IRS. If you want to authorize an individual to represent you, use Form 2848, Power of Attorney and Declaration of Representative.

Use Form 4506, Request for Copy of Tax Return, to get a copy of your tax return.

Use new Form 4506-T, Request for Transcript of Tax Return, to order: (a) transcript of tax account information and (b) Form W-2 and Form 1099 series information.

Use Form 56, Notice Concerning Fiduciary Relationship, to notify the IRS of the existence of a fiduciary relationship. A fiduciary (trustee, executor, administrator, receiver, or guardian) stands in the position of a taxpayer and acts as the taxpayer. Therefore, a fiduciary does not act as an appointee and should not file Form 8821. If a fiduciary wishes to authorize an appointee to inspect and/or receive confidential tax information on behalf of the fiduciary, Form 8821 must be filed and signed by the fiduciary acting in the position of the taxpayer.

When To File

Form 8821 must be received by the IRS within 60 days of the date it was signed and dated by the taxpayer.

Where To File Chart

IF you live in . . .	THEN use this address . . .	Fax Number*
Alabama, Arkansas, Connecticut, Delaware, District of Columbia, Florida, Georgia, Illinois, Indiana, Kentucky, Louisiana, Maine, Maryland, Massachusetts, Michigan, Mississippi, New Hampshire, New Jersey, New York, North Carolina, Ohio, Pennsylvania, Rhode Island, South Carolina, Tennessee, Vermont, Virginia, or West Virginia	Internal Revenue Service Memphis Accounts Management Center Stop 8423 5333 Getwell Road Memphis, TN 38118	901-546-4115
Alaska, Arizona, California, Colorado, Hawaii, Idaho, Iowa, Kansas, Minnesota, Missouri, Montana, Nebraska, Nevada, New Mexico, North Dakota, Oklahoma, Oregon, South Dakota, Texas, Utah, Washington, Wisconsin, or Wyoming	Internal Revenue Service Ogden Accounts Management Center 1973 N. Rulon White Blvd. Mail Stop 6737 Ogden, UT 84404	801-620-4249
All APO and FPO addresses, American Samoa, nonpermanent residents of Guam or the Virgin Islands**, Puerto Rico (or if excluding income under Internal Revenue Code section 933), a foreign country: U.S. citizens and those filing Form 2555, 2555-EZ, or 4563.	Internal Revenue Service Philadelphia Accounts Management Center DPSW 312 11601 Roosevelt Blvd. Philadelphia, PA 19255	215-516-1017

*These numbers may change without notice.

**Permanent residents of Guam should use Department of Taxation, Government of Guam, P.O. Box 23607, GMF, GU 96921; permanent residents of the Virgin Islands should use: V.I. Bureau of Internal Revenue, 9601 Estate Thomas Charlotte Amaile, St. Thomas, V.I. 00802.

¶253   Exhibit 2-3

Excerpts from Form 1040—Check the Box

Third Party Designee	Do you want to allow another person to discuss this return with the IRS (see page 58)? ☐ **Yes.** Complete the following. ☐ **No**

	Designee's name ▶	Phone no. ▶ ( )	Personal identification number (PIN) ▶	☐☐☐☐☐

Sign Here	Under penalties of perjury, I declare that I have examined this return and accompanying schedules and statements, and to the best of my knowledge and belief, they are true, correct, and complete. Declaration of preparer (other than taxpayer) is based on all information of which preparer has any knowledge.
Joint return? See page 20.	Your signature Date Your occupation Daytime phone number ( )
Keep a copy for your records.	Spouse's signature. If a joint return, **both** must sign. Date Spouse's occupation

Paid Preparer's Use Only	Preparer's signature ▶	Date Check if self-employed ☐	Preparer's SSN or PTIN
	Firm's name (or yours if self-employed), address, and ZIP code ▶	EIN Phone no. ( )	

Form **1040** (2003)

Third Party Designee

If you want to allow a friend, family member, or any other person you choose to discuss your 2003 tax return with the IRS, check the "Yes" box in the "Third Party Designee" area of your return. Also, enter the designee's name, phone number, and any five numbers the designee chooses as his or her personal identification number (PIN). **But** if you want to allow the paid preparer who signed your return to discuss it with the IRS, just enter "Preparer" in the space for the designee's name. You do not have to provide the other information requested.

If you check the "Yes" box, you, and your spouse if filing a joint return, are authorizing the IRS to call the designee to answer any questions that may arise during the processing of your return. You are also authorizing the designee to:

• Give the IRS any information that is missing from your return,

• Call the IRS for information about the processing of your return or the status of your refund or payment(s),

• Receive copies of notices or transcripts related to your return, upon request, and

• Respond to certain IRS notices about math errors, offsets, and return preparation.

You are not authorizing the designee to receive any refund check, bind you to anything (including any additional tax liability), or otherwise represent you before the IRS. If you want to expand the designee's authorization, see **Pub. 947.**

The authorization will automatically end no later than the due date (without regard to extensions) for filing your 2004 tax return. This is April 15, 2005, for most people. If you wish to revoke the authorization before it ends, see Pub. 947.

¶254 Exhibit 2-4

Form **2848**	**Power of Attorney**	OMB No. 1545-0150
(Rev. March 2004) Department of the Treasury Internal Revenue Service	**and Declaration of Representative** ▶ Type or print. ▶ See the separate instructions.	**For IRS Use Only** Received by: Name Telephone Function Date / /

Part I **Power of Attorney**
Caution: *Form 2848 will not be honored for any purpose other than representation before the IRS.*

1 **Taxpayer information.** Taxpayer(s) must sign and date this form on page 2, line 9.

Taxpayer name(s) and address	Social security number(s)	Employer identification number
	Daytime telephone number ( )	Plan number (if applicable)

hereby appoint(s) the following representative(s) as attorney(s)-in-fact:

2 **Representative(s)** must sign and date this form on page 2, Part II.

Name and address	CAF No. .... Telephone No. .... Fax No. .... Check if new: Address ☐ Telephone No. ☐ Fax No. ☐
Name and address	CAF No. .... Telephone No. .... Fax No. .... Check if new: Address ☐ Telephone No. ☐ Fax No. ☐
Name and address	CAF No. .... Telephone No. .... Fax No. .... Check if new: Address ☐ Telephone No. ☐ Fax No. ☐

to represent the taxpayer(s) before the Internal Revenue Service for the following tax matters:

3 **Tax matters**

Type of Tax (Income, Employment, Excise, etc.) or Civil Penalty (see the instructions for line 3)	Tax Form Number (1040, 941, 720, etc.)	Year(s) or Period(s) (see the instructions for line 3)

4 **Specific use not recorded on Centralized Authorization File (CAF).** If the power of attorney is for a specific use not recorded on CAF, check this box. See the instructions for **Line 4. Specific uses not recorded on CAF.** . . . . ▶ ☐

5 **Acts authorized.** The representatives are authorized to receive and inspect confidential tax information and to perform any and all acts that I (we) can perform with respect to the tax matters described on line 3, for example, the authority to sign any agreements, consents, or other documents. The authority does not include the power to receive refund checks (see line 6 below), the power to substitute another representative, the power to sign certain returns, or the power to execute a request for disclosure of tax returns or return information to a third party. See the line 5 instructions for more information.

Exceptions. An unenrolled return preparer cannot sign any document for a taxpayer and may only represent taxpayers in limited situations. See **Unenrolled Return Preparer** on page 2 of the instructions. An enrolled actuary may only represent taxpayers to the extent provided in section 10.3(d) of Circular 230. See the line 5 instructions for restrictions on tax matters partners.

List any specific additions or deletions to the acts otherwise authorized in this power of attorney: ....
....
....
....

6 **Receipt of refund checks.** If you want to authorize a representative named on line 2 to receive, **BUT NOT TO ENDORSE OR CASH**, refund checks, initial here _____ and list the name of that representative below.

Name of representative to receive refund check(s) ▶

For Privacy Act and Paperwork Reduction Notice, see page 4 of the instructions.   Cat. No. 11980J   Form **2848** (Rev. 3-2004)

7   **Notices and communications.** Original notices and other written communications will be sent to you and a copy to the first representative listed on line 2.

a   If you also want the second representative listed to receive a copy of notices and communications, check this box   .   . ▶ ☐

b   If you do not want any notices or communications sent to your representative(s), check this box   .   .   .   . ▶ ☐

8   **Retention/revocation of prior power(s) of attorney.** The filing of this power of attorney automatically revokes all earlier power(s) of attorney on file with the Internal Revenue Service for the same tax matters and years or periods covered by this document. If you **do not** want to revoke a prior power of attorney, check here.   .   .   .   . ▶ ☐
YOU MUST ATTACH A COPY OF ANY POWER OF ATTORNEY YOU WANT TO REMAIN IN EFFECT.

9   **Signature of taxpayer(s).** If a tax matter concerns a joint return, **both** husband and wife must sign if joint representation is requested, otherwise, see the instructions. If signed by a corporate officer, partner, guardian, tax matters partner, executor, receiver, administrator, or trustee on behalf of the taxpayer, I certify that I have the authority to execute this form on behalf of the taxpayer.

▶ **IF NOT SIGNED AND DATED, THIS POWER OF ATTORNEY WILL BE RETURNED.**

Signature	Date	Title (if applicable)
Print Name	PIN Number	Print name of taxpayer from line 1 if other than individual
Signature	Date	Title (if applicable)
Print Name	PIN Number	

Part II   **Declaration of Representative**

Caution: *Students with a special order to represent taxpayers in Qualified Low Income Taxpayer Clinics or the Student Tax Clinic Program, see the instructions for Part II.*

Under penalties of perjury, I declare that:

- I am not currently under suspension or disbarment from practice before the Internal Revenue Service;
- I am aware of regulations contained in Treasury Department Circular No. 230 (31 CFR, Part 10), as amended, concerning the practice of attorneys, certified public accountants, enrolled agents, enrolled actuaries, and others;
- I am authorized to represent the taxpayer(s) identified in Part I for the tax matter(s) specified there; and
- I am one of the following:

    a   Attorney—a member in good standing of the bar of the highest court of the jurisdiction shown below.

    b   Certified Public Accountant—duly qualified to practice as a certified public accountant in the jurisdiction shown below.

    c   Enrolled Agent—enrolled as an agent under the requirements of Treasury Department Circular No. 230.

    d   Officer—a bona fide officer of the taxpayer's organization.

    e   Full-Time Employee—a full-time employee of the taxpayer.

    f   Family Member—a member of the taxpayer's immediate family (i.e., spouse, parent, child, brother, or sister).

    g   Enrolled Actuary—enrolled as an actuary by the Joint Board for the Enrollment of Actuaries under 29 U.S.C. 1242 (the authority to practice before the Service is limited by section 10.3(d) of Treasury Department Circular No. 230).

    h   Unenrolled Return Preparer—the authority to practice before the Internal Revenue Service is limited by Treasury Department Circular No. 230, section 10.7(c)(1)(viii). You must have prepared the return in question and the return must be under examination by the IRS. See **Unenrolled Return Preparer** on page 2 of the instructions.

▶ **IF THIS DECLARATION OF REPRESENTATIVE IS NOT SIGNED AND DATED, THE POWER OF ATTORNEY WILL BE RETURNED.** See the Part II instructions.

Designation—Insert above letter **(a–h)**	Jurisdiction (state) or identification	Signature	Date

Form **2848** (Rev. 3-2004)

¶255 Exhibit 2-5

Form **56**		
(Rev. April 2002)	**Notice Concerning Fiduciary Relationship**	OMB No. 1545-0013
Department of the Treasury Internal Revenue Service	(Internal Revenue Code sections 6036 and 6903)	

Part I Identification

Name of person for whom you are acting (as shown on the tax return)	Identifying number	Decedent's social security no.

Address of person for whom you are acting (number, street, and room or suite no.)

City or town, state, and ZIP code (If a foreign address, see instructions.)

Fiduciary's name

Address of fiduciary (number, street, and room or suite no.)

City or town, state, and ZIP code	Telephone number (optional) ( )

Part II Authority

1 Authority for fiduciary relationship. Check applicable box:

a(1) ☐ Will and codicils or court order appointing fiduciary . . . . (2) Date of death ....

b(1) ☐ Court order appointing fiduciary . . . . (2) Date (see instructions) ....

c ☐ Valid trust instrument and amendments

d ☐ Other. Describe ▶ ....

Part III Tax Notices

Send to the fiduciary listed in Part I all notices and other written communications involving the following tax matters:

2 Type of tax (estate, gift, generation-skipping transfer, income, excise, etc.) ▶ ....

3 Federal tax form number (706, 1040, 1041, 1120, etc.) ▶ ....

4 Year(s) or period(s) (if estate tax, date of death) ▶ ....

Part IV Revocation or Termination of Notice

Section A—Total Revocation or Termination

5 Check this box if you are revoking or terminating all prior notices concerning fiduciary relationships on file with the Internal Revenue Service for the same tax matters and years or periods covered by this notice concerning fiduciary relationship . ▶ ☐

Reason for termination of fiduciary relationship. Check applicable box:

a ☐ Court order revoking fiduciary authority

b ☐ Certificate of dissolution or termination of a business entity

c ☐ Other. Describe ▶

Section B—Partial Revocation

6a Check this box if you are revoking earlier notices concerning fiduciary relationships on file with the Internal Revenue Service for the same tax matters and years or periods covered by this notice concerning fiduciary relationship . . . . ▶ ☐

b Specify to whom granted, date, and address, including ZIP code.

▶ ....

Section C—Substitute Fiduciary

7 Check this box if a new fiduciary or fiduciaries have been or will be substituted for the revoking or terminating fiduciary(ies) and specify the name(s) and address(es), including ZIP code(s), of the new fiduciary(ies) . . . . ▶ ☐

Part V Court and Administrative Proceedings

Name of court (if other than a court proceeding, identify the type of proceeding and name of agency)	Date proceeding initiated
Address of court	Docket number of proceeding

City or town, state, and ZIP code	Date	Time	a.m. p.m.	Place of other proceedings

I certify that I have the authority to execute this notice concerning fiduciary relationship on behalf of the taxpayer.

Please Sign Here	Fiduciary's signature	Title, if applicable	Date
	Fiduciary's signature	Title, if applicable	Date

For Paperwork Reduction Act and Privacy Act Notice, see back page.   Cat. No. 16375I   Form **56** (Rev. 4-2002)

General Instructions

Section references are to the Internal Revenue Code unless otherwise noted.

Purpose of Form

You may use Form 56 to notify the IRS of the creation or termination of a fiduciary relationship under section 6903 and to give notice of qualification under section 6036.

Who Should File

The fiduciary (see **Definitions** below) uses Form 56 to notify the IRS of the creation, or termination, of a fiduciary relationship under section 6903. For example, if you are acting as fiduciary for an individual, a decedent's estate, or a trust, you may file Form 56. If notification is not given to the IRS, notices sent to the last known address of the taxable entity, transferee, or other person subject to tax liability are sufficient to satisfy the requirements of the Internal Revenue Code.

Receivers and assignees for the benefit of creditors also file Form 56 to give notice of qualification under section 6036. However, a bankruptcy trustee, debtor in possession, or other like fiduciary in a bankruptcy proceeding is not required to give notice of qualification under section 6036. Trustees, etc., in bankruptcy proceedings are subject to the notice requirements under title 11 of the United States Code (Bankruptcy Rules).

Definitions

Fiduciary. A fiduciary is any person acting in a fiduciary capacity for any other person (or terminating entity), such as an administrator, conservator, designee, executor, guardian, receiver, trustee of a trust, trustee in bankruptcy, personal representative, person in possession of property of a decedent's estate, or debtor in possession of assets in any bankruptcy proceeding by order of the court.

Person. A person is any individual, trust, estate, partnership, association, company or corporation.

Decedent's estate. A decedent's estate is a taxable entity separate from the decedent that comes into existence at the time of the decedent's death. It generally continues to exist until the final distribution of the assets of the estate is made to the heirs and other beneficiaries.

Terminating entities. A terminating entity, such as a corporation, partnership, trust, etc., only has the legal capacity to establish a fiduciary relationship while it is in existence. Establishing a fiduciary relationship prior to termination of the entity allows the fiduciary to represent the entity on all tax matters after it is terminated.

When and Where To File

Notice of fiduciary relationship. Generally, you should file Form 56 when you create (or terminate) a fiduciary relationship. To receive tax notices upon creation of a fiduciary relationship, file Form 56 with the Internal Revenue Service Center where the person for whom you are acting is required to file tax returns. If you wish to receive tax notices for more than one form and one of the forms is Form 1040, file Form 56 with the Internal Revenue Service Center where the person for whom you are acting is required to file Form 1040.

Proceedings (other than bankruptcy) and assignments for the benefit of creditors. A fiduciary who is appointed or authorized to act as:

- A receiver in a receivership proceeding or similar fiduciary (including a fiduciary in aid of foreclosure), or

- An assignee for the benefit of creditors, must file Form 56 on, or within 10 days of, the date of appointment with the Chief, Special Procedures Staff, of the area office of the IRS having jurisdiction over the person for whom you are acting.

The receiver or assignee may also file a separate Form 56 with the service center where the person for whom the fiduciary is acting is required to file tax returns to provide the notice required by section 6903.

Specific Instructions

Part I—Identification

Provide all the information called for in this part.

Identifying number. If you are acting for an individual, an individual debtor, or other person whose assets are controlled, the identifying number is the social security number (SSN). If you are acting for a person other than an individual, including an estate or trust, the identifying number is the employer identification number (EIN).

Decedent's SSN. If you are acting on behalf of a decedent, enter the decedent's SSN shown on his or her final Form 1040 in the space provided.

Address. Include the suite, room, or other unit number after the street address.

If the postal service does not deliver mail to the street address and the fiduciary (or person) has a P.O. box, show the box number instead of the street address.

For a foreign address, enter the information in the following order: city, province or state, and country. Follow the country's practice for entering the postal code. Please **do not** abbreviate the country name.

Part II—Authority

Line 1a. Check the box on line 1a if the decedent died **testate** (i.e., having left a valid will) and enter the decedent's date of death.

Line 1b. Check the box on line 1b if the decedent died **intestate** (i.e., without leaving a valid will). Also, enter the decedent's date of death and write "Date of Death" next to the date.

Assignment for the benefit of creditors. Enter the date the assets were assigned to you and write "Assignment Date" after the date.

Proceedings other than bankruptcy. Enter the date you were appointed or took possession of the assets of the debtor or other person whose assets are controlled.

Caution: You must be prepared to furnish evidence that substantiates your authority to act as a fiduciary for the person for whom you are acting.

Part III—Tax Notices

Complete this part if you want the IRS to send you tax notices regarding the person for whom you are acting.

Line 2. Specify the type of tax involved. This line should also identify a transferee tax liability under section 6901 or fiduciary tax liability under 31 U.S.C. 3713(b) when either exists.

Part IV—Revocation or Termination of Notice

Complete this part only if you are revoking or terminating a prior notice concerning a fiduciary relationship. Completing this part will relieve you of any further duty or liability as a fiduciary if used as a notice of termination.

Part V—Court and Administrative Proceedings

Complete this part only if you have been appointed a receiver, trustee, or fiduciary by a court or other governmental unit in a proceeding other than a bankruptcy proceeding.

If proceedings are scheduled for more than one date, time, or place, attach a separate schedule of the proceedings.

Assignment for the benefit of creditors. You must attach the following information:

1. A brief description of the assets that were assigned and

2. An explanation of the action to be taken regarding such assets, including any hearings, meetings of creditors, sale, or other scheduled action.

Signature

Sign Form 56 and enter a title describing your role as a fiduciary (e.g., assignee, executor, guardian, trustee, personal representative, receiver, or conservator).

Paperwork Reduction Act and Privacy Act Notice. We ask for the information on this form to carry out the Internal Revenue laws of the United States. Form 56 is provided for your convenience and its use is voluntary. Under section 6109 you must disclose the social security number or employer identification number of the individual or entity for which you are acting. The principal purpose of this disclosure is to secure proper identification of the taxpayer. We also need this information to gain access to the tax information in our files and properly respond to your request. If you do not disclose this information, we may suspend processing the notice of fiduciary relationship and not consider this as proper notification until you provide the information.

You are not required to provide the information requested on a form that is subject to the Paperwork Reduction Act unless the form displays a valid OMB control number. Books or records relating to a form or its instructions must be retained as long as their contents may become material in the administration of any Internal Revenue law. Generally, tax returns and return information are confidential as required by section 6103.

The time needed to complete and file this form will vary depending on individual circumstances. The estimated average time is:

Recordkeeping	8 min.
Learning about the law or the form	32 min.
Preparing the form	46 min.
Copying, assembling, and sending the form to the IRS . .	15 min.

If you have comments concerning the accuracy of these time estimates or suggestions for making this form simpler, we would be happy to hear from you. You can write to the Tax Forms Committee, Western Area Distribution Center, Rancho Cordova, CA 95743-0001. **Do not** send Form 56 to this address. Instead, see **When and Where To File** on this page.

¶257 DISCUSSION QUESTIONS

1. You prepared Henry Helpless' tax return for 2003 and Helpless has been called in by a Revenue Agent. He asks you to attend the meeting.

   (A) Assume that you are Friendly Frank, Helpless' neighbor, who has prepared the return *without compensation*. What document(s), if any, must you file with the IRS *to accompany the taxpayer* and act in the capacities described below?

      (1) To receive or inspect confidential tax information.

      (2) To act as an advocate on behalf of Helpless and perform acts as described in Reg. § 601.504(a).

   (B) Assume the same facts in (A), except that Helpless *is not present* at the meeting. What document(s), if any, must you file in the following capacities:

      (1) To receive or inspect confidential tax information.

      (2) To act as an advocate on behalf of Helpless and perform acts as described in Reg. § 601.504(a).

   (C) Assume that Henry Helpless compensates you for preparing his return. Would your answers to the questions in (A) and (B), above, differ? Why?

2. Assume that you *did not* prepare Henry Helpless' return in Question 1 but that Helpless still wants you to represent him at the audit. What do you need to file in the following situations?

   (A) You are Helpless' representative and he is present at the meeting.

   (B) You are Helpless' representative and he is not present at the meeting.

   (C) You are Helpless' representative and he is not present and the Agent has indicated that he wishes to have the statute of limitations on assessment extended.

3. Your employer, Seville, Inc., is being audited by the IRS. You are assigned to coordinate the responses given to the IRS and to handle any negotiations with them. Assuming you have been granted carte blanche corporate authority, what acts can you perform and what decisions can you make if your status is:

   (A) Bookkeeper for Seville, Inc.?

   (B) Internal auditor for Seville, Inc., and a graduate of High Standards University with a Masters in Taxation?

   (C) Comptroller of Seville, Inc., and a Certified Public Accountant?

   (D) Corporate Counsel for Seville, Inc., and an attorney with a Masters of Law in Taxation?

4. Tammy Terrified received a notice from the IRS Center demanding payment in full of $50,000 of additional tax, $10,000 in penalties and $5,000 in statutory interest. The computerized statement sets out in bold,

¶257

capital letters "Final Notice—Payment Due Within Ten (10) Days." Tammy Terrified looks in the Yellow Pages and finds that representation in tax matters seems to be touted by a number of different professions. She seeks your help in deciding which ones she could call for her problem. Terrified tells you that she does owe the tax, penalties and interest, but that she and her nine children have been abandoned, left penniless and are on welfare.

The phone book has the following listings:

ACCOUNTANT—noncertified—enrolled to practice before the IRS.

ACCOUNTANT—Certified Public—licensed to practice in this state.

ATTORNEY—licensed to practice in this state—divorce, real estate, tax, personal injury and Workers' Compensation cases accepted.

BOOKKEEPING SERVICE—accounting and bookkeeping service, general ledger, profit and loss and financial statements, and tax return preparation.

CONSULTANT—tax and related matters, mergers, acquisitions and business closings—MBA and MS in Taxation, High Standards University.

TAXMAN—preparation of Forms 1040EZ, 1040A, 1040, 1040X, 1120, 1120S, 940, 941 and other federal tax forms—inexpensive but good—We talk tax!

(A) Explain in detail which one(s) Tammy Terrified could call, and explain the powers and authority of each representative.

(B) Explain in detail the reason for rejecting any individual, including lack of authority.

(C) If Tammy Terrified asks you to make a single choice, which one would you choose and why?

5. Oscar Obnoxious is a CPA and an ardent champion of taxpayers' rights. He specializes in representing taxpayers in audits and boasts that he has been extremely successful either in resolving audits with little or no tax due or in delaying them so long that the IRS finally gives up. Oscar's aggressive television advertising has resulted in his having many clients whose cases need his attention.

In 2003, on four separate occasions, the IRS has not been able to get information from Oscar in a timely fashion and it has resorted to contacting his clients directly, following the bypass procedure described in IRM 5.1.1.7.6. In two instances the IRS found Oscar had never contacted the taxpayer to get the information; in the other two, the taxpayers had given Oscar the information several months before.

Oscar is concerned that the IRS's use of the bypass procedure will hamper his ability to effectively resolve his clients' situations and will eventually destroy his practice. He wishes to sue the IRS for an injunction against their using the bypass procedure and also for damages for impairing his contracts with his clients and for violations of his constitutional rights. He wants to know his chances in this litigation.

CHAPTER 3
ETHICAL RESPONSIBILITIES

Prohibitions and Duties Regarding Practice

¶301 CODE OF CONDUCT

Subpart B of Circular 230[1] sets forth a code of conduct which representatives must follow in representing taxpayers. Subpart C[2] contains the procedural rules for disciplinary proceedings when the Treasury Department seeks to suspend or disbar an attorney, certified public accountant, enrolled agent or enrolled actuary from practice before the Internal Revenue Service (IRS).

¶302 PRACTITIONER'S DUTIES TO CORRECT ERRORS

Historically, one of the most ambiguous areas concerning the ethical duties of a tax preparer was the problem created by the preparer's knowledge that a client had underpaid a tax liability either in the current year or in prior years. Section 10.21 of Circular 230, as modified by the 2002 final regulations, helps clarify this ambiguity by requiring that a practitioner not only advise a client promptly of any noncompliance with the revenue law, but also inform the client about the possible consequences for failing to take corrective action.

The American Bar Association (ABA) and the American Institute of Certified Public Accountants (AICPA) periodically issue statements describing the ethical responsibilities of their respective members in these areas. The ABA Standards of Tax Practice Statement 2000-1 (see Exhibit 3-1 at ¶351) addresses the ethical issues resulting from the difference between the income tax return accuracy standards for taxpayers and their lawyers. The AICPA issues Statements on Standards for Tax Services.[3] Statement No. 6, issued August 2000, addresses a CPA's knowledge of error in cases of failure to file or errors in previously filed returns, while Statement No. 7 discusses appropriate action where the error is discovered in a return that is the subject of an administrative (noncriminal) proceeding.

Conversely, occasions arise where there are computational errors in favor of the taxpayer in IRS settlements and/or court cases. These mistakes could cause a reduced deficiency or an erroneous refund if not corrected. The ABA has issued ethical guidance to its practitioner members in these situations in Standards of Tax Practice Statement 1999-1 (see Exhibit 3-2 at ¶352).

---

[1] 31 CFR §§10.20–10.34.
[2] *Id.* §§10.50–10.76

[3] See http://www.aicpa.org/download/tax/SSTSfinal.pdf.

¶303   DENIAL OF RIGHT TO PRACTICE BEFORE THE INTERNAL REVENUE SERVICE

The disciplinary proceedings under Subpart C of Circular 230 are conducted by the Office of Professional Responsibility.[4] The only effective sanction that the Director of Professional Responsibility can impose is the suspension or disbarment of a person who is entitled to practice before the IRS. For many professionals their ability to represent taxpayers before the IRS constitutes a substantial portion of their practice. Denial of the right to practice would not only have a significant economic effect on them but would also result in their loss of professional standing and esteem.

Section 10.51 of Circular 230 lists specific instances of incompetence and disreputable conduct which may be grounds for disbarment from practice before the IRS. The list contained in Section 10.51 does not purport to be exhaustive and should be read in conjunction with the grounds set forth in Section 10.52. That section provides for censure, suspension or disbarment from practice for willful violation of any of the regulations contained in Circular 230 or for recklessness through gross incompetence violating Sections 10.33[5] or 10.34, relating to the standards for advising with respect to tax return positions and for preparing and signing returns.

¶304   CIRCULAR 230, SUBPARTS B AND C

Set forth below is the current text of the relevant portions of Subpart B and Subpart C of Circulare 230, Rules of Practice Before the IRS. The changes made to Circular 230 by the 2002 final regulations are discussed in ¶305, and the 2004 proposed amendments to Circular 230 are discussed in ¶306.

PART 10—PRACTICE BEFORE THE INTERNAL REVENUE SERVICE

* * * * *

Subpart B—Duties and Restrictions Relating to Practice Before the Internal Revenue Service

---

[4] As part of its ongoing modernization effort, the IRS created a new office, the Office of Professional Responsibility. This office replaces the Office of the Director of Practice. With twice the staff of the Office of the Director of Practice, the Office of Professional Responsibility will continue to enforce the standards of practice of those tax professionals who represent taxpayers and hopes to further its commitment to ensuring the integrity of the system. IR-2003-3 (1/8/2003).

[5] The final regulations reserve Section 10.33 of Circular 230 for provisions relating to tax shelter opinions. The Addendum to the final regulations sets forth the text of Section 10.33, as it read prior to adoption of the final regulations.

§ 10.20. Information to be furnished. (a) *To the Internal Revenue Service.* (1) A practitioner must, on a proper and lawful request by a duly authorized officer or employee of the Internal Revenue Service, promptly submit records or information in any matter before the Internal Revenue Service unless the practitioner believes in good faith and on reasonable grounds that the records or information are privileged.

(2) Where the requested records or information are not in the possession of, or subject to the control of, the practitioner or the practitioner's client, the practitioner must promptly notify the requesting Internal Revenue Service officer or employee and the practitioner must provide any information that the practitioner has regarding the identity of any person who the practitioner believes may have possession or control of the requested records or information. The practitioner must make reasonable inquiry of his or her client regarding the identity of any person who may have possession or control of the requested records or information, but the practitioner is not required to make inquiry of any other person or independently verify any information provided by the practitioner's client regarding the identity of such persons.

(b) *To the Director of Practice.* When a proper and lawful request is made by the Director of Practice, a practitioner must provide the Director of Practice with any information the practitioner has concerning an inquiry by the Director of Practice into an alleged violation of the regulations in this part by any person, and to testify regarding this information in any proceeding instituted under this part, un-less the practitioner believes in good faith and on reasonable grounds that the information is privileged.

(c) *Interference with a proper and lawful request for records or information.* A practitioner may not interfere, or attempt to interfere, with any proper and lawful effort by the Internal Revenue Service, its officers or employees, or the Director of Practice, or his or her employees, to obtain any record or information unless the practitioner believes in good faith and on reasonable grounds that the record or information is privileged.

§ 10.21. Knowledge of client's omission. A practitioner who, having been retained by a client with respect to a matter administered by the Internal Revenue Service, knows that the client has not complied with the revenue laws of the United States or has made an error in or omission from any return, document, affidavit, or other paper which the client submitted or executed under the revenue laws of the United States, must advise the client promptly of the fact of such noncompliance, error, or omission. The practitioner must advise the client of the consequences as provided under the Code and regulations of such noncompliance, error, or omission.

§ 10.22. Diligence as to accuracy. (a) In general. A practitioner must exercise due diligence—

(1) In preparing or assisting in the preparation of, approving, and filing tax returns, documents, affidavits, and other papers relating to Internal Revenue Service matters;

(2) In determining the correctness of oral or written representations

¶304

made by thepractitioner to the Department of the Treasury; and

(3) In determining the correctness of oral or written representations made by the practitioner to clients with reference to any matter administered by the Internal Revenue Service.

(b) Reliance on others. Except as provided in §10.33 and §10.34, a practitioner will be presumed to have exercised due diligence for purposes of this section if the practitioner relies on the work product of another person and the practitioner used reasonable care in engaging, supervising, training, and evaluating the person, taking proper account of the nature of the relationship between the practitioner and the person.

§10.23. **Prompt disposition of pending matters.** A practitioner may not unreasonably delay the prompt disposition of any matter before the Internal Revenue Service.

§10.24. **Assistance from disbarred or suspended persons and former Internal Revenue Service employees.** A practitioner may not, knowingly and directly or indirectly:

(a) Accept assistance from or assist any person who is under disbarment or suspension from practice before the Internal Revenue Service if the assistance relates to a matter or matters constituting practice before the Internal Revenue Service.

(b) Accept assistance from any former government employee where theprovisions of §10.25 or any Federal law would be violated.

§10.25. **Practice by former Government employees, their partners and their associates.** (a) *Definitions.* For purposes of this section—

(1) *Assist* means to act in such a way as to advise, furnish information to, or otherwise aid another person, directly or indirectly.

(2) *Government employee* is an officer or employee of the United States or any agency of the United States, including a *special government employee* as defined in 18 U.S.C. 202(a), or of the District of Columbia, or of any State, or a member of Congress or of any State legislature.

(3) Member of a firm is a sole practitioner or an employee or associate thereof, or a partner, stockholder, associate, affiliate or employee of a partnership, joint venture, corporation, professional association or other affiliation of two or more practitioners who represent nongovernmental parties.

(4) *Practitioner* includes any individual described in paragraph (f) of §10.2.

(5) *Official responsibility* means the direct administrative or operating authority, whether intermediate or final, and either exercisable alone or with others, and either personally or through subordinates, to approve, disapprove, or otherwise direct Government action, with or without knowledge of the action.

(6) *Participate or participation* means substantial involvement as a Government employee by making decisions, or preparing or reviewing documents with or without the right to exercise a judgment of approval or disapproval, or participating in conferences or investigations, or rendering advice of a substantial nature.

(7) Rule includes Treasury Regulations, whether issued or under preparation for issuance as Notices of Proposed Rule Making or as Treasury Decisions; revenue rulings; and revenue procedures published in the Internal Revenue Bulletin. Rule does not include a transaction as defined in paragraph (a)(8) of this section.

(8) *Transaction* means any decision, determination, finding, letter ruling,technical advice, Chief Counsel advice, or contract or the approval or disapprovalthereof, relating to a particular factual situation or situations involving a specific party or parties whose rights, privileges, or liabilities under laws or regulations administered by the Internal Revenue Service, or other legal rights, are determined or immediately affected therein and to which the United States is a party or in which it has a direct and substantial interest, whether or not the same taxable periods are involved. Transaction does not include rule as defined in paragraph (a)(7) of this section.

(b) *General rules.* (1) No former Government employee may, subsequent to his or her Government employment, represent anyone in any matter administered by the Internal Revenue Service if the representation would violate 18 U.S.C. 207 or any other laws of the United States.

(2) No former Government employee who participated in a transaction may, subsequent to his Government employment, represent or knowingly assist, in that transaction, any person who is or was a specific party to that transaction.

(3) A former Government employee who within a period of one year prior to the termination of his Government employment had official responsibility for a transaction may not, within one year after his Government employment is ended, represent or knowingly assist in that transaction any person who is or was a specific party to that transaction.

(4) No former Government employee may, within one year after his Government employment is ended, appear before any employee of the Treasury Department in connection with the publication, withdrawal, amendment, modification, or interpretation of a rule in the development of which the former Government employee participated or for which, within a period of one year prior to the termination of his or her Government employment, he or she had official responsibility. This paragraph (b)(4) does not, however, preclude such former employee from appearing on his or her own behalf or from representing a taxpayer before the Internal Revenue Service in connection with a transaction involving the application or interpretation of such a rule with respect to that transaction, provided that such former employee does not utilize or disclose any confidential information acquired by the former employee in the development of the rule.

(c) *Firm representation.* (1) No member of a firm of which a former Government employee is a member may represent or knowingly assist a person who was or is a specific party in any transaction with respect to which the restrictions of paragraph (b)(2) or (3) of this section apply to the former Government employee, in that transaction, unless the firm isolates the former Government employee in such a way to ensure that the former Goverment

employee cannot assist in the representation.

(2) When isolation of a former Government employee is required under paragraph (c)(1) of this section, a statement affirming the fact of such isolation must be executed under oath by the former Government employee and by another member of the firm acting on behalf of the firm. The statement must clearly identify the firm, the former Government employee, and the transaction(s) requiring isolation and it must be filed with the Director of Practice (and at such other place(s) directed by the Director of Practice) and in such other place and in the manner prescribed by rule or regulation.

(d) *Pending representation.* Practice by former Government employees, their partners and associates with respect to representation in specific matters where actual representation commenced before July 26, 2002, is governed by the regulations set forth at 31 CFR Part 10 revised as of July 1, 2002. The burden of showing that represenation commenced before July 26, 2002, lies with the former Government employee, and their partners and associates.

§10.26. Notaries. A practitioner may not take acknowledgments, administer oaths, certify papers, or perform any official act as a notary public with respect to any matter administered by the Internal Revenue Service and for which he or she is employed as counsel, attorney, or agent, or in which he or she may be in any way interested.

§10.27. Fees. (a) *Generally.* A practitioner may not charge an unconscionable fee for representing a client in a matter before the Internal Revenue Service.

(b) *Contingent fees.* (1) For purposes of this section, a contingent fee is any fee that is based, in whole or in part, on whether or not a position taken on a tax return or other filing avoids challenge by the Internal Revenue Service or is sustained either by the Internal Revenue Service or in litigation. A contingent fee includes any fee arrangement in which the practitioner will reimburse the client for all or a portion of the client's fee in the event that a position taken on a tax return or other filing is challenged by the Internal Revenue Service or is not sustained, whether pursuant to an indemnity agreement, a guarantee, rescission rights, or any other arrangement with a similar effect.

(2) A practitioner may not charge a contingent fee for preparing an original tax return or for any advice rendered in connection with a position taken or to be taken on an original tax return.

(3) A contingent fee may be charged for preparation of or advice in connection with an amended tax return or a claim for refund (other than a claim for refund made on an original tax return), but only if the practitioner reasonably anticipates at the time the fee arrangement is entered into that the amended tax return or refund claim will receive substantive review by the Internal Revenue Service.

§ 10.28 Return of client's records.

(a) In general, a practitioner must, at the request of a client, promptly return any and all records of the client that are necessary for the client to comply with his or her Federal tax obligations. The practitioner may retain copies of the records returned to a client. The existence of a dispute over fees generally does not relieve the practitioner of his or her responsibility under this section. Nevertheless, if applicable state law allows or permits the retention of a client's records by a practitioner in the case of a dispute over fees for services rendered, the practitioner need only return those records that must be attached to the taxpayer's return. The practitioner, however, must provide the client with reasonable access to review and copy any additional records of the client retained by the practitioner under state law that are necessary for the client to comply with his or her Federal tax obligations.

(b) For purposes of this section. *Records of the client* include all documents or written or electronic materials provided to the practitioner, or obtained by the practitioner in the course of the practitioner's representation of the client, that preexisted the retention of the practitioner by the client. The term also includes materials that were prepared by the client or a third party (not including an employee or agent of the practitioner) at any time and provided to

the practitioner with respect to the subject matter of the representation. The term also includes any return, claim for refund, schedule, affidavit, appraisal or any other document prepared by the practitioner, or his or her employee or agent, that was presented to the client with respect to a prior representation if such document is necessary for the taxpayer to comply with his or her current Federal tax obligations. The term does not include any return, claim for refund, schedule, affidavit, appraisal or any other document prepared by the practitioner or the practitioner's firm, employees or agents if the practitioner is withholding such document pending the client's performance of its contractual obligation to pay fees with respect to such document.

§ 10.29. Conflicting interests.

(a) Except as provided by paragraph (b) of this section, a practitioner shall not represent a client in his or her practice before the Internal Revenue Service if the representation involves a conflict of interest. A conflict of interest exists if:

(1) The representation of one client will be directly adverse to another client; or

(2) There is a significant risk that the representation of one or more clients will be materially limited by the practitioner's responsibilities to another client, a former client or a third person or by a personal interest of the practitioner.

(b) Notwithstanding the existence of a conflict of interest under paragraph (a) of this section, the practitioner may represent a client if:

(1) The practitioner reasonably believes that the practitioner will be able to provide competent and diligent representation to each affected client;

(2) The representation is not prohibited by law;

(3) Each affected client gives informed consent, confirmed in writing.

(c) Copies of the written consents must be retained by the practitioner for at least 36 months from the date of the conclusion of the representation of the affected clients and the written consents must be provided to any officer or employee of the Internal Revenue Service on request. (Approved by the Office of Management and Budget under Control No. 1545-1726)

§10.30. Solicitation. (a) *Advertising and Solicitation Restrictions.* (1) A practitioner may not, with respect to any Internal Revenue Service matter, in any way use or participate in the use of any form of public communication or private solicitation containing a false, fraudulent, or coercive statement or claim; or a misleading or deceptive statement or claim.

Enrolled agents, in describing their professional designation, may not utilize the term of art "certified" or imply an employer/employee relationship with the Internal Revenue Service. Examples of acceptable descriptions are "enrolled to represent taxpayers before the Internal Revenue Service," "enrolled to practice before the Internal Revenue Service," and "admitted to practice before the Internal Revenue Service."

(2) A practitioner may not make, directly or indirectly, an uninvited written or oral solicitation of employment in matters related to the Internal Revenue Service if the solicitation violates Federal or State law or other applicable rule, e.g., attorneys are precluded from making a solicitation that is prohibited by conduct rules applicable to all attorneys in their State(s) of licensure. Any lawful solicitation made by or on behalf of a practitioner eligible to practice before the Internal Revenue Service must, nevertheless, clearly identify the solicitation as such and, if applicable, identify the source of the information used in choosing the recipient.

(b) *Fee Information.* (1)(i) A practitioner may publish the availability of a writtenschedule of fees and disseminate the following fee information—

(A) Fixed fees for specific routine services.

(B) Hourly rates.

(C) Range of fees for particular services.

(D) Fee charged for an initial consultation.

(i) Any statement of fee information concerning matters in which costs may be incurred must include a statement disclosing whether clients will be responsible for such costs.

(2) A practitioner may charge no more than the rate(s) published underparagraph (b)(1) of this section for at least 30 calendar days after the last date on which the schedule of fees was published.

(c) *Communication of fee information.* Fee information may be communicated in professional lists, telephone directories, print media, mailings, electronic mail, facsimile, hand delivered flyers, radio, television, and any other method. The method chosen, however, must not cause the communication to become untruthful, deceptive, or otherwise in violation of this part. A practitioner may not persist in attempting to contact a prospective client if the prospective client has made it known to the practitioner that he or she does not desire to be solicited. In the case of radio and television broadcasting, the broadcast must be recorded and the practitioner must retain a recording of the actual transmission. In the case of direct mail and e-commerce communications, the practitioner must retain a copy of the actual communication, along with a list or other description of persons to whom the communication was mailed or otherwise distributed. The copy must be retained by the practitioner for a period of at least 36 months from the date of the last transmission or use.

(d) *Improper Associations.* A practitioner may not, in matters related to the Internal Revenue Service, assist, or accept assistance from, any person or entity who, to the knowledge of the practitioner, obtains clients or otherwise practices in a manner forbidden under this section.

(Approved by the Office of Management and Budget under Control No. 1545-1726)

§10.31. Negotiation of taxpayer refund checks. A practitioner who prepares tax returns may not endorse or otherwise negotiate any check issued to a client by the government in respect of a Federal tax liability.

§10.32. Practice of law. Nothing in the regulations in this part may be construed as authorizing persons not members of the bar to practice law.

* * *

¶304

§ 10.34. Standards for advising with respect to tax return positions and for preparing or signing returns. (a) *Realistic possibility standard.* A practitioner may not sign a return as a preparer if the practitioner determines that the return contains a position that does not have a realistic possibility of being sustained on its merits (the realistic possibility standard) unless the position is not frivolous and is adequately disclosed to the Service. A practitioner may not advise a client to take a position on a return, or prepare the portion of a return on which a position is taken, unless—

(1) The practitioner determines that the position satisfies the realistic possibility standard; or

(2) The position is not frivolous and the practitioner advises the client of any opportunity to avoid the accuracy-related penalty in section 6662 of the Internal Revenue Code by adequately disclosing the position and of the requirements for adequate disclosure.

(b) *Advising clients on potential penalties.* A practitioner advising a client to take a position on a return, or preparing or signing a return as a preparer, must inform the client of the penalties reasonably likely to apply to the client with respect to the position advised, prepared, or reported. The practitioner also must inform the client of any opportunity to avoid any such penalty by disclosure, if relevant, and of the requirements for adequate disclosure. This paragraph (b applies even if the practi-

tioner is not subject to a penalty with respect to the position.

(c) *Relying on information furnished by clients.* A practitioner advising a client to take a position on a return, or preparing or signing a return as a preparer, generally may rely in good faith without verification upon information furnished by the client. The practitioner may not, however, ignorethe implications of information furnished to, or actually known by, the the practitioner, and must make reasonable inquiries if the information as furnished appears to be incorrect, inconsistent with an important fact or another factual assumption, or incomplete.

(d) *Definitions.* For purposes of this section—

(1) *Realistic possibility.* A position is considered to have a realistic possibility of being sustained on its merits if a reasonable and well-informed analysis by a person knowledgeable in the tax law would lead such a person to conclude that the position has approximately a one in three, or greater, likelihood of being sustained on its merits. The authorities described in 26 CFR 1.6662-4(d)(3)(iii), or any successor provision, of the substantial understatement penalty regulations may be taken into account for purposes of this analysis. The possibility that a tax return will not be audited, that an issue will not be raised on audit, or that an issue will be settled may not be taken into account.

(2) *Frivolous.* A position is frivolous if it is patently improper.

Subpart C—Sanctions for Violation of the Regulations

§ 10.50 Sanctions. (a) *Authority to censure, suspend, or disbar.* The Secretary of the Treasury, or his or her delegate, after notice and an opportunity for a proceeding, may censure, suspend or disbar any practitioner from practice before the Internal Revenue Service if the practitioner is

shown to be incompetent or disreputable, fails to comply with any regulation in this part, or with intent to defraud, willfully and knowingly misleads or threatens a client or prospective client. Censure is a public reprimand.

(b) *Authority to disqualify.* The Secretary of the Treasury, or his or her delegate, after due notice and opportunity for hearing, may disqualify any appraiser with respect to whom a penalty has been assessed under section 6701(a) of the Internal Revenue Code.

(1) If any appraiser is disqualified pursuant to this subpart C, such appraiser is barred from presenting evidence or testimony in any administrative proceeding before the Department of Treasury or the Internal Revenue Service, unless and until authorized to do so by the Director of Practice pursuant to '10.81, regardless of whether such evidence or testimony would pertain to an appraisal made prior to or after such date.

(2) Any appraisal made by a disqualified appraiser after the effective date of disqualification will not have any probative effect in any administrative proceeding before the Department of the Treasury or the Internal Revenue Service. An appraisal otherwise barred from admission into evidence pursuant to this section may be admitted into evidence solely for the purpose of determining the taxpayer's reliance in good faith on such appraisal.

§10.51. Incompetence and disreputable conduct. Incompetence and disreputable conduct for which a practitioner may becensured, suspended or disbarred from practice before the Internal Revenue Service includes, but is not limited to—

(a) Conviction of any criminal offense under the revenue laws of the United States;

(b) Conviction of any criminal offense involving dishonesty or breach of trust;

(c) Conviction of any felony under Federal or State law for which the conductinvolved renders the practitioner unfit to practice before the Internal Revenue Service;

(d) Giving false or misleading information, or participating in any way in the giving of false or misleading information to the Department of the Treasury or any officer or employee thereof, or to any tribunal authorized to pass upon Federal tax matters, in connection with any matter pending or likely to be pending before them, knowing such information to be false or misleading. Facts or other matters contained in testimony, Federal tax returns, financial statements, applications for enrollment, affidavits, declarations, or any other document or statement, written or oral, are included in the term information.

(e) Solicitation of employment as prohibited under § 10.30, the use of false or misleading representations with intent to deceive a client or prospective client in order to procure employment, or intimating that the practitioner is able improperly to obtain special consideration or action from the Internal Revenue Service or officer or employee thereof.

(f) Willfully failing to make a Federal tax return in violation of the revenue laws of the United States, willfully evading, attempting to evade, or participating in any way in evading or attempting to evade any assessment or payment of any Federal tax, or knowingly counseling or suggesting to a client or prospective client an illegal plan to evade Federal taxes or payment thereof.

(g) Misappropriation of, or failure properly and promptly to remit funds received from a client for the purpose of payment of taxes or other obligations due the United States.

(h) Directly or indirectly attempting to influence, or offering or agreeing to attempt to influence, the official action of any officer or employee of the Internal Revenue Service by the use of threats, false accusations, duress or coercion, by the offer of any special inducement or promise of advantage or by the bestowing of any gift, favor or thing of value.

(i) Disbarment or suspension from practice as an attorney, certified public accountant, public accountant, or actuary by any duly constituted authority of any State, territory, possession of the United States, including a Commonwealth, or the District of Columbia, any Federal court of record or any Federal agency, body or board.

(j) Knowingly aiding and abetting another person to practice before the Internal Revenue Service during a period of suspension, disbarment, or ineligibility of such other person.

(k) Contemptuous conduct in connection with practice before the Internal Revenue Service, including the use of abusive language, making false accusations and statements, knowing them to be false, or circulating or publishing malicious or libelous matter.

(l) Giving a false opinion, knowingly, recklessly, or through gross incompetence, including an opinion which is intentionally or recklessly misleading, or engaging in a pattern of providing incompetent opinions on questions arising under the Federal tax laws. False opinions described in this paragraph (l) include those which reflect or result from a knowing misstatement of fact or law, from an assertion of a position known to be unwarranted under existing law, from counseling or assisting in conduct known to be illegal or fraudulent, from concealing matters required by law to be revealed, or from consciously disregarding information indicating that material facts expressed in the tax opinion or offering material are false or misleading. For purposes of this paragraph (l), reckless conduct is a highly unreasonable omission or misrepresentation involving an extreme departure from the standards of ordinary care that a practitioner should observe under the circumstances. A pattern of conduct is a factorthat will be taken into account in determining whether a practitioner acted knowingly, recklessly, or through gross incompetence. Gross incompetence includes conduct that reflects gross indifference, preparation which is grossly inadequate under the circumstances, and a consistent failure to perform obligations to the client.

§10.52. Violation of regulations. A practitioner may be censured, suspended or disbarred from practice before the Internal Revenue Service for any of the following:

(a) Willfully violating any of the regulations contained in this part.

(b) Recklessly or through gross incompetence (within the meaning of §10.51(l)) violating §10.33 or §10.34.

§10.53. Receipt of information concerning practitioner. (a) *Officer or employee of the Internal Revenue Service.* If an officer or employee of the Internal Revenue Service has reason to believe that a practitioner has violated any provision of this part, the officer or employee will promptly make a written report to the Director of Practice of the suspected violation. The report will explain the facts and reasons upon which the officer's or employee's belief rests.

(b) *Other persons.* Any person other than an officer or employee of the Internal Revenue Service having information of a violation of any provision of this part may make an oral or written report of the alleged violation to the Director of Practice or any officer or employee of the Internal Revenue Service. If the report is made to an officer or employee of the Internal Revenue Service, the officer or employee will make a written report of the suspected violation to the Director of Practice.

(c) *Destruction of report.* No report made under paragraph (a) or (b) of this section shall be maintained by the Director of Practice unless retention of such record is permissible under the applicable records control schedule as approved by the National Archives and Records Administration and designated in the Internal Revenue Manual. The Director of Practice must destroy such reports as soon as permissible under the applicable records control schedule.

(d) *Effect on proceedings under subpart D.* The destruction of any report will not bar any proceeding under subpart D of this part, but precludes the Director of Practice's use of a copy of such report in a proceeding under subpart D of this part.

¶305 CIRCULAR 230-FINAL REGULATIONS

In July, 2002, the Department of Treasury finalized the regulations governing practice before the IRS (Circular 230). These final regulations adopted many of the amendments relating to practice before the IRS involving non-tax shelter related cases that were proposed in 2001 and made additional changes and clarifications to Circular 230. Some of the more significant changes are discussed below.

Among the more significant changes are those made by Section 10.20 of Circular 230, which clarifies that a practitioner is required to properly respond to a request for documents or information by either submitting the information or advising the requesting IRS employee why the information can not be provided. If the documents are not controlled by either the practitioner or the practitioner's client, the practitioner is required, to the extent possible, to identify any person who may have the requested documents. In Section 10.22, the due diligence burden of a practitioner who has relied on the work project of another person is eased. This section now provides that a practitioner who uses reasonable care in engaging, supervising, training and evaluating the third person is presumed to have exercised due diligence.

Concerned with contingent fees, Section 10.27 clarifies the rules governing the prohibition on a practitioner receiving a contingent fee for the advice rendered in connection with a position taken or to be taken on an original return. The final regulations to Circular 230 also clarify the rules governing when a practitioner may retain a client's records in the event of a fee dispute. When a practitioner does retain the records, Section 10.28 requires that the practitioner permit the client to review and copy any of the records retained by the practitioner.

Section 10.50 now permits censure as a lesser sanction. Prior to these regulations, suspension or disbarment were the only sanctions available.

¶306 PROPOSED AMENDMENTS CIRCULAR 230

In 2004, the Treasury Department issued new proposed amendments to Circular 230 that address the standards of practice for tax shelter cases. These revisions have not yet been finalized. The proposed version of Circular 230 is reproduced at Appendix B. Comments on the proposed rulemaking, prepared by the Joint Task Force Committee on Standards of Tax Practice and the Tax Shelter Task Force of the Section are set forth in Exhibit 3-3 at ¶353.

The new proposed amendments seek to accomplish three goals: promote and maintain the public's confidence in tax professionals by establishing "best practices" for tax advisors; modify the requirements for practitioners regarding tax shelter matters; and ensure compliance with the "best practices" for tax advisors and the rules governing practice before the IRS relating to tax-shelter matters.

The "best practices" for tax advisors are set forth in Section 10.33. Best practices include: (a) communicating clearly with the client regarding the terms of the engagement and the form and scope of the advice or assistance to be rendered; (b) establishing the relevant facts, including evaluating the reasonableness of any assumptions or representations; (c) relating applicable law, including potentially applicable judicial doctrines, to the relevant facts; (d) arriving at a conclusion supported by the law and the facts; (e) advising the client regarding the conclusions reached, including whether the taxpayer may avoid penalties under Section 6662(d); and (f) acting fairly before the IRS.

Tax shelter opinions are no longer addressed in Section 10.33 of Circular 230. The 2004 proposed amendments modified the rules governing tax shelter opinions and relocated those rules to a new section, Section 10.35. This paragraph sets forth the requirements for practitioners providing "more likely than not" and "marketed" tax shelter opinions. A "more likely than not" tax shelter opinion is one that reaches a conclusion of at least more likely than not with respect to one or more material federal tax issues. This is in contrast to the prior proposed regulations, which did not define a "more likely than not" tax shelter opinion with reference to a "material federal tax issue."

A "marketed" tax shelter opinion is an opinion, including a "more likely than not" tax shelter opinion, that a practitioner knows or has reason to know will be used or referred to by a person in promoting, marketing or recommending a tax shelter. This is a change from the prior proposed regulations, which defined a "marketed" tax shelter opinion as a tax shelter opinion that does **not** conclude that the Federal tax treatment of a tax shelter item or items is more likely than not the proper treatment.

The proposed requirements for "more likely than not" and "marketed" tax shelter opinions are as follows:

1. The practitioner must use reasonable efforts to identify the facts and determine which facts are relevant. The relevant facts must be identified in the opinion. However, the practitioner is not expected to identify or ascertain facts peculiar to a taxpayer to whom the transaction may be marketed.

2. The practitioner must not base the opinion on any unreasonable factual or legal assumptions, representations, statements for findings that the practitioner knows or should know are incorrect or incomplete.

3. The practitioner must set forth in the opinion how the applicable law relates to the facts.

4. The opinion must include the practitioner's conclusion on the likelihood of the taxpayer to prevail on the merits of each Federal tax issue, the reasons for such conclusions and an overall conclusion as to the likelihood that the Federal tax treatment of the tax shelter item or items is proper.

5. There are certain disclosures that each opinion must contain. These disclosures are set forth in Section 10.35(d).

The proposed regulations define "tax shelter" in the same manner as Section 6662 of the Code, except that it excludes preliminary advice given pursuant to an engagement in which the practitioner is expected to later provide an opinion that satisfies the requirements of Section 10.35.

The provisions of Section 10.35 would also permit a practitioner to provide an opinion that is limited to some material Federal tax issues that may be relevant to the treatment of a tax shelter item if the taxpayer and the practitioner agree to limit the scope of the opinion. Such a limited scope opinion must contain the required disclosures provided in Section 10.35(d), and can not be a marketed shelter opinion.

To ensure compliance with "best practices" for tax advisors and the rules governing practice before the IRS in tax shelter matters, a new section, Section 10.36, was added. This section requires that tax advisors with responsibility for overseeing a firm's practice before the IRS take reasonable steps to ensure that the firm's procedures for its members, associates and employees, are consistent withthe proposed "best practice" rules set forth in Section 10.33, and that the firm has adequate procedures in effect for the purposes of complying with the requirements of Section 10.35 for "more likely than not" and "marketed" opinions. Practitioners who fail to take reasonable steps to ensure adequate procedures are in place or who fail to correct the non-compliance of a member or employee of the firm whom the practitioner knows or has reason to know has engaged in a practice that does not comply with Circular 230 will be disciplined.

The final regulations also added a new section 10.37, which authorizes the Director of Professional Responsibility to create advisory committees to review and make recommendations regarding processional standards or best practices for tax advisors. Such committees may also advise the Director whether a practitioner may have violated Sections 10.35 or 10.36.

¶351 Exhibit 3-1

ABA SECTION OF TAXATION STANDARD OF TAX PRACTICE STATEMENT 2000-1

The following Standard of Tax Practice Statement is issued for the guidance of tax practitioners. It was prepared by the Committee on Standards of Tax Practice of the Section of Taxation of the American Bar Association. The Statement was reviewed before issuance by the Council of the Section of Taxation. The Statement has not been approved by the Section or by the American Bar Association and should not be construed as policy of those entities. The ABA Standing Committee on Ethics and Professional Responsibility has indicated that it has no objection to the issuance of the Statement. The Reporter for this Statement was Deborah Schenk of New York, New York. The Chair of the Committee on Standards of Tax Practice was Linda Galler of Hempstead, New York; the Vice Chair was Donald P. Lan, Jr., of Dallas, Texas; and the Chair of its Subcommittee on Standards of Tax Practice Statements was Charles Pulaski of Phoenix, Arizona.[*]

Issue Presented

This standard addresses whether differences between the income tax return accuracy standards for taxpayers and the lawyers who advise them result in conflicts of interest between clients and their lawyers. Specifically, this standard explores whether the benefits of adequately disclosing return positions, which may affect taxpayers and advisers differently, generate conflicts of interest.

---

[*] Copyright © 2000 by The American Bar Association. All Rights Reserved. Reprinted by Permission. Statement can be found at http://www.abanet.org/ftp/pub/tax/stp00-1.pdf.

The text below first describes the relevant tax return accuracy standards and the professional standards for conflicts of interest. It then identifies a variety of factual situations and determines in each whether there is a conflict between theinterests of the client and lawyer. Finally, the text discusses the ethical options available to the lawyer in those situations where a conflict exists.

Applicable Rules

Tax Return Accuracy Standards Applicable to Taxpayers

The accuracy-related penalty of Code section 6662 articulates the tax return accuracy standard governing taxpayers. The twenty percent accuracy-related penalty applies if an underpayment of tax exists as a consequence of any one of three component elements of the penalty: (1) a disregard of rules and regulations, (2) an act of negligence, or (3) a substantial understatement of income tax.[1]

Disregard of rules and regulations will generally not expose the taxpayer to the accuracy-related penalty if the taxpayer has a reasonable basis for the return position and makes adequate disclosure. I.R.C. § 6662(d)(2)(B); Reg. § 1.6662-3(c). *Negligence* occurs where a return position lacks a reasonable basis. Reg. § 1.6662-3(b)(1). Accordingly, a position having a reasonable basis will not expose the taxpayer to the negligence component of the accuracy-related penalty, even if the position is not adequately disclosed.

A *substantial understatement* of income tax exists if the understatement exceeds the greater of ten percent of the correct tax liability or $5,000 ($10,000 for C corporations). If there is a substantial understatement, the taxpayer may avoid the accuracy-related penalty by establishing either (1) that there was substantial authority for the position or (2) that the position had a reasonable basis and was adequately disclosed. I.R.C. § 6662(b)(2); Reg. § 1.6662-4(d), -4(e). However, substantial understatements attributable to tax shelter positions are subject to more stringent rules. If an individual taxpayer has a substantial understatement as a result of a tax shelter position, adequate disclosure is not effective to avoid the penalty; the taxpayer must establish both substantial authority and a reasonable belief that the position taken was more likely than not the correct position in order to avoid the penalty. I.R.C. § 6662(d)(2)(C)(i). If a corporate taxpayer has a substantial understatement as a result of a tax shelter position, the accuracy-related penalty automatically applies.[2] I.R.C. § 6662(d)(2)(C)(ii).

No accuracy-related penalty applies to any portion of an underpayment if the taxpayer is able to establish that there was reasonable cause for that portion and that the taxpayer acted in good faith with respect to it. I.R.C. § 6664(c). Reliance on the advice of counsel, although not determinative, is a factor in assessing whether reasonable cause and good faith exist. Reg. § 1.6664-4(c).

---

[1] Other components of the accuracy-related penalty, *i.e.,* valuation and pension liability misstatements, are not addressed here because adequate disclosure generally does not play a role in the application or nonapplication of these components of the penalty.

[2] A corporation, like other taxpayers, may avoid the application of the accuracy-related penalty by establishing reasonable cause and good faith under § 6664(c), as noted in the next paragraph.

Tax Return Accuracy Standards Applicable to Lawyers

ABA Formal Opinion 85-352 concludes: "A lawyer may advise reporting a position on a tax return so long as the lawyer believes in good faith that theposition is warranted in existing law or can be supported by a good faith argument for an extension, modification or reversal of existing law and there is some realistic possibility of success if the matter is litigated." In addition, the Opinion states that the lawyer should "refer to potential penalties and other legal consequences should the client take the position advised." Although the Opinion does not define "realistic possibility of success," a task force of the ABA Tax Section has taken the position that "a position having a likelihood of success closely approximating one-third should meet the standard."[3]

Formal Opinion 85-352 does not expressly state that a lawyer may advise a position not satisfying the realistic possibility standard if that position is adequately disclosed on the return. However, the Opinion summarizes its holding as follows: "In summary, a lawyer may advise reporting a position on a return even where the lawyer believes the position probably will not prevail, there is no 'substantial authority' in support of the position, *and there will be no disclosure of the position in the return*," so long as the realistic possibility standard is satisfied. (emphasis supplied.) Given the legislative and regulatory refinements to the accuracy-related penalty since the issuance of ABA Opinion 85-352, we believe that it may fairly be read to permit a lawyer to advise a position not meeting the realistic possibility standard so long as that position is adequately disclosed on the return and satisfies the not frivolous standard set forth in Model Rule 3.1.[4]

Circular 230 § 10.34(a) provides that a practitioner may not sign a return as a preparer if the return contains a position not adequately disclosed that does not have a realistic possibility of being sustained on its merits. A position is considered to have a realistic possibility of being sustained on its merits "if a reasonable and well-informed analysis by a person knowledgeable in the tax law would lead such a person to conclude that the position has approximately a one in three, or greater, likelihood of being sustained on its merits." Circular 230 § 10.34(a)(4)(i). However, the practitioner may sign a return containing a position that does not meet the realistic possibility standard so long as the position is not frivolous and is adequately disclosed. A practitioner may not advise a client to take a return position, or prepare a portion of a return containing a position, if that position does not meet the realistic possibility standard unless the position is not frivolous and the practitioner advises the client of any opportunity to avoid the accuracy-related penalty by making adequate disclosure.

---

[3] 39 Tax Law. 635, 638-39 (1986).

[4] Model Rule 3.1 provides in part that a "lawyer shall not bring or defend a proceeding, or assert or controvert an issue therein, unless there is a basis for doing so that is not frivolous, which includes a good faith argument for an extension, modification or reversal of existing law." Although the ABA Tax Section task force report denies the existence of a disclosure option where the realistic possibility standard is not satisfied (*id.* at 639), the ABA Tax Section advocated such an option for not frivolous positions in comments communicated to the Director of Practice on proposed amendments to Circular 230, ultimately reflected in § 10.34 and discussed below. Letter from John B. Jones, ABA Tax Section Chair, to Leslie B. Shapiro, Director of Practice (February 12, 1987).

Under Code section 6694(a)(1), a penalty may be imposed on the preparer of a return that shows an understatement due to a position that does not have a realistic possibility of being sustained on its merits. For purposes of this penalty, the realistic possibility standard is also deemed satisfied by a one-in-three possibility of being sustained on its merits. Reg. § 1.6694-2(b)(1). The penalty will not apply if the position is not frivolous and is adequately disclosed. In the case of a signing preparer, actual disclosure is required. In the case of a nonsigning preparer, the penalty may be avoided if the nonsigning preparer advises the taxpayer or the signing preparer of the need for or effects of adequate disclosure. Reg. § 1.6694-2(c).

Conflict of Interest and Withdrawal Standards Applicable to Lawyers

Model Rule 1.7(b) provides: "A lawyer shall not represent a client if the representation of that client may be materially limited by the lawyer's responsibilities to another client or to a third person, or by the lawyer's own interests, unless: (1) the lawyer reasonably believes the representation will not be adversely affected; and (2) the client consents after consultation."

Comment [4] to Model Rule 1.7(b) provides: "Loyalty to a client is also impaired when a lawyer cannot consider, recommend or carry out an appropriate course of action for the client because of the lawyer's other responsibilities or interests." Comment [6] to Model Rule 1.7(b) provides: "The lawyer's own interests should not be permitted to have adverse effect on representation of a client . . . If the probity of a lawyer's own conduct in a transaction is in serious question, it may be difficult or impossible for the lawyer to give a client detached advice."

Circular 230 section 10.29 provides that "no attorney . . . shall represent conflicting interests in his practice before the Internal Revenue Service, except by express consent of all directly interested parties after full disclosure has been made."

Model Rule 1.16(a) provides that "a lawyer shall not represent a client or, where representation has commenced, shall withdraw from the representation of a client if: (1) the representation will result in violation of the rules of professional conduct or other law . . . "

Discussion

Presentation of Hypothetical Situations

The following discussion identifies some of the situations in which a conflict exists between the interests of the client and lawyer. It is assumed that the hierarchy of tax return accuracy standards is as follows, listed from highest to lowest: more likely than not, substantial authority, realistic possibility, reasonable basis, and not frivolous. It is also assumed that the lawyer is advising the client with respect to a return position and/or preparing the return.

1. Taxpayer Exposure to the Disregard Component

(1) Adoption of a tax return position that disregards rules or regulations but has a reasonable basis and does not expose the taxpayer to the disregard

¶351

component of the accuracy-related penalty if the position is adequately disclosed and, in the case of a regulation, the taxpayer in good faith seeks tochallenge the validity of the regulation. Reg. § 1.6662-3(c). Accordingly, disclosure will benefit the taxpayer, and the lawyer should advise disclosure. Disclosure also would benefit the lawyer because the position is not frivolous. If the position is contrary to a revenue ruling or notice and satisfies the realistic possibility standard, disclosure is not necessary to protect the taxpayer or the lawyer from the disregard penalty and is not required by the lawyer's professional standards. There is no conflict between the client and lawyer because disclosure either will benefit, or is not necessary for both the client and the lawyer.

(2) Adoption of a tax return position that disregards rules and regulations, does not have a reasonable basis, and is not frivolous exposes the taxpayer to the disregard component of the accuracy-related penalty. Disclosure will not benefit the taxpayer. The lawyer will violate professional standards and be exposed to a penalty unless the position is adequately disclosed, and thus disclosure is of benefit to the lawyer. There is a conflict between the interests of the client and lawyer.

2. Taxpayer Exposure to the Negligence and Substantial Understatement Components

(3) Adoption of a return position supported by substantial authority does not expose the taxpayer to either the negligence or substantial understatement component of the accuracy-related penalty, and disclosure does not benefit the taxpayer.[5] In addition, since the return position will satisfy the realistic possibility standard, the lawyer does not violate professional standards or incur a penalty, and disclosure does not benefit the lawyer. Accordingly, there is no conflict between the interests of the client and lawyer.

(4) Adoption of a return position not supported by substantial authority, but satisfying the realistic possibility standard, exposes the taxpayer to the substantial understatement component of the accuracy-related penalty unless adequate disclosure is made. There is no exposure to the negligence component even if no disclosure is made (because reasonable basis will exist). The lawyer does not violate professional standards or incur a penalty because the realistic possibility standard is satisfied. There is no conflict between the interests of the client and lawyer because disclosure benefits the client and does not disadvantage the lawyer.

(5) If a return position has a reasonable basis (but is not supported by substantial authority and does not meet the realistic possibility standard), the taxpayer is in the same position as in (4) above, *i.e.*, adequate disclosure is necessary to avoid exposure to the substantial understatement component of the accuracy-related penalty. The realistic possibility standard is not satisfied,but the lawyer does not violate professional standards or become exposed to a penalty if the position is adequately disclosed. There is no conflict between the interests of the client and lawyer because disclosure benefits both.

(6) Adoption of a return position that lacks a reasonable basis (but is not frivolous) exposes the taxpayer to both the negligence and substantial understatement components of the accuracy-related penalty. Disclosure will not serve to avoid the penalty because reasonable basis is not present. The realistic

---

[5] We assume here that the understatement of income tax is "substantial" and that the return position does not relate to a tax shelter. For situations where the understatement is not substantial, see (8), (9), and (10) below. For situations where the return position is related to a tax shelter, see (11) and (12) below.

possibility standard is not satisfied, but the lawyer (as in situation (5) above) does not violate professional standards or become exposed to a penalty if the position is adequately disclosed. There is a conflict between the interests of the client and lawyer because disclosure does not benefit the client but does benefit the lawyer.

(7) Adoption of a frivolous return position exposes the taxpayer to the accuracy-related penalty and causes the lawyer to violate professional standards and to become exposed to a penalty. There is no conflict between the interests of the client and lawyer.[6]

3. Taxpayer Exposure Where an Understatement of Income Tax is Not Substantial

(8) The facts are the same as in situation (4) (no substantial authority, realistic possibility satisfied) except that the understatement of income tax is not "substantial," *i.e.*, it does not exceed the greater of 10 percent of liability or $5,000 ($10,000 for a C corporation). The taxpayer is not exposed to either the substantial understatement component (because the threshold amount is not present) or the negligence component (because reasonable basis exists), and disclosure does not benefit the taxpayer. Disclosure does not benefit the lawyer because the realistic possibility standard is satisfied. There is no conflict between the interests of the client and lawyer because disclosure benefits neither.

(9) The facts are the same as in situation (5) (reasonable basis, but no substantial authority and realistic possibility not satisfied) except that the understatement of income tax is again not "substantial." The taxpayer is exposed to neither the substantial understatement component (because the threshold amount is not present) nor the negligence component (because there is reasonable basis), and disclosure does not benefit the client. Disclosure, however, benefits the lawyer because the realistic possibility standard is not satisfied. There is a conflict between the interests of the client and lawyer.

(10) The facts are the same as in situation (6) (no reasonable basis but not frivolous) except that the understatement of income tax is again not "substantial." The taxpayer avoids exposure to the substantial understatement component (because the threshold amount is not present) but is exposed to the negligence component (because reasonable basis does not exist). Disclosuredoes not benefit the taxpayer (because disclosure is not effective where reasonable basis does not exist). Since the realistic possibility standard is not satisfied, disclosure benefits the lawyer. There is a conflict between the interests of the client and lawyer.

4. Taxpayer Exposure Where the Proposed Return Position Relates to a Tax Shelter

(11) The facts are the same as in either situation (3) (substantial authority exists) or situation (4) (no substantial authority but realistic possibility satisfied) except that the proposed tax return position relates to a tax shelter. In both situations, the taxpayer is exposed to the substantial understatement component, and disclosure does not benefit the taxpayer (because disclosure is not effective with regard to a tax shelter position).[7] The lawyer does not violate professional standards or become exposed to a penalty because the

---

[6] The lawyer should advise the client against taking the return position and, if the client persists, should withdraw.

[7] The taxpayer may escape the application of the substantial understatement component of the penalty if substantial authority exists and she is able to establish a good faith belief that the position was more likely than not the correct position. However, this opportunity is independent of disclosure.

realistic possibility standard is satisfied, and disclosure does not benefit the lawyer. There is no conflict between the interests of the client and lawyer.

(12) The facts are the same as in either situation (5) (reasonable basis, no substantial authority, and realistic possibility not satisfied) or situation (6) (no reasonable basis, not frivolous, realistic possibility not satisfied) except that the return position relates to a tax shelter. The taxpayer is again subject to the substantial understatement component of the accuracy-related penalty, and disclosure does not benefit her. The realistic possibility standard is not satisfied, and disclosure does benefit the lawyer. There is a conflict between the interests of the client and lawyer.

Discussion of Lawyer's Ethical Options Where Conflict Exists

In situations 2, 6, 9, 10, and 12, a conflict exists between the interests of the client and the lawyer. In each of these situations, the client will not benefit from adequate disclosure of the proposed return position (either because the taxpayer has no penalty exposure [9 and 10] or because disclosure will not avoid the taxpayer's existing penalty exposure [2, 6 and 12]), but disclosure will protect the lawyer (because the position disregards a rule or regulation or the realistic possibility standard is not satisfied).

In determining whether the lawyer will actually benefit from disclosure, it is necessary to consider whether the lawyer acts only as advisor or nonsigning preparer of the return, or whether, in contrast, the lawyer acts as a signing preparer of the return. Where the lawyer acts only as advisor or nonsigning preparer, both Circular 230 and Code section 6694(a) permit him to advise a return position that does not satisfy the realistic possibility standard so long as he advises the taxpayer of any opportunity to avoid the accuracy-related penaltythrough disclosure. Although disclosure will not in fact affect the taxpayer's penalty exposure in these five factual situations, the lawyer discharges his responsibility under Circular 230 and Code section 6694(a) by advising the taxpayer that adequate disclosure will not be effective to avoid penalty exposure. Circular 230 § 10.34(a)(1)(ii); Reg. § 1.6694-2(c)(3)(ii). Although Formal Opinion 85-352 does not explicitly permit the lawyer to advise in these circumstances, it is reasonable to construe it as allowing the lawyer to advise with respect to the position. Certainly, that should be true where the taxpayer faces no penalty exposure (9 and 10). While less clear where there is taxpayer penalty exposure that will not be eliminated by disclosure (2, 6 and 12), we believe that the lawyer who does not act as a signing preparer of the return in these circumstances discharges his professional responsibility and satisfies the penalty standard by advising the taxpayer that adequate disclosure will not benefit the taxpayer.

If the lawyer acts as signing preparer of the return in any of the five situations where a conflict exists between client and lawyer, the lawyer should advise the client fully concerning the penalty aspects of adopting the proposed return position and the fact that adequate disclosure will not benefit the taxpayer. The lawyer should advise the client that the client's decision regarding disclosure will affect the lawyer's ability to sign the return as preparer, as well as the reasons why that decision impacts the lawyer's ability to act in these capacities. However, the lawyer must make it clear to the taxpayer that disclo-

¶351

sure will not advance the client's interests and may even be detrimental to those interests. The lawyer should advise the client that it may be in the client's best interests to seek independent legal counsel on the question whether to make adequate disclosure of the tax return position.[8] The lawyer may not advise the client to make adequate disclosure where the only purpose is to benefit the lawyer. See Model Rule 1.7(b), relative to conflicts of interest attributable to the lawyer's own interests.

If the client seeks independent counsel, the client and lawyer should be guided by the opinion of that counsel. If the client, after having been fully informed, declines to seek independent counsel and decides to make adequate disclosure, the lawyer may proceed with the representation. If the client, after having been fully informed, determines, either with or without the advice of independent counsel, not to make adequate disclosure, the lawyer must withdraw from further assisting the client with regard to the tax return engagement in question. To proceed in situations where the taxpayer does not disclose the position and the position either disregards a rule or regulation or does not satisfy the realistic possibility standard and the taxpayer does not disclose the position would cause the lawyer to violate both professional standards and penalty standards. See Model Rule 1.16(a), relative to withdrawal from representations in violation of the rules of professional conduct.

¶352 Exhibit 3-2

ABA SECTION OF TAXATION STANDARD OF TAX PRACTICE
STATEMENT 1999-1 (Updated March 2000)

The following Standard of Tax Practice Statement is issued for the guidance of tax practitioners. It was prepared by the Committee on Standards of Tax Practice of the Section of Taxation of the American Bar Association. The Statement was reviewed before issuance by the Council of the Section of Taxation. The Statement has not been approved by the Section or by the American Bar Association and should not be construed as policy of those entities. The ABA Standing Committee on Ethics and Professional Responsibility has indicated that it has no objection to the issuance of the Statement. The Reporter for this Statement was Donald P. Lan, Jr. of Dallas, Texas. The Chair of the Committee on Standards of Tax Practice was Leslie S. Shapiro of Washington, D.C., the Vice Chair was Linda Galler of Hempstead, New York, and the Chair of its Subcommittee on Standards of Tax Practice Statements was Charles Pulaski of Phoenix, Arizona.[**]

Issue Presented

This Statement addresses the issue of counsel's responsibilities upon discovering a computational error made by the Internal Revenue Service in the client's

---

[8] We do not believe that a lawyer consulted solely to advise a taxpayer whether to disclose a tax return position should be viewed as an income tax return preparer under Code section 6694 or be subject to Circular 230 §10.34 with respect to that issue. To conclude otherwise effectively would deprive the taxpayer of the opportunity to seek legal counsel from a lawyer free of conflicts of interest.

[**] Copyright © 2000 by The American Bar Association. All Rights Reserved. Reprinted by Permission. Statement can be found at http://www.abanet.org/tax/groups/stp/stp_stmt99-1.html.

favor that is unrelated to any affirmative representation or omission of either the client or counsel.

The issue arises in a number of contexts. A computational error may surface either before or after the client has determined the correct tax calculation. A computational error may involve a tribunal, as in the settlement or decision in a docketed tax case. Documents filed by the parties with the court may carry the error, as in a stipulated decision document filed in Tax Court, or may not, as in general stipulations for dismissal filed in District Court. Computational errors by the Internal Revenue Service may create a reduced deficiency, but can also result in an erroneous refund being received by the client.

Applicable Rules

- Rule 1.6(a) of the ABA Model Rules prevents a lawyer from revealing confidential information relating to representation of a client, unless the client consents to disclosure after consultation or there is implied authorization to disclose in order to carry out the representation.

- Rule 4.1(a) prevents a lawyer from knowingly making a false statement of material fact to a third person. Rule 4.1(b) prevents a lawyerfrom knowingly failing to disclose a material fact to a third person, but only where disclosure is necessary to avoid assisting a fraudulent act by the client and then only if disclosure is not prohibited by Rule 1.6.

- Rule 1.2(d) prevents a lawyer from knowingly counseling a client to engage in, or assist a client in, conduct that is criminal or fraudulent. In this regard, Rule 8.4(c) proscribes conduct involving dishonesty, fraud, deceit or misrepresentation.

- Under Rule 3.3(a), a lawyer may not knowingly make a false statement of material fact to a tribunal or fail to disclose to a tribunal a material fact necessary to avoid assisting a client in a fraudulent act. These duties to a tribunal continue through the conclusion of the proceedings and specifically apply even if compliance requires a lawyer to disclose a confidence otherwise protected under Rule 1.6.

- Rules 1.4(a) and (b) require a lawyer to keep the client reasonably informed about the status of the matter and to explain the matter to the client, to the extent reasonably necessary to permit the client to make informed decisions.

- Rule 1.16(a) requires a lawyer to withdraw from representation if called upon to act in violation of the rules of professional conduct. Under Rule 1.16(b), a lawyer may (but need not) withdraw if withdrawal is without material adverse effect on the client, or if the client (i) persists in action involving the lawyer's service that counsel believes to be fraudulent or (ii) persists in pursuing an objective that counsel considers repugnant or imprudent.

An error in calculating the correct tax liability can be computational, such as an arithmetic mistake, or clerical, such as a typographical mistake. Computational errors can also be conceptual, such as where the calculation depends on

¶352

the application or interpretation of a particular Code section. The computational error need not relate to the tax liability, but can occur with respect to penalties or interest. Courts generally have not been reluctant to correct clerical errors. *See Holland v. Commissioner,* 64 T.C.M. (CCH) 1433 (1992); *In re Catt,* 96-2 U.S.T.C. ¶ 50,422 (E.D. Wash. 1996). An arithmetic error, rather than a conceptual error, can be corrected by the Internal Revenue Service without the need for a statutory notice of deficiency. I.R.C. section 6213(b)(1) and (g)(2). An arithmetic error generally is not subject to dispute. This is not necessarily the case with conceptual errors, where the courts are more reluctant to permit correction. In *Stamm International Corp. v. Commissioner,* 90 T.C. 315 (1988), for example, the Tax Court refused to allow the Internal Revenue Service to withdraw a stipulated settlement upon discovering its unilateral mistake of not considering the application of a Code provision in calculating the settlement amount. The Tax Court held that silence by the taxpayer's counsel, although misleading, was not the equivalent of a misrepresentation in that case.

Two local bar association opinions have held that a computational error in a client's favor constituted a client confidence under the applicable state professional rules of conduct and thus counsel was not permitted to disclose. Chicago Bar Ass'n Op. 86-4; Dallas Bar Ass'n Op. (8-23-89) (apparently involving a tribunal.)

The ABA has opined that a lawyer may not deliberately or affirmatively mislead the IRS in settlement negotiations, either by affirmative misstatements or by silence and may not permit the client to mislead, while at the same time noting that a lawyer need not disclose weaknesses in a client's case even if an unjust result occurs. Formal Opinion 314 (April 27, 1965). This Opinion is also explicit that the Internal Revenue Service is not a tribunal.

In *United States v. McRee,* 7 F.3d 976 (11th Cir. 1993), a taxpayer was convicted for converting government property by cashing an erroneously issued refund check, even though the taxpayer did nothing to induce issuance of the refund.

ABA Informal Opinion 86-1518 (Feb. 9, 1986) determined that counsel had a duty to disclose an inadvertently omitted provision from a contract when presented for signature because the omission involved merely a scrivener's error. The ABA assumed for purposes of discussion that the scrivener's error was a client confidence and reasoned that counsel had implied authority to disclose under Model Rule 1.6 because the parties had already reached a meeting of the minds. The Informal Opinion did not address counsel's duty if the client wished to exploit the error.

Discussion

When counsel learns that the Internal Revenue Service has made a computational error of tax, penalty or interest in the client's favor, the information gained is a client confidence under Rule 1.6(a), which generally may not be disclosed without the client's consent, unless otherwise provided in the Model Rules or by other law. Confidentiality applies to all information obtained about the client relating to the representation and not just communications from the client. But Model Rule 8.4(c) provides that a lawyer may not engage in conduct that is dishonest.

The lawyer's ethical obligations will depend on the circumstances; thus, this Statement recognizes that different conclusions should be reached in different factual situations. There is nonetheless a common theme. A client should not profit from a clear unilateral arithmetic or clerical error made by the Internal Revenue Service, and a lawyer may not knowingly assist the client in doing so. This is not the case, however, if the computational error is conceptual, such that a reasonable dispute still exists concerning the calculation.

DOCKETED CASE

If the parties in a docketed case are required to document the amount of the client's tax liability or overpayment, such as in a decision document filed in Tax Court or in a judgment entered on a counterclaim in U. S. District Court or the U. S. Court of Federal Claims, counsel must disclose an error to the court. Model Rule3.3(a)(1). Because counsel knows that the deficiency is understated, or refund overstated, counsel cannot file a document with the Court that contains an incorrect deficiency or overpayment without making a false statement to a tribunal. Disclosure of the error may be made in this situation without the consent of, or consultation with, the client. Rule 3.3(b) specifically requires disclosure notwithstanding that the error is a client confidence under Rule 1.6.

Where the parties need not document the amount of the tax liability or refund, as is generally the case in the U.S. District Courts or the U.S. Court of Federal Claims, the dismissal document generally does not contain the false statement of material fact. Nonetheless, under Model Rule 3.3, counsel owes a greater duty to a tribunal than is owed to an opposing party, and the rules of conduct should not vary depending on the particular forum. Disclosure is required, and may be made without consulting the client.

SETTLEMENT OF NON-DOCKETED CASE

A lawyer must disclose a clear arithmetic or clerical calculation error (but not a conceptual error) the amount of which is not de minimis to the Internal Revenue Service, if there exists express or implied authority from the client to make the disclosure. Whether implied authority exists is a question of fact. Implied authority will generally exist where the terms of a settlement have been reached and the Internal Revenue Service then commits a unilateral arithmetic or clerical error in the computation of the tax, penalty or interest owed or refund due. Implied authority generally will not exist if the calculation error is conceptual; that is, for example, it depends on the application or interpretation of a Code section for which a reasonable dispute could exist.

In refund situations, the cashing of an erroneous refund check can constitute a criminal violation for converting government property. A lawyer who knows that a miscalculation will result in an erroneous refund cannot become an instrumentality in creating the erroneous refund. However, the potential crime is

¶352

a client confidence that generally cannot be disclosed, unless express or implied authority to do so exists.

Therefore, in non-docketed cases involving refunds or deficiencies, if the client refuses to consent where there is no implied authorization, counsel must withdraw from the engagement because the failure to act would constitute a violation of Rule 8.4(c) and Rule 1.2(d). *See* Rule 1.16(a). Counsel need not withdraw if express consent is withheld and the error is conceptual.

These principles can be illustrated by the following examples:

- *Example 1:* After the terms of a settlement in a non-docketed case have been reached, the Internal Revenue Service in calculating the deficiency inadvertently misplaces a decimal point so that the recomputed deficiency is reflected as $25,189.01, instead of $251,890.10. This error is entirely clerical. Implied authority to disclose ordinarily would exist, absent an extraordinary circumstance such as the client's prior express direction to the contrary. Therefore counsel must disclose and need not consult with the client. *See* Example 3. If impliedauthority to disclose does not exist and express consent is withheld by the client, counsel must withdraw. Where the case is docketed, disclosure is required irrespective of the client's express or implied consent.

- *Example 2:* As part of the terms of a settlement reached with the Internal Revenue Service Office of Appeals, the client is entitled to claim a $100,000 deduction, which was originally reflected on Schedule C of his federal income tax return. Counsel believes that this deduction is more likely attributable to a passive activity, but the issue was not raised at Appeals and the Internal Revenue Service computation treated the deduction as non-passive. The taxpayer would not currently benefit from the deduction if it was related to a passive activity. This error is conceptual, as the application of Section 469 to the settlement computation is highly factual and is subject to some reasonable dispute. Counsel may not disclose this error without express consent from the client. Implied authority to consent does not exist because the issue was not addressed in the settlement negotiations and there was no meeting of the minds on the point. The result does not change where the failure to consider Section 469 resulted in a refund or if the case was docketed.

- *Example 3:* The client agrees to settle a non-docketed tax case after the client calculates the deficiency to be approximately $150,000. Counsel later receives the Internal Revenue Service recomputation reflecting a deficiency of only $125,000 and learns that the difference resulted from a multiplication error. Because this error is entirely arithmetical, as to which there can be no reasonable dispute, counsel must disclose the error. Implied authority to disclose exists because the client agreed to settle knowing that the revised deficiency would be approximately $150,000. If the multiplication error resulted in a revised deficiency of $149,900, disclosure would not be necessary because the error is de minimis.

- *Example 4:* In Example 3, assume the client accepted the settlement terms in principle, subject to the Internal Revenue Service recomputation, but estimated a $100,000 revised deficiency. Upon receiving the Internal Revenue Service recomputation, the client and counsel learn that the Internal Revenue Service erroneously determined the deficiency to be $125,000 and the correct revised deficiency was actually $150,000. Implied authority does not exist here because the correct amount is not consistent with the client's stated expectation. This is so notwithstanding that the IRS computational error is entirely arithmetic. Under these circumstances, the lawyer may not disclose the error to the Internal Revenue Service absent express consent from the client. If the client refuses to consent, the lawyer must withdraw.

Conclusion

A lawyer must disclose a clear arithmetic or clerical error in the client's favor in a case docketed in court. In a non-docketed case, a lawyer must disclose a clear unilateral arithmetic or clerical error if there exists express or implied consent. If the client refuses express consent where there is no implied authorization, counsel must withdraw.

¶353 Exhibit 3-3

COMMENTS ON PROPOSED RULEMAKING CIRCULAR 230 ABA SECTION OF TAXATION February 12, 2004

The views expressed herein are presented on behalf of the Section of Taxation (the "Section"). These comments have not been approved by the Board of Governors or the House of Delegates of the American Bar Association and should not be construed as representing the policy of the American Bar Association.[1]

The Section regularly has commented on proposed revisions to Circular 230. Most recently the Section commented extensively on April 23, 2001, August 13, 2001 and April 24, 2002. The Section enjoys a long rich history as a leader in matter involving the improvement of the tax system by regulating the conduct of practitioners pursuant to Circular 230. The Tax Section first proposed rules governing tax shelter opinions nearly 25 years ago, leading the American Bar Association to issue Opinion 346, which was largely incorporated into Circular

---

[1] The comments were prepared by a Joint Task Force Committee on Standards of Tax Practice and the Tax Shelter Task Force of the Section. Members of the Joint Task Force were Federic L. Ballard, Jr., Dennis B. Drapkin, Miriam L. Fisher, Steve R. Johnson, Phillip L. Mann, Ronald A. Pearlman, Charles A. Pulaski, and Paul J. Sax. Principal drafting responsibility was exercised by Paul J. Sax and reviewed by Michael B. Lang, Chair of the Committee of Standards of Tax Practice; Herbert N. Beller, Council Director for the Tax Shelter Task Force; Mark L. Yecies, Council Director for the Standards of Tax Practice Committee; and Richard A. Shaw, Chair of the Section. Although many of the members of the Section who have participated in preparing these comments have clients that would be affected by the principles addressed by these comments or have advised clients in the application of said principles, and all would be affected in their capacity as practitioners, no such member (or the firm or organization to which such member belongs) has been engaged by a client to make, or has a specific individual interest in making, a government submission with respect to, or otherwise to influence the development or outcome of, the specific subject matter of these comments.

230 as Section 10.33. Because Section 10.33 would be repeated by the proposal, and replaced by a new Section 10.35, the Tax Section has a keen interest in assuring a comprehensive and effective transition.

The Section is pleased to be able to supply these comments within the short response period that was provided. In view of the difficulty of some of the questions we address below, we intend to continue our consideration, and look forward to such additional communications as time permits.

Summary

The Section welcomes the proposed rulemaking. The statements included as "best practices" for tax advisors are a useful addition to practice guidelines. To avoid misuse, it should be made clear that the statement of "best practices" is aspirational and that the "best practices" are not intended to state minimum standards of conduct intended to be enforced.

The Section strongly believes that in addition to such guidelines, rules stating minimum standards of conduct are necessary. It is important that such rules be enforceable and that in fact they be enforced.

We believe that it is essential that rules applicable to "more likely than not tax shelter opinions" apply only to formal opinions. Application of the rules to informal advice would burden and disrupt traditional tax planning advice to the detriment of the tax system, by discouraging taxpayers for requesting (and practitioners from providing) written advice.

The opinion requirements that are proposed to apply to certain tax shelter opinions are reasonable and follow logically from the experience with Section 10.33. There is a proper role exempting form the requirements limited opinions and advice reasonably expected to be followed by an opinion, and we offer clarifications that we hope will be helpful. We believe, however, that the proposal requires modification so as not to allow self-marketing of limited opinions free of the requirements that are proposed to apply to certain tax shelter opinions. Failure to address this serious potential gap in coverage of the proposal could have serious consequences, as it could lead to a return to the limited opinion abuses of the 1970's that were corrected in the provisions of Section 10.33 of Circular 230 that would be repealed by the proposal.

We oppose the proposed delegation of authority to practitioner members of the Advisory Committee to single out other practitioners for discipline. Such a delegation has a prohibitive potential for abuse and error.

Best Practices. We welcome the articulation of best practices for tax advisors set forth in proposed Section 10.33(a). We note that the best practices in their most general form are derivative of the American Bar Association Model Rules of Professional Conduct, including Rule 1.1, The Duty of Competence; Rule 1.2, Scope of Representational Rule 2.3, Evaluation for Use by Third Person; Rule 3.4, Fairness to Opposing Party and Counsel; and Rule 5.1, Responsibilities of a Partner or Supervisory Lawyer. More specifically, the American Bar Association has issued Formal Opinions addressing application to tax practice, including

Opinion 314 delineating the relationship between lawyers and the Internal Revenue Service, Opinion 346 prohibiting forms of limited opinion in tax shelter opinions to non-clients adopted in Section 10.33 of Circular 230, and Opinion 85-352 stating the minimum standard for asserting a position in a tax return adopted in Section 10.34 of Circular 230.

The list of best practices makes no reference to applicable professional standards. Nor does the best practices list include reference to practicing competently (the proposal opinion requirements specifically impose a duty of competence, in proposed section 10.35(b)(1)). We suggest the addition of new paragraph (a)(7), as follows: "Practicing competently and otherwise in accordance with the principles and guidelines recognized by the practitioner's profession."

In any statement of best practices we believe that it is important to be clear that best practices are solely aspirational. Otherwise that statement is vulnerable to misuse, by mischaracterizing what is intended as an aspirational guideline as aminimum standard of conduct. We encourage inclusion of a specific recitation that the best practices do not constitute minimum standards of conduct intended to be enforced. We recommend substituting the "endeavor" for "take reasonable steps" in the first sentence of paragraph 10.36(a), and adding the following sentence at the end of that paragraph: "Evidence that a practitioner has endeavored to comply with procedures of the type contemplated by this paragraph (a) will be considered to be substantial mitigation in any case in which a violation of paragraph (b) may have occurred."

We do not intend to diminish the value of a statement of best practices. There is value to such a statement, properly done, and we welcome it. But in today's circumstances, aspirational standards cannot be a substitute for rules that can be enforced, and that are enforced. The Section strongly believes that there is no substitute for rules in today's tax shelter context, and welcomes requirements that practitioners must follow.

We advocate the adoption of rules because they are necessary to end practices that we view as damaging to the tax system, even though those practices have been engaged in by only a relatively small number of firms. We believe that the vast majority of our members understand and abide by the principles embodied in the statement of best practices. But the adverse effect of untoward opinion practices by some on the administration of the tax system, in our view, mandates the action represented by the proposal.

Requirements For Certain Tax Shelter Opinions. As applied to formal tax opinions, the requirements that apply to "more likely than not tax shelter opinions" and "marketed tax shelter opinions" are reasonable and fair. We view them essentially applying the requirements of Opinion 346, as incorporated in existing Section 10.33 applicable to third party tax shelter opinions. We make only a few suggestions in the interest of clarity.

Subparagraph (a)(1)(ii) should be clarified to provide that, although a practitioner rendering a marketed tax shelter opinion in not expected to identify or ascertain facts peculiar to the taxpayer to whom the transaction is marketed, the facts that the practitioner in not expected to identify related to the taxpayer's particular tax status, such as a PHC, CFC, REIT and the like. Our concern is that the sentence could be read to qualify the remainder of subparagraph(a)(2)(ii), in which event marketed tax shelter opinions would be exempted from the proposed prohibition against assuming the transaction has a business purpose or is potentially profitable apart form tax benefits. Under no circumstance should a practitioner rendering a marketed tax shelter opinion be allowed "to assume that a transaction has a business purpose or that a transaction is potentially profitable apart from tax benefits, or to make an assumption with respect to a material valuation issue." The ambiguity might be remedied by stating that in the case of any marketed tax shelter opinion, the practitioner is not "otherwise" expected to identify or ascertain facts peculiar to a taxpayer, and by stating explicitly that apractitioner rendering a marketed tax shelter opinion may not indulge such assumptions.

In subparagraph (a)(3)(iv) practitioners are foreclosed from taking into account the possibility that a return will not be audited, an issue will not be raised on audit, or that an issue will be settled, in providing opinions on material tax issues. It should be made clear that this requirement applies also the overall conclusion described in subparagraph (a)(4), such that the overall conclusion also must address the merits rather than the vagaries of the audit selection and settlement process.

Subparagraph (b) allows the practitioner to rely upon the opinion of another practitioner only if the practitioner is not sufficiently knowledgeable to render an informed opinion with respect to the material federal tax issue. This precludes a practitioner from sharing responsibility with another practitioner for and reason other that a lack of knowledge, even though all issues are addressed by a practitioner and an overall conclusion is reached. We view this as a reasonable requirement, but submit that it also would be reasonable to allow a practitioner who is knowledgeable with respect to all issues to involve another practitioner on a discrete issue, provided that in the aggregate, all requirements are met.

Limited Opinions. The concept of the limited scope opinion is helpful but may prove difficult to apply in practice. We concur that the required disclosure should be stated "at the beginning of the opinion" and that it should be recited that the opinion cannot be used by the recipient to avoid the substantial understatement penalty as to issues outside the scope of the opinion. To eliminate all doubt, it should be explicitly stated that limited opinions need not provide the overall conclusion required by paragraph (a)(4). We agree with the approach of the proposal to preclude the use of limited opinions in the context of tax shelter marketing—the "marketed tax shelter opinion."

However, we further believe there is great potential for abuse inherent in the use of limited opinions. We recall the Opinion 346 and Section 10.33 were written as a direct response to the abuses represented by limited opinions given to third parties in the context of tax shelters marketed to non-client investors in the 1970's. The "reasonable basis" opinion, the "hypothetical facts" opinion, and the "memorandum of law" that discussed issues but drew no conclusion were all forms of limited opinion. The abuses were well chronicled. Taking history as a guide, the use of limited opinions should be very carefully circumscribed, as discussed below, by specifically subjecting all "self-marketed" opinions to the coverage and diligence requirements of Section 10.35.

The concept of limited opinions does not alter the need, discussed below, to limit application of the proposal to "more likely than not tax shelter opinions" that are formal tax opinions, in order to avoid unwanted application to traditional forms of tax planning advice. The proposal required that a practitioner rendering a limited opinion ascertain the actual facts, relate the law to those facts, recite the agreed-upon limitation of scope, make specific disclosures as to reliance for penalty protection, and make specific disclosures as the existence of certain arrangements. Compliance with these requirements is often wholly impractical in the context of informal advice. Taken together, these requirements greatly diminish the practical utility of the limited opinion concept to the extent it was intended to provide a general exception for informal advice.

"More Likely Than Not Tax Shelter Opinions." We agree with the approach of the proposal to impose the tax shelter opinion requirements on "more likely than not tax shelter opinions." Such opinions are assumed by investors to offer at least some level of penalty protection, even though absent compliance with the proposed requirements (that they address all material tax issues, relate the law to the actual facts, and draw an overall conclusion) they would offer little if any such protection. We caution, however, that absent a carefully drawn definition of "more likely than not tax shelter opinion" that excludes advice of an informal nature, the proposal could have unintended consequences, placing impossible burdens on traditional tax planning advice necessary to the functioning of our tax system, and deterring taxpayers from seeking advice they need.

"Excluded Advice." The proposed rulemaking provides that excluded advice consists of written tax advice that is expected subsequently to be followed by written advice that satisfies the requirements. To avoid abuse, it should be required not only that there be such an expectation in fact, but that the expectation written advice will subsequently be provided be "reasonable" as evidenced by objective facts. A pattern of alleged but failed such expectations would render the claimed expectation unreasonable. The regulatory exception should be available whether the subsequent advice is expected to be provided by the practitioner or by another.

We not also that advice concerning the qualification of a qualified plan is excluded advice, and exclusion that we welcome. There are other potential exclusions that we believe have merit, as we have discussed in prior comments. Advice that will be subject to review by the Internal Revenue Service prior to implementation, such as advice that a proposed transaction that is subject of a private letter ruling issued by the Service or an accounting method change that is approved by the Service, should be and excluded opinion. Advice in SEC registered offerings should be considered for exclusion, by reason of SEC review. An opinion that interest is excludable from income under Section 103 of the Code should be excluded, by reason of the relatively higher standard of certainty embodied in opinions as to the issuance or remarketing of state and local government obligations.[2] Consideration should be given to more expansive exclusion in and "angel list" of tax-favored transaction, excluding opinions in categories that the Service agrees are rarely the subject of abuse (such as those enumerated in Treas. Reg. § 1.6662-4(g)(2)(ii)).

Marketed Tax Shelter Opinion. We note the application of the opinion requirements to "marketed tax shelter opinions," using a definition that is the same as that proposed in our comments of April 24, 2002. At that time, however, we also proposed that opinions be subjected to these requirements if any of a number of other factors were met, including one determined by reference to the payment of fees that targeted marketed tax shelters. As proposed, the definition or marketed tax shelter opinion would not include self-marketed tax shelter opinions. Experience reveals that many abusive tax shelter transactions have been self-marketed. Exempting such opinions form the requirements of the proposal would lead to assertions that the proposal does more to encourage, that to stem, abusive tax shelter activity.

We understand the difficulty of determining when a self-marketed tax shelter opinion should be subject to the requirements of the proposal. This asks the question of when an "idea memorandum" shown to a client should be required to address all material issues, related the law to the fact and draw an overall conclusion.

We previously urged that certain tests or indicators be used to subject opinions to the opinion requirements, such as the presence of conditions of confidentiality, a principal purpose of tax avoidance, contractual protections against liability and a fee arrangement not reasonably related to reasonable hourly rates. We understand the difficulty of applying those rules, and accept that the proposal has chosen not to adopt them.

Nonetheless, by allowing limited opinions and exempting self-marketing of opinions other than "more likely than not" opinions, a path is laid for a return to pro-Opinion 346 practices in which opinions were widely employed that stated only a reasonable basis for the position rather than stating any prospect for success, opinions that assumed facts that could not be true, and opinions that discussed issues but drew no conclusions. Such opinions rarely, if ever, would afford any basis for penalty protection. Nonetheless, based upon both history and understanding of practices today, we know that such opinions can be widely and successfully used in marketing. The reason is that tax opinions are not used solely to provide penalty protection. Instead, the fact of the association of a professional reputation of a law firm or a large multidisciplinary professional services firm lends legitimacy to the transaction which is important in the investment process, whether in the boardroom, or the chief financial officer, or to

---

[2] We are concerned that failure to exempt these opinions ultimately would lead to a degradation of "Section 103" opinions. This is not to say there are no abuses in "Section 103 opinions." Rather, our concern is that such opinions would, in the guise of compliance with the rule requiring that material tax issues be addressed, be used to put transactions onto the market that would not be approved under present standards.

an individual investor. The fact of association with the transaction by such a firm is taken in the marketplace as an imprimatur and speaks more loudly to investors than a lengthy substantive law discourse in the opinion.

As discussed above, we have previously suggested a variety of indicators that can be used to determine when an opinion should be subjected to the requirements included in the proposal. Perhaps an even more filling and com prehensive solution than the use of such indicators would be to include in the definition of "marketed tax shelter opinion" any tax shelter opinion that is actively marketed, whether by the practitioners who prepared it, the practitioner's own firm or others. To that end we recommend that paragraph (c)(6) be amended to read as follows: "A marketedtax shelter opinion is a tax shelter opinion that the practitioner knows or has reason to know will be used or referred to in marketing the tax shelter." We find both useful symmetry and desirable common sense in treating any opinion that is in fact actively marketed as a "marketed tax shelter opinion."

We appreciate that there may be uncertainty inherent in what is marketing and what is not. One obvious remedy to uncertainty is, when in doubt, to comply with the opinion requirements. In addition, the proposal might draw from our prior comments of August 13, 2001 to explain that an opinion is not considered marketed solely because the practitioner or the practitioner's firm send clients a letter or memorandum informing them of new developments or tax planning opportunities, or provides similar tax planning advice to multiple clients solely in response to the clients' requests for assistance. All fact and circumstances would be taken into account, including activities by the practitioner, the practitioner's firm and others, to determine if the activities with respect to the transaction constitute marketing. Consideration also could be given to a conclusive presumption that marketing has occurred when substantially the same advice has been given to three or more clients that id not initiate the requests for assistance. Client inquiries that have been solicited as part of the marketing effort would be disregarded for this purpose. Useful reference may be made to the securities law experience and concepts used in determining if a series of ostensibly unrelated private placements constitute and integrated public offering, where there is industry acceptance of reference to relevant facts and circumstances in determining application of securities regulations.

Definitions. In order for the proposal to regulate tax shelter opinion practices without undue burden on the preponderance of ordinary written tax advice, it is essential that the term "more likely than not tax shelter opinion" include only formal opinions. This should be done in a way that is certain and unambiguous. The term should be limited to written opinions that on their face provide formal advice of a type that usually is rendered only on the final and complete form of a transaction.

Practitioners are deeply concerned that the term "more likely than not tax shelter opinion" might be read to encompass any written advice, however informal, that expressly or implicitly states a conclusion as to particular tax consequences that does or could be interpreted to indicate a "more likely than not" or higher level confidence. Such advice is an essential part of many written communications that comprise traditional tax planning of ordinary business transactions. Like a formal opinion, such tax planning advice is intended to be relied upon, but only in a way appropriate to the circumstances, and rarely for penalty protection. Often it addresses alternatives, or is hypothetical, or preliminary, or merely describes what the law is. Were the proposal to apply to such forms of advice, serious adverse consequences to the tax system would result, in that clients would either have to pay for costly and less quickly delivered formal advice that they did not feel was necessary or, more likely, would be deterred form obtaining the basic advice they need to comply with the tax law.

If no way can be found to differentiate formal opinions form lesser forms of written advice, alternatives should be considered. For example, it may be possible to distinguish pre-transactional planning advice, where the rules would apply only to formal opinions, from advice not given prior to (or in connection with) consummation of the transaction, which presumptively may be viewed as issued for penalty protection purposed and therefore more broadly subjected to the proposed rules.

Another alternative may be to conform these rules with applicable penalty regulations, such that penalty protection would be afforded only by an opinion bearing a legend stating that the opinion was intended to be relied upon for purposes of penalty protection, and which otherwise complied with these proposed rules. An advantage of such an approach is that it would relieve the pressure now placed by the proposal by the combination of the broad definition of "tax shelter" to include a "significant purpose" of tax avoidance or evasion and the potential for including informal advice as a "more likely than not tax shelter opinion." On the other hand, this approach might be of limited effectiveness, because it is not clear that it would (or should) preclude taxpayers from asserting that opinions not complying with the rules should be taken into account in assessing the taxpayer's reasonable cause and good faith.

We therefore urge that, as finalized, the regulations unambiguously limit "more likely than not tax shelters opinions" to formal written advice that purports to be the opinion of the practitioner or firm, of a type which ordinarily addressed the final and complete form of a transaction. Such a limitation need not apply to "marketed tax shelter opinions," where the threat to the system represented by active marketing of tax products justifies additional burdens, and history reflects a potential for abuse in forms of advice other than formal opinions.

We previously suggested that a material tax issue be defined as one as to which the Service position enjoyed a "realistic possibility of success." The proposal lowers the standard to "reasonable basis." We understand the desire to broaden the category of material tax issues required to be addressed. But if "reasonable basis" is to be employed, the meaning of the term should be further clarified. The reason that Opinion 85-352 was issued later was and adopted in Section 10.34 was that "reasonable basis" had come to have different meanings, requiring restatement in the form of the "realistic possibility of success" standard, which per Regulation section 1.6694-2(b)(1) implies an approximately one in three or greater likelihood of success. The definition of "reasonable basis" in Regulation section 1.6662-3(b)(3) has the effect of narrowing the uncertainty but is nonetheless vague. One solution would be to state that a position has a "reasonable basis" if it enjoys an approximately one in five likelihood of success on the merits.

The definition of "tax shelter opinion" requires written advice. It should be made clear that advice is written advice even though it communicated only electronically.

The definition of "tax shelter item" might be expanded to address employment tax concepts such as inclusion in "wages". Application to employment taxesappears intended, as the definition of tax shelter reaches any tax imposed by the Internal Revenue Code.

We agree that an opinion should be included even if the name of the practitioner or the practitioner's firm is not referred to in the offering materials or in connection with the sales promotion efforts. Likewise, we agree that the requirements should apply where the practitioner is an officer or employee of the taxpayer.

Disclosures. We agree with the proposed disclosures required to be made with respect to fee sharing arrangements and referral arrangements. But we question whether there is a need to require disclosure of customary fee arrangements; no useful purpose is served by requiring a recitation at the beginning of the opinion that the author was compensated at its regular and usual hourly rates for the time employed or otherwise in accordance with industry custom and practice.

Procedures To Ensure Compliance. In addition to the necessary conforming amendment to section 10.52, Treasury should make clear in the preamble to the final regulations, or through other published guidance, that discipline will not lie for isolated, technical failures to comply, or for good faith misinterpretations of the rules. Practitioners ought not have the slightest reason to fear that they could be subjected to the cost and burden of defending a charge of violating Circular 230 merely by reason of unintentional misapplication of these rules.

We welcome the inclusion of rules applicable to person having responsibility for a firm's tax practice. We note that the rule for persons having responsibility for a firm's tax practice. We note that the rule for persons having responsibility applies only to practitioners who have "principal" authority and responsibility for overseeing a firm's practice. That is too narrowly limited, to the extent principal means of "first importance." The rules should not be limited to the topmost person in a large professional organization, but rather made applicable to practitioners who have supervisory authority and responsibility. We submit that ABA Model Rule of Professional Conduct 5.1, Responsibilities of a Partner of Supervisory Lawyer, would be useful as a guide. Individual practitioners having supervisory responsibility should be subject to discipline if they fail to take reasonable steps to assure compliance, if the failure is willful, reckless or through gross incompetence as provided in Section 10.52.

Some believe that Treasury should give serious consideration to strengthening the proposal by providing for appropriate sanctions against firms that fail to take reasonable steps to have and maintain policies and procedures that assure compliance with these rules, and whose members engage in a pattern or practice of violations. They assert that it is the firm that enjoys the financial benefits of improper opinion practices, and concomitantly, it is the firm which should be given a strong incentive to assure compliance with the proposed rules. Others believe that authority for firmwide discipline not only put at risk practitioners wholly unrelated to any offense, but give rise to a prohibitive risk of abuse in actual application. Particularly in the case of smaller firms, the mere threat may be sufficient toobtain acquiescence in a position no matter how wrong or unjustified the firm may believe that position to be. All agree that any such sanctions should be measured fairly against the offense, and that because the mere threat of firmwide suspension may have draconian consequences, it should be provided that, except in extraordinary circumstances, the sanction appropriate to an entire firm would be in the form of private or public censure or reprimand, not suspension or disbarment. Given the significant division of views on the subject, we do not make a specific recommendation.

Advisory Committee. We note in Section 10.37(a) the suggestion that there be an advisory committee. This has long been a provision in Section 10.33(d). However, the proposal would have the advisory committee make recommendations regarding "whether a practitioner" may have violated Section 10.35 and 10.36. That is a new concept. We view it as appropriate for an advisory committee to make recommendations of general application. But absent an extraordinary circumstance, members of an advisory committee would not be positioned appropriately to conduct examinations or investigations sufficient to warrant recommendations for individual discipline. There is prohibitive potential for conflicts of interest, abuse and error inherent in some practitioners singling out others for discipline by the Service. We strongly urge that such responsibility is better undertaken by the Director of Practice and the professional personnel of the Director's office.

Effective Date. We recommend that the final proposal not be made effective until at least thirty days after publication, in order to avoid disruption to pending transactions and offerings in circulation.

¶354 Exhibit 3-4

AICPA Tax Division Recommendations for a Section 10.37 Advisory Committee February 18, 2004

Circular 230, section 10.37: "(a) Advisory committees. To promote and maintain the public's confidence in tax advisors, the Director of the Office of Professional Responsibility is authorized to establish one or more advisory committees composed of at least five individuals authorized to practice before the Internal Revenue Service. Under procedures prescribed by the Director, an advisory committee may review and make recommendations regarding professional standards or best practices for tax advisors, or more particularly, whether a practitioner may have violated sections 10.35 or 10.36."

AICPA Recommendations:

- A Section 10.37 Advisory Committee, containing six enrolled agents, six lawyers and six CPAs, should be formed under the auspices of the Office of Professional Responsibility (OPR).

- The Advisory Committee would be created and operated in accordance with the *Federal Advisory Committee Act* (FACA), 5 U.S.C. Appendix 2.

- Advisory Committee service should be for three years with a one-third rotation each year of equal numbers of representatives from each professional category. OPR would provide staff support.

- The Advisory Committee's purpose would be to (1) consult with and advise OPR with regard to alleged violations of Circular 230, section 10.35 (Tax Shelter Opinions) and section 10.36 (Compliance Procedures); and (2) to advise OPR with regard to the application of standards and other relevant matters.

- The entire Section 10.37 Advisory Committee should convene at least once each year to: (1) review its operating procedures; (2) discuss "generic" violation and investigation issues; (3) consider recommendations for areas needing additional IRS/Treasury guidance; and (4) consider appropriate follow-up activities, such as Circular 230 changes, discussing and recommending changes to the sanctioning guidelines and best practices, and recommendations to professional organizations. These policy-oriented meetings would be open to the public.

- For each alleged violation being investigated by OPR for which advice is sought, a working group of six should be impaneled, composed of two enrolled agents, two lawyers, and two CPAs. Conflicts of interest will be taken into account in choosing working group members. A majority (four) of the working group must agree to render advice to OPR; otherwise the case is returned to OPR with no advice rendered.

- Information about taxpayers involved with tax shelter opinions at issue may be disclosed to investigating group members, as "special government employees," in accordance with section 6103.

- The working group could accomplish its work through e-mails and conference calls, with meetings held at the discretion of the Advisory Committee.

- Case-related conference calls, meetings, and hearings would not be open to the public to protect the confidentiality of tax return information under section 6103.

¶354

¶355 DISCUSSION QUESTIONS

1. PUB Corp. is a publicly held company, and for several years its certified audit has been done by Final 4, a nationally known accounting firm. Annabel Aggressive, certified public accountant, a recent graduate of a Master of Taxation program and the self-styled "fireball" of Final 4, has just received a summons from the IRS. Annabel worked on the certified audit of PUB Corp. and prepared the tax accrual workpapers regarding PUB Corp. The summons seeks production of the tax accrual workpapers, a step the agent has resorted to because Annabel refuses to produce them (or anything else if she can get away with it) voluntarily.

   Annabel knows that you are still a student in the Master of Taxation program and also knows that in your course you are discussing the FATP privilege and the *Arthur Young* case, 465 U.S. 805, 104 S.Ct. 1475 (1984), 84-1 USTC ¶9305, concerning a privilege for accountant's tax accrual workpapers. (Chapter 6, IRS position on seeking accrual workpapers, and Chapter 7, discussion of the AICPA position on accrual workpapers). Annabel wants to claim privilege solely to delay the agent in his audit. She wants to know whether her actions are prohibited by Circular 230.

2. You normally prepare the tax return for ABC Manufacturing, an S corporation. The sole shareholder of the corporation submits all of the year-end figures except the closing inventory. The owner tells you that they are still in the process of extending the inventory, but that you should start working on those portions of the return that you can do without the closing inventory. He suggests you use $250,000 as an estimate for the closing inventory.

   After you have the return sketched out, you call the owner to get the closing inventory figures. The conversation goes as follows:

   You: I have sketched out your return using the $250,000 estimate for the closing inventory. Do you have any accurate figures for the closing inventory yet?

   Owner: No, we're just finishing that up right now. Tell me, how does the year look using the estimated figure?

   You: Well, it looks like you had a pretty good profit. It's hard to say without all the figures, but I would guess your profit could be as high as $145,000 this year.

   Owner: You say that I could have a $145,000 profit this year?

   You: That assumes that your inventory will close at $250,000.

   Owner: What will my profit be if the closing inventory is only $175,000?

   You: It looks like your profit will only be $70,000.

   Owner: What if the ending inventory is only $125,000?

   You: Then your profit will probably be about $20,000. Why do you ask?

About an hour later the owner comes in. He says, "I just got the figures for the closing inventory. We had to do a lot of computing to come up with an accurate figure, but I'm pretty sure this is it." He hands you a sheet of paper showing the closing inventory to be $95,000.

(A) What does Circular 230 tell you to do in such a situation?

(B) As a practical matter, what should you do in this situation?

3. Alex Alert is the in-house Certified Public Accountant for a large manufacturing firm. He is asked to prepare a pro forma schedule to be used by the president's personal tax preparer in the preparation of the president's individual income tax return.

When Alert receives the figures from the president, he notes that the only income items are the president's already sizable salary and two cash dividends paid to all stockholders during that year. Alert knows that the maintenance staff of the company has rebuilt the president's summer cottage during that year with "surplus goods" rerouted from the plant expansion site. Alert has been reviewing some of the cost overruns on the plant expansion, and he estimates that the cost of labor and materials that went into the president's four-bedroom, three-bath "cottage" is approximately $50,000.

(A) What, if anything, does Circular 230 require Alert to do in this situation?

(B) What should be done as a practical matter?

4. You work for Modmfg as an internal accountant. Modmfg is a very successful sole proprietorship. During the year, Peter Proprietor sells his business, Modmfg, to Newton Owner. Owner asks you to stay on as internal accountant and you agree. At the same time, Proprietor wishes you to continue to prepare his personal tax returns, something you have done for fifteen years.

When it comes time to prepare Peter Proprietor's personal return, you review the contract for the sale of the business. You notice for the first time that the contract drafted by Owner's attorney has allocated 100% of the purchase price to the tangible assets of the business, with no amount allocated to good will at all. You believe that this is an unreasonable allocation, so in reporting the gain on Proprietor's return, you allocate 50% of the purchase price to good will. You are not involved in the preparation of the personal return for Newton Owner, since that task is handled by the outside accountant who worked with Owner's attorney in drafting the contract for the purchase of the business.

Approximately a year later, Proprietor receives a notice that he has been called in for an office examination for a review of the sale of the business. Proprietor asks you to represent him before the IRS in connection with this audit. At the same time, your responsibilities at Modmfg have been growing and Newton Owner has just asked you to be its senior representative in dealing with the IRS in connection with a field

¶355

audit that is about to be conducted of the operations of Modmfg. You realize that Proprietor's and Owner's interests are adverse as to the allocation of the purchase price and that you may have a potential conflict of interest in seeking to represent both of them.

(A) Under Circular 230, can you represent both of them?

(B) What could you do if you wish to represent them both?

(C) Can they agree on an allocation of the purchase price between themselves prior to the time that the audits are scheduled?

5. Bob Beaner is the independent accountant for Lima Enterprise, an S corporation. Bob prepares the corporate tax return based on the ledgers given to him by the internal bookkeepers. During his current year review of the ledgers, he discovered an error in a year-end adjusting entry which was posted two years earlier. The entry was made to record the return of $100,000 worth of merchandise to a supplier. Rather than credit the purchases account, the bookkeeper credited the accounts payable officers' account for $100,000. As a result, cost of goods sold was overstated and income was understated. Furthermore, the corporation subsequently reduced the accounts payable by making a distribution to the officers. The officers thought the distribution was nontaxable and therefore, did not report it as income.

The statute of limitations will run in 10 months, Bob wants to know whether he should advise his client of the error. Does Bob have any further obligations under Circular 230 to amend the prior year's tax return?

CHAPTER 4
EXAMINATION OF RETURNS

¶401 INTRODUCTION

Under the federal taxation system, the taxpayer files a return disclosing income and expenses and pays the tax based on the taxable income shown on the return. While the Internal Revenue Service (IRS) depends primarily on voluntary compliance with the self-assessment system, it also examines and audits returns. For many taxpayers the possibility that the IRS will examine their returns encourages voluntary compliance. The actual chances of examination vary depending on geographical location, type of return and adjusted gross income.

Audit Procedures

¶405 SERVICE CENTER

The audit process begins at the Internal Revenue Service Center where computers and personnel routinely check for such obvious errors as missing signatures and social security numbers and mathematical mistakes. A magnetic tape with pertinent information from each return is sent to the national computer center in Martinsburg, West Virginia, where each return is rated by computer for potential errors by means of a mathematically-based technique known as Discriminate Function (DiF). Numerical weights are assigned to items on the return and the computers produce a composite score for each return. All individual returns are rated under the DiF system. The higher the DiF score, the greater the probability of error on the return.[1]

A number of different formulas for computing a return's error potential exist, but the exact makeup of the formula is not publicly disclosed.[2] Variables probably include amount of income and its source, number and type of dependents, size and nature of certain itemized deductions, and the taxpayer's marital status.

When the computer selects a return with a high DiF score, a classifying officer inspects the return for some obvious or innocent explanation. If the classifyingofficer sees no ready explanation, the questionable return is forwarded for examination.

In addition to computer selected returns, other returns are manually selected under various IRS programs designed to probe for specific tax problems. Manual

---

[1] IRS Pub. 556 (2001).

[2] Code Sec. 6103(b)(2) provides that nothing "shall be construed to require the disclosure of standards used or to be used for the selection of returns for examination, or data used or to be used for determining such standards, if the Secretary determines that such disclosure will seriously impair assessment, collection, or enforcement under the Internal Revenue Laws." This provision was added by Act §701(a) of the Economic Recovery Tax Act of 1981, P.L. 97-34, and was intended to reverse the result in cases such as *Long v. Bureau of Economic Analysts,* 646 F2d 1310 (9th Cir. 1981), 81-1 USTC ¶9439.

identification includes tax returns made available for classification other than by computer identification—e.g., amended returns, information reports (Form 1099 matching program), claims for refund, etc. When a return reviewed by a classifying officer does not warrant examination, it is stamped "Accepted as Filed by Classification" on the face of the return to indicate its status.[3]

¶406 UNALLOWABLE ITEMS PROGRAM

The IRS presently conducts five major types of audit programs. The first, the Unallowable Items Program, is the simplest audit and is conducted at the Service Center. Personnel at the Service Center review returns for items that are obviously not permissible under the law. Some common items include incorrect tax computations, incorrect claims of head of household status, claims of charitable contributions to non-qualifying organizations and excessive child care credits. As part of this same process the return will be screened against information returns that have been filed concerning the taxpayer to make certain that all income reported on the information returns has been reported as income by the taxpayer.[4] The taxpayer audited under this program receives a computer-printed notice proposing a correction in the tax. (The IRS, through the screening of information returns, also detects those taxpayers who failed to file income tax returns for the year.)

¶407 CORRESPONDENCE EXAMINATION

The second of the five major types of audit programs is a correspondence examination. This type of audit is usually conducted by Service Centers. As its name implies, the IRS sends a letter questioning a single tax issue. The types of issues handled by correspondence include: payments to a Keogh plan, payments to an IRA, interest penalty on early withdrawal of savings, disability income exclusion, employee business expenses of less than $1,000, casualty or theft loss of less than $2,000, itemized deductions for interest, taxes, contributions, medical expenses and miscellaneous deductions other than office in home, travel and entertainment or education and credits for child care, elderly, residential energy and political contributions.[5] The letter indicates what item on the return is in doubt and asks the taxpayer to mail supporting documents to the IRS.

Substantiation by the taxpayer might be a receipt or cancelled check or a written explanation of how the person arrived at a particular figure entered on the return. In a correspondence examination, the IRS will wait for the taxpayer to submit substantiation before proposing any changes on the return. Unless specifically required to produce originals, a taxpayer should only produce copies of documents to the IRS.

¶408 OFFICE EXAMINATION

The third of the five major types of audit programs is the office examination. In this audit the taxpayer is asked to visit the IRS. The taxpayer receives a letter (see Exhibit 4-1 at ¶451) which specifies the date and time for the appointment. The

---

[3] IRM Handbook 4.1.5.1.1.   [5] IRM Handbook 4.1.5.9.1.
[4] IRM Handbook 1.3.22.3.4.

letter also indicates the areas under audit and the records and information that the taxpayer should bring to the appointment. Some IRS offices issue audit letters to taxpayers requesting that they call the office and arrange a time and date that is convenient to them. The audit letter also provides the taxpayer with the office location for the interview.

The place of the examination will be based upon the address shown on the tax return.[6] This will be the IRS office closest to the taxpayer's residence. In those situations where the nearest IRS office does not have the appropriate personnel, it will be considered reasonable to conduct the audit at the closest office that has such personnel.

Although office examinations are generally conducted at the nearest IRS office, it is possible to have them held at another location. As an example, if the taxpayer can show a clear need for the audit to take place somewhere else, the IRS will accommodate that situation. Such would be the case if a taxpayer was of advanced age, was infirm or where the taxpayer's books, records and source documents were too cumbersome to bring to an IRS office.[7] A request to change the place of examination should be in writing. The IRS normally will not consider a request that is based on the location of the taxpayer's representative or requires the reassignment of the case to an office that would have difficulty accommodating the audit. The taxpayer must agree to extend the statute of limitations for up to one year if it would expire within thirteen months of the requested transfer.[8]

The office examination is conducted by an interview with the taxpayer, his representative or both.[9] If the taxpayer attends alone, the interview will be suspended at any time the taxpayer asks to consult with an attorney, a CPA or any other person permitted to represent that taxpayer before the IRS.[10] The taxpayer also is permitted to make an audio recording of the interview, provided he or she makes the request at least ten days in advance of the interview, bears the cost of such recording and allows the IRS to make its own recording.[11] If the taxpayer does not record the interview, the IRS nevertheless may make its own recording, but only upon giving at least ten days advance notice to the taxpayer.[12]

Typical issues covered at an office examination include income from tips, capital gains, charitable contributions, dependency exemptions, travel and entertainment expenses, education expenses, medical expenses and bad debts. Although the entire return is technically subject to audit, the IRS generally stays close to the items in question unless a very obvious issue comes up at the examination.

---

[6] Reg. § 301.7605-1(d).

[7] Reg. § 301.7605-1(c)(2)

[8] Reg. § 301.7605-1(e)(4).

[9] Code Sec. 7521(c) provides that the taxpayer need not attend with his representative unless required to do so by an IRS summons.

[10] Code Sec. 7521(b)(2).

[11] Code Sec. 7521(a)(1); Notice 89-51, 1989-1 CB 691.

[12] Code Sec. 7521(a)(2); Notice 89-51, 1989-1 CB 691.

Previously, an office examination was generally limited to individuals who did not have significant business income. The complexity of business returns being audited in this program has been expanded in recent years.

As part of any examination of a business return, the examiner[13] will probe gross receipts.[14] The taxpayer will be questioned regarding sources of income, standard of living, purchases of assets, balances of cash on hand, loan payments and the receipt of borrowed funds. If, based on the answers to these questions, the examiner has a reasonable indication of unreported income, the examiner will probe further by use of one of the indirect methods for reconstructing income.[15] In office audits, this is most commonly the cash transaction or T-account method. The bank-deposits method or source-and-application-of-funds method also may be used by the examiner.

If the T-account or other analysis discloses no discrepancy in reported income, the examination will proceed to a verification of the specific items requested in the appointment letter (see Exhibit 4-1 at ¶451). After all the evidence has been presented, the examiner will afford the taxpayer or his representative an opportunity for a conference. During the conference the examiner will explain the findings and the amount of any additional tax to be proposed. When the examiner and the taxpayer are unable to agree on all the adjustments, the examiner will submit a Form 4549, Income Tax Examination Changes (see Exhibit 4-2 at ¶452), to the taxpayer using either Transmittal Letter 915 (see Exhibit 4-3 at ¶453) or Letter 950 (see Exhibit 4-4 at ¶454). The first letter gives the taxpayer an opportunity to submit additional evidence or information within thirty days, or to request a review by the Appeals Officer. This letter is generally used in connection with a correspondence examination or an office audit when very little interviewer contact has been had with the taxpayer. When the examiner and the taxpayer have had a full discussion of the issues, Letter 950 is submitted to the taxpayer, together with a Form 870, Waiver of Restrictions on Assessment (see Exhibit 4-5 at ¶455). Publication 5, Appeal Rights and Preparation of Protests for Unagreed Cases, which explains a taxpayer's appeal rights, is enclosed with both letters (see Exhibit 4-6 at ¶456).

¶410 FIELD EXAMINATION

The field examination, the fourth type of the five types of audit programs, is used for most business returns and the larger, more complex individual returns. The revenue agent normally advises the taxpayer that the return has been assigned for examination and schedules an appointment at a mutually convenient time, date and place (see Exhibit 4-5 at ¶455). Generally, the examination must be scheduled during the IRS's normal workday and business hours. The IRS may schedule examinations without regard to seasonal fluctuations of the taxpayer's

---

[13] The title of the examiner in the Office Examination program has been changed from "Office Auditor" or "Office Examiner" to "Tax Compliance Officer" (TCO) as part of the IRS reorganization.

[14] IRM Handbook 4.2.4.3.

[15] Code Sec. 7602(e) limits the use of these indirect methods without a "reasonable indication that there is a likelihood of unreported income." See Chapter 19, *infra,* for discussion of these indirect methods.

¶410

business, but will attempt to accommodate the taxpayer to minimize any adverse effects an examination might have on the taxpayer's business.[16]

A field examination normally is required to be conducted at the location where the taxpayer's books, records and other relevant documents are maintained. Typically, this will be the taxpayer's principal place of business or personal residence. However, if a business is so small that an on-site examination would essentially require the business to close or unduly disrupt its operations, the IRS will change the place of examination to an IRS office.[17] The IRS may also move the examination to an IRS office if a taxpayer conditions access to the audit site on IRS employees' compliance with requests for personal identification, surrender of credentials or permission to copy such credentials.[18] Regardless of where the audit occurs, the IRS reserves the right to visit the business premises or the taxpayer's residence to verify facts that can only be established by such a visit.

A taxpayer's written request to change the place of examination will be considered by the IRS on a case-by-case basis.[19] Such a request normally will be granted if the taxpayer has moved or the books and records are being maintained at some other location. No consideration will be given, however, to the location or convenience of the taxpayer's representative. The IRS will take into account the place at which the examination can be performed most efficiently and the resources that are available at the IRS office to which the transfer is requested. A change also will be considered if other factors indicate that examination at the location set by the IRS could pose undue inconvenience to the taxpayer. As a condition for granting a request for transfer, the taxpayer must agree to extend the statute of limitations for up to one year if it will expire within thirteen months of the transfer.[20]

When an IRS agent contacts a taxpayer to examine a return, the agent is required to furnish an explanation of the audit process and the taxpayer's rights relating to that process.[21] If the taxpayer wishes to consult with a representative, the agent must hold the interview in abeyance to allow time for the taxpayer to meet with his or her representative. In many instances, the agent will ask the representative to have the taxpayer present at the meeting. The taxpayer is notrequired to attend the meeting, however, unless he or she has been given a summons to appear.[22] A taxpayer may make an audio recording of the meeting, provided that ten days advance notice be given to the IRS that the taxpayer intends to record the interview. The recording must be done with the taxpayer's equipment and at the taxpayer's own expense. In these situations, the IRS may also record the interview.[23] To fully appreciate the scope of the field examination, it is helpful to reflect on the power given to the IRS to examine returns. Section 7602 of the Internal Revenue Code (the Code) authorizes the Treasury Depart-

---

[16] Reg. § 301.7605-1(b)(1).

[17] Reg. § 301.7605-1(d)(3)(ii).

[18] CCA 200206054. The only information required to be provided by an IRS employee is the employee's name and unique identifying number.

[19] Reg. § 301.7605-1(e)(1).

[20] Reg. § 301.7605-1(e)(4).

[21] Code Sec. 7521(b)(1).

[22] Code Sec. 7521(c).

[23] Code Sec. 7521(a).

ment to examine any books, papers, records or other data which may be relevant or material to ascertaining the correctness of any return. A field examination conducted by a revenue agent is in essence a complete review of the entire financial workings of the taxpayer. The agent will examine the history of the taxpayer, including a study of any pertinent business agreements or documents. In the case of a corporation, the corporate minutes and any other written documentation of the actions of the corporation for the years under audit will be examined.

Determining the scope of an examination is the process by which an examiner selects issues warranting examination. Examiners should select issues so that, with reasonable certainty, all items necessary for a substantially proper determination of the tax liability have been considered. Examiners must assess the facts and apply judgment in determining the scope of the examination. The scope of the examination will be determined by the revenue agent. Examiners are expected to continually exercise judgment throughout the examination process to expand or contract the scope as needed. If, during the course of the examination, the scope of the examination is expanded to include another tax period and the taxpayer has representation, the taxpayer should be notified of the expansion and given time to secure a power-of-attorney for the additional tax period, before any examination action is taken.[24]

The revenue agent will look into the method of accounting employed by the taxpayer (cash or accrual) and determine whether income and expenses have been reported consistently with that method. A comparison of the original books of entry with the tax return will also be made. The agent will seek to reconcile book income with tax return income. Usually this reconciliation will require an analysis of the year-end adjusting entries as well as the journals and ledgers. Special analysis of reserve accounts for bad debts and depreciation can be expected. A test of gross receipts either through the use of a simple T-account, a bank deposit analysis or a spot check is usually required. The agent may also seek inventory verification in the case of a business in which inventory is a material income producing factor. Compensation of officers, accumulation of earnings and related-party transactions are three other prime objects of field examination verification. In these instances, the taxpayer will be asked to furnish the foundation for deductions taken on the return.

An item that is common to both field and office audits is the verification of travel and entertainment expenses. Under Code Sec. 274, specific criteria must be met before a deduction can be taken for these expenses. The revenue agent will be interested in verifying not only the amount of the expenditure but also whether the expenditure meets the requirements of Code Sec. 274.

As part of an audit, the revenue agent may request file copies of a variety of other tax returns. It ensures that all required returns have been filed and the information correctly reported. As an example, a revenue agent auditing a corporation may ask the principal officers for copies of their individual returns.

---

[24] IRM Handbook 4.2.2.6.1.

¶410

The "inspection" of these file copies does not constitute an audit but is merely a verification to ensure that a return was filed and that income on that return corresponds to those items from the corporate audit that should be reported by the individual. In the event of a discrepancy on the individual return, the agent generally will open that return for examination and conduct an audit of the individual taxpayer. In a "package audit" of a business, the agent also will ask for copies of employment tax returns to determine that such returns have been filed and that the reported information reconciles with the tax return deductions of the business.

During an audit, questions frequently arise concerning the valuation, depreciation, obsolescence or depletion of particular assets. Such issues are often referred to an engineering group which services the local examination area.

¶412 RESEARCH AUDIT

The final type of the five audit programs is a research audit. Returns are chosen at random from a scientific sample based on the ending digits of the taxpayer's social security number. Referred to as TCMP (Taxpayer Compliance Measurement Program) audits, they represent fewer than two percent of all returns audited. Under the TCMP, the return is subjected to a thorough audit in which every item on the return is covered regardless of dollar amount. Although some taxpayers have objected to such an in-depth scrutiny for research purposes, both *United States v. Flagg*[25] and *United States v. First National Bank of Dallas*[26] have held that a taxpayer cannot refuse to comply with the requirements of a TCMP audit.

In order to protect the validity of the statistical sample, revenue agents are required to complete an assigned TCMP audit, even though there is no apparent error on the tax return. The failure to complete the audit would impair the sampling technique, since one audit reflects a sample universe of approximately 30,000 tax returns.

The last TCMP audit program was conducted on returns for 1988. Another TCMP audit program scheduled for 1994 was cancelled due to budget constraints and because it was thought to be too intrusive on taxpayers. The DiF formula updated in 1993 based upon 1988 return data is being updated each year for tax law and tax form changes and is still being used to select returns for audit. One of the IRS's improvement priorities is to design a national compliance survey as an effective alternative to TCMP.[27]

¶413 TAXPAYER RIGHTS

The Secretary of the Treasury is required to prepare and distribute a statement explaining in simple language the rights of taxpayers when dealing with the IRS. That statement must be furnished to all taxpayers contacted by the IRS for the purpose of determining or collecting taxes. Publication No. 1, Your Rights as a Taxpayer (see Exhibit 4-8 at ¶1458) issued by the IRS, sets forth in nontechnical terms the following rights:

---

[25] 634 F2d 1087 (8th Cir. 1980), 80-2 USTC ¶9795 cert. denied, 451 U.S. 909 (1981).

[26] 635 F2d 391 (5th Cir. 1981), 81-1 USTC ¶9159.
[27] CCH Federal Tax Day, 9/27/2000, Item #I.2.

1. The rights of the taxpayer and obligations of the IRS during the audit;

2. The right to a representative;

3. How adverse decisions are appealed;

4. How refunds can be claimed;

5. How the taxpayers may file complaints; and

6. How and by what procedures the IRS assesses and collects tax.

At the initial interview, revenue agents and auditors also are required to orally explain to the taxpayer the audit process and the rights of the taxpayer with respect to such process. They must clearly advise the taxpayer of his or her right to appeal.

In addition, the IRS is now prohibited from contacting any person, other than the taxpayer, regarding the determination or collection of the taxpayer's tax liability without providing reasonable advance notice to the taxpayer.[28] However, disclosure need not be made for any contact (1) authorized by the taxpayer; (2) situations where notice would jeopardize collection; and (3) contacts during a pending criminal investigation.

¶414 INTERNAL REVENUE MANUAL

A number of auditing techniques or procedures, which are provided to and followed by IRS personnel who examine tax returns, are contained in the Internal Revenue Manual. A brief description of some of the more important techniques and their use is contained in the following handbooks:

1. *Examination of Returns Handbook.*[29] This handbook contains guidelines that are followed by examiners of individual and corporate income tax returns. This handbook is used for reference purposes in dealing with various problems encountered in day-to-day work.

2. *Specialty Handbook.*[30] There are various handbooks for various types of tax returns, various industries, and special features or programs.

3. *Fraud Handbook.*[31] This handbook contains a number of examination procedures and techniques that are principally used in in-depth fraud examinations or investigations (see Chapters 18 and 19.) The handbook's guidelines are not all-inclusive and are permissive.

¶415 BURDEN OF PROOF

An audit is basically an adversary proceeding, but unlike a criminal trial in which the defendant is presumed innocent until proven guilty, historically, an audit placed the burden of proof on the taxpayer. In one of its most publicized provisions, the IRS Restructuring and Reform Act of 1998[32] altered the historical rule[33] that the IRS will have the burden of proof in any court proceedings arising out of examinations beginning after July 22, 1998, if the taxpayer introduces

---

[28] Code Sec. 7602(c).

[29] IRM Handbook 4.2.

[30] See Exhibit 4-9 at ¶1459 for a list of specialty handbooks.

[31] IRM Handbook 104.2.

[32] P.L. 105-206.

[33] Code Sec. 7491.

"credible evidence" on any factual issue relevant to ascertaining the taxpayer's liability for any income, estate, or gift tax, provided that (1) the taxpayer has complied with any requirement to substantiate any item,[34] (2) the taxpayer has maintained records required under the Code and has cooperated with reasonable requests by the IRS for witnesses, information, documents, meetings and interviews, and (3) in the case of a partnership, corporation, or trust, the taxpayer has a net worth of no more than seven million dollars. The term "credible evidence" is the "quality of evidence which, after the critical analysis, the court would find sufficient upon which to base a decision if no contrary evidence were submitted (without regard to the judicial presumption of Internal Revenue Service correctness)."[35] Code Sec. 7491's cooperation requirement demands that, among other things, the taxpayer exhaust all administrative remedies, including any appeal rights. The taxpayer is not, however, required to agree to extend the statute of limitations. The taxpayer must establish the applicability of any claimed privilege. The taxpayer has the burden of proving that he or she meets the requirements for shifting the burden of proof under Code Sec. 7491.

The IRS will also have the burden of proof on any item of income that is reconstructed through the use of statistical information of unrelated taxpayers.[36] In addition, under Code Sec. 7491(c), the IRS will have the burden of proof in any court proceeding involving imposition of a civil penalty on any individual.

The perceived importance of the burden shift from the taxpayer makes it critical for accountants, attorneys, and others who represent taxpayers during audits to ensure that the prerequisites for the burden shift are met, if possible. However, in situations where the taxpayer failed to shift the burden, it will benecessary to present a persuasive defense. A practitioner should prepare for an audit in the same way an attorney prepares for a courtroom appearance. The practitioner should marshal all the evidence and should have all receipts and cancelled checks classified and verified with adding machine tapes. The practitioner also should verify that all books of account correspond with the items in the tax return.

Generally, it is better for the practitioner not to volunteer any extraneous information and only to present evidence or documents pertaining to those areas about which the agent has inquired. After the agent completes the examination, he or she will tell the taxpayer or practitioner what the results are. At this stage, depending on the nature of the issue, arguments can be presented in an attempt to settle the case.

¶416 SETTLEMENT EFFORTS

While no general rule can be formulated for the best time or procedure to be followed in settling a tax case, it is helpful to attempt to dispose of a case at the lowest possible level, that is, with the revenue agent. The agent who has

---

[34] *Sowards v. Comm'r*, T.C. Memo 2003-180

[35] Sen. Comm. Rep. to P.L. 105-206; *Higbee v. Comm'r*, 116 T.C. 438, 442-3 (2001); *Forste v. Comm'r*, T.C. Memo 2003-103.

[36] Code Sec. 7491(b).

conducted the examination will be completely familiar with all the facts and circumstances surrounding the items in issue. In most cases, the taxpayer has nothing to lose by an intensive effort to settle a tax controversy immediately. If negotiations are unsuccessful, at least the taxpayer will know what issues are in doubt and where he or she stands. This will allow the taxpayer time to prepare the case and to consider the various alternative actions available.

Although a revenue agent technically has no settlement authority, in practice, the agent has discretion in a number of areas. However, a revenue agent does not have authority or discretion in areas where the Commissioner has indicated that the IRS will not follow a court decision or has issued adverse regulations or revenue rulings. Therefore, it is important to determine whether the issues raised by the agent are of a factual or a legal nature. For example, reasonableness of compensation and deductibility of travel and entertainment expenses are factual issues. On such issues, the agent may have substantial authority to settle a case.

When a legal issue is involved and the IRS has clearly articulated its position, an impasse will quickly be reached in any settlement attempt. In such a situation, the practitioner should indicate that the agent's opinion is respected and that the representative realizes the agent has no choice on the issue. At the same time, the practitioner should explain that he or she must disagree in order to represent the client's best interests. The practitioner should attempt to isolate the agreed from the unagreed issues and, if possible, to have the agent's report reflect only the unagreed issues. Finally, the practitioner should make sure that the agent has a complete and accurate picture of each transaction, because the statement of facts in the agent's report will be relied upon by the IRS in all future settlement discussions.

Another means of settling legal issues is to obtain a National Office Technical Advice Memorandum. Technical advice is furnished by the National Office of the Internal Revenue Service to help IRS personnel close cases and to establish and maintain consistent holdings on issues. Such advice can be obtained during the course of the examination or when the case has been forwarded to the Appeals Office for review. A technical advice conclusion that is adverse to the taxpayer does not preclude the taxpayer from litigating the issue. The rules for obtaining a Technical Advice Memorandum are discussed in Chapter 16.

If a full settlement has been reached, the revenue agent will prepare a Form 4549, Income Tax Examination Changes (see Exhibit 4-2 at ¶452). This form will set forth in summary the adjustments to income or expenses that have been made as a result of the audit, the years being adjusted, the amount of additional tax and penalties, if any, and with whom the examination changes were discussed. The Form 4549 is to be signed by the examiner and consented to by the taxpayer. Execution of a Form 4549 constitutes a consent to the assessment of the deficiencies shown on the form and eliminates the need for the IRS to follow the formal assessment procedures required by Code Sec. 6212. The execution of Form

¶416

4549 at this stage of the proceedings will stop the running of interest thirty days after the consent to assessment is filed with the IRS.[37]

In cases in which there has been a partial agreement, the revenue agent may request that the taxpayer sign a Form 870, Waiver of Restrictions on Assessment and Collection of Deficiency in Tax and Acceptance of Overassessment (see Exhibit 4-5 at ¶455). Execution of this waiver by the taxpayer will allow the immediate assessment of the tax on agreed issues without the need to issue a formal statutory notice of deficiency. Since Form 870 generally does not detail the audit changes, it will be accompanied by a Form 4549-A, Income Tax Examination Changes (see Exhibit 4-10 at ¶460 and Exhibit 4-11 at ¶461, Form 886-A, Explanation of Items).

Any agreement reached with the revenue agent or auditor is not binding on the IRS. It is subject to review by the Quality Measurement Staff (QMS) servicing the local office. QMS checks the report and the workpapers prepared by the agent to see if all relevant issues have been examined. QMS will also review the recommended treatment of items by the agent to see if such treatment conforms to the IRS rules. This is an extension of the IRS's attempt to apply the law uniformly throughout the country to all taxpayers. At times, QMS will question whether the agent's proposed allowance or disallowance of a deduction or exclusion of income is appropriate. In such a situation, the case may be sent back to the examiner to develop further facts supporting the conclusion reached. At other times, the review staff will instruct the agent that the proposed treatment is wrong because of an error in the agent's interpretation of the law. Cases subject to mandatory review by QMS include: Taxpayer Compliance Measurement Program (TCMP) cases, Joint Committee cases, Employee audits, and Innocent Spouse cases. Although there are a limited number of identified mandatory review categories, territory managershave the discretion to designate any type or group of cases as a 100-percent review category if reviews are considered essential.[38] In addition, cases are reviewed on a random sample basis.

It is only when the local office issues a report accepting the return as filed or notifying the taxpayer of any agreed adjustment to his or her tax liability that any settlement reached with the agent can be considered final. The letter notifying the taxpayer of final action is set forth as Exhibit 4-12 at ¶462.[39]

¶418 UNAGREED CASES

If a settlement cannot be reached with the examiner, a report is prepared detailing the reasons for the inclusion of additional income or disallowance of expenses. A summary of the changes is reflected on Form 4549-A (see Exhibit 4-10 at ¶460). This form along with the full explanation of adjustments is sent to the taxpayer along with a Form 870. A transmittal letter commonly known as a "30-day letter" (see Exhibit 4-4 at ¶454) also accompanies this report. The transmittal letter sets out the following options:

---

[37] Code Sec. 6601(c).
[38] IRM Handbook 4.8.4.2.

[39] IRM Handbook 104.3.7.4.4.

1. The taxpayer can accept the findings of the examiner and execute a Waiver of Restrictions on Assessment (Form 870). If this course is followed, the taxpayer is billed for any additional tax resulting from the examination. This does not preclude the taxpayer from contesting the deficiency in court, but it does mean that the tax will have to be paid and then a claim for refund filed.[40]

2. The taxpayer can request a conference with the local Appeals office. This request normally must be received within thirty days of the issuance of the transmittal letter. When the deficiency in tax is more than $25,000, the request must include a written protest setting forth the taxpayer's position.[41] The examiner will then forward the file along with the protest to the Appeals Office.

3. The taxpayer can do nothing, in which case the taxpayer will receive a "Statutory Notice of Deficiency," commonly referred to as a "90-day letter" (see Exhibit 4-13 at ¶463). This form indicates that the tax will be assessed unless a petition is filed with the Tax Court of the United States. A waiver, Form 4089, is enclosed with the 90-day letter (see Exhibit 4-14 at ¶464).

---

[40] See Chapter 15, *infra.*   [41] See Chapter 12, *infra.*

¶451 Exhibit 4-1

Internal Revenue Service	Department of the Treasury

Date:

Taxpayer Identification Number:

Tax Year:

Form Number:

Person to Contact:

Employee Identification Number:

Contact Telephone Number:

Fax Number:

Dear

Your federal income tax return for the year shown above has been selected for examination. We examine tax returns to verify the correctness of income, deductions, exemptions, and credits.

WHAT YOU NEED TO DO
Please call our appointment clerk **WITHIN 10 DAYS** to schedule an appointment. For your convenience we have provided space below to record your appointment.

Place: Date:

Time:

Attached to this letter is a list of the items on your return which will be examined. In an effort to save time, you should organize your records according to the category as deducted on your return. For further information see the enclosed Publication 1, *Your Rights as a Taxpayer,* and Notice 609, *Privacy Act Notice.*

WHAT TO EXPECT AT THE EXAMINATION
Generally an examination is scheduled to last two to four hours. After the completion of the initial interview, additional information still may be needed. You may submit this information by mail or by scheduling a follow-up appointment. When the examination is completed, you may owe additional tax, be due a refund, or there may be no change to your return.

WHO MAY COME TO THE EXAMINATION
If you filed a joint return, you and/or your spouse may attend. You also may elect to have someone else represent you. If you will not attend with your representative, you must provide a completed Form 2848, *Power of Attorney,* or Form 8821, *Tax Information Authorization,* by the start of the examination. You can get these forms from our office.

(over)

Letter 2201 (DO) (Rev. 12-1999)
Catalog Number 63748H

WHAT WILL HAPPEN IF YOU DO NOT RESPOND

If you do not keep your appointment or provide the requested records, we will issue an examination report showing additional tax due. Therefore, it is to your advantage to keep your appointment and to provide the records. If you are uncertain about the records needed or the examination process, we will answer your questions when you call to schedule your appointment.

Sincerely yours,

Enclosures:
Publication 1
Notice 609

Letter 2201 (DO) (Rev. 12-1999)
Catalog Number 63748H

Please bring records to support the following items reported on your tax return for _____ .

☐ Automobile Expenses	☐ Energy Credit	☐ Sale or Exchange of Residence
☐ Bad Debts	☐ Exemptions (Child/Children, Other)	☐ Taxes
☐ Capital Gains and Losses	☐ Filing Status	☐ Uniform, Equipment, and Tools
☐ Casualty Losses	☐ Income	☐
☐ Contributions	☐ Interest Expenses	☐
☐ Credit for Child and	☐ Medical and Dental Expenses	☐
Dependent Care Expenses	☐ Miscellaneous Expenses	☐
☐ Education Expenses	☐ Moving Expenses	
☐ Employee Business Expenses	☐ Rental Income and Expenses	

Schedule C

☐ Books and records about your income, expenses, and deductions
☐ Workpapers used in preparing your return
☐ Savings account passbooks, brokerage statements, and other information related to foreign and domestic investments
☐ Bank statements, canceled checks, and duplicate deposit slips covering the period from _____ to_____ .
☐ Information on loans, repayments, and other nontaxable sources of income

☐ All Business Expenses	☐ Gross Receipts	☐ Salaries and Wages
☐ Bad Debts	☐ Insurance	☐ Supplies
☐ Car and Truck Expenses	☐ Interest	☐ Taxes
☐ Commissions	☐ Legal and Professional Services	☐ Travel and Entertainment
☐ Cost of Goods Sold	☐ Rent	
☐ Depreciation	☐ Repairs	
☐		

Schedule F

☐ Books and records about your income, expenses, and deductions
☐ Workpapers used in preparing your return
☐ Savings account passbooks, brokerage statements, and other information related to foreign and domestic investments
☐ Bank statements, canceled checks, and duplicate deposit slips covering the period from _____ to_____ .
☐ Information on loans, repayments, and other nontaxable sources of income

☐ All Farm Expenses	☐ Insurance	☐ Repairs and Maintenance
☐ Depreciation	☐ Inventories	☐ Supplies Purchases
☐ Feed Purchases	☐ Labor Hired	☐ Taxes
☐ Fertilizers and Lime	☐ Machine Hire	☐
☐ Gross Receipts	☐ Other Farm income	☐
☐		

Letter 2201 (DO) (Rev. 12-1999)
Catalog Number 63748H

¶451

¶452 Exhibit 4-2

		Page _____ of _____ Pages

Form **4549** (Rev. 11-93)	Department of the Treasury — Internal Revenue Service **Income Tax Examination Changes**	Return Form No.

Name and Address of Taxpayers	S.S. or E.I. Number		Filing Status
	Person With Whom Examination Changes Were Discussed	Name and Title	

1. Adjustments to Income	Year:	Year:	Year:
a.			
b.			
c.			
d.			
e.			
f.			
g.			
2. Total Adjustments			
3. Adjusted Gross or Taxable Income Shown on Return or as Previously Adjusted			
4. Corrected Adjusted Gross or Taxable Income			
5. Corrected Tax			
6. Less Credits a.			
b.			
c.			
7. Balance (Line 5 less total of lines 6a through 6c)			
8. Plus Other Taxes a.			
b.			
c.			
9. Total Corrected Tax Liability (Line 7 plus total of lines 8a through 8c)			
10. Total Tax Shown on Return or as Previously Adjusted			
11. Adjustments to EIC/Fuels Credits - increase (decrease)			
12. Deficiency - Increase in Tax (Line 9 adjusted by lines 10 and 11)			
13. Overassessment - Decrease in Tax (Line 9 adjusted by lines 10 & 11)			
14. Adjustments to Prepayment Credits - increase (decrease)			
15. Balance Due, Excluding Interest and Penalties (Line 12 adjusted by line 14)			
16. Overpayment (Line 13 adjusted by line 14)			
17. Penalties Code Section			
A.			
B.			
C.			
D.			
18. Prepayment on Balance Due Check #			

Examiner's Signature	District	Date

Consent to Assessment and Collection — I do not wish to exercise my appeal rights with the Internal Revenue Service or to contest in the United States Tax Court the findings in this report. Therefore, I give my consent to the immediate assessment and collection of any increase in tax and penalties, and accept any decrease in tax and penalties shown above, plus any interest as provided by law. I understand that this report is subject to acceptance by the District Director.

NOTE: If a joint return was filed, both taxpayers must sign.	Signature of Taxpayer	Date	Signature	Date
		Title		Date
By				

¶452

The Internal Revenue Service has agreements with State tax agencies under which information about Federal tax, including increases or decreases, is exchanged with the States. If th is change affects the amount of your State income tax, you should file the required State form.

You may be subject to backup withholding if you underreport your interest, dividend, or patronage dividend income and do not pay the required tax. The IRS may order backup withholding at 31 percent after four notices have been issued to you over a 120-day period and the tax has been assessed and remains unpaid.

Form 4549 (Rev. 11-93)

¶452

¶453 Exhibit 4-3

Internal Revenue Service   **Department of the Treasury**

Date:

Taxpayer Identification Number:

Form:

Tax Period(s) Ended:

Person to Contact:

Contact Telephone Number:

Employee Identification Number:

Refer Reply to:

Last Date to Respond to this Letter:

Dear

We have enclosed two copies of our examination report showing the changes we made to your tax for the period(s) shown above. Please read the report and tell us whether you agree or disagree with the changes. (This report may not reflect the results of later examinations of partnerships, "S" Corporations, trusts, etc., in which you have an interest. Changes made to those tax returns could affect your tax.)

IF YOU AGREE with the changes in the report please sign, date, and return one copy to us by the response date shown above. If you filed a joint return, both taxpayers must sign the report. If you owe additional tax, please include payment for the full amount to limit penalty and interest charges to your account.

IF YOU CAN'T PAY the full amount you owe now, pay as much as you can. If you want us to consider an installment agreement, please complete and return the enclosed Form 9465, *Installment Agreement Request*. If we approve your request, we will charge a $43.00 fee to help offset the cost of providing this service. We will continue to charge penalties and interest until you pay the full amount you owe.

IF YOU DON'T AGREE with the changes shown in the examination report, you should do one of the following by the response date.

- Mail us any additional information that you would like us to consider

- Discuss the report with the examiner

- Discuss your position with the examiner's supervisor

- Request a conference with an Appeals Officer, as explained in the enclosed Publication 3498, *The Examination Process*. Publication 3498 also explains *Your Rights as a Taxpayer* and *The Collection Process.*

Letter 915 (DO) (Rev. 9-2000)
Catalog Number 62712V

¶453

IF YOU DON'T TAKE ANY ACTION by the response date indicated in the heading of this letter, we will process your case based on the information shown in the report. We will send you a statutory notice of deficiency that gives you 90 days to petition the United States Tax Court. If you allow the 90-day period to expire without petitioning the tax court, we will bill you for any additional tax, interest, and penalties.

If you have any questions, please contact the person whose name and telephone number are shown in the heading of this letter. When you write to us, please include your telephone number and the best time for us to call you if we need more information. We have enclosed an envelope for your convenience.

Thank you for your cooperation.

Sincerely yours,

Enclosures:
Examination Report (2)
Form 9465
Publication 3498
Envelope

¶454 Exhibit 4-4

Internal Revenue Service	**Department of the Treasury**

Taxpayer Identification Number:

Date: Form:

Tax Period(s) Ended and Deficiency Amount(s):

Person to Contact:

Contact Telephone Number:

Employee Identification Number:

Last Date to Respond to this Letter:

Dear

We have enclosed an examination report showing proposed changes to your tax for the period(s) shown above. Please read the report, and tell us whether you agree or disagree with the changes by the date shown above. (This report may not reflect the results of later examinations of partnerships, "S" Corporations, trusts, etc., in which you may have an interest. Changes to those accounts could also affect your tax.)

If you agree with the proposed changes...

1. Sign and date the enclosed agreement form. If you filed a joint return, both taxpayers must sign the form.

2. Return the signed agreement form to us.

3. Enclose payment for tax, interest and any penalties due. Make your check or money order payable to the **United States Treasury.** You can call the person identified above to determine the total amount due as of the date you intend to make payment.

4. After we receive your signed agreement form, we will close your case.

If you pay the full amount due now, you will limit the amount of interest and penalties charged to your account. If you agree with our findings, but can only pay part of the bill, please call the person identified above to discuss different payment options. We may ask you to complete a collection information statement to determine your payment options, such as paying in installments. You can also write to us or visit your nearest IRS office to explain your circumstances. If you don't enclose payment for the additional tax, interest, and any penalties, we will bill you for the unpaid amounts.

Letter 950 (DO) (Rev. 9-2000)
Catalog Number 40390D

If you are a "C" Corporation, Section 6621 (c) of the Internal Revenue Code provides that an interest rate 2% higher than the standard rate of interest will be charged on deficiencies of $100,000 or more.

If you don't agree with the proposed changes...

1. You may request a meeting or telephone conference with the supervisor of the person identified in the heading of this letter. If you still don't agree after the meeting or telephone conference, you can:

2. Request a conference with our Appeals Office. If the total proposed change to your tax is:

    * $25,000 or less for *each* referenced tax period, send us a letter requesting consideration by Appeals. Indicate the issues you don't agree with and the reasons why you don't agree. If you don't want to write a separate letter, you can complete the Statement of Disputed Issues at the end of this letter and return it to us.

    *   More than $25,000 for *any* referenced tax period; you must submit a formal protest.

The requirements for filing a formal protest are explained in the enclosed Publication 3498, *The Examination Process.* Publication 3498 also includes information on your *Rights as a Taxpayer* and the *IRS Collection Process.*

If you request a conference with our Appeals Office, an Appeals Officer will call you (if necessary) for an appointment to take a fresh look at your case. The Appeals Office is an independent office and most disputes considered by the Appeals Office are resolved informally and promptly. By requesting a conference with our Appeals Office you may avoid court costs (such as the Tax Court $60 filing fee), resolve the matter sooner, and/or prevent interest and any penalties from increasing on your account.

If you decide to bypass the Appeals Office and petition the Tax Court directly, your case will usually be sent to an Appeals Office first to try to resolve the issue. Certain procedures and rights in court (for example, the burden of proof and potential recovery of litigation costs) depend on you fully participating in the administrative consideration of your case, including consideration by the IRS Appeals Office.

If you don't reach an agreement with our Appeals Office or if you don't respond to this letter, we will send you another letter that will tell you how to obtain Tax Court Review of your case.

You must mail your signed agreement form, completed Statement of Disputed Issues, or a formal protest to us by the response date shown in the heading of this letter. If you decide to request a conference with the examiner's supervisor, your request should also be made by the response date indicated.

MAIL RESPONSES TO: **Internal Revenue Service**
Attn:

Letter 950 (DO) (Rev. 9-2000)
Catalog Number 40390D

¶454

If you have any questions, please contact the person identified in the heading of this letter. We will be glad to discuss your options with you.

Sincerely yours,

Enclosures:
Copy of this letter
Examination Report
Agreement Form
Publication 3498
Envelope

Letter 950 (DO) (Rev. 9-2000)
Catalog Number 40390D

¶454

STATEMENT OF DISPUTED ISSUES

☐ THE PROPOSED CHANGE IS $25,000 or less for each of the REFERENCED TAX PERIOD(S).

Issue(s) I Disagree With: Reasons for Disagreement:

_____   _____
_____   _____
_____   _____
_____   _____
_____   _____
_____   _____
_____   _____
_____   _____
_____   _____
_____   _____
_____   _____

(if more space is needed, attach a separate sheet)

_____   _____
Signature   Date

Letter 950 (DO) (Rev. 9-2000)
Catalog Number 40390D

¶454

¶455 Exhibit 4-5

Form **870** (Rev. March 1992)	Department of the Treasury — Internal Revenue Service **Waiver of Restrictions on Assessment and Collection of Deficiency in Tax and Acceptance of Overassessment**	Date received by Internal Revenue Service

Names and address of taxpayers *(Number, street, city or town, State, ZIP code)*	Social security or employer identification number

Increase (Decrease) in Tax and Penalties

Tax year ended	Tax	Penalties			
	$	$	$	$	$
	$	$	$	$	$
	$	$	$	$	$
	$	$	$	$	$
	$	$	$	$	$
	$	$	$	$	$
	$	$	$	$	$

(For instructions, see back of form)

Consent to Assessment and Collection

I consent to the immediate assessment and collection of any deficiencies *(increase in tax and penalties)* and accept any overassessment *(decrease in tax and penalties)* shown above, plus any interest provided by law. I understand that by signing this waiver, I will not be able to contest these years in the United States Tax Court, unless additional deficiencies are determined for these years.

YOUR SIGNATURE——▶ HERE		Date
SPOUSE'S SIGNATURE——▶		Date
TAXPAYER'S REPRESENTATIVE HERE ———————▶		Date
CORPORATE NAME ——————▶		
CORPORATE OFFICER(S) SIGN HERE		Title	Date
		Title	Date

Catalog Number 16894U   Form **870** (Rev. 3-92)

Instructions

General Information

If you consent to the assessment of the deficiencies shown in this waiver, please sign and return the form in order to limit any interest charge and expedite the adjustment to your account. Your consent will not prevent you from filing a claim for refund *(after you have paid the tax)* if you later believe you are so entitled. It will not prevent us from later determining, if necessary, that you owe additional tax; nor extend the time provided by law for either action.

We have agreements with State tax agencies under which information about Federal tax, including increases or decreases, is exchanged with the States. If this change affects the amount of your State income tax, you should file the required State form.

If you later file a claim and the Service disallows it, you may file suit for refund in a district court or in the United States Claims Court, but you may not file a petition with the United States Tax Court.

We will consider this waiver a valid claim for refund or credit of any overpayment due you resulting from any decrease in tax and penalties shown above, provided you sign and file it within the period established by law for making such a claim.

Who Must Sign

If you filed jointly, both you and your spouse must sign. If this waiver is for a corporation, it should be signed with the corporation name, followed by the signatures and titles of the corporate officers authorized to sign. An attorney or agent may sign this waiver provided such action is specifically authorized by a power of attorney which, if not previously filed, must accompany this form.

If this waiver is signed by a person acting in a fiduciary capacity *(for example, an executor, administrator, or a trustee)* Form 56, Notice Concerning Fiduciary Relationship, should, unless previously filed, accompany this form.

*U.S. GPO:1992-312-711/50896

¶456 Exhibit 4-6

Your Appeal Rights and How To Prepare a Protest If You Don't Agree

Department of the Treasury
Internal Revenue Service

www.irs.ustreas.gov

Publication 5 **(Rev. 01-1999)**
Catalog Number 46074I

Introduction

This Publication tells you how to appeal your tax case if you don't agree with the Internal Revenue Service (IRS) findings.

If You Don't Agree

If you don't agree with any or all of the IRS findings given you, you may request a meeting or a telephone conference with the supervisor of the person who issued the findings. If you still don't agree, you may appeal your case to the Appeals Office of IRS.

If you decide to do nothing and your case involves an examination of your income, estate, gift, and certain excise taxes or penalties, you will receive a formal Notice of Deficiency. The Notice of Deficiency allows you to go to the Tax Court and tells you the procedure to follow. If you do not go to the Tax Court, we will send you a bill for the amount due.

If you decide to do nothing and your case involves a trust fund recovery penalty, or certain employment tax liabilities, the IRS will send you a bill for the penalty. If you do not appeal a denial of an offer in compromise or a denial of a penalty abatement, the IRS will continue collection action.

If you don't agree, we urge you to appeal your case to the Appeals Office of IRS. The Office of Appeals can settle most differences without expensive and time-consuming court trials. [Note: Appeals can not consider your reasons for not agreeing if they don't come within the scope of the tax laws (for example, if you disagree solely on moral, religious, political, constitutional, conscientious, or similar grounds.)]

The following general rules tell you how to appeal your case.

Appeals Within the IRS

Appeals is the administrative appeals office for the IRS. You may appeal most IRS decisions with your local Appeals Office. The Appeals Office is separate from - and independent of - the IRS Office taking the action you disagree with. The Appeals Office is the only level of administrative appeal within the IRS.

Conferences with Appeals Office personnel are held in an informal manner by correspondence, by telephone or at a personal conference. There is no need for you to have representation for an Appeals conference, but if you choose to have a representative, see the requirements under **Representation.**

If you want an Appeals conference, follow the instructions in our letter to you. Your request will be sent to the Appeals Office to arrange a conference at a convenient time and place. You or your representative should prepare to discuss all issues you don't agree with at the conference. Most differences are settled at this level.

In most instances, you may be eligible to take your case to court if you don't reach an agreement at your Appeals conference, or if you don't want to appeal your case to the IRS Office of Appeals. See the later section *Appeals To The Courts.*

Protests

When you request an appeals conference, you may also need to file a formal written protest or a small case request with the office named in our letter to you. Also, see the special appeal request procedures in Publication 1660, Collection Appeal Rights, if you disagree with lien, levy, seizure, or denial or termination of an installment agreement.

You need to file a written protest:

- In all employee plan and exempt organization cases without regard to the dollar amount at issue.

- In all partnership and S corporation cases without regard to the dollar amount at issue.

- In all other cases, unless you qualify for the small case request procedure, or other special appeal procedures such as requesting Appeals consideration of liens, levies, seizures, or installment agreements. See Publication 1660.

How to prepare a protest:

When a protest is required, **send it within the time limit specified in the letter you received.** Include in your protest:

1) Your name and address, and a daytime telephone number,

2) A statement that you want to appeal the IRS findings to the Appeals Office,

3) A copy of the letter showing the proposed changes and findings you don't agree with (or the date and symbols from the letter),

4) The tax periods or years involved,

5) A list of the changes that you don't agree with, and why you don't agree,

6) The facts supporting your position on any issue that you don't agree with,

7) The law or authority, if any, on which you are relying.

8) You must sign the written protest, stating that it is true, under the penalties of perjury as follows:

"**Under the penalties of perjury, I declare that I examined the facts stated in this protest, including any accompanying documents, and, to the best of my knowledge and belief, they are true, correct, and complete.**"

If your representative prepares and signs the protest for you, he or she must substitute a declaration stating:

1) That he or she submitted the protest and accompanying documents and

2) Whether he or she knows personally that the facts stated in the protest and accompanying documents are true and correct.

We urge you to provide as much information as you can, as this will help us speed up your appeal. This will save you both time and money.

Small Case Request:

If the total amount for any tax period is not more than $25,000, you may make a small case request instead of filing a formal written protest. In computing the total amount, include a proposed increase or decrease in tax (including penalties), or claimed refund. For an offer in compromise, in calculating the total amount, include total unpaid tax, penalty and interest due. For a small case request, follow the instructions in our letter to you by: sending a letter requesting Appeals consideration, indicating the changes you don't agree with, and the reasons why you don't agree.

Representation

You may represent yourself at your appeals conference, or you may have an attorney, certified public accountant, or an individual enrolled to practice before the IRS represent you. Your representative must be qualified to practice before the IRS. If you want your representative to appear without you, you must provide a properly completed power of attorney to the IRS before the representative can receive or inspect confidential information. Form 2848, Power of Attorney and Declaration of Representative, or any other properly written power of attorney or authorization may be used for this purpose. You can get copies of Form 2848 from an IRS office, or by calling 1-800-TAX-FORM (1-800-829-3676).

You may also bring another person(s) with you to support your position.

Appeals To The Courts

If you and Appeals don't agree on some or all of the issues after your Appeals conference, or if you skipped our appeals system, you may take your case to the United States Tax Court, the United States Court of Federal Claims, or your United States District Court, after satisfying certain procedural and jurisdictional requirements as described below under each court. (However, if you are a nonresident alien, you cannot take your case to a United States District Court.) These courts are independent judicial bodies and have no connection with the IRS.

Tax Court

If your disagreement with the IRS is over whether you owe additional income tax, estate tax, gift tax, certain excise taxes or penalties related to these proposed liabilities, you can go to the United States Tax Court. (Other types of tax controversies, such as those involving some employment tax issues or manufacturers' excise taxes, cannot be heard by the Tax Court.) You can do this after the IRS issues a formal letter, stating the amounts that the IRS believes you owe. This letter is called a notice of deficiency. You have 90 days from the date this notice is mailed to you to file a petition with the Tax Court (or 150 days if the notice is addressed to you outside the United States). The last date to file your petition will be entered on the notice of deficiency issued to you by the IRS. If you don't file the petition within the 90-day period (or 150 days, as the case may be), we will assess the proposed liability and send you a bill. You may also have the right to take your case to the Tax Court in some other situations, for example, following collection action by the IRS in certain cases. See Publication 1660.

If you discuss your case with the IRS during the 90-day period (150-day period), the discussion will not extend the period in which you may file a petition with the Tax Court.

The court will schedule your case for trial at a location convenient to you. You may represent yourself before the Tax Court, or you may be represented by anyone permitted to practice before that court.

Note: If you don't choose to go to the IRS Appeals Office before going to court, normally you will have an opportunity to attempt settlement with Appeals before your trial date.

If you dispute not more than $50,000 for any one tax year, there are simplified procedures. You can get information about these procedures and

other matters from the Clerk of the Tax Court, 400 Second St. NW, Washington, DC 20217.

Frivolous Filing Penalty

Caution: If the Tax Court determines that your case is intended primarily to cause a delay, or that your position is frivolous or groundless, the Tax Court may award a penalty of up to $25,000 to the United States in its decision.

District Court and Court of Federal Claims

If your claim is for a refund of any type of tax, you may take your case to your United States District Court or to the United States Court of Federal Claims. Certain types of cases, such as those involving some employment tax issues or manufacturers' excise taxes, can be heard only by these courts.

Generally, your District Court and the Court of Federal Claims hear tax cases only after you have paid the tax and filed a claim for refund with the IRS. You can get information about procedures for filing suit in either court by contacting the Clerk of your District Court or the Clerk of the Court of Federal Claims.

If you file a formal refund claim with the IRS, and we haven't responded to you on your claim within 6 months from the date you filed it, you may file suit for a refund immediately in your District Court or the Court of Federal Claims. If we send you a letter that proposes disallowing or disallows your claim, you may request Appeals review of the disallowance. If you wish to file a refund suit, you must file your suit no later than 2 years from the date of our notice of claim disallowance letter.

Note: Appeals review of a disallowed claim doesn't extend the 2 year period for filing suit. However, it may be extended by mutual agreement.

Recovering Administrative and Litigation Costs

You may be able to recover your reasonable litigation and administrative costs if you are the prevailing party, and if you meet the other requirements. You must exhaust your administrative remedies within the IRS to receive reasonable litigation costs. You must not unreasonably delay the administrative or court proceedings.

Administrative costs include costs incurred on or after the date you receive the Appeals decision letter, the date of the first letter of proposed deficiency, or the date of the notice of deficiency, whichever is earliest.

Recoverable litigation or administrative costs may include:

■ Attorney fees that generally do not exceed $125 per hour. This amount will be indexed for a cost of living adjustment.

■ Reasonable amounts for court costs or any administrative fees or similar charges by the IRS.

■ Reasonable expenses of expert witnesses.

■ Reasonable costs of studies, analyses, tests, or engineering reports that are necessary to prepare your case.

You are the prevailing party if you meet all the following requirements:

■ You substantially prevailed on the amount in controversy, or on the most significant tax issue or issues in question.

■ You meet the net worth requirement. For individuals or estates, the net worth cannot exceed $2,000,000 on the date from which costs are recoverable. Charities and certain cooperatives must not have more than 500 employees on the date from which costs are recoverable. And taxpayers other than the two categories listed above must not have net worth exceeding $7,000,000 and cannot have more than 500 employees on the date from which costs are recoverable.

You are not the prevailing party if:

■ The United States establishes that its position was substantially justified. If the IRS does not follow applicable published guidance, the United States is presumed to not be substantially justified. This presumption is rebuttable. Applicable published guidance means regulations, revenue rulings, revenue procedures, information releases, notices, announcements, and, if they are issued to you, private letter rulings, technical advice memoranda and determination letters. The court will also take into account whether the Government has won or lost in the courts of appeals for other circuits on substantially similar issues, in determining if the United States is substantially justified.

You are also the prevailing party if:

■ The final judgment on your case is less than or equal to a "qualified offer" which the IRS rejected, and if you meet the net worth requirements referred to above.

A court will generally decide who is the prevailing party, but the IRS makes a final determination of liability at the administrative level. This means you may receive administrative costs from the IRS without going to court. You must file your claim for administrative costs no later than the 90th day after the final determination of tax, penalty or interest is mailed to you. The Appeals Office makes determinations for the IRS on administrative costs. A denial of administrative costs may be appealed to the Tax Court no later than the 90th day after the denial.

¶457 Exhibit 4-7

Internal Revenue Service	**Department of the Treasury**

Date:

Taxpayer Name:

Taxpayer Identification Number:

Tax Form:

Tax Period(s):

Person to Contact:

Employee Identification Number:

Telephone Number:

FAX Number:

Dear Taxpayer:

The purpose of this letter is to let you know that I have scheduled the following appointment to meet with you and examine the above referenced tax return:

Place: Date:

                                          Time:

Should you need to change this date, please contact me to arrange a more convenient meeting. I will consider the above appointment confirmed if I don't hear from you by _____ .

In order to minimize the time we need to complete the examination, please have available the items listed on the attached Form 4564, *Information Document Request*, at our first appointment.

You may have someone represent you during any part of this examination. Should you want someone to represent you, please give us a completed Form 2848, *Power of Attorney and Declaration of Representative*, at our first meeting. We will delay examination activity to allow you time later to secure a representative if you choose.

We encourage you to read the enclosed Publication 1, *Your Rights as a Taxpayer*, and Notice 609, *Privacy Act and Paperwork Reduction Act.* Thank you for your cooperation.

Sincerely yours,

Enclosures: Internal Revenue Agent
Publication 1
Notice 609
Form 4564

Letter 2205 (DO) (Rev. 10-1999)
Catalog Number 63744P

¶458 Exhibit 4-8

Department of the Treasury
Internal Revenue Service

Publication 1
(Rev. August 2000)

Catalog Number 64731W

www.irs.gov

Your Rights as a Taxpayer

The first part of this publication explains some of your most important rights as a taxpayer. The second part explains the examination, appeal, collection, and refund processes. This publication is also available in Spanish.

Declaration of Taxpayer Rights

I. Protection of Your Rights

IRS employees will explain and protect your rights as a taxpayer throughout your contact with us.

II. Privacy and Confidentiality

The IRS will not disclose to anyone the information you give us, except as authorized by law. You have the right to know why we are asking you for information, how we will use it, and what happens if you do not provide requested information.

III. Professional and Courteous Service

If you believe that an IRS employee has not treated you in a professional, fair, and courteous manner, you should tell that employee's supervisor. If the supervisor's response is not satisfactory, you should write to the IRS director for your area or the center where you file your return.

IV. Representation

You may either represent yourself or, with proper written authorization, have someone else represent you in your place. Your representative must be a person allowed to practice before the IRS, such as an attorney, certified public accountant, or enrolled agent. If you are in an interview and ask to consult such a person, then we must stop and reschedule the interview in most cases.

You can have someone accompany you at an interview. You may make sound recordings of any meetings with our examination, appeal, or collection personnel, provided you tell us in writing 10 days before the meeting.

V. Payment of Only the Correct Amount of Tax

You are responsible for paying only the correct amount of tax due under the law—no more, no less. If you cannot pay all of your tax when it is due, you may be able to make monthly installment payments.

VI. Help With Unresolved Tax Problems

The Taxpayer Advocate Service can help you if you have tried unsuccessfully to resolve a problem with the IRS. Your local Taxpayer Advocate can offer you special help if you have a significant hardship as a result of a tax problem. For more information, call toll free 1–877–777–4778 (1–800–829–4059 for TTY/TDD) or write to the Taxpayer Advocate at the IRS office that last contacted you.

VII. Appeals and Judicial Review

If you disagree with us about the amount of your tax liability or certain collection actions, you have the right to ask the Appeals Office to review your case. You may also ask a court to review your case.

VIII. Relief From Certain Penalties and Interest

The IRS will waive penalties when allowed by law if you can show you acted reasonably and in good faith or relied on the incorrect advice of an IRS employee. We will waive interest that is the result of certain errors or delays caused by an IRS employee.

THE IRS MISSION

PROVIDE AMERICA'S TAXPAYERS TOP QUALITY SERVICE BY HELPING THEM UNDERSTAND AND MEET THEIR TAX RESPONSIBILITIES AND BY APPLYING THE TAX LAW WITH INTEGRITY AND FAIRNESS TO ALL.

¶458

Examinations, Appeals, Collections, and Refunds

Examinations (Audits)

We accept most taxpayers' returns as filed. If we inquire about your return or select it for examination, it does not suggest that you are dishonest. The inquiry or examination may or may not result in more tax. We may close your case without change; or, you may receive a refund.

The process of selecting a return for examination usually begins in one of two ways. First, we use computer programs to identify returns that may have incorrect amounts. These programs may be based on information returns, such as Forms 1099 and W-2, on studies of past examinations, or on certain issues identified by compliance projects. Second, we use information from outside sources that indicates that a return may have incorrect amounts. These sources may include newspapers, public records, and individuals. If we determine that the information is accurate and reliable, we may use it to select a return for examination.

Publication 556, *Examination of Returns, Appeal Rights, and Claims for Refund,* explains the rules and procedures that we follow in examinations. The following sections give an overview of how we conduct examinations.

By Mail

We handle many examinations and inquiries by mail. We will send you a letter with either a request for more information or a reason why we believe a change to your return may be needed. You can respond by mail or you can request a personal interview with an examiner. If you mail us the requested information or provide an explanation, we may or may not agree with you, and we will explain the reasons for any changes. Please do not hesitate to write to us about anything you do not understand.

By Interview

If we notify you that we will conduct your examination through a personal interview, or you request such an interview, you have the right to ask that the examination take place at a reasonable time and place that is convenient for both you and the IRS. If our examiner proposes any changes to your return, he or she will explain the reasons for the changes. If you do not

agree with these changes, you can meet with the examiner's supervisor.

Repeat Examinations

If we examined your return for the same items in either of the 2 previous years and proposed no change to your tax liability, please contact us as soon as possible so we can see if we should discontinue the examination.

Appeals

If you do not agree with the examiner's proposed changes, you can appeal them to the Appeals Office of IRS. Most differences can be settled without expensive and time-consuming court trials. Your appeal rights are explained in detail in both Publication 5, *Your Appeal Rights and How To Prepare a Protest If You Don't Agree,* and Publication 556, *Examination of Returns, Appeal Rights, and Claims for Refund.*

If you do not wish to use the Appeals Office or disagree with its findings, you may be able to take your case to the U.S. Tax Court, U.S. Court of Federal Claims, or the U.S. District Court where you live. If you take your case to court, the IRS will have the burden of proving certain facts if you kept adequate records to show your tax liability, cooperated with the IRS, and meet certain other conditions. If the court agrees with you on most issues in your case and finds that our position was largely unjustified, you may be able to recover some of your administrative and litigation costs. You will not be eligible to recover these costs unless you tried to resolve your case administratively, including going through the appeals system, and you gave us the information necessary to resolve the case.

Collections

Publication 594, *The IRS Collection Process,* explains your rights and responsibilities regarding payment of federal taxes. It describes:

- What to do when you owe taxes. It describes what to do if you get a tax bill and what to do if you think your bill is wrong. It also covers making installment payments, delaying collection action, and submitting an offer in compromise.

- IRS collection actions. It covers liens, releasing a lien, levies, releasing a levy, seizures and sales, and release of property.

Your collection appeal rights are explained in detail in Publication 1660, *Collection Appeal Rights.*

Innocent Spouse Relief

Generally, both you and your spouse are responsible, jointly and individually, for paying the full amount of any tax, interest, or penalties due on your joint return. However, if you qualify for innocent spouse relief, you may not have to pay the tax, interest, and penalties related to your spouse (or former spouse). For information on innocent spouse relief and two other ways to get relief, see Publication 971, *Innocent Spouse Relief,* and Form 8857, *Request for Innocent Spouse Relief (And Separation of Liability and Equitable Relief).*

Refunds

You may file a claim for refund if you think you paid too much tax. You must generally file the claim within 3 years from the date you filed your original return or 2 years from the date you paid the tax, whichever is later. The law generally provides for interest on your refund if it is not paid within 45 days of the date you filed your return or claim for refund. Publication 556, *Examination of Returns, Appeal Rights, and Claims for Refund,* has more information on refunds.

If you were due a refund but you did not file a return, you must file within 3 years from the date the return was originally due to get that refund.

Tax Information

The IRS provides a great deal of free information. The following are sources for forms, publications, and additional information.

- *Tax Questions: 1–800–829–1040* (1–800–829–4059 for TTY/TDD)

- *Forms and Publications: 1–800–829–3676* (1–800–829–4059 for TTY/TDD)

- *Internet:* **www.irs.gov**

- *TaxFax Service:* From your fax machine, dial **703–368–9694.**

- *Small Business Ombudsman:* If you are a small business entity, you can participate in the regulatory process and comment on enforcement actions of IRS by calling **1–888–REG–FAIR.**

- *Treasury Inspector General for Tax Administration:* If you want to confidentially report misconduct, waste, fraud, or abuse by an IRS employee, you can call **1–800–366–4484** (1–800–877–8339 for TTY/TDD). You can remain anonymous.

¶459 Exhibit 4-9

List of Specialty Handbooks

IRM Handbook No. 4.3.1.1, International Procedures Handbook

IRM Handbook No. 4.3.1.2, International Audit Guidelines Handbook

IRM Handbook No. 4.3.1.5, Partnership and S. Corporation Handbook

IRM Handbook No. 4.3.2, Examination Collectibility Handbook

IRM Handbook No. 4.3.3, Excise Tax Handbook

IRM Handbook No. 4.3.4, Anti-Money Laundering Handbook

IRM Handbook No. 4.3.5, Joint Committee Handbook

IRM Handbook No. 4.3.6, Audit Reconsideration Handbook

IRM Handbook No. 4.3.7, Market Segment Specialization Program Handbook

IRM Handbook No. 4.3.8, Estate and Gift Tax Handbook

IRM Handbook No. 4.3.9, Jeopardy/Termination Assessments Handbook

IRM Handbook No. 4.3.10, Bankruptcy Handbook

IRM Handbook No. 4.3.11, Coordinated Examination Program Case Manager Handbook

IRM Handbook No. 4.3.12, Coordinated Examination Program Team Member Handbook

IRM Handbook No. 4.3.13, Computer Assisted Audit Program Handbook

IRM Handbook No. 4.3.14, Nonfiled Returns Handbook

IRM Handbook No. 4.3.16, Engineering Program Handbook

IRM Handbook No. 4.3.17, Economist Program Handbook

IRM Handbook No. 4.3.19, Statutory Notices of Deficiency

IRM Handbook No. 4.3.20, Frivolous Filers/Non-filers Handbook

IRM Handbook No. 4.3.21, Exam Offer-in-Compromise

IRM Handbook No. 4.4, Industry Specialization Program Handbook

IRM Handbook No. 4.4.1, Oil and Gas Industry Handbook

IRM Handbook No. 4.4.2, Insurance Industry Handbook

IRM Handbook No. 4.4.3, Retail Industry Handbook

IRM Handbook No. 4.7, Examination Returns Control System (ECRS)

IRM Handbook No. 4.8, Quality Measurement Handbook

IRM Handbook No. 4.9, Examination Technical Time Reporting Handbook

IRM Handbook No. 104.1, Fed State Relations Handbook

IRM Handbook No. 104.3, AIMS/Processing Handbook

IRM Handbook No. 104.4, Information and Informants' Rewards Handbook

IRM Handbook No. 104.5, Exam Relief from Joint and Several Liability

IRM Handbook No. 104.6, Employment Tax Handbook

IRM Handbook No. 104.7, Financial Products and Transactions Handbook

IRM Handbook No. 104.8, Interest

IRM Handbook No. 104.9, Midwest Automated Compliance System Handbook

IRM Handbook No. 104.11, Electronic Filing Program

IRM Handbook No. 104.12, Audit Reconsideration

¶460 Exhibit 4-10

Page _____ of _____ pages

Form **4549-A** (Rev. June 1994)	Department of the Treasury — Internal Revenue Service **Income Tax Examination Changes**		Return Form No.
Name and Address of Taxpayers	S.S. or E.I. Number		Filing Status
	Person With Whom Examination Charges Were Discussed	Name and Title	

1. Adjustments to Income	Year:	Year:	Year:
a.			
b.			
c.			
d.			
e.			
f.			
g.			
2. Total Adjustments			
3. Adjusted Gross or Taxable Income Shown on Return or as Previously Adjusted			
4. Corrected Adjusted Gross or Taxable Income			
5. Corrected Tax			
6. Less Credits a.			
b.			
c.			
7. Balance (Line 5 less total of lines 6a through 6c)			
8. Plus Other Taxes a.			
b.			
c.			
9. Total Corrected Tax Liability (line 7 plus total of lines 8a through 8c)			
10. Total Tax Shown on Return or as Previously Adjusted			
11. Adjustments to EIC/Fuels Credits - increase (decrease)			
12. Deficiency - Increase in Tax (Line 9 adjusted by lines 10 and 11)			
13. Overassessment - Decrease in Tax (Line 9 adjusted by lines 10 and 11)			
14. Adjustments to Prepayment Credits - increase (decrease)			
15. Balance Due, Excluding Interest and Penalties (Line 12 adjusted by Line 14)			
16. Overpayment (Line 13 adjusted by Line 14)			
17. Penalties Code Section a.			
b.			
c.			
d.			

Other Information (See the back of this form.)

Examiner's Signature	District	Date

Cat. No. 23110T   Form **4549-A** (Rev. 5-94)

Form **4549-A** (Rev. 5-94)   *(back of the form)*

The Internal Revenue Service has agreements with state tax agencies to exchange information with them about federal tax, including increases or decreases in tax. If there is a change that affects the amount of your state income tax, you should file the required state form.

You may be subject to backup withholding if you don't report all of the interest, dividend, or patronage dividend income you earned and don't pay the required tax. The IRS will first tell you the amount of tax you may owe by sending you four notices over a 120-day period. Then, if this assessed tax remains unpaid, IRS may begin or continue to withhold 31 percent of your divident and/or interest payments.

*U.S. GPO: 1994-301-643/12190

¶461 Exhibit 4-11

Form **886-A** (REV JANUARY 1994	**EXPLANATIONS OF ITEMS**	SCHEDULE NO. OR EXHIBIT
NAME OF TAXPAYER	TAX IDENTIFICATION NUMBER	YEAR/PERIOD ENDED

¶462 Exhibit 4-12

Internal Revenue Service   **Department of the Treasury**

Taxpayer Identification Number:

Form:

Date:

Tax Period(s) Ended and Tax Deficiency:

Person to Contact:

Employee Identification Number:

Contact Telephone Number:

Examiner:

Refer Reply to:

Dear

The examiner whose name appears above gave you an examination report showing changes to your tax return(s) and discussed the changes with you. Based on your request, we've reviewed the report and have taken the action indicated below.

☐   We have made no changes to the original report.

☐   We have made the changes indicated on the enclosed corrected report.

(We won't make further changes to your return unless we examine and change the return of a partnership, S corporation, trust, or estate in which you have an interest. Changes made to those returns could later affect your return.)

If you owe additional tax, please send us payment for the full amount. If you can't pay the full amount now, pay as much as you can. If you want us to consider an installment agreement, please complete and return the enclosed Form 9465, Installment Agreement Request. If we approve your request, we will charge you a $43 user fee to help offset the cost of providing this service. We will take the fee from your first installment payment. If your request includes amounts for more than one tax period, you will have to pay the $43 fee only one time. We will continue to charge penalties and interest until you pay the full amount you owe.

If you have overpaid your tax, we will send you a refund with any interest we owe you. It may take us up to 8 weeks to do this.

Letter 987 (DO) (Rev. 4-1999)
Cat. No. 40421R

If you have any questions, please contact the person whose name and telephone number are shown in the heading of this letter. Thank you for your cooperation.

Sincerely yours,

Enclosures:
☐ Corrected Examination Report
☐ Form 9465
☐ Envelope

Letter 987 (DO) (Rev. 4-1999)
Cat. No. 40421R

¶462

¶463 Exhibit 4-13

Department of the Treasury
Internal Revenue Service

Letter Number: 531 (DO)

Form Number:

Person to Contact:

Telephone Number:

Date:

Employee Identification Number

Taxpayer Identifying Number:

Refer Reply To:

Last Day to File a Petition With
the United States Tax Court:

Tax Year Ended:

Deficiency:
Increase in tax

Dear

NOTICE OF DEFICIENCY

We have determined that you owe additional tax or other amounts, or both, for the tax year(s) identified above. This letter is your NOTICE OF DEFICIENCY, as required by law. The enclosed statement shows how we figured the deficiency.

If you want to contest this determination in court before making any payment, you have 90 days from the date of this letter (150 days if this letter is addressed to you outside of the United States) to file a petition with the United States Tax Court for a redetermination of the deficiency. You can get a copy of the rules for filing a petition and a petition form you can use by writing to the address below.

United States Tax Court, 400 Second Street, NW Washington, DC 20217

The Tax Court has a simplified procedure for small tax cases when the amount in dispute is $50,000 or less for any one tax year. You can also get information about this procedure by writing to the Tax Court. You should write promptly if you intend to file a petition with the Tax Court

Letter 531 (DO) (Rev. 3-1999)
Cat. No. 40222A

¶463

Send the completed petition form, a copy of this letter, and copies of all statements and/or schedules you received with this letter to the Tax Court at the above address. The Court cannot consider your case if the petition is filed late. The petition is considered timely filed if the postmark date falls within the prescribed 90 or 150 day period and the envelope containing the petition is properly addressed with the correct postage.

The time you have to file a petition with the court is set by law and cannot be extended or suspended. Thus, contacting the Internal Revenue Service (IRS) for more information, or receiving other correspondence from the IRS won't change the allowable period for filing a petition with the Tax Court.

As required by law, separate notices are sent to husbands and wives. If this letter is addressed to both husband and wife, and both want to petition the Tax Court, both must sign and file the petition or each must file a separate, signed petition. If more than one tax year is shown above, you may file one petition form showing all of the years you are contesting.

You may represent yourself before the Tax Court, or you may be represented by anyone admitted to practice before the Tax Court.

If you decide not to file a petition with the Tax Court, please sign the enclosed waiver form and return it to us at the IRS address on the top of the front of this letter. This will permit us to assess the deficiency quickly and can help limit the accumulation of interest.

If you decide not to sign and return the waiver, and you do not file a petition with the Tax Court within the time limit, the law requires us to assess and bill you for the deficiency after 90 days from the date of this letter (150 days if this letter is addressed to you outside the United States)

NOTE: If you are a C-corporation, section 6621(c) of the Internal Revenue Code requires that we charge an interest rate two percent higher than the normal rate on large corporate underpayments of $100,000 or more.

If you have questions about this letter, you may write to or call the contact person whose name, telephone number, and IRS address are shown on the front of this letter. If you write, please include your telephone number, the best time for us to call you if we need more information, and a copy of this letter to help us identify your account. Keep the original letter for your records. If you prefer to call and the telephone number is outside your local calling area, there will be a long distance charge to you.

The contact person can access your tax information and help you get answers. You also have the right to contact the office of the Taxpayer Advocate. Taxpayer Advocate assistance is not a substitute for established IRS procedures such as the formal appeals process. The Taxpayer Advocate is not able to reverse legally correct tax determinations, nor extend the time fixed by law that you have to file a petition in the U.S. Tax Court. The Taxpayer Advocate can, however, see that a tax matter that may not have been resolved through normal channels gets prompt and proper handling. If you want Taxpayer Advocate assistance, please contact the Taxpayer Advocate for the IRS office that issued this notice of deficiency. See the enclosed Notice 1214, *Helpful Contacts for Your "Notice of Deficiency"*, for Taxpayer Advocate telephone numbers and addresses.

Thank you for your cooperation.

Sincerely,

Commissioner
By

Enclosures:
Explanation of tax changes
Waiver
Notice 1214

Letter 531 (DO) (Rev. 3-1999)
Cat. No. 40222A

¶463

¶464 Exhibit 4-14

Form **4089** (Rev. January 1983)	Department of the Treasury — Internal Revenue Service **Notice of Deficiency-Waiver**	Symbols

Name, SSN or EIN, and Address of Taxpayer(s)

Kind of Tax	☐ Copy to Authorized Representative	

	Deficiency	
Tax Year Ended	Increase in Tax	Penalties

See the attached explanation for the above deficiencies

I consent to the immediate assessment and collection of the deficiencies (increase in tax and penalties) shown above, plus any interest provided by law.

Your Signature	▶ _____	_____
		(Date signed)
Spouse's Signature, If A Joint Return Was Filed	▶ _____	_____
		(Date signed)
Taxpayer's Representative Sign Here	▶ _____	_____
		(Date signed)

Corporate Name: _____

Corporate Officers Sign Here	▶ _____	_____	_____
	(Signature)	*(Title)*	*(Date signed)*
	▶ _____	_____	_____
	(Signature)	*(Title)*	*(Date signed)*

Note:

If you consent to the assessment of the amounts shown in this waiver, please sign and return it in order to limit the accumulation of interest and expedite our bill to you. Your consent will not prevent you from filing a claim for refund (after you have paid the tax) if you later believe you are entitled to a refund. It will not prevent us from later determining, if necessary, that you owe additional tax; nor will it extend the time provided by law for either action.

If you later file a claim and the Internal Revenue Service disallows it, you may file suit for refund in a district court or in the United States Claims Court, but you may not file petition with the United States Tax Court.

Who Must Sign

If this waiver is for any year(s) for which you filed a joint return,

both you and your spouse must sign the original and duplicate of this form. Sign your name exactly as it appears on the return. If you are acting under power of attorney for your spouse, you may sign as agent for him or her.

For an agent or attorney acting under a power of attorney, a power of attorney must be sent with this form if not previously filed.

For a person acting in a fiduciary capacity (executor, administrator, trustee), file Form 56, Notice Concerning Fiduciary Relationship, with this form if not previously filed.

For a corporation, enter the name of the corporation followed by the signature and title of the officer(s) authorized to sign.

If you agree, please sign one copy and return it; keep the other copy for your records.

Form **4089** (Rev. 1-83)

¶465 DISCUSSION QUESTIONS

1. Andy Antagonistic comes to your office with a letter he has received from the IRS scheduling an examination by the tax compliance officer. The letter explains that among the items to be reviewed at the examination is the verification of gross receipts from Andy's business (retailer of used automobiles). Andy explains that his operation is not very large but that he does not want to have to transport the records to the suburban office of the IRS where the examination is scheduled. Andy assumes that revenue agents of the IRS are more experienced and more reasonable to deal with and asks you to request that the audit be transferred to a revenue agent in SB/SE. What is your advice?

2. You have been just retained by Nick L. Nockdown in connection with the examination of his return. Nick runs a tavern with reported gross sales of $250,000. Nick has met with the IRS on numerous occasions. You attend the first conference with the examiner and he runs a preliminary "T-account" to attempt to verify gross receipts. Because Nick is not with you at the conference, there is no information available as to his "cash on hand." The examiner also does not have much information regarding personal expenses (other than the listed itemized deductions), but a reasonable estimate is $10,000. The preliminary T-account reflects a potential understatement of gross receipts of $50,000.

   You return to your office and discuss the potential understatement with the taxpayer. Nick explains that his wife has worked as a restroom custodian at the Big Bucks Hotel for the past 25 years. She receives nominal wages and "cash tips". She has always been able to save a substantial portion of her cash tips. When they were putting an addition on the tavern, Nick's wife took her money out of the mason jars in the basement and paid the contractor for the addition. The amount paid was approximately $50,000, and Nick explains that this is where the understatement must be coming from.

   (A) If you are representing Nick, how do you deal with the information that he has given you regarding the explanation of the understatement?

   (B) If this story is presented to the examiner, will the statement of the taxpayer given under oath be sufficient or must other evidence be submitted to back it up?

   (C) Who will bear the burden of proof on the reliability of the explanation?

   (D) Can an explanation like this be used in court as a defense to an assessment by the IRS?

3. Assume in Question 2 that the examiner has also requested the individual checks and bank statements to confirm the estimated personal expenses. Must you provide the information? What can happen if you do not?

4. If you are consulted regarding a field audit and you discover that the agent and the taxpayer have already met at the place of business, how do you proceed in each of the following circumstances:

   (A) The president of the corporation tells you that he had a personality conflict with the examiner and threw the examiner out of the office?

   (B) You have had previous dealings with the IRS Agent, Oscar Obnoxious, and you have found him to be arrogant, insufferable and completely impossible to work with?

   (C) The audit is disrupting the business operations of the taxpayer.

5. You are contacted to represent a taxpayer in a field audit. Bob Butcher, the bookkeeper, prepared the return. In reviewing the records, you find substantial errors which will be very obvious to the agent, i.e., income improperly posted and not included in gross receipts, duplicated expenditures and depreciation claimed on retired assets. The Agent is scheduled to come in the following day. When, if at all, do you disclose these errors to the Agent?

6. At the conclusion of his corporate audit, the Revenue Agent questions the reasonableness of the corporation's accumulated earnings. For the current year, the corporation has total additions to accumulated earnings of $300,000. The balance at the beginning of the year was $750,000, and there is a plethora of liquid assets reflected on the corporate balance sheet. The corporation manufactures computer parts and has two shareholders, Mr. Greed and Mr. Glutt. Dividends have not been declared in the last 10 years. However, the corporate minutes reflect various anticipated needs of the business as reasons for the accumulation of earnings, including an acquisition of or an expansion into other businesses.

   (A) Should you discuss with the agent the grounds on which the corporation relies to establish the reasonableness of its accumulated earnings?

   (B) Should you wait to discuss the issue with the Appeals Office? See Code Sec. 534.

CHAPTER 5
LARGE CASE AUDITS

¶500 LARGE AND MID-SIZE BUSINESS DIVISION

The Large and Mid-Size Business (LMSB) Division serves taxpayers with assets over $5 million. This operating division is organized into industry segments. These businesses generally have large employee bases and "in-house" tax organizations. They also have access to large legal and accounting organizations for the most complex issues.

Within the LMSB program is the Office of Tax Shelter Analysis, which is to serve as a clearinghouse of information relating to potentially improper tax shelter activities by corporate and noncorporate taxpayers.[1]

¶501 COORDINATED INDUSTRY CASES

The Coordinated Industry case program[2] was established by the Internal Revenue Service (IRS) to provide a team approach to the examination of very large corporate cases which meet specific criteria for size and complexity of audit.[3]

This program brings together as one unit for audit purposes the primary taxpayer and all of the taxpayer's effectively controlled corporations and other entities. A Coordinated Industry case, therefore, will usually involve a large group of closely affiliated, centrally controlled, widely dispersed and highly diversified business entities. Domestic and foreign corporations, partnerships, joint ventures, syndicates, unincorporated businesses, individuals, trusts, estates, foundations, pension and profit sharing trusts and other exempt organizations may be included within the coordinated audit group.[4] The Coordinated Industry case is identified by the name of the primary taxpayer, usually a large corporation, which exerts control over all of the other corporations and entities in the audit group. Effective control by the primary taxpayer is determined by such factors as stock ownership, economic domination and significant influence over the tax objectivity of the other entity.[5]

¶502 COORDINATED INDUSTRY CASE PROCESS

The Coordinated Industry case team manager is responsible for organizing, controlling and directing the team examination. The supporting team usually includes not only groups of revenue agents throughout the country, but also industry and otherspecialists, such as engineers, excise tax agents, economists, international examiners, computer audit specialists, employment tax agents and employee and exempt organization specialists.[6] The team manager organizes and

---

[1] IRS Announcement 2000-55, IRB 2000-25.

[2] The program was previously known as the Coordinated Examination Program (CEP).

[3] The fixed formula and point value requirements used in selecting CEP cases has been eliminated.

Assignment is now based on the Industry Territory Manager's discretion.

[4] IRM Handbook 4.3.1.3.

[5] IRM Handbook 4.3.11.1.6.

[6] IRM Handbook 4.3.11.1.2.

sets the scope of the examination in a three-step process. In the first step, the general scope and depth of the examination is established by reviewing all of the related returns, reviewing the planning files of previous examinations, and discussing the case with the team mangers of previous examinations.[7] The second step involves the review of certain taxpayer records in order to aid in (1) determining the procedures to be employed in examining noncompliance areas, (2) determining other areas or issues not apparent in the preliminary review, and (3) modifying decisions made during the preliminary review.[8] In the third step, questionable items are further defined and audit procedures are developed with respect to specific accounts.[9] After this three-step initial review has taken place, a pre-examination conference is held with representatives of the taxpayer. The meeting permits the parties to discuss the scope of the audit and to consider any accommodations that may be possible to facilitate the audit or minimize the disruption to business operations.[10]

¶503 SCOPE OF PRE-EXAMINATION

The scope of any Coordinated Industry case examination should consider concurrently all returns of the various entities included in the Coordinated Industry case group. In addition to income tax returns, this may encompass employment and excise tax returns, and pension and profit sharing plans.[11] In every Coordinated Industry case examination there is one area which is always tested for compliance with the law: lobbying and political campaign expenses.[12] The Coordinated Industry team manager may include in the examination plan any other areas that are believed to require compliance checks.

Improper payments by corporations relating to bribes, kickbacks, illegal political contributions and the use of slush funds and secret bank accounts also may be given special attention during a large case audit. When considered appropriate, selected officers and key employees are asked five specific questions concerning these matters.[13] If any of the questions are answered in the affirmative, the IRS will continue to probe until all details have been obtained. If the questions are not answered voluntarily, the IRS will issue an administrative summons to compel such testimony.[14]

Also during the pre-examination conference, the accuracy related penalty under Code Sec. 6662(b)(2) is discussed. The taxpayer is allowed to make anycorrections to the return or make adequate disclosure as to items that may cause the taxpayer to be subject to the negligence and the substantial understatement penalty. Under these special procedures the penalty will be waived if the taxpayer makes adequate disclosure within fifteen days of a request for such a statement by the IRS.[15]

---

[7] IRM Handbook 4.3.11.3.4.

[8] IRM Handbook 4.3.11.6.2.2.1. The records to be reviewed in this step include the Schedule M, corporate minutes, internal management reports and accounting manuals and systems analysis.

[9] IRM Handbook 4.3.11.6.2.2.2.

[10] IRM 4.3.11.7.4.

[11] IRM 4.3.11.2.3.

[12] IRM 4.3.12.5.4.

[13] IRM Handbook 4.3.12. Exhibit 5.1.

[14] See Chapter 6, *infra*.

[15] Rev. Proc. 1994-69, 1994-2 CB 804.

¶504 WRITTEN PLAN

Following the pre-examination conference, a written plan is formulated and provided to the taxpayer. The purpose of this document is twofold. First, it formalizes the general examination procedures to be followed. Second, it prevents any misunderstanding as to agreements reached between the taxpayer and the IRS. To avoid misunderstandings, agreements reached during the pre examination conference should be included in the plan.[16] This written plan provides for the general scope of the examination and it clearly apprises the taxpayer that it may be modified to meet the needs of the examination.

¶505 EXAMINATION

During Coordinated Industry case examinations, IRS attorneys in the Chief Counsel's local office are more directly involved. Officially, they are available to offer legal advice on complex issues and to provide assistance in the development of facts relating to those issues. Although taxpayers have voiced concern regarding such intimate involvement by Counsel attorneys during the examination phase, the IRS maintains that such involvement promotes early development and resolution of the significant legal issues.[17]

The Tax Court has been critical of the active participation by an IRS attorney in an ongoing examination at the same time the attorney was acting as trial counsel in a docketed case against the same taxpayer for earlier years involving identical issues. In *Westreco, Inc. v. Commissioner*,[18] the IRS trial attorney was ordered to discontinue participation in the audit. The IRS was further ordered not to use in the Tax Court proceedings any evidence obtained by summons or any other means during the examination of the more recent years. The Tax Court was concerned that the IRS was attempting to circumvent the Court's limited discovery rules by allowing trial attorneys to obtain testimony and other evidence during an examination by use of broad investigative powers not available to the IRS in pretrial discovery under the Rules of the Tax Court. However, in a 1996 case, *Mary Kay Ash v. Commissioner*,[19] the Tax Court modified its position in *Westreco* and denied petitioner's motion for a protective order. The court noted that while the compelling facts in *Westreco* justified a protective order, not all cases could be seen as an attempt to circumvent the Tax Court's discovery rules. The summonses in *Mary Kay Ash* were issued before any litigation commenced andthus the dangers of information being used improperly by an IRS attorney in a proceeding were not present. The court did not rule that a protective order could never be granted, but that a protective order would only be justified when the facts of a particular case warranted.

Upon completion of the Coordinated Industry case examination, the taxpayer may object to any proposed tax adjustments by filing a protest with the Appeals Office.[20] Unlike normal audit and appeal procedures, however, in a Coordinated Industry case, personnel from the offices of LMSB and Appeals are

---

[16] IRM Handbook 4.3.11.6.4.

[17] Daily Tax Report, BNA, at E-1 (Mar. 4, 1991).

[18] 60 TCM 824, TC Memo. 1990-501, CCH Dec. 46,882(M).

[19] 96 TC 459 (1991), CCH Dec. 47,221.

[20] See Chapter 11, *infra*.

authorized and, in some instances, required to hold a conference before Appeals Office personnel meet with the taxpayer.[21] The purpose of this unique pre-conference is to discuss the issues, the taxpayer's protest and the written rebuttal to the protest prepared by the LMSB team. Such a conference also serves to identify the need for additional information and development of issues.

It is expected at this pre-conference that lines of communication will be established between the Offices of Appeals and LMSB that will be maintained throughout the case. Although the LMSB is encouraged during this meeting to share its views on the issues, including its assessment of litigating hazards, the parties are specifically instructed that the conference is not to be used as a means for securing a commitment from Appeals that any particular issue should be defended or the manner in which the case should be settled.[22] In substance, despite such intimate discussions of the case, the parties to the pre-conference are reminded that the detached objectivity of Appeals is not to be compromised. Counsel must be invited to participate in pre-conferences in all docketed cases and may be invited to attend in other Coordinated Industry cases.

¶506 SETTLING ISSUES

Once the audit has begun, the IRS will use Form 4564, Information Document Request (see Exhibit 5-1 at ¶551), to make any information requests.[23] As the IRS makes each adjustment during the audit, it will give the taxpayer notice on Form 5701, Notice of Proposed Adjustment (see Exhibit 5-2 at ¶552). Presented with Form 5701, the taxpayer may either sign the form indicating that it agrees with the adjustment, or file a written protest if it disagrees.[24] Certain issues on which there is disagreement may be settled by the team manager under the authority of Code Sec. 7121. This authority exists where the Appeals Office has previously approved a settlement agreement involving the same issue in a Coordinated Industry case examination in a prior year involving the same taxpayer or a taxpayer directly involved in the taxable transaction.[25] The following conditions must be present for the team manager to have jurisdiction to settle an issue: (1) substantially the same facts must be involved in both examination years,(2) the legal authority must not have changed, (3) the issue must have been settled on its merits and not have been settled in exchange for the taxpayer's concession on another issue, and (4) the issue must concern the same taxpayer or a taxpayer who was directly involved in the settled transaction.

¶507 TAXPAYER OPTIONS

LMSB Pre-Filing Requirements. Taxpayers may request the examination of specific issues relating to a tax return before the return is filed.[26] If the taxpayer and the IRS are able to resolve the issues prior to the filing of the return, the taxpayer and the IRS may finalize their resolution by executing an LMSB Pre-Filing Agreement (LMSB PFA). A taxpayer may request an LMSB PFA with

---

[21] IRM Handbook 8.6.1.2.7.
[22] *Id.*
[23] IRM Handbook 4.3.11.12.4.9.

[24] IRM Handbook 4.3.11.7.3.
[25] IRM Handbook 4.3.11.14.3.
[26] Rev. Proc. 2001-22, IRB 2001-9.

¶506

respect to the current taxable year or any prior taxable year for which the return is not yet due (including extensions) and is not yet filed.

This procedure applies only to issues involving the application of well settled principles of law and is not intended to resolve issues involving questions of law and facts. Thus, the valuation of a specific asset during an eligible year is generally an eligible issue for the LMSB PFA program, whereas the valuation of an asset during a prior or subsequent taxable year is not.

A nonexclusive list of domestic issues that are likely to be suitable for resolution through the LMSB PFA program are contained in Rev. Proc. 2001-22 and include:

1. The current valuation of specific assets (except in the context of transfer pricing), but not the appropriateness of a valuation methodology;

2. The allocation of the purchase or sale of a business among the assets acquired or sold;

3. The allocation of costs among the different categories of deductible and capital items, in contexts where there is a published revenue ruling, e.g., repairs,[27] advertising,[28] and Y2K costs;[29]

4. Whether a taxpayer's financial statement presentation of its last-in, first-out (LIFO) inventory is consistent with the LIFO conformity requirement under Reg. § 1.472-2(e);

5. Whether a security became worthless during the eligible taxable year, for purposes of Code Sec. 165.[30]

The IRS generally will not enter into an LMSB PFA on the following types of issues:

1. Issues that can be resolved by requesting a change in method of accounting on Form 3115, Application for Change in Accounting Method.

2. Issues that have been designated for litigation by the Office of Chief Counsel.

3. Issues involving a tax shelter described in Code Sec. 6662(d)(2)(C)(iii).[31]

A request for an LMSB PFA must contain:

1. Names, addresses, telephone numbers, and taxpayer identification numbers of all interested parties;

2. The name, title, address and telephone number of a person to contact (if the person to contact is an authorized representative of the taxpayer, a properly executed Form 2848, Power of Attorney and Declaration of Representative, must accompany the request);

3. The annual accounting period and the overall method of accounting (e.g., cash receipts and disbursement or accrual) for maintaining the

[27] See Rev. Rul. 94-12, 1994-1 CB 36.
[28] See Rev. Rul. 92-80, 1992-2 CB 57.
[29] See Rev. Proc. 97-50, 1997-2 CB 515, modified by Rev. Proc. 2000-50, 2000-52 I.R.B. 1, 601.
[30] List of international issues that are likely to be suitable for resolution through the LMSB PFA program is discussed in Rev. Proc. 2001-22 IRB 2001-9, Section 3.05. See also Chapter 17.
[31] For a complete listing see Rev. Proc. 2001-22.

accounting books and filing the federal income tax return of all interested parties;

4. The location of the taxpayer's tax staff and records;

5. A brief description of the taxpayer's business operations, including the NAICS (North American Industry Code System) classification used by the taxpayer on its last filed return; and

6. The taxable period for which the LMSB PFA is sought, the last date on which the taxpayer may file (with extensions) a timely return for that period, and (if earlier) the date on which the taxpayer intends to file that return.

A request for an LMSB PFA must contain a separate written statement for each proposed issue that concisely:

1. Describes the issue;

2. Summarizes all the facts that are relevant and material to the issue;

3. Discuss whether the LMSB PFA will have any effect in taxable periods either before or after the taxable period for which the LMSB PFA is sought.

4. Discusses whether the issue can be resolved by the date on which the taxpayer intends to file its return for the taxable period in question.[32]

A request for an LMSB PFA, and any supplemental submissions (including additional documents), must include a declaration, signed by a person currently authorized to sign the taxpayer's federal income tax return, in the following form:

> Under penalties of perjury, I declare that I have examined this request, including accompanying documents, and to the best of my knowledge and belief, the facts presented in support of the request for the Pre-Filing Agreement are true, correct and complete.

The request for a LMSB PFA must also contain a statement by the taxpayer that it agrees that the inspection of records and testimony under the LMSB PFA procedures will not preclude or impede (under Code Sec. 7605(b) or any administrative provisions adopted by the IRS) a later examination of a return or inspection of records with respect to any taxable year needed to resolve the issue in the request for LMSB PFA, and that the IRS need not comply with any applicable procedural restrictions (such as providing notice under Code Sec. 7605(b) before beginning such examination or inspection).

The LMSB Industry Director with jurisdiction over the taxpayer will make the final decision whether to proceed with the taxpayer's request for an LMSB PFA. A representative of LMSB will contact the taxpayer within 14 business days of receipt of the taxpayer's request for an LMSB PFA to discuss the potential suitability of the issue(s) for inclusion in the LMSB PFA program. A taxpayer is not entitled to a conference to appeal a decision not to go forward with the LMSB PFA process. A taxpayer not selected for the LMSB PFA program remains eligible

---

[32] Rev. Proc. 2001-22 lists 11 specific criteria that must be met.

for other procedures for early issue resolution, including the Accelerated Issue Resolution (AIR) program.

If the IRS and the taxpayer cannot agree with respect to an issue, either before or after the filing of the return to which the LMSB PFA relates, and the IRS subsequently disagrees with the taxpayer's treatment of the issue, the taxpayer and the IRS may continue their efforts to reach an agreement using Accelerated Issue Resolution (AIR)[33] or the taxpayer may appeal either by requesting an Early Referral to Appeals or by protesting any proposed deficiency related to the issue.[34]

Early Referral Program. If the issue is one that is not within the team manager's settlement jurisdiction, the taxpayer may elect to use the early appeals referral procedures and have the issue considered by the Appeals Office while the audit work continues in other areas. The IRS has instituted the early referral program for Coordinated Industry cases in order to expedite the resolution of unagreed issues. Early referral is optional, it must be initiated by the taxpayer and it is subject to the approval of the Team Manager.[35] The taxpayer will be notified whether the early referral was granted. If the request is granted, the file is forwarded to Appeals. The taxpayer cannot appeal a refusal to grant early referral (see ¶ 1210).

Accelerated Issue Resolution. Another option available in Coordinated Industry cases for unresolved issues is the accelerated issue resolution (AIR) program. The purpose of this program is to advance the resolution of issues from one tax period to another. Under this program, the taxpayer enters into an AIR agreement which acts as a closing agreement with respect to one or more issues present in a Coordinated Industry examination for one or more periods ending before the date of the agreement.[36] Revenue Procedure 94-67 explains the scope and procedure for obtaining an AIR agreement. An AIR agreement may only be entered into for issues which fall under the jurisdiction of the Director and which relate to other items in another tax period. An AIR agreement may not be entered into for transfer pricing transactions, partnership items or any item designated for litigation by the Office of Chief Counsel.[37] Because the AIR program is voluntary, the taxpayer must submit a written request to the team manager which has jurisdiction over the taxpayer's returns. If the request is denied, the taxpayer has no right to appeal an AIR determination.

---

[33] ¶ 506, *infra.*
[34] ¶ 1210, *infra.*
[35] Rev. Proc. 99-28, IRB 1999-29.

[36] Rev. Proc. 94-67, 1994-2 CB 800.
[37] *Id.*

¶551 Exhibit 5-1

Form **4564** (Rev. June 1988)	Department of the Treasury — Internal Revenue Service **Information Document Request**	Request Number 15
To: *(Name of Taxpayer and Company Division or Branch)* OFFSHORE EXPORTERS LTD. Please return Part 2 with listed documents to requester identified below.	Subject Corporate Return 9609	
	SAIN Number	Submitted to: POA
	Dates of Previous Requests None	

Description of Documents Requested

1. Please provide a listing of projects worked during the fiscal year under audit.

2. At what point is revenue reported? What makes up the unbilled work-in-process on the balance sheet?

3. What is the average length of a project?

4. Does the corporation have any foreign bank accounts?

5. Please provide the loan documents for the 2.9 million dollar loan dated August 26, 1996.

Information Due By _____2-12-98_____   At Next Appointment ☐   Mail In ☐

From:	Name and Title of Requester Larry Lukenfer	Date 1-15-98
	Office Location Downtown District	Telephone Number 555-1212

Catalog No. 23145K   Part 1 — Taxpayer's File Copy   Form **4564** (Rev. 6-88)

¶552 Exhibit 5-2

Form **5701**	Department of the Treasury — Internal Revenue Service
(Rev. December 1983)	**Notice of Proposed Adjustment**

Name of taxpayer	Issue No.

Name and title of person to whom delivered	Date

Entity for this proposed adjustment

Based on the information we now have available and our discussions with you, we believe the proposed adjustment listed below should be included in the revenue agent's report. However, if you have additional information that would alter or reverse this proposal, please furnish this information as soon as possible.

Years	Amount	Account or return line	SAIN NO.	Issue Code

Issue

Reasons for Proposed Adjustment

If the explanation of the adjustment will be longer than the space provided below,
the entire explanation should begin on Form 886 — A (Explanation of Items.)

Taxpayer Representative's action
☐ Agreed   ☐ Agreed in Part   ☐ Disagreed   ☐ Have additional information; will submit by:

Case Manager	Date

Form **5701** (Rev. 12-83)

Part 1 - Taxpayer's File Copy

¶553 DISCUSSION QUESTIONS

1. ABC Corporation, a calendar year taxpayer, purchased a business in January 2004. The tax department wants to authoritatively determine the basis for the acquired assets prior to filing its 2004 return. What course of action would you advise? What are the appeal rights for your suggested course of action?

2. During an examination, the IRS proposes an adjustment based upon a revenue ruling which appears to be squarely in point. However, taxpayer contends that the revenue ruling is contrary to established tax law. How can taxpayer expedite resolution of this matter?

3. XYZ Corporation, a large multi-national entity, "managed" the prior IRS examination as follows. The IRS audit team, including a member of IRS Counsel, was housed in a large comfortable room adjoining the accounting department. The Controller, an especially busy person, dealt directly with the various IRS auditors. These interactions were friendly and informal. The modus operandi for handling IRS written requests for records was for the Controller to assign the Revenue Agents to deal directly with the accounting personnel responsible for the applicable records. This worked well for the IRS because it resulted in a prompt receipt of requested information. Furthermore, the Revenue Agents informally obtained additional information and records from the recordkeepers and, thereby, developed many issues well beyond the scope of the original written requests. The company kept no records with respect to information or records turned over to the IRS.

   On the other hand, this "system" did not work well for the taxpayer. At the end of the audit, the IRS raised numerous, often meritorious, issues which generally came as a complete surprise to the Controller. Some of the issues were later resolved at Appeals, but other issues currently await trial in Tax Court.

   XYZ Corporation has been informed that the IRS is commencing a new audit cycle. What advice would you give XYZ Corporation on how to establish procedures for this new IRS audit?

CHAPTER 6

INVESTIGATIVE AUTHORITY OF THE INTERNAL REVENUE SERVICE

¶601 GENERAL AUTHORITY TO EXAMINE

The Internal Revenue Service (IRS) has been granted broad powers to examine records and question individuals for the purpose of determining whether there has been compliance with the tax laws. Internal Revenue Code Section 7602(a)(1) specifically authorizes the IRS to examine any books, papers, records or other data that may be relevant or material to ascertaining the correctness of any return, determining the tax liability of any person or collecting any tax. Since most taxpayers and other individuals voluntarily produce records and answer questions when requested to do so by the IRS, this general authority in itself is normally sufficient to obtain the necessary information.

During an audit, a taxpayer may be asked informally for certain records or documents. Although such requests may be verbal, written requests specifically describing the documents or information to be produced frequently are made on Form 4564, Information Document Request. This form provides a permanent record of what was requested, received and returned to the taxpayer.

¶602 NOTICE OF THIRD-PARTY CONTACT

As part of its enforcement efforts, the IRS may also seek to gather information from third parties in connection with the examination of a taxpayer. Prior to the enactment of the IRS Restructuring and Reform Act of 1998[1] no prior notice in advance of a third-party contact was required. The lack of notice, Congress believed, often led to a chilling affect on a taxpayer's business or damaged the taxpayer's reputation, because the taxpayer was denied the opportunity to resolve issues and volunteer information before the IRS actually contacted third parties for such information.

The IRS is now required to provide reasonable notice of the fact that "a third party" will be contacted with respect to the examination or collection activities regarding the taxpayer.[2] However, the service is not under an obligation to provide the names or identity of the third parties prior to actual contact. Upon the taxpayer's request, or at least annually, the IRS is to provide a taxpayer with a record of persons contacted during the period by the IRS.[3]

A third-party contact is considered as having been made when an employee of the IRS contacts a person other than the taxpayer and asks questions about aspecific taxpayer with respect to the determination or collection of that tax-payer's tax liability.[4] The receipt of unsolicited information from a third party, a

---

[1] P.L. 105-206.
[2] Code Sec. 7602(c)(1).

[3] Code Sec. 7602(c)(2).
[4] IRM Handbook 4.2.1.6.12.1.

foreign country pursuant to an exchange of information clause or contacts made by the IRS to respond to a request from a treaty partner, are not considered third-party contacts. Furthermore, searches made on computer databases which do not require any personal involvement on the other end (e.g., Lexis or Information America), or contacts made for the purpose of obtaining information about an industry or market segment where specific taxpayers have not been identified, are also not considered third-party contacts within the context of Code Sec. 7602(c).[5]

If a third-party contact is necessary, a Letter 3164 must be provided to the taxpayer. If the tax liability is due to a jointly filed return, a separate Letter 3164 must be provided to each spouse. In order to allow the United States Post Office sufficient time to deliver the notice, IRS employees are instructed not to make any third-party contacts until ten days from the date Letter 3164 was mailed. If the letter was handed to the taxpayer, contacts may be made immediately. A copy of Letter 3164 should also be provided to the Power of Attorney.[6] When a third-party contact is made, the IRS employee is also to complete a Form 12175, Third Party Contact Report.[7]

Four situations are excluded from the notification requirements of Code Sec. 7602(c). The situations are: when the taxpayer (verbally or in writing) authorizes a third-party contact; when notice of such contact would jeopardize collection of any tax; when notice may involve reprisals against any person (an abusive spouse situation); and when there is a pending criminal investigation.[8] If a taxpayer authorizes a third-party contact, the IRS employee is to prepare Form 12180, Third Party Contact Authorization (see Exhibit 6-1 at ¶651) or obtain other written evidence listing the names of all third parties the taxpayer has authorized the employee to contact. For joint returns, both spouses must authorize contacts.

Taxpayer representatives who are attorneys, CPAs and enrolled agents can authorize third-party contacts on behalf of their clients. This authority does not extend to other types of representatives such as family members, unenrolled agents or tax return preparers.[9]

¶603 THE SUMMONS POWER

To give force and meaning to this general authority to examine, the IRS has been granted the power to compel a taxpayer or any other person to produce records and to testify under oath. This compulsory process is the administrative summons authorized by Code Sec. 7602(a)(2). The IRS may summon any person to appear at a time and place named in the summons for the purpose of giving testimony under oath and producing books, papers, records or other data. The

---

[5] IRM Handbook 4.2.1.6.12.1.
[6] IRM Handbook 4.2.1.6.12.2.1.
[7] IRM Handbook 4.2.1.6.12.3.1.
[8] IRM Handbook 4.2.1.6.12.4.
[9] IRM Handbook 13.1.7.3.3.3. The taxpayer and the representative must have executed a valid Form 2848, Power of Attorney and Declaration of Repre-

sentative. Form 2848 provides that "the representatives are authorized to . . . perform any and all acts that I (we) can perform with respect to tax matters described on line 3 [Form 2848], for example, the authority to sign any agreement, consent or other documents." This language is considered sufficient to allow a taxpayer's representative to authorize a Code Sec. 7602(c) third-party contact.

authority to issue summonses has been delegated generally to those agents and other personnel within the IRS who are responsible for the examination of returns, collection of taxes and investigation of tax offenses.[10] Thus, revenue agents, tax auditors, revenue officers and special agents are all permitted to issue a summons.

The summons must be served either by handing an attested copy to the person to whom it is directed or by leaving it at that person's "last and usual place of abode."[11] If personal service cannot be made, the summons is to be left at the place of residence either with some other person who is present or in a place where the person summoned will be likely to find it.[12] Several Courts of Appeals have held that the summons need not be left with someone of suitable age and discretion when personal service is not possible.[13] Simply leaving the summons at the last and usual place of residence is sufficient.

When a corporation is under examination, the summons may be directed to either a specific corporate officer or the corporation itself. The officer's corporate position or title should be indicated on the summons. When a summons is directed to the corporation, service must be made upon an officer, director, managing agent or other person authorized to accept service of process on behalf of the corporation.[14]

After service of the summons, the individual serving the summons prepares and signs a certificate of service on the reverse side of the Form 2039, Summons, retained by the IRS (see Exhibit 6-2 at ¶ 652). The date, time and manner of service are entered on the certificate. Code Sec. 7603(a) provides that the signed certificate of service is evidence of the facts it states in any proceeding to enforce the summons.

¶605 SCOPE OF THE POWER

The scope of the summons power in Code Sec. 7602 has been held to extend to the production of records stored on magnetic tape.[15] It has also been held to require the production of videotapes,[16] tax preparation software[17] and microfiche copies of records.[18] The United States Supreme Court has even approved the use of a summons to compel an individual to prepare handwriting exemplars before the examining agent.[19] However, the summons cannot require a person to create any documents, such as lists or schedules of factual information, that did not exist at the time the summons was issued.[20]

---

[10] IRM Handbook 1.2.2.2 Order Number 4.

[11] Code Sec. 7603(a).

[12] IRM Handbook 5.17.6.7.

[13] *United States v. Bichara*, 826 F.2d 1037 (11th Cir. 1987); *United States v. Gilleran*, 992 F.2d 232 (9th Cir. 1993), 93-1 USTC ¶ 50,356.

[14] IRM Handbook 109.1.3.2.

[15] *United States v. Davey*, 543 F.2d 996 (2d Cir. 1976), 76-1 USTC ¶ 9724.

[16] *United States v. Schenk*, 581 F. Supp. 218 (S.D. Ind. 1984), 84-1 USTC ¶ 9197; *United States v. Norton*, 81-1 USTC ¶ 9398 (N.D. Cal. 1981).

[17] *United States v. Norwest Corp.*, 116 F.3d 1227 (8th Cir. 1997), 97-2 USTC ¶ 50,510.

[18] *United States v. Mobil Corp.*, 543 F. Supp. 507 (N.D. Tex. 1982), 82-1 USTC ¶ 9242.

[19] *United States v. Euge*, 444 U.S. 707 (1980), 80-1 USTC ¶ 9222.

[20] *United States v. Davey, supra.*

Although the authority to summon and to examine books and records is very extensive, it is not without limits. Code Sec. 7605(b) provides that no taxpayer shall be subjected to unnecessary examination; it also prohibits more than one inspection of the taxpayer's books for each taxable year unless the taxpayer requests otherwise or unless the IRS notifies the taxpayer in writing that an additional inspection is necessary. The courts, as well as the IRS, generally have taken the position that there is no second inspection, even though the requested records were inspected previously, if the examination or investigation for the taxable year has not been completed or closed.[21]

The date fixed in the summons for compliance cannot be less than ten days from the date of the summons.[22] Revenue agents are instructed that the time set for appearance should not be less than eleven full calendar days from the date the summons is served.[23] This minimum allowable time for compliance is for the benefit of the summoned party and may be waived by an earlier voluntary compliance.

¶606 PROTECTION OF INTELLECTUAL PROPERTY RIGHTS

In order to protect the intellectual and property rights of the developers and owners of computer programs, the IRS is generally prohibited from issuing a summons or enforcing a summons to produce or analyze any tax related computer software and source code.[24] In addition, there are specific protections against the disclosure and improper use of trade secrets and other confidential information related to computer programs and source code in the possession of the IRS as the result of an examination of any taxpayer.[25]

A summons, however, may be issued for tax related computer source code in connection with an inquiry into any offense connected with the administration or enforcement of federal tax laws.[26] The general prohibition likewise does not apply to any tax related computer software source code acquired or developed by thetaxpayer or a related person primarily for internal use rather than commercial distribution.[27] Finally, the IRS may issue or begin an action to enforce a summons for tax-related computer software source code if the IRS is unable to otherwise reasonably ascertain the correctness of any return.[28]

¶607 REPRESENTATION AND RECORDING OF TESTIMONY

The individual to whom a summons is directed is entitled to have a representative present when appearing in response to a summons. When a third-party witness is summoned, other persons may be present at the interview as observers if the witness requests their presence and obtains a waiver of the taxpayer's right to confidentiality.[29] The taxpayer and his or her representative, however, generally have been held to have no right to be present during the interview of a third-

---

[21] IRM Handbook 109.1.4.4.3.

[22] Code Sec. 7605(a). A longer period is required for third-party recordkeeper summonses. See ¶ 615, *infra*.

[23] IRM Handbook 109.1.1.5.

[24] Code Sec. 7612(a)(1).

[25] Code Sec. 7612(a)(2).

[26] Code Sec. 7612(b)(2)(A).

[27] Code Sec. 7612(b)(2)(B).

[28] Code Sec. 7612(b)(1).

[29] *United States v. Finch*, 434 F. Supp. 1085 (D. Colo. 1977), 78-1 USTC ¶ 9135.

party witness.[30] When a witness requests or consents to be represented at an appearance by the same attorney or other representative who has been retained by the taxpayer, a conflict-of-interest may arise. If such a question of dual representation occurs, the representative normally will not be excluded from the interview of the witness unless the representative does something which impedes or obstructs the investigation.[31]

A taxpayer appearing in response to a summons has the right to make an audio or stenographic recording, provided advance notice is given to the IRS of such intention.[32] If the IRS makes its own recording, the taxpayer normally is entitled to a copy or transcript upon request. However, the IRS must be reimbursed for the cost of reproducing such copy or transcript. In criminal tax investigations, a witness also will be furnished a copy of a transcript of his or her testimony (or affidavit) upon request, except when it is determined that release should be delayed until such time as it will not interfere with the development or successful prosecution of the case.[33]

¶609 PROPER USE OF INTERNAL REVENUE SERVICE SUMMONS

An IRS summons may be used only for the purposes set forth in Code Sec. 7602. These purposes include the verification, determination and collection of the taxliability of any person. Since 1982, the IRS also has been specifically authorized to issue summonses for the purpose of investigating any criminal tax offense.[34]

The Supreme Court has stated that a summons will not be enforced if it has been issued for an improper purpose, such as to harass the taxpayer, pressure settlement of a collateral dispute, or for any other purpose reflecting on the good faith of the particular investigation.[35] Enforcement of such a summons constitutes an abuse of the court's process.[36]

Criminal Tax Investigations. For many years prior to 1982, a controversy existed as to whether it was proper to use an administrative summons in a criminal tax investigation. At the time, the specific purposes for which a summons was authorized by the Code appeared to be restricted solely to the determination or collection of the *civil* tax liability. There was nothing which suggested that a summons could be used for criminal tax investigations. The

---

[30] *United States v. Newman*, 441 F.2d 165 (5th Cir. 1971), 71-1 USTC ¶9329; *United States v. Nemetz*, 450 F.2d 924 (3d Cir. 1971), 71-2 USTC ¶9725.

[31] IRM Handbook 109.1.5.5, IRM Handbook 9781, Section 343.6. To avoid censure for unethical conduct, there must be full disclosure of the potential conflict to the witness, and the witness must thereafter consent to such dual representation. See Circular 230, §10.29.

[32] Code Sec. 7521(a); IRM Handbook 109.1.5.4.

[33] Reg. §601.107(b); IRM Handbook 9781, Section 343.3.

[34] Code Sec. 7602(b).

[35] *United States v. Powell*, 379 U.S. 48 (1964), 64-2 USTC ¶9858.

[36] For an excellent discussion of the possible abuse of process and improper use of an IRS summons demanding appearance at a police station for the taking of fingerprints, see *United States v. Michaud*, 907 F.2d 750 (7th Cir. 1990), 90-2 USTC ¶50,425.

Supreme Court attempted to resolve this question, but the vague guideline which it established only generated more litigation.[37]

In 1982, Congress amended Code Sec. 7602 to establish a bright-line rule for the use of summonses in criminal tax investigations. Code Sec. 7602(b) now specifically provides that a summons may be issued for "the purpose of inquiring into any offense connected with the administration or enforcement of the internal revenue laws."[38] Under Code Sec. 7602(c), the authority to issue a summons in a criminal investigation terminates once there is a "Justice Department referral in effect" with respect to the person under investigation. Such a "referral" is in effect when the IRS recommends to the Attorney General either the criminal prosecution or a grand jury investigation of such person. A "referral" is also in effect if any request is made in writing by the Attorney General to the IRS for the disclosure of any tax return or return information relating to such person.

This limitation on the issuance of a summons is removed once the Attorney General notifies the IRS in writing that the person involved will not be prosecuted or will not be the subject of a grand jury investigation. The limitation also ceaseswhen there has been a final disposition of any criminal proceeding instituted against such person.

Tax Court Proceedings. The use of administrative summonses by the IRS during Tax Court proceedings has raised objections by taxpayers. The Tax Court discovery rules permitting both parties to obtain relevant information before trial are much more restricted in their scope than the summons power available to the IRS. In certain situations, the Tax Court has held that to allow the IRS in a pending case to use evidence obtained by the issuance of a summons would give the government an unfair advantage over the taxpayer. In substance, such use of the summons would permit the IRS to circumvent the limitations of the Tax Court's discovery rules. The Tax Court will issue protective orders to preclude the IRS from using information obtained by such abusive use of the administrative summons.[39]

In *Ash v. Commissioner*,[40] the Tax Court set forth guidelines which it would follow in determining whether such a protective order should be issued when the IRS obtains information during a pending case by means of a summons. In one situation, where litigation has commenced by the filing of a petition by the taxpayer, and a summons is then issued with regard to the same taxpayer and taxable year involved in the case, the Tax Court will issue a protective order to prevent the IRS from using any of the summoned evidence in the litigation.[41]

---

[37] In *United States v. LaSalle National Bank*, 437 U.S. 298 (1978), 78-2 USTC ¶9501, the Supreme Court held that a criminal tax investigation was not solely for criminal enforcement purposes until criminal prosecution was recommended or *an institutional commitment had been made to recommend prosecution*. Until such time, the Court indicated, the criminal investigation also had a civil purpose related to the determination of the civil tax liability. The ensuing litigation revolved around the question of when an "institutional" commitment had been made to recommend prosecution.

[38] See Chapter 17, Criminal Tax Procedure, *infra*, for a discussion of the various criminal tax offenses.

[39] Tax Court Rule 103.

[40] 96 TC 459 (1991), CCH Dec. 47,221.

[41] The Tax Court issued such an order in *Universal Manufacturing Co. v. Comm'r*, 93 TC 589 (1989), CCH Dec. 46,154.

However, in such a situation, the Court will not issue a protective order if the IRS can show that the summons was issued for a sufficient reason that was independent of the pending litigation.

In another situation, in those cases where the summons is issued before the taxpayer files a Tax Court petition, no order will be issued with respect to any information obtained as a result of the summons. The Tax Court in *Ash* explained that, before a petition is filed, the Court has no jurisdiction and there is no basis for viewing the summons as an attempt to undermine the Court's discovery rules.

In a third situation dealt with in *Ash*, where litigation has commenced, and an administrative summons is issued with regard to a different taxpayer or a different taxable year, the Tax Court normally will not issue a protective order.[42] However, the Court stated that it would do so if the taxpayer could show that the IRS lacked an independent and sufficient reason for the summons.

Other Objections. In addition to the potential challenges to a summons for improper use, a summoned individual also may raise other objections based on constitutional rights or common-law privileges. These include, among others, theFourth Amendment protection against unreasonable searches and seizures,[43] the Fifth Amendment privilege against self-incrimination,[44] and the common-law privilege which protects confidential communications between attorney and client. These rights and privileges are discussed in Chapter 17, Criminal Tax Procedure, *infra*.

¶611 ENFORCEMENT OF SUMMONS

When a summons is issued and the summoned person refuses to comply, the government can seek enforcement of the summons in the United States District Court for the district in which the summoned party lives.[45] Before the Court may order the summoned person to comply, the IRS is initially required to prove the following elements:

1. The information sought by the summons is relevant;

2. The purpose of the inquiry is legitimate;

3. The information sought is not already in the government's possession; and

---

[42] In an earlier case involving this type of situation, the issuance of a protective order was justified by the "compelling facts." *Westreco, Inc. v. Comm'r,* 60 TCM 824 (1990), CCH Dec. 46,882(M).

[43] *Vaughn v. Baldwin,* 950 F.2d 331 (6th Cir. 1991). Taxpayer's Fourth Amendment rights were violated when the IRS refused to return the taxpayer's papers, which he had voluntarily turned over to the IRS pursuant to a summons, after the taxpayer had formally demanded their return and revoked his consent to have them copied.

[44] *U.S. v. Wirenius,* 94-1 USTC ¶50,132. The court upheld the taxpayer's Fifth Amendment claim and refused to enforce an IRS summons, because testi-

mony by the taxpayer could have lead to criminal prosecution, and the taxpayer reasonably and legitimately feared his testimony would lead to criminal prosecution.

[45] Code Secs. 7604(a) and 7402(b). Failure to comply with a summons will not be punished as a criminal offense under Code Sec. 7210, nor subject a person to attachment and arrest under Code Sec. 7604(b), if goodfaith objections to the summons have been raised and there has not been a complete default or contumacious refusal to comply. *Reisman v. Caplin,* 375 U.S. 440 (1964), 64-1 USTC ¶9202. For a discussion of the suspension of the statute of limitations on assessment when a "designated summons" to a corporation is contested, see Chapter 8, *infra.*

4. The administrative steps required by the Code have been followed.[46]

If the government meets this initial burden of proof, and the defenses raised by the summoned party are rejected, the Court will order compliance with the summons. The civil and criminal contempt powers of the Court are available to enforce compliance with the order. A finding of contempt can result in the imposition of monetary penalties[47] or incarceration.[48]

¶615 THIRD-PARTY RECORDKEEPER SUMMONS

Prior to 1976, a taxpayer could not raise objections to summonses issued to third parties. The Supreme Court had held that a taxpayer could not stay compliance with such a summons because he had no proprietary interest in the records that the summons sought.[49] In 1976, Congress acted to change this result. It created a limited class of "third-party recordkeepers" and gave taxpayers a legal right to object to summonses issued to such third parties.[50] In addition to the notice requirements under Code Sec. 7602(c)(1) (see ¶601), new Code Sec. 7609 provides that a taxpayer must also be given notice of a summons issued to any third party.[51] Nonetheless, in certain situations, the IRS need not provide taxpayer notice of a third-party summons. These exemptions include (1) a summons served on the person with respect to whose tax liability the summons issued or any officer or employee of the person; (2) a summons issued to determine whether or not records of the business transactions or affairs of an identified person have been made or kept; (3) a summons issued by a criminal investigator of the IRS in connection with the investigation of an offense connected with the administration or enforcement of the revenue laws; and (4) a collection summons.

A summons issued under Code Sec. 7602 can be served by either handing an attested copy of the summons to the person to whom it is directed or leaving the attested copy at the person's last and usual place of abode.[52] When a third-party recordkeeper is summoned by the IRS, the summons can also be served by Certified or Registered Mail to the last known address of the third-party recordkeeper.[53] Providing service of summonses by mail is an option available only to the IRS when the person on whom the summons is served is a "third-party recordkeeper" as defined in Code Sec. 7603(b)(2).

---

[46] *United States v. Powell,* 379 U.S. 48 (1964), 64-2 USTC ¶9858.

[47] See, for example, *United States v. Chase Manhattan Bank,* 590 F. Supp. 1160 (S.D.N.Y. 1984), 84-2 USTC ¶9749, and *United States v. Darwin Construction Co.,* 873 F.2d 730 (4th Cir. 1989), 89-2 USTC ¶9425, imposing a fine of $5,000 per day for failure to comply with a summons enforcement order.

[48] See, for example, *Ex Parte Tammen,* 438 F. Supp. 349 (N.D. Tex. 1977), 78-1 USTC ¶9302, and *United States v. Lillibridge,* 80-2 USTC ¶9694 (6th Cir. 1980).

[49] *United States v. Donaldson,* 400 U.S. 517 (1971), 71-1 USTC ¶9173.

[50] Former Code Sec. 7609 applicable to summonses served on or before July 22, 1998.

[51] The notice must be accompanied by a copy of the summons and must be given to the taxpayer within three days of service on the third party, but no later than the twenty-third day before the date fixed for examination of the records. The notice may be served in the same manner as a summons or mailed by certified or registered mail. Code Sec. 7609(a).

[52] Code Sec. 7603(a).

[53] Code Sec. 7603(b)(1).

Within twenty days after the taxpayer receives the notice, the taxpayer may then file a petition to quash the summons in the district court. The petition must be served upon both the IRS and the third party within the twenty-day period. The third party has the right to intervene in the proceedings, but is not required to do so. In any event, the recordkeeper will be bound by the ruling on the petition to quash.[54]

If a taxpayer files a petition to quash the summons, the statutes of limitations for assessment and for criminal prosecution are suspended during the period that the proceeding regarding the summons is pending.[55] Further, even if the taxpayer does not attempt to quash, the statute can be suspended if the third party delaysproduction of the records or disputes the summons. Code Sec. 7609(e)(2) provides that if issues raised by a third-party response to the summons are not resolved within six months after the summons is issued, the statute is suspended beginning six months after issuance until the date the dispute is finally resolved (see ¶940).

If a petition to quash is not filed, the IRS may not begin examining the documents until the twenty-fourth day following notice to the taxpayer that the summons was issued. The third party is required to begin assembling the records at the time the original summons is received, so that there is no further delay once it is clear that the IRS is entitled to them. If a petition to quash is filed, the IRS will be permitted to examine the records only upon order of the court or with the consent of the taxpayer.[56]

Code Sec. 7603(b)(2) provides the definition of the term "third-party recordkeeper." This definition of a third-party recordkeeper is the same as the definition of a third-party recordkeeper formerly provided by Code Sec. 7609(a)(3) before amendment in 1998. Included in that definition are any bank, savings and loan, or credit union, any consumer reporting agency, any person extending credit through the use of credit cards or similar devices, any broker, any attorney, any accountant, any barter exchange, and after the Taxpayer Bill of Rights 2 of 1996,[57] any enrolled agent. Employers are not included within the definition of third-party recordkeepers.[58]

¶618 JOHN DOE SUMMONSES FOR "LISTED TRANSACTIONS" OR"TAX SHELTERS"

The government has resorted to, and been quite successful, in using John Doe Summonses under Section 7609 in its investigations of "listed transactions" or "tax shelters." *In Re: Does*, 93 AFTR 2d 2004-742 (John Doe Summons authorized

---

[54] Code Sec. 7609(b)(2)(c).

[55] Code Sec. 7609(e). See discussion in Chapter 8, *infra*. Code Sec. 7609(e) only suspends the statute of limitations on assessment in the case of summonses issued to third-party recordkeepers. The statute of limitations may also be tolled in the case of a summons issued to a corporation if the summons is a "designated summons." A designated summons is any summons issued for the purpose of determin-ing the amount of tax due, issued at least sixty days before the day on which the assessment period is to end and which clearly states that it is a designated summons. Code Sec. 6503(j).

[56] Code Sec. 7609(d).

[57] P.L. 104-188.

[58] It should be noted that the third party summoned in the *Donaldson* case was the taxpayer's employer.

with respect to Sidley Austin Brown & Wood). In order to serve a John Doe Summons, the IRS must obtain court approval and show to the Court that (1) the summons relates to the investigation of a particular person or ascertainable group or class of persons, (2) there is a reasonable basis for believing that such person or group or class of persons may fail or may have failed to comply with any provision of any internal revenue law, and (3) the information sought to be obtained from the examination of the records or testimony (and the identity of the person or persons with respect to whose liabilty the summons is issued) is not readily available fromother sources.[59] The provisions of Section 7609(e)(2) regarding suspension of the statute of limitations also apply to John Doe Summonses. In addition, the summoned party must provide notice of such suspension to the John Doe(s).[60]

Power to Summon Accountants' Workpapers

¶621 AUDIT AND TAX ACCRUAL PAPERS

In light of the uncertainty of the application of the new privilege (see ¶701), tax professionals may want to carefully consider the IRS "positions" and "decisions" issued prior to the new legislation as this may be applicable to the "nonprivileged" information or documents sought by the IRS. The American Institute of Certified Public Accountants (AICPA) Tax Guides and Checklists, 2000 Edition, provides the following commentary with respect to tax returns, tax accrual workpapers and technical memorandum:

> **Tax returns:** Because Federal returns are intended to be disclosed to revenue officials, and are not intended to be confidential, the Confidentiality Privilege generally does not extend to any of these returns, nor to the calculations included in the returns.

> **Tax reconciliation workpapers:** These are usually workpapers used in assembling and compiling financial data preparatory to placing it on a return. Because this is financial data, not tax advice, the Confidentiality Privilege does not likely apply.

> **Tax accrual workpapers:** These are financial statement audit workpapers that reflect the estimate of a company's tax contingency liability. The decision in *Arthur Young** held that when an independent CPA firm prepared them, the workpapers were being prepared for the public and shareholders, and were not subject to an accountant-client privilege. These workpapers would not be viewed as tax advice because the CPA's public role in preparing the workpapers. Because they are not communicated in confidence, they would not be protected by the Confidentiality Privilege

> **Technical memorandums:** This is usually a detailed memorandum discussing items reflected on the return, in which the ultimate tax treatment is unclear. This may contain mental impressions, thought processes and speculations of possible adverse IRS positions, the likelihood of success on the issues if challenged by the IRS, and various negotiation and settlement positions. This type of document may be distinguishable from return reparation, and may be viewed as tax planning. If the CPA communicated this document to the taxpayer, it might be tax advice protected by the Confidentiality Privilege.

---

[59] Code Sec. 7609(f).   [60] Code Sec. 7609(i)(4).

Alternatively, this may be protected as CPA work product prepared in antici-pation of litigation.

U.S. v. Young & Co., Arthur, (1984, S Ct) 465 US 805, 79 L Ed 2d 826

One issue that had been extensively litigated was the power of the IRS, by use of the summons power, to gain access to audit workpapers and tax accrual papers prepared by accountants. The IRS believes such workpapers are not protected from disclosure as "privileged communications." IRS Ann. 2002-63, 2002-2 CB 72. The following abstract from the Internal Revenue Manual describes the types of documents that have been sought by the IRS.

Definitions

1. The term "tax reconciliation workpapers" means workpapers used in assembling and compiling financial data preparatory to placing it on a tax return. Typically these will include final trial balances for each entity and/or a schedule of consolidating and adjusting entries. They include information used to trace financial information to the tax return.

2. The term "audit workpapers" means workpapers retained by the indepen-dent accountant as to the procedures followed, the tests performed, the information obtained, and the conclusions reached pertinent to his/her exam-ination. Workpapers may include work programs, analyses, memorandums, letters of confirmation and representation, abstracts of company documents, and schedules or commentaries prepared or obtained by the auditor. These workpapers provide an important support for the independent certified pub-lic accountant's opinion as to the fairness of the presentation of the financial statements, in conformity with generally accepted accounting principles and demonstrate compliance with the generally accepted auditing standards. (See Sections 338.02 and .03 of the Codification of Statements on Auditing Stan-dards, as issued by the American Institute of Certified Public Accountants.)[61]

[3. The term "tax accrual workpapers" means workpapers that reflect the estimate of a company's tax contingency liability. Tax accrual workpapers are sometimes referred to as the tax pool analysis, tax liability contingency analysis, tax cushion or tax contingency reserve. These workpapers are gener-ally prepared and maintained by the taxpayer but, in some cases, all or portions of them may be maintained by the independent accountant. The specific objective of the tax accrual process is to obtain a figure representing a reasonable estimate of the income tax properly attributable to all items of income and expense for a given year and an accrued balance to cover the estimated tax liabilities as of the balance sheet date. Tax accrual workpapers may include the following:

(a) A summary of the transactions recorded in the taxpayer's general ledger with respect to income tax accounts;

(b) A computation of the tax provision for the current year, whether or not the tax is payable in that year; and

(c) A memorandum discussing items reflected in the financial state-ments income or expense where the ultimate tax treatment is unclear.][62]

---

[61] IRM Handbook 34.12.3.13.1.

[62] Former IRM 4024.2. The present section of the IRM relative to this subject is Handbook 109.1.4.4.7 states "Reserved".

The Internal Revenue Manual makes it clear that the requesting of tax accrual workpapers is not a routine examination procedure and is to be restricted "to those cases when unusual circumstances make it necessary to have access to the workpapers to complete an examination."[63] The Internal Revenue Manual instructions regarding accountants' workpapers distinguish between tax reconciliation workpapers and audit or tax accrual workpapers. The manual provides that no special circumstances need be shown to request tax reconciliation workpapers. In fact such workpapers are to be requested at the beginning of an examination so they can be used to trace financial information to the tax return. However, the tax accrual workpapers which normally would be prepared by an outside accountant are only to be requested after the agent has substantially completed an examination, has reconciled Schedule M-1 of Form 1120, U.S. Corporation Income Tax Return, and has identified specific issues for which the tax accrual papers are needed.[64]

In connection with its investigation of "tax shelters," the IRS has expanded the circumstances under which it will request tax accrual workpapers. For returns filed on or after July 1, 2002, the IRS may request workpapers when examining any return which claims benefit for a transaction determined to be a "listed transaction" under the Regulations under Section 6011. IRS Ann. 2002-63, 2002-2 CB 72.

In edition, the Office of Chief Council has provided specific guidelines for requesting tax accrual and other financial audit workpapers relating to the tax reserve for deferred tax liabilities and to footnotes disclosing contingent tax liabilities appearing on audited financial statements (see Exhibit 6-3 at ¶ 653 and Exhibit 6-4 at ¶ 654).

The limits on an agent's discretion to resort to the tax accrual workpapers also do not apply when a case has been referred to the Criminal Investigation Division. Special Agents have no restrictions on their ability to obtain tax accrual workpapers in criminal investigations. At the first hint of criminal activity (either apparent directly from the taxpayer or its records, or indicated by the appearance of a Special Agent of the IRS) a tax practitioner should recommend that the client consult with an attorney experienced in criminal tax matters.[65]

When an attorney hires an agent to assist him in a tax controversy, any work product produced by the accountant subsequent to such employment will be protected in the same manner as if it was prepared by the attorney. To aid in the protection of such information, a written engagement letter should be prepared confirming that the attorney is retaining the accountant and that the accountant will be working under his direction and control. This engagement letter is commonly known as a *Kovel Letter* (see Exhibit 6-5 at ¶ 655).[66] The reason for using a *Kovel Letter* is that the presence of an accountant may be necessary to "translate" a taxpayer's story to an attorney who may not be as well versed as

---

[63] IRM Handbook 34.12.3.13.1.

[64] IRM 4024.3 and 4.

[65] AICPA Tax Guides and Checklists, 2000 Edition

[66] *United States v. Kovel*, 296 F.2d 918 (2nd Cir. 1961) 62-1 USTC ¶ 9111; *In the Matter of Grand Jury Proceedings*, 220 F.3d 568 (7th Cir. 2000), 2000-2 USTC ¶ 50,598.

the accountant in tax matters. It has been held that the accountant must be "necessary, or at least highly useful" in facilitating the attorney's provision of legal advice in order to be protected by the attorney client privilege.[67]

Communications made to the accountant prior to the retention of the attorney will not be privileged information. It is better practice, therefore, not to hire an accountant who has previously worked on the matter thus avoiding the stringent burden of separating what was communicated to him before and after being retained by the attorney.

An engagement letter should be issued from the attorney to the accountant and it should include the following: (1) a recital that the attorney is hiring the accountant-agent to assist him in rending legal advice; (2) the nature and scope of the accountant-agent's engagement; (3) acknowledge that payment will come from the law firm (and that the ultimate client is not to be billed); (4) acknowledgement that all records, schedules, documents, etc., of the accountant-agent will be the sole property of the attorney; and (5) a recital that once the assignment is completed, all of the accountant-agent's files will be delivered to the attorney and copies will not be retained.

To insure the communications between the client and the accountant will continue to be privileged under *Kovel*, the attorney as opposed to the accountant must act as the taxpayer's primary representative and play a visible role.

---

[67] *Cavallaro v. U.S.*, 284 F.3d 236 (1st Cir. 2002).

¶651 Exhibit 6-1

THIRD PARTY CONTACT AUTHORIZATION FORM
Internal Revenue Code Section 7602(c)

Under section 7602(c) of the Internal Revenue Code, the Internal Revenue Service (IRS) is required to provide taxpayers with reasonable advance notice that contacts with persons other than the taxpayer may be made with respect to the determination or collection of the tax liability of such taxpayer. Additionally, IRS is required to provide the taxpayer with a record of persons contacted on a periodic basis. IRS will also provide this record to the taxpayer upon request. However, IRS is not required to provide advance notice or a record of persons contacted with respect to any contacts which the taxpayer has authorized.

By signing this form, you are waiving your rights under section 7602(c) with respect to the persons you have authorized IRS to contact. Accordingly, IRS will not be required to maintain a record of these contacts. If no third party contacts are made other than those authorized by you, IRS will not be required to provide you with advance notice ~~that contacts with third parties may be made~~ or provide you with a record of persons contacted.

Authorization of Third Party Contact(s)

I authorize an officer or employee of the Internal Revenue Service to contact the following third person(s) with respect to the determination or collection of my tax liability.

Name(s) of Third Person(s) _____

_____

_____

I understand that ~~in signing~~ this form, I am waiving my rights under section 7602(c) with respect to contacts made by an officer or employee of the Internal Revenue Service with the above listed person(s).

TAXPAYER'S SIGNATURE   _____ DATE _____

TAXPAYER IDENTIFICATION NUMBER _____

SPOUSE'S SIGNATURE   _____ DATE _____

TAXPAYER REPRESENTATIVE   _____ DATE _____

CORPORATE NAME   _____ DATE _____

CORPORATE OFFICER(S)   _____ DATE _____

FORM 12180 (01-1999)

¶652 Exhibit 6-2

Summons

In the matter of _____

Internal Revenue District of _____   Periods _____

The Commissioner of Internal Revenue

To: _____

At: _____
_____

You are hereby summoned and required to appear before _____,
an officer of the Internal Revenue Service, to give testimony and to bring with you and to produce for examination the following books, records, papers, and other data relating to the tax liability or the collection of the tax liability or for the purpose of inquiring into any offense connected with the administration or enforcement of the internal revenue laws concerning the person identified above for the periods shown.

SAMPLE

SAMPLE Do not write in this space

Business address and telephone number of IRS officer before whom you are to appear:

_____

Place and time for appearance at _____

IRS

on the _____ day of _____ , _____ at _____ o'clock _____ m.
(year)

Issued under authority of the Internal Revenue Code this _____ day of _____ , _____ .
(year)

Department of the Treasury
Internal Revenue Service

w w w . i r s . u s t r e a s . g o v

_____   _____
Signature of issuing officer   Title

Form 2039 (Rev. 9-1999)

_____   _____
Signature of approving officer _(if applicable)_   Title

Original — to be kept by IRS

¶652

Service of Summons, Notice and Recordkeeper Certificates

(Pursuant to section 7603, Internal Revenue Code)

I certify that I served the summons shown on the front of this form on:

Date	Time

How Summons Was Served

1. ☐ I certify that I handed a copy of the summons, which contained the attestation required by § 7603, to the person to whom it was directed.

2. ☐ I certify that I left a copy of the summons, which contained the attestation required by § 7603, at the last and usual place of abode of the person to whom it was directed. I left the copy with the following person (if any): _____

3. ☐ I certify that I sent a copy of the summons, which contained the attestation required by § 7603, by certified or registered mail to the last known address of the person to whom it was directed, that person being a third-party recordkeeper within the meaning of § 7603(b). I sent the summons to the following address: _____

SAMPLE

Signature	Title

4. This certificate is made to show compliance with IRC Section 7609. This certificate does not apply to summonses served on any officer or employee of the person to whose liability the summons relates nor to summonses in aid of collection, to determine the identity of a person having a numbered account or similar arrangement, or to determine whether or not records of the business transactions or affairs of an identified person have been made or kept.

I certify that, within 3 days of serving the summons, I gave notice (Part D of Form 2039) to the person named below on the date and in the manner indicated.

SAMPLE

Date of giving notice: _____   Time: _____

Name of Noticee: _____

Address of Noticee (if mailed): _____

How Notice Was Given

☐ I gave notice by certified or registered mail to the last known address of the noticee.

☐ I left the notice at the last and usual place of abode of the noticee. I left the copy with the following person (if any).

☐ I gave notice by handing it to the noticee.

☐ In the absence of a last known address of the noticee, I left the notice with the person summoned.

☐ No notice is required.

Signature	Title

I certify that the period prescribed for beginning a proceeding to quash this summons has expired and that no such proceeding was instituted or that the noticee consents to the examination.

Signature	Title

Form **2039** (Rev. 9-1999)

Summons

In the matter of _____

Internal Revenue District of _____ Periods _____

The Commissioner of Internal Revenue

To: _____

At: _____

You are hereby summoned and required to appear before _____,
an officer of the Internal Revenue Service, to give testimony and to bring with you and to produce for examination the following books, records, papers, and other data relating to the tax liability or the collection of the tax liability or for the purpose of inquiring into any offense connected with the administration or enforcement of the internal revenue laws concerning the person identified above for the periods shown.

SAMPLE

SAMPLE

Attestation

I hereby certify that I have examined and compared this copy of the summons with the original and that it is a true and correct copy of the original.

_____   _____
Signature of IRS officer serving the summons   Title

Business address and telephone number of IRS officer before whom you are to appear:

_____

Place and time for appearance at _____

_____

IRS

Department of the Treasury
Internal Revenue Service

www.irs.ustreas.gov

Form 2039 (Rev. 9-1999)

on the _____ day of _____ , _____ at _____ o'clock _____ m.
(year)
Issued under authority of the Internal Revenue Code this _____ day of _____ , _____ .
(year)

_____   _____
Signature of issuing officer   Title

_____   _____
Signature of approving officer *(if applicable)*   Title

Part A — to be given to person summoned

¶652

Provisions of the Internal Revenue Code

Sec. 7602. Examination of books and witnesses

(a) Authority to Summon, etc. — For the purpose of ascertaining the correctness of any return, making a return where none has been made, determining the liability of any person for any internal revenue tax or the liability at law or in equity of any transferee or fiduciary of any person in respect of any internal revenue tax, or collecting any such liability, the Secretary is authorized —

(1) To examine any books, papers, records, or other data which may be relevant or material to such inquiry.

(2) To summon the person liable for tax or required to perform the act, or any officer or employee of such person, or any person having possession, custody, or care of books of account containing entries relating to the business of the person liable for tax or required to perform the act, or any other person the Secretary may deem proper, to appear before the Secretary at a time and place named in the summons and to produce such books, papers, records, or other data, and to give such testimony, under oath, as may be relevant or material to such inquiry; and

(3) To take such testimony of the person concerned, under oath, as may be relevant or material to such inquiry.

(b) Purpose may include inquiry into offense. — The purposes for which the Secretary may take any action described in paragraph (1), (2), or (3) of subsection (a) include the purpose of inquiring into any offense connected with the administration or enforcement of the internal revenue laws.

(c) Notice of contact of third parties. —

(1) General Notice. — An officer or employee of the Internal Revenue Service may not contact any person other than the taxpayer with respect to the determination or collection of the tax liability of such taxpayer without providing reasonable notice in advance to the taxpayer that contacts with persons other than the taxpayer may be made.

(2) Notice of specific contacts. — The Secretary shall periodically provide to a taxpayer a record of persons contacted during such period by the Secretary with respect to the determination or collection of the tax liability of such taxpayer. Such record shall also be provided upon request of the taxpayer.

(3) Exceptions. — This subsection shall not apply —

(A) to any contact which the taxpayer has authorized,

(B) if the Secretary determines for good cause shown that such notice would jeopardize collection of any tax or such notice may involve reprisal against any person, or

(C) with respect to any pending criminal investigation.

(d) No administrative summons when there is Justice Department referral. —

(1) Limitation of authority. — No summons may be issued under this title, and the Secretary may not begin any action under section 7604 to enforce any summons, with respect to any person if a Justice Department referral is in effect with respect to such person.

(2) Justice Department referral in effect. — For purposes of this subsection —

(A) In general. — A Justice Department referral is in effect with respect to any person if —

(i) the Secretary has recommended to the Attorney General a grand jury investigation of, or the criminal prosecution of, such person for any offense connected with the administration or enforcement of the internal revenue laws, or

(ii) any request is made under section 6103(h)(3)(B) for the disclosure of any return or return information (within the meaning of section 6103(b)) relating to such person.

(B) Termination. — A Justice Department referral shall cease to be in effect with respect to a person when—

(i) the Attorney General notifies the Secretary, in writing, that —

(I) he will not prosecute such person for any offense connected with the administration or enforcement of the internal revenue laws,

(II) he will not authorize a grand jury investigation of such person with respect to such an offense, or

(III) he will discontinue such a grand jury investigation.

(ii) a final disposition has been made of any criminal proceeding pertaining to the enforcement of the internal revenue laws which was instituted by the Attorney General against such person, or

(iii) the Attorney General notifies the Secretary, in writing, that he will not prosecute such person for any offense connected with the administration or enforcement of the internal revenue laws relating to the request described in subparagraph (A)(ii).

(3) Taxable years, etc., treated separately. — For purposes of this subsection, each taxable period (or, if there is no taxable period, each taxable event) and each tax imposed by a separate chapter of this title shall be treated separately.

(e) Limitation on examination on unreported income. — The Secretary shall not use financial status or economic reality examination techniques to determine the existence of unreported income of any taxpayer unless the Secretary has a reasonable indication that there is a likelihood of such unreported income.

Authority to examine books and witness is also provided under sec. 6420 (e)(2) — Gasoline used on farms: sec. 6421(g)(2) — Gasoline used for certain nonhighway purposes by local transit systems, or sold for certain exempt purposes; and sec. 6427(j)(2) — Fuels not used for taxable purposes

★ ★ ★ ★ ★

Sec. 7603. Service of summons

(a) In general — A summons issued under section 6420(e)(2), 6421(g)(2), 6427(j)(2), or 7602 shall be served by the Secretary, by an attested copy delivered in hand to the person

to whom it is directed, or left at his last and usual place of abode; and the certificate of service signed by the person serving the summons shall be evidence of the facts it states on the hearing of an application for the enforcement of the summons. When the summons requires the production of books, papers, records, or other data, it shall be sufficient if such books, papers, records, or other data are described with reasonable certainty.

(b) Service by mail to third-party recordkeepers. —

(1) In general. — A summons referred to in subsection (a) for the production of books, papers, records, or other data by a third-party recordkeeper may also be served by certified or registered mail to the last known address of such recordkeeper.

(2) Third party recordkeeper. — For purposes of paragraph (1), the term *third-party recordkeeper* means —

(A) any mutual savings bank, cooperative bank, domestic building and loan association, or other savings institution chartered and supervised as a savings and loan or similar association under Federal or State law, any bank (as defined in section 581), or any credit union (within the meaning of section 501(c)(14)(A));

(B) any consumer reporting agency (as defined under section 603(f) of the Fair Credit Reporting Act (15 U.S.C. 1681 a(f));

(C) any person extending credit through the use of credit cards or similar devices;

(D) any broker (as defined in section 3(a)(4) of the Securities Exchange Act of 1934 (15 U.S.C. 78c(a)(4));

(E) any attorney;

(F) any accountant;

(G) any barter exchange (as defined in section 6045(c)(3));

(H) any regulated investment company (as defined in section 851) and any agent of such regulated investment company when acting as an agent thereof;

(I) any enrolled agent; and

(J) any owner or developer of a computer software source code (as defined in section 7612(d)(2)). Subparagraph (J) shall apply only with respect to a summons requiring the production of the source code referred to in subparagraph (J) or the program and data described in section 7612(b)(1)(A)(ii) to which source code relates.

Sec. 7604. Enforcement of summons

(a) Jurisdiction of District Court. — If any person is summoned under the internal revenue laws to appear, to testify, or to produce books, papers, records, or other data, the United States district court for the district in which such person resides or is found shall have jurisdiction by appropriate process to compel such attendance, testimony, or production of books, papers, records, or other data.

(b) Enforcement. — Whenever any person summoned under section 6420(e)(2), 6421(g), 6427(j)(2), or 7602 neglects or refuses to obey such summons, or to produce books, papers, records, or other data, or to give testimony, as required, the Secretary may apply to the judge of the district court or to a United States Commissioner[1] for the district within which the person so summoned resides or is found for an attachment against him as for a contempt, it shall be the duty of the judge or commissioner[1] to hear the application, and, if satisfactory proof is made, to issue an attachment, directed to some proper officer, for the arrest of such person, and upon his being brought before him to proceed to a hearing of the case; and upon such hearing the judge or the United States Commissioner[1] shall have power to make such order as he shall deem proper, not inconsistent with the law for the punishment of contempts, to enforce obedience to the requirements of the summons and to punish such person for his default or disobedience.

★ ★ ★ ★ ★

Sec. 7605. Time and place of examination

(a) Time and place. — The time and place of examination pursuant to the provisions of section 6420(e)(2), 6421(g)(2), 6427(j)(2), or 7602 shall be such time and place as may be fixed by the Secretary and as are reasonable under the circumstances. In the case of a summons under authority of paragraph (2) of section 7602, or under the provisions of authority of section 6420(e)(2), 6421(g)(2), or 6427(j)(2), the date fixed for appearance before the Secretary shall not be less than 10 days from the date of the summons.

[1]Or United States magistrate, pursuant to P.L. 90-578.

Sec. 7610. Fees and costs for witnesses

(a) In general. — The Secretary shall by regulations establish the rates and conditions under which payment may be made of —

(1) fees and mileage to persons who are summoned to appear before the Secretary, and

(2) reimbursement for such costs that are reasonably necessary which have been directly incurred in searching for, reproducing, or transporting books, papers, records, or other data required to be produced by summons.

(b) Exceptions. — No payment may be made under paragraph (2) of subsection (a) if —

(1) the person with respect to whose liability the summons is issued has a proprietary interest in the books, papers, records or other data required to be produced, or

(2) the person summoned is the person with respect to whose liability the summons is issued or an officer, employee, agent, accountant, or attorney of such person who, at the time the summons is served, is acting as such.

(c) Summons to which section applies. — This section applies with respect to any summons authorized under section 6420(e)(2), 6421(g)(2), 6427(j)(2), or 7602.

Sec. 7210. Failure to obey summons

Any person who, being duly summoned to appear to testify, or to appear and produce books, accounts, records, memoranda, or other papers, as required under sections 6420(e)(2), 6421(g)(2), 6427(j)(2), 7602, 7603, and 7604(b), neglects to appear or to produce such books, accounts, records, memoranda, or other papers, shall, upon conviction thereof, be fined not more than $1,000, or imprisoned not more than 1 year, or both, together with costs of prosecution.

Form **2039** (Rev. 9-1999)

Notice to Third Party
Recipient of IRS Summons

As a third-party recipient of a summons, you may be entitled to receive payment for certain costs directly incurred which are reasonably necessary to search for, reproduce, or transport records in order to comply with a summons.

This payment is made only at the rates established by the Internal Revenue Service to certain persons served with a summons to produce records or information in which the taxpayer does not have an ownership interest. The taxpayer to whose liability the summons relates and the taxpayer's officer, employee, agent, accountant, or attorney are not entitled to this payment. No payment will be made for any costs which you have charged or billed to other persons.

The rate for search costs is $8.50 an hour or fraction of an hour and is limited to the total amount of personnel time spent in locating and extracting documents or information requested by the summons. Specific salaries of such persons may not be included in search costs. In addition, search costs do not include salaries, fees, or similar costs for analysis of material or for managerial or legal advice, expertise, research, or time spent for any of these activities. If itemized separately, search costs may include the actual costs of extracting information stored by computer in the format in which it is normally produced, based on computer time and necessary supplies; however, personnel time for computer search may be paid for only at the Internal Revenue Service rate specified above.

The rate for reproduction costs for making copies or duplicates of summoned documents, transcripts, and other similar material is 20 cents for each page. Photographs, films, and other material are reimbursed at cost.

The rate for transportation costs is the same as the actual cost necessary to transport personnel to locate and retrieve summoned records or information but only costs incurred solely by the need to transport the summoned material to the place of examination.

In addition to payment for search, reproduction, and transportation costs, persons who appear before an Internal Revenue Service officer in response to a summons may request payment for authorized witness fees and mileage fees. You may make this request by contacting the Internal Revenue Service officer or by claiming these costs separately on the itemized bill or invoice as explained below.

Instructions for requesting payment

After the summons is served, you should keep an accurate record of personnel search time, computer costs, number of reproductions made, and transportation costs. Upon satisfactory compliance, you may submit an itemized bill or invoice to the Internal Revenue Service officer before whom you were summoned to appear, either in person or by mail to the address furnished by the Internal Revenue Service officer. Please write on the itemized bill or invoice the name of the taxpayer to whose liability the summons relates.

If you wish, Form 6863, Invoice and Authorization for Payment of Administrative Summons Expenses, may be used to request payment for search, reproduction, and transportation costs. Standard Form 1157, Claims for Witness Attendance Fees, Travel, and Miscellaneous Expenses, may be used to request payment for authorized witness fees and mileage fees. These forms are available from the Internal Revenue Service officer who issued the summons.

If you have any questions about the payment, please contact the Internal Revenue Service officer before whom you were summoned to appear.

Anyone submitting false claims for payment is subject to possible criminal prosecution.

Department of the Treasury
Internal Revenue Service

w w w . i r s . u s t r e a s . g o v

Form 2039 (Rev. 9-1999)

Part B — to be given to person summoned

¶652

Summons

In the matter of _____

Internal Revenue District of _____ Periods _____
The Commissioner of Internal Revenue

To: _____

At: _____
     _____

You are hereby summoned and required to appear before _____,
an officer of the Internal Revenue Service, to give testimony and to bring with you and to produce for examination the following books, records, papers, and other data relating to the tax liability or the collection of the tax liability or for the purpose of inquiring into any offense connected with the administration or enforcement of the internal revenue laws concerning the person identified above for the periods shown.

SAMPLE

SAMPLE Do not write in this space

Business address and telephone number of IRS officer before whom you are to appear:

_____

Place and time for appearance at _____

_____

on the _____ day of _____ , _____ at _____ o'clock _____ m.
                                                           (year)

Issued under authority of the Internal Revenue Code this _____ **day of** _____ , _____ .
                                                                  (year)

IRS
Department of the Treasury
Internal Revenue Service
w w w . i r s . u s t r e a s . g o v

Form 2039 (Rev. 9-1999)

_____
      Signature of issuing officer   Title

_____
Signature of approving officer *(if applicable)*   Title

Part C — to be given to noticee

¶652

To: Date:

Address:

Enclosed is a copy of a summons served by the IRS to examine records or to request testimony relating to records which have been made or kept of your business transactions or affairs by the person summoned. If you object to the summons, you are permitted to file a lawsuit in the United States district court in the form of a petition to quash the summons in order to contest the merits of the summons.

General Directions

1. You must file your petition to quash in the United States district court for the district where the person summoned resides or is found.

2. You must file your petition within 20 days from the date of this notice and pay a filing fee as may be required by the clerk of the court.

3. You must comply with the Federal Rules of Civil Procedure and local rules of the United States district court.

Instructions for Preparing Petition to Quash

1. Entitle your petition "Petition to Quash Summons."

2. Name the person or entity to whom this notice is directed as the petitioner.

3. Name the United States as the respondent.

4. State the basis for the court's jurisdiction, as required by Federal Rule of Civil Procedure. See Internal Revenue Code Section 7609(h).

5. State the name and address of the person or entity to whom this notice is directed and state that the records sought by the summons relate to that person or entity.

6. Identify and attach a copy of the summons.

7. State in detail every legal argument supporting the relief requested in your petition. See Federal Rules of Civil Procedure. Note that in some courts you may be required to support your request for relief by a sworn declaration or affidavit supporting any issue you wish to contest.

8. Your petition must be signed as required by Federal Rule of Civil Procedure 11.

9. Your petition must be served upon the appropriate parties, including the United States, as required by Federal Rule of Civil Procedure 4.

10. At the same time you file your petition with the court, you must mail a copy of your petition by certified or registered mail to the person summoned and to the IRS. Mail the copy for the IRS to the officer whose name and address are shown on the face of this summons. See Internal Revenue Code Section 7609(b)(2)(B).

The court will decide whether the person summoned should be required to comply with the summons request. Your filing of a petition to quash may suspend the running of the statute of limitations for civil liability or for criminal prosecution for offenses under the tax laws for the tax periods to which the summons relates. Such suspension would be in effect while any proceeding (or appeal) with respect to the summons is pending.

The relevant provisions of the Internal Revenue Code are enclosed with this notice. If you have any questions, please contact the Internal Revenue Service officer before whom the person summoned is to appear. The officer's name and telephone number are shown on the summons.

IRS

Department of the Treasury
Internal Revenue Service

www.irs.ustreas.gov

Form 2039 (Rev. 9-1999)

Part D — to be given to noticee

¶653 Exhibit 6-3

Department of the Treasury	Internal Revenue Service	Office of Chief Counsel **N o t i c e**

CC-2003-012

April 9, 2003

Upon Incorporation
Subject: Obtaining Tax Accrual Workpapers   Cancel Date: into CCDM

Purpose

This notice sets out procedures to be used in connection with the Service's policy regarding requests for tax accrual and other financial audit workpapers relating to the tax reserve for deferred tax liabilities and to footnotes disclosing contingent tax liabilities appearing on audited financial statements. It also modifies existing procedures for requests for audit and tax accrual workpapers that are not affected by Announcement 2002-63.

New Procedures for Examination of Returns Involving Listed Transactions

Announcement 2002-63 provides that the Service may request Tax Accrual Workpapers in the course of examining any return filed on or after July 1, 2002, that claims any tax benefit arising out of a transaction that the Service has determined to be a listed transaction at the time of the request within the meaning of Treas. Reg. § 1.6011-4(b)(2). (Treas. Reg § 1.6011-4(b)(2) defines listed transactions to include substantially similar transactions.) If the listed transaction was disclosed under Treas. Reg. § 1.6011-4, the Service will routinely request the tax accrual workpapers pertaining only to the listed transaction. If the listed transaction was not disclosed, the Service will routinely request all tax accrual workpapers. In addition, if the Service determines that tax benefits from multiple investments in listed transactions are claimed on a return, regardless of whether the listed transactions were disclosed, the Service, as a discretionary matter, will request all tax accrual workpapers. Similarly, if, in connection with the examination of a return claiming tax benefits from a listed transaction that was disclosed, there are reported financial accounting irregularities, such as those requiring restatement of earnings, the Service, as a discretionary matter, will request all tax accrual workpapers. In general, these requests will be limited to the tax accrual workpapers for the years under examination but may extend to other years if directly relevant to the years under examination.

Filing Instructions: Binder Part ( )   Master Sets: NO X   RO X
NO: Circulate___Distribute X__to: All Personnel__ X__ Attorneys___In: all NO functions
Field: Circulate___Distribute X__to: All Personnel X__Attorneys___In: all field offices
Other: _FOIA Reading Room
Electronic Filename: TaxAccru.pdf____ Original signed copy in: CC:F&M:PM:P

- 2 -

For a return filed prior to July 1, 2002, that claims any tax benefit arising out of a listed transaction, the Service may request tax accrual workpapers pertaining to the listed transaction, if the taxpayer had an obligation to disclose the transaction under Treas. Reg. § 1.6011-4, and failed to do so. The required disclosure may have been made (1) on the return; (2) under Rev. Proc. 94-69, 1994-2 C.B. 804, if applicable; or (3) pursuant to Announcement 2002-2, 2002-2 I.R.B. 304 (Jan. 14, 2002).

In general, the information document request (IDR) will be limited to the tax accrual workpapers related to the listed transaction for the years under examination. It will be directed to the taxpayer or the independent accounting firm, based on the Service's determination as to the location of the tax accrual workpapers. The Service will, however, request all tax accrual workpapers for those years, if (1) the taxpayer failed to disclose a listed transaction on a return filed after July 1, 2002; (2) the taxpayer claimed benefits from multiple investments in listed transactions on a return filed after July 1, 2001, regardless of whether the transactions are disclosed, or (3) there are reported financial irregularities. The announcement provides that circumstances (2) and (3) will lead to a request for all tax accrual workpapers as a discretionary matter.

The initial request for tax accrual workpapers should be coordinated with field counsel and prior approval must be obtained from the Director Field Operations, LMSB, or the Area Compliance Director, with the concurrence of the Director of Compliance Policy, SB/SE. Field counsel should coordinate the requests for tax accrual workpapers with Branch 3 of the Collection Bankruptcy and Summonses Division in the office of the Associate Chief Counsel (Procedure & Administration). They can be reached at 202-622-3630. Counsel will treat the review of the IDR as a high priority matter and complete the review as soon as possible so as not to delay the examination process.

To the extent the Service must use a summons to obtain the information, Counsel will review the summons before it is issued to ensure that it is addressed to the proper party, that any claims of privilege have been identified and addressed, and that the summons would otherwise be enforceable. The summons will be directed to the taxpayer or to the independent accounting firm based on a determination as to the location of the tax accrual workpapers.

All summonses will be approved prior to issuance by the Director of Field Operations, LMSB, or the Area Compliance Director, with the concurrence of the Director of Compliance Policy, SB/SE, and reviewed by Counsel. Counsel's review of the summons will be coordinated by field counsel through the appropriate Division Counsel and the Associate Chief Counsel (Procedure & Administration). Counsel will treat the review of the summons as a high priority matter and complete the review as soon as possible so as not to delay the examination process.

If neither the taxpayer nor the accounting firm comply with the summons, the Service will refer the matter to Counsel for enforcement of the summons. The summons enforcement letter will be approved by the Deputy Chief Counsel (Operations) after review by the responsible Division Counsel and coordination with the Associate Chief Counsel (Procedure & Administration).

- 3 -

Procedures Applicable to Requests for Audit and Tax Accrual Workpapers Not Covered by the Announcement

Examiners normally request audit and tax accrual workpapers only in unusual circumstances and when the necessary factual data used to support the return cannot be obtained from the taxpayer's records. If a decision is made to seek this information, the examiner's request should be limited to the portion of the workpapers that are material and relevant to the examination. Whether an item is considered to be material is based on the examiner's judgment and an evaluation of the facts and circumstances in the case. Any request for tax accrual workpapers requires the prior written approval of the Director of Field Operations, LMSB or the Area Compliance Director with the concurrence of the Director of Compliance Policy, SB/SE. See Memorandum from Commissioner, Large and Mid-Size Business Division and Commissioner, Small Business/Self-Employed Division, *Obtaining Tax Accrual Workpapers Related to Abusive Tax Avoidance Transactions* dated June 17, 2002.

If a determination is made that a summons for tax accrual workpapers will be issued, the summons should be submitted to field counsel for review and comment. Field counsel will then coordinate issuance of the summons with the Associate Chief Counsel (Procedure & Administration). To the extent the summons is not complied with, any summons enforcement letter to the Department of Justice must be coordinated with, and prereviewed by, the Associate Chief Counsel (Procedure & Administration). CCDM 34.12.3.7.2.

Applicability of Procedures to Tax Reconciliation and Audit Workpapers

Neither existing procedures nor those set out in Announcement 2002-63 apply to requests for tax reconciliation workpapers. *See* CCDM 34.12.3.13.2(c). Tax reconciliation workpapers are used in assembling and compiling financial data preparatory to placing it on a tax return. Tax reconciliation workpapers may be routinely requested in the course of an examination. Typically these workpapers will include final trial balances for each entity and a schedule of consolidating and adjusting entries. They include information used to trace financial information to the tax return.

Announcement 2002-63 also does not apply to audit workpapers. Audit workpapers are retained by the independent accountant to establish the procedures followed, the tests performed, the information obtained, and the conclusions reached pertinent to its examination. Audit workpapers may include work programs, analyses, memoranda, letters of confirmation and representation, abstracts of company documents, and schedules or commentaries prepared or obtained by the auditor. The audit workpapers provide important support for the independent certified public accountant's opinion as to the fairness of the presentation of the financial statements in conformity with generally accepted auditing standards. Any summons for the audit workpapers should be coordinated with Counsel prior to the issuance of the summons. *See* CCDM 34.12.3.13.1(2)a.

- 4 -

Discovery of Tax Accrual Workpapers

Existing CCDM procedures require discovery requests and subpoenas for tax accrual workpapers to be coordinated with Branch 3 of the Administrative Provisions and Judicial Practice Division in the office of the Associate Chief Counsel (Procedure & Administration). Discovery requests for tax accrual workpapers that are subject to Announcement 2002-63 will be coordinated through Division Counsel with the Associate Chief Counsel (Procedure & Administration). Subpoenas for tax accrual workpapers subject to the Announcement directed to third party accounting firms will also be coordinated through Division Counsel with the Associate Chief Counsel (Procedure & Administration).

Any questions about this notice should be directed to the Office of the Associate Chief Counsel (Procedure & Administration): with regard to summonses, Branch 3, Collection, Bankruptcy and Summonses, at 202-622-3630, or with regard to discovery matters, Branch 3, Administrative Provisions and Judicial Practice, at 202-622-7940. Documents sent for review by, or coordination with, the office of the Associate Chief Counsel (Procedure & Administration) should be sent to TSS4510 for assignment.

_____/s/_____
DEBORAH A. BUTLER
Associate Chief Counsel
(Procedure and Administration)

¶654 Exhibit 6-4

Department of the Treasury	Internal Revenue Service	Office of Chief Counsel	**N o t i c e**

[CC-2004-010]

January 22, 2004

Subject:	Requests for Tax Accrual Workpapers	**Cancel Date:** Upon incorporation into CCDM

Purpose

This Notice supplements CC-2003-012, "Obtaining Tax Accrual Workpapers" with respect to clarifying the definition of tax accrual workpapers.

Background

The term "tax accrual workpapers" means those audit workpapers relating to the tax reserve for current, deferred and potential or contingent tax liabilities, however classified or reported on audited financial statements, and to footnotes disclosing those tax liabilities appearing on audited financial statements. The Supreme Court upheld the Service's authority, under section 7602, to summon tax accrual workpapers. United States v. Arthur Young & Co., 465 U.S. 805 (1984). Subsequent to the Arthur Young opinion, however, the Service announced that it would continue its policy of not routinely requesting tax accrual workpapers during examinations. Announcement 84-46, 1984-18 I.R.B. 18. In 2002, the Service announced that it was modifying its policy with respect to tax accrual workpapers. In general, the modified policy applies to returns filed by taxpayers who failed to disclose their involvement in listed transactions as required by Treas. Reg. § 1.6011-4. Announcement 2002-63, 2002-2 C.B. 72. See also Memorandum from Commissioner, Large and Mid-Size Business Division and Commissioner, Small Business/Self-Employed Division, Obtaining Tax Accrual Workpapers Related to Abusive Tax Avoidance Transactions dated June 17, 2002, which discusses both the new policy with respect to listed transactions and describes the requirements for requesting audit workpapers and tax accrual workpapers in all other cases.

Discussion

Some questions have been raised regarding the definition of tax accrual workpapers. Tax accrual workpapers are those audit workpapers, whether prepared by the taxpayer or by an independent accountant, relating to the tax reserve for current, deferred and potential or contingent tax liabilities, however classified or reported on audited financial statements, and to footnotes disclosing those tax liabilities on audited financial statements. They reflect an estimate of a company's tax liabilities and may also be referred to as the tax pool analysis, tax liability contingency analysis, tax cushion analysis, or tax contingency reserve analysis.

Electronic Filename: CC-2004-010.pdf

-2-

The name given the workpapers by the taxpayer or its accountant is not determinative as to whether the papers are tax accrual workpapers. Rather, if the papers are described by the definition given above, the papers are tax accrual workpapers. The Service's policy of restraint in not requesting tax accrual workpapers is limited to papers falling within this definition.

The definition does not include documents created prior to or outside of the consideration of whether reserves should be created, even though these documents may have been subsequently used in the preparation of the tax accrual workpapers or are attached to workpapers. These preexisting documents likely fall within the scope of the general IDRs issued at the beginning of an examination and should be produced by the taxpayer or the accountant even though no request for the tax accrual workpapers has been made.

Workpapers and tax return preparation documents that reconcile net income per books or financial statements to taxable income also do not fall within the definition of tax accrual workpapers since these documents are part of the tax return preparation process, and the information is required to be reported on income tax returns, usually on schedules designed to report those reconciliations. Reconciling workpapers are also within the scope of the general IDRs issued during an examination.

Additionally, the existence of, and the amount of, reserve accounts are not within the scope of the definition of tax accrual workpapers.

Finally, this Notice is limited to clarifying the definition of tax accrual workpapers. The Notice neither addresses the definition of the more general category of audit workpapers nor reflects any change in the policy regarding tax accrual workpapers or when audit workpapers will be requested by the Service.

Because of the sensitive nature of requests for tax accrual workpapers, field attorneys are to work with the operating divisions in preparing any requests for tax accrual workpapers and will review proposed summonses for tax accrual workpapers. Field attorneys should coordinate with the office of the Associate Chief Counsel (Procedure & Administration) with respect to questions regarding the definition of tax accrual workpapers and prior to the issuance of any administrative summons or discovery request for tax accrual workpapers. Counsel will review questions regarding tax accrual workpapers and proposed summonses as a high priority matter and complete the review as soon as possible so as not to delay the examination process.

Any questions about the provisions of this Notice should be directed to the Office of the Associate Chief Counsel (Procedure & Administration): with regard to summonses, Branch 3, Collection, Bankruptcy & Summonses, at 202-622-3630; with regard to discovery matters, Branch 3, Administrative Provisions & Judicial Practice, at 202-622-7940; and with regard to general questions about the Notice, George Bowden or

-3-

Kathryn Zuba at 202-622-3400. Documents sent for review by, or coordination with, the office of the Associate Chief Counsel (Procedure & Administration) should be sent to TSS4510 for assignment.

_____/s/_____
DEBORAH A. BUTLER
Associate Chief Counsel
(Procedure & Administration)

¶655 Exhibit 6-5

SAMPLE *"KOVEL*-TYPE" LETTER

[DATE]

Privileged and Confidential Tax Advice Attorney-Client and Work-Product Doctrine

[NAME OF ACCOUNTANT]

[ADDRESS]

Re: Investigation Agreement

Dear Mr. Accountant:

This letter will memorialize the terms and conditions of the engagement of _____ (hereinafter referred to as the "Investigation Firm") by the law office of _____ (hereinafter referred to as the "Law Firm"). The Law Firm represents _____ (hereinafter referred to as the "Client"). The Investigation Firm will assist the Law Firm in connection with the rendering of legal services by the Law Firm to Client, and, in particular, with certain matters involving the examination of the correct amount of Federal and State income tax liability, as well as the location and interview of certain individuals, including, without limitation, the performance of investigative, advisory, and consulting services (collectively "investigative services") for the Law Firm. The engagement also includes all steps that are necessary to assist in the analysis, documentation, and review of the various individuals to be located and interviewed.

Investigation Firm shall undertake such examination of books, records, papers and documents, and other items as Law Firm may request, and all of the Investigation Firm's findings with respect to the services performed pursuant to this Agreement shall be submitted directly and exclusively to the Law Firm. In addition, the Investigation Firm may be called upon to participate in conferences with the Client, as well as members of the Law Firm, and to conduct or participate in meetings with other persons pursuant to instructions from the Law Firm.

The Investigation Firm shall keep the Law Firm advised of the steps that are being taken in the performance of the requested services, and the Investigation Firm and shall receive permissions from the Law Firm prior to incurring any extraordinary expenses (including, but without limitation, travel outside of the immediate area) with regard to this equipment.

It is understood that the Investigation Firm shall be compensated for their work for the Law Firm in these matters in accordance with the Investigation Firm's letter dated _____ attached as Exhibit A. It is also understood that all billings from the Investigation Firm shall be made monthly in writing and directed to the Law Firm at the above address. Law Firm shall make immediate payment to the Investigation Firm.

It is expressly agreed between the Investigation Firm and the Law Firm that all originals and copies of statements, records, schedules, work papers, memoranda, reports, and all other documents prepared by the Investigation Firm, incident to or in accordance with the professional services rendered to the Law Firm, shall be, and at all times remain, the property of the Law Firm and the Client and shall be considered privileged matters, not to be disclosed to any other person(s). Any and all originals and copies of statements, records, schedules, work papers, memoranda, reports, and any other documents belonging to the Client or the Law Firm which is directly or indirectly placed in the Investigation Firm's possession or which the Law Firm directs the Investigation Firm to take possession of with respect to this matter shall be given temporarily and solely for the purpose of enabling the Investigation Firm to assist the Law Firm in making legal decisions. Custody thereof shall be retained by the Investigation Firm only to the extent necessary and for the period of time necessary to perform those assignments given to the Investigation Firm. Furthermore, the statements, records, schedules, work papers, memoranda, and other documents shall at all times remain the property of the Client or the Law Firm and shall be considered privileged matters, not to be disclosed to any other person(s). All original and copies of all of the items referred to in this paragraph shall be turned over to the Client or a member of the Law Firm immediately upon either oral or written demand. None of the foregoing material or information referred to in this paragraph shall be revealed to any third party without the advance written consent of a member of the Law Firm. In the event that the Law Firm requests the Investigation Firm to turn over all documents relating to this matter to either the Client or the Law Firm, the Investigation Firm further agrees that no photocopies or reproductions of the documents shall be retained by the Investigation Firm without express written approval of the Law Firm. The Investigation Firm shall be responsible for its compliance with the terms of this Agreement.

All oral and written communications between the Law Firm and all other persons representing or acting on behalf of the Client and the Investigation Firm, or between the Client and the investigation Firm as a result of this engagement, shall be strictly confidential and privileged and shall be safeguarded so as to protect the attorney/client privilege and work product doctrine which attached to such information and documentation.

As part of its Agreement to provide investigative services in this matter, Investigation Firm will immediately notify the Law Firm of the happening of any one of the following events: (a) the exhibition or surrender of any documents or records prepared by or submitted to Investigation Firm or someone under Investigative Firm's direction, in a manner not expressly authorized by the Law Firm; (b) a request by anyone to examine, inspect, or copy such documents or records; (c) any attempt to serve, or the actual service of, any court order, subpoena, or summons upon Investigation Firm which requires the production of any such documents or records.

If this letter accurately sets forth our understanding and agreement, please date and sign the enclosed original of this letter and return it to us for our files.

Yours very truly,

_____

Law Firm

Accepted and Agreed To:

_____

Accountant

_____

Date

¶656 DISCUSSION QUESTIONS

1. You are an accountant and a client of yours is under audit by the IRS. The Revenue Agent contacts you after she has spent some time investigating the taxpayer's records. She says that there are certain items that she has not been able to locate and she wishes to review your workpapers, retained copies of returns and files.

   (A) Do you grant her request?

   (B) Assume that the Revenue Agent sent you a letter stating that under Code Sec. 7602 she has the right to request, review and copy the records and that she is formally requesting them. Do you comply with her request at this point?

   (C) If you turn the records over under either of these circumstances, do you expose yourself to any potential liability to your client?

2. Assume that you receive an IRS summons in the matter of the tax liability of a client of yours. The taxpayer takes action to stay compliance with the summons under Code Sec. 7609(b). A period of 18 months passes in which the IRS takes no action to enforce the summons. Because of economic conditions, the client is forced to relocate his business in another part of the country. He no longer requires your services as his accountant either for the business or for his personal records. You would like to return his records to him because they take up a great deal of space in your office. How long must you keep the client's records available?

3. On September 15, 2004, Special Agent Randy Rambunctious of the IRS issued a summons to Rudy Recordkeeper, a certified public accountant. The summons sought production of Recordkeeper's workpapers regarding Gilbert Giltiasin, who was then under examination. Within the time prescribed by law, Giltiasin took steps to stay compliance by Recordkeeper.

   On October 8, 2004, a petition to quash the summons was filed with the District Court in the district in which Recordkeeper resides. On the same day, Rambunctious called Recordkeeper and asked him how long it would take to assemble the records if the summons was enforced. Recordkeeper estimated that it would take approximately 100 hours to put together the records. Rambunctious asked Recordkeeper to begin assembling the records immediately so that if the summons was enforced, there would not be a long delay before he could get the records. Must Recordkeeper comply with this request?

4. Randy Rambunctious also wishes to review the personal records of Gilbert Giltiasin. He issues a summons properly addressed to Giltiasin and serves it by taking it to Giltiasin's house and handing it toGiltiasin's three-year-old daughter. Unfortunately, she uses it to cut out paper dolls and never gives it to her father. Later, the IRS seeks to hold Gilbert in

contempt for failing to comply with the summons. Does Gilbert have a defense because the summons was improperly served?

5. Wanda Withheld is the president of Wexley's, Inc. She failed to pay over her social security and withholding taxes for the last quarter of 2004. Wanda has acknowledged her personal liability and consented to an assessment under Code Sec. 6672 of an amount equal to the trust fund portion of these taxes. Wanda has failed to respond to the series of notices from the IRS seeking payment of the balance due plus interest. She has also ignored the telephone calls and repeated attempts by the Revenue Officer to meet with her in person. The revenue officer has also sought a financial statement from Wanda, but to no avail.

   Assume that you are a new Revenue Officer and you seek to enforce collection against Wanda. What actions, if any, are you authorized to take to discover the value and location of any assets held by Wanda which are available for collection?

6. If the Revenue Officer in Problem 5, above, issues a summons to the third-party recordkeepers, is Wexley's, Inc., entitled to notice under Code Sec. 7609?

7. Tilda Taxpayer and her CPA, I.M. Careful, prepare a comprehensive amended return but ultimately decide not file it. If the IRS issues a summons with regard to that draft document, does Tilda have to submit it?

CHAPTER 7
EVIDENTIARY PRIVILEGE FOR FEDERALLY AUTHORIZED TAX PRACTITIONERS

¶701 INTRODUCTION

Historically, accountants' workpapers have not been privileged because an accountant has been viewed as a neutral advisor and not an advocate.[1] On the other hand, communications between an attorney and a client with respect to legal advice are protected by a common-law privilege of confidentiality.

Effective for communications on or after July 22, 1998, with some exceptions, the IRS Restructuring and Reform Act of 1998[2] extended the attorney/client privilege to communications between clients and individuals who are authorized to practice before the Internal Revenue Service (IRS). Code Sec. 7525(a) provides that with respect to tax advice, the same common law protections of confidentiality which apply to a communication between a taxpayer and an attorney shall also apply to a communication between a taxpayer and certain tax practitioners to the extent the communication would be considered a privileged communication if it were between a taxpayer and an attorney.

¶703 CODE SECTION 7525(a) PRIVILEGE

The Code Sec. 7525(a) "privilege" only applies to tax advice between a taxpayer and a federally authorized tax practitioner (FATP), i.e., one who is authorized to practice before the IRS. Tax advice means advice given by a FATP with respect to a matter that is within the scope of the practitioner's authority to practice.[3] Circular 230 (see Chapter 3) defines a practitioner's authority to practice as encompassing "all matters connected with presentation to the Internal Revenue Service or any of its officers or employees relating to a client's rights, privileges or liabilities under the laws or regulations administered by the Internal Revenue Service."

Under Circular 230, tax advice means advice that requires presentation of information to the IRS given after an event has occurred. Since planning advice does not necessitate presenting anything to the IRS and because a tax practitioner technically does not have to be authorized to practice before the IRS to give planning advice, such advice would not be privileged under the Code Sec. 7525(a)statute. For example, communications regarding a corporation's value for estate tax given by a FATP will not be privileged under Code Sec. 7525(a) since it does not meet the narrow definition of tax advice.

---

[1] *United States v. Arthur Young & Co.*, 465 U.S. 805 (1984), 84-1 USTC ¶9305.

[2] P.L. 105-206.

[3] Code Sec. 7525(a)(3).

Only communications subject to the attorney/client privilege are protected communications. They must be based on facts that the client provides the attorney for the purpose of receiving a legal opinion, legal services or assistance in some legal proceeding and the communication is made in confidence and by the client. The confidentiality privilege applies only to advice on legal matters and is not applicable where the attorney is acting in another capacity such as a scrivener engaged to prepare a tax return.[4] The privilege is that of the client and may be waived by the client or waived by disclosure to a third party. Courts have rejected the claim that Section 7525 protects a client's identity in the context of IRS investigations of tax shelter activity.[5]

Limited to noncriminal proceedings before the IRS or in a federal court, the privilege does not extend to proceedings before other federal or state administrative agencies or in connection with issues arising out of transactions and lawsuits brought by third parties. Thus, regulatory bodies other than the IRS may continue to compel the production of information pertaining to accountant/client communications. Finally, it does not apply to any written communication between an accountant, director, shareholder, officer, employee, agent or representative of the corporation in connection with the promotion or the direct or indirect participation of that corporation in a tax shelter.[6]

Although very little is known about the extent to which accounting firms have changed their office procedures as a result of the confidentiality privilege, based upon survey responses in a recent study,[7] the accounting practitioners have not made major changes in their office practices and procedures in response to the new confidentiality privilege. However, to assist tax practitioners in maintaining the confidentiality privilege, the American Institute of Certified Public Accountants (AICPA), in its Tax Guides and Checklists, 2000 Edition, has included a sample"Privileged and Confidential Tax Advice (Under Sec. 7525) Engagement Checklist" as well as sample "Tax Advice" and "Tax Controversy" Engagement Letters.[8] The sample letters attempt to segregate tax matters covered by the confidentiality privilege and describe to the client the cautions regarding waiver of the privilege. The AICPA has also constructed a summary of the likely effects of the confidentiality privilege in the context of:

Tax Planning

Tax advice directly to the client: These are items such as personal discussions, letters, memoranda, notes, reports, etc. This direct tax advice and the tax

---

[4] *United States v. Frederick,* 182 F.3d 496 (7th Cir. 1999), 99-1 USTC ¶50,465. In theory, the attorney/client privilege does not distinguish between in-house and outside counsel. *Upjohn Co. v. United States,* 449 U.S. 383 (1981), 1-1 USTC ¶9138; *Hartz Mountain Industries v. Comm'r,* 93 TC 521 (1989), CCH Dec. 46,126. In practice, however, courts apply greater scrutiny to privilege claims asserted by in-house attorneys. This is because only legal advice—not business advice—is protected by the privilege. Given that in-house counsel are resolving legal issues, in a business setting, it is often difficult to divorce the legal from the business communications.

In-house tax counsel have it doubly hard. Like all in-house counsel, they must establish they have provided legal services rather than business advice. They also have the added burden of proving that the tax advice they provided does not constitute accounting services or tax return preparation because neither is protected by the privilege.

[5] *U.S. v. BDO Seidman,* 337 F.3d 802 (7th Cir. 2003).

[6] Code Sec. 7525(b).

[7] Bauman, C.C. and A.C. Fowler. January 2001. *The Expanded Tax Confidentiality Privilege: A Review and Assessment of IRC Section 7525.* Working Paper, University of Wisconsin-Milwaukee.

[8] AICPA Tax Guides and Checklist, 2000 Edition.

¶703

advice documents describing tax interpretations, opinions, mental processes, thoughts, tax positions, likelihood of success, etc., should be eligible for the Confidentiality Privilege.

Tax memoranda and other documents to the file: These tax advice documents also should be eligible for the Confidentiality Privilege if they are relevant to tax advice communications to the client and if disclosure of these documents would tend to reveal the nature of the actual communications. The likelihood of protection under the Confidentiality Privilege is increased if these documents are kept in a separate file and access is limited to the CPA, appropriate staff and the client.

Tax opinions: These tax advice documents are eligible for protection under the confidentiality Privilege, provided the communication is limited to the client. If the tax opinions are disclosed to bankers, securities brokers, financial advisers and others, the privilege may be waived unless they have a role in the tax advice process. Also, a written tax opinion relating to a tax shelter may not be subject to the Confidentiality Privilege.

Tax Controversies

Information responses to the IRS, protests, appeals, briefs: When these documents are sent to the IRS, they may be treated as similar to a tax return. Thus, the basis for numbers, calculations, statements of facts and other information made to support a position in these documents may be subject to discovery by the IRS. However, any backup research or memoranda reflecting mental impressions, thought processes, likelihood of success, etc., may be eligible for the Confidentiality Privilege; alternatively, the work-product doctrine may protect these items, because the controversy with the IRS may help to indicate that they were prepared for litigation.[9]

The privileged communication between the taxpayer and the FATP does not encompass the so-called work-product doctrine and, therefore, does not apply to such items as workpapers or an accountant's opinion on a taxpayer's financial statements.[10]

¶705 WORK-PRODUCT DOCTRINE

Generally, work product would be made up of two classes of documents. First, interviews and written statements of witnesses. Secondly, correspondence andmemoranda in which the practitioner put in written form his mental impressions and legal theories with respect to a litigated or potentially litigated matter. Although not an evidentiary privilege, an attorney's work product is conditionally *protected from compulsory disclosure in a tax controversy.* However, work product may be discoverable by the IRS in a tax controversy if there is a showing of absolute necessity for the IRS to have the information or the denial of discovery would unfairly prejudice the IRS's preparation of the case.

While courts have allowed the IRS access to certain work products by the requisite showing of necessity or unfair prejudice, the Supreme Court has indicated that such showing would never require one to produce his mental impressions and theories of the case. If an otherwise discoverable document were to

---

[9] *Id.*

[10] *United States v. Frederick,* 182 F.3d 496 (7th Cir. 1999), 99-1 USTC ¶ 50,465.

contain such information, the court would have to allow such information to be redacted before completing its production.

The work-product doctrine applies once it is reasonable to assume that litigation involving the particular issue to which the work product relates is inevitable, even if no litigation is pending at the time information is produced. In tax controversies, the work-product doctrine generally will attach when an administrative dispute with the IRS is anticipated.[11]

However, an accountant's work may, in some circumstances, be protected under the attorney-client privilege or the attorney work-product doctrine. The Tax Court in *Bernardo v. Commissioner*[12] addressed these issues and held that the attorney-client privilege protects third-party communications or reports when they are made to the client's attorney at the request of the client and are made for the purpose of obtaining legal advice from the attorney. As to the work-product doctrine, the court held that documents prepared in anticipation of litigation by a client's representatives, whether or not the representative was retained by the client directly or by his attorney, are protected. In *Bernardo*, the taxpayers claimed a charitable contribution deduction for the donation of a granite sculpture to a transit authority. In challenging both the validity and the amount of the deduction, the IRS sought the production of documents prepared by an accountant which the taxpayers claimed were privileged under either the attorney-client privilege, the work-product doctrine or both. The communications which the IRS had sought production of were generated by the accountant during IRS audits and subsequently provided to the attorney to aid in the structuring of the charitable contribution. The Tax Court found that the attorney-client privilege did not apply because the accountant had not been engaged to assist the attorney in providing legal advice. The Court did find, however, that certain documents which were prepared in anticipation of litigation were protected under the work-product doctrine.

The work-product doctrine can only relate to information produced when it is reasonable to assume that litigation could ensue. Therefore, one cannot employ the work-product doctrine to shield information on behalf of a client when a possibility of litigation is remote or the records in question were prepared in the ordinary course of business as opposed to prepared in preparation for litigation. For example, one would not be entitled to claim a work-product privilege with respect to workpapers used in the preparation of a client's original or amended tax returns.

Voluntary disclosure to third parties of information which would otherwise be conditionally protected under the work-product doctrine by either the taxpayer or the practitioner constitutes a waiver of the work-product doctrine. Once information is obtained which is subject to either the attorney/client or work-product privilege, taxpayers must act to insure that such information is kept confidential. If the taxpayer acts in a way which could be interpreted as not trying to keep the information confidential, it may lose the privilege through waiver.

---

[11] *U.S. v. Adlman*, 134 F.3d 1194 (2nd Cir. 1998), 98-1 USTC ¶ 50,230.

[12] *Bernardo v. Comm'r*, 104 TC 677 (1995), CCH Dec. 50,705.

¶706 DISCUSSION QUESTIONS

1. You are an accountant. A sole proprietor client of yours asks you to prepare a tax advice memorandum with regard to the prospective purchase of a business. You do so. Several years later, during an examination, an IRS agent issues a summons for said memorandum. Is there an accountant privilege for said memorandum?

   (A) Assume that the summons was instead issued by a Special Agent.

   (B) Assume that the summons was instead issued by the Labor Department (with respect to a pension issue).

2. You are an accountant. A corporate client asks you to give tax advice with respect to its recently completed corporate merger. You conclude that the merger qualifies as a tax free reorganization and deliver your memorandum exclusively to the client. Subsequently, the client confidentially sends your memorandum to a concerned creditor. Can you and/or the client claim accountant's privilege?

3. You are an accountant. Your client, an individual, hires you to investigate the tax treatment of a particular transaction reported on a prior return (which has been prepared by another accountant). The client is concerned that the treatment was erroneous and, therefore, she might be subject to some kind of penalty. Is your tax advice memorandum privileged under either an attorney-client privilege or attorney work-product doctrine?

4. Assume that a client is looking for tax advice from an accountant which will be privileged. Under what circumstances would it be reasonable for a client to rely upon an accountant's privilege?

CHAPTER 8
PARTNERSHIP AUDIT PROCEDURES

Partnerships in General

¶801 INTRODUCTION

Under general concepts of tax law, a partnership is not a taxable entity. For this reason, the law prior to 1982 provided that tax adjustments to partnership items were made at the partner level. The Internal Revenue Service (IRS) would audit each partner's return to adjust partnership items, and the adjustment of one partner's return could not be based on the audit of another partner.

The Tax Equity and Fiscal Responsibility Act of 1982[1] (TEFRA) significantly changed this process. Under TEFRA, proceedings for the assessment or refund of a tax arising out of a partner's distributive share of income or loss are now conducted at the partnership level. The Taxpayer Relief Act of 1997 (the 1997 Act) further refined the partnership audit procedure and created a set of procedural rules for an "electing large partnership" (see ¶824) by enacting Code Secs. 6240 through 6255 and amending various other relevant sections.[2]

Any partnership[3] required under Section 6031(a) of the Internal Revenue Code (the Code) to file a return is treated as a "partnership" subject to the new procedural rules. However, an exception exists for "small partnerships" having ten or fewer partners each of whom is an individual, a C corporation, or the estate of a deceased partner.[4] A partner that is a Section 501(a) tax-exempt organization that meets the definition of a C corporation is considered a C corporation.[5] For purposes of the small partnership exception, the statute treats a husband and wife (and their estates) as one partner. Regardless of the size of a partnership, if another partnership, a trust, or a non-C corporation is a partner, the entity will not be classified as a "small partnership."

Although normally exempt, a qualifying "small partnership" may elect to be governed by the TEFRA audit provisions. The election can be made for any taxable year and will become binding as to all subsequent taxable years unless revoked with the consent of the IRS. The election normally would be made if it is more economical to have only one proceeding instead of separate audits of each partner.

Congress originally extended TEFRA partnership treatment to S corporation items as well.[6] However, in 1996, Congress repealed Code Secs. 6241–6245 for tax years beginning after December 31, 1996.[7]

---

[1] P.L. 97-248, Title IV, §§401-06, 96 Stat. 324.

[2] The Taxpayer Relief Act of 1997, P.L. 105-34, Title XII, §§111 Stat. 788 (1997).

[3] Code Sec. 761(a).

[4] Code Sec. 6231(a)(1)(B).

[5] Rev. Rul. 2003-69, 2003-26 IRB 1118.

[6] Subchapter S Revision Act of 1982, P.L. 97-354, §4(a), 96 Stat. 1691.

[7] Small Business Job Protection Act of 1996, P.L. 104-188, Title I, §1307(c)(1), 110 Stat. 1781.

¶803 CONSISTENCY REQUIREMENT

A cornerstone of the provisions is the requirement that a partner treat all "partnership item[s]" consistently with the treatment on the partnership return.[8] If the partner chooses to report an item inconsistently with the partnership return, the partner is required to disclose the inconsistency in the filing of his or her return. To facilitate consistent reporting, the Code requires each partnership to furnish a copy of the information contained in the partnership return to each partner.

If a partner fails to report an item consistently with the partnership return, and if the inconsistency results in a deficiency in tax, the IRS can make an immediate assessment of the deficiency (a computational adjustment) without issuing a notice of deficiency to the partner. In addition, this assessment can be made prior to the commencement of a partnership audit proceeding and prior to the issuance of any notice to any other partner. Finally, the underpayment resulting from the inconsistent reporting will be subject to the penalties under Code Secs. 6662–6664 relating to inaccuracy and fraud.[9]

Partnership Audit Procedures

¶805 NOTICE REQUIREMENTS

Partnership items are audited at the partnership level by an examination of the partnership return. This audit is commenced by issuance of a notice of commencement of an administrative proceeding.[10] If the proper notice requirements are met, the audit at the partnership level will apply to all partners. The notice of the commencement of the audit must be mailed to the tax matters partner (TMP) and to each notice partner in the partnership.

¶807 TAX MATTERS PARTNER

The TMP is the general partner who has been designated by the partnership to act as the TMP.[11] This individual will be treated by the IRS as the primary representative of the partnership. If no general partner has been designated by the partnership itself, the Code provides that the general partner having the largestprofit interest at the close of the tax year involved will be the TMP.[12] If more than one general partner has the same largest profit percentage at the end of the year involved, then the partner first in alphabetical order will be the TMP. Finally, if no partner can be chosen under these methods, the IRS has the power to choose a TMP. Where the IRS selects the TMP or requires the resignation of a TMP, it must, within 30 days, notify all partners required to receive notice under Code Sec. 6223(a) of the name and address of the individual selected.[13]

There are also circumstances where a partner, having been designated as the TMP for the tax year under audit, will continue to have authority to act as the TMP even after having resigned as a partner in the partnership or where under

---

[8] Code Sec. 6222.

[9] *Id.*

[10] Code Sec. 6223(a).

[11] Code Sec. 6231(a)(7)(A).

[12] Code Sec. 6231(a)(7)(B).

[13] *Id.*

criminal investigation. For example, in *Monetary II Limited Partnership v. Commissioner*[14] the Court of Appeals upheld a Tax Court determination that a former partner's consent to extend the statute of limitations for assessment of tax was valid. In another situation involving authority to extend the limitations period, a TMP who was cooperating with the IRS in a criminal tax fraud investigation of the partnership where his cooperation could influence his own sentence and who had signed the partnership returns for the years under audit was held not to have lost his TMP status thereby.[15]

The responsibilities of the TMP include receiving notice of the commencement of a partnership audit and of final partnership administrative adjustments, forwarding that notice to partners who do not receive notice, keeping all partners informed of all administrative and judicial proceedings regarding the partnership, extending the statute of limitations with respect to all partners, and entering into settlements which will bind all partners who are not notice partners. Further, after the IRS proposes final partnership adjustments, the TMP has sole authority to seek judicial review of the audit adjustment during the first 90 days after the notice of final partnership audit adjustment.

Generally, the IRS will deal with the TMP in obtaining the books and records of the partnership and in verifying any items that come up during the audit. The TMP is required to keep all partners informed of administrative and judicial proceedings relating to the adjustment of partnership items. However, the TMP's failure to inform the other partners will not affect the validity of the partnership proceedings as to such partners.

¶809 NOTIFICATION OF PARTNERS

The IRS is required to send notice of the commencement and completion of the partnership audit to each "notice partner."[16] A notice partner is one whose name, address, and profit interest appear on the partnership return or whose identity hasbeen furnished to the IRS at least 30 days prior to the giving of notice to the TMP. If a partnership has more than one hundred partners, the IRS is not required to give notice to any single partner who has less than a one percent interest in the profits of the partnership determined as of the end of the relevant taxable year. However, a group of partners in a partnership of more than one hundred persons may band together and designate one of their members to receive notice provided that the group as an aggregate has a five percent or more interest in the profits.

If the IRS receives notice that an indirect partner has an interest in the profits by ownership of a beneficial interest of a passthrough partner (a partnership, S corporation, or trust), then the IRS will give notice to the indirect partner rather than to the passthrough partner. A passthrough partner is required to forward notices from the IRS to its indirect partners within 30 days of receiving the notice.

---

[14] 47 F.3d 342 (9th Cir. 1995), 95-1 USTC ¶ 50,073.

[15] *Transpac Drilling Venture v. United States,* 32 Fed. Cl. 810 (1995), 95-1 USTC ¶ 50,192, *aff'd on other grounds,* 83 F.3d 1410 (1995), 96-1 USTC ¶ 50,271.

[16] Code Sec. 6223(a).

¶811 PARTNERS' DEALINGS WITH THE INTERNAL REVENUE SERVICE

All partners, whether or not notice partners, have the right to participate in the partnership proceedings regarding the tax treatment of any partnership item.[17] A partner will be able to attend any meeting with the IRS to discuss the matter; however, the time and place of that meeting is determined by the IRS and the TMP. A partner may waive any right he or she has under the unified audit procedures, including the restrictions on assessment or collection. This waiver is made by filing a signed statement with the IRS.

If during the conduct of the audit any partner enters into a settlement agreement with the IRS, that agreement will be binding on the IRS and on the partners participating in the settlement unless the settlement document otherwise provides or unless there is fraud, malfeasance, or misrepresentation of fact.[18] (See Form 870-P, Agreement to Assessment and Collection of Deficiency in Tax for Partnership Adjustments, Exhibit 8-1 at ¶851.) Nonparticipating partners who make a request will be offered settlement terms that are consistent with such agreement. The offer of consistent settlement terms will not be available, however, unless the initial agreement was entered into before a final partnership audit notice was mailed to the TMP and the request for consistent terms was made within 150 days of such mailing.

An indirect partner will be bound by any settlement entered into by the passthrough partner from which he or she derives his or her interest, unless the indirect ownership has been disclosed to the IRS. If the TMP enters into a settlement, that settlement will be binding on any partner who is not a notice partner (or a member of a five-percent notice group) if the settlement expressly states that it is to be binding on other partners. However, if a partner who is not a notice partner has filed a statement with the IRS that the TMP has no authority to enter into a settlement on his or her behalf, then the settlement is not binding as to that partner.

Upon completion of a TEFRA partnership audit, the revenue agent will provide the TMP with a summary report detailing the proposed adjustments. The TMP will be offered a closing conference to discuss the report. After the closing conference, the agent will prepare a report utilizing the same procedure as in an individual examination.

The report will be reviewed by the local QMS staff and, when approved, will be sent to the TMP along with a 60-day letter explaining the partners' appeal rights. A Form 870-P will also accompany the report. Copies of the 60-day letter and the Form 870-P are sent to all partners at the same time to give them an opportunity to agree with the proposed determination. If the TMP agrees with the IRS determination, he or she can execute the Form 870-P. However, if any

---

[17] Code Sec. 6224(a).

[18] The IRS Restructuring and Reform Act of 1998 (P.L. 105-206) has incorporated into the partnership audit procedures provisions for raising the innocent spouse defense of Code Sec. 6015(e). These provisions allow an innocent spouse of a partner to be relieved of liability for tax, penalties and interest if certain conditions are met. See Code Sec. 6230(c)(5).

partner submits an acceptable written protest, the entire partnership case file will be transferred to the appropriate Appeals Office for the partnership, the settlement reached with the TMP will be temporarily suspended, and the consolidated appeals procedure outlined at ¶812 is then followed. The 60-day letter does not constitute a final partnership administrative adjustment (see ¶813 below) and does not confer jurisdiction on the Tax Court to resolve the matter.[19]

¶812 PARTNERSHIP APPEAL PROCEDURES

Appeals Office procedures exist for partnerships in TEFRA proceedings. Under the Appeals Office procedures, if any partner requests an Appeals conference regarding the proposed partnership adjustments, Appeals will hold a consolidated conference in the Appeals Office servicing the area where the partnership has its principal place of business. All partners have the right to attend this conference, but any partner planning to attend must notify the TMP of his or her plan to be present.[20]

Prior to the conference the TMP must furnish the names of the partners or representatives who will be attending and must submit valid power of attorney forms for those partners who send representatives. Appeals then schedules the conference and communicates the time, date, and location to the TMP who must furnish the information to all other persons planning to attend.

If the Appeals proceedings result in a change in the original settlement proposal, a revised Form 870-P is given to the TMP, who must send a copy to all partners who did not assent to the original report. The TMP is responsible for advising all nonassenting partners of any settlement terms. If a partner executes the revised Form 870-P, he or she is bound by that settlement. The form will beforwarded to the Service Center, which will release that partner's return from the suspense unit for assessment of any resulting deficiency.

If the TMP executes the revised Form 870-P, that settlement will be binding on all non-notice partners, unless the non-notice partner has filed a statement with the IRS denying the TMP authority to bind him or her.

If any partner does not agree to the settlement, Appeals is responsible for preparation of the final partnership administrative adjustment (FPAA). This commences the 90-day period in which the TMP can file a suit regarding the FPAA.

¶813 FINAL PARTNERSHIP ADMINISTRATIVE ADJUSTMENT

No deficiency in tax attributable to partnership items may be assessed until 150 days after the mailing of the final partnership administrative adjustment (FPAA) to the TMP.[21] The FPAA may not be mailed to the TMP until 120 days after the notice of commencement of the partnership audit. The FPAA is similar to a

---

[19] See *Clovis I v. Comm'r*, 88 TC 980 (1987), CCH Dec. 43,856.

[20] IRM Handbook 8113 Section 632.

[21] Mailing to the TMP at the address of the partnership is sufficient. Temp. Treas. Reg. §301.6223(a)-1T (1987). To be valid, an FPAA need not be mailed to a specifically named TMP. See *Seneca, Ltd. v. Comm'r*, 92 TC 363, 366-68 (1989), CCH Dec. 45,492; *Chomp Assocs. v. Comm'r*, 91 TC 1069, 1072-74 (1988), CCH Dec. 45,217.

statutory notice of deficiency, and the mailing of the FPAA tolls the statute of limitations on assessment of partnership items. The IRS must also send notice of the FPAA to each notice partner within 60 days of sending it to the TMP. Finally, the IRS may issue only one FPAA per partnership per taxable year.

¶815 JUDICIAL REVIEW OF FPAA

Within 90 days of the mailing of the FPAA, the TMP may file a petition for readjustment of the partnership items with the United States Tax Court, the United States District Court for the district in which the partnership's principal place of business is located, or the United States Court of Federal Claims. During this period, no other partner may file a petition for judicial review.[22]

If the TMP does not file a readjustment petition within ninety days, any notice partner or any five-percent group may file a petition in the Tax Court, the District Court, or the Court of Federal Claims within the next sixty days. However, if a notice partner or five-percent group files prematurely within the ninety-day period allowed for the TMP, and no action is otherwise brought within the sixty-day period which is not dismissed, the prematurely-filed petition will be treated as filed on the last day of the sixty-day period.[23] If more than one partner files a petition for readjustment, then the first petition filed in the Tax Court obtains priority. If no Tax Court action is brought, the first action in either the Court of Federal Claims or the District Court is given priority and all other actions are dismissed. The TMP may intervene in any such proceedings.[24]

To file a petition in either the District Court or the Court of Federal Claims, the TMP must deposit with the IRS an amount equal to the deficiency in tax that would result if the FPAA were upheld.[25] The court that acquires jurisdiction of the FPAA has authority to determine all partnership items of the partnership taxable year to which the FPAA relates. If a partner has already been involved in a judicial determination of tax liability resulting from nonpartnership items, an adjustment of the partner's liability for partnership items still may be made following resolution of the FPAA.

¶817 PARTNERSHIP ITEMS

The partnership audit provisions apply only to partnership items. The term "partnership item" includes any item to the extent that regulations provide that such item is more appropriately determined at the partnership level than at the partner level.[26] The regulations include as partnership items virtually all income, expenditures, credits, assets, liabilities, investments, transactions, accounting practices and other items which relate to the operation of the partnership and which may affect the individual partners' tax liabilities.[27]

A partnership item may become a nonpartnership item under the following circumstances:

1. The IRS fails to give notice of the commencement of a partnership audit.

---

[22] Code Secs. 6226(a).
[23] *Id.* Code Sec. 6226(b)(1).
[24] Code Sec. 6226(b)(5).

[25] *Id.* Code Sec. 6226(e)(1).
[26] *Id.* Code Sec. 6231(a)(3).
[27] Reg. § 301.6231(a)(3)-1.

2. The IRS mails to a partner a notice that an item is to be treated as a nonpartnership item.

3. The IRS enters into a settlement agreement with a partner regarding such item.

4. A partner files suit regarding the failure of the IRS to allow an administrative adjustment request with respect to any such item.

5. When a partner treats an item inconsistently with the partnership return and notifies the IRS of the inconsistency, then the IRS has the discretion to treat that item as a nonpartnership item.

6. If a partner has filed a request for administrative adjustment which would result in the item's being treated inconsistently with the treatment on the partnership return, the IRS has discretion to treat that item as a nonpartnership item.

7. If a husband and wife hold partnership interests as community property, partnership items of the husband will be treated as nonpartnership items where the husband is named as a debtor in a bankruptcy proceeding.[28]

If a partnership item becomes a nonpartnership item, the normal deficiency procedures may be used with respect to that item.

¶819 REQUEST FOR ADMINISTRATIVE ADJUSTMENT

Within three years of the time the partnership return was filed, any partner may file a request for administrative adjustment (RAA) for any partnership item for that year.[29] This request must be filed before the mailing of a notice of FPAA to the TMP for that taxable year. However, where the limitations period has been extended under a settlement agreement made pursuant to Code Sec. 6229(b), the time for filing the RAA will equal the extension of time under the agreement, plus six months. The time for filing an RAA relating to deductions for bad debts and worthless securities is seven years and before the mailing of the FPAA for the taxable year.[30] The RAA is analogous to an amended return or a claim for refund.

If the RAA is filed by the TMP and the TMP requests that the IRS treat it as a substitute return, then the IRS may assess any additional tax on the basis of the changes in the RAA without issuance of a notice of deficiency to any partner. The changes are treated as a correction of a clerical or mathematical error for which no notice of deficiency is required. If the TMP does not designate the RAA as a substitute return, the IRS may either allow the changes requested, commence a partnership audit proceeding or take no action on the request. If the IRS does not allow the RAA in full, the TMP may file a petition for readjustment of the disallowed items with the Tax Court, the District Court or the Court of Federal Claims. The petition may not be filed until six months after the date the RAA was filed and must be filed before two years after the date the RAA was filed. No

---

[28] See *Dubin v. Comm'r*, 99 TC 325 (1992), CCH Dec. 48,500; Acq. In Result, IRB 1999-40.

[29] Code Sec. 6227(a).

[30] Code Sec. 6227(e).

petition may be filed if the IRS has notified the TMP that it is conducting a partnership proceeding.

If the petition for review of the RAA has been filed and a timely notice of FPAA is mailed, the proceeding will be treated as a proceeding with respect to the FPAA. However, a deposit will not be required to establish jurisdiction in the appropriate District Court or Court of Federal Claims. Judicial review of an RAA filed by the TMP is limited to those items which the IRS disallows or asserts as an offset to the requested adjustments.

Parties to an action for review of the RAA are the same parties eligible as parties for review of an FPAA. Thus, all partners who were partners at any time during the tax year in question may be parties to the action.

If the RAA is filed by a partner other than the TMP, the IRS has four options: (1) it may treat the request as though it were a claim for refund based on nonpartnership items, (2) it may assess any additional tax resulting from the adjustments, (3) it may notify the partner that all partnership items of that partner for that year are being converted to nonpartnership items, or (4) it may commence a partnership audit proceeding. A partner who is notified that the partnership items are being treated as nonpartnership items may file a claim for refund attributable to those items within two years of receiving the notice from the IRS. If any portion of the request for administrative adjustment is not allowed, suit may be commenced after the expiration of six months from the date of filing the RAA and must be brought within two years of such filing date. Unlike a suit on an RAA filed by a TMP, a suit filed by an individual partner will not bind other partners.

¶821 STATUTE OF LIMITATIONS ON ASSESSMENTS

The general period for assessment against any person with respect to partnership items for any partnership taxable year is three years from the date of the filing of the partnership return or, if later, the last date prescribed for filing such return determined without extension.[31] An individual partner may enter into an agreement with the Secretary to extend the assessment period for that partner. Additionally, the filing of a Title 11 bankruptcy petition naming the partner as a debtor will toll the running of the limitations period for the time during which the Secretary is prohibited from making an assessment because of the bankruptcy proceeding, plus sixty days.[32]

For partnership items that become nonpartnership items for an individual partner as the result of a settlement agreement covering those items, the period for assessing tax is one year after the date the partnership items convert to nonpartnership items. However, where a settlement agreement relates only to some, but not all, of the disputed partnership items, the period for assessing tax attributable to the settled items is determined as though the settlement agreement had not been entered into.[33] The practical effect is that the limitations

---

[31] Code Sec. 6229(a).
[32] Code Sec. 6229(h).

[33] Code Sec. 6229(f).

period applicable to the last item resolved by settlement will control with respect to the remaining disputed partnership items.[34]

The assessment period will be suspended where the TMP files a petition for readjustment of partnership items following receipt of the FPAA.[35] Under TEFRA, only the filing of a *timely* petition tolls the running of the statute of limitations. In a deficiency case, however, the filing of *any* petition, whether timely or not, or valid or not, tolls the statute.

The TMP, or any other person authorized in writing by the partnership, has authority to extend the assessment period for all partners.[36] Code Sec. 6229(b) provides that if the TMP is a debtor in bankruptcy at the time the agreement is signed, the agreement will bind all partners unless the Secretary has been notified pursuant to Treasury Regulations of the bankruptcy proceeding.

An extension agreement must be entered into before the expiration of the statute. Form 872-P (see Exhibit 10-5 at ¶ 1055) is used to extend the statute to a specific date. As an alternative, the partnership can use Form 872-O (see Exhibit 10-6 at ¶ 1056) which extends the statute until ninety days after the extension is terminated by submitting Form 872-N (see Exhibit 10-7 at ¶ 1057).

Assessments may be made at any time against partners who sign or actively participate in the preparation of a fraudulent return with the intent to evade tax. The period is also extended from three years to six years with respect to all other partners in the case of a false partnership return.[37] Similarly, if the partnership omits an amount from gross income which exceeds twenty-five percent of reported gross income, the assessment period is extended to six years.[38] When no partnership return has been filed, assessment may be made at any time.

If a partner is not properly identified on the partnership return and the IRS timely mails a notice of the FPAA to the TMP, the period for assessment does not expire until one year after the name, address and taxpayer identification number of the partner are mailed to the IRS.[39] The IRS has ruled that partners may be assessed based upon a TEFRA proceeding in year 2 even though the period for assessing tax has expired for year 1, where the losses that are subject of the assessment in year 2 arose in year 1.[40]

¶823 ERRONEOUS INTERNAL REVENUE SERVICE COMPUTATIONAL ADJUSTMENTS

Once the proper treatment of partnership items has been determined at the partnership level, the IRS must then convert these items into tax adjustments for each of the individual partners.[41] When the IRS errs in making these "computa-

---

[34] See H.R. Rep. No. 105-34. (Found at 143 Cong. Rec. H6470, H6586 [daily ed. July 30, 1997].)

[35] Code Sec. 6229(d).

[36] Code Sec. 6229(b); *see generally* Ronald A. Stein, *Statutes of Limitation: Who May Extend Them for TEFRA Partners?*, TAXES, Sept. 1994, 560.

[37] Code Sec. 6229(c)(1).

[38] Code Sec. 6229(c)(2); See Chapter 9, Statute of Limitations on Assessment, *infra*.

[39] Code Sec. 6229(e).

[40] CCA 200414045.

[41] Where there is a delay in making a computational adjustment following a settlement under Code Sec. 6224(c) in which partnership items are converted to nonpartnership items pursuant to Code Sec. 6231(b)(1)(C), interest on any deficiency

tional adjustments" to reflect the proper treatment of the partnership items on the individual returns of the partners, special rules permit a partner to file a claim for refund of the tax attributable to such error.[42] If the IRS mails a notice of the computational adjustment to a partner, a claim for refund due to an error in the computation must be filed within six months after the notice was mailed. On the other hand, if the IRS does not make a computational adjustment and thereby fails to allow a proper refund or credit, a partner must file a claim for refund within two years after: (1) the date the settlement was entered into, (2) the date on which the period expired to file a petition in response to the FPAA, or (3) the date on which the decision of the court became final. If the claim is disallowed by the IRS, the partner may file a suit for refund within two years after the notice of disallowance is mailed out.

¶824 ELECTING LARGE PARTNERSHIPS

A partnership with more than 100 partners during the preceding tax year, not counting "service partners,"[43] may elect to be governed by simplified procedural rules, unless the partnership's principal business is either dealing in commodities or the performance of services, with all partners performing such services on behalf of the partnership.[44]

Adjustments to the income or deductions of an electing large partnership will ordinarily affect only the persons who are partners in the year that the adjustment becomes final, rather than the persons who were partners when the adjusted item actually arose.[45] An electing large partnership may either pass through the adjustment to the partners in the year the adjustment becomes final, in which case the partners report the adjustment on their personal income tax returns like any other operating or capital item of the partnership,[46] or it may pay directly the deficiency, interest and penalties associated with the adjustment,[47] so that the partners do not report any of the adjustment on their personal returns. If the partnership chooses to pay the deficiency, the deficiency will be based on the highest personal or corporate income tax rate in effect in the year the adjustment becomes final. Only one type of adjustment must flow through to the persons who were partners in the year to which the adjustment relates; that is, an adjustment to the partners' respective distributive shares, under Code Sec. 704, must be picked up by the partners whose distributive shares are adjusted and must be reflected in the partners' personal income tax returns for the year to which the adjustment relates.[48]

Although most of the procedural rules and deadlines discussed above also apply to an electing large partnership, the differences are nonetheless significant and generally enhance the ability of the partnership and the IRS to dispose of partnership item disputes more simply, at the cost of eliminating the individual

---

(Footnote Continued)

will be suspended in those circumstances provided in Code Sec. 6601(c).

[42] Code Sec. 6230(c).

[43] Code Sec. 775(b)(1).

[44] Code Secs. 775 and 6240.

[45] Code Sec. 6241(c)(1).

[46] Code Sec. 6242(a).

[47] Code Sec. 6242(b).

[48] Code Sec. 6241(c)(2).

partners' ability to influence the outcome of the dispute either at the partnership level or with regard to the partner's personal income tax return. Thus, a partner in an electing large partnership *must* report all partnership items consistently with the partnership's reporting.[49] Disclosure will not relieve the partner of penalties and the IRS can unilaterally and unappealably assess additional taxes and negligence and fraud penalties against a partner who takes inconsistent positions.Furthermore, the IRS is not required to notify partners of the beginning of a partnership audit or inform them of the terms of proposed adjustments to partnership items.[50] The IRS can select a representative for the partnership, without regard to the representative's relative partnership interest and, unless the partnership designates a different person to represent it, the IRS's representative can bind the partnership and all of its current and past partners.[51] In addition, only the partnership can file for judicial review of a proposed IRS adjustment or for a request for administrative adjustment.[52] If the partnership fails to do so, none of the individual partners have the right to seek judicial review or request an administrative adjustment.

Lastly, an electing large partnership *must* provide its partners with the Form 1065, Schedule K-1, Beneficiary's Share of Income, Deductions, Credits, etc., information returns on or before March 15th following the close of the partnership's taxable year, regardless of whether the partnership itself will file its own information return on that date.[53]

¶825 DECLARATORY JUDGMENT PROCEEDINGS

A taxpayer whose "oversheltered return" has been audited can obtain judicial review of the proposed adjustment even if the proposed adjustment does not produce a tax deficiency. An "oversheltered return" is a return that (1) contains both partnership and nonpartnership items, (2) shows no taxable income for the year, and (3) shows a net loss from partnership items that are subject to the partnership audit rules described above.[54] If the IRS audits such a return and adjusts the nonpartnership items, and the adjustments, if correct, would lead to a deficiency in taxes in the absence of the partnership net losses, the taxpayer can seek a declaratory judgment in Tax Court to determine the correctness of the proposed nonpartnership item adjustments.[55]

If the IRS follows this audit procedure, it must issue a notice of adjustment, rather than the notice of deficiency of the conventional audit. If the taxpayer timely petitions the Tax Court with respect to the notice of adjustment, the IRS cannot issue either a second notice of adjustment or a notice of deficiency (except to the extent of a later adjustment of the taxpayer's partnership items) with respect to that tax year absent fraud, malfeasance or misrepresentation of a material fact.[56]

---

[49] Code Sec. 6241(a) and (b).
[50] Code Sec. 6245(b).
[51] Code Sec. 6255(b).
[52] Code Sec. 6247(a).

[53] Code Sec. 6031(b).
[54] Code Sec. 6234(b).
[55] Code Sec. 6234(a) and (c).
[56] Code Sec. 6234(f).

The procedural rules for Tax Court review are the same as those governing review of a notice of deficiency. Once the taxpayer is in Tax Court for review of a notice of adjustment, the Tax Court may exercise its authority to address all items on the taxpayer's return, except for partnership items. Ordinarily, no tax willbecome due merely because the notice of adjustment is upheld, because the taxpayer still will be in a net loss position owing to the net loss on his or her partnership items. If the partnership items are later finally adjusted to change the taxpayer's position from a net loss to net taxable income, however, the taxpayer will be assessed for additional tax reflecting both the nonpartnership items in the notice of adjustment and the subsequent partnership item adjustments.[57]

An oversheltered taxpayer has a second chance to contest items in the notice of adjustment if the taxpayer failed to seek a declaratory judgment review in the Tax Court. If and when the taxpayer's partnership items are finally determined, leading to an underpayment of tax reflecting both the partnership items and the nonpartnership items in the notice of adjustment, the taxpayer may file for a refund claim with the IRS, based on the nonpartnership items in the notice of adjustment, and is entitled to the full panoply of judicial review if the IRS denies the claim.[58]

Tax Shelter Audit Techniques

¶833 TAX SHELTER REGISTRATION REQUIREMENTS

Over the years a major portion of the administrative resources of the IRS was directed toward abusive tax shelters. New programs were developed to combat this problem both legislatively and administratively. The procedures that have evolved as a result are discussed below.

An organizer of a tax shelter that is required to register under Code Sec. 6111, including a confidential corporate tax shelter, must file a Form 8264, Application for Registration of a Tax Shelter (See Exhibit 8-2 at ¶852). Generally, a Form 8264 must be filed prior to the time that an interest in the tax shelter is first offered for sale. Once a Form 8264 is filed, the organizer will receive a tax shelter registration number from the IRS. This number must be furnished to any individual invests in the tax shelter at the time of the sale or transfer of the interest, unless a number has not yet been assigned to the tax shelter. In that case, the investor must be given a written statement stating that a tax shelter registration number has been applied for and such number will be furnished when available, no later than 20 days after the number is received by the seller/transferor. If an investor claims any deduction, loss, credit or other tax benefit, he or she must report the tax shelter registration number on his or her tax return using a Form 8271, Investor Reporting of Tax Shelter Registration Number (See Exhibit 8-3 at ¶853).

Certain tax shelters are required to register with the IRS on Form 8271, Investor Reporting of Tax Shelter Registration Numbers (see Exhibit 8-3 at ¶853),

---

[57] Code Sec. 6234(g).   [58] Code Sec. 6234(d)(2).

prior to the time that interests in the shelter are offered for sale.[59] The tax shelter is considered "registered" when Form 8271 is mailed to or otherwise filed with the IRS.

Tax shelters are required to register if:

1. They represent at the time of sale that they will produce a tax shelter ratio, as of the close of any of the first five years, of greater than two to one; and

2. They are required to register with federal or state securities authorities but are offered for sale pursuant to an exemption from registration, or are a substantial investment. An investment is substantial if the aggregate amount offered for sale exceeds $250,000 and five or more investors are expected. Similar investments organized by the same person are aggregated to determine whether they are to be treated as a substantial investment.

Under final regulations issued in February 2003, confidential arrangements that meet the following requirements must also be treated as tax shelters for purposes of the registration requirements of Code Sec. 6111:[60]

1. A significant purpose of the structure of the investment is the avoidance or evasion of Federal income tax for a direct or indirect corporate participant; which means that the transaction is either a listed transaction[61] or the transaction has been structured to produce Federal income tax benefits that constitute an important part of the intended results of the transaction and the organizer, tax shelter promoter or other person responsible for registering the tax shelter reasonably expects the transaction to be presented to more than one potential participant in substantially similar form.

2. The tax shelter will be offered under conditions of confidentiality; and

3. The promoter of the tax shelter may receive fees greater than $100,000 in the aggregate.

The tax shelter ratio equals the ratio which the total amount of deductions claimed plus 350 percent of the credits potentially allowable to any investor bears to the total amount of money and the adjusted basis of other property (reduced by any liabilities the property may have) contributed by the investor as of the close of any of the first five taxable years.[62]

In computing this ratio, amounts borrowed from anyone who is a participant in the organization, sale, or management of the shelter, or from a person related to a participant, are not to be considered as money contributed by the investor.

Although the duty to register is imposed upon any person who organizes the tax shelter, for these purposes the term "tax shelter organizer" includes any

---

[59] Code Sec. 6111(a).
[60] Code Sec. 6011(d).

[61] See ¶ 835, below, which discusses what a listed transaction is.
[62] Code Sec. 6111(c).

persons who participated in the organization of the shelter or any persons participating in the sale or management of the investment.[63] If the person who organizes a shelter does not register it and another person in the chain of distribution does, the fact of registration does not relieve the organizer or the promoter of liability for penalties for failure to register.

The information required for registration includes the following: identification of the tax shelter and the organizer, the type of business organization of the shelter and its accounting method, the business activities and principal asset of the shelter, the form and source of financing, data regarding federal or state securities registration, the number and cost of investment units available, the acquisition costs per unit, the date the first unit may be offered for sale and the tax shelter ratio.[64]

The penalty for failure to register the partnership is the greater of $500 or one percent of the aggregate amount invested in the venture.[65] If the failure to register is due to reasonable cause, the penalty can be abated.

After the registration form is filed with the IRS, the IRS will issue a tax shelter identification number to the person who organized the shelter. The promoter is required to furnish this number to each investor and the investor must use that number on the tax return on which the benefits from the partnership are claimed. The penalty for each failure by the promoter to furnish the number to investors is $100. If an investor fails to provide the number on his or her tax return, the penalty is $250, unless the failure is due to reasonable cause.[66]

Any person who organizes or sells an interest in a potentially abusive tax shelter also is required to maintain a list of persons to whom interests in the tax shelter were sold.[67] Failure to maintain such a list subjects the organizer or seller to a penalty of $50 limited to a maximum of $100,000 per year per shelter.[68]

Recently, legislation has been introduced into the House and the Senate that would broaden the ability of the IRS to enjoin tax shelter promoters and impose other penalties, such as suspension or disbarment. The pending legislation also increases the amount of the penalty for failure to comply with the registration, disclosure and list maintenance requirements set forth in the Code.[69] In particular, the amount of the penalty for failure to register would increase to $50,000 unless the transaction is a listed transaction, in which case the amount of the penalty would be the greater of $200,000 or 50 percent of the gross income derived by such person.

¶835 TAX SHELTER DISCLOSURE REQUIREMENTS

A second element in the IRS's attack on abusive tax shelters is the requirement of disclosure. In the past, the IRS used an "after the fact" approach to identify tax

---

[63] Code Sec. 6111(d).

[64] Code Sec. 6111(a).

[65] Code Sec. 6707(a).

[66] Code Sec. 6707(b).

[67] Code Sec. 6112.

[68] Code Sec. 6708.

[69] See H. 1555, The Abusive Tax Shelter Shutdown and Taxpayer Accountability Act, introduced on April 2, 2003 and S. 1937, Tax Shelter Transparency and Enforcement Act, introduced on November 24, 2003.

shelters. With publication of final regulations in 2003, the IRS imposed disclosure requirements on tax shelters. The regulations generally apply to tax returns filed after February 28, 2003, and other reporting requirements are imposed on earlier-filed returns. In general, every taxpayer who has "participated" in a "reportable transaction" must attach a "disclosure statement" (Form 8886) (See Exhibit 8-4 at ¶ 854) to the tax return filed for the year in which the reportable transaction occurred. The term "transaction" is very broad, including all of the factual elements "relevant to the expected tax treatment of any investment, entity, plan or arrangement," and also "includes any series of steps carried out as part of a plan."

Reportable Transaction. There are six categories of reportable transactions:

1. Listed Transactions.

2. Confidential Transactions.

3. Transactions with Contractual Protection.

4. Loss transactions.

5. Transactions with Significant Book-Tax Difference.

6. Transactions Involving Brief Asset Holding Period.

Listed Transactions. A "listed transaction" is a transaction that is the same as or substantially similar to certain transactions publicly identified by the IRS to be tax avoidance transactions. A transaction will be considered the same as or substantially similar to a listed transaction if such transaction is expected to obtain the same or similar tax consequence and is either factually similar or it uses the same or similar tax strategy. As of April 2004, the IRS has identified 31 listed transactions.[70]

Confidential Transactions. A "confidential transaction" is a transaction where the taxpayer places a limitation on disclosure of the tax treatment or tax structure of the transaction. Two exceptions to the confidentiality rules exist. First, a transaction is not considered a confidential transaction if disclosure would violate securities law. Second, the acquisition of a non-public corporation is not a confidential transaction if the taxpayer discloses the tax treatment and structure as soon as the acquisition is disclosed to the public.

Transactions with Contractual Protection. A "transaction with contractual protection" is a transaction where the taxpayer or a related third party is entitled to receive a refund of all or any part of the fees paid for tax advice if the intended tax benefits are not achieved.

Loss Transactions. A "loss transaction" is a transaction that results in a taxpayer claiming a loss under Code Sec. 165 that exceeds certain thresholds. For corporations and partnerships having only corporate partners, the threshold is a $10 million dollar loss in any single year or a loss that is reasonably expected to exceed $20 million over a several year period. In general, losses on the sale or

---

[70] A list of the 31 identified listed transactions, with citations to published guidance and court cases, can be found at www.irs.gov/businesses/ corporations/article/0,,id=120633,00.html.

exchange of an asset with a "qualifying basis," as defined in Revenue Procedure 2003-24,[71] is not a loss transaction if certain requirements are met. These requirements, along with other exceptions to the loss transaction rule, are also discussed in Rev. Proc. 2003-24.[72]

Transactions with Significant Book-Tax Difference. A "transaction with significant book-tax difference" is a transaction where the treatment of any item for federal income tax purposes differs by more than $10 million from the book treatment of that same item. The $10 million is determined on a gross basis, without netting offsetting items or adjusting reserves for taxes. This provision is generally applicable only to publicly held companies and large companies (those with gross assets in excess of $250 million).

Revenue Procedure 2003-25 lists numerous book-tax differences that are not taken into account when determining if a transaction is reportable for purposes of the disclosure rules.[73]

Transactions Involving Brief Asset Holding Period. A "transaction involving brief asset holding period" is a transaction that involves an asset that is held by a taxpayer for less than 45 days and such asset is expected to give rise to a tax credit of more than $250,000.

Participation in Reportable Transactions. Participation in a reportable transaction may be direct or indirect. A taxpayer whose return reflects a tax consequence from a reportable transaction is considered to have participated directly. A taxpayer who knows or has reason to know that the tax benefits claimed on a return are derived from a reportable transaction is considered to have participated indirectly. Shareholders in a foreign corporation are considered to be indirect participants if the shareholders would be considered participants if the foreign corporation were instead a domestic corporation filing a tax return reflecting the same transaction.

Other Disclosure Rules. As noted above, disclosure of a reportable transaction must be made on a Form 8886, Reportable Transactions Disclosure Statement. A Form 8886 must be attached to a taxpayer's return for each year in which the taxpayer has participated in a reportable transaction. If the IRS designates a transaction as a listed transaction, a taxpayer who has participated in such a transaction but already filed a return must attach a disclosure statement to the taxpayer's next return. Likewise, if the cumulative losses under Code Sec. 165 cause a transaction to become a loss transaction, a taxpayer must report the transaction. Reportable transactions that result in a loss that is carried back to a prior year must be disclosed on an amended tax return.

Penalties for Failure to Disclose. Currently, there is no explicit monetary penalty for the failure to disclose a reportable transaction. However, pending legislation would impose a monetary penalty in the amount of $50,000 for each transaction, unless such transaction is a listed transaction, in which case the

---

[71] IRB 2003-11, 599, Section 4.02.   [73] IRB 2003-11, 601.

[72] Id.

penalty would increase to $100,000.[74] For large entities and high net worth individuals, the amount of the penalty is double.

¶837 TAX SHELTER LIST MAINTENANCE REQUIREMENTS

In addition to the onerous disclosure requirements placed on taxpayers, the IRS also finalized regulations in February 2003 that subject all tax professionals to burdensome "list maintenance" requirements. These regulations require that each "organizer or seller" of "potentially abusive tax shelters" maintain a list of the persons involved with such transaction. A separate list must be maintained that identifies all substantially similar transactions.

The regulations define "potentially abusive tax shelter" as any transaction that is (a) listed among one of the six categories of reportable transactions listed under Code Sec. 6011; (b) subject to registration under Code Sec. 6111; or (c) transferred if the transferor knows or reasonably expects that the transferee will sell or transfer the interest in a reportable transaction.

A person is an "organizer or seller" of a potentially abusive tax shelter if that person is a "material advisor" with respect to such a transaction. Any person who makes any statement, oral or written, as to the potential tax consequences of that transaction before the tax return reflecting the tax benefit is filed and receives or expects to receive a minimum fee[75] with respect to that transaction is a "material advisor." However, a person who makes a tax statement solely in the person's capacity as an employee, shareholder, partner or agent is not considered a material advisor.

For each transaction, the "list" must contain certain information, including the name and address of each person required to be on the list,[76] and must be retained for a period of 7 years. Upon request by the IRS, such list must be furnished to the IRS. Currently, the penalty for failure to comply with the list maintenance rules is $50 for each person not properly included on a list, with a maximum penalty of $100,000 per advisor per calendar year.[77] Under pending legislation, any individual who fails to provide to the IRS the list required to be provided under Code Sec. 6112 within 20 days of a request to furnish the IRS with such list is subject to a penalty of $10,000 a day after the 20th day for each failure, without limitation.[78]

¶839 INJUNCTIONS AGAINST TAX PROMOTERS

The IRS employs injunctions against promoters as a means of curbing abusive tax shelters.[79] An "injunction" is generally a legal action in which a court forbids a person from performing some act. In the case of tax shelters, the injunction is intended to prevent widespread marketing of the tax shelter by the promoter. Thus, in most cases, the injunction prohibits the promoter from organizing and

---

[74] Sec. 102 of S. 1937.

[75] Generally the minimum fee is $250,000 for a transaction in which all participants are C corporations, and $50,000 for any other type of person or entity, See. Reg. 301.6112-1(c)(3)(ii).

[76] Each piece of information the list must contain is set forth in Reg. 301.6112-1(e)(3).

[77] Code Sec. 6708.

[78] Sec. 109 of S. 1937.

[79] Code Sec. 7408.

selling the abusive tax shelter. The promoter also may be enjoined from organizing, promoting or selling interests in other abusive tax shelters. As part of the injunctive relief, the promoter may be required to notify the IRS of its involvement in any type of tax shelter and to submit all promotional materials related to tax shelters to the IRS for a specified period of time.

The injunction may be applied against all persons engaged in the promotion of the abusive tax shelter. Such persons include the entity or organization that set up the shelter (for example, a partnership or corporation), the officers of such entity or organization and the salespersons who market the shelter for the promoter. Furthermore, the IRS will enforce the injunction on a nationwide basis and not just in the locality where the injunction was obtained. Thus, the use of the injunction is a most potent technique for curbing abusive tax shelters, and it has been used with increasing frequency by the IRS.[80]

---

[80] In a recent release, the Justice Department indicated that it expected to block twice as many promoters from selling illegal tax shelters in 2004 as it did in 2003.

¶851 Exhibit 8-1

Form **870-P** (Rev. 6-93)	Department of the Treasury — Internal Revenue Service **AGREEMENT TO ASSESSMENT AND COLLECTION OF** **DEFICIENCY IN TAX FOR PARTNERSHIP ADJUSTMENTS**	IN REPLY REFER TO:
Taxpayer(s) name(s), address and ZIP code Taxpayer Identifying Number ▶	Name of partnership Taxpayer identifying number Name of tax matters partner	Tax year(s) ended

OFFER OF AGREEMENT FOR PARTNERSHIP ITEMS

Under the provisions of section 6224(c) of the Internal Revenue Code, the Commissioner of Internal Revenue and the undersigned taxpayer(s) agree to the determination of partnership items of the partnership for the years shown on the attached schedule of adjustments. The undersigned taxpayer(s), in accordance with section 6224(b), also waive(s) the restrictions on assessment and collection of any deficiency attributable to partnership items (with interest as required by law) provided in section 6225(a).

This agreement is conditional, and will not become effective or final until this agreement form is returned to Internal Revenue and is signed for the Commissioner. The one year extension of the period of limitations on assessment under section 6229(f) will not begin to run until the date the Commissioner's representative signs this form for the Commissioner.

If this agreement form is signed for the Commissioner, the treatment of partnership items under this agreement will not be reopened in the absence of fraud, malfeasance, or misrepresentation of fact; and no claim for an adjustment of partnership items or for a refund or credit based on any change in the treatment of partnership items may be filed or prosecuted.

Signature of taxpayer	Date
Signature of taxpayer	Date
By *(Signature and title)*	Date

(See Instructions For Signing On Next Page)

FOR INTERNAL REVENUE USE ONLY	Date accepted for Commissioner	Signature
	Office	Title

Cat. Number 611750   Form **870-P** (Rev. 6-93)

Instructions for signing this agreement:

1. Sign the agreement if you wish to agree to the partnership items as shown on the attached Schedule of Adjustments.

2. If a JOINT RETURN OF A HUSBAND AND WIFE was filed, both spouses must sign, unless one spouse, acting under a power of attorney, signs as agent for the other.

3. If you are a corporation, the officer authorized to sign must sign with the corporate name followed by his/her signature and title.

4. Your attorney or agent may sign for you provided we have received a power of attorney, which if not previously filed, must accompany this form.

Form **870-P** (Rev. 6-93)

Department of the Treasury — Internal Revenue Service

AGREEMENT TO ASSESSMENT AND COLLECTION OF
DEFICIENCY IN TAX FOR PARTNERSHIP ADJUSTMENTS

SCHEDULE OF ADJUSTMENTS

NAME OF PARTNERSHIP	TAX YEAR(S) ENDED		
TAXPAYER IDENTIFYING NUMBER			
DETAIL OF ADJUSTMENTS TO ORDINARY INCOME			
TOTAL ADJUSTMENTS TO ORDINARY INCOME			
OTHER ADJUSTMENTS			
A.			
(1) ADJUSTMENT			
(2) AS REPORTED			
(3) CORRECTED			
B.			
(1) ADJUSTMENT			
(2) AS REPORTED			
(3) CORRECTED			

REMARKS

Form **870-P** (Rev. 6-93)
*U.S.GPO:1993-0-343-049/82159

¶852 Exhibit 8-2

Form **8264**	**Application for Registration of a Tax Shelter**	OMB No. 1545-0865
(Rev. March 2004) Department of the Treasury Internal Revenue Service	▶ **See separate instructions.**	For IRS use only ☐

If this is an amended form, enter the tax shelter registration number previously issued to the tax shelter. See **Amended Forms 8264** on page 4 of the instructions . . . . ▶

Part I **General Information**	**Note:** *The tax shelter registration number will be sent to the organizer's address below.*

Tax shelter name	Tax shelter organizer's name	If you are not a principal organizer, check this box ▶ ☐
Number, street, and room or suite no.	Number, street, and room or suite no.	

City or town	State	ZIP code	City or town	State	ZIP code

Identifying number	Telephone number ( )	Identifying number	Telephone number ( )

1a Type of business organization: ☐ Partnership (including a limited partnership)   **b** Is this offering subject
☐ Trust   ☐ S corporation   ☐ Schedule C or F activity (Form 1040)   to the aggregation rules
☐ Other (specify) ▶   in the regulations?   ☐ Yes   ☐ No

2a Principal business activity code. See page 5 of the instructions.   **b** Secondary business activity code. If not applicable, enter N/A.

3a Type of principal asset acquired (or to be acquired)   **b** Was acquisition from a related party?   ☐ Yes   ☐ No

c(1) Cost (actual or projected) to tax shelter   **c(2)** Cost to related party   **d** Is the asset located in a foreign country?
$ $ ☐ Yes   ☐ No   Country ▶

e Means of acquisition: ☐ Purchase   ☐ Construction   **f(1)** Date acquired   **f(2)** Date placed in service
☐ Lease   ☐ Other (specify) ▶

4 Accounting method: ☐ Cash   ☐ Accrual   ☐ Hybrid   ☐ Other (specify) ▶

5a Is the tax shelter offering required to be registered with Federal or state agencies?   ☐ Yes   ☐ No   **b** Is the tax shelter offering exempt from Federal or state agency registration but filing of notice is required?   ☐ Yes   ☐ No

c If you checked "Yes" in either item 5a or 5b, check the appropriate boxes in item c(1) and/or enter the names of the states in item c(2).
c(1) Federal: ☐ SEC   ☐ HUD   ☐ CFTC   ☐ Other   **c(2)** States

6 Tax shelter registration number of other registered tax shelters. See page 6 of the instructions.

7 Date an interest in the tax shelter was first offered for sale

8 Describe the tax shelter, including its structure and the specific tax benefits intended. For confidential corporate tax shelters, attach any written material presented to potential participants (see instructions on page 6).

Part II   **Tax Shelter Information Under Section 6111(c)**

Note: *Complete items 9a through 11e for a minimum investment unit. See instructions for item 9a on page 6.*

9a Method of financing. Check applicable box and enter dollar amount.   **b** Length of financing   **c** Is any financing collateralized by letters of credit?
☐ **(1)** Cash $ ☐ Yes   ☐ No
☐ **(2)** Property contributions $ **d** Source of financing
☐ **(3)** Recourse debt $ ☐ Unrelated party . . . . %
☐ **(4)** Nonrecourse debt $ ☐ Related party   %
☐ **(5)** Other (specify) . . . . $ **e** Foreign-connected financing. If none, check this box ☐ ; otherwise, enter:
(6) Total. Add items 9a(1)-(5) $ $ Country ▶

10a Gross deductions   **b** Deduction codes   **c** Total credits   **d** Credit codes
$ $

11 Tax shelter ratio. Complete Part III on page 2.
a Year 1   **b** Year 2   **c** Year 3   **d** Year 4   **e** Year 5

12 Aggregate amount from sale of interests in the tax shelter . . . . ▶ $

13a Maximum number of investors   **b** Maximum number of investment units

For Privacy Act and Paperwork Reduction Act Notice, see separate instructions.   Cat. No. 61863D   Form **8264** (Rev. 3-2004)

Form 8264 (Rev. 3-2004)

Page **2**

Part III — Tax Shelter Ratio Computation

Tax Benefits	(a) Year 1	(b) Year 2	(c) Year 3	(d) Year 4	(e) Year 5
14 Current year's gross deductions	////////	line 16, col. (a)	line 16, col. (b)	line 16, col. (c)	line 16, col. (d)
15 Prior years' gross deductions					
16 Cumulative gross deductions. Add lines 14 and 15					
17 Current year's credits	////////	line 19a, col. (a)	line 19a, col. (b)	line 19a, col. (c)	line 19a, col. (d)
18 Prior years' credits					
19a Cumulative credits. Add lines 17 and 18					
b Statutory factor	3.5	3.5	3.5	3.5	3.5
c Multiply line 19a by line 19b					
20 Cumulative tax benefits. Add lines 16 and 19c . .					
Investment Base	////////	////////	////////	////////	////////
21 Cash contributed					
22 Adjusted basis of property contributed					
23 Tentative investment base. Add lines 21 and 22 .					
24 Reductions to investment base					
25 Current year's investment base. Subtract line 24 from line 23	////////	line 27, col. (a)	line 27, col. (b)	line 27, col. (c)	line 27, col. (d)
26 Prior years' investment base					
27 Cumulative investment base. Add lines 25 and 26 .					
28 Tax shelter ratio. Divide line 20 by line 27. Enter in the appropriate space on line 11 on the front of this form					

Part IV — Confidential Corporate Tax Shelter Information

29 Aggregate organizer(s) fees

$

30a Is the transaction the same as or substantially similar to a "listed transaction"? (see instructions) ☐ Yes ☐ No

b If "Yes," identify the listed transaction

Part V — Explanation of Items

Sign Here

▶ _____ Signature of tax shelter organizer Date

▶ Title

▶ _____ Print Name

Paid Preparer's Use Only

Preparer's signature ▶ Date Check if self-employed ▶ ☐ Preparer's SSN or PTIN

Firm's name (or yours if self-employed), address, and ZIP code ▶ EIN ▶ Phone no. ▶ ( )

Form **8264** (Rev. 3-2004)

¶853 Exhibit 8-3

Form **8271**	Investor Reporting of Tax Shelter Registration Number	OMB No. 1545-0881
(Rev. July 1998)	► Attach to your tax return.	
Department of the Treasury Internal Revenue Service	► If you received this form from a partnership, S corporation, or trust, see the instructions.	Attachment Sequence No. **71**

Investor's name(s) shown on return		Investor's identifying number	Investor's tax year ended

	(a) Tax Shelter Name	(b) Tax Shelter Registration Number (11-digit number)	(c) Tax Shelter Identifying Number
1			
2			
3			
4			
5			
6			
7			
8			
9			
10			

General Instructions

Section references are to the Internal Revenue Code.

Purpose of Form

Use Form 8271 to report the tax shelter registration number the IRS assigns to certain tax shelters required to be registered under section 6111 ("registration- required tax shelters") and to report the name and identifying number of the tax shelter. This information must be reported even if the particular interest is producing net income for the filer of Form 8271. Use additional forms to report more than 10 tax shelter registration numbers.

Note: *A tax shelter registration number does not indicate that the tax shelter or its claimed tax benefits have been reviewed, examined, or approved by the IRS.*

Who Must File

Any person claiming or reporting any deduction, loss, credit, or other tax benefit, or reporting any income on any tax return from an interest purchased or otherwise acquired in a registration-required tax shelter must file Form 8271. If you are an investor in a partnership or an S corporation, look at item G, Schedule K-1 (Form 1065), or item C, Schedule K-1 (Form 1120S). If a tax shelter registration number or the words "Applied for" appear there, then the entity is a registration-required tax shelter. If the interest is purchased or otherwise acquired by a pass-through entity, both the pass-through entity and its partners, shareholders, or beneficiaries must file Form 8271.

A pass-through entity that is the registration-required tax shelter does not have to prepare Form 8271 and give copies to its partners, shareholders, or beneficiaries unless the pass-through entity itself has invested in a registration-required tax shelter.

In certain cases, a tax shelter that does not expect to reduce the cumulative tax liability of any investor during the 5-year period ending after the date the investment is first offered for sale may be considered a "projected income investment." Such a tax shelter will not have to register, and thus not have to furnish a tax shelter registration number to investors, unless and until it ceases to be a projected income investment. It is possible, therefore, that you may not be furnished a tax shelter registration number, and not have to report it, for several years after you purchase or otherwise acquire your interest in the tax shelter. If you are later furnished a tax shelter registration number because the tax shelter ceased to be a projected income investment, follow these instructions. However, you must file Form 8271 only for tax years ending on or after the date the tax shelter ceases to be a projected income investment.

Note: *Even if you have an interest in a registration-required tax shelter, you do not have to file Form 8271 if you did not claim or report any deduction, loss, credit, or other tax benefit, or report any income on your tax return from an interest in the registration-required tax shelter. This could occur, for example, if for a particular year you are unable to claim any portion of a loss because of the passive activity loss limitations, and that loss is the only tax item reported to you from the shelter.*

Filing Form 8271

Attach Form 8271 to any return on which a deduction, loss, credit, or other tax benefit is claimed or reported, or any income reported, from an interest in a registration-required tax shelter. These returns include applications for tentative refunds (Forms 1045 and 1139) and amended returns (Forms 1040X and 1120X).

Furnishing Copies of Form 8271 to Investors

A pass-through entity that has invested in a registration-required tax shelter must furnish copies of its Form 8271 to its partners, shareholders, or beneficiaries.

However, in the case where **(a)** the pass-through entity acquired at least a 50% interest in one tax year in a registered tax shelter (and in which it had not held an interest in a prior year), and **(b)** the investment would not meet the definition of a tax shelter immediately following the acquisition if it had been offered for sale at that time, the pass-through entity need not distribute copies of Form 8271 to its investors. The pass-through entity alone is required to prepare Form 8271 and include it with the entity tax return.

Penalty For Not Including Registration Number on Return

A $250 penalty will be charged for each failure to include a tax shelter registration number on a return on which it is required to be included unless the failure is due to reasonable cause.

Specific Instructions

Investor's Identifying Number

Enter the social security number or employer identification number shown on the return to which this Form 8271 is attached.

Investor's Tax Year Ended

Enter the date the tax year ended for the return to which this Form 8271 is attached.

Cat. No. 61924F   Form **8271** (Rev. 7-98)

Columns (a) Through (c)

Enter the name, the 11-digit tax shelter registration number, and the identifying number of the tax shelter in the columns provided.

You must be given the tax shelter registration number at the time of your purchase or acquisition of an interest in a registration-required tax shelter or (if later) within 20 days after the seller or transferor receives the registration number. The seller or transferor of the interest in the tax shelter must give you the tax shelter registration number in a written statement that also provides the other information needed to complete columns (a) and (c) of Form 8271.

If you acquired your interest in the tax shelter from a pass-through entity that has invested in a tax shelter, the entity must give you a copy of its Form 8271. The copy of the entity's Form 8271 contains the information needed to complete columns (a) through (c) of your Form 8271.

If the person from whom you purchased or otherwise acquired an interest in the tax shelter notifies you that a registration number has been applied for, but has not yet been received, enter "Applied for" in column (b). Also enter in column (b) the name of the person who has applied for registration of the tax shelter, and complete columns (a) and (c). This notification must be in a written statement that includes the information you need to complete columns (a) through (c). If you have not received any notification, enter "No notification" in column (b) and complete columns (a) and (c) if you have this information.

Paperwork Reduction Act Notice. We ask for the information on this form to carry out the Internal Revenue laws of the United States. You are required to give us the information. We need it to ensure that you are complying with these laws and to allow us to figure and collect the right amount of tax.

You are not required to provide the information requested on a form that is subject to the Paperwork Reduction Act unless the form displays a valid OMB control number. Books or records relating to a form or its instructions must be retained as long as their contents may become material in the administration of any Internal Revenue law. Generally, tax returns and return information are confidential, as required by section 6103.

The time needed to complete and file this form will vary depending on individual circumstances. The estimated average time is:

Recordkeeping . . . . . . 7 min.

Learning about the law or the form . . . . 7 min.

Preparing the form . . . . 17 min.

Copying, assembling, and sending the form to the IRS . . . . 14 min.

If you have comments concerning the accuracy of these time estimates or suggestions for making this form simpler, we would be happy to hear from you. See the instructions for the tax return with which this form is filed.

¶853

¶854 Exhibit 8-4

Form **8886** (March 2003) Department of the Treasury Internal Revenue Service	**Reportable Transaction Disclosure Statement** ▶ **Attach to your tax return.** ▶ **See separate instructions.**	OMB No. 1545-1800 Attachment Sequence No. **137**

Name(s) shown on return	Identifying number

Number, street, and room or suite no.

City or town, state, and ZIP code

1a Name of reportable transaction	**1b** Tax shelter registration number (11-digits) (if any)

2 Identify the type of reportable transaction. Check the box(es) that apply. (see instructions)

   a ☐ Listed transaction   **d** ☐ Loss transaction

   b ☐ Confidential transaction   **e** ☐ Transaction with significant book-tax difference

   c ☐ Transaction with contractual protection   **f** ☐ Transaction with brief asset holding period

3 If the transaction is a "listed transaction" or substantially similar to a listed transaction, identify the listed transaction (see instructions) ▶ ....

4 Enter the number of transactions reported on this form . . . . ▶ _____

5 If you invested in the transaction through another entity, such as a partnership, an S corporation, or a foreign corporation, identify the name and employer identification number (EIN) (if any) of that entity . . . . ▶ ....
....

6 Enter in **columns (a) and (b)** below, the name and address of each person to whom you paid a fee with regard to the transaction if that person promoted, solicited, or recommended your participation in the transaction, or provided tax advice related to the transaction.

(a) Name	(b) Address

Cat. No. 34654G

Form **8886** (3-2003)

¶854

7   Facts. Describe the facts of the transaction that relate to the expected tax benefits, including your participation in the transaction.

....

....

....

....

....

....

....

....

8   Expected tax benefits. Describe the expected tax benefits, including deductions, exclusions from gross income, nonrecognition of gain, tax credits, adjustments (or the absence of adjustments) to the basis of property, etc. See instructions for more details.

....

....

....

....

....

....

....

....

9   Estimated tax benefits. Provide a separate estimate of the amount of each of the expected tax benefits described above for each affected tax year (including prior and future years).

....

....

....

....

....

....

....

....

Form **8886** (3-2003)

¶855 DISCUSSION QUESTIONS

1. The IRS is conducting an examination of the returns of Aggressivity, Ltd., a partnership in which Nellie Neglect is a 10-percent partner and also the designated Tax Matters Partner (TMP). The Tax Equity and Fiscal Responsibility Act of 1982 (TEFRA; P.L. 97-248) procedures have been scrupulously followed by the IRS, and a Final Partnership Administrative Adjustment (FPAA) was issued to Nellie on June 18, 2004, for the 2002 taxable year. The FPAA provided that the TMP had 90 days in which to file a petition for judicial review of the FPAA.

   On the same day, the IRS sent copies of the FPAA to all notice partners as required by the TEFRA provisions. All of these partners assume that Nellie would be filing a petition for judicial review on behalf of the partnership, because she had previously advised them of that strategy. For that reason, none of the other partners ever filed a petition for judicial review.

   Unfortunately, Nellie got occupied with other things and failed to file the petition by September 17, 2004. However, on November 12, 2004, Nellie realized her error and quickly filed a petition for judicial review of the FPAA with the Court of Federal Claims.

   The IRS, in responding to the petition, files a motion to dismiss for lack of jurisdiction with the Court on two separate grounds:

   (A) Nellie did not file a petition for readjustment within the 90 days of the FPAA as required by Code Sec. 6226(a).

   (B) Nellie in petitioning the Court only made a deposit of the tax liability, not the interest. Thus, she failed the TMP to meet the jurisdictional requirements of Code Sec. 6226(e)(1).

   Which party should prevail?

2. Constance C. Enshus, the limited partner in Bilda Brickhouse, a real estate partnership, received a copy of financial information prepared by the general partners of the partnership. In reviewing the information, Connie finds what she believes should be an additional deduction for the partnership for the preceding year. Connie writes to the general partner (who is also the TMP) asking that he prepare an amended return. The general partner disagrees with Connie and informs her of his decision. Connie still believes she is right and proceeds to file a Request for Administrative Adjustment (RAA) seeking a refund of $4,050, her proportionate share of the refund due as a result of the adjustment at the partnership level. Connie is notified by the IRS on September 15, 2004, that her RAA has been treated as requesting a refund for a nonpartnership item.

   (A) Assuming the IRS decides the TMP was correct and no refund is allowable, what is the last day that Connie can commence an action in federal court to litigate the matter?

(B) What action, if any, is required as a condition precedent to Connie's commencing legal action?

(C) Does it matter that the partnership has elected to be governed by the large partnership rules?

3. Larry Landowner is a partner in Water Street Ventures. The partnership has been undergoing an audit of its 2003 tax return. In an agreement with the tax matters partner and all other partners, Larry signs the Form 870-P—Agreement to Assessment and Collection of Deficiency in Tax for Partnership Adjustments, and pays his portion of the proposed deficiency.

Later that day Larry attends the O.P.E. (Overpaid Executives) luncheon. The speaker is discussing ways to deal with the IRS. He described a situation where a taxpayer entered an agreement with an Appeals Officer by executing a Form 870-AD—Offer to Waive Restrictions on Assessment and Collection of Tax Deficiency and to Accept Overassessment (see Chapter 12), which states that "no claim for refund or credit shall be filed or prosecuted" for the years involved. In the form, the IRS also promises that the case will not be reopened by the Commissioner "in the absence of fraud, malfeasance, concealment or misrepresentation of fact." Despite this language, the speaker explains that some courts have allowed claims for refund even though a Form 870-AD was signed by the taxpayer.

Recognizing that the same language is incorporated in Form 870-P, Larry would like to know whether he would be able to reopen his case on the same basis as Form 870-AD.

4. The IRS has recently concluded an examination of the returns of WWW.Com.Ltd, a partnership in which HTTP, Inc., is the Tax Matters Partner (TMP). HTTP, Inc. is an S corporation. It owns a 10% interest in the partnership. HTTP, Inc.'s shareholders are John E. Mail and his brother Jack E. Mail. As a result of the audit of the partnership, the ultimate tax liability of John E. Mail will be $50,000. Jack E. Mail, on the other hand, due to other investment losses, will have no tax liability as a result of this audit.

The partnership has directed the TMP not to file a petition for judicial review of the FPAA with the Tax Court of the United States. It desires to either go to the United States District Court or the United States Court of Federal Claims. The TMP has asked what amount, if any, it must deposit in order to acquire jurisdiction in the United States District Court or the United States Court of Federal Claims.

CHAPTER 9
PENALTIES AND INTEREST

¶901 INTRODUCTION

A deficiency in tax does not result merely in an increase in tax but also in the assessment of interest. In addition, various civil penalties may be imposed on taxpayers for failure to correctly report the tax, file a return or pay the tax when due. Tax return preparers and tax shelter promoters also may be subject to special penalties. This chapter discusses the application of these interest and penalty provisions. These penalties may be revised under proposals pending in Congress aimed at curbing tax shelters.[1]

Interest

¶903 INTEREST ON DEFICIENCIES

When a tax deficiency is assessed by the Internal Revenue Service (IRS), the IRS also will assess interest on the deficiency. This interest is compensation to the government for being deprived of the use of the tax revenue for the period of time that the tax was not paid and is personal interest which is not deductible under Section 163 of the Internal Revenue Code (the Code).[2] Until the 1980s, interest on taxes was not a major concern because the rates were considerably below market. However, changes in the law have resulted in interest rates that are considerably above "the Federal short-term rate."[3] For this reason, it is important to understand how interest is computed.

Interest is assessed from the date the taxes are required to be paid (generally, the due date of the return) until the date payment is actually made.[4] However, when a deficiency in tax is determined and the taxpayer consents to the assessment of the deficiency by executing a Form 870, Waiver of Restrictions on Assessment and Collection of Deficiency in Tax and Acceptance of Overassessment (see Exhibit 4-5 at ¶455), the interest is suspended for a period beginning thirty days after the Form 870 is filed[5] until twenty-one days (if the amount is less than $100,000 or ten days if it is greater) after notice and demand is sent to the taxpayer.[6] If the taxpayer does not timely pay the assessment at that time, the accrual of interest will resume. A taxpayer who is granted an extension of time to pay the tax or whoagrees to an installment payment arrangement with the Collection Division is not excused from paying interest. The interest continues until the time the tax is paid.

---

[1] S. 1937, Tax Shelter Transparency and Enforcement Act.

[2] Temp. Reg. §1.163-9T(b)(2)(i)(A), Accord. *Fitzmaurice v. U.S.*, 2001-1 USTC ¶50,198 (USDC SD Tex., Houston Div.).

[3] Code Sec. 1274(d).

[4] Code Sec. 6601(a).

[5] Code Sec. 6601(c).

[6] Code Sec. 6601(e)(2)(A).

There is no statutory provision for the suspension of interest on a deficiency while the Tax Court is considering the merits of the deficiency. However, the IRS has provided a procedure by which the accrual of interest can be stopped. Under Rev. Proc. 84-58,[7] if a taxpayer makes a remittance after the mailing of a Notice of Deficiency, the accrual of interest on the amount remitted will be suspended from the date of payment. The fact that the payment is made does not deprive the Tax Court of jurisdiction.[8] The remittance will either be credited as a payment of tax or held as a deposit in the nature of a cash bond. In either event, the running of the interest will stop. However, if the amount remitted does not take into account the interest that would have accrued to the date of payment, then the compounding rules in Code Sec. 6622 will require that interest continue to accrue on the interest portion even though the underlying tax has been paid.

In addition to interest on the unpaid taxes, Code Sec. 6601(e)(2) imposes interest on certain penalties from the due date of the return. For tax returns due prior to 1989, this provision applied to the failure-to-file penalty under Code Sec. 6651(a), the penalties for erroneous valuation under former Code Secs. 6659 and 6660, and the substantial understatement penalty under former Code Sec. 6661. For tax returns due after 1988, the Technical and Miscellaneous Revenue Act of 1988[9] extended this interest provision to the negligence and fraud penalties under former Code Sec. 6653. The Revenue Reconciliation Act of 1989[10] retained this provision, but incorporated all of the accuracy-related penalties (former Code Secs. 6653, 6659, 6660 and 6661) into one new Code section—Sec. 6662.[11] With the exception of the failure-to-file penalty, the fraud penalty and the accuracy-related penalties, all other penalties begin to accrue interest upon assessment if they are not paid within twenty-one days of the date of notice and demand if the amount is less than $100,000, otherwise, interest will begin to accrue ten days after the notice and demand.

¶905 SPECIAL RULE FOR EMPLOYMENT TAXES

While the general rule is that interest is assessed on all deficiencies in tax, under certain circumstances it may be possible to obtain an interest-free adjustment for an erroneous reporting of employment taxes. Code Sec. 6205(a) provides that if less than the correct amount of Federal Insurance Contributions Act (FICA), Railroad Retirement Tax Act or Federal Withholding tax is paid with respect to wages or compensation, proper adjustments can be made without interest. Treasury Regulation §31.6205-1 provides the procedure for making such corrections. Interest will not accrue on the additional tax provided the adjustment and payment of the taxare made by the due date of the Federal Employment Tax Return for the quarter during which the error is first determined or "ascertained."[12]

---

[7] 1984-2 CB 501.

[8] Code Sec. 6213(b)(4).

[9] P.L. 100-647.

[10] P.L. 101-239.

[11] See ¶917, *infra*.

[12] Rev. Rul. 75-464, 1975-2 CB 474.

¶907 COMPUTATION OF INTEREST RATE

The interest rate for overpayments and underpayments of taxes is established on a quarterly basis and is reported in the Internal Revenue Bulletin. The rate is determined in the first month of each quarter, effective for the following quarter. The rate is based on the short-term federal rate established under Code Sec. 1274(d), rounded to the nearest full percent, and generally represents the average yield on marketable obligations of the United States that have a maturity of less than three years. This rate is then increased by three percentage points for interest due or an overpayment.[13]

Effective January 1, 1983, with respect to deficiencies, refunds or overpayments (regardless of the taxable year generating the tax), interest payable to or by the IRS is compounded daily.[14] Thus, where only the principal portion of a tax deficiency is paid, interest will continue to be compounded on the outstanding interest due.

Interest rates on underpayments of tax have varied since 1992 from seven percent to ten percent, while rates on overpayments have fluctuated between six percent and nine percent during the same period. The interest rate applicable to a deficiency or an overpayment is the rate in effect during any intervening period. If an amount due is unpaid during a period when the interest rate changes, the new rate will apply from the date of the change until the rate again changes. Normally, therefore, the total amount of interest must be calculated by using various rates. The changing interest rates and the daily compounding create complex computational problems. However, computer software programs used by the IRS and available to the practitioner provide a fast and accurate means for calculating interest. For those without such resources, Rev. Proc. 95-17[15] provides uniform tables and procedures for the daily compounding of interest at the various rates that may apply during any period.

Since 1986, individual and corporate taxpayers have paid higher interest rates on underpayments of tax than the IRS paid on overpayments. Code Sec. 6621(a)(1) has now equalized the interest rates for *noncorporate taxpayers*. Simultaneously, Congress also codified an administrative service practice of netting tax due and refunds[16] by creating Code Sec. 6621(d). This "netting" is available for any type of tax imposed by the Internal Revenue Code. For example, income taxes can be netted against self-employment taxes, and employment taxes can be netted against excise taxes.[17]

¶908 INCREASED RATE ON LARGE CORPORATE UNDERPAYMENTS

The Revenue Reconciliation Act of 1990[18] increased the interest rate applicable to "large corporate underpayments" by two percent over the normal rate for

---

[13] Code Sec. 6621(a).

[14] Code Sec. 6622(a).

[15] 1995-1 CB 556.

[16] Rev. Proc 99-43.

[17] See Rev. Proc. 2000-26, IRM 2000-24 offering guidance for application of the zero net interest note on overlapping tax underpayments and overpayments.

[18] P.L. 101-508.

underpayments.[19] Thus, if the effective interest rate is ten percent for ordinary underpayments, a large corporate underpayment would be subject to an interest rate of twelve percent. A "large corporate underpayment" is defined as any underpayment of tax by a C corporation[20] which exceeds $100,000 for any taxable period. For the purpose of determining whether this "threshold underpayment" has been reached, only the tax itself is considered.[21] Any penalties, additions to tax, or interest are excluded in determining whether the $100,000 threshold underpayment of tax has been exceeded. However, once this threshold test has been met, the increased interest rate applies to the total underpayment, including all interest and additions to tax.

The increased interest rate for such large corporate underpayments only becomes applicable thirty days after the date on which the IRS sends specific notices or letters informing the taxpayer of an assessment, a proposed deficiency or a proposed assessment. With respect to those underpayments to which the deficiency procedures apply, this thirty-day period begins to run from the earlier of (1) the date on which the IRS sends a thirty-day letter proposing a deficiency and offering an Appeals Office review, or (2) the date on which a statutory Notice of Deficiency is sent. In situations where the deficiency procedures do not apply, such as the failure to pay the tax reported on the tax return, the thirty-day period is measured from the date the IRS sends a notice or letter which informs the taxpayer of the amount due or the proposed assessment of a tax. If, within the thirty-day period, payment is made in full of the amount shown as due, the notice or letter sent by the IRS will be disregarded for purposes of determining the date on which the increased interest rate will begin to apply.

The "threshold underpayment" of $100,000 is determined by aggregating all amounts of taxes that have not been timely paid for the taxable year or period involved. For example, a late payment of a portion of the tax shown on the tax return will be added to any subsequently assessed deficiency in tax determined upon examination of that return.[22] Thus, if a corporation is one week late in paying $60,000 of its reported tax for 1990 and is later assessed a $50,000 tax deficiency for the same year, the total underpayment of $110,000 would exceed the $100,000 "threshold" level required to trigger the increased rate of interest. In this example, if the corporation was first notified of the proposed deficiency by a thirty-day letter sent on June 1, 1992, the date on which the increased interest rate firstbegins to apply would be July 1, 1992. It also should be noted that in this illustration the amount of the underpayment subject to the increased interest rate would be substantially less than $100,000 ($50,000, plus any penalties and accrued interest).

¶911 ALLOCATION OF PAYMENT

When a partial payment is made to the IRS and the taxpayer does not designate the manner in which the funds should be allocated, the IRS will apply the

---

[19] Code Sec. 6621(c).

[20] As opposed to an "S corporation," Code Sec. 6621(c)(3).

[21] Reg. § 301.6621-3T(b)(2)(ii).

[22] See examples in Temp. Reg. § 301.6621-3.

payment in its best interest, first to the tax, then to the penalties and finally to the interest for the earliest year. Any remaining balance will then be applied in the same order to each succeeding year until the entire payment is exhausted. However, a designation by the taxpayer as to how the payment is to be applied will be honored by the IRS.[23] This rule does not apply to an involuntary payment, which would include any payments resulting from levies or from court actions.

¶913 REVIEW OF INTEREST LIABILITY

The imposition of interest on underpayments of tax is expressly provided for in Code Sec. 6601. The IRS does not have discretion as to when to compute interest or to excuse anyone from paying interest. If the taxpayer disagrees with the amount of interest due and is unable to convince the IRS to reassess or eliminate the interest liability, the taxpayer must pay the amount determined. The taxpayer can thereafter file a claim for refund for the amount of interest disputed. If the taxpayer is able to recover interest pursuant to a claim for refund, the taxpayer is entitled to interest from the date the liability arose (either the due date or the assessment date) to the date of judgment.

When a deficiency has been determined by the Tax Court, the taxpayer also may file a petition in the Tax Court to claim that excessive interest was assessed on the deficiency.[24] Such a petition must be filed within one year after the initial decision of the Tax Court becomes final and may not be filed unless the taxpayer first pays in full the amount of the assessed deficiency and interest.

¶915 ABATEMENT OF INTEREST DUE TO INTERNAL REVENUE SERVICE ERROR

The Tax Reform Act of 1986[25] and the Taxpayer Bill of Rights 2 (1996)[26] authorize the IRS to abate any unpaid interest on a deficiency to the extent that the interest is attributable to unreasonable errors or delays resulting from the failure of an IRS official to perform a ministerial or managerial act. The abatement may be made with respect to adjustment directly to the taxpayer's return or when the tax is the result of a flow-through adjustment of a Tax Equity and Fiscal Responsibility Act of 1982 (TEFRA)[27] partnership item.[28] For interest to qualify under Code Sec. 6404(e)(1), no significant aspect of any error or delay may be attributable to the taxpayer. Further, the error or delay must have occurred after the IRS contacted the taxpayer in writing. Thus, this provision cannot be used to abate interest prior to the time an audit has commenced.

The regulations define the scope of a "ministerial act" as one that does not involve the exercise of judgment or discretion, and that occurs during the processing of a taxpayer's case after all prerequisites to the act, such as conferences and review by supervisors, have taken place. A decision concerning the proper application of federal or state law is not a ministerial act.[29] The regulations

---

[23] Rev. Proc. 2002-26, 2002-1 CB 746.

[24] Code Sec. 7481(c).

[25] P.L. 99-514.

[26] P.L. 104-168.

[27] P.L. 97-248.

[28] Field Service Advice 199941010 (July 2, 1999).

[29] Reg. § 301.6404-2(b)(2).

give several examples of delays in the performance of managerial and ministerial acts, including a delay in transferring an audit to the district office to which the taxpayer has moved and a delay in the issuance of a notice of deficiency after all issues in a case have been agreed to and the entire review process has been completed.[30]

Claims for interest abatement must be filed on Form 843, Claim for Refund and Request for Abatement, and should be labeled "Request for Abatement of Interest under Section 6404(e)." The instructions to Form 843 provide further information on such claims, which should be filed with the IRS Service Center where the tax return that was affected was filed.

The Tax Reform Act of 1986 contains another provision allowing for the abatement of interest. Code Sec. 6404(e)(2) provides that interest is to be abated on any erroneous refund sent to the taxpayer up until the time the IRS demands repayment of the refund. To qualify for this relief, the taxpayer cannot have caused the erroneous refund in any way. Further, no abatement of interest applies if the erroneous refund exceeds $50,000.

The Taxpayer Bill of Rights 2 (1996) gives the Tax Court jurisdiction over any action brought by the taxpayer to determine whether the IRS's refusal to abate the interest was an abuse of discretion. Such an action must be brought within 180 days after the mailing of the IRS's final determination not to abate the interest.

Penalties

¶916 SUSPENSION OF INTEREST AND PENALTIES FOR FAILURE TO SEND NOTICE

Interest and penalties generally accrue during periods for which taxes are unpaid, regardless of whether the taxpayer is aware that there is an additional tax due. Prompted by a concern that accrual of interest and penalties absent prompt resolution of tax deficiencies may lead to the perception that the IRS is more concerned about collecting revenue than in resolving taxpayer's problems, Congress has suspended the accrual of penalties of interest if the IRS fails to send propernotice to the taxpayer. This suspension of interest and penalties is available only if the tax relates to timely filed returns (including extensions) by individuals with respect to income taxes.

Under Code Sec. 6751, for notices issued and penalties assessed after December 31, 2000, the IRS must include the name of any penalty assessed, the Code section that authorizes the penalty, and computation explaining the penalty shown on the notice. In addition, Code Sec. 6751 prohibits the IRS from assessing a penalty unless the initial determination of the assessment is personally approved in writing by either the immediate supervisor of the individual making the determination or a designated higher-level official. The preassessment approval rules do not apply to delinquency penalties under Code Sec. 6651,

---

[30] Reg. § 301.6404-2(c).

estimated tax penalties under Code Secs. 6654 and 6655, or any other penalties automatically calculated through electronic means.

The statute provides for the suspension of the accrual of certain penalties and interest if the IRS does not send the taxpayer a notice specifically stating the taxpayer's liability for additional taxes and the basis for the liability within 18 months following the date that is the later of (1) the original due date of the return, or (2) the date on which the individual taxpayer timely filed the return.[31] It does not apply to the failure-to-pay penalty, the fraud penalty, or with respect to criminal penalties. Interest and penalties will resume accruing twenty-one days after the IRS sends appropriate notice. This provision is effective for taxable years ending after July 22, 1998. The 18-month period is reduced to 12 months for tax years beginning after January 1, 2004.

¶917 ADDITIONS TO TAX

When a deficiency in tax results from culpable conduct on the part of the taxpayer, the IRS can impose penalties in the form of additions to the tax. These civil penalties are designed to deter taxpayers from understating their tax liabilities. For more flagrant violations, criminal penalties[32] exist as an additional deterrent. Since 1976, civil tax penalties in the Internal Revenue Code have increased in number and severity, and the IRS has asserted these penalties with increasing regularity.

The procedure for assessing and collecting civil penalties is the same as that used for taxes. The Tax Court,[33] district court, and Court of Federal Claims all have jurisdiction to determine the propriety of the assessment of any of these civil penalties. The more significant civil penalties are described in the following paragraphs. No deduction is allowed to a taxpayer for the amount of any penalty paid.

¶919 ACCURACY-RELATED PENALTY

Code Sec. 6662, entitled "Imposition of Accuracy-Related Penalty" (ARP), includes the following violations:

1. Negligence or Disregard of Rules or Regulations.

2. Substantial Understatement of Income Tax.

3. Substantial Valuation Misstatement.

4. Substantial Overstatement of Pension Liabilities.

5. Substantial Estate or Gift Tax Valuation Understatement.

A uniform penalty of twenty percent applies to any portion of an underpayment of tax attributable to "one or more" of the accuracy-related violations.[34] No overlapping or "stacking" of these penalties is permitted. The twenty percent

---

[31] Code Sec. 6404(g).

[32] See Chapter 18, *infra.*

[33] The Tax Court's jurisdiction for civil penalties is limited to those penalties which are contained in a notice of deficiency and which are included in a timely petition; see Code Sec. 6213(a).

[34] However, if there is a "gross valuation misstatement" with respect to items 3, 4 and 5 above, a 40-percent penalty applies. Code Sec. 6662(h).

ARP does not apply to any portion of an underpayment on which the fraud penalty is imposed.[35]

The accuracy-related penalty will not be imposed if it is shown that there is reasonable cause for the underpayment and the taxpayer acted in good faith.[36] Interest on the ARP and the fraud penalty is computed from the due date of the return.[37] Neither the ARP nor the fraud penalty may be imposed in any case where the 100-percent penalty under Code Sec. 6672 is asserted for failure to collect or pay over tax. The ARP applies to all taxes imposed by the Code.

A uniform definition of "underpayment" upon which the penalty is imposed applies to all accuracy-related and fraud penalties.[38] The "underpayment" is the amount by which the correct tax exceeds the tax shown on the return, plus any additional assessments not shown on the return, less the amount of any "rebates" (an abatement, credit, refund or other repayment). This is the same definition as that of a "deficiency" found in Code Sec. 6211. As a result, if a return is filed late, the penalty for fraud or negligence will no longer apply to the entire tax liability without reduction for the tax shown on the delinquent return.

The accuracy-related and fraud penalties apply only where a tax return has been filed.[39] The components of the accuracy-related penalty, as well as the fraud penalty and other civil penalties, will be discussed below.

¶921 UNDERPAYMENT DUE TO FRAUD

Code Sec. 6663(a) provides that if any underpayment of tax is due to fraud, a penalty is imposed equal to seventy-five percent of the portion of the underpayment due to fraud.[40] Statutory interest on the penalty accrues from the due date of the return.

For purposes of Code Sec. 6663, a portion of the underpayment will be considered to be due to fraud where it is the result of an intent to evade tax. An underpayment that results from mere negligence or intentional disregard of rules or regulations will not subject the taxpayer to the fraud penalty. Moreover, the existence of an understatement of income, standing alone, generally will not be sufficient to justify the fraud penalty unless there is some showing of intentional wrongdoing on the part of the taxpayer.

Under Code Sec. 7454(a), the burden of proof is on the IRS in any proceeding in which the existence of fraud is an issue. The IRS is required to prove that the taxpayer's conduct was fraudulent by clear and convincing evidence. However, where the taxpayer has been convicted or has entered a guilty plea to a charge of willfully attempting to evade tax,[41] the taxpayer will be collaterally estopped

[35] Code Sec. 6662(b).
[36] Code Sec. 6664(c).
[37] Code Sec. 6601(e).
[38] Code Sec. 6664(a).
[39] Code Sec. 6664(b).
[40] The seventy-five percent fraud penalty applies to taxable years beginning after December 31, 1986.

For years prior thereto, the penalty was fifty percent of the understatement plus fifty percent of the interest on that portion of the deficiency attributable to fraud. Unlike current law, the base penalty (fifty percent) applied to the entire understatement, even though not all of the understatement resulted from fraudulent conduct.
[41] Code Sec. 7201.

from denying that fraud existed and the IRS will have met its burden of proof.[42] Once the government proves that any portion of an underpayment is due to fraud, the fraud penalty will apply to the entire underpayment unless the taxpayer is able to prove by a preponderance of the evidence that some portion is not attributable to fraud.[43]

There are two instances where the IRS does not have the burden of proving fraud even though it proposes to assess the fraud penalty. The first is where the taxpayer fails to pay the filing fee when a petition is filed in the Tax Court. The failure to pay the fee prevents the joining of the issue of fraud and results in the Tax Court's dismissal of the petition. Where the petition is dismissed for failure to pay the filing fee, not only is the deficiency presumed correct, but the addition to tax under the fraud penalty is also presumed correct. The second instance is where allegations of fraud are made in the answer to the taxpayer's petition in the Tax Court. Where the taxpayer fails to reply to the fraud issue, the taxpayer is deemed to have admitted it. Thus, the Commissioner need not prove that any portion of the understatement was due to fraud. If the petitioner files a reply denying that there was fraud, the burden of proving the existence of fraud remains with the Commissioner.[44]

¶923 NEGLIGENCE PENALTY

When an underpayment of tax is due to negligence or disregard of rules and regulations, Code Sec. 6662(b)(1) provides for an accuracy-related penalty (ARP) of twenty percent. The penalty applies only to the portion of the underpayment attributable to such negligence or disregard. The twenty-percent ARP is applicable to tax returns due after 1989. Statutory interest on the penalty accrues from the due date of the return.

"Negligence" is defined under Code Sec. 6662(c) as "any failure to make a reasonable attempt to comply with the provisions of [the Code]." The term "disregard" includes any "careless, reckless, or intentional disregard." If a position taken by a taxpayer with respect to an item on a tax return "lacks a reasonable basis," the negligence penalty will apply.[45] However, a taxpayer who takes a position that is contrary to a revenue ruling or an IRS notice will not be subject to the penalty if the position has "a realistic possibility of being sustained on its merits."[46]

The negligence penalty may be imposed in addition to the delinquency penalty provided by Code Sec. 6651(a).

---

[42] See *Charles Ray Considine v. Comm'r,* 68 TC 52 (1977), CCH Dec. 34,365 (the Tax Court held that a taxpayer was collaterally estopped to deny fraud where he had been convicted of willfully making a false return under Code Sec. 7206(1). But see *Considine v. Comm'r,* 683 F.2d 1285, 1287 (9th Cir. 1982), 82-2 USTC ¶9537 (criticized the Tax Court view); *John T. Wright v. Comm'r,* 84 TC 636 (1985), CCH Dec. 42,013 (Tax Court overruled *Considine* and held that there is no collateral estoppel where the offense charged was the filing of a false return under Code Sec. 7206(1).

[43] Code Sec. 6663(b).

[44] Tax Court Rule 123(a); *Hicks v. Comm'r,* 46 TCM 1135, TC Memo. 1983-496, CCH Dec. 40,371(M). See *Rechtzigel v. Comm'r,* 79 TC 132 (1982), CCH Dec. 39,204, *aff'd,* 703 F.2d 1063 (8th Cir. 1983), 83-1 USTC ¶9281.

[45] Reg. §1.6662-3(b)(1).

[46] Reg. §1.6662-3(a). This is the same test applied to tax return preparers to determine whether the preparer penalty should be imposed. See Reg. §1.6694-2(b) and ¶939, *infra*.

When the IRS proposes an addition to tax for negligence or disregard of rules and regulations, that determination is presumed correct and the taxpayer has the burden of proving that the penalty is not warranted. In any situation where the taxpayer shows that the underpayment is due to reasonable cause and that he acted in good faith, the penalty should be abated under Code Sec. 6664(c)(1). According to the recently amended regulations under Code Sec. 6664(c), whether the reasonable cause and good faith exception applies is a facts and circumstances determination. The regulations state that the most important factor will be the efforts of the taxpayer in determining the correct tax liability.[47] Further, the regulations identify two sets of circumstances which would qualify for the exception: (1) an honest misunderstanding of fact or law that is reasonable, taking into consideration the taxpayers education and experience,[48] and (2) an isolated computational error. Relying on the advice of a tax professional, in and of itself, does not necessarily demonstrate reasonable cause and good faith. Reliance on a tax professional will qualify for the exception if the advice is based on all the pertinent facts and applicable law and does not rely on unreasonable assumptions.[49] If the taxpayer fails to disclose pertinent facts or circumstances that he or she knows or should know to be relevant, the taxpayer will not qualify for the exception.[50] Similarly, if the professional advice unreasonably relies on the representations, statements or findings of the taxpayer or any other person, the exception will not apply.

Up until the Omnibus Budget Reconciliation Act of 1993 (the 1993 Act),[51] the negligence and the disregard-of-the-rules penalties could have been avoided by a complete and adequate disclosure of the questionable item or position on Form 8275 or Form 8275-R attached to the tax return (see Exhibit 9-1 at ¶951 and Exhibit 9-2 at ¶952).[52] Since the passage of this law, the disclosure defense is no longer available to taxpayers who are subject to the negligence penalty. However, it is still a viable defense for the disregard-of-the-rules penalty. In the case of an item or position other than one that is contrary to a regulation, disclosure must be made on Form 8275, Disclosure Statement. If the position taken on the tax return is contrary to a regulation, disclosure must be made on Form 8275-R, Regulation Disclosure Statement, and must represent a good faith challenge to the validity of the regulation. The 1993 Act also requires that the position disclosed have a reasonable basis and that adequate books and records be kept, whereas prior to 1993 a disclosed position need only have been not frivolous.

---

[47] Reg. § 1.6664-4(b).

[48] See *U.S. v. Boyle*, 469 U.S. 241 (1985), 85-1 USTC ¶13,602 (relying on a tax professional for filing deadlines is not reasonable as it is a simple matter of which a layperson should have knowledge); *Olsen v. U.S.*, 853 F.Supp. 396 (D.C. Fla. 1993) (corporate president's reliance on a CPA's misleading advice was not reasonable given that complex tax concepts were not involved).

[49] *Mauerman v. Comm'r*, 22 F.3d 1001 (10th Cir. 1994), 94-1 USTC ¶50,222 (reliance on advice of tax professional to deduct fees instead of capitalizing was reasonable).

[50] *Baugh v. Comm'r*, 71 TCM 2140, TC Memo. 1996-70, CCH Dec. 51,173(M) (lack of full disclosure to an accountant precluded qualifying for the reasonable cause and good faith exception).

[51] P.L. 103-66.

[52] Reg. § 1.6662-3(c)(2).

¶925 SUBSTANTIAL UNDERSTATEMENT OF TAX

If there is a substantial understatement of tax, Code Sec. 6662(b)(2) provides that the twenty-percent accuracy-related penalty (ARP) may apply. The penalty applies only to that portion of the underpayment due to such "substantial understatement." For an understatement to be substantial, it must exceed the greater of ten percent of the tax required to be shown on the return or $5,000 ($10,000 for corporations).

The substantial understatement penalty will not be imposed if the taxpayer can show that there was reasonable cause for such understatement and that he or she acted in good faith.[53] The penalty also does not apply if there was substantial authority for the taxpayer's treatment of the item or if the relevant facts with respect to such item have been disclosed on the return or in a statement attached to the return.

In determining whether there is substantial authority for the taxpayer's position, the taxpayer can rely on court decisions, revenue rulings, regulations, congressional committee reports, private letter rulings, technical advice memoranda, general counsel memoranda, IRS information or press releases and other IRS announcements published in the Internal Revenue Bulletin.[54] Conclusions reached in treatises, legal periodicals, legal opinions or opinions by tax professionals are not authority. However, the authorities underlying such conclusions or opinions may provide substantial authority for the tax treatment of the item in question. The IRS must publish in the Federal Register and revise, at least annually, a list of positions for which the IRS believes there is not substantial authority and which affect a substantial number of taxpayers.[55]

If substantial authority does not exist, but the position has a reasonable basis, as defined in Reg. §1.6662-3(b)(3), the substantial understatement penalty can still be avoided by adequate disclosure of the relevant facts. The IRS issues annual revenue procedures which set forth the circumstances under which disclosure on a return of information relating to an item will be treated as adequate.[56] This revenue procedure lists the specific items that must be identified for various itemized deductions, trade or business expenses, Schedule M-1 adjustments, foreign tax items and various other matters. If the revenue procedure does not include the questionable item as one which can be adequately disclosed on the return, disclosure must be made on Form 8275 or Form 8275-R. For disclosures relating to an item or position that is not contrary to a regulation, Form 8275 must be used. When the position is contrary to a regulation, Form 8275-R is to be used.[57]

If the understatement relates to a tax shelter (an investment the principal purpose of which is the avoidance of federal income tax), then even adequate disclosure of the item will not relieve the taxpayer from the penalty. The

---

[53] Code Sec. 6664(c)(1); see ¶923, *infra*.

[54] Reg. §1.6662-4(d)(3)(iii).

[55] Code Sec. 6662(d)(2)(D).

[56] Rev. Proc. 95-55, 1995-2 CB 457.

[57] Reg. §1.6662-4(f).

taxpayer must have both substantial authority and a reasonable belief that it was more likely than not that the treatment was proper.[58]

¶927 SUBSTANTIAL VALUATION MISSTATEMENTS

Penalties may be imposed for substantial errors in valuing property on income, estate or gift tax returns. Substantial overstatements of pension liabilities resulting in underpayments of tax also may be subject to penalty. There is a two-tier penalty rate structure of twenty percent and forty percent for substantial valuation errors[59]

Overvaluation on Income Tax Returns	*Undervaluation on Estate and Gift Tax Returns*	*Penalty*
200% or more, but less than 400%	50% or less, but not less than 25%	20%
400% or more	25% or less	40%

The underpayment of tax due to valuation misstatements also must meet certain threshold levels before the penalty will apply:

Type Of Valuation Misstatement	*Underpayment Must Exceed*
Substantial Valuation Misstatement	$5,000 ($10,000 in the case of a corporation)
Substantial Overstatement of Pension Liability	$1,000
Substantial Estate or Gift Tax Valuation Understatement	$5,000

The Revenue Reconciliation Act of 1990 extended the valuation overstatement penalty to certain valuation misstatements relating to Code Sec. 482 transactions.[60] Valuation questions are frequently involved in disputes with the IRS regarding the allocation of income, credits, deductions, or other items between commonly owned or controlled taxpayers under Code Sec. 482. The twenty-percent penalty applies to the understatement resulting from the valuation misstatement when either of the following threshold levels is reached:

1. The price for any property or services (or for the use of property) claimed on the return is 200 percent or more (or fifty percent or less) of the correct amount determined under Code Sec. 482 (referred to as the transactional penalty); or

2. The "net Section 482 transfer price adjustment" exceeds the lesser of $5,000,000 or ten percent of the taxpayer's receipts. (This amount is defined as the net increase in taxable income resulting from adjustments to prices under Code Sec. 482) (referred to as the net adjustment penalty).

If either of the above threshold levels reaches 400 percent or more (or twenty-five percent or less), or exceeds the lesser of $20,000,000 or twenty percent of the taxpayer's receipts, the penalty increases to forty percent.

The accuracy-related penalty, including all of the valuation misstatement components, is applicable to all taxpayers.

---

[58] Reg. § 1.6662-4(e)(2); Reg. § 1.6662-4(g)(1).
[59] Code Sec. 6662(e), (f), (g) and (h).
[60] P.L. 101-508, Act § 11312.

The substantial valuation misstatement penalties will not be applied if it is shown that there was reasonable cause for such misstatement and that the taxpayer acted in good faith in making such valuation.[61] If the valuation misstatement penalty involves a Code Sec. 482 transaction, the reasonable cause exception in Code Sec. 6664(c) may or may not be applicable. Reg. §1.6662-6 specifies that a different reasonable cause standard is to be employed in certain circumstances. The standard under Reg. §1.6662-6(d) must be met where transactions in which a valuation misstatement under the transactional penalty constitutes or is part of a valuation misstatement under the net adjustment penalty for the penalty to bereduced or abated. Further, in transactions in which the Code Sec. 6664(c) reasonable cause standard is applicable, it is satisfied by meeting the standard provided under Reg. §1.6662-6(d). Reasonable cause under Reg. §1.6662-6(d) is met under two alternatives. The first alternative requires the taxpayer to show that he or she used a specified method under Code Sec. 482 for valuing the transaction and that the method was applied reasonably. Further, the taxpayer must maintain sufficient documentation to demonstrate that the method applied provided the most reliable measure of an arm's-length transaction. The second alternative, labeled the unspecified method, is met if the taxpayer can show that the use of a method specified under Code Sec. 482 would not produce a reliable result, and that the unspecified method employed was reliable in obtaining an arm's-length result. Again, sufficient documentation must be maintained to demonstrate that the unspecified method was reliable. If a transaction involves a charitable contribution, reasonable cause and good faith will not abate the penalty for a substantial valuation overstatement unless the value of the property was based on a qualified appraisal and the taxpayer made a good faith investigation of the value.[62]

¶928 FRIVOLOUS TAX RETURNS

A frivolous return penalty of $500 is imposed, in addition to any other penalties provided by law, against any individual taxpayer who, to further a frivolous position or with a clear intent to impede administration of the law, files a purported return that either fails to contain sufficient information from which a reasonably correct tax liability can be determined or clearly indicates that the tax liability reflected is substantially incorrect.[63] The first Code Sec. 6702 rule is directed at incomplete tax protester returns, and the second applies to individuals who claim tax protest deductions. This penalty can be assessed without resort to the deficiency procedures and is immediately payable. However, taxpayers may contest the penalty in federal district court by paying the amount assessed. If a taxpayer does contest the penalty in court, Code Sec. 6703(a) provides that the burden of proof is on the government.

¶929 FAILURE TO FILE OR PAY

Failure to file any required return may subject the taxpayer to civil penalties and possible criminal prosecution. Code Sec. 6651(a)(1) provides that, in the case of a

---

[61] Code Sec. 6664(c)(1).
[62] Code Sec. 6664(c)(2).

[63] Code Sec. 6702.

failure to file a return on the date prescribed, a penalty of five percent of the tax required to be shown on the return will be imposed for each month that the return is late. However, this penalty cannot exceed twenty-five percent of the amount required to be shown as tax on the return. A minimum penalty, equal to the lesser of $100 or the tax due, is imposed if the return is not filed within sixty days from the due date. If the taxpayer can establish that the failure to file the return wasdue to reasonable cause and not due to willful neglect, the penalty may be abated. In determining the tax required to be shown on the return, any tax paid in advance of the return is not treated as an amount subject to the penalty. The five percent penalty for each month, or part thereof, during which a delinquency continues, is increased to fifteen percent per month for any failure to file due to fraud. The maximum penalty of twenty-five percent for failure to file is increased to seventy-five percent when the failure is fraudulent.[64]

The Code also provides a penalty for taxpayers, who do not timely pay the tax shown on the return. Code Sec. 6651(a)(2) imposes a penalty equal to one-half of one percent of the balance for each month that the tax shown on the return is not paid, not to exceed twenty-five percent in the aggregate. For any month in which penalties apply under both Code Sec. 6651(a)(1) and (a)(2), the penalty under Code Sec. 6651(a)(1) is reduced by an amount equal to the penalty under Code Sec. 6651(a)(2).[65] The maximum aggregate penalty under Code Sec. 6651(a)(1) and (a)(2) is forty-seven and one-half percent.

Another failure to pay penalty under Code Sec 6651(a)(3) of one-half of one percent a month applies to additional tax deficiencies. The maximum penalty under Code Sec. 6651(a)(3) is twenty-five percent.

If the IRS notifies the taxpayer of its intention to levy or to resort to enforced collection, the penalties under Code Secs. 6651(a)(2) and 6651(a)(3) increase to one percent per month.[66] The penalties under Code Secs. 6651(a)(2) and 6651(a)(3) are decreased to one quarter of one percent a month during the period an installment agreement is in effect. The penalties under Code Sec. 6651(a) can be abated if the failure to pay is due to reasonable cause.

For months beginning after December 31, 1999, the monthly increase in the failure to pay penalty for timely filed individual returns is reduced from .5% to .25% during the period that any installment agreement is in effect.[67]

¶931 FAILURE TO FILE INFORMATION RETURNS OR PROVIDE CORRECT INFORMATION

Code Sec. 6721 imposes penalties for failure to file information returns and for failure to include correct information on such returns. Both failure to file and to provide correct information are subject to the following three-tier penalty structure for returns due after 1989:

---

[64] Code Sec. 6651(f).
[65] Code Sec. 6651(c)(1).
[66] Code Sec. 6651(d).

[67] Code Sec. 6651(h). This section applies to months beginning after December 31, 1999, and only applies to timely filed returns.

Correction of Failure	Penalty
Within 30 days	$15 per failure ($75,000 maximum)
After 30 days, but before August 1	$30 per failure ($150,000 maximum)
After August 1	$50 per failure ($250,000 maximum)

There is a substantially higher penalty for failures due to intentional disregard of the filing or reporting requirements.

Code Sec. 6721 provides a *de minimis* exception to relieve taxpayers from any penalty if they correct erroneous information on filed information returns before August 1, provided that the number of such corrected returns does not exceed the greater of ten or one-half of one percent of the total information returns filed. In addition, if a taxpayer's average annual gross receipts for the most recent three years do not exceed $5,000,000, the maximum penalties that may be imposed during any year under the new three-tier penalty structure are reduced to $25,000, $50,000 and $100,000, respectively.

Code Sec. 6722 combines the penalty for failure to furnish payee statements and the penalty for failure to include correct information on such statements. A $50 penalty applies to each failure to furnish a payee statement and to each failure to include correct information on such statement. The total amount of such penalties that can be imposed during any one year is limited to $100,000.

Code Sec. 6723 provides the penalty for failure to supply identifying numbers. All failures to comply with the specified information reporting requirements are subject to a fifty dollar penalty. The total of all such penalties that may be imposed during any year is limited to $100,000. The failure of a transferor of a partnership interest to promptly notify the partnership of such exchange under Code Sec. 6050K(c)(1) is made subject to the penalty.

Under Code Sec. 6724(a), no penalty is imposed with respect to any information reporting requirement if it is shown that such failure is due to reasonable cause and not to willful neglect. The law also specifically provides that if a taxpayer or preparer includes on a return incorrect information provided by another, that person will not be subject to the penalty if he or she had no reason to believe such information was incorrect.

The IRS may not require that information returns be filed on magnetic media unless at least 250 returns are required to be filed during the year.[68] Furthermore, no penalty will be imposed for failure to file on magnetic media except to the extent such failure occurs with respect to more than 250 information returns.[69]

¶933 FAILURE TO TIMELY DEPOSIT

Code Sec. 6656 provides a penalty for failure to make timely deposits[70] of employment and other taxes. This penalty is designed to encourage taxpayers to make a delinquent deposit as soon as possible after the due date. The penalty rates are as follows:

---

[68] Code Sec. 6011(e).
[69] Code Sec. 6724(c).

[70] The penalty under this section also pertains to payments not made electronically when required by Code Sec. 6302(h).

Days Elapsed After Due Date	Rate
Not more than 5 days	2%
More than 5 days, but not more than 15 days	5%
More than 15 days	10%

A special fifteen-percent penalty rate applies when the deposit is not made within ten days after the date of the first delinquency notice to the taxpayer or, if a jeopardy assessment is made, on or before the day on which notice and demand for payment is given. Code Sec. 6656(c) provides relief for first-time depositors and for the first period subsequent to a change in the frequency of deposits. Code Sec 6656(e) provides relief for cascading penalties, which occur if a taxpayer misses a deposit early in a return period but makes succeeding deposits on time.[71]

¶935 PREPARER PENALTIES

Along with those penalties that can be imposed on taxpayers who file inaccurate returns, the Code provides civil penalties for tax return preparers who prepare inaccurate returns. The first penalties were enacted by the Tax Reform Act of 1976,[72] which also defined the class of "income tax return preparers" to whom these penalties could be applied. The Tax Equity and Fiscal Responsibility Act of 1982 (TEFRA)[73] enacted other more stringent penalties that also apply to preparers. Unlike the 1976 provisions, the later penalties are not limited to income tax return preparers as defined in the Code. The later penalties can be imposed on any person who advises or participates in the preparation of any false return that results in an understatement of a person's tax liability. The Revenue Reconciliation Act of 1989[74] further amended and broadened the application of the preparer penalties.

Code Sec. 6694 applies where there is an understatement of a tax liability that is due to a position taken on the tax return for which there is no realistic possibility of being sustained on its merits or where the understatement is due either to a willful attempt to understate the tax liability or to a reckless or intentional disregard of rules or regulations. These penalties can only be assessed where the person who prepared the return is an "income tax return preparer" as defined in Section 7701(a)(36) of the Code.

Where the understatement results from taking an unrealistic position, Code Sec. 6694(a) imposes a $250 penalty for each return or claim resulting in an understatement.

If the understatement is due to a willful attempt to understate, or a reckless or intentional disregard of rules or regulations, the penalty under Code Sec. 6694(b) is $1,000. Where both penalties under Code Sec. 6694 apply to the

---

[71] Code Sec. 6656(e) applies to deposits required to be made after December 31, 2001. For deposits that are required to be made after January 18, 1999 and relate to deposit periods ending on or before December 31, 2001 see Rev. Proc. 99-10, 11 IRB 1999-2.

[72] P.L. 94-455.

[73] P.L. 97-248.

[74] P.L. 101-508.

proscribed conduct, the larger penalty under Code Sec. 6694(b) is reduced by the amount of the lesser penalty paid under Code Sec. 6694(a).

Code Sec. 6695 imposes other penalties for technical violations by income tax return preparers. For failure either to furnish a copy of a return to a taxpayer, to retain a copy or list of returns prepared, to sign a return, to furnish the preparer's identifying number, or to file a correct information return regarding others employed to prepare returns, the penalty for each such failure is $50 and the maximum annual penalty for each type of failure is $25,000. There is a $50 penalty for failure to retain copies of the returns or a list of the names and identification numbers of taxpayers for whom such returns were prepared. Code Sec. 6695 also imposes a $500 penalty on any income tax return preparer who endorses or negotiates any refund check issued to a taxpayer.

Code Sec. 6713 imposes a $250 penalty for return preparers who make unauthorized disclosures of tax return information. Under Code Sec. 7216(b), disclosures are exempt from the penalty if they are made pursuant to either a court order, other provisions of the Code or Treasury regulations. These exemptions include the disclosure or use of such information "for quality or peer reviews," so a return preparer may disclose tax information to another return preparer for the purpose of such reviews.

¶937 DEFINITION OF INCOME TAX RETURN PREPARER

Because the preparer penalties only apply to an "income tax return preparer" as defined in Code Sec. 7701(a)(36), the statutory definition takes on great importance. The Code definition includes any person who *for compensation* prepares an income tax return or claim for refund. It also includes any person who employs another person to prepare income tax returns for compensation. It is not necessary that the preparer have been directly compensated for the return in question if other circumstances indicate that the return was not prepared gratuitously. Thus, an accountant who prepared tax returns for individual shareholders of a corporation, but did not charge the shareholders, was held to be an income tax return preparer where he also prepared the corporate return for compensation.[75] The compensation was treated as payment for a package deal which included preparation of both the corporate and individual returns.

A person who prepares a *substantial portion* of a return or claim is considered to be a preparer.[76] The regulations indicate that providing advice with respect to an entry on a return or any portion of a return will constitute preparation of the return if the item involved is a *substantial portion* of the return.[77] Whether a portion of a return is substantial is determined by comparing that portion with the complete return on the basis of length, complexity and tax liability involved.Specific safe harbor guidelines are provided in the regulations to exempt as tax return preparers those who prepare or give advice with respect to a portion of a tax return or claim which has relatively nominal tax consequences.[78]

---

[75] *Papermaster v. United States*, 81-1 USTC ¶9217 (E.D. Wis. 1980).

[76] Code Sec. 7701(a)(36)(A).

[77] Reg. § 301.7701-15(b).

[78] *Id.*

A portion of a return is not considered substantial if it involves gross income or deductions (or amounts on the basis of which credits are determined) which are either (1) less than $2,000, or (2) less than $100,000, and also less than twenty percent of the gross income (or adjusted gross income if the taxpayer is an individual) shown on the return or claim. Thus, under these guidelines, advice concerning a $99,000 deduction on a return reporting $500,000 of adjusted gross income would not cause the adviser to be treated as a preparer.

Because of the wide sweep of the literal terms of the return preparer definition, the statute contains a number of exceptions. For example, an employee who types the final form of the return would be a person who is employed to prepare a return for compensation. However, Code Sec. 7701(a)(36)(B)(i) provides that a person is not an income tax return preparer merely because the person furnishes typing, reproducing or other mechanical assistance.[79] A corporate employee who prepares a return for his employer (or for an officer or employee of the employer) is not considered an income tax return preparer so long as the corporation is one by whom he is regularly and continuously employed.[80] Also excluded from the definition is a fiduciary of an estate or trust who prepares an income tax return for the estate or trust. A final exception is a person who prepares a claim for refund after an audit of the taxpayer's return has produced a deficiency determination.

A number of rulings have been issued that illustrate the scope of the definition of "income tax return preparer." In Rev. Rul. 84-3, a tax consultant who was asked to review a return prepared by the taxpayer and to recommend possible changes was held to be a tax return preparer.[81] A firm that furnished computerized tax return preparation services to tax practitioners also was determined to be an income tax return preparer where the software program went beyond mere mechanical assistance.[82] In a similar vein, software companies that sold taxpayers computer programs that furnished more than mechanical assistance and, in effect, provided substantive tax advice were held to come within the definition of a return preparer.[83] In another ruling, a farmers' cooperative was found to be a return preparer where it prepared a Form 1040, Schedule F, as part of a computerized data processing service provided to members, and the schedule was a substantial portion of the member's return.[84] In Rev. Rul. 86-55, a used car dealership that offered free income tax preparation on the condition that any refund be applied to a down payment on a car was an income tax return preparer where the dealershipreviewed or completed the tax return.[85] The same ruling held that a firm that offered discounted cash payments for tax refunds was a preparer where the firm's employees either reviewed or completed the return. Even though no separate fee was charged for the tax preparation in either

---

[79] Priv. Ltr. Rul. 8416024, January 13, 1984; Priv. Ltr. Rul. 8416025, January 13, 1984. Both held that a computer tax processing firm that received computer input sheets from an insurance agency and then processed the input sheets into a completed return was not an income tax return preparer.

[80] Code Sec. 7701(a)(36)(B)(ii).
[81] Rev. Rul. 84-3, 1984-1 CB 264.
[82] Rev. Rul. 85-187, 1985-2 CB 338.
[83] Rev. Rul. 85-189, 1985-2 CB 341.
[84] Rev. Rul. 85-188, 1985-2 CB 339.
[85] Rev. Rul. 86-55, 1986-1 CB 373.

¶937

situation, the IRS found that the customer was offered a "package deal" that included the tax return.

¶939 UNREALISTIC POSITIONS

Code Sec. 6694(a) imposes a $250 penalty on a "tax return preparer" if any part of an understatement is due to a position taken on the return or refund claim for which there is no "realistic possibility" of being sustained on its merits. This standard does not require certainty or that the preparer conclude that the position is more likely than not to succeed. The regulations define this "realistic possibility standard" as follows:

> A position is considered to have a realistic possibility of being sustained on its merits if a reasonable and well-informed analysis by a person knowledgeable in the tax law would lead such a person to conclude that *the position has approximately a one-in-three, or greater, likelihood of being sustained on its merits.*[86]

The authorities to be analyzed in determining whether a position satisfies the realistic possibility of success standard are the same authorities which may be relied upon in determining whether substantial authority exists for purposes of avoiding the substantial understatement penalty under Code Sec. 6662(b)(2).[87]

If the realistic possibility standard is not met, the penalty still will not be imposed if there is either (1) an adequate disclosure of the questionable position on the return, or (2) a showing that there was reasonable cause for the under-statement and that the preparer acted in good faith. If either of these defenses is claimed in any proceeding involving the penalty under Code Sec. 6694(a), the preparer has the burden of proving that there was adequate disclosure or reasonable cause and good faith.[88]

If the unrealistic position taken on the return is not "frivolous," proper disclosure of the questionable position will relieve the preparer from the penalty under Code Sec. 6694(a). The regulations define a "frivolous position" as one that is "patently improper."[89] The type of disclosure required to avoid the penalty depends on whether the preparer is a signing or nonsigning preparer. If the preparer is one who signed the return, disclosure is adequate only if made on a Form 8275 or 8275-R, whichever is appropriate, or on the tax return itself with respect to those items specifically permitted to be disclosed in such a manner by anannual revenue procedure.[90] This is the same disclosure a taxpayer is required to make in order to avoid the substantial understatement penalty under Code Sec. 6662(d) (see ¶825).

If the preparer did not sign the return, but merely gave oral or written advice to the taxpayer or to another return preparer, disclosure also is adequate if made in the same manner required of a signing preparer. In addition, if the nonsigning preparer gave the advice to a taxpayer, disclosure is adequate if such

---

[86] Reg. § 1.6694-2(b), emphasis added.

[87] Reg. § 1.6694-2(b), citing Reg. § 1.6662-4(d)(3)(ii); see ¶825, *supra,* for a listing of authorities. Examples of situations which meet, or do not meet, the realistic possibility standard are set forth in Reg. § 1.6694-2(b)(3).

[88] Reg. § 1.6694-2(e).

[89] Reg. § 1.6694-2(c)(2).

[90] Note 47, *supra,* and accompanying text.

advice also includes a statement that the position lacks substantial authority and, therefore, may be subject to the substantial understatement penalty under Code Sec. 6662(d) unless properly disclosed.[91] The cautionary statement to the taxpayer must be in writing if the advice was in writing. If the advice was orally given to the taxpayer, the warning regarding the potential penalty and the need for disclosure also may be oral.

When a nonsigning preparer advises another preparer with respect to a position that does not meet the realistic possibility standard, disclosure is adequate if the advice to the other preparer includes a statement that disclosure is required under Code Sec. 6694(a). As in the case of advice to a taxpayer, if the advice to the other preparer was in writing, the warning with respect to disclosure also must be in writing. An oral warning to the preparer is sufficient if the advice was orally given.[92] However, a cautious tax adviser may wish to document the fact that these required statements were made to the other preparer or to the taxpayer.

The penalty under Code Sec. 6694(a) will not be imposed if the understatement was due to reasonable cause and the preparer acted in good faith. In making this determination, the IRS will consider all facts and circumstances. The regulations provide some guidance concerning the factors that will be considered. These include:

1. *Nature of the error causing the understatement.* The IRS will consider whether or not the error resulted from a provision that was so complex, uncommon, or highly technical that a competent preparer of returns or claims of the type at issue reasonably could have made the error. The reasonable cause and good faith exception does not apply to an error that would have been apparent from a general review of the return or claim for refund by the preparer.

2. *Frequency of errors.* The IRS will consider whether or not the understatement was the result of an isolated error (such as an inadvertent mathematical or clerical error) rather than a number of errors. Although the reasonable cause and good faith exception generally applies to an isolated error, it does not apply if the isolated error is so obvious, flagrant or material that it should have been discovered during a review of the return or claim. Furthermore, the reasonable cause andgood faith exception does not apply if there is a pattern of errors on a return or claim for refund even though any one error, in isolation, would have qualified for the reasonable cause and good faith exception.

3. *Materiality of errors.* The IRS will consider whether or not the understatement was material in relation to the correct tax liability. The reasonable cause and good faith exception generally applies if the understatement is of a relatively immaterial amount. Nevertheless, even an immaterial

---

[91] Reg. §1.6694-2(c)(3)(ii)(A). If the questionable position relates to a tax shelter item, the taxpayer must be advised that the penalty may apply regardless of disclosure.

[92] Reg. §1.6694-2(c)(3)(ii)(B).

understatement may not qualify for the reasonable cause and good faith exception if the error or errors creating the understatement are sufficiently obvious or numerous.

4. *Preparer's normal office practice.* The IRS will consider whether or not the preparer's normal office practice, when considered together with other facts and circumstances such as the knowledge of the preparer, indicates that the error in question would rarely occur and the normal office practice was followed in preparing the return or claim in question. Such a normal office practice must be a system for promoting accuracy and consistency in the preparation of returns or claims and generally would include, in the case of a signing preparer, checklists, methods for obtaining necessary information from the taxpayer, a review of the prior year's return and review procedures. Notwithstanding the above, the reasonable cause and good faith exception does not apply if there is a flagrant error on a return or claim for refund, a pattern of errors on a return or claim for refund, or a repetition of the same or similar errors on numerous returns or claims.

5. *Reliance on advice of another preparer.* The IRS will consider whether or not the preparer relied on the advice ("advice") of or schedules prepared by another preparer as defined in Reg. §1.6694-1(b). The reasonable cause and good faith exception applies if the preparer relied in good faith on the advice of another preparer (or a person who would be considered a preparer under Reg. §1.6694-1(b) had the advice constituted preparation of a substantial portion of the return or claim for refund) whom the relying preparer had reason to believe was competent to render such advice. A preparer is not considered to have relied in good faith if—

   i. The advice is unreasonable on its face;

   ii. The preparer knew or should have known that the other preparer was not aware of all relevant facts; or

   iii. The preparer knew or should have known (given the nature of the preparer's practice), at the time the return or claim for refund was prepared, that the advice was no longer reliable due to developments in the law since the time the advice was given.

The advice may be written or oral, but in either case the burden of establishing that the advice was received is on the preparer.[93]

¶940 WILLFUL, RECKLESS OR INTENTIONAL CONDUCT

A more severe penalty of $1,000 is imposed on a return preparer under Code Sec. 6694(b) for any understatement on a return or refund claim which is due either to a willful attempt to understate tax or to a reckless or intentional disregard of rules or regulations. A preparer who attempts wrongfully to reduce the tax liability of a taxpayer by disregarding information furnished to him, or fabricates items or amounts on the return, is subject to the penalty for a willful attempt to

---

[93] Reg. §1.6694-2(d).

understate tax.[94] Thus, if a taxpayer informs the preparer of certain items of income, but the preparer intentionally omits such income from the return, the penalty will apply. The penalty also will be imposed if the preparer is informed that the taxpayer has two dependents but the preparer wrongfully reports six dependents.[95] In any proceeding involving the penalty, the government bears the burden of proving that the preparer willfully attempted to understate the tax liability.[96]

The penalty under Code Sec. 6694(b) also applies when a preparer *recklessly* or *intentionally* disregards a rule or regulation.[97] Such conduct is reckless or intentional if the preparer takes a position on a return or refund claim that is contrary to a rule or regulation and the preparer knows of, or is reckless in not knowing of, such rule or regulation.[98] A preparer is reckless if he or she makes little or no effort to determine whether a rule or regulation exists under circumstances which indicate a substantial departure from what a "reasonable preparer" would do.[99] Thus, the failure of a preparer to research the law for rules and regulations will be judged for purposes of the penalty by a "reasonable preparer" standard of conduct.

The regulations provide that the penalty for reckless or intentional disregard of rules or regulations will not apply in two specific situations. In the first of these, when the position taken by the preparer is contrary to a revenue ruling or notice published in the Internal Revenue Bulletin, the penalty will not be imposed if the position has a realistic possibility of being sustained on its merits.[100] his is the same test applied in determining whether the penalty under Code Sec. 6694(a) applies. Thus, a position adopted which is contrary to a revenue ruling or published notice will not warrant a penalty if the position has a one-in-three, or greater, chance of being sustained. In some instances, the realistic possibility standard will not avoidthe penalty under Code Sec. 6694(b) when the position taken is contrary to a Treasury regulation.[101]

The penalty for reckless or intentional conduct also may be avoided by adequate disclosure of the questionable position taken on the return. Although there are some differences, the disclosure requirements are similar in most respects to the disclosure required under Code Sec. 6694(a) to avoid the penalty for adopting an "unrealistic position."[102] Disclosure under Code Sec. 6694(b), unlike Code Sec. 6694(a), is not adequate if made only on the tax return itself with respect to those items which otherwise are permitted to be disclosed in such manner by an annual revenue procedure.[103] Only Forms 8275 and 8275-R may be used, and the disclosure must identify the rule or regulation that is being

---

[94] Criminal sanctions also may apply. See Chapter 18, *infra.*

[95] Reg. § 1.6694-3(b).

[96] Reg. § 1.6694-3(h).

[97] The regulations define the term "rules or regulations" to include the Internal Revenue Code, temporary or final Treasury Regulations, and revenue rulings or notices published in the Internal Revenue Bulletin. Reg. § 1.6694-3(f).

[98] Reg. § 1.6694-3(c)(1).

[99] *Id.*

[100] Reg. § 1.6694-3(c)(3).

[101] Reg. § 1.6694-3(d), Ex. 4.

[102] See ¶ 939, *supra.*

[103] Note 47, *supra,* and accompanying text.

challenged. Under Code Sec. 6694(b), moreover, if the position taken by the preparer is contrary to a regulation, disclosure is adequate only if the position represents a good-faith challenge to the validity of the regulation.[104]

Both signing and nonsigning return preparers may make a disclosure on Forms 8275 or 8275-R. However, a nonsigning preparer who merely gives advice to a taxpayer or another return preparer may, in the alternative, satisfy the disclosure requirements by informing those who received the tax advice that penalties may be imposed and that disclosure is required.[105] When the advice is given to a taxpayer, the nonsigning preparer must inform the taxpayer that the position is contrary to a specific rule or regulation and subject to the negligence penalty under Code Sec. 6662(c) unless adequately disclosed. If another preparer has been given advice, that preparer must be informed that disclosure under Code Sec. 6694(b) is required. These statements regarding the potential penalties and need for disclosure must be in writing if the tax advice is in writing. If the advice is oral, such statements also may be made orally.

When there is a controversy involving the penalty under Code Sec. 6694(b), the preparer has the burden of proving that he did not recklessly or intentionally disregard a rule or regulation. He also carries the burden of establishing that any challenge to the validity of a regulation was made in good faith and that any disclosure was adequate.[106]

¶941 COMMON PRINCIPLES

Both of the preparer penalties under Code Sec. 6694 have certain principles in common. One of the most significant relates to reliance by a preparer on the information furnished by the taxpayer. The regulations state that a preparer is not required to verify what he receives from a taxpayer and may rely on such information if he does so in good faith.[107] Thus, the preparer is not required to audit, examine or review books and records, business operations or documents in order to independently verify such information. A preparer, however, may not ignore either the implications of the information he receives or what he actually knows. He must make reasonable inquiries if the information appears to be incorrect or incomplete. He also must ask questions to determine the existence of certain facts and circumstances required by the Code or regulations as a condition to the claiming of a deduction. The latter requirement is met with respect to travel and entertainment expenses if the preparer asks the taxpayer whether he has adequate records to substantiate such expenses and the preparer is reasonably satisfied that such records exist.

Another principle common to both penalties under Code Sec. 6694 is that no more than one individual associated with a firm (a sole proprietorship, partnership or corporation) that prepares tax returns is treated as a return preparer with respect to any one return or claim for refund.[108] If two or more individuals in a firm are involved in the preparation of a return, only the signing preparer will be

---

[104] Reg. § 1.6694-3(c)(2).
[105] Reg. § 1.6694-3(e)(2).
[106] Reg. § 1.6694-3(h).

[107] Reg. § 1.6694-1(e).
[108] Reg. § 1.6694-1(b).

treated as a preparer for penalty purposes. If none of the participating individuals in the firm is a signing preparer, the individual in the firm who has overall supervisory responsibility for advice given by the firm with respect to the return or claim will be treated as the preparer.

Under certain circumstances, the preparer penalties will apply not only to the individual preparer but also to the employer of the preparer or the partnership in which the preparer is a partner. The regulations state that the employer or partnership, in addition to the individual preparer, will be liable for the penalty in the following situations:

1. One or more members of the principal management (or principal officers) of the firm or a branch office participated in or knew of the conduct proscribed by Code Sec. 6694(b) or (a);

2. The employer or partnership failed to provide reasonable and appropriate procedures for review of the position for which the penalty is imposed; or

3. Such review procedures were disregarded in the formulation of the advice, or the preparation of the return or claim for refund, that included the position for which the penalty is imposed.[109]

¶943 INJUNCTION AGAINST RETURN PREPARERS

Section 7407 of the Code authorizes the IRS to seek an injunction against any income tax return preparer who is found to have violated certain rules of conduct contained in Code Sec. 7407(b). Included among those rules is conduct subject to penalty under Code Secs. 6694 and 6695. The court has jurisdiction to enjoin the individual from engaging in such conduct, and, if the individual has repeatedly engaged in such conduct, the court can enjoin the individual from acting as anincome tax return preparer. This injunction has been entered on a permanent basis by various courts.[110]

Any one of the following types of conduct may be grounds for injunctive relief:

1. Engaging in any conduct subject to penalty under Code Secs. 6694 or 6695, or subject to any criminal penalty provided by Title 26, United States Code.

2. Misrepresenting the preparer's eligibility to practice before the IRS or otherwise misrepresenting his or her experience or education as an income tax return preparer.

3. Guaranteeing the payment of any tax refund or the allowance of any tax credit.

---

[109] Reg. §§ 1.6694-2(a)(2) and 1.6694-3(a)(2).

[110] *United States v. Owens, Jr.,* 79-2 USTC ¶9742 (C.D. Cal. 1979); *United States v. May,* 83-1 USTC ¶9220 (E.D. Mich. 1983); *United States v. Hutchinson,* 83-1 USTC ¶9322 (S.D. Cal. 1983); *United States v. Bullard,* 89-2 USTC ¶9620 (E.D. Tex. 1989).

4. Engaging in any other fraudulent or deceptive conduct which substantially interferes with the proper administration of the Internal Revenue Laws.

In addition to finding one of these grounds to be present, the court must also find that injunctive relief is appropriate to prevent the recurrence of such conduct.[111]

¶946 AIDING AND ABETTING UNDERSTATEMENT

Section 6701 of the Code imposes a penalty of $1,000 on any person who aids or assists in the preparation of any portion of a return, claim, affidavit or other document, who knows (or has reason to believe) that such portion will be used in connection with any matter arising under the Internal Revenue laws, and who knows that the use of such portion would result in an understatement of tax liability. If the tax liability of a corporation is involved, the penalty is increased to $10,000. This civil penalty is comparable in most respects to the criminal penalty under Code Sec. 7206(2) for willfully aiding or assisting in the preparation or presentation of a false or fraudulent return or document.

The scope of the penalty is extremely broad. It covers not only one who aids or assists, but also any person who advises or procures the preparation of a return or any portion of a return that such person knows will result in an understatement of tax. It includes advice by an attorney or accountant who knowingly counsels such a course of action. One of the purposes of the penalty is to protect taxpayers from advisors who seek to profit by leading innocent taxpayers into fraudulent conduct. The penalty will apply even if the taxpayer does not know the return is false.[112]

The term "procures" includes ordering or causing a subordinate to prepare or present a false return or document. A subordinate is any other person over whose activities the person subject to the penalty has direction, supervision or control. The Code specifically provides that an individual may be a subordinate even though he is a director, officer, employee or agent of the taxpayer involved.[113] Thus, if the president of a corporation instructs the comptroller to prepare false inventory sheets but does not actually prepare the inventory sheets himself, the penalty can be imposed on the president. In fact, because the term "procures" is expanded to include knowing that a subordinate is preparing a false document and failing to prevent the subordinate from doing so, the president could be liable if he merely knew of the false inventory and did nothing to prevent it.

Only one such penalty for each taxable period is to be imposed on the person who is liable, even though there may be more than one item on the return which could be the basis for the penalty. However, a separate penalty may be assessed for each taxpayer whose tax liability was understated.

---

[111] Code Sec. 7407(b)(1) and (2).
[112] Code Secs. 6701(d).
[113] Code Sec. 6701(c)(2).

If a penalty is assessed under Code Sec. 6701, the preparer penalties under Code Sec. 6694 and the penalty for promoting abusive tax shelters under Code Sec. 6700 are not to be imposed. This gives the IRS discretion as to which penalty to assert when some or all of these penalties would be warranted. The Code provides that the burden of proof will be on the IRS in any proceeding to determine liability for the penalty.

¶947 PROMOTING ABUSIVE TAX SHELTERS

A second penalty is aimed at those who organize or promote abusive tax shelters. To be subject to the penalty under Code Sec. 6700, the person must either help organize the tax shelter (partnership or other entity, any investment plan or arrangement or any other plan or arrangement) or participate, directly or indirectly, in its sale. In addition, the person must make or furnish, or cause another person to make or furnish, either a false statement as to the allowability of the tax benefits sought from the shelter or a gross valuation overstatement with respect to the shelter.

For false statements or gross valuation overstatements made or furnished after 1989, the penalty is equal to the lesser of $1,000 for each proscribed tax shelter activity or 100 percent of the gross income derived or to be derived from such activity. For years prior to 1990, the penalty was the greater of $1,000 or twenty percent of the gross income derived or to be derived from such activity. While this penalty is not specifically aimed at return preparers, the scope of the penalty is so broad that it could apply to some activities of professional tax advisors.

In computing this penalty, each sale of an interest in a tax shelter, as well as the organization of each tax shelter plan or entity, will constitute a separate activity subject to the $1,000 penalty.

A statement concerning the tax benefits of the shelter cannot be the basis for the penalty unless the person knows or has reason to know that the statement is false. Such knowledge will be presumed if facts contained in the sales materials indicate that the statement is false. However, if the sales material does not contain such information, the salesperson is not under a duty to make further inquiry. The penalty can be imposed even though there is no reliance on the false statement by the purchasing taxpayer or no actual underpayment of tax. Thus, the penalty can be based on the offering materials alone without the necessity of auditing any returns.

A gross valuation overstatement of the value of property or services occurs when the stated value exceeds two hundred percent of the correct valuation as finally determined. The value of the property or services involved must be directly related to the amount of some deduction or credit allowable to partici-pants in the shelter.[114] The IRS is not required to show an intent to overstate the value in order to sustain the penalty. The penalty, or any part of the penalty, may

---

[114] Code Sec. 6700(b)(1).

be waived by the IRS upon a showing that there was a "reasonable basis for the valuation" and that such valuation was made in good faith.[115]

¶948 PROCEDURAL ASPECTS OF PREPARER PENALTIES

The Internal Revenue Manual instructs examiners that during every field and office examination, the examiner is to determine if return preparer violations exist. The review of the preparer's conduct is separate from the examination of the return, and no discussion of the proposed penalty is to occur in the presence of a taxpayer.[116] Generally, the return preparer penalty is not proposed until the income tax examination is completed.

If indications of conduct violations are found, the examiner is instructed to develop the facts to a point where a determination can be made if a penalty investigation should be opened. This is to be done without discussing the conduct penalty with the preparer. If the examiner concludes that the penalty should be pursued, the case will then be discussed with the examiner's group manager. It is only at such time that a decision is made on whether to begin an investigation. When the examiner is authorized to conduct a penalty investigation, he or she is to contact the preparer to fully develop and document the facts and circumstances with respect to the preparation of the return. The examiner's workpapers must reflect the position of the preparer.

If the examiner determines that a penalty should be asserted, the preparer is given an opportunity to agree to the assessment. The agreement is formalized by executing a Form 5816, Report of Income Tax Return Preparer Penalty Case (see Exhibit 9-3 at ¶953). The same form is used for an unagreed case.

The IRS is not bound by the notice of deficiency requirements prior to the assessment of a preparer penalty. However, an opportunity for an Appeals Office conference is offered. Notice of the proposed assertion of the penalty is given in a thirty-day letter (see Exhibit 9-4 at ¶954) from which the preparer can request an appeal. The IRS will not assess the penalty until the determination of the Appeals Office is final.

If the Appeals Office rejects the preparer's contentions, a notice of assessment of the penalty and demand for payment is sent to the preparer. The preparer can then pay fifteen percent of the penalty assessed within thirty days of assessment and file a claim for refund. If the claim is disallowed, suit may be brought in the district court.

The IRS has three years from the date the return is filed in which to assess any penalty under Code Secs. 6694(a) or 6695. However, in the event the penalty is for willful, reckless or intentional conduct under Code Sec. 6694(b), the Code provides that the penalty may be assessed at any time.[117]

---

[115] Code Sec. 6700(b)(2).
[116] IRM Handbook 4.2.6.8.2.

[117] Code Sec. 6696(d)(1).

¶949 BURDEN OF PROOF

In any proceeding regarding a penalty asserted under Code Secs. 6700 and 6701, the Secretary must bear the burden of proof in establishing that the person is liable for such penalty.[118] To contest the penalties under these provisions, the person assessed may pay fifteen percent of the penalty within thirty days of assessment and file a claim for refund of the amount paid. If this is done, no further proceeding or levy to collect the balance is to commence until final resolution of the proceeding. If the claim is denied, the person assessed may sue in the district court to determine liability for the penalty. However, suit must be brought within the earlier of (1) thirty days after the day on which the claim for refund is denied, or (2) thirty days after the expiration of six months after the day on which the claim for refund was filed. The statute of limitations on collection is suspended while the refund action is pending and the IRS is barred from collecting the penalty.[119]

---

[118] Code Sec. 6703(a).   [119] Code Sec. 6703(c).

¶951 Exhibit 9-1

Form **8275** (Rev. May 2001) Department of the Treasury Internal Revenue Service	**Disclosure Statement** Do not use this form to disclose items or positions that are contrary to Treasury regulations. Instead, use Form 8275-R, Regulation Disclosure Statement. See separate instructions. ▶ **Attach to your tax return.**	OMB No. 1545-0889 Attachment Sequence No. **92**
Name(s) shown on return		Identifying number shown on return

Part I   General Information (see instructions)

	(a) Rev. Rul., Rev. Proc., etc.	(b) Item or Group of Items	(c) Detailed Description of Items	(d) Form or Schedule	(e) Line No.	(f) Amount
1						
2						
3						

Part II   Detailed Explanation (see instructions)

1

2

3

Part III   **Information About Pass-Through Entity.** To be completed by partners, shareholders, beneficiaries, or residual interest holders.

Complete this part only if you are making adequate disclosure for a pass-through item.

Note: *A pass-through entity is a partnership, S corporation, estate, trust, regulated investment company (RIC), real estate investment trust (REIT), or real estate mortgage investment conduit (REMIC).*

1 Name, address, and ZIP code of pass-through entity	**2** Identifying number of pass-through entity
	3 Tax year of pass-through entity / / to / /
	4 Internal Revenue Service Center where the pass-through entity filed its return

For Paperwork Reduction Act Notice, see separate instructions.   Cat. No. 61935M   Form **8275** (Rev. 5-2001)

Form 8275 (Rev. 5-2001)   Page **2**

Part IV	**Explanations** *(continued from Parts I and/or II)*

Form **8275** (Rev. 5-2001)

¶952 Exhibit 9-2

Form **8275-R**	**Regulation Disclosure Statement**	OMB No. 1545-0889
(Rev. February 2002)	Use this form only to disclose items or positions that are contrary to Treasury regulations. For other disclosures, use Form 8275, Disclosure Statement. See separate instructions.	Attachment
Department of the Treasury Internal Revenue Service	▶ **Attach to your tax return.**	Sequence No. **92A**

Name(s) shown on return	Identifying number shown on return

Part I General Information (See instructions.)

(a) Regulation Section	(b) Item or Group of Items	(c) Detailed Description of Items	(d) Form or Schedule	(e) Line No.	(f) Amount
1					
2					
3					

Part II Detailed Explanation (See instructions.)

1

2

3

Part III Information About Pass-Through Entity. To be completed by partners, shareholders, beneficiaries, or residual interest holders.

Complete this part only if you are making adequate disclosure for a pass-through item.

Note: *A pass-through entity is a partnership, S corporation, estate, trust, regulated investment company (RIC), real estate investment trust (REIT), or real estate mortgage investment conduit (REMIC).*

1 Name, address, and ZIP code of pass-through entity	2 Identifying number of pass-through entity
	3 Tax year of pass-through entity / / to / /
	4 Internal Revenue Service Center where the pass-through entity filed its return

For Paperwork Reduction Act Notice, see separate instructions.	Cat. No. 14594X	Form **8275-R** (Rev. 2-2002)

Form 8275-R (Rev. 2-2002)   Page **2**

Part IV	**Explanations** *(continued from Parts I and/or II)*

¶953 Exhibit 9-3

Form **5816** (Rev. August 1990)	Department of the Treasury — Internal Revenue Service **Report of Income Tax Return Preparer Penalty Case**

Name and address of preparer	Check one box below
	 Preparer is:
	     Employer preparer ☐
	     Self-employed preparer ☐
	     Employee preparer ☐

Preparer's social security or employer identification number	Examining district	Agreement ☐ Full ☐ None

Name and title of person with whom penalty was discussed	Date of report	In reply refer to:

The following information identifies the tax return or claim for which penalty is being charged:

Taxpayer's name and address	Taxpayer's social security or employer identification number	Tax period	Master file tax code

Kind of Preparer Penalty Charged	Amount
A. Understatement of tax due to unrealistic positions	
B. Understatement of tax due to willful or reckless conduct.	
C. Negotiating or endorsing a Federal income tax check issued to a taxpayer (other than the preparer)	
D. Failure to keep a copy or list of the returns or claims prepared	
E. Failure to sign return or claim	
F. Failure to provide preparer's social security or employer identification number on return or claim	
G. Failure to furnish a copy of the return or claim to the taxpayer by the time it was presented for taxpayer's signature	
H. Disclosure or use of information, other than to prepare or assist in preparing returns.	
Total penalties	

Other Information	Examiner's signature

- -

Note: Examiner Remove Appeals Message on Unagreed Cases

    I have read the information on the back of this form that explains these penalties as they relate to income tax return preparers. I agree to comply with those provisions in the future.

Consent to Assessment and Collection — I do not wish to exercise my appeal rights with the Internal Revenue Service or to contest in the United States District Court the findings in this report, therefore, I give my consent to the immediate assessment and collection of the tax return preparer penalty.

Preparer's signature and date

PART 1

Form **5816** (Rev. 8-90)

In general, under IRC 7701(a)(36), any person who prepares for compensation, or who employs one or more persons to prepare for compensation, any return of tax or any claim for refund, is considered an income tax return preparer.

A. A penalty is charged the income tax return preparer for understating a taxpayer's tax liability when the understatement is due to unrealistic positions. The penalty is $250 for each return or claim that shows such understatement. (IRC 6694(a).)

B. The penalty for understatement of tax due to willful or reckless conduct is $1,000 for each return or claim, less any penalty paid under IRC 6694(a) unless reasonable cause can be shown and the person charged with the penalty acted in good faith. (IRC 6694(b).)

C. A penalty is charged the income tax preparer for negotiating or endorsing a Federal income tax check issued to a taxpayer (other than the preparer). The penalty is $500 for each check. (IRC 6695(f).)

In addition to the above penalties, the penalties in D through G will also be imposed unless it can be shown that the failure to comply was due to reasonable cause and not due to willful neglect.

D. A penalty is charged the income tax preparer for not keeping a copy or list of the returns or claims prepared. These records must be kept for 3 years. The penalty is $50 for each return or claim not recorded, with a maximum penalty of $25,000 for each return period. (IRC 6695(d).)

E. An income tax preparer can be charged a penalty for each failure to sign a return or claim. The penalty is $50 for each return or claim not manually signed. The maximum penalty, with respect to documents filed during any calendar year, shall not exceed $25,000. (IRC 6695(b).)

F. A penalty is charged income tax return preparers for not providing their identification numbers. The penalty is $50 for each return or claim that does not show an identifying number, to a maximum of $25,000, with respect to documents filed in any calendar year. An individual preparer should use his or her social security number. An individual who is employed by another preparer should show his or her identification number, the identification number of his or her employer and the business address where the return or claim was prepared. For this purpose, the partner in a partnership is considered an employee and should use the partnership's employer identification number. The number must be entered on the return or claim in the space provided. (IRC 6695(c).)

G. A penalty is charged the income tax preparer for not furnishing a copy of the return or claim to the taxpayer by the time it is present for the taxpayer's signature. The penalty is $50 for each return or claim not so provided, to a maximum of $25,000, with respect to documents filed in any calendar year. (IRC 6695(a).)

H. A penalty is charged the income tax preparer if information furnished to him for, or in connection with the preparation of returns of tax is disclosed or used for any other purpose other than to prepare, or to assist in preparing returns. The penalty is $250 for each disclosure or use, to a maximum of $1,000 per person for any calendar year. (IRC 6713(a)(1) and 6713(a)(2).)

Under section 7407 of the Code, the Department of Treasury may seek a court injunction against preparers to either bar them from conduct described in that section or to bar them from acting as income tax return preparers.

¶954 Exhibit 9-4

Internal Revenue Service
District Director

Department of the Treasury

Date:

Information Copy Only

In Reply Refer To:

Person to Contact:

Contact Telephone Number:

>

—

    We have enclosed a copy of our examination report explaining why we are proposing the tax return preparer penalty.

    If you accept our findings, please sign and return the enclosed Form 5838. If a penalty amount is due, you may want to pay it now. Otherwise, we will bill you.

    If you do not accept our findings, we recommend that you request a hearing with the Office of Regional Director of Appeals. If the total penalties in our report are $2,500 or less, a written protest is unnecessary. You may, however, want to send us a statement of your reasons for not accepting our findings along with your request for a hearing. To arrange a hearing in the case of total penalties of more than $2,500, a written protest is necessary.

    The written protest should contain:

    1. A statement that you want to appeal the findings of the examining officer to the Office of Regional Director of Appeals;

    2. Your name and address;

    3. The date and symbols from this letter;

    4. Information to identify the taxpayer's return for which the penalty is being charged;

    5. A statement of facts explaining your position and outlining the law or other authority upon which you rely.

    A statement of facts, under 5 above, must be declared true under penalties of perjury. This may be done by adding to the protest the following signed declaration:

    "Under the penalties of perjury, I declare that I have examined the statement of facts presented in this protest and in any accompanying schedules and statements and, to the best of my knowledge and belief, they are true, correct, and complete."

(over)

Letter 1125(DO) (Rev. 7–80)

If your representative submits the protest for you, a declaration may be substituted stating:

(1) That the representative prepared the protest and accompanying documents; and

(2) Whether the representative knows personally that the statements of fact contained in the protest and accompanying documents are true and correct.

Your representative must have a power of attorney if he or she attends a hearing without you.

Appeals to the court will be to a United States District Court. We will be glad to explain how to appeal to the court.

If we do not hear from you within 30 days, we will have to process your case on the basis of the findings in the examination report. If you have any questions, please contact the person whose name and telephone number are shown in the heading of this letter.

An addressed envelope is enclosed for your convenience.

Thank you for your cooperation.

                                        Sincerely yours,

                                        District Director

Enclosures:
Examination Report
Form 5838
Envelope

¶955 DISCUSSION QUESTIONS

1. Peter Procrastinator forgot to file his 2001 tax return. Eventually the collection function of the IRS contacted him and after several delays was able to secure a tax return early in 2004. The return showed a liability in tax of $5,500, which Peter tendered along with the return. Peter also sent a second check which was computed to pay all of the interest due to date.

   Approximately two months later, Peter received an assessment notice from the Service Center. The notice showed an assessment of tax of $5,500, interest in the approximate amount that Peter had computed, delinquency penalties, and a substantial understatement penalty. Peter wishes to challenge the assessment of the penalties. What are his chances?

2. In August 2003, Paula Preparer was retained as accountant and tax return preparer for a new corporate client. In reviewing the prior returns of the client, Paula noticed that substantial deductions for travel and entertainment expenses had been claimed. She asked the client if the corporation had ever been audited and was told that it had not. Paula knew that the president of the corporation spent a great deal of time traveling and promoting the business, and so in setting up their procedures for the new client, she stressed the importance of keeping adequate records for any travel and entertainment expenses. Paula also discussed the sort of recordkeeping procedures that should be followed by the bookkeeper of the corporation.

   The first fiscal year of the corporation for which Paula prepared its return was the fiscal year ending August 2003. In reviewing the records that were submitted to her, Paula noticed that expenses of $9,500 were claimed for travel and entertainment by the president. Because the sales of the corporation were approximately $750,000 for that year, Paula did not think that the $9,500 figure was out of line. Since Paula had spent so much time stressing the Code Sec. 274 recordkeeping requirements when she was initially retained, she assumed that the taxpayer had followed through on her insistence that adequate records be kept. Paula did not inquire into the adequacy of the T&E records before she prepared the return.

   In 2004, the corporation's return is audited. The agent discovered that included in the $9,500 was approximately $2,000 that constituted personal expenditures of the president and approximately $5,500 for which adequate substantiation did not exist. The IRS has disallowed $7,500 of the deduction to the corporation and is also proposing toassess the penalty under Code Sec. 6694(a) against Paula. Is the proposed penalty assessment justified?

3. Ned Negligent, a not overly careful accountant, has retained you for tax advice. During 2002, in preparing tax returns for several clients, he overlooked the mileage rules and reported deductions based on com-

muting mileage. The IRS audited the returns and assessed penalties under Code Sec. 6694(a).

In preparing the 2004 returns for two of his remaining clients (both of whom had been audited for 2002 and had commuting disallowed), Ned finds that one client forgot to inform him of an IRA he had created in 2002 for which no deduction was taken. The refund for the IRA deduction will be greater than the tax assessed for the mileage deduction. Further, Ned finds that the other client has incurred a net operating loss that will be available for carryback to 2001 (1999 and 2000 also being loss years) and totally eliminate any tax liability for that year. Can the penalty assessed for 2002 against Ned be abated under either of these circumstances?

4. Sterling Clampett is the president and sole shareholder of Spoonful, Inc., a manufacturer of fine flatware. Sterling has always made it his job to sell the scrap silver which remains after the flatware is manufactured. The problem is that Sterling has been selling the scrap as his own, rather than on behalf of the corporation.

   During their recent audit of Spoonful, Inc., the IRS has also discovered Sterling's personal silver sales. The government has enough evidence to sustain a civil fraud penalty. For the tax year 2003, Spoonful, Inc., reported a tax of $125,500. After taking into consideration the adjustments related to the silver sales, the IRS calculated the correct tax for 2003 to be $200,500. Sterling would like to know the maximum amount of penalties that could be imposed against the corporation due to its understatement of tax in 2003.

5. Motoco, Inc., manufactures and designs mopeds which it sells throughout the world. In valuing its inventory for tax purposes, the corporation is subject to the uniform capitalization rules under Code Sec. 263A. Pursuant to the rules, Motoco must include not only direct costs, but also a portion of certain indirect costs in their inventory costs. The president of the corporation argues that the government is wrong in expecting the corporation to treat some of the compensation paid to its officers as inventoriable costs. Therefore, he refuses to capitalize such costs. Is the corporation subject to any penalties as a result of the failure to capitalize the indirect costs?

6. George Baily is the sole shareholder of Building and Loan, Inc. The IRS is conducting an audit and is scrutinizing withdrawals thatGeorge made from the corporation which were used to pay his personal expenses. George has argued that the withdrawals were loans that he had taken from the corporation rather than taxable income to him. He points to the fact that the withdrawals were reflected on the corporation's books and records as "Loans to Stockholders." George also attached Form W-2 to his tax return, disclosing the imputed interest income on his claimed interest-free loan. In addition, he disclosed the interest expense associ-

ated with the claimed loans on various schedules attached to the corporation's return.

Despite George's arguments, the IRS has ultimately determined that George had no intent to repay the withdrawals and, therefore, that amounts withdrawn represent taxable income to him. The deficiencies calculated by the IRS result in a substantial understatement of income tax. George wants to know whether he can avoid any additions to tax due to the deficiencies.

7. The 2003 tax return of Sam Short is being examined by the IRS. His return reported tax due in the amount of $60,000. The Revenue Agent has determined that Sam understated his tax for 2003 by $22,000 and is proposing to assess the substantial understatement penalty. What arguments might Sam make that the penalty should not be imposed?

CHAPTER 10
STATUTE OF LIMITATIONS ON ASSESSMENT

¶1001 INTRODUCTION

In most instances, any tax due must be paid at the time the return is filed. However, if income has not been reported on the return, or if an improper deduction has been taken, the Internal Revenue Service (IRS) can examine the return and seek additional tax in the form of a deficiency. Tax policy suggests that at some point, a taxpayer should be relieved of the responsibility for, and the government should no longer be required to expend its resources in locating, additional amounts of tax from a given year. In the legal system, this function is served by statutes of limitations—laws which specify the amount of time within which an act must be performed to be legally binding.

The Internal Revenue Code (the Code) contains a number of statutes of limitations. In general, these provisions are contained in Subtitle F of the Code, Sections 6501 through 6533. Many other provisions can have an effect on the statute of limitations in different circumstances.

Normally, the IRS must make any assessment of additional tax within three years of the time a return is filed.[1] A return filed prior to the due date is treated for purposes of the statute of limitations as though the return was filed on the due date.[2] If the return is filed after the due date, then the actual date of filing is used.[3] If the return is not filed when due, then the filing date for limitations purposes is the date on which it is actually delivered to the IRS.[4] When a return is filed with the wrong Service Center, moreover, the statute does not begin to run until the redirected return is received by the correct Service Center.[5]

¶1002 TIMELY MAILING IS TIMELY FILING

A return can be deemed timely filed for purposes of determining the commencement of the limitations period when it is postmarked. Thus, even if a return is actually received after the last date prescribed for filing, the return is considered as timely filed if postmarked on or before the due date.[6] Code Sec. 7502, however, isapplicable only to returns timely filed where the envelope containing the return has been properly addressed and bears the proper postage. Since July 30, 1996, the timely-mailing-is-timely-filing rule of Code Sec. 7502 has applied to private delivery services (PDS) as well as to returns sent by the United States

---

[1] Code Sec. 6501(a).

[2] Code Sec. 6501(b)(1).

[3] *Burnet v. Willingham Loan & Trust Co.,* 282 U.S. 437 (1931), S.Ct., 2 USTC ¶655.

[4] *Emmons v. Comm'r,* 92 TC 342 (1989), CCH Dec. 45,490, *aff'd,* 898 F.2d 50 (5th Cir. 1990), 90-1 USTC ¶50,217.

[5] *Winnett v. Comm'r,* 96 TC 802 (1991), CCH Dec. 47,409; Reg. §1.6091-2(a)(2)(C).

[6] Code Sec. 7502.

Postal Service.[7] The IRS has designated a list of approved PDSs.[8] In addition to the transmittal of returns by conventional means a special provision has been made for documents electronically filed. An electronically filed document by an electronic return transmitter is deemed to be filed on the date of the electronic postmark.[9] The timely filing rule of Code Sec. 7502 is equally applicable to foreign postmarks. A return bearing an official foreign postmark dated on or before midnight as of the last date prescribed for filing, including any extensions of time, will be treated as timely filed.[10] The IRS's position is not based on Code Sec. 7502, but on the general authority granted in Code Sec. 6081(a) for the IRS to "grant a reasonable extension of time for filing any return." The decision to accept a return as timely when it is mailed and officially postmarked in a foreign country is a reasonable and proper exercise of the IRS Commissioner's administrative authority.[11]

The IRS has determined that in certain situations, a claim for credit or refund made on a late-filed original return should be treated under Code Sec. 7502 as timely filed on the postmarked date for purposes of Code Sec. 6511(b)(2)(A). This is consistent with the opinion of the United States Court of Appeals for the Second Circuit in *Weisbart v. United States Department of Treasury and Internal Revenue Service*.[12]

¶1003 COMPUTATION OF TIME

In computing the three-year period, the date that the return is actually filed is excluded. When the due date falls on a Saturday, Sunday or legal holiday, Code Sec. 7503 provides that the return will be considered timely filed if it is filed on the next business day. In such an instance, the statute of limitations begins to run on the actual date of filing. For example, if April 15 is a Saturday, a return filed onApril 17, the next business day, is considered timely filed. The IRS has three years from April 17 to assess any additional tax.[13]

The general three-year statute for assessment applies to all income tax returns, as well as estate and gift tax returns. However, in many cases, the three-year statute of limitations will not apply. For example, a deficiency attributable to the carryback of a net operating loss, capital loss or unused tax credit may be assessed within three years of the date of filing the return for the year of loss or

---

[7] Code Sec. 7502(f).

[8] Effective September 1, 1999, the list of designated PDSs was: Airborne Express (Airborne); DHL Worldwide Express (DHL); Federal Express (Fedex); United Parcel Service (UPS). Rev. Proc. 97-19, 1997-1 CB 644.

[9] Reg. §301.7502-1(d); TD 8932. Note the electronic return filing regulation is effective on and after January 11, 2001.

[10] ITA 200012085. But see Reg. §301.7502-1(c)(ii); *Cespedes v. Comm'r*, 33 TC 214 (1959), CCH Dec. 23,833; *Madison v. Comm'r*, 28 TC 1301 (1957), CCH Dec. 22,596; *Electronic Automation Sys., Inc. v. Comm'r*, 35 TCM 1183, TC Memo. 1976-270, CCH Dec. 33,995(M).

[11] ITA 200012085, at p.3.

[12] 222 F.3d 93 (2nd Cir. 2000), 2000-2 USTC ¶50,641. This is applicable for claims for credit or refund made on late-filed original tax returns other than income tax returns. This would include Form 720, Quarterly Federal Excise Tax Returns, and Form 706, U.S. Estate Tax Returns. Moreover the IRS had determined that the late-filed original tax returns as well as the claim for credit or refund should also be treated as filed on the postmarked date. Reg. §301.7502-1(f).

[13] *Brown v. U.S.*, 391 F.2d 653 (Ct. Cl. 1968), 68-1 USTC ¶9275.

credit, even though such date may be well beyond the normal statute of limitations for the year to which the loss or credit was carried.[14]

The passthrough adjustments to an individual's reported income resulting from the IRS examination of S corporations and partnerships raise an interesting question regarding the period of limitations for assessment. Does the limitations period begin to run from the filing date of the return for the passthrough entity or from the date the individual return of the shareholder or partner was filed? With respect to partnerships with more than ten partners and S corporations with more than five shareholders (prior to 1/1/97)[15], this question was specifically answered by the unified audit and litigation procedures for these passthrough entities adopted by the Tax Equity and Fiscal Responsibility Act of 1982 (TEFRA).[16] In general, the statute of limitations for assessments arising from adjustments to the income of these larger passthrough entities is measured from the filing date of the entity's tax return.[17]

For smaller partnerships and other S corporations not subject to the unified audit rules, the answer to the foregoing question was not as clear. With respect to S corporations, the answer was provided by the United States Supreme Court.[18] In *Bufferd v. Commissioner,* the Court held that the period for assessing the income tax liability of an S corporation runs from the date the shareholder files his or her return. With respect to partnerships not covered by the unified audit procedures of TEFRA, the courts have uniformly held that the period of limitations is determined solely on the basis of the partner's individual return.[19] Therefore, the statute of limitations is triggered by the filing of the return of the individual reporting the passthrough entity income and not the return of the entity.

Adopting the Supreme Court's reasoning in *Bufferd,* Congress in 1997 amended the statutory language of Code Sec. 6501(a) by providing that a "return" for the purposes of the statute of limitations on assessment is "the return required to be filed by the taxpayer (and does not include a return of any person from whom the taxpayer has received any item of income, gain, loss, deduction or credit)."[20]

Substantial Understatement

¶1005 OMISSION OF INCOME

If the taxpayer omits income exceeding twenty-five percent of the gross income reported on his or her return, the IRS has a six-year period to assess any

---

[14] Code Sec. 6501(h) and (j).

[15] The Small Business Job Protection Act of 1996, P.L. 104-188; § 1307(c)(1) repealed the application of TEFRA (P.L. 97-248) to S Corporations for the tax years beginning after December 31, 1996.

[16] P.L. 97-248; Code Secs. 6221–6245. For the exclusion of smaller entities from these unified audit rules, see Code Sec. 6231(a)(1)(B), Temp. Reg. § 301.6241-1T(c)(2)(i), and *Eastern States Casualty Agency, Inc. v. Comm'r,* 96 TC 773 (1991), CCH Dec. 47,379.

[17] Code Secs. 6229 and 6244. Further discussion of these special limitations provisions is found in Chapter 7, "Partnership Audit Procedures," *supra.*

[18] *Bufferd v. Comm'r,* 506 U.S. 523 (1993), 93-1 USTC ¶ 50,038.

[19] *Siben v. Comm'r,* 930 F.2d 1034 (2d Cir. 1991), 91-1 USTC ¶ 50,215; *Stahl v. Comm'r,* 96 TC 798 (1991), CCH Dec. 47,395.

[20] Code Sec. 6501(a), as amended by the Taxpayer Relief Act of 1997, P.L. 105-34, § 1284(a), for tax years beginning after August 5, 1997.

additional tax. A similar rule applies to estate tax or gift tax returns where an amount is omitted that exceeds twenty-five percent of the amount of the gross estate or total gifts reported.[21]

On an income tax return reflecting a trade or business, the term "gross income" refers to gross receipts (defined as the total of the amounts received or accrued from the sale of goods or services prior to reduction for the cost of such sales or services). Thus, in determining whether there has been in excess of a twenty-five percent omission, the larger gross receipts figure is used, not the smaller gross profit figure. For example, if a taxpayer has sales of $100,000, costs of goods of $40,000, and gross profit of $60,000, more than $25,000 must be omitted from income for the six-year statute to apply.[22] However, income from the sale of stock or other capital assets is not treated in a similar fashion. For purposes of the six-year statute, gross income from the sale of stock is only the gain actually reported and not the gross proceeds of the sale.[23]

If the net income or loss from a partnership or S corporation is reported on a taxpayer's individual return, his or her share of the gross income reported on the separate tax return of the passthrough entity is added to the gross income reported on that individual's return to determine the amount of gross income to which the twenty-five percent test applies.[24] This is consistent with the repeal of the unified audit rules for S corporations and treatment of subchapter S items at the shareholder level.[25]

The six-year statute of limitations provision has been strictly interpreted to require an omission from gross income. Even if deductions are overstated, thus producing a tax deficiency as significant as would occur with a failure to report gross income, the six-year statute of limitations will not apply.[26] Similarly, where the cost basis of property sold by a dealer has been overstated, thus reducing the profit on sale, the three-year statute of limitations has been held applicable, even though overstating the cost had the same effect as if twenty-five percent of the gross sale proceeds had not been reported.[27] The rationale for this result is that claiming the deductions fully apprises the Secretary of the nature of the items. If there is a substantial omission of gross income, however, the six-year statute of limitations applies to the entire deficiency irrespective of the fact that some items of the deficiency were not included in calculating the omission.[28]

---

[21] Code Sec. 6501(e)(1) and (2).

[22] Code Sec. 6501(e)(1)(A)(i).

[23] *Insulglass Corp. v. Comm'r*, 84 TC 203 (1985), CCH Dec. 41,880.

[24] Rev. Rul. 55-415, 1955-1 CB 412; *Davenport v. Comm'r*, 48 TC 921 (1967), CCH Dec. 28,615. However, if partnership items (or S corporation items) are being adjusted, the special limitations provisions of the TEFRA unified audit procedures may apply. See footnotes 7 and 8, *supra*. Code Sec. 6229(c)(2) provides that, with respect to partnerships subject to the unified audit rules (more than ten partners), the six-year statute applies if more than twenty-five percent of the partnership's gross income is omitted.

[25] For tax years beginning after 1996, rules requiring consistency between the returns of an S corporation and its shareholders are provided at Code Sec. 6037(c).

[26] For instance, in the example above, an overstatement of the cost of goods sold by $30,000 would understate gross profit by $30,000. Similarly, an omission of gross receipts of $30,000 would also understate gross profit by $30,000.

[27] *Colony, Inc. v. Comm'r*, 357 U.S. 28, 78 S.Ct. 1033 (1958), 58-2 USTC ¶9593.

[28] *Colestock v. Comm'r*, 102 TC 380 (1994), CCH Dec. 49,703. In the example above, where there is $100,000 worth of sales and $25,000 is omitted from income, if the IRS disallowed $5,000 of the deduc-

An item is not considered omitted if its existence has been disclosed in the return, or in a statement attached to the return, in a manner that apprises the IRS of the nature and amount of the item.[29] For example, if the return discloses the existence of an item (e.g., a settlement received in litigation) but erroneously takes the position that the amount is not includible in gross income, then the six-year statute of limitations will not apply, even though the omission is more than twenty-five percent of the gross income. Generally, the disclosure must be made on the taxpayer's own return and the fact that a return of a related entity or taxpayer may have disclosed the existence of the item has been held to be insufficient to avoid the six-year statute of limitations.[30]

However, with respect to smaller partnerships not subject to the unified audit procedures of TEFRA and S corporations, disclosure of an item on the partnership or S corporation return constitutes sufficient disclosure on the individual return of the partner or shareholder to avoid the provisions of Code Sec. 6501(e).[31] For larger partnerships covered by the unified rules, the audit is conducted at the partnership level. Special statutes of limitations apply at that level.[32]

False or Fraudulent Return

¶1011 INTENT

Code Sec. 6501(c) provides that when a false or fraudulent return is filed with the intent to evade tax, an additional assessment may be made at any time. The government, however, has the burden of proving by clear and convincing evidence that the taxpayer intended to evade tax. The conviction of the taxpayer in a tax evasion prosecution under Code Sec. 7201 is sufficient to meet this burden of proof and collaterally estops the taxpayer from contending that he did not intend to evade tax.[33]

¶1012 AMENDING A FALSE RETURN

When a taxpayer originally files a false or fraudulent return but later files an amended nonfraudulent return, does the three-year statute of limitations begin to run from the filing of the amended return or does the statute never begin to run? The answer to this question had divided the courts of appeals in several circuits. The United States Supreme Court finally resolved the matter in *Badaracco v. Commissioner*.[34] The Court, in that case, held that the Internal Revenue Code does

---

(Footnote Continued)

tions in the cost of goods, the six-year statute of limitations would not only apply to the $25,000 omitted but also the $5,000 of disallowed deductions.

[29] Code Sec. 6501(e)(1)(A)(ii); Rev. Proc. 2001-11, IRB 2001-2 applicable to any return filed on 2000 tax forms for tax years beginning in 2000. (Guidelines for adequate disclosure).

[30] See *Reuter v. Comm'r*, 51 TCM 99, TC Memo. 1985-607, CCH Dec. 42,536(M).

[31] *Roschuni v. Comm'r*, 44 TC 80 (1965), CCH Dec. 27,345; *Ketchum v. United States*, 697 F.2d 466 (2d Cir.

1982), 83-1 USTC ¶9122 (S corporations); *Walker v. Comm'r*, 46 TC 630 (1966), CCH Dec. 28,080; *Rose v. Comm'r*, 24 TC 755 (1955), CCH Dec. 21,160 (partnerships).

[32] See footnotes 7 and 8, *supra*.

[33] *Taylor v. Comm'r*, 73 TCM 2028, TC Memo. 1997-82, CCH Dec. 51,887(M); *DiLeo v. Comm'r*, 96 TC 858, 885-886 (1991), CCH Dec. 47,423, *aff'd*, 959 F.2d 16 (2nd Cir. 1992), 92-1 USTC ¶50,197.

[34] *Badaracco v. Comm'r*, 464 U.S. 386 (1984), 84-1 USTC ¶9150.

not explicitly provide for either the filing or acceptance of an amended return and that an amended return is merely a creature of administrative origin and grace. It is only the original return, not an amended return, the Court said, which determines which statute of limitations on assessment applies under Code Sec. 6501.[35] An amended return, therefore, does not trigger the three-year statute of limitations. The time to assess remains open on the basis of the fraud in the original return.

No Return Filed

¶1015 STATUTE OF LIMITATIONS

If no return is filed or if an incomplete return is filed, the Internal Revenue Code provides that the tax may be assessed at any time.[36] A return which the IRS prepares and executes on behalf of a nonfiling taxpayer under the authority ofCode Sec. 6020(b) is not treated as a return that will start the running of the statute of limitations.[37] Even if a document denominated as a "return" is filed by the taxpayer, it may not constitute a return that is sufficient to trigger the statute of limitations.

A return sufficient to start the running of the period of limitations generally must be properly signed and contain substantial information as to gross income, deductions and credits.[38] A document described as a "tentative" return, which failed to include items of gross income or any deductions or credits, was held not to be a proper return.[39] The fact that a tentative return is properly signed, moreover, does not validate an improperly signed final return.[40] Even a return which computed the taxable income was held by the Tax Court to be insufficient to commence the running of the statute of limitations where the taxpayer's social security number and occupation were omitted, no information as to personal exemptions was provided and the return was marked "tentative."[41]

On the other hand, the IRS has determined that a Form 1040, U.S. Individual Tax Return, that reports zeroes on each line and is signed by the taxpayer without modification to the attestation statement should be treated as a return for statute of limitation purposes.[42] Alteration of the jurat on the return, however, was sufficient for a finding that the document filed did not constitute a properly executed U.S. Individual Tax Return.[43]

---

[35] See *supra* note 8. The Court noted that courts have consistently held that the filing of an amended return does not serve either to extend the statute of limitations on assessments and refunds or to reduce the six-year limitations period triggered by the omission of gross income in the original return.

[36] Code Sec. 6501(c)(3).

[37] Code Sec. 6501(b)(3).

[38] *Zellerbach Paper Co. Helvering*, 293 US 172 (1934), 35-1 USTC ¶9003.

[39] *Chesterfield Textile Corp. v. Comm'r*, 29 TC 651 (1958), CCH Dec. 22,802.

[40] *General Instrument Corp. v. Comm'r*, 35 TC 803 (1961), CCH Dec. 24,686.

[41] *Foutz v. Comm'r*, 24 TC 1109 (1955), CCH Dec. 21,244. A tampered Form 1040 which deleted various margin and item captions, in whole or in part, and which replaced them with language fabricated by the taxpayer, was also held not to be a valid return (for purposes of the failure to file penalty). *Beard v. Comm'r*, 82 TC 766 (1984), CCH Dec. 41,237, *aff'd per curiam*, 793 F.2d 139 (6th Cir. 1986), 86-2 USTC ¶9496.

[42] SCA 200028033.

[43] *Letscher v. United States*, DC-NY, 2000-2 USTC ¶50,723.

Gift Tax Provision

¶1016 GIFT OMISSION

If a gift has been erroneously omitted from a gift tax return, the tax on such gift may be assessed at any time or a proceeding begun in court for collection of such tax may be begun without assessment at any time. In other words, the statute of limitations does not run on omitted gifts regardless of the fact that a gift tax return was filed for other transfers in the same period.[44] This rule does not apply if the gift tax return discloses the transfer in a manner that adequately apprises the IRS of the nature of the omitted item.[45]

Mitigation Provisions

¶1021 REOPENING A CLOSED TAX YEAR

There are occasions when fairness requires that the taxpayer or the IRS be permitted to reopen a taxable year to avoid the harsh results of the statute of limitations. In 1938, Congress enacted mitigation provisions in an attempt to remedy such inequities. These provisions, as subsequently amended, are now contained in Code Secs. 1311 through 1314. When they apply, they allow the assessment of a deficiency or the refund of an overpayment for a year which would otherwise be barred by the statute of limitations.

These mitigation Code sections are designed essentially to permit the taxpayer or the government to correct the erroneous treatment of income, deductions or credits in a barred year in order to prevent the other party from later gaining an unfair tax benefit by taking an inconsistent position in an open year with respect to the proper year to which such items belong. For example, a taxpayer who has erroneously reported an item of income in a barred year will be entitled to a refund for that year if there is a later determination which adopts the government's position that such income should have been reported in a different year open to assessment. The mitigation provisions similarly would permit the IRS to disallow a deduction and assess the tax for a barred year where a taxpayer claims the same deduction in both the barred year and an open year which is later determined to be the proper year for taking the deduction.

¶1022 MITIGATION FLOWCHARTS

Set forth on the following pages are flowcharts showing the operation of Code Secs. 1311 through 1314. These flowcharts were designed by the IRS and are reprinted from the Internal Revenue Agent Basic Training Coursebook.[46]

---

[44] Code Sec. 6501(c)(9) applicable to gifts made after August 5, 1997.

[45] Rev. Proc. 2000-34, IRB 2000-34, 186, provides guidance for submitting information adequate to meet the disclosure requirement.

[46] For a thorough discussion of the mitigation provisions, see the article written by the drafters of the Code provisions: Surry and Traynor, *§ 820 of the Revenue Act of 1938,* 48 YALE LAW J. 509, 719 (1939). See also, John D. Rice, *When and How Will the Courts Apply the Mitigation Provisions?,* 69 J. OF TAXATION 106 (August 1988).

Figure 24-C(1)
Mitigation of the Statute of Limitations §§ 1311–1314

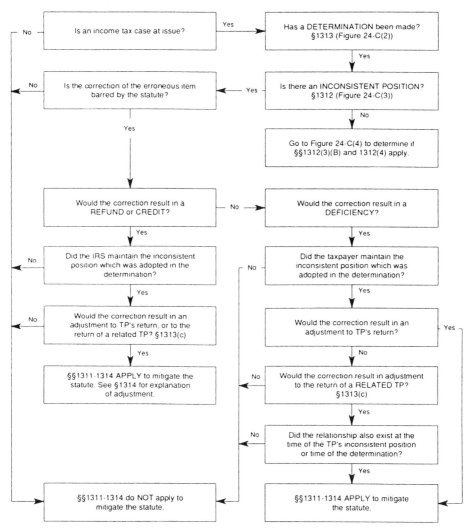

Figure 24-C(2)
Has a Determination Been Made?

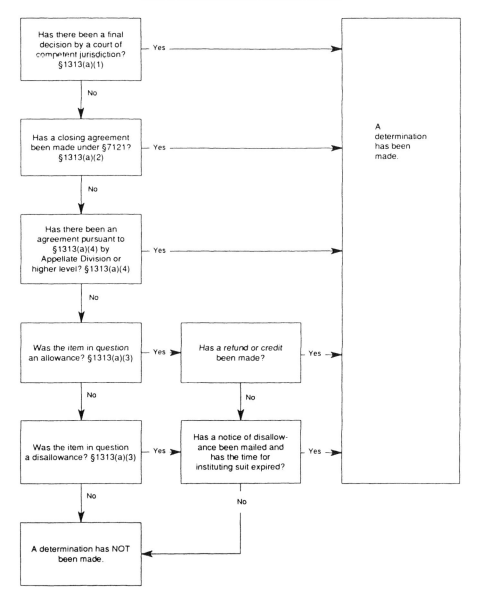

Figure 24-C(3)
Is There an Inconsistent Position?

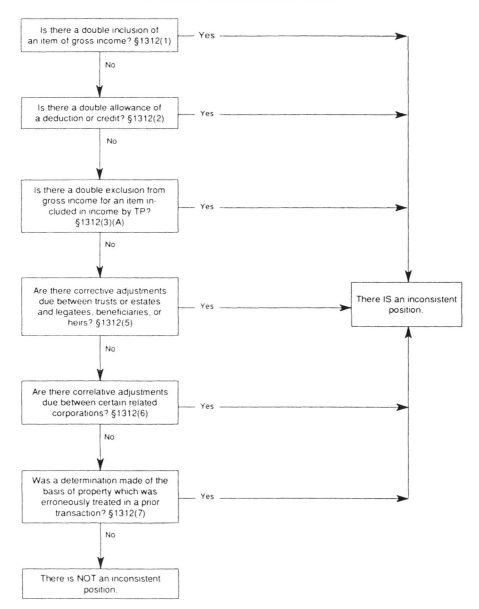

Figure 24-C(4)
Are Situations Described in §1312(3)(B) or 1312(4) Met to Mitigate the Statute of Limitations?

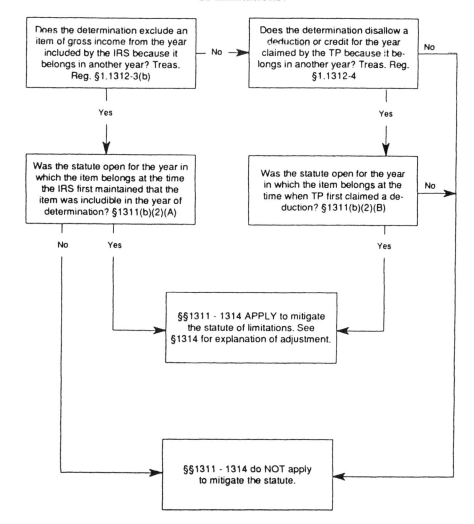

¶1024 REQUIREMENTS FOR MITIGATION

Correction of the erroneous treatment of an item in a barred year is permitted only when the specific requirements of the mitigation provisions of the Code are met. One of the most important prerequisites is a determination, defined in Code Sec. 1313(a), which finally resolves in an open year the proper treatment of the item that was incorrectly included or excluded in the barred year. The law further requires that the determination in the open year and the error in the barred year must result in the double inclusion, exclusion, allowance or disallowance of the item in question or must fall within one of the other sets of circumstances specifically described in Code Sec. 1312.

The third basic requirement that must be met to qualify for mitigation is the adoption of an inconsistent position.[47] The determination of the correct treatment of the questioned item must adopt the position of the party who would benefit from the error in the barred year, and that position must be inconsistent with the erroneous treatment of the item in the barred year. Thus, if the taxpayer takes the same deduction in both a barred year and an open year, a later determination that the taxpayer correctly claimed the deduction in the open year would permit the IRS to disallow the deduction and assess the resulting tax in the barred year.

There are two specific sets of circumstances in which an inconsistent position is not required. These exceptions and the basic prerequisites for mitigation mentioned above are discussed more fully in the following paragraphs (¶1025–¶1034).

¶1025 A DETERMINATION

To qualify for mitigation, a determination in an open year is essential to establish the correct treatment of the item that was erroneously excluded or included in the barred year. A "determination" is defined in Code Sec. 1313(a) to include the following:

1. A final decision or judgment by the Tax Court or any other court;

2. A closing agreement under Code Sec. 7121;[48]

3. A final disposition by the IRS of a claim for refund; and

4. A special agreement between the taxpayer and the IRS which serves as a determination for purposes of mitigation (see Exhibit 10-1 at ¶1051 (Form 2259)).

Final Decision of a Court. A decision of the Tax Court or any other court becomes final when the time for appeal expires. The rules of the various courts establish the period within which an appeal must be taken. If either party appeals, the decision or order of the Court of Appeals becomes final when the time for filing a petition for certiorari to the United States Supreme Court expires or, if filed,when such petition is denied. If certiorari is granted, the decision of

---

[47] Code Sec. 1311(b).

[48] See Chapter 12, The Appeals Office, for further discussion of closing agreements which are final determinations of tax liability binding on both the taxpayer and the IRS.

the Supreme Court becomes final upon issuance of the Supreme Court's mandate.

Final Disposition of a Claim for Refund. The time at which the disposition of a taxpayer's claim for refund becomes final depends initially on whether the claim has been allowed or disallowed. If a refund is *allowed* with respect to an item which is the subject of mitigation, the disposition of the claim becomes final on the date of allowance of the refund. Even if other items included in a claim are denied, or the IRS offsets adjustments to reduce the claim, the disposition becomes final if there is a *net* refund and the item subject to mitigation has been allowed in full. In the unusual situation where there is a full allowance of the item subject to mitigation, but the entire refund is disallowed as a result of other offsetting adjustments by the IRS, the date of final disposition is the date the notice of disallowance is mailed to the taxpayer.[49]

If a refund is *disallowed* with respect to the item subject to mitigation, the disposition generally becomes final when the two-year period for filing a suit for refund expires, unless the taxpayer commences an earlier refund action.[50] This general rule applies even though there is only a partial disallowance of the item subject to mitigation and even though the allowance of other items included in the claim results in a partial refund. In the event the taxpayer files a refund suit, there is no determination until there is a final decision or judgment by the court. As an alternative to either a refund suit or a two-year wait after disallowance of the claim, a taxpayer may obtain a determination by entering into a closing agreement or special determination agreement with the IRS.

When a taxpayer does not include an item subject to mitigation in a claim for refund, but the IRS determines that such an item should be applied to offset or reduce the taxpayer's claim, special rules determine the time at which there is a final disposition with respect to such item. If the net result of the offset or reduction by the IRS is a refund, the disposition becomes final upon expiration of the two-year period within which a suit for refund must be filed, unless the taxpayer institutes an earlier refund action. On the other hand, if the IRS asserts a tax deficiency as a result of applying the item subject to mitigation against the taxpayer's claim, such action does not constitute a final disposition of a claim for refund.[51] The determination of the item causing the deficiency may be obtained only by means of a closing agreement, a special determination agreement or a final court decision.

Special Determination Agreement. Sec. 1313(a)(4) of the Internal Revenue Code provides that a special agreement between the IRS and the taxpayer relating to the tax liability of the taxpayer will serve as a determination for purposes of mitigation. The specific terms and conditions required in such anagreement are prescribed by regulation.[52] Form 2259, Agreement as a Determi-

---

[49] Reg. § 1.1313(a)-3(b).
[50] Reg. § 1.1313(a)-3(c). See Chapter 15, Claims for Refund or Abatement, *infra*.

[51] Reg. § 1.1313(a)-3(d).
[52] Reg. § 1.1313(a)-4.

nation Pursuant to Sec. 1313(a)(4) of the Internal Revenue Code (see Exhibit 10-1 at ¶1051), is the form provided by the IRS for this purpose.

This special agreement permits an expeditious method of obtaining the determination required for mitigation. Although the parties agree to the amount of the income tax liability for the open taxable year, the agreement does not establish and is not binding with respect to such tax liability. The determination becomes final only when the tax liability for the open year becomes final.[53] Until such finality, the IRS and the taxpayer may attempt to change or modify the stated liability. Thus, a taxpayer may file a claim for refund or the IRS may issue a notice of deficiency asserting a different tax liability for the open year. A subsequent determination adopting a modified tax liability for the open year will provide the basis for a change in the mitigation adjustment for the barred year. Despite the lack of finality with respect to the tax liability stated in the agreement, such an agreement does permit the immediate allowance of a refund or assessment of a deficiency.

In addition to the agreed-upon tax liability for the open year, the special agreement also must contain the following:

1. A reference to any concurrently executed documents, such as a waiver of the restrictions on assessment or a Tax Court stipulation, which affect the stated tax liability for the open year;

2. A concise statement of the material facts with respect to the erroneously treated item in the closed year, including a statement of the manner in which such item was treated in the open year;

3. A statement of the amount of the mitigation adjustment to tax liability resulting from correction of the erroneously treated item in the barred year; and

4. A waiver of restrictions on assessment and collection of any deficiencies resulting from the mitigation adjustments in the barred year.[54]

The amount of tax stated in the determination agreement for the open year may be the amount shown on the tax return. Such an agreement, however, is frequently executed concurrently with documents modifying the open-year tax liability. Typical examples of such documents would include a waiver of restrictions on assessment and collection of a deficiency or acceptance of an overassessment, as well as a Tax Court stipulation resolving an item subject to mitigation. The execution of such documents in conjunction with the determination agreement not only expedites the mitigation adjustment, but often permits refunds and deficiencies in open and barred years to be offset against one another.[55]

¶1026 QUALIFYING CIRCUMSTANCES

The determination in the open year and the erroneous treatment of the item subject to mitigation in the barred year must involve one of the following "circumstances of adjustment" set forth in Code Sec. 1312:

---

[53] Reg. § 1.1313(a)-4(d).
[54] Reg. § 1.1313(a)-4(b).
[55] Reg. § 1.1313(a)-4(a)(2).

1. *Double inclusion of an item of income* resulting from the inclusion of an item of income in the open year and the erroneous inclusion of the same item in the barred year;

2. *Double allowance of a deduction or credit* caused by the allowance of a deduction or credit in the open year and the erroneous allowance of the same item in the barred year;

3. *Double exclusion of an item of income* which occurs when an item of income is reported or included in the open year and erroneously omitted in the barred year, and a subsequent determination adopts the position that the item was erroneously reported in the open year and should be excluded;

4. *Double exclusion of an item of income* which results when an item of income is not reported or taxed in either the open year or the barred year, and a subsequent determination adopts the position that the item was properly excluded from income in the open year;

5. *Double disallowance of a deduction or credit* which occurs when the determination disallows a deduction or credit which should have been allowed, but was not allowed, for another taxable year;

6. *Correlative deductions and inclusions for trusts or estates and legatees, beneficiaries, or heirs* are also circumstances which permit mitigation when a determination disallows, allows, includes, or excludes a deduction or item of income with respect to a trust or estate and any of their distributees, and such determination has a correlative tax effect on a barred year of the other related party or parties;

7. *Correlative deductions and credits for certain related corporations* similarly permit mitigation when a determination allows or disallows a deduction or credit to a corporation, and a correlative deduction or credit has been erroneously allowed or disallowed with respect to a related corporation belonging to the affiliated group (as defined in Code Sec. 1504); or

8. *A determination of the basis of property after erroneous treatment of a prior transaction* permits mitigation and the correction of the following errors which may have occurred in barred years in respect to any transaction on which such basis depends or in respect to any transaction which was erroneously treated as affecting such basis:

    a. an erroneous inclusion in, or omission from, gross income,

    b. an erroneous recognition or nonrecognition of gain or loss, or

    c. an erroneous deduction of an item properly chargeable to a capital account or an erroneous charge to a capital account of an item properly deductible.

Mitigation relief from the above errors is available only to the following three classes of taxpayers:

1. The taxpayer with respect to whom the determination of basis is made;

¶1026

2. The taxpayer who acquired title to the property in the erroneously treated transaction and from whom (either mediately or immediately) the taxpayer, with respect to whom the determination is made, derived title; or

3. The taxpayer who had title to the property at the time of the erroneously treated transaction and from whom (either mediately or immediately) the taxpayer, with respect to whom the determination is made, acquired title to the property as a gift with a carryover basis.[56]

Exceptions and Special Restrictions. In all of the above circumstances of adjustment, with two important exceptions, it is also essential to establish that an inconsistent position was maintained by the party who would benefit from the error in the barred year and that this position was adopted in the determination.[57] The two exceptions to the inconsistent position requirement are set forth in items four and five, above. Thus, where the determination rejects the position of the government that an item of income should be included in an open year, and the taxpayer has not reported the income in either that year or a prior year where such income properly belongs, existence of an inconsistent position is irrelevant. This is also true when the determination disallows a deduction or credit claimed by the taxpayer in an open year, and the deduction or credit was not allowed, but should have been allowed, in a prior year.

Although these two circumstances of adjustment are excluded from the inconsistent position requirement, they must meet a much more stringent test before mitigation will be permitted. In the case of the double exclusion of an item of income never taxed or reported by the taxpayer, a determination rejecting the government's position that the income should be included in an open year will not permit the government to open a barred year unless the statute of limitations with respect to the barred year was still open at the time the government first maintained its position in a notice of deficiency sent to the taxpayer.[58]

The purpose of this requirement is to prevent the government from attempting to open a barred year by manipulating the mitigation provisions whenever-omitted income is discovered after the period of limitations on assessment has run. Without the special restriction, an unfounded claim by the government that the income should have been reported in an open year would force the taxpayer to take an inconsistent position. The anticipated determination rejecting the government's baseless claim would then trigger mitigation relief and permit assessment of tax on the income omitted in the barred year.

For similar reasons, a special restriction also is imposed when the double disallowance of a deduction or credit is involved. If a determination disallows in an open year a deduction claimed by the taxpayer which was properly allowable in an earlier year, the mitigation provisions will not apply unless a refund for the earlier year was not barred at the time the taxpayer first maintained in writing

---

[56] See Reg. §1.1312-7 for examples of the manner in which the mitigation provisions are applied to erroneously treated transactions relating to basis.

[57] Code Sec. 1311(b)(1).
[58] Code Sec. 1311(b)(2)(A).

before the IRS or before the Tax Court that he or she was entitled to such deduction or credit in the open year.[59] Writings that will determine the time at which the deduction was first claimed include tax returns, claims for refund, protests and Tax Court petitions.

This restriction in the case of double disallowances is imposed to prevent a taxpayer from improperly using the mitigation provisions to obtain a refund for a deduction that he or she belatedly discovers should have been taken in a barred year. By claiming such a deduction in a current tax return or in a claim for refund for an open year, the taxpayer would force the IRS to take an inconsistent position with respect to the proper year of deduction. In the absence of the special restriction, a subsequent determination disallowing the deduction in the open year would then permit the taxpayer to open the barred year and obtain a refund. In substance, these restrictions ensure that only those who make good-faith claims regarding the proper year for taking a deduction or reporting income are allowed relief under the mitigation statutes.

Related Taxpayers. Although the mitigation provisions are most commonly applied in order to correct errors relating to the proper year in which an item should be included or allowed, they also provide relief when the error involves the proper allocation of an item between certain related taxpayers. Mitigation is available only when one of the following relationships exists:

1. Husband and wife;

2. Grantor and fiduciary;

3. Grantor and beneficiary;

4. Fiduciary and beneficiary, legatee or heir;

5. Decedent and decedent's estate;

6. Partner; or

7. Member of an affiliated group of corporations (as defined in Code Sec. 1504).[60]

The same mitigation rules applicable to the correction of an error resulting from selection of an improper year also apply to correction of an error caused by the incorrect allocation of items between related taxpayers. A determination is essential and, except for the two instances previously discussed, so is an inconsistent position. The situation requiring relief also must fall within one of the circumstances of adjustment involving the double inclusion or exclusion of an item of income or the double allowance or disallowance of a deduction or credit.[61]

The application of the mitigation provisions to related taxpayers may be illustrated by the following example: Partner A deducts 100 percent of a partnership loss, while Partner B deducts none of the loss. Partner B later decides he is entitled to a deduction of fifty percent of the loss and files a claim for refund

---

[59] Code Sec. 1311(b)(2)(B).
[60] Code Sec. 1313(c).
[61] Reg. § 1.1313(c)-1.

based on his share of the loss. The IRS allows the refund claim but discovers that the statute of limitations is no longer open for an assessment against Partner A to recover the tax on his erroneous deduction.

In the above example, the IRS will be permitted to open the barred year and make the assessment against Partner A. The requirements for mitigation have been met. The allowance of the claim for refund by the IRS constitutes a determination. The allowance of the same fifty-percent portion of the loss to both partners would be a "double allowance of a deduction," one of the circumstances of adjustment. Finally, Partner B successfully maintained in his refund claim an inconsistent position with respect to the deduction erroneously claimed by Partner A in the barred year.

When the related taxpayer is the party seeking mitigation relief, the relationship must have been in existence at some time during the year in which the erroneous treatment occurred.[62] The relationship need not exist throughout the entire year of the error.[63] If such relationship exists, moreover, it is not essential that the error result from a transaction made possible only because of such relationship. For example, if one partner erroneously assigns rent income to his partner, and such rent is not connected in any way to their partnership, the partner relationship in itself is sufficient to afford mitigation relief.[64]

When the government is the party attempting to open a barred year to assess tax against a related taxpayer, the time at which the relationship was in existence must meet a more stringent test. For the IRS to obtain such relief, the relationship must exist not only at some time during the year of the error, but also at the time the taxpayer first maintains the inconsistent position in a tax return, claim for refund or petition to the Tax Court.[65] If none of these documents have been filed, then the relationship must exist at the time the determination adopts the inconsistent position.

¶1028 INCONSISTENT POSITION

An inconsistent position is an essential requirement for mitigation relief in all but two of the situations described as circumstances of adjustment in Code Sec. 1312. The two situations excepted from the inconsistent position requirement involve the double disallowance of a deduction and the double exclusion of an item of income not previously reported or taxed.[66]

In all other cases, the party who would benefit from the error in the barred year must maintain a position with respect to the treatment of an item in an open year, and that position must be adopted in the determination and must be inconsistent with the erroneous treatment of the item in the barred year.[67] To avoid the confusion that sometimes occurs, it is important to emphasize the

---

[62] Code Sec. 1313(c).

[63] Reg. § 1.1313(c)-1.

[64] *Id.*

[65] Code Sec. 1311(b)(3). The courts are divided on whether or not an "active" inconsistency is required for this purpose. *Yagoda v. Comm'r*, 331 F.2d 485 (2d Cir. 1964), 64-1 USTC ¶9448 (not required); *Estate of Weinrich v. Comm'r*, 316 F.2d 97 (9th Cir. 1963), 63-1 USTC ¶9420 (required).

[66] See ¶926 for previous discussion of these exceptions.

[67] Code Sec. 1311(b)(1).

specific requirement that the inconsistent position must not only be maintained, but must also be "adopted" in the determination. Regardless of what position the government or taxpayer may maintain at any other time and for any other purpose, it is only the position which is both maintained *and* adopted in the determination which is controlling. Thus, a position taken by the government in a ruling or unrelated proceeding is irrelevant if the determination adopts a contrary position advanced by the government.

The inconsistent position must be that of the party who would benefit from the error in the barred year. It cannot be that of the party who is seeking to correct the error. Thus, if the taxpayer is attempting to obtain a refund for a barred year, the IRS is the party who must have successfully maintained the inconsistent position in the open year. Conversely, if the government is seeking to assess a tax in a closed year, it is the taxpayer's inconsistent position which must have been adopted in the determination.

The inconsistent position is always attributed to the party who successfully advanced and maintained that position. It is irrelevant that the prevailing party may have been forced to raise the position as a defense. Furthermore, a party does not become the party who maintained the inconsistent position simply by agreeing to the position initially advanced by the adverse party. For example, if the government agrees to the position of the taxpayer in allowing a claim for refund, such agreement does not constitute an inconsistent position attributable to the government.

¶1030 MITIGATION ADJUSTMENT

Once it is determined the mitigation provisions apply, the increase or decrease in tax liability for the barred year must be determined. With several importantexceptions, the computation follows the normal procedures for determining a deficiency or overpayment of tax for an open year. The most important distinction is the requirement that the adjustment of tax in the barred year must be based solely on the erroneously treated item which is the subject of mitigation.[68] No other items that may have been incorrectly reported or treated in the barred year may be included in the computation or utilized by way of setoff or credit to reduce or increase the deficiency or overpayment.[69] The equitable principle of setoff, which normally permits a tax claim to be reduced by other errors discovered in the return, does not apply. Although other erroneous items in the barred year must be ignored, this does not prevent the eventual overpayment or deficiency determined under the mitigation provisions from being credited against, or offset by, overpayments or tax liabilities for other years.[70]

The deficiency or overpayment of tax resulting from the mitigation computation is subject to the same interest and penalty provisions that would apply to an open year. All penalty and tax determinations, however, are made in accordance with the tax law in effect for the year of adjustment. If the mitigation computation produces a net operating loss or capital loss which may be carried

---

[68] Code Sec. 1314(a)(2).

[69] Code Sec. 1314(c).

[70] Reg. § 1.1314(c)-1(e).

back or forward to other barred years, the resulting overpayment or deficiency in those years is also allowable as a mitigation adjustment subject to assessment or refund.[71]

In order to recover the overpayment or assess the deficiency for the barred year, the normal refund and assessment procedures must be followed. Thus, a refund claim must be filed by the taxpayer or a deficiency notice must be issued by the government unless the matter is resolved earlier by agreement or consent of the parties.

A special *one-year statute of limitations* applies to the recovery or assessment of tax for the mitigation year.[72] The one-year period of limitations begins to run on the date of the determination which adopts the inconsistent position triggering the mitigation relief. Therefore, a refund claim must be filed by the taxpayer within one year of the determination date. The government also must issue its notice of deficiency within the same one-year period.

¶1034 JUDICIAL MITIGATION

Before the statutory mitigation provisions were enacted in 1938, those who sought to open a barred year were required to rely on the judicially created doctrine of equitable recoupment. That doctrine is no longer applicable to income tax cases now covered by the statutory provisions.[73] Equitable recoupment, however, continues to offer relief from the statute of limitations in cases involving estate, gift and excise taxes.

Other principles also have been developed by the courts to permit the avoidance of the statutory bar. These equitable and judicial doctrines are discussed below.[74]

Equitable Recoupment. The underlying purpose of this equitable doctrine is similar to that of the statutory mitigation provisions. That purpose is to prevent a party from gaining an unfair tax benefit from the statutory bar by inconsistently treating a single transaction or item in different years or between related taxpayers.[75] The doctrine also applies when inconsistent legal theories may permit the imposition of two different taxes on the same transaction. Thus, a barred income tax overpayment may be offset against an excise tax deficiency, and an overpaid, but barred, estate tax may be applied against an income tax deficiency.[76]

---

[71] Reg. § 1.1314(a)-1 and -2.

[72] Code Sec. 1314(b).

[73] The Ninth Circuit has indicated that the equitable recoupment doctrine may have continued vitality in those income tax situations not technically subject to statutory relief. *Kolom v. United States*, 791 F.2d 762 (9th Cir. 1986), 86-1 USTC ¶9471. In the words of the Supreme Court, however, this might be "little more than overriding Congress' judgment as to when equity requires that there be an exception to the limitations bar." *United States v. Dalm*, 494 U.S. 596 (1990), 90-1 USTC ¶50,154.

[74] See Camilla E. Watson, *Equitable Recoupment: Revisiting an Old and Inconsistent Remedy*, 65 FORD-HAM L. REV. 691 (1996).

[75] *Stone v. White*, 301 U.S. 532 (1937), 37-1 USTC ¶9303. Unpaid tax on trust income taxable to beneficiaries could be recouped by the IRS against claim for refund of income tax paid by trust on same income.

[76] *Bull v. United States*, 295 U.S. 247 (1935), 35-1 USTC ¶9346—estate tax overpayment could be recouped by estate against income tax on same payment reported on both the estate tax and income tax returns; Rev. Rul. 71-56, 1971-1 CB 404—estate tax overpayment attributable to an income tax deficiency of the decedent could be offset against the deficiency; Ltr. Rul. 8333007 (May 16, 1983)—overpayment of income tax could be applied against an

When such inconsistency occurs, the party who has been unfairly treated is permitted to recoup or offset an erroneous underpayment or overpayment of tax in a barred year against a claimed refund or assessment in the open year. Equitable recoupment is a defensive doctrine which affords relief only by way of offset and only against a tax claim which itself is not time-barred.[77] It may not be used affirmatively to initiate an independent suit for the refund of a barred tax. Moreover, if the amount of the erroneous tax exceeds the tax against which recoupment is sought, the excess amount is not recoverable.

Setoff. The doctrine of setoff applies in those instances where the taxpayer files a timely claim for refund at a time when the statute of limitations bars the government from assessing tax for the year to which the refund relates. Despite the statutory bar, this doctrine permits the government to offset against the claimed refund any adjustments for errors discovered in the refund year which are favorable to the government.[78] A return may be reaudited for the purpose ofdiscovering such offsetting errors. Should the amount of such errors exceed the refund claimed, however, the statute of limitations bars any additional assessment.

Equitable Estoppel. Estoppel is a broad equitable doctrine which extends into many areas of tax law and applies to both the IRS and the taxpayer. In general, it prevents or estops a party from taking unfair advantage of another party's action or failure to act which has been caused by the misrepresentation or concealment of material facts by the party to be estopped.[79]

The doctrine of equitable estoppel finds limited application with respect to the statute of limitations. It has been utilized principally by the government in cases involving the alteration of consent forms agreeing to the extension of the statute of limitations (see ¶1038, *infra*). In such cases, the IRS may contend that it relied on the intentional misrepresentation or misleading silence by the taxpayer with respect to the alteration of the consent and that the taxpayer should be equitably estopped from claiming that the statute of limitations has expired.

¶1036 CONSENT

The taxpayer can voluntarily agree with the IRS to extend the time within which the tax may be assessed. This extension by consent, however, is not available in the case of estate tax assessments.[80]

Form 872, Consent to Extend the Time to Assess Tax (see Exhibit 10-2 at ¶1052), is the form normally used by the IRS when a taxpayer voluntarily agrees to extend to a specified date the period in which an assessment can be made. If an extension on a Form 872 is limited to specific issues, the IRS must adhere to

---

(Footnote Continued)

outstanding excise tax deficiency which caused the overpayment.

[77] In *United States v. Dalm, supra,* note 56, the Supreme Court held that the doctrine of equitable recoupment does not confer upon a court the jurisdiction necessary to hear a time-barred refund suit for the recovery of gift taxes erroneously paid on the

receipt of funds that were subsequently taxed as income.

[78] *Lewis v. Reynolds,* 284 U.S. 281 (1932), 3 USTC ¶856.

[79] *Sangers Home for Chronic Patients v. Comm'r,* 72 TC 105 (1979), CCH Dec. 36,001.

[80] Code Sec. 6501(c)(4).

the restrictions agreed upon in the extension.[81] Form 872 should be contrasted with the provisions in Form 872-A, Special Consent to Extend the Time to Assess Tax (see Exhibit 10-3 at ¶1053). A Form 872-A is normally used by the Appeals Office and indefinitely extends the time within which the tax may be assessed. The extension will not terminate until ninety days after (1) the IRS receives a notice of termination on Form 872-T (see Exhibit 10-4 at ¶1054) executed by the taxpayer, or (2) the IRS mails either a notice of deficiency or a Form 872-T, Notice of Termination of Special Consent to Extend the Time to Assess Tax, to the taxpayer. An extension on Form 872-A can be terminated only in accordance with its terms and will not expire by operation of law simply as a result of the passage of a reasonable period of time.[82] The execution of a closing agreement will not terminate a Form 872-A extension,[83] nor will a letter sent by the IRS or the taxpayer be sufficient.[84] Even the mailing of a deficiency notice will not serve to terminate theconsent after ninety days unless the notice is mailed to the correct address of the taxpayer.[85] A thirty-day letter also will not commence the running of the ninety-day termination period after thirty days, even though the letter indicates that a notice of deficiency will be issued if there is not a timely response.[86]

By executing a Form 872-A, the taxpayer gives an open-ended extension of the statute of limitations to the IRS. Either the taxpayer or the IRS can use a Form 872-T to terminate the extension of time given by a Form 872-A. Revenue Procedure 79-22[87] specifically provides that written notification of termination can only be made by using Form 872-T. The notification form, moreover, must be sent to the IRS office considering the case, and delivery to another IRS office or representative may not be sufficient to start the running of the ninety-day period following notice of termination. In *Burke v. Commissioner*,[88] the Tax Court held that delivery of a termination notice to an IRS Collection Division representative was insufficient.

Special consent forms are used by the IRS to extend the limitations period with respect to partnerships and S corporations subject to the unified audit procedures of Code Secs. 6221 to 6245. These forms are similar in effect to Forms 872 and 872-A, but are given special letter designations (e.g., 872-P). They extend the time to assess the individual partners or shareholders for any tax resulting from audit adjustments to partnership or S corporation items (see Exhibit 10-5 at ¶1055, Exhibit 10-6 at ¶1056, Exhibit 10-7 at ¶1057, and Exhibit 10-8 at ¶1058). Other special consent forms are available for extending the time to assess

---

[81] *Ripley v. Comm'r*, 103 F.3d 332 (4th Cir. 1996), 96-2 USTC ¶60,253.

[82] *Estate of Camara v. Comm'r*, 91 TC 957 (1988), CCH Dec. 45,181; *Wall v. Comm'r*, 875 F.2d 812 (10th Cir. 1989), 89-1 USTC ¶9343.

[83] *Silverman v. Comm'r*, 105 TC 157 (1995), CCH Dec. 50,878, *aff'd* 86 F.3d 260 (1996), 96-2 USTC ¶50,327.

[84] *Grunwald v. Comm'r*, 86 TC 85 (1986), CCH Dec. 42,841; *Myers v. Comm'r*, 52 TCM 841, TC Memo.

1986-518, CCH Dec. 43,447(M), and *Aronson v. Comm'r*, 989 F.2d 105 (2nd Cir. 1993), 93-1 USTC ¶50,174.

[85] *Roszkos v. Comm'r*, 850 F.2d 514 (9th Cir. 1988); *Coffey v. Comm'r*, 96 TC 161 (1991), CCH Dec. 47,135.

[86] *Kinsey v. Comm'r*, 859 F.2d 1361 (9th Cir. 1988), 88-2 USTC ¶9563.

[87] 1979-1 CB 563.

[88] 53 TCM 1279, TC Memo. 1987-325, CCH Dec. 44,015(M).

¶1036

miscellaneous excise taxes (see Exhibit 10-9 at ¶1059) or to assess the tax return preparer penalty (see Exhibit 10-10 at ¶1060).

The forms for the extension of the limitations period require execution both by the taxpayer (or the taxpayer's representative) and by an authorized representative of the Internal Revenue Service.[89] Both parties must execute the extension prior to expiration of the time within which the assessment can be made. If the taxpayer executes the consent prior to the expiration of the statute of limitations but the IRS does not execute it until after the expiration, the extension will not be valid. An extension may be further extended by an additional consent properly executed before the expiration of the previously extended time to assess the tax.

An extension of the statute of limitations is invalid if the consent of the taxpayer is obtained by coercion or under duress. For example, where consent was coerced by threat of seizure of property, the Tax Court treated the extension as void.[90] Similarly, where the imposition of the fraud penalty was threatened in order to secure an extension, the assessment was rejected as untimely.[91]

If, in the course of an examination, there is one issue which cannot be resolved prior to the expiration of the statute of limitations, even though all other issues have been resolved, the IRS will generally request that the taxpayer extend the statute of limitations. The taxpayer normally will be reluctant to subject the entire return to the possibility of additional assessment when only one issue remains in controversy. In such a situation, a procedure exists for the IRS to secure a restricted consent. Under such a consent, the statute of limitations will be extended only with regard to the remaining unagreed issue. Restricted consents are executed on Form 872 and, in some cases, on Form 872-A.

Revenue Procedures 68-31 and 77-6 set forth the circumstances under which the IRS will seek a restricted consent.

Revenue Procedure 68-31

Section 1. PURPOSE.

This issuance supersedes Revenue Procedure 68-3, C.B. 1968-1, 745, which contains procedures under which the scope of a consent, Form 872, extending the limitation period for assessment under sec. 6501(c) of the Internal Revenue Code of 1954 may be restricted to one or more issues.[92]

Sec. 2. BACKGROUND.

.01 Occasionally in the course of examination of a tax return or during Appellate proceedings, issues are confronted which cannot be resolved within the normal limitation period, or prior extensions thereof, because of the need to await establishment of an interpretative position through court decision, regulation, ruling or other National Office action.

---

[89] Reg. §301.6501(c)-1(d); IRM 1.2.2.24, Order Number 42.

[90] *Robertson v. Comm'r,* 32 TCM 955, TC Memo. 1973-205, CCH Dec. 32,136(M).

[91] *Alfred J. Diescher,* 18 BTA 353, 358 (1929), CCH Dec. 5658.

[92] 1968-2 CB 917.

.02 Generally, in cases described in .01 above, where there is agreement on other issues, if any, it serves the interests of both the taxpayer and the Service to conclude the action on agreed issues and to restrict the scope of extensions of the period for assessment to the issue or issues held in suspense.

Sec. 3. PROCEDURE.

.01 Restricted consents referred to herein will be entered into only under circumstances described in section 2.01 or where other equally meritorious circumstances exist.

.02 The use of a restricted consent at the district level must be approved by the Chief, Audit Division, and at the Appellate level by the Chief, Associate Chief, or Assistant Chief of the Branch Office.

.03 Where there are issues other than the one or more subject to the restricted consent such issues must be agreed and a partial waiver executed on Form 870 (or Form 870 AD where appropriate).

.04 Where resolution of the principle [sic] issues subject to the restricted consent has an automatic effect on other items (e.g., foreign tax credit which may be changed in reaching a decision on an international issue; medical expense or contribution deductions which must be changed upon an increase or decrease in income), the restricted consent will cover both the principal issues and the related or automatic items.

Sec. 4. EFFECTIVE DATE.

This Revenue Procedure is effective August 26, 1968.

Revenue Procedure 77-6

Section 1. PURPOSE.

The purpose of this Revenue Procedure is to modify section 3.04 of Rev. Proc. 68-31, 1968-2 C.B. 917, concerning the language of a restricted consent on Form 872, Consent Fixing Period of Limitation Upon Assessment of Income Tax.[93]

Sec. 2. BACKGROUND.

.01 Section 3104 of Rev. Proc. 68-31 provides that where resolution of the principal issues subject to the restricted consent has an "automatic effect" on other items, the restricted consent will cover both the principal issues and the "related or automatic items". Automatic effect means any direct or indirect effect on other items caused by an adjustment to the principal issues. In order to avoid any misunderstanding of the above quoted phrases, they are being changed to read "a direct or indirect effect" and "consequential changes", respectively.

.02 To illustrate the principle of consequential changes, assume the principal issue subject to a restricted consent involves the allowability of an exemption for a claimed dependent. If resolution of the issue results in an adjustment to disallow the exemption, the *prime* effect of the adjustment is an increase in taxable income in the amount of the exemption. One possible *direct* consequence

---

[93] 1977-1 CB 539.

of the adjustment is the disallowance of any medical expenses claimed for the disallowed dependent. If this direct consequence reduces the total itemized deductions to the point that the standard deduction is greater, the disallowance of all itemized deductions and the allowance of the standard deduction would be *indirect* consequences of the adjustment to the principal issue.

.03 To illustrate further, any adjustment to a principal issue that increases adjusted gross income can have a *direct* consequence on a deduction for medical expenses and contributions due to the statutory limitations on those items based on a percentage of adjusted gross income.

Sec. 3. MODIFIED PROCEDURE.

In order to reflect the above clarifications, section 3.04 of Rev. Proc. 68-31 is modified to read as follows:

.04 Where resolution of the principal issues subject to the restricted consent has a direct or indirect effect on other items, the restricted consent will cover both the principal issues and the consequential changes to other items.

Sec. 4. EFFECT ON OTHER DOCUMENTS.

This Revenue Procedure modifies Rev. Proc. 68-31.

Sec. 5. EFFECTIVE DATE.

This Revenue Procedure is effective February 7, 1977.

¶1038 UNILATERAL ALTERATION OF EXTENSION

Unilateral alteration of an extension by either the government or the taxpayer has been grounds for disregarding the agreement. Because the statute requires any extension to be in writing, there can be no implied consent either on the part of the IRS Commissioner or on the part of the taxpayer to such an alteration.[94]

Where the taxpayer alters the consent form before it is executed by the IRS and there is no evidence that the taxpayer is attempting to mislead, the Tax Court has upheld the validity of altered forms. In an unusual case,[95] the taxpayer altered a Form 872-A by erasing the figure "9" from the "90" day grace period to assess tax after notice of termination. Replacing the figure "9" with a "0," the "90" then became "00." The taxpayer subsequently filed a notice of termination. The Tax Court held that the altered Form 872-A was valid and that the government's right to assess tax was immediately terminated upon receipt of the notice of termination.

In holding for the taxpayer in *Schenk*, the Court relied heavily upon the fact that the taxpayer had previously attempted to file another altered Form 872 which the IRS rejected. This fact, the Court indicated, would have led the taxpayer to believe that his subsequent alteration of the Form 872-A also would have been rejected if not acceptable. The Court found no evidence that the taxpayer was attempting to mislead. It further noted that the IRS official who

---

[94] *Cary v. Comm'r,* 48 TC 754 (1967), CCH Dec. 28,588.

[95] *Schenk v. Comm'r,* 35 TCM 1652, TC Memo. 1976-363, CCH Dec. 34,126(M).

signed the 872-A had failed to testify as to his awareness of the alteration at the time he signed the form. As an alternative ground for barring assessment, the Court stated that, if the IRS were not aware of the alteration, the consent was invalid because there was no meeting of the minds to constitute a contract and, therefore, the period of limitations had expired because there was no extension.

In another case involving more obvious alterations, the taxpayer inserted on two Forms 872-A specific restrictions setting forth the dates on which the consents would terminate.[96] The typewritten restrictions were in larger type and in a different style than the printed material on the forms. The IRS officials who requested and signed the consent forms did not notice the alterations. The Tax Court rejected the government's argument that the doctrine of equitable estoppel should preclude the taxpayer from raising the statute of limitations as a defense. Equitable estoppel did not apply, the Court decided, because there was no false representation or wrongful misleading silence on the part of the taxpayer. In the absence of proof of one of the essential elements necessary to establish equitable estoppel, the court held that assessment was barred by the statute of limitations.

In contrast to the foregoing cases, the Tax Court in *Huene v. Commissioner*[97] found that the taxpayer's sophisticated efforts to alter a Form 872-A were "tantamount to fraud." The taxpayer had substituted his own computer generated "Form872-M" for the Form 872-A sent to him by the IRS. The modified form, visually identical in most respects to a Form 872-A, limited his potential liability for additional tax to fifty dollars. The government did not discover the alteration until the statute of limitations had expired. The court concluded that the taxpayer's conduct constituted "concealment or wrongful misleading silence concerning a mistake that he knew had occurred upon the part of the government." Finding all of the elements necessary to apply the doctrine of equitable estoppel, the Court held that the taxpayer was precluded from raising the statute of limitations as a defense.

Alterations of a consent form by the IRS after it has been signed by the taxpayer also will invalidate the extension. This is true even though the alteration merely corrects a clerical error by the IRS in typing in the wrong year to which the consent applies, and the taxpayer, knowing of the error, signs and returns the form without advising the IRS of the error.[98] In a more complex situation, the Tax Court in *Piarulle v. Commissioner*[99] held that the striking of one taxable year from a multi-year Form 872 previously signed by the taxpayers invalidated the consent with respect to all the years to which the extension applied.

The Form 872 in *Piarulle* related to the years 1974, 1975 and 1977 and was restricted to issues arising from one of the taxpayer's joint ventures. After receiving the signed Form 872, the IRS learned that another of the taxpayer's joint ventures was under examination and that the taxpayer had claimed a loss from that joint venture on the 1977 return. To avoid the original restriction, the IRS

---

[96] *Estate of Taft v. Comm'r*, 57 TCM 1291, TC Memo. 1989-427, CCH Dec. 45,940(M).

[97] 58 TCM 456, TC Memo. 1989-570, CCH Dec. 46,102(M).

[98] See *Cary v. Comm'r, supra.*

[99] 80 TC 1035 (1983), CCH Dec. 40,130.

¶1038

crossed out the year 1977 on the signed Form 872 and returned a copy of the altered form to the taxpayer together with a new Form 872 for 1977. The taxpayer told the IRS he would not sign the consent for 1977 and strongly objected to the alteration of the original consent. The Tax Court said that the altered consent covering two years was "materially different" from the original extension for three years to which the taxpayers had agreed. Such a "different" consent, the Court held, was invalid and could not be enforced against the taxpayers. In rejecting the government's equitable estoppel argument, the Court also found that the taxpayer had not attempted to mislead by his failure to advise the IRS that the altered consent was invalid.

The IRS may not mislead a taxpayer into providing an extension and if it does, the IRS may be equitably estopped from relying on the improperly obtained extension.[100] In January of 1981, a revenue agent contacted Fredericks and asked him to extend the assessment period for the year 1977 by executing Form 872, Consent to Extend the Time to Assess Tax. The taxpayer had already signed a Form 872-A at the request of another agent. The current agent replied that there was no Form 872-A in his file and that the former was probably lost in the mail. The taxpayer thereafter executed a number of Forms 872. At some point, the IRS located the original Form 872-A, however, the taxpayer was not notified and theIRS did not contact the taxpayer for eight years. A Notice of Deficiency for the tax year 1977 was issued to the taxpayer in July of 1992. The Third Circuit concluded that the agent's statement that the Form 872-A was not in his file, confirmed by the repeated requests for single-year extensions, constitute a false representation of fact that no Form 872-A existed. Furthermore, the IRS's silence regarding the reappearance of the Form 872-A further misled the taxpayer. On the basis, the Court of Appeals found that the taxpayer had established sufficient grounds for estoppel in that the IRS's actions amounted to affirmative misconduct.[101]

¶1040 SUSPENSION OF THE STATUTE

In addition to those exceptions discussed above, where a period of limitations longer than the normal three-year period is applicable, there are also situations where the running of the statute of limitations will be suspended for a stated period of time. One of the most significant of these occurs when a statutory notice of deficiency is issued to the taxpayer under Code Sec. 6212. Code Sec. 6503(a) provides that the running of the statute of limitations upon assessment is suspended after the mailing of a deficiency notice during the period of time the IRS is prohibited from making an assessment and for sixty days thereafter. Thus, on issuance of a ninety-day letter (Statutory Notice of Deficiency), the statute of limitations is suspended for the ninety-day period during which a petition to the Tax Court can be filed. If a petition to the Tax Court is filed, the statute of limitations is further suspended until 60 days after the decision of the Tax Court becomes final.

---

[100] *Fredericks v. Comm'r*, 126 F.3d 433 (3rd Cir. 1997), 97-2 USTC ¶50,692, Acq. *rev'g* 71 TCM 2998, TC Memo. 1996-222, CCH Dec. 51,338(M); AOD 1998-004.

[101] *Id.*

Another situation where the statute will be suspended is set forth in Code Sec. 7609(e). Under Code Sec. 7609(b), when a third-party recordkeeper (a bank, a broker, an attorney, an accountant or any other person extending credit through the use of credit cards or similar devices) receives a summons, the taxpayer is entitled to begin a proceeding to quash such summons, and the IRS cannot examine the records summoned until the proceeding to quash is resolved. Code Sec. 7609(e) provides that where an action to quash is filed, the statute of limitations is suspended for the period during which the proceeding and any appeals are pending.

Code Sec. 7609(e) also provides for suspension of the statute when a summons is issued to a third-party recordkeeper and a dispute arises between the recordkeeper and the IRS. Even though the taxpayer has not sought to quash the summons, the statute against the taxpayer is suspended if the dispute is not resolved within six months of the time the summons is issued. The dispute is not considered resolved during the time any action to enforce the summons is pending. Because the taxpayer would not normally know about the dispute, the Code requires the recordkeeper to notify the taxpayer of the suspension of the statute. However, the fact that the taxpayer is not notified would not prevent the suspension of the statute.

Another important suspension provision of the Code is Code Sec. 6503(j) which suspends all periods of limitations when the IRS is required to enforce in court a "designated" summons issued to a corporation under examination. This provision does not apply to summonses issued with respect to the audits of individuals. A "designated" summons to a corporation is one which is issued at least sixty days before the statute of limitations on assessment expires and which clearly states that it is a designated summons issued under Code Sec. 6503(j). The period of limitations is suspended during the judicial enforcement period and for an additional 120 days after final resolution of the matter if the court orders compliance. If the court does not order compliance, the limitations period is suspended for only an additional sixty days.

Only one designated summons is permitted to be issued under Code Sec. 6503(j) for any taxable year of a corporation. However, additional summonses, which are issued within thirty days after the issuance of the designated summons and which relate to the examination of the same corporate tax liability, are treated the same as the designated summons for the purpose of suspending the period of limitations. Such additional summonses may be issued to obtain further information or records from shareholders, employees and others, including the audited corporation itself. If enforcement of these supplemental summonses is required, the statute of limitations is suspended during the judicial enforcement period.

A final provision temporarily suspending the statute of limitations is contained in Code Sec. 6501(c)(7), which only applies to those situations where the taxpayer submits an amended return increasing his tax liability for a given year within sixty days of the time the assessment statute would expire for that year. Under such circumstances, the IRS is given a full sixty days from receipt of the

¶1040

amended return to make the additional assessment, regardless of how much sooner the period of limitations otherwise would have run.

Request for Prompt Assessment

¶1042 EIGHTEEN-MONTH PERIOD

The Internal Revenue Code gives estates the ability to reduce the normal three-year statute of limitations to an eighteen-month period for income tax returns.[102] This privilege can be exercised by filing Form 4810, Request for Prompt Assessment under Internal Revenue Code Sec. 6501(d) (see Exhibit 10-11 at ¶1061). The request must be filed after the income tax return has been filed and it must set forth the type of tax (i.e., income, employment, excise, etc.) and the taxable period for which the prompt assessment is requested. If Form 4810 is not used to make the request, an individually prepared request must clearly indicate that it is a request for prompt assessment under the provisions of Code Sec. 6501(d) and must containall of the requisite information. A separate request must be made for each succeeding taxable period because a request filed prior to the filing of a return has no effect.[103]

This special privilege also applies to corporations which have dissolved, are in the process of dissolution or are contemplating dissolution on or before the expiration of the eighteen-month limitations period. The request must specifically include this information.[104] Form 4810 provides appropriate boxes to be checked for this purpose.

A Request for Prompt Assessment filed when the normal three-year statute of limitations has less than eighteen months to run will not lengthen the normal period. Such a request, moreover, does not shorten the extended assessment period in the case of fraud or in the case of a twenty-five-percent omission from gross income.[105]

Transferee Liability

¶1044 CONSIDERATION

If assets are transferred for less than full and adequate consideration by a taxpayer, an estate or a donor (the transferor), Code Sec. 6901(a) provides for the assessment against the transferee of any income, estate or gift taxes for which the transferor is liable. For these purposes, the statute of limitations for assessing the tax against the transferee extends until one year after the expiration of the statute of limitations for assessment against the transferor. If the transferee has further transferred the property, then an additional one-year period can be added to the statute; however, in no event can the assessment against transferees be made more than three years after the expiration of the period for assessment against the initial transferor.[106]

---

[102] Code Sec. 6501(d). With the exception of the estate tax return itself, this right also extends to all other returns required to be filed by the estate.

[103] Reg. §301.6501(d)-1(b).

[104] Reg. §301.6501(d)-1(a)(2) and (c).

[105] Code Sec. 6501(d).

[106] Code Sec. 6901(c).

The IRS may seek to assess transferee liability against stockholders based on the receipt of liquidating distributions. Where a liquidating corporation files a request for prompt assessment, the period of limitations against the stockholders for transferee liability expires one year after the eighteen-month period involved in the request.

¶1051 Exhibit 10-1

Form **2259** (Rev. May 1980)	Department of the Treasury — Internal Revenue Service **Agreement as a Determination Pursuant to Section 1313(a)(4)** **of the Internal Revenue Code**	
Name of Taxpayers		Taxable Year Ended

Address of Taxpayers

We, the above-named taxpayers, and the Commissioner of Internal Revenue agree that the income tax liability for the taxable year shown above is $ _____ This liability was established by *(to complete this statement, see Income Tax Regulations section 1.1313(a)-4(b)(1) printed on the back of this form):*

We have attached as a part of this agreement the statement required by Income Tax Regulations sections 1.1313(a)-4(b)(2) and (3) that are printed on the back of this form. This statement consists of _____ pages.

Upon approval of this agreement for the Commissioner of Internal Revenue, we further agree to the assessment and collection of any deficiency (increase in tax) and accept any overassessment (decrease in tax) shown below, plus interest provided by law. We understand that by signing this agreement we will not be able to contest these years in the United States Tax Court, unless additional deficiencies are determined for these years.

Taxpayers	Taxable Year Ended	Kind of Tax	Increase in Tax	Decrease in Tax

We further agree that the determination date will be the date on which this agreement is signed for the Commissioner.

Signature of Taxpayers	Date
Signature of Related Taxpayers, if any	Date
Signature for the Commissioner	Date
Title	

Note: Your agreement will not prevent you from filing a claim for refund (after you have paid the tax) if you later believe you are so entitled; nor prevent us from later determining, if necessary, that you owe additional tax; nor extend the time provided by law for either action.

If this agreement is for a year for which a joint return was filed, both husband and wife must sign unless one, acting under a power of attorney, signs as agent for the other.

If the taxpayer is a corporation, this agreement must be signed with the corporate name followed by the signatures and titles of the officers authorized to sign.

This agreement may be signed by an attorney or agent of the taxpayers, provided this action is specifically authorized by a power of attorney which, if not previously filed, must accompany this form.

(See applicable regulations on the back) Form **2259** (Rev. 5-80)

Instructions

The original of this agreement will be associated with the return of the taxpayer to whom the determination is made. An additional executed copy will be furnished to each taxpayer involved and one will also be associated with each related tax return.

The statement required by section 1.1313(a) - 4(b)(2) and (3) of the regulations must be headed "Statement to be Attached to, and Made a Part of, Form 2259 in the Case of   ", and must be securely attached to this form.

Provisions of the Internal Revenue Code and the Regulations Issued Thereunder Covering the Preparation of an Agreement as a Determination

Code section 1313(a)(4):*Determination.* [For purposes of this part, the term "determination" means. . .] under regulations prescribed by the Secretary, an agreement for purposes of this part, signed by the Secretary and by any person, relating to the liability of such person (or the person for whom he acts) in respect of a tax under this subtitle for any taxable period.

Regulations section 1.1313(a) - 4:*Agreement pursuant to section 1313(a)(4) as a determination - -(a) In general.*

(1) A determination may take the form of an agreement made pursuant to this section. This section is intended to provide an expeditious method for obtaining an adjustment under section 1311 and for offsetting deficiencies and refunds whenever possible. The provisions of part II (section 1311 and following), subchapter Q, Chapter 1 of the Code, must be strictly complied with in any such agreement.

(2) An agreement made pursuant to this section will not, in itself, establish the tax liability for the open taxable year to which it relates, but it will state the amount of the tax, as then determined, for such open year. The tax may be the amount of tax shown on the return as filed by the taxpayer, but if any changes in the amount have been made, or if any are being made by documents executed concurrently with the execution of said agreement, such changes must be taken into account. For example, an agreement pursuant to this section may be executed concurrently with the execution of a waiver of restrictions on assessment and collection of a deficiency or acceptance of an overassessment with respect to the open taxable year, or concurrently with the execution and filing of a stipulation in a proceeding before the Tax Court of the United States, where an item which is to be the subject of an adjustment under section 1311 is disposed of by the stipulation and is not left for determination by the court.

(b) *Contents of agreement.* An agreement made pursuant to this section shall be so designated in the heading of the agreement, and it shall contain the following:

(1) A statement of the amount of the tax determined for the open taxable year to which the agreement relates, and if said liability is established or altered by a document executed concurrently with the execution of the agreement, a reference to said document.

(2) A concise statement of the material facts with respect to the item that was the subject of the error in the closed taxable year or years, and a statement of the manner in which such item was treated in computing the tax liability set forth pursuant to subparagraph (1) of this paragraph.

(3) A statement as to the amount of the adjustment ascertained pursuant to section 1.1314(a) - 1 for the taxable year with respect to which the error was made and, where applicable, a statement as to the amount of the adjustment or adjustments ascertained pursuant to section 1.1314(a) - 2 with respect to any other taxable year or years; and

(4) A waiver of restrictions on assessment and collection of any deficiencies set forth pursuant to subparagraph (3) of this paragraph.

(c) *Execution and effect of agreement.* An agreement made pursuant to this section shall be signed by the taxpayer with respect to whom the determination is made, or on the taxpayer's behalf by an agent or attorney acting pursuant to a power of attorney on file with the Internal Revenue Service. If an adjustment is to be made in a case of a related taxpayer, the agreement shall be signed also by the related taxpayer, or on the related taxpayer's behalf by an agent or attorney acting pursuant to a power of attorney on file with the Internal Revenue Service. It may be signed on behalf of the Commissioner by the district director, or such other person as is authorized by the Commissioner. When duly executed, such agreement will constitute the authority for an allowance of any refund or credit agreed to therein, and for the immediate assessment of any deficiency agreed to therein for the taxable year with respect to which the error was made, or any closed taxable year or years affected, or treated as affected, by a net operating loss deduction or capital loss carryover determined with reference to the taxable year with respect to which the error was made.

(d) *Finality of determination.* A determination made by an agreement pursuant to this section becomes final when the tax liability for the open taxable year to which the determination relates becomes final. During the period, if any, that a deficiency may be assessed or a refund or credit allowed with respect to such year, either the taxpayer or the Commissioner may properly pursue any of the procedures provided by law to secure a further modification of the tax liability for such year. For example, if the taxpayer subsequently files a claim for refund, or if the Commissioner subsequently issues a notice of deficiency with respect to such year, either may adopt a position with respect to the item that was the subject of the adjustment that is at variance with the manner in which said item was treated in the agreement. Any assessment, refund, or credit that is subsequently made with respect to the tax liability for such open taxable year, to the extent that it is based upon a revision in the treatment of the item that was the subject of the adjustment, shall constitute an alteration of revocation of the determination for the purpose of a redetermination of the adjustment pursuant to paragraph (d) of section 1.1314(b) - 1.

Form 2259 (Rev. 5-80)

¶1052 Exhibit 10-2

Form **872** (Rev. January 2001)	Department of the Treasury-Internal Revenue Service **Consent to Extend the Time to Assess Tax**	In reply refer to:
		Taxpayer Identification Number

_____
(Name(s))

taxpayer(s) of _____
(Number, Street, City or Town, State, ZIP Code)

and the Commissioner of Internal Revenue consent and agree to the following:

(1) The amount of any Federal _____ tax due on any return(s) made by or
(Kind of tax)

for the above taxpayer(s) for the period(s) ended _____

may be assessed at any time on or before _____ . However, if
(Expiration date)

a notice of deficiency in tax for any such period(s) is sent to the taxpayer(s) on or before that date, then the time for assessing the tax will be further extended by the number of days the assessment was previously prohibited, plus 60 days.

(2) The taxpayer(s) may file a claim for credit or refund and the Service may credit or refund the tax within 6 months after this agreement ends.

MAKING THIS CONSENT WILL NOT DEPRIVE THE TAXPAYER(S) OF ANY APPEAL RIGHTS TO WHICH THEY WOULD OTHERWISE BE ENTITLED.

YOUR SIGNATURE HERE ➤ ....
(Date signed)

SPOUSE'S SIGNATURE ➤ ....
(Date signed)

TAXPAYER'S REPRESENTATIVE

SIGN HERE ➤ ....
(Date signed)

CORPORATE NAME ➤ ....

CORPORATE OFFICER(S) SIGN HERE ➤ ....
(Title) *(Date signed)*

➤ ....
(Title) *(Date signed)*

INTERNAL REVENUE SERVICE SIGNATURE AND TITLE

....
(Division Executive Name - see instructions) *(Division Executive Title - see instructions)*

BY ....
(Authorized Official Signature and Title - see instructions) *(Date signed)*

| *(Signature instructions are on the back of this form)* | www.irs.gov | Catalog Number 20755I | Form **872** (Rev. 1-2001) |

Instructions

If this consent is for income tax, self-employment tax, or FICA tax on tips and is made for any year(s) for which a joint return was filed, both husband and wife must sign the original and copy of this form unless one, acting under a power of attorney, signs as agent for the other. The signatures must match the names as they appear on the front of this form.

If this consent is for gift tax and the donor and the donor's spouse elected to have gifts to third persons considered as made one-half by each, both husband and wife must sign the original and copy of this form unless one, acting under a power of attorney, signs as agent for the other. The signatures must match the names as they appear on the front of this form.

If this consent is for Chapter 41, 42, or 43 taxes involving a partnership or is for a partnership return, only one authorized partner need sign.

If this consent is for Chapter 42 taxes, a separate Form 872 should be completed for each potential disqualified person, entity, or foundation manager that may be involved in a taxable transaction during the related tax year. See Revenue Ruling 75-391, 1975-2 C.B. 446.

If you are an attorney or agent of the taxpayer(s), you may sign this consent provided the action is specifically authorized by a power of attorney. If the power of attorney was not previously filed, you must include it with this form.

If you are acting as a fiduciary (such as executor, administrator, trustee, etc.) and you sign this consent, attach Form 56, Notice Concerning Fiduciary Relationship, unless it was previously filed. If the taxpayer is a corporation, sign this consent with the corporate name followed by the signature and title of the officer(s) authorized to sign.

Instructions for Internal Revenue Service Employees

Complete the Division Executive's name and title depending upon your division.

If you are in the Small Business /Self-Employed Division, enter the name and title for the appropriate division executive for your business unit (e.g., Area Director for your area; Director, Compliance Policy; Director, Compliance Services).

If you are in the Wage and Investment Division, enter the name and title for the appropriate division executive for your business unit (e.g., Area Director for your area; Director, Field Compliance Services).

If you are in the Large and Mid-Size Business Division, enter the name and title of the Director, Field Operations for your industry.

If you are in the Tax Exempt and Government Entities Division, enter the name and title for the appropriate division executive for your business unit (e.g., Director, Exempt Organizations; Director, Employee Plans; Director, Federal, State and Local Governments; Director, Indian Tribal Governments; Director, Tax Exempt Bonds).

If you are in Appeals, enter the name and title of the appropriate Director, Appeals Operating Unit.

The signature and title line will be signed and dated by the appropriate authorized official within your division.

¶1052

¶1053 Exhibit 10-3

Form **872-A** (Rev. October 1987)	Department of the Treasury — Internal Revenue Service **Special Consent to Extend the Time to Assess Tax**	In reply refer to: SSN or EIN

_____
(Name(s))

taxpayer(s) of _____
(Number, Street, City or Town, State, ZIP Code)

and the District Director of Internal Revenue or Regional Director of Appeals consent and agree as follows:

(1) The amount(s) of any Federal_____tax due on any return(s) made by or
(Kind of tax)

for the above taxpayer(s) for the period(s) ended _____
may be assessed on or before the 90th (ninetieth) day after: (a) the Internal Revenue Service office considering the case receives Form 872-T, Notice of Termination of Special Consent to Extend the Time to Assess Tax, from the taxpayer(s); or (b) the Internal Revenue Service mails Form 872-T to the taxpayer(s); or (c) the Internal Revenue Service mails a notice of deficiency for such period(s); except that if a notice of deficiency is sent to the taxpayer(s), the time for assessing the tax for the period(s) stated in the notice of deficiency will end 60 days after the period during which the making of an assessment is prohibited. A final adverse determination subject to declaratory judgment under sections 7428, 7476, or 7477 of the Internal Revenue Code will not terminate this agreement.

(2) This agreement ends on the earlier of the above expiration date or the assessment date of an increase in the above tax or the overassessment date of a decrease in the above tax that reflects the final determination of tax and the final administrative appeals consideration. An assessment or overassessment for one period covered by this agreement will not end this agreement for any other period it covers. Some assessments do not reflect a final determination and appeals consideration and therefore will not terminate the agreement before the expiration date. Examples are assessments of: (a) tax under a partial agreement; (b) tax in jeopardy; (c) tax to correct mathematical or clerical errors; (d) tax reported on amended returns; and (e) advance payments. In addition, unassessed payments, such as amounts treated by the Service as cash bonds and advance payments not assessed by the Service, will not terminate this agreement before the expiration date determined in (1) above. This agreement ends on the date determined in (1) above regardless of any assessment for any period includible in a report to the Joint Committee on Taxation submitted under section 6405 of the Internal Revenue Code.

(3) This agreement will not reduce the period of time otherwise provided by law for making such assessment.

(4) The taxpayer(s) may file a claim for credit or refund and the Service may credit or refund the tax within 6 (six) months after this agreement ends.

_____

(Signature instructions and space for signature are on the back of this form)   Form **872-A** (Rev. 10-87)

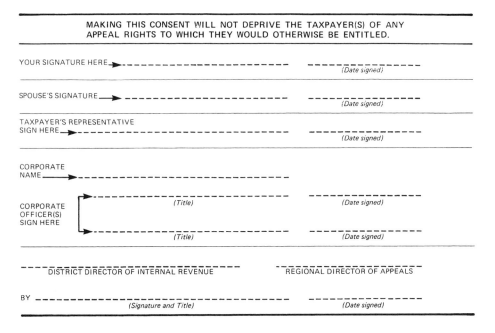

MAKING THIS CONSENT WILL NOT DEPRIVE THE TAXPAYER(S) OF ANY
APPEAL RIGHTS TO WHICH THEY WOULD OTHERWISE BE ENTITLED.

YOUR SIGNATURE HERE ➤ _____   _____
                                                              (Date signed)

SPOUSE'S SIGNATURE ➤ _____   _____
                                                              (Date signed)

TAXPAYER'S REPRESENTATIVE
SIGN HERE ➤ _____   _____
                                                              (Date signed)

CORPORATE
NAME ➤ _____

CORPORATE   _____   _____
OFFICER(S)   *(Title)*   *(Date signed)*
SIGN HERE
                  _____   _____
                              (Title)   *(Date signed)*

_____   _____
DISTRICT DIRECTOR OF INTERNAL REVENUE   REGIONAL DIRECTOR OF APPEALS

BY _____   _____
              (Signature and Title)   *(Date signed)*

Instructions

If this consent is for income tax, self-employment tax, or FICA tax on tips and is made for any year(s) for which a joint return was filed, both husband and wife must sign the original and copy of this form unless one, acting under a power of attorney, signs as agent for the other. The signatures must match the names as they appear on the front of this form.

If this consent is for gift tax and the donor and the donor's spouse elected to have gifts to third persons considered as made one-half by each, both husband and wife must sign the original and copy of this form unless one, acting under a power of attorney, signs as agent for the other. The signatures must match the names as they appear on the front of this form.

If this consent is for Chapter 41, 42, or 43 taxes involving a partnership, only one authorized partner need sign.

If you are an attorney or agent of the taxpayer(s), you may sign this consent provided the action is specifically authorized by a power of attorney. If the power of attorney was not previously filed, you must include it with this form.

If you are acting as a fiduciary *(such as executor, administrator, trustee, etc.)* and you sign this consent, attach Form 56, Notice Concerning Fiduciary Relationship, unless it was previously filed.

If the taxpayer is a corporation, sign this consent with the corporate name followed by the signature and title of the officer(s) authorized to sign.

If this consent is for Chapter 42 taxes, a separate Form 872-A should be completed for each potential disqualified person or entity that may have been involved in a taxable transaction during the related tax year. See Revenue Ruling 75-391, 1975-2 C.B. 446.

Form **872-A** (Rev. 10-87)

¶1053

¶1054 Exhibit 10-4

Form **872-T** (Rev. Oct. 90)	Department of the Treasury — Internal Revenue Service **Notice of Termination of Special Consent to Extend the Time to Assess Tax**	In reply refer to:
Taxpayer(s) Name(s)		Termination By: ☐ Taxpayer ☐ IRS
Taxpayer(s) Address		Taxpayer Identifying Number
Kind of Tax	Tax Period(s) Covered by this Notice	Issuing Office Code
		Service Center Code

Under the agreement dated _____ , between the above taxpayer(s) and the Internal Revenue Service, this form is written notification of termination of Form 872-A, Special Consent to Extend the Time to Assess Tax, for the kind of tax and tax period(s) indicated above.

Signature and mailing instructions are on the back of this form.
Signing this notice will not deprive the taxpayer(s) of any appeal rights to which they otherwise been entitled.

Your Signature	Date Signed
Spouse's Signature	Date Signed
Taxpayer's Representative's Signature	Date Signed

Corporate Name

Corporate Officer(s) Signature	Name and Title	Date Signed
	Name and Title	Date Signed

District Director of Internal Revenue	Regional Director of Appeals
By (Signature and Title)	Date Signed

Cat. No. 20775A   Form **872-T** (Rev. 10-90)

Instructions

This notice may be made by either the taxpayer(s) or the Internal Revenue Service.

Please enter, in the space provided on the front of this form, the date Form 872-A was signed for the Internal Revenue Service.

If this notice is for income tax, self-employment tax, or FICA tax on tips and is made for any year(s) for which a joint return was filed, both husband and wife must sign this form unless one, acting under a power of attorney, signs as agent for the other. The signatures must match the names as they appear on the Form 872-A.

If this notice is for gift tax and the donor and the donor's spouse elected to have gifts to third persons considered as made one-half by each, both husband and wife must sign this form unless one, acting under a power of attorney, signs as agent for the other. The signatures must match the names as they appear on the Form 872-A.

If this notice is for Chapter 41, 42, or 43 taxes involving a partnership, only one authorized partner need sign.

If you are an attorney or agent of the taxpayer(s), you may sign this notice provided the action is specifically authorized by a power of attorney. If the power of attorney was not previously filed, you must include it with this form.

If you are acting as a fiduciary (such as executor, administrator, trustee, etc.) and you sign this notice, attach Form 56, Notice Concerning Fiduciary Relationship, unless it was previously filed.

If the taxpayer is a corporation, sign this notice with the corporate name followed by the signature and title of the officer(s) authorized to sign.

If the tax return(s) to which this notice applies is under consideration by the Examination Division, mail this notice to the District Director of Internal Revenue having jurisdiction over the return(s), Attention: Chief, Examination Division.

If the tax return(s) to which this notice applies is under consideration by the Employee Plans and Exempt Organizations Division, mail this notice to the District Director of Internal Revenue for the key district having jurisdiction over the return(s), Attention: Chief, EP/EO Division. See Rev. Proc. 85-32, 1985-2 C.B. 414, for a listing of the key district offices and the districts covered by each.

If the tax return(s) to which this notice applies is under consideration by Appeals, mail this notice to the Chief, Appeals Office, having jurisdiction over the return(s).

Form 872-T (Rev. 10-90)

¶1055 Exhibit 10-5

Form **872-P** (Rev. November 1992)	Department of the Treasury—Internal Revenue Service **Consent to Extend the Time to Assess Tax Attributable to Items of a Partnership**	In reply refer to: _____ Taxpayer Identification Number

_____, a partnership of
(Name)

_____ and the
(Number, street, city or town, state, and ZIP code)

District Director of Internal Revenue or the Regional Director of Appeals consent and agree as follows:

The amount(s) of any Federal income tax with respect to all partners attributable to any partnership item(s) for the above named partnership for the period(s) ended _____

may be assessed at any time on or before _____.

If a notice of Final Partnership Administrative Adjustment is mailed to the Tax Matters Partner, the time for assessing the tax for the period(s) stated in the notice of Final Partnership Administrative Adjustment shall be suspended for the period during which an action may be brought under section 6226 of the Internal Revenue Code (and, if an action with respect to such administrative adjustment is brought during such period, until the decision of the court in such action becomes final) and for 1 year thereafter.

Signature instructions are on the back of this form.
Making this consent will not deprive the partnership or partners of any appeal rights to which they would otherwise be entitled.

Partnership
Name _____

Under penalties of perjury, I declare that I am not currently in bankruptcy nor have I previously been named as a debtor in a bankruptcy proceeding in which the United States could have filed a claim for income tax due with respect to any partnership taxable year covered by this consent.

Tax Matters Partner
Sign Here _____   _____
                                                                                    (Date signed)

Authorized Person
Sign Here _____   _____
                (You must also attach written authorization   (Date signed)
                as stated in the instructions on the back of this form.)

District Director of Internal Revenue	Regional Director of Appeals
By (Signature and Title)	Date Signed

Cat. No. 16910J   Form **872-P** (Rev. 11-92)

Instructions for Signing

1. The consent generally applies to partnership returns filed for partnership tax years beginning after September 3, 1982.

2. The consent may be signed for the partnership in the appropriate space by either:

   a. The tax matters partners for the partnership for the year(s) covered by the consent, or

   b. Any other person authorized by the partnership in writing to sign the consent (see item 5 below).

3. If the Tax Matters Partner is not an individual and the consent is signed by a person acting in a representative capacity for the tax matters partner, for example, the trustee of a trust, the declaration above the signature line for the tax matters partner refers to the bankruptcy of the tax matters partner, not the person who actually signed the consent.

4. If the tax matters partner has filed a joint return with his or her spouse for the taxable year(s) covered by the consent and the consent is signed by the tax matters partner, the declaration above the signature line for the tax matter(s) partner refers to the bankruptcy of either spouse, not just to the person who actually signed the consent.

5. If the consent is signed by any person other than the tax matter(s) partner, a copy of the written authorization from the partnership must be attached to the consent. The information that must be included in the authorization is described in Temporary Regulation 301.6229(b)-1 and is listed below. The written authorization must:

   a. Provide that it is an authorization for a person other than the tax matters partner to extend the assessment period with respect to all partners.

   b. Identify the partnership and the person being authorized by name, address, and taxpayer identification number.

   c. Specify the partnership tax year or years for which the authorization is effective, and

   d. Include the signatures of all persons who were general partners at any time during the year or years for which the authorization is effective.

¶1055

¶1056 Exhibit 10-6

Form **872-O** (Rev. February 1993)	Department of the Treasury—Internal Revenue Service **Special Consent to Extend the Time to Assess Tax Attributable to Items of a Partnership**	In reply refer to: Taxpayer Identification Number

_____ , an
(Name)

Partnership of _____
(Number, street, city or town, state, and ZIP code)

and the District Director of Internal Revenue or the Regional Director of Appeals consent and agree as follows:

(1) The amount(s) of any Federal income tax with respect to all partners attributable to any partnership item(s) for the above named partnership for the period(s) ended _____
may be assessed at any time on or before the 90th (ninetieth) day after:

    (a) the date Form 872-N, Notice of Termination of Special Consent to Extend the Time to Assess Tax Attributable to Items of a Partnership, is received by the Internal Revenue Service Office from which the Form 872-O originated; or

    (b) the Internal Revenue Service mails a Form 872-N to the Tax Matters Partner.

If a notice of Final Partnership Administrative Adjustment is mailed to the Tax Matters Partner, the time for assessing the tax for the period(s) stated in that notice shall be suspended:

    (a) for the period during which an action may be brought under section 6226 of the Internal Revenue Code and,

    (b) if an action with respect to such administrative adjustment is brought during such period, until the decision of the court becomes final, and

    (c) for 1 (one) year thereafter.

(2) This agreement will not reduce the period of time otherwise provided by law for making such assessment.

(3) This agreement may be terminated by either the taxpayer or the Internal Revenue Service with the use of Form 872-N which is available from the office considering the taxpayer's case. For the termination to be valid, Form 872-N must be delivered to one of the following addresses.

    If MAILING Form 872-N, send to: If HAND CARRYING Form 872-N deliver to:

(Signature instructions and space for signature are on back of this form.)   Cat. No. 61178V   Form **872-O** (Rev. 2-93)

¶1056

MAKING THIS CONSENT WILL NOT DEPRIVE THE PARTNERSHIP OR THE PARTNERS
OF ANY APPEAL RIGHTS TO WHICH THEY WOULD OTHERWISE BE ENTITLED.

Under penalties of perjury, I declare that I am not currently in bankruptcy nor have I previously been named as a debtor in a bankruptcy proceeding in which the United States could have filed a claim for income tax due with respect to any partnership taxable year covered by this consent.

Tax Matters Partner
Sign Here _____   _____

(Date signed)

Authorized Person
Sign Here _____   _____

(You must also attach written authorization   *(Date signed)*
as stated in the instructions on the back of this form.)

_____   _____
District Director of Internal Revenue   Regional Director of Appeals

By _____   _____
(Signature and Title)   *(Date Signed)*

Instructions for Signing

1. The consent generally applies to partnership returns filed for partnership tax years beginning after September 3, 1982.

2. The consent may be signed for the partnership in the appropriate space by either:

    a. The tax matters partner for the partnership for the year(s) covered by the consent, or

    b. Any other person authorized by the partnership in writing to sign the consent (see # 5 below).

3. If the Tax Matters Partner is not an individual and the consent is signed by a person acting in a representative capacity for the tax matters partner, for example, the trustee of a trust, the declaration above the signature line for the tax matters person refers to the bankruptcy of the tax matters partner, not the person who actually signed the consent.

4. If the tax matters partner has filed a joint return with his or her spouse for the taxable year(s) covered by the consent and the consent is signed by the tax matters partner, the declaration above the signature line for the tax matters partner refers to the bankruptcy of either spouse, not just to the person who actually signed the consent.

5. If the consent is signed by any person other than the tax matters partner, a copy of the written authorization from the partnership must be attached to the consent. The written authorization is described in Temporary Regulation 301.6229(b)-1 and listed below. The authorization must:

    a. Provide that it is an authorization for a person other than the tax matters partner to extend the assessment period with respect to all partners.

    b. Identify the partnership and the person being authorized by name, address, and taxpayer identification number.

    c. Specify the partnership taxable year or years for which the authorization is effective, and

    d. Be signed by all persons who were general partners at any time during the year or years for which the authorization is effective.

☆ U.S. GPO:1993-343-049/72004   Form **872-O** (Rev. 2-93)

¶1057 Exhibit 10-7

Form **872-N** (Rev. 10-88)	Department of the Treasury — Internal Revenue Service **Notice of Termination of Special Consent to Extend the Time to Assess Tax Attributable to Items of a Partnership**	In reply refer to:
Partnership Name		Termination By: ☐ Tax Matters Partner ☐ IRS
Partnership Address		Taxpayer Identification Number
Tax Period(s) Covered by this Notice		Office Where Form 872-O Originated:
		Service Center Where Partnership Return Filed:

Under the agreement dated _____ , between the above partnership and the Internal Revenue Service, this form is written notification of termination of Form 872-O, Special Consent to Extend the Time to Assess Tax Attributable to Items of a Partnership.

Signature and mailing instructions are on the bottom of this form.
Signing this notice may alter the partnership's or partner's appeal rights to which they would otherwise be entitled.

TAX MATTERS PARTNER
SIGNATURE HERE _____   _____
                                                                                            (Date signed)

AUTHORIZED PERSON
SIGN HERE _____   _____
          (You must also attach written authorization as stated in the   *(Date signed)*
          instructions on this form.)

_____   _____
District Director of Internal Revenue   Regional Director of Appeals

BY _____   _____
          (Signature and Title)   *(Date signed)*

Form **872-N** (Rev. 10-88)

Instructions for Signing

1. This notice may be made by any of the following signing in the appropriate space:

    a. The tax matters partner for the partnership for the year(s) covered by the consent (Form 872-O),

    b. Any other person authorized by the partnership in writing (see item 2 below), or

    c. The Internal Revenue Service.

2. If the notice is signed by any person other than the tax matters partner, a copy of the written authorization from the partnership must be attached to the notice. The information that must be included in the authorization is described in Temporary Regulation 301.6229(b)-1 and is listed below. The written authorization must:

    a. Provide that it is an authorization for a person other than the tax matters partner to extend the assessment period with respect to all partners.

    b. Identify the partnership and the person being authorized by name, address, and taxpayer identification number.

    c. Specify the partnership tax year or years for which the authorization is effective, and

    d. Include the signatures of all persons who were general partners at any time during the year or years for which the authorization is effective.

3. MAILING INSTRUCTIONS: This notice must be received by the Internal Revenue Service office from which the original Form 872-O originated. See Form 872-O item (3) for the proper address to mail this notice. Until the notice is received by that office, it has no force or effect.

    HAND DELIVERY: See Form 872-O item (3) for the address to hand deliver this notice.

4. In preparing Form 872-N, please do not omit any of the required information.

☆ U.S. GPO:1988-242-483/91482   Form **872-N** (Rev. 10-88)

¶1058 Exhibit 10-8

Form **872-F** (Rev. 10-90)	Department of the Treasury — Internal Revenue Service **Consent to Extend the Time to Assess Tax Attributable to Items of a Partnership or S Corporation That Have Converted Under Section 6231(b) of the Internal Revenue Code** (Signature instructions are on the back of this form)	In reply refer to: Taxpayer Identification Number

_____ , of
(Name(s))

_____ , a partner (Shareholder)
(Number, Street, City or Town, State, Zip Code)

in _____ and the
(Name of Partnership/S Corporation)

District Director, Director of Service Center, or Regional Director of Appeals consent and agrees as follows:

    The amount of any Federal income tax with respect to the above named taxpayer(s) on any partnership (subchapter S) item(s) for the above named partnership (S corporation) that have converted by reason of one or more of the events described in subsection (b) of section 6231 of the Internal Revenue Code or any item affected by such item(s) for the period(s) ended _____

may be assessed at any time on or before _____ .

If a statutory notice of deficiency is sent to the taxpayer pursuant to section 6230(a)(2)(A)(ii) of the Code with respect to the above tax on or before that date, the running of the period of limitations provided in section 6229(f) of the Code on assessment of any tax attributable to such converted items (or any item affected by such item(s)) shall be suspended for the period during which an action may be brought in the Tax Court under section 6213 of the Code (and, if an action with respect to such notice is brought in the Tax Court during such period, until the decision of the Court in such action becomes final pursuant to section 7481 of the Code), and for 60 days thereafter.

Cat. No. 16907M   Form **872-F** (Rev. 10-90)

Making this consent will not deprive the taxpayer(s) of any appeal rights to which they would otherwise be entitled.

Partner's (Shareholder's) Signature	Date Signed

Spouse's Signature	Date Signed

Name of Taxpayer's Representative (Please Type or Print)

Signature of Taxpayer's Representative	Date Signed

(Attach Form 2848 - Power of Attorney and Declaration of Representative)

For Internal Revenue Service Use Only

District Director of Internal Revenue	Director of Service Center	Regional Director of Appeals

By: (Signature and Title)	Date Signed

Instructions for Signing

1. The consent can only apply to partnership (subchapter S) item(s) (or any item affected by such item(s)) that have converted to nonpartnership (subchapter S) items for partnership tax years beginning after September 3, 1982 or to an S corporation beginning after December 31, 1982.

2. The Tax Matters Partner (Person) of the partnership (S corporation) in which the items arose (or any person authorized by the partnership in writing) may not consent to extend the period of limitations for a partner (shareholder).

3. If this consent is made for any year(s) for which a joint return was filed, both the husband and wife must sign, unless one spouse, acting under a power of attorney, signs as agent for the other.

4. If you are acting as an authorized representative (attorney, CPA, enrolled actuary, or enrolled agent) of the taxpayer(s), you may sign this consent provided a valid power of attorney has been executed by the taxpayer. If the power of attorney was not previously filed, please include it with this form.

5. Partnerships with Tiers: If the partner is a partnership, corporation, or trust of the partnership in which the converted items arose, only the person authorized or the Tax Matters Partner (Person) or Trustee for the tiered entity may sign this consent.

6. S Corporation: Shareholders must be an individual, estate or trust as defined in section 1361(c)(2).

¶1058

¶1059 Exhibit 10-9

Form **872-B** (Rev. January 2001)	Department of the Treasury - Internal Revenue Service **Consent to Extend the Time to Assess Miscellaneous Excise Taxes**	In reply refer to: Taxpayer Identification Number

_____ , taxpayer(s)
(Name(s))

of _____ and the
(Number, Street, City or Town, State, ZIP Code)

Commissioner of Internal Revenue consent and agree to the following:

(1) The amount of liability for _____ tax, imposed on the taxpayer(s) by
(Kind)

section _____ of the _____ due for the period _____
(Internal Revenue Code, Revenue Act, etc.)

_____ may be assessed at any time on or before_____
(Expiration date)

(2) The collection provisions and limitations now in effect will also apply to any tax assessed within the extended period.

(3) The taxpayer(s) may file a claim for credit or refund and the Service may credit or refund the tax within 6 months after this agreement ends.

**MAKING THIS CONSENT WILL NOT DEPRIVE THE TAXPAYER(S) OF ANY APPEAL
RIGHTS TO WHICH THEY WOULD OTHERWISE BE ENTITLED.**

YOUR SIGNATURE HERE ➤ ....
(Date signed)

TAXPAYER'S REPRESENTATIVE
SIGN HERE ➤ ....
(Date signed)

CORPORATE
NAME ➤ ....

CORPORATE
OFFICER(S)
SIGN HERE ➤ ....
(Title) *(Date signed)*

➤ ....
(Title) *(Date signed)*

INTERNAL REVENUE SERVICE SIGNATURE AND TITLE

....
(Division Executive Name - see instructions) *(Division Executive Title - see instructions)*

BY ....
(Authorized Official Signature and Title - see instructions) *(Date signed)*

| *(Signature instructions are on the back of this form)* | www.irs.gov | Catalog No. 61485N | Form **872-B** (Rev. 1-2001) |

Instructions

If this consent is for a partnership return, only one authorized partner need sign.

If you are an attorney or agent of the taxpayer(s), you may sign this consent provided the action is specifically authorized by a power of attorney. If the power of attorney was not previously filed, you must include it with this form.

If you are acting as a fiduciary (such as executor, administrator, trustee, etc.) and you sign this consent, attach Form 56, Notice Concerning Fiduciary Relationship, unless it was previously filed.

If the taxpayer is a corporation, sign this consent with the corporate name followed by the signature and title of the officer(s) authorized to sign.

Instructions for Internal Revenue Service Employees

Complete the Division Executive's name and title depending upon your division.

If you are in the Small Business /Self-Employed Division, enter the name and title for the appropriate division executive for your business unit (e.g., Area Director for your area; Director, Compliance Policy; Director, Compliance Services).

If you are in the Wage and Investment Division, enter the name and title for the appropriate division executive for your business unit (e.g., Area Director for your area; Director, Field Compliance Services).

If you are in the Large and Mid-Size Business Division, enter the name and title of the Director, Field Operations for your industry.

If you are in the Tax Exempt and Government Entities Division, enter the name and title for the appropriate division executive for your business unit (e.g., Director, Exempt Organizations; Director, Employee Plans; Director, Federal, State and Local Governments; Director, Indian Tribal Governments; Director, Tax Exempt Bonds).

If you are in Appeals, enter the name and title of the appropriate Director, Appeals Operating Unit.

The signature and title line will be signed and dated by the appropriate authorized official within your division.

¶1059

¶1060 Exhibit 10-10

Form **872-D** (Rev. January 2001)	Department of the Treasury - Internal Revenue Service **Consent to Extend the Time on Assessment of Tax Return Preparer Penalty**	In reply refer to: Taxpayer Identification Number

_____

(Name)

a tax return preparer, of _____

(Number, Street, Town or City, State, and ZIP Code)

and the Commissioner of Internal Revenue consent and agree to the following:

(1) The penalty imposed by section 6694(a) and/or 6695 of the Internal Revenue Code may be assessed against the above named tax return preparer at any time on or before _____ with respect to the tax return(s) for claim(s) for refund of the taxpayers named below.

(2) The tax return preparer may file a claim for credit or refund and the Internal Revenue Service may credit or refund the penalty(ies) within 6 months after this agreement ends.

Form number of return for which penalty is being charged	Taxpayer's name as shown on return	Taxpayer's identification number	Tax period

**MAKING THIS CONSENT WILL NOT DEPRIVE THE TAXPAYER(S) OF ANY APPEAL
RIGHTS TO WHICH THEY WOULD OTHERWISE BE ENTITLED.**

WHO MUST SIGN The consent should be signed by the preparer. An attorney or agent may sign this consent if specifically authorized by a power of attorney which, if not previously filed, must accompany this form.	
	_____ _____
	(Signature) (Date signed)

INTERNAL REVENUE SERVICE SIGNATURE and TITLE

_____   _____

(Division Executive Name - see instructions)   (Division Executive Title - see instructions)

BY _____   _____

(Authorized Official Signature and Title - see instructions)   (Date signed)

(Signature instructions for Internal Revenue Service Employees are on the back of this form)   www.irs.gov   Catalog No. 61634Y   Form **872-D** (Rev. 1-2001)

Instructions for Internal Revenue Service Employees

Complete the Division Executive's name and title depending upon your division.

If you are in the Small Business /Self-Employed Division, enter the name and title for the appropriate division executive for your business unit (e.g., Area Director for your area; Director, Compliance Policy; Director, Compliance Services).

If you are in the Wage and Investment Division, enter the name and title for the appropriate division executive for your business unit (e.g., Area Director for your area; Director, Field Compliance Services).

If you are in the Large and Mid-Size Business Division, enter the name and title of the Director, Field Operations for your industry.

If you are in the Tax Exempt and Government Entities Division, enter the name and title for the appropriate division executive for your business unit (e.g., Director, Exempt Organizations; Director, Employee Plans; Director, Federal, State and Local Governments; Director, Indian Tribal Governments; Director, Tax Exempt Bonds).

If you are in Appeals, enter the name and title of the appropriate Director, Appeals Operating Unit.

The signature and title line will be signed and dated by the appropriate authorized official within your division.

¶1060

¶1061 Exhibit 10-11

Form **4810** (Rev. Dec 1999)	Department of the Treasury Internal Revenue Service **Request for Prompt Assessment** **Under Internal Revenue Code Section 6501(d)** *(Please see instructions on reverse)*	OMB Clearance Number 1545-0430

TO Director, Internal Revenue Service	Kind of tax

Tax returns for which prompt assessment of any additional tax is requested

Form Number	Tax Period Ended	Social Security or Employer Identification Number	Name and Address Shown on Return	Internal Revenue Service Office Where filed	Date Filed

Remarks

If applicable, please provide the following Information ▶	Spouse's name *(surviving or deceased)*	Spouse's social security number

If the forms listed above are corporation income tax returns, please check one of the boxes below

☐ Dissolution has been completed.

☐ Dissolution has begun and will be completed either before or after the 18-month period of limitation.

☐ Dissolution has not begun but is expected by the expiration of the 18-month period of limitation; dissolution will begin before the period expires and will be completed either before or after that period expires.

I have attached the following item (s) to help expedite action on my request: ☐ Letters testamentary, or ☐ Letters of administration ☐ Copies of returns listed above *(See "What to File" on the back)* ☐ Other:	Requester's name and address

I request a prompt assessment of any additional tax for the kind of tax and periods shown above, as provided by section 6501 (d) of the Internal Revenue Code.	Requester's signature	Date
	Title	

Cat. No. 42022S

Form **4810** (Rev. 12-1999)

¶1061

Information and Instructions

General Information

Ordinarily, the Internal Revenue Service has 3 years after you file an income tax return to assess additional tax or to begin court action to collect the tax. The fiduciary representing a dissolving corporation or a decedent's estate may request a prompt assessment of tax under the Internal Revenue Code (IRC)§ 6501(d). This will limit the time to 18 months from the date the fiduciary files the request, but not beyond 3 years from the date you filed your return.

The prompt assessment of tax will not shorten the period for assessing the tax, or for beginning court action to collect it if:

- the taxpayer or fiduciary did not report substantial amounts of gross income, or the
- taxpayer or fiduciary filed false or fraudulent tax returns.

When to file

You should not file Form 4810 until after you file the tax returns listed on the front of this form. **Note:** The special limitation period applies only to the returns you list on this form. You must submit a separate request for prompt assessment for any tax returns you file after you file Form 481 0.

Where to file

Send your request to the Internal Revenue Service office where you filed your returns.

What to file

This Form 481 0 provides spaces for all information required to process a request for prompt assessment. If you prefer to use your own format, you must file the request by itself and it must clearly show:

- that it is a request for prompt assessment under I RC§ 6501(d)

- the kind of tax and tax periods

- the name and social security number or employer identification number shown on the return *(copies of returns maybe attached to help identify your* return; write *at top of* return: **"Copy-Do not process as original"**)

- the date and location of the IRS office where you filed the returns

- verification of your authority to act for the taxpayers, such as letters testamentary, letters of administration, etc.

Paperwork Reduction Act Notice - We ask for the information on this form to ensure compliance with the Internal Revenue laws of the United States. These laws require you to give us this information so that we can compute and collect the correct amount of tax.

You are not required to provide the information requested on a form that is subject to the Paperwork Reduction Act unless the form displays a valid OMB control number. Books or records relating to a form or its instructions must be related as long as their contents may become material in the administration of any Internal Revenue law. Generally, tax returns and return information are confidential, as required by code section 6103.

The time needed to complete and file this form will vary depending on individual circumstances. The estimated average time is: **30 minutes**

If you have comments about the accuracy of this estimated time of completion, or have suggestions for making this form simpler, we would be happy to hear from you. You may write to the:

Tax Forms Committee
Western Area Distribution Center
Rancho Cordova, CA 95743-0001

DO NOT send the tax form to this office. Instead, see the instruction above for information on where to file.

Cat. No. 42022S   Form **4810** (Rev. 12-1999)

¶1062 DISCUSSION QUESTIONS

1. You are dealing with a Revenue Agent in the audit of one of your clients. The Agent requests that you as the taxpayer's representative execute a Form 872, extending the statute of limitations on behalf of your client.

   (A) Under what circumstances should *you* personally (as opposed to your client) sign the Form 872?

   (B) Under what circumstances should you recommend to your clients that they do not sign a Form 872?

2. Is it more favorable for the taxpayer to sign a Form 872-A than to sign a Form 872?

3. If you are called in as a representative during an audit and you find out that your client has executed a Form 872-A, what steps, if any, should you take?

4. The taxpayer, a corporation with an April 30 fiscal year, mails its return for the year 2004 to the Any City Service Center on July 14, 2004. The return is received at the Service Center on July 16, 2004. Three years later, on July 16, 2007, the IRS mails the taxpayer a notice of deficiency seeking additional tax for the 2004 year. Is the proposed assessment barred by the statute of limitations?

5. (A) If the IRS prepares a return under Code Sec. 6020(b) for an individual's taxable year 2004, when would the statute of limitations expire with respect to that return?

   (B) How can the taxpayer in (A) cause the statute of limitations to expire earlier?

6. Harry Hardluck incurred a net operating loss in 2004 and carried it back to 2001. In auditing the 2004 return and its net operating loss, the year 2001 is also examined. An error in the 2001 return is found resulting in a deficiency. Assuming that the 2001 return was filed on April 15, 2002, and that the 2004 return was filed on April 15, 2005, what is the last date the IRS can assess and collect additional tax for the 2001 year? Explain in full.

7. Backhand Berg, an accrual basis taxpayer, is a sole proprietor operating a tennis and sporting goods store in Sportville, U.S.A. Berg reported the following items of income and expense on his federal tax return for the calendar year 2004:

Gross Business Receipts		$200,000
Cost of Goods Sold		90,000
Gross Profit		$110,000
Expenses		
Wages	$(70,000)	
Other	(15,000)	
		(85,000)

Net Profit	$25,000
Interest Income (from bank account)	5,000
Adjusted Gross Income	$30,000

Assuming that Berg's return is filed on January 6, 2005, on what date will the statute of limitations on assessment of tax expire in each of the following situations? Explain.

(A) An IRS audit later reveals that Berg's Cost of Goods Sold was actually $30,000.

(B) An IRS audit later reveals that Berg failed to report $60,000 in gross business receipts.

(C) Berg attached the following note to his return:

Dear Sir:

In April of 2004, I sold certain tennis equipment to Don Deadbeat in return for his $60,000 promissory note. Since Don has a reputation as a poor credit risk, I am not going to report this amount as income until he redeems the note in 2005.

Sincerely,

Backhand Berg

(D) An IRS audit later reveals that Berg failed to report certain dividends paid to him by the Racquet Corp. The corporation's books clearly show that Berg received $54,000 in dividend income in 2004.

(E) Berg was on a tennis vacation in Australia during April of 2005 and completely forgot to file a tax return for 2004.

8. On March 12, 2004, Understatement, Inc., a new corporation, files its first corporate income tax return for the calendar year 2003. The return shows gross receipts of $700,000, expenses of $200,000, and no other transactions. However, Schedule L, the balance sheet to the return, shows the sole asset at the beginning of the tax year as being land with a cost of $300,000. The sole asset shown on the balance sheet at the end of the tax year is cash of $1,000,000. What the return did not disclose was that the land with a cost basis of $300,000 was sold for $500,000 cash during the year in question.

On April 1, 2009, the IRS issues a notice of deficiency to assess the tax on the unreported sale of the land. The taxpayer contends that theassessment is barred by the statute of limitations under Code Sec. 6501(a). The IRS argues that the failure to report the sale of the land has resulted in a substantial omission of gross income which renders the six-year statute under Code Sec. 6501(e) applicable. The taxpayer counters with the contention that a comparison of the beginning and ending balance sheet for the corporation clearly discloses that the property had been sold and thus that there is an adequate disclosure of the income apprising the

Commissioner of the nature and amount of the item omitted. Is the notice of deficiency valid?

9. Brite Bros., Inc., is a consulting company which keeps its books on the cash basis method and operates on a calendar year. In 2003, the corporation erroneously included in income the amount realized on a project completed in December 2003. The corporation did not receive payment from the client until January 2004. The income, however, was reported on the 2003 corporate tax return filed on March 15, 2004.

On August 2, 2007, the IRS commenced an audit of Brite Bros. for the tax year 2004. During the audit the revenue agent discovered the error and included the amount in income for 2004. The 2004 tax return was filed on March 15, 2005.

(A) Can Brite Bros. file a claim for refund for the tax year 2003? If not, what would you advise them to do?

(B) Assume there was no audit and that Brite Bros. discovered on August 2, 2007, that they erroneously deducted the cost of certain materials in 2003 which should have been deducted on their 2004 return. If the corporation files a claim for refund for the 2004 tax year, what recourse would the IRS have?

¶1062

CHAPTER 11
ACCESS TO INTERNAL REVENUE SERVICE INFORMATION

¶1101 INTRODUCTION

In the process of administering the Internal Revenue Code (the Code), the Internal Revenue Service (IRS) obtains and generates a substantial amount of information. This may take the form of workpapers, memoranda, records and other documents gathered or produced during examinations of taxpayers. Such information also may include determinations, rules, procedures and legal positions developed within the IRS or adopted by Chief Counsel. Congress has enacted specific laws to require disclosure of such information to taxpayers in appropriate situations. Superimposed on these provisions for liberal disclosure is additional legislation which seeks to protect the privacy and confidentiality of tax information furnished to the IRS. At times, these protective provisions and disclosure requirements appear to work at cross purposes.

In addition to the access to IRS information provided by specific legislation, taxpayers involved in civil tax litigation may obtain relevant information from the IRS under the pretrial discovery rules available in these proceedings. The Tax Court, the Court of Federal Claims and the district courts all permit such discovery under their own rules of procedure.

¶1103 THE FREEDOM OF INFORMATION ACT

The most important legislation permitting taxpayer access to IRS information was enacted in 1967. Commonly known as the Freedom of Information Act (FOIA), this law provides that, with certain exceptions and exclusions, every government agency is required to make available to the public all information and records in the possession of such agency.[1] The Act sets forth three methods by which certain types of information will be made available. The first requires current publication in the Federal Register of the agency's procedural and operating rules, substantive rules, general policy statements and descriptions of its organization.[2] The second method of disclosure requires that each agency permit inspection and copying of final opinions and orders in litigated cases, policy statements and interpretations not published in the Federal Register and administrative staff manuals and instructions that affect the public.[3] Most of the relevant information made available for inspection or published in the Federal Register by the IRS has been reproduced by commercial publishers and may be found in most tax libraries.

---

[1] 5 U.S.C. §552.
[2] 5 U.S.C. §552(a)(1).
[3] 5 U.S.C. §552(a)(2). Such material relating to the IRS is generally available in the public reading rooms at the National Office and regional offices. Copies will be mailed upon request, but such service is subject to standard fees. Reg. §601.702(b)(3).

The third method for making information available to the public is probably the most significant to tax practitioners. Any person may request access to any records maintained by the IRS.[4] The right to disclosure under FOIA, however, is limited by nine specific exemptions and three exclusions (see ¶1105). In addition, the restrictions relating to confidentiality of tax returns and return information under Code Sec. 6103 further limit the information the IRS is permitted to disclose.

¶1104 RULINGS, DETERMINATION LETTERS AND TECHNICAL ADVICE MEMORANDA

In 1976, Congress enacted Code Sec. 6110 to permit open public inspection of private letter rulings, determination letters and technical advice memoranda issued by the IRS.[5] This enactment preempted and superseded all requirements of FOIA to make such information available to the public.[6] Under Code Sec. 6110, the text of any ruling, determination letter, or technical advice memorandum is made available after identifying details and confidential information regarding the taxpayer have been deleted.[7] Any background information in the IRS files relating to the request for a ruling or determination will be made available only upon special request.[8] Revenue Procedure 95-15 sets forth the procedure for making requests for background file documents relating to a ruling or technical advice memorandum. Any technical advice memorandum involving a matter that is the subject of a civil or criminal fraud investigation or a jeopardy or termination assessment is not subject to inspection until all actions relating to such investigation or assessment are completed.[9]

The rulings or determinations required to be disclosed may not be used or cited as precedent in any proceeding.[10] There must be deleted from such disclosures all identifying details regarding the person requesting the determination as well as all information generally exempted under FOIA.[11]

Private letter rulings and technical advice memoranda are open to inspection and copying at the public reading rooms of the National Office of the IRS.[12] Determination letters may be inspected and copied at the reading rooms of theregional offices of the districts which issued the letters.[13] Written requests for copies of such material may be made to the IRS reading rooms holding such material for inspection.[14]

---

[4] 5 U.S.C. §552(a)(3). See ¶1107, *infra,* for procedures relating to the formal request for such information.

[5] See Chapter 16, *infra,* for discussion of procedures relating to issuance of private letter rulings and determination letters.

[6] Code Sec. 6110(l).

[7] Code Sec. 6110(c).

[8] Code Sec. 6110(e); Reg. §§301.6110-1(b) and 301.6110-5(d).

[9] Reg. §301.6110-1(b)(2).

[10] Reg. §301.6110-7(b). However, private letter rulings may be cited to avoid the substantial understatement penalty under Code Sec. 6662(d)(2)(B)(i).

[11] See ¶1105.

[12] These rulings and memoranda are now commercially published and are available in most tax libraries.

[13] Reg. §301.6110-1(c).

[14] *Id.*

¶1105 EXEMPTIONS AND EXCLUSIONS UNDER FOIA

The Freedom of Information Act provides nine specific exemptions from required disclosure.[15] Only five of these are relevant to the typical disclosure requested by a taxpayer.[16]

Internal Personnel Rules and Practices. In general, rules which only affect the conduct of IRS personnel as employees and do not relate to their conduct with respect to the public are exempted from disclosure. However, if an internal personnel rule or practice affects interests outside of the IRS, it must be made available to the public.[17] Major portions of the Internal Revenue Manual have been made available to the public despite this exemption.[18] Such information will be made available unless the information would assist an individual in evading the law or would endanger the safety of law enforcement agents.[19]

Information Exempt by Statute. Information need not be disclosed under FOIA if it is specifically exempted from disclosure by some other statute. Such statutes must (1) require that the matter be withheld from the public in such a manner as to leave no discretion on the issue, or (2) establish particular criteria for withholding or references to particular matters to be withheld.[20] The most important tax statute exempting such information from disclosure is Code Sec. 6103, which makes tax returns and return information confidential.[21]

Confidentiality Under Code Sec. 6103. No tax returns or return information may be disclosed to anyone unless such disclosure is specifically authorized by Code Sec. 6103.[22] The definition of return information protected from unauthorized disclosure is extremely broad. In addition to a taxpayer's identity and the information reported on tax returns, return information also includes all information obtained during, or relating to, any tax examination or investigation of the taxpayer.[23] Tax shelter registration applications, the fact of registration, the registration letters that the IRS sends to registrants and the tax shelter registration number all constitute "return information."[24] Data which does not directly or indirectly identify a particular taxpayer, however, does not constitute return information. Despite this exception to the confidentiality coverage, standards used by the IRS for the selection of returns for audit or data used in determining such standards need not be disclosed if the IRS determines that such disclosure will seriously impair assessment, collection or enforcement under the Internal Revenue laws.[25]

---

[15] 5 U.S.C. § 552(b).

[16] The four exemptions which are normally irrelevant to the usual request for tax information include (1) matters involving national security, (2) personnel and medical files, (3) information relating to the regulation of financial institutions, and (4) geological and geophysical information concerning wells.

[17] See *Dept. of Air Force v. Rose*, 425 U.S. 352 (1976).

[18] *Long v. IRS*, 339 F.Supp. 1266 (W.D. Wash. 1971), 72-1 USTC ¶ 9110.

[19] *Crooker v. Bureau of Alcohol, Tobacco & Firearms*, 670 F.2d 1051 (D.C. Cir. 1981).

[20] 5 U.S.C. § 552(b)(3).

[21] The disclosure of such information under FOIA is controlled by Code Sec. 6103.

[22] Unauthorized disclosure is subject to criminal prosecution under Code Sec. 7216, and the injured taxpayer may file suit for civil damages under Code Sec. 7431.

[23] Code Sec. 6103(b)(2).

[24] CCA 200336029.

[25] *Buckner v. IRS*, 25 F.Supp2.d 893 (1998) USDC NO. D. Ind., 98-2 USTC ¶ 50,640; *Coolman v. United States*, US-CT-APP-8, 2000-1 USTC ¶ 50,113.

A taxpayer's returns and return information, of course, may be disclosed to the individual taxpayer. Such disclosure also may be made to the taxpayer's authorized representative or to any other person designated in writing to receive such information.[26] However, return information will not be disclosed even to the taxpayer or those authorized by the taxpayer if the IRS determines "that such disclosures would seriously impair Federal tax administration."[27] "Tax administration" is broadly defined to cover all governmental functions relating to the tax laws, including the formulation of tax policy and the assessment, collection and enforcement activities of the IRS. This restriction on disclosure is primarily relied upon to deny a taxpayer access to information gathered by the Criminal Investigation Division of the IRS during an investigation of the taxpayer for violations of the tax laws. Disclosure of documents and information relating to a taxpayer's own tax liability have been denied under these circumstances on the ground that such disclosure would prematurely reveal the scope, direction and level of the government's investigation.[28] The government contends in these situations that such early disclosure might permit the taxpayer to interfere with potential witnesses or tailor a defense to counter the information in the IRS files.[29]

Trade Secrets and Commercial or Financial Information. For tax purposes, the FOIA exemption from disclosure of "trade secrets and commercial or financial information" is reinforced by Code Secs. 6103 and 6110.[30] Any such data obtained by the IRS which constitutes "return information" may not be disclosed unless disclosure is specifically permitted by Code Sec. 6103. If such information was submitted to the IRS for the purpose of obtaining a private letter ruling, a determination or technical advice, Code Sec. 6110(c)(4) explicitly exempts this confidential business data from disclosure. Treasury regulations provide specific procedures for promptly notifying a business submitter of such information that an FOIA request for this data has been made.[31] Procedures for objecting to such a request and litigating any administrative determination are also set forth in the regulation.

Inter-Agency or Intra-Agency Memoranda or Letters. This exemption denies access to IRS memoranda and letters that relate to the IRS's deliberative or policy-making processes that would not be subject to discovery in any tax litigation.[32] The purpose of the exemption is to protect the open exchange of ideas during the deliberative process that occurs *prior* to a final decision on a matter by the IRS. Any memoranda issued after the final decision to explain that decision, however, are not exempt.[33]

---

[26] Code Sec. 6103(c); Reg. § 301.6103(c)-1.

[27] *Id.*

[28] *Youngblood v. Comm'r,* 2000-1 USTC ¶ 50,457 CD Cal 2000 (Special Agents Report); *Anderson v. United States,* 83 AFTR 2d 99-2051 WD Tenn. 1999, checkspread shown to taxpayer during interview. However, in *Grasso v. IRS,* 785 F.2d 70 (3d Cir. 1986), 86-1 USTC ¶ 9263, the court affirmed an order to disclose IRS memoranda of interviews with the taxpayer conducted during an investigation of his civil and criminal tax liability.

[29] *Holbrook v. IRS,* 914 F.Supp 314 (SD Iowa 1996).

[30] 5 U.S.C. § 552(b)(4).

[31] Reg. § 601.702(h).

[32] 5 U.S.C. § 552(b)(5).

[33] *NLRB v. Sears, Roebuck & Co.,* 421 U.S. 132 (1975); *Taxation With Representation Fund v. IRS,* 646 F.2d 666 (D.C. Cir. 1981), 81-1 USTC ¶ 9252 (General Counsel's memoranda and technical memoranda); *Tax Analysts v. IRS,* 117 F.3d 607 (DC Cir. 1997) (Field Service Advice Memoranda, i.e., FSAs).

Investigatory Records and Information. FOIA exempts records or information compiled for law enforcement purposes, but only to the extent that the disclosure of such material:

> (A) could reasonably be expected to interfere with enforcement proceedings, (B) would deprive a person of a right to a fair trial or an impartial adjudication, (C) could reasonably be expected to constitute an unwarranted invasion of personal privacy, (D) could reasonably be expected to disclose the identity of a confidential source, including a State, local or foreign agency or authority or any private institution which furnished information on a confidential basis, and, in the case of a record or information compiled by criminal law enforcement authority in the course of a criminal investigation or by an agency conducting a lawful national security intelligence investigation, information furnished by a confidential source, (E) would disclose techniques and procedures for law enforcement investigations or prosecutions, or would disclose guidelines for law enforcement investigations or prosecutions if such disclosure could reasonably be expected to risk circumvention of the law or (F) could reasonably be expected to endanger the life or physical safety of any individual.[34]

This exemption is usually asserted by the IRS when a taxpayer under criminal investigation requests disclosure of all workpapers, memoranda, records and other information gathered by the IRS during the investigation. With the exception of memoranda or records of the taxpayer's own statements, normally such investigatory information is exempt from disclosure.[35] The refusal to produce such records and information is generally based on the belief by the IRS that such disclosure would interfere with the criminal investigation, would reveal the identity of a confidential informant or would disclose investigation or prosecution techniques and procedures.

General Exclusions. In criminal tax investigations, certain records may be treated as though they were not subject to the requirements of FOIA.[36] These exclusions were added to the Act in 1986 to permit a government agency, including the IRS, to ignore requests for records and information when a response to the request would disclose that a criminal investigation is in progress, and the target of the investigation is not aware that he or she is being investigated. Requests for records relating to a confidential informant may also be ignored when the existence of the informant has not been officially confirmed. A response denying such requests would reveal, in substance, that there was an ongoing investigation or confidential informant.

¶1107 REQUESTS FOR INFORMATION

During the administrative processing of civil tax cases and the investigation of criminal tax cases, taxpayers may resort to FOIA to request records and information from the examination and investigation files of the IRS. Other information maintained by the IRS may also be specifically requested if such material is not published in the Federal Register or made available at the IRS national and regional offices. As a practical matter, however, tax practitioners will be primar-

---

[34] 5 U.S.C. § 552(b)(7).
[35] See notes 27 and 32.

[36] 5 U.S.C. § 552(c).

ily concerned with records and information obtained by the IRS during examinations and investigations of the taxpayer.

All requests for records and information must be made in writing to the disclosure officer in the appropriate office. The procedure to be followed and the contents of the letter requesting such information are set forth in the Statement of Procedural Rules.[37] Such a letter (see Exhibit 11-1 at ¶1151) must contain the following information:

1. A statement that the request is being made pursuant to FOIA, 5 U.S.C. §552.

2. The address of the IRS disclosure officer who will handle the request.[38]

3. A reasonable description of the records requested to enable the IRS to locate the records.

4. If the requested records contain information which is restricted or limited as to disclosure, sufficient identification or authorization to establish the right to disclosure. A notarized statement affirming identity or a photocopy of a driver's license is sufficient.

5. The address of the person(s) to whom the information and notice of the action on the request should be sent.

6. A request for either inspection or copies of the requested information.

7. A statement agreeing to pay the official fees for copying and research.[39]

8. A statement which identifies the requester as either a commercial use requester, media requester, educational institution requester, noncommercial scientific institution requester or other requester.

A tax practitioner who requests records and files relating to an examination or investigation of a taxpayer is classified as an "other requester." A representative filing a request on behalf of a taxpayer should include a properly executed Power of Attorney (Form 2848, see Exhibit 2-4 at ¶254) or Tax Information Authorization (Form 8821, see Exhibit 2-3 at ¶253).

In responding to the request, the disclosure officer will indicate which portions of the requested material have been deleted or removed. A typical IRS letter responding to the request is included as Exhibit 11-2 at ¶1152. Although the IRS is required by law to respond within ten working days, in most situations the disclosure officer requests additional time to locate and review the records. Such delay could be contested in court, but normally a taxpayer will permit the additional time if the request is reasonable.

As a general rule, in civil cases all examination files will be made available to the requester after deletion or removal of any return information relating to third parties and other information exempt from disclosure under FOIA. If exempt

---

[37] Reg. §601.702(c). See also, IRM Handbook 1.3.13.5.

[38] The mailing addresses of the disclosure officers who will respond to the request are set forth in Reg. §601.702(g).

[39] The fees for copying and research are set forth in Reg. §601.702(f).

¶1107

information can be separated and deleted from the requested information, the remainder must be disclosed.[40]

Specific fees for search time and copying the requested material are set forth in the regulations.[41] Those who are classified as other requesters, a category into which most taxpayers' requests will fall, are not charged for the first two hours of search time or the first 100 copies. To avoid unexpectedly high fees, the request may include a dollar limit which should not be exceeded unless the requester is first notified of the anticipated charges. If the costs will exceed $250, advance payment may be required.[42]

¶1109 ADMINISTRATIVE APPEALS AND JUDICIAL REVIEW

If the request for information under FOIA is either denied or partially denied, an appeal may be filed with the Commissioner of Internal Revenue within thirty-five days after notice of denial.[43] The letter of appeal should be addressed to:

> Freedom of Information Appeal
> Commissioner of Internal Revenue
> Ben Franklin Station
> P.O. Box 929
> Washington, DC 20044

The letter should describe the records requested, indicate the date of the original request and the office to which it was submitted and enclose copies of the initial request and the letter denying the request. Arguments in support of the appeal should be set forth in the letter. Generally, these arguments will attempt to establish that the FOIA exemptions cited for denial of the request do not apply to the records in question.

The Commissioner must issue a decision on such administrative appeals within twenty working days after receipt of the appeal.[44] If the appeal is either denied or partially denied, or if the Commissioner has not acted timely in responding to the appeal, a suit requesting judicial review may be commenced in a United States District Court.[45] The court will determine the matter *de novo* on the basis of the evidence and arguments presented to the court. In these proceedings, the burden of proof is on the IRS to justify withholding the records under one or more of the FOIA exemptions.[46] The court may ask to examine the

---

[40] 5 U.S.C. § 552(b); Reg. § 601.701(b)(3).

[41] Reg. § 601.702(f).

[42] Reg. § 601.702(f)(4).

[43] Reg. § 601.702(c)(8).

[44] Up to an additional ten days may be allowed under certain circumstances. Reg. § 601.702(c)(9).

[45] The action may be brought in the district where the requester resides or has his or her principal place of business, in the district where the requested records are located or in the District of Columbia. 5 U.S.C. § 552(a)(4)(B). For the district court to have jurisdiction, the requester must show that the agency has improperly withheld agency records.

Gabel v. Comm'r, 61 F.3d 910 (9th Cir. 1995), 95-1 USTC ¶ 50,289.

[46] When the confidentiality restrictions of Code Sec. 6103 apply, there is a split of authority among the courts of appeals as to whether this specific Code provision supersedes the disclosure requirements of FOIA. For a discussion of these conflicting views, see *DeSalvo v. IRS*, 861 F.2d 1217 (10th Cir. 1988), 88-2 USTC ¶ 9609; *Church of Scientology v. IRS*, 792 F.2d 146 (DC Cir. 1986), *en banc aff'd* 484 US 9 (1987), 87-2 USTC ¶ 9604; *Grasso v. IRS*, 785 F.2d 70 (3rd Cir. 1986), 86-1 USTC ¶ 9263; *Long v. IRS*, 596 F.2d 362 (9th Cir. 1979), 79-1 USTC ¶ 9381; *Linsteadt v. IRS*, 729 F.2d 998 (CA 5, 1984), 84-1 USTC ¶ 9392. The minority view that Code Sec. 6103 is controlling

requested records *in camera* to determine whether any of them, or any part of them, should be withheld. To avoid the judicial burden of such *in camera* inspections, the courts have frequently ordered the government to submit a detailed listing of the items withheld which specifically describes each record and explains the exemption which is claimed to apply. This listing is known as a "*Vaughn* index," named after the case in which it was first required.[47]

¶1111 THE PRIVACY ACT

The Privacy Act was enacted in 1974 for the purpose of regulating the disclosure and management of records maintained by a government agency with respect to any individual.[48] In general, the Privacy Act permits disclosure only for limited purposes, allows access by the individual to his or her records, requires an accounting of disclosures made by the agency to other parties, permits an individual to correct erroneous information in his or her records, and requires the agency to explain its authority and reason when requesting information. In addition, an agency generally must inform an individual upon request about any disclosures of his records made by the agency to other parties. The Privacy Act also prevents an agency from maintaining in its files any information about an individual that is not relevant and necessary to the purpose to be accomplished by the agency.

Despite these elaborate provisions designed to protect an individual from improper government disclosure of records and permitting an individual access to such records, the Privacy Act has very little, if any, real importance in the area of taxation. The restrictions on disclosure have been essentially preempted by the confidentiality provisions of Code Sec. 6103 relating to "return information." The Secretary of the Treasury, moreover, has issued regulations specifically exempting from the disclosure and other requirements of the Privacy Act all IRS records and files accumulated for purposes of examination, investigation, collection and appeals.[49] Any meaningful access to such IRS records and information is available only under FOIA. In addition, Code Sec. 7852(e) precludes a taxpayer from resorting to the Privacy Act in an attempt to correct any erroneous information in his or her IRS files when such information relates directly or indirectly to the existence or determination of that individual's liability under the tax laws.

The Privacy Act does not impose any additional exemptions from, or restrictions on, disclosure under FOIA. If FOIA permits access to records or informa-

---

(Footnote Continued)

eliminates the heavy burden of proof on the government under FOIA and merely requires the court to determine if the decision not to disclose was "arbitrary, capricious, an abuse of discretion, or otherwise not in accordance with law." 5 U.S.C. §706(2)(A). See *Aronson v. IRS*, 973 F.2d 962 (1st Cir. 1992), 92-2 USTC ¶50,366.

[47] *Vaughn v. Rosen*, 484 F.2d 820 (D.C. Cir. 1973). See also, *Osborn v. IRS*, 754 F.2d 195 (6th Cir. 1985), 85-1 USTC ¶9187. Indexing each document may be unnecessary in some cases, and a category by cate-

gory listing may be sufficient if the categories are sufficiently distinct to enable a court to make a determination. *Vaughn v. IRS*, 936 F.2d 862 (6th Cir. 1991).

[48] 5 U.S.C. §552(a).

[49] 31 CFR §1.36 (IRS Notice of Exempt Systems). Specific procedures for making requests for nonexempt IRS records under the Privacy Act are set forth in 31 CFR, Subtitle A, Part I, Subpart C, Appendix B. See also, IRM Handbook 1.3.14.

tion, the Privacy Act specifically allows such disclosure.[50] As a result of the specific statutory provisions and regulations limiting the application of the Privacy Act, a taxpayer's request for IRS records or information under FOIA will not be affected, either favorably or unfavorably, by the access requirements or disclosure restrictions of the Privacy Act.

¶1113 PRETRIAL DISCOVERY

When tax cases go to trial, the taxpayer has additional opportunity to obtain information from the IRS by resorting to the pretrial discovery rules applicable to proceedings in the Tax Court, the Court of Federal Claims and federal district courts.[51] The rules generally provide that, prior to trial, a party may obtain discovery of any information which is not privileged and which is relevant to the subject matter involved in the pending action. The methods for obtaining such discovery include depositions (formal questioning of witness with opportunity to cross-examine by opposing counsel), written interrogatories (questions requiring written responses) and requests for production of documents.[52]

The government may object to discovery of IRS records and information on the ground that such matters are privileged or are not relevant to the issues in the tax case. The privileges commonly raised as objections include the attorney-client privilege, the work-product doctrine and the qualified executive privilege.[53] With the exception of the qualified executive privilege, the courts have generally held such privileges to be inapplicable to IRS documents and information acquired or generated during the administrative stages of a tax case.[54]

The qualified executive privilege protects the confidentiality of the deliberative or policy-making process of the executive branch of the government and the various agencies involved. Congress intended to incorporate this rule of privilege in the FOIA exemption from disclosure of "interagency or intraagency memoranda or letters."[55] The purpose of the privilege and the FOIA exemption is to promote the free exchange of ideas during preliminary deliberations within government agencies. Knowledge that information and memoranda relating to such deliberations might be readily accessible to the public would obviously discourage open discussion. The privilege is not absolute, however, and discovery will be permitted when the information involves purely factual material or when there is a compelling evidentiary need for such information.[56]

---

[50] 5 U.S.C. § 552(a)(b)(2).

[51] Tax Court Rules of Practice and Procedure, Rules 70 through 90, 15 CCH STANDARD FEDERAL TAX REPORTER, ¶ 42,930, *et seq.*; Rules of the United States Court of Federal Claims, Rules 26 through 37, 28 U.S.C.A.; Federal Rules of Civil Procedure, Rules 26 through 37, 28 U.S.C.A.

[52] The conditions upon which depositions may be taken are far more restrictive in the Tax Court than in the other federal courts. See Tax Court Rules 74 through 85.

[53] *P.T. & L. Construction Co. v. Comm'r*, 63 TC 404 (1974), CCH Dec. 32,993; *Branerton Corp. v. Comm'r*,

64 TC 191 (1975), CCH Dec. 33,178; *Barger v. Comm'r*, 65 TC 925 (1976), CCH Dec. 33,650.

[54] *Id.*

[55] 5 U.S.C. § 552(b)(5); *EPA v. Mink*, 410 U.S. 73, 86 (1973). See discussion at ¶ 1105, *supra.*

[56] *EPA v. Mink*, 410 U.S. at 91, *supra*, note 53; cases cited *supra*, note 51. *Linsteadt v. IRS*, 729 F.2d 998 (5th Cir. 1984), 84-1 USTC ¶ 9392. The minority view that Code Sec. 6103 is controlling eliminates the heavy burden of proof on the government under FOIA and merely requires the court to determine if the decision not to disclose was "arbitrary, capricious, an abuse of discretion, or otherwise not in accordance with law." 5 U.S.C. § 706(2)(A). See *Ar-*

¶1151 Exhibit 11-1

FOIA Request
June 18, 2001

Disclosure Officer

Internal Revenue Service

(Address)

Re: (Taxpayer's Name)

S.S. No.:_____

Years:_____

Dear _____:

This request for information under the Freedom of Information Act, 5 U.S.C. § 552, is made by _____, attorney for the taxpayer. A Power of Attorney and Declaration accompany this request. The records requested are as follows:

(a) All workpapers, correspondance, and other documents pertinent to the examination and investigation of the federal income tax liability of the above-named taxpayer for the years (specify years) including, but not limited to: (describe records in detail).

(b) All statements given by the taxpayer to the Internal Revenue Service during the course of its examination, including all written statements, all oral statements recorded by any mechanical recording device, all oral statements reduced to writing by Internal Revenue Agents, whether verbatim or not, and whether or not signed by the taxpayer.

My return address is:

(Attorney's Name and Address)

_____

_____

I am authorized and agree to pay the current fee per copy for each copy obtained pursuant to this request and also the currently hourly search fee. I attest under penalty of perjury that I am **not** a (a) commercial use requester, (b) media requester, (c) educational institutions requester, or (d) noncommercial scientific institution requester, but that I am an (e) other requester.

Yours very truly,

(Attorney for Taxpayer)

(Footnote Continued)

onson v. IRS, 973 F.2d 962 (1st Cir. 1992), 92-2 USTC ¶ 50,366.

¶1151

¶1152 Exhibit 11-2

FOIA Reply

Internal Revenue Service	Department of the Treasury
Disclosure Office	Person to Contact:
	Telephone Number:
	Refer Reply to:
	Date:

Dear _____:

We are replying to your Freedom of Information request of _____, regarding your client, _____. We are enclosing copies of all nonexempt documents found in their examination file. Your payment of $__ for our copying costs has been received.

Certain information was removed from the file since it is exempt from disclosure under the provisions of the Freedom of Information Act. We have listed this material below and cited the appropriate exemptions at the end of this letter.

1. The Discriminant Function (DIF) Score has been deleted from eight pages because DIF scores are solely related to internal practices and their release would reveal guidelines used in our investigations.[1]

2. Information related to years not covered by your power of attorney has been deleted.[2]

3. Confidential tax information of third-party taxpayers has been deleted.[3]

4. Information which could impair tax administration has been deleted.[4]

Since we withheld information from your client's file, your request has been partially denied. However, you may appeal this decision. We have enclosed Notice 393 which provides information concerning your appeal rights.

If you have any questions, please contact _____ at _____.

Sincerely yours,

Disclosure Officer

Enclosures

---

[1] FOIA Subsection (b)(2), (b)(7)(E), and (b)(3) with IRC Section 6103(b)(2).

[2] FOIA Subsection (b)(3) with IRC Section 6103(a).

[3] FOIA Subsection (b)(7)(C) and (b)(3) with IRC Section 6103(a).

[4] FOIA Subsection (b)(2) and (b)(7)(E) with IRC Section 6103(e)(7).

Notice 393 (Rev. 4-94)
Information on an IRS Determination to Withhold Records Exempt From The Freedom Of Information Act — 5 U.S.C. 552

Appeal Rights

You may file an appeal with the Internal Revenue Service within 35 days after we (1) determine to withhold records, (2) determine that no records exist, or (3) deny a fee waiver or a favorable fee category. If some records are released at a later date, you may file within 35 days after the date the last records were released.

The appeal must be in writing, must be signed by you, and must contain the following information:

> Your name and address
>
> description of the requested records
>
> date of the request (and a copy, if possible)
>
> date of the letter denying the request (and a copy, if possible)

Mail your appeal to:

> Internal Revenue Service
> Richmond Appeals Office—FOIA Appeal
> 2727 Enterprise parkway Suite 100
> Richmond, VA 23229

Judicial Review

If we deny your appeal, or if we do not send you a reply within 20 days (not counting Saturdays, Sundays, or legal public holidays) after the date we received the appeal, you may file a complaint with the U.S. District Court in the district where (1) you reside, (2) your principal place of business is located, or (3) the records are located. You may also file in the District Court for the District of Columbia.

The court will treat your complaint according to the Federal Rules of Civil Procedure (F.R.C.P.). Service of process is governed by Rule 4(d)(4) and (5), which requires that a copy of the summons and complaint be (1) personally served on the United States Attorney for the district in which the lawsuit is brought; (2) sent by registered or certified mail to the Attorney General of the United States at Washington, D.C., and (3) sent by registered or certified mail to the Commissioner of Internal Revenue, Attn: CC:EL:D, 1111 Constitution Avenue, N.W., Washington, D.C. 20224.

In such a court case, the burden is on the Internal Revenue Service to justify withholding the requested records, determining that no records exist, or denying a fee waiver or a favorable fee category. The court may assess against the United States reasonable attorney fees and other litigation costs incurred by the person who takes the case to court and who substantially prevails. You will have substantially prevailed if the court determines, among other factors, that you had to file the lawsuit to obtain the records you requested and that the Internal

¶1152

Revenue Service had no reasonable grounds to withhold the records. See Internal Revenue Service Regulations 26 CFR 601.702 for further details.

Exemptions

The Freedom of Information Act, 5 U.S.C. 552, does not apply to matters that are—

(b)(1) • (A) specifically authorized under criteria established by an Executive Order to be kept secret in the interest of national defense or foreign policy and

(B) are in fact properly classified under such an Executive Order;

(b)(2) • related solely to the internal personnel rules and practices of an agency;

(b)(3) • specifically exempt from disclosure by statute (other than section 552b of this title), provided that the statute

(A) requires that the matters be withheld from the public in such a manner as to leave no discretion on the issue, or

(B) establishes particular criteria for withholding or refers to particular types of matters to be withheld;

Note: subsection (b)(3) protects information exempted by certain qualifying statutes, such as Internal Revenue Code section 6103, which protects tax returns and information generated by and collected by the IRS with regard to a taxpayer.

(b)(4) • trade secrets and commercial or financial information obtained from a person and privileged or confidential;

(b)(5) • inter-agency or intra-agency memorandums or letters which would not be available by law to a party other than an agency in litigation with the agency;

(b)(6) • personnel and medical files and similar files the disclosure of which would constitute a clearly unwarranted invasion of personal privacy;

(b)(7) • records or information compiled for law enforcement purposes, but only to the extent that the production of such law enforcement records or information

(A) could reasonably be expected to interfere with enforcement proceedings,

(B) would deprive a person of a right to a fair trial or an impartial adjudication,

(C) could reasonably be expected to constitute an unwarranted invasion of personal privacy,

(D) could reasonably be expected to disclose the identity of a confidential source, including a State, local or foreign agency or authority or any private institution which furnished information on a confidential basis, and, in the case of a record or information compiled by a criminal law enforcement authority in the course of a criminal investigation, or by an agency conducting a lawful national security intelligence investigation, information furnished by a confidential source,

(E) would disclose techniques and procedures for law enforcement investigations or prosecutions, or would disclose guidelines for law enforcement investigations or prosecutions if such disclosure could reasonably be expected to risk circumvention of the law, or

(F) could reasonably be expected to endanger the life or physical safety of any individual;

(b)(8) • contained in or related to examination, operating, or condition reports prepared by, on behalf of, or for the use of an agency responsible for the regulation or supervision of financial institutions; or

(b)(9) • geological and geophysical information and data, including maps, concerning wells.

¶1152

¶1153 DISCUSSION QUESTIONS

1. Danny Delinquent is an American citizen who has been working for an oil company in Saudi Arabia for the past seven years. Danny has failed to file timely income tax returns for the years 1998 through 2004 under the mistaken impression that the Code Sec. 911 foreign earned income credit offset his tax liability. What he did not realize was that the credit is available only if he makes a timely election. Danny received a Notice of Assessment in the amount of $175,000 and has asked for your help in dealing with the Revenue Officer who is pursuing collection.

   In reviewing the matter you discover that there may be doubt as to Danny's liability and, therefore, you intend to file an Offer in Compromise as soon as possible. However, you need information from the IRS files and, therefore, you filed a request pursuant to the Freedom of Information Act (FOIA). The IRS Disclosure Officer has sent you a letter asking for an additional thirty days to locate and consider releasing the requested records. The letter reads as follows:

   Dear Representative:

   We are sorry, but we must ask for additional time to locate and consider releasing the IRS records of Danny Delinquent, because we are still searching for the 1998 through 2004 records. We will make every effort to respond within thirty days from the date of this letter.

   If you agree to this extension of time, no reply to this letter is necessary. You will still have the right to file an appeal if we subsequently deny your request.

   We hope you will agree to a voluntary extension of time. If you do not agree, you have the right to consider this letter as a denial and, if you wish, immediately file an appeal. If you have any question-sor need information about the status of your request, please contact the person whose name and telephone number are shown above.

   Thank you for your cooperation.

   Sincerely yours,

   Internal Revenue Service Disclosure Officer

   Do you voluntarily grant the extension to locate the records or file an appeal?

2. In January 2005, Sam Skimmer was interviewed by two special agents of the IRS in the course of a criminal tax investigation. In May 2005, Sam retained an attorney who in turn has hired you to assist him as his agent. A request was made under FOIA for the Special Agents' notes and memoranda prepared during the interview. The IRS Disclosure Officer responded by providing a copy of their memoranda of the interview.

However, significant portions had been deleted. The IRS stated that the deleted information is exempt from disclosure since such information would impair federal tax administration under Code Sec. 6103. Are there any grounds for appeal?

3. Attorney Larry Litigatee has been retained to represent a client in the U.S. Tax Court. As part of his pretrial discovery, Larry served the IRS with a Request for the Production of Documents under Tax Court Rule 72. Larry's request called for the production of the following documents:

(A) Copies of a statement made by his client in the presence of an IRS special agent and revenue agent.

(B) Copies of statements made by third parties who were interviewed by the IRS agents.

(C) Copies of a statement made by his client to a third party concerning issues to be addressed during the trial.

(D) Copies of all special agents' reports and revenue agents' reports concerning the case.

Can the IRS object to the production of any of the documents? If so, why? If not, why?

CHAPTER 12
THE APPEALS OFFICE

¶1201 INTRODUCTION

If an audit adjustment cannot be resolved at the Examination level, the Internal Revenue Service (IRS) provides a further opportunity to resolve tax controversies without litigation. This activity is conducted by the Appeals Office. As part of the IRS Restructuring and Reform Act of 1998,[1] the IRS Appeals Office has been realigned to coordinate with the new operating divisions of the IRS but maintain the current geographical alignment. Similar to the rest of the IRS, appeals officers will focus on taxpayers with similar concerns and issues.

Wage and Investment appeal officers will be centralized and conduct appeals primarily by telephone or correspondence; Small Business and Self-Employed (SB/SE) and Tax Exempt and Government Entities (TE/GE) appeals officers will be disbursed throughout the country to mirror the geographic disbursement of SB/SE staff. Due to the heavy concentration of large and mid-sized business (LMSB) taxpayers in large metropolitan areas, LMSB appeals officers will be concentrated in those large cities with limited representation elsewhere.[2]

¶1205 PROTEST REQUIREMENTS

Upon receipt of a thirty-day letter from an operating division proposing a deficiency, the taxpayer may request a conference with the Appeals Office. If the total amount of proposed additional tax is under $25,000 for each year or taxable period under consideration, the taxpayer may make a small case request. The small case request should be in writing and contain a brief statement of disputed issues for Appeals Office consideration.

A formal protest is required to obtain Appeals Office review of all other proposed deficiencies, all employee plan and exempt organization cases, and of all partnership and S corporation cases.[3] The formal protest must be in writing and must include certain elements that meet the requirements of the Appeals Office (see Exhibit 12-1 at ¶1251).[4]

Exhibit 12-1 at ¶1251 is a sample protest. In particular, the protest must contain a statement of facts supporting the taxpayer's position. This statement of facts must be declared true under the penalties of perjury—this is the function of the last paragraph of the protest, where the taxpayer declares that he or she hasexamined the statement of facts and that, to the best of his or her knowledge and belief, they are true, correct and complete.

---

[1] P.L. 105-206.
[2] Internal Revenue Organization Blueprint: 1999 Phase IIA, Document 11052 (5-1999).

[3] Appeals has also been given jurisdiction to review certain collection actions. See Chapter 13 for details.
[4] Prop. Reg. § 601.106(d).

If the protest has been prepared by the representative and not by the taxpayer, normally it will not be possible for the representative to sign such a declaration under penalties of perjury. Instead, a declaration may be substituted which states that the representative has prepared the protest, and states whether or not he or she knows of his or her own knowledge and belief that the statement of facts is true, correct and complete. In addition, the representative may wish to go on to state that upon information and belief he or she believes the statement of facts to be true, correct and complete.

The protest is to be filed with the IRS office designated in the thirty-day letter. The protest also will be reviewed by the examining agent who made the initial determination. The administrative file will then be assembled and forwarded with all pertinent documents, including the workpapers of the auditor or revenue agent, to the Appeals Office. The appeals officer makes a preliminary review to determine whether the case should be heard by Appeals. The appeals officer is not to act as an investigator or an examining officer, and therefore, if the case requires further significant factual development, the appeals officer may return the case to the appropriate operating division.

¶1207 PROCEDURE AT APPEALS

Proceedings before the Appeals Office are informal. Testimony is not taken under oath, although the Appeals Office may require matters alleged to be true to be submitted in the form of affidavits or declarations under the penalties of perjury. The taxpayer or the representative will meet with the appeals officer and informally discuss the pros and cons of the various positions taken by the taxpayer and the IRS. Under the Regulation, Appeals will follow the law and the recognized standards of legal construction in determining facts and applying the law. Appeals will determine the correct amount of the tax with strict impartiality as between the taxpayer and the Government, and without favoritism or discrimination between taxpayers.[5]

Although an appeals officer is to maintain the standard of impartiality set forth in the Regulations, he or she must, nevertheless, protect the rights of the IRS and act as an advocate on its behalf. Therefore, an appeals officer can raise a new issue or propose a new theory in support of the examining agent's proposed adjustment. However, an appeals officer generally should not do so unless the grounds for raising such new issues are substantial and the effect on the tax liability is material.[6]

¶1208 EX PARTE COMMUNICATIONS

The IRS Restructuring and Reconciliation Act of 1998 sought to insure an independent appeals function and prohibits ex parte communication between appeals officers and other IRS employees.[7] The IRS published Rev. Proc. 2000-43 setting out the prohibited and permitted ex parte communications.

---

[5] Reg. §601.106(f)(1).
[6] IRM 8.6.1.4.

[7] Code Sec. 1001(a)(4).

¶1209 REVENUE PROCEDURE 2000-43

Below are excerpts from Revenue procedure 2000-43, IRB 2000-43.

TABLE OF CONTENTS

SECTION 1. PURPOSE AND SCOPE

SECTION 2. BACKGROUND

SECTION 3. GUIDANCE CONCERNING THE EX PARTE COMMUNICA-TIONS PROHIBITION DESCRIBED IN SECTION 1001(a)(4) OF THE INTER-NAL REVENUE SERVICE RESTRUCTURING AND REFORM ACT OF 1998

SECTION 4. EFFECTIVE DATE

SECTION 1. PURPOSE AND SCOPE

* * *

SECTION 2. BACKGROUND

* * *

SECTION 3. GUIDANCE CONCERNING THE EX PARTE COMMUNICA-TIONS PROHIBITION DESCRIBED IN § 1001(a)(4) OF THE INTERNAL REV-ENUE SERVICE RESTRUCTURING AND REFORM ACT OF 1998

Q-1 What is "ex parte communication" and when is it prohibited?

A-1 For the purposes of this revenue procedure, ex parte communications are communications that take place between Appeals and another Service function without the participation of the taxpayer or the taxpayer's representative (taxpayer/representative). While the legislation refers to "appeals officers," the overall intent of the ex parte provision is to ensure the independence of the entire Appeals organization. Ex parte communications between any Appeals employee, e.g., Appeals Officers, Appeals Team Case Leaders, Appeals Tax Computation Specialists, and employees of other Internal Revenue Service offices are prohibited to the extent that such communications appear to compromise the independence of Appeals.

Q-2 Is the prohibition on ex parte communications limited to oral communications?

A-2 No. The prohibition is not limited to oral communications. It applies to any form of communication, oral or written (manually or computer generated).

Q-3 Are communications between Appeals Officers and other Appeals employees subject to the prohibition on ex parte communications?

A-3 No. As indicated in A-1 above, the ex parte communication prohibition was intended to preserve the independence of the Appeals organization as a whole. IntraAppeals communications during the deliberation process do not compromiseor appear to compromise that independence. Appeals employees may communicate freely with other Appeals employees without inviting the taxpayer/representative to participate.

Q-4 Is the administrative file transmitted to Appeals by the office that made the determination which is subject to the Appeals process (the originating function) considered to be an ex parte communication within the context of this revenue procedure?

A-4 No. The administrative file is not considered to be an ex parte communication within the context of this revenue procedure. The administrative file, containing the proposed determination and the taxpayer's protest or other approved means of communicating disagreement with the proposed determination, sets forth the boundaries of the dispute between the taxpayer and the Service and forms the basis for Appeals to assume jurisdiction.

Q-5 Does the prohibition on ex parte communications extend to discussions between Appeals employees and the originating function during the course of preliminary review of a newly assigned case?

A-5 It depends on the nature of the communication. During the preliminary review of a newly assigned case, officials in Appeals may ask questions that involve ministerial, administrative, or procedural matters and do not address the substance of the issues or positions taken in the case. For example, Appeals employees may make the following types of inquiries without involving the taxpayer/representative:

- Questions about whether certain information was requested and whether it was received.
- Questions about whether a document referred to in the workpapers that the Appeals Officer cannot locate in the file is available.
- Questions to clarify the content of illegible documents or writings.
- Questions about case controls on the IRS's management information systems.
- Questions relating to tax calculations that are solely mathematical in nature.

Communications with the originating function which extend beyond matters of the type described above and address the substance of the issues in the case are prohibited unless the taxpayer is given the opportunity to participate. Examples of prohibited communications include:

- Discussions about the accuracy of the facts presented by the taxpayer and the relative importance of the facts to the determination.
- Discussions of the relative merits or alternative legal interpretations of authorities cited in a protest or in a report prepared by the originating function.
- Discussions of the originating function's perception of the demeanor or credibility of the taxpayer or taxpayer's representative.

Q-6 Does the ex parte communications prohibition apply to Appeals consideration of cases which originated in the Collection function, e.g., collection due process (CDP) appeals, collection appeals program (CAP) cases, offers in compromise, trust fund recovery penalty cases, etc.?

A-6 Yes. The principles applicable to discussions between Appeals employees and officials in other originating functions also apply to discussions between Appeals and Collection employees. Appeals may not engage in discussions of the strengths and weaknesses of the issues and positions in the case, which would appear to compromise Appeals' independence. The taxpayer/representative should be given an opportunity to participate in any discussion that involves matters other than ministerial, administrative or procedural matters.

Section 3401 of RRA 98 (§§6320 and 6330 of the Internal Revenue Code), regarding due process in IRS collection actions, states that at a hearing, the Appeals Officer must obtain verification that the requirements of any applicable law or administrative procedure have been met. Communications seeking to verify compliance with legal and administrative requirements are similar to the ministerial, administrative or procedural inquiries discussed in A-5 above. Therefore, such communications are not subject to the prohibition on ex parte communications.

Q-7 Does the prohibition on ex parte communications change the criteria for premature referrals?

A-7 As a general rule, there is no change to current criteria or procedures. In essence, RRA 98 reinforces the instructions in Section 8.2.1.2 of the Internal Revenue Manual (IRM) and reaffirms Appeals' role as the settlement arm of the Service. If a case is not ready for Appeals consideration, Appeals may return it for further development or for other reasons described in IRM 8.2.1.2. Appeals may communicate with the originating function regarding the anticipated return of the case, but may not engage in a discussion of matters beyond the types of ministerial, administrative or procedural matters set forth in A-5 as part of a discussion of whether the premature referral guidelines require further activity by the originating function.

Q-8 Is there any change to the Appeals new issue policy?

A-8 No. The prohibition against ex parte communications does not affect Appeals' existing policy about raising new issues in Appeals. However, any new issue must first satisfy Appeals' new issue policy. New issues must continue to meet the "material" and "substantial" tests of IRM 8.6.1.4 and succeeding sections. If discussions with the originating function are needed in order to evaluate the strengths and weaknesses of the possible new issue, the taxpayer/representative must be given an opportunity to participate in such discussions. Appeals will continue to follow the principles of Policy Statement P-8-49 and the "General Guidelines" outlined in IRM 8.6.1.4.2 in deciding whether or not to raise a new issue.

Q-9 May Appeals continue to have ongoing communication with the originating function during the course of an appeal?

A-9 Yes. However, the prohibition on ex parte communications will affect the manner in which Appeals has traditionally operated during the course of the appeal. Appeals must give the taxpayer/representative the opportunity to participate in any discussions with the originating function which concern matters beyond the ministerial, administrative or procedural matters described in A-5 above.

Q-10 What should Appeals do if new information or evidence is submitted? Can Appeals still return the new material to the originating function for review and comment?

A-10 There is no change to existing procedures. The principles in IRM 8.2.1.2.2 remain in effect. The originating function should be given the opportunity totimely review and comment on significant new information presented by the taxpayer. "Significant new information" is information of a nonroutine nature which, in the judgment of Appeals, may have had an impact on the originating function's findings or which may impact on the Appeals' independent evaluation of the litigating hazards. Generally, the review can be accomplished by sending the material to the originating function while Appeals retains jurisdiction of the case and proceeds with resolution of other issues. However, if it appears that important new information or evidence was purposely withheld from the originating function, the entire case should be returned to the originating function and jurisdiction relinquished pursuant to IRM 8.2.1.2.2(3). The taxpayer/representative must be notified when a case is returned to the originating function or new material not available during

¶1209

initial consideration has been sent to the originating function. The results of the originating function's review of the new information will be communicated to the taxpayer/representative.

Q-11 Does the prohibition on ex parte communications have any impact on the relationship between Appeals and Counsel?

A-11 Chief Counsel is the legal adviser to the Commissioner of Internal Revenue and his or her officers and employees (including employees of Appeals) on all matters pertaining to the interpretation, administration and enforcement of the internal revenue laws and related statutes. Attorneys in the Office of Chief Counsel are expected to provide legal advice based on a determination of "the reasonable meaning of various Code provisions in light of the Congressional purpose in enacting them," without bias in favor of either the Government or the taxpayer. Rev. Proc. 64-22, 1964-1 C.B. 689. To balance Appeals employees' need to obtain legal advice with the requirement that they avoid ex parte communications that would appear to compromise Appeals' independence, the following limitations will apply to communications between Appeals employees and attorneys in the Office of Chief Counsel in cases not docketed in the United States Tax Court:

- Appeals employees should not communicate ex parte regarding an issue in a case pending before them with Counsel field attorneys who have previously provided advice on that issue in the case to the IRS employees who made the determination Appeals is reviewing. Counsel will assign a different attorney to provide assistance to Appeals. If an Appeals employee believes it is necessary to seek advice from any Counsel field attorney who previously provided advice to the originating function regarding that issue in the case, the taxpayer/representative will be provided an opportunity to participate in any such communications.

- Appeals' requests for legal advice that raise questions that cannot be answered with a high degree of certainty by application of established principles of law to particular facts will be referred to the Chief Counsel National Office and will be handled as requests for field service advice or technical advice, as appropriate, in accordance with applicable procedures. The response of the National Office to Appeals will be disclosed to the taxpayer in accordance with § 6110.

Appeals employees are cautioned that, while they may obtain legal advice from the Office of Chief Counsel, they remain responsible for independently evaluating the strengths and weaknesses of the specific issues presented by the cases assignedto them, and for making independent judgments concerning the overall strengths and weaknesses of the cases and the hazards of litigation. Consistent with this assignment of responsibility, Counsel attorneys will not provide advice that includes recommendations of settlement ranges for an issue in a case pending before Appeals or for the case as a whole.

The foregoing limitations on ex parte communications do not apply to cases docketed in the United States Tax Court. Docketed cases will be handled in accordance with Rev. Proc. 87-24, 1987-1 C.B. 720, and the Tax Court Rules of Practice and Procedure.

Q-12 Appeals is required to submit certain cases to the Joint Committee on Taxation for review. On occasion, the Joint Committee (or its staff) will question a settlement or raise a new issue. Are communications with the

Joint Committee (or its staff) covered by the ex parte communications prohibition?

A-12 No. The prohibition applies only to communications between Appeals and other Internal Revenue Service employees.

Q-13 Does the prohibition on ex parte communications have any impact on the requirement that Industry Specialization Program (ISP) issues in cases in Appeals jurisdiction be reviewed and approved by the Appeals ISP Coordinator?

A-13 No. Existing procedures for review and approval remain in place. The Appeals ISP Coordinator serves as a resource person for the Appeals organization. The purpose of the review is to ensure consistency of settlements and adherence to approved settlement guidelines. Communications between Appeals employees and the Appeals ISP Coordinator are entirely internal within Appeals, and consequently, the ex parte communications prohibition does not apply.

* * *

Q-21 Several responses in this document refer to the taxpayer/representative being given an "opportunity to participate." What does this phrase mean?

A-21 It means that the taxpayer/representative will be given a reasonable opportunity to attend a meeting or be a participant in a conference call between Appeals and the originating function when the strengths and weaknesses of issues or positions in the taxpayer's case are discussed. The taxpayer/representative will be notified of a scheduled meeting or conference call and invited to participate. If the taxpayer/representative is unable to participate at the scheduled time, reasonable accommodations will be made to reschedule. This does not mean that the Service will delay scheduling a meeting for a protracted period of time to accommodate the taxpayer/representative. Facts and circumstances will govern what constitutes a reasonable delay.

Q-22 May the taxpayer/representative waive the prohibition on ex parte communications?

A-22 Yes. If the taxpayer/representative is given an opportunity to participate in a discussion, but decides that such participation is unnecessary, the prohibition can be waived. Generally, a waiver will be granted on a communication-by-communication basis. However, if the taxpayer/representative so desires, the waiver could encompass all communications that might occur during the course of Appeals' consideration of a specified case. The Appeals Officer should document the waiver in the Case Activity Record.

Q-23 What if the taxpayer/representative declines to participate or seeks to delay the meeting/conference call beyond a reasonable time?

A-23 Appeals should proceed with the meeting or discussion and document the taxpayer/representative's declination or the reason for proceeding in the absence of the taxpayer/representative. This could be accomplished by an entry in the Case Activity Record and a letter to the taxpayer/representative documenting the reason for proceeding.

* * *

Q-25 Does the prohibition on ex parte communications apply to pre-conference meetings between Appeals and Examination?

A-25 Yes. This is clearly a situation where the intended communications could appear to compromise the independence of Appeals. Pre-conference meetings should not be held unless the taxpayer/representative is given the opportunity to participate.

Q-26 Does the prohibition on ex parte communications apply to post-settlement conferences between Appeals and Examination?

A-26 No. The post-settlement conference with Examination is intended to inform Examination about the settlement of issues and to supply information that may be helpful in the examination of subsequent cycles. Appeals' objective is to ensure that Examination fully understands the settlement and the rationale for the resolution. In addition, the conference provides an opportunity for Appeals to discuss with Examination the application of Delegation Orders 236 and 247 (i.e., settlement by Examination consistent with prior Appeals settlement or ISP settlement guidelines) to issues settled by Appeals.

The tax periods that are the subject of the post-settlement conference have been finalized, and the participants are cautioned to limit discussion to the results in the closed cycle. Discussion of the resolution of issues present in the closed periods does not jeopardize the independence of Appeals. Any discussion that addresses open cycles of the same taxpayer should be postponed, and the guidance provided in this revenue procedure relating to ongoing disputes should be followed.

* * *

¶1210 EARLY REFERRAL TO APPEALS

Early referral to Appeals is optional, available to any taxpayer and is intended to resolve cases more expeditiously through the operating divisions and appeals working together. The procedures are effective for requests filed after July 19, 1999.[8] Early referral may be made with respect to issues involving involuntary change of accounting methods, employment tax, employee plans, exempt organizations, as well as income tax matters.[9]

Early referral is initiated by the taxpayer with reference to any developed unagreed issue under the jurisdiction of an operating division. The operating division will continue to develop other issues that have not been referred to appeals.

Appropriate issues for early referral are limited to those issues which (1) are *fully developed* and, if resolved, can reasonably be expected to result in a quicker-resolution of the entire case, and (2) both the taxpayer and the operating division agree should be referred to appeals early. Whip-saw transactions (situations produced when the government is subjected to conflicting claims of taxpayers), issues designated for litigation by the Office of Chief Counsel and those for which the taxpayer has filed a request for Competent Authority Assistance may not be referred to appeals for early resolution.

---

[8] Code Sec. 7123.   [9] Rev. Proc. 99-28, 1999-29 IRB 109.

¶1210

In a manner similar to the formal protest, a request for early referral must be submitted in writing by the taxpayer to the team leader/group manager. The taxpayer's early referral request must contain: (1) identity of the taxpayer and the tax periods to which those issues relate; (2) each issue for which early referral is requested; and (3) the taxpayer's position with regard to the relevant early referral issue, including a brief discussion of the material facts and an analysis of the facts and law as they apply to each referral issue. The early referral request and any supplemental submissions (including additional documents) must include a declaration similar to the jurat required for a protest.

There is no formal taxpayer appeal. If the early referral request is denied or if the team leader/group manager does not approve the early referral request with respect to any issue, the taxpayer retains the right to pursue the normal administrative appeal of any proposed deficiency relating to that issue at a later date.

In situations where the operating division concurs with the referral of an issue for early disposition, the operating division is to complete a Form 5701, Notice of Proposed Adjustment (see Exhibit 5-2 at ¶ 552), or an equivalent form for each early referral issue approved. The operating division is then to send the notification form to the taxpayer within thirty days from the date the early referral request was accepted. The notification form is to describe the issue and explain the operating division's proposed adjustment. The taxpayer must respond in writing to each of the operating divisions' proposed adjustments set forth in the notification form. The response must contain an explanation of the taxpayer's position regarding the issues. The response is to be submitted to the team leader/group manager within thirty days (unless extended) from the date that the proposed adjustment (the notification form) is sent to the taxpayer. The procedural requirements for a statement executed under the penalties of perjury and appropriate signature similar to those used in a protest also apply to the taxpayer's response to the notification form. If a response is not received for any issue within the time provided, the taxpayer's early referral request will be considered withdrawn regarding that particular issue.

The taxpayer's written response to the notification form generally serves the same purpose as a protest to appeals. Established appeals procedures including those governing submissions and taxpayer's conferences apply to early referral issues.[10]

If an agreement is reached with respect to an early referral issue, generally a Form 906, Closing Agreement on Final Determination, covering specific matters is prepared. If early referral negotiations are unsuccessful and an agreement is notreached with respect to an early referral issue, appeals will not consider an unagreed early referral issue again if the entire case is later protested to appeals.

---

[10] Prop. Reg. § 601.106(b)(4).

¶1211 SETTLEMENT AGREEMENTS

The IRS describes the "appeals mission" as one to resolve tax controversies without litigation, on a basis which is fair and impartial to both the government and the taxpayer and in a manner that will enhance voluntary compliance and public confidence in the integrity and efficiency of the IRS.[11] Thus, the appeals officer can split or trade issues where there are substantial uncertainties as to the law, the facts or both. In splitting a "legal issue," the appeals officer will ordinarily consider the hazards which would exist if the case were litigated. The appeals officer will weigh the testimony of the proposed witnesses, judge the trends that the court has been following in similar cases and generally try to predict the outcome of the matter if the case were actually tried. Where a case involves concessions by both the government and the taxpayer "for purposes of settlement," and where there is substantial uncertainty as to how the courts would interpret and apply the law or what facts the court would find, a settlement is classified as a "mutual concession settlement." According to the regulations, no settlement is to be made simply on nuisance value.

Where a taxpayer and the appeals officer have reached an agreement as to some or all of the issues in controversy, generally the appeals officer will request the taxpayer to sign a Form 870, Waiver of Restrictions on Assessment and Collection of Deficiency in Tax and Acceptance of Overassessment (see Exhibit 4-5 at ¶455), the same agreement used at the district level. However, when neither party with justification is willing to concede in full the unresolved area of disagreement and a resolution of the dispute involves concessions for the purposes of settlement by both parties based on the relative strengths of the opposing positions, a "mutual concession settlement" is reached, and a Form 870-AD type of agreement is to be used.[12]

The special appeals Form 870-AD (see Exhibit 12-2 at ¶1252) differs from the normal Form 870 in several ways. The Form 870-AD agreement contains pledges against reopening which the usual agreement does not. Furthermore, the normal Form 870 becomes effective as a Waiver of Restrictions on Assessment when *received by the IRS*, whereas the special Form 870-AD is effective only upon *acceptance by or on behalf of the Commissioner of Internal Revenue*. Finally, under Sec. 6601(c) of the Internal Revenue Code (the Code), the running of interest is suspended thirty days after a Form 870 is received, whereas with a Form 870-AD, interest is not suspended until thirty days after the agreement is executed by the government.

The finality of the Form 870-AD has been the subject of substantial litigation. The form provides that upon acceptance by or on behalf of the Commissioner,

> the case shall not be reopened in the absence of fraud, malfeasance, concealment or misrepresentation of material fact, [or] an important mistake in mathematical calculation . . . and no claim for refund or credit shall be filed or prosecuted for the year(s) stated . . .

---

[11] IRM 8.1.3.2.   [12] IRM 8.6.1.3.1.

¶1211

Furthermore, the form states in language similar to that contained in a normal Form 870 that it *is not* a final closing agreement under Code Sec. 7121 and does not extend the statutory period of limitations on refund, assessment or collection of tax. The controversy arises where a taxpayer, after executing a Form 870-AD, pays the tax, files a claim for refund and brings suit in district court or the Court of Federal Claims. The taxpayer takes the position that Code Sec. 7121 is the exclusive method by which the IRS may enter into a final and binding agreement, and since the Form 870-AD specifically repudiates reference to this section, the taxpayer is not bound by the agreement.

¶1213 REFUND CLAIMS

Generally, the courts have held that a Form 870-AD, standing alone, is insufficient to bar a claim for refund.[13] However, other Courts have denied the taxpayer relief after the execution of a Form 870-AD on the ground of collateral estoppel.[14]

The decision whether the taxpayer should file a claim for refund after the execution of a Form 870-AD may be more a practical than a legal decision. Under Procedural Reg. § 601.106(h)(2), a taxpayer may apply to reopen a case. This approval will be granted "under certain unusual circumstances favorable to the taxpayer such as retroactive legislation." Compare the following views expressed in two relatively authoritative works to see the differences in approach.

REDMAN AND QUIGGLE

As a practical matter, however, it is not frequent that a taxpayer executes an agreement in settlement of a case with the thought of awaiting the lapse of the statute of limitations on assessment by the Government and then filing a claim for refund.[33] There is a great natural reluctance of lawyers and accountants versed in tax procedure to participate in any such maneuver. This repugnance is not lessened by the knowledge that the refund claim would be routed to the same service office and probably the same individual with whom the settlement had been consummated. There seems something immoral (or better, perhaps, sneaky) in reneging upon either Form 870 or 870-AD after a settlement has been hammered out by the ardor of both parties.[34] To a different degree is a person conscience-stricken if the agreement is upset because of fraud or mistake and perhaps subsequently discovered evidence or a retroactive change in the law. This discussion was not begun to teach the reader how to renege on settlement agreements, but to inform him of (1) his chances if he should, in litigation, be faced with an agreement of which he is unaware and (2) the consequences of signing it in the first place.[15]

Footnotes

[33] One related device does not bear the same stigma of sharp practice. Taxpayers who discover errors in the Government's favor on unaudited returns may prefer to wait until just before the statute of limitations on assessment runs to file refund claims. By the time the Service has received and considered the claim, it is too late to assess a deficiency. The Service may offset the refund claim, but no more, under the doctrine of equitable overpayment. *Lewis v. Reynolds*, 284 U.S. 281 (1932).

---

[13] *Arch Engineering Co., Inc.*, 783 F.2d 190, CA-FC, 86-1 USTC ¶9275; *D.J. Lignos*, (2nd Cir.), 71-1 USTC ¶9302; and *Uinta Livestock Corp.*, (10th Cir.), 66-1 USTC ¶9193.

[14] *M.R. Flynn*, 786 F.2d 586 (3rd Cir.), 86-1 USTC ¶9285; *Elbo Coals, Inc.*, 763 F.2d 818 (6th Cir.), 85-2 USTC ¶9454; *Stair v. United States*, 516 F.2d 560 (CA 2, 1975), 75-1 USTC ¶9463; *Kretchmar v. United States*, 91 Cl. Ct. 191 (1985); see also *McGraw-Hill, Inc. v. United States*, 90-1 USTC ¶50,053 (SD Ny. 1990); 65 FORDHAM L. REV. 691 (1996), fn. 56.

[15] *Procedure Before the Internal Revenue*, 6th Edition, American Law Institute, 1984, p. 137.

[34] The Procedural Rulings concede that a nondocketed case closed by the Appellate Division not involving concessions by both parties (i.e., Form 870) may be reopened by the taxpayer "by any appropriate means" as by the filing of a refund claim. Treasury Reg. §601.106(h)(4). At the same time the rules promise that the Service will not reopen any such case absent "fraud, malfeasance, concealment or misrepresentation of material fact, an important mistake in mathematical calculation or such other circumstances that indicates [sic] that failure to take such action would be a serious administrative omission." Treas. Reg. §601.106(h)(3).

THOMAS J. DONELLY

Where to Litigate

The split of authority therefore is quite clear. The Court of Federal Claims will enforce the Form 870-AD and similar agreements, and the courts of appeals will not. These tribunals are in conflict on both the statutory requirements and the estoppel issue. The solution is simple: if it is desired to overturn a Form 870-AD or similar agreement, do not attempt to do so in the Court of Claims.[16]

Government Should Not Be Permitted to Plead Estoppel

While the decisions of the courts of appeal have always favored the taxpayer on this issue, it is not quite clear whether the estoppel defense might ever be available to the government. If the government can show a false representation by the taxpayer, relied upon it and that it has allowed the statute of limitations to expire on further deficiencies against the taxpayer for the years involved, should the government then be allowed to interpose the defense of estoppel?

It would appear that even in this situation the government has suffered no detriment, an essential element of estoppel. The maximum burden the government might suffer as a result of permitting the taxpayer to proceed with his or her refund suit is the amount of the taxpayer's recovery. However, this may be offset in full by the government, notwithstanding the running of the statute of limitations against it. Consequently, it would appear that an estoppel argument should never prevail.

A Proposed Remedy

It is unfortunate that there is not a higher degree of finality to most of the settlements made by the Internal Revenue Service. In the great majority of cases, the "settlement" which the taxpayer considers a final disposition of his matter is in fact not what it purports to be. It is hardly good practice for the taxpayers andthe Commissioner to enter into agreements which purport to legally bind them, but which in fact do not. There would seem to be little reason why the Appellate Division should not be authorized to enter into binding agreements with taxpayers. A slight change in the Code would accomplish this.

¶1215 CLOSING AGREEMENT

Some tax cases may involve matters which have a direct effect on other taxes, related taxpayers or other years. Settlement of this type of case may require an additional agreement. Sec. 7121 of the Code authorizes the Secretary to enter into an agreement in writing with any person regarding that person's tax liability for any period.

> **Example:** WEMALE Corporation, a C corporation, involved in the sale of household products through mail order catalogs, acquired all the assets of FEMALE Corporation along with a covenant not to compete agreement from

---

[16] "How Binding Are Stipulations With the Commissioner," 27 NEW YORK UNIV. INST. ON FED. TAX. 1371, at 1380-1381.

Jane Jones, the founder and sole shareholder of FEMALE. The date of the sale was 12/31/1999. The parties assigned a value of $1,500,000 to the covenant, which is the amount amortized by MALE under Code Sec. 197 as an intangible asset to be amortized over 15 years. Simultaneously with the sale, Ms. Jones entered into an employment contract for $4,500,000 at $1,500,000 a year for three years and an option to renew for an additional 5 years for $750,000 a year. An audit of the 2000 return of WEMALE Corporation by Internal Revenue resulted in the disallowance of the compensation of $1,500,000 to Ms. Jones as a "sham transaction". WEMALE Corporation filed a protest with Appeals and the case was settled on December 31, 2001.

- For the year 2000, the value of the covenant was agreed upon at $4,500,000 and an amortization deduction under Code Sec. 197 of $300,000 is allowed.

- For purposes of the settlement the amounts of $600,000, $500,000, and $400,000 are to be treated as compensation for the first three years of the agreement.

- No value was assigned to the option years.

WEMALE Corporation is concerned that the Internal Revenue Service may refuse to allow the increased amortization of $300,000 in later years or will attempt to disallow more of the compensation to Ms. Jones. Therefore in order to bind the Internal Revenue Service with regard to the settlement, a closing agreement was entered into. (See Exhibit 12-3 at ¶1253).

The above example illustrates the following process. While Regional Appeals Offices do not have the authority in closing agreements to bind the Internal Revenue Service with regard to transactions in future years, closing agreements can characterize transactions for the years in issue so as to avoid disputes with regard to carry-over effects of the same issue in future years. It should be noted,that this closing agreement does not impact upon Ms. Jones, as she was not a party to the agreement.

A closing agreement can only be consummated pursuant to the statute. Regulation § 301.7121-1(a) provides that:

> A closing agreement may be entered into in any case in which there appears to be an advantage in having the case permanently and conclusively closed or if good and sufficient reasons are shown by the taxpayer for desiring a closing agreement and it is determined by the Commissioner that the United States will sustain no disadvantage by consummation of such an agreement.

Other examples of the use of closing agreements are where a corporate taxpayer wishes to definitely establish its tax liability to facilitate a transaction, such as the sale of its stock; a corporation in the process of liquidation or dissolution desires a closing agreement in order to wind up its affairs; or a taxpayer may wish to fulfill his or her creditors' demands for authentic evidence as to the status of that individual's tax liability.[17]

---

[17] See Rev. Proc. 68-16, 1968-1 CB 770, for closing agreement procedures, forms, and additional examples. Closing agreement forms for the final determination of tax liability (Form 866) or the final

¶1221 COLLATERAL AGREEMENTS AND CLOSING AGREEMENTS DISTINGUISHED

Although in the broadest nontechnical sense, closing agreements, waivers and consents can be characterized as collateral agreements, the term as used by the IRS has reference to some matter related to a tax controversy but collateral to the amount of tax to be assessed or the amount of a refund to be received in the instant case. For example, a collateral agreement may commit a trustee or a beneficiary to use the same valuation for income tax purposes as was used for federal estate tax purposes. One important distinction between collateral agreements and closing agreements is that the collateral agreement does not purport to bind the IRS. It is a one-sided commitment. The IRS does not enter into the agreement nor does the IRS sign as a party. Furthermore, collateral agreements, unlike closing agreements, are administrative in nature and not expressly provided for by the Internal Revenue Code.

¶1225 POST-ASSESSMENT PENALTY APPEALS

The Internal Revenue Manual contains provisions for post-assessment review by the Appeals Office of certain penalties. These are generally penalties which may be immediately assessed without the usual deficiency procedures which would otherwise permit appeal to the Tax Court before assessment. A post-assessment appeal right exists for virtually any penalty that may be avoided by a showing of reasonable cause or reasonable basis.[18] Penalty Appeal consideration generallyoccurs after assessment of such penalties but before payment. Collection action is normally suspended during the Appeal process

The penalty appeal action generally begins with the Service Center. Usually, penalties for late filing, late payment and other penalties associated with the filing of a tax return are assessed by the Service Center. Taxpayers may protest the penalty charges upon receipt of the billing notice. The notice provides information on how to request elimination of the penalty when the taxpayer believes reasonable cause exists. If the Service Center agrees with the taxpayer's position, it has authority to abate the penalty. If it rejects the explanation, an 854(C) Letter (see Exhibit 12-4 at ¶1254) is sent to the taxpayer explaining the reasons for denying the request and explaining how to file a written protest to the Appeals Office.[19]

A similar procedure is used when penalties are originally assessed by customer service representatives in the local offices.

The Appeals Office generally is required to dispose of a penalty case within ninety days of receipt of the case file.[20] The Internal Revenue Manual provides that most penalty appeals should be resolved with only written or telephone communication with the taxpayer. A conference is only to be granted upon

---

(Footnote Continued)

determination of specific matters (Form 906) are available. These forms need not be used, however, provided the agreement includes the standard provisions set forth in the IRS forms.

[18] IRM 8.11.1.2(d).

[19] IRM 8.11.1.7.1.

[20] IRM 8.11.1.7.2.1.

request by the taxpayer and only when deemed necessary by the appeals officer. In general, it is only the more complex reasonable cause determinations that are to be handled by the penalty appeal procedure.[21] Each case is to be considered on its own facts, and the appeals officer can consider hazards of litigation in determining whether to abate all or part of the penalties asserted.[22]

---

[21] *Id.*   [22] IRM 8.11.1.3.

¶1251 Exhibit 12-1

SAMPLE PROTEST

CERTIFIED MAIL—RETURN RECEIPT REQUESTED

Internal Revenue Service
1234 Main Street
Milwaukee, WI 53201

Re: Frozen Tundra Meat Co., Inc. EIN 39–0000000

PROTEST

The above-named taxpayer hereby protests the proposed adjustments to its taxable income and corporation income taxes for the calendar years 2000, 2001, and 2002 as set forth in the report enclosed with your letter dated June 19, 2003.

The following information is submitted in support of this Protest:

1. Appeal and Request for Hearing.

It is requested that this case be transferred to the Appeals Office at Milwaukee, Wisconsin, and that a conference be arranged at a time convenient to that office.

2. Name and Address of Taxpayers.

Frozen Tundra Meat Co., Inc.
101 Lombardi Drive
Packers Grove, WI 55555-0000

3. Date and Symbol of Transmittal Letter.

Date: June 19, 2003

Person to Contact: Ira Agent

4. Tax Periods or Years Involved.

Form 1120 Corporation Income Taxes for the calendar years 2000, 2001, and 2002.

5. Unagreed Adjustments.

(a) The disallowance of auto/truck expenses in the amount of $42,150 for the year 2000.

(b) The disallowance of cost of goods sold in the amount of $56,320 for the year 2000.

(c) The additional allowance of depreciation for the calendar year 2001 in the amount of $18,052.

(d) The disallowance of officer's compensation in the amount of $1,740,906 for the year 2001.

(e) The additional allowance of depreciation in the amount of $10,831 for the year 2002.

(f) The disallowance of officer's compensation in the amount of $1,742,698 for the year 2002.

(g) The determination that the taxpayer was liable for the negligence portion of the accuracy related penalty under Section 6662(c) in the amount of $6,892 for the year 2000.

(h) The determination that the taxpayer was liable for the negligence portion of the accuracy related penalty under Section 6662(c) in the amount of $120,600 for the year 2001.

(i) The determination that the taxpayer was liable for the negligence portion of the accuracy related penalty under Section 6662(c) in the amount of $121,989 for the year 2002.

(j) The determination that, should it be finally determined that the taxpayer is not liable for the negligence portion of the accuracy related penalty for the year 2000, then in the alternative the taxpayer is liable for the substantial understatement portion of the accuracy related penalty under Section 6662(d) in the amount of $6,892 for the year 2000.

(k) The determination that, should it be finally determined that the taxpayer is not liable for the negligence portion of the accuracy related penalty for the year 2001, then in the alternative the taxpayer is liable for the substantial understatement portion of the accuracy related penalty under Section 6662(d) in the amount of $120,600 for the year 2001.

(l) The determination that, should it be finally determined that the taxpayer is not liable for the negligence portion of the accuracy related penalty for the year 2002, then in the alternative the taxpayer is liable for the substantial understatement portion of the accuracy related penalty under Section 6662(d) in the amount of $121,989 for the year 2002.

6. Facts Supporting Position.

(a) Taxpayer alleges that the auto/truck expenses paid or incurred in the amount of $42,150 for the year 2000 constituted ordinary and necessary business expenses deductible under Section 162 of the Internal Revenue Code of 1986 as Amended.

(b) Taxpayer alleges that the expenses paid or incurred in the amount of $56,320 in repairing certain trailers constituted ordinary and necessary business expenses deductible under Section 162 of the Internal Revenue Code of 1986 as Amended and did not constitute a permanent improvement or betterment made to increase the value of property.

(c) Taxpayer alleges that the additional depreciation deduction of $18,052 for 2001 is erroneous in that the taxpayer did not make a permanent improvement or betterment to a depreciable asset subject to depreciation.

(d) Taxpayer alleges that the amounts paid or incurred as compensation to officers during the year 2001 constituted an ordinary and necessary business expense deductible under Section 162 of the Internal Revenue Code of 1986 as Amended

¶1251

(e) Taxpayer alleges that the additional depreciation deduction of $10,831 for 2002 is erroneous in that the taxpayer did not make a permanent improvement or betterment to a depreciable asset subject to depreciation.

(f) Taxpayer alleges that the amounts paid or incurred as compensation to officers during the year 2002 constituted an ordinary and necessary business expense deductible under Section 162 of the Internal Revenue Code of 1986 as Amended.

(g) Taxpayer alleges that any underpayment that may have occurred for the calendar year 2000 was due to reasonable cause and not negligence or disregard of rules or regulations and that a penalty under § 6662(c) is inapplicable.

(h) Taxpayer alleges that any underpayment that may have occurred for the calendar year 2001 was due to reasonable cause and not negligence or disregard of rules or regulations and that a penalty under § 6662(c) is inapplicable.

(i) Taxpayer alleges that any underpayment that may have occurred for the calendar year 2002 was due to reasonable cause and not negligence or disregard of rules or regulations and that a penalty under § 6662(c) is inapplicable.

(j) Taxpayer alleges that there was no substantial understatement of tax for 2000. However, in the alternative, should it be finally determined that there was such understatement then and in that event, taxpayer alleges that it had reasonable cause for the underpayment and it acted in good faith.

(k) Taxpayer alleges that there was no substantial understatement of tax for 2001. However, in the alternative, should it be finally determined that there was such understatement then and in that event, taxpayer alleges that it had reasonable cause for the underpayment and it acted in good faith.

(l) Taxpayer alleges that there was no substantial understatement of tax for 2002. However, in the alternative, should it be finally determined that there was such understatement then and in that event, taxpayer alleges that it had reasonable cause for the underpayment and it acted in good faith.

7. Statement Outlining Authority.

All of the issues raised by the protest are of a factual nature and will be presented in further detail at the conference with the appeals officer.

8. Taxpayer's Representation.

(a) Seeno Evil and Hearno Evil are the representatives of the taxpayer named in the Protest. A Power of Attorney with respect to each of these years is on file with the Internal Revenue Service.

¶1251

(b) Taxpayer's representatives have prepared this Protest on the basis of records and statements furnished by the taxpayer.

(c) Taxpayer's representatives have no personal knowledge of whether the statements of fact contained in this Protest are true and correct, but upon information and belief, they believe them to be true and correct.

Respectfully submitted,

Evil and Evil S.C.

Date: July 1, 2003

By_____

Seeno Evil

_____

Hearno Evil

¶1252 Exhibit 12-2

Form **870-AD** (Rev. April 1992)	Department of the Treasury—Internal Revenue Service **Offer to Waive Restrictions on Assessment and Collection of Tax Deficiency and to Accept Overassessment**	
Symbols	Name of Taxpayer	SSN or EIN

Under the provisions of section 6213(d) of the Internal Revenue Code of 1986 (the Code), or corresponding provisions of prior internal revenue laws, the undersigned offers to waive the restrictions provided in section 6213(a) of the Code or corresponding provisions of prior internal revenue laws, and to consent to the assessment and collection of the following deficiencies and additions to tax, if any, with interest as provided by law. The undersigned offers also to accept the following overassessments, if any, as correct. Any waiver or acceptance of an overassessment is subject to any terms and conditions stated below and on the reverse side of this form.

		Deficiencies (Overassessments) and Additions to Tax				
Year Ended	Kind of Tax	Tax				
		$	$	$		
		$	$	$		
		$	$	$		
		$	$	$		
		$	$	$		
		$	$	$		

Signature of Taxpayer	Date
Signature of Taxpayer	Date
Signature of Taxpayer's Representative	Date
Corporate Name	Date
By Corporate Officer Title	Date

For Internal Revenue Use Only	Date Accepted for Commissioner	Signature
	Office	Title

Cat. No. 16896Q   (See Reverse Side)   Form **870-AD** (Rev. 4-92)

This offer must be accepted for the Commissioner of Internal Revenue and will take effect on the date it is accepted. Unless and until it is accepted, it will have no force or effect.

If this offer is accepted, the case will not be reopened by the Commissioner unless there was:

- fraud, malfeasance, concealment or misrepresentation of a material fact
- an important mistake in mathematical calculation
- a deficiency or overassessment resulting from adjustments made under Subchapters C and D of Chapter 63 concerning the tax treatment of partnership and subchapter S items determined at the partnership and corporate level
- an excessive tentative allowance of a carryback provided by law

No claim for refund or credit will be filed or prosecuted by the taxpayer for the years stated on this form, other than for amounts attributed to carrybacks provided by law.

The proper filing of this offer, when accepted, will expedite assessment and billing (or overassessment, credit or refund) by adjusting the tax liability. This offer, when executed and timely submitted, will be considered a claim for refund for the above overassessment(s), if any.

This offer may be executed by the taxpayer's attorney, certified public accountant, or agent provided this is specifically authorized by a power of attorney which, if not previously filed, must accompany this form. If this offer is signed by a person acting in a fiduciary capacity (for example: an executor, administrator, or a trustee) Form 56, Notice Concerning Fiduciary Relationship, must accompany this form, unless previously filed.

If this offer is executed for a year for which a joint return was filed, it must be signed by both spouses unless one spouse, acting under a power of attorney, signs as agent for the other.

If this offer is executed by a corporation, it must be signed with the corporate name followed by the signature and title of the officer(s) authorized to sign. If the offer is accepted, as a condition of acceptance, any signature by or for a corporate officer will be considered a representation by that person and the corporation, to induce reliance, that such signature is binding under law for the corporation to be assessed the deficiencies or receive credit or refund under this agreement. If the corporation later contests the signature as being unauthorized on its behalf, the person who signed may be subject to criminal penalties for representing that he or she had authority to sign this agreement on behalf of the corporation.

¶1253 Exhibit 12-3

CLOSING AGREEMENT ON FINAL DETERMINATION COVERING SPECIFIC MATTERS

Under section 7121 of the Internal Revenue Code, WEMALE Corporation, 123 Main Street, Milwaukee, WI 55555-0000, 39–0000000, and the Commissioner of Internal Revenue make the following agreement:

WHEREAS, the Taxpayer acquired all the assets of FEMALE Corporation (Seller) on December 31, 2000;

WHEREAS, the Taxpayer and Seller assigned a value of $1,500,000 to a covenant to compete agreement from the founder and sole shareholder (Seller Shareholder), which amount was treated by the Taxpayer as an intangible asset to be amortized over 15 years under Section 197 of the Internal Revenue Code;

WHEREAS, the Taxpayer and Seller Shareholder have entered into an employment contract whereby Taxpayer will pay Seller Shareholder $1,500,000 a year during 2001, 2002, and 2003 with Taxpayer having an option to renew at $750,000 a year for 2004 through 2008;

WHEREAS, the parties wish to determine (a) the amount to be allowed as an amortization deduction under Section 197 of the Internal Revenue Code for the year 2000 and succeeding years, (b) the amount deductible as compensation paid to Seller Shareholder for years 2001, 2002, and 2003, and (c) the treatment of payments to Seller Shareholder during the option years 2004 through 2008; and

WHEREAS, the parties have determined that the agreement set forth herein is in their best interests;

NOW, IT IS HEREBY DETERMINED AND AGREED, for Federal income tax purposes, that:

1. The amount to be amortized under Section 197 of the Internal Revenue Code by Taxpayer is $4,500,000, which consists of $1,500,000 which was paid to Seller and $900,000, $1,000,000, and $1,100,000 to be paid to Seller Shareholder during the years 2001, 2002, and 2003, respectively.

2. The amount to be allowed as deductible compensation to taxpayer for payments to Seller Shareholder for years 2001, 2002, and 2003 shall be limited to amounts paid reduced by the amounts to be treated as amounts to be amortized under Section 197 of the Internal Revenue Code as stated above.

3. Any amounts paid to Seller Shareholder by the Taxpayer in accordance with the employment contract should the renewal option be exercised for years after 2003 shall be allowed as deductible compensation.

This agreement is final and conclusive except:

(a) the matter it relates to may be reopened in event of fraud, malfeasance, or misrepresentation of material facts;

(b) it is subject to the Internal Revenue Code sections that expressly provide that effect be given to their provisions (including any stated exception for Code section 7122) notwithstanding any other law or rule of law; and

(c) if it relates to a tax period ending after the date of this agreement, it is subject to any law, enacted after this agreement date, that applies to that tax period.

By signing, the above parties certify that they have read and agree to the terms of this document.

Taxpayer (other than individual)

By _____ Date Signed ____

Title _____

Commissioner of Internal Revenue

By _____ Date Signed ____

Title _____

¶1254 Exhibit 12-4

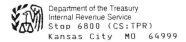

Department of the Treasury
Internal Revenue Service
Stop 6800 (CS:TPR)
Kansas City MO 64999

```
                                    In reply refer to:  0957921848
                                    Aug. 28, 2000    LTR 854C
                                         200003 01 000    1
                                         0957921848      01751
```

```
        Taxpayer Identification Number:  39-
                         Tax Period(s):  Mar. 31, 2000

                                  Form:  941

                       Kind of Penalty:  EFTPS
```

Dear Taxpayer:

Thank you for the inquiry dated June 20, 2000.

We are sorry, but the information submitted does not establish reasonable cause or show due diligence. Therefore, we must deny your request for penalty adjustment.

. Our records show that you were mandated to file electronically in 1999. Taxpayers were issued three letters informing and reminding them of the requirement date. This is required for all tax forms.

. We will be sending you a current balance due notice in two to three weeks.

If you want to appeal or give us more information, the following will be helpful.

APPEALS PROCEDURES

If you have additional information and want your case to receive further consideration by an Appeals Officer, please provide a brief written statement of the disputed issues to the Service Center Appeals Coordinator. It should include:

1. Your name and address;
2. Your social security number or employer identification number;
3. A statement that you want to appeal the findings;
4. A statement of facts supporting your position on the issues you are appealing,
5. If possible, a statement outlining the law or other authority on which you rely.

0957921848
Aug. 28, 2000   LTR 854C
200003 01 000   1
0957921848   01752

---

6. A copy of this letter.

The statement of facts, under 4 above, should be detailed and complete, including specific dates, names, amounts, and locations. It must be declared true under penalties of perjury. You may do this by adding to your statement the following signed declaration:

> "Under penalties of perjury, I declare that the facts presented in my written protest, which are set out in the accompanying statement of facts, schedules, and other statements are, to the best of my knowledge and belief, true, correct, and complete."

If your authorized representative sends us the protest for you, he or she may substitute a declaration stating that he or she prepared the statement and accompanying documents and whether he or she knows that the statement and accompanying documents are true and correct.

Please send your response to:

    Internal Revenue Service
    Service Center Penalty Appeals Coordinator
    Attn: Pete Seamans
           P.O. BOX 24551 (ADMIN.)
           KANSAS CITY MO 64999

The Service Center Appeals Coordinator will review your appeal information to determine whether the penalty should be removed or reduced. If your appeal can't be resolved immediately with the additional information, the coordinator will send your written statement to the Appeals Office serving your district.

REPRESENTATION

An attorney, certified public accountant, or person enrolled to practice before the Internal Revenue Service may represent you. To have someone represent you, attach a Form 2848, Power of Attorney and Declaration of Representative, (or similar written authorization) to your written statement.

Forms, instructions, and Treasury Department Circular 230, Regulations Governing the Practice of Attorneys, Certified Public Accountants, and Enrolled Agents Before the Internal Revenue Service, are available from any Internal Revenue Service office.

OTHER INFORMATION

0957921848
Aug. 28, 2000   LTR 854C
200003 01 000   1
0957921848   01753

If taxes are overdue on your account, you will continue to receive
bills even if you appeal the penalty. If you decide to appeal,
you may pay the penalty to avoid further interest charges on the
penalty amount. If you appeal the penalty and the Appeals Officer
determines that you are not required to pay it, we will adjust your
account and send you a refund.

If you don't appeal, you may file a claim for refund after you pay
the penalty. If you want to take your case to court immediately, you
should request in writing that your claim for refund be immediately
rejected. Then you will be issued a notice of disallowance. You
have two years from the date of the notice of disallowance to bring
suit in the United States District Court having jurisdiction or in
the United States Claims Court.

If you have any questions, please call our Customer Service area at
1-800-829-8815 between the hours of 12:00 AM and 11:59 PM.
If you prefer, you may write to us at the address shown at the top of
the first page of this letter.

Whenever you write, please include this letter and, in the spaces
below, give us your telephone number with the hours we can reach you.
Keep a copy of this letter for your records.

Telephone Number (   )_____ Hours_____

Sincerely yours,

Patricia E. Manes

Patricia E. Manes
Chief, Taxpayer Relations Branch

Enclosures:
Copy of this letter
Envelope

¶1255 DISCUSSION QUESTIONS

1. The Appeals Office and the taxpayer reach a settlement in a tax case. A Form 870-AD is executed by the taxpayer and is accepted on behalf of the Commissioner of Internal Revenue. The taxpayer pays the tax and interest in full. The taxpayer, still believing that he deserves a better deal, comes to you and asks that you file on his behalf a claim for refund to recover the full tax and interest paid with the Form 870-AD. Should you file the claim for refund for the taxpayer?

2. Should the ethical and moral considerations of filing a claim for refund after the execution of Form 870-AD at the Appeals Office level be any different than with a Form 870 at the examination level?

3. Leroy Loser's return has been examined and the IRS has disallowed losses claimed in his chinchilla farm operation as an activity not entered into for profit. Leroy wants you to appeal the Revenue Agent's determination. He explains to you that his intention in entering into the venture was to make a profit and that it was only bad luck and poor economic conditions that caused him to show a loss for the last six years. During the entire six-year period, Leroy was also a highly paid consultant to a nationwide engineering firm.

    (A) Should Leroy attend the conference with the Appeals Officer "to help establish the profit motive?"

    (B) If not, how else can he "prove" his profit motive?

4. You have been assigned to be the mentor for Betty Beancounter, a summer intern. Betty has been asked to prepare a protest on behalf of a major client of the firm. The client received a 30-day letter from the IRS proposing a deficiency of $195,000, including interest and penalties. The proposed deficiency is based on the IRS's argument that the client should account for its manufacturing contracts on the percentage of completion method. The client argues that it is not subject to long-term contract treatment since the items they produce are not unique and normally require less than 12 months to complete.

    Both the tax and audit partners handling the client's matters have approached Betty on different occasions regarding their theory on preparing this protest. One partner believes that brevity is best. His theory is that a simple protest should be filed and then see what the appeals officer thinks before giving any more information. The other partner takes an exhaustive approach. She believes that a protest should contain all the arguments which could be presented and the case cites to support the arguments. Betty has come to you for advice in preparing the protest.

    Which theory should she adopt and why?

5. You have appealed a determination by the District Director that gains on various installment sales of real estate constitutes ordinary income rather than capital gain. Upon careful review of the case law, you conclude that the taxpayer has an overall 50% chance of prevailing in

court. Explain how you would present your case to the Appeals Officer. What approach would you utilize to guarantee that the District Director does not subsequently raise the same issue with respect to future install-ment payments on said sales.

CHAPTER 13
ASSESSMENT PROCEDURE

¶1301 INTRODUCTION

When the Internal Revenue Service (IRS) determines that additional taxes are due, it must first make a formal assessment of the additional tax (the "deficiency") to put the collection process in motion. Sec. 6213 of the Internal Revenue Code (the Code) provides that no assessment of any deficiency may be made until after the notice of deficiency described in Code Sec. 6212 is mailed by registered or certified mail to the taxpayer. The document prescribed by Code Sec. 6212 through which the IRS notifies the taxpayer is referred to as a Statutory Notice of Deficiency or a ninety-day letter (see Exhibit 4-13 at ¶463). The Statutory Notice of Deficiency is accompanied by a relevant portion of the agent's report explaining in abbreviated form the reasons for the proposed adjustments along with a detailed computation of the tax effect of the adjustments (see Exhibit 13-1 at ¶1351).

The term "90-day letter" stems from Code Sec. 6213(a), which allows the taxpayer ninety days after the mailing of the notice to file a Petition for Redetermination of the deficiency with the United States Tax Court. During the ninety-day period and, if a petition to the Tax Court is filed, until the decision of the Tax Court becomes final, the IRS may not assess a deficiency and may not levy or attempt to collect a deficiency. In the event the IRS makes an assessment before a decision is rendered, the Tax Court has authority under Code Sec. 6213(a) to restrain the assessment and collection of tax.

Under Code Sec. 6211, the term "deficiency" refers to the amount of tax (income, estate, gift and certain excise taxes) determined to be due in excess of the amount shown as tax on the return. If no return has been filed or if the return does not show any tax liability, then for purposes of computing the deficiency, the amount shown as tax is considered to be zero. However, any amount shown as additional tax on an amended return filed after the due date of the return is treated as an amount shown on the return in computing the amount of deficiency. Thus, any additional tax shown on an amended return may be assessed without the formal requirement of a notice of deficiency.[1]

¶1303 RESCISSION OF STATUTORY NOTICE

Under Code Sec. 6212(d), the IRS, with the consent of the taxpayer, is authorized to rescind a Statutory Notice after it has been issued. Revenue Procedure 98-54[2] has been issued by the IRS to provide instructions for agreements for the rescission of a Statutory Notice.[3] The Revenue Procedure indicates that rescission is purelydiscretionary with the Commissioner of Internal Revenue and that the

---

[1] Reg. § 301.6211-1(a).
[2] 1998-2 CB 531.

[3] See also IRM Handbook 4.3.19.1.24.

Statutory Notice can only be rescinded with the consent of the taxpayer. The Revenue Procedure suggests that the following reasons would be sufficient for rescission of a Statutory Notice:

1. If the Statutory Notice was issued as a result of an administrative error (e.g., for the wrong taxpayer, the wrong year or without recognizing that an extension of the statute had been executed);

2. If the taxpayer submits information establishing that the actual tax liability is less than that shown in the Statutory Notice; or

3. If the taxpayer specifically requests an Appeals Conference to enter into settlement negotiations (for this procedure to be used, the Appeals Office must confirm that the case is susceptible to settlement.)

If fewer than ninety days remain before the statute of limitations for assessment expires, the Statutory Notice can only be rescinded if an agreement to extend the statute (see Form 872, Exhibit 10-2 at ¶1052) is executed by the taxpayer. If an unlimited extension has been given on Form 872-A, the rescission procedure cannot be used. Finally, if a petition to the Tax Court has been filed, or if the period to file a petition has expired, no rescission is allowed.

Form 8626, Agreement to Rescind Notice of Deficiency (see Exhibit 13-2 at ¶1352), is the form used by the IRS when a taxpayer wishes to consent to a rescission of the Statutory Notice. The taxpayer must first contact the office that issued the Statutory Notice and explain the reasons that rescission is sought. If the taxpayer wishes an Appeals Conference, that taxpayer will be informed as to how to contact the Appeals Office to see if they concur in the request.

If the Statutory Notice is rescinded, the IRS can later issue another Statutory Notice, and nothing prohibits the IRS from issuing a subsequent notice for an amount greater than that reflected in the original Statutory Notice. The running of the statute of limitations on assessment is suspended during the period the rescinded Statutory Notice is outstanding.

¶1305 MAILING TO LAST KNOWN ADDRESS

Under Code Sec. 6212(b), mailing of a Statutory Notice to the taxpayer's last known address is sufficient to commence the running of the ninety-day period. This is the case even if the taxpayer is deceased or under a legal disability or, if a corporation, has terminated its existence. The statute does not require actual notice, only mailing to the last known address by certified or registered mail. Therefore, a notice sent by certified mail to the proper address is effective even though never actually received by the taxpayer.[4]

The issue of what is the taxpayer's "last known address" has been the subject of voluminous litigation. In a significant reversal of position, the Tax Court held in *Abeles v. Commissioner*[5] that a taxpayer's last known address is that address which appears on the taxpayer's most recently filed return, unless the IRS has been given clear and concise notification of a different address. The most

---

[4] *M.P. Gam v. Comm'r*, 79 TCM 1798, TC Memo. 2000-115, CCH Dec. 53,831(M).

[5] 91 TC 1019 (1988), CCH Dec. 45,203.

recently filed return, the Court said, is that return which has been properly processed by the IRS center so that the address on that return is available to the agent who prepares the notice of deficiency with respect to an examination of a previously filed return. The address must be obtainable at such time by a computer generation of an IRS transcript using the taxpayer's Taxpayer Identification Number (TIN) (i.e, Social Security or employer identification number).

In *Abeles*, a wife was held to have properly notified the IRS of her last known address by filing a separate return after the years under examination. This test for determining the "last known address" was approved by the Ninth Circuit in *Williams v. Commissioner*.[6]

Generally, a representative filing a Form 2848, Power of Attorney (see Chapter 2), will request that copies of correspondence from the IRS be sent to his or her office. The IRS has stated that its practice will be to treat the address of the taxpayer's attorney as the "last known address" of the taxpayer only where the Power of Attorney requires that all communications be mailed to the representative.[7] This practice does not extend to a situation where, as with the printed form of the Power of Attorney, the power merely requires that copies of communications be sent to the attorney.[8]

A husband and wife filing a joint Form 1040, U.S. Individual Income Tax Return, are considered to have the same address for purposes of their last known address unless either spouse has given the IRS notice of a separate residence.[9] Regulation § 301.6212-1 provides that a duplicate original Statutory Notice of Deficiency must be sent to each spouse at his or her last known address.[10]

Where a Statutory Notice is incompletely or incorrectly addressed and the notice does not reach the taxpayer, the Tax Court lacks jurisdiction. The taxpayer who receives a defective Statutory Notice of Deficiency has a choice of ignoring the notice or responding by filing a petition with the Tax Court together with a motion to dismiss on the grounds that the Court is without jurisdiction. However, the filing of the petition with the Tax Court, even though untimely, may disclose the claimed defect in time to permit the Commissioner to issue a new Notice of Deficiency to correct the error.[11] On the other hand, if the deficiency notice is ignored because of its possible defect, the taxpayer has the remedy of seeking injunctive relief in the United States District Court for purposes of prohibiting an assessment by the Commissioner. If the district court finds the

---

[6] 935 F.2d 1066 (9th Cir. 1991), 91-2 USTC ¶ 50,317.

[7] Rev. Proc. 61-18, 1961-2 CB 550; *Honts v. Comm'r*, 70 TCM 1256, TC Memo. 1995-532, CCH Dec. 50,990(M).

[8] The Tax Court has held that receipt of a copy of a Notice of Deficiency by the taxpayer's accountant who had filed a Form 2848, Power of Attorney, did not constitute the mailing of a Notice of Deficiency to the taxpayer's last known address and, thus, that the Notice of Deficiency was not valid. See *Mulvania v. Comm'r*, 47 TCM 1187, TC Memo. 1984-98, CCH Dec. 41,026(M), *aff'd* 769 F.2d 1376 (9th Cir. 1985), 85-2 USTC ¶ 9634.

[9] Code Sec. 6212(b)(2).

[10] *Monge v. Comm'r*, 93 TC 22 (1989), CCH 45,827 (Tax Court lacked jurisdiction because the IRS had notice of a separate residence for the wife and failed to send a duplicate original of the notice of deficiency to her).

[11] The statute of limitations will not be suspended if the Notice of Deficiency is held invalid. Where the Notice is mailed to an incorrect address and never delivered to the taxpayer, the Notice will be considered a nullity which will not suspend the Statute. *Mulvania, supra*, note 8. See ¶ 940, *supra*.

notice was not defective and refuses to enjoin, the taxpayer will have foregone his right to file a petition with the Tax Court and then must pay the tax, file the claim for refund and commence a suit either in the district court or the Court of Federal Claims.

The courts have generally held that an incorrect address will not nullify a Notice of Deficiency if in fact the taxpayer receives the notice without delay.[12] Even if the incorrect address causes a delay in delivering the notice, the defect may be waived by the taxpayer's filing a timely petition with the Tax Court. No case has held a notice insufficient where it was sent by registered or certified mail to the wrong address but was received by the taxpayer in due course.

¶1306 NOTIFYING THE INTERNAL REVENUE SERVICE OF ADDRESS CHANGE

To avoid the dispute as to whether a Statutory Notice of Deficiency was mailed to the last known address, a taxpayer should ensure that the IRS has the current address on file. The address of record for IRS purposes is the address that appears on the gummed, peel-off label of the income tax return package which is mailed to taxpayers each year. If the address on the peel-off label is not correct, taxpayers are instructed to use the peel-off label but to correct the address. This correction serves to update the tax account so that all future correspondence will go to thecurrent address. In situations where taxpayers have moved after the return has been filed, there have been some problems in notifying the IRS of a current address. In order to deal with these problems, the IRS has developed Form 8822, Change of Address (see Exhibit 13-3 at ¶1353), for use in notifying the IRS of a new address. Form 8822 should be filed with the Internal Revenue Service Center for the old address.

The most recent pronouncement by the IRS regarding change of address is contained in Revenue Procedure 2001-18.[13] The IRS generally will use the address on the most recently filed and properly processed return as the address of record for all notices. However, under new regulations, the IRS may update the tax-payer's address of record using United States Postal Service's (USPS) National Change of Address Database (NCOAD) in accordance with Regulation §301.6212-2 (effective January 29, 2001). If a taxpayer wishes to change the address of record, he or she must give clear and concise notification of a different address. Citing *Abeles* (*discussed supra*), the Rev. Proc. states that the address on the most recently filed and properly processed return will be considered the "last known address." A return will be considered "properly processed" after a forty-five-day processing period which begins the day after the date of the receipt of the return by the Service Center.[14] Due to the high volume of returns received

---

[12] *Miller v. Comm'r*, 94 TC 316 (1990), CCH Dec. 46,435 (although IRS failed to send a duplicate original to the wife, the notice of deficiency was timely because she received actual notice of the deficiency and was not prejudiced). Also physical receipt is actual receipt and a taxpayer cannot claim he or she did not receive notice by refusing to accept delivery.

Erhard v. Comm'r, 87 F.3d 273 (9th Cir. 1996), 96-2 USTC ¶50,331.

[13] IRB 2001-8.

[14] However, if a return is received prior to the due date for the return, the 45-day processing period will begin the day after the due date of the return. Returns that are not filed in a processable form may

during a normal filing season, a taxpayer providing new address information on any of the Forms 1040[15] that is received by the IRS after February 14 and before June 1 will be considered properly processed on July 16. A taxpayer filing Form 8822, Change of Address, will be considered to have complied with the requirements for a clear and concise notification and will be considered properly processed after a forty-five-day processing period beginning on the day after the date of receipt by the IRS.

¶1307 TAX COURT REVIEW

Tax Court Rule 200 provides that an applicant for admission to the Court must establish that he or she is of good moral character and repute, and that he or she possesses requisite qualifications to represent others in the preparation and trial of cases. An attorney can be admitted to practice by showing that he or she is a member in good standing of the Bar of the Supreme Court of the United States or the highest Court of any state, territory or the District of Columbia. Other applicants must pass a written examination. An individual taxpayer may appear on his or her own behalf and, with the permission of the Court, an officer of a corporation may appear on behalf of the corporation.

The initial paper to be filed in the Tax Court is the petition.[16] The contents of a petition are prescribed by Tax Court Rule 34(b) and generally consist of six paragraphs, the first five of which are numbered. The first paragraph should contain the name and address of the taxpayer along with his or her identification number (social security or employer identification), and the office of the IRS with which the tax return for the period in controversy was filed. The second paragraph, which is the basis of the Tax Court's jurisdiction, must state the date of the mailing of the Statutory Notice, the city and state of the IRS office which issued the notice and any other proper allegations demonstrating the jurisdiction of the Court. A copy of the Statutory Notice of Deficiency should be referred to in this paragraph and should be attached as an exhibit to the petition. The third paragraph relates the type of tax in dispute (income, gift or estate), and the year or periods for which the determination was made, as well as the appropriate amount in controversy. The fourth paragraph sets forth in detail the errors which the petitioner contends the Commissioner made rendering a determination. Each assignment is to be lettered and concisely stated. The fifth paragraph must contain a clear and concise statement of the facts upon which the petitioner relies in support of his or her assignments of error. The final paragraph, unnumbered, is the prayer for relief and the request that the Court grant the relief sought by the petitioner.

(Footnote Continued)

require additional processing time. In such cases, the 45-day processing period for address change will begin the day after the error that caused the return to be unprocessable is corrected.

[15] 1040A, 1040EZ, 1040NR, 1040PR, 1040SS or 1040X.

[16] A taxpayer has the option of not filing a petition and paying the assessed amount and then filing a claim for refund which, if denied, may be litigated in a district court or the Court of Federal Claims. The choice of forum for litigating a tax controversy is discussed in Chapter 14, *infra*.

The petition itself must be signed by the taxpayer or his or her counsel, and attached to the petition should be a designation of place of trial (Official Form 4). A sample petition is included as Exhibit 13-4 at ¶ 1354.

Following the filing of the petition by the taxpayer, the Commissioner of Internal Revenue, through the local office of Chief Counsel, will file an answer within sixty days. If the IRS makes an affirmative allegation, such as fraud, the taxpayer must respond with a secondary pleading referred to as a reply. In the reply the taxpayer admits or denies facts or allegations of fact affirmatively made by the Commissioner in his or her answer.

The Appeals Office possesses complete settlement jurisdiction of all docketed cases after the issuance of a Statutory Notice, unless it issued the Notice of Deficiency. If the Deficiency Notice in a docketed case was issued by the examination function and there is no recommendation for criminal prosecution pending, the Office of Chief Counsel will refer the case to the Appeals Office for settlement as soon as it has filed its answer in the Tax Court. The Appeals Office has exclusive settlement jurisdiction over the case until the case is returned to Chief Counsel for preparation for trial. Upon the taxpayer's request, the Appeals Office will grant the taxpayer a hearing and consider any case for settlement purposes where the notice has been issued by the examination function. Except in unusual circumstances, no hearing will be granted in the period after the issuance of the Statutory Notice of Deficiency and prior to the filing of a petition with the Tax Court.

If an agreement is reached between the taxpayer and the Appeals Office after the filing of a petition in the Tax Court, a stipulation of settlement is prepared and executed by the parties. This stipulation is then filed with the Tax Court which will enter its order in conformity with the stipulation. The taxpayer may also receive an "audit statement" setting forth the adjustments based on the settlement, a computation of the revised tax liability and the resulting deficiency or overpayment. These documents are not filed with the Tax Court and are for the information of the taxpayer only.

The Tax Court has jurisdiction under Code Sec. 6512(b)(2) to order a refund if its determination results in an overpayment. The Court also has jurisdiction under Code Sec. 7481(c) to determine whether interest on a deficiency resulting from its decision has been computed correctly. The taxpayer desiring a review of the interest computation must petition the Tax Court within one year of the decision. Such review is permitted, however, only if all the assessed tax and interest has been paid.

Reasonable litigation costs, including attorneys' fees, will be awarded by the Tax Court to a prevailing taxpayer who is able to establish that the position of the IRS in the proceeding was not substantially justified.[17] To recover such costs, the prevailing party must have exhausted all of the administrative remedies available within the IRS before petitioning the Tax Court. A protest, therefore, must have been filed with the Appeals Office. The prevailing party is defined as one

---

[17] Code Sec. 7430.

who has substantially prevailed either with respect to the amount in controversy or with respect to the most significant issue or set of issues.

To provide taxpayers with a simplified and relatively informal procedure for handling small tax cases, the Tax Court created the Small Claims Division in 1969. Under Code Sec. 7463(a), when neither the amount of the deficiency nor the amount of any claimed overpayment exceeds $50,000.00,[18] the taxpayer may request to have the proceedings conducted under the small tax case procedure at the time the petition is filed. Proceedings conducted in the Small Claims Division are informal, and any evidence deemed by the Court to have probative value will be admissible. A decision entered in a case in the Small Claims Division is not subject to review by any other court, nor is it treated as precedent for any other case. Cases considered under the procedures are generally referred to as "S" cases due to the presence of "S" in the docket number. Beginning in January 2001, decisions on "S" cases are being released on the Tax Court's website (http://www.ustaxcourt.gov). In the past these opinions could only be viewed by requesting them by case name from the court's Public Files Section. At this time, there are no plans to add features to the court's website that would permit text searching of court opinions.[19]

¶1310 SPECIAL ASSESSMENTS

Congress has given the IRS power to take whatever measures are necessary to collect unpaid taxes. Normally, these efforts do not begin until an assessment is made. This could either be the assessment of the tax shown as due on the return or the assessment of a deficiency after an examination of the return. However, in certain instances Congress has decided that the normal assessment procedures should not be followed because the delay from doing so will endanger the collection of the taxes.

¶1315 JEOPARDY ASSESSMENT: SECTION 6861

Under Code Sec. 6861(a), if the IRS has reason to believe that the assessment or collection of a deficiency will be jeopardized by delay, by the departure of the taxpayer or by the removal of his or her assets, the IRS may make a jeopardy assessment, notwithstanding the restrictions upon assessment of Code Sec. 6213(a). In making such an assessment, the IRS is not bound by the requirement that a Notice of Deficiency be sent before any assessment is made or any effort to collect a tax is undertaken.

For the IRS to make a jeopardy assessment, a determination must be made that at least one of the following conditions exists:

1. The taxpayer is or appears to be designing quickly to depart from the United States or to conceal himself or herself;

2. The taxpayer is or appears to be designing quickly to place his or her property beyond the reach of the government either by removing it from

---

[18] For proceedings commenced prior to July 23, 1998, the limit was $10,000.

[19] 2001 CCH Tax Day, 01/21/2001, Item J.6.

the United States, by concealing it, by dissipating it or by transferring it to other persons; or

3. The taxpayer's financial solvency is or appears to be imperiled (for purposes of determining solvency, the proposed assessment of taxes, interest and penalty is not considered).[20]

Jeopardy assessments concerning trust-fund recovery penalty assessments under Code Sec. 6672, employment or excise tax assessments, or income tax assessments (where there is no question as to the amount of the liability) can be initiated and processed by the collection function. The examination function initiates jeopardy assessments of income taxes (where liability may be in question), estate taxes and gift taxes.

Whether the jeopardy assessment is initiated by the Examination or collection function, the recommendation must be reviewed by the jeopardy assessment coordinator in the Collection Technical Support unit, the Criminal Investigation area director, and the local office of Chief Counsel prior to approval by the Director.[21]

A jeopardy assessment can be made for virtually any reasonable amount that the Director sees fit (see Exhibit 13-5 at ¶1355). Even if a Notice of Deficiency has been issued, a jeopardy assessment can be made for an amount greater than that set forth in the prior notice.[22]

Once a jeopardy assessment has been made, the taxpayer's property can be seized to satisfy the amount of the assessment, including any penalties and interest. Jeopardy assessments are made sparingly.[23]

¶1317 REMEDIES OF TAXPAYER

After the jeopardy assessment is made, the taxpayer is given a Notice and Demand to pay the tax, a Notice of Jeopardy Assessment and Right of Appeal, and a computation of the tax. The Notice of Jeopardy Assessment and Right of Appeal (see Exhibit 13-5 at ¶1355) is in a letter from the director and informs the taxpayer that he may file a protest seeking redetermination whether the making of the assessment is reasonable and whether the amount assessed is appropriate under the circumstances.

Code Sec. 7429 provides expedited administrative and judicial review of jeopardy and termination assessments. Under this provision, within five days after the jeopardy or termination assessment, the IRS must give the taxpayer a written statement of the information upon which it relies in making the assessment. Within thirty days thereafter, the taxpayer may request the IRS to review the assessment and determine whether under the circumstances the assessment was reasonable and the amount assessed was appropriate. Such a request for review will be given immediate consideration, and the results of the redetermina-

---

[20] Reg. §1.6851-1(a)(1). See also IRM 1.2.1.4.27 P-4-88.

[21] IRM 1.2.2.122 Order Number 219.

[22] Code Sec. 6861(c).

[23] Policy Statement P-4-88.

tion are to be provided within sixteen days from the date of the receipt of the taxpayer's request.[24]

If the Director makes an unfavorable determination or fails to make any review within the sixteen-day period, the taxpayer has ninety days to bring a civil action in the United States District Court to determine the reasonableness of the assessment and the appropriateness of the amount. This is to be a priority item on the court's calendar, and the court must render a decision within twenty days unless the taxpayer requests an extension and establishes reasonable grounds for such additional time. The decision of the court is final and unappealable. Under Code Sec. 7429, the court may order the assessment abated in whole or in part or may require such other action as the court finds appropriate. The Tax Court has concurrent jurisdiction with the federal district courts if a petition for redetermination of the deficiency has been filed with the Tax Court before the jeopardy assessment was made.

Although the regulations provide only the three grounds for making jeopardy assessments that are detailed in ¶1315, the courts have generally interpreted these requirements very broadly.[25] For example, although Reg. §1.6851-1(a)(1)(ii) requires the IRS to show that the taxpayer is concealing his assets, the courts generally have been willing to draw the inference of concealment of assets from any evidence of illegal activity.[26] The general standard of review followed by the courts was articulated in *Loretto v. United States*,[27] one of the first reported decisions under Code Sec. 7429. According to *Loretto*, the court is not to give great weight to the judgment of the IRS, but rather it should make an independent de novo determination. In determining whether it was reasonable to make the assessment under the circumstances, the court must find the IRS actions to be something more than arbitrary and capricious but not necessarily supported by substantial evidence. The court can and should consider information that was not available to the IRS at the time it made its assessment to determine whether the IRS's actions were reasonable.

Because of the unusual nature of a jeopardy assessment, a statutory right to stay collection exists. The collection of a jeopardy assessment may be stayed by the taxpayer upon the filing of a bond with the Director. The bond can be filed at any time before actual levy is made on any property or property rights.[28] The amount of the bond to be filed must be equal to the full amount of tax, penalties and interest calculated to be due by the Director as of the date of the jeopardy

---

[24] Rev. Proc. 78-12, 1978-1 CB 590.

[25] *Park v. U.S.*, 1992 WL 136622 4 (C.D. Cal. 1992), 92-1 USTC ¶50,270 (government was reasonable in concluding that taxpayer was planning to leave the country when he liquidated substantially all of his real property). But see *Modern Bookkeeping v. U.S.*, 854 F.Supp 475 (D.C. Minn. 1994), 94-2 USTC ¶50,310 (jeopardy assessment was unreasonable because the taxpayer filed corporate returns and declared distributions received in the form of precious metals).

[26] See *Hamilton v. United States*, 81-1 USTC ¶9325 (E.D. Va. 1981), and *Prather v. United States*, 84-2

USTC ¶9730 (M.D. Pa. 1984). Such illegal activity does not include the intentional failure to report income. *Burd v. United States*, 774 F. Supp. 903 (D.N.J. 1991), 91-2 USTC ¶50,530.

[27] 440 F. Supp. 1168 (E.D. Pa. 1978), 78-1 USTC ¶9110.

[28] Under Reg. §301.6863-1(a)(2)(iii), a bond may also be filed "in the discretion of the district director, after any such levy has been made and before the expiration of the period of limitations on collection."

¶1317

assessment. Furthermore, the bond must be conditioned upon the payment of the full amount of tax, penalty and interest. After a bond has been filed, collection of the assessment covered by the bond will be stayed. The taxpayer then will have an opportunity to allow the Tax Court to determine whether the amount assessed is more or less than the correct amount of tax due.

If a Notice of Deficiency has not been sent to the taxpayer, then a Special Notice of Deficiency must be mailed to the taxpayer within sixty days following the jeopardy assessment.[29] The mailing of the Notice of Deficiency within this sixty-day period is necessary to make the jeopardy assessment enforceable. As is the case with a regular ninety-day Notice of Deficiency, a taxpayer may appeal to the Tax Court. In addition to issuing a Notice of Deficiency, the IRS must also send the taxpayer a "Notice and Demand" for payment. Under Reg. § 301.6861-1(d), payment of the full amount of the assessment is to be made within ten days after the Notice and Demand is sent.

¶1320 JEOPARDY LEVIES: SECTION 6331(a)

The administrative and judicial review provisions of Code Sec. 7429 are also available for jeopardy levies. Under Code Sec. 6331(a), the IRS may demand immediate payment of assessed taxes and levy upon and seize any property or right to property, including wages and commissions, if collection is determined to be in jeopardy. Without this jeopardy provision for an immediate levy, the IRS would not be permitted to make a levy until thirty days after the taxpayer had been notified by certified or registered mail of the intention to levy.[30] The grounds for making a jeopardy levy are the same as those for a jeopardy assessment. If such a levy is contested, the burden is on the government to establish the reasonableness of the levy. The jeopardy levy is frequently used in conjunction with the jeopardy assessment so as to permit the IRS not only to make an immediate assessment, but also to seize or levy upon property at the same time without having to wait thirty days after the issuance of a notice of intent to levy.

¶1322 ALTERNATIVE JEOPARDY ASSESSMENT: SECTION 6867

Code Sec. 6867 provides what is effectively an alternative jeopardy assessment procedure. Primarily aimed at the situation where law enforcement officials discover a large amount of cash and where the person holding the cash does not admit to ownership, it provides a mechanism by which that cash can be seized and an assessment of tax made immediately. The statute presumes that the cash represents gross income of the person in possession and that it is taxable at the highest allowable rate.[31] An assessment notice and statement setting out the information upon which the IRS relies in making the assessment are given to the person in possession.

---

[29] Code Sec. 6861(b).

[30] Code Sec. 6331(d). See Chapter 14, *infra,* for detailed discussion of the IRS right to levy.

[31] Code Sec. 6867(b)(2).

Where such an assessment is made, the true owner can come forward and contest the assessment. In that case, the original assessment will be abated; however, a jeopardy assessment will probably be made against the true owner. For the special assessment provision to apply, a person must be found in possession of cash or its equivalent in excess of $10,000.00 and that person must not claim the cash or identify the person to whom it belongs. For purposes of these provisions, cash equivalent can include any foreign currency, any bearer obligation and any medium of exchange commonly used in illegal activities. Where these requirements are met, it is presumed that collection of the tax will be jeopardized by delay and an immediate assessment and levy upon the cash will be made.

¶1324 TERMINATION ASSESSMENT: SECTION 6851

Another type of immediate assessment available to the IRS is a termination assessment. Code Sec. 6851 empowers the Director to terminate the taxable year of the taxpayer if he or she determines that the taxpayer is planning to act in such amanner as will prejudice or make ineffectual proceedings to collect income tax for the current or preceding year. A termination assessment for the current year is based on a short taxable year ending on the date of assessment. A letter informing the taxpayer of the termination of the taxable period (see Exhibit 13-6 at ¶1356) is not a "Notice of Deficiency," and, therefore, the Tax Court has no jurisdiction.

The circumstances under which a termination assessment can be made are similar to those for a jeopardy assessment. However, a termination assessment can only be made as to income tax liability for the current or the immediately preceding taxable year. Further, no termination assessment can be made after the due date of the taxpayer's return for the immediately preceding year. If no return has been filed, then at that point a jeopardy assessment of the delinquency could be made and immediate collection measures pursued.

The Internal Revenue Manual requires that the termination assessment be based on a reasonable computation of tax liability and further provides that the basis on which adjusted gross income is computed (for example, source and application of funds statement or net worth computation) must be stated. If appropriate, a reasonable estimate is to be made of the expenses of the taxpayer in arriving at the adjusted gross income figure.[32]

¶1325 ASSESSMENT IN BANKRUPTCY CASES

Under the Federal Bankruptcy Code, the commencement of a bankruptcy case creates a bankruptcy estate generally consisting of the debtor's property. The commencement of such a case also creates an automatic stay generally prohibiting a wide variety of acts including the collection of taxes. Under the Bankruptcy Tax Act of 1980,[33] when a taxpayer filed for bankruptcy, the government was permitted to assess taxes only under very limited circumstances. This procedure

---

[32] IRM Handbook 4.3.9.2.4.1.3.2. [33] P.L. 96-589.

was changed by the 1994 amendments[34] to the Bankruptcy Code. The changes clarified the government's right to audit the taxpayer, to demand the filing of tax returns, and to issue statutory notices of deficiency. They also authorized the government to assess taxes and issue notices and demands for payment. However, the provisions of the bankruptcy law still prohibit actual collection of the tax during administration of the bankruptcy case absent permission from the Bankruptcy Court. The tax lien that would otherwise attach to the debtor's property by reason of an assessment made during the administration of a bankruptcy case does not take effect unless the tax (1) will not be discharged in the bankruptcy case, and (2) the property to which the lien would attach is transferred out of the bankruptcy estate to or revested in the taxpayer.

A special form of Notice of Deficiency (see Exhibit 13-7 at ¶1357) is used when the taxpayer is in bankruptcy proceedings. If the taxpayer wishes to petition the United States Tax Court, he or she will first have to obtain relief from theautomatic stay to file the petition. However, the taxpayer has an alternative to filing a petition in the Tax Court; the taxpayer can elect to have the merits of the tax case heard in the Bankruptcy Court.

The collection function is responsible for ascertaining the commencement of bankruptcy and receivership proceedings. Once it is determined that a bankruptcy proceeding has been filed, a determination is made whether the case is an "asset" or "no asset" case. A no-asset case is one in which the assets of an individual taxpayer are valued at an amount less than allowable exemptions plus the cost of administration.[35] A no asset case also includes a situation in which the Bankruptcy Court has issued a notice that no dividend to creditors will be issued. When it is determined that a case is a no-asset case, usually the only action taken on it will be to freeze the account so that no notices or collection efforts are undertaken during the period that the stay imposed by the Bankruptcy Court is in effect.

When it is determined that there may be assets available in a case, the examination function is contacted to determine whether the taxpayer's returns are presently under examination. If the returns are not presently being examined, the returns are reviewed and, if examination is warranted, assigned immediately. If examination is not warranted, the returns will be accepted as filed.

The examination function is to expeditiously determine the taxpayer's liability for federal taxes in each asset case assigned for examination. After the examination is completed, the collection function is notified so that a proof of claim (see Exhibit 13-8 at ¶1358) can be filed. In preparing the proof of claim, the IRS is to include not only amounts determined to be due by examination function but also any other taxes that have not been paid by the debtor. The proof of claim is to set forth the type of tax and also the nature of the claim as secured or unsecured and as a priority claim or a general claim. The proof of claim will include the calculation of any interest or penalties accrued before the filing of the bankruptcy petition.

---

[34] P.L. 103-394.　　　　　[35] IRM Handbook 5.5.1.4.1.

Claims of creditors in bankruptcy proceedings generally fall into three categories: secured, priority and unsecured. Secured creditors generally have specific assets that can be distributed to them in satisfaction of their claim, and thus, their claims are paid first in order of priority. Priority claims are governed by Sec. 507 of the Bankruptcy Code and are entitled to priority in distribution over unsecured creditor claims. Tax claims generally are assigned to eighth priority among the priority claims. However, tax claims representing taxes incurred in the administration of the bankrupt estate can be first priority because they are treated as administrative expense claims.

The trustee is required to file a U.S. Income Tax Return for Estates and Trusts, Form 1041, covering the income and expenses of the bankruptcy estate during the period of administration. When the final Form 1041 is filed, the trustee can request an immediate determination of any unpaid tax liability of the estate. The IRS has sixty days to notify the trustee whether it accepts the returns as filed or whether it wishes to audit the returns. If an audit is performed, any deficiencymust be proposed within 180 days after the original audit request. If the trustee disagrees with the proposed deficiency, the jurisdiction of the Bankruptcy Court can be invoked to resolve the disagreement.

¶1331 TRUST-FUND RECOVERY PENALTY ASSESSMENT

The United States government in its tax collection process relies heavily upon the withholding of taxes at the source by an employer. The primary responsibility for withholding is that of the employing entity and those individuals who are responsible for its management. To protect against failure to discharge this duty properly, Code Sec. 6672 provides that when a designated collection entity fails to perform its statutory duty to collect, truthfully account for, and pay over the amount of taxes due, those individuals who are responsible for the performance of those duties and who willfully fail to do so become personally liable for a penalty equal to 100 percent of the amount which should have been withheld and paid over.[36] The Code Sec. 6672 "penalty" is not a penalty in the conventional sense; rather, it is more in the nature of a recompense to the government for funds which were withheld or should have been withheld from employees which the responsible individual has failed to remit as taxes held in trust for the government. Investigations concerning the penalty are conducted by revenue officers.

The two primary factors in the imposition of a 100-percent penalty are (1) the responsible person and (2) willfulness. If the person against whom the 100-percent penalty is assessed is not a "person required to collect, truthfully account for, and pay over," the individual in question is not liable for the penalty. However, even if that person is such an individual, if the failure to collect, account for, or pay over was not willful, he or she is not liable for the penalties under Code Sec. 6672. Generally, the courts have determined that if a person is

---

[36] This penalty only enforces personal liability for the withheld taxes; no *personal* liability will exist under Code Sec. 6672 for the corporate FICA tax or employment tax penalties and interest assessed against the corporation. See IRM 5.17.7.1.6.

¶1331

able to exercise full authority over the financial affairs of an entity required to collect, withhold or pay over trust-fund taxes, he or she is "a responsible person" regardless of what formal title or connection he or she may have with the entity. Furthermore, even a director who is neither an officer nor an employee of the corporation may be found liable as a responsible person if the Board of Directors has the final decision on what corporate debts are to be paid, to whom and when.[37]

The Internal Revenue Manual indicates that a responsible person may be an officer, an employee, a director or a shareholder of a corporation, or some other person[38] with sufficient control over the funds to direct disbursement of suchfunds. This does not preclude another person, such as a lender, from also being treated as a responsible person if that person exercises significant control over corporation operations.[39] In a 1993 revision of their policy, the IRS stated that an employee who performs his or her duties under the dominion and control of others and who does not make decisions on behalf of the corporation will not be subject to the trust-fund penalty.[40] In conducting the investigation to determine who is a responsible officer, the revenue officer is to review the corporation's charter, by-laws and minute books. A review of the actual opera-tion and control of the corporation is also significant. The Manual indicates that the authority to sign or co-sign checks is a significant factor to be considered; however, the fact that an employee signed corporate checks by itself is not enough to establish responsibility.[41]

The Manual also provides that, if it cannot be conclusively determined which person is responsible for withholding, collecting or paying over taxes, the IRS will look to the president, secretary and the treasurer as responsible officers. Case law has established that it is possible for more than one officer to be a responsible person for the same quarter.[42]

Under Code Sec. 6672, the term "willfulness" is used in the broadest sense of the term. It includes a voluntary, conscious and intentional act. The actions of the responsible person need not be malicious nor stem from bad motives or evil purposes. The mere voluntary act of preferring any creditor over the United States is sufficient to make an individual a responsible person willfully failing to pay over or collect taxes under Code Sec. 6672.[43] The Manual describes willful-

---

[37] *Wood v. U.S.*, 808 F.2d 411 (5th Cir. 1987), 87-1 USTC ¶9165 (board member who had authority to sign checks, was active in decision making, and had control over the corporation was a responsible per-son); but see Code Sec. 6672(e) for voluntary board members of Tax Exempt Organizations.

[38] *In Re Thomas*, 187 B.R. 471 (Bankr. E.D. Pa. 1995), 95-2 USTC ¶50,490 (an accountant was held to be a responsible person because he had knowledge that the company did not pay over its payroll tax and he preferred certain creditors over the government).

[39] *Merchants National Bank of Mobile v. U.S.*, 878 F.2d 1382 (11th Cir. 1989), 89-2 USTC ¶9511 (a bank

was held to be a responsible person because it had the right to oversee substantially all of the corpora-tion's significant operations).

[40] IRM 1.2.1.5.14.

[41] IRM Handbook 5.7.3.3.

[42] *Brown v. United States*, 591 F.2d 1136 (5th Cir. 1979), 79-1 USTC ¶9285.

[43] *Purcell v. U.S.*, 1 F.3d 932 (9th Cir. 1993), 93-2 USTC ¶50,460 (taxpayer who had knowledge that the withholding taxes had not been paid over and con-sciously directed payment to other creditors was held to be willful).

ness as the attitude of a person who, having a free will or choice, either intentionally disregards the law or is plainly indifferent to its requirements.[44]

As a practical matter, in most 100-percent penalty cases involving officers of corporations, the revenue officer conducting the investigation must determine which officer or officers were actually under a duty to see that the taxes were withheld, collected or paid over to the government. An analysis of the operation and control of the corporation's affairs normally will disclose which officer or officers were responsible individuals under Code Sec. 6672. As a tool in making this determination, a revenue officer will conduct interviews with the individuals involved. Form 4180 (see Exhibit 13-9 at ¶ 1359) is a guide used by the revenue officer in these interviews.

Once a revenue officer has determined willfulness and responsibility, he or she will make a 100-percent assessment recommendation against all those who are so identified. This is to assure that the penalty is asserted in an even-handed manner against all parties regardless of considerations such as the degree of responsibility or collectibility. Each responsible person is jointly and severally liable for the full amount of the penalty. The IRS may collect all or any part of the penalty from any one of the responsible parties. It is the policy of the IRS, however, not to collect more than the total unpaid trust-fund taxes when several responsible parties are involved.[45] Further, Code Sec. 6103, which involves disclosure to persons having a material interest, was amended by the Taxpayer Bill of Rights 2 (1996),[46] and now provides that a taxpayer subject to the Code Sec. 6672 penalty shall, upon request, receive in writing the names of any other parties the IRS has determined to be liable for the penalty and whether the IRS has attempted to collect the penalty from such parties. This 1996 legislation also amended Code Sec. 6672 to provide a taxpayer subject to the penalty the right to contribution when more than one person is liable for the penalty. The factor of collectibility will be considered as a basis for nonassertion of the 100-percent penalty only in those cases where future collection potential is obviously nonexistent because of advanced age or deteriorating physical or mental condition.

Code Sec. 6671 provides that the penalty under Code Sec. 6672 is to be assessed and collected in the same manner as taxes. Under this provision, the statute of limitations for assessment of the penalty is that which applies to the assessment of the tax: it must be assessed within three years from the time the employment tax return is deemed to have been filed. If such returns are timely filed, the returns are considered to have been filed on April fifteenth of the succeeding year.[47] The Internal Revenue Manual indicates that every effort must be made to collect the liability from the corporation before asserting the Code Sec. 6672 liability. However, as a practical matter, if the assets of the corporation are not readily available to pay the withholding tax liability, often the potential

---

[44] IRMHandbook 5.7.3.4. See *In re Slodov*, 436 U.S. 238 (1978), 78-1 USTC ¶ 9447, for discussion of willfulness when an individual acquires control of a corporation with pre-existing employment tax liabilities.

[45] IRM 1.2.1.5.14.

[46] P.L. 104-168.

[47] Code Sec. 6501(b)(2).

expiration of the statute of limitations will force the revenue officer to assert the Code Sec. 6672 liability even though there is a possibility that the corporation might be able to satisfy the delinquency at some point in the future. The assessment against the individual is abated to the extent that the corporation does pay withheld taxes. It should be noted that any property of the corporation levied upon by the IRS will not be applied to the trust-fund portion of the employment tax liability. Because the payment does not constitute a voluntary payment, it must be applied in the best interests of the government, which in this instance would require application of the levied amount first to the corporate FICA(Federal Insurance Contributions Act) expense and any employment tax penalties and interest assessed against the corporation.

The Taxpayer Bill of Rights 2 amended Code Sec. 6672 to require the IRS to notify the taxpayer in writing that he or she is subject to assessment for the trust-fund penalty at least sixty days before a notice and demand letter is sent. If the initial notice is sent before the expiration of the three-year statute of limitations, the period for assessment will not expire before the later of ninety days after the mailing of such notice, or if there is a timely protest, thirty days after the IRS makes a final determination with respect to such protest.

When a revenue officer determines that a person is a potentially responsible person, he or she will send the taxpayer a letter (see Exhibit 13-10 at ¶ 1360) advising that the penalty is being proposed. The letter requests that the taxpayer agree to the penalty by executing Form 2751, Proposed Assessment of 100-Percent Penalty (see Exhibit 13-11 at ¶ 1361). If the taxpayer does not agree, he or she is given opportunities to discuss the matter with the collection function Group Manager and to appeal the proposed penalty through the Appeals office. However, if there are fewer than 120 days remaining before the expiration of the statutory period for assessment, the case cannot be transferred to the Appeals Office prior to assessment unless the taxpayer executes a Form 2750, Waiver of Statutory Period (see Exhibit 13-12 at ¶ 1362), to extend the time for assessment.

A liability somewhat similar to that under Code Sec. 6672 exists under Code Sec. 3505(b), which provides that any lender, surety or other person who supplies funds for the account of an employer for the purpose of paying wages of the employer can be personally liable for any taxes not withheld or paid over to the government from those wages. However, such liability can only be asserted if the lender has actual notice or knowledge that the withholding taxes will not be paid over. Further, this liability is limited to twenty-five percent of the amount loaned to the employer for purposes of making wage payments.

¶1331

¶1351 Exhibit 13-1

Form **5278** (Rev. July 1992)	Department of the Treasury—Internal Revenue Service **Statement—Income Tax Change**	1. Office symbols

2. Name(s) of taxpayer(s)	3. ☐ Notice of Deficiency ☐ Other (specify) ☐ Settlement computation

4. Social security number	5. Form number	6. Court docket number

7. Adjustment to income	Tax years ended		
a.			
b.			
c.			
d.			
e.			
f.			
g.			
h.			
8. Total adjustments			
9. a. ☐ Taxable income ☐ Adjusted gross income b. As shown in: ☐ Preliminary letter dated_____ ☐ Notice of deficiency dated_____ ☐ Return as filed			
10. ☐ Taxable income as revised ☐ Adjusted gross income as revised			
11. Tax from: ☐ tax tables ☐ tax rate schedules ☐ other			
12. Alternative tax if applicable *(from page _____)*			
13. Corrected tax liability *(lesser of line 11 or 12)*			
14. Less credits a. *(specify)* b. c.			
15. Balance *(line 13 less amounts on lines 14a through 14c)*			
16. Plus a. b. c.			
17. Total corrected income tax liability *(line 15 plus amounts on lines 16a through 16c)*			
18. Total tax shown on return or as previously adjusted			
19. Adjustments to EIC/Fuels Credit increase *(decrease)*			
20. Increase in Tax or *(Overassessment - Decrease in Tax)* *(Line 17 adjusted by lines 18 and 19)*			
21. Additions/Adjustments to the Tax *(listed below)*			

Form **5278** (Rev. July 1992)

¶1352 Exhibit 13-2

Form **8626** (Rev. September 1987)	Department of the Treasury — Internal Revenue Service **Agreement to Rescind Notice of Deficiency** *(See instructions on reverse)*	In reply refer to: SSN or EIN:

Pursuant to section 6212(d) of the Internal Revenue Code, the parties, _____ ,
Name(s)

taxpayers of _____ , and the District Director of
(Number, Street, City or Town, State, Zip Code)

Internal Revenue, Regional Director of Appeals or Service Center Director consent and agree to the following:

1. The parties mutually agree to rescind the notice of deficiency issued on _____

to the above taxpayer(s) stating a deficiency in Federal _____ tax due and, where applicable,
Kind of tax

additions to the tax for the year(s) as follows:

		Additions to Tax:	Additions to Tax:
Tax Year Ended	Deficiency	_____	_____

2. The parties agree that the statute of limitations has not expired as to the above tax year(s) and can be further extended at the time of this agreement or at a later date under applicable provisions of the Internal Revenue Code.

3. The parties agree that good reasons have been shown to exist for the action being taken in this agreement. The parties agree that the effect of this rescission is as if the notice of deficiency had never been issued. The parties are returned to the rights and obligations existing on the day immediately prior to the date on which the rescinded notice of deficiency was issued. Included among those rights and obligations is the right of the Commissioner or his delegate to issue a later notice of deficiency in an amount that exceeds, or is the same as, or is less than the amount previously determined, from which amount the taxpayer(s) may exercise all administrative and statutory appeal rights.

4. The taxpayers affirmatively state that at the time of signing this agreement they have not petitioned the United States Tax Court contesting the deficiencies in the notice of deficiency.

Your Signature	Date
Spouse's Signature	Date
Taxpayers' Representative	Date
Corporate Name	
Corporate Officer Title	Date
Commissioner of Internal Revenue or Delegate	Date

Instructions

If the rescission of the notice of deficiency is for income tax for which a joint return was filed, and a joint notice of deficiency was issued both husband and wife must sign the original and copy of this form unless one, acting under a power of attorney, signs as agent for the other. The signature must match the names as they appear on the front of this form.

If you are an attorney or agent of the taxpayer(s), you may sign this agreement provided the action is specifically authorized by a power of attorney. If a power of attorney was not previously filed, it must be included with this form.

If you are acting as a fiduciary (such as executor, administrator, trustee, etc.) and you sign this agreement, attach Form 56, Notice Concerning Fiduciary Relationship, unless it was previously filed.

If the taxpayer is a corporation, sign this agreement with the corporate name followed by the signature and title of the officer(s) authorized to sign.

The effective date of this agreement shall be the date on which the Commissioner or his delegate signs this form.

Form **8626** (Rev. 9-87)

¶1353 Exhibit 13-3

Form **8822**	**Change of Address**	
(Rev. December 2003)	▶ Please type or print.	OMB No. 1545-1163
Department of the Treasury Internal Revenue Service	▶ See instructions on back. ▶ Do not attach this form to your return.	

Part I	**Complete This Part To Change Your Home Mailing Address**

Check **all** boxes this change affects:

1 ☐   Individual income tax returns (Forms 1040, 1040A, 1040EZ, TeleFile, 1040NR, etc.)

     ▶ If your last return was a joint return and you are now establishing a residence separate
     from the spouse with whom you filed that return, check here . . . .   ▶   ☐

2 ☐   Gift, estate, or generation-skipping transfer tax returns (Forms 706, 709, etc.)

     ▶ For Forms 706 and 706-NA, enter the decedent's name and social security number below.

▶ Decedent's name	▶ Social security number	
3a Your name (first name, initial, and last name)		**3b** Your social security number
4a Spouse's name (first name, initial, and last name)		**4b** Spouse's social security number

5   Prior name(s). See instructions.

6a Old address (no., street, city or town, state, and ZIP code). If a P.O. box or foreign address, see instructions.	Apt. no.
6b Spouse's old address, if different from line 6a (no., street, city or town, state, and ZIP code). If a P.O. box or foreign address, see instructions.	Apt. no.
7 New address (no., street, city or town, state, and ZIP code). If a P.O. box or foreign address, see instructions.	Apt. no.

Part II	**Complete This Part To Change Your Business Mailing Address or Business Location**

Check **all** boxes this change affects:

8 ☐   Employment, excise, income, and other business returns (Forms 720, 940, 940-EZ, 941, 990, 1041, 1065, 1120, etc.)
9 ☐   Employee plan returns (Forms 5500, 5500-EZ, etc.).
10 ☐   Business location

11a Business name	**11b** Employer identification number
12 Old mailing address (no., street, city or town, state, and ZIP code). If a P.O. box or foreign address, see instructions.	Room or suite no.
13 New mailing address (no., street, city or town, state, and ZIP code). If a P.O. box or foreign address, see instructions.	Room or suite no.
14 New business location (no., street, city or town, state, and ZIP code). If a foreign address, see instructions.	Room or suite no.

Part III	**Signature**

Daytime telephone number of person to contact (optional) ▶ (   ) _____

Sign **Here**	▶ _____	▶ _____
	Your signature Date	If Part II completed, signature of owner, officer, or representative Date
	▶ _____	▶ _____
	If joint return, spouse's signature Date	Title

For Privacy Act and Paperwork Reduction Act Notice, see back of form.   Cat. No. 12081V   Form **8822** (Rev. 12-2003)

Purpose of Form

You may use Form 8822 to notify the Internal Revenue Service if you changed your home or business mailing address or your business location. If this change also affects the mailing address for your children who filed income tax returns, complete and file a separate Form 8822 for each child. If you are a representative signing for the taxpayer, attach to Form 8822 a copy of your power of attorney.

Changing Both Home and Business Addresses? If you are, use a separate Form 8822 to show each change.

Prior Name(s)

If you or your spouse changed your name because of marriage, divorce, etc., complete line 5. Also, be sure to notify the **Social Security Administration** of your new name so that it has the same name in its records that you have on your tax return. This prevents delays in processing your return and issuing refunds. It also safeguards your future social security benefits.

Addresses

Be sure to include any apartment, room, or suite number in the space provided.

P.O. Box

Enter your box number instead of your street address **only** if your post office does not deliver mail to your street address.

Foreign Address

Enter the information in the following order: city, province or state, and country. Follow the country's practice for entering the postal code. Please **do not** abbreviate the country name.

Signature

If you are completing Part II, the owner, an officer, or a representative must sign. An officer is the president, vice president, treasurer, chief accounting officer, etc. A representative is a person who has a valid power of attorney to handle tax matters or is otherwise authorized to sign tax returns for the business.

Where To File

Send this form to the **Internal Revenue Service Center** shown next that applies to you.

 If you checked the box on line 2, see **Filers Who Checked the Box on Line 2 or Completed Part II** for where to file this form.

Filers Who Checked the Box on Line 1 and Completed Part I

IF your old home mailing address was in . . .	THEN use this address . . .
Alabama, Florida, Georgia, Mississippi, North Carolina, Rhode Island, South Carolina, West Virginia	Atlanta, GA 39901
Arkansas, Colorado, Kentucky, Louisiana, New Mexico, Oklahoma, Tennessee, Texas	Austin, TX 73301
Alaska, Arizona, California, Hawaii, Idaho, Montana, Nevada, Oregon, Utah, Washington, Wyoming	Fresno, CA 93888
Maine, Massachusetts, New Hampshire, New York, Vermont	Andover, MA 05501
Delaware, Illinois, Indiana, Iowa, Kansas, Michigan, Minnesota, Missouri, Nebraska, North Dakota, South Dakota, Wisconsin	Kansas City, MO 64999
Ohio, Virginia	Memphis, TN 37501
Connecticut, District of Columbia, Maryland, New Jersey, Pennsylvania	Philadelphia, PA 19255
American Samoa	Philadelphia, PA 19255
Guam: Permanent residents	Department of Revenue and Taxation Government of Guam P.O. Box 23607 GMF, GU 96921
Guam: Nonpermanent residents Puerto Rico (or if excluding income under Internal Revenue Code section 933) Virgin Islands: Nonpermanent residents	Philadelphia, PA 19255
Virgin Islands: Permanent residents	V. I. Bureau of Internal Revenue 9601 Estate Thomas Charlotte Amalie St. Thomas, VI 00802
Foreign country: U.S. citizens and those filing Form 2555, Form 2555-EZ, or Form 4563 Dual-status aliens All APO and FPO addresses	Philadelphia, PA 19255

Filers Who Checked the Box on Line 2 or Completed Part II

IF your old business address was in . . .	THEN use this address . . .
Connecticut, Delaware, District of Columbia, Illinois, Indiana, Kentucky, Maine, Maryland, Massachusetts, Michigan, New Hampshire, New Jersey, New York, North Carolina, Ohio, Pennsylvania, Rhode Island, South Carolina, Vermont, Virginia, West Virginia, Wisconsin	Cincinnati, OH 45999

Alabama, Alaska, Arizona, Arkansas, California, Colorado, Florida, Georgia, Hawaii, Idaho, Iowa, Kansas, Louisiana, Minnesota, Mississippi, Missouri, Montana, Nebraska, Nevada, New Mexico, North Dakota, Oklahoma, Oregon, South Dakota, Tennessee, Texas, Utah, Washington, Wyoming	Ogden, UT 84201
Outside the United States	Philadelphia, PA 19255

Privacy Act and Paperwork Reduction Act Notice. We ask for the information on this form to carry out the Internal Revenue laws of the United States. We may give the information to the Department of Justice and to other Federal agencies, as provided by law. We may give it to cities, states, the District of Columbia, and U.S. commonwealths or possessions to carry out their tax laws. We may give it to foreign governments because of tax treaties they have with the United States. We may also give this information to Federal and state agencies to enforce Federal nontax criminal laws and to combat terrorism.

Our legal right to ask for information is Internal Revenue Code sections 6001 and 6011, which require you to file a statement with us for any tax for which you are liable. Section 6109 requires that you provide your social security number on what you file. This is so we know who you are, and can process your form and other papers.

You are not required to provide the information requested on a form that is subject to the Paperwork Reduction Act unless the form displays a valid OMB control number. Books or records relating to a form or its instructions must be retained as long as their contents may become material in the administration of any Internal Revenue law. Generally, tax returns and return information are confidential, as required by section 6103.

The use of this form is voluntary. However, if you fail to provide the Internal Revenue Service with your current mailing address, you may not receive a notice of deficiency or a notice and demand for tax. Despite the failure to receive such notices, penalties and interest will continue to accrue on the tax deficiencies.

The time needed to complete and file this form will vary depending on individual circumstances. The estimated average time is 16 minutes.

If you have comments concerning the accuracy of this time estimate or suggestions for making this form simpler, we would be happy to hear from you. You can write to the Tax Products Coordinating Committee, Western Area Distribution Center, Rancho Cordova, CA 95743-0001. **Do not** send the form to this address. Instead, see **Where To File** on this page.

¶1354 Exhibit 13-4

UNITED STATES TAX COURT

XYZ MANUFACTURING COMPANY,	:	
Petitioner,	:	
		Docket
v.	:	
		No._____
COMMISSIONER OF INTERNAL REVENUE,	:	
Respondent.	:	

PETITION

The above-named Petitioner, hereby petitions for redetermination of the deficiencies set forth by the Commissioner of Internal Revenue in his Notice of Deficiency dated December 21, 2001, and as a basis for this proceeding alleges as follows:

1. Petitioner is a Wisconsin corporation presently located at 103 Favre Drive, Lambeau Lake, Wisconsin, 55555. The Petitioner's employer identification number is 39-0000000. The returns for the periods herein involved were filed with the Internal Revenue Service Center at Kansas City, Missouri.

2. The Notice of Deficiency, (a copy of which is attached and marked Exhibit A), was mailed to Petitioner under date of December 21, 2001 by the Internal Revenue Service at Milwaukee, Wisconsin.

3. The Commissioner has determined deficiencies in income tax and penalties for the calendar 2000, all of which are in dispute, as follows:

Tax Year	Tax	Penalties Under § 6662(b)
2000	$14,019,431	$2,803,886

4. The determination set forth in the Notice of Deficiency is based upon the following errors by the Commissioner:

 A. In determining the taxable income, the Commissioner increased the income in the amount of $40,055,518 by erroneously disallowing expenses from rental activities.

 B. In his alternative claim in which the Commissioner asserted that the sale of the lease receivable (the "Assignment" as defined below) was a financing arrangement, which increased taxable income by $27,585,814.

 C. In erroneously determining that the Petitioner was negligent or that there was a substantial understatement of tax, the Commissioner asserted a penalty under IRC § 6662(b) in the amount of $2,803,886.

5. The facts upon which Petitioner relies in support of the foregoing assignments of error are as follows:

(A) 1. Prior to May 4, 2000, ABC Corporation (ABC) was the owner of certain construction equipment with a fair market value of $97,932,610.

2. ABC sold construction equipment to the petitioner on May 4, 2000, for its fair market value of $97,932,610.

3. The purchase of the construction equipment was financed by the petitioner by borrowing $11,996,745 from the Banco Internationale, Cayman Islands—Green Bay Branch, giving promissory notes totaling $15,992,410 to ABC, and borrowing $81,940,200 from ABC.

4. The petitioner immediately leased the construction equipment back ABC at a fair market rent pursuant to a net lease between the petitioner and ABC dated May 4, 2000. Under the lease, the construction equipment was leased to ABC for a period of 38 to 44 months, depending on the category of construction equipment.

5. The petitioner reasonably anticipated that the construction equipment would have a residual value at the termination of the lease of at least 20% of the construction equipment's value at the inception of the lease, and that each item of construction equipment would have a remaining useful life of approximately three years at the end of the lease term.

(B) 1. The petitioner alleges and incorporates all of the facts set forth in paragraph 5 (A) above.

2. The assignment, referred to by the Commissioner as the sale of the lease receivable, to Kiln Leasing (Kiln) occurred on May 4, 2000, prior to the time Kiln was part of the consolidated group. The proceeds of the assignment were paid to ABC to satisfy the ABC loan.

(C) No part of any underpayment of tax was due to negligence or substantial understatement. Underpayment of tax, if any, was due to reasonable basis and, therefore, the imposition of the penalty under Sec.6662 of the Internal Revenue Code is inappropriate.

WHEREFORE, Petitioner prays that the Court may hear this case and determine that there is no deficiency in income tax from the Petitioner.

Dated at Milwaukee, Wisconsin, this 15th day of March, 2002.

Evil and Evil, S.C.
1234 North Main Street, Suite 100
Milwaukee, Wisconsin 55555-0000
414-555-1212

Mailing Address:
P.O. Box 000000
Milwaukee, WI 55555-0000

_____
Seeno Evil
Tax Court No. ES0000
Attorney for Petitioner

_____
Hearno Evil
Tax Court No. EH0000
Attorney for Petitioner

¶1355 Exhibit 13-5

IRM Handbook No. 5.1 Exhibit 5.1.4-1

Date Document last amended: 5-27-1999

Pattern Letter P-513 (Rev. 5-78) (Reference: IRM 5.1.4.6)

[Internal Revenue Service]	[Department of the Treasury]
[Director]	
[Taxpayer Name:]	[Person to Contact:]
[Taxpayer Address:]	[Telephone Number:]
	[Refer Reply to:]
	[Date:]

NOTICE OF JEOPARDY ASSESSMENT AND RIGHT OF APPEAL

Dear Taxpayer:

Under section (insert 6861, 6862 or 6867) of the Internal Revenue Code, you are notified that I have found you (insert reason for asserting the jeopardy assessment), thereby tending to prejudice or render ineffectual collection of (insert type of tax) for the period ____. Accordingly, based on the information available at this time, I have approved assessment of tax and additional amounts determined to be due as reflected in the attached computations:

Taxable Period	Tax	Penalty	Interest
[Dates]	[Amount]	[Amount]	[Amount]

Under sec. 7429 of the Internal Revenue Code, you are entitled to request administrative and judicial reviews of this assessment action.

For an administrative review, you may file a written protest with the District Director within 30 days from the date of this letter, requesting redetermination of whether or not:

1. the making of the assessment is reasonable under the circumstances, and

2. the amount so assessed or demanded as a result of the action is appropriate under the circumstances.

A conference will be held on an expedite basis to consider your protest. Your protest will be forwarded to the Regional Appeals Office where a conference will be held.

If you submit new information or documentation for the first time at an Appeals conference, the Appeals Office may request comment from the District Director on such evidence or documents.

Enforced collection action may proceed during any administrative appeal process unless arrangements are made regarding collection of the amount assessed. To make such arrangements, please contact (insert name and telephone number of appropriate district office official).

You may request a judicial review of this assessment by bringing a civil suit against the United States in the U.S. District Court in the judicial district in which you reside, or in which your principal office is located. However, in order to have

¶1355

this action reviewed by the District Court, you must request administrative reviewwithin 30 days of the date of this letter. Such suit must be filed within 30 days after the earlier of (1) the day the Service notifies you of its decision on your protest, or (2) the 16th day after your protest. The Court will make an early determination of the same points raised in your protest to determine whether the making of the assessment is reasonable under the circumstances, and whether the amount assessed or demanded is appropriate under the circumstances. The Court's determination is final and not reviewable by any other court.

Appeal to the Courts in Case of Income, Estate, Gift and Certain Excise Taxes

If an agreement is not reached with the Internal Revenue Service, a notice of deficiency is required by law to be issued within 60 days from the date of jeopardy assessment made under sec. 6861 of the Internal Revenue Code. You will then have 90 days (150 days if outside the United States) from the date the notice is mailed to file a petition with the United States Tax Court.

Appeal to Courts in Case of Other Taxes Assessed Under IRC § 6862

Claim for credit or refund of taxes assessed under sec. 6862 of the Internal Revenue Code may be filed in accordance with sec. 6511(a) of the Code of administrative and judicial review of the merits of the liability assessed. An administrative decision on the claim may be appealed to the courts under the provisions of sec. 7422(a) of the Code.

Very truly yours,

District Director

¶1356 Exhibit 13-6

IRM Handbook No. 5.1 Exhibit 5.1.4-2

Date document last amended: 5-27-1999

Pattern Letter 1583(P) (Rev. 8-81)

[Internal Revenue Service]   [Department of the Treasury]
[Director]
[Taxpayer Name:]   [Person to Contact:]
[Taxpayer Address:]   [Telephone Number:]
                                        [Refer Reply to:]
                                        [Date:]

NOTICE OF TERMINATION ASSESSMENT OF INCOME TAX

Dear Taxpayer:

Under sec. 6851 of the Internal Revenue Code, you are notified that I have found you (insert specific facts and reasons for termination assessment action), thereby tending to prejudice or render ineffectual collection of income tax for the (current/preceding) taxable year. Accordingly, the income tax, as set forth below, is due and payable immediately.

Taxable Year	Tax	Penalty
[Dates]	[Amount]	[Amount]

Based on information available at this time, tax and penalty, if any, reflected in the attached computations, have been assessed.

This action does not relieve you of the responsibility for filing a return for your usual annual accounting period under sec.6012 of the Code. Such return must be filed with the office of the District Director of the district in which you reside, or the district in which your principal office is located, not with the Internal Revenue Service Center. A copy of this letter should accompany the return so that any amount collected as a result of this termination assessment will be applied against the tax finally determined to be due on your annual return or to be credited or refunded.

Under sec. 7429 of the Internal Revenue Code, you are entitled to request administrative and judicial reviews of this assessment action.

For an administrative review, you may file a written protest with the District Director within 30 days from the date of this letter, requesting redetermination of whether or not:

1. the making of the assessment is reasonable under the circumstances, and

2. the amount so assessed or demanded as a result of the action is appropriate under the circumstances.

When feasible, a conference will be held on an expedite basis by the Regional Appeals Office to consider your protest.

If you submit information or documentation for the first time at an Appeals conference, the Appeals Office may request comment from the District Director on such evidence or documents.

As indicated above, enforced collection action may proceed during any administrative appeal process unless arrangements are made regarding collection of the amount assessed. To make such arrangements, please contact (insert name and telephone number of appropriate district office official).

You may request a judicial review of this assessment by bringing a civil suit against the United States in the U.S. District Court in the judicial district in which you reside or in which your principal office is located. However, in order to have this action reviewed by the District Court, you must first request administrative review within 30 days of the date of this letter. Such suit must be filed within 30 days after the earlier of (1) the day the Service notifies you of its decision on your protest, or (2) the 16th day after your protest. The Court will make an early determination of the same points raised in your protest to determine whether the making of the assessment is reasonable under the circumstances and to determine whether the amount assessed or demanded as a result of the action is appropriate under the circumstances. The Court's determination is final and not reviewable by any other court.

Very truly yours,

District Director

¶1357 Exhibit 13-7

Internal Revenue Service   **Department of the Treasury**

Date:

CERTIFIED / REGISTERED MAIL

Employee to Contact:

Employee Identification Number:

Contact Telephone Number:

Taxpayer Identification Number:

Notice of Deficiency

| | | | Penalties or Additions to Tax | | |
Tax Year Ended	Type of Tax	Deficiency	IRC Section	IRC Section	IRC Section

Dear

The last date to file a petition with the United States Tax Court is _____ if the filing of the tax court petition is not prohibited by the automatic stay imposed by the bankruptcy code. If the automatic stay was in effect on the date of this letter or comes into effect during the period from the date of this letter through _____ , see the description of how to calculate the last date to file a petition below.

We have determined that you owe additional tax, other amounts, or both for the tax year(s) identified above. This letter is your NOTICE OF DEFICIENCY, as required by law and permitted by Bankruptcy Code § 362(b)(9). The enclosed statement shows how we figured the deficiency. If you are a C-corporation, section 6621(c) of the Internal Revenue Code requires that we charge an interest rate two percent higher than the normal rate on large corporate underpayments of $100,000 or more.

You and/or your spouse have various options in responding to this letter. The **first** option is to agree with the amount of proposed deficiency listed above. *If you agree,* sign the enclosed waiver form and return it in the enclosed envelope addressed to the IRS. This will permit us to assess the deficiency quickly and can limit the accumulation of interest. If you choose this option, you do not need to read any further.

A **second** option is to petition the United States Tax Court by the date shown above, *if the automatic stay was not in effect from the date of this letter through the date shown above as the last date to file a petition.* A stay is a temporary suspension of proceedings. If we issue a notice of deficiency and the automatic stay is in effect, the automatic stay prohibits a person in bankruptcy from filing a petition with the Tax Court until the automatic stay is lifted or terminated by operation of law.

A **third** option is to request the Bankruptcy Court to lift the automatic stay under Bankruptcy Code section 362(d)(1) so that you can file a Tax Court petition while you are still in bankruptcy. *If you file a Tax Court petition while the automatic stay is still in effect, the Tax Court will dismiss your petition for lack of jurisdiction.*

Letter 1384 (DO) (Rev. 9-2000)
Catalog Number 40693N

A **fourth** option is to petition the Tax Court *after* the automatic stay is no longer in effect by operation of law. Generally, the automatic stay terminates by operation of law at the earliest of the time the bankruptcy case is closed, the time the bankruptcy case is dismissed, or in an individual Chapter 7 case or a case under Chapters 9, 11, 12 or 13, the time a discharge is granted or denied by the Bankruptcy Court.

WHEN TO FILE A PETITION

Second Option — File by the date shown above as "the last date to file a petition," *if the automatic stay was* **never** *in effect for the time period from the date of this letter through the date listed above as the "last date to file a petition."*

Third and Fourth Options — If the automatic **stay is in effect** as of the date of this letter and prohibits the filing of a Tax Court petition, you may file a Tax Court petition after the automatic stay is lifted by the Bankruptcy Court or when the automatic stay is no longer in effect by operation of law. If the automatic stay was in effect as of the date of this letter, then once the automatic stay is terminated you have 90 days from the date it was terminated (150 days if we mailed this letter to an address outside of the United States), plus the additional 60 day period set out in section 6213(f)(1) of the Internal Revenue Code, to file your Tax Court petition asking for a redetermination of the deficiency.

If the automatic **stay was not in effect** as of the date of this letter but you file a bankruptcy petition within the 90 day (or if applicable, 150 day) period to file a Tax Court petition but prior to filing your Tax Court petition, then once the automatic stay is terminated, you have 90 days (or if applicable, 150 days) less the number of days between the date of this letter and the date of filing the bankruptcy petition, plus the additional 60 day period set out in section 6213(f)(1), to file your Tax Court petition. However, we suggest that you file your petition as soon as possible after the Bankruptcy Court lifts the automatic stay or the automatic stay is no longer in effect.

HOW TO FILE A PETITION

If this letter is addressed to a husband and wife, both want to petition the Tax Court, **and** neither is in bankruptcy with an automatic stay in effect, you may file a joint petition that both of you must sign, or you may each file a separately signed petition.

If both spouses are in bankruptcy and the automatic stay is in effect, each spouse should request the Bankruptcy Court to lift the automatic stay before filing a Tax Court petition. If only one spouse has the automatic stay lifted, then only that spouse can file a Tax Court petition. If only one spouse is in bankruptcy and the automatic stay is in effect, the spouse in bankruptcy must request the Bankruptcy Court to lift the stay before filing a petition with the Tax Court. The spouse not in bankruptcy can file a separate petition to the Tax Court. The extension of time given the spouse in bankruptcy does not extend the time to file a petition for the spouse not in bankruptcy.

All petitions to the Tax Court for a redetermination of this deficiency must be sent to: **United States Tax Court, 400 Second Street, N.W., Washington, D.C. 20217.** Attach a copy of this letter and copies of all statements and/or schedules you received with this letter. You can get a copy of the rules for filing a petition and a petition form by writing to the Clerk of the Tax Court at the same address. If more than one tax year is shown above, you may file one petition form showing all of the years you are contesting. You may represent yourself or you may be represented by anyone admitted to practice before the Tax Court.

The Tax Court has a simplified procedure for cases when the amount in dispute is $50,000 or less for any one tax year. You can get information about this procedure by writing to the Tax Court at the address listed above. Write promptly if you intend to file a timely petition with the Tax Court.

Letter 1384 (DO) (Rev. 9-2000)
Catalog Number 40693N

The Court cannot consider your case if the petition is filed late. The petition is considered timely filed if the U. S. postmark date falls within the 90 (or 150) day period stated above and as extended by I.R.C. § 6213(f)(1), if applicable, and the envelope containing the petition is properly addressed to the Tax Court with the correct postage affixed. Contacting the Internal Revenue Service (IRS) for more information, or receiving other correspondence from the IRS will not change the allowable period for filing a petition with the Tax Court. If you decide not to sign and return the enclosed waiver form, and you do not file a petition with the Tax Court within the applicable time limits discussed above, the law requires us to assess the proposed deficiency and send you a request for payment.

BANKRUPTCY COURT CONSIDERATIONS AND OPTIONS

Whether you file a petition with the Tax Court, contest the deficiency in the Bankruptcy Court, or sign and return the waiver form, the IRS is authorized to file a proof of claim with the Bankruptcy Court for the deficiency, interest and additions to tax provided by law.

You have the option of filing an objection in the Bankruptcy Court to any proof of claim the IRS may file or of initiating a proceeding under section 505 of the Bankruptcy Code to determine the amount of the proposed deficiency, interest and additions to tax provided by law that are due from you. You can initiate a section 505 proceeding even if the IRS has not filed a proof of claim in your bankruptcy case. If the Bankruptcy Court or the Tax Court determines your tax liability, you can not petition the other Court to redetermine the same liability at some later date.

GETTING ANSWERS TO ANY QUESTIONS

If you have questions about this letter, you may write to or call the contact person whose name, telephone number, employee identification number and IRS address are shown on the front of this letter. If you write, please include your telephone number, the best time for us to call, and a copy of this letter to help us to identify your account. You may wish to keep the original letter for your records. If you prefer to call and the telephone number is outside your local calling area, there will be a long distance charge to you.

The contact person can access your tax information and help you to get answers. Also you have the right to contact the office of the Taxpayer Advocate. Taxpayer Advocate assistance is not a substitute for established IRS procedures such as the formal appeals process. The Taxpayer Advocate is not able to reverse legally correct tax determinations, nor extend the time fixed by law that you have to file a petition with the Tax Court. The Taxpayer Advocate can ensure that a tax matter gets prompt and proper handling when it may not have been resolved through normal channels. If you want Taxpayer Advocate assistance, please contact the Taxpayer Advocate for the IRS office that issued this notice of deficiency. For a list of Taxpayer Advocate telephone numbers and addresses, see the enclosed Notice 1214, Helpful Contacts for Your "Notice of Deficiency".

Thank you for your cooperation.

Sincerely yours,

Commissioner

Enclosures: By
Statement
Copy of this letter
Attachments to this letter
Waiver
Notice 1214
Envelope   **Letter 1384 (DO) (Rev. 9-2000)**
                                                     Catalog Number 40693N

¶1358 Exhibit 13-8

Form **6338** (Rev. September, 1982)	Department of the Treasury — Internal Revenue Service **Proof of Claim for Internal Revenue Taxes** (Bankruptcy Code Cases)	Case Number
		Type of Bankruptcy Case

United States Bankruptcy Court for the _____ District of _____

In the Matter of:

	Date of Petition
	Social Security Number
	Employer Identification Number

1. The undersigned, whose business address is _____ is the agent of the Department of Treasury. Internal Revenue Service. and is authorized to make this proof of claim on behalf of the United States
2. The debtor is indebted to the United States in the sum of $ _____ as of the petition date.
3. The amount of all payments on this claim has been credited and deducted for the purpose of making this claim.
4. The ground of liability is taxes due under the internal revenue laws of the United States.

A. Secured Claims (Notice of Federal tax lien filed under internal revenue laws before petition date)

Kind of Tax	Tax Period	Date Tax Assessed	Tax Due	Penalty to Petition Date	Interest to Petition Date	Notice of Tax Lien Filed: Date	Office Location
			$	$	$		

For the purposes of section 506(b) of the Bankruptcy Code, post petition interest may be payable.

B. Unsecured Priority Claims under section 507 (a) (6) of the Bankruptcy Code

Kind of Tax	Tax Period	Date Tax Assessed	Tax Due	Interest to Petition Date
			$	$

C. Unsecured General Claims

Kind of Tax	Tax Period	Date Tax Assessed	Tax Due	Interest to Petition Date
			$	$

Penalty to date of petition on unsecured priority claims .... $ _____

Penalty to date of petition on unsecured general claims .... $ _____

5. No note or other negotiable instrument has been received for the account or any part of it, except _____
6. No judgment has been rendered on this claim, except _____ .
7. This claim is not subject to any set off or counterclaim, except _____
8. No security interest is held, except for the secured claims listed in item 4A above and _____
9. To the extent that post petition penalties and interest are nondischargeable and remain unpaid, they may be collectible from the debtor.

Penalty for Presenting Fraudulent Claim—Fine of not more than $5,000 or imprisonment for not more than 5 years or both—Title 18, U.S.C. Section 152.	Signature	Date
	Title	Telephone Number

Part 1—For Court (or Fiduciary, if required by local procedures)

Form 6338 (Rev. 9-82)

¶1358

¶1359 Exhibit 13-9

Report of Interview with Individual Relative to Trust Fund Recovery Penalty or Personal Liability for Excise Tax	Date of Interview
Notice 609 was furnished during the interview. (Check here) [ ] (See instructions below.)	Name of Interviewer

INSTRUCTIONS TO INTERVIEWER: The questions which follow are to be used as a guide as you conduct the interview. Other questions may be asked. You must prepare this form personally, recording the interviewee's answers. Where a question is not applicable, write "N/A." Do not leave any blocks or lines blank. Attach additional sheets if necessary.

Notice 609, Privacy Act and Paperwork Reduction Act Notice, must be given to persons who haven't received notice of their right to privacy. If furnished during the interview, check the box above. If not, explain in the case history.

IRC 6672, failure to collect and pay tax from *(date)* _____ to *(date)* _____

IRC 4103, failure to pay tax from *(date)* _____ to *(date)* _____

Section I—Background Information

1.	a.	Person interviewed *(name)*	
	b.	*(address)*	
	c.	Telephone number *(home)*	d. Telephone number *(work)*
	e.	Social Security number	
2.	a.	Taxpayer (Corporation) *(name)*	
	b.	*(address)*	
	c.	Incorporation *(date)*	d. State where incorporated
	e.	Has the state revoked the corporation franchise? ☐ yes ☐ no	f. If so, when?
	g.	Has the corporation ever filed bankruptcy? ☐ yes ☐ no	h. If so, when?

3. Was any of the property of the corporation sold, transferred, quitclaimed, donated or otherwise disposed of, for less than fair market value, since the accrual of the tax liability? ☐ yes ☐ no
What happened to the corporate assets?

4.	a.	How were you associated with this corporation?
	b.	Describe your duties/responsibilities.
	c.	By whom were you hired?
	d.	What were the dates of your employment with the corporation?

Form **4180** (Rev. 2-93) Cat. No. 22710P Department of the Treasury — Internal Revenue Service

Page 1

¶1359

e.	Did you resign from the corporation? ☐ yes ☐ no	f. In writing?			☐ yes	☐ no
g.	When?	h. Is a copy of your resignation available? ☐ yes ☐ no				
i.	To whom was your resignation submitted?					
j.	Did you have your name removed from the bank signature cards? ☐ yes ☐ no			k.	When?	
h.	Do you have any money invested in the corporation? ☐ yes ☐ no			m.	Amount $	

5.
a.	Have you ever been involved with another company which had tax problems? ☐ yes ☐ no
b.	If so, explain. *(Corporate name, EIN, etc.)*

6. With what banks or financial institutions did the corporation have transactions such as checking and other accounts, loans, financing agreements, etc.? *(attach additional sheet, if necessary)*

Financial Institution	Transaction(s)	Address	Date(s)

7. Where are the financial records located?

8. Please indicate the names, dates of service and percentage of ownership for the positions indicated below.

Position	Name	Dates of Service	% Ownership
Chairman of the board			
Other Directors *(list)*			
President			
Vice President			
Secretary			
Treasurer			
Others *(shareholders, owners)*			

Page 2

¶1359

Section II—Ability to Direct	Interviewee

Please indicate whether you performed any of the duties/functions indicated below for the corporation and the time periods during which you performed them. If another person performed these duties, please list names and time periods.

Did you...	Yes	No	Dates		Did anyone else? (name)	Dates	
			from	to		from	to
1. Hire/fire employees							
2. Manage employees							
3. Direct (authorize) payment of bills							
4. Deal with major suppliers and customers							
5. Negotiate large corporate purchases, contracts, loans							
6. Open/close corporate bank accounts							
7. Sign/countersign corporate checks							
8. Guarantee/co-sign corporate bank loans							
9. Make/authorize bank deposits							
10. Authorize payroll checks							
11. Prepare federal payroll tax returns							

Page 3

¶1359

Did you...	Yes	No	Dates		Did anyone else? *(name)*	Dates	
			from	to		from	to
12. Prepare federal excise tax returns							
13. Sign federal excise tax returns							
14. Authorize payment of federal tax deposits							
15. Review federal income tax returns							
16. Determine Company financial policy							

17. Please provide the information requested below for each person, other than yourself, listed for the above questions. Also, please provide any additional information indicating their knowledge and/or control over the corporation's financial affairs. *(Attach additional sheets if necessary.)*

Name | Address

Phone Number | Social Security number

Additional information

Name | Address

Phone Number | Social Security number

Additional information

Name | Address

Phone Number | Social Security number

Additional information

Name | Address

Phone Number | Social Security number

Additional information

¶1359

Section III—Knowledge	Interviewee

1. When and how did you first become aware of the delinquent taxes?

2. What action did you take to see that the tax liabilities were paid?

3. Were discussions or meetings ever held by stockholders, officers or other interested parties regarding the non-payment of the taxes? ☐ yes ☐ no
   Identify who attended, the dates of the meetings, and any decisions reached.
   (Attach additional sheets, if necessary.)

4. Are minutes available from any meetings described in question 3 above? ☐ yes ☐ no

5. Who maintained or has access to the books and records of the corporation? When?
   (Please provide name, address and phone number, if possible)

6. Were financial statements ever prepared for the corporation? ☐ yes ☐ no
   If so, by whom? Who reviewed them and to whom were they submitted?
   (Please provide time periods.)

7. Did the corporation employ an outside accountant? ☐ yes ☐ no
   If so, please provide the name, address and phone number of the person or firm.

¶1359

8. Who in the corporation had the responsibility of dealing with the outside accountant?

9. Did you personally have discussions with the accountant or bookkeeper of the corporation regarding the tax liability?
□ yes □ no

If so, when?
What was discussed?

10. Who reviewed the payroll tax returns or tax payments?

11. Who reviewed the excise tax returns or tax payments?

12. Who handled IRS contacts, such as IRS correspondence, phone calls from IRS, or visits by IRS personnel?

When?
What were the results of these contacts?

13. During the time the delinquent taxes were increasing, or at any time thereafter, were any financial obligation of the corporation paid?
□ yes □ no
If so, which ones?

14. Which individual or individuals authorized or allowed any of these obligations to be paid?

15. During the time that the delinquent taxes were increasing, or at any time thereafter, were all or a portion of the payrolls met?
□ yes □ no

16. When there was not enough money to pay all the bills, what decisions were made and what actions were taken to deal with the situation? Who made the decisions?

17. Did any person or organization provide funds to pay net corporate payrolls?   □ yes □ no
If so, explain in detail.

¶1359

Section IV—Special Circumstances

1. Is the corporation required to file federal excise tax returns?   □ yes   □ no
   If so, are you aware of any required excise tax returns which have not been filed?   □ yes   □ no
   (If either response is negative, do not complete remaining questions in Section IV.)

2. With respect to excise taxes, were the patrons or customers informed that the tax was included in the sales price?
        □ yes   □ no

3. If the tax liability is one of the so-called "collected" taxes—transportation of persons or property and communications:

   a. Was the tax collected?   □ yes   □ no

   b. Were you aware, during the period tax accrued, that the law required collection of the tax?   □ yes   □ no

Continue answers from Sections I through III below. Identify by section and item number.

¶1359

Section V—Additional Comments

Is there anyone else who may have been involved or who could provide additional information regarding this matter?

☐ yes   ☐ no

Please add any comments you may wish to make regarding this matter.

_____

_____

_____

_____

_____

_____

_____

_____

_____

_____

_____

_____

_____

_____

_____

_____

I declare that I have examined the information given in this statement and, to the best of my knowledge and belief, it is true, correct and complete.

Person interviewed *(signature)*	Date
Interviewer *(signature)*	Date

Date copy given to person interviewed

¶1359

¶1360 Exhibit 13-10

Internal Revenue Service

Department of the Treasury

Date:

Number of This Letter:

Person to Contact:

IRS Contact Address:

IRS Telephone Number:

Employer Identification Number:

Business Name and Address:

Dear

The business named above owes Federal taxes described in the enclosed Form 2751, Proposed Assessment of Trust Fund Recovery Penalty. Our efforts to collect these taxes haven't been successful, so we plan to assess a penalty against you.

The law provides that individuals who were required to collect, account for, and pay taxes for the business may be personally liable for a penalty if the business doesn't pay the taxes. These taxes, which consist of employment taxes you withheld or should have withheld from employees' wages and didn't pay, or excise taxes you collected or should have collected from patrons and didn't pay, are commonly referred to as trust fund taxes.

We plan to charge you an amount equal to the unpaid trust fund taxes which the business still owes the government. This personal liability is called the trust fund recovery penalty. We will assess and collect the penalty as though it were a tax you owed.

If you agree with this penalty, please sign Part 1 of the enclosed Form 2751 and return it to me in the enclosed envelope.

If you don't agree, have additional information to support your case, and wish to try to resolve the matter informally, contact the person named at the top of this letter within ten days from the date of this letter.

You have the right to appeal or protest this action, and you may also have the right to a delay before we collect the money. You may request either of these within 60 days from the date of this letter (90 days if this letter is addressed to you outside the United States). The instructions below explain how to make the request.

(over)

Letter 1153(DO) (Rev. 3-93)
Cat. No. 40545C

¶1360

APPEALS

You may appeal your case to the office of the Regional Director of Appeals. To do this, address your request to the Group Manager, to the attention of the Person to Contact and the address shown at the top of this letter. The dollar amount you are protesting affects the form your request should take.

If the amount is:	You should:
$2,500 or less	Verbally request an Appeals conference.
More than $2,500, but not more than $10,000	Submit a brief written statement of the issues You disagree with.
Over $10,000	Submit a written protest.

Include any additional information that you want the Appeals Officer to consider. You may still appeal without additional information, but including it at this stage will help us to process your request promptly.

A BRIEF WRITTEN STATEMENT should include:

1. Your name, address, and social security number;

2. A statement that you want a conference;

3. The date and number of this letter;

4. The tax periods or years involved; and

5. A list of the issues you disagree with. These issues could include responsibility, willfulness, and the way we applied payments to the business tax liability.

Please submit two copies of your statement.

A WRITTEN PROTEST should include the items below. Pay particular attention to item 6 and the note which follows it.

1. Your name, address, and social security number;

2. A statement that you want a conference;

3. The date and number of this letter;

4. The tax periods or years involved (see Form 2751);

5. A list of the findings you disagree with;

6. A statement of fact, signed under penalties of perjury, that explains why you disagree and why you believe you shouldn't be charged the penalty. Include specific dates, names, amounts, locations, etc.

(over)

Letter 1153(DO) (Rev. 3-93)
Cat. No. 40545C

NOTE: Usually, penalty cases like this one involve issues of responsibility and willfulness. Therefore, your statement should include a clear explanation of your duties and responsibilities within the business. (Responsibility in this case means possessing the status, duty, and authority to collect, account for, and pay the trust fund taxes. Willfulness means that an action was intentional, deliberate, or voluntary and not an accident or mistake.)

To declare that the statement in item 6 is true under penalties of perjury, you must add the following to your statement and sign it:

"Under penalties of perjury, I declare that I have examined the facts presented in this statement and any accompanying information, and, to the best of my knowledge and belief, they are true, correct, and complete."

7. If you rely on a law or other authority to support your arguments, explain what it is and how it applies.

REPRESENTATION

You may represent yourself at your conference or have someone who is qualified to practice before the Internal Revenue Service represent you. This may be your attorney, a certified public accountant, or another individual enrolled to practice before the IRS. If your representative attends a conference without you, he or she must file a power of attorney or tax information authorization before receiving or inspecting confidential tax information. **Form 2848,** Power of Attorney and Declaration of Representative, or **Form 8821**, Tax Information Authorization, may be used for this purpose. -Both forms are available from any IRS office. A properly written power of attorney or authorization is also acceptable.

CONSIDERATION BY THE COURTS

If you and the IRS still disagree after your conference, we will send you a till. However, you may take your case to the United States Claims Court or to your United States District Court. These courts have no connection with the IRS.

Generally, the courts will hear tax cases only after you have paid the tax and filed a claim for a refund. The claim for a refund is an additional, informal review. To request this additional review, do the following:

1. Pay the tax for one employee for one quarter of liability, if we have based the amount of the penalty on unpaid employment taxes; or pay the tax for one transaction, if we have based the amount of the penalty on unpaid excise taxes.

2. File a claim for a refund of the amount you paid, using Form 843, Refund and Claim for Request for Abatement.

DELAY IN COLLECTION

To request a delay in collection of the penalty, you must take the following additional actions within 30 days of the date of the official notice of assessment.

1. Pay a portion of the tax and file a claim for a refund as explained above.

2. Post a bond with the IRS for one and one half times the amount of the penalty that is left after you have made the payment in item 1.

(over)

Letter 1153(DO) (Rev. 3-93)
Cat. No. 40545C

You should be aware that, if IRS finds that the collection of this penalty is in jeopardy, we may take immediate action to collect it without regard to the 60 day period for submitting a protest mentioned above.

If IRS denies your claim, you have the right to appeal the denial. You may wish to appeal before filing suit. To do this, follow the instructions above for <u>APPEALS.</u>

If IRS hasn't acted on your claim within 6 months from the date you filed it, you can then file suit for a refund. You can also file suit for a refund any time within 2 years after IRS has disallowed your claim. For further information about filing a suit you may contact the Clerk of your District Court or the Clerk of the Claims Court, 717 Madison Place, NW., Washington, DC 20005.

If we don't hear from you within 60 days from the date of this letter (or 90 days, if this letter is addressed to you outside the United States), we will begin collection action.

Sincerely yours,

Group Manager

Enclosures:
Form 2751
Publication 1
Envelope

Letter 1153(DO) (Rev. 3-93)
Cat. No. 40545C

¶1360

¶1361 Exhibit 13-11

Form **2751** (Rev. January, 1998)	Department of the Treasury - Internal Revenue Service **Proposed Assessment of Trust Fund Recovery Penalty** (Sec. 6672, Internal Revenue Code, or corresponding provisions of prior internal revenue laws)

Report of Business's Unpaid Tax Liability

Name and address of business

Tax Return Form No.	Tax Period Ended	Date Return Filed	Date Tax Assessed	Identifying Number	Amount Outstanding	Penalty
					$	$
					Total Penalty	$

Agreement to Assessment and Collection of Trust Fund Recover Penalty

Name, address, and social security number of person responsible

I consent to the assessment and collection of the total penalty shown, which is equal either to the amount of Federal employment taxes withheld from employees' wages or to the amount of Federal excise taxes collected from patrons or members, and which was not paid over to the Government by the business named above. I waive the 60 day restriction on notice and demand set forth in Internal Revenue Code § 6672(b) and I waive the privilege of filing a claim for abatement after assessment.

Signature of person responsible	Date

Part 1 — This copy to be signed and returned to Internal Revenue Service | Form **2751** (Rev. 1-98)

Form **2751** (Rev. January, 1998)	Department of the Treasury - Internal Revenue Service **Proposed Assessment of Trust Fund Recovery Penalty** (Sec. 6672, Internal Revenue Code, or corresponding provisions of prior internal revenue laws)

Report of Business's Unpaid Tax Liability

Name and address of business

Tax Return Form No.	Tax Period Ended	Date Return Filed	Date Tax Assessed	Identifying Number	Amount Outstanding	Penalty
					$	$
					Total Penalty	$

Agreement to Assessment and Collection of Trust Fund Recover Penalty

Name, address, and social security number of person responsible

I consent to the assessment and collection of the total penalty shown, which is equal either to the amount of Federal employment taxes withheld from employees' wages or to the amount of Federal excise taxes collected from patrons or members, and which was not paid over to the Government by the business named above. I waive the 60 day restriction on notice and demand set forth in Internal Revenue Code § 6672(b) and I waive the privilege of filing a claim for abatement after assessment.

Signature of person responsible	Date

Part 2 — Keep this copy for your records | Form **2751** (Rev. 1-98)

¶1362   Exhibit 13-12

Form **2750** (Rev. February 1993)	Department of the Treasury — Internal Revenue Service **Waiver Extending Statutory Period for Assessment of Trust Fund Recovery Penalty** *(Section 6672, Internal Revenue Code, or corresponding provisions of prior internal revenue laws)*

1. Name and Address of Person Potentially Responsible	Social Security Number

The person named above and the District Director of Internal Revenue or the Regional Director of Appeals agree that the penalty under Internal Revenue Code section 6672 (applicable to the tax for the periods shown below) may be assessed against that person on or before the date shown at the right. This agreement extends the statutory period for assessing the penalty; it does not mean that the person named accepts responsibility for the penalty. ⟶	2. Statutory Period Extended To

3.   Description

Name and Address of Taxpayer *(Employer or Collecting Agency)* (a)	Form Number (b)	Tax Period Ended (c)

4. Signature of Person Potentially Responsible	4a. Date

5. District Director	or	5a. Regional Director of Appeals

5b. By *(Signature and title)*	5c. Date

Cat. No. 18857L   Part 1 — IRS COPY   Form **2750** (Rev. 2-93)

Form **2750** (Rev. February 1993)	Department of the Treasury — Internal Revenue Service **Waiver Extending Statutory Period for Assessment of Trust Fund Recovery Penalty** *(Section 6672, Internal Revenue Code, or corresponding provisions of prior internal revenue laws)*

1. Name and Address of Person Potentially Responsible	Social Security Number

The person named above and the District Director of Internal Revenue or the Regional Director of Appeals agree that the penalty under Internal Revenue Code section 6672 (applicable to the tax for the periods shown below) may be assessed against that person on or before the date shown at the right. This agreement extends the statutory period for assessing the penalty; it does not mean that the person named accepts responsibility for the penalty. ⟶	2. Statutory Period Extended To

3.   Description

Name and Address of Taxpayer *(Employer or Collecting Agency)* (a)	Form Number (b)	Tax Period Ended (c)

4. Signature of Person Potentially Responsible	4a. Date

5. District Director	or	5a. Regional Director of Appeals

5b. By *(Signature and title)*	5c. Date

Cat. No. 18857L   Part 2 — Copy For Person Potentially Responsible   Form **2750** (Rev. 2-93)

¶1362

¶1363 DISCUSSION QUESTIONS

1. Peter Procrastinator, who resides in Detroit, Michigan, was audited for the years 2003 and 2004. On September 13, 2006, a notice of deficiency was mailed to Procrastinator's last known address in Detroit. On September 14, Procrastinator traveled to Windsor, Ontario, Canada, to visit relatives. The Notice arrived in the United States mail at Procrastinator's home on September 17, 2006. He remained in Canada for a couple of days and returned to his residence in Detroit on the evening of September 17, 2006. When he returned, Procrastinator received the notice of deficiency.

   On December 31, 2006, Procrastinator sent by certified mail a petition to the United States Tax Court. The government has filed a motion to dismiss the petition, alleging that it was not filed within the 90-day period required under Code Sec. 6213. Procrastinator responds by alleging that he had 150 days to file his petition.

   Should Procrastinator's petition be dismissed for lack of jurisdiction?

2. Leroy Loser is in the scrap metal business. During the years 2003 and 2004, he "allegedly" purchased scrap from the Drill-a-Bit Manufacturing Corporation. Leroy deducted all of the "purchases" on his Schedule C for each year. However, Drill-a-Bit has not reflected any "sales" to Leroy on their returns. Following an audit of both taxpayers, the IRS disallows Leroy's purchases and increases Drill-a-Bit sales by an identical amount. Leroy receives a notice of deficiency for 2003 and 2004 and files a petition with the U.S. Tax Court. At the same time, Drill-a-Bit receives a notice of deficiency resulting from the increase on sales. Drill-a-Bit defaults on the notice, pays the tax, files a claim for refund, and eventually sues for refund. It loses its case in the U.S. District Court in the area in which Leroy resides.

   Leroy now wants to dismiss his Tax Court Petition, pay the tax, and file a claim for refund and sue in the same district court. What advice can you give him?

3. Harry Hardluck and his ex-wife, Hortense Hapless Hardluck, were divorced in 2001. Under the divorce decree, Harry was required to make payments of $600 a month (for the support of Hortense and their children). Because the decree labels these payments as alimony, Harry had deducted them on his 2002, 2003 and 2004 income tax returns. At the same time, Hortense has taken the position that these are child support payments and has not reported them as income for the years in question.

   The IRS has audited Harry and Hortense. They have issued a notice of deficiency to Harry disallowing the deduction claimed for alimony payments. At the same time, they have sent a notice of deficiency toHortense claiming that the payments were alimony and should have been reported as income. Harry and Hortense's respective attorneys consult you as a noted tax expert in tax procedure to find out whether the IRS can actually make assessments in such an "inconsistent" fashion. What advice do you give them?

4. B.N. Krupt Company, Inc., timely filed its first quarter 2003 withholding tax return (Form 941) on April 29, 2003. On May 1, 2003, Mr. Scatterbrain, the president of the corporation, resigned. Scatterbrain normally signed all corporate checks and approved all financial transactions. No successor was appointed, but Mr. Disorganized, the vice president, and Ms. Slipshod, the treasurer, were given co-check-signing authority and together assumed Scatterbrain's financial duties. Ms. Neglectful, the corporation's sole shareholder and director, assumed the acting presidency.

Ten days before the second quarter 2003 withholding tax return (Form 941) was due, Mr. Diligent, the accounts payable clerk, prepared the Form 941 and a check for the total amount due. The check and the Form 941 were given to the treasurer, Ms. Slipshod, to be signed and forwarded to Mr. Disorganized for cosignature of the check. Because of the corporation's poor financial condition that month, Mr. Disorganized decided to sign only certain checks and failed to cosign the tax check. Mr. Disorganized returned all of the checks to Mr. Diligent. Mr. Diligent noticed that several checks were not cosigned and adjusted his cash disbursement journal accordingly. Mr. Disorganized resigned two days prior to the due date for filing the return. No tax was paid for the second quarter. Ms. Neglectful had no knowledge of the nonpayment of the Form 941 taxes.

(A) For each person involved, state whether you think the person is liable for the 100% penalty under Code Sec. 6672. Why or why not?

(B) The corporation's portion of the FICA tax was also not paid. Is this amount included in the 100% penalty?

5. You are consulted by Kal Koke regarding the following situation. Kal tells you that he is an unregistered "pharmacist" dealing primarily in certain controlled substances. He explains that he has just received a termination assessment of income tax under Code Sec. 6851. The assessment resulted from a raid upon Kal's home on July 1, 2003. In that raid, $500,000 in cash was seized. As Kal explains it, the IRS determined that $500,000 constituted his gross receipts for that week. They have now made an assessment against him of income tax for the period January 1 through July 1, 2003. The IRS has computed his income to be $13,000,000 and is seeking tax of approximately$6,000,000. In addition, the IRS is holding the $500,000 seized for eventual application to the tax liability for the year.

Kal said that he objected to this assessment and that he asked for review. His grounds for review were as follows: (1) $500,000 only constituted his gross receipts for a month, not for a week; and (2) the IRS failed to give any effect to his cost of goods sold, which he estimates to be approximately $260,000 per month. The request for review of the assessment has been denied. Kal wants to know what he can do next! He is willing to pay for "successful" advice.

6. Assume that you are a Revenue Officer with the IRS. You are assigned to investigate unpaid withholding taxes from Delilah's Deli, Inc. Your investigation discloses the following facts. The corporation has operated a delicatessen for two years. During that period of time, Delilah Delinquent was the president, treasurer, sole director and shareholder of the corporation. Her husband, David Delinquent, was the corporate vice president and secretary; however, David had very little to do with the business because he was gainfully employed elsewhere. The corporation is approximately $35,000 behind in its withholding taxes from the past two quarters, and at present is on the verge of bankruptcy.

Your investigation further discloses that Delilah Delinquent signed all corporate checks and that no second signature was needed on any check. She also prepared the Forms 941 for the business; however, she had her husband sign those forms because the Delinquents were under the impression that the corporate secretary had to sign the withholding tax returns. The Forms 941 that were filed showed that the amount of tax withheld had been deposited to the IRS. Your investigation further discloses that David had little reason to believe that those deposits had not been made.

A review of the assets of the corporation shows that it is virtually bankrupt. After reviewing the Delinquents' personal assets, you find that their sole significant asset is a personal residence with a fair market value of $110,000 and a mortgage of $70,000.

Your group manager asks for your recommendations regarding the possible assessment of a Code Sec. 6672 liability. Whom would you recommend that the IRS treat as a responsible person? Should the practical consideration of "collectibility" enter into your decision? State your reasons for your recommendation.

7. You are consulted by the court-appointed guardian of Sam Strate regarding the following situation. In 2002, Sam sold a piece of property that had a basis of $35,000 for $235,000. Under the terms of the contract of sale, Sam received $35,000 in 2002 with the balance of the proceeds being placed in escrow. The escrowee was to pay the remaining $200,000 out in four equal installments over the four years after the closing of the sale. However, the escrowee was given authority to pay out the balance to Sam if Sam were to request acceleration of the pay out and were to cite changed circumstances that would convince his nephew, the escrowee, that acceleration was warranted.

In 2004, Seymour Sharpeyes audited Sam's return. Sharpeyes determined that Sam was in constructive receipt of the entire sale proceeds and, thus, disallowed the installment treatment claimed on the 2002 return. He sought to tax Sam upon the entire gain in 2002. At his final conference with the agent, Sam was informed that the understatement of tax would be at least $35,000.

The very evening that Sam had his final conference with the agent, he happened to attend a cocktail party. He mentioned to one of the persons there that he had the conference with the IRS, and his acquaintance told him about the terrible things the IRS can do. He referred to something called a jeopardy assessment which he said the IRS can use to tie up all of his property if he does not pay the tax. Sam was very nervous about this, and a week later he became so distraught that he had a nervous breakdown and was hospitalized. Because of his stay in the hospital, all correspondence from the IRS went unanswered. Finally, a guardian was appointed to look into Sam's affairs. The guardian consults you to see whether the IRS can make a jeopardy assessment of the taxes and whether they can seize all of Sam's property on the basis of the circumstances that he has described.

CHAPTER 14
THE COLLECTION PROCESS

¶1401 INTRODUCTION

Revenue officers possess perhaps the widest range of authority of all federal government employees. They possess all the powers enjoyed by the Internal Revenue Service (IRS) to collect or abate delinquent accounts. They also have the authority to seize and sell property, impose and enforce major penalties for failure to comply with the revenue laws and recommend compromises of accounts for less than the balance due. A revenue officer may also make the initial recommendation whether to relieve property from the effect of federal tax liens or protect the government's interest by lawsuit or jeopardy assessment. In addition to these powers, revenue officers possess a wide range of investigative tools. However, the IRS must abide by provisions of the Fair Debt Collection Practices Act. For example, the IRS may generally not communicate with the taxpayer at an inconvenient time or place.[1]

The Internal Revenue Manual recognizes that at times taxpayers are not immediately able to pay the entire amount of tax that is due. Therefore, the manual states that installment agreements must be considered.[2] In many situations, a short-term installment agreement will be entered into, the payments made and the entire matter handled without any threats of levy on property or other enforced collection measures. The key to such a result is good communication with the revenue officer.

Generally, the initial step in the collection process is the assessment of tax against the taxpayer. The assessment may arise under various provisions of law, but usually results from a return filed by the taxpayer. Under Section 6201 of the Internal Revenue Code (the Code) and the accompanying regulations, the IRS has broad authority to assess taxes either determined by the taxpayer on a self-assessing basis or as a result of a subsequent examination of the return. However, with the exceptions noted,[3] no collection action can be taken until a tax assessment has been made.

After a return has been processed, the actual assessment of the tax itself is made by an assessment officer. The assessment officer signs a Form 23-C, Assessment Certificate. This record provides identification of the taxpayer by name and number, taxable period, the nature of the tax and the amount assessed.

---

[1] Code Sec. 6304.

[2] IRM Handbook 5.14.1.2.

[3] Under Code Sec. 6201(a)(3), the IRS has been given the authority to assess erroneous income tax prepayment credits. If the amount of income tax withheld or the amount of estimated tax paid is overstated by a taxpayer on a return or a claim for refund, the overstated amount can be automatically assessed in the same manner as a mathematical error under Code Sec. 6213(b)(1). Also, any income tax assessed against a child (to the extent the amount is attributable to income included in the gross income of the child solely by reason of Code Sec. 73(a)), if not paid by the child, may be considered as having also been properly assessed against the parents under Code Sec. 6201(c).

The "date of assessment" is the date that the Form 23-C is actually signed by the assessment officer. This date becomes particularly important in the collection process, since it establishes the beginning of the ten-year statutory period for collection and is the date on which the statutory lien provided for under Code Sec. 6321 arises.

The first billing notice generally will come from the Internal Revenue Service Center. The computer in the Service Center will generate a notice of amount due and ask for payment within ten days. Often taxpayers will ignore the notice. They then receive a series of notices, each more threatening than the previous one. Eventually someone will contact the taxpayer, either in person or by telephone. Even at that point, the IRS will generally only ask for information as to how the taxpayer proposes to take care of the delinquency. If the taxpayer indicates that he or she cannot pay the full amount due at that time, the IRS will ask for a financial statement from which ability to pay the taxes can be determined. Often at this time, an installment arrangement will be entered into based on the payments that the financial statement indicates the taxpayer can afford.

¶1405 DOCUMENT LOCATOR NUMBER

The IRS uses a Document Locator Number (DLN) as a means to control returns and documents. A DLN is a controlled, 13-digit number assigned to every return or document that is input through the Service Centers. DLNs are used to control, identify, and locate documents and appear on all notices sent to taxpayers, usually situated in the upper right-hand corner of the document.

The following is an example of a DLN, and explains how information is tracked by the specific digits contained in a DLN.

28 210-105-60025

These first two digits identify the IRS Service Center; Service Center codes are:

07=Atlanta	08=Andover	09=Kansas City
17=Cincinnati	18=Austin	19=Brookhaven
28=Philadelphia	29=Ogden	49=Memphis
89=Fresno[4]		

282 10-105-60025

The third digit identifies the tax class code for the documents. Some sample codes are:

1=Withholding and FICA
2=Individual
3=Corporate and Partnership
6=Fiduciary and Non-Master File (NMF)
8=FUTA

---

[4] Older returns or documents have a district code rather than a Service Center code.

28210-105-60025

The fourth and fifth digits are document codes. Sample document codes are:

    10=Form 1040
    36=Form 1041
    41=Form 941

28210-**105**-60025

The sixth through eighth digits indicate the Julian date with which the return was numbered.

28210-105-**600** 25

The ninth through eleventh digits indicate the block of 100 that contains the document.

28210-105-600**25**

The twelfth and thirteenth digits are the serial numbers—from 00 through 99—of the document with the block of 100.[5]

See Exhibit 14-1 at ¶1451 for a partial list of tax classes and document codes.

¶1411 SERVICE CENTER BILLING PROCESS

The actual billing process for the IRS is done on a regional basis by the various Service Centers. A taxpayer will receive a series of notices from the Service Center requesting payment before a demand for payment is received. Unless unusual circumstances exist, there generally will be three notices requesting payment (see Exhibit 14-2 at ¶1452) before a final notice is received (see Exhibit 14-3 at ¶1453). The final notice is sent by certified mail and informs the taxpayer that the IRS intends to levy on his or her assets if payment is not made within thirty days.

If a balance due condition still exists on the account after the mailing of the fourth and final notice, a taxpayer's delinquent account (TDA) will be created by the Service Center and transmitted to the field office. The TDA also serves as a case assignment to the revenue officer who then assumes responsibility for the account.

¶1412 TRANSCRIPTS

A taxpayer or representative may at times request a transcript or copy of the taxpayer's account maintained at the Service Center to verify the balance due and to determine whether assessments and payments have been properly charged or credited to the account. Generally, the IRS will provide what is called a "literal translation transcript." This transcript must be ordered by the local office from theService Center and therefore is not immediately available. The local office has online access to a transcript with transaction codes rather than the

---

[5] IRS Pub. 1966, section 2.

literal translation of the codes. For a partial listing of transaction codes, see exhibit 14-4 at ¶1454.

¶1413 STATUTE OF LIMITATIONS ON COLLECTION

Under Code Sec. 6502(a)(1), the IRS has ten years from the date of assessment to collect the amount of tax assessed. During the period the tax may be collected by levy or by a proceeding in court. Under Code Sec. 6502(a)(2), requests to extend the period of time in which the IRS may collect, made on or before December 31, 1999, can be done by an agreement in writing executed prior to the expiration of the time to collect. If, however, any such agreement extends the collection period of limitations beyond ten years, the extension expires automatically on the later of (1) the last day of the ten-year period under Code Sec. 6502(a), (2) December 31, 2002, or (3) in the case of an extension with an installment agreement, the 90th day after the end of the period of such extension.[6]

After December 31, 1999, the IRS cannot request waivers to extend collection statutes in connection with an installment agreement. The collection statute will automatically expire 90 days after any period for collection agreed upon in writing at the time at which the installment agreement was entered. On the other hand, if a suit in a U.S. District Court to collect the tax is begun before the expiration of the ten-year period, and a judgment against the taxpayer is obtained, the period for collecting the tax by levy is extended until the judgment is satisfied or becomes unenforceable.

In order to insure the taxpayers are aware that they have a right to refuse to extend the limitations period for tax assessments, the IRS must notify each taxpayer of this right. More specifically, the IRS must notify the taxpayer that he or she may (1) refuse to extend the limitation period, or (2) limit the extension to particular issues or a particular period of time. These provisions are equally applicable to the assessment of additional taxes generally as well as a requested waiver of the statute of limitations entered in connection with an installment agreement. The Congressional Committee Reports accompanying the IRS Restructuring and Reform Act of 1998,[7] in relation to Act Sec. 3461, provide:

> The statute of limitations on collection, however, continues to be suspended by various acts specified in Section 6503. For example, under Section 6503(b), if assets of the taxpayer are in the control or custody of any court, the statute is suspended until six months after the termination of those proceedings. Section 6503(c) provides that, if the taxpayer is outside the United States for a continuous period of six months, the statute of limitations is suspended until six months after the return of the taxpayer to the United Sates. Prior to December 31, 1999, the filing of an Offer in Compromise ("Offer") by the taxpayer represented an agreement between the taxpayer and the Internal Revenue Service that the statute of limitations on collection was to be suspended during the period that an Offer was pending or during the period that installments remained unpaid and for one year thereafter.[8] After December 31, 1999, the collection statute will only be suspended from the time the Offer

---

[6] P.L. 101-206, Act §3461(c)(2).
[7] P.L. 105-206.

[8] See Item 8 of Form 656 (Rev. 1-2000) (Exhibit 14-5 at ¶1455).

is considered pending.[9] The term pending is the date it is determined processable, lasting until it is accepted, rejected or withdrawn, plus a 30-day period following rejection of the Offer. This period is further extended during the time a timely filed appeal of the rejection is being heard and considered.[10]

¶1415 FIELD COLLECTION PROCESS

The first step in the field collection process involves a referral of the account to one of the twenty-one automated collection system (ACS) sites, where the on-site computers determine which cases receive priority attention, monitor the case until full payment is made or until the case is referred to a field officer, and display current information regarding the status of the account. A contact person from ACS will call the taxpayer to review sources from which payment can be made. The contact person can enter into an installment agreement or can initiate a levy action. If an installment agreement is entered into, the case will remain within ACS jurisdiction until the liability is paid or until there is a default on one of the installments. If it is not possible for ACS to contact the taxpayer, the case will be assigned to the field office.

Generally, a revenue officer assigned to the field office will attempt to contact the taxpayer for either a telephone interview or person-to-person interview. The purpose of the interview is to request full payment of the tax as well as to determine the means of payment and sources from which collection can be made if full payment is not possible.

When a taxpayer is requested to appear for an interview, he or she is usually asked to bring all documents necessary to resolve the tax matter. If the taxpayer alleges an inability to pay, for example, that individual will be requested to bring a copy of his or her latest income tax return as well as information necessary to establish his or her financial condition, such as earnings statements and records of outstanding debts. Revenue officers are instructed to conduct such interviews in a courteous and businesslike manner (see Exhibit 14-6 at ¶1456).

To aid the interview process, a number of forms have been developed for summarizing essential financial information necessary in evaluating collection cases. Generally, in smaller cases, a Form 433-A, Collection Information Statement for Individuals (see Exhibit 14-7 at ¶1457 and Exhibit 14-8 at ¶1458), is sufficient. This form provides information needed to determine how an individual taxpayer can satisfy a tax liability. It is generally used in connection with Form 433-B when the taxpayer operates a business. The Form 433-B, Collection Information Statement for Businesses (see Exhibit 14-9 at ¶1459), is used to determine how a business taxpayer can satisfy a tax liability. It includes such information as a profit and loss statement and balance sheet. In addition to these formal IRS forms, taxpayers can submit any similar forms that adequately reflect their true and complete financial condition. Each form should contain a statement to the effect that: "Under the penalties of perjury, I declare that to the best of my knowledge and belief the statement of assets, liabilities, and other informa-

---

[9] *Id.* [10] See IRM 8.13.2.1.2.

tion is true, correct, and complete." The taxpayer should sign and date the statement and indicate a title, if applicable.

If the taxpayer refuses to voluntarily produce financial information, the revenue officer may use the summons authority contained in Code Sec. 7602 to require the taxpayer to produce books and records. For these purposes a special summons, Form 6639 (see Exhibit 14-10 at ¶1460), is used. If the summons is to be served upon the taxpayer, the revenue officer need not obtain approval prior to issuing the summons. However, if the summons is to be issued to a third party, then supervisory approval is required.[11]

Following an interview with the taxpayer, the revenue officer prepares a Collection Information Statement. The information to be secured depends on the taxpayer's financial condition and the unpaid liability. For example, if the taxpayer has assets which can readily satisfy the liability, an income and expense analysis is unnecessary. The analysis of the taxpayer's financial condition should provide the revenue officer with a basis for deciding whether to secure a short-term payment agreement (sixty days or less), or whether a longer installment agreement is necessary. In analyzing the financial information submitted, the revenue officer is to determine the manner in which assets can be liquidated. If necessary, the revenue officer is to review any unencumbered assets, any equity in encumbered assets, any interests in estates or trusts and any lines of credit from which money can be secured to make payment. If such items exist, the taxpayer is advised of the possibilities of obtaining money from these sources and full payment is requested.

When this analysis does not disclose any obvious means to liquidate the liability, the taxpayer's income and expenses are to be analyzed. Take-home pay and net business income in excess of necessary living expenses are considered available for payment of the tax liability. In analyzing the taxpayer's expenses, the revenue officer is instructed to use prudent judgment in determining which are necessary or excessive living expenses. The dates that payments on loans and installment purchases terminate are noted so that additional funds can be made available to pay the tax liability. If the items on the Collection Information Statement appear overstated, understated or unusual, the taxpayer is to be asked for an explanation or substantiation.

In arriving at the value of assets, the revenue officer is to consider the forced sales value of assets. The forced sales value is the amount which would be realizedas the result of a seizure and sale. The depreciated cost of the asset, its going concern value and other bases of valuation commonly relied on may not reflect the forced sales value of the assets. Because of this possibility, current sales of similar property in the locality or any recent appraisals made of the property are considered. If machinery and equipment of large size is involved, its state of depreciation or obsolescence and its movability are factors to be considered because they affect its marketability in the event of seizure.

---

[11] IRM 1.2.2.1, Order Number 4 (Rev. 8-18-97).

¶1415

¶1421 FEDERAL TAX LIENS

Notice of Federal Tax Lien. The IRS Restructuring and Reform Act of 1998 (the Act) requires the IRS to develop procedures whereby revenue officers generally obtain a supervisor's approval prior to issuing a Notice of Lien, serving a Notice of Levy or seizing property. Information with respect to adhering to these service procedures are to be subject to disclosure under the Freedom of Information Act. Revenue officers and supervisors are subject to disciplinary action for failure to adhere to these procedures. These procedures apply generally as of July 22, 1998, but not to the automated collection system until December 31, 2000.[12]

The Act also added Section 6320 to the Internal Revenue Code which provides that the IRS must notify the taxpayer within five business days after the filing of a Notice of Lien. The Notice must include certain information, including the amount of the unpaid tax, the right of the person to request a hearing during the 30-day period beginning on the day after the five-day period described above and their right to an IRS hearing and Tax Court review (see Exhibit 14-11 at ¶1461 (Form Letter 3172)).

Withdrawal of Notice of Federal Tax Lien. The IRS under Code Sec. 6323(j) is allowed to withdraw a notice of lien in certain circumstances. A notice may be withdrawn if (1) the filing was premature or was not in accordance with administrative procedures; (2) the taxpayer entered into an installment agreement under Code Sec. 6159; (3) the withdrawal of the notice will facilitate the collection of the tax; or (4) it is in the best interests of the taxpayer and the United States as determined by the National Taxpayer Advocate. If the IRS withdraws a notice of a lien, it must file a notice of the withdrawal at each office where the notice of the lien was filed.

Filing of Federal Tax Lien. Under Code Sec. 6321, a "statutory lien" attaches to a taxpayer's property in an amount equal to the liability for the tax assessment due and owing. The statutory lien arises automatically when three events occur:

1. An assessment of tax is made pursuant to Code Sec. 6203;

2. A demand for payment as prescribed in Code Sec. 6303(a) is made, unless waived by the taxpayer; and

3. The taxpayer neglects or refuses to pay the tax.

The lien attaches to all property and rights to property belonging to the taxpayer at any time during the period of the lien, including any property or rights to property acquired after the lien arises. The lien may be satisfied by payment or abatement, allowance of a claim, an audit adjustment or discharge in bankruptcy proceedings.

Under Code Sec. 6322, the statutory lien for federal taxes arises at the time the assessment is made, which is the date the summary record of assessment is signed by an assessment officer. This statutory lien only gives the government a right to the taxpayer's property which is superior to that of the taxpayer. Until a

---

[12] Act Sec. 3421.

Notice of Lien is filed, this statutory lien does not provide the IRS with a right to property which is superior to the rights of third parties who later acquire an interest in the property.

The form used by the IRS to file the notice of lien is Form 668, Notice of Federal Tax Lien (see Exhibit 14-12 at ¶1462). The Notice of Federal Tax Lien is required to be filed and recorded at various locations, depending upon the nature of the property affected. For example, in the case of real property, the notice is to be filed in the office within the state designated by the laws of such state for real property filings. In the case of personal property (whether tangible or intangible property), the lien notice is to be filed in the office within the state as designated by the laws of such state in which the property subject to the lien is situated. If the state has not designated any particular office within its jurisdiction for filing, the Notice of Federal Tax Lien is to be filed in the office of the clerk of the United States District Court.

Priority of tax liens is determined under Code Sec. 6323(a). This section provides that until a lien notice has been filed, the tax lien is not valid against prior purchasers, holders of security interests, mechanic liens or judgment lien creditors. To keep the lien notice effective (if the limitation period on collection has not expired), Code Sec. 6323(g) requires that the lien notice must be refiled within a one-year period ending ten years and thirty days after the date of the assessment. Failure to refile the lien notice does not affect the validity of the lien itself. However, if a member of the "protected group" (holders of security interests, purchasers, mechanic lien creditors) acquires an interest in property subject to the tax lien after the filing of the prior lien notice but before the late refiling, that interest obtains a priority, as a result of the late refiling, to the same extent as if no tax lien notice had been filed. The tax lien will be subordinated to the interest acquired by the purchaser or other member of a protected group.

Even if the Notice of Federal Tax Lien has not been filed, the government's claim receives priority in some special cases (for example, if the taxpayer is insolvent or the estate of a decedent is insufficient to pay all the decedent's debts).[13] Furthermore, if no special rules apply, the first-in-time, first-in-right-principle governs. This means that liens of equal standing have priority according to the date on which they were actually perfected.

Even though a proper Notice of Federal Tax Lien is filed, the lien is neither valid against certain purchases made nor against security interests arising after such filing.[14] These classifications are known as "super priorities" and include: (1) purchases of securities; (2) motor vehicle purchases; (3) retail purchases; (4) purchases in casual sales; (5) possessory liens; (6) real property and special assessment liens; (7) liens for small repairs and improvements of residential real property; (8) attorneys' liens; (9) certain insurance contracts; and (10) savings passbook loans. In addition to these "super priorities," certain other security

---

[13] 31 U.S.C. §3713(a)(1).   [14] Code Sec. 6323(b).

interests may take priority over a filed tax lien if they result from financing agreements entered into prior to the filing of the tax lien.[15]

Discharge of Property from Federal Tax Lien. Often a taxpayer will have an opportunity to sell property or borrow against property to obtain funds to pay a delinquent tax liability. A problem created in this situation is to give clear title to the purchaser or to protect the security interest of the lender. Because the lien will attach to all property of the taxpayer, and because the lien has been filed before the contemplated transaction occurs, the transaction designed to give the taxpayer the funds needed to satisfy the tax liability can be threatened.

In such a situation, the IRS is authorized to discharge a portion of the taxpayer's property from the lien under Code Sec. 6325(b) if either of the following circumstances exist:

1. The remaining property covered by the lien has a fair market value at least twice the unpaid tax liability plus the sum of all encumbrances that have priority over the tax lien;[16] or

2. There is paid, in part satisfaction of the liability secured by the lien, an amount determined to be not less than the value of the interest of the United States in the property to be discharged.[17]

Code Sec. 6325 authorizes the IRS to release a federal tax lien or discharge property from the lien if certain conditions are met. The release of a tax lien operates to completely extinguish the lien, while a discharge operates only to discharge specific property from the reach of the lien. A lien can be released when an acceptable bond has been filed. The lien must be released no later than thirty days after the day on which any of these events has occurred (see Exhibit 14-13 at ¶1463 (Pub. 1450)).[18]

The Act also amends Code Sec. 6325(b)(4) to create an administrative procedure whereby a third-party record owner of property against which a tax lien has been filed can obtain a certificate of discharge of the property from the lien. Toobtain such a discharge the owner must (1) deposit an amount of money equal to the value of the IRS's interest in the property (as determined by the IRS), or (2) furnish a bond acceptable to the IRS in a like amount. After receipt of the certificate of discharge, the record owner may bring a civil action against the United States to redetermine the value of the government's interest in the property.[19] Finally, the District Director has the authority to grant the discharge of specific property from the lien if the taxpayer agrees to have the proceeds from the sale of such property substituted for the discharged property and subject to the same lien (see Exhibit 14-14 at ¶1464 (Form 669-A) and Exhibit 14-15 at ¶1465 (Pub. 783)).[20]

---

[15] Code Sec. 6323(c).

[16] Code Sec. 6325(b)(1).

[17] Code Sec. 6325(b)(2)(A).

[18] IRM 5.12.2.1 (Rev. 5-28-98). Under Code Sec. 7432, a taxpayer may bring a civil action for dam-

ages if the IRS knowingly or negligently fails to release a lien.

[19] Code Sec. 7426(a)(4).

[20] Code Sec. 6325(b)(3).

In addition, Code Sec. 6325(d) authorizes the IRS to subordinate the federal tax lien to a new security interest if the proceeds of the new loan are paid over to the government, or if it believes that subordination of the tax liability will ultimately increase the amount realizable from the property in question. To obtain a subordination of lien (see Exhibit 14-16 at ¶1466 (Form 669-D) and Exhibit 14-17 at ¶1467 (Pub. 784)), a written application must be submitted and must contain such information as may be required.[21]

Code Sec. 7425(b) requires that a sale (or foreclosure) of property on which the United States has a valid tax lien does not extinguish the lien and is made subject to the lien unless notice of the sale is given to the IRS. Code Sec. 7425(c)(4) specifically extends this rule to require notice of any forfeiture of a land contract.

¶1423 ADMINISTRATIVE APPEAL OF LIENS

Under Code Sec. 6326, taxpayers have a right to an administrative appeal if a federal tax lien has been erroneously filed on their property. An appeal is permitted only if one of the following errors occurred:

1. The tax liability that gave rise to the lien was paid prior to the filing of the lien;

2. The tax liability that was the basis for the lien was assessed in violation of the deficiency procedures set forth in Code Sec. 6213;

3. The tax liability underlying the lien was assessed in violation of the Bankruptcy Code (11 U.S.C.); or

4. The statute of limitations on collection of the tax liability that gave rise to the lien expired before the lien was filed.[22]

No consideration will be given during an appeal to any questions regarding the correctness of the underlying tax deficiency.

The appeal must be made within one year after the taxpayer becomes aware of the erroneous filing. If the filing was incorrect, the IRS must expeditiously issuea certificate of release and, to the extent practicable, the certificate must be issued within fourteen days after such determination. The release must acknowledge that the filing was erroneous and was not the fault of the taxpayer. This statement is to ensure that the taxpayer's credit rating will not be affected by the erroneous filing.

The appeal must be in writing and should include a copy of the erroneous lien. It also must include the taxpayer's name, current address and identification number. The appeal should state why the lien is erroneous and, if the claim is made that the tax liability was previously paid, copies of receipts or cancelled checks showing full payment should be included.[23]

---

[21] Reg. §301.6325-1(b)(4).
[22] Reg. §301.6326-1(b).
[23] Reg. §301.6326-1(e).

¶1425 LEVY AND SALE

Under Internal Revenue Code Section 6331(b), a levy is defined as the power to collect taxes by distraint or seizure of the taxpayer's assets. Through a levy, the IRS can attach property in the possession of third parties or payments to be made by third parties to the taxpayer. The IRS is required to give notice by certified or registered mail to the taxpayer thirty days prior to the time it levies upon any property (see Exhibit 14-18 at ¶1468).[24]

The notice of levy must describe in simple nontechnical terms:

1. The amount of unpaid tax;

2. The right to request a hearing during the 30-day period before the day of levy; and

3. The proposed action by the IRS and the taxpayer's rights with respect to:

    a. the Code section relating to levy and sale;

    b. the procedures that apply to levy and sale of the property;

    c. the administrative and judicial appeals available to the taxpayer;

    d. the alternatives available which could prevent a levy, including installment agreements; and

    e. the procedures relating to redemption of property and release of liens.

The appeal provisions are more fully discussed at ¶1439.

The levy authority of the IRS is far reaching. It permits a continuous attachment of the nonexempt portion of wages or salary payments due to a taxpayer, and the seizure and sale of all the taxpayer's assets except certain property that is specifically exempt by law. However, with the exception of wages, salaries and commissions, no "continuing levy" exists. The levy only reaches property held by the taxpayer or a third party at the time of the levy itself.[25]

Under Code Sec. 6334(d), a minimum amount of salaries and wages is exempt from levy. The weekly amount of wages exempt from levy is equal to the taxpayer's standard deduction and personal exemptions for the taxable year, divided by fifty-two. If such wages or other income are received on other than a weekly basis, the exemption from levy will be determined in such a manner that the exemption will be comparable to what it would have been on a weekly basis. When a taxpayer receives a notice of levy upon his or her wages, that individual should be advised to file a statement claiming the number of exemptions from levy to which he or she is entitled. If that statement is not filed, the exemption from levy will be computed as if the taxpayer were a married individual filing a separate return claiming only one personal exemption.

A levy on salary or wages is often used by the IRS as a last resort when a delinquent taxpayer will not respond to notices or otherwise cooperate in the

---

[24] Code Sec. 6331(d).   [25] Code Sec. 6331(b).

liquidating of a tax delinquency. Generally, when the taxpayer receives the notice of levy on wages, he or she will decide to cooperate with the IRS, file an appropriate financial statement and enter into a realistic installment arrangement. However, IRS policy is not to release the levy on the wages until at least one payment from the employer has been received. This policy can work a hardship on a taxpayer in certain circumstances.

Certain other property is exempt from levy. Code Sec. 6334(a) exempts wearing apparel, schoolbooks, unemployment benefits, undelivered mail, certain railroad and service-related annuity and pension benefits, payments needed for child support, service-connected disability payments, welfare payments and job training program payments. The Code further exempts books and tools of the taxpayer's trade, business or profession which, for levies issued after July 22, 1998, do not exceed $3,125.00 in total value.[26] If the taxpayer is the head of a family, fuel, provisions, furniture and personal effects not exceeding $6,250.00 in value also are exempt.[27]

In order to prevent undue disruption to the occupants of any residence, the IRS may not seize any real property used as a residence by the taxpayer or any real property of the taxpayer (other than rented property) that is used as a residence by another person in order to satisfy a liability of $5,000 or less (including tax, penalties and interest).[28] In the case of the taxpayer's principal residence, the IRS may not seize the residence without written approval of a U.S. District Court Judge or Magistrate.[29]

In addition to these statutory exemptions, IRS policy as contained in the Internal Revenue Manual is to use discretion before levying on retirement income.[30]

Code Sec. 6332(a) provides that any person in possession of property or rights to property upon which a levy has been made shall, upon demand, surrender such property or rights to the IRS. Anything which has been attached or upon which execution has been had under any judicial process need not be surrendered. Normally, the service of a levy and demand requires immediate surrender of the property or rights to property. However, as a result of numerous claims that bank account deposits seized by levy belonged to someone other than the taxpayer, Congress provided in Code Sec. 6332(c) that banks are not allowed to surrender a taxpayer's deposits until twenty-one days after service of the levy.

Any person who fails or refuses upon demand to surrender any property or rights to property subject to levy is personally liable to the United States in a sum equal to the value of the property or rights not so surrendered (not exceeding the amount of the taxes for the collection of which the levy has been made together with costs and interest). In addition, a civil penalty equal to fifty percent of the

---

[26] Code Sec. 6334(a)(3). For levies issued before July 22, 1998, the exemption is not to exceed $1,250.00 in total value.

[27] Code Sec. 6334(a)(2). For levies issued before July 22, 1998, the exemption is not to exceed $2,500.00.

[28] Code Sec. 6334(a)(13)(A).

[29] Code Sec. 6334(a)(13)(B) and (e)(1).

[30] IRM 5.11.6.1 (Rev. 11-5-99).

amount recoverable is provided where the holder of property fails or refuses to surrender it without reasonable cause.[31] A bona fide dispute over the amount of the property to be surrendered or the legal effectiveness of the levy itself constitutes reasonable cause.[32] When collected, the fifty-percent penalty, however, is not credited against the delinquent tax liability but is deposited as a collection of miscellaneous revenue.

Code Sec. 6343(a) sets forth the circumstances under which the IRS is required to release a levy. A levy must be released if any one of the following conditions exist:

1. The tax liability underlying the levy has been paid or collection of the tax has become barred by the statute of limitations;

2. Release of the levy would facilitate collection of the taxes;

3. The taxpayer has entered into an installment agreement under Code Sec. 6159 to pay the tax liability (unless such agreement provides to the contrary or release of the levy would jeopardize the creditor status of the IRS);

4. The IRS has determined that the levy is creating an economic hardship due to the financial condition of the taxpayer; or

5. The fair market value of the property exceeds the tax liability and release of the levy could be made without hindering the collection of the liability.

A levy will be released on the grounds of economic hardship if the levy causes the taxpayer to be unable to pay his or her "reasonable basic living expenses."[33]

A taxpayer who wishes to obtain the release of a levy must submit such request in writing to the appropriate IRS personnel.[34] The request must include the taxpayer's name, address, identification number and a statement of the grounds for release. It also should describe the property levied upon and set forth the date of the levy, the type of tax and the period for which the tax is due. The written request must normally be made more than five days prior to any scheduled sale of the property to which the levy relates. The Area Manager is required to make a determination promptly, and this generally should be within thirty days. In the case of a levy on personal property essential to the operation of a taxpayer's business, where such levy would prevent the taxpayer from carrying on his or her business, the Area Manager is required to provide an expedited determination of the taxpayer's request for release of the levy. This determination must be made within ten business days of receipt of the written request or, if later, receipt of any necessary supporting data.[35] If it is determined that release of a levy is justified, a revenue officer will issue a Form 668-D, Release of Levy/Release of Property from Levy (see Exhibit 14-19 at ¶1469).

---

[31] Code Sec. 6332(d)(2).
[32] Reg. § 301.6332-1(b)(2).
[33] Reg. § 301.6343-1(b)(4).

[34] Reg. § 301.6343-1(c).
[35] Reg. § 301.6343-1(d).

If any property is actually seized by levy, the Area Manager is required to give the taxpayer immediate notice of the tax demanded and the description of the seized property. The IRS is also required to give notice to the taxpayer and to publish the time, place, manner and conditions for a sale of the seized property. The sale must take place not less than ten days and not more than forty days after the public notice. It must be by public auction or by public sale under sealed bids.[36] The owner of the seized property may request the IRS to sell the property within sixty days (or some longer period) after such request. The IRS must comply with the request for such early sale unless it is determined that to do so would not be in the best interest of the government.[37]

When property is seized to be sold for delinquent taxes, the IRS is required to determine a minimum bid price and also to determine whether the purchase of the property at that price by the United States is in the best interest of the government. Code Sec. 6335(e)(1) provides that if there are no bids at the sale that exceed the minimum bid price, and if the IRS has determined to purchase, the property will be sold to the United States at that price. If the IRS determines not to purchase the property, the property can be released to the owner, although it will remain subject to the tax lien.

Under Code Sec. 6337(a), the taxpayer may reacquire any property before sale by payment of the outstanding tax liability and expenses. The taxpayer mayalso redeem real estate within a 180-day period after the sale by payment of the purchase price plus interest at the rate of twenty percent per annum.[38]

Under Code Sec. 6343(d), the IRS may return property to a taxpayer under certain circumstances. These circumstances are the same as those under which a notice of a lien may be withdrawn.[39] The IRS is also required to provide a taxpayer the opportunity to appeal a levy or a seizure administratively.

¶1427 FORCED SALE AND HOMESTEAD RIGHTS OF NONDELINQUENT SPOUSE

The United States Supreme Court has held that state homestead laws do not exempt real property from a forced sale by the IRS to satisfy the delinquent tax liability of one co-owner.[40] The Court did temper the effect of this holding, however, by formally recognizing that district courts may exercise limited discretion in ordering a sale and that the nondelinquent spouse is entitled to full

---

[36] Reg. § 301.6335-1; Code Sec. 6335.

[37] Code Sec. 6335(f); see Reg. § 301.6335-1(d) for the procedural requirements for making a written request.

[38] Code Sec. 6337(b).

[39] See ¶1421, *supra*.

[40] *United States v. Rodgers,* 461 U.S. 677 (1983), 83-1 USTC ¶9374. Some courts have held that where state law creates an undivided interest in the house, one spouse cannot unilaterally convey his or her interest without the consent of the other, and thus the IRS may not sell the interest without consent as it steps into the shoes of the delinquent taxpayer. *Marshall v.*

Marshall, 921 F.Supp. 641 (D.C. Minn. 1995), 96-1 USTC ¶50,122; *O'Hagan v. U.S.,* 1995 WL 113417 (D.C. Minn. 1994), 95-1 USTC ¶50,082; *Elfelt v. Cooper,* 168 Wis.2d 1008 (1992), 92-2 USTC ¶50,338. The Supreme Court has extended the result in *Rodgers* to recognize the ability of the IRS to levy on a joint bank account to satisfy tax delinquencies of one of the joint owners. See *United States v. National Bank of Commerce,* 472 U.S. 713 (1985), 85-2 USTC ¶9482. But see *I.R.S. v. Gaster,* 42 F.3d 787 (3rd Cir. 1994), 94-2 USTC ¶50,622. IRS could not levy a joint bank account because under state law the taxpayer could not unilaterally withdraw funds.

compensation for the separate homestead interest of such spouse. Unfortunately, such compensation may be in monetary form and may not seem adequate to spouses required to move from their homes. The nondelinquent spouse, however, generally will have a property interest in the home and, thus, will be able to redeem the property during the 180-day period specified in Code Sec. 6337(b), assuming the spouse can obtain the financing to do so. When such spouse does redeem, he or she obtains an equity in the property up to the amount paid to redeem. Such equity will be a superior interest to the IRS lien. If both spouses redeem, the status of their equity following redemption *vis-á-vis* the tax lien is not clear.

¶1429 INNOCENT SPOUSE RELIEF

Code Sec. 6015 substantially alters and expands the circumstances under which a person may qualify for "innocent spouse" treatment, which releases them from what otherwise would be a joint liability. Former Code Sec. 6013(e) is eliminated. Code Sec. 6015 provides that an "innocent spouse" election must be made within two years after collection activities begin. "Innocent spouse" relief is now available for *all* understatements of tax (rather than only "substantial" understatements) attributable to erroneous items (rather than only *grossly* erroneous items) of theother spouse. A person seeking "innocent spouse" relief must still establish that, in signing the return, he or she did not know and had no reason to know of the understatement.[41] If the lack of knowledge is only as to the extent of the understatement, relief is available on an apportioned basis. Code Sec. 6015(f) permits the IRS to grant equitable relief to taxpayers who do not satisfy the stated tests.[42]

In addition, Code Sec. 6015(c) now allows an individual to elect separate tax liability, despite having filed a joint return, if the taxpayers are (1) divorced or legally separated, or (2) have been living apart for more than one year. This election must be made no later than two years after the IRS has started collection action.

The new "innocent spouse" provisions are applicable to any tax liability arising after July 22, 1998, and any tax liability arising on or before that date, but remaining unpaid as of July 22, 1998.

Subparagraph (e)(1) of Code Sec. 6015 grants the Tax Court jurisdiction to review IRS decisions regarding "innocent spouse" status and separate liability elections.

¶1435 BANKRUPTCY PROCEEDINGS

A petition in bankruptcy acts as an automatic stay of any Tax Court proceeding and of any judicial or nonjudicial action for the collection of taxes. Jurisdiction to determine taxes lies with the Bankruptcy Court unless it lifts the stay. Generally, a claim for taxes is entitled to an eighth-level priority among competing claims in bankruptcy.[43] Further, if the tax is one for which an income tax return was due

---

[41] *Johnson v. Comm'r*, 118 T.C. 106 (2002).
[42] Rev. Proc. 2003-61, 2003-32 IRB.

[43] 11 U.S.C. § 507(a)(7).

within three years of the date of bankruptcy filing, or if the tax was assessed within 240 days before the date of such filing, the debt is not subject to discharge in bankruptcy.[44] Discharge also is not available if the taxpayer made a fraudulent return or willfully attempted to evade the tax.

¶1437 TAXPAYER ASSISTANCE ORDERS

The IRS Restructuring and Reform Act of 1998 renames the Office of Taxpayer Advocate as the National Taxpayer Advocate, which is now appointed by the Secretary of the Treasury. The duties of the Advocate remain to (1) assist taxpayers in resolving problems with the IRS; (2) identify areas in which taxpayers have difficulty in dealing with the IRS; (3) propose changes in administrative practices of the IRS to decrease the aforementioned problems; and (4) identify potential legislation which might decrease taxpayers' problems in dealing with the IRS. In assisting taxpayers suffering significant hardships as a result of *how* the revenuelaws are being enforced, the National Taxpayer Advocate may issue Taxpayer Assistance Orders.[45] Such hardships commonly occur during the collection process. The local taxpayer advocate's office under the authority of the National Taxpayer Advocate, is primarily responsible for issuing such orders. The order may require the IRS to release levied property or stop any action, or refrain from taking further action, under *any* section of the Internal Revenue Code.

An application for a Taxpayer Assistance Order (TAO) should be made on Form 911 (see Exhibit 14-20 at ¶1470) and filed with the local National Taxpayer Advocate's office (formerly the problem resolution office) in the area where the taxpayer resides. The application may be filed by the taxpayer or the taxpayer's duly authorized representative. If filed by a representative, Form 911 should be accompanied by a Form 2848, Power of Attorney and Declaration of Representative, or other power of attorney in proper form.

An application for a TAO on Form 911, however, is not essential. National Taxpayer Advocate officers, as well as personnel in other divisions of the IRS, are directed to prepare Forms 911 on behalf of taxpayers in response to requests for assistance received by telephone, correspondence or personal contact. These informal requests for relief must meet certain basic hardship guidelines. However, if the taxpayer or the taxpayer's representative insists that the matter requires this form of special consideration by the problem resolution officer, a Form 911 will be prepared by the IRS personnel involved.

What constitutes a "significant hardship" warranting the issuance of a TAO is a very subjective determination which must be made on a case-by-case basis. Such hardship could include the exceptional emotional stress of a taxpayer in dealing with tax problems, the threat of a poor credit rating caused by erroneous enforcement action, gross disserve to a taxpayer, pending eviction, possible loss of job, significant personal emergencies or other equally serious situations.

---

[44] 11 U.S.C. §§ 523(a)(1) and 507(a)(7)(A). A similar rule applies where the assessment is for the Code

Sec. 6672 penalty. See *United States v. Sotelo*, 436 U.S. 268 (1978), 78-1 USTC ¶ 9446.

[45] Code Sec. 7811.

Imminent bankruptcy, failure to meet payroll and inability to buy needed prescription medication are cited as other examples of what may be considered to be significant hardships.

The regulations define "significant hardship" as a "serious privation caused or about to be caused to the taxpayer as the result of the particular manner in which the revenue laws are being administered by the Internal Revenue Service."[46] Such hardship does not include "mere economic or personal inconvenience."[47] The Act now allows the National Taxpayer Advocate to issue a TAO if it is determined that the taxpayer is suffering, or is about to suffer, a significant hardship as a result of the manner in which the Internal Revenue laws are being administered by the IRS or if the taxpayer meets such other requirements as may be set forth in any future regulations.[48] Specifically, the National Taxpayer Advocate must consider among other things the following four specific facts when determining whether there is a "significant hardship" and whether a TAO should be issued:

1. Whether there is an immediate threat of adverse action;

2. Whether there has been a delay of more than 30 days in resolving the taxpayer's account problems;

3. Whether the taxpayer will have to pay significant costs (including fees for professional representation) if relief is not granted; or

4. Whether the taxpayer will suffer irreparable injury or a long term adverse upset if relief is not granted.

The TAO may not require any action or restraint that is not permitted by law. The order also may not be issued to contest the merits of any tax liability or as a substitute for any established administrative or judicial review procedure. A TAO may require the IRS, within a specified period of time, to take any action permitted by law which relates to collection or other tax matters to relieve a taxpayer's hardship. For example, a TAO may require the IRS to pay a refund to an eligible taxpayer who faces a hardship.

An application for a TAO filed by a taxpayer suspends the running of any statute of limitations affected by the action required by the assistance order. However, if the Form 911 is prepared by the IRS on the basis of an informal request for relief, and is not filed or signed by the taxpayer, the statute of limitations is not suspended.

The law authorizing the issuance of TAOs replaces earlier informal practices with a defined procedure for obtaining relief in certain hardship situations. It assures the taxpayer of a prompt response in accordance with strict time constraints established by the IRS for processing applications for such assistance orders.

---

[46] Reg. § 301.7811-1(a)(4).
[47] IRM 7.10.2.5 (4-13-99).

[48] Code Sec. 7811(a)(1).

¶1439 ADMINISTRATIVE AND JUDICIAL APPEAL AND REVIEW OF NOTICE OF LIEN OR LEVY

A person who receives a Notice of Lien or Levy[49] may, within 30 days, request a Collection Due Process Hearing (see Exhibit 14-21 at ¶1471 (Form 12153)) which is held by the IRS Office of Appeals.[50] The hearing must be conducted by an officer or employee who had no prior involvement with respect to that unpaid tax.[51] The appeals officer at the hearing must obtain verification from the IRS that the requirements of any applicable law or administrative procedure have been met. This would include but not be limited to a showing that the revenue officer recommending the collection action has verified the taxpayer's tax liability, that the estimated expenses of levy and sale will not exceed the value of the property to be seized and that the revenue officer has determined that there is sufficient equity in the property to be seized to yield net proceeds from sale to apply to the unpaid tax liability. If the seizure of assets is of a going business, the revenue officers recommending the collection action must thoroughly have considered the facts and circumstances of the case including the availability of alternative collection methods before recommending the collection action.

The taxpayer or an affected third party may raise any relevant issues at the hearing regarding the unpaid tax or proposed lien or levy including but not limited to appropriate spousal defenses (innocent spouse status), challenges to the appropriateness of collection actions, offers of collection alternatives which may include the posting of a bond, the substitution of other assets, an installment agreement, an Offer in Compromise, or challenges to the existence of the amount of the underlying tax liability for any tax period. The IRS Office of Appeals is to retain jurisdiction over any determination that it makes at a hearing. This includes jurisdiction to hold a further hearing as requested by the person who sought the original hearing on issues regarding (1) collection actions taken or proposed with respect to the determination and after the person has exhausted all administrative remedies, or (2) a change in circumstances with respect to such action which affects the determination.

If the hearing officer, after verifying that all the applicable laws are satisfied and considering all of the issues raised by the taxpayer, determines that the collection action balances efficient tax collection with the taxpayer's legitimate concerns, the officer may issue an order upholding the filing of the Notice of Tax Lien. The person subject to the Notice of Tax Lien may, within 30 days of the date of the determination, appeal to the Tax Court (if the Tax Court has jurisdiction to hear the matter)[52] or a U.S. District Court.[53] The Tax Court has generally upheld the IRS's action in Collection Due Process cases.[54] If a court determines that the

---

[49] Code Sec. 6330(a).

[50] Code Sec. 6330(b)(1); Reg §301.6330-1.

[51] However, a taxpayer may waive this requirement. Code Sec. 6330(b)(3). See CAP (Collection Appeals Program) at ¶1449, *infra,* and Exhibit 14-24 at ¶1474 (Collection Appeal Rights).

[52] Code Sec. 6330(d)(1)(A).

[53] If the Tax Court does not have jurisdiction of the underlying tax liability. Code Sec. 6330(d)(1)(B).

[54] *Willis v. Comm'r,* T.C. Memo 2003-302; *Crisan v. Comm'r,* T.C. Memo 2003-318; *Van Vlaenderen v. Comm'r,* T.C. Memo 2003-346; *Goldman v. Comm'r,* T.C. Memo 2004-3.

appeal was to an incorrect court, a person shall have 30 days after the court determination to file an appeal with the correct court.[55]

The Chief Judge of the Tax Court may assign an appeal from a IRS determination regarding a lien or levy to be heard by a special trial judge and may authorize the special trial judge to make a decision of the court with respect to the appeal.

¶1441 ACTIONS TO ENJOIN COLLECTION

The Internal Revenue Code generally denies a taxpayer any right to interfere with the assessment or collection of taxes. Under Code Sec. 7421(a),

> [N]o suit for the purpose of restraining the assessment or collection of any tax shall be maintained in any Court by any person, whether or not such person is the person against whom such tax was assessed.

Despite the absolute nature of the statutory language used in Code Sec. 7421, the Supreme Court of the United States has ruled that an injunction against collection may be granted where "it is clear that under no circumstances can the government ultimately prevail"[56] and then only if a refund suit would be an inadequate remedy "because collection would cause irreparable injury, such as the ruination of the taxpayer's enterprise."[57]

The right of taxpayers and third parties[58] to bring an action against the United States for civil damages stemming from reckless or intentional disregard of the statutory collection provisions has been expanded to include negligence on the part of a IRS employee. Claimants are required to exhaust all administrative remedies. The liability is limited to $1 million, except in the case of negligence where the limitation is $100,000.

¶1443 INSTALLMENT AGREEMENTS

Generally, when taxpayers claim inability to pay due to financial reasons, installment agreements are considered. Under Code Sec. 6159(a), the IRS is specifically authorized to enter into installment agreements if such agreements will facilitate collection of the tax liability. Form 9465, Installment Agreement Request (see Exhibit 14-22 at ¶1472), may be attached to the return if the taxpayer cannot pay the full amount due when filing the return. However, before any installment agreements are considered, future compliance with the tax laws will be addressed, and any returns or tax due within the prescribed period of the agreement must be timely filed and timely paid.

There are a number of possible installment agreements. Under Internal Revenue Code Sec. 6159(c), the IRS is required to accept the proposals of installment agreements under certain circumstances. These "guaranteed installment agreements" must be accepted by the IRS if the taxpayer: (1) owes income

---

[55] Code Sec. 6330(d)(1).

[56] *Enochs v. Williams Packing & Navigation Co., Inc.,* 370 U.S. 1 (1962), 62-2 USTC ¶9545.

[57] *Hillyer v. Comm'r,* 817 F.Supp 532 (M.D. Pa. 1993), 93-1 USTC ¶50,184. The court enjoined the sale

of a lot containing the taxpayer's residence because he was unemployed and would suffer irreparable damage.

[58] Under Code Secs. 7433 and 7426(h).

tax only of $10,000 or less; (2) has filed and paid all tax returns during the five-year period prior to the year of the liability; (3) cannot pay the tax immediately; (4) agrees to fully pay the tax liability within three years; (5) files and pays all tax returns during the term of the agreement; and (6) did not have an installment agreement during the prior five-year period. Unlike the criteria for "streamlined agreements" (discussed below), the $10,000 limit for "guaranteed installment agreements" applies to tax only. The taxpayer may owe additional amounts in penalty and interest (both assessed and accrued) but qualify for a guaranteed installment agreement, so long as the tax alone is not greater than $10,000.

"Guaranteed installment agreements" may be granted by revenue officers. No approval beyond the revenue-officer level is required unless the collection statute expiration date (CSED) needs to be extended. CSED extensions require branch chief approval.[59]

The second type of installment agreement generally calls for full payment within five years. These "streamlined installment agreements" may be approved for taxpayers where: (1) the unpaid balance of assessments is $25,000 or less; (the unpaid balance includes tax, assessed penalty and interest, and all other assessments—it does not include accrued penalty and interest); (2) the "streamlined installment agreement" must be fully paid in 60 months or prior to the CSED, whichever comes first; and (3) the taxpayer must have filed all tax returns that are due prior to entering into the agreement.

Taxpayers may request an installment payment agreement by completing Form 9465, Installment Agreement Request (see Exhibit 14-22 at ¶1472). The IRS will normally notify the taxpayer within 30 days if the proposal is acceptable and a Form 433-D, Installment Agreement (see Exhibit 14-23 at ¶1473), will then be executed. For individuals, the penalty amount for failure to pay tax is limited by the IRS Restructuring and Reform Act of 1998 (the Act) to one-half the usual rates (one-fourth of one percent rather than one-half of one percent) for any month in which an installment payment agreement with the IRS is in effect.[60] This provision applies in determining additions to tax for the months beginning after December 31, 1999.

The Act also requires the IRS, beginning no later than July 1, 2000, to provide every taxpayer who has an installment agreement in effect under Code Sec. 6159 an annual statement showing the initial balance of the account at the beginning of the year, the payments made during the year and the remaining balance in the account at the end of the year.

Under Code Sec. 6159(d), if a taxpayer's request for an installment agreement is denied, the taxpayer will be informed of the rejection and the right to appeal it to the Office of Appeals within 30 days of the date of the rejection.

---

[59] IRM, Handbook No. 5.14; Installment Agreement Handbook, Section 1.7; Collection Statute Expiration Date (CSED): Law Policy and Procedures.

[60] Code Sec. 6651(h): The failure to pay penalty reduction is only applicable if the individual timely filed (including extensions) the return relating to the liability that is subject to the installment agreement.

Although it is the revenue officer's duty to insure that the interests of the government are protected during any extended payment period, the Act placed a number of restrictions on the IRS's ability to secure their interests. Under Code Sec. 6331(k)(2) certain levy restrictions have been imposed during the period that an installment agreement is pending and/or in effect. No levy may be made on taxpayer accounts: (1) while requests for installment agreements are pending; (2) while installment agreements are in effect; (3) for 30 days after requests for installment agreements are rejected; (4) for 30 days after agreements are terminated; and (5) while an appeal of a termination or rejection of an installment agreement is pending or unresolved. Exceptions to this general rule allow a levy if a taxpayer waives the restrictions in writing or if the IRS believes that its collection is in jeopardy. If an installment agreement is pending and a levy is outstanding, the levy may be released but it is not required that the levy be released. If an installment agreement is approved and there is a levy outstanding, the levy must be released unless the installment agreement otherwise provides. For example, with the taxpayer's written consent reflected in the "additional conditions block" of Form 433-D, where a levy has attached to funds in the taxpayer's bank account and an installment agreement is prepared *before* the proceeds are received, the levy need not be released. Similarly, if a wage levy is to remain open while a taxpayer is making installment payments, such concurrence must be reflected in writing in the "additional conditions block" of Form 433-D in order to allow the levy to remain open until the liability is satisfied.

¶1445 AUDIT RECONSIDERATION AFTER ASSESSMENT

Often a practitioner will be consulted by a taxpayer faced with the collection of delinquent tax. In most instances, the revenue officer's job is to collect the amount of the tax shown as due. The revenue officer generally has no authority to reexamine the return and determine if the deficiency assessed was proper.

However, in those instances where the taxpayer has ignored a Statutory Notice of Deficiency or where there has been a breakdown in communications between the IRS and the taxpayer, the Internal Revenue Manual permits audits of returns after the collection process has begun. Such an audit is available to the individual only after having received a balance due notice and when one of the following conditions is present:

1. The taxpayer has not received any notification from the IRS prior to the billing;

2. The taxpayer has moved since filing the return in question; or

3. The taxpayer has not had an opportunity to submit required substantiation and now has the necessary documents or documentation.

Office audits can be obtained through employees assigned to the SB & SE (see ¶105) division who will review and evaluate information submitted by the taxpayer, including copies of the tax return and examination reports. If these employees determine that an audit should be made, the case is forwarded to a revenue agent for resolution. Collection efforts are suspended while the case is in examination.

¶1447 OFFERS IN COMPROMISE

As early as 1831, the Treasury Department was authorized to compromise tax liabilities. This authority is currently vested in the Secretary of the Treasury pursuant to Code Sec. 7122. The IRS liberalized its policies on the use andacceptance of Offers in Compromise in 1992. Policy Statement P-5-100 set forth the IRS's position. To comply with a Congressional mandate of the IRS Restructuring and Reform Act of 1998 to become more reasonable in its collection efforts, the IRS revised its Internal Revenue Manual provisions that deal with Offers in Compromise. The revised manual supplement consists of ten concise chapters called *The Internal Revenue Manual 5.18 (the Offer in Compromise Handbook)*. The IRS begins its discussion of the Offer in Compromise (OIC) by citing Policy Statement P-5-100, summarized below.[61] The current procedures for submitting an Offer in Compromise are set forth in Rev. Proc. 2003-71, 2003-36 IRB 517, effective August 21, 2003.

The IRS will accept an Offer in Compromise when it is unlikely that the tax liability can be collected in full and the amount offered reasonably reflects collection potential. An Offer in Compromise is a legitimate alternative to declaring a case as currently not collectible or as a protracted installment agreement. The goal is to achieve collection of what is potentially collectible at the earliest possible time and at the least cost to the government.

In cases where an Offer in Compromise appears to be a viable solution to a tax delinquency, the IRS employee assigned to the case will discuss the compromise alternative with the taxpayer and, when necessary, assist in preparing the required forms. The taxpayer will be responsible for initiating the first specific proposal for compromise.

The success of the compromise program will be assured only if taxpayers make adequate compromise proposals consistent with their ability to pay and the IRS makes prompt and reasonable decisions. Taxpayers are expected to provide reasonable documentation to verify their ability to pay. The ultimate goal is a compromise which is in the best interest of both the taxpayer and the IRS. Acceptance of an adequate offer will also result in creating, for the taxpayer, an expectation of, and a fresh start toward, compliance with all future filing and payment requirements.

When an Offer in Compromise is submitted, it is first reviewed by the revenue officer assigned to the delinquent account. Collection activity will be suspended during the pendency of the offer if it is not deemed frivolous and there is no indication that the filing of the offer was solely for purposes of delaying collection or that a delay would jeopardize the government's interest.[62]

In rare instances an offer may be rejected on public policy grounds even though the amount offered is otherwise acceptable. The rejection on public policy grounds is generally limited to situations where public knowledge of the accepted offer would have a seriously harmful effect on voluntary compliance with

---

[61] IRM 5.8.1.1.1.   [62] IRM 5.8.3.

¶1447

the tax laws. The Internal Revenue Manual[63] dictates that such decisions should be *extremely rare*. Rejections of this nature include cases not only of negative public reaction and undermining voluntary compliance but also cases of criminal activityinvolving a taxpayer submitting an offer or attempting to compromise tax liabilities arising from egregious criminal activity.[64] The Manual, however, provides that an offer will not be rejected on public policy grounds *solely* because it might generate substantial critical public interest and/or a taxpayer who was criminally prosecuted for a tax or nontax violation.

Offers in Compromise will be considered if there is doubt as to liability, collectibility or both liability and collectibility. The Examination Division is responsible for the investigation and processing of offers based solely on doubt as to liability. Frequently, such offers result from the failure of the taxpayer to take advantage of opportunities to contest proposed adjustments before an assessment is made. Evidence which has not previously been submitted by the taxpayer to correct errors in the assessment will be considered by the revenue agent assigned to investigate the offer.

The Revenue Officers have the responsibility for processing and investigating all Offers in Compromise based solely on doubt as to collectibility. They also have initial jurisdiction over offers based on doubt as to both liability and collectibility.[65] A Form 656, Offer in Compromise (see Exhibit 14-5 at ¶1455), must be submitted. A comprehensive financial statement detailing the taxpayer's assets, liabilities, income and expenses must accompany an offer that is based on doubt as to collectibility. Official forms for providing such financial information are normally used for this purpose. See Form 433-A, Collection Information Statement for Individuals (see Exhibit 14-7 at ¶1457) and Form 433-B, Collection Information Statement for Businesses (see Exhibit 14-9 at ¶1459). The latter two forms are now the ones most commonly submitted with an Offer in Compromise.

These forms and accompanying instructions were revised in 2000 to meet the requirements of the IRS Regulations under Code Sec. 7122 pertaining to offers in compromise (see Exhibit 14-5 at ¶1455). An Offer in Compromise now also requires an application fee of $150. See Form 656-A (see Exhibit 14-5 at ¶1455).

The IRS places Offers in Compromise into three categories: (1) cash offers, (2) short-term deferred payment offers, and (3) deferred payment offers. The amount considered acceptable for each type of offer is different. In each case, the amount of the offer must include the "quick sale value" (QSV) of the taxpayer's assets.[66] In addition, in each case the offer must also include the total amount the IRS could collect from available income of the taxpayer.[67] The IRS is also to advise the taxpayer of his or her right to appeal any rejection of an Offer in Compromise.

---

[63] IRM 5.8.7.
[64] IRM 5.8.7.3 (2).
[65] IRM 4.3.21 (Sec. 4.2).

[66] Normally eighty percent of the equity of the asset.
[67] IRM 5.8.1.5.4.1(1); IRM 5.8.1.5.4.2(1); IRM 5.8.1.5.4.3(1).

¶1447

Generally, the excess of the taxpayer's income over his or her expenses and current tax payment is what the IRS expects that it can collect. Expenses for housing and transportation are determined from tables of "allowable standards" for specific geographic areas.[68] Other monthly expenses generally need to be justified on an item-by-item basis.

The Internal Revenue Manual now also includes a new table titled "Deferred Payment Offer Chart" which is based on the time remaining before the expiration of the collection statute and adjusted to reflect current IRS interest rates that are applicable to deferred payment offers of more than twenty-four months (see Exhibit 14-5 at ¶1455).

Submission of an Offer in Compromise.

Cash offers. In the case of a cash offer, the offer amount must include an amount equal to forty-eight months of the "collectible amount" in addition to the quick sale value of assets. A short-term deferred payment offer requires that the offer amount will include sixty months of the "collectible amount" in addition to the quick sale value of assets, and that full payment will occur later than ninety days but within two years from acceptance.

A deferred payment offer requires that the offer amount will include an amount (in addition to the quick sale value of assets) equivalent to the monthly "collectible amount" multiplied by the number of months remaining on the collection statute. For deferred payment offers, a taxpayer can elect: (1) to make full payment of the quick sale value of assets within ninety days of acceptance of the offer, and the amount the IRS could expect to collect during the lifetime of the statute; (2) to make payment of a portion of the quick sale value of assets within ninety days of acceptance and the remainder of the quick sale value and the amount the IRS could expect to collect during the lifetime of the statute; or (3) payment of the entire offer amount over the lifetime of the statute.

Generally, the manual supplement requires consideration of the filing of federal tax liens in the case of each type of Offer in Compromise and provides, that if liens are filed, they are released when the taxpayer satisfies the terms and conditions of the offer.[69] Furthermore, it also instructs IRS personnel to inform the taxpayer that interest accrues on the offered amount from the date of acceptance until it is paid in full.

Offers in Compromise based on economic hardship. In late July 1999, the Treasury Department issued temporary regulations under Code Sec. 7122 governing offers in compromise. These regulations ostensibly were made in response to the Congressional Directive in Offer in Compromise Committee Reports, adding a new category for "economic hardship" to the long standing doubt-as-to-liability and doubt-as-to-collectibility reasons for accepting Offers in Compromise. The temporary regulations[70] provide for examples of situations where collection of the full liability is considered to create economic hardship for the taxpayer

---

[68] See www.irs.gov/ind_info/coll_stds/index.html.

[69] IRM 5.8.1.5.4; IRM 5.8.1.5.4; IRM 5.8.1.5.4.

[70] Temp. Reg. §301.7122-1T(b)(4)(D).

sufficient to meet the criteria for offer acceptance, and two examples of situations where, regardless of the taxpayer's financial circumstances, exceptional conditions existthat make collection of the full amount detrimental to voluntary compliance by taxpayers.

In all the situations described, the Treasury Regulations conclude that the requirement is met and that compromise of the liability will not undermine compliance by taxpayers with the tax laws.[71]

¶1449 INTERNAL REVIEW WITHIN THE INTERNAL REVENUE SERVICE

Review of Offers in Compromise and Installment Agreements. The IRS must subject any proposals for an installment agreement and/or an offer in compromise that it is considering rejecting to an internal review. This IRS "self examination" must occur before communicating the rejection to the taxpayer.[72]

Appeal of Offers in Compromise and Installment Agreements. The right to appeal denials or termination of installment agreements and/or offers in compromise is a matter of right rather than administrative grace (see Exhibit 14-24 at ¶1474).[73] These appeals are governed by the Collection Appeals Program (CAP). Taxpayers who disagree with the decision of the Revenue Officer must first request a conference with a Collection Manager. If they are unable to resolve their disagreement, then consideration by the Appeals Office is made by completion of Form 9423, Collection Appeal Request (see Exhibit 14-25 at ¶1475). The appeal must be received by the collection office within:

1. Two days of the taxpayer's conference with the collection manager on appeals of liens, levies or seizures; or

2. Thirty days from the date of denial or termination of an installment agreement and/or an offer in compromise.

Decisions by the Appeals Officer are binding on both the taxpayer and the IRS and are not subject to judicial review.

---

[71] Temp. Reg. § 301.7122-1T(b)(1)(iii).
[72] Code Sec. 7122(d)(1).
[73] Code Secs. 6159(d) and 7122(d)(2).

¶1451 Exhibit 14-1

Partial Table of Tax Class and Document Codes

Form No.	Title	Tax Class	Doc. Code
CP2000	Proposed Changes to Income or Withholding Tax	2	54
CTR	Currency Transaction	5	15
SS-4	Application for Employer TIN	9	04
W-2	Wage and Tax Statement	5	11
W-4	Employee's Withholding Certificate	5	42
706	U.S. Estate Tax Return	5	06
709	U.S. Gift Tax Return	5	09
720	Quarterly Federal Excise Tax Return	4	20
730	Tax on Wagering	4	13
940	FUTA (Paper)	8	40
940	FUTA (Magnetic Tape)	8	39
941	FICA (Paper)	1	41
941	FICA (Magnetic Tape)	1	35
942	Employer's Quarterly Return for Household Employee	1	42
943	Employer's Annual Return for Agricultural Employee	1	43
990	Tax Exempt Organization Return	4	90
1040	U.S. Individual Income Tax Return	2	11
1040A	U.S. Individual Income Tax Return	2	09
1040X	Amended U.S. Individual Income Tax	2	11
1099-INT	Statement of Interest Income	5	92
1120	U.S. Corporation Income Tax Return	3	10
1120-S	U.S. Small Business Corporation Income Tax	3	16
1139	Corporation Application for Tentative Refund	3	84
4868	Automatic Extension of Time to File	2	17
5500	Annual Report of Employee Benefit Plan	0	37
5713	Internation Boycott Report	6	08
7004	Corporation Automatic Extension to File	3	04

¶1452 Exhibit 14-2

Department of the Treasury
Internal Revenue Service
KANSAS CITY   MO   64999

Date of this notice: SEP. 11, 2000
Taxpayer Identifying Number   39-
Form.   941   Tax Period: JUNE 30, 2000

For assistance you may
call us at:

1-800-829-8815

.ıll

```
WE CHANGED YOUR RETURN -- YOU HAVE AN AMOUNT DUE IRS

     WE CHANGED YOUR EMPLOYMENT TAX RETURN FOR THE ABOVE TAX PERIOD.  YOU MAY
WANT TO CHECK YOUR FIGURES AGAINST THOSE SHOWN BELOW:

ADJUSTED TOTAL OF FEDERAL INCOME TAX WITHHELD        $40,016.47
TAX ON SOCIAL SECURITY WAGES            46,753.27
TAX ON MEDICARE WAGES AND TIPS                       $10,934.23
ADJUSTED TOTAL OF SOCIAL SECURITY AND MEDICARE TAXES               57,799.96
TOTAL TAXES                                                       $97,816.45
TOTAL TAX DEPOSITED FOR THE QUARTER                 $97,717.38-
OVERPAYMENT FROM THE PREVIOUS QUARTER                      .00
OTHER CREDITS AND PAYMENTS                                 .00
TOTAL CREDITS AND PAYMENTS                                        $97,717.38-
     UNDERPAYMENT                                                     $99.07
PLUS:*PENALTY                                              $.99
     *INTEREST                                            $1.03
     TOTAL AMOUNT YOU OWE                                            $101.09

WE MADE THE CHANGES FOR THE FOLLOWING REASON(S):
THERE WAS A DISCREPANCY IN THE AMOUNT REPORTED AS TOTAL FEDERAL TAX
DEPOSITS FOR THE QUARTER AND THE AMOUNT SHOWN ON OUR RECORDS.

THE FOLLOWING IS A LIST OF PAYMENTS WE HAVE CREDITED TO YOUR ACCOUNT FOR THE ABOVE
TAX AND TAX PERIOD.
DATE OF PAYMENT     AMOUNT     DATE OF PAYMENT     AMOUNT     DATE OF PAYMENT     AMOUNT
APR. 11, 2000      7,723.38   APR. 17, 2000      7,537.25   APR. 24, 2000      7,132.07
MAY   1, 2000      7,390.09   MAY   8, 2000      7,400.48   MAY  15, 2000      7,030.77
MAY  22, 2000      9,031.20   MAY  30, 2000      6,736.13   JUNE  5, 2000      7,102.16
JUNE 12, 2000      7,966.32   JUNE 19, 2000      7,130.67   JUNE 26, 2000      8,804.13
JULY  3, 2000      6,696.40   JULY 31, 2000         36.33

     TO AVOID ADDITIONAL FAILURE TO PAY PENALTY AND INTEREST, PLEASE ALLOW ENOUGH MAILING
TIME SO THAT WE RECEIVE YOUR PAYMENT BY OCT.  2, 2000.  MAKE YOUR CHECK OR MONEY ORDER
PAYABLE TO THE UNITED STATES TREASURY.  SHOW YOUR TAXPAYER IDENTIFICATION NUMBER OR
YOUR IDENTIFYING NUMBER ON YOUR PAYMENT AND MAIL IT WITH THE STUB PORTION OF THIS NOTICE.

IF YOU THINK WE MADE A MISTAKE, PLEASE CALL US AT THE NUMBER LISTED ABOVE.  WHEN YOU
CALL, PLEASE HAVE YOUR PAYMENT INFORMATION AND A COPY OF YOUR TAX RETURN AVAILABLE.
THIS INFORMATION WILL HELP US FIND ANY PAYMENT YOU MADE THAT WE HAVEN'T APPLIED.

ABOUT YOUR NOTICE.  YOU MAY CALL YOUR LOCAL IRS TELEPHONE NUMBER IF THE NUMBER
SHOWN ON YOUR NOTICE IS A LONG-DISTANCE CALL FOR YOU.  ALL DAYS MENTIONED IN
THE PARAGRAPHS BELOW ARE CALENDAR DAYS, UNLESS SPECIFICALLY STATED OTHERWISE.

          $.99   PAYING LATE

WE CHARGED A PENALTY BECAUSE, ACCORDING TO OUR RECORDS, YOU DIDN'T PAY YOUR TAX
ON TIME.  INITIALLY, THE PENALTY IS 1/2% OF THE UNPAID TAX FOR EACH MONTH OR
PART OF A MONTH YOU DIDN'T PAY YOUR TAX.

NOTE:  EFFECTIVE FOR MONTHS BEGINNING AFTER DECEMBER 31, 1999, THE FAILURE TO
PAY TAX PENALTY (FTP) FOR INDIVIDUALS, WHO FILE A TAX RETURN ON OR BEFORE THE
DUE DATE (INCLUDING EXTENSIONS), IS LIMITED TO HALF THE USUAL RATE (0.25% RATHER
THAN 0.5%) FOR ANY MONTH IN WHICH AN INSTALLMENT PAYMENT AGREEMENT IS IN EFFECT.
```

PAGE 1

¶1452

```
        TIN              FORM: 941      TAX PERIOD: JUNE 30, 2000
```

IF WE ISSUE A NOTICE OF INTENT TO LEVY AND YOU DON'T PAY THE BALANCE DUE WITHIN
10 DAYS FROM THE DATE OF THE NOTICE, THE PENALTY INCREASES TO 1% A MONTH.
NOTE: WE WILL NOT REDUCE THE 1% FTP EVEN IF YOU FILED TIMELY AND HAVE A VALID
INSTALLMENT AGREEMENT.

THE PENALTY CAN'T BE MORE THAN 25% OF THE TAX PAID LATE. IF YOU THINK WE SHOULD
REMOVE OR REDUCE THIS PENALTY, SEE "REMOVAL OF PENALTIES - REASONABLE CAUSE."

___ REMOVAL OF PENALTIES

REASONABLE CAUSE. THE LAW LETS US REMOVE OR REDUCE THE PENALTIES WE EXPLAIN IN
THIS NOTICE IF YOU HAVE AN ACCEPTABLE REASON. IF YOU BELIEVE YOU HAVE AN
___ ACCEPTABLE REASON, YOU MAY SEND US A SIGNED STATEMENT EXPLAINING YOUR REASON. WE
WILL REVIEW IT AND LET YOU KNOW IF WE ACCEPT YOUR EXPLANATION AS REASONABLE CAUSE
TO REMOVE OR REDUCE YOUR PENALTY. THIS PROCEDURE DOESN'T APPLY TO INTEREST AND,
IN SOME CASES, WE MAY ASK YOU TO PAY THE TAX IN FULL BEFORE WE REDUCE OR REMOVE
THE PENALTY FOR PAYING LATE.

ERRONEOUS WRITTEN ADVICE FROM IRS

WE WILL ALSO REMOVE YOUR PENALTY IF:

   -YOU WROTE TO IRS AND ASKED FOR ADVICE ON A SPECIFIC ISSUE,
   -YOU GAVE IRS COMPLETE AND ACCURATE INFORMATION,
   -IRS WROTE BACK TO YOU AND GAVE YOU A SPECIFIC COURSE OF
    ACTION TO TAKE OR EXPLAINED WHAT ACTIONS NOT TO TAKE,
   -YOU FOLLOWED OUR WRITTEN ADVICE IN THE MANNER WE OUTLINED, AND
   -YOU WERE PENALIZED FOR THE WRITTEN ADVICE WE GAVE YOU.

TO HAVE THE PENALTY REMOVED BECAUSE OF ERRONEOUS WRITTEN ADVICE FROM IRS,
YOU SHOULD:

   -COMPLETE FORM 843, CLAIM FOR REFUND AND REQUEST FOR ABATEMENT,
   -REQUEST THAT IRS REMOVE THE PENALTY, AND
   -SEND FORM 843 TO THE IRS SERVICE CENTER WHERE YOU FILED YOUR
    RETURN FOR THE YEAR YOU RELIED ON ERRONEOUS ADVICE FROM THE IRS.

THE THREE DOCUMENTS YOU MUST ATTACH TO YOUR FORM 843 ARE:

   -A COPY OF YOUR ORIGINAL REQUEST FOR ADVICE FROM IRS,
   -A COPY OF THE ERRONEOUS WRITTEN ADVICE FROM IRS, AND
   -A NOTICE (IF ANY) SHOWING THE PENALTY WE CHARGED THAT
    YOU NOW WISH US TO REMOVE.

THE INTEREST RATES ON UNDERPAYMENT AND OVERPAYMENT OF TAXES ARE AS FOLLOWS:

PERIODS   PERCENTAGE RATES

	UNDERPAYMENT	OVERPAYMENT
OCTOBER 1, 1988 THROUGH MARCH 31, 1989	11	10
APRIL 1, 1989 THROUGH SEPTEMBER 30, 1989	12	11
OCTOBER 1, 1989 THROUGH MARCH 31, 1991	11	10
APRIL 1, 1991 THROUGH DECEMBER 31, 1991	10	9
JANUARY 1, 1992 THROUGH MARCH 31, 1992	9	8
APRIL 1, 1992 THROUGH SEPTEMBER 30, 1992	8	7
OCTOBER 1, 1992 THROUGH JUNE 30, 1994	7	6
JULY 1, 1994 THROUGH SEPTEMBER 30, 1994	8	7
OCTOBER 1, 1994 THROUGH MARCH 31, 1995	9	8
APRIL 1, 1995 THROUGH JUNE 30, 1995	10	9
JULY 1, 1995 THROUGH MARCH 31, 1996	9	8
APRIL 1, 1996 THROUGH JUNE 30, 1996	8	7
JULY 1, 1996 THROUGH MARCH 31, 1998	9	8
APRIL 1, 1998 THROUGH DECEMBER 31, 1998	8	7
JANUARY 1, 1999 THROUGH MARCH 31, 1999	7	7
APRIL 1, 1999 THROUGH MARCH 31, 2000	8	8
BEGINNING APRIL 1, 2000	9	9

PAGE 2

¶1452

TIN   FORM: 941   TAX PERIOD: JUNE 30, 2000

BEGINNING JANUARY 1, 1999, THE INTEREST RATE WE PAY ON OVERPAYMENT OF TAXES, EXCEPT FOR CORPORATE TAXES, IS THE SAME AS THE RATE OF INTEREST WE CHARGE ON THE UNDERPAYMENT OF TAXES. THE LAW REQUIRES US TO REDETERMINE THESE INTEREST RATES QUARTERLY. FROM JANUARY 1, 1987 THROUGH DECEMBER 31, 1998, THE INTEREST RATE WE PAID ON AN OVERPAYMENT OF TAXES WAS ONE PERCENT LESS THAN THE RATE OF INTEREST WE CHARGED ON YOUR UNDERPAYMENT OF TAXES.

WE COMPOUND INTEREST DAILY EXCEPT ON LATE OR UNDERPAID ESTIMATED TAXES FOR INDIVIDUALS OR CORPORATIONS.

WE CHARGE A SPECIAL INTEREST RATE OF 120 PERCENT OF THE UNDERPAYMENT RATE IF:

- THE RETURN, NOT INCLUDING EXTENSIONS, WAS DUE BEFORE JANUARY 1, 1990,
- THE UNDERPAYMENT WAS MORE THAN $1,000, AND
- THE UNDERPAYMENT CAME FROM A TAX-MOTIVATED TRANSACTION.

WE CHARGE INTEREST ON PENALTIES FOR LATE FILING, OVER OR UNDERSTATING VALUATIONS, AND SUBSTANTIALLY UNDERSTATING THE TAX YOU OWE. ALSO, WE CHARGE INTEREST ON FRAUD AND NEGLIGENCE PENALTIES IF THE TAX RETURNS, INCLUDING EXTENSIONS, ARE DUE AFTER DECEMBER 31, 1988.

WE CONTINUE TO CHARGE INTEREST UNTIL YOU PAY THE AMOUNT YOU OWE IN FULL.

AFTER DECEMBER 31, 1990, THE LAW ALLOWS US TO CHARGE INTEREST AT THE UNDERPAYMENT RATE PLUS TWO PERCENT ON UNDERPAYMENTS OF MORE THAN $100,000 FOR LARGE CORPORATIONS.

$1.03   INTEREST

WE CHARGED INTEREST BECAUSE, ACCORDING TO OUR RECORDS, YOU DIDN'T PAY YOUR TAX ON TIME. WE FIGURED INTEREST FROM THE DUE DATE OF YOUR RETURN (REGARDLESS OF EXTENSIONS) TO THE DATE WE RECEIVE YOUR FULL PAYMENTS OR THE DATE OF THIS NOTICE.

CORPORATE INTEREST - WE CHARGE ADDITIONAL INTEREST OF 2% BECAUSE, ACCORDING TO OUR RECORDS, YOU DIDN'T MAKE YOUR CORPORATE TAX PAYMENT WITHIN 30 DAYS AFTER THE IRS NOTIFIED YOU OF THE UNDERPAYMENT OF TAX. THIS INTEREST BEGINS ON THE 31ST DAY AFTER WE NOTIFY YOU OF THE UNDERPAYMENT ON TAX AMOUNTS YOU OWE OVER $100,000, MINUS YOUR TIMELY PAYMENTS AND CREDITS.

INTEREST REDUCED

IF WE REDUCE INTEREST THAT YOU PREVIOUSLY REPORTED AS A DEDUCTION ON YOUR TAX RETURN, YOU MUST REPORT THIS REDUCTION OF INTEREST AS INCOME ON YOUR TAX RETURN FOR THE YEAR WE REDUCE IT.

INTEREST REMOVED - ERRONEOUS REFUND

THE LAW REQUIRES US TO REMOVE INTEREST UP TO THE DATE WE REQUEST YOU TO REPAY THE ERRONEOUS REFUND WHEN:

- YOU DIDN'T CAUSE THE ERRONEOUS REFUND IN ANY WAY, AND
- THE REFUND DOESN'T EXCEED $50,000.

THE IRS MAY REMOVE OR REDUCE INTEREST ON OTHER ERRONEOUS REFUNDS BASED ON THE FACTS AND CIRCUMSTANCES INVOLVED IN EACH CASE.

ANNUAL INTEREST NETTING

EFFECTIVE JANUARY 1, 1987, THROUGH DECEMBER 31, 1998, THE INTEREST RATE WE PAID ON THE OVERPAYMENT OF TAXES WAS 1% LESS THAN THE INTEREST RATE WE CHARGED ON THE UNDERPAYMENT OF TAXES. AS OF JANUARY 1, 1999, THE OVERPAYMENT AND UNDERPAYMENT RATES OF INTEREST THAT WE PAY AND CHARGE ARE THE SAME, EXCEPT FOR CORPORATE OVERPAYMENTS. IF WE REFUND AN OVERPAYMENT WITH INTEREST AND WE HAVE TO INCREASE THE TAX AT A LATER DATE, WE GIVE SPECIAL CONSIDERATION TO THE INTEREST ON THAT ACCOUNT.

ON THE TAX INCREASE MADE AFTER THE REFUND, WE WILL CHARGE THE LOWER REFUND RATE OF INTEREST (UP TO THE AMOUNT OF THE REFUND) FOR THE SAME TIME PERIOD THAT WE PAID INTEREST ON THE OVERPAYMENT.

¶1452

```
            TIN          FORM: 941      TAX PERIOD: JUNE 30, 2000

      REQUEST FOR NET INTEREST RATE OF ZERO

      GENERAL RULE - IF YOU OWE INTEREST TO THE IRS ON AN UNDERPAYMENT FOR THE SAME
      PERIOD OF TIME THAT THE IRS OWES YOU INTEREST ON AN OVERPAYMENT, YOU MAY BE
      ENTITLED TO RECEIVE A NET INTEREST RATE OF ZERO (THE SAME RATE OF INTEREST
      APPLIES TO YOUR UNDERPAYMENT AS YOUR OVERPAYMENT).

      TO RECEIVE THE NET INTEREST RATE OF ZERO FOR INTEREST YOU OWED (OR PAID) THE
      IRS, OR INTEREST THAT WE OWED (OR PAID) YOU BEFORE OCTOBER 1, 1998, YOU MUST
      FILE A FORM 843, CLAIM FOR REFUND AND REQUEST FOR ABATEMENT. FOR MORE
      INFORMATION ON THE FILING REQUIREMENTS FOR THE FORM 843, SEE REVENUE PROCEDURE
      99-43, 1999-47 I.R.B. 579. REVENUE PROCEDURE 99-43 AND FORM 843 ARE AVAILABLE
      ON THE WORLD WIDE WEB AT WWW.IRS.USTREAS.GOV.

      TO QUALIFY FOR THE NET INTEREST RATE OF ZERO, THE PERIOD OF LIMITATION FOR
      CLAIMING A REFUND OF INTEREST ON AN UNDERPAYMENT AND THE PERIOD OF LIMITATION
      FOR CLAIMING ADDITIONAL INTEREST ON AN OVERPAYMENT MUST HAVE BEEN OPEN ON
      JULY 22, 1998. GENERALLY, THE PERIOD OF LIMITATION FOR CLAIMING A REFUND OF
      INTEREST ON AN UNDERPAYMENT IS 3 YEARS FROM THE TIME YOU FILED YOUR TAX
      RETURN, OR 2 YEARS FROM THE TIME YOU PAID THE INTEREST, WHICHEVER IS LATER.
      THE PERIOD OF LIMITATION TO REQUEST ADDITIONAL INTEREST ON AN OVERPAYMENT IS
      6 YEARS FROM THE DATE OF THE REFUND.

      YOU MUST FILE FORM 843 ON OR BEFORE THE CLOSING DATE OF THE LATER STATUE OF
      LIMITATION PERIOD. MAIL FORM 843 TO:

      U.S. MAIL
      INTERNAL REVENUE SERVICE
      NET RATE INTEREST NETTING CLAIM
      P.O. BOX 9987
      MAIL STOP 6800
      OGDEN, UT  84409

      OTHER THAN U.S. MAIL
      INTERNAL REVENUE SERVICE
      NET RATE INTEREST NETTING CLAIM
      1160 WEST 1200 SOUTH
      MAIL STOP 6800
      OGDEN, UT  84201

      FOR INTEREST YOU OWED THE IRS OR THAT THE IRS OWED YOU ON OR AFTER OCTOBER 1,
      1998, THE IRS WILL TAKE REASONABLE STEPS TO IDENTIFY THESE PERIODS AND APPLY
      THE NET INTEREST RATE OF ZERO. HOWEVER, TO ENSURE THAT YOU RECEIVE THE NET
      INTEREST RATE OF ZERO FOR OVERLAPPING PERIODS, YOU SHOULD FILE A FORM 843
      FOLLOWING THE PROCEDURES DESCRIBED ABOVE.
```

```
RETURN THIS PART TO US WITH YOUR CHECK OR INQUIRY
YOUR TELEPHONE NUMBER     BEST TIME TO CALL
 (    )    -
                                    AMOUNT YOU OWE....................$101.09

                                    LESS PAYMENTS NOT INCLUDED.$_____
 24
                                    PAY ADJUSTED AMOUNT........$_____

              I.I

                       670    0000010109


 102
          INTERNAL REVENUE SERVICE
          KANSAS CITY  MO   64999


 200035 0709            09141-213-12192-0
```

¶1453 Exhibit 14-3

POA COPY

Internal Revenue Service   Department of the Treasury

Letter Number:

Letter Date:

Employer Identification No.:

--CERTIFIED MAIL - RETURN RECEIPT   Person to Contact:

Contact Telephone Number:

Employee Identification No.:

FINAL NOTICE
NOTICE OF INTENT TO LEVY AND NOTICE OF YOUR RIGHT TO A HEARING
PLEASE RESPOND IMMEDIATELY

Your Federal tax is still not paid. We previously asked you to pay this, but we still haven't received your payment. This letter is your notice of our intent to levy under Internal Revenue Code(IRC) Section 6331 and your right to receive Appeals consideration under IRC Section 6330.

We may file a Notice of Federal Tax Lien at any time to protect the government's interest. A lien is a public notice to your creditors that the government has a right to your current assets, including any assets you acquire after we file the lien.

If you don't pay the amount you owe, make alternative arrangements to pay, or request Appeals consideration within 30 days from the date of this letter, we may take your property, or rights to property, such as real estate, automobiles, business assets, bank accounts, wages, commissions, and other income. We've enclosed Publication 594 with more information, Publication 1660 explaining your right to appeal, and Form 12153 to request a Collection Due Process Hearing with Appeals.

To prevent collection action, please send your full payment today. Make your check or money order payable to U.S. Treasury. Write your social security number or employer identification number on your payment. Send your payment to us in the enclosed envelope with a copy of this letter.

The amount you owe is listed on the following page(s).

Page 1

Letter 1058(DO) (Rev. 1-1999) Cat. No. 40488S

```
                              POA COPY
     Internal Revenue Service              Department of the Treasury

                                           Letter Number:

                                           Letter Date:


   Form        Tax      Unpaid Amount        Additional
  Number      Period    from Prior Notices  Penalty & Interest   Amount You Owe
  _____     _____   _____   _____   _____



                                           Total:
```

If you have recently paid this tax or you can't pay it, call us immediately at the telephone number shown at the top of this letter and let us know.

The unpaid amount from prior notices may include tax, penalties and interest you still owe. It also includes any credits and payments we've received since we sent our last notice to you.

Enclosures:
Copy of letter
Pub. 594
Pub. 1660
Form 12153

Letter 1058(DO) (Rev. 1-1999) Cat. No. 40488S

¶1454 Exhibit 14-4

IRS Transaction Codes

A transcript of a taxpayer's account with the IRS may contain numerous transaction codes. The following list will assist in interpreting such codes.

Code	Description	Code	Description
000	Establish an Account	350	Negligence Penalty
013	Name Change	351	Reversal of TC 350
014	Address Change	360	Fees and Collection Costs
150	Return Filed/Tax Assessed	361	Abatement of Fees and Collection Costs
160	Delinquent Return Penalty	420	Examination Indicator
161	Reversal of TC 160, 166	430	Estimated Tax Payment
166	Delinquent Return Penalty	459	Prior Quarter Liability
167	Reversal of TC 166	460	Extension of Time for Filing
170	Estimated Tax Penalty	470	Taxpayer Claim Pending
171	Reversal of TC 170, 176	480	Offer in Compromise Pending
176	Estimated Tax Penalty	481	Offer in Compromise Rejected
177	Reversal of TC 176	482	Offer in Compromise Withdrawn
180	Deposit (FTD) Penalty	488	Installment or Manual Billing
181	Reversal of TC 180, 186	520	IRS Litigation Instituted
186	Deposit (FTD) Penalty	550	Waiver of Extension of Collection Statute
187	Reversal of TC 186	560	Waiver of Extension of Assessment Statute
190	Interest Assessed	570	Additional Liability Pending
191	Reversal of TC 190	582	Lien Indicator
196	Interest Assessed	610	Remittance With Return
197	Reversal of TC 196	611	Remittance With Return Dishonored
270	Late Payment Penalty	612	Correction to TC 610 Error
271	Reversal of TC 270, 276	620	Installment Payment
276	Late Payment Penalty	621	Installment Payment Dishonored
277	Reversal of TC 276	622	Correction to TC 620 Error
280	Bad Check Penalty	640	Advanced Payment-Determined Deficiency
281	Reversal of TC 280, 286	641	Payment Dishonored
286	Bad Check Penalty	642	Correction to TC 640 Error
290	Additional Tax Assessed	650	Depository Receipt/FTD Credit
291	Abatement of Prior Tax	651	Invalid TC 650
294	Additional Tax/Reverses TC 295	652	Correction to TC 650
295	Tentative Allowance/Tax Decrease	660	Estimated Tax Payment
298	Additional Tax/TC 299	661	Estimated Tax Payment
299	Carryback Allow/Tax Decrease	662	Correction to TC 660
300	Additional Tax by Examination	670	Subsequent Payment
301	Abatement by Examination	671	Subsequent Payment Dishonored
308	Additional Tax by Examination	672	Correction to TC 670
309	Abatement by Examination	700	Credit Applied
320	Fraud Penalty	701	Reversal of TC 700 and 706
321	Reversal of TC 320	702	Correction to TC 700
336	Interest Assessed	706	Credit Applied
340	Interest Assessed	710	Credit From Prior Period
341	Interest Abated		

Code	Description	Code	Description
712	Correction to 710 or 716	800	Credit for Withheld Tax
716	Credit From Prior Period	806	Credit for Withheld Tax
720	Refund Payment	807	Reversal of TC 800 and 806
721	Refund Repayment Check Dishonored	820	Credit Transferred Out
730	Interest Overpayment Credit Applied	821	Reversal of TC 820 and 826
732	Correction to TC 730	826	Credit Transferred Out
736	Overpayment Interest Applied by Computer	830	Overpayment Transferred to Next Period
740	Undelivered Refund Check	832	Correction to TC 830
742	Correction to TC 740	836	Overpayment Transferred to Next Period
764	Earned Income Credit	840	Refund Issued
765	Reversal of TC 764 and 768	841	Refund Cancelled/Credit to Account
766	Refundable Credit	842	Refund Deleted
767	Reversal of TC 766	844	Erroneous Refund Identified
768	Earned Income Credit	846	Refund Issued
770	Interest Due Taxpayer	850	Overpayment Interest Transfer
772	Reversal of TC 770	856	Overpayment Interest Transferred
776	Interest Due Taxpayer	960	Add Centralized Authorization
777	Reversal of TC 776	976	Duplicate Return
		977	Amended Return Filed

Most other transaction codes append administrative data to accounts. A minus sign (–) designates a credit transaction.

¶1455 Exhibit 14-5

Department of the Treasury
Internal Revenue Service

www.irs.gov

Form 656 (Rev. 5-2001)
Catalog Number 16728N

Form 656

Offer in Compromise

This Offer in Compromise package includes:

■ Information you need to know before submitting an offer in compromise

■ Instructions on the type of offers you can submit

■ Form 433-A, Collection Information Statement for Wage Earners and Self-Employed Individuals, and Form 433-B, Collection Information Statement for Businesses

■ A worksheet that wage earners and self-employed individuals can use to calculate their offer amount

■ Instructions on completing an offer in compromise form

■ Two copies of Form 656

Note: You can get forms and publications by calling 1–800–829–1040 or 1–800–829–FORM, or by visiting your local Internal Revenue Service (IRS) office or our website at *www.irs.gov.*

What You Need to Know Before Submitting an Offer in Compromise

What is an Offer in Compromise?

An *Offer in Compromise* (OIC) is an agreement between a taxpayer and the Internal Revenue Service (IRS) that resolves the taxpayer's tax liability. The IRS has the authority to settle, or *compromise*, federal tax liabilities by accepting less than full payment under certain circumstances. The IRS may legally compromise for one of the following reasons:

■ **Doubt as to Liability** — Doubt exists that the assessed tax is correct.

■ **Doubt as to Collectibility** — Doubt exists that you could ever pay the full amount of tax owed.

■ **Effective Tax Administration** — There is no doubt the tax is correct and no doubt the amount owed could be collected, but an exceptional circumstance exists that allows us to consider your offer. To be eligible for compromise on this basis, you must demonstrate that collection of the tax would create an economic hardship or would be unfair and inequitable.

Form 656, Offer in Compromise, and Substitute Forms

Form 656, *Offer in Compromise*, is the official compromise agreement. Substitute forms, whether computer-generated or photocopies, must affirm that:

1. The substitute form is a verbatim duplicate of the official Form 656, and

2. You agree to be bound by all terms and conditions set forth in the official Form 656.

You must initial and date all pages of the substitute form, in addition to signing and dating the signature page.

You can get Form 656 by calling 1–800–829–1040 or 1–800–829–FORM, by visiting your local Internal Revenue Service (IRS) office, or by accessing our website at www.irs.gov

Am I Eligible for Consideration of an Offer in Compromise?

You may be eligible for consideration of an *Offer in Compromise* if:

1. In your judgment, you don't owe the tax liability (**Doubt as to Liability**). You must submit a detailed written statement explaining why you believe you don't owe the tax liability you want to compromise. You won't be required to submit a collection information statement if you're submitting an offer on this basis alone.

2. In your judgment, you can't pay the entire tax liability in full (**Doubt as to Collectibility**). You must submit a collection information statement showing your current financial situation.

3. You agree the tax liability is correct and you're able to pay the balance due in full, but you have exceptional circumstances you'd like us to consider (**Effective Tax Administration**). To receive consideration on this basis, you must submit:

a. a collection information statement, and

b. a detailed written narrative. The narrative must explain your exceptional circumstances and why paying the tax liability in full would either create an economic hardship or would be unfair and inequitable.

We'll also consider your overall history of filing and paying taxes.

Note: If you request consideration on the basis of effective tax administration, we're first required to establish that there is no doubt as to liability and no doubt as to collectibility. We can only consider an offer on the basis of effective tax administration after we've determined the liability is correct and collectible.

1

When Am I Not Eligible for Consideration of an Offer in Compromise?

You are not eligible for consideration of an *Offer in Compromise* on the basis of **doubt as to collectibility** or **effective tax administration** if:

1. You haven't filed all required federal tax returns, or

2. You're involved in an open bankruptcy proceeding.

Note: If you are an in-business taxpayer, you must have filed and deposited all employment taxes on time for the two (2) quarters preceding your offer, as well as, deposit all employment taxes on time during the quarter you submit your offer.

What We Need to Process Your Offer in Compromise

For us to process your offer, you must provide a complete and correct Form 656 and:

■ Form 433-A, *Collection Information Statement for Wage Earners and Self-Employed Individuals*, if you are submitting an offer as an **individual** or **self-employed taxpayer**.

■ Form 433-B, *Collection Information Statement for Businesses*, if you are submitting an offer as a **corporation** or **other business** taxpayer. We may also require Forms 433-A from corporate officers or individual partners.

For a more detailed explanation of the information required to complete these forms, see the section entitled, "Financial Information" on page 3.

Note: We don't need a collection information statement for an offer based solely on doubt as to liability.

Please complete all applicable items on Form 656 and provide all required documentation. We may contact you for any missing required information. If we don't receive a response to our request or receive the required information, we won't recommend your offer for acceptance and will return your Form 656 to you by mail. We will explain our reason(s) for returning your offer in our letter. The reasons for return are:

■ The pre-printed terms and conditions listed on Form 656 have changed

■ A taxpayer name is missing

■ A Social Security Number or Employer Identification Number is missing, incomplete, or incorrect

■ An offer amount or payment term is unstated

■ A signature is missing

■ A collection information statement (Form 433-A or Form 433-B) is missing or incomplete, if your offer is based on doubt as to collectibility or effective tax administration

■ We did not receive collection information statement verification

■ Our records show you don't have a tax liability

■ Your offer is submitted to delay collection or cause a delay which will jeopardize our ability to collect the tax

Note: You should personally sign your offer and any required collection information statements unless unusual circumstances prevent you from doing so. If someone with an authorized power of attorney signs your offer because of unusual circumstances, you must include a completed Form 2848, Power of Attorney and Declaration of Representative, with your offer.

2

¶1455

What You Should Do If You Want to Submit an Offer in Compromise

Determine Your Offer Amount

All offer amounts (**doubt as to liability**, **doubt as to collectibility**, or **effective tax administration**) must exceed $0.00.

■ **Doubt as to Liability**

Complete Item 9, *Explanation of Circumstances*, on Form 656, explaining why, in your judgment, you don't owe the tax liability you want to compromise. Offer the correct tax, penalty, and interest owed based on your judgment.

■ **Doubt as to Collectibility**

Complete Form 433-A, *Collection Information Statement for Wage Earners and Self-Employed Individuals*, or Form 433-B, *Collection Information Statement for Businesses*, as appropriate, and attach to your Form 656. For assistance in determining your offer amount, visit our website at www.irs.ustreas.gov/ind_info/oic/index.html. If you are a wage earner or self-employed individual, figure your offer amount by completing the worksheet on pages 10–11.

You must offer an amount greater than or equal to the "reasonable collection potential" (RCP). The RCP equals the net equity of your assets plus the amount we could collect from your future income. Please see page 8, **Terms and Definitions**, for more detailed definitions of these and other terms.

If special circumstances cause you to offer an amount less than the RCP, you must also complete Item 9, *Explanation of Circumstances*, on Form 656, explaining your situation. Special circumstances may include factors such as advanced age, serious illness from which recovery is unlikely, or unusual circumstances that impact upon your ability to pay the total RCP and continue to provide for the necessary expenses for you and your family.

■ **Effective Tax Administration**

Complete Form 433-A or Form 433-B, as appropriate, and attach to Form 656.

Complete Item 9, *Explanation of Circumstances*, on Form 656, explaining your exceptional circumstances and why requiring payment of the tax liability in full would either create an economic hardship or would be unfair and inequitable.

Enter your offer amount on Item 7 of Form 656.

Financial Information

Note: We do not require this information if your offer is based solely on doubt as to liability.

You must provide financial information when you submit offers based on **doubt as to collectibility** and **effective tax administration**.

If you are submitting an offer as a wage earner or self-employed individual, you must file Form 433-A, *Collection Information Statement for Wage Earners and Self-Employed Individuals*, with your Form 656. If you are a corporation or other business taxpayer, you must file Form 433-B, *Collection Information Statement for Businesses*. We may also request Forms 433-A from corporate officers or individual partners.

You must send us current information that reflects your financial situation for at least the past six months. Collection information statements must show all your assets and income, even those unavailable to us through direct collection action, because you can use them to fund your offer. The offer examiner needs this information to evaluate your offer and may ask you to update it or verify certain financial information. We may also return offer packages without complete collection information statements.

3

When only one spouse has a tax liability but both have incomes, only the spouse responsible for the debt is required to prepare the necessary collection information statements. In states with community property laws, however, we require collection information statements from both spouses. We may also request financial information on the non-liable spouse for offer verification purposes, even when community property laws do not apply.

Determine Your Payment Terms

There are three payment plans you and the IRS may agree to:

- **Cash** (paid in 90 days or less)

- **Short-Term Deferred Payment** (more than 90 days, up to 24 months)

- **Deferred Payment** (offers with payment terms over the remaining statutory period for collecting the tax).

Cash Offer

You must pay cash offers within 90 days of acceptance.

You should offer the realizable value of your assets plus the total amount we could collect over 48 months of payments (or the remainder of the ten-year statutory period for collection, whichever is less).

Note: We require full payment of accepted doubt as to liability offers at the time of mutual agreement of the corrected liability. If you're unable to pay the corrected amount, you must also request compromise on the basis of doubt as to collectibility.

Short-Term Deferred Payment Offer

This payment plan requires you to pay the offer within two years of acceptance.

The offer must include the realizable value of your assets plus the amount we could collect over 60 months of payments (or the remainder of the ten-year statutory period for collection, whichever is less).

You can pay the short-term deferred payment plan in three ways:

Plan One

- Full payment of the realizable value of your assets within 90 days from the date we accept your offer, and

- Payment within two years of acceptance of the amount we could collect over 60 months (future income) or the remaining life of the collection statute, whichever is less.

Plan Two

- Cash payment for a portion of the realizable value of your assets within 90 days from the date we accept your offer, and

- The balance of the realizable value plus the amount we could collect over 60 months (future income) or the remaining life of the collection statute, whichever is less, within two years of acceptance.

Plan Three

- The entire offer amount in monthly payments extending over a period not to exceed two years from date of acceptance (e.g., four payments within 120 days of acceptance).

For example, on a short-term deferred payment total offer of $16,000, you might propose to pay your realizable value of assets (e.g., $13,000) within 90 days of

4

acceptance and the amount of your future income (e.g., $50 per month for 60 months, or $3,000) over 6 monthly payments of $500 each, beginning the first month after acceptance.

We may file a Notice of Federal Tax Lien on tax liabilities compromised under short-term deferred payment offers.

Deferred Payment Offer

This payment plan requires you to pay the offer amount over the remaining statutory period for collecting the tax.

The offer must include the realizable value of your assets plus the amount we could collect through monthly payments during the remaining life of the collection statute.

For wage earners and self-employed individuals who want to submit a deferred payment offer, we will help you determine your future income amount. To compute this amount, we must calculate the remaining time left on the collection statute for each period of the tax liability.

- Call 1–800–829–1040 to assist you in this calculation.

- Using Form 433-A Worksheet, multiply the amount from Item 12, Box O, by the number of months remaining on the collection statute. Add that amount to Item 11, Box N, and use the total as the basis for your offer amount in Item 7 of Form 656.

You can pay the deferred payment plan in three ways:

Plan One

- Full payment of the realizable value of your assets within 90 days from the date we accept your offer, and

- Your "future income" in monthly payments during the remaining life of the collection statute

Plan Two

- Cash payment for a portion of the realizable value of your assets within 90 days from the date we accept your offer, and

- Monthly payments during the remaining life of the collection statute for both the balance of the realizable value and your future income

Plan Three

- The entire offer amount in monthly payments over the life of the collection statute

For example, on a deferred payment offer with 7 years (84 months) remaining on the statutory period for collection and a total offer of $25,000, you might propose to pay your realizable value of assets (e.g., $10,000) within 90 days and your future income (e.g., $179 per month for 7 years, or $15,000) in 84 monthly installments of $179. Alternately, you could also pay the same total $25,000 offer in 84 monthly installments of $298.

Just as with short-term deferred payment offers, we may file a Notice of Federal Tax Lien.

Note: The worksheet on page 10 instructs wage earners and self-employed individuals how to figure the appropriate amount for a Cash, Short-Term Deferred Payment, or Deferred Payment Offer.

5

¶1455

How We Consider Your Offer	An offer examiner will evaluate your offer and may request additional documentation from you to verify financial or other information you provide. The examiner will then make a recommendation to accept it or reject the offer. The examiner may also	return your offer if you don't provide the requested information. The examiner may decide that a larger offer amount is necessary to justify acceptance. You will have the opportunity to amend your offer.
Additional Agreements	When you submit certain offers, we may also request that you sign an additional agreement requiring you to:	■ Pay a percentage of your future earnings ■ Waive certain present or future tax benefits
Withholding Collection Activities	We will withhold collection activities while we consider your offer. We will not act to collect the tax liability: ■ While we investigate and evaluate your offer ■ For 30 days after we reject an offer ■ While you appeal an offer rejection	The above do not apply if we find any indication that you submitted your offer to delay collection or cause a delay which will jeopardize our ability to collect the tax. If you currently have an installment agreement when you submit an offer, you must continue making the agreed upon monthly payments while we consider your offer.
If We Accept Your Offer	If we accept your offer, we will notify you by mail. When you receive your acceptance letter, you must: ■ Promptly pay any unpaid amounts that become due under the terms of the offer agreement ■ Comply with all the terms and conditions of the offer, along with those of any additional agreement ■ Promptly notify us of any change of address until you meet the conditions of your offer. Your acceptance letter will indicate which IRS office to contact if your address changes. Your notification allows us to contact you immediately regarding the status of your offer We will release all Notices of Federal Tax Lien when you satisfy the payment terms of the offered amount. For an immediate	release of a lien, you can submit certified funds with a request letter. In the future, not filing returns or paying taxes when due could result in the default of an accepted offer (see Form 656, Item 8(d), the *future compliance provision*). If you default your agreement, we will reinstate the unpaid amount of the original tax liability, file a Notice of Federal Tax Lien on any tax liability without a filed notice, and resume collection activities. The future compliance provision applies to offers based on **doubt as to collectibility**. In certain cases, the future compliance provision may apply to offers based on **effective tax administration**. We won't default your offer agreement when you have filed a joint offer with your spouse or ex-spouse as long as you've kept or are keeping all the terms of the agreement, even if your spouse or ex-spouse violates the future compliance provision.

6

¶1455

Except for offers based on **doubt as to liability**, the offer agreement requires you to forego certain refunds, and to return those refunds to us if they are issued to you by mistake. These conditions are also listed on Form 656, Items 8(g) and 8(h).

Note: *The law requires us to make certain information from accepted Offers in Compromise available for public inspection and review in your local IRS Territory Office. Therefore, information regarding your Offer in Compromise may become publicly known.*

If We Reject Your Offer

We'll notify you by mail if we reject your offer. In our letter, we will explain our reason for the rejection. If your offer is rejected, you have the right to:

■ Appeal our decision to the Office of Appeals within thirty days from the date of our letter. The letter will include detailed instructions on how to appeal the rejection.

■ Submit another offer. You must increase an offer we've rejected as being too low, when your financial situation remains unchanged. However, you must provide updated financial information when your financial situation has changed or when the original offer is more than six months old.

7

Terms and Definitions

An understanding of the following terms and conditions will help you to prepare your offer.

Fair Market Value (FMV) – The amount you could reasonably expect from the sale of an asset. Provide an accurate valuation of each asset. Determine value from realtors, used car dealers, publications, furniture dealers, or other experts on specific types of assets. Please include a copy of any written estimate with your Collection Information Statement.

Quick Sale Value (QSV) – The amount you could reasonably expect from the sale of an asset if you sold it quickly, typically in ninety days or less. This amount generally is less than fair market value, but may be equal to or higher, based on local circumstances.

Realizable Value – The quick sale value amount minus what you owe to a secured creditor. The creditor must have priority over a filed Notice of Federal Tax Lien before we allow a subtraction from the asset's value.

Future Income – We generally determine the amount we could collect from your future income by subtracting necessary living expenses from your monthly income over a set number of months. For a cash offer, you must offer what you could pay in monthly payments over forty-eight months (or the remainder of the ten-year statutory period for collection, whichever is less). For a short-term deferred offer, you must offer what you could pay in monthly payments over sixty months (or the remainder of the statutory period for collection, whichever is less). For a deferred payment offer, you must offer what you could pay in monthly payments during the remaining time we could legally receive payments.

Reasonable Collection Potential (RCP) – The total realizable value of your assets plus your future income. The total is generally your minimum offer amount.

Necessary Expenses – The allowable payments you make to support you and your family's health and welfare and/or the production of income. This expense allowance does not apply to business entities. Our Publication 1854 explains the National Standard Expenses and gives the allowable amounts. We derive these amounts from the Bureau of Labor Statistics (BLS) Consumer Expenditure Survey. We also use information from the Bureau of the Census to determine local expenses for housing, utilities, and transportation.

Note: If the IRS determines that the facts and circumstances of your situation indicate that using the scheduled allowance of necessary expenses is inadequate, we will allow you an adequate means for providing basic living expenses. However, you must provide documentation that supports a determination that using national and local expense standards leaves you an inadequate means of providing for basic living expenses.

Expenses Not Generally Allowed – We typically do not allow you to claim tuition for private schools, public or private college expenses, charitable contributions, voluntary retirement contributions, payments on unsecured debts such as credit card bills, cable television charges and other similar expenses as necessary living expenses. However, we can allow these expenses when you can prove that they are necessary for the health and welfare of you or your family or for the production of income.

8

¶1455

For use by Wage Earners and Self-Employed Individuals.

Keep this worksheet for your records.
Do not send to IRS.

Form 433-A Worksheet

Use this Worksheet to calculate an offer amount using information from Form 433-A.

1. Enter total checking accounts from Item 11c   `A` _____

2. Enter total other accounts from Item 12c   `B` _____

       If less than "0", enter "0"

3. Enter total investments from Item 13d   `C` _____

4. Enter total cash on hand from Item 14a   `D` _____

5. Enter life insurance cash value from Item 16f   `E` _____

6. Enter total accounts/notes receivable from Item 23m   `F` _____

       Subtotal: Add boxes A through F = `G` _____

---

7. **Purchased Automobiles, Trucks, and Other Licensed Assets**

	Enter current value for each asset		Enter loan balance for each asset	Individual asset value (if less than "0", enter "0")
From line 18a	$_____	x .8 = $_____	− $_____	= _____
From line 18b	$_____	x .8 = $_____	− $_____	= _____
From line 18c	$_____	x .8 = $_____	− $_____	= _____

       Subtotal = `H` _____

---

8. **Real Estate**

	Enter current value for each asset		Enter loan balance for each asset	Individual asset value (if less than "0", enter "0")
From line 20a	$_____	x .8 = $_____	− $_____	= _____
From line 20b	$_____	x .8 = $_____	− $_____	= _____

       Subtotal = `I` _____

---

9. **Personal Assets**

	Enter current value for each asset		Enter loan balance for each asset	Individual asset value (if less than "0", enter "0")
From line 21b	$_____	x .8 = $_____	− $_____	= _____
From line 21c	$_____	x .8 = $_____	− $_____	= _____
From line 21d	$_____	x .8 = $_____	− $_____	= _____
From line 21e	$_____	x .8 = $_____	− $_____	= _____

       Subtotal = `J` _____

| From line 21a | $_____ | x .8 = $_____ | − $_____ | = _____ |

       Subtract − $ 6560.00

       Subtotal = `K` _____

---

10. **Business Assets**

	Enter current value for each asset		Enter loan balance for each asset	Individual asset value (if less than "0", enter "0")
From line 22b	$_____	x .8 = $_____	− $_____	= _____
From line 22c	$_____	x .8 = $_____	− $_____	= _____
From line 22d	$_____	x .8 = $_____	− $_____	= _____
From line 22e	$_____	x .8 = $_____	− $_____	= _____

       Subtotal = `L` _____

| From line 22a | $_____ | x .8 = $_____ | − $_____ | = _____ |

       Subtract − $ 3280.00

       Subtotal = `M` _____

10

11. Add amounts in Boxes G through M to obtain your total equity and assets

$= \boxed{\text{N}}$

12. Enter amount from Item 34 $\$\underline{\hspace{3cm}}$

Enter amount from Item 45 and subtract $-\ \$\underline{\hspace{2cm}}$

Net Difference $= \boxed{\text{O}}$

This amount would be available to pay monthly on your tax liability.

If Box O is "0" or less, STOP. Use the amount from Box N and to base your offer amount in Item 7 of Form 656. Your offer amount must equal or exceed (*) the amount shown in Box N.

$\$\underline{\hspace{3cm}}$

Enter amount from Box N $+$

Add amounts in Box P and Box Q $=$

$= \boxed{\text{P}}$

$\boxed{\text{Q}}$

$\boxed{\text{R}}$

Use the amount from Box R to base your offer amount in Item 7 of Form 656.
Note: Your offer amount must equal or exceed (*) the amount shown in Box R.

Enter amount from Box O $\$\underline{\hspace{3cm}}$

Multiply by

$= \boxed{\text{S}}$

$+$ $\boxed{\text{T}}$

$= \boxed{\text{U}}$

Use the amount from Box U to base your offer amount in Item 7 of Form 656.
Note: Your offer amount must equal or exceed (*) the amount shown in Box U.

Note: Do not compute your offer amount using 13a or 13b if your statute expiration date(s) is less than 5 years from the date of your offer. Instead, refer to page 5 under "Deferred Payment Offer" options 1 through 3.

* Unless you are submitting an offer under effective tax administration or doubt as to collectibility with special circumstances considerations, as described on page 3.

11

¶1455

Completing Form 656, Offer in Compromise

We have included two Offer in Compromise forms. Use one form to submit your offer in compromise. You may use the other form as a worksheet and retain it for your personal records.

Note: If you have any questions about completing this form, you may call 1–800–829–1040 or visit your local IRS office or our website at www.irs.ustreas.gov/ind_info/oic/index.html. We may return your offer if you don't follow these instructions.

Item 1:

Enter your name and home or business address. You should also include a mailing address, if it is different from your street address.

Show both names on joint offers for joint liabilities. If you owe one liability by yourself (such as employment taxes), and other liabilities jointly (such as income taxes), but only you are submitting an offer, list all tax liabilities on one Form 656. If you owe one liability yourself and another jointly, and both parties submit an offer, **complete two Forms 656**, one for the individual liability and one for the joint liability.

Item 2:

Enter the social security number(s) for the person(s) submitting the offer. For example, enter the social security number of both spouses when submitting a joint offer for a joint tax liability. However, when only one spouse submits an offer, enter only that spouse's social security number.

Item 3:

Enter the employer identification number for offers from businesses.

Item 4:

Show the employer identification numbers for all other businesses (excluding corporate entities) that you own or in which you have an ownership interest.

Item 5:

Identify your tax liability and enter the tax year or period. Letters and notices from us and Notices of Federal Tax Lien show the tax periods for trust fund recovery penalties.

Item 6:

Check the appropriate box (es) describing the basis for your offer.

Doubt as to Liability offers require a statement describing in detail why you think you do not owe the liability. Complete Item 9, "Explanation of Circumstances," explaining your situation.

Doubt as to Collectibility offers require you to complete a Form 433-A, *Collection Information Statement for Wage Earners and Self-Employed Individuals*, if you are an individual taxpayer, or a Form 433-B, *Collection Information Statement for Businesses*, if you are a corporation or other business taxpayer.

Effective Tax Administration offers require you to complete a Form 433-A, *Collection Information Statement for Wage Earners and Self-Employed Individuals*, if you are an individual taxpayer, or a Form 433-B, *Collection Information Statement for Businesses*, if you are a corporation or other business taxpayer. Complete Item 9, "Explanation of Circumstances."

Note: Staple in the upper left corner the six (6) pages of the collection information statement before you send it to us.

12

¶1455

Item 7:	Enter the total amount of your offer (see page 3, "Determine Your Offer Amount"). Your offer amount cannot include a refund we owe you or amounts you have already paid.	Check the appropriate payment box (cash, short-term deferred payment or deferred payment — see page 4, "Determine Your Payment Terms") and describe your payment plan in the spaces provided.
Item 8:	It is important that you understand the requirements listed in this section. Pay particular attention to Items 8(d)	and 8(g), as they address the future compliance provision and refunds.
Item 9:	Explain your reason(s) for submitting your offer in the "Explanation of	Circumstances." You may attach additional sheets if necessary.
Item 10:	Explain where you will get the funds to pay the amount you are offering.	
Item 11:	All persons submitting the offer must sign and date Form 656. Include titles of authorized corporate officers, executors, trustees, Powers of Attorney, etc. where applicable.	*Note: Staple in the upper left corner the four (4) pages of Form 656 before you send it to us.*

Where to File

IF YOU RESIDE IN

the states of Alaska, Alabama, Arizona, California, Colorado, Hawaii, Idaho, Kentucky, Louisiana, Mississippi, Montana, Nevada, New Mexico, Oregon, Tennessee, Texas, Utah, Washington, Wisconsin or Wyoming,

AND	AND
You are a wage earner or a self-employed individual without employees,	You are **OTHER** than wage earner or a self-employed individual without employees,
THEN MAIL	THEN MAIL
Form 656 and attachments to:	Form 656 and attachments to:
Memphis Internal Revenue Service Center COIC Unit **PO Box 30803, AMC** Memphis, TN 38130-0803	Memphis Internal Revenue Service Center COIC Unit **PO Box 30804, AMC** Memphis, TN 38130-0804

IF YOU RESIDE IN

Arkansas, Connecticut, Delaware, District of Columbia, Florida, Georgia, Illinois, Indiana, Iowa, Kansas, Maine, Maryland, Massachusetts, Michigan, Minnesota, Missouri, Nebraska, New Hampshire, New Jersey, New York, North Carolina, North Dakota, Ohio, Oklahoma, Pennsylvania, Puerto Rico, Rhode Island, South Carolina, South Dakota, Vermont, Virginia, West Virginia or have a foreign address,

AND	AND
You are a wage earner or a self-employed individual without employees,	You are **OTHER** than wage earner or a self-employed individual without employees,
THEN MAIL	THEN MAIL
Form 656 and attachments to:	Form 656 and attachments to:
Brookhaven Internal Revenue Service Center COIC Unit **PO Box 9007** Holtsville, NY 11742-9007	Brookhaven Internal Revenue Service Center COIC Unit **PO Box 9008** Holtsville, NY 11742-9008

13

¶1455

IRS

Department of the Treasury
Internal Revenue Service

www.irs.gov

Form 656 (Rev. 5-2001)
Catalog Number 16728N

Form 656

Offer in Compromise

IRS RECEIVED DATE

Item 1 — Taxpayer's Name and Home or Business Address

Name
_____

Name
_____

Street Address
_____

City _____ State _____ ZIP Code _____

Mailing Address *(if different from above)*

DATE RETURNED

Street Address
_____

City _____ State _____ ZIP Code _____

Item 2 — Social Security Numbers

(a) Primary _____

(b) Secondary _____

Item 3 — Employer Identification Number *(included in offer)*

_____

Item 4 — Other Employer Identification Numbers *(not included in offer)* _____
_____
_____

Item 5 — To: Commissioner of Internal Revenue Service

I/We (includes all types of taxpayers) submit this offer to compromise the tax liabilities plus any interest, penalties, additions to tax, and additional amounts required by law (tax liability) for the tax type and period marked below: (Please mark an "X" in the box for the correct description and fill-in the correct tax period(s), adding additional periods if needed).

❏ **1040/1120 Income Tax** — Year(s) _____

❏ **941 Employer's Quarterly Federal Tax Return** — Quarterly period(s) _____

❏ **940 Employer's Annual Federal Unemployment (FUTA) Tax Return** — Year(s) _____

❏ **Trust Fund Recovery Penalty** as a responsible person of (enter corporation name) _____ ,

for failure to pay withholding and Federal Insurance Contributions Act Taxes (Social Security taxes), for period(s) ending _____ .

❏ **Other Federal Tax(es)** [specify type(s) and period(s)] _____
_____

Note: If you need more space, use another sheet titled "Attachment to Form 656 Dated_____ ." Sign and date the attachment following the listing of the tax periods.

Item 6 — I/We submit this offer for the reason(s) checked below:

❏ **Doubt as to Liability** — "I do not believe I owe this amount." You must include a detailed explanation of the reason(s) why you believe you do not owe the tax in Item 9.

❏ **Doubt as to Collectibility** — "I have insufficient assets and income to pay the full amount." You must include a complete Collection Information Statement, Form 433-A and/or Form 433-B.

❏ **Effective Tax Administration** — "I owe this amount and have sufficient assets to pay the full amount, but due to my exceptional circumstances, requiring full payment would cause an economic hardship or would be unfair and inequitable." You must include a complete Collection Information Statement, Form 433-A and/or Form 433B **and** complete Item 9.

Item 7

I/We offer to pay $ _____ (must be more than zero). Complete item 10 to explain where you will obtain the funds to make this offer.

Check one of the following:

❏ **Cash Offer (Offered amount will be paid in 90 days or less.)**

Balance to be paid in: ❏ 10; ❏ 30; ❏ 60; or ❏ 90 days from written notice of acceptance of the offer.

❏ **Short-Term Deferred Payment Offer (Offered amount will be paid in MORE than 90 days but within 24 months from written notice of acceptance of the offer.)**

$_____ within_____ days (not more than 90 — See Instructions Section, **Determine Your Payment Terms**) from written notice of acceptance of the offer; and

beginning in the _____ month after written notice of acceptance of the offer, $_____ on the _____ day of each month for a total of _____ months. (Cannot extend more than 24 months from written notice of acceptance of the offer.)

❏ **Deferred Payment Offer (Offered amount will be paid over the life of the collection statute.)**

$_____ within_____ days (not more than 90 — See Instructions Section, **Determine Your Payment Terms**) from written notice of acceptance of the offer; and

beginning in the first month after written notice of acceptance of the offer, $_____ on the _____ day of each month for a total of _____ months.

NOTE: Signature(s) of taxpayer required on last page of Form 656

Item 8 — By submitting this offer, I/we understand and agree to the following conditions:

(a) I/We voluntarily submit all payments made on this offer.

(b) The IRS will apply payments made under the terms of this offer in the best interest of the government.

(c) If the IRS rejects or returns the offer or I/we withdraw the offer, the IRS will return any amount paid with the offer. If I/we agree in writing, IRS will apply the amount paid with the offer to the amount owed. If I/we agree to apply the payment, the date the IRS received the offer remittance will be considered the date of payment. I/We understand that the IRS will not pay interest on any amount I/we submit with the offer.

(d) I/We will comply with all provisions of the Internal Revenue Code relating to filing my/our returns and paying my/our required taxes for 5 years or until the offered amount is paid in full, whichever is longer. In the case of a jointly submitted offer to compromise joint tax liabilities, I/we understand that default with respect to the compliance provisions described in this paragraph by one party to this agreement will not result in the default of the entire agreement. The default provisions described in Item 8(n) of this agreement will be applied only to the party failing to comply with the requirements of this paragraph. This provision does not apply to offers based on Doubt as to Liability.

(e) I/We waive and agree to the suspension of any statutory periods of limitation (time limits provided for by law) for the IRS assessment of the tax liability for the periods identified in Item 5. I/We understand that I/we have the right not to waive these statutory periods or to limit the waiver to a certain length or to certain issues. I/We understand, however, that the IRS may not consider this offer if I/we refuse to waive the statutory periods for assessment or if we provide only a limited waiver. The amount of any Federal tax due for the periods described in Item 5 may be assessed at any time prior to the acceptance of this offer or within one year of the rejection of this offer.

(f) The IRS will keep all payments and credits made, received or applied to the total original tax liability before submission of this offer. The IRS may keep any proceeds from a levy served prior to submission of the offer, but not received at the time the offer is submitted. If I/we have an installment agreement prior to submitting the offer, I/we must continue to make the payments as agreed while this offer is pending. Installment agreement payments will not be applied against the amount offered.

(g) As additional consideration beyond the amount of my/our offer, the IRS will keep any refund, including interest, due to me/us because of overpayment of any tax or other liability, for tax periods extending through the calendar year that the IRS accepts the offer. I/We may not designate an overpayment ordinarily subject to refund, to which the IRS is entitled, to be applied to estimated tax payments for the following year. This condition does not apply if the offer is based on Doubt as to Liability.

(h) I/We will return to the IRS any refund identified in (g) received after submission of this offer. This condition does not apply to offers based on Doubt as to Liability.

(i) The IRS cannot collect more than the full amount of the tax liability under this offer.

(j) I/We understand that I/we remain responsible for the full amount of the tax liability, unless and until the IRS accepts the offer in writing and I/we have met all the terms and conditions of the offer. The IRS will not remove the original amount of the tax liability from its records until I/we have met all the terms of the offer.

NOTE: Signature(s) of taxpayer required on last page of Form 656

(k) I/We understand that the tax I/we offer to compromise is and will remain a tax liability until I/we meet all the terms and conditions of this offer. If I/we file bankruptcy before the terms and conditions of this offer are completed, any claim the IRS files in the bankruptcy proceedings will be a tax claim.

(l) Once the IRS accepts the offer in writing, I/we have no right to contest, in court or otherwise, the amount of the tax liability.

(m) The offer is pending starting with the date an authorized IRS official signs this form. The offer remains pending until an authorized IRS official accepts, rejects, returns or acknowledges withdrawal of the offer in writing. If I/we appeal an IRS rejection decision on the offer, the IRS will continue to treat the offer as pending until the Appeals Office accepts or rejects the offer in writing. If I/we don't file a protest within 30 days of the date the IRS notifies me/us of the right to protest the decision, I/we waive the right to a hearing before the Appeals Office about the offer in compromise.

(n) If I/We fail to meet any of the terms and conditions of the offer and the offer defaults, then the IRS may:

- immediately file suit to collect the entire unpaid balance of the offer

- immediately file suit to collect an amount equal to the original amount of the tax liability as liquidating damages, minus any payment already received under the terms of this offer

- disregard the amount of the offer and apply all amounts already paid under the offer against the original amount of the tax liability

- file suit or levy to collect the original amount of the tax liability, without further notice of any kind.

The IRS will continue to add interest, as Section 6601 of the Internal Revenue Code requires, on the amount the IRS determines is due after default. The IRS will add interest from the date the offer is defaulted until I/we completely satisfy the amount owed.

(o) The IRS generally files a Notice of Federal Tax Lien to protect the Government's interest on deferred payment offers. This tax lien will be released when the payment terms of the offer agreement have been satisfied.

(p) I/We understand that the IRS employees may contact third parties in order to respond to this request and I authorize the IRS to make such contacts. Further, by authorizing the Internal Revenue Service to contact third parties, I understand that I will not receive notice, pursuant to section 7602(c) of the Internal Revenue Code, of third parties contacted in connection with this request.

NOTE: Signature(s) of taxpayer required on last page of Form 656

Item 9 — Explanation of Circumstances

I am requesting an offer in compromise for the reason(s) listed below:

Note: If you are requesting compromise based on doubt as to liability, explain why you don't believe you owe the tax. If you believe you have special circumstances affecting your ability to fully pay the amount due, explain your situation. You may attach additional sheets if necessary.

_____

_____

_____

_____

_____

_____

_____

_____

_____

_____

_____

_____

_____

_____

_____

_____

_____

_____

Item 10 — Source of Funds

I/we shall obtain the funds to make this offer from the following source(s):

_____

_____

_____

Item 11

If I/we submit this offer on a substitute form, I/we affirm that this form is a verbatim duplicate of the official Form 656, and I/we agree to be bound by all the terms and conditions set forth in the official Form 656.

Under penalties of perjury, I declare that I have examined this offer, including accompanying schedules and statements, and to the best of my knowledge and belief, it is true, correct and complete.

_____
11(a) Signature of Taxpayer

_____
Date

_____
11(b) Signature of Taxpayer

_____
Date

For Official Use Only

I accept the waiver of the statutory period of limitations for the Internal Revenue Service.

_____
Signature of Authorized Internal Revenue Service Official

_____
Title

_____
Date

NOTE: Signature(s) of taxpayer required on last page of Form 656

¶1455

¶1456 Exhibit 14-6

IRS Mission:

Provide America's
taxpayers top quality
service by helping them
understand and meet
their tax responsibilities
and by applying the tax
law with integrity and
fairness to all.

What You Should Know About

The IRS Collection Process

Keep this publication for future reference   **Publication 594**

If our records show that you owe us, we usually send this publication with your final bill. If you owe the tax shown on the bill we sent to you, please arrange to pay it immediately. If you believe the bill is incorrect, call us now so that we may correct the mistake. We urge you to settle your tax account now so that we don't have to take any further action to collect the taxes you owe.

This publication tells you the steps the Internal Revenue Service (IRS) may take to collect overdue taxes. **This publication includes a summary of your rights and responsibilities concerning paying your federal taxes.**

Inside you will find a number of titles of IRS forms and publications that apply to the various situations discussed. For a complete list of these documents, see page 12. For copies of these documents, please call us, write to us, visit your local library or IRS office, or contact us at our web site. See the next page for the contact information that you'll need. Please contact us right away; we will work with you to solve your tax problem.

Please note that the information in this document applies to all taxpayers — for example, individuals who owe income tax and employers who owe employment tax. At the end of this publication, we've included a separate section for special rules that apply to employers only.

This document is for information only. Although it discusses the legal authority that allows the IRS to collect taxes, it is not a precise and technical analysis of the law.

Department of the Treasury
Internal Revenue Service

w w w . i r s . g o v

Publication 594 (Rev. 2-2004)
Catalog Number 46596B

---

en español

Existe una versión de esta publicación en español, la Publicación 594SP, que puede obtener en la oficina local del Servicio de Impuestos Internos.

What's inside. . .

Do you have questions or need help right away? Call us. We're here to help you.

For tax information and help:

Call the number on the bill you received.

For tax forms and publications:

1–800–829–3676

1–800–829–4059 / TDD

Internet: www.irs.gov

- FTP — ftp.irs.ustreas.gov

- Telnet — iris.irs.ustreas.gov

- Interactive calculator on IRS
  Installment Agreement (IA) URL

You'll find answers to frequently asked tax questions, tax forms online, publications, hot tax issues and news, and help through e-mail.

If you prefer to write to us. . .

Enclose a copy of your tax bill. If you do not have a copy of your bill, print your name, social security number or taxpayer identification number, and the tax form and period shown on your bill. Write to us at the address shown on your tax bill.

You can also visit your nearest IRS office.

You'll find the exact address in your local phone book under U.S. Government.

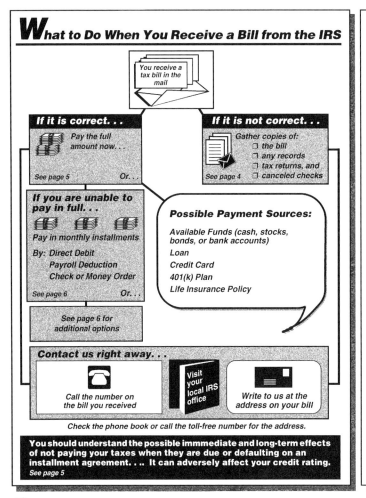

What to Do When You Receive a Bill from the IRS

You receive a tax bill in the mail

If it is correct. . .

Pay the full amount now. . .

See page 5   Or. . .

If you are unable to pay in full. . .

Pay in monthly installments

By: Direct Debit
     Payroll Deduction
     Check or Money Order

See page 6   Or. . .

See page 6 for additional options

If it is not correct. . .

Gather copies of:
☐ the bill
☐ any records
☐ tax returns, and
See page 4   ☐ canceled checks

Possible Payment Sources:

Available Funds (cash, stocks, bonds, or bank accounts)
Loan
Credit Card
401(k) Plan
Life Insurance Policy

Contact us right away. . .

Call the number on the bill you received

Visit your local IRS office

Write to us at the address on your bill

Check the phone book or call the toll-free number for the address.

You should understand the possible immmediate and long-term effects of not paying your taxes when they are due or defaulting on an installment agreement. . .. It can adversely affect your credit rating.
See page 5

Avoid Having Overdue Taxes Next Year

▶ If you owe taxes because you did not have enough money withheld from your income, you should claim a lower number of allowances on your Form W-4 or Form W-4P. See Publication 919, *Is My Withholding Correct?*

▶ Take advantage of the Electronic Federal Tax Payment System. See Publication 966, check website at: *www.eftps.gov.*, call 1–800–555–4477 or 1–800–945–8400.

▶ If you owe tax, you should increase your estimated tax payments. See Publication 505, *Tax Withholding and Estimated Tax.*

▶ If you are an employer, see Publication 15, *Circular E, Employer's Tax Guide.*

*I*mportant Information You Should Know

You have the right to be treated professionally, fairly, promptly, and courteously by IRS employees. Among other rights, you have the right to:

▶ disagree with your tax bill,

▶ meet with an IRS manager if you disagree with the IRS employee who handles your tax case,

▶ appeal most IRS collection actions,

▶ have your case transferred to a different IRS office if you have a valid reason (such as if you move),

▶ be represented by someone when dealing with IRS matters, and

▶ receive a receipt for any payment you make.

For details about your rights, see Publication 1, *Your Rights as a Taxpayer.* You received a copy of it with your first bill.

– 3 –

¶1456

If you disagree with our decisions. . .

Fast Track Mediation Process

If you disagree with any or all of the IRS findings, you may request the Fast Track Mediation services to help you resolve disputes resulting from collection or examination. The Fast Track Mediation offers an expedited process with a trained mediator, who will help facilitate communication, in a neutral setting. The mediator will work within the law to resolve the issues, but does not have the authority to require either party to accept the resolution.

Most cases qualify for the Fast Track Mediation. To begin the process, you may request the IRS representative arrange a mediation meeting. Both you and the IRS representative must agree to participate in mediation, and sign an agreement to mediate form. The IRS representative will send the signed agreement to the local Appeals Office, which will assign a mediator. Generally, within a week, the mediator will contact you and the IRS representative to schedule a meeting. The mediator will give you a brief explanation of the Fast Track Mediation process and set up a mutually agreeable time and place to hold your mediation session.

For additional information, refer to Publication 3605, *Fast Tract Mediation — A Process for Prompt Resolution of Tax Issues*.

If any issues remain unresolved, or if you decide not to use the Fast Track Mediation process, you still have the right to use the normal appeal process.

Appeal Process

If you disagree with the decision of an IRS employee at any time during the collection process, you can ask that employee's manager to review your case.

When you ask for a review, the employee will refer you to a manager. The manager will either speak with you then or will return your call by the next work day.

If you disagree with the manager's decision, you have the right to file an appeal under the Collection Appeals Program. This program enables you to appeal most collection actions we may take, including filing a lien, placing a levy on your wages or bank account, or seizing your property. You also will have an opportunity to request a Collection Due Process (CDP) hearing with the Office of Appeals after the initial filing of a Notice of Federal Tax Lien. This opportunity takes place prior to the initial levy action, unless collection of the tax is in jeopardy or the levy is on your state tax refund. In these two cases, you can ask for a CDP hearing after the levy. See Publication 1660, *Collection Appeal Rights* for more information.

If you want someone to represent you. . .

When dealing with the IRS, you may choose to represent yourself, or you may have an attorney, a certified public accountant, an enrolled agent, or any person enrolled to practice before the IRS represent you. For example, you may want your representative to respond to a tax bill that you believe is incorrect.

If your representative appears without you, he or she must file a Form 2848, *Power of Attorney and Declaration of Representative*, or Form 8821, *Tax Information Authorization*, before being allowed to receive or inspect confidential material.

Other items to note. . .

- ▶ **The IRS can share your tax information** — By law, the IRS can share your tax information with city and state tax agencies, and in some cases with the Department of Justice, other federal agencies, and people you authorize. We can also share it with certain foreign governments under tax treaty provisions.

- ▶ **We may contact a third party** — The law allows us to contact someone else, such as neighbors, banks, employers, or employees, to investigate your case.

- ▶ **If you are involved in bankruptcy proceedings** — Contact your local IRS office. While the proceeding may not eliminate your tax debt, it may temporarily stop IRS enforcement action from collecting a debt related to the bankruptcy.

- ▶ **Help for an innocent spouse** — In some cases, you may not be responsible for taxes, interest, and penalties on a joint income tax return. Contact your local IRS office for more information. For information about your rights as an innocent spouse, see Publication 971, *Innocent Spouse Relief*. For information on three ways to get help with the amount you owe, see Form 8857, *Request for Innocent Spouse Relief (And Separation of Liability and Equitable Relief)*.

What if you believe your bill is wrong?

If you believe your bill is wrong, let us know as soon as possible.

- Write to the IRS office that sent you the bill,
- Call the IRS office that sent you the bill, or
- Visit your local IRS office.

To help us correct the problem, gather a copy of the bill along with copies of any records, tax returns, and canceled checks, etc., that will help us understand why you believe your bill is wrong.

If you write to us, tell us why you believe your bill is wrong. With your letter, include copies of all the documents you gathered to explain your case. Please do not send original documents. If we find you are correct, we will adjust your account and, if necessary, send you a corrected bill.

¶1456

What to Do When You Owe Taxes

Options to Pay Your Taxes

When you file your tax return, we check to see if the math is accurate and if you have paid the correct amount. If you have not paid all you owe, we send a bill called a *Notice of Tax Due and Demand for Payment*. The bill includes the taxes, plus interest and penalties. We encourage you to pay as soon as possible. You may pay your taxes by credit card, electronic funds transfer, check, money order or cash. Take advantage of the Electronic Federal Tax Payment System (EFTPS) to pay by electronic funds transfer. See Publication 966, check website at *www.eftps.gov* or call 1–800–555–4477 or 1–800–945–8400.

Taxpayers may initiate a credit card payment by contacting:

▶ Official Payments Corporation at 1–800–2PAYTAX (1–800–272–9829) or online at *www.officialpayments.com*, or

▶ Link2Gov at 1–888–PAY1040 (1–888–729–1040) or online at *www.pay1040.com*.

It is in your best interest to pay your tax liability in full to minimize the amount of interest and penalty charged. The interest rate your credit card issuer or bank charges may be lower than the combination of interest and penalties imposed by the Internal Revenue Code. For further information on interest and penalty rates, see Alternative Payment Options Truth in Lending, which is available at *www.irs.gov*.

What If You Cannot Fully Pay Your Taxes?

If you cannot pay all your taxes now, pay as much as you can. By paying now, you reduce the amount of interest and penalty you will owe. Then immediately call, write, or visit the nearest IRS office to explain your situation.

After you explain your situation, we may ask you to fill out a Collection Information Statement to help us compare your monthly income with your expenses to determine the amount you can pay. Based on your situation, we may work with you to consider several different ways to pay:

▶ You may be able to make monthly payments through an installment agreement. We can set up a direct debit from your financial institution or a payroll deduction from your wages or salary.

▶ You may qualify for a temporary delay if your case is considered a significant hardship. (See page 6.)

▶ In some cases, you may qualify for an Offer in Compromise. (See page 6.)

By law, the IRS has the authority to collect outstanding federal taxes for ten years from the date your liability is due.

There is a special program to help you with tax problems that cannot be resolved through normal IRS channels. . .

The **Taxpayer Advocate Function** is an IRS program that provides an independent system to assure that tax problems, which have not been resolved through normal channels, are promptly and fairly handled. Each state and service center has at least one local Taxpayer Advocate, who is independent of the local IRS office and reports directly to the National Taxpayer Advocate. The Taxpayer Advocate can help if:

▶ You are suffering, or are about to suffer, a significant hardship,

▶ You are facing an immediate threat of adverse action,

▶ You will incur significant cost (including fees for professional representation),

▶ You will suffer irreparable injury or long-term adverse impact,

▶ You have experienced a delay of more than 30 days to resolve the issue,

▶ You have not received a response or resolution by the date promised, or

▶ Established systems or procedures have failed to operate as intended to resolve the problem or dispute.

You may apply for Taxpayer Advocate Function assistance by:

▶ Completing Form 911, *Application For Taxpayer Assistance Order* (ATAO),

▶ Completing a written request for assistance (if Form 911 is not available),

▶ Requesting an IRS employee complete a Form 911 on your behalf (in person or over the phone), or

▶ Sending (or FAX) Form 911 to your local Taxpayer Advocate. Refer to Publication 1546, *The Taxpayer Advocate Service of the IRS*, for your local Taxpayer Advocate's address, phone and FAX number. Call the Taxpayer Advocate Service's toll-free number: 1–877–777–4778; TDD 800–829–4059.

¶1456

If you enter into an installment agreement and you cannot fully pay the amount you owe within the normal collection period, the IRS may request you to sign a waiver to extend the collection period. The collection period is automatically extended when a taxpayer files for bankruptcy or an Offer in Compromise.

If you do not pay the taxes you owe and if you make no effort to pay them, we can ask you to take action to pay your taxes, such as selling or mortgaging any assets you have or getting a loan. If you still make no effort to pay your bill or to work out a payment plan, we may also take more serious action, such as levying your bank account, wages, or other income or assets. (See pages 7–10.)

Installment Agreements

Installment agreements allow the full payment of your debt in smaller, more manageable amounts. Installment agreements generally require equal monthly payments. The amount of your installment payment will be based on the amount you owe and your ability to pay that amount within the time available to the IRS to collect the tax debt from you. To be eligible for an installment agreement, you must file all returns that are required to be filed, and you should make your current estimated tax payment (if required). If you are an employer, you must be current with federal tax deposits.

A $43 user fee will be charged to set up your installment agreement. When you arrange for an installment agreement, you should pay by Direct Deposit (Form 9465) from your bank account or Payroll Deduction (Form 2159) from your wages. These two types of payment agreements will help you avoid defaulting your agreement by ensuring timely payments and preventing enforced collection action. These types of agreements will reduce the burden of you mailing the payments and save you postage.

You can secure:

> ▶ Form 9465: *Installment Agreement Request*, at *www.irs.gov*; by calling us at 1–800–TAX–FORM or visiting your local IRS office.

> ▶ Form 2159, *Payroll Deduction Agreement*, by calling the number on your notice or visiting your local IRS office. You should mail these completed forms to the address listed on your bill.

A Notice of Federal Tax Lien may be filed to secure the government's interest against other creditors. We cannot levy against your property:

> ▶ while your request for an installment agreement is being considered,

> ▶ while your agreement is in effect,

> ▶ for 30 days after your request for an agreement has been rejected, or

> ▶ for any period while an appeal of the rejection is being evaluated.

If you already have an approved installment agreement from a previous tax debt and your financial situation has changed, we may be able modify your monthly amount. A reinstatement fee of $24 may be charged. You may have to complete a Collection Information Statement explaining your financial situation.

A default of your installment agreement may cause the filing of a Notice of Federal Tax Lien and/or an IRS levy action. Either can be very damaging to your credit worthiness and cause financial difficulties.

Apply for an Offer in Compromise

The Internal Revenue Service (IRS) may accept an Offer in Compromise to settle unpaid tax accounts for less than the full amount of the balance due. This applies to all taxes, including any interest, penalties, or additional amounts arising under the internal revenue laws. We will charge you a $150.00 user fee for submitting an offer. To be considered for an Offer in Compromise, you must file all of your returns that are due and, if applicable, be current with all Federal Tax Deposits for the last two quarters.

The IRS may legally compromise a tax liability for one of the following reasons:

> ▶ *Doubt as to liability* — there is doubt as to whether or not the assessed tax is correct,

> ▶ *Doubt as to collectibility* — there is doubt that you could ever pay the full amount of the tax owed. In these cases, the total amount you owe must be greater than the sum of your assets and future income, or

> ▶ *Promote effective tax administration* — there is no doubt that the assessed tax is correct and no doubt that the amount owed could be collected, but you have an economic hardship or other special circumstances which may allow the IRS to accept less than the total balance due.

You may submit an Offer in Compromise by completing Form 656, *Offer in Compromise*. If you are basing your offer on doubt as to collectibility or promotion of effective tax administration, you must also submit Form 433-A, *Collection Information Statement for Individuals*. After acceptance of an offer, you must remain current with filing and paying requirements for five years.

Temporarily Delay the Collection Process

If we determine that you cannot pay any of your tax debt, we may temporarily delay collection until your financial condition improves. You should know that if we do delay collecting from you, your debt will increase because penalties and interest are charged until you pay the full amount. During a temporary delay, we will again review your ability to pay. We may also file a *Notice of Federal Tax Lien* (see page 7) to protect the government's interest in your assets.

About IRS Collection Actions

Before we take any action explained in this section, we will contact you to give you a chance to voluntarily pay what you owe. But if you do not pay your taxes in full and do not contact us to let us know why you cannot pay or why you disagree with our decision to take enforcement action, the law requires us to take action. We may:

- **File a lien** against your property (Make a legal claim to your property as security or payment for your tax debt) *(See the information below)*,

- **Serve a levy** on your property or salary (Legally seize your property to satisfy a tax debt) *(See page 8)*, or

- **Assess a trust fund recovery penalty** for employment taxes *(See page 11)*.

These *enforced collection actions* are the means by which we can enforce the *Notice and Demand for Tax Payment*. On the following pages, we explain these collection actions and the rules that govern them.

Liens

Liens give us a legal claim to your property as security for payment of your tax debt. The federal tax lien arises when:

- We assess the liability,

- We send you a *Notice and Demand for Payment*, a bill that tells you how much you owe in taxes, and

- You neglect or refuse to fully pay the debt within 10 days after we notify you about it.

We then may file a Notice of Federal Tax Lien. By filing a Notice of Federal Tax Lien, your creditors are publicly notified that we have a claim against all your property, including property you acquire after the lien was filed.

The lien attaches to all your property (such as your house or car) and to all your rights to property (such as your accounts receivable, if you are an employer).

Caution   Once a lien is filed, your credit rating may be harmed. You may not be able to get a loan to buy a house or a car, get a new credit card, or sign a lease.

Releasing a lien

We will issue a *Release of the Notice of Federal Tax Lien*:

- Within 30 days after you satisfy the tax due (including interest and other additions) by paying the debt or by having it adjusted, or

- Within 30 days after we accept a bond that you submit, guaranteeing payment of the debt.

In addition, you must pay all fees that a state or other jurisdiction charges you to file and release the lien. These fees will be added to the amount you owe. See Publication 1450, *Request for Release of Federal Tax Lien*.

Usually 10 years after a tax is assessed, a lien releases automatically if we have not filed it again. If we knowingly or negligently do not release a *Notice of Federal Tax Lien* when it should be released, you may sue the federal government, but not IRS employees, for damages.

Payoff amount

The full amount of your lien will remain a matter of public record until it is paid in full. However, at any time you may request an updated lien payoff amount to show the remaining balance due. An IRS employee (either over the toll-free customer service telephone line, or at a walk-in counter service site, or your local IRS lien desk) can issue you a letter with the current amount that must be paid before we release the Notice of Federal Lien.

¶1456

Applying for a discharge of a Notice of Federal Tax Lien

If you are giving up ownership of property, such as when you sell your home, you may apply for a *Certificate of Discharge*. Each application for a discharge of a tax lien releases the effects of the lien against one piece of property. Note that when certain conditions exist, a third party may also request a *Certificate of Discharge*. If you're selling your primary residence, you may apply for a taxpayer relocation expense allowance. Certain conditions and limitations apply. See Publication 783, *Instructions on How to Apply for a Certificate of Discharge of Property from the Federal Tax Lien.*

Making the IRS lien secondary to another lien

In some cases, a creditor may refuse to extend credit to you unless their lien will be satisfied before the Notice of Federal Tax Lien. Subordination is the process that can make a federal tax lien secondary to another lien. For more information, see Publication 784, *How to Prepare Application for Certificate of Subordination of Federal Tax Lien.*

Withdrawing liens

We may, at our discretion, withdraw a filed Notice of Federal Tax Lien if:

- the notice was filed too soon or not according to IRS procedures,

- you entered into an installment agreement to pay the debt on the notice of lien (unless the agreement provides otherwise),

- withdrawal will speed collecting the tax, or

- withdrawal would be in your best interest (as determined by the Taxpayer Advocate) and the best interest of the government.

We will give you a copy of the withdrawal, and if you send us a written request, we will send a copy to other institutions you name.

Appealing the filing of a lien

The law requires us to notify you in writing not more than 5 business days after the filing of a lien. We may give you this notice in person, leave it at your home or your usual place of business, or send it by certified or registered mail to your last known address. You may (except if you are designated as a nominee and/or alter-ego) ask an IRS manager to review your case, or you may request a Collection Due Process hearing with the Office of Appeals, by filing a request for a hearing with the office listed on your notice. You must file your request by the date shown on your notice. Some of the issues you may discuss include:

- You paid all you owed before we filed the lien,

- We assessed the tax and filed the lien when you were in bankruptcy and subject to the automatic stay during bankruptcy,

- We made a procedural error in an assessment,

- The time to collect the tax (called the Statute of Limitations) expired before we filed the lien,

- You did not have an opportunity to dispute the assessed liability,

- You wish to discuss the collection options, or

- You wish help, as an innocent spouse.

At the conclusion of your Collection Due Process hearing, the IRS Office of Appeals will issue a determination. That determination may support the continued existence of the filed federal tax lien or it may determine that the lien should be released or withdrawn. You will have a 30-day period, starting with the date of the determination, to bring a suit to contest the determination. See Publication 1660, *Collection Appeal Rights*, for more information.

Levies

A levy is a legal seizure of your property to satisfy a tax debt. Levies are different from liens. A lien is a claim *used as security* for the tax debt, while a levy actually *takes the property* to satisfy the tax debt.

If you do not pay your taxes (or make arrangements to settle your debt), the IRS may seize and sell any type of real or personal property that you own or have an interest in. For instance:

- We could seize and sell property that you hold (such as your car, boat, or house), or

- We could levy property that is yours but is held by someone else (such as your wages, retirement accounts, dividends, bank accounts, rental income, accounts receivables, the cash value of your life insurance, or commissions).

We usually levy only after these three requirements are met:

- We assessed the tax and sent you a *Notice and Demand for Payment*,

- You neglected or refused to pay the tax, and

⬧ We sent you a *Final Notice of Intent to Levy* and *Notice of Your Right to A Hearing* (levy notice) at least 30 days before the levy. We may give you this notice in person, leave it at your home or your usual place of business, or send it to your last known address by certified mail, return receipt requested. Please note: if we levy your state tax refund, you may receive a Notice of Levy on Your State Tax Refund, Notice of Your Right to Hearing after the levy.

You may ask an IRS manager to review your case, or you may request a Collection Due Process hearing with the Office of Appeals by filing a request for a Collection Due Process hearing with the IRS office listed on your notice. You must file your request within 30 days of the date on your notice. Some of the issues you may discuss include:

⬧ You paid all you owed before we sent the levy notice,

⬧ We assessed the tax and sent the levy notice when you were in bankruptcy and subject to the automatic stay during bankruptcy,

⬧ We made a procedural error in an assessment,

⬧ The time to collect the tax (called the statute of limitations) expired before we sent the levy notice,

⬧ You did not have an opportunity to dispute the assessed liability,

⬧ You wish to discuss the collection options, or

⬧ You wish to make a spousal defense.

At the conclusion of your hearing, the Office of Appeals will issue a determination. You will have 30-days after the determination date to bring a suit to contest the determination. See Publication 1660, *Collection Appeal Rights*, for more information.

If your property is levied or seized, contact the employee who took the action. You also may ask the manager to review your case. If the matter is still unresolved, the manager can explain your rights to appeal to the Office of Appeals.

Levying your wages, federal payments, such as federal retirement or federal vendor payments, or your bank account

If we levy your wages or federal payments, the levy will end when:

⬧ The levy is released,

⬧ You pay your tax debt, or

⬧ The time expires for legally collecting the tax.

If we levy your bank account, for 21 days your bank must hold funds you have on deposit — up to the amount you owe. This period allows you time to solve any problems from the levy. After 21 days, the bank must send the money, plus interest if it applies, to the IRS.

To discuss your case, call the IRS employee whose name is shown on the *Notice of Levy*.

Filing a claim for reimbursement when we made a mistake in levying your account

If you paid bank charges because of a mistake we made when we levied your account, you may be entitled to a reimbursement. To be reimbursed, you must file a claim with us within 1 year after your bank charged you the fee. Use Form 8546, *Claim for Reimbursement of Bank Charges Incurred Due to Erroneous Service Levy or Misplaced Payment Check*.

Levying your federal payments through the Federal Payment Levy Program

Under the Federal Payment Levy Program, if you owe the IRS, in order to pay that debt, we may levy (take) monies from the following federal payments that you may receive: retirement from the Office of Personnel Management, social security benefits, federal vendor payments, federal employee salaries, or federal employee travel advances and reimbursements. This program electronically levies your federal payments paid through the Department of Treasury, Financial Management Service (FMS). If we electronically levy your federal payments, the levy will take 15% from each of the payments until the account is resolved. If you already are working with an IRS employee, call that employee for assistance. If you are not working with an employee, and you receive federal vendor payments, please call 1–800–829–3903 for assistance. If you are not working with an employee, and you receive any other federal payment, please call 1–800–829–7650 for assistance.

Releasing a levy

We must release your levy if any of the following occur:

⬧ You pay the tax, penalty, and interest you owe,

⬧ We discover that the time for collection (the *statute of limitations*) ended before the levy was served,

⬧ We decide that the documentation you provided proves that releasing the levy will help us to collect the tax,

⬧ You have an installment agreement, or enter into one, unless the agreement says the levy does not have to be released,

⬧ We determine that the levy is creating a significant economic hardship for you, or

⬧ The fair market value of the property exceeds the liability for which the levy was made, and release of the levy on part of the property can be made without hindering the collection of the liability.

Releasing your property

Before the sale date, we may release the property if:

⬧ You pay the amount of the government's interest in the property,

¶1456

- You enter into an escrow arrangement,
- You furnish an acceptable bond,
- You make an acceptable agreement for paying the tax, or
- The expense of selling your property would be greater than the Government's interest in the property.

Returning levied property

If you request the return of levied property within nine months from the date of the levy, we can consider returning the property if:

- We levy before we send you the two required notices or before your time for responding to them has passed (ten days for the *Notice and Demand*; 30 days for the *Notice of Intent to Levy* and the *Notice of Right to Hearing*),
- We did not follow our own procedures,
- We agree to let you pay in installments, but we still levy, and the agreement does not say that we can do so,
- Returning the property will help you pay your taxes, or
- Returning the property is in both your best interests (as determined by the National Taxpayer Advocate) and the government's best interest.

Selling your property

We will post a public notice of a pending sale, usually in local newspapers or flyers. We will deliver the original notice of sale to you or send it to you by certified mail.

After placing the notice, we must wait at least ten days before conducting the sale, unless the property is perishable and must be sold immediately.

Before the sale, we will compute a *minimum bid price*. This bid is usually 80% or more of the forced sale value of the property, after subtracting any liens.

If you disagree with this price, you can appeal it. Ask that the price be computed again by either an IRS or private appraiser.

You may also ask that we sell the seized property within 60 days. For information about how to do so, call the IRS employee who made the seizure. We will grant your request, unless it is in the government's best interest to hold the property for a later sale. We will send you a letter telling you of our decision on your request. After the sale, we first use the proceeds to pay the expenses of the levy and sale. Then we use any remaining amount to pay the tax bill.

- ***If the proceeds of the sale are less than the total of the tax bill and the expenses of levy and sale***, you will still have to pay the unpaid tax.

- ***If the proceeds of the sale are more than the total of the tax bill and the expenses of the levy and sale***, we will notify you about the surplus money and will tell you how to ask for a refund. However, if someone, such as a mortgagee or other lienholder, makes a claim that is superior to yours, we will pay that claim before we refund any money to you.

Redeeming your real estate

You (or anyone with an interest in the property) may redeem your real estate within 180 days after the sale. You must pay the purchaser the amount paid for the property, plus interest at 20% annually.

Some property cannot be levied or seized

By law, some property cannot be levied or seized. We may not seize any of your property unless we have determined that we expect there to be net proceeds to apply to the liability. In addition, we may not seize or levy your property on the day you attend a collection interview because of a summons.

Other items we may not levy or seize include:

- School books and certain clothing,
- Fuel, provisions, furniture, and personal effects for a household totaling $6,890,[*]
- Books and tools you use in your trade, business, or profession, totaling $3,440,[*]
- Unemployment benefits,
- Undelivered mail,
- Certain annuity and pension benefits,
- Certain service-connected disability payments,
- Workmen's compensation,
- Salary, wages, or income included in a judgment for court-ordered child support payments,
- Certain public assistance payments, or
- A minimum weekly exemption for wages, salary, and other income.

Use Publication 1494, *Table of Figuring Amount Exempt from Levy on Wages, Salary and Other Income* (Forms 668-W(c)(DO) and 668-W(c)), to determine the amount of earned income exempt from levy.

---

[*]These amounts are indexed annually for inflation (these amounts are for calendar year 2003).

Employment Taxes for Employers

To encourage prompt payment of withheld income and employment taxes, including social security taxes, railroad retirement taxes, or collected excise taxes, Congress passed a law that provides for the Trust Fund Recovery Penalty. (These taxes are called *trust fund taxes* because you actually hold the employee's money in trust until you make a federal tax deposit in that amount.)

If we plan to assess you for the trust fund recovery penalty, we will send you a letter stating that you are a *responsible* person. You have 60 days after we send our letter to appeal our proposal. If you do not respond to our letter, we will assess the penalty against you and send you a *Notice and Demand for Payment*. Also, we can apply this penalty whether or not you are out of business.

A responsible person is an individual or group of people who had the duty to perform and the power to direct the collecting, accounting, and paying of trust fund taxes. This person may be:

- an officer or an employee of a corporation,

- a member or employee of a partnership,

- a corporate director or shareholder,

- a member of a board of trustees of a nonprofit organization, or

- another person with authority and control to direct the disbursement of funds.

Assessing the Trust Fund Recovery Penalty

We may assess the penalty against anyone:

- who is responsible for collecting or paying withheld income and employment taxes, or for paying collected excise taxes, and

- who willfully fails to collect or pay them.

Willfulness exists if the responsible person:

- knew about the unpaid taxes, and

- used the funds to keep the business going or allowed available funds to be paid to other creditors.

Especially for employers. . .

Employment taxes are:

- The amount you should withhold from your employees for both income and social security tax, plus

- The amount of social security tax you pay on behalf of each employee.

Caution   *If you ignore the federal tax deposit and filing requirements, the amount you owe can increase dramatically.*

If you do not pay your employment taxes on time, or if you were required to and did not include your payment with your return, we will charge you interest and penalties on any unpaid balance. We may charge you penalties of up to 15% of the amount not deposited, depending on how many days late you are.

If you do not pay withheld trust fund taxes, we may take additional collection action. We may require you to:

- File and pay your taxes monthly rather than quarterly, or

- Open a special bank account for the withheld amounts, under penalty of prosecution. See Form 8109, *Federal Tax Deposit Coupon* and Circular E, *Employer's Tax Guide*.

See publication 535, *Business Expenses*, for information on how to deduct interest paid as a business deduction.

– 11 –

Figuring the Penalty Amount

The amount of the penalty is equal to the unpaid balance of the trust fund tax. The penalty is computed based on:

▶ The unpaid income taxes that should have been withheld, or were withheld but not paid over, plus

▶ The employee's portion of the FICA tax that should have been withheld, or was withheld but not paid over.

For collected taxes, the penalty is based on the unpaid amount of collected excise taxes.

Caution Once we assert the penalty, we can take collection action against your personal assets. For instance, we can file a Notice of Federal Tax Lien against you, if you are a responsible person.

Appealing the Decision

You have the right to appeal a proposed assessment of the Trust Fund Recovery Penalty. [See Publication 5, *(Your Appeal Rights and How to Prepare a Protest if You Don't Agree)*, for a clear outline of the appeals process.]

We offer you a number of free publications and forms. . .

These IRS forms and publications mentioned in this document give you more information about the various situations discussed. For copies of these documents, call us, write to us, visit your local library or IRS office, or contact us at our website at **www.irs.gov**.

Forms

▶ Form 433-F, *Collection Information Statement*

▶ Form 911, *Application for Taxpayer Assistance Order*

▶ Form 656, *Offer in Compromise*

▶ Form 2159, *Payroll Deduction Agreement*

▶ Form 2848, *Power of Attorney and Declaration of Representative*

▶ Form 8109, *Federal Tax Deposit Coupon*

▶ Form 8821, *Tax Information Authorization*

▶ Form 8546, *Claim for Reimbursement of Bank Charges Incurred Due to Erroneous Service Levy or Misplaced Payment Check*

▶ Form 9465, *Installment Agreement Request*

Publications

▶ Publication 1, *Your Rights as a Taxpayer*

▶ Publication 5, *Your Appeal Rights and How to Prepare a Protest if You Don't Agree*

▶ Publication 15, *Circular E, Employer Tax Guide*

▶ Publication 783, *Instructions on How to Apply for a Certificate of Discharge of Property from the Federal Tax Lien*

▶ Publication 784, *How to Prepare Application for Certificate of Subordination of Federal Tax Lien*

▶ Publication 908, *Bankruptcy Tax Guide*

▶ Publication 919, *Is My Withholding Correct?*

▶ Publication 966, *Electronic Choices to Pay All Your Federal Taxes*

▶ Publication 1450, *Request for Release of Federal Tax Lien*

▶ Publication 1494, *Table of Figuring Amount Exempt from Levy on Wages, Salary and Other Income*

▶ Publication 1546, *The Taxpayer Advocate Service of the IRS*

▶ Publication 1660, *Collection Appeal Rights*

▶ Publication 3959, *EFTPS CD-Rom for Tax Practitioner & Financial Institutions*

– 12 –

¶1456

¶1457 Exhibit 14-7

Department of the Treasury
Internal Revenue Service

www.irs.gov

Form 433-A (Rev. 5-2001)
Catalog Number 20312N

Collection Information Statement for Wage Earners and Self-Employed Individuals

Complete all entry spaces with the most current data available.

Important! Write "N/A" (not applicable) in spaces that do not apply. We may require additional information to support "N/A" entries.

Failure to complete all entry spaces may result in rejection or significant delay in the resolution of your account.

Section 1
Personal Information

☐ Check this box when all spaces in Sect. 1 are filled in.

1. Full Name(s) _____

Street Address _____
City _____ State _____ Zip _____
County of Residence _____
How long at this address? _____

1a. Home
Telephone (___) _____

Best Time To Call:
_____ am _____ pm
(Enter Hour)

2. Marital Status:
☐ Married   ☐ Separated
☐ Unmarried (single, divorced, widowed)

3. Your Social Security No.(SSN) _____
4. Spouse's Social Security No. _____

3a. Your Date of Birth (mm/dd/yyyy) _____
4a. Spouse's Date of Birth (mm/dd/yyyy) _____

5. ☐ Own Home   ☐ Rent   ☐ Other (specify, i.e. share rent, live with relative) _____

6. List the dependents you can claim on your tax return: (Attach sheet if more space is needed.)

First Name	Relationship	Age	Does this person live with you?	First Name	Relationship	Age	Does this person live with you?
_____			☐ No ☐ Yes	_____			☐ No ☐ Yes
_____			☐ No ☐ Yes	_____			☐ No ☐ Yes

Section 2
Your Business Information

☐ Check this box when all spaces in Sect. 2 are filled in and attachments provided.

7. Are you or your spouse self-employed or operate a business? (Check "Yes" if either applies)

☐ No   ☐ Yes   If yes, provide the following information:

7a. Name of Business _____
7b. Street Address _____
City _____ State _____ Zip _____

7c. Employer Identification No., if available : _____
7d. Do you have employees?   ☐ No ☐ Yes
7e. Do you have accounts/notes receivable?   ☐ No ☐ Yes
If yes, please complete Section 8 on page 5.

ATTACHMENTS REQUIRED: Please include proof of self-employment income for the **prior 3 months** (e.g., invoices, commissions, sales records, income statement).

Section 3
Employment Information

☐ Check this box when all spaces in Sect. 3 are filled in and attachments provided.

8. Your Employer
Street Address _____
City _____ State _____ Zip _____
Work telephone no. (___) _____
May we contact you at work?   ☐ No ☐ Yes
8a. How long with this employer? _____
8b. Occupation

9. Spouse's Employer
Street Address _____
City _____ State _____ Zip _____
Work telephone no. (___)
May we contact you at work?   ☐ No ☐ Yes
9a. How long with this employer? _____
9b. Occupation

ATTACHMENTS REQUIRED: Please provide proof of gross earnings and deductions for the past 3 months from each employer (e.g., pay stubs, earnings statements). If year-to-date information is available, send only 1 such statement as long as a **minimum of 3 months** is represented.

Section 4
Other Income Information

☐ Check this box when all spaces in Sect. 4 are filled in and attachments provided.

10. Do you receive income from sources other than your own business or your employer? (Check all that apply.)

☐ Pension   ☐ Social Security   ☐ Other (specify, i.e. child support, alimony, rental) _____

ATTACHMENTS REQUIRED: Please provide proof of pension/social security/other income for the past 3 months from each payor, including any statements showing deductions. If year-to-date information is available, send only 1 such statement as long as a **minimum of 3 months** is represented.

Page 1 of 6

Section 5 begins on page 2 →
(Rev. 5-2001)

Collection Information Statement for Wage Earners and Self-Employed Individuals   Form 433-A

Name_____ SSN_____

Section 5

Banking,
Investment,
Cash, Credit,
and Life
Insurance
Information

*Complete all
entry spaces
with the most
current data
available.*

11. CHECKING ACCOUNTS. List all checking accounts. (If you need additional space, attach a separate sheet.)

Type of Account	Full Name of Bank, Savings & Loan, Credit Union or Financial Institution	Bank Routing No.	Bank Account No.	Current Account Balance
11a. Checking	Name ___ Street Address ___ City/State/Zip ___			$
11b. Checking	Name ___ Street Address ___ City/State/Zip ___		11c. Total Checking Account Balances	$ ___ / $

12. OTHER ACCOUNTS. List all accounts, including brokerage, savings, and money market, not listed on line 11.

Type of Account	Full Name of Bank, Savings & Loan, Credit Union or Financial Institution	Bank Routing No.	Bank Account No.	Current Account Balance
12a.	Name ___ Street Address ___ City/State/Zip ___			$
12b.	Name ___ Street Address ___ City/State/Zip ___		12c. Total Other Account Balances	$ ___ / $

ATTACHMENTS REQUIRED: Please include your current bank statements (checking, savings, money market, and brokerage accounts) for the past three months for all accounts.

13. INVESTMENTS. List all investment assets below. Include stocks, bonds, mutual funds, stock options, certificates of deposits, and retirement assets such as IRAs, Keogh, and 401(k) plans. (If you need additional space, attach a separate sheet.)

¤ **Current Value:** Indicate the amount you could sell the asset for today.

Name of Company	Number of Shares / Units	¤ Current Value	Loan Amount	Used as collateral on loan?
13a.		$	$	☐ No ☐ Yes
13b.				☐ No ☐ Yes
13c.				☐ No ☐ Yes
13d. Total Investments		$		

14. CASH ON HAND. Include any money that you have that is not in the bank.

14a. Total Cash on Hand $

15. AVAILABLE CREDIT. List all lines of credit, including credit cards.

Full Name of Credit Institution	Credit Limit	Amount Owed	Available Credit
15a. Name ___ Street Address ___ City/State/Zip ___			$
15b. Name ___ Street Address ___ City/State/Zip ___			$
	15c. Total Credit Available		$

Section 5 continued on page 3 →
(Rev. 5-2001)

Collection Information Statement for Wage Earners and Self-Employed Individuals	Form 433-A

Name _____   SSN _____

Section 5
continued

16. LIFE INSURANCE. Do you have life insurance with a cash value? ☐ No ☐ Yes
(Term Life insurance does not have a cash value.)
If yes:

16a. Name of Insurance Company _____

16b. Policy Number(s) _____

16c. Owner of Policy _____

16d. Current Cash Value $ _____   **16e.** Outstanding Loan Balance $ _____

Subtract "Outstanding Loan Balance" line 16e from "Current Cash Value" line 16d = 16f $ _____

☐ Check this box when all spaces in Sect. 5 are filled in and attachments provided.

ATTACHMENTS REQUIRED: Please include a statement from the life insurance companies that includes type and cash/loan value amounts. If currently borrowed against, include loan amount and date of loan.

Section 6
Other Information

17. OTHER INFORMATION. Respond to the following questions related to your financial condition: (Attach sheet if you need more space.)

17a. Are there any garnishments against your wages? ☐ No ☐ Yes
If yes, who is the creditor? _____ Date creditor obtained judgement _____ Amount of debt $ _____

17b. Are there any judgments against you? ☐ No ☐ Yes
If yes, who is the creditor? _____ Date creditor obtained judgement _____ Amount of debt $ _____

17c. Are you a party in a lawsuit? ☐ No ☐ Yes
If yes, amount of suit $ _____ Possible completion date _____ Subject matter of suit _____

17d. Did you ever file bankruptcy? ☐ No ☐ Yes
If yes, date filed _____ Date discharged _____

17e. In the past 10 years did you transfer any assets out of your name for less than their actual value? ☐ No ☐ Yes
If yes, what asset? _____ Value of asset at time of transfer $ _____
When was it transferred? _____ To whom was it transferred? _____

17f. Do you anticipate any increase in household income in the next two years? ☐ No ☐ Yes
If yes, why will the income increase? _____ (Attach sheet if you need more space.)
How much will it increase? $ _____

17g. Are you a beneficiary of a trust or an estate? ☐ No ☐ Yes
If yes, name of the trust or estate _____ Anticipated amount to be received $ _____
When will the amount be received? _____

☐ Check this box when all spaces in Sect. 6 are filled in.

17h. Are you a participant in a profit sharing plan? ☐ No ☐ Yes
If yes, name of plan _____ Value in plan $ _____

Section 7
Assets and Liabilities

18. PURCHASED AUTOMOBILES, TRUCKS AND OTHER LICENSED ASSETS. Include boats, RV's, motorcycles, trailers, etc.
(If you need additional space, attach a separate sheet.)

⊐ **Current Value:** Indicate the amount you could sell the asset for today.

Description (Year, Make, Model, Mileage)	⊐ Current Value	Current Loan Balance	Name of Lender	Purchase Date	Amount of Monthly Payment
18a. Year Make/Model Mileage	$	$			$
18b. Year Make/Model Mileage	$	$			$
18c. Year Make/Model Mileage	$	$			$

Collection Information Statement for Wage Earners and Self-Employed Individuals   Form 433-A

Name_____   SSN_____

Section 7
continued

19. **LEASED AUTOMOBILES, TRUCKS AND OTHER LICENSED ASSETS.** Include boats, RV's, motorcycles, trailers, etc.
(If you need additional space, attach a separate sheet.)

Description (Year, Make, Model)	Lease Balance	Name and Address of Lessor	Lease Date	Amount of Monthly Payment
19a. Year				
Make/Model	$			$
19b. Year				
Make/Model	$			$

ATTACHMENTS REQUIRED: Please include your current statement from lender with monthly car payment amount and current balance of the loan for each vehicle purchased or leased.

20. **REAL ESTATE.** List all real estate you own. (If you need additional space, attach a separate sheet.)

▯ **Current Value:** Indicate the amount you could sell the asset for today.

✳ **Date of Final Payment:** Enter the date the loan or lease will be fully paid.

Street Address, City, State, Zip, and County	Date Purchased	Purchase Price	▯Current Value	Loan Balance	Name of Lender or Lien Holder	Amount of Monthly Payment	✳Date of Final Payment
20a.		$	$	$		$	
20b.		$	$	$		$	

ATTACHMENTS REQUIRED: Please include your current statement from lender with monthly payment amount and current balance for each piece of real estate owned.

21. **PERSONAL ASSETS.** List all Personal assets below. (If you need additional space, attach separate sheet.)
Furniture/Personal Effects includes the total current market value of your household such as furniture and appliances. *Other Personal Assets* includes all artwork, jewelry, collections (coin/gun, etc.), antiques or other assets.

Description	▯Current Value	Loan Balance	Name of Lender	Amount of Monthly Payment	✳Date of Final Payment
21a. Furniture/Personal Effects	$	$		$	
Other: (List below)					
21b. Artwork	$	$		$	
21c. Jewelry					
21d.					
21e.					

22. **BUSINESS ASSETS.** List all business assets and encumbrances below, include Uniform Commercial Code (UCC) filings. (If you need additional space, attach a separate sheet.) *Tools used in Trade or Business* includes the basic tools or books used to conduct your business, excluding automobiles. *Other Business Assets* includes any other machinery, equipment, inventory or other assets.

☐ Check this box when all spaces in Sect. 7 are filled in and attachments provided.

Description	▯Current Value	Loan Balance	Name of Lender	Amount of Monthly Payment	✳Date of Final Payment
22a. Tools used in Trade/Business	$	$		$	
Other: (List below)					
22b. Machinery	$	$		$	
22c. Equipment					
22d.					
22e.					

Section 8 begins on page 5 →
(Rev. 5-2001)

¶1457

Collection Information Statement for Wage Earners and Self-Employed Individuals | Form 433-A

Name_____ SSN_____

Section 8

Accounts/ Notes Receivable

Use only if needed.

☐ *Check this box if Section 8 not needed.*

23. **ACCOUNTS/NOTES RECEIVABLE**. List all accounts separately, including contracts awarded, but not started. (If you need additional space, attach a separate sheet.)

Description	Amount Due	Date Due	Age of Account
23a. Name _____ Street Address _____ City/State/Zip _____	$_____	_____	☐ 0 - 30 days ☐ 30 - 60 days ☐ 60 - 90 days ☐ 90+ days
23b. Name _____ Street Address _____ City/State/Zip _____	$_____	_____	☐ 0 - 30 days ☐ 30 - 60 days ☐ 60 - 90 days ☐ 90+ days
23c. Name _____ Street Address _____ City/State/Zip _____	$_____	_____	☐ 0 - 30 days ☐ 30 - 60 days ☐ 60 - 90 days ☐ 90+ days
23d. Name _____ Street Address _____ City/State/Zip _____	$_____	_____	☐ 0 - 30 days ☐ 30 - 60 days ☐ 60 - 90 days ☐ 90+ days
23e. Name _____ Street Address _____ City/State/Zip _____	$_____	_____	☐ 0 - 30 days ☐ 30 - 60 days ☐ 60 - 90 days ☐ 90+ days
23f. Name _____ Street Address _____ City/State/Zip _____	$_____	_____	☐ 0 - 30 days ☐ 30 - 60 days ☐ 60 - 90 days ☐ 90+ days
23g. Name _____ Street Address _____ City/State/Zip _____	$_____	_____	☐ 0 - 30 days ☐ 30 - 60 days ☐ 60 - 90 days ☐ 90+ days
23h. Name _____ Street Address _____ City/State/Zip _____	$_____	_____	☐ 0 - 30 days ☐ 30 - 60 days ☐ 60 - 90 days ☐ 90+ days
23i. Name _____ Street Address _____ City/State/Zip _____	$_____	_____	☐ 0 - 30 days ☐ 30 - 60 days ☐ 60 - 90 days ☐ 90+ days
23j. Name _____ Street Address _____ City/State/Zip _____	$_____	_____	☐ 0 - 30 days ☐ 30 - 60 days ☐ 60 - 90 days ☐ 90+ days
23k. Name _____ Street Address _____ City/State/Zip _____	$_____	_____	☐ 0 - 30 days ☐ 30 - 60 days ☐ 60 - 90 days ☐ 90+ days
23l. Name _____ Street Address _____ City/State/Zip _____	$_____	_____	☐ 0 - 30 days ☐ 30 - 60 days ☐ 60 - 90 days ☐ 90+ days

☐ Check this box when all spaces in Sect. 8 are filled in.

Add "Amount Due" from lines 23a through 23l = 23m $_____

Collection Information Statement for Wage Earners and Self-Employed Individuals **Form 433-A**

Name_____ SSN_____

Section 9	**Total Income**			**Total Living Expenses**		
Monthly Income and Expense Analysis	Source	Gross Monthly		Expense Items [4]	Actual Monthly	
	24. Wages (Yourself)[1]	$		35. Food, Clothing and Misc.[5]	$	
	25. Wages (Spouse)[1]			36. Housing and Utilities[6]		
	26. Interest - Dividends			37. Transportation[7]		
	27. Net Income from Business[2]			38. Health Care		
If only one spouse has a tax liability, but both have income, list the total household income and expenses.	28. Net Rental Income[3]			39. Taxes (Income and FICA)		
	29. Pension/Social Security (Yourself)			40. Court ordered payments		
	30. Pension/Social Security (Spouse)			41. Child/dependent care		
	31. Child Support			42. Life insurance		
	32. Alimony			43. Other secured debt		
	33. Other			44. Other expenses		
	34. **Total Income**	$		45. **Total Living Expenses**	$	

[1] **Wages, salaries, pensions, and social security:** Enter your gross monthly wages and/or salaries. Do not deduct withholding or allotments you elect to take out of your pay, such as insurance payments, credit union deductions, car payments etc.
To calculate your gross monthly wages and/or salaries:
  If paid weekly - multiply weekly gross wages by 4.3. Example: $425.89 x 4.3 = $1,831.33
  If paid bi-weekly (every 2 weeks) - multiply bi-weekly gross wages by 2.17. Example: $972.45 x 2.17 = $2,110.22
  If paid semi-monthly (twice each month) - multiply semi-monthly gross wages by 2. Example: $856.23 x 2 = $1,712.46

[2] **Net Income from Business:** Enter your monthly net business income. This is the amount you earn after you pay ordinary and necessary monthly business expenses. This figure should relate to the yearly net profit from your Form 1040 Schedule C. If it is more or less than the previous year, you should attach an explanation. If your net business income is a loss, enter "0". Do not enter a negative number.

[3] **Net Rental Income:** Enter your monthly net rental income. This is the amount you earn after you pay ordinary and necessary monthly rental expenses. If your net rental income is a loss, enter "0". Do not enter a negative number.

[4] **Expenses not generally allowed:** We generally do not allow you to claim tuition for private schools, public or private college expenses, charitable contributions, voluntary retirement contributions, payments on unsecured debts such as credit card bills, cable television and other similar expenses. However, we may allow these expenses, if you can prove that they are necessary for the health and welfare of you or your family or for the production of income.

[5] **Food, Clothing and Misc.:** Total of clothing, food, housekeeping supplies and personal care products for one month.

[6] **Housing and Utilities:** For your principal residence: Total of rent or mortgage payment. Add the average monthly expenses for the following: property taxes, home owner's or renter's insurance, maintenance, dues, fees, and utilities. Utilities include gas, electricity, water, fuel, oil, other fuels, trash collection and telephone.

[7] **Transportation:** Total of lease or purchase payments, vehicle insurance, registration fees, normal maintenance, fuel, public transportation, parking and tolls for one month.

ATTACHMENTS REQUIRED: Please include:

A copy of your last Form 1040 with all Schedules.

Proof of all current expenses that you paid for the past 3 months, including utilities, rent, insurance, property taxes, etc.

Proof of all non-business transportation expenses (e.g., car payments, lease payments, fuel, oil, insurance, parking, registration).

Proof of payments for health care, including health insurance premiums, co-payments, and other out-of-pocket expenses, for the past 3 months.

☐ Check this box when all spaces in Sect. 9 are filled in and attachments provided.

Copies of any court order requiring payment and proof of such payments (e.g., cancelled checks, money orders, earning statements showing such deductions) for the past 3 months.

☐ Check this box when all spaces in all sections are filled in and all attachments provided.

⚠ **CAUTION**

Failure to complete all entry spaces may result in rejection or significant delay in the resolution of your account.

Certification: *Under penalties of perjury, I declare that to the best of my knowledge and belief this statement of assets, liabilities, and other information is true, correct and complete.*

✍

_____ _____ _____
Your Signature Spouse's Signature Date

¶1457

¶1458 Exhibit 14-8

How to prepare a
Collection Information Statement (Form 433-A)

Complete all blocks, except shaded areas. Write "N/A" *(Not Applicable)* in those blocks that do not apply to you. **If you don't complete the form, we won't be able to help determine the best method for you to pay the amount due.** The areas explained below are the ones we have found to be the most confusing to people completing the form.

Section 5

Items 11 – Checking Accounts, and 12 – Other Accounts
Enter all accounts, even if there is currently no balance. *Do Not* enter bank loans.

Item 15 – Available Credit
Enter only credit issued by a bank, credit union, or savings and loan *(MasterCard, Visa, overdraft protection, etc.).*

Section 7

Items 18, 20, 21, and 22 – Automobiles, Trucks, Other Licensed Assets, Real Estate, Personal Assets, and Business Assets

Current Value – Indicate the amount you could sell the asset for today.

Date of Final Payment – Enter the date the loan or lease will be fully paid.

Item 20 – Real Estate
List all property that you own or are purchasing.

Item 21 – Personal Assets
List other assets you own such as artwork, jewelry, antiques, etc.

Section 9

If only one spouse has a tax liability, but both have income, list the total household income and expenses.

TOTAL INCOME

Items 24 and 25 – Wages
Enter your *gross* monthly wages and/or salaries. Do not deduct withholding or allotments you elect to take out of your pay such as insurance payments, credit union deductions, car payments, etc. List these expenses in Items 38 through 44.

Item 27 – Net Business Income
Enter your monthly *net* business income. The net is what you earn after you have paid your ordinary and necessary monthly business expenses.

TOTAL LIVING EXPENSES *(necessary)*

To be necessary, expenses must provide for the health and welfare of you and your family and/or provide for the production of income, and must be reasonable in amount. We may ask you to provide substantiation of certain expenses.

Item 35 – Food, Clothing, and Misc.
This category includes clothing and clothing services, food, housekeeping supplies, personal care products amount from the chart on the back of these instructions, based on your total monthly gross income and the size of your family. If you claim a higher amount, you must substantiate why a higher amount is necessary for each item included in a category.

Item 36 – Housing and Utilities
Enter the monthly rent or mortgage payment for your principal residence. Add the average monthly payment for the following expenses, if they are *not* included in your rent or mortgage payments: property taxes, homeowner's or renter's insurance, parking, necessary maintenance and repair, homeowner dues, condominium fees, and utilities. Utilities includes gas, electricity, water, fuel oil, coal, bottled gas, trash and garbage collection, wood and other fuels, septic cleaning and telephone.

Item 37 –Transportation
Enter your average monthly transportation expenses. Transportation expenses include: lease or purchase payments, insurance, registration fees, normal maintenance, fuel, public transportation, parking and tolls.

Item 43 – Other Secured Debt
Do not enter mortgage payment entered in Item 43, or lease or purchase payments entered in Item 44.

Item 44 – Other Expenses
Enter your average monthly payments for any other *necessary* expenses.

Certification
For joint income tax liabilities, both husband and wife should sign the statement.

Department of the Treasury
Internal Revenue Service

www.irs.gov

Publication 1854 (Rev. 1-2003)
Catalog Number 21563Q

Total Monthly National Standards
(Except Alaska and Hawaii*)
Effective 01/01/03

TOTAL GROSS MONTHLY INCOME	NUMBER OF PERSONS				
	One	Two	Three	Four	Over Four
Less than $830	344	493	675	838	+125
$831 to $1,249	393	554	679	847	+135
$1,250 to $1,669	456	642	741	877	+145
$1,670 to $2,499	514	716	834	902	+155
$2,500 to $3,329	598	782	895	969	+165
$3,330 to $4,169	670	879	982	1,175	+175
$4,170 to $5,829	701	940	1,020	1,249	+185
$5,830 and over	1,016	1,290	1,414	1,497	+195

Total Monthly Standards for Alaska
Effective 01/01/03

TOTAL GROSS MONTHLY INCOME	NUMBER OF PERSONS				
	One	Two	Three	Four	Over Four
Less than $830	455	651	891	1,106	+165
$831 to $1,249	519	731	895	1,118	+178
$1,250 to $1,669	602	848	978	1,157	+191
$1,670 to $2,499	678	944	1,101	1,190	+205
$2,500 to $3,329	790	1,033	1,181	1,279	+218
$3,330 to $4,169	885	1,161	1,297	1,551	+231
$4,170 to $5,829	925	1,242	1,346	1,649	+244
$5,830 and over	1,342	1,702	1,867	1,976	+257

Total Monthly Standards for Hawaii
Effective 01/01/03

TOTAL GROSS MONTHLY INCOME	NUMBER OF PERSONS				
	One	Two	Three	Four	Over Four
Less than $830	358	512	702	872	+130
$831 to $1,249	409	575	706	881	+140
$1,250 to $1,669	474	667	771	912	+151
$1,670 to $2,499	534	745	867	939	+161
$2,500 to $3,329	622	813	930	1,008	+172
$3,330 to $4,169	697	914	1,021	1,223	+182
$4,170 to $5,829	729	977	1,061	1,299	+192
$5,830 and over	1,056	1,341	1,469	1,557	+203

Expenses include:
Housekeeping supplies
Clothing and clothing services
Personal care products and services
Food
Miscellaneous

To find the amount of expenses we can allow you, please read down the Total Gross Monthly Income column until you find your income, then read across to the column that matches the number of persons in your family.

When you have more than four persons in your family, you need to multiply the amount of additional persons over four by the dollar amount in the "Over Four" column; then add the answer to the dollar amount in the "Four" column. For example: when your total monthly income is between $830 and $1,249 and you have six persons in your family, you would multiply $135 by the two members of your family over four to get $270. You then would add this $270 to the $847 allowed to a family of four in your income bracket. As a result, your allowed expenses would equal $1,117 ($270+$847).

* Residents of either Alaska or Hawaii should use the table that outlines the expenses allowed for their state.

¶1458

¶1459 Exhibit 14-9

 IRS   ## Collection Information Statement for Businesses

Department of the Treasury
Internal Revenue Service

www.irs.gov

Form 433-B (Rev. 5-2001)
Catalog Number 16649P

Complete all entry spaces with the most current data available.

Important! Write "N/A" (not applicable) in spaces that do not apply. We may require additional information to support "N/A" entries.

Failure to complete all entry spaces may result in rejection or significant delay in the resolution of your account.

Section 1 **Business Information**	**1a.** Business Name _____
	Business Street Address _____
	_____
	City _____ State _____ Zip _____
	County _____
	1b. Business Telephone (___) _____
	2a. Employer Identification No. (EIN) _____
	2b. Type of Entity (Check appropriate box below)
☐ Check this box when all spaces in Sect. 1 are filled in.	☐ Partnership ☐ Corporation ☐ Other
	2c. Type of Business _____

3a. Contact Name _____
3b. Contact's Business Telephone (___) _____
    Extension _____
    Best Time To Call _____ am _____ pm (Enter Hour)
3c. Contact's Home Telephone   (___) _____
    Best Time To Call _____ am _____ pm (Enter Hour)
3d. Contact's Other Telephone (___) _____
    Telephone Type (i.e. fax, cellular, pager) _____
3e. Contact's E-mail Address _____

Section 2
Business Personnel and Contacts

4. PERSON RESPONSIBLE FOR DEPOSITING PAYROLL TAXES

4a. Full Name _____ Title _____
    Home Street Address _____
    City _____ State _____ Zip _____

Social Security Number _____ | _____ |
Home Telephone (___) _____
Ownership Percentage & Shares or Interest _____

5. PARTNERS, OFFICERS, MAJOR SHAREHOLDERS, ETC.

5a. Full Name _____ Title _____
    Home Street Address _____
    City _____ State _____ Zip _____

Social Security Number _____ | _____ |
Home Telephone (___) _____
Ownership Percentage & Shares or Interest _____

5b. Full Name _____ Title _____
    Home Street Address _____
    City _____ State _____ Zip _____

Social Security Number _____ | _____ |
Home Telephone (___) _____
Ownership Percentage & Shares or Interest _____

5c. Full Name _____ Title _____
    Home Street Address _____
    City _____ State _____ Zip _____

Social Security Number _____ | _____ |
Home Telephone (___) _____
Ownership Percentage & Shares or Interest _____

5d. Full Name _____ Title _____
    Home Street Address _____
    City _____ State _____ Zip _____

Social Security Number _____ | _____ |
Home Telephone (___) _____
Ownership Percentage & Shares or Interest _____

☐ Check this box when all spaces in Sect. 2 are filled in.

Section 3
Accounts/ Notes Receivable

See page 6 for additional space, if needed.

6. ACCOUNTS/NOTES RECEIVABLE. List all contracts separately, including contracts awarded, but not started.

Description	Amount Due	Date Due	Age of Account
6a. Name _____ Street Address _____ City/State/Zip _____	$ _____	_____	☐ 0 - 30 days ☐ 30 - 60 days ☐ 60 - 90 days ☐ 90+ days
6b. Name _____ Street Address _____ City/State/Zip _____	$ _____	_____	☐ 0 - 30 days ☐ 30 - 60 days ☐ 60 - 90 days ☐ 90+ days

6a + 6b = 6c   **6c** $ _____

Amount from Page 6   **6p** + _____

6q. Total Accounts/ Notes Receivable   **6c + 6p = 6q** = $ _____

☐ Check this box when all spaces in Sect. 3 are filled in.

Page 1 of 6

Section 4 begins on page 2 →
(Rev. 5-2001)

Collection Information Statement for Businesses   Form 433-B

Business Name _____   EIN _____

Section 4	**7.** **OTHER FINANCIAL INFORMATION.** Respond to the following business financial questions.

Section 4

Other Financial Information

7a. Does this business have other business relationships (e.g. subsidiary or parent, corporation, partnership, etc.)? .... ☐ No ☐ Yes
If yes, list related EIN _____   Additional EIN _____

7b. Does anyone (e.g. officer, stockholder, partner or employees) have an outstanding loan borrowed from the business? .... ☐ No ☐ Yes
If yes, amount of loan $ _____   Date of loan _____   Current balance $____

7c. Are there any judgments or liens against your business? .... ☐ No ☐ Yes
If yes, who is the creditor?_____   Date creditor obtained judgment/lien _____   Amount of debt $ _____

7d. Is your business a party in a lawsuit? .... ☐ No ☐ Yes
If yes, amount of suit $ _____   Possible completion date _____   Subject matter of suit_____

7e. Has your business ever filed bankruptcy? .... ☐ No ☐ Yes
If yes, date filed _____   Date discharged _____   Petition No._____

7f. In the past 10 years have you transferred any assets from your business name for less than their actual value? .... ☐ No ☐ Yes
If yes, what asset? _____   Value of asset at time of transfer $_____
When was it transferred? _____   To whom or where was it transferred?_____

7g. Do you anticipate any increase in business income (e.g. contracts bid but not yet awarded)? .... ☐ No ☐ Yes
If yes, why will the income increase? _____ ..... (Attach sheet if you need additional space.)
How much will it increase? _____   When will the business income increase?_____

☐ Check this box when all spaces in Sect. 4 are filled in.

7h. Is your business a beneficiary of a trust, an estate or a life insurance policy? .... ☐ No ☐ Yes
If yes, name of the trust, estate or policy? _____   Anticipated amount to be received?_____
When will the amount be received?_____

Section 5

Business Assets

⌶ **Current Value:** Indicate the amount you could sell the asset for today.

8. **PURCHASED AUTOMOBILES, TRUCKS AND OTHER LICENSED ASSETS.** Include boats, RV's, motorcycles, trailers, etc.
(If you need additional space, attach a separate sheet.)

Description (Year, Make, Model, Mileage)	⌶ Current Value	Loan Balance	Name of Lender	Purchase Date	Amount of Monthly Payment
8a. Year _____ Make/Model _____ Mileage _____	$	$	_____	_____	$ _____
8b. Year _____ Make/Model _____ Mileage _____	$	$	_____	_____	$ _____
8c. Year _____ Make/Model _____ Mileage _____	$	$	_____	_____	$ _____

9. **LEASED AUTOMOBILES, TRUCKS AND OTHER LICENSED ASSETS.** Include boats, RV's, motorcycles, trailers, etc.
(If you need additional space, attach a separate sheet.)

Description (Year, Make, Model)	Lease Balance	Name of Lessor	Lease Date	Amount of Monthly Payment
9a. Year _____ Make/Model _____	$	_____	_____	$ _____
9b. Year _____ Make/Model _____	$	_____	_____	$ _____

ATTACHMENTS REQUIRED: Please include your current statement from lender with monthly car payment amount and current balance of the loan for each vehicle purchased or leased.

                    Section 5 continued on page 3 →
(Rev. 5-2001)

¶1459

Collection Information Statement for Businesses   Form 433-B

Business Name _____   EIN _____

Section 5	10. **REAL ESTATE.** List all real estate owned by the business. (If you need additional space, attach a separate sheet.)

Section 5 continued

¤ **Current Value:** Indicate the amount you could sell the asset for today.

✱ **Date of Final Payment:** Enter the date the loan or lease will be fully paid.

	Street Address, City, State, Zip, and County	Date Purchased	Purchase Price	¤ Current Value	Loan Balance	Name of Lender or Lien Holder	Amount of Monthly Payment	✱ Date of Final Payment
10a.			$	$	$		$	
10b.			$	$	$		$	

📎 **ATTACHMENTS REQUIRED:** Please include your current statement from lender with monthly payment amount and current balance for each piece of real estate owned.

☐ *Check this box if you are attaching a depreciation schedule for machinery/ equipment in lieu of completing line 11.*

11. **BUSINESS ASSETS.** List all business assets and encumbrances below, include Uniform Commercial Code (UCC) filings. (If you need additional space, attach a separate sheet.)   Note: If attaching a depreciation schedule, the attachment must include all of the information requested below.

	Description	¤ Current Value	Loan Balance	Name of Lender	Amount of Monthly Payment	✱ Date of Final Payment
11a.	Machinery	$	$		$	
	Equipment					
	Merchandise					
	Other Assets: (List below)					
11b.		$	$		$	
11c.						

☐ Check this box when all spaces in Sect. 5 are filled in and attachments provided.

📎 **ATTACHMENTS REQUIRED:** Please include your current statement from lender with monthly payment amount and current loan balance for assets listed which have an encumbrance.

Section 6

Investment, Banking and Cash Information

12. **INVESTMENTS.** List all investment assets below. Include stocks, bonds, mutual funds, stock options and certificates of deposits.

	Name of Company	Number of Shares / Units	¤ Current Value	Loan Amount	Used as collateral on loan?
12a.			$	$	☐ No ☐ Yes
12b.					☐ No ☐ Yes
	12c. **Total Investments**		$		

Section 6 continued on page 4 →
(Rev. 5-2001)

¶1459

Collection Information Statement for Businesses   Form 433-B

Business Name _____   EIN _____

Section 6

continued

Complete all entry spaces with the most current data available.

13. BANK ACCOUNTS. List all checking and savings accounts. (If you need additional space, attach a separate sheet.)

	Type of Account	Full Name of Bank, Savings & Loan, Credit Union or Financial Institution	Bank Routing No.	Bank Account No.	Current Account Balance
13a. Checking		Name _____	_____	_____	$ _____
		Street Address _____			
		City/State/Zip _____			
13b. Checking		Name _____	_____	_____	$ _____
		Street Address _____			
		City/State/Zip _____			
13c. Savings		Name _____	_____	_____	$ _____
		Street Address _____			
		City/State/Zip _____	**13d. Total Bank Account Balances**		$ _____

ATTACHMENTS REQUIRED: Please include your current bank statements (checking and savings) for the past three months for all accounts.

14. OTHER ACCOUNTS. List all accounts including brokerage accounts, money market, additional checking and savings accounts not listed on line #13 and any other accounts not listed in this section.

	Type of Account	Full Name of Bank, Savings & Loan, Credit Union or Financial Institution	Bank Routing No.	Bank Account No.	Current Account Balance
14a. _____		Name _____	_____	_____	$ _____
		Street Address _____			
		City/State/Zip _____			
14b. _____		Name _____	_____	_____	$ _____
		Street Address _____			
		City/State/Zip _____	**14c. Total Other Account Balances**		$ _____

ATTACHMENTS REQUIRED: Please include your current bank statements (checking, savings, money market, and brokerage accounts) for the past three months for all accounts.

15. CASH ON HAND. Include any money that you have that is not in the bank.

15a. Total Cash on Hand $ _____

16. AVAILABLE CREDIT. List all lines of credit, including credit cards.

	Full Name of Credit Institution	Credit Limit	Amount Owed	Available Credit
16a. Name _____		_____	_____	$ _____
	Street Address _____			
	City/State/Zip _____			
16b. Name _____		_____	_____	$ _____
	Street Address _____			
	City/State/Zip _____	**16c. Total Credit Available**		$ _____

☐ Check this box when all spaces in Sect. 6 are filled in and attachments provided.

¶1459

Collection Information Statement for Businesses   **Form 433-B**

Business Name _____   EIN _____

Section 7   **17.** The following information applies to income and expenses from your most recently filed Form 1120 or Form 1065.

Monthly   Fiscal Year Period _____ to _____

Income and   **18.** Accounting Method Used: ☐ Cash   ☐ Accrual

Expenses

*Complete all
entry spaces
with the most
current data
available.*

The information included on lines 19 through 39 should reconcile to your business federal tax return.

Total Income			*Total Expenses*	
Source	Gross Monthly		Expense Items	Actual Monthly
19. Gross Receipts	$		**27.** Materials Purchased [1]	$
20. Gross Rental Income			**28.** Inventory Purchased [2]	
21. Interest			**29.** Gross Wages & Salaries	
22. Dividends			**30.** Rent	
Other Income (specify in lines 23-25)			**31.** Supplies [3]	
23.			**32.** Utilities / Telephone [4]	
24.			**33.** Vehicle Gasoline / Oil	
25.			**34.** Repairs & Maintenance	
(Add lines 19 through 25)			**35.** Insurance	
26. **TOTAL INCOME**	$		**36.** Current Taxes [5]	
			Other Expenses (include installment payments, specify in lines 37-38)	
			37.	
			38.	
			(Add lines 27 through 38)	
			39. **TOTAL EXPENSES**	$

[1] **Materials Purchased:** Materials are items directly related to the production of a product or service.

[2] **Inventory Purchased:** Goods bought for resale.

[3] **Supplies:** Supplies are items used in your business that are consumed or used up within one year, this could be the cost of books, office supplies, professional instruments, etc.

[4] **Utilities:** Utilities include gas, electricity, water, fuel, oil, other fuels, trash collection and telephone.

☐ Check this box when all spaces in Sect. 7 are filled in.   [5] **Current Taxes:** Real estate, state and local income tax, excise, franchise, occupational, personal property, sales and the employer's portion of employment taxes.

☐ Check this box when all spaces in all sections are filled in and all attachments provided.

⚠ **CAUTION**   *Failure to complete all entry spaces may result in rejection or significant delay in the resolution of your account.*

Certification: Under penalties of perjury, I declare that to the best of my knowledge and belief this statement of assets, liabilities, and other information is true, correct and complete.

_____   _____

Print Name   Title

_____   _____

Your Signature   Date

Page 5 of 6   *Accounts/Notes Receivable Continuation on page 6* →
(Rev. 5-2001)

Collection Information Statement for Businesses   **Form 433-B**

Business Name _____ EIN _____

Section 3	ACCOUNTS/NOTES RECEIVABLE CONTINUATION PAGE. List all contracts separately, including contracts awarded, but not

Accounts/ Notes Receivable continued

started. (If you need additional space, copy this page and attach to the 433-B package.)

Use only if needed.

☐ *Check this box if this page is not needed.*

	Description	Amount Due	Date Due	Age of Account
6d.	Name _____	$ _____ _____		☐ 0 - 30 days ☐ 30 - 60 days ☐ 60 - 90 days ☐ 90+ days
	Street Address _____			
	City/State/Zip _____			
6e.	Name _____	$ _____	_____	☐ 0 - 30 days ☐ 30 - 60 days ☐ 60 - 90 days ☐ 90+ days
	Street Address _____			
	City/State/Zip _____			
6f.	Name _____	$ _____	_____	☐ 0 - 30 days ☐ 30 - 60 days ☐ 60 - 90 days ☐ 90+ days
	Street Address _____			
	City/State/Zip _____			
6g.	Name _____	$ _____	_____	☐ 0 - 30 days ☐ 30 - 60 days ☐ 60 - 90 days ☐ 90+ days
	Street Address _____			
	City/State/Zip _____			
6h.	Name _____	$ _____	_____	☐ 0 - 30 days ☐ 30 - 60 days ☐ 60 - 90 days ☐ 90+ days
	Street Address _____			
	City/State/Zip _____			
6i.	Name _____	$ _____	_____	☐ 0 - 30 days ☐ 30 - 60 days ☐ 60 - 90 days ☐ 90+ days
	Street Address _____			
	City/State/Zip _____			
6j.	Name _____	$ _____	_____	☐ 0 - 30 days ☐ 30 - 60 days ☐ 60 - 90 days ☐ 90+ days
	Street Address _____			
	City/State/Zip _____			
6k.	Name _____	$ _____	_____	☐ 0 - 30 days ☐ 30 - 60 days ☐ 60 - 90 days ☐ 90+ days
	Street Address _____			
	City/State/Zip _____			
6l.	Name _____	$ _____	_____	☐ 0 - 30 days ☐ 30 - 60 days ☐ 60 - 90 days ☐ 90+ days
	Street Address _____			
	City/State/Zip _____			
6m.	Name _____	$ _____	_____	☐ 0 - 30 days ☐ 30 - 60 days ☐ 60 - 90 days ☐ 90+ days
	Street Address _____			
	City/State/Zip _____			
6n.	Name _____	$ _____	_____	☐ 0 - 30 days ☐ 30 - 60 days ☐ 60 - 90 days ☐ 90+ days
	Street Address _____			
	City/State/Zip _____			
6o.	Name _____	$ _____	_____	☐ 0 - 30 days ☐ 30 - 60 days ☐ 60 - 90 days ☐ 90+ days
	Street Address _____			
	City/State/Zip _____			

☐ Check this box when all spaces in Sect. 3 are filled in.

Add lines 6d through 6o = 6p $ _____   *(Add this amount to amount on line 6c, Section 3, page 1)*

Page 6 of 6

(Rev. 5-2001)

¶1459

¶1460 Exhibit 14-10

Form 6639
(Rev. October 1993)

Summons
Financial Records

Department of the Treasury
Internal Revenue Service

In the matter of _____

Internal Revenue District of _____ Periods _____

The Commissioner of Internal Revenue

To _____

At _____

You are hearby summoned and required to appear before _____ ,
an Internal Revenue Service (IRS) officer, to give testimony and to bring for examination the following information related
to the collection of the tax liability of the person identified above for the periods shown:

Copies of documents and records that you possess or control that concern banking matters of the taxpayer named above,
as described in the subparagraphs checked below for the periods shown:

☐   bank signature cards in effect . . . . from _____ to _____

☐   corporate resolutions in effect . . . . from _____ to _____

☐   bank statements . . . . from _____ to _____

☐   _____ cancelled checks issued by
(NUMBER)   the taxpayer for each month
             of the period . . . . from _____ to _____

☐   loan applications, agreements, and
    related records, including corporate
    financial statements, submitted,
    entered into, or in effect . . . . from _____ to _____

Do not write in this space

Business address and telephone number of Internal Revenue Service officer named above:

_____

Place and time for appearance:
at _____
on the _____ day of _____ , 19 _____ at _____ o'clock _____m.
Issued under authority of the Internal Revenue Code this _____ day of _____ , 19 ____

_____   _____
Signature of Issuing Officer   Title

_____   _____
Signature of Approving Officer (If applicable)   Title

Original to be kept by IRS   Catalog No. 25004I   Form **6639** (Rev. 10-93)

Form 6639 (Rev. 10-93)

Certificate of
Service of Summons
(Pursuant to section 7603, Internal Revenue Code)

I certify that I served the summons shown on
the front of this form on:

Date	Time

How Summons Was Served

☐ I handed an attested copy of the summons to the person to whom it was directed.

☐ I left an attested copy of the summons at the last and usual place of abode of th person to whom it was directed. I left the copy with the following person (if any):

Signature	Title

I certify that the copy of the summons served contained the required certification.

Signature	Title

Form **6639** (Rev. 10-93)

¶1460

¶1461 Exhibit 14-11

Internal Revenue Service	**Department of the Treasury**
District Director	

Date:

Social Security or Employer
Identification Number:

Person to Contact:

Telephone Number:

┘

Notice of Federal Tax Lien Filing and Your Right to a Hearing Under IRC 6320

This letter is to inform you that we have filed a Notice of Federal Tax Lien and that you have a right to a hearing to discuss collection options and liability issues. The enclosed Publication 1660, Collection Appeal Rights, explains your right to a hearing.

The amount of the unpaid tax is:

Type of Tax	**Period**	**Amount**

In order to exercise your right to a hearing, you must file your request by _____. A copy of the request form is attached. It must be sent to

A Notice of Federal Tax Lien was filed on_____, with respect to these taxes. The total amount you owe for the period(s) includes interest and other additions such as penalties and lien fees. You must pay all of the taxes, interest and other additions in order to obtain release of the lien. Call the number above to obtain your current balance.

The lien attaches to all property you currently own and to all property you may acquire in the future. It also may damage your credit rating and hinder your ability to obtain additional credit.

We will issue a Certificate of Release of Notice of Federal Tax Lien within 30 days after you pay the debt or have us adjust it. We will release the lien within 30 days after we accept a bond that you submit, guaranteeing payment of the debt.

(over)

Letter 3172(DO) (01-1999)
Cat. No. 26767I

¶1461

Procedures for requesting a certificate of release are in the enclosed Publication 14560, Request of Federal Tax Lien.

Sincerely,

Chief, Special Procedures

Enclosures:
    Publication 1660
    Publication 1450
    Form 668Y, Notice Of federal Tax Lien
    Form 12153, Request for Collection Due Process Hearing

Letter 3172(DO) (01-1999)
Cat. No. 267671

¶1461

¶1462 Exhibit 14-12

Form 668 (Y)(c) (Rev. August 1997)	Department of the Treasury - Internal Revenue Service **Notice of Federal Tax Lien**	
District	Serial Number	For Optional Use by Recording Office

As provided by section 6321, 6322, and 6323 of the Internal Revenue Code, we are giving a notice that taxes (including interest and penalties) have been assessed against the following-named taxpayer. We have made a demand for payment of this liability, but it remains unpaid. Therefore, there is a lien in favor of the United States on all property and rights to property belonging to this taxpayer for the amount of these taxes, and additional penalties, interest, and costs that may accrue.

● This Notice of Federal Tax Lien has been filed as a matter of public record.

● IRS will continue to charge penalty and interest until you satisfy the amount you owe.

● Contact the District Office Collection Division for information on the amount you must pay before we can release this lien.

● See the back of this page for an explanation of your Administrative Appeal rights.

Name of Taxpayer

Residence

> **IMPORTANT RELEASE INFORMATION:** For each assessment listed below, unless notice of the lien is refiled by the date given in column (e), this notice shall, on the day following such date, operate as a certificate of release as defined in IRC 6325(a).

Kind of Tax (a)	Tax Period Ending (b)	Identifying Number (c)	Date of Assessment (d)	Last Day for Refiling (e)	Unpaid Balance of Assessment (f)

Place of Filing

Total $

This notice was prepared and signed at _____ , on this,

the _____ day of _____, _____.

Signature	Title

(**NOTE:** Certificate of officer authorized by law to take acknowledgment is not essential to the validity of Notice of Federal Tax lien Rev. Rul. 71-466, 1971 - 2 C.B. 409)

Part 3 - Taxpayer's Copy

Form **668(Y)(c)** (Rev. 8-97)
CAT. NO 60025X

¶1462

Lien

This Notice of Federal Tax Lien gives public notice that the government has a lien on all your property (such as your house or car), all your rights to property (such as money owed to you) and to property you acquire after this lien is filed.

Your Administrative Appeal Rights

If you believe the IRS filed this Notice of Federal Tax Lien in error, you may appeal if any of the following conditions apply:

● you had paid all tax, penalty and interest before the lien was filed;

● IRS assessed tax after the date you filed a petition for bankruptcy;

● IRS mailed your notice of deficiency to the wrong address;

● you have already filed a timely petition with the Tax Court;

● the statute of limitations for collection ended before IRS filed the notice of lien.

Your appeal request must be in writing and contain the following:

● your name, current address and SSN/EIN;

● a copy of this notice of lien, if available;

● the specific reason(s) why you think the IRS is in error;

● proof that you paid the amount due (such as a cancelled check);

● proof that you filed a bankruptcy petition before this lien was filed.

Send your written request to the District Director, Attention: Chief, Special Procedures Function, in the district where this notice of lien was filed.

When This Lien Can Be Released

The IRS will issue a Certificate of Release of Federal Tax Lien within 30 days after:

● you pay the tax due, including penalties, interest, and any other additions under law, or IRS adjusts the amount due, or;

● we accept a bond that you submit guaranteeing payment of your debt, or;

● the end of the time period during which we can collect the tax (usually 10 years).

Publication 1450, Request for Release of Federal Tax Lien, available at IRS District offices, describes this process.

When a Lien against Property can be Removed

The IRS may remove the lien from a specific piece of property if any of the following conditions apply:

● you have other property subject to this lien that is worth at least two times the total of the tax you owe, including penalties and interest, plus the amount of any other debts you owe on the property (such as a mortgage);

● you give up ownership in the property and IRS receives the value of the government's interest in the property;

● IRS decides the government's interest in the property has no value when you give up ownership;

● the property in question is being sold;, there is a dispute about who is entitled to the sale proceeds; and the proceeds are placed in escrow while the dispute is being resolved.

Publication 783, Instructions on How to Apply for a Certificate of Discharge of Property from a Federal Tax Lien, available at IRS District offices, describes this process.

Gravamen

Este Aviso de Gravamen del Impuesto Federal da aviso público que el gobierno tiene un gravamen en toda su propiedad (tal como su casa o carro), todo sus derechos a propiedad (tal como dinero que le deben) y propiedad que se adquiere después que se radicó este gravamen.

Sus Derechos de Apelación Administrativos

Si usted cree que el IRS radicó este Aviso de Gravamen del Impuesto Federal por error, usted debe apelar si cualquiera de las condiciones siguientes le aplican:

● usted pagó todos los impuestos (contribuciones), penalidades e interéses antes de que el gravamen fuera radicado.

● IRS tasó el impuesto después del la fecha que se radicó una petición de quiebra.

● IRS envió por correo el aviso de deficiencia a una dirección incorrecta.

● usted radicó a tiempo una petición ante el Tribunal Tributario;
● el IRS radicó el aviso de gravamen despues que expiró el término de prescripción.

Su petición de apelación debe de estar por escrito e incluir lo siguiente:

● su nombre, dirección actual y SSN/EIN;

● una copia de este aviso de gravamen, si está disponible;

● la razón (o razones) específica(s) porqué piensa que el IRS está erróneo;

● prueba que usted pagó la cantidad adeudada (tal como un cheque cancelado)

● prueba que radicó una petición de quiebra antes de que se radicara el gravamen.

Envie su petición por escrito al Director de Distrito, atención Jefe, Procedimientos Especiales del distrito donde esté gravamen fué radicado.

Cuándo Este Gravamen Se Puede Condonar

El IRS condonará un Aviso de Gravamen del Impuesto Federal dentro de los 30 días después de que:

● usted paga el impuesto (tributo) pagadero, incluyendo penalidades, intereses, y otras sumas adicionales según la ley, o el IRS ajusta la cantidad adeudada, o;

● aceptamos una fianza que nos garantice el pago de su deuda, o;

● la expiración del término en que podemos cobrar el impuesto (tributo) (usualmente 10 años).

Publicación 1450, Petición para Condonar el Gravamen del Impuesto Federal, disponible en las oficinas de Distrito del IRS describe este proceso.

Cuándo el Gravamen contra la Propiedad se puede Eliminar

El IRS puede eliminar el gravamen de una propiedad específica si cualquiera de las condiciones siguientes aplican:

● usted tiene otra propiedad sujeta a este gravamen cuyo valor es por lo menos dos veces el total del impuesto (tributo) que usted debe, incluyendo penalidades e intereses, más la cantidad de cualquiera de las otras deudas que usted debe en la propiedad (tal como una hipoteca);

● usted deja de ser el propietario y el IRS recibe el valor del interés del gobierno en la propiedad;

● el IRS decide que el interés del gobierno en la propiedad no tiene valor alguno cuando usted dejó de ser el propietario;

● la propiedad gravada será vendida; existe una controversia acerca de quien tiene el derecho a los resultados de la venta; y se depositan los fondos recibidos en la venta en una cuenta especial en lo que se resuelve la controversia.

Publicación 783, Instrucciones en Cómo Solicitar un Certificado de Relevo de la Propiedad de un Gravamen del Impuesto Federal, disponible en las oficinas de Distrito del IRS, describen este proceso.

Form **668(Y)(c)** (Rev. 8-97)

¶1463 Exhibit 14-13

Instructions on Requesting

A Certificate of Release of Federal Tax Lien

Section 6325(a) of the Internal Revenue Code directs us to release a Federal Tax Lien after a tax liability becomes fully paid or legally unenforceable. We also must release a lien when we accept a bond for payment of the tax.

If we haven't released the lien within thirty days, you can ask for a Certificate of Release of Lien. Send your written request with any required documents to:

District Director of Internal Revenue Service
(Address to District in which the lien is filed)

Attention: Chief, Special Procedures

We need your request to contain the following information:

A. The date of your request;

B. The name and address of the taxpayer;

C. One copy of each notice of Federal Tax Lien you want released; and

D. Why you want us to release the lien.

If you've paid the tax, enclose a copy of either of the following:

1. An Internal Revenue Service receipt;

2. A canceled check;

3. Any other acceptable proof.

Please include a telephone number with the best time for us to call you should we need information.

We may need to research your account to confirm you no longer have a liability. We will provide a release once we have done so.

For an immediate or urgent Certificate of Release of Federal Tax Lien, visit or telephone the district office that filed the Notice of Federal Tax Lien. Be prepared to show proof of payment.

You can pay any unpaid tax with a certified check, cashier's check, or money order to receive a release.

 **IRS**   Department of the Treasury   Publication 1450 (Rev. 3-1999)
Internal Revenue Service   Catalog Number 10665H

¶1464 Exhibit 14-14

FORM **669-A** (Rev. February 1992)	DEPARTMENT OF THE TREASURY - INTERNAL REVENUE SERVICE **CERTIFICATE OF DISCHARGE OF PROPERTY FROM FEDERAL TAX LIEN** *(Sec. 6325(b)(1) of the Internal Revenue Code)*

WHEREAS, _____

Of _____ , City of _____ ,

County of _____ , State of _____ ,

is indebted to the United States for unpaid internal revenue tax in the sum of _____

_____ Dollars ($ _____)

as evidenced by:

NOTICE OF FEDERAL TAX LIEN SERIAL NUMBER (a)	RECORDING INFORMATION (b)	DATE RECORDED (c)	TAXPAYER IDENTIFICATION NUMBER (d)	AMOUNT SHOWN ON LIEN (e)

Sample

WHEREAS, to secure the collection of said tax, notice of the lien of the United States, attaching to all the property and rights to property of the said taxpayer on account of said tax indebtedness, was filed with the

_____ for the

_____ , and also with the _____

_____ , in accordance with the applicable provisions of law.

WHEREAS, the lien of the United States, listed above, for said tax has attached to certain property described as:

Catalog No. 16751C

FORM **669-A** (Rev. 2-92)

¶1464

(Use this space for continued description of property)

WHEREAS, the District Director of Internal Revenue has determined that if the certificate of discharge is issued with respect to the foregoing property, the other property which will remain subject to the lien of the United States has a fair market value at this time of at least double the sum of: (1) the amount of the liability remaining unsatisfied in respect of such tax and (2) the amount of all prior liens upon such property;

NOW, THEREFORE, THIS INSTRUMENT WITNESSETH, That I, _____ ,

District Director of Internal Revenue at _____ , charged by law with the duty of collecting and enforcing the collection of internal revenue taxes due the United States, and charged with the assessment hereinbefore stated, do, pursuant to the provisions of section 6325(b)(1), of the Internal Revenue Code discharge the property heretofore described from the aforesaid tax lien, saving and reserving, however, the force and effect of said tax lien against and upon all other property or rights to property to which said lien is attached, wheresoever situated.

WITNESS my hand at _____ , on this,

the _____ day of _____ , 19 ___ .

SIGNATURE	TITLE

(NOTE: Certificate of officer authorized by law to take acknowledgments is not essential to the validity of Discharge of Federal Tax Lien. Rev. Rul 71-466, 1971-2, C.B. 409)

¶1464

FORM **669-B** (Rev. February 1992)	DEPARTMENT OF THE TREASURY - INTERNAL REVENUE SERVICE **Certificate of Discharge of Property from Federal Tax Lien** *(Section 6325(b)(2)(A) of the Internal Revenue Code)*

Whereas, _____

Of _____ , City of _____ ,

County of _____ , State of _____ ,

is indebted to the United States for unpaid internal revenue tax in the sum of _____

_____ Dollars *($* _____ *)*

as evidenced by:

NOTICE OF FEDERAL TAX LIEN SERIAL NUMBER (a)	RECORDING INFORMATION (b)	DATE RECORDED (c)	TAXPAYER IDENTIFICATION NUMBER (d)	AMOUNT SHOWN ON LIEN (e)

Whereas, to secure the collection of said tax, notice of the lien of the United States, attaching to all the property

and rights to property of the said taxpayer on account of said tax indebtedness, was filed with the _____

_____ for the

_____ , and also with the _____

_____ , in accordance with the applicable provisions of law.

Whereas, the lien of the United States, listed above, for said tax has attached to certain property described as:

Catalog No. 16752N   Form **669-B** (Rev. 2-92)

¶1464

¶1465 Exhibit 14-15

Instructions on how to apply for

Certificate of Discharge of Property From Federal Tax Lien

Department of the Treasury

Internal Revenue Service

Publication 783 (Rev 9-91)
Cat. No. 46755I

Since there is no standard form available for an application for a certificate of discharge of property from a Federal Tax Lien, a typewritten request will be considered as an application. Submit your typewritten request and all accompanying documents in duplicate to:

District Director of Internal Revenue
(Address to District in which the property is located)

Attention of: Chief, Special Procedures Staff

Give Date of Application

Information required on application

Please give the name and address of the person applying, under section 6325(b) of the Internal Revenue Code, for a certificate of discharge. See the reverse of this publication for applicable Internal Revenue Code sections. Give the name and address of the taxpayer, and describe the property as follows:

1. Give a detailed description, including the location of the property for which you are requesting the certificate of discharge. If real property is involved, submit a legible copy of the title or deed to the property, and the complete address (street, city, State). If the certificate is requested under section 6325(b)(1), also give a description of all the taxpayer's remaining subject to the lien.

2. Show how and when the taxpayer has been, or will be, divested of all rights, title and interest in an to the property for which a certificate of discharge is requested.

3. Attach a copy of each notice of Federal tax lien, or furnish the following information as it appears on each filed notice of Federal tax lien:
   a. The name of the Internal Revenue District;
   b. The name and address of the taxpayer against whom the notice was filed;
   c. Serial number shown on the lien;
   d. Taxpayer's identification number shown on the lien;
   e. The date and place the notice was filed;
   f. In lieu of the above, a preliminary title report may be substituted listing the required information.

4. List the encumbrances (or attach a copy of the instrument that created each encumbrance) on the property which you believe have priority over the Federal tax lien. For each encumbrance show:
   a. The name and address of the holder;
   b. A description of the encumbrance;
   c. The date of the agreement;
   d. The date and place of the recording, if any;
   e. The original principal amount and the interest rate;
   f. The amount due as of the date of the application, if known (show costs and accrued interest separately);
   g. Your family relationship, if any, to the taxpayer and to the holders of any other encumbrances on the property.

h. In lieu of the above, a preliminary title report may be substituted listing the required information.

5. Itemize all proposed or actual costs, commissions and expenses of any transfer or sale of the property.

6. Furnish information to establish the value of the property for which you are applying for a certificate of discharge. If the certificate is requested under section 6325(b)(1) furnish an estimate of the fair market value of the property which will remain subject to the lien. In addition,
   a. If private sale—Submit written appraisals by two disinterested people qualified to appraise the property, and a brief statement of each appraiser's qualifications.
   b. If public sale (auction) already held—Give the date and place the sale was held, and the amount for which the property was sold.
   c. If public sale (auction) to be held—Give the proposed date and place of the sale, and include a statement that the United States will be paid in its proper priority from the proceeds of the sale.

7. Give any other information that might, in your opinion, have bearing upon the application, such as pending judicial actions.

8. The District Director may request you to furnish additional information.

9. If you are submitting the application under the provisions of section 6325(b)(3), dealing with the substitution of proceeds of sale, attach a copy of the proposed agreement containing the following:
   a. Name and address of proposed escrow agent;
   b. Caption, type of account, name and address of depositary for the account;
   c. Conditions under which the escrow fund is to be held;
   d. Conditions under which payment will be made from escrow, including the limitation for negotiated settlement of claims against the fund;
   e. Estimated costs of escrow;
   f. Name and address of any other party you and the District Director determine to be a party to the escrow agreement;
   g. Your signature, and those of the escrow agent, District Director and any other party to the escrow agreement;
   h. Any other specific information the District Director requests.

10. Give a daytime telephone number where you may be reached.

11. Give the name, address and telephone number of your attorney or other representative, if any.

12. Make the following declaration over your signature and title: "Under penalties of perjury, I declare that I have examined this application, including any accompanying schedules, exhibits, affidavits, and statements, and to the best of my knowledge and belief it is true, correct, and complete."

Additional Information

Please follow the instructions in this publication when applying for a Certificate of Discharge of Property From Federal Tax Lien.

The District Director has the authority to issue a certificate of discharge of a lien that is filed on any part of a taxpayer's property subject to the lien. The following sections and provisions of the Internal Revenue Code apply:

Section 6325(b)(1), a specific property may be discharged; if the taxpayer's property remaining subject to the lien has a Fair Market Value (FMV) which is double the sum of the balance due a) all Federal Tax Liens b) all other liens. (FMV=(a + b) x 2)

Section 6325(b)(2)(A), if there is paid in partial satisfaction of the liability secured by the lien an amount determined to be not less than the value of the interest of the United States in the property to be discharged.

Section 6325(b)(2)(B), if it is determined that the interest of the United States in the property to be discharged has no value.

Section 6325(b)(3), if the property subject to the lien is sold and, under an agreement with the Internal Revenue Service, the proceeds from the sale are to be held as a fund subject to the liens and claims of the United States in the same manner, and with the same priority, as the liens and claims on the discharged property.

1. No payment is required for the issuance of a certificate under **section 6325(b)(1) or section 6325(b)(2)(B)** of the Code. Payment is required for certificates issued under **section 6325(b)(2)(A)**. Do not send the payment with your application, however. The District Director will notify you after determining the amount due.

2. The District Director will have your application investigated to determine whether to issue the certificate, and will let you know the outcome.

3. A certificate of discharge under **section 6325 (b)(2)(A)** will be issued upon receipt of the amount determined to be the interest of the United States in the subject property under the Federal tax lien. Make remittances in cash, or by a certified, cashier's, or treasurer's check drawn on any bank or trust company incorporated under the laws of the United States or of any State, or possession of the United States, or by United States postal, bank, express, or telegraph money order. (If you pay by uncertified personal check, issuance of the certificate of discharge will be delayed until the bank honors the check.)

4. If application is made under **section 6325(b)(2)(A)** or **6325(b)(2)(B)** because a mortgage foreclosure is contemplated, there will be a determination of the amount required for discharge or a determination that the Federal tax lien interest in the property is valueless.

Within 30 days from the date of the application, the applicant will receive a written conditional commitment for a certificate of discharge. When the foreclosure proceeding has been concluded, a certificate of discharge will be issued in accordance with the terms of the commitment letter. Also see, Application Requesting the United States to Release Its Right to Redeem Property Secured by a Federal Tax Lien, Publication 487.

5. If application is made under the provisions of **section 6325(b)(3)**, the District Director has the authority to approve an escrow agent selected by the applicant. Any reasonable expenses incurred in connection with the sale of the property, the holding of the fund, or the distribution of the fund shall be paid by the applicant or from the proceeds of the sale before satisfaction of any claims and liens. Submit a copy of the proposed escrow agreement as part of the application.

Publication 783 (Rev. 9-91)
*U.S. GPO: 1995-402-283/39051

¶1466 Exhibit 14-16

Form **669-D** (Rev. February 1992)	DEPARTMENT OF THE TREASURY - INTERNAL REVENUE SERVICE **Certificate of Subordination of Federal Tax Lien** *(Section 6325(d)(1) of the Internal Revenue Code)*

Whereas, _____

Of _____ , City of _____ ,

County of _____ , State of _____ ,

is indebted to the United States for unpaid internal revenue tax in the sum of _____

_____ Dollars *($* _____ *)*

as evidenced by:

NOTICE OF FEDERAL TAX LIEN SERIAL NUMBER (a)	RECORDING INFORMATION (b)	DATE RECORDED (c)	TAXPAYER IDENTIFICATION NUMBER (d)	AMOUNT SHOWN ON LIEN (e)

Whereas, to secure the collection of said tax, notice of the lien of the United States, attaching to all the property

and rights to property of the said taxpayer on account of said tax indebtedness, was filed with the _____

_____ _____ for the

_____ , and also with the _____ ,

_____ , in accordance with the applicable provisions of law.

Whereas, the lien of the United States, listed above, for said tax has attached to certain property described as:

Catalog No. 16754J   FORM **669-D** (Rev. 2-92)

(Use this space for continued description of property)

Whereas, the District Director of Internal Revenue has determined that upon the payment of the sum of _____ dollars *($_____)* which amount is equal to the amount with respect to which the tax lien is subordinated and is to be applied in part satisfaction of the liability in respect of the tax hereinbefore stated which sum has been paid to be so applied, and the receipt of which sum by me is hereby acknowledged; _____ , has authorized the issuance, under the provisions of **section 6325(d)(1)** of the Internal Revenue Code, of a certificate subordinating the tax lien of the United States;

   Now, therefore, this instrument witnesseth, that I, _____ ,

District Director of Internal Revenue at _____ , charged by law with the duty of collecting and enforcing the collection of internal revenue taxes due the United States, and charged with the assessment hereinbefore stated, do, pursuant to the provisions of section 6325(d)(1) of the Internal Revenue Code, subordinate the aforesaid tax lien, in the amount heretofore stated to the instrument herein described as _____

_____ ,

saving and reserving, however, the force and effect of said tax lien against and upon all other property or rights to property to which said lien is attached, wherever situated.

   Witness my hand at _____ , on this,

the _____ day of _____ , 19 ____ .

Signature	Title

Note: Certificate of officer authorized by law to take acknowledgments is not essential to the validity of Subordination of Federal Tax Lien. Rev. Rul 71-466, 1971-2, C.B. 409.

Form **669-D** (Rev. 2-92)

¶1466

¶1467 Exhibit 14-17

How to Prepare an Application for a

Certificate of Subordination of Federal Tax Lien

Since there is no standard form available for an application for a Certificate of Subordination of Federal tax lien, a computer generated request will be considered as an application *(please, no handwritten request).* **Submit your request and all accompanying documents in duplicate to:**

IRS, Attn: Technical Services Group Manager

(Address to the IRS office in which the lien was filed. Use **Publication 4235**, *Technical Services Group Addresses, to determine where to mail your request.)*

Information Required on Application

Give date of the application.

Please **give the name and address of the person applying** for the certificate of subordination under either **section 6325(d)(1) or 6325(d)(2)** of the Internal Revenue Code. See the "*Additional Information*" section of this publication for applicable Internal Revenue Code sections. Give the name and address of the taxpayer, and describe the property as follows:

1. Give a detailed description, including the location of the property for which you are requesting the certificate of subordination. **If real property is involved,** give the description contained in the title or deed of the property and the complete address *(street, city, state, and ZIP code).*

2. **Attach a copy of each notice of Federal tax lien,** or furnish the following information as it appears on each filed notice of Federal tax lien:
   a. The name of the Internal Revenue Office;
   b. The name and address of the taxpayer against whom the notice was filed; and
   c. The date and place the notice was filed.

3. Submit a copy of each instrument to which you believe an encumbrance exists or describe the encumbrance to which the Federal tax lien is to be subordinated, including:
   a. The present amount of the encumbrance;
   b. The nature of the encumbrance *(such as mortgage, assignment, etc.)*; and
   c. The date the transaction is to be completed.

4. List the encumbrances *(or attach a copy of the instrument that created each encumbrance)* on the property that you believe has priority over the Federal tax lien. For each encumbrance show:
   a. The name and address of the holder;
   b. A description of the encumbrance;
   c. The date of the agreement;
   d. The date and place of the recording, if any;
   e. The original principal amount and the interest rate;
   f. The amount due as of the date of the application, if known *(show costs and accrued interest separately)*; and
   g. Your family relationship, if any, to the taxpayer and to the holders of any other encumbrances on the property.

5. Furnish an estimate of the fair market value of the property for which you would like a certificate of subordination.

6. If you are submitting the application under **section 6325(d)(1)**, show the amount to be paid to the United States.

7. If you are submitting the application under **section 6325(d)(2)**, attach a complete statement showing how the amount the United States may realize will ultimately increase and how collection of the tax liability will be made easier.

8. Furnish any other information that might help the Technical Services Group Manager decide whether to issue a certificate of subordination.

9. The Technical Services Group Manager may request that you furnish additional information.

10. Give a daytime telephone number where you may be reached.

11. Give the name, address and telephone number of your attorney or other representative, if any.

12. **Write the following declaration over your signature and title:** "Under penalties of perjury, I declare that I have examined this application, including any accompanying schedules, exhibits, affidavits, and statements, and to the best of my knowledge and belief it is true, correct, and complete."

(over)

Additional Information

Please follow the instructions in this publication when applying for a Certificate of Subordination of Federal Tax Lien.

The Technical Services Group Manager has the authority to issue a certificate of subordination of a lien that is filed on any part of a taxpayer's property subject to the lien. The following sections and provisions of the Internal Revenue Code apply:

Section 6325(d)(1) - If you pay an amount equal to the lien or interest to which the certificate subordinates the lien of the United States.

Section 6325(d)(2) - If the Technical Services Group Manager believes that issuance of the certificate will increase the amount the United States may realize, or the collection of the tax liability will be easier. This applies to the property that the certificate is for or any other property subject to the lien.

1. No payment is required for the issuance of a certificate under **section 6325(d)(2)** of the Code. Payment is required for certificates issued under **section 6325(d)(1)**. However, do not send the payment with your application. The Technical Services Group Manager will notify you after determining the amount due.

2. The Technical Services Group Manager will have your application investigated to determine whether to issue the certificate and will let you know the outcome.

3. A certificate of subordination under **section 6325(d)(1)** will be issued upon receipt of the amount determined to be the interest of the United States in the subject property under the Federal tax lien. Make payments in cash, or by a certified, cashier's, or treasurer's check. It must be drawn on any bank or trust company incorporated under the laws of the United States, or of any state, or possession of the United States. Payment can also be made by United States postal, bank, express, or telegraph money order. *(If you pay by personal check, issuance of the certificate of subordination will be delayed until the bank honors the check.)*

4. In certain cases the Technical Services Group Manager may require additional information such as written appraisals by disinterested third parties, a list of all the taxpayer's property, or other information needed to make a determination.

Department of Treasury
Internal Revenue Service

www.irs.gov

Publication 784 (Rev. 1-2004)
Catalog Number 46756T

¶1467

¶1468 Exhibit 14-18

Form **668-A(c) (DO)** (Rev. Sept. 1997)	Department of the Treasury — **Internal Revenue Service** **Notice of Levy**

DATE: DISTRICT: TELEPHONE NUMBER
                                            OF IRS OFFICE:
REPLY TO:

NAME AND ADDRESS OF TAXPAYER:

TO:

IDENTIFYING NUMBER(S):

THIS ISN'T A BILL FOR TAXES YOU OWE. THIS IS A NOTICE OF LEVY WE ARE USING TO COLLECT MONEY OWED BY THE TAXPAYER NAMED ABOVE.

Kind of Tax	Tax Period Ended	Unpaid Balance of Assessment	Statutory Additions	Total

THIS LEVY WON'T ATTACH FUNDS IN IRAs, SELF-EMPLOYED INDIVIDUALS' RETIREMENT PLANS, OR ANY OTHER RETIREMENT PLANS IN YOUR POSSESSION OR CONTROL, UNLESS IT IS SIGNED IN THE BLOCK TO THE RIGHT. ⟶

| Total Amount Due ▶ | |

We figured the interest and late payment penalty to _____

The Internal Revenue Code provides that there is a lien for the amount that is owed. Although we have given the notice and demand required by the Code, the amount owed hasn't been paid. This levy requires you to turn over to us this person's property and rights to property (such as money, credits, and bank deposits) that you have or which you are already obligated to pay this person. However, don't send us more than the "Total Amount Due."

Money in banks, credit unions, savings and loans, and similar institutions described in section 408(n) of the Internal Revenue Code must be held for 21 calendar days from the day you receive this levy before you send us the money. Include any interest the person earns during the 21 days. Turn over any other money, property, credits, etc. that you have or are already obligated to pay the taxpayer, when you would have paid it if this person asked for payment.

Make a reasonable effort to identify all property and rights to property belonging to this person. At a minimum, search your records using the taxpayer's name, address, and identifying numbers(s) shown on this form. Don't offset money this person owes you without contacting us at the telephone number shown above for instructions. You may not subtract a processing fee from the amount you send us.

To respond to this levy:
1. Make your check or money order payable to Internal Revenue Service.
2. Write the taxpayer's name, identifying number(s), kind of tax and tax period shown on this form, and "LEVY PROCEEDS" on your check or money order (not on a detachable stub.).
3. Complete the back of Part 3 of this form and mail it to us with your payment in the enclosed envelope.
4. Keep Part 1 of this form for your records and give the taxpayer Part 2 within 2 days.

If you don't owe any money to the taxpayer, please complete the back of Part 3, and mail that part back to us in the enclosed envelope.

Signature of Service Representative	Title

Part 1 - FOR ADDRESSEE   FORM **668-A(c) (DO)** (Rev. 9-97)   15704T

¶1469 Exhibit 14-19

Form **668-D** (Rev. May 1997)	Department of the Treasury — Internal Revenue Service ## Release of Levy/Release of Property from Levy

To	Taxpayer(s)
	Identifying Number(s)

A notice of levy was served on you and demand was made for the surrender of:

☐ all property, rights to property, money, credits and bank deposits of the taxpayer(s) named above, except as provided in 6332(c) of the Internal Revenue Code—"Special Rule For Banks." See the back of this form regarding this exception.

☐ wages, salary and other income, now owed to or becoming payable to the taxpayer(s) named above.

The box checked below applies to the levy we served on you.

Release of Levy

☐ Under the provisions of Internal Revenue Code section 6343, all property, rights to property, money, credits, and bank deposits of the taxpayer(s) named above are released from the levy.

☐ Under the provisions of Internal Revenue Code section 6343, all wages, salary and other income now owed to or becoming payable to the taxpayer(s) named above are released from the levy.

Release of Property from Levy

☐ Under the provisions of Internal Revenue Code section 6343, all property, rights to property, money, credits, and bank deposits greater than $ _____ are released from the levy. The levy now attaches only to this amount.

☐ The last payment we received from you was $ _____ dated _____ . The amount the taxpayer still owes is $ _____ . When this amount is paid to the Internal Revenue Service, the levy is released. If you sent us a payment after the last payment date shown, subtract that from the amount you send now.

☐ Under the provisions of Internal Revenue code section 6343, all wages, salary and other income ☐ **greater than** ☐ **less than** $ _____ each _____ now owed to or becoming payable to the taxpayer(s) named above are released from the levy.

Dated at _____   _____ , 19 ____
       (Place)   (Date)

Signature	Telephone Number	Title

Part 1 — To Addressee   Cat. No. 20450C   Form **668-D** (Rev. 05-97)

¶1469

Excerpts from the Internal Revenue Code

Sec. 6332 Surrender of Property Subject to Levy

(c) **Special Rule for Banks.**—Any bank *(as defined in section 408(n))* shall surrender *(subject to an attachment or execution under judicial process)* any deposits *(including interest thereon)* in such bank only after 21 days after service of levy.

* * * * * * *

Sec. 6343. Authority to Release Levy and Return Property

(a) **Release of Levy and Notice of Release.**—

(1) **In general.**—Under regulations prescribed by the Secretary, the Secretary shall release the levy upon all, or part of, the property or rights to property levied upon and shall promptly notify the person upon whom such levy was made *(if any)* that such levy has been released if—

(A) the liability for which such levy was made is satisfied or becomes unenforceable by reason of lapse of time,

(B) release of such levy will facilitate the collection of such liability,

(C) the taxpayer has entered into an agreement under section 6159 to satisfy such liability by means of installment payments, unless such agreement provides otherwise,

(D) the Secretary has determined that such levy is creating an economic hardship due to the financial condition of the taxpayer, or

(E) the fair market value of the property exceeds such liability and release of the levy on a part of such property could be made without hindering the collection of such liability.

For purposes of subparagraph (C), the Secretary is not required to release such levy if such release would jeopardize the secured creditor status of the Secretary.

(2) **Expedited determination of certain business property.**—In the case of any tangible personal property essential in carrying on the trade or business of the taxpayer, the Secretary shall provide for an expedited determination under paragraph (1) if levy on such tangible personal property would prevent the taxpayer from carrying on such trade or business.

(3) **Subsequent levy.**—The release of levy on any property under paragraph (1) shall not prevent any subsequent levy on such property.

(b) **Return of property.**—

If the Secretary determines that property has been wrongfully levied upon, it shall be lawful for the Secretary to return . . . an amount equal to the amount of money levied upon . . . any time before the expiration of 9 months from the date of such levy . . . .

(d) **Return of Property in Certain Cases.**—If—

(1) any property has been levied upon, and

(2) the Secretary determines that—

(A) the levy on such property was premature or otherwise not in accordance with administrative procedures of the Secretary,

(B) the taxpayer has entered into an agreement under section 6159 to satisfy the tax liability for which the levy was imposed by means of installment payments, unless such agreement provides otherwise,

(C) the return of such property will facilitate the collection of the tax liability, or

(D) with the consent of the taxpayer or the Taxpayer Advocate, the return of such property would be in the best interests of the taxpayer (as determined by the Taxpayer Advocate) and the United States,

the provisions of subsection (b) shall apply in the same manner as if such property had been wrongly levied upon, except that no interest shall be allowed . . . .

Form **668-D** (Rev. 05-97)

¶1470 Exhibit 14-20

OMB No. 1545-1504

Department of the Treasury – Internal Revenue Service

TAXPAYER ADVOCATE SERVICE

Application for Taxpayer Assistance Order (ATAO)

Form **911** (Rev. 3-2000)

Section I.	Taxpayer Information	

1. Name(s) as shown on tax return	4. Your Social Security Number	6. Tax Form(s)
	5. Social Security No. of Spouse	7. Tax Period(s)
2. Current mailing address (Number, Street & Apartment Number)	8. Employer Identification Number (if applicable)	
	9. E-Mail address	
3. City, Town or Post Office, State and ZIP Code	10. Fax number	
11. Person to contact	12. Daytime telephone number	13. Best time to call

14. Please describe the problem and the significant hardship it is creating. *(If more space is needed, attach additional sheets.)*

15. Please describe the relief you are requesting. *(If more space is needed, attach additional sheets.)*

I understand that Taxpayer Advocate employees may contact third parties in order to respond to this request and I authorize such contacts to be made. Further, by authorizing the Taxpayer Advocate Service to contact third parties, I understand that I will not receive notice, pursuant to section 7602(c) of the Internal Revenue Code, of third parties contacted in connection with this request.

16. Signature of taxpayer or corporate officer	17. Date	18. Signature of spouse	19. Date

Section II.	Representative Information (if applicable)	

1. Name of Authorized Representative	3. Centralized Authorization File Number (CAF)
2. Mailing Address	4. Daytime telephone number
	5. Fax number
6. Signature of Representative	7. Date

Cat. No. 16965S

Form **911** (Rev. 3-2000)

Section III.   **(For Internal Revenue Service only)**

Taxpayer Name	Taxpayer Identification Number (TIN)

1. Name of Initiating Employee	2. Employee Telephone Number	3. Operating Division or Function	4. Office

5. How Identified & Received (Check the appropriate box)	6. IRS Received Date

IRS Function Identified Issue as Meeting TAS Criteria
❑ (r) Functional referral (Functional area identified TP/Rep issue as meeting TAS criteria)
❑ (x) Congressional correspondence/inquiry not addressed to TAS but referred for TAS handling

Taxpayer or Representative Requested TAS Assistance
❑ (c) Taxpayer or representative filed Form 911 or sent other correspondence to TAS
❑ (n) Taxpayer or representative called into a National Taxpayer Advocate (NTA) Toll-Free site
❑ (p) Taxpayer or representative called TAS (other than NTA Toll-Free)
❑ (s) Functional referral (Taxpayer or representative specifically requested TAS assistance)
❑ (w) Taxpayer or representative sought TAS assistance in a TAS walk-in area
❑ (y) Congressional corresp/inquiry addressed to TAS or any Congressional specifically requesting TAS assistance

7. TAS Criteria (Check the appropriate box)
❑ (1) Taxpayer is suffering or about to suffer a significant hardship
❑ (2) Taxpayer is facing an immediate threat of adverse action
❑ (3) Taxpayer will incur significant costs, including fees for professional representation, if relief is not granted
❑ (4) Taxpayer will suffer irreparable injury or long-term adverse impact if relief is not granted
❑ (5) Taxpayer experienced an IRS delay of more than 30 calendar days in resolving an account-related problem or inquiry
❑ (6) Taxpayer did not receive a response or resolution to their problem by the date promised
❑ (7) A system or procedure has either failed to operate as intended or failed to resolve a taxpayer problem or dispute with the IRS
❑ (8) Congressional Duplicate of any criteria or non-criteria case already in TAS or on TAMIS
❑ (9) Any issue/problem not meeting the above TAS criteria but kept in TAS for handling and resolution

8. Initiating Employee: What actions did you take to help resolve the problem?

9. Initiating Employee: State reason(s) why relief was not provided.

Section III Instructions (For Internal Revenue Service only)
1. Enter your name.
2. Enter your telephone number.
3. Enter your function (i.e.; ACS, Collection, Examination, Customer Service, etc.). If you are now part of one of the new Business Operating Divisions (Wage & Investment Income, Small Business/Self-Employed, Large/Mid-Size Business, Tax-Exempt/Govt Entity), enter the name of the division.
4. Enter the number/Organization Code for your office. (e.g.; 18 for AUSC, 95 for Los Angeles).
5. Check the appropriate box that best reflects how the taxpayer informed us of the problem. For example, did TP call or write an IRS function or TAS? Did TP specifically request TAS assistance/handling or did the function identify the issue as meeting TAS criteria?
6. The IRS Received Date is the date TP/Rep first informed the IRS of the problem. Enter the date the TP/Rep first called, walked in or wrote the IRS to seek assistance with getting the problem resolved.
7. Check the box that best describes the reason/justification for Taxpayer Advocate Service (TAS) assistance and handling.
8. Indicate the actions you took to help resolve taxpayer's problem.
9. State the reason(s) that prevented you from resolving taxpayer's problem and from providing relief. For example, levy proceeds cannot be returned since they were already applied to a valid liability; an overpayment cannot be refunded since the refund statute expired; or current law precludes a specific interest abatement.

Section IV.   **(For Taxpayer Advocate Service only)**

1. TAMIS CF#	2. BOD/Client	3. How Recd Code	4. Criteria Code	5. IRS Recd Date	6. TAS Recd Date
7. Reopen Ind	8. Func/Unit Assigned	9. Employee Assigned	10. Major Issue Code	11. ATAO Code/Subcode	12. PSD Code
13. Special Case Code	14. Complexity Code	15. Outreach	16. Local Use Code TP _|_|_|_|_| Case __|	17. Relief Date	18. TAS Clsd Date
19. Cust Satisfact Cde	20. Root Cause Code				

Hardship ❑ Yes ❑ No	Taxpayer Advocate Signature	Date

Cat. No. 16965S   Form **911** (Rev. 3-2000)

Instructions

When to use this form: Use this form to request relief if any of the following apply to you:

1. You are suffering or about to suffer a significant hardship;
2. You are facing an immediate threat of adverse action;
3. You will incur significant costs, including fees for professional representation, if relief is not granted;
4. You will suffer irreparable injury or long-term adverse impact if relief is not granted;
5. You experienced an IRS delay of more than 30 calendar days in resolving an account-related problem or inquiry;
6. You did not receive a response or resolution to your problem by the date promised;
7. A system or procedure has either failed to operate as intended or failed to resolve your problem or dispute with the IRS.

If an IRS office will not grant the relief requested or will not grant the relief in time to avoid the significant hardship, you may submit this form. No enforcement action will be taken while we are reviewing your application.

Where to Submit This Form: Submit this application to the Taxpayer Advocate office located in the state or city where you reside. For the address of the Taxpayer Advocate in your state or city or for additional information call the National Taxpayer Advocate Toll-Free Number 1-877-777-4778.

Third Party Contact: You should understand that in order to respond to this request you are also authorizing the Taxpayer Advocate Service to contact third parties when necessary and that you will not receive further notice regarding contacted parties. See IRC 7602(c).

Overseas Taxpayers: Taxpayers residing overseas can submit this application by mail to the Taxpayer Advocate, Internal Revenue Service, PO Box 193479, San Juan, Puerto Rico 00919 or in person at 2 Ponce de Leon Avenue, Mercantil Plaza Building, Room GF05A, Hato Rey PR 00918. The application can also be faxed to (787) 759-4535.

Caution: Incomplete applications or applications submitted to an Advocate office outside of your geographical location may result in delays. If you do not hear from us within one week of submitting Form 911, please contact the Taxpayer Advocate office where you originally submitted your application.

Section I Instructions--Taxpayer Information

1. Enter your name(s) as shown on the tax return that relates to this application for relief.
2. Enter your current mailing address, including street number and name and apartment number.
3. Enter your city, town or post office, state and ZIP code.
4. Enter your Social Security Number.
5. Enter the Social Security Number of your spouse if this application relates to a jointly filed return.
6. Enter the number of the Federal tax return or form that relates to this application. For example, an individual taxpayer with an income tax issue would enter Form 1040.
7. Enter the quarterly, annual or other tax period that relates to this application. For example, if this request involves an income tax issue, enter the calendar or fiscal year; if an employment tax issue, enter the calendar quarter.
8. Enter your Employer Identification Number if this relief request involves a business or non-individual entity (e.g.; a partnership, corporation, trust, self-employed individual with employees).
9. Enter your E-mail address.
10. Enter your fax number including the area code.
11. Enter the name of the individual we should contact. For partnerships, corporations, trusts, etc., enter the name of the individual authorized to act on the entity's behalf.
12. Enter your daytime telephone number including the area code.
13. Indicate the best time to call you. Please specify a.m. or p.m. hours.
14. Describe the problem and the significant hardship it is creating for you. Specify the actions that the IRS has taken (or not taken) to cause the problem and ensuing hardship. **If the problem involves an IRS delay of more than 30 days in resolving your issue, indicate the date you first contacted the IRS for assistance in resolving your problem.**
15. Describe the relief you are seeking. Specify the actions that you want taken and that you believe necessary to relieve the significant hardship. Furnish if applicable any relevant proof and corroboration as to why relief is warranted or why you cannot or should not meet current IRS demands to satisfy your tax obligations.

16.&18. If this application is a joint relief request relating to a joint tax liability, both spouses should sign in the appropriate blocks. If only one spouse is requesting relief relating to a joint tax liability, only the requesting spouse has to sign the application. If this application is being submitted for another individual, only a person authorized and empowered to act on that individual's behalf should sign the application.
    NOTE: The signing of this application allows the IRS by law to suspend, for the period of time it takes the Advocate to review and decide upon your request, any applicable statutory periods of limitation relating to the assessment or collection of taxes..

17.&19. Enter the date the application was signed.

Section II Instructions--Representative Information

Taxpayers: If you wish to have a representative act on your behalf, you must give him/her power of attorney or tax information authorization for the tax return(s) and period(s)involved. For additional information see Form 2848, Power of Attorney and Declaration of Representative or Form 8821, Tax Information Authorization, and the accompanying instructions.

Representatives: If you are an authorized representative submitting this request on behalf of the taxpayer identified in Section I, complete Blocks 1 through 7 of Section II. Attach a copy of Form 2848, Form 8821 or other power of attorney. Enter your Centralized Authorization File (CAF) number in Block 3 of Section II. The CAF number is the unique number that the IRS assigns to a representative after Form 2848 or Form 8821 is filed with an IRS office.

Paperwork Reduction Act Notice: We ask for the information on this form to carry out the Internal Revenue laws of the United States. Your response is voluntary. You are not required to provide the information requested on a form that is subject to the Paperwork Reduction Act unless the form displays a valid OMB control number. Books or records relating to a form or its instructions must be retained as long as their contents may become material in the administration of any Internal Revenue law. Generally, tax returns and return information are confidential, as required by Code section 6103. Although the time needed to complete this form may vary depending on individual circumstances, the estimated average time is 30 minutes. Should you have comments concerning the accuracy of this time estimate or suggestions for making this form simpler, please write to the Internal Revenue Service, Attention: Tax Forms Committee, Western Area Distribution Center, Rancho Cordova, CA 95743-0001.

Cat. No. 16965S   Form **911** (Rev. 3-2000)

¶1471 Exhibit 14-21

Request for a Collection Due Process Hearing

Use this form to request a hearing with the IRS Office of Appeals only when you receive a **Notice of Federal Tax Lien Filing & Your Right To A Hearing Under IRC 6320**, a **Final Notice - Notice Of Intent to Levy & Your Notice Of a Right To A Hearing**, or a **Notice of Jeopardy Levy and Right of Appeal**. Complete this form and send it to the address shown on your lien or levy notice for expeditious handling. Include a copy of your lien or levy notice(s) to ensure proper handling of your request.

(Print) Taxpayer Name(s):_____

(Print) Address: _____

Daytime Telephone Number:_____ Type of Tax/Tax Form Number(s):_____

Taxable Period(s):_____

Social Security Number/Employer Identification Number(s):_____

Check the IRS action(s) that you do not agree with. Provide specific reasons why you don't agree. If you believe that your spouse or former spouse should be responsible for all or a portion of the tax liability from your tax return, check here [__] and attach Form 8857, Request for Innocent Spouse Relief, to this request.

_____ **Filed Notice of Federal Tax Lien (Explain why you don't agree. Use extra sheets if necessary.)**

_____ **Notice of Levy/Seizure (Explain why you don't agree. Use extra sheets if necessary.)**

I/we understand that the statutory period of limitations for collection is suspended during the Collection Due Process Hearing and any subsequent judicial review.

Taxpayer's or Authorized Representative's Signature and Date:_____

Taxpayer's or Authorized Representative's Signature and Date:_____

IRS Use Only:

IRS Employee *(Print)*: _____ IRS Received Date:_____

Employee Telephone Number: _____

Form **12153** (01-1999)   Catalog Number 26685D   Department of the Treasury – Internal Revenue Service

(Over)

¶1471

Where to File Your Request

It is important that you file your request using the address shown on your lien or levy notice. If you have been working with a specific IRS employee on your case, you should file the request with that employee.

How to Complete Form 12153

1. Enter your full name and address. If the tax liability is owed jointly by a husband and wife, and both wish to request a Collection Due Process Hearing, show both names.

2. Enter a daytime telephone number where we can contact you regarding your request for a hearing.

3. List the type(s) of tax or the number of the tax form(s) for which you are requesting a hearing (e.g. Form 1040, Form 941, Trust Fund Recovery Penalty, etc.).

4. List the taxable periods for the type(s) of tax or the tax form(s) that you listed for item 3 above (e.g., year ending 12-31-98, quarter ending 3-31-98).

5. Show the social security number of the individual(s) and/or the employer identification number of the business(s) that are requesting a hearing.

6. Check the IRS action(s) that you do not agree with (Filed Notice of Federal Tax Lien and/or Notice of Levy/Seizure). You may check both actions if applicable.

7. Provide the specific reason(s) why you do not agree with the filing of the Notice of Federal Tax Lien or the proposed Notice of Levy/Seizure action. One specific issue that you may raise at the hearing is whether income taxes should be abated because you believe that your spouse or former spouse should be responsible for all or a portion of the tax liability from your tax return. You must, however, elect such relief. You can do this by checking the indicated box and attaching Form 8857 to this request for a hearing. If you previously filed Form 8857, please indicate when and with whom you filed the Form.

8. You, or your authorized representative, must sign the Form 12153. If the tax liability is joint and both spouses are requesting a hearing, both spouses, or their authorized representative(s), must sign.

9. It is important that you understand that we are required by statute to suspend the statutory period for collection during a Collection Due Process Hearing.

¶1472   Exhibit 14-22

Form **9465**		**Installment Agreement Request**		
(Rev. December 2003)				OMB No. 1545-1350
Department of the Treasury Internal Revenue Service		▶ If you are filing this form with your tax return, attach it to the front of the return. Otherwise, see instructions.		

Caution: *Do not file this form if you are currently making payments on an installment agreement. Instead, call 1-800-829-1040. If you are in bankruptcy or we have accepted your offer-in-compromise, see* **Bankruptcy or Offer-in-Compromise** *below.*

1	Your first name and initial	Last name		Your social security number
	If a joint return, spouse's first name and initial	Last name		Spouse's social security number
	Your current address (number and street). If you have a P.O. box and no home delivery, enter your box number.			Apt. number
	City, town or post office, state, and ZIP code. If a foreign address, enter city, province or state, and country. Follow the country's practice for entering the postal code.			

2   If this address is new since you filed your last tax return, check here   . . . . ▶ ☐

3	( )		4	( )		
	Your home phone number Best time for us to call			Your work phone number Ext. Best time for us to call		
5	Name of your bank or other financial institution:		6	Your employer's name:		
	Address			Address		
	City, state, and ZIP code			City, state, and ZIP code		

7   Enter the tax return for which you are making this request (for example, Form 1040) . . . . ▶ _____

8   Enter the tax year for which you are making this request (for example, 2003) . . . . ▶ _____

9   Enter the total amount you owe as shown on your tax return . . . . | **9** | |

10   Enter the amount of any payment you are making with your tax return (or notice). See instructions | **10** | |

11   Enter the amount you can pay each month. **Make your payments as large as possible to limit interest and penalty charges.** The charges will continue until you pay in full . . . . | **11** | |

12   Enter the date you want to make your payment each month. **Do not** enter a date later than the 28th.   . ▶

13   If you want to make your payments by electronic funds withdrawal from your checking account, see the instructions and fill in lines 13a and 13b.

▶   **a**   Routing number   ☐☐☐☐☐☐☐☐☐

▶   **b**   Account number   ☐☐☐☐☐☐☐☐☐☐☐☐☐☐☐☐☐

I authorize the U.S. Treasury and its designated Financial Agent to initiate a monthly ACH electronic funds withdrawal entry to the financial institution account indicated for payments of my Federal taxes owed, and the financial institution to debit the entry to this account. This authorization is to remain in full force and effect until I notify the U.S. Treasury Financial Agent to terminate the authorization. To revoke payment, I must contact the U.S. Treasury Financial Agent at **1-800-829-1040** no later than 7 business days prior to the payment (settlement) date. I also authorize the financial institutions involved in the processing of the electronic payments of taxes to receive confidential information necessary to answer inquiries and resolve issues related to the payments.

Your signature	Date	Spouse's signature. If a joint return, **both** must sign.	Date

General Instructions

Section references are to the Internal Revenue Code.

Purpose of Form

Use Form 9465 to request a monthly installment plan if you cannot pay the full amount you owe shown on your tax return (or on a notice we sent you). Generally, you may have up to 60 months to pay. But before requesting an installment agreement, you should consider other less costly alternatives, such as a bank loan. If you have any questions about this request, call 1-800-829-1040.

Guaranteed Installment Agreement. Your request for an installment agreement cannot be turned down if the tax you owe is not more than $10,000 and **all three** of the following apply.

1. During the past 5 tax years, you (and your spouse if you are making a request for a joint tax return) have timely filed all income tax returns and

paid any income tax due, and have not entered into an installment agreement for payment of income tax.

2. The IRS determines that you cannot pay the tax owed in full when it is due and you give the IRS any information needed to make that determination.

3. You agree to pay the full amount you owe within 3 years and to comply with the tax laws while the agreement is in effect.

⚠   *A Notice of Federal Tax Lien may be filed to protect the government's interest until you pay in full.*

Bankruptcy or Offer-in-Compromise. If you are in bankruptcy or we have accepted your offer-in-compromise, **do not** file this form. Instead, call 1-800-829-1040 to get the number of your local IRS Insolvency function for bankruptcy or Technical Support function for offer-in-compromise.

For Privacy Act and Paperwork Reduction Act Notice, see back of form.   Cat. No. 14842Y   Form **9465** (Rev. 12-2003)

What Will You Be Charged

You will be charged a $43 fee if your request is approved. **Do not include the fee with this form.** After approving your request, we will bill you for the fee with your first payment.

You will also be charged interest and may be charged a late payment penalty on any tax not paid by its due date, even if your request to pay in installments is granted. To limit interest and penalty charges, file your return on time and pay as much of the tax as possible with your return (or notice).

How Does the Installment Agreement Work

If we approve your request, we will send you a letter. It will tell you how to pay the fee and make your first installment payment. We will usually let you know within 30 days after we receive your request whether it is approved or denied. But if this request is for tax due on a return you filed after March 31, it may take us longer than 30 days to reply.

By approving your request, we agree to let you pay the tax you owe in monthly installments instead of immediately paying the amount in full. In return, you agree to make your monthly payments on time. **You also agree to meet all your future tax liabilities.** This means that you must have enough withholding or estimated tax payments so that your tax liability for future years is paid in full when you timely file your return. Your request for an installment agreement will be denied if all required tax returns have not been filed. Any refund due you in a future year will be applied against the amount you owe.

After we receive each payment, we will send you a letter showing the remaining amount you owe, and the due date and amount of your next payment. But if you choose to have your payments automatically withdrawn from your checking account, you will not receive a letter. Your bank statement is your record of payment. You can also make your payments by credit card. For details on how to pay, see your tax return instructions or visit **www.irs.gov.** We will also give you a statement showing the amount you owe at the beginning of the year, all payments made during the year, and the amount you owe at the end of the year.

If you **do not** make your payments on time or you have an outstanding past-due amount in a future year, you will be in default on your agreement and we may take enforcement actions, such as a Notice of Federal Tax Lien or an IRS levy, to collect the entire amount you owe. To ensure that your payments are made timely, you should consider making them by electronic funds withdrawal (see the instructions for lines 13a and 13b).

Where To File

Attach Form 9465 to the front of your return and send it to the address shown in your tax return booklet. If you have already filed your return or you are filing this form in response to a notice, file Form 9465 by itself with the **Internal Revenue Service Center** at the address below for the place where you live. No street address is needed.

IF you live in . . .	THEN use this address . . .
Alabama, Florida, Georgia, Mississippi, North Carolina, Rhode Island, South Carolina, West Virginia	Atlanta, GA 39901
Maine, Massachusetts, New Hampshire, New York, Vermont	Andover, MA 05501
Delaware, Illinois, Indiana, Iowa, Kansas, Michigan, Minnesota, Missouri, Nebraska, North Dakota, South Dakota, Wisconsin	Kansas City, MO 64999
Connecticut, District of Columbia, Maryland, New Jersey, Pennsylvania	Philadelphia, PA 19255
Arkansas, Colorado, Kentucky, Louisiana, New Mexico, Oklahoma, Tennessee, Texas	Austin, TX 73301
Alaska, Arizona, California, Hawaii, Idaho, Montana, Nevada, Oregon, Utah, Washington, Wyoming	Fresno, CA 93888
Ohio, Virginia	Memphis, TN 37501

If you live in American Samoa or Puerto Rico *(or exclude income under section 933)*; are a nonpermanent resident of Guam or the Virgin Islands*; have an APO, FPO, or foreign address; are a dual-status alien; or file Form 2555, 2555-EZ, or 4563, use this address: *Internal Revenue Service Center, Philadelphia, PA 19255.*

* Permanent residents of Guam and the Virgin Islands cannot use Form 9465.

Specific Instructions

Line 1

If you are making this request for a joint tax return, show the names and social security numbers (SSNs) in the same order as on your tax return.

Line 10

Even if you cannot pay the full amount you owe now, you should pay as much as possible to limit penalty and interest charges. If you are filing this form with your tax return, make the payment with your return. For details on how to pay, see your tax return instructions.

If you are filing this form **by itself**, such as in response to a notice, attach a check or money order payable to the **"United States Treasury."** **Do not send cash.** Be sure to include:

- Your name, address, SSN, and daytime phone number.
- The tax year and tax return (for example, "2003 Form 1040") for which you are making this request.

Line 11

You should try to make your payments large enough so that your balance due will be paid off by the due date of your next tax return.

Line 12

You can choose the date your monthly payment is due. For example, if your rent or mortgage payment is due on the first of the month, you may want to make your installment payments on the 15th. When we approve your request, we will tell you the month and date that your first payment is due.

If we have not replied by the date you chose for your first payment, you may send the first payment to the Internal Revenue Service Center at the address shown on this page that applies to you. See the instructions for line 10 to find out what to write on your payment.

Lines 13a and 13b

To pay by electronic funds withdrawal from your checking account at a bank or other financial institution (such as mutual fund, brokerage firm, or credit union), fill in lines 13a and 13b. Check with your financial institution to make sure that an electronic funds withdrawal is allowed and to get the correct routing and account numbers.

Note: *We will send you a bill for the first payment and the fee. All other payments will be electronically withdrawn.*

Line 13a. The routing number **must** be **nine** digits. The first two digits of the routing number must be 01 through 12 or 21 through 32. Use a check to verify the routing numbers. But if your check is payable through a financial institution different from the one at which you have your checking account, do not use the routing numbers on that check. Instead, contact your financial institution for the correct routing numbers.

Line 13b. The account number can be up to 17 characters (both numbers and letters). Include hyphens but omit spaces and special symbols. Enter the number from left to right and leave any unused boxes blank. Be sure **not** to include the check number.

Privacy Act and Paperwork Reduction Act Notice. Our legal right to ask for the information on this form is sections 6001, 6011, 6012(a), 6109, and 6159 and their regulations. We will use the information to process your request for an installment agreement. The reason we need your name and social security number is to secure proper identification. We require this information to gain access to the tax information in our files and properly respond to your request. If you do not enter the information, we may not be able to process your request.

You are not required to provide the information requested on a form that is subject to the Paperwork Reduction Act unless the form displays a valid OMB control number. Books or records relating to a form or its instructions must be retained as long as their contents may become material in the administration of any Internal Revenue law. Generally, tax returns and return information are confidential, as required by section 6103. However, we may give this information to the Department of Justice for civil and criminal litigation, and to cities, states, and the District of Columbia to carry out their tax laws. We may also disclose this information to other countries under a tax treaty, to Federal and state agencies to enforce Federal nontax criminal laws and to combat terrorism.

The time needed to complete and file this form will vary depending on individual circumstances. The estimated average time is: **Learning about the law or the form,** 16 min.; **Preparing the form,** 26 min.; and **Copying, assembling, and sending the form to the IRS,** 20 min.

If you have comments concerning the accuracy of this time estimate or suggestions for making this form simpler, we would be happy to hear from you. You can write to the Tax Products Coordinating Committee, Western Area Distribution Center, Rancho Cordova, CA 95743-0001. **Do not** send the form to this address. Instead, see **Where To File** on this page.

¶1473 Exhibit 14-23

Form **433-D** (Rev. May 1996)	Department of the Treasury — Internal Revenue Service **Installment Agreement**	check box if installment agreement fee was paid ☐

Name and address of taxpayer(s) ┌ └	Social security or employer identification number (primary) (secondary)
	Telephone number (home) (business)
	Kinds of taxes (form numbers) | Tax periods
	Amount owed as of _____ $ | Earliest CSED

Employer (name and address)	Financial institutions (names and addresses)	For assistance: Call 1-800-829-1040 or write: _____ Service Ctr. _____ City, State and Zip Code

I/We agree that the federal taxes shown above, PLUS ALL PENALTIES AND INTEREST PROVIDED BY LAW, will be paid as follows:

$ _____ will be paid on _____ and $ _____ will be paid

no later than the _____ of each month thereafter until the total liability is paid in full. I/we also agree that the above

installment payment will be increased or decreased as follows:

check box if pre-assessed modules included ☐

Date of increase (or decrease)	/ /	/ /
Amount of increase (or decrease)	$	
New installment amount	$	

AGREEMENT LOCATOR NUMBER: ___ ___ ___ ___
(circle)
0   No future action is required
5   Financial review date: ___ ___ / ___ ___
6   Monitor ES compliance:
         Indicator: 1st Qtr___ 2nd Qtr___ 3rd Qtr___
         ES payment: $_____ $_____ $_____

Conditions of this agreement:
- We must receive each payment by the date shown above; if you have a problem, contact us immediately.
- This agreement is based on your current financial condition. We may change or cancel it if our information shows that your ability to pay has changed significantly.
- We may cancel this agreement if you don't give us updated financial information when we ask for it.
- While this agreement is in effect, you must file all federal tax returns and pay any taxes you owe on time.
- We will apply your federal or state tax refunds (if any) to the amount you owe until it is fully paid. (This includes the Alaska Permanent Fund dividend for Alaska residents.)
- You must pay a $43 installment agreement fee, which we have authority to deduct from the first payment.
- If agreement defaults, you must pay a $24 reinstatement fee if agreement is reinstated, which we have authority to deduct from the first payment.

Additional Conditions: (To be completed by IRS)

- If you don't meet the conditions of this agreement, we will cancel it, and may collect the entire amount you owe by levy on your income, bank accounts or other assets, or by seizing your property.
- We will cancel this agreement at any time if we find that collection of the tax is in jeopardy.
- We will apply all payments on this agreement in the best interest of the United States.
- This agreement may require managerial approval. If it is not approved, you will be notified.
- **A NOTICE OF FEDERAL TAX LIEN** (check one)
  - ☐ **HAS ALREADY BEEN FILED**
  - ☐ **WILL BE FILED IMMEDIATELY**
  - ☐ **WILL BE FILED WHEN TAX IS ASSESSED**
  - ☐ **MAY BE FILED IF THIS AGREEMENT DEFAULTS**

Your signature	Title (if corporate officer or partner)	Date	Originator's name, title and IDRS assignment number (or district):
Spouse's signature (if a joint liability)		Date	
Agreement examined or approved by (signature, title, function)		Date	Originator Code:

YOU MAY HAVE YOUR INSTALLMENT AGREEMENT PAYMENT DEDUCTED FROM YOUR CHECKING ACCOUNT EACH MONTH (DIRECT DEBIT); IF YOU CHOOSE THIS OPTION, FOLLOW THE DIRECTIONS ON THE BACK OF YOUR COPY OF THIS FORM.

If you agree to Direct Debit, initial here: _____ and attach a blank voided check.	• I (we) authorize the IRS and the depository (bank) identified on the attached voided check to deduct payments (debit) from my (our) checking account or correct errors on the account. This authorization remains in effect until I (or either of us) notify IRS in writing to stop or until the liability covered by this agreement is satisfied. • I (we) understand that if the depository is unable to honor IRS's request for payment due to insufficient funds in my (our) account on the payment due date I (we) will be charged a penalty of $15 or two percent of the payment request, whichever is greater. If the payment request is for less than $15, the penalty is the amount of the request.

CAT. NO. 16644M   Part 1 — IRS Copy   Form **433-D** (Rev. 5-96)

¶1473

¶1474 **Exhibit 14-24**

Collection Appeal Rights

You can appeal many IRS collection actions. There are various collection appeal procedures available to you. The two main procedures are **Collection Due Process (CDP)** and **Collection Appeals Program (CAP)**. There are other collection actions which have their own specific appeal procedures. These other actions are discussed at the bottom of page four of this publication.

Collection Due Process (CDP) is available if you receive one of the following notices: Notice of Federal Tax Lien Filing and Your Right to a Hearing Under IRC 6320 (Lien Notice), *a Final Notice - Notice of Intent to Levy and Notice of Your Right to A Hearing, a Notice of Jeopardy Levy and Right of Appeal, a Notice of Levy on Your State Tax Refund – Notice of Your Right to a Hearing (Levy Notices)*. If you disagree with the CDP decision, you can go to court. CDP is more thoroughly described on pages one and two of this publication.

Collection Appeals Program (CAP) is generally quicker and available for a broader range of collection actions. However, you can't go to court if you disagree with the CAP decision. CAP procedures are described on pages three and four of this publication.

You may represent yourself at CDP, CAP and other Appeals proceedings. Or, you can have an attorney, certified public accountant, or a person enrolled to practice before the IRS represent you. If you want your representative to appear without you, you must provide a properly completed Form 2848, *Power of Attorney and Declaration of Representative*. This form is available at your local IRS office, or by calling 1-800-829-3676, or from our web site at **www.irs.gov**.

HEARING AVAILABLE UNDER COLLECTION DUE PROCESS (CDP)
For Lien and Levy Notices

You have the right to a CDP hearing by the IRS Office of Appeals for these collection actions: the first time a Notice of Federal Tax Lien is filed on a tax period; before we send the first levy on your property for a tax period; when we levy your state refund; and when we issue a jeopardy levy. You may contest the CDP decision in the Tax Court or an U.S. District Court, as appropriate.

Lien Notice: The IRS is required to notify you the first time a Notice of Federal Tax Lien is filed for each tax period. We have to notify you within 5 days after the lien notice filing. You then have 30 days, after that 5-day period, to request a hearing with the Office of Appeals. The lien notice you receive will indicate the date this 30-day period expires.

Levy Notice: For each tax period, the IRS is required to notify you the first time we intend to collect a tax liability by taking your property or rights to property. We do this by sending you a levy notice. We can't levy or seize your property within 30 days from the date this notice is mailed, or given to you, or left at your home or office. During that 30-day period, you may request a hearing with the Office of Appeals. There are two exceptions to this notice of intent to levy provision. We may issue a levy without sending this notice or waiting 30 days when collection of the tax is in jeopardy. We may also levy on your state tax refund without sending a notice or waiting 30 days. You can request a hearing after the levy action for both of these instances.

How do you request a hearing under Collection Due Process with the Office of Appeals?

Complete Form 12153, *Request for a Collection Due Process Hearing*, and send it to us at the address shown on your lien or levy notice within 30 days. Check the IRS action(s) you disagree with, and explain why you disagree. If you received both a lien and a levy notice, you may appeal both actions. You must identify all of your reasons for disagreement with us at this time. You may raise issues relating to the unpaid tax including:

- Appropriateness of collection actions
- Collection alternatives such as installment agreement, offer in compromise, posting a bond or substitution of other assets
- Appropriate spousal defenses
- The existence or amount of the tax, but only if you did not receive a notice of deficiency or did not otherwise have an opportunity to dispute the tax liability.

You may not raise an issue that was raised and considered at a prior administrative or judicial hearing, if you participated meaningfully in the prior hearing or proceeding.

To preserve your right to go to court, you must send us the Form 12153 within 30 days. Form 12153 is also available by calling 1-800-829-3676, or from our web site at **www.irs.gov**. Include a copy of your lien and/or levy notice. List all taxes and tax periods for which you are requesting a hearing. Under CDP, you are entitled to only one hearing relating to a lien notice and one hearing relating to a levy notice, for each taxable period. If you receive a subsequent lien or levy notice after you request a hearing on an earlier notice, Appeals can consider both matters at the same time

Before you formally appeal a lien or levy notice by sending us Form 12153, you may be able to work out a solution with the Collection function that took the action. To do so, contact the IRS employee whose name appears on the lien or levy notice and explain why you disagree with the action. This contact, however, does NOT extend the 30-day period to make a written request for a CDP hearing.

What will happen when you request a CDP hearing with the Office of Appeals?

After you request a hearing, you can still discuss your concerns with the office collecting the tax or filing the Notice of Federal Tax Lien. If you are able to resolve the issues with that office, you may withdraw your request for a hearing.

The Office of Appeals will contact you to schedule a hearing. Your hearing may be held either in person, by telephone or by correspondence.

Unless we have reason to believe that collection of the tax is in jeopardy, we will stop levy action during the 30 days after the levy notice and, if your appeal is timely, during the appeal process.

Your appeal is timely if you mail your request for a hearing to the address shown on our notice on or before the 30th day after the date of the levy notice or the date shown on the lien notice. If we receive a timely filed Form 12153, we will also suspend the 10-year collection statute of limitations until the date the determination is final or you withdraw, in writing, your request for a hearing.

At the conclusion of the hearing, Appeals will issue a written determination letter. If you agree with Appeals' determination, both you and the IRS are required to live up to the terms of the determination.

If you don't agree with Appeals' determination, you may request judicial review of the determination by initiating a case in a court of proper jurisdiction (United States Tax Court or United States District Court, depending on the circumstances) on or before the 30th day after the date of Appeals' determination. Once the Court rules, its decision will be binding on both you and the IRS.

The Office of Appeals will retain jurisdiction over its determinations and how they are carried out. You may also return to Appeals if your circumstances change and impact the original determination. However, you must exhaust your administrative remedies first.

If your appeal request is not timely, you will be allowed a hearing, but there will be no statutory suspension of collection action and you can't go to court if you disagree with Appeals' decision.

¶1474

ADMINISTRATIVE COLLECTION APPEAL RIGHTS
COLLECTION APPEALS PROGRAM (CAP)

For liens, levies, seizures and installment agreements
under the CAP procedure, you don't have the right to a judicial review of Appeals' decision.

The CAP procedure is available under more circumstances than the Collection Due Process hearing procedure. It is important to note that you can't proceed to court if you don't agree with Appeals' decision in your CAP case. Collection actions you can appeal are:

Notice of Federal Tax Lien. You may appeal before or after the IRS files a lien. You may also appeal denied requests to withdraw a Notice of Federal Tax Lien, and denied discharges, subordinations, and non-attachments of a lien. If the IRS files a Notice of Federal Tax Lien, you may have additional Collection Due Process appeal rights. See the preceding information regarding Hearing Available under Collection Due Process.

Notice of Levy. You may appeal before or after the IRS places a levy on your wages, bank account or other property. Before a levy is issued, you may have additional Collection Due Process appeal rights. See the preceding information regarding Hearing Available Under Collection Due Process.

Seizure of Property. You may appeal before or after the IRS makes a seizure. If you request an appeal after the IRS makes a seizure, you must appeal to the Collection manager within 10 business days after the Notice of Seizure is provided to you, or left at your home or business.

Denial or Termination of Installment Agreement. You may appeal when you are notified that the IIRS intends to deny you an installment agreement. You may also appeal when we propose to terminate or terminate your installment agreement. The right to appeal denials or terminations of installment agreements is provided by law rather than provided by IRS administratively. As such, there are some differences between CAP for installment agreements and other CAP cases, such as levies etc.

How do you appeal one of these IRS actions if your only collection contact has been a notice or telephone call?

1. Call the IRS at the telephone number shown on your notice. Be prepared to explain which action(s) you disagree with and why you disagree. You must also offer your solution to your tax problem.
2. If you can't reach an agreement with the employee, tell the employee that you want to appeal their decision. The employee must honor your request and will refer you to a manager. The manager will either speak with you then, or will return your call within 24 hours.
3. Explain which action(s) you disagree with and why you disagree to the manager. The manager will make a decision on the case. If you don't agree with the manager's decision, your case will be forwarded to an Appeals Officer for review.

How do you appeal one of these IRS collection actions if you have been contacted by a Revenue Officer?

1. If you disagree with the decision of the Revenue Officer, and wish to appeal under CAP, you must first request a conference with a Collection manager.
2. If you do not resolve your disagreement with the Collection manager, you may request Appeals consideration by completing Form 9423, *Collection Appeal Request*. This form is available by calling 1-800-829-3676, or from our web site at www.irs.gov. Check the action(s) you disagree with and explain why you disagree. You must also explain your solution to resolve your tax problem.
3. Submit the Form 9423 to that Collection Office.
4. The Collection Office must receive your appeal request for a lien, levy or seizure within 2 days of your conference with the Collection manager or we will resume collection action. For an appeal request for a denial or termination of an installment agreement, you have 30 days from the date of denial or termination of your installment agreement, to submit your request to the Collection Office.

Page 3

Important: The IRS can not levy until 30 days after the denial or termination of an Installment Agreement. If you appeal the denial or termination of an installment agreement within that 30-day period, we must stop levy action until your appeal is completed.

What will happen when you appeal your case?

Lien, Levy and Seizure: Normally, we will stop collection action on the tax periods the Appeal Officer is considering, unless we believe the collection of the tax is at risk.

Installment Agreements: The IRS can't levy until 30 days after the denial or termination of your agreement. If you appeal within that 30-day period, we will stop levy action until your appeal is completed.

Once the Appeals Officer makes a decision on your case, that decision is binding on both you and the IRS. This means that both you and the IRS are required to accept the decision and live up to its terms. You cannot obtain judicial review of an Appeals Officer's decision following a CAP hearing.

Note: Providing false information, failure to provide all pertinent information or fraud will void Appeals' decision.

APPEAL OF OTHER COLLECTION ACTIONS

You may also appeal other Collection actions such as denied Offers in Compromise (OIC) or Trust Fund Recovery Penalties (TFRP) that the IRS is proposing. Other penalties are also appealable, if you made an abatement request that was denied.

For OICs and TFRPs, follow the protest requirements in Publication 5, *Your Appeal Rights and How To Prepare A Protest If You Don't Agree.* The correspondence you receive on these types of cases will explain where you should send your protest. For other penalties, follow the instructions in the letter that denies your abatement

Department of the Treasury
Internal Revenue Service

www.irs.gov

Publication **1660** (Rev. 05-2000)
Catalog Number **14376Z**

Page 4

¶1475 Exhibit 14-25

Collection Appeal Request

1. Taxpayer's Name	2. Representative: (Form 2848, Power of Attorney Attached)		
3. SSN/EIN	4. Taxpayer's Business Phone	5. Taxpayer's Home Phone	6. Representative's Phone
7. Taxpayer's Street Address			

8. City	9. State	10. Zip Code	
11. Type of Tax (Tax Form)	12. Tax Periods Being Appealed		13. Tax Due

Collection Action(s) Appealed

14. Please Check the Collection Action(s) You're Appealing:

☐ Federal Tax Lien   ☐ Denial of Installment Agreement

☐ Levy or Notice of Levy   ☐ Termination of Installment Agreement

☐ Seizure

Explanation

15. Please explain why you disagree with the collection action(s) you checked above and explain how you would resolve your tax problem. Attach additional pages if needed. Attach copies of any documents that you think will support your position.

Under penalties of perjury, I declare that I have examined this request and the attached documents, and to the best of my knowledge and belief, they are true, correct and complete. A submission by a representative, other than the taxpayer, is based on all information of which preparer has any knowledge.

16. Taxpayer's or Authorized Representative's Signature	17. Date
18. Collection Manager's Signature	19. Date Received

Form **9423** (Rev. 01-1999)   Catalog Number 14169I   **(Over)**   Department of the Treasury – Internal Revenue Service

¶1475

Collection Appeal Rights

FOR LIENS, LEVIES, SEIZURES, AND DENIAL OR TERMINATION OF INSTALLMENT AGREEMENT

You may appeal a Notice of Federal Tax Lien, levy, seizure, or denial or termination of an installment agreement under these procedures. However, if you request an appeal after IRS makes a seizure, you must appeal to the Collection manager within 10 business days after the Notice of Seizure is provided to you or left at your home or business.

How to Appeal If You Disagree With One of These Actions

1. If you disagree with the decision of the Revenue Officer, and wish to appeal, you must first request a conference with a Collection manager.

2. If you do not resolve your disagreement with the Collection manager, you may request Appeals consideration by completing Form 9423, Collection Appeal Request.

3. On the Form 9423, check the Collection action(s) you disagree with and explain why you disagree. You must also explain your solution to resolve your tax problem. **THE COLLECTION OFFICE MUST RECEIVE YOUR REQUEST FOR AN APPEAL WITHIN 2 DAYS OF YOUR CONFERENCE WITH THE COLLECTION MANAGER OR WE WILL RESUME COLLECTION ACTION.**

What will happen when you appeal your case

Normally, we will stop the collection action(s) you disagree with until your appeal is settled, unless we have reason to believe that collection of the amount owed is at risk.

You may have a representative

You may represent yourself at your Appeals conference or you may be represented by an attorney, certified public accountant, or a person enrolled to practice before the IRS. If you want your representative to appear without you, you must provide a properly completed Form 2848, Power of Attorney and Declaration of Representative. You can obtain Form 2848 from your local IRS office or by calling 1-800-829-3676.

Decision on the appeal

Once the Appeals Officer makes a decision on your case, that decision is binding on both you and the IRS. This means that both you and the IRS are required to accept the decision and live up to its terms.

Note: Providing false information, failing to provide all pertinent information, or fraud will void Appeal's decision.

¶1476 DISCUSSION QUESTIONS

1. Oscar Oppressed consults you regarding his tax problems. Oscar tells you that he has not paid the $20,000 balance due on his 2003 income tax return. He had sent some information to the Collection Division of the IRS showing them that he had no money aside from the wages he earned as a janitor at the local packing plant. Oscar mailed in the information approximately six months ago and heard nothing further until he went to pick up his paycheck last Friday. The paymaster informed him that they had received a levy and had paid over the amount of his check to the IRS.

   (A) Is the levy proper?

   (B) Can the IRS take Oscar's entire check or must they leave something for Oscar and his three minor children to live on?

2. Bill and Betty Bankrupt have received a notice of seizure on their home. Title to the home is jointly held, and they have owned it for five years. They give you the following information regarding the home:

Fair market value	$165,000
Mortgage	$125,000
Equity	$40,000

   Bill and Betty want to know what will happen to the mortgage if the house is sold and they want to know whether the IRS will pay off the first mortgage for them. They also want to know whether the IRS can levy on their joint equity in the house or only on Bill's equity.

   In answering this question, assume that the tax being collected by the seizure is as follows:

   (A) The assessment is $45,000, representing the balance due on their joint 2000 and 2001 federal income tax returns.

   (B) The assessment is $45,000 and represents the balance due on Bill's separate returns for 2002 and 2003. Bill had filed using the married filing separate status because the marriage was on the rocks at the time. The time to elect to file a joint return has not yet expired, and filing jointly would save them approximately $3,000.

   (C) The assessment is $45,000 resulting from an audit of their 2002 and 2003 income tax return. The auditor found that Betty had not reported approximately $40,000 of gross receipts each year resulting from her real estate business. Bill did not know how successful Betty's real estate business was, and he never saw any of the money because Betty was always reinvesting it in new properties. The assessment was made jointly against Bill and Betty.

3. Carl Cashflow consults you regarding a tax lien in the amount of $25,000 for delinquent employment taxes of his corporation. Carl tells you that his sole asset is his residence, and he gives you the following information:

Fair market value	$125,000
Mortgage	$115,000
Equity	$10,000

Carl is paying $800 per month on the mortgage, and he finds that this is more than he can afford. He has an offer to purchase his home for $125,000. He would like to buy a condominium for $75,000 after he sells his home, but he needs $7,500 for a down payment. He figures buying the condominium will bring his monthly housing payment to $550.

(A) Can anything be done to prevent the IRS from levying on the proceeds of the sale of the house?

(B) What can you suggest to Carl to get the IRS to go along with this arrangement?

4. Daryl Deadbeat owes the IRS $75,000 for delinquent income taxes. He owns real property with appraised equities of $85,000. The IRS seizes the properties and sets a minimum bid price of $75,000. Because no one trusts Daryl not to start legal hassles if they buy the properties, no one shows up to bid. Finally, the United States buys the properties at the minimum bid price and credits Daryl's account as being paid in full. All tax liens are released at the time of sale.

Seven months after the sale, the United States receives an offer to purchase the properties. Because oil has been discovered on one of the parcels, the offer is in the amount of $150,000. Obviously the offer is accepted and the transaction closes. Does the IRS have to share the profit on the sale with Daryl?

5. David Developer owes approximately $250,000 in employment taxes. David owns a large tract of land which has been subdivided into 100 lots. Liens were filed by the IRS in 2000 which attached to his interest in the land. It is now 2004, and David's subdivision has become a prime location. He has a purchaser who will buy one lot for $50,000, but he needs to get the lien released. He is afraid that the buyer's attorney will not let the buyer go ahead unless you can assure him that title will not be clouded by the lien.

(A) Will the IRS have a lien on title in the hands of the purchaser? Will the purchaser have priority over the IRS? If the purchaser gets a mortgage to buy the property, which lien is in first place?

(B) Can anything be done to improve the situation?

6. Danny Disorganized is the sole shareholder of Envigrow, Inc., a corporation which markets environmentally safe lawn products. The IRS has completed an audit of Envigrow's 2002 tax return, which was filed on March 15, 2003. The revenue agent disallowed a majority of the deductions taken for travel and entertainment due to Danny's inability to substantiate the expenses. Apparently, Danny misplaced the box which contained the travel and entertainment records. As a result, Danny

consented to the adjustments and the corporation was assessed an additional tax of $55,000 in February 2004.

In May 2004, as the corporation was completing its move to a new high-rise on Milwaukee's skyline, Danny found the box containing the 2002 travel and entertainment records. Since the time has past to file a claim for refund, Danny would like to know what, if anything, he can do to suspend collection efforts and abate the additional assessment?

7. Sam Spendthrift just completed the bankruptcy filing of Belly-Up, Inc., the most recent of his failed ventures. Sam was left with tax claims in the amount of $200,000, consisting of trust fund employment taxes which are nondischargeable in bankruptcy. Since his current job at Paupers, Inc., only pays minimum wage, he plans to pay off the debt by taking out a $200,000 loan. All Sam has to do is convince his wealthy uncle, Milton Megabucks, to co-sign for the loan. Milton calculates, however, that a 15-year loan at 9% would cost approximately $365,000. Knowing Sam's earning capabilities, Milton figures that there must be a cheaper way out.

To fully analyze the situation, Milton has asked Sam to compile a financial statement detailing any additional assets and liabilities. Sam came up with the following:

Assets

1998 Pinto Wagon	$700
Baseball card collection	$1,000
Cash in bank	$500

Liabilities

University of Wisconsin student loans	$15,000
Credit card debt	$2,500
Unpaid rent	$1,200

Unfortunately, Milton has not found it in his heart to grant Sam any right to his estate. He is a bit disappointed that, at 33 years old, all Sam has managed to do is increase his negative net worth.

What can Milton and Sam do to abate the tax claim? What factors would the IRS consider in evaluating any proposals by Sam?

8. Felisha Fitness is the sole shareholder of LaSpa, Inc., a corporation which operates three health clubs. As of January 2004, LaSpa, Inc., owed approximately $150,000 in corporate income taxes which were assessed in February 2003 for the tax years 2001 and 2002. The corporation has always filed its tax returns on a timely basis. Felisha has failed to respond to the assessment and demands for payment by the IRS due to the fact that business has been slow and she has been inundated with other bills. As a consequence, the IRS filed a tax lien which attached to all of the exercise equipment owned by LaSpa, Inc. On April 1, 2004, the IRS seized the equipment, intending to proceed with a tax sale. Is there anything Felisha can do to block the IRS's sale of the equipment? In the

¶1476

event that Felisha is unable to pay any of the taxes, can any portion of the assessment be discharged?

9. Owen Ozelot has received a Notice of Intent to Levy with respect to his unpaid income tax liability of $100,000. Owen comes to you and asks what his options are.

CHAPTER 15

CLAIMS FOR REFUND

¶1501 INTRODUCTION

When an audit results in a tax deficiency, the taxpayer can either contest the liability in the United States Tax Court or pay the deficiency and file a claim for refund. If the claim for refund is disallowed by the Internal Revenue Service (IRS) or if a period of six months from the date of filing passes without any action being taken, the taxpayer may then bring suit to recover the overpayment of tax in either the United States District Court or the United States Court of Federal Claims.[1] This alternative procedure can be employed at any stage of the audit process: when the agent first proposes the deficiency, after an appeals conference or after a formal notice of deficiency.

Execution of Refund Claim

¶1505 GOVERNMENT NOTICE

The principal function of a claim for refund is to put the government on notice that the taxpayer believes the tax has been overpaid and to describe the grounds upon which the taxpayer relies. The filing of the claim gives the IRS an opportunity to examine the taxpayer's contention and to determine whether there has been an overpayment. The filing of a claim for refund is also a prerequisite to bringing a legal action for a refund of any taxes alleged to have been overpaid.[2]

The IRS has prescribed forms to be used in seeking a refund of tax. While it is not absolutely necessary to use such forms, some courts have rejected informal claims which failed to contain the requisite elements of a Claim for Refund. For example, where the taxpayer failed to provide the IRS sufficient indication that a refund was being sought, courts have held that the statutory elements of a Claim for Refund had not been met.[3] While not all courts have been this strict in testing the sufficiency of an informal claim for refund, a cautious practitioner will generally utilize the prescribed forms to avoid unnecessary litigation.

The three principal Claim for Refund forms are included at the end of this chapter. Form 1040X (see Exhibit 15-1 at ¶1551) is used to claim a refund of individual income taxes. Form 1120X (see Exhibit 15-2 at ¶1552) is used to claim a refund of an overpayment of corporate income tax. Finally, Form 843 (seeExhibit 15-3 at ¶1553) is used to claim a refund of any tax other than income tax. Form 843 can be used to claim a refund of estate tax, gift tax, excise tax or employment taxes and to claim refunds of penalties and interest.

---

[1] Code Sec. 6532(a).
[2] Code Sec. 7422(a).

[3] *BCS Financial Corp. v. U.S.*, 118 F.3d 522 (7th Cir. 1997), 97-2 USTC ¶50,514; *Pala, Inc. v. U.S.*, 234 F.3d 873 (5th Cir. 2000), 2000-2 USTC ¶50,864.

A number of cases have established certain requirements which must be met for a valid refund claim:

1. The claim must be in writing;

2. The claim must be signed by the person entitled to recover the overpayment;

3. The claim must demand that the overpayment be refunded;

4. The claim must specify the grounds upon which it is based; and

5. The statement of the grounds and facts upon which the refund of a claim is based must be verified by a written declaration made under the penalties of perjury.[4]

The courts will only allow the taxpayer to bring suit to recover a refund of taxes *on a ground which has been raised in the claim for refund*.[5] Thus, considerable care should be taken to assure that all grounds have been stated in the claim for refund that is filed so that all possible theories for recovery have been presented.

Because of the limitations on the time in which a refund claim must be filed (see ¶1511, below), it may be important to document when a claim was filed. While the IRS keeps records of all returns and claims it receives, the burden of proof to show actual filing is on the taxpayer. If for some reason the claim was not delivered to the IRS, the taxpayer may not be able to prove filing unless the claim was sent certified or registered mail. For this reason, all claims for refund should be filed either by physical delivery, with the taxpayer or representative obtaining a receipted copy of the claim, or by mailing certified or registered mail. Failure to do so can deny the taxpayer the right to recover on the refund claim.[6]

Statute of Limitations on Refund Claim

¶1511 FILING PERIODS

Sec. 6511 of the Internal Revenue Code (the Code) provides that a claim for credit or refund must be filed within three years of the time the return was filed or within two years of the time the tax was paid, whichever period ends later.[7] If noreturn was filed, then the claim for refund must be made within two years of the time the tax is paid. For tax years ending after August 5, 1997, the Tax Court, which has authority to order refunds in cases under its jurisdiction, can do so for taxes paid less than three years before a notice of deficiency is issued if the taxpayer has not filed a tax return on the date when the notice of deficiency is

---

[4] Reg. § 301.6402-2(b)(1).

[5] *Boyles v. U.S.*, 2000-1 USTC ¶50,243; *Parma v. U.S.*, 45 Fed. Cl. 124 (1999), 99-2 USTC ¶50,919.

[6] For examples, see *Miller v. United States*, 784 F.2d 728 (6th Cir. 1986), 86-1 USTC ¶9261; and *Wiggins v. United States*, (D. Md. 1986), 87-1 USTC ¶9180.

[7] There are exceptions to this general rule. One example of this is an overpayment resulting from the deduction for a bad debt or a worthless security. In such case, a claim for refund may be filed at any time within seven years from the date on which

the return was due. Code Sec. 6511(d)(1). Other examples include net operating loss or capital loss carrybacks and unused tax credit carrybacks where the time for a claim for refund resulting from such carrybacks begins to run from the taxable year in which the net operating loss, capital loss or unused tax credit arose. Code Sec. 6511(d)(2) and (4). The United States Supreme Court has held that courts cannot toll the statute of limitations of refund claims for nonstatutory, equitable reasons. *United States v. Brockamp*, 117 S.Ct. 849 (1996), 97-1 USTC ¶50,216.

¶1511

issued.[8] If the taxpayer files a return prior to the due date, or if the tax itself is paid prior to the due date, for purposes of the statute of limitations the return is treated as filed and the tax is treated as paid on "the last possible day." However, "the last possible day" for this purpose does not include any extensions of time to file the return.[9]

The rule regarding early payment of the tax often comes into play when the taxpayer's wages are subject to withholding or estimated tax payments are made. Under Code Sec. 6513(b)(1), any tax deducted and withheld by the taxpayer's employer will be deemed to be paid against the taxpayer's income tax liability on the fifteenth day of the fourth month following the close of that taxable year. In addition, any payments towards a taxpayer's estimated income tax are considered paid on the last day prescribed for filing the return for the taxable year for which the estimates are being made.

> **Example:** The taxpayer is entitled to a refund of income taxes for the taxable year ending December 31, 2000. The taxpayer requests that this amount be applied toward estimated income tax payments to be made during 2001. In addition, the taxpayer makes other estimated tax payments during 2001, and the wages made during that year are subject to withholding under the requirements of Code Secs. 3401 through 3404. The taxpayer's return is due on April 15, 2002. Under Code Sec. 6513, all of the payments credited against the taxpayer's income tax liability (including the refund of the 2000 overpayment) are considered to be made on April 15, 2002.

If the taxpayer consents to extend the period in which the IRS may assess any tax (generally by a Form 872, Consent to Extend Time to Assess Tax (see Exhibit 10-2 at ¶ 1052)), the time within which the taxpayer may file a claim for refund isalso extended for an additional six months from the date that the extension expires.[10]

The mitigation provisions of Code Secs. 1311 through 1314 also may apply to permit a refund which would otherwise be barred by the statute of limitations. These and other judicially created mitigation provisions are discussed in Chapter 10 beginning at ¶ 1021.

Amount Recoverable

¶ 1515 TWO OR THREE-YEAR STATUTE

To determine the amount that can be recovered through a refund claim, it is important first to determine under which statute of limitations the taxpayer is filing. If the claim is filed within three years from the date the return was filed, the amount refundable cannot exceed the total tax paid within the three years plus any extension period that was granted for filing the return.

---

[8] Code Sec. 6512(b)(3). Taxpayer Relief Act of 1997, P.L. 105-34, Act § 1282. For tax years ending before August 5, 1997, where no return was filed, the Tax Court has jurisdiction to order refunds for taxes paid within two years before a notice of deficiency is issued. *Comm'r v. Lundy*, 116 S.Ct. 647 (1996), 96-1 USTC ¶ 50,035.

[9] Code Sec. 6513(a).

[10] Code Sec. 6511(c)(1).

Example: If the return was due on April 16, 2000, but an extension to August 15, 2000, was obtained, then the claim for refund must be filed by August 15, 2003. The amount which the taxpayer can seek through a claim for refund will include all payments of tax made during the calendar year 1999, plus any payments made through August 15, 2003.

On the other hand, if the claim for refund is filed under the two-year statute of limitations, then the amount recoverable is limited to the tax paid during the two years immediately preceding the filing of the claim.

Example: Taxpayer files a 1999 return on April 17, 2000, and pays a tax of $3,000 at that time. In June 2002, an audit is performed which results in a deficiency of $2,000, which he pays. Upon reviewing the return, taxpayer discovers that he forgot to claim $2,500 in tax credit for 1999. If he files a claim for refund on April 15, 2003, he can recover $2,500. However, if he does not file until April 16, 2003, he can only recover $2,000, the amount paid within two years of filing. Code Sec. 7503 allows returns filed after the due date to be deemed as filed on the due date. A claim for refund of tax on the return must be filed within three years of the due date.[11]

Interest on Refund Claims

¶1521 OVERPAYMENT OF TAX

Under Code Sec. 6611, the IRS is to pay interest on any overpayment of any Internal Revenue tax. Where an overpayment is refunded, the interest is to be computed from the date of the overpayment to a date preceding the date of the refund check by no more than thirty days. Normally the tax would be considered to be overpaid from the due date of the return. However, if a return has been filed late, the due date of the return is ignored and interest is only computed from the day on which the return is actually filed.[12]

If a refund results from the carryback of a net operating loss or a capital loss, interest runs only from the day on which the return generating the loss is filed.[13]

If a taxpayer is entitled to a refund of income tax which has been withheld or paid in the form of estimated tax payments during the year, no interest is required to be paid on that refund if the overpayment is refunded within forty-five days of the due date of the return or the day on which the return is actually filed, whichever is later.

Procedure on Refund Claims

¶1525 CLAIM PROCESSING

Under most circumstances a claim for refund will be filed with the Service Center serving the state in which the tax was paid. The claims are recorded at the Service Center, reviewed and assigned for examination at the district level if that

---

[11] *Hannahs v. U.S.*, W. Dist. Tenn., 95-1 USTC ¶ 50,111.

[12] Code Sec. 6611(b)(3).

[13] Code Sec. 6611(f)(1).

is warranted. The review of the claim for refund at the Service Center level is conducted to determine a number of issues:

1. Whether the claim was timely filed;

2. Whether the claim is based on the alleged unconstitutionality of the Internal Revenue laws;

3. Whether the taxpayer has waived the right to a refund in having the IRS compromise a tax liability;

4. Whether the claim for refund covers a taxable year which was the subject of a closing agreement under Code Sec. 7121 or in which the tax liability was compromised under Code Sec. 7122; or

5. Whether the claim for refund relates to a return closed on the basis of a final order of the Tax Court or other court.

If any of these circumstances are found, the Service Center will generally issue a letter to the taxpayer (see Exhibit 15-4 at ¶1554) which advises the taxpayerthat no consideration can be given to the claim.[14] In addition, if the claim is one which the taxpayer has requested be withdrawn, or if it is one for which the taxpayer has requested in writing that a statutory notice of claim disallowance be immediately issued, then the certified notice of claim disallowance will be issued (see Exhibit 15-5 at ¶1555). If the claim for refund does not fit into any of these classifications, it will be referred to an examiner for further review.[15]

Often when the claim for refund is assigned to an examiner, it is returned to the same agent who originally examined the return. If the claim for refund refers to a deficiency in which the Appeals Office had previously acquired jurisdiction, the concurrence of the Appeals Office in any modification of the item is required. If the closing of the matter with the Appeals Office involved the execution of a Form 870-AD, Offer to Waive Restrictions on Assessment and Collection of Tax Deficiency and to Accept Overassessment (see Chapter 12 and Exhibit 12-2 at ¶1252), then the claim for refund and the case file are generally forwarded to the Appeals Office for any further action.[16] If the only issue in dispute is identical or similar to an issue pending in a case before the Tax Court or any other court, the case will be placed in a suspense file until the court case is resolved.[17]

After the claim for refund is reviewed, if the examiner determines that the claim should not be allowed, a report will be sent to the taxpayer proposing disallowance of the claim (see Exhibit 15-6 at ¶1556). That report will propose either partial disallowance or full disallowance and will also seek the execution of a Form 2297, Waiver of Statutory Notification of Claim Disallowance (see Exhibit 15-7 at ¶1557). In addition, the taxpayer is given the opportunity to appeal the proposed disallowance of the claim and to request a hearing with the Appeals Office.

---

[14] IRM Handbook 4.3.3.7.4, IRM Handbook 104.6.12.4.

[15] IRM Handbook 4.1.4.6.

[16] IRM 8.5.1.7.

[17] IRM Handbook 4.8.2.10.1.

If the Form 2297 is not secured from the taxpayer, then a certified notice of disallowance (see Exhibit 15-7 at ¶1557) will be issued to the taxpayer. The issuance of the certified notice of claim disallowance or the execution of the waiver of statutory notification of claim disallowance is a significant event because it begins the two-year statute of limitations under Code Sec. 6532(a) governing the time in which any suit for refund based on the claim must be brought.[18] Unless either a waiver has been executed or a notice of disallowance has been received, the taxpayer must wait until at least six months after the filing of the claim for refund before filing a suit for refund.[19]

If the examining agent decides to allow the claim after reviewing it, normally the taxpayer will receive a check representing the overpayment from the Department of the Treasury. In some instances, because Code Sec. 6402(a) allows theTreasury to credit the overpayment against any other liabilities of the taxpayer, the taxpayer will receive a Form 4356 (see Exhibit 15-9 at ¶1559), which states that the overpayment may be applied to unpaid taxes.

If a claim for refund is allowed which would produce a refund or credit of tax in excess of $2,000,000,[20] Code Sec. 6405(a) requires that a final decision on such refund be made only after referral of the facts and the IRS's recommendation to the Joint Committee on Taxation. It is only after the Joint Committee finishes its review that a refund can be issued to the taxpayer.

Miscellaneous

¶1531 FORMS

If a taxpayer has a carryback resulting from a net operating loss, a capital loss or an unused general business credit, the taxpayer may file a Form 1045, Application for Tentative Refund (see Exhibit 15-10 at ¶1560). Corporations apply for a tentative refund of these amounts by filing Form 1139, Corporation Application for Tentative Refund (see Exhibit 15-11 at ¶1561). Also, corporations expecting refunds from carryback claims may extend the time to pay their income tax for the preceding year by filing Form 1138, Extension of Time for Payment of Taxes by a Corporation Expecting a Net Operating Loss Carryback (see Exhibit 15-12 at ¶1562). Code Sec. 6411 authorizes the Secretary of the Treasury to refund the excess tax within a period of ninety days from the date of filing of the application for tentative carryback adjustment. If the Commissioner finds that the information presented in Form 1045 or Form 1139 is incomplete or inaccurate, he or she has the authority not to allow the tentative refund. In such a case, a formal claim for refund should be filed to protect the right of the taxpayer to recover the excess payment. The tentative application is not a claim for refund, and if the application is disallowed, no suit may be maintained to recover the tax unless a formal claim has been filed.[21] In addition, the filing of the application does not

---

[18] With the concurrence of the IRS, the two year period during which a suit can be filed can be extended with the filing of a Form 907 (Exhibit 15-8 at ¶1558).

[19] Code Sec. 6532(a)(1).

[20] Amount was increased from $1,000,000 on December 21, 2000.

[21] Code Sec. 6411(a).

constitute the filing of a claim for refund for purposes of determining if a claim was timely filed within the statute of limitations.[22]

Form 1310, Statement of Person Claiming Refund Due a Deceased Taxpayer (see Exhibit 15-13 at ¶1563), is generally used by a decedent's spouse or personal representative to claim a refund of tax owed to the decedent.

One other claim for refund with which the practitioner should be familiar is Form 6118, Claim for Refund of Income Tax Return Preparer Penalties (see Exhibit 15-14 at ¶1564). This form is used when a preparer penalty has been assessed against an income tax return preparer which the preparer wishes to litigate (see Chapter 8, *supra*).

¶1533 CHOICE OF JUDICIAL FORUM

When contested adjustments to tax are the result of an IRS examination, a taxpayer has a choice of three judicial forums in which to litigate the tax controversy. As discussed in Chapter 13, the taxpayer may challenge a proposed deficiency by filing a petition in the Tax Court without first paying the tax. In the alternative, the taxpayer may pay the assessed deficiency, file a claim for refund and then file suit in either the United States District Court or the United States Court of Federal Claims.

In choosing the court in which to litigate, consideration should be given to the controlling legal precedents in each of the forums as well as the procedural differences that exist. One important factor, of course, is the ability of the taxpayer to pay the full amount of the assessed deficiency before filing suit. If financial problems exist, the only forum realistically open to the taxpayer may be the Tax Court. If a jury trial appears to offer advantages, the district court would be the only appropriate forum. Trial by jury is not available in either the Tax Court or Court of Federal Claims.

The IRS has the right to assert additional deficiencies after a petition is filed in the Tax Court, whereas new adjustments to taxable income may be utilized by the government in defending a refund suit only by way of setoff against the amount of the claimed refund. If a taxpayer is concerned that the IRS may raise new issues that would increase the deficiency proposed in the statutory notice, the Tax Court should be avoided as the litigating forum. However, in such a situation it should be kept in mind that the filing of a claim for refund does not prevent the IRS from attempting to assess an additional deficiency on newly discovered adjustments if the statute of limitations on assessment has not expired. To reduce this possibility, if the assessment period is still open, it may be advisable not to file the claim for refund too soon.

Settlement negotiations in the Tax Court are the responsibility of the Appeals Office and District Counsel. Settlement discussion and trial in the district court and Court of Federal Claims are handled by attorneys from the Tax Division of the Department of Justice. Pretrial discovery is available to both parties in all

---

[22] Reg. § 1.6411-1(b)(2).

three of the forums, but is more limited in the Tax Court (see ¶1113). The need for, or fear of, extensive discovery may influence a taxpayer's choice of forum.

¶1535 PREREQUISITES FOR LEGAL ACTION

Code Sec. 7422 provides that no suit for the recovery of any Internal Revenue tax shall be maintained until after a claim for refund has been filed with the IRS. The taxpayer may only recover in a suit for refund on a ground which was presented in the claim for refund. The Code also provides that no suit may be commenced within six months of the time the claim is filed unless the claim has been disallowed during that period of time.

In addition, Code Sec. 6532(a) provides that no suit shall be filed after two years from the time of mailing by certified mail or registered mail of a notice ofdisallowance to the taxpayer. If the taxpayer has waived the requirement of mailing the notice of disallowance, then the two-year limitations period begins with the execution of the waiver on Form 2297, Waiver of Statutory Notification of Claim Disallowance (see Exhibit 15-7 at ¶1557).

The taxpayer also can be barred from filing a suit for refund by undertaking other proceedings. For example, if a timely petition to the Tax Court was filed, then the Tax Court acquires exclusive jurisdiction for that taxable year, and under most circumstances a suit for refund regarding that year cannot be prosecuted.[23] In addition, if the taxpayer previously filed a suit to recover any tax alleged to have been erroneously assessed, any finding that the taxpayer was not entitled to recover in that proceeding will be binding in any later refund action under the doctrine of *res judicata*.

¶1536 PAYMENT OF TAX IN FULL

An additional prerequisite for a suit for refund is that the entire tax must be paid in full prior to the time that the claim for refund is filed. Failure to pay the entire amount of tax can result in a dismissal of the case for lack of jurisdiction, as illustrated by the landmark case of *Flora v. United States*.[24]

However, the Court of Appeals for the Federal Circuit has ruled that the full payment rule of *Flora* does not require the taxpayer to pay interest or penalties before filing a claim for refund.[25]

¶1537 PARTIAL PAYMENT OF TAX

The "full payment" rule enunciated in *Flora* remains binding in all income, gift, or estate tax cases. However, the rule of *Flora* does not apply to a responsible officer assessment under Code Sec. 6672. The 100-percent penalty tax is classified as an excise tax and, therefore, is "divisible." The essential theory of divisibility is that any assessment of a divisible tax is considered to consist of the assessment of a separate tax liability for each separate tax transaction or event. Therefore, to meet the full payment rule and the jurisdictional prerequisite for a tax refund

---

[23] Code Sec. 7422(e).
[24] 362 U.S. 145 (1960), 80 S.Ct. 630, 60-1 USTC ¶9347.

[25] *Shore v. U.S.*, 9 F.3d 1524 (Fed. Cir. 1993), 93-2 USTC ¶50,623.

suit[26] as to these taxes, the taxpayer need not pay the full amount assessed for the taxable period but only the tax due with respect to one allegedly taxable transaction or event.[27] For example, assume that the IRS has made an assessment under Code Sec. 6672 of $75,000 covering the first, second and third quarters of 2000. If a taxpayer makes a token payment representing a divisible portion of that assessment, he or she may file a claim for refund and then file a refund suit. Generally, the divisible portion of a Code Sec. 6672 penalty assessment is the amount of tax tobe withheld for one employee for one quarter. However, making an arbitrary payment of $50 or $100 may not be sufficient to meet the judicial jurisdiction test as illustrated by the following case:

United States District Court, S.D. New York.

47TH STREET SETTING CORP., Plaintiff,

v.

The United States of America, Defendant.

No. 98 CIV. 2704(RMB).

July 27, 1999.

ORDER

BERMAN, D.J.

*1 Plaintiff, 47th Street Setting Corporation ("Setting Corp." or "Plaintiff"), brought the underlying action pursuant to 28 U.S.C. §1346(a) to recover $43.25 paid to the Internal Revenue Service ("IRS") in employment taxes, plus interest, and to avoid $32,570.04 in employment taxes assessed by the IRS against Setting Corp. for the 1993 tax year, pursuant to 26 U.S.C. §§3101, 3111. [FN1] (Taxpayer's Mem. at 9). The Government moves to dismiss the complaint pursuant to Federal Rule of Civil Procedure ("Fed. R. Civ.P.") 12(b)(1) for lack of subject matter jurisdiction, alleging that Plaintiff has failed, before filing the lawsuit, to pay the requisite amount of employment tax liabilities attributable to one employee for one quarter and to file a claim for refund in accordance with IRS rules and regulations. (Govt's Mem. at 2).

FN1. Under the Internal Revenue Code, 26 U.S.C. §§3101, 3111, Setting Corp. is required to pay employment taxes, Federal Insurance Contributions Act ("FICA") and Medicare wage adjustments, for each of its employees. (Govt's Mem. at 2).

For the reasons set forth below, the Government's motion to dismiss is granted.

I. *Background*

The following facts, which are set forth in the Government's Memorandum of Law in Support of its Motion to Dismiss the Complaint ("Government's Motion") and Setting Corp.'s Memorandum of Law in Support of its Opposition to the Government's Motion to Dismiss the Taxpayer's Complaint ("Taxpayer's Response"), are largely undisputed and are taken as true for the purposes of this motion. *See, e.g., Atlantic Mut. Ins. Co. v. Balfour Maclaine Int'l Ltd.,* 968 F.2d 196, 198 (2d Cir.1992) (finding that in considering a motion to dismiss for lack of subject matter jurisdiction under Rule 12(b)(1), a court "must accept as true all material factual allegations in the complaint"); *Sierra v. United States,* 1998 WL 599715 at *2 (S.D.N.Y. Sept.10, 1998), *reconsideration denied,* 1998 WL 851598 (S.D.N.Y. Dec.8, 1998)("[t]he court must examine the substance of the allegations and any other

---

[26] *Flora v. U.S., supra* note 24; IRM Handbook 5.7.7.7; *Steele v. U.S.,* 280 F.2d 89 (9th Cir. 1960), 60-2 USTC ¶9573; *Magone v. U.S.,* 902 F.2d 192 (2nd Cir. 1990), 90-1 USTC ¶50,253.

[27] *ACT Restoration, Inc. v. U.S.,* 99-2 USTC ¶50,911.

evidence before it in resolving the jurisdictional dispute . . . [h]owever, the Court will not draw inferences favorable to the party asserting jurisdiction").

Setting Corp. is, among other things, a gem-setting business which employs jewelers, polishers and office workers and which also utilizes the services of seventeen gem setters. According to Setting Corp.'s Response, fifteen of these gem-setters are independent contractors who do not necessarily work exclusively for Setting Corp. (Taxpayer's Mem. at 3). Setting Corp. claims that, under the Internal Revenue Code, it is not required to pay employment taxes for independent contractors; that its' gem setters are independent contractors, and thus it has never been obligated to withhold employment taxes with respect to its' gem setters; and that, apart from the $43.25 paid to initiate the instant proceeding, it has never paid employment taxes with respect to any of its' gem setters. (Taxpayer's Mem. at 3).

By letter dated May 23, 1995, the IRS notified Setting Corp. of a forthcoming IRS employment tax compliance check which would include review of Setting Corp.'s "basis for the determination of independent contractor status." (Govt's Mem. at 3). From June through October 1995, an IRS Revenue Officer Examiner ("IRS Officer") visited Setting Corp., reviewed documents, and met with representatives of Setting Corp. On October 31, 1995, the IRS Officer met with Marc Forman, a representative of Setting Corp., to discuss the classification of the gem setters. (Taxpayer's Mem. at 4) (Forman Aff., §3). The details of that conversation are disputed by the parties. The Government claims that the IRS Officer stated that the IRS considered the gem setters to be "employees" rather than "independent contractors," but as a courtesy to Setting Corp., the IRS would only pursue reclassification of eight (out of fifteen) gem setters; i.e., those who earned more than $20,000 in 1993. (Govt's Mem. at 4). Setting Corp. claims that "Mr. Forman has no recollection of any such oral agreement with [the IRS Officer.]" (Taxpayer's Mem. at 4) (Forman Aff., §3). On or about November 22, 1995, the IRS assessed against Plaintiff additional employment taxes and interest due for the quarters and amounts as follows:

1st Quarter (1993)	$ 8,142.51
2nd Quarter (1993)	$ 8,142.51
3rd Quarter (1993)	$ 8,142.51
4th Quarter (1993)	$ 8,142.51
Total (1993)	$32,570.04

*2 By letter dated December 21, 1995, counsel for Setting Corp. submitted a protest to the IRS contesting any additional liability for employment taxes for all four quarters in 1993. (Taxpayer's Mem. at 4). In that protest letter, Setting Corp. challenged the IRS's reclassification of fifteen gem setters as "employees" rather than "independent contractors." (Govt's Mem. at 4). Setting Corp.'s protest letter does not identify which fifteen gem setters are the subject of protest. (Govt.'s Mem. at 5). The Government claims that by letter dated March 13, 1996, IRS Appeals Officer Anthony J. Santoro proposed that Setting Corp. attend an appeals conference on April 3, 1996, at 10:00 a.m. [FN2] (Govt's Mem. at 5). By letter dated February 11, 1997, the IRS notified Setting Corp. that, because no agreement had been reached regarding the proposed 1993 employment tax liability assessment, Setting Corp.'s account would be adjusted and it would receive a bill for assessed employment tax liability. (Taxpayer's Mem. at 4)(Govt's. Mem. at 5).

> FN2. There is no indication in either parties' written submissions as to whether or not a Setting Corp. representative attended the conference.

On March 17, 1997, the IRS assessed Setting Corp. for FICA and Medicare tax liabilities totaling $8,142.51, plus interest, for each of the four quarters of the 1993 tax year. (Govt's Mem. at 5). Of the eight gem setters whom the IRS reclassified as employees, Jorge Rivas had the lowest reported earnings in 1993 (i.e., $21,731.00). Mr. Rivas' compensation was the basis for $415.60, plus interest, of Setting Corp.'s employment tax liabilities for one quarter of tax year 1993. (Govt's Mem. at 5).

The IRS sent Setting Corp. a notice of collection on March 17, 1997 and a notice of delinquent account on July 14, 1997. (Govt's Mem. at 5). On or about July 24, 1997, Setting Corp. filed a Form 941C (Supporting Statement to Correct Information) and submitted payment of $43.25 to the IRS, representing the assessed employment tax for one "independent contractor" for the tax period ending December 31, 1993. (Taxpayer's Mem. at 4). Setting Corp. noted that $43.25 was being remitted "under protest" for one of its workers. (Taxpayer's Mem. at 4). In fact, this amount corresponds to the amount "owed" for Brian Jijon, a gem setter who worked for Setting Corp. during 1993. (Taxpayer's Mem. at 4). Setting Corp. claims that this particular gem setter was selected because the amount of employment taxes allegedly due for the work he performed during 1993 was the lowest amount due of any of the gem setters in 1993. [FN3] (Taxpayer's Mem. at 4). In its Motion to Dismiss, the Government contends that Brian Jijon was not one of the gem setters classified by the IRS as an employee. According to the Government's Motion, workers who were reclassified by the IRS as employees were individuals who earned more than $20,000 in 1993. (Govt's Mem. at 4). Setting Corp claims that "there was no reasonable way for Setting Corp. to have known that this particular gem setter [Brian Jijon] was allegedly excluded from the IRS's assessment." (Taxpayer's Mem. at 8).

> FN3. Simultaneous with the filing of the Form 941C and the $43.25 payment, Plaintiff filed a Form 843 (Claim for Refund and Request for Abatement) and a memorandum of law setting forth Plaintiff's position that it was not required to pay employment taxes for its gem setters because the gem setters are independent contractors. (Compl. §9). On or about October 27, 1997, the IRS issued a letter denying Plaintiff's claim for refund, stating that Plaintiff had previously waived its rights by entering into a settlement agreement (stipulation) with the IRS. The IRS denied Plaintiff's refund based on the alleged stipulation. (Compl. §9). Plaintiff immediately contacted the IRS Problem Resolution Office in Holtsville, NY, and on or about January 26, 1998, Plaintiff received a letter from the IRS Problem resolution office stating that Plaintiff had not, in fact, waived its right to an appeal and that Plaintiff may exercise its right to file a lawsuit for the refund. (Compl. §9).

*3 Setting Corp. then filed the instant action, on April 16, 1998, seeking to recover the $43.25 it paid to the IRS. In it's Response to the Government's Motion, Setting Corp. alleges that it "did not deliberately underpay the minimum amount allegedly required to be paid in order to initiate suit in this Court" and that the alleged underpayment "was based on the taxpayer's reasonable reliance on the IRS's assessment." (Taxpayer's Mem. at 16). The Government argues that the Court lacks subject matter jurisdiction to consider Setting Corp.'s claim because Setting Corp. failed to pay the requisite amount of employment tax liabilities attributable to one (affected) employee for one quarter. (Govt's Mem. at 7). Accordingly, the Government seeks to dismiss Setting Corp.'s refund claim pursuant to Fed.R.Civ.P. 12(b)(1) for lack of subject matter jurisdiction. [FN4]

> FN4. The Government further asserts that the Court lacks subject matter jurisdiction over this refund suit pursuant to 26 U.S.C. §7422(a) because Setting Corp. failed to file a refund claim in accordance with IRS rules and regulations. (Govt's Mem. at 8-10). Under Sec. 7422(a),
>
> No suit or proceeding shall be maintained in any court for the recovery of any internal revenue tax alleged to have been erroneously or illegally assessed or collected . . . until a claim for refund or credit has been duly filed with the Secretary, according to the provisions of law in that regard, and the regulations of the Secretary established in pursuance thereof. 26 U.S.C. §7422(a). The Government claims that Setting Corp. failed to satisfy the requirements for a refund suit because it did not provide all the necessary information in its July,

1997 refund claim and submission as required by Treasury Regulation ("Treas.Reg.") §31.6402(a)-2(a)(2); Treas. Reg. §31.6402(a)-2(c), and Revenue Ruling ("Rev.Rul.") 83-136. Setting Corp. argues that it did, in fact, follow proper procedure in filing its claim for refund. (Taxpayer's Mem. at 11-15).

The Government claims, for example, that Setting Corp. failed to comply with Treas. Reg. §31.6402(a)-2(a)(2) which requires, as a prerequisite to a refund suit, that an employer file a refund claim which includes a statement by the employer that it has repaid taxes to its employees or secured its employees' consent if no taxes have ever been collected. (Govt's Mem. at 9). Setting Corp. argues that this section only applies to employers who have withheld the employee's share of FICA taxes. Setting Corp. claims that "[i]f the employer did not withhold the employee's share, obviously the employee's consent is not required as there is nothing to be repaid to such employee." (Taxpayer's Mem. at 12).

The Government also claims that Setting Corp. failed to identify one employee (i.e., a reclassified gem setter) whose wages formed the basis of the employment tax dispute. (Govt's Mem. at 9). Setting Corp. contends there is no such requirement. (Taxpayer's Mem. at 12). Finally, the Government claims that according to Rev. Rul. 83-136, an "employer must submit with the refund claim a written statement, signed under penalty of perjury, stating that the employer did not deduct the employees' share of FICA tax from their pay." (Govt's Mem. at 9 citing Rev. Rul. 83-136, 1983-2 C.B. 244, 1983 WL 190160 (September 12, 1983)). The Government claims that Setting Corp. failed to comply with this Revenue Ruling because it did not supply any statement or certify on its Forms 843 or 941c that it had not withheld the employment taxes that are the subject of the claim for refund. (Govt's Mem. at 9). Setting Corp. argues, however, that Rev. Rul. 83-136 is not applicable to the instant case because the revenue ruling involves a "very peculiar set of facts" that are "distinct from the present situation where Setting Corp. has never paid employment taxes for its gem setters, paid under protest the amount allegedly due for one gem setter and simultaneously filed a claim for refund." (Taxpayer's Mem. at 13).

As this Court has decided to dismiss this motion on other grounds, it is not necessary to rule on these issues.

II. *Discussion*

The United States Supreme Court has held that "the United States, as sovereign, 'is immune from suit save as it consents to be sued . . . and the terms of its consent to be sued in any court define that court's jurisdiction to entertain the suit.'" *United States v. Testan,* 424 U.S. 392, 399, 96 S.Ct. 948, 47 L.Ed.2d 114 (1941) (citation omitted). *See also United States v. Forma,* 42 F.3d 759, 763 (2d Cir.1994); *Morton v. Granite,* 1991 WL 33333 at *5 (S.D.N.Y. Mar.5, 1991). Such a waiver of sovereign immunity must be " 'unequivocally expressed.'" *Morton,* 1991 WL 33333 at *5 (citations omitted). "Where waiver has been expressed unequivocally, the relevant 'authorizations for suits against the Government must be strictly construed in its favor.'" *Id.* (citing *Office of Personnel Management v. Richmond,* 496 U.S. 414, 110 S.Ct. 2465, 2475, 110 L.Ed.2d 387 (1990)) (emphasis added).

By statute, United States District Courts are vested with original jurisdiction over any "civil action against the United States for the recovery of any internal revenue tax alleged to have been erroneously or illegally assessed or collected" 28 U.S.C. §1346(a)(1). The statute "has been read by the Supreme Court to require full payment of an assessed tax before a taxpayer can invoke the jurisdiction of the district courts for the refund of such tax." *United States v. Forma,* 42 F.3d at 763 (citing *Flora v. United States,* 357 U.S. 63, 78 S.Ct. 1079, 2 L.Ed.2d 1165 (1958), *aff'd on reh'g,* 362 U.S. 145, 80 S.Ct. 630, 4 L.Ed.2d 623 (1960)). In order to file a tax refund action in District Court under 28 U.S.C.

§ 1346(a)(1), the taxpayer must, among other things, make full payment of the disputed tax assessment, including all penalties and accrued interest. *See Magnone v. United States,* 902 F.2d 192, 193 (2d. Cir.1990), *cert. denied,* 498 U.S. 853, 111 S.Ct. 147, 112 L.Ed.2d 113 (1990) (citing *Flora v. United States,* 357 U.S. 63, 78 S.Ct. 1079, 2 L.Ed.2d 1165 (1958)). Employment tax liabilities, however, may be the subject of a refund suit if the employer pays the smallest divisible unit of taxes, meaning that amount which is attributable to one employee for one quarter. *See Steele v. United States,* 280 F.2d 89, 90-91 (8th Cir.1960); *Magnone v. United States,* 733 F.Supp. 613, 615 n. 3 (S.D.N.Y.1989), *aff'd,* 902 F.2d 192 (2d Cir.1990), *cert. denied,* 498 U.S. 853, 111 S.Ct. 147, 112 L.Ed.2d 113 (1990).

*4 Courts in this Judicial District have strictly construed the requirements for filing a tax refund action under 28 U.S.C. § 1346(a)(1). For example, in *Spivak v. United States,* the government made (100%) Penalty assessments against plaintiffs by reason of allegedly unpaid income withholding and FICA taxes due for the first quarter of 1955 and the first quarter of 1956 from Lincoln Industries, Inc., a corporation of which the plaintiffs were officers. *See Spivak v. United States,* 254 F.Supp. 517, 519 (S.D.N.Y. May 2, 1966) *aff'd,* 370 F.2d 612 (2d Cir.1967), *cert. denied,* 387 U.S. 908, 87 S.Ct. 1690, 18 L.Ed.2d 625 (1967). Plaintiffs paid what they asserted were the taxes due for one employee for each period ($50 and $60, respectively), and sued for a refund of that amount. *Id.* at 522. Plaintiffs claimed that they acted pursuant to *Steele v. United States,* 280 F.2d 89 (8th Cir.1960), which held that the taxes involved were "divisible" taxes and that the tax due for a single employee for one period could be paid and an action maintained for a refund of just that amount. *See Spivak,* 254 F.Supp. at 522. Upholding the *Steele* doctrine, Judge Levet found that the plaintiffs failed to sustain the burden of proving, "by a fair preponderance of the credible evidence that the sums they paid were in fact the taxes due for one employee for each quarter here involved." Spivak, 254 F.Supp. at 522. The Court dismissed the complaint "[s]ince proof that plaintiffs have paid the amount of tax due for one employee for one period is absent, plaintiffs have not shown facts necessary to the subject matter jurisdiction of this court." *Id.* at 522-23.

Similarly, in *Morton v. U.S.,* the plaintiffs instituted an action for a refund of taxes allegedly overpaid and an abatement of taxes allegedly wrongfully assessed for the years 1971 through 1976. *See Morton v. U.S.,* 1991 WL 33333 at *6 (S.D.N.Y. March 5, 1991). The plaintiffs acknowledged that they had not made the requisite payment of tax assessments for the years 1974, 1975 and 1976, but asked that the Court make an exception to the filing requirements for a tax refund action because the assessments made against them were "fraudulently secured" and were made without issuing a Notice of Deficiency. *See Morton,* 1991 WL 33333 at *5. The Court refused plaintiffs' request and "decline[d] to disturb the settled law in this area." *Id.*

Here, it is undisputed that Setting Corp. has paid only $43.25 of the total disputed employment tax liabilities assessed for tax year 1993. (Taxpayer's Mem. at 4) (Govt.'s Mem. at 8). The Government argues that Setting Corp. has not made full payment of the total disputed employment tax liabilities for 1993 or of those taxes attributable to one affected employee for one quarter, and, thus, cannot maintain this challenge to the assessment of tax liabilities. Specifically, the Government contends that because the amount paid by Plaintiff is less than the amount of additional employment tax liabilities assessed for one quarter (i.e., $8,142.51 plus interest) and is also less than the amount of total employment tax liabilities associated with one employee for one quarter (i.e., $415.60 plus interest), Setting Corp. has failed to make payment of either the entire disputed employment tax liability or the smallest divisible unit of that liability for the tax year 1993, before filing the instant lawsuit. (Govt.'s Mem. at 8).

*5 Setting Corp. contends that the decision by the IRS to classify certain gem setters (i.e., those who earned more than $20,000) as "employees", while others, such as Brian Jijon, were classified as "independent contractors" was not appropriate. Setting Corp. asserts that all gem setters should be classified in the same category. Thus, Setting Corp. argues that by submitting payment of $43.25 to the IRS, representing the amount "owed" for

Brian Jijon for one quarter of 1993, it has satisfied the requirements for bringing this action. (Taxpayer's Mem. at 7-8). The Government claims, however, that it decided not to reclassify Brian Jijon as an employee "as a courtesy to Setting Corp." and because he earned less than $20,000 in 1993. (Govt's Mem. at 4). Setting Corp. responds that this classification fails to comport with the guidelines contained in Internal Revenue Code and Treasury Regulations for determining whether a worker is an "employee" or an "independent contractor." (Taxpayer's Mem. at 7). Setting Corp. asserts "how much an individual earns in a particular tax year is not listed as a factor to consider in determining worker status," and that the Government's decision to use yearly earnings as a factor to determine worker status was not "appropriate." (Taxpayer's Mem. at 7).

According to Setting Corp's Response, in addition to the IRS' failure to follow it's own guidelines, the IRS, in its assessment, did not list the individuals upon whom it based it's assessment and made no distinction between gem setters who earned more than $20,000 in 1993 and those who earned $20,000 or less. Setting Corp. contends that it, therefore, had no way of knowing about the IRS's classification of Brian Jijon as an "independent contractor" rather than an "employee." [FN5]

> FN5. Setting Corp.'s argument that "[i]f the IRS has determined, as the Government contends, that some of Setting Corp.'s gem setters are not employees, then Setting Corp. should be able to treat all of its gem setters as independent contractors" (Taxpayer's Mem. at 6), while potentially applicable to Setting Corp.'s underlying claim that its gem setters are "independent contractors" and not "employees," is not relevant to the instant motion to dismiss. Here, the relevant issue is whether or not Setting Corp. has satisfied the (strict) requirements for bringing a tax refund action in District Court.

This does not appear to be a case where clearly the taxpayer deliberately circumvented the required procedure by not paying taxes owed. However, as stated above, Courts in this District have strictly construed the requirements for filing a tax refund action under 28 U.S.C. § 1346(a). This Court will also do so. *See Spivak,* 254 F.Supp. at 522-23; Morton, 1991 WL 33333 at *5. Here, the IRS classified Brian Jijon as an "independent contractor," not an "employee." With this in mind, the Court is unwilling to disturb the well settled law in this area which requires that an employer wishing to bring a refund suit under § 1346(a)(1) must pay either the entire disputed tax assessment or the payment associated with one employee for one quarter. *See Steele v. United States,* 280 F.2d 89, 90-91 (8th Cir.1960); Morton, 1991 WL 33333 at *6; *Magnone,* 733 F.Supp. at 615 n. 3. [FN6] Plaintiff has not satisfied this requirement.

> FN6. The Court further declines to relieve Setting Corp. of the requirements of 26 U.S.C. § 7422(a). "It is undisputed that § 7422 requires administrative exhaustion." *United States v. Williams,* 514 U.S. 527, 533, 115 S.Ct. 1611, 131 L.Ed.2d 608 (1995). The Court further notes that "[t]he Supreme Court has long recognized the importance of requiring full compliance with Treasury Regulations in filing tax claims." *Morton,* 1991 WL 33333 at *7. *See also United States v. Felt & Tarrant Mfg. Co.,* 283 U.S. 269, 273, 51 S.Ct. 376, 75 L.Ed. 1025 (1931)("[t]he necessity for filing a claim [for refund] such as the statute requires is not dispensed with because the claim may be rejected. It is the rejection which makes the suit necessary. An anticipated rejection of the claim, which the statute contemplates, is not a ground for superseding its operation").

III. *Conclusion*

Accordingly, the Government's motion to dismiss is granted. Clerk to enter judgment. (It is recommended that the parties endeavor in good faith to settle the underlying issues involved here).

¶1551 Exhibit 15-1

Form **1040X** (Rev. November 2003)	Department of the Treasury—Internal Revenue Service **Amended U.S. Individual Income Tax Return** ► See separate instructions.	OMB No. 1545-0091

This return is for calendar year ► _____ , or fiscal year ended ► _____ , _____ .

Please print or type

Your first name and initial	Last name	Your social security number
If a joint return, spouse's first name and initial	Last name	Spouse's social security number
Home address (no. and street) or P.O. box if mail is not delivered to your home	Apt. no.	Phone number ( )
City, town or post office, state, and ZIP code. If you have a foreign address, see page 2 of the instructions.		For Paperwork Reduction Act Notice, see page 6.

A If the name or address shown above is different from that shown on the original return, check here . . . . ► ☐

B Has the original return been changed or audited by the IRS or have you been notified that it will be? . . ☐ Yes ☐ No

C Filing status. Be sure to complete this line. **Note.** You cannot change from joint to separate returns after the due date.

On original return ► ☐ Single ☐ Married filing jointly ☐ Married filing separately ☐ Head of household ☐ Qualifying widow(er)

On this return ► ☐ Single ☐ Married filing jointly ☐ Married filing separately ☐ Head of household* ☐ Qualifying widow(er)

*If the qualifying person is a child but not your dependent, see page 2.

Use Part II on the back to explain any changes

				A. Original amount or as previously adjusted (see page 2)	B. Net change—amount of increase or (decrease)—explain in Part II	C. Correct amount
	Income and Deductions (see pages 2–6)					
1	Adjusted gross income (see page 3)	**1**				
2	Itemized deductions or standard deduction (see page 3) .	**2**				
3	Subtract line 2 from line 1	**3**				
4	Exemptions. If changing, fill in Parts I and II on the back	**4**				
5	Taxable income. Subtract line 4 from line 3	**5**				
6	Tax (see page 4). Method used in col. C........................	**6**				
7	Credits (see page 4)	**7**				
8	Subtract line 7 from line 6. Enter the result but not less than zero .	**8**				
9	Other taxes (see page 4)	**9**				
10	Total tax. Add lines 8 and 9	**10**				
11	Federal income tax withheld and excess social security and tier 1 RRTA tax withheld. If changing, see page 4	**11**				
12	Estimated tax payments, including amount applied from prior year's return	**12**				
13	Earned income credit (EIC)	**13**				
14	Additional child tax credit from Form 8812	**14**				
15	Credits from Form 2439, Form 4136, or Form 8885 . . .	**15**				
16	Amount paid with request for extension of time to file (see page 4)		**16**		
17	Amount of tax paid with original return plus additional tax paid after it was filed		**17**		
18	Total payments. Add lines 11 through 17 in column C		**18**		

Refund or Amount You Owe

19	Overpayment, if any, as shown on original return or as previously adjusted by the IRS . . .	**19**	
20	Subtract line 19 from line 18 (see page 5)	**20**	
21	**Amount you owe.** If line 10, column C, is more than line 20, enter the difference and see page 5 .	**21**	
22	If line 10, column C, is less than line 20, enter the difference	**22**	
23	Amount of line 22 you want **refunded to you**	**23**	
24	Amount of line 22 you want **applied to your** estimated tax ► **24**		

Sign Here
Joint return? See page 2.
Keep a copy for your records.

Under penalties of perjury, I declare that I have filed an original return and that I have examined this amended return, including accompanying schedules and statements, and to the best of my knowledge and belief, this amended return is true, correct, and complete. Declaration of preparer (other than taxpayer) is based on all information of which the preparer has any knowledge.

► Your signature	Date	► Spouse's signature. If a joint return, **both** must sign.	Date

Paid Preparer's Use Only

Preparer's signature ►		Date	Check if self-employed ☐	Preparer's SSN or PTIN
Firm's name (or yours if self-employed), address, and ZIP code ►			EIN	
			Phone no. ( )	

Cat. No. 11360L   Form **1040X** (Rev. 11-2003)

¶1551

Form 1040X (Rev. 11-2003)   Page **2**

Part I   **Exemptions.** See Form 1040 or 1040A instructions.

If you are **not changing your exemptions,** do not complete this part.
If claiming **more exemptions,** complete lines 25–31.
If claiming **fewer exemptions,** complete lines 25–30.

			A. Original number of exemptions reported or as previously adjusted	B. Net change	C. Correct number of exemptions
25	Yourself and spouse	25			
	Caution. If your parents (or someone else) can claim you as a dependent (even if they chose not to), you cannot claim an exemption for yourself.				
26	Your dependent children who lived with you	26			
27	Your dependent children who did not live with you due to divorce or separation	27			
28	Other dependents	28			
29	Total number of exemptions. Add lines 25 through 28	29			
30	Multiply the number of exemptions claimed on line 29 by the amount listed below for the tax year you are amending. Enter the result here and on line 4.	30			

Tax year	Exemption amount	But see the instructions for line 4 on page 3 if the amount on line 1 is over:
2003	$3,050	$104,625
2002	3,000	103,000
2001	2,900	99,725
2000	2,800	96,700

31   Dependents (children and other) not claimed on original (or adjusted) return:

(a) First name Last name	(b) Dependent's social security number	(c) Dependent's relationship to you	(d) ✓ if qualifying child for child tax credit (see page 5)
			☐
			☐
			☐
			☐
			☐
			☐

No. of your children on line 31 who:
- **lived with** you . . ▶ ☐
- **did not** live with you due to divorce or separation (see page 5) . . ▶ ☐

Dependents on line 31 not entered above ▶ ☐

Part II   **Explanation of Changes to Income, Deductions, and Credits**

Enter the line number from the front of the form for each item you are changing and give the reason for each change. Attach only the supporting forms and schedules for the items changed. If you do not attach the required information, your Form 1040X may be returned. Be sure to include your name and social security number on any attachments.

If the change relates to a net operating loss carryback or a general business credit carryback, attach the schedule or form that shows the year in which the loss or credit occurred. See page 2 of the instructions. Also, check here . . . . . . ▶ ☐

Part III   **Presidential Election Campaign Fund.** Checking below will not increase your tax or reduce your refund.

If you did not previously want $3 to go to the fund but now want to, check here . . . . ▶ ☐
If a joint return and your spouse did not previously want $3 to go to the fund but now wants to, check here . . . . ▶ ☐

Form **1040X** (Rev. 11-2003)

¶1552 Exhibit 15-2

Form **1120X** (Rev. December 2001) Department of the Treasury Internal Revenue Service	**Amended U.S. Corporation Income Tax Return**	OMB No. 1545-0132
		For tax year ending ▶ .... (Enter month and year.)

Please Type or Print	Name	Employer identification number
	Number, street, and room or suite no. (If a P.O. box, see instructions.)	
	City or town, state, and ZIP code	Telephone number (optional) ( )

Enter name and address used on original return (If same as above, write "Same.")

Internal Revenue Service Center ▶
where original return was filed

Fill in Applicable Items and Use Part II To Explain Any Changes

Part I Income and Deductions (see instructions)	**(a)** As originally reported or as previously adjusted	**(b)** Net change— increase or (decrease)— explain in Part II	**(c)** Correct amount
1 Total income (Form 1120 or 1120-A, line 11) . . . **1**			
2 Total deductions (total of lines 27 and 29c, Form 1120, or lines 23 and 25c, Form 1120-A) **2**			
3 Taxable income. Subtract line 2 from line 1 . . . . **3**			
4 Tax (Form 1120, line 31, or Form 1120-A, line 27) . **4**			

Payments and Credits (see instructions)

5a Overpayment in prior year allowed as a credit . . . **5a**			
b Estimated tax payments . . . . **b**			
c Refund applied for on Form 4466 . . . . **c**			
d Subtract line 5c from the sum of lines 5a and 5b . . **d**			
e Tax deposited with Form 7004 . . . . **e**			
f Credit from Form 2439 . . . . **f**			
g Credit for Federal tax on fuels . . . . **g**			
6 Tax deposited or paid with (or after) the filing of the original return **6**			
7 Add lines 5d through 6, column (c) **7**			
8 Overpayment, if any, as shown on original return or as later adjusted **8**			
9 Subtract line 8 from line 7 . . . . **9**			

Tax Due or Overpayment (see instructions)

10 **Tax due.** Subtract line 9 from line 4, column (c). If paying by check, make it payable to the "**United States Treasury.**" . . . . ▶ **10**	
11 **Overpayment.** Subtract line 4, column (c), from line 9 . . . . ▶ **11**	
12 Enter the amount of line 11 you want: **Credited to 20___estimated tax ▶** Refunded ▶ **12**	

Sign Here	Under penalties of perjury, I declare that I have filed an original return and that I have examined this amended return, including accompanying schedules and statements, and to the best of my knowledge and belief, this amended return is true, correct, and complete. Declaration of preparer (other than taxpayer) is based on all information of which preparer has any knowledge.

Sign Here	▶ Signature of officer	Date	▶ Title

Paid Preparer's Use Only	Preparer's ▶ signature	Date	Check if self-employed ☐	Preparer's SSN or PTIN
	Firm's name (or yours if self-employed), address, and ZIP code ▶		EIN	
			Phone no. ( )	

For Paperwork Reduction Act Notice, see page 4.   Cat. No. 11530Z   Form **1120X** (Rev. 12-2001)

Form 1120X (Rev. 12-2001)   Page **2**

Part II   **Explanation of Changes to Items in Part I** (Enter the line number from page 1 for the items you are changing, and give the reason for each change. Show any computation in detail. Also, see **What To Attach** on page 3 of the instructions.)

If the change is due to a net operating loss carryback, a capital loss carryback, or a general business credit carryback, see **Carryback Claims** on page 3, and check here . . . . ▶ ☐

Form **1120X** (Rev. 12-2001)

Form 1120X (Rev. 12-2001)   Page **3**

General Instructions

Section references are to the Internal Revenue Code unless otherwise noted.

Purpose of Form

Use Form 1120X to:
- Correct a previously filed* Form 1120 or 1120-A or
- Make certain elections after the prescribed deadline (see Regulations section 301.9100-1 through 3).

Use Form 1120X to correct the return as originally filed, or as later adjusted by an amended return, a claim for refund, or an examination.

Do not use Form 1120X to...	Instead, use...
Apply for a quick refund of estimated tax	**Form 4466,** Corporation Application for Quick Refund of Estimated Tax
Obtain a tentative refund of taxes due to: • A net operating loss (NOL) carryback • A net capital loss carryback • An unused general business credit carryback • A claim of right adjustment under section 1341(b)(1)	**Form 1139,** Corporation Application for Tentative Refund **Note:** *Use Form 1139 only if 1 year or less has passed since the tax year in which the carryback or adjustment occurred. Otherwise, use Form 1120X.*
Request IRS approval for a change in accounting method	**Form 3115,** Application for Change in Accounting Method

When To File

File Form 1120X only after the corporation has filed its original return. Generally, Form 1120X must be filed within 3 years after the date the original return was due or 3 years after the date the corporation filed it, whichever is later. A Form 1120X based on an NOL carryback, a capital loss carryback, or a general business credit carryback, generally must be filed within 3 years after the due date (including extensions) of the return for the tax year of the NOL, capital loss, or unused credit. Other claims for refund must be filed within 3 years after the date the original return was due, 3 years after the date the corporation filed it, or 2 years after the date the tax was paid, whichever is later.

Note: *It often takes 3 to 4 months to process Form 1120X.*

Private delivery services. See the instructions for the corporation's income tax return for information on certain private delivery services designated by the IRS to meet the "timely mailing as timely filing/paying" rule for tax returns and payments.

Caution: *Private delivery services cannot deliver items to P.O. boxes. Use the U.S. Postal Service to send any item to an IRS P.O. box address.*

What To Attach

If the corrected amount involves an item of income, deduction, or credit that must be supported with a schedule, statement, or form, attach the appropriate schedule, statement, or form to Form 1120X. Include the corporation's name and employer identification number on any attachments.

In addition, if the corporation requests a direct deposit of a refund of $1 million or more, attach **Form 8302,** Direct Deposit of Tax Refund of $1 Million or More.

Tax Shelters

If the corporation's return is being amended to include any item (loss, credit, deduction, other tax benefit, or income) relating to a tax shelter required to be registered, attach **Form 8271,** Investor Reporting of Tax Shelter Registration Number.

Carryback Claims

If Form 1120X is used as a carryback claim, attach copies of Form 1120 (pages 1 and 3) or Form 1120-A (pages 1 and 2), for both the year the loss or credit originated and for the carryback year. Also attach any other forms, schedules, or statements that are necessary to support the claim, including a statement that shows all adjustments required to figure any NOL that was carried back. At the top of the forms or schedules attached, write "Copy Only—Do Not Process."

Information on Income, Deductions, Tax Computation, etc.

For information on income, deductions, tax computation, etc., see the Instructions for Forms 1120 and 1120-A for the tax year being amended.

Caution: *Deductions for such items as charitable contributions and the dividends-received deduction may have to be refigured because of changes made to items of income or expense.*

Where To File

File this form at the applicable Internal Revenue Service Center where the corporation filed its original return.

Specific Instructions

Tax Year

In the space above the employer identification number, enter the ending month and year of the calendar or fiscal year for the tax return being amended.

P.O. Box

If the post office does not deliver mail to the street address and the corporation has a P.O. box, show the box number instead of the street address.

Column (a)

Enter the amounts from the corporation's return as originally filed or as it was later amended. If the return was changed or audited by the IRS, enter the amounts as adjusted.

Column (b)

Enter the net increase or net decrease for each line being changed. Use parentheses around all amounts that are decreases. Explain the increase or decrease in Part II.

Column (c)

Lines 1 and 2. Add the increase in column (b) to the amount in column (a) or subtract the column (b) decrease from column (a). Enter the result in column (c). For an item that did not change, enter the amount from column (a) in column (c).

Line 4. Figure the new amount of tax using the taxable income on line 3, column (c). Use Schedule J, Form 1120, or Part I, Form 1120-A, of the original return to make the necessary tax computation.

Line 5e. Enter the amount of tax deposited with **Form 7004,** Application for Automatic Extension of Time To File Corporation Income Tax Return.

Line 5g. Include on line 5g any write-in credits or payments, such as the credit for ozone-depleting chemicals or backup withholding.

Line 8. Enter the amount from the "Overpayment" line of the original return, even if the corporation chose to credit all or part of this amount to the next year's estimated tax. This amount must be considered in preparing Form 1120X because any refund due from the original return will be refunded separately (or credited to estimated tax) from any additional refund claimed on Form 1120X.

Line 10—Tax due. If the corporation does not use the Electronic Federal Tax Payment System (EFTPS), enclose a check with this form and make it payable to the **"United States Treasury."** Do not use the depository method of payment.

Line 11—Overpayment. If the corporation is entitled to a refund larger than the amount claimed on the original return, line 11 will show only the additional amount of overpayment. This additional amount will be refunded separately from the amount claimed on the original return. The IRS will figure any interest due and include it in the refund.

Line 12. Enter the amount, if any, to be applied to the estimated tax for the next tax period. Also, enter that tax period. No interest will be paid on this amount. The election to apply part or all of the overpayment to the next year's estimated tax is irrevocable.

Who Must Sign

The return must be signed and dated by:

- The president, vice president, treasurer, assistant treasurer, chief accounting officer or
- Any other corporate officer (such as tax officer) authorized to sign.

A receiver, trustee, or assignee must also sign and date any return filed on behalf of a corporation.

If a corporate officer completes Form 1120X, the paid preparer's space should remain blank. Anyone who prepares Form 1120X but does not charge the corporation should not sign the return. Generally, anyone who is paid to prepare the return must sign it and fill in the "Paid Preparer's Use Only" area. See the Instructions for Forms 1120 and 1120-A for more information.

Paperwork Reduction Act Notice. We ask for the information on this form to carry out the Internal Revenue laws of the United States. You are required to give us the information. We need it to ensure that you are complying with these laws and to allow us to figure and collect the right amount of tax.

You are not required to provide the information requested on a form that is subject to the Paperwork Reduction Act unless the form displays a valid OMB control number. Books or records relating to a form or its instructions must be retained as long as their contents may become material in the administration of any Internal Revenue law. Generally, tax returns and return information are confidential, as required by section 6103.

The time needed to complete and file this form will vary depending on individual circumstances. The estimated average time is:

Recordkeeping	13 hr., 9 min.
Learning about the law or the form	1 hr., 14 min.
Preparing the form	3 hr., 22 min.
Copying, assembling, and sending the form to the IRS	32 min.

If you have comments concerning the accuracy of these time estimates or suggestions for making this form simpler, we would be happy to hear from you. You can write to the Tax Forms Committee, Western Area Distribution Center, Rancho Cordova, CA 95743-0001. **Do not** send the form to this address. Instead, see **Where To File** above.

¶1553 Exhibit 15-3

| Form **843** (Rev. November 2002) Department of the Treasury Internal Revenue Service | **Claim for Refund and Request for Abatement** ▶ See separate instructions. | OMB No. 1545-0024 |

*Use Form 843 only if your claim involves **(a)** one of the taxes shown on line 3a or **(b)** a refund or abatement of interest, penalties, or additions to tax on line 4a.*

Do not *use Form 843 if your claim is for—*
- *An overpayment of income taxes;*
- *A refund for nontaxable use (or sales) of fuel; or*
- *An overpayment of excise taxes reported on Form(s) 11-C, 720, 730, or 2290.*

Type or print

Name of claimant	Your SSN or ITIN
Address (number, street, and room or suite no.)	Spouse's SSN or ITIN
City or town, state, and ZIP code	Employer identification number (EIN)
Name and address shown on return if different from above	Daytime telephone number ( )

1 Period. Prepare a separate Form 843 for each tax period
From / / to / /

2 Amount to be refunded or abated
$

3a Type of tax, penalty, or addition to tax:
☐ Employment ☐ Estate ☐ Gift ☐ Excise (see instructions)
☐ Penalty—IRC section ▶ _____

b Type of return filed (see instructions):
☐ 706 ☐ 709 ☐ 940 ☐ 941 ☐ 943 ☐ 945 ☐ 990-PF ☐ 4720 ☐ Other (specify)

4a Request for abatement or refund of:
☐ Interest as a result of IRS errors or delays.
☐ A penalty or addition to tax as a result of erroneous advice from the IRS.

b Dates of payment ▶

5 **Explanation and additional claims.** Explain why you believe this claim should be allowed, and show computation of tax refund or abatement of interest, penalty, or addition to tax. If you need more space, attach additional sheets.

Signature. If you are filing Form 843 to request a refund or abatement relating to a joint return, both you and your spouse must sign the claim. Claims filed by corporations must be signed by a corporate officer authorized to sign, and the signature must be accompanied by the officer's title.

Under penalties of perjury, I declare that I have examined this claim, including accompanying schedules and statements, and, to the best of my knowledge and belief, it is true, correct, and complete.

Signature (Title, if applicable. Claims by corporations must be signed by an officer.)   Date

Signature   Date

For Privacy Act and Paperwork Reduction Act Notice, see separate instructions. Cat. No. 10180R   Form **843** (Rev. 11-2002)

¶1553

¶1554 Exhibit 15-4

Internal Revenue Service
District Director

Department of the Treasury

Date:

Refund Claimed:

Kind of Tax:

Tax Period Ended:

Person to Contact:

Contact Telephone Number:

CERTIFIED MAIL

We have reviewed your claim for refund, and we cannot consider it for the reason checked below.

☐ It was received after the deadline for filing.

☐ As consideration in a previous settlement, you waived your right to claim the refund.

☐ It is based upon your failure or refusal to comply with tax laws because of moral, religious, political, constitutional, conscientious, or similar grounds. The Internal Revenue Service does not have the authority to consider such grounds in administering the tax laws.

☐ This matter has already been settled under the terms of a Closing Agreement we made for the tax period in question. (See section 7121 of the Internal Revenue Code.)

☐ This matter was disposed of by a final order of the United States Tax Court or other court.

☐ This matter was settled in your favor in an earlier determination of your liability.

This letter is your legal notice that we cannot consider your claim.

If you want to bring suit or proceedings for the recovery of any tax, penalties, or other moneys for which this disallowance notice is issued, you may do so by filing such a suit with the United States District Court having jurisdiction, or the United States Claims Court. The law permits you to do this within 2 years from the mailing date of this letter.

(over)

Letter 916(DO) (Rev. 12–84)

If you have any questions, please contact the person whose name and address are shown in the heading of this letter. If you write, please include your telephone number and the most convenient time for us to call if we need more information.

Thank you for your cooperation.

Sincerely yours,

District Director

¶1555 Exhibit 15-5

Internal Revenue Service   **Department of the Treasury**

Taxpayer Identification Number:

Kind of Tax:

Tax Period(s) Ended

Amount of Claim:

Date Claim Received:

Date: Person to Contact:

Contact Telephone Number:

Employee Identification Number:

Dear

We are sorry, but we cannot allow your claim for an adjustment to your tax, for the reasons stated below. This letter is your legal notice that we have fully disallowed your claim.

If you wish to bring suit or proceedings for the recovery of any tax, penalties, or other moneys for which this disallowance notice is issued, you may do so by filing suit with the United States District Court having jurisdiction, or the United States Claims Court. The law permits you to do this within 2 years from the mailing date of this letter. However, if you signed a *Waiver of Statutory Notification of Claim Disallowance*, Form 2297, the period for bringing suit began to run on the date you filed the waiver.

We have enclosed Publication 5, *Your Appeal Rights and How to Prepare a Protest If You Don't Agree*, and Publication 594, *The IRS Collection Process*, if additional tax is due.

(over)   **Letter 906 (DO) (Rev. 6-2000)**
                                                Cat. No. 14978B

If you have any questions, please contact the person whose name and telephone number are shown in the heading of this letter. Thank you for your cooperation.

Sincerely yours,

Enclosures:
Publication 5
☐ Publication 594

Reasons for disallowance:

Letter 906 (DO) (Rev. 6-2000)
Cat. No. 14978B

¶1555

¶1556 Exhibit 15-6

Internal Revenue Service   **Department of the Treasury**

Date:

Taxpayer Identification Number:

Form:

Tax Period(s) Ended and Claim Amount:

Date Claim Received:

Person to Contact:

Contact Telephone Number:

Employee Identification Number:

Last date to Respond to this Letter:

Dear

We examined your claim and propose:

☐   Partial disallowance, as shown in the enclosed examination report. If you accept our findings, please sign and return the enclosed Form 2297, *Waiver Form* and Form 3363, *Acceptance Form.*

☐   Full disallowance, as shown in the enclosed examination report or at the end of this letter. If you accept our findings, please sign and return the enclosed Form 2297, *Waiver Form* and Form 3363, *Acceptance Form.*

☐   Full disallowance with additional tax due, as shown in the enclosed examination report. If you accept our findings, please sign and return the enclosed Form 2297, *Waiver Form* and the examination report.

Note: If your claim involves a joint return, both taxpayers must sign the form(s).

If you are a "C" Corporation filer, Section 6621(c) of the Internal Revenue Code provides for an interest rate 2% higher than the standard interest rate on deficiencies of $100,000 or more.

If you don't agree with our findings, you may request a meeting or telephone conference with the supervisor of the person identified in the heading of this letter. If you still don't agree with our findings, we recommend that you request a conference with our Appeals Office. If you request a conference, we will forward your request to the Appeals Office and they will contact you to schedule an appointment.

Letter 569 (DO) (Rev. 9-2000)
Catalog Number 40248G

¶1556

If the proposed change to tax is:

- $25,000 or less for *each* referenced tax period; you may send us a letter requesting Appeals consideration, indicating what you don't agree with and the reasons why you don't agree.

- More than $25,000 for *any* referenced tax period; you must submit a formal protest.

The requirements for filing a formal protest are explained in the enclosed Publication 3498, *The Examination Process.* Publication 3498 also includes information on your *Rights as a Taxpayer* and the *IRS Collection Process.*

If you don't respond by the date shown in the heading of this letter, we will process your case based on the adjustments shown in the enclosed examination report or the explanations given at the end of this letter.

If you have any questions, please contact the person whose name and telephone number are shown in the heading of this letter. Thank you for your cooperation.

Sincerely yours,

Enclosures:
☐ Examination Report
Form 2297
☐ Form 3363
Publication 3498
Envelope

Letter 569 (DO) (Rev. 9-2000)
Catalog Number 40248G

¶1556

Reason for Disallowance:

Letter 569 (DO) (Rev. 9-2000)
Catalog Number 40248G

¶1556

¶1557 Exhibit 15-7

Form **2297** (Rev. March 1982)	Department of the Treasury — Internal Revenue Service **Waiver of Statutory Notification of Claim Disallowance**

I, _____ of _____

      (Name, SSN or EIN)   *(Number, Street, City or Town, State, ZIP Code)*

waive the requirement under Internal Revenue Code section 6532(a)(1) that a notice of claim disallowance be sent to me by certified or registered mail for the claims for credit or refund shown in column (d), below.

    I understand that the filing of this waiver is irrevocable and it will begin the 2-year period for filing suit for refund of the claims disallowed as if the notice of disallowance had been sent by certified or registered mail.

Claims

(a) Taxable Period Ended	(b) Kind of Tax	(c) Amount of Claim	(d) Amount of Claim Disallowed

If you file this waiver for a joint return, both you and your spouse must sign the original and duplicate of this form. Sign your name exactly as it appears on the return. If you are acting under power of attorney for your spouse, you may sign as agent for him or her.

    For an agent or attorney acting under a power of attorney, a power of attorney must be sent with this form if not previously filed.

    For a partnership with excise or employment tax liability, all partners must sign. However, one partner may sign with appropriate evidence of authorization to act for the partnership.

    For a person acting in a fiduciary capacity (executor, administrator, trustee), file Form 56, Notice Concerning Fiduciary Relationship with this form if not previously filed.

    For a corporation, enter the name of the corporation followed by the signature and title of the officer(s) authorized to sign.

Your Signature ——▶ _____   *(Date signed)*

Spouse's Signature If A Joint Return Was Filed ——▶ _____   *(Date signed)*

Taxpayer's Representative Sign Here ——▶ _____   *(Date signed)*

Partnership/ Corporate Name: _____

Partners/ Corporate Officers Sign Here _____ *(Title)*   *(Date signed)*

_____ *(Title)*   *(Date signed)*

NOTE - Filing this waiver within 6 months from the date the claim was filed will not permit filing a suit for refund before the 6-month period has elapsed unless a decision is made by the Service within that time disallowing the claims.

Form **2297** (Rev. 3-82)

¶1558 Exhibit 15-8

Form **907** (Revised January 2001)	Department of the Treasury - Internal Revenue Service **Agreement to Extend the Time to Bring Suit**	In reply refer to: _____ Taxpayer Identification Number

_____, taxpayer(s) of
(Name(s))

_____
(Number, street, city or town, State, ZIP code)

and the Commissioner of Internal Revenue agree that the taxpayer(s) may bring suit to recover the taxes described below, on or before

_____ .
(Expiration date)

Claims for the amounts shown below have been timely filed by the taxpayer(s), and these claims have been disallowed in whole or in part. A notice of disallowance has been mailed to the taxpayer(s) by certified or registered mail, unless the taxpayer(s) waived the requirement that the notice be issued.

	Period Ended	Kind of Tax	Amount of Tax	Date Notice of Disallowance Mailed or Waiver Filed
Refund Credit				

IMPORTANT:

You must submit with this agreement a statement of the issues involved in the claims for refund or credit of the taxes listed above.

You may request in writing that the claims be reopened and reconsidered at any time before the expiration date shown.
You should state the particular circumstances on which you base the request. Please identify the claims in the request by stating the amounts claimed, the periods involved, and the date and symbols appearing on the letter in which notice of disallowance was given, or the date the waiver (Form 2297) was filed. Attach a copy of this agreement to your request.

This agreement will not be effective until the appropriate Internal Revenue Service official signs this form on behalf of the Commissioner of Internal Revenue. You should therefore be prepared to protect your interests by bringing suit, if desired, at any time before this agreement is signed.
If the appropriate Internal Revenue Service official signs this agreement on behalf of the Commissioner of Internal Revenue , the final decision in any case now in litigation does not bind that official in the disposition, of the issues on the taxes covered by this agreement.

YOUR SIGNATURE HERE ➤ _____ _____
(Date signed)

SPOUSE'S SIGNATURE ➤ _____ _____
(Date signed)

TAXPAYER'S REPRESENTATIVE

SIGN HERE ➤ _____ _____
(Date signed)

CORPORATE NAME ➤ _____

CORPORATE OFFICER(S) SIGN HERE ➤ _____ _____ _____
(Title)   (Date signed)

➤ _____ _____ _____
(Title)   (Date signed)

INTERNAL REVENUE SERVICE SIGNATURE AND TITLE

_____   _____
(Division Executive Name - see instructions)   (Division Executive Title - see instructions)

BY _____ _____
(Authorized Official Signature and Title - see instructions)   (Date signed)

(Signature instructions are on the back of this form)	www.irs.gov	Catalog Number 16963W	Form **907** (Rev. 1-2001)

Instructions

If this agreement is for any year(s) you filed a joint return, both husband and wife must sign the original and copy of this form unless one, acting under a power of attorney, signs as agent for the other. The signatures must match the names as they appear on this form.

If you are an attorney or agent of the taxpayer(s), you may sign this agreement provided the action is specifically authorized by a power of attorney. If you didn't previously file the power of attorney, please include it with this form.

If you are acting as a fiduciary (such as executor, administrator, trustee, etc.) and you sign this agreement, also attach a completed Form 56, Notice Concerning Fiduciary Relationship, if you haven't already filed one.

If the taxpayer is a corporation, sign this agreement with the corporate name followed by the signature and title of the officer(s) authorized to sign.

Instructions for Internal Revenue Service Employees

Complete the Division Executive's name and title depending upon your division.

If you are in the Small Business /Self-Employed Division, enter the name and title for the appropriate division executive for your business unit (e.g., Area Director for your area; Director, Compliance Policy; Director, Compliance Services).

If you are in the Wage and Investment Division, enter the name and title for the appropriate division executive for your business unit (e.g., Area Director for your area; Director, Field Compliance Services).

If you are in the Large and Mid-Size Business Division, enter the name and title of the Director, Field Operations for your industry.

If you are in the Tax Exempt and Government Entities Division, enter the name and title for the appropriate division executive for your business unit (e.g., Director, Exempt Organizations; Director, Employee Plans; Director, Federal, State and Local Governments; Director, Indian Tribal Governments; Director, Tax Exempt Bonds).

If you are in Appeals, enter the name and title of the appropriate Director, Appeals Operating Unit.

The signature and title line will be signed and dated by the appropriate authorized official within your division.

Catalog Number 16963W   Form **907** (Rev. 1-2001)

¶1558

¶1559 Exhibit 15-9

Department of the Treasury
Internal Revenue Service

If you have any questions, refer to this information:

Date of This Notice:
Taxpayer Identifying Number:
Document Locator Number:
Form　　　　　　　Tax Period:

Call:

or

Write:　Chief, Service Center Collection Branch
　　　　　Internal Revenue Service Center

Delay in Processing Your Refund

This copy is for your records.

We are sorry, but there is a delay in processing your overpayment for the above tax period because we must check to make sure you do not owe other Federal taxes. This will take about 6 to 8 weeks.　　　Your Overpaid Tax Shown on Return. $ _____

If you owe other Federal taxes, all or part of your overpaid taxes may be applied to those taxes. We will let you know how the overpaid tax is applied. If you requested a refund and do not owe other Federal taxes, a check will be sent to you for the amount you overpaid. Any interest due you will be included in the check.

No further action is required of you, but if you have any questions you can call or write us -- see the information in the upper right corner. To make sure that IRS employees give courteous responses and correct information to taxpayers, a second employee sometimes listens in on telephone calls.

Form 4356 (Part 1) (Rev. 5-93)

¶1560 Exhibit 15-10

Form **1045**	**Application for Tentative Refund**	OMB No. 1545-0098

Application for Tentative Refund

▶ See separate instructions.
▶ Do not attach to your income tax return—mail in a separate envelope.
▶ For use by individuals, estates, or trusts.

Department of the Treasury
Internal Revenue Service

20**03**

Type or print		
Name(s) shown on return	Social security or employer identification number	
Number, street, and apt. or suite no. If a P.O. box, see page 2 of the instructions.	Spouse's social security number (SSN)	
City, town or post office, state, and ZIP code. If a foreign address, see page 2 of the instructions.	Daytime phone number ( )	

1	This application is filed to carry back:	**a** Net operating loss (NOL) (Sch. A, line 27, page 2) $	**b** Unused general business credit $	**c** Net section 1256 contracts loss $

2a For the calendar year 2003, or other tax year
beginning , 2003, ending , 20   **b** Date tax return was filed

3 If this application is for an unused credit created by another carryback, enter year of first carryback ▶ ....

4 If you filed a joint return (or separate return) for some, but not all, of the tax years involved in figuring the carryback, list the years and specify whether joint (J) or separate (S) return for each ▶ ....

5 If SSN for carryback year is different from above, enter **a** SSN ▶ .... and **b** Year(s) ▶ ....

6 If you changed your accounting period, give date permission to change was granted ▶ ....

7 Have you filed a petition in Tax Court for the year(s) to which the carryback is to be applied? . . . . . ☐ Yes ☐ No

8 Is any part of the decrease in tax due to a loss or credit from a tax shelter required to be registered? . . ☐ Yes ☐ No

9 If you are carrying back an NOL or net section 1256 contracts loss, did this cause the release of foreign tax credits or the release of other credits due to the release of the foreign tax credit (see page 3 of the instructions)? . . ☐ Yes ☐ No

	Computation of Decrease in Tax (see page 3 of the instructions) **Note:** *If 1a and 1c are blank, skip lines 10 through 16.*	____ preceding tax year ended ▶		____ preceding tax year ended ▶		____ preceding tax year ended ▶	
		Before carryback	After carryback	Before carryback	After carryback	Before carryback	After carryback
10	Adjusted gross income						
11	NOL deduction after carryback (see page 3 of the instructions)						
12	Subtract line 11 from line 10 . . .						
13	Deductions (see page 4 of the instructions)						
14	Subtract line 13 from line 12 . . .						
15	Exemptions (see page 4 of the instructions)						
16	Taxable income. Line 14 minus line 15						
17	Income tax. See page 5 of the instructions and attach an explanation						
18	Alternative minimum tax						
19	Add lines 17 and 18						
20	General business credit (see page 5 of the instructions)						
21	Other credits. Identify						
22	Total credits. Add lines 20 and 21 .						
23	Subtract line 22 from line 19 . . .						
24	Self-employment tax						
25	Other taxes						
26	Total tax. Add lines 23 through 25 .						
27	Enter the amount from the "After carryback" column on line 26 for each year						
28	Decrease in tax. Line 26 minus line 27						

29 Overpayment of tax due to a claim of right adjustment under section 1341(b)(1) (attach computation) . .

Sign Here

Keep a copy of this application for your records.

Under penalties of perjury, I declare that I have examined this application and accompanying schedules and statements, and to the best of my knowledge and belief, they are true, correct, and complete.

Your signature	Date
Spouse's signature. If Form 1045 is filed jointly, **both** must sign.	Date

Preparer Other Than Taxpayer	Name ▶	Date
	Address ▶	

For Disclosure, Privacy Act, and Paperwork Reduction Act Notice, see page 7 of the instructions.   Cat. No. 10670A   Form **1045** (2003)

Form 1045 (2003)   Page **2**

Schedule A—NOL (see page 5 of the instructions)

1. Adjusted gross income from your 2003 Form 1040, line 35. Estates and trusts, skip lines 1 and 2 . . . . **1**

2. Deductions:
   a. Enter the amount from your 2003 Form 1040, line 37 . . . . **2a**
   b. Enter your deduction for exemptions from your 2003 Form 1040, line 39 . . . . **2b**
   c. Add lines 2a and 2b **2c**

3. Subtract line 2c from line 1. Estates and trusts, enter taxable income increased by the sum of the charitable deduction and income distribution deduction **3**

   Note: *If line 3 is zero or more, do not complete the rest of the schedule. You **do not** have an NOL.*

4. Deduction for exemptions from line 2b above. Estates and trusts, enter the exemption amount from tax return **4**

5. Total nonbusiness capital losses before limitation. Enter as a positive number **5**

6. Total nonbusiness capital gains (without regard to any section 1202 exclusion) **6**

7. If line 5 is more than line 6, enter the difference; otherwise, enter -0- . **7**

8. If line 6 is more than line 5, enter the difference; otherwise, enter -0- **8**

9. Nonbusiness deductions (see page 5 of the instructions) **9**

10. Nonbusiness income other than capital gains (see page 5 of the instructions) **10**

11. Add lines 8 and 10 . . . . **11**

12. If line 9 is more than line 11, enter the difference; otherwise, enter -0- **12**

13. If line 11 is more than line 9, enter the difference; otherwise, enter -0-. **But do not enter more than line 8** **13**

14. Total business capital losses before limitation. Enter as a positive number **14**

15. Total business capital gains (without regard to any section 1202 exclusion) **15**

16. Add lines 13 and 15 . . . . **16**

17. Subtract line 16 from line 14. If zero or less, enter -0- **17**

18. Add lines 7 and 17 . . . . **18**

19. Enter the loss, if any, from line 17a of Schedule D (Form 1040). (Estates and trusts, enter the loss, if any, from line 16a, column (3), of Schedule D (Form 1041).) Enter as a positive number. If you do not have a loss on that line (and do not have a section 1202 exclusion), skip lines 19 through 24 and enter on line 25 the amount from line 18 . . . . **19**

20. Section 1202 exclusion. Enter as a positive number **20**

21. Subtract line 20 from line 19. If zero or less, enter -0- **21**

22. Enter the loss, if any, from line 18 of Schedule D (Form 1040). (Estates and trusts, enter the loss, if any, from line 17 of Schedule D (Form 1041).) Enter as a positive number **22**

23. If line 21 is more than line 22, enter the difference; otherwise, enter -0- **23**

24. If line 22 is more than line 21, enter the difference; otherwise, enter -0- **24**

25. Subtract line 23 from line 18. If zero or less, enter -0- **25**

26. NOL deduction for losses from other years. Enter as a positive number **26**

27. **NOL.** Combine lines 3, 4, 12, 20, 24, 25, and 26. If the result is less than zero, enter it here and on page 1, line 1a. If the result is zero or more, you **do not** have an NOL **27**

Form **1045** (2003)

Schedule B—NOL Carryover (see page 6 of the instructions)

Complete one column before going to the next column. Start with the earliest carryback year.	_____ preceding tax year ended ►		_____ preceding tax year ended ►		_____ preceding tax year ended ►	
1 **NOL deduction** (see page 6 of the instructions). Enter as a positive number						
2 Taxable income before 2003 NOL carryback (see page 6 of the instructions). Estates and trusts, increase this amount by the sum of the charitable deduction and income distribution deduction						
3 Net capital loss deduction (see page 6 of the instructions)						
4 Section 1202 exclusion. Enter as a positive number						
5 Adjustments to adjusted gross income (see page 6 of the instructions)						
6 Adjustment to itemized deductions (see page 6 of the instructions) . .						
7 Deduction for exemptions. Estates and trusts, enter exemption amount						
8 Modified taxable income. Combine lines 2 through 7. If zero or less, enter -0-						
9 **NOL carryover** (see page 7 of the instructions). Subtract line 8 from line 1. If zero or less, enter -0- . .						
Adjustment to Itemized Deductions (Individuals Only)						
Complete lines 10 through 34 for the carryback year(s) for which you itemized deductions **only** if line 3 or line 4 above is more than zero.						
10 Adjusted gross income before 2003 NOL carryback						
11 Add lines 3 through 5 above . . .						
12 Modified adjusted gross income. Add lines 10 and 11						
13 Medical expenses from Sch. A (Form 1040), line 4 (or as previously adjusted)						
14 Medical expenses from Sch. A (Form 1040), line 1 (or as previously adjusted)						
15 Multiply line 12 by 7.5% (.075) . .						
16 Subtract line 15 from line 14. If zero or less, enter -0-						
17 Subtract line 16 from line 13 . . .						

Form **1045** (2003)

Schedule B—NOL Carryover *(Continued)*

Complete one column before going to the next column. Start with the earliest carryback year.	____ preceding tax year ended ▶	____ preceding tax year ended ▶	____ preceding tax year ended ▶
18 Modified adjusted gross income from line 12 on page 3			
19 Enter as a positive number any NOL carryback from a year before 2003 that was deducted to figure line 10 on page 3			
20 Add lines 18 and 19			
21 Charitable contributions from Sch. A (Form 1040), line 18 (line 16 for 1993) (or as previously adjusted) . . .			
22 Refigured charitable contributions (see page 7 of the instructions) . .			
23 Subtract line 22 from line 21 . . .			
24 Casualty and theft losses from Form 4684, line 18 (or as previously adjusted)			
25 Casualty and theft losses from Form 4684, line 16 (or as previously adjusted)			
26 Multiply line 18 by 10% (.10) . . .			
27 Subtract line 26 from line 25. If zero or less, enter -0-			
28 Subtract line 27 from line 24 . . .			
29 Miscellaneous itemized deductions from Sch. A (Form 1040), line 26 (line 24 for 1993) (or as previously adjusted)			
30 Miscellaneous itemized deductions from Sch. A (Form 1040), line 23 (line 21 for 1993) (or as previously adjusted)			
31 Multiply line 18 by 2% (.02) . . .			
32 Subtract line 31 from line 30. If zero or less, enter -0-			
33 Subtract line 32 from line 29 . . .			
34 Complete the worksheet on page 8 of the instructions if line 18 is **more than** the applicable amount shown below (more than one-half that amount if married filing separately for that year).			

- $108,450 for 1993.
- $111,800 for 1994.
- $114,700 for 1995.
- $117,950 for 1996.
- $121,200 for 1997.
- $124,500 for 1998.
- $126,600 for 1999.
- $128,950 for 2000.
- $132,950 for 2001.
- $137,300 for 2002.

Otherwise, combine lines 17, 23, 28, and 33; enter the result here and on line 6 (page 3) . . . .

¶1560

¶1561 Exhibit 15-11

Form **1139**	**Corporation Application for Tentative Refund**	
(Rev. June 2002)	▶ Read the separate instructions before completing this form.	OMB No. 1545-0582
Department of the Treasury Internal Revenue Service	▶ Do not attach to the corporation's income tax return—mail in a separate envelope.	

Name	Employer identification number
Number, street, and room or suite no. (If a P.O. box, see instructions.)	Date of incorporation
City or town, state, and ZIP code	Daytime phone number ( )

1	This application is filed to carry back:	**a** Net operating loss (NOL) (attach computation) ▶	$	**c** Unused general business credit (attach computation) ▶	$
		b Net capital loss (attach computation) . . . ▶	$		
2	Return for year of loss, unused credit, or overpayment under section 1341(b)(1) ▶	**a** Tax year ended	**b** Date tax return filed	**c** Service center where filed	

3   If this application is for an unused credit created by another carryback, enter ending date for the tax year of the first carryback ▶ ....

4   Did an NOL or net capital loss result in the release of a foreign tax credit, or is the corporation carrying back a general business credit that was released because of the release of a foreign tax credit (see instructions)? If "Yes," the corporation must file an amended return to carry back the released credits. . . . . ☐ Yes ☐ No

5a   Was a consolidated return filed for any carryback year or did the corporation join a consolidated group (see instructions)? ☐ Yes ☐ No

  b   If "Yes," enter the tax year ending date and the name of the common parent and its EIN, if different from above (see instructions) ▶ ......

6a   If Form 1138 has been filed, was an extension of time granted for filing the return for the tax year of the NOL? . . . . ☐ Yes ☐ No

  b   If "Yes," enter the date to which extension was granted ▶ .... **c** Enter the date Form 1138 was filed ▶ ....

  d   Unpaid tax for which Form 1138 is in effect . . . . ▶ ....

7   If the corporation changed its accounting period, enter the date permission to change was granted . . . ▶ ....

8   If this is an application for a dissolved corporation, enter date of dissolution . . . . ▶ ....

9   Has the corporation filed a petition in Tax Court for the year or years to which the carryback is to be applied? ☐ Yes ☐ No

10   Does this application include a loss or credit from a tax shelter required to be registered? If "Yes," attach Form(s) 8271 ☐ Yes ☐ No

Computation of Decrease in Tax See page 2 of the instructions.	.... preceding tax year ended ▶		.... preceding tax year ended ▶		.... preceding tax year ended ▶	
Note: If lines **1a** and **1b** are blank, skip lines 11 through 15.	**(a)** Before carryback	**(b)** After carryback	**(c)** Before carryback	**(d)** After carryback	**(e)** Before carryback	**(f)** After carryback
11 Taxable income from tax return . . .						
12 **Capital loss carryback (see instructions)**	/////		/////		/////	
13 Subtract line 12 from line 11						
14 **NOL deduction (see instructions)** . .						
15 Taxable income. Subtract line 14 from line 13	/////					
16 **Income tax**						
17 Alternative minimum tax						
18 Add lines 16 and 17						
19 General business credit (see instructions)						
20 Other credits (see instructions) . . .						
21 Total credits. Add lines 19 and 20 . .						
22 Subtract line 21 from line 18						
23 Personal holding company tax (Sch. PH (Form 1120))						
24 Other taxes (see instructions)						
25 Total tax liability. Add lines 22 through 24						
26 Enter amount from "After carryback" column on line 25 for each year		/////		/////		/////
27 Decrease in tax. Subtract line 26 from line 25 .						
28 Overpayment of tax due to a claim of right adjustment under section 1341(b)(1) (attach computation)						

Sign Here	Under penalties of perjury, I declare that I have examined this application and accompanying schedules and statements, and to the best of my knowledge and belief, they are true, correct, and complete.		
Keep a copy of this application for your records.	▶ Signature of officer	▶ Date	▶ Title

Preparer Other Than Taxpayer	Name ▶	Date
	Address ▶	

For Paperwork Reduction Act Notice, see separate instructions.   Cat. No. 11170F   Form **1139** (Rev. 6-2002)

¶1562 Exhibit 15-12

Form **1138**	**Extension of Time for Payment of Taxes by a Corporation Expecting a Net Operating Loss Carryback**	OMB No. 1545-0135

(Rev. February 1998)
Department of the Treasury
Internal Revenue Service

(Under Section 6164 of the Internal Revenue Code)

Name	Employer identification number

Number, street, and room or suite no. (If a P.O. box, see instructions.)

City or town, state, and ZIP code

1	Ending date of the tax year of the expected net operating loss (NOL)	**2** Amount of expected NOL $
3	Reduction of previously determined tax attributable to the expected NOL carryback. **Attach a schedule.** See instructions . . . . ▶	$
4	Ending date of the tax year immediately preceding the tax year of the expected NOL	

5 Give the reasons, facts, and circumstances that cause the corporation to expect an NOL.

6 Amount for Which Payment Is To Be Extended:

a Enter the total tax shown on the return, plus any amount assessed as a deficiency, interest, or penalty. See instructions . . . . | **6a** |

b Enter amounts from line 6a that were already paid or were required to have been paid, plus refunds, credits, and abatements. See instructions . . . . | **6b** |

c Subtract line 6b from line 6a. Do not enter more than the amount on line 3 above. This is the amount of tax for which the time for payment is extended . . . . | **6c** |

Sign Here

Under penalties of perjury, I declare that I have examined this form, including any accompanying schedules and statements, and to the best of my knowledge and belief it is true, correct, and complete.

Keep a copy of this form for your records.

▶ _____ ▶ _____ ▶ _____
Signature of officer   Date   Title

For Paperwork Reduction Act Notice, see instructions on back.   Cat. No. 17250W   Form **1138** (Rev. 2-98)

¶1562

General Instructions

Section references are to the Internal Revenue Code.

Purpose of Form. A corporation that expects a net operating loss (NOL) in the current tax year may file Form 1138 to extend the time for payment of tax for the immediately preceding tax year. This includes extending the time for payment of a tax deficiency. The payment of tax that may be postponed cannot exceed the expected overpayment from the carryback of the NOL.

Only payments of tax that are required to be paid after the filing of Form 1138 are eligible for extension. Do not file this form if all the required payments have been paid or were required to have been paid.

If the corporation previously filed Form 1138 and later finds information that will change the amount of the expected NOL, the corporation may file a revised Form 1138. If the amount of the NOL is increased based on the new information, the corporation may postpone the payment of a larger amount of tax as long as the larger amount has not yet been paid or is not yet required to be paid. If the amount of the NOL is reduced because of the new information, the corporation must pay the tax to the extent that the amount of tax postponed on the original filing exceeds the amount of tax postponed on the revised filing.

When and Where To File. File Form 1138 after the start of the tax year of the expected NOL but before the tax of the preceding tax year is required to be paid.

File Form 1138 with the Internal Revenue Service Center where the corporation files its income tax return.

Period of Extension. In general, the extension for paying the tax expires at the end of the month in which the return for the tax year of the expected NOL is required to be filed (including extensions).

The corporation may further extend the time for payment by filing **Form 1139,** Corporation Application for Tentative Refund, before the period of extension ends. The period will be further extended until the date the IRS informs the corporation that it has allowed or disallowed the application in whole or in part.

Termination of Extension. The IRS may terminate the extension if it believes that any part of the form contains erroneous or unreasonable information. The IRS may also terminate the extension if it believes it may not be able to collect the tax.

Interest. Interest is charged on postponed amounts from the dates that the payments would normally be due. The interest is figured at the underpayment rate specified in section 6621.

Additional Information. A corporation may file Form 1138 separately or with **Form 7004,** Application for Automatic Extension of Time To File Corporation Income Tax Return. If Form 1138 and Form 7004 are filed together, Form 1138 will reduce or eliminate the amount of tax to be deposited when Form 7004 is filed.

Specific Instructions

Address. Include the suite, room, or other unit number after the street address. If the Post Office does not deliver mail to the street address and the corporation has a P.O. box, show the box number instead of the street address.

If your address is outside the United States or its possessions or territories, fill in the line for "City or town, state, and ZIP code" in the following order: city, province or state, and country. Follow the foreign country's practice for entering the postal code, if any. Do not abbreviate the country name.

Line 2. The amount of the expected NOL must be based on all of the facts relating to the operation of the corporation. Consider the following items when estimating the amount of the expected NOL:

1. The number and dollar amounts of the corporation's Government contracts that have been canceled,

2. Profit and loss statements, and

3. Other factors peculiar to the corporation's operations.

See section 172 and **Pub. 536,** Net Operating Losses, to help determine the amount of the expected NOL. Limitations apply to **(a)** the amount of taxable income of a new loss corporation for any tax year ending after an ownership change that may be offset by any pre-change NOLs and **(b)** the use of preacquisition losses of one corporation to offset recognized built-in gains of another corporation. See sections 382 and 384 for details.

Line 3. Enter the reduction of previously determined tax attributable to the carryback, for tax years before the tax year of the NOL. Figure the previously determined tax according to section 1314(a). This is generally the amount shown on the return, plus any amounts assessed as deficiencies before Form 1138 is filed minus any abatements, credits, or refunds allowed or made before Form 1138 is filed.

Attach a schedule showing how the reduction was figured. See the instructions for the corporate income tax return for information on figuring the NOL deduction and recomputing the tax.

Line 6a. For the year shown on line 4, enter on line 6a the total of the following:

1. The total tax shown on the return, **plus**

2. Any amount assessed as a deficiency (or as interest or a penalty) prior to the filing of this Form 1138.

Line 6b. Enter the total of the following:

1. The amount of tax paid or required to be paid before the date this form is filed. This includes any amount assessed as a deficiency (or as interest or a penalty) if this form is filed more than 21 calendar days after notice and demand for payment was made (more than 10 business days if the amount for which the notice and demand for payment was made equals or exceeds $100,000). An amount of tax for which the corporation has received an extension of time to pay (under section 6161) is not considered required to be paid before the end of the extension, **plus**

2. The amount of refunds, credits, and abatements made before the date this form is filed.

Paperwork Reduction Act Notice. We ask for the information on this form to carry out the Internal Revenue laws of the United States. You are required to give us the information. We need it to ensure that you are complying with these laws and to allow us to figure and collect the right amount of tax.

You are not required to provide the information requested on a form that is subject to the Paperwork Reduction Act unless the form displays a valid OMB control number. Books or records relating to a form or its instructions must be retained as long as their contents may become material in the administration of any Internal Revenue law. Generally, tax returns and return information are confidential, as required by section 6103.

The time needed to complete and file this form will vary depending on individual circumstances. The estimated average time is:

Recordkeeping . . . . 3 hr., 21 min.

Learning about the law or the form . . . . 42 min.

Preparing and sending the form to the IRS . . . . . 47 min.

If you have comments concerning the accuracy of these time estimates or suggestions for making this form simpler, we would be happy to hear from you. You can write to the Tax Forms Committee, Western Area Distribution Center, Rancho Cordova, CA 95743-0001. **DO NOT** send Form 1138 to this office. Instead, see **When and Where To File** above.

¶1563 Exhibit 15-13

Form **1310**	**Statement of Person Claiming**	OMB No. 1545-0073
(Rev. November 2002) Department of the Treasury Internal Revenue Service	**Refund Due a Deceased Taxpayer** ▶ See instructions below and on back.	Attachment Sequence No. **87**

Tax year decedent was due a refund:

Calendar year _____ , or other tax year beginning _____ , 20 _____ , and ending _____ , 20 _____

	Name of decedent	Date of death	Decedent's social security number
Please type or print	Name of person claiming refund		Your social security number
	Home address (number and street). If you have a P.O. box, see instructions.		Apt. no.
	City, town or post office, state, and ZIP code. If you have a foreign address, see instructions.		

Part I   Check the box that applies to you. Check only one box. **Be sure to complete Part III below.**

A ☐ Surviving spouse requesting reissuance of a refund check (see instructions).

B ☐ Court-appointed or certified personal representative. Attach a court certificate showing your appointment, unless previously filed (see instructions).

C ☐ Person, **other** than A or B, claiming refund for the decedent's estate (see instructions). Also, complete Part II.

Part II   Complete this part only if you checked the box on line C above.

		Yes	No
1	Did the decedent leave a will?		
2a	Has a court appointed a personal representative for the estate of the decedent?		
b	If you answered **"No"** to 2a, will one be appointed?		
	If you answered **"Yes"** to 2a or 2b, the personal representative must file for the refund.		
3	As the person claiming the refund for the decedent's estate, will you pay out the refund according to the laws of the state where the decedent was a legal resident?		
	If you answered **"No"** to 3, a refund cannot be made until you submit a court certificate showing your appointment as personal representative or other evidence that you are entitled under state law to receive the refund.		

Part III   Signature and verification. All filers must complete this part.

I request a refund of taxes overpaid by or on behalf of the decedent. Under penalties of perjury, I declare that I have examined this claim, and to the best of my knowledge and belief, it is true, correct, and complete.

Signature of person claiming refund ▶ _____   **Date** ▶ _____

General Instructions

Purpose of Form

Use Form 1310 to claim a refund on behalf of a deceased taxpayer.

Who Must File

If you are claiming a refund on behalf of a deceased taxpayer, you must file Form 1310 unless **either** of the following applies:

● You are a surviving spouse filing an original or amended joint return with the decedent or

● You are a personal representative (defined on this page) filing an original Form 1040, Form 1040A, Form 1040EZ, or Form 1040NR for the decedent and a court certificate showing your appointment is attached to the return.

Example. Assume Mr. Green died on January 4 before filing his tax return. On April 3 of the same year, you were appointed by the court as the personal representative for Mr. Green's estate and you file Form 1040 for Mr. Green. You do not need to file Form 1310 to claim the refund on Mr. Green's

tax return. However, you must attach to his return a copy of the court certificate showing your appointment.

Where To File

If you checked the box on line A, you can return the joint-name check with Form 1310 to your local IRS office or the Internal Revenue Service Center where you filed your return. If you checked the box on line B or line C then:

● Follow the instructions for the form to which you are attaching Form 1310 or

● Send it to the same Internal Revenue Service Center where the original return was filed if you are filing Form 1310 separately.

Personal Representative

For purposes of this form, a personal representative is the executor or administrator of the decedent's estate, as certified or appointed by the court. A copy of the decedent's will **cannot** be accepted as evidence that you are the personal representative.

For Privacy Act and Paperwork Reduction Act Notice, see page 2.   Cat. No. 11566B   Form **1310** (Rev. 11-2002)

Additional Information

For more details, see **Death of Taxpayer** in the index to the Form 1040, Form 1040A, or Form 1040EZ instructions, or get **Pub. 559,** Survivors, Executors, and Administrators. If the taxpayer died as a result of a terrorist act, see **Pub. 3920,** Tax Relief for Victims of Terrorist Attacks.

Specific Instructions

P.O. Box

Enter your box number **only** if your post office does not deliver mail to your home.

Foreign Address

If your address is outside the United States or its possessions or territories, enter the information in the following order: City, province or state, and country. Follow the country's practice for entering the postal code. **Do not** abbreviate the country name.

Line A

Check the box on line A if you received a refund check in your name and your deceased spouse's name. You can return the joint-name check with Form 1310 to your local IRS office or the Internal Revenue Service Center where you filed your return. A new check will be issued in your name and mailed to you.

Line B

Check the box on line B **only** if you are the decedent's court-appointed personal representative claiming a refund for the decedent on **Form 1040X,** Amended U.S. Individual Income Tax Return, or **Form 843,** Claim for Refund and Request for Abatement. You **must** attach a copy of the court certificate showing your appointment. But if you have already sent the court certificate to the IRS, complete Form 1310 and write "Certificate Previously Filed" at the bottom of the form.

Line C

Check the box on line C if you are not a surviving spouse claiming a refund based on a joint return **and** there is no court-appointed personal representative. You must also complete Part II. If you check the box on line C, you **must** have proof of death.

The proof of death **must** be an authentic copy of **either** of the following:

- The death certificate or
- The formal notification from the appropriate government office (such as, Department of Defense) informing the next of kin of the decedent's death.

Do not attach the death certificate or other proof of death to Form 1310. Instead, keep it for your records and provide it if requested.

Example. Your father died on August 25. You are his sole survivor. Your father did not have a will and the court did not

appoint a personal representative for his estate. Your father is entitled to a $300 refund. To get the refund, you must complete and attach Form 1310 to your father's final return. You should check the box on line C of Form 1310, answer all the questions in Part II, and sign your name in Part III. You must also keep a copy of the death certificate or other proof of death for your records.

Lines 1–3

If you checked the box on line C, you must complete lines 1 through 3.

Privacy Act and Paperwork Reduction Act Notice

We ask for the information on this form to carry out the Internal Revenue laws of the United States. This information will be used to determine your eligibility pursuant to Internal Revenue Code section 6012 to claim the refund due the decedent. Code section 6109 requires you to provide your social security number and that of the decedent. You are not required to claim the refund due the decedent, but if you do so you must provide the information requested on this form. Failure to provide this information may delay or prevent processing of your claim. Providing false or fraudulent information may subject you to penalties. Routine uses of this information include providing it to the Department of Justice for use in civil and criminal litigation, to the Social Security Administration for the aministration of Social Security programs, and to cities, states, and the District of Columbia for the administration of their tax laws. We may also disclose this information to other countries under a tax treaty or to Federal and state agencies to enforce Federal nontax criminal laws and to combat terrorism.

You are not required to provide the information requested on a form unless the form displays a valid OMB control number. Books or records relating to a form or its instructions must be retained as long as their contents may become material in the administration of any Internal Revenue law. Generally, tax returns and return information are confidential, as required by Code section 6103.

The time needed to complete and file this form will vary depending on individual circumstances. The estimated average time is:

Recordkeeping	6 min.
Learning about the law or the form	3 min.
Preparing the form	15 min.
Copying, assembling, and sending the form to the IRS	16 min.

If you have comments concerning the accuracy of these time estimates or suggestions for making this form simpler, we would be happy to hear from you. You can write to the Tax Forms Committee, Western Area Distribution Center, Rancho Cordova, CA 95743-0001. **Do not** send the form to this address.

¶1563

¶1564 Exhibit 15-14

Form **6118** (Rev. January 2001) Department of the Treasury Internal Revenue Service	**Claim for Refund of Income Tax Return Preparer Penalties** ▶ For Penalties Assessed Under IRC Sections 6694 and 6695. ▶ See instructions on page 2.	OMB No. 1545-0240

<table>
<tr><td rowspan="4">Print or Type</td><td>Name of preparer</td><td>Taxpayer identification number
See instructions.</td></tr>
<tr><td>Address to which statement(s) of notice and demand were mailed</td><td rowspan="2"></td></tr>
<tr><td>City, town or post office, state, and ZIP code</td></tr>
<tr><td>Address of preparer shown on return(s) for which penalties were assessed (if different from above)</td><td>IRS office that sent statement(s)</td></tr>
</table>

Type of Penalty. Enter letter in column (c) below.

A Understatements due to unrealistic positions—section 6694(a)

B Willful or reckless conduct (intentional disregard of rules and regulations)—section 6694(b)

C Failure to furnish copy of return or claim for refund to taxpayer—section 6695(a)

D Failure to sign return or claim for refund—section 6695(b)

E Failure to furnish identifying number—section 6695(c)

F Failure to retain copy or list—section 6695(d)

G Failure to file a record of return preparers—section 6695(e)(1)

H Failure to include an item in the required record of return preparers—section 6695(e)(2)

I Negotiation of check—section 6695(f)

J Failure to exercise due diligence in determining eligibility for, and/or amount of, the earned income credit—section 6695(g)

K Other (specify) (see instructions) ▶

Identification of Penalties. Enter the information from your statement.

	(a) Statement document locator number (DLN)	(b) Date of statement	(c) Type of penalty	(d) Name(s) of taxpayer(s)
1				
2				
3				
4				
5				
6				
7				
8				
9				
10				
11				
12				

	(e) Taxpayer's identification number	(f) Form number	(g) Tax year	(h) Amount assessed	(i) Amount paid	(j) Date paid (mo., day, yr.)
1						
2						
3						
4						
5						
6						
7						
8						
9						
10						
11						
12						

Amount of Claim. Enter the total of column (i), lines 1 through 12 . . . . . ▶

Sign Here   Under penalties of perjury, I declare that I have examined this claim, including accompanying schedules and statements, and to the best of my knowledge and belief, it is true, correct, and complete.

▶ _____ Signature   ▶ _____ Date

For Privacy Act and Paperwork Reduction Act Notice, see back of form.   Cat. No. 24415J   Form **6118** (Rev. 1-2001)

General Instructions

Section references are to the Internal Revenue Code unless otherwise noted.

Purpose of Form

Use Form 6118 if you are a tax return preparer and want to claim a refund of preparer penalties you paid but that you believe were incorrectly charged.

Claims for More Than One Penalty

If you are claiming a refund for more than one of the penalties listed, you may be able to combine some of the penalties on one Form 6118. Follow the chart below for combining the penalties.

IF you were billed...	THEN combine penalties...
On the same statement	G and H only
On separate statements but by the same IRS office or service center	C, D, E, and F only **Note:** *Be sure to group the penalties from each statement together.*

You **cannot** combine:

• Penalties from different IRS offices or service centers. See **When and Where To File** below.

• Penalties A, B, I, J, and K. You must file a separate Form 6118 for each of these even if you were charged for two or more of the same type.

Where and When To File

File Form 6118 with the IRS service center or IRS office that sent you the statement(s). Generally, your claim must be filed within 3 years from the date you paid the penalty.

Specific Instructions

Taxpayer Identification Number (TIN)

If you are self-employed or employed by another preparer, enter your social security number. If you are the employer of other preparers, enter your employer identification number.

Type of Penalty

For **K,** enter the name of the penalty and the corresponding Internal Revenue Code section. These other penalties include promoting abusive tax shelters under section 6700 and aiding and abetting an understatement of tax liability under section 6701.

Additional Information

You may want to attach a copy of the penalty statements to your claim. In addition to completing the form, you must give your reasons for claiming a refund for each penalty listed. Identify each penalty by its line number and write your explanation in the space below.

For additional information about refunds of preparer penalties, see Regulations section 1.6696–1.

Privacy Act and Paperwork Reduction Act Notice. We ask for the information on this form to carry out the Internal Revenue laws of the United States. Subtitle F, Procedure and Administration, allows for Additions to Tax, Additional Amounts, and Assessable Penalties. This form is used by return preparers to make a claim for refund of any overpaid penalty amount. Section 6696 requires the return preparer to provide the requested information including his taxpayer identification number (SSN or EIN) within the prescribed time for filing a claim for refund. Routine uses of this information include giving it to the Department of Justice for civil and criminal litigation, and to cities, states, and the District of Columbia for use in administering their tax laws.

You are not required to provide the information requested on a form that is subject to the Paperwork Reduction Act unless the form displays a valid OMB control number. Books or records relating to a form or its instructions must be retained as long as their contents may become material in the administration of any Internal Revenue law. Generally, tax returns and return information are confidential, as required by section 6103.

The time needed to complete and file this form will vary depending on individual circumstances. The estimated average time is: **Recordkeeping,** 13 min.; **Learning about the law or the form,** 16 min.; **Preparing the form,** 10 min.; and **Copying, assembling, and sending the form to the IRS,** 20 min.

If you have comments concerning the accuracy of these time estimates or suggestions for making this form simpler, we would be happy to hear from you. You can write to the Tax Forms Committee, Western Area Distribution Center, Rancho Cordova, CA 95743-0001. **Do not** send this form to this address. Instead, see **Where and When To File** above.

Reasons for claiming refund. Attach additional sheets if more space is needed. Write your name and TIN on each sheet.

¶1565 DISCUSSION QUESTIONS

1. Paul Perplexed's 2002 income tax return was audited in January 2004. An assessment was made and the tax, interest and penalties were paid by Paul on August 2, 2004. On August 13, 2004, Paul filed a Form 1040X—Claim for Refund to recover the full amount that he had paid.

   Paul consults you today to see what further action he can take to get his money back. He has lived at the same address for the entire period since he filed his claim for refund and he has never received any correspondence from the IRS either allowing or disallowing the claim for refund.

   (A) What is the last date on which Paul can successfully bring a lawsuit against the IRS to recover his taxes, penalties and interest paid in 2002?

   (B) What is the earliest date on which a law suit could have been brought on the claim?

2. Following an audit of his 2003 income tax return, an assessment was made against Charlie Cheapskate as a result of the disallowance of certain deductions. In addition to the tax, interest and a negligence penalty were also assessed. Charlie wishes to dispute the propriety of this assessment and he consults you regarding the most economical way in which to do it. He has heard that the deduction challenged has been consistently allowed by the Court of Federal Claims and consistently disallowed by the Tax Court. Charlie tells you that he only has enough money to pay the tax. He cannot pay the interest and penalty. Charlie wants to know whether he can take his case to the Court of Federal Claims.

3. Steve Skimmer operates a tavern which has been very successful over the years. For 2001, 2002, and 2003, Steve reported taxable income of $12,000 from the operation of the tavern in each year. Steve's returns have been audited and, because of the inadequacy of the books and records, the agent has used the net worth method to determine his income. The agent has found the following information:

Date	Net Worth
12/31/00	$175,000
12/31/01	$220,000
12/31/02	$255,000

   Because the agent has not discovered, nor has Steve offered, any explanations for the increase in his net worth, the agent has made an assessment taxing Steve on the difference between his reported taxableincome and the increase in net worth for each of the years. The assessments are as follows:

Year	Tax	Interest	Penalty	Total
2001	$11,550.00	$3,000.00	$7,275.00	$21,825.00
2002	8,050.00	2,200.00	5,075.00	15,375.00
2003	11,000.00	1,700.00	6,350.00	19,050.00

Steve receives the assessment notice on October 15, 2004. He wishes to dispute the adjustments, but he does not have the cash available to pay all of the assessments. He wants to know whether he can just pay the tax, interest and penalties for just one year and then file a claim for refund and sue for recovery. He has a maximum of $22,000 available excluding any fees you may charge. What is your advice? Why? Explain in full.

4. Amanda Amendor filed her 2001, 2002, and 2003 income tax returns with the Central West Internal Revenue Service Center. In preparing those returns, Amanda omitted significant amounts of her gross income. In 2004, Amanda filed amended returns showing the correct gross income. She also computed the additional tax for the three years. Because Amanda was nervous about filing the amended returns, she sent a check to the IRS for the amount of the tax and asked that they send her a statement for the interest to the date of payment.

When the returns were received at the Service Center, Susie Suspicious thought that they looked suspect. She referred the returns to Criminal Investigation (CI) at the Service Center, and CI eventually referred the case for a criminal investigation. Because of the pending criminal investigation, Amanda's amended returns were not processed. Rather, the following letter was sent to Amanda Amendor:

November 4, 2004

Dear Ms. Amendor:

We received your amended returns for the years shown above. We are not assessing additional tax at this time, pending a final determination of your tax liability.

We will accept the payment you sent with your returns as a cash bond. Acceptance of the payment as a cash bond means that (1) interest charges will stop, at the date the payment was received, on that part of any assessment later satisfied by the payment; (2) the payment is not subject to a claim for credit or refund as an overpayment of tax, penalties, or interest; and (3) interest will not be paid to you on any of the payment returned to you if it is more than any additional tax, penalties, or interest later assessed.

If these conditions are not satisfactory to you and you would like us to return your payment, please sign the statement at the end of this letter and send it to us within 30 days. An addressed envelope is enclosed for your convenience. The copy of this letter is for your records.

Thank you for your cooperation.

Sincerely yours,

I.M. Evilminded, Chief Criminal Investigation

Amanda now wishes to hire expert legal and accounting help to represent her in the criminal investigation. However, she has no cash available to retain anyone, and she wishes she had not sent the check to the IRS. She consults with you to see whether she can get her money back from the IRS even though the 30 days in the letter have passed. What advice do you give her? See Rev. Proc. 84-58, 1984-2 CB 501.

5. On September 16, 2002, the estate tax return for Paul Postmortem was filed with the IRS. On December 30, 2003, an assessment of additional estate tax in the amount of $300,000 was made by the IRS. This assessment resulted from the IRS including in the gross estate a gift in the amount of $1,500,000 which was determined to be a transfer with a retained life estate. The additional estate tax resulting from the inclusion of the gift in the gross estate was actually $500,000, but the estate was given a credit under Code Sec. 2012 for the $200,000 of gift tax paid at the time of the filing of the gift tax return. The $300,000 plus interest was paid by the estate on January 2, 2004.

   On October 3, 2005, the estate filed a claim for refund on an amended return, alleging that the gift was not a transfer with a retained life interest and also seeking a refund of estate taxes for the allowance of additional administrative expenses. The amount of the claim for refund was $325,000. Assume that the estate is correct on the merits and that it is entitled to a recovery of the $300,000 of estate tax from the inclusion of the gift and the $25,000 of estate tax resulting from the allowance of the administration expenses. Is the recovery limited to $300,000, the amount of estate tax paid within two years of the filing of the claim?

6. Correcto Corp.'s 2002 income tax return is audited by the IRS. In 2004, the corporation pays an assessment of $100,000 of additional tax resulting from the disallowance of travel and entertainment expenses. Three weeks later the corporation files a claim for refund seeking a refund of $100,000 resulting from the denial of deductions for ordinary and necessary business expenses deductible under Code Secs. 161 through 169. The claim for refund is denied and a lawsuit is filed. After the suit is filed, the accountant determines that the substantiation for the travel and entertainment expenses in fact was insufficient, but also determines that the depreciation deduction for the corporation should have been $300,000 greater than the amount claimed on the return. Because the agent had disallowed $300,000 in travel and entertainment, the accountant is of the opinion that the claim for refund should be allowed. The government opposes the suit for refund. Who wins?

7. Brian Brinksmanship consults you regarding the following situation. Brian's 2003 income tax return was due on April 15, 2004. Because the information was not available, no return was filed on that date. Instead, Brian filed a request for extension and tendered the sum of $5,000 in payment of the tax anticipated to be due. On October 17, 2004, the extension ran out, but still no return was filed. On that date, Brian

tendered another $5,000 towards the eventual tax liability. On November 15, 2004, the return was finally filed. At that time, an additional $5,000 in tax was paid. Finally, the return was audited during 2005 and on November 1, 2005, a deficiency of $5,000 was also paid.

Brian consults you on October 2, 2006. In reviewing his records, you discover that a tax credit for 2003 in the amount of $20,000 has not been claimed. You inform Brian of this and suggest that he file a claim for refund. Brian wants to hold off until the very last possible date to file a claim for refund because he knows that interest on the refund is presently higher than market rates of interest. Brian instructs you to prepare the claim for refund and hold it until the very last day on which it can be filed. He tells you to play it safe, but to get him every possible bit of interest that you can. On which day should the claim for refund be filed?

8. NOL Corporation filed its 2003 tax return on March 15, 2004, reporting a loss of $100,000. The corporate accountant simply chose to use the loss to offset income earned in 2004 rather than carry the loss back to years 2001 and 2002.

The IRS is currently auditing the 2003 tax return. On May 11, 2007, the Revenue Agent proposed to disallow the loss carried forward to 2004 because the taxpayer did not make an affirmative election to forego the carryback. See Code Sec. 172(b)(3). Is there anything the accountant can do to preserve the use of the net operating loss that was carried forward? Would your answer change if the revenue agent proposed to disallow the carryforward loss on March 13, 2007?

CHAPTER 16
PRIVATE RULINGS AND DETERMINATION LETTERS

¶1601 IN GENERAL

Because of the inherent complexity of the Internal Revenue Code (the Code) and the time lag between the completion of a transaction and any examination of it by the Internal Revenue Service (IRS), the IRS has made it a practice to answer inquiries of individuals and organizations as to their status for tax purposes and as to the tax effects of their acts or transactions. The inquiries are submitted by means of letters to the Commissioner, and the Commissioner's responses to these inquiries—in the form of letters—are known as rulings.[1]

The IRS issues rulings whenever appropriate for sound tax administration. To this end, the IRS has published rules and guidelines as to how a ruling is requested and when a ruling may or may not be issued. Assuming the IRS continues its long standing practice, the first eight Revenue Procedures issued every year relate to Rulings and Technical Advice. They are as follows:

1. Procedure for requesting letter rulings, determination letters;[2]
2. Procedures for requesting technical advice;
3. Areas in which advance rulings will not be issued (domestic areas);
4. Procedures for requesting ruling letter, information letter, etc., on matters relating to sections of the Code currently under the jurisdiction of the Commissioner, Tax Exempt and Government Entities Division;
5. Procedures for requesting technical advice for matters under the jurisdiction of the Commissioner, Tax Exempt and Government Entities Division;
6. Procedures for requesting determination letters on the qualified status of employee plans;
7. Areas in which advance rulings will not be issued (International); and
8. User fees and guidance for employee plans and exempt organization requests for letter rulings, determination letters, etc.

The IRS has issued a list of topics upon which it will decline to issue advance rulings or determination letters.[3] There are four categories of topics on the list:

1. Areas involving inherently factual matters in which rulings or determination letters will not be issued;[4]

---

[1] These rulings are also known within the tax profession as private rulings or private letter rulings because they are issued to specific taxpayers as opposed to the general public.

[2] Rev. Proc. 2004-1, IRB 2004-1, 1, is printed in part as Exhibit 16-1 at ¶1651.

[3] Rev. Proc. 2004-3, IRB 2004-3, 114, Sec. 2.

[4] Id., Sec. 3.

2. Areas in which rulings and determination letters will "not ordinarily" be issued. "Not ordinarily" means that unique and compelling reasons must be demonstrated to justify a ruling in these areas;[5]

3. Areas in which the IRS is temporarily not issuing advance rulings and determinations because the matters are under extensive study;[6] and

4. Areas where the IRS will not ordinarily issue advance rulings because the IRS has provided automatic approval procedures for these matters.[7]

In the *Tax Analysts and Advocates* case,[8] the IRS was required under the Freedom of Information Act to publish the results of its ruling determinations. In 1976, Congress codified this decision and enacted Code Sec. 6110, which required the disclosure of private letter rulings (written determinations). Congress specifically provided that any identifying information be deleted from a ruling before it is published. Regulation §601.201(e)(5) requires a taxpayer to state what deletions he or she proposes in a document submitted with a ruling request (see ¶1521).

¶1605 DEFINITION

Rulings. By definition, a "ruling" is a written statement issued to a taxpayer or a taxpayer's authorized representative by the National Office of the IRS.[9] The National Office interprets and applies the tax laws to a specific set of facts set out in a ruling request. Rulings are issued under the general supervision of the Associate Chief Counsels (which include Corporate, Financial Institutions & Products, Income Tax & Accounting, International, Passthrough & Special Industries, Procedure & Administration, and Division Counsel/Associate Chief Counsel—Tax Exempt and Government Entities) (Associate Office)[10] who can redelegate authority to the technical advisors of the corporation tax division and the individual tax division in their respective areas.[11] Issues under the jurisdiction of the various Associate Chief Counsels are listed in Section 3 of Rev. Proc. 2004-1 (see Exhibit 16-1 at ¶1651).

In income, gift and private foundation tax matters, the Associate Office issues rulings on prospective transactions and on completed transactions before the return is filed. However, rulings are ordinarily not issued if the identical issue exists in a return of the taxpayer for a prior year which is under examination by a district office or which is being considered by any Appeals Office.[12]

In estate tax matters, the Associate Office issues rulings with respect to transactions affecting the estate tax of a decedent before the estate tax return is filed. No rulings will be issued after the estate tax return has been filed unless the ruling request was submitted prior to the filing of the return, nor will one be issued on the application of the estate tax to property or the estate of a living

---

[5] *Id.*, Sec. 4.

[6] *Id.*, Sec. 5.

[7] *Id.*, Sec. 6.

[8] 405 F. Supp. 1065 (D.C.-D.C. 1975), 75-2 USTC ¶9869.

[9] Reg. §301.6110-2(d).

[10] This is a change from the past, when the term "National Office" was used to describe the Offices of the Associate Chief Counsels. See Rev. Proc. 2004-1.

[11] Rev. Proc 2004-1, IRB 2004-1, 1.

[12] Rev. Proc. 2004-1, IRB 2004-1, 1, Sec. 6.01(1).

person. Practical problems can arise from this position of the Associate Office because of the relatively short time following a decedent's death before the due date of the estate tax return and the time period it takes to prepare, review and have the Associate Office process a ruling request. In the event a ruling is sought concerning an estate tax matter, special attention should be given to obtaining any necessary extensions for filing the estate tax return in order to avoid incurring a penalty.[13]

In employment and excise tax matters, the Associate Office will rule on prospective and completed transactions either before or after the return is filed. However, the Associate Office will not ordinarily rule on an issue if it knows an identical issue is before any field office (including Appeals) in connection with an examination or audit of the liability of the same taxpayer for the same or a prior period.[14]

The IRS will not rule on requests of business, trade or industrial associations or other similar groups relating to the application of the tax laws to members of the group. However, rulings may be issued to groups or associations relating to their own tax status or liability, provided the issue is not before any field office (including Appeals) in connection with an examination or audit of the liability of the same taxpayer for the same or a prior period.[15]

When new tax laws are enacted, pending the adoption of regulations, the issuance of a ruling will be considered under certain conditions:

1. If an inquiry presents an issue on which the answer seems to be clear from an application of the provisions of the statute to the facts described, a ruling will be issued in accordance with usual procedures.

2. If an inquiry presents an issue on which the answer seems reasonably certain, but not entirely free from doubt, a ruling will be issued only if it is established that a business emergency requires a ruling or that unusual hardship will result from failure to obtain a ruling.

3. If an inquiry presents an issue that cannot be reasonably resolved prior to the issuance of regulations, a ruling will not be issued.

4. In any case in which the taxpayer believes that a business emergency exists or that an unusual hardship will result from failure to obtain a ruling, he or she should submit with the request a separate letter setting forth the facts necessary for the IRS to make a determination regarding the emergency or hardship. The IRS will not deem a "business emergency" to result from circumstances within the control of the taxpayer.[16]

Determination Letters. The IRS also issues determination letters to taxpayers. A "determination letter" is a written statement issued by a director in response to a written inquiry by an individual or an organization that applies the principles and precedents previously announced by the Associate Office to the

---

[13] See Rev. Proc. 2004-1, IRB 2004-1, 1, Sec. 5.05.

[14] *Id.*, Sec. 6.01.

[15] *Id.*, Sec. 5.11.

[16] Statement of Procedural Rules, Reg. § 601.201(b)(5).

particular facts involved. A determination letter is issued only where a determination can be made on the basis of clearly established rules set forth in the Code, a Treasury decision or a regulation, or by a ruling, opinion or court decision published in the Internal Revenue Bulletin. Where such a determination cannot be made, perhaps because the question involves a novel issue or because the matter is excluded from the director's jurisdiction, a determination letter will not be issued.[17]

The IRS also issues determination letters with respect to the qualification of an organization for exempt status under Code Sec. 501(c)(3). Organizations seeking exempt status under Code Sec. 501 must apply for a determination letter from the Exempt Organizations (EO) Determination Office, Covington, Kentucky.[18]

Organizations seeking exempt status under Code Sec. 501(c)(3), which encompasses organizations to which contributions qualify for the charitable donation deduction under Code Sec. 170, apply for a determination letter on Form 1023 (see Exhibit 16-2 at ¶1652), while organizations seeking exempt status under some other subsection of Code Sec. 501(c) apply by means of Form 1024 (see Exhibit 16-3 at ¶1653). Both of these forms are issued as booklets and request that the applicant supply detailed factual and financial data along with documentation to show that the organization is operated within the law and regulations.

The IRS also issues determination letters to applicants with respect to the qualification of their retirement plans (including pension and profit-sharing plans) under Code Sec. 401. Applications in this instance are made on Form 5300, Application for Determination for Employee Benefit Plan (see Exhibit 16-4 at ¶1654). The issuance of determination letters regarding retirement plans is handled by the Employee Plans (EP) Determination Office, Covington, Kentucky.[19]

In income, gift and private foundation tax matters, operating division directors issue determination letters regarding completed transactions that affect returns over which they have audit jurisdiction, but only if the answer to the question presented is covered specifically by a statute, Treasury decision or regulation, or covered specifically by a ruling, opinion or court decision published in the Internal Revenue Bulletin. A determination letter will not usually be issued with respect to a question which involves a return to be filed by the taxpayer if the identical question is involved in a return or returns already filed by the taxpayer. Directors may not issue determination letters as to the tax consequences of prospective or proposed transactions, with certain exceptions to be discussed later in this portion of the chapter.

---

[17] Rev. Proc. 2004-1, IRB 2004-1, 1, Sec. 6.

[18] The procedures for seeking determination letters as to exempt status are set forth in Rev. Proc. 2004-8, IRB 2004-1, 240.

[19] Rev. Proc. 2004-6, IRB 2004-1, 197.

¶1605

In estate and gift tax matters, directors issue determination letters regarding estate tax returns of decedents that will be audited by their offices, but only if the answers to the questions presented are specifically covered by the same kinds of authority mentioned in the preceding paragraph. Directors will not issue determination letters relating to matters involving the application of the estate tax to property or the estate of a living person.

In employment and excise tax matters, directors issue determination letters to taxpayers who have filed or who are required to file returns over which the directors have audit jurisdiction, but only if the answers to the questions presented are covered specifically by the previously mentioned authorities. Because of the impact of these taxes upon the business operation of the taxpayer and because of special problems of administration both to the IRS and to the taxpayer, directors may take appropriate action in regard to such requests, whether they relate to completed or prospective transactions or returns previously filed or to be filed.

In spite of the areas mentioned in the preceding paragraphs, a director will not issue a determination letter in response to an inquiry where the following circumstances are present:

1. It appears that the taxpayer has directed a similar inquiry to the Associate Office;

2. An identical issue involving the same taxpayer is pending in a case before the Appeals Office;

3. The determination letter is requested by an industry, trade association or similar group; or

4. The request involves an industry-wide problem.[20]

Under no circumstances will the director issue a determination letter unless the inquiry is with regard to a taxpayer or taxpayers who have filed or are required to file returns over which that director's office has or will have audit jurisdiction. Also, a director will not issue a determination letter on an employment tax questionwhen the specific question involved has been or is being considered by the central office of the Social Security Administration or the Railroad Retirement Board.

Other Determinations. Other correspondence written by the IRS is mentioned here for reference only and will not be discussed in further detail. "Opinion letters" are written statements issued by the Director of EP Rulings and Agreements as to the acceptability of the form of a master or prototype plan and any related trust or custodian account under Code Secs. 401 and 501(a).[21] An "information letter" is a statement issued either by the National Office or by a director that does no more than call attention to a well-established interpretation or principle of tax law, without applying it to a specific set of facts. An information letter may be issued when a ruling request seeks general information, or

---

[20] Statement of Procedural Rules, Reg. § 601.201(c)(4).

[21] Rev. Proc. 2004-4, IRB 2004-1, 125, Sec. 3.05.

where it does not meet all the requirements for the issuance of a ruling or determination letter, and the IRS believes that such general information will assist the requester.[22]

A "revenue ruling," as opposed to a private ruling, is an official interpretation by the IRS which has been published in the Internal Revenue Bulletin. Revenue rulings are issued only by the National Office and are published for the information and guidance of taxpayers, IRS officials and others concerned.[23]

A "closing agreement" is an agreement between the IRS and a taxpayer with respect to a specific issue or issues entered into pursuant to the authority contained in Code Sec. 7121. A closing agreement is based on a private ruling which has been signed by the Commissioner or the Commissioner's delegate and which indicates that a closing agreement will be entered into on the basis of the holding of the ruling letter. A closing agreement is final and conclusive except upon a showing of fraud, malfeasance or misrepresentation of material fact. It is used where it is advantageous to have the matter permanently and conclusively closed, or where a taxpayer can show good and sufficient reasons for an agreement and the government will sustain no disadvantage by its consummation. In certain cases, taxpayers may be required to enter into a closing agreement as a condition to the issuance of a ruling.[24] A closing agreement will not be entered into in cases where it is requested on behalf of more than 25 taxpayers. However, in cases where the issue and holding are identical as to all of the taxpayers and the number of taxpayers exceeds 25, a Mass Closing Agreement can be entered into with the taxpayer who is authorized by the others to represent the entire group.[25]

Technical advice is issued by the National Office in the form of a memorandum to a director, in connection with the examination of a return or consideration of a claim for refund or credit. The memorandum gives advice or guidance as to the interpretation and proper application of Internal Revenue regulations, related statutes and regulations to a specific set of facts. It is furnished as a means of assisting IRS personnel in closing cases and establishing and maintaining consistent holdings in the various districts. Seeking technical advice from the National Office is discretionary with a director.

A director may request technical advice on any technical or procedural question that develops during the audit of a return or claim for refund of a taxpayer. In addition, while the case is under the jurisdiction of a director, a taxpayer (or representative) may request that an issue be referred to the National Office for technical advice on the grounds that a lack of uniformity exists as to the disposition of the issue, or that the issue is so unusual or complex as to warrant consideration by the National Office. Although a written request by a taxpayer for technical advice is preferred, it may be made orally.

---

[22] Rev. Proc. 2004-1, IRB 2004-1, 1, Sec. 2.04.

[23] Rev. Proc. 2004-4, IRB 2004-1, Sec. 3.07.

[24] For examples, see Rev. Proc. 78-15, 1978-2 CB 488, and Rev. Proc. 85-44, 1985-2 CB 504.

[25] Rev. Proc. 2004-1, IRB 2004-1, 1, Sec. 3.03.

¶1605

Different rules exist for obtaining technical advice on income tax issues than on questions involving employee plans and exempt organizations. There are also separate technical advice rules for cases under the jurisdiction of an appeals officer.[26]

¶1613 USER FEES FOR RULING REQUESTS

The Revenue Act of 1987[27] modified the ruling procedure in one significant respect: It required the Secretary of the Treasury to establish a program requiring the payment of user fees for requests for rulings, opinion letters, determination letters and similar services. The fees set forth in Section 10511 of that Act were effective until October 1, 2003. Section 7528 of the Internal Revenue Code, enacted on that date, is effective for requests made after October 1, 2003.[28] Code Sec. 7528 requires the fees to vary according to categories, taking into account the average time needed for, and difficulty of complying with, requests in each category. Such fees are to be paid in advance.

Rev. Proc. 2004-1 provides guidance regarding user fees for ruling requests. Section 15 of that Revenue Procedure indicates that the user fee must accompany all requests for rulings, determination letters or opinion letters. The fees range from $45 to $6,000, depending on the type of ruling sought. If the fee is not paid, the entire file submitted will be returned to the requester. In general, no refund of the user fee will be made unless the IRS declines to rule on all issues for which a ruling is requested. The Revenue Procedure specifically notes that no refund will be given if the request for a ruling is withdrawn.

¶1615 REQUIREMENTS FOR RULING REQUESTS

Each request for a ruling or determination letter must contain a complete statement of all relevant facts relating to the transaction. Such facts include (1) names, addresses and taxpayer identification numbers of all interested parties; (2) a full and precise statement of the business reasons for the transaction; and (3) a carefully detailed description of the transaction. (The term "all interested parties" does not require the listing of all shareholders of a widely held corporation or all employees under a qualified plan.)[29]

If a taxpayer is contending for a particular determination, that individual must furnish an explanation of the grounds for the stated contentions, together with a statement from relevant authorities in support of his views. Even if the taxpayer is urging no particular determination with regard to a proposed or prospective transaction, the individual must state his or her views as to the tax results of the proposed action and furnish a statement from relevant authorities to support such views.

---

[26] If further information is desired with respect to technical advice memoranda, consult § 601.105(b)(5) of the Statement of Procedural Rules in the Appendix. See also Rev. Proc. 2001-2, IRB 2001-1, 79, and Rev. Proc. 2001-5, IRB 2001-1, 164.

[27] P.L. 100-203.

[28] P.L. 108-89, Sec 202(a), added Code Sec. 7528.

[29] As a rule of thumb, the practitioner can assume that the listing of all shareholders or employees is not required if more than 25 taxpayers are involved.

In addition, true copies of all contracts, wills, deeds, instruments and other documents involved in the transaction must be submitted with the request. Relevant facts reflected in documents submitted should be included in the taxpayer's statement and not merely incorporated by reference. The documents must be accompanied by an analysis of their bearing on the issue or issues, specifying the pertinent provisions.

The importance of including relevant facts in the taxpayer's statement of the facts in the ruling request is evidenced by private Letter Ruling 8026012 (see Exhibit 16-5 at ¶1655). In that ruling, the taxpayer used the two-part ruling option (discussed below) and indicated that one corporation was going to assume the debt of a second corporation in connection with a reorganization. A favorable ruling was issued to the taxpayer, even though a balance sheet accompanying the ruling request indicated in a note that advances to the first corporation were to be converted to a promissory note. The first corporation was then going to borrow funds to pay the note to the second corporation.

In response to a request for technical advice upon examination of the transaction, the IRS retroactively revoked the earlier favorable ruling because there had been a clear misstatement of material fact and because the facts as subsequently developed differed materially from the facts on which the ruling letter was based. Although the true nature of the transaction was disclosed in documents submitted with the ruling request (the balance sheet), the IRS found no obligation to ferret out material or relevant facts reflected in documents accompanying the ruling request or to reconcile seemingly inconsistent data as it might bear on a particular issue.

When it is necessary to submit documents with a ruling request, the original documents should not be submitted, because documents and exhibits submitted as a part of a ruling request become part of the IRS file and cannot be returned to the requester. If the request is with respect to a corporate distribution, reorganization or other similar or related transaction, the corporate balance sheet nearest the dateof the transaction should be submitted. (If the request relates to the prospective transaction, the most recent balance sheet should be submitted.)

The request must also contain a statement of whether, to the best of the knowledge of the taxpayer or the taxpayer's representative, the identical issue is being considered by any IRS field office in connection with an active examination or audit of a tax return of the taxpayer already filed (including Appeals). The taxpayer or a representative should indicate in writing when filing the request if he or she desires a discussion of the issues involved, so that a conference may be arranged at that stage of consideration when it will be most helpful. Where the request pertains to only one step of a larger integrated transaction, the facts and circumstances must be submitted with respect to the entire transaction.

A request for a ruling or determination letter is to be submitted in duplicate. However, if (1) more than one issue is presented in the request, or (2) a closing agreement is requested with respect to the issue presented, then the original and two copies must be submitted. A specific declaration must accompany the request in the following form:

¶1615

> Under penalties of perjury, I declare that I have examined this request, including accompanying documents, and to the best of my knowledge and belief, the request contains all the relevant facts relating to the request, and such facts are true, correct and complete.

The declaration must be signed by the person or persons on whose behalf the request is made, not by the requester's representative.[30]

The task of drafting an advance ruling request under Code Secs. 302, 332, 346, 351 and 355 is simplified by revenue procedures[31] that set forth the information that the IRS considers important enough to be included in ruling requests regarding those sections. See Exhibit 16-6 at ¶1656 for a sample format of a letter ruling request,[32] and Exhibit 16-7 at ¶1657 for a checklist to use when requesting a letter ruling.[33]

¶1621 DISCLOSURE OF RULING REQUESTS

To assist the IRS in deleting identifying information[34] from the text of rulings and determination letters, requests for rulings and determination letters must include as a separate document either a statement of the deletions proposed by the requester or a statement that no information other than names, addresses and taxpayer identification numbers need be deleted. If additional deletions are proposed, the requester should specify the statutory basis for the deletion. When additional deletions are proposed, a copy of the request should be submitted which indicates, by use of brackets, the material which the person proposes to have deleted. The statement of proposed deletions is not to be referred to anywhere in the request. If the person making the request decides to request additionaldeletions prior to the time the ruling or determination letter is issued, additional statements may be submitted.

Generally, prior to issuing the ruling or determination letter, the National Office or director informs the requester of any material likely to appear in the ruling or determination letter which such person proposed to delete but which the IRS determines should be included. The requester may then submit further information, arguments or other material to support deletion within twenty days. The IRS attempts to resolve all disagreements with respect to proposed deletions prior to the issuance of the ruling or determination letter. The requester does not have any right to a conference to resolve disagreements concerning material to be deleted from the text of the ruling or determination letter, but such matters may be considered at any other conference scheduled with respect to the ruling request. Exhibit 16-8 at ¶1658 is a sample of how a ruling letter appears after deletions.

¶1625 TWO-PART RULINGS

To expedite prospective transactions, the Associate Office provides an alternative procedure for the issuance of rulings. The taxpayer submits a summary state-

---

[30] Reg. §601.201(e)(1); Rev. Proc. 2004-1, 2004-1, 1, Sec. 7.01(15)(b).

[31] Rev. Procs. include 86-18, 90-52, 81-42, 83-59 and 96-30, respectively.

[32] Rev. Proc. 2004-1, IRB 2004-1, 1, Appendix B.

[33] *Id.*, Appendix C.

[34] Code Sec. 6110(c).

ment of the facts considered to control the issue, in addition to the complete statement of facts required for ruling requests. If the IRS agrees with the taxpayer's summary statement of the facts, it is used as a basis for the ruling. The ruling is based on the facts in the statement, and ordinarily only this statement is incorporated into the ruling letter.

This procedure is elective with the taxpayer, and the taxpayer's rights and responsibilities are the same as under the normal procedure. Under this procedure, the IRS reserves the right to rule on the basis of a more complete statement of facts it considers controlling and to seek further information in developing facts and restating them for ruling purposes. The two-part ruling request procedure does not apply where it is inconsistent with other procedures applicable to specific situations, such as requests for permission to change accounting method or rulings on employment tax status.

¶1631 FAULTY REQUESTS

Any request for a ruling or determination letter that does not comply with all of the requirements of the IRS is acknowledged, and the requirements that have not been met are delineated. If a request lacks essential information, the taxpayer or the taxpayer's representative is advised that the request will be closed if the information is not forthcoming within 21 days. If the information is received after the request is closed, the request will be reopened and treated as a new request as of the date of the receipt of the essential information. Because the Associate Office processes ruling requests on a first-come, first-served basis, delay in providingessential information within the 21-day period can result in substantial and possibly disastrous delay of receipt of a ruling.

Priority treatment of a ruling request is granted only in rare cases. To obtain such approval a taxpayer must submit an independent request for priority treatment and demonstrate that the need for priority treatment is beyond the control of the requesting taxpayer.

¶1635 ASSOCIATE OFFICE CONFERENCES

A taxpayer is entitled, as a matter of right, to only one conference with respect to a ruling request in the Associate Office. If a conference has been requested, the taxpayer will be notified of the time and place of the conference, although a conference is normally scheduled only when the IRS deems it helpful in deciding the case or when it appears the IRS will issue an adverse ruling. The conference is usually held at the branch level and will be attended by a person who has authority to act for the branch chief.

The conference is usually held after the branch has had an opportunity to study the case so that there can be a free and open discussion of the issues. Because a taxpayer has no right to appeal the action of a branch chief to a division director or to any other official of the IRS, unless special circumstances are present, there is no real advantage to requesting a conference before the IRS has a chance to study the case.

¶1641 WITHDRAWALS OF RULING REQUESTS

A taxpayer may withdraw a request for a ruling (or a determination letter) at any time prior to the signing of the letter by the IRS. When the request is withdrawn, the Associate Office may furnish its views to the director whose office has or will have audit jurisdiction of the return. The information submitted can be considered by the director in a subsequent audit or examination of the taxpayer's return. Even though a request is withdrawn, all correspondence and exhibits are retained by the IRS and may not be returned to the taxpayer. The taxpayer should consider the potential for referral of a withdrawn request to a director before a ruling is requested from the IRS.

¶1645 EFFECT OF RULINGS

The effect of a private ruling is very limited: one taxpayer may not rely on a ruling issued to another, and a ruling with respect to a particular transaction represents a holding of the IRS only on that transaction. If the ruling is later found to be in error or no longer in accord with the position of the IRS, it will afford the taxpayer no protection with respect to a similar transaction in the same or subsequent year. However, if a ruling relates to a continuing action or a series of actions, the ruling will control until specifically withdrawn or until applicable regulations or revenue rulings are issued. A ruling, except to the extent that it is incorporated in a closing agreement, may be revoked or modified at any time. If a ruling is revoked or modified, the revocation or modification applies to all open years under the statutes, unless the Commissioner exercises discretionary authority under Code Sec. 7805(b) of the Code to limit the retroactive effect of the revocation or modification.

In determining a taxpayer's liability, a director is to ascertain whether any ruling previously issued to the taxpayer has been properly applied. An examiner will determine whether the representations upon which the ruling was based reflected an accurate statement of the material facts and whether the transaction actually was carried out substantially as proposed. If, in the course of determining tax liability, a director concludes that a ruling previously issued to the taxpayer should be modified or revoked, the findings and recommendations of that office are forwarded to the Associate Office for consideration prior to further action. The reference to the Associate Office is treated as a request for technical advice (see discussion, *supra*). Otherwise, the ruling is to be applied by a director in its determination of the taxpayer's liability.[35]

A ruling found to be in error or not in accord with the current views of the IRS may be modified or revoked. Modification or revocation may be effected by a notice to the taxpayer to whom the ruling originally was issued or by a revenue ruling or other statement published in the Internal Revenue Bulletin. Except in

---

[35] For an example affecting many taxpayers as the result of the retroactive revocation of a ruling based upon a determination that representations had not been complied with, see *Heverly v. Comm'r*, 621 F.2d 1227 (1980), 80-1 USTC ¶9322, and *Chapman v.* *Comm'r*, 618 F.2d 856 (1980), 80-1 USTC ¶9330, involving International Telephone and Telegraph Corporation's acquisition of Hartford Insurance Company.

rare or unusual circumstances, the revocation or modification of a ruling is not applied retroactively with respect to the taxpayer to whom the ruling was originally issued or to a taxpayer whose tax liability was directly involved in that ruling if five circumstances are present:

1. There has been no misstatement or omission of material facts;

2. The facts subsequently developed are not materially different from the facts on which the ruling was based;

3. There has been no change in the applicable law;

4. The ruling was originally issued with respect to a prospective or proposed transaction; and

5. The taxpayer directly involved in a ruling acted in good faith in reliance upon the ruling and the retroactive revocation would be to his or her detriment.[36]

When a ruling to a taxpayer is revoked with retroactive effect,[37] the notice to that taxpayer, except in fraud cases, sets forth the grounds upon which the revocation is being made and the reasons that the revocation is being applied retroactively. In the case of rulings involving completed transactions, taxpayers are not afforded the protection against retroactive revocation available in the case of proposed transactions. For this reason it is generally better to obtain a ruling for a proposed transaction than for a completed transaction.

¶1647 EFFECT OF DETERMINATION LETTERS

A determination letter issued by a director will be given the same effect upon examination of the return of the taxpayer to whom the determination letter was issued as a private ruling, except that reference to the Associate Office is not necessary where, upon examination of the return, it is the opinion of the director that a conclusion contrary to that expressed in the determination letter is indicated. A director may not limit the retroactive effect of the modification or revocation of a determination letter. However, if a director believes it necessary to limit the retroactive effect of a modification or revocation, the matter must be referred to the Associate Office for approval.

---

[36] § 601.201(l)(5) of the Statement of Procedural Rules.

[37] See, for example, IRS Ltr. Rul. 8506003 (Nov. 1, 1984), in which a ruling was revoked with retroactive effect for omission of a material fact in failing to disclose that most of the taxpayer's business was conducted with a parent corporation.

¶1651 Exhibit 16-1

Revenue Procedure 2004-1, IRB 2004-1, 1 (Jan. 5, 2004)

TABLE OF CONTENTS

SECTION 5. UNDER WHAT CIRCUMSTANCES DOES THE NATIONAL OFFICE ISSUE LETTER RULINGS?

.01 In income and gift tax matters

.02 A §301.9100 request for extension of time for making an election or for other relief

.03 Determinations under §999(d) of the Internal Revenue Code

.04 In matters involving §367

.05 In estate tax matters

.06 In matters involving additional estate tax under §2032A(c)

.07 In matters involving qualified domestic trusts under §2056A

.08 In generation-skipping transfer tax matters

.09 In employment and excise tax matters

.10 In administrative provisions matters

.11 In Indian tribal government matters

.12 On constructive sales price under §4216(b) or §4218(c)

.13 May be issued before the issuance of a regulation or other published guidance

SECTION 6. UNDER WHAT CIRCUMSTANCES DOES THE SERVICE NOT ISSUE LETTER RULINGS OR DETERMINATION LETTERS?

.01 Ordinarily not if issue involves an issue under examination, or consideration, or in litigation

.02 Ordinarily not in certain areas because of factual nature of the problem

.03 Ordinarily not on part of an integrated transaction

.04 Ordinarily not on which of two entities is a common law employer

.05 Generally not to business associations or groups

.06 Generally not to foreign governments

.07 Ordinarily not on federal tax consequences of proposed legislation

.08 Not before issuance of a regulation or other published guidance

.09 Not on frivolous issues

.10 No "comfort" letter rulings

.11 Not on alternative plans or hypothetical situations

.12 Not on property conversion after return filed

.13 Circumstances under which determination letters are not issued by a director

SECTION 7. WHAT ARE THE GENERAL INSTRUCTIONS FOR REQUESTING LETTER RULINGS AND DETERMINATION LETTERS?

.01 Certain information required in all requests

    (1) Complete statement of facts and other information

(2) Copies of all contracts, wills, deeds, agreements, instruments, other documents, and foreign laws

(3) Analysis of material facts

(4) Statement regarding whether same issue is in an earlier return

(5) Statement regarding whether same or similar issue was previously ruled on or requested, or is currently pending

(6) Statement regarding interpretation of a substantive provision of an income or estate tax treaty

(7) Letter from Bureau of Indian Affairs relating to a letter ruling request for recognition of Indian tribal government status or status as a political subdivision of an Indian tribal government

(8) Statement of supporting authorities

(9) Statement of contrary authorities

(10) Statement identifying pending legislation

(11) Statement identifying information to be deleted from copy of letter ruling or determination letter for public inspection

(12) Signature by taxpayer or authorized representative

(13) Authorized representatives

(14) Power of attorney and declaration of representative

(15) Penalties of perjury statement

(16) Number of copies of request to be submitted

(17) Sample format for a letter ruling request

(18) Checklist for letter ruling requests

.02 Additional procedural information required with request

(1) To request separate letter rulings for multiple issues in a single situation

(2) To indicate recipient of original or copy of letter ruling or determination letter

(3) To request a particular conclusion on a proposed transaction

(4) To request expedited handling

(5) Taxpayer requests to receive any document related to the letter ruling request by facsimile transmission (fax)

(6) To request a conference

.03 Address to send the request

.04 Pending letter ruling requests

.05 When to attach ruling to return

.06 How to check on status of request

.07 Request may be withdrawn or Associate office may decline to issue letter ruling

¶1651

SECTION 8. HOW DOES THE ASSOCIATE OFFICE HANDLE LETTER RULING REQUESTS?

.01 Controls request and refers it to appropriate Associate Chief Counsel's office

.02 Branch representative contacts taxpayer within 21 days

.03 Determines if transaction can be modified to obtain favorable letter ruling

.04 Is not bound by informal opinion expressed

.05 Additional information

    (1) Additional information must be submitted within 21 days

    (2) Extension of reply period

    (3) Letter ruling request closed if the taxpayer does not submit additional information

    (4) Penalties of perjury statement

    (5) Faxing request and additional information

    (6) Address to send additional information

    (7) Identifying information

    (8) Number of copies

.06 Near the completion of the ruling process, advises the taxpayer of conclusions and, if the Associate office will rule adversely, offers the taxpayer the opportunity to withdraw the letter ruling request

.07 May request draft of proposed letter ruling near the completion of the ruling process

.08 Issues separate letter rulings for substantially identical letter rulings and generally issues a single letter ruling for related § 301.9100 letter

.09 Sends a copy of the letter ruling to appropriate Service official

SECTION 9. WHAT ARE THE SPECIFIC AND ADDITIONAL PROCEDURES FOR A REQUEST FOR A CHANGE IN ACCOUNTING METHOD FROM THE ASSOCIATE OFFICE?

.01 Automatic and advance consent change in accounting method requests

    (1) Automatic change in accounting method request procedures

    (2) Advance consent letter ruling requests

.02 Ordinarily only one change in accounting method on a Form 3115

.03 Information required with Form 3115

    (1) Facts and other information requested on Form 3115 and in applicable revenue procedures

    (2) Statement of contrary authorities

    (3) Copies of all contracts, agreements, and other documents

    (4) Analysis of material facts

.16 Letter ruling ordinarily not issued for one of two or more interrelated items or submethods

.17 Consent Agreement

.18 Sends a copy of the change in accounting method letter ruling to appropriate Service official

.19 Consent to change an accounting method may be relied on subject to limitations

.20 Change in accounting method letter ruling will not apply to another taxpayer

.21 Associate office discretion to permit requested change in accounting method

.22 List of automatic change in accounting method request procedures

.23 Other sections of this revenue procedure that are applicable to a Form 3115

SECTION 10. HOW ARE CONFERENCES FOR LETTER RULINGS SCHEDULED?

.01 Schedules a conference if requested by taxpayer

.02 Permits taxpayer one conference of right

.03 Disallows verbatim recording of conferences

.04 Makes tentative recommendations on substantive issues

.05 May offer additional conferences

.06 Requires written confirmation of information presented at conference

.07 May schedule a pre-submission conference

.08 May schedule a conference to be held by telephone

SECTION 11. WHAT EFFECT WILL A LETTER RULING HAVE?

.01 May be relied on subject to limitations

.02 Will not apply to another taxpayer

.03 Will be used by a field office in examining the taxpayer's return

.04 May be revoked or modified if found to be in error

.05 Letter ruling revoked or modified based on material change in facts applied retroactively

.06 Not otherwise generally revoked or modified retroactively

.07 Retroactive effect of revocation or modification applied to a particular transaction

.08 Retroactive effect of revocation or modification applied to a continuing action or series of actions

.09 Generally not retroactively revoked or modified if related to sale or lease subject to excise tax

.10 May be retroactively revoked or modified when transaction is entered into before the issuance of the letter ruling

.11 Taxpayer may request that retroactivity be limited

> (1) Request for relief under §7805(b) must be made in required format
>
> (2) Taxpayer may request a conference on application of §7805(b)

SECTION 12. UNDER WHAT CIRCUMSTANCES DO DIRECTORS ISSUE DETERMINATION LETTERS?

.01 In income and gift tax matters

.02 In estate tax matters

.03 In generation-skipping transfer tax matters

.04 In employment and excise tax matters

.05 Requests concerning income, estate, or gift tax returns

.06 Attach a copy of determination letter to taxpayer's return

.07 Review of determination letters

.08 Addresses to send determination letter requests

SECTION 13. WHAT EFFECT WILL A DETERMINATION LETTER HAVE?

.01 Has same effect as a letter ruling

.02 Taxpayer may request that retroactive effect of revocation or modification be limited

> (1) Request for relief under §7805(b) must be made in required format
>
> (2) Taxpayer may request a conference on application of §7805(b)

SECTION 14. UNDER WHAT CIRCUMSTANCES ARE MATTERS REFERRED BETWEEN A FIELD OFFICE AND AN ASSOCIATE OFFICE?

.01 Requests for determination letters

.02 No-rule areas

.03 Requests for letter rulings

.04 Letter ruling request mistakenly sent to a director

SECTION 15. WHAT ARE THE USER FEE REQUIREMENTS FOR REQUESTS FOR LETTER RULINGS AND DETERMINATION LETTERS?

.01 Legislation authorizing user fees

.02 Requests to which a user fee applies

.03 Requests to which a user fee does not apply

.04 Exemptions from the user fee requirements

.05 Fee schedule

.06 Applicable user fee for a request involving multiple offices, fee categories, issues, transactions, or entities

.07 Applicable user fee for substantially identical letter rulings or identical accounting method changes

.08 Method of payment

.09 Effect of nonpayment or payment of incorrect amount

.10 Refunds of user fee

.11 Request for reconsideration of user fee

SECTION 16. WHAT SIGNIFICANT CHANGES HAVE BEEN MADE TO REV. PROC. 2003-1?

SECTION 17. WHAT IS THE EFFECT OF THIS REVENUE PROCEDURE ON OTHER DOCUMENTS?

SECTION 18. WHAT IS THE EFFECTIVE DATE OF THIS REVENUE PROCEDURE?

SECTION 19. PAPERWORK REDUCTION ACT

DRAFTING INFORMATION

INDEX

APPENDIX A—SCHEDULE OF USER FEES

APPENDIX B—SAMPLE FORMAT FOR A LETTER RULING REQUEST

APPENDIX C—CHECKLIST FOR A LETTER RULING REQUEST

APPENDIX D—LIST OF SMALL BUSINESS/SELF-EMPLOYED DIVISION (SB/SE) COMPLIANCE AREA DIRECTORS FOR REQUESTING DETERMINATION LETTERS

APPENDIX E—CHECKLISTS, GUIDELINE REVENUE PROCEDURES, NOTICES, SAFE HARBOR REVENUE PROCEDURES, AND AUTOMATIC CHANGE REVENUE PROCEDURES

.01 Checklists, guideline revenue procedures, and notices

.02 Safe harbor revenue procedures

.03 Automatic change in accounting period revenue procedures

SECTION 1. WHAT IS THE PURPOSE OF THIS REVENUE PROCEDURE?

This revenue procedure explains how the Service provides advice to taxpayers on issues under the jurisdiction of the Associate Chief Counsel (Corporate), the Associate Chief Counsel (Financial Institutions and Products), the Associate Chief Counsel (Income Tax and Accounting), the Associate Chief Counsel (International), the Associate Chief Counsel (Passthroughs and Special Industries), the Associate Chief Counsel (Procedure and Administration), and the Division Counsel/Associate Chief Counsel (Tax Exempt and Government Entities). It explains the forms of advice and the manner in which advice is requested by taxpayers and provided by the Service. A sample format of a request for a letter ruling is provided in Appendix B.

¶1651

Operating divisions of the Service

The Service includes four operating divisions that are responsible for meeting the needs of the taxpayers they serve. These operating divisions are:

(1) Large and Mid-Size Business Division (LMSB), which generally serves corporations; S corporations, and partnerships with assets in excess of $10 million;

(2) Small Business/Self-Employed Division (SB/SE), which generally serves corporations, including S corporations, and partnerships, with assets less than or equal to $10 million; estates and trusts; individuals filing an individual federal income tax return with accompanying Schedule C (Profit or Loss From Business (Sole Proprietorship)), Schedule E (Supplemental Income and Loss), Schedule F (Profit or Loss From Farming), Form 2106 (Employee Business Expenses) or Form 2106-EZ (Unreimbursed Employee Business Expenses); and individuals with international tax returns;

(3) Wage and Investment Division (WI), which generally serves individuals with wage and investment income only (and with no international tax returns) filing an individual federal income tax return without accompanying Schedule C, E, or F, or Form 2106 or Form 2106-EZ; and

(4) Tax Exempt and Government Entities Division (TE/GE), which serves three distinct taxpayer segments: employee plans, exempt organizations, and government entities.

Description of terms used in this revenue procedure

For purposes of this revenue procedure—

(1) any reference to director or field office refers to the Director, Field Operations, LMSB; the Area Director, Field Compliance, SB/SE; or the Director, Compliance, W&I, as appropriate, and their respective offices or, when appropriate, the Director, International, LMSB; the Director, Employee Plans Examinations; the Director, Exempt Organizations Examinations; the Director, Federal, State & Local Governments; the Director, Tax Exempt Bonds; or the Director, Indian Tribal Governments, and their respective offices;

(2) the term "taxpayer" includes all persons subject to any provision of the Internal Revenue Code (including issuers of ?03 obligations) and, when appropriate, their representatives; and

(3) the term "Associate office" refers to the Office of Associate Chief Counsel (Corporate), the Office of Associate Chief Counsel (Financial Institutions and Products), the Office of Associate Chief Counsel (Income Tax and Accounting), the Office of Associate Chief Counsel (International), the Office of Associate Chief Counsel (Passthroughs and Special Industries), the Office of Associate Chief Counsel (Procedure and Administration), or the Office of Division Counsel/Associate Chief Counsel (Tax Exempt and Government Entities), as appropriate.

¶1651

Updated annually

The revenue procedure is updated annually as the first revenue procedure of the year, but may be modified or amplified during the year.

SECTION 2. IN WHAT FORM IS ADVICE PROVIDED BY THE OFFICES OF ASSOCIATE CHIEF COUNSEL (CORPORATE), ASSOCIATE CHIEF COUNSEL (FINANCIAL INSTITUTIONS AND PRODUCTS), ASSOCIATE CHIEF COUNSEL (INCOME TAX AND ACCOUNTING), ASSOCIATE CHIEF COUNSEL (INTERNATIONAL), ASSOCIATE CHIEF COUNSEL (PASSTHROUGHS AND SPECIAL INDUSTRIES), ASSOCIATE CHIEF COUNSEL (PROCEDURE AND ADMINISTRATION), AND DIVISION COUNSEL/ASSOCIATE CHIEF COUNSEL (TAX EXEMPT AND GOVERNMENT ENTITIES)?

The Service provides advice in the form of letter rulings, closing agreements, determination letters, information letters, and oral advice.

Letter ruling

.01 A "letter ruling" is a written determination issued to a taxpayer by the Associate office that interprets and applies the tax laws to the taxpayer's specific set of facts. A letter ruling includes the written permission or denial of permission by the Associate office to a request for a change in a taxpayer's accounting method or accounting period. Once issued, a letter ruling may be revoked or modified for any number of reasons, as explained in section 11 (section 9.19 for a change in accounting method letter ruling) of this revenue procedure, unless it is accompanied by a "closing agreement."

Closing agreement

.02 A "closing agreement" is a final agreement between the Service and a taxpayer on a specific issue or liability. It is entered into under the authority in § 7121 and is final unless fraud, malfeasance, or misrepresentation of a material fact can be shown.

A taxpayer may request a closing agreement with the letter ruling, or in lieu of a letter ruling, with respect to a transaction that would be eligible for a letter ruling.

A closing agreement may be entered into when it is advantageous to have the matter permanently and conclusively closed or when a taxpayer can show that there are good reasons for an agreement and that making the agreement will not prejudice the interests of the Government. In appropriate cases, a taxpayer may be asked to enter into a closing agreement as a condition to the issuance of a letter ruling.

If, in a single case, a closing agreement is requested for each person in a class of taxpayers, separate agreements are entered into only if the class consists of 25 or fewer taxpayers. If the issue and holding are identical for the class and there are more than 25 taxpayers in the class, a "mass closing agreement" will be entered into with the taxpayer who is authorized by the others to represent the class.

Determination letter

.03 A "determination letter" is a written determination issued by a director that applies the principles and precedents previously announced by the Associate office to a specific set of facts. It is issued only when a determination can be made based on clearly established rules in the statute, a tax treaty, the regulations, a conclusion in a revenue ruling, or an opinion or court decision that represents the position of the Service.

Information letter

.04 An "information letter" is a statement issued either by the Associate office or by a director. It calls attention to a well-established interpretation or principle of tax law (including a tax treaty) without applying it to a specific set of facts. An information letter may be issued if the taxpayer's inquiry indicates a need for general information or if the taxpayer's request does not meet the requirements of this revenue procedure and the Service thinks general information will help the taxpayer. The taxpayer should provide a daytime telephone number with the taxpayer's request for an information letter. An information letter is advisory only and has no binding effect on the Service. If the Associate office issues an information letter in response to a request for a letter ruling that does not meet the requirements of this revenue procedure, the information letter is not a substitute for a letter ruling.

Information letters that are issued by the Associate office to members of the public are made available to the public. Information letters that are issued by the field or a director are not made available to the public.

The following documents also will not be available for public inspection as part of this process:

(1) letters that merely transmit Service publications or other publicly available material, without significant legal discussion;

(2) responses to taxpayer or third party contacts that are inquiries with respect to a pending request for a letter ruling, technical advice memorandum, or Chief Counsel Advice (whose public inspection is subject to § 6110); and

(3) responses to taxpayer or third party communications with respect to any investigation, audit, litigation, or other enforcement action.

Before any information letter is made available to the public, the Associate office will delete any name, address, and other identifying information as appropriate under the Freedom of Information Act ("FOIA") (for example, FOIA personal privacy exemption of 5 U.S.C. § 552(b)(6) and tax details exempt pursuant to § 6103, as incorporated into FOIA by 5 U.S.C. § 552(b)(3)). Because information letters do not constitute written determinations (including Chief Counsel Advice) as defined in § 6110, these documents are not subject to public inspection under § 6110.

Oral advice

.05

(1) No oral rulings, and no written rulings in response to oral requests.

The Service does not orally issue letter rulings or determination letters, nor does it issue letter rulings or determination letters in response to oral requests from taxpayers. Service employees ordinarily will discuss with taxpayers or their representatives inquiries regarding whether the Service will rule on particular issues and questions relating to procedural matters about submitting requests for letter rulings or determination letters for a particular case.

(2) Discussion possible on substantive issues.

At the discretion of the Service and as time permits, substantive issues also may be discussed. Such a discussion will not be binding on the Service in general or on the Office of Chief Counsel in particular and cannot be relied upon as a basis for obtaining retroactive relief under the provisions of §7805(b).

Substantive tax issues involving the taxpayer that are under examination, in Appeals, or in litigation will not be discussed by Service employees not directly involved in the examination, appeal, or litigation of the issues unless the discussion is coordinated with those Service employees who are directly involved in the examination, appeal, or litigation of the issues. The taxpayer or the taxpayer's representative ordinarily will be asked whether the oral request for advice or information relates to a matter pending before another office of the Service or before a federal court.

If a tax issue is not under examination, in appeals, or in litigation, the tax issue may be discussed even though the issue is affected by a nontax issue pending in litigation.

A taxpayer may seek oral technical guidance from a taxpayer service representative in a field office or service center when preparing a return or report. Oralguidance is advisory only, and the Service is not bound to recognize it, for example, in the examination of the taxpayer's return.

The Service does not respond to letters seeking to confirm the substance of oral discussions and the absence of a response to such a letter is not confirmation.

SECTION 3. ON WHAT ISSUES MAY TAXPAYERS REQUEST WRITTEN ADVICE UNDER THIS PROCEDURE?

Taxpayers may request letter rulings, information letters, and closing agreements under this revenue procedure on issues within the jurisdiction of the Associates' offices. The Associate offices issue letter rulings to answer written inquiries of individuals and organizations about their status for tax purposes and the tax effects of their acts or transactions when appropriate in the interest of sound tax administration.

¶1651

Taxpayers also may request determination letters from the director in the appropriate division on subjects that relate to the Code sections under the jurisdiction of the respective Associate offices.

Issues under the jurisdiction of the Associate Chief Counsel (Corporate)

.01 Issues under the jurisdiction of the Associate Chief Counsel (Corporate) include those that involve consolidated returns, corporate acquisitions, reorganizations, liquidations, redemptions, spinoffs, transfers to controlled corporations, distributions to shareholders, corporate bankruptcies, the effect of certain ownership changes on net operating loss carryovers and other tax attributes, debt vs. equity determinations, allocation of income and deductions among taxpayers, acquisitions made to evade or avoid income tax, and certain earnings and profits questions.

Issues under the jurisdiction of the Associate Chief Counsel (Financial Institutions & Products)

.02 Issues under the jurisdiction of the Associate Chief Counsel (Financial Institutions and Products) include those that involve income taxes and accounting method changes of banks, savings and loan associations, real estate investment trusts (REITs), regulated investment companies (RICs), real estate mortgage investment conduits (REMICs), insurance companies and products, and financial products.

Issues under the jurisdiction of the Associate Chief Counsel (Income Tax & Accounting)

.03 Issues under the jurisdiction of the Associate Chief Counsel (Income Tax and Accounting) include those that involve recognition and timing of income and deductions of individuals and corporations, sales and exchanges, capital gains and losses, installment sales, equipment leasing, long-term contracts, inventories, the alternative minimum tax, net operating losses generally, including accounting method changes for these issues, and accounting periods.

Issues under the jurisdiction of the Associate Chief Counsel (International)

.04 Issues under the jurisdiction of the Associate Chief Counsel (International) include the tax treatment of nonresident aliens and foreign corporations, withholding of tax on nonresident aliens and foreign corporations, foreign tax credit, determination of sources of income, income from sources without the United States,subpart F questions, domestic international sales corporations (DISCs), foreign sales corporations (FSCs), exclusions under § 114 for extraterritorial income (ETI) pursuant to § 941(a)(5)(A), international boycott determinations, treatment of certain passive foreign investment companies, income affected by treaty, and other matters relating to the activities of non-U.S. persons within the United States or U.S.- related persons outside the United States, and accounting method changes.

For the procedures to obtain advance pricing agreements under § 482, see Rev. Proc. 96-53, 1996-2 C.B. 375, as modified by Notice 98-65, 1998-2 C.B. 803 and amplified by Rev. Proc. 2002-52, 2002-2 C.B. 242.

For the procedures concerning competent authority relief arising under the application and interpretation of tax treaties between the United States and other countries, see Rev. Proc. 96-13, 1996-1 C.B. 616. Competent authority consideration for an advance pricing agreement should be requested under Rev. Proc. 96-53.

¶1651

Issues under the jurisdiction of the Associate Chief Counsel (Passthroughs & Special Industries)

.05 Issues under the jurisdiction of the Associate Chief Counsel (Passthroughs and Special Industries) include those that involve income taxes of S corporations (except accounting periods and methods) and certain noncorporate taxpayers (including partnerships, common trust funds, and trusts), entity classification, estate, gift, generation-skipping transfer, and certain excise taxes, amortization, depreciation, depletion, and other engineering issues, accounting method changes for depreciation and amortization, cooperative housing corporations, farmers' cooperatives (under §521), the low-income housing, disabled access, and qualified electric vehicle credits, research and experimental expenditures, shipowners' protection and indemnity associations (under §526), and certain homeowners associations (under §528).

Issues under the jurisdiction of the Associate Chief Counsel (Procedure and Administration)

.06 Issues under the jurisdiction of the Associate Chief Counsel (Procedure and Administration) include those that involve federal tax procedure and administration, disclosure and privacy law, reporting and paying taxes, assessing and collecting taxes (including interest and penalties), abating, crediting, or refunding overassessments or overpayments of tax, and filing information returns.

Issues under the jurisdiction of the Division Counsel/Associate Chief Counsel (Tax Exempt and Government Entities)

.07 Issues under the jurisdiction of the Division Counsel/Associate Chief Counsel (Tax Exempt and Government Entities) include those that involve income tax and other tax aspects of executive compensation and employee benefit programs, including accounting method changes for these issues (other than those within the jurisdiction of the Commissioner, Tax Exempt and Government Entities Division), employment taxes, taxes on self-employment income, tax-exempt obligations, mortgage credit certificates, qualified zone academy bonds (QZABS), and federal, state, local, and Indian tribal governments.

SECTION 4. ON WHAT ISSUES MUST WRITTEN ADVICE BE REQUESTED UNDER DIFFERENT PROCEDURES?

Alcohol, tobacco, and firearms taxes

.01 The procedures for obtaining letter rulings, etc., that apply to federal alcohol, tobacco, and firearms taxes under subtitle E of the Code are under the jurisdiction of the Alcohol and Tobacco Tax and Trade Bureau of the Department of the Treasury.

Employee plans and exempt organizations

.02 The procedures for obtaining letter rulings, determination letters, etc., on employee plans and exempt organizations are under the jurisdiction of the Commissioner, Tax Exempt and Government Entities Division. See Rev. Proc. 2004-4, this Bulletin. See also Rev. Proc. 2004-6, this Bulletin, for the procedures for issuing determination letters on the qualified status of pension, profit-shar-

¶1651

ing, stock bonus, annuity, and employee stock ownership plans under §§ 401, 403(a), 409, and 4975(e)(7), and the status for exemption of any related trusts or custodial accounts under § 501(a).

For the user fee requirements applicable to requests for letter rulings, determination letters, etc., under the jurisdiction of the Commissioner, Tax Exempt and Government Entities Division, see Rev. Proc. 2004 8, this Bulletin.

SECTION 5. UNDER WHAT CIRCUMSTANCES DOES THE ASSOCIATE OFFICE ISSUE LETTER RULINGS?

In income and gift tax matters

.01 In income and gift tax matters, the Associate office generally issues a letter ruling on a proposed transaction and on a completed transaction if the letter ruling request is submitted before the return is filed for the year in which the transaction that is the subject of the request was completed.

In lieu of requesting a letter ruling under this revenue procedure, a taxpayer may obtain relief for certain late S corporation and related elections by following the procedures in Rev. Proc. 2003-43, 2003-1 C.B. 998, or Rev. Proc. 97-48, 1997-2 C.B. 521. A request made pursuant to Rev. Proc. 2003-43 or Rev. Proc. 97-48 does not require payment of any user fee. See section 3.01 of Rev. Proc. 2003-43, section 3 of Rev. Proc. 97-48, and section 15.03(2) of this revenue procedure.

A § 301.9100 request for extension of time for making an election or for other relief

.02 The Associate office will consider a request for an extension of time for making an election or other application for relief under § 301.9100-3 of the Regulations on Procedure and Administration. Even if submitted after the return covering the issue presented in the § 301.9100 request has been filed and even if submitted after an examination of the return has begun or after the issues in the return are being considered by Appeals or a federal court, a § 301.9100 request is a letter ruling request. Therefore, the § 301.9100 request should be submitted pursuant to this revenue procedure. An election made pursuant to § 301.9100-2 is not a letter ruling request and does not require payment of any user fee. See§ 301.9100-2(d) and section 15.03(1) of this revenue procedure. Such an election pertains to an automatic extension of time.

(1) Format of request. A § 301.9100 request (other than an election made pursuant to § 301.9100-2) must be in the general form of, and meet the general requirements for, a letter ruling request. These requirements are given in section 7 of this revenue procedure. In addition, the § 301.9100 request must include the information required by § 301.9100-3(e).

(2) Period of limitations. The running of any applicable period of limitations is not suspended for the period during which a § 301.9100 request has been filed. *See* § 301.9100-3(d)(2). If the period of limitation on assessment under § 6501(a) for the taxable year in which an election should have been made or any taxable year that would have been affected by the election had it been timely made will expire before receipt of a § 301.9100 letter ruling, the Service ordinarily will not issue a §301.9100 ruling. *See* §301.9100-3(c)(1)(ii). Therefore, the taxpayer must secure a consent under §6501(c)(4) to extend the period of limitation on assessment. Note that the filing of a claim for refund under §6511 does not extend the period of limitation on assessment. If §301.9100 relief is granted, the Service may require the taxpayer to consent to an extension of the period of limitation on assessment. *See* §301.9100-3(d)(2).

(3) **Taxpayer must notify Associate office if examination of return begins while request is pending.** If the Service starts an examination of the taxpayer's return for the taxable year in which an election should have been made or any taxable year that would have been affected by the election had it been timely made while a §301.9100 request is pending, the taxpayer must notify the Associate office. This notification includes the name and telephone number of the examining agent. *See* §301.9100-3(e)(4)(i) and section 7.04(1)(b) of this revenue procedure.

(4) **Associate office will notify examination agents, appeals officer, or government counsel of a §301.9100 request if return is being examined by a field office or is being considered by Appeals or a federal court.** If the taxpayer's return for the taxable year in which an election should have been made or any taxable year that would have been affected by the election had it been timely made is being examined by a field office or considered by Appeals or a federal court, the Associate office will notify the appropriate examining agent, appeals officer, or government counsel that a §301.9100 request has been submitted to the Associate office. The examining officer, appeals officer, or government counsel is not authorized to deny consideration of a §301.9100 request. The letter ruling will be mailed to the taxpayer and a copy will be sent to the appropriate Service official in the operating division that has examination jurisdiction of the taxpayer's tax return, appeals officer, or government counsel.

Determinations under §999(d) of the Internal Revenue Code

.03 Under Rev. Proc. 77-9, 1977-1 C.B. 542, the Office of Associate Chief Counsel (International) issues determinations under §999(d) that may deny certain benefits of the foreign tax credit, deferral of earnings of foreign subsidiaries and domestic international sales corporations (DISCs) to a person, if that person, is a member of a controlled group (within the meaning of §993(a)(3)) that includes the person, or a foreign corporation of which a member of the controlled group is a United States shareholder, agrees to participate in, or cooperate with, an international boycott. The same principles shall apply with respect to tax exemption for foreign trade income of a foreign sales corporation or a small foreign sales corporation (FSC or small FSC) and exclusions under §114 for exterritorial income (ETI) pursuant to §941(a)(5)(A). Requests for determinations under Rev. Proc. 77-9 are letter ruling requests and, therefore, should be submitted to the Associate Chief Counsel (International) pursuant to this revenue procedure.

In matters involving §367

.04 Unless the issue is covered by section 6 of this revenue procedure, the Office of Associate Chief Counsel (International) may issue a letter ruling under §367 even if the taxpayer does not request a letter ruling as to the characterization of the transaction under the reorganization provisions of the Code. The Office of Associate Chief Counsel (International) will determine the §367 consequences of a transaction based on the taxpayer's characterization of the transaction but will indicate in the letter ruling that it expresses no opinion as to the characterization of the transaction under the reorganization. The Office of Associate Chief Counsel (International) may decline to issue a §367 ruling in situations in which the taxpayer inappropriately characterizes the transaction under the reorganization provisions.

In estate tax matters

.05 In general, the Associate office issues prospective letter rulings on transactions affecting the estate tax on the prospective estate of a living person and affecting the estate tax on the estate of a decedent before the decedent's estate tax return is filed. The Associate office will not issue letter rulings for prospective estates on computations of tax, actuarial factors, and factual matters.

If the taxpayer is requesting a letter ruling regarding a decedent's estate tax and the estate tax return is due to be filed before the letter ruling is expected to be issued, the taxpayer should obtain an extension of time for filing the return and should notify the Associate office branch considering the letter ruling request that an extension has been obtained.

If the return is filed before the letter ruling is received from the Associate office, the taxpayer must disclose on the return that a letter ruling has been requested, attach a copy of the pending letter ruling request to the return, and notify the Associate office that the return has been filed. *See* section 7.04 of this revenue procedure. The Associate office will make every effort to issue the letter ruling within 3 months of the date the return was filed.

If the taxpayer requests a letter ruling after the return is filed, but before the return is examined, the taxpayer must notify the director having jurisdiction over the return that a letter ruling has been requested, attach a copy of the pending letter ruling request, and notify the Associate office that a return has been filed.*See* section 7.04 of this revenue procedure. The Associate office will make every effort to issue the letter ruling within 3 months of the date the return has been filed.

If the letter ruling cannot be issued within that 3-month period, the Associate office will notify the field office having jurisdiction over the return, who may, by memorandum to the Associate office, grant an additional period for the issuance of the letter ruling.

In matters involving additional estate tax under §2032A(c)

.06 In matters involving additional estate tax under §2032A(c), the Associate office issues letter rulings on proposed transactions and on completed transactions that occurred before the return is filed.

In matters involving qualified domestic trusts under § 2056A

.07 In matters involving qualified domestic trusts under § 2056A, the Associate office issues letter rulings on proposed transactions and on completed transactions that occurred before the return is filed.

In generation-skipping transfer tax matters

.08 In general, the Associate office issues letter rulings on proposed transactions that affect the generation-skipping transfer tax and on completed transactions that occurred before the return is filed. In the case of a generation-skipping trust or trust equivalent, letter rulings are issued either before or after the trust or trust equivalent has been established.

In employment and excise tax matters

.09 In employment and excise tax matters, the Associate office issues letter rulings on proposed transactions and on completed transactions either before or after the return is filed for those transactions.

Requests regarding employment status (employer/employee relationship) from federal agencies and instrumentalities should be submitted directly to the Associate office. Requests regarding employment status from other taxpayers must first be submitted to the appropriate Service office listed on the current Form SS-8 (Rev. June 2003). *See* section 12.04 of this revenue procedure. Generally, the employer is the taxpayer and requests the letter ruling. If the worker asks for the letter ruling, both the worker and the employer are considered to be the taxpayer and both are entitled to the letter ruling.

In administrative provisions matters

.10 The Associate office issues letter rulings on matters arising under the Code and related statutes and regulations that involve—

(1) the time, place, manner, and procedures for reporting and paying taxes;

(2) the assessment and collection of taxes (including interest and penalties);

(3) the abatement, credit, or refund of an overassessment or overpayment of tax; or

(4) the filing of information returns.

In Indian tribal government matters

.11 Pursuant to Rev. Proc. 84-37, 1984-1 C.B. 513, as modified by Rev. Proc. 86-17, 1986-1 C.B. 550, and Rev. Proc. 2004-1 (this revenue procedure), the Office of Division Counsel/Associate Chief Counsel (Tax Exempt and Government Entities) issues determinations recognizing a tribal entity as an Indian tribal government within the meaning of § 7701(a)(40) or as a political subdivision of an Indian tribal government under § 7871(d) if it determines, after consultation with the Secretary of the Interior, that the entity satisfies the statutory definition of an Indian tribal government or has been delegated governmental functions of an Indian tribal government. Requests for determinations under Rev. Proc. 84-37 are letter ruling requests, and, therefore, should be submitted to the Office of

Division Counsel/Associate Chief Counsel (Tax Exempt and Government Entities) pursuant to this revenue procedure.

(1) Definition of Indian tribal government. The term "Indian tribal government" is defined under §7701(a)(40) to mean the governing body of any tribe, band, community, village or group of Indians, or (if applicable) Alaska Natives, that is determined by the Secretary of the Treasury, after consultation with the Secretary of the Interior, to exercise governmental functions. Section 7871(d) provides that, for purposes of §7871, a subdivision of an Indian tribal government shall be treated as a political subdivision of a state if the Secretary of the Treasury determines, after consultation with the Secretary of the Interior, that the subdivision has been delegated the right to exercise one or more of the substantial governmental functions of the Indian tribal government.

(2) Inclusion in list of tribal governments. Rev. Proc. 2002-64, 2002-2 C.B. 717, provides a list of Indian tribal governments that are treated similarly to states for certain federal tax purposes. Rev. Proc. 84-36, 1984-1 C.B. 510, as modified by Rev. Proc. 86-17, provides a list of political subdivisions of Indian tribal governments that are treated as political subdivisions of states for certain federal tax purposes. Under Rev. Proc. 84-37, tribal governments or subdivisions recognized under §7701(a)(40) or §7871(d) will be included on the list of recognized tribal government entities in revised versions of Rev. Proc. 2002-64 or Rev. Proc. 84-36.

On constructive sales price under §4216(b) or §4218(c)

.12 The Associate office will issue letter rulings in all cases on the determination of a constructive sales price under §4216(b) or §4218(c) and in all other cases on prospective transactions if the law or regulations require a determination of the effect of a proposed transaction for tax purposes.

May be issued before the issuance of a regulation or other published guidance

.13 Unless the issue is covered by section 6 of this revenue procedure, Rev. Proc. 2004-3, this Bulletin, or Rev. Proc. 2004-7, this Bulletin, a letter ruling may be issued before the issuance of a temporary or final regulation or other published guidance that interprets the provisions of any act under the following conditions:

(1) Answer is clear or is reasonably certain. If the letter ruling request presents an issue for which the answer seems clear by applying the statute to thefacts or for which the answer seems reasonably certain but not entirely free from doubt, a letter ruling may be issued.

(2) Answer is not reasonably certain. The Associate office will consider all letter ruling requests and use its best efforts to issue a letter ruling even if the answer does not seem reasonably certain where the issuance of a letter ruling is in the best interests of tax administration. But see section 6.08 of this revenue procedure.

SECTION 6. UNDER WHAT CIRCUMSTANCES DOES THE SERVICE NOT ISSUE LETTER RULINGS OR DETERMINATION LETTERS?

Ordinarily not if issue involves an issue under examination, or consideration, or in litigation

.01 The Service ordinarily does not issue a letter ruling or a determination letter if, at the time of the request the identical issue is involved in the taxpayer's return for an earlier period and that issue—

(1) is being examined by a field office;

(2) is being considered by Appeals;

(3) is pending in litigation in a case involving the taxpayer or a related taxpayer;

(4) has been examined by a field office or considered by Appeals and the statutory period of limitations on assessment or on filing a claim for refund or credit of tax has not expired; or

(5) has been examined by a field office or considered by Appeals and a closing agreement covering the issue or liability has not been entered into by a field office or by Appeals.

If a return dealing with an issue for a particular year is filed while a request for a letter ruling on that issue is pending, the Associate office will issue the letter ruling unless it is notified by the taxpayer or otherwise learns that an examination of that issue or the identical issue on an earlier year's return has been started by a field office. *See* section 7.04 of this revenue procedure. In income and gift tax matters, even if an examination has begun, the Associate office ordinarily will issue the letter ruling if the field office agrees, by memorandum, to the issuance of the letter ruling.

Ordinarily not in certain areas because of factual nature of the problem

.02 The Service ordinarily does not issue letter rulings or determination letters in certain areas because of the factual nature of the problem involved or because of other reasons. Rev. Proc. 2004-3 and Rev. Proc. 2004-7, this Bulletin, provide a list of these areas. This list is not all-inclusive because the Service may decline to issue a letter ruling or a determination letter when appropriate in the interest of sound tax administration or on other grounds whenever warranted by the facts or circumstances of a particular case.

Instead of issuing a letter ruling or determination letter, the Associate office or a director may, when it is considered appropriate and in the best interests of the Service, issue an information letter calling attention to well-established principles of tax law.

Ordinarily not on part of an integrated transaction

.03 The Associate office ordinarily will not issue a letter ruling on only part of an integrated transaction. If a part of a transaction falls under a no-rule area, a letter ruling on other parts of the transaction may be issued. Before preparing the letter ruling request, a taxpayer should call the branch having jurisdiction for the matters on which the taxpayer is seeking a letter ruling to discuss whether the Associate office will issue a letter ruling on part of the transaction.

Ordinarily not on which of two entities is a common law employer

.04 The Service does not ordinarily issue a letter ruling or a determination letter on which of two entities, under common law rules applicable in determining the employer-employee relationship, is the employer, when one entity is treating the worker as an employee.

Generally not to business associations or groups

.05 The Service does not issue letter rulings or determination letters to business, trade, or industrial associations or to similar groups concerning the application of the tax laws to members of the group. But groups and associations may submit suggestions of generic issues that would be appropriately addressed in revenue rulings. See Rev. Proc. 89-14, 1989-1 C.B. 814, which states the objectives of, and standards for, the publication of revenue rulings and revenue procedures in the Internal Revenue Bulletin.

The Service may issue letter rulings or determination letters to groups or associations on their own tax status or liability if the request meets the requirements of this revenue procedure.

Generally not to foreign governments

.06 The Service does not issue letter rulings or determination letters to foreign governments or their political subdivisions about the U.S. tax effects of their laws. The Associate office also does not issue letter rulings on the effect of a tax treaty on the tax laws of a treaty country for purposes of determining the tax of the treaty country. *See* section 13.02 of Rev. Proc. 2002-52, 2002-2 C.B. 242 at 252. Treaty partners can continue to address matters such as these under the provisions of the applicable tax treaty. In addition, the Associate office may issue letter rulings to foreign governments or their political subdivisions on their own tax status or liability under U.S. law if the request meets the requirements of this revenue procedure.

Ordinarily not on federal tax consequences of proposed legislation

.07 The Service ordinarily does not issue letter rulings on a matter involving the federal tax consequences of any proposed federal, state, local, municipal, or foreign legislation. The Office of Division Counsel/Associate Chief Counsel (Tax Exempt and Government Entities) may issue letter rulings regarding the effect of proposed state, local, or municipal legislation upon an eligible deferred compensation plan under § 457(b) provided that the letter ruling request relating to the plan complies with the other requirements of this revenue procedure. The Associate office also may provide general information in response to an inquiry.

Not before issuance of a regulation or other published guidance

.08 The Service will not issue a letter ruling or a determination letter if the request presents an issue that cannot be readily resolved before a regulation or any other published guidance is issued. When the Service has closed a regulation project or any other published guidance project that might have answered the

¶1651

issue or decides not to open a regulation project or any other published guidance project, the Associate office may consider all letter ruling requests unless the issue is covered by section 6 of this revenue procedure, Rev. Proc. 2004-3, or Rev. Proc. 2004-7, this Bulletin.

Not on frivolous issues

.09 The Service will not issue a letter ruling or a determination letter on frivolous issues. A "frivolous issue" is one without basis in fact or law, or that espouses a position which has been held by the courts to be frivolous or groundless. Examples of frivolous or groundless issues include, but are not limited to:

(1) frivolous "constitutional" claims, such as claims that the requirement to file tax returns and pay taxes constitutes an unreasonable search barred by the Fourth Amendment; violates Fifth and Fourteenth Amendment protections of due process; violates Thirteenth Amendment protections against involuntary servitude; or is unenforceable because the Sixteenth Amendment does not authorize nonapportioned direct taxes or was never ratified;

(2) claims that income taxes are voluntary, that the term "income" is not defined in the Internal Revenue Code, or that preparation and filing of income tax returns violates the Paperwork Reduction Act;

(3) claims that tax may be imposed only on coins minted under a gold or silver standard or that receipt of Federal Reserve Notes does not cause an accretion to wealth;

(4) claims that a person is not taxable on income because he or she falls within a class entitled to "reparation claims" or an extra-statutory class of individuals exempt from tax, e.g., "free-born" individuals;

(5) claims that a taxpayer can refuse to pay taxes on the basis of opposition to certain governmental expenditures;

(6) claims that taxes apply only to federal employees; only to residents of Puerto Rico, Guam, the U.S. Virgin Islands, the District of Columbia, or "federal enclaves"; or that sections 861 through 865 or any other provision of the Internal Revenue Code imposes taxes on U.S. citizens and residents only on income derived from foreign based activities;

(7) claims that wages or personal service income are not "income," are "nontaxable receipts," or "are a nontaxable exchange for labor;"

(8) claims that income tax withholding by an employer on wages is optional; or

(9) other claims the courts have characterized as frivolous or groundless.

No "comfort" letter rulings

.10 Except as otherwise provided in Rev. Proc. 2004-3, this Bulletin, (e.g., under section 3.01 (29), where the Associate office already is ruling on a significant issue in the same transaction), a letter ruling will not be issued with respect to an issue that is clearly and adequately addressed by statute, regulations, decisions of a court, revenue rulings, revenue procedures, notices, or other authority published in the Internal Revenue Bulletin. The Associate office may in its discretion determine to issue a letter ruling on such an issue if the Associate office is otherwise issuing a ruling on another issue arising in the same transaction.

Not on alternative plans or hypothetical situations

.11 The Service will not issue a letter ruling or a determination letter on alternative plans of proposed transactions or on hypothetical situations.

Not on property conversion after return filed

.12 The Associate office will not issue a letter ruling on the replacement of involuntarily converted property, whether or not the property has been replaced, if the taxpayer has already filed a return for the taxable year in which the property was converted. The field office may issue a determination letter in this case. *See* section 12.01 of this revenue procedure.

Circumstances under which determination letters are not issued by a director

.13 A director will not issue a determination letter if—

(1) it appears that the taxpayer has directed a similar inquiry to the Associate office;

(2) the same issue involving the same taxpayer or a related taxpayer is pending in a case in litigation or before Appeals;

(3) the request involves an industry-wide problem;

(4) the specific employment tax question at issue in the request has been, or is being, considered by the Central Office of the Social Security Administration or the Railroad Retirement Board for the same taxpayer or a related taxpayer; or

(5) the request is for a determination of constructive sales price under §4216(b) or §4218(c), which deal with special provisions applicable to the manufacturers excise tax. The Associate office will issue letter rulings in this area. *See* section 5.12 of this revenue procedure.

SECTION 7. WHAT ARE THE GENERAL INSTRUCTIONS FOR REQUESTING LETTER RULINGS AND DETERMINATION LETTERS?

This section explains the general instructions for requesting letter rulings and determination letters. See section 9 of this revenue procedure for the specific and additional procedures for requesting a change in accounting method.

Requests for letter rulings except for certain changes in accounting methods under the automatic change request procedures (see section 9.01(1) of this revenue procedure) and certain changes in accounting periods made under automatic change request procedures (see Appendix E of this revenue procedure), closing agreements, and determination letters require the payment of the applicable user fee listed in Appendix A of this revenue procedure. For additional user fee requirements, see section 15 of this revenue procedure.

¶1651

Specific and additional instructions also apply to requests for letter rulings and determination letters on certain matters. Those matters are listed in Appendix E of this revenue procedure followed by a reference (usually to another revenue procedure) where more information can be obtained.

Certain information required in all requests

.01

Facts

(1) Complete statement of facts and other information. Each request for a letter ruling or a determination letter must contain a complete statement of all facts relating to the transaction. These facts include—

(a) names, addresses, telephone numbers, and taxpayer identification numbers of all interested parties. (The term "all interested parties" does not mean all shareholders of a widely held corporation requesting a letter ruling relating to a reorganization or all employees where a large number may be involved.);

(b) the annual accounting period, and the overall method of accounting (cash or accrual) for maintaining the accounting books and filing the federal income tax return, of all interested parties;

(c) a description of the taxpayer's business operations;

(d) a complete statement of the business reasons for the transaction; and

(e) a detailed description of the transaction.

Documents and foreign laws

(2) Copies of all contracts, wills, deeds, agreements, instruments, other documents, and foreign laws.

(a) Documents. True copies of all contracts, wills, deeds, agreements, instruments, trust documents, proposed disclaimers, and other documents pertinent to the transaction must be submitted with the request.

If the request concerns a corporate distribution, reorganization, or similar transaction, the corporate balance sheet and profit and loss statement should also be submitted. If the request relates to a prospective transaction, the most recent balance sheet and profit and loss statement should be submitted.

If any document, including any balance sheet and profit and loss statement, is in a language other than English, the taxpayer must also submit a certified English translation of the document, along with a true copy of the document. For guidelines on the acceptability of such documents, see paragraph (c) of this section 7.01(2).

Each document, other than the request, should be labeled and attached to the request in alphabetical sequence. Original documents, such as contracts, wills, etc., should not be submitted because they become part of the Service's file and will not be returned.

(b) Foreign laws. The taxpayer must submit with the request a copy of the relevant parts of all foreign laws, including statutes, regulations, administrative

¶1651

pronouncements, and any other relevant legal authority. The documents submitted must be in the official language of the country involved and must be copied from an official publication of the foreign government or another widely available, generally accepted publication. If English is not the official language of the country involved, the taxpayer must also submit a copy of an English language version of the relevant parts of all foreign laws. This translation must be: (i) from an official publication of the foreign government or another widely available, generally accepted publication; or (ii) a certified English translation submitted in accordance with paragraph (c) of this section 7.01(2).

The taxpayer must identify the title and date of publication, including updates, of any widely available, generally accepted publication that the taxpayer (or the taxpayer's qualified translator) uses as a source for the relevant parts of the foreign law.

(c) Standards for acceptability of submissions of documents in a language other than English and certified English translations of laws in a language other than English. The taxpayer must submit with the request an accurate and complete certified English translation of the relevant parts of all contracts, wills, deeds, agreements, instruments, trust documents, proposed disclaimers, or other documents in a language other than English. If the taxpayer chooses to submit certified English translations of foreign laws, those translations must be based on an official publication of the foreign government or another widely available, generally accepted publication. In either case, the translation must be that of a qualified translator and must be attested to by the translator. The attestation must contain: (i) a statement that the translation submitted is a true and accurate translation of the foreign language document or law; (ii) a statement as to the attestant's qualifications as a translator and as to that attestant's qualifications and knowledge regarding tax matters or foreign law if the law is not a tax law; and (iii) the attestant's name and address.

Analysis of material facts

(3) Analysis of material facts. All material facts in documents must be included, rather than merely incorporated by reference, in the taxpayer's initial request or in supplemental letters. These facts must be accompanied by an analysis of their bearing on the issue or issues, specifying the provisions that apply.

Same issue in an earlier return

(4) Statement regarding whether same issue is in an earlier return. The request must state whether, to the best of the knowledge of both the taxpayer and the taxpayer's representatives, any return of the taxpayer (or any return of a related taxpayer within the meaning of §267 or of a member of an affiliated group of which the taxpayer is also a member within the meaning of §1504) that would be affected by the requested letter ruling or determination letter is under examination, before Appeals, or before a federal court.

Same or similar issue previously submitted or currently pending

(5) Statement regarding whether same or similar issue was previously ruled on or requested, or is currently pending. The request must also state whether, to the best of the knowledge of both the taxpayer and the taxpayer's representatives—

(a) the Service previously ruled on the same or a similar issue for the taxpayer (or a related taxpayer within the meaning of §267 or a member of an affiliated group of which the taxpayer is also a member within the meaning of §1504) or a predecessor;

(b) the taxpayer, a related taxpayer, a predecessor, or any representatives previously submitted a request (including an application for change in accounting method) involving the same or a similar issue to the Service but withdrew the request before a letter ruling or determination letter was issued;

(c) the taxpayer, a related taxpayer, or a predecessor previously submitted a request (including an application for change in accounting method) involving the same or a similar issue that is currently pending with the Service; or

(d) at the same time as this request, the taxpayer or a related taxpayer is presently submitting another request (including an application for change in accounting method) involving the same or a similar issue to the Service.

If the statement is affirmative for (a), (b), (c), or (d) of this section 8.01(5), the statement must give the date the request was submitted, the date the request was withdrawn or ruled on, if applicable, and other details of the Service's consideration of the issue.

Interpretation of a substantive provision of an income or estate tax treaty

(6) Statement regarding interpretation of a substantive provision of an income or estate tax treaty. If the request involves the interpretation of a substantive provision of an income or estate tax treaty, the request must also state whether—

(a) the tax authority of the treaty jurisdiction has issued a ruling on the same or similar issue for the taxpayer, a related taxpayer (within the meaning of §267 or a member of an affiliated group of which the taxpayer is also a member within the meaning of §1504), or any predecessor;

(b) the same or similar issue for the taxpayer, a related taxpayer, or any predecessor is being examined, or has been settled, by the tax authority of the treaty jurisdiction or is otherwise the subject of a closing agreement in that jurisdiction; and

(c) the same or similar issue for the taxpayer, a related taxpayer, or any predecessor is being considered by the competent authority of the treaty jurisdiction.

Letter from Bureau of Indian Affairs relating to Indian tribal government

(7) Letter from Bureau of Indian Affairs relating to a letter ruling request for recognition of Indian tribal government status or status as a political subdivision of an Indian tribal government. To facilitate prompt action on a

¶1651

letter ruling request for recognition of Indian tribal government status or status as a political subdivision of an Indian tribal government, the taxpayer is encouraged to submit with the letter ruling request a letter from the Department of the Interior, Bureau of Indian Affairs ("BIA"), verifying that the tribe is recognized by BIA as an Indian tribe and that the tribal government exercises governmental functions or that the political subdivision of the Indian tribal government has been delegated substantial governmental functions. A letter ruling request that does not contain this letter from BIA cannot be resolved until the Service obtains a letter from BIA regarding the tribe's status.

The taxpayer should send a request to verify tribal status to the following address:

> Branch of Tribal Government & Alaska
> Division of Indian Affairs
> Office of the Solicitor, Room 6456
> U.S. Department of the Interior
> 1849 C Street, N.W.
> Washington, D.C. 20240

Statement of authorities supporting taxpayer's views

(8) Statement of supporting authorities. If the taxpayer advocates a particular conclusion, an explanation of the grounds for that conclusion and the relevant authorities to support it must be included. Even if not advocating a particular tax treatment of a proposed transaction, the taxpayer must still furnish views on the tax results of the proposed transaction and a statement of relevant authorities to support those views.

In all events, the request must include a statement of whether the law in connection with the request is uncertain and whether the issue is adequately addressed by relevant authorities.

Statement of authorities contrary to taxpayer's views

(9) Statement of contrary authorities. The taxpayer is also encouraged to inform the Service about, and discuss the implications of, any authority believed to be contrary to the position advanced, such as legislation (or pending legislation), tax treaties, court decisions, regulations, notices, revenue rulings, revenue procedures, or announcements. If the taxpayer determines that there are no contrary authorities, a statement in the request to this effect would be helpful. If the taxpayer does not furnish either contrary authorities or a statement that none exists, the Service in complex cases or those presenting difficult or novel issues may request submission of contrary authorities or a statement that none exists. Failure to comply with this request may result in the Service's refusal to issue a letter ruling or determination letter.

Identifying and discussing contrary authorities will generally enable Service personnel to understand the issue and relevant authorities more quickly. When Service personnel receive the request, they will have before them the taxpayer's thinking on the effect and applicability of contrary authorities. This information should make research easier and lead to earlier action by the Service. If the taxpayer does not disclose and distinguish significant contrary authorities, the Service may need to request additional information, which will delay action on the request.

Statement identifying pending legislation

(10) Statement identifying pending legislation. At the time of filing the request, the taxpayer must identify any pending legislation that may affect the proposed transaction. In addition, if legislation is introduced after the request is filed but before a letter ruling or determination letter is issued, the taxpayer must notify the Service.

Deletions statement required by § 6110

(11) Statement identifying information to be deleted from copy of letter ruling or determination letter for public inspection. The text of letter rulings and determination letters is open to public inspection under § 6110. The Service makes deletions from the text before it is made available for inspection. To help the Service make the deletions required by § 6110(c), a request for a letter ruling or determination letter must be accompanied by a statement indicating the deletions desired ("deletions statement"). If the deletions statement is not submitted with the request, a Service representative will tell the taxpayer that the request will be closed if the Service does not receive the deletions statement within 21 calendar days. *See* section 8.05 of this revenue procedure.

(a) Format of deletions statement. A taxpayer who wants only names, addresses, and identifying numbers to be deleted should state this in the deletion statement. If the taxpayer wants more information deleted, the deletion statement must be accompanied by a copy of the request and supporting documents on which the taxpayer should bracket the material to be deleted. The deletion statement must include the statutory basis under § 6110(c) for each proposed deletion.

If the taxpayer decides to ask for additional deletions before the letter ruling or determination letter is issued, additional deletions statements may be submitted.

(b) Location of deletions statement. The deletions statement must not appear in the request, but instead must be made in a separate document and placed on top of the request for a letter ruling or determination letter.

(c) Signature. The deletions statement must be signed and dated by the taxpayer or the taxpayer's authorized representative. A stamped signature is not permitted.

(d) Additional information. The taxpayer should follow the same procedures above to propose deletions from any additional information submitted after the initial request. An additional deletion statement is not required with eachsubmission of additional information if the taxpayer's initial deletions statement requests that only names, addresses, and identifying numbers are to be deleted and the taxpayer wants only the same information deleted from the additional information.

¶1651

(e) Taxpayer may protest deletions not made. After receiving from the Service the notice under §6110(f)(1) of intention to disclose the letter ruling or determination letter (including a copy of the version proposed to be open to public inspection and notation of third-party communications under §6110(d)), the taxpayer may protest the disclosure of certain information in the letter ruling or determination letter. The taxpayer must send a written statement within 20 calendar days to the Service office indicated on the notice of intention to disclose. The statement must identify those deletions that the Service has not made and that the taxpayer believes should have been made. The taxpayer must also submit a copy of the version of the letter ruling or determination letter and bracket the deletions proposed that have not been made by the Service. Generally, the Service will not consider deleting any material that the taxpayer did not propose to be deleted before the letter ruling or determination letter was issued.

Within 20 calendar days after the Service receives the response to the notice under §6110(f)(1), the Service will mail to the taxpayer its final administrative conclusion regarding the deletions to be made. The taxpayer does not have the right to a conference to resolve any disagreements concerning material to be deleted from the text of the letter ruling or determination letter. However, these matters may be taken up at any conference that is otherwise scheduled regarding the request.

(f) Taxpayer may request delay of public inspection. After receiving the notice under §6110(f)(1) of intention to disclose, but within 60 calendar days after the date of notice, the taxpayer may send a request for delay of public inspection under either §6110(g)(3) or (4). The request for delay must be sent to the Service office indicated on the notice of intention to disclose. A request for delay under §6110(g)(3) must contain the date on which it is expected that the underlying transaction will be completed. The request for delay under §6110(g)(4) must contain a statement from which the Commissioner of Internal Revenue may determine that there are good reasons for the delay.

Signature on request

(12) Signature by taxpayer or authorized representative. The request for a letter ruling or determination letter must be signed and dated by the taxpayer or the taxpayer's authorized representative. A stamped signature or faxed signature is not permitted.

Authorized representatives

(13) (a) Authorized representatives. To sign the request or to appear before the Service in connection with the request, the taxpayer's authorized representative (for rules on who may practice before the Service, see Treasury Department Circular No. 230 (31 C.F.R. part 10, July 26, 2002) must be:

Attorney

(1) An attorney who is a member in good standing of the bar of the highest court of any state, possession, territory, commonwealth, or the District of Columbia and who is not currently under suspension or disbarment from practice before the Service. He or she must file a written declaration with the Service

showing current qualification as an attorney and current authorization to represent the taxpayer;

Certified public accountant

(2) A certified public accountant who is duly qualified to practice in any state, possession, territory, commonwealth, or the District of Columbia and who is not currently under suspension or disbarment from practice before the Service. He or she must file a written declaration with the Service showing current qualification as a certified public accountant and current authorization to represent the taxpayer;

Enrolled agent

(3) An enrolled agent who is a person, other than an attorney or certified public accountant, that is currently enrolled to practice before the Service and is not currently under suspension or disbarment from practice before the Service. He or she must file a written declaration with the Service showing current enrollment and authorization to represent the taxpayer. Either the enrollment number or the expiration date of the enrollment card must be included in the declaration;

Enrolled actuary

(4) An enrolled actuary who is a person, other than an attorney or certified public accountant, that is currently enrolled as an actuary by the Joint Board for the Enrollment of Actuaries pursuant to 29 U.S.C. § 1242 and who is not currently under suspension or disbarment from practice before the Service. He or she must file a written declaration with the Service showing current qualification as an enrolled actuary and current authorization to represent the taxpayer. Practice before the Service as an enrolled actuary is limited to representation with respect to issues involving §§ 401, 403(a), 404, 412, 413, 414, 419, 419A, 420, 4971, 4972, 4976, 4980, 6057, 6058, 6059, 6652(e), 6652(f), 6692, and 7805(b); former § 405; and 29 U.S.C. § 1083; or

A person with a "Letter of Authorization"

(5) Any other person, including a foreign representative, who has received a "Letter of Authorization" from the Director of the Office of Professional Responsibility under section 10.7(d) of Treasury Department Circular No. 230. A person may make a written request for a "Letter of Authorization" to: Office of Professional Responsibility, N:S:SC, Internal Revenue Service, 1111 Constitution Avenue, N.W., Washington, D.C. 20224. Section 10.7(d) of Circular No. 230 authorizes the Commissioner to allow an individual who is not otherwise eligible to practice before the Service to represent another person in a particular matter.

Employee, general partner, bona fide officer, administrator, trustee, etc.

(b) The requirements of section 7.01(13)(a) of this revenue procedure do not apply to a regular full-time employee representing his or her employer; to a general partner representing his or her partnership; to a bona fide officer representing hisor her corporation, association, or organized group; to a regular full-

¶1651

time employee representing a trust, receivership, guardianship, or estate; or to an individual representing his or her immediate family. A preparer of a return (other than a person referred to in paragraph (a)(1), (2), (3), (4), or (5) of this section 7.01(13)) who is not a full-time employee, general partner, bona fide officer, an administrator, a trustee, etc., or an individual representing his or her immediate family may not represent a taxpayer in connection with a letter ruling or a determination letter. *See* section 10.7(c) of Treasury Department Circular No. 230.

Foreign representative

(c) A foreign representative (other than a person referred to in paragraph (a)(1), (2), (3), (4), or (5) of this section 7.01(13)) is not authorized to practice before the Service and, therefore, must withdraw from representing a taxpayer in a request for a letter ruling or a determination letter. In this situation, the nonresident alien or foreign entity must submit the request for a letter ruling or a determination letter on the individual's or the entity's own behalf or through a person referred to in paragraph (a)(1), (2), (3), (4), or (5) of this section 7.01(13); see also Rev. Proc. 81-38, 1981-2 C.B. 592.

Power of attorney and declaration of representative

(14) **Power of attorney and declaration of representative.** Any authorized representative, whether or not enrolled to practice, must also comply with the conference and practice requirements of the Statement of Procedural Rules (26 C.F.R. § 601.501-601.509 (2002)), which provide the rules for representing a tax-payer before the Service. It is preferred that Form 2848, Power of Attorney and Declaration of Representative, be used to provide the representative's authority (Part I of Form 2848, Power of Attorney) and the representative's qualification (Part II of Form 2848, Declaration of Representative). The name of the person signing Part I of Form 2848 should also be typed or printed on this form. A stamped signature is not permitted. An original, a copy, or a facsimile transmission (fax) of the power of attorney is acceptable so long as its authenticity is not reasonably disputed. For additional information regarding the power of attorney form, see section 7.02(2) of this revenue procedure.

The taxpayer's authorized representative, whether or not enrolled, must comply with Treasury Department Circular No. 230, which provides the rules for practice before the Service. In situations when the Service believes that the taxpayer's representative is not in compliance with Circular 230, the Service will bring the matter to the attention of the Office of Professional Responsibility.

Penalties of perjury statement

(15) **Penalties of perjury statement.**

(a) **Format of penalties of perjury statement.** A request for a letter ruling or determination letter and any change in the request submitted at a later time must be accompanied by the following declaration: **"Under penalties of perjury, I declare that I have examined [Insert, as appropriate: this request or this modification to the request], including accompanying documents, and, to the best of my knowledge and belief, [Insert, as appropriate: the request orthe** modification] contains all the relevant facts relating to the request, and such facts are true, correct, and complete."

See section 8.05(4) of this revenue procedure for the penalties of perjury statement applicable for submissions of additional information.

(b) Signature by taxpayer. The declaration must be signed and dated by the taxpayer, not the taxpayer's representative. A stamped signature or faxed signature is not permitted.

The person who signs for a corporate taxpayer must be an officer of the corporate taxpayer who has personal knowledge of the facts and whose duties are not limited to obtaining a letter ruling or determination letter from the Service. If the corporate taxpayer is a member of an affiliated group filing consolidated returns, a penalties of perjury statement must also be signed and submitted by an officer of the common parent of the group.

The person signing for a trust, a state law partnership, or a limited liability company must be, respectively, a trustee, general partner, or member-manager who has personal knowledge of the facts.

Number of copies of request to be submitted

(16) Number of copies of request to be submitted. Generally, a taxpayer needs only to submit one copy of the request for a letter ruling or determination letter. If, however, more than one issue is presented in the letter ruling request, the taxpayer is encouraged to submit additional copies of the request.

Further, two copies of the request for a letter ruling or determination letter are required if—

(a) the taxpayer is requesting separate letter rulings or determination letters on different issues as explained later under section 7.02(1) of this revenue procedure; or

(b) the taxpayer is requesting deletions other than names, addresses, and identifying numbers, as explained in section 7.01(11)(a) of this revenue procedure (one copy is the request for the letter ruling or determination letter and the second copy is the deleted version of such request); or

(c) a closing agreement (as defined in section 2.02 of this revenue procedure) is being requested on the issue presented.

Sample of a letter ruling request

(17) Sample format for a letter ruling request. Sample format for a letter ruling request. To assist a taxpayer or the taxpayer's representative in preparing a letter ruling request, a sample format for a letter ruling request is provided in Appendix B of this revenue procedure. This format is not required to be used by the taxpayer or the taxpayer's representative.

Checklist

(18) Checklist for letter ruling requests. Checklist for letter ruling requests. The Associate office will be able to respond more quickly to a taxpayer's letter ruling request if the request is carefully prepared and complete. Thechecklist in

¶1651

Appendix C of this revenue procedure is designed to assist taxpayers in preparing a request by reminding them of the essential information and documents to be furnished with the request. The checklist in Appendix C must be completed to the extent required by the instructions in the checklist, signed and dated by the taxpayer or the taxpayer's representative, and placed on top of the letter ruling request. If the checklist in Appendix C is not received, a branch representative will ask the taxpayer or the taxpayer's representative to submit the checklist, which may delay action on the letter ruling request.

For letter ruling requests on certain matters, specific checklists supplement the checklist in Appendix C. These checklists are listed in section 1 of Appendix E of this revenue procedure and must also be completed and placed on top of the letter ruling request along with the checklist in Appendix C.

Copies of the checklist in Appendix C can be obtained by calling (202) 622-7560 (not a toll-free call) or a copy can be obtained from this revenue procedure in Internal Revenue Bulletin 2004-1 on the IRS web site at www.irs.gov by accessing the Newsroom link, and then the IRS Guidance link, to obtain Internal Revenue Bulletin 2004-1. A photocopy of this checklist may be used.

Additional information required in certain circumstances

.02

Multiple issues

(1) To request separate letter rulings for multiple issues in a single situation. If more than one issue is presented in a request for a letter ruling, the Associate office generally will issue a single letter ruling covering all the issues. If the taxpayer requests separate letter rulings on any of the issues (because, for example, one letter ruling is needed sooner than another), the Associate office usually will comply with the request unless it is not feasible or not in the best interests of the Associate office to do so. A taxpayer who wants separate letter rulings on multiple issues should make this clear in the request and submit the original and two copies of the request.

In issuing each letter ruling, the Associate office will state that it has issued separate letter rulings or that requests for other letter rulings are pending.

Power of attorney used to indicate recipient of original or copy

(2) To indicate recipient of original or copy of letter ruling or determination letter. Unless the most recent power of attorney provides otherwise, the Service will send the original of the letter ruling or determination letter to the taxpayer and a copy of the letter ruling or determination letter to the taxpayer's representative. In this case, the letter ruling or determination letter is addressed to the taxpayer. It is preferred that Form 2848, Power of Attorney and Declaration of Representative, be used to provide the representative's authority.

When a taxpayer has more than one representative, the Service will send the copy of the letter ruling or determination letter to the first representative named on the most recent power of attorney. If the taxpayer wants an additional copy of the letter ruling or determination letter sent to the second representative listed in the power of attorney, the taxpayer must check the appropriate box on Form 2848. If this form is not used, the taxpayer must state in the power of attorney that a copy of the letter ruling or determination letter is also to be sent to the second representative listed in the power of attorney. Copies of the letter ruling or determination letter will be sent to no more than two representatives.

The taxpayer may check the appropriate box on Form 2848 or indicate in a power of attorney that the taxpayer does not want a copy of the letter ruling or determination letter to be sent to the taxpayer's representative.

The taxpayer may check the appropriate box on Form 2848 or indicate in a power of attorney that the taxpayer requests that the original of the letter ruling or determination letter be sent to the taxpayer's representative. In this case, a copy of the letter ruling or determination letter will be sent to the taxpayer.

"Two-Part" letter ruling requests

(3) To request a particular conclusion on a proposed transaction. A taxpayer who is requesting a particular conclusion on a proposed transaction may make the request for a letter ruling in two parts. This type of request is referred to as a "two-part" letter ruling request. The first part must include the complete statement of facts and related documents described in section 7.01 of this revenue procedure. The second part must include a summary statement of the facts the taxpayer believes to be controlling in reaching the conclusion requested.

If the Associate office accepts the taxpayer's statement of controlling facts, it will base its letter ruling on these facts. Ordinarily, this statement will be incorporated into the letter ruling. The Associate office reserves the right to rule on the basis of a more complete statement of the facts and to seek more information in developing the facts and restating them.

A taxpayer who chooses this two-part procedure has all the rights and responsibilities provided in this revenue procedure.

Taxpayers may not use the two-part procedure if it is inconsistent with other procedures, such as those dealing with requests for permission to change accounting methods or periods, applications for recognition of exempt status under § 521, or rulings on employment tax status.

After the Associate office has resolved the issues presented by a letter ruling request, the Associate office representative may request that the taxpayer submit a proposed draft of the letter ruling to expedite the issuance of the ruling. See section 8.07 of this revenue procedure.

Expedited handling

(4) To request expedited handling. The Service ordinarily processes requests for letter rulings and determination letters in order of the date received. Expedited handling means that a request is processed ahead of the regular order. Expedited handling is granted only in rare and unusual cases, both out of fairness to other taxpayers and because the Service seeks to process all requests as expeditiously as possible and to give appropriate deference to normal business exigencies in all cases not involving expedited handling.

A taxpayer who has a compelling need to have a request processed ahead of the regular order may request expedited handling. This request must explain in detail the need for expedited handling. The request must be made in writing, preferably in a separate letter with, or soon after filing, the request for the letter ruling or determination letter. If the request is not made in a separate letter, then the letter in which the letter ruling or determination letter request is made should say, at the top of the first page: **"Expedited Handling Is Requested. See page _ of this letter."**

A request for expedited handling will not be forwarded to a rulings branch for action until the check for the user fee is received.

Whether a request for expedited handling will be granted is within the Service's discretion. The Service may grant the request when a factor outside a taxpayer's control creates a real business need to obtain a letter ruling or determination letter before a certain time in order to avoid serious business consequences. Examples include situations in which a court or governmental agency has imposed a specific deadline for the completion of a transaction, or a transaction must be completed expeditiously to avoid an imminent business emergency (such as the hostile takeover of a corporate taxpayer), provided that the taxpayer can demonstrate that the deadline or business emergency, and the need for expedited handling, resulted from circumstances that could not reasonably have been anticipated or controlled by the taxpayer. To qualify for expedited handling in such situations, the taxpayer must also demonstrate that the taxpayer submitted the request as promptly as possible after becoming aware of the deadline or emergency. The extent to which the letter ruling or determination letter complies with all of the applicable requirements of this revenue procedure, and fully and clearly presents the issues, is a factor in determining whether expedited treatment will be granted. When the Service agrees to process a request out of order, it cannot give assurance that any letter ruling or determination letter will be processed by the time requested.

The scheduling of a closing date for a transaction or a meeting of the board of directors or shareholders of a corporation, without regard for the time it may take to obtain a letter ruling or determination letter, will not be considered a sufficient reason to process a request ahead of its regular order. Also, the possible effect of fluctuation in the market price of stocks on a transaction will not be considered a sufficient reason to process a request out of order.

Because most requests for letter rulings and determination letters cannot be processed ahead of the regular order, the Service urges all taxpayers to submit their requests well in advance of the contemplated transaction. In addition, to facilitate prompt action on letter ruling requests, taxpayers are encouraged to ensure that their initial submissions comply with all of the requirements of this revenue procedure (including the requirements of other applicable guidelines set forth in section 9 of this revenue procedure), to prepare "two-part" requests described in section 7.02(3) of this revenue procedure when possible, and to provide any additional information requested by the Service promptly.

Facsimile transmission (fax) to taxpayer or taxpayer's authorized representative of any document related to the letter ruling request

(5) Taxpayer requests to receive any document related to the letter ruling request by facsimile transmission (fax). If the taxpayer requests, a copy of any document related to the letter ruling request may be faxed to the taxpayer or the taxpayer's authorized representative (for example, a request for additional information or the letter ruling).

A request to fax a copy of any document related to the letter ruling request to the taxpayer or the taxpayer's authorized representative must be made in writing, either as part of the original letter ruling request or prior to the mailing, or with respect to the letter ruling prior to the signing, of the document. The request must contain the fax number of the taxpayer or the taxpayer's authorized representative to whom the document is to be faxed.

A document other than the letter ruling will be faxed by a branch representative. The letter ruling may be faxed by either a branch representative or the Docket, Records, and User Fee Branch of the Legal Processing Division (CC:PA:LPD:DRU). For purposes of § 301.6110-2(h), a letter ruling is not issued until the ruling is mailed.

Requesting a conference

(6) To request a conference. A taxpayer who wants to have a conference on the issues involved should indicate this in writing when, or soon after, filing the request. *See also* sections 10.01, 10.02, and 11.11(2) of this revenue procedure.

Address to send the request

.03 Original letter ruling requests must be sent to the appropriate Associate office. The package should be marked: RULING REQUEST SUBMISSION.

(1) Requests for letter rulings should be sent to the following address:

Internal Revenue Service
Attn: CC:PA:LPD:DRU
P.O. Box 7604
Ben Franklin Station
Washington, D.C. 20044

If a private delivery service is used, the address is:

Internal Revenue Service
Attn: CC:PA:LPD:DRU, Room 5336
1111 Constitution Avenue, N.W.
Washington, D.C. 20044

(2) Requests for letter rulings may also be hand delivered between the hours of 8:00 a.m. and 4:00 p.m. to the courier's desk at the loading dock (behind the 12th Street security station) of 1111 Constitution Avenue, N.W., Washington, D.C. A receipt will be given at the courier's desk. The package should be addressed to:

¶1651

Courier's Desk
Internal Revenue Service
Attn: CC:PA:LPD:DRU, Room 5336
1111 Constitution Avenue, N.W.
Washington, D.C. 20044

Requests for determination letters

(3) Requests for letter rulings must not be submitted by fax

Pending letter ruling requests

.04

(1) Circumstances under which the taxpayer must notify the Associate office. The taxpayer must notify the Associate office if, after the letter ruling request is filed but before a letter ruling is issued, the taxpayer knows that—

(a) an examination of the issue or the identical issue on an earlier year's return has been started by a field office;

(b) in the case of a §301.9100 request, an examination of the return for the taxable year in which an election should have been made or any taxable year that would have been affected by the election had it been timely made, has been started by a field office. *See* §301.9100-3(e)(4)(i) and section 5.02(3) of this revenue procedure;

(c) legislation that may affect the transaction has been introduced. *See* section 7.01(10) of this revenue procedure; or

(d) another letter ruling request (including an application for change in accounting method) has been submitted by the taxpayer (or a related party within the meaning of §267 or a member of an affiliated group of which the taxpayer is also a member within the meaning of §1504) involving the same or similar issue that is currently pending with the Service.

(2) Taxpayer must notify the Associate office if a return is filed and must attach the request to the return. If the taxpayer files a return before a letter ruling is received from the Associate office concerning the issue, the taxpayer must notify the Associate office that the return has been filed. The taxpayer must also attach a copy of the letter ruling request to the return to alert the field office and thereby avoid premature field action on the issue.

If the taxpayer requests a letter ruling after the return is filed, but before the return is examined, the taxpayer must notify the Associate office that the returnhas been filed. The taxpayer must also notify the field office having jurisdiction over the return and attach a copy of the letter ruling request to the notification to alert the field office and thereby avoid premature field action on the issue.

This section 7.04 also applies to pending requests for a closing agreement on a transaction for which a letter ruling is not requested or issued.

When to attach ruling to return

.05 A taxpayer who receives a letter ruling before filing a return about any transaction that is relevant to the return being filed must attach a copy of the letter ruling to the return when it is filed.

How to check on status of request

.06 The taxpayer or the taxpayer's authorized representative may obtain information regarding the status of a request by calling the person whose name and telephone number are shown on the acknowledgment of receipt of the request or the appropriate branch representative who contacts the taxpayer as explained in section 8.02 of this revenue procedure.

Request may be withdrawn or Associate office may decline to issue letter ruling

.07

(1) **In general.** A taxpayer may withdraw a request for a letter ruling or determination letter at any time before the letter ruling or determination letter is signed by the Service. Correspondence and exhibits related to a request that is withdrawn or related to a letter ruling request for which the Associate office declines to issue a letter ruling will not be returned to the taxpayer. See section 7.01(2) of this revenue procedure. In appropriate cases, the Service may publish its conclusions in a revenue ruling or revenue procedure.

(2) **Notification of appropriate Service official.**

(a) **Letter ruling requests.** If a taxpayer withdraws a letter ruling request or if the Associate office declines to issue a letter ruling, the Associate office generally will notify, by memorandum, the appropriate Service official in the operating division that has examination jurisdiction of the taxpayer's tax return and may give its views on the issues in the request to the Service official to consider in any later examination of the return. This section 7.07(2)(a) generally does not apply if the taxpayer withdraws the letter ruling request and submits a written statement that the transaction has been, or is being, abandoned and if the Associate office has not already formed an adverse opinion. See, in appropriate cases, section 7.07(1) above.

(b) **Notification of Service official may constitute Chief Counsel Advice.** If the memorandum to the Service official referred to in paragraph (a) of this section 7.07(2) provides more than the fact that the request was withdrawn and the Associate office was tentatively adverse, or that the Associate office declines to issue a letter ruling, the memorandum may constitute Chief Counsel Advice, as defined in §6110(i)(1), subject to disclosure under §6110.

(3) **Refund of user fee.** Ordinarily, the user fee will not be returned for a letter ruling request that is withdrawn. If the Associate office declines to issue a letter ruling on all of the issues in the request, the user fee will be returned. If the Associate office issues a letter ruling on some, but not all, of the issues, the user fee will not be returned. See section 15.10 of this revenue procedure for additional information regarding the refunds of user fees.

SECTION 8. HOW DOES THE ASSOCIATE OFFICE HANDLE LETTER RULING REQUESTS?

The Associate office will issue letter rulings on the matters and under the circumstances explained in sections 3 and 5 of this revenue procedure and in the manner explained in this section and section 11 of this revenue procedure. See section 9 of this revenue procedure for procedures for change in accounting method requests.

Controls request and refers it to appropriate Associate Chief Counsel's office

.01 All requests for letter rulings will be controlled by the Docket, Records, and User Fee Branch of the Legal Processing Division of the Associate Chief Counsel (Procedure and Administration) (CC:PA:LPD:DRU). That office will process the incoming documents and the user fee and will forward the file to the appropriate Associate Chief Counsel's office for assignment.

Branch representative contacts taxpayer within 21 days

.02 Within 21 calendar days after a letter ruling request has been received in the branch having jurisdiction, a representative of the branch will discuss the procedural issues in the letter ruling request with the taxpayer or, if the request includes a properly executed power of attorney, with the authorized representative unless the power of attorney provides otherwise. If the case is complex or a number of issues are involved, it may not be possible for the branch representative to discuss the substantive issues during this initial contact. When possible, for each issue within the branch's jurisdiction, the branch representative will tell the taxpayer—

(1) whether the branch representative will recommend that the Associate office rule as the taxpayer requested, rule adversely on the matter, or not rule;

(2) whether the taxpayer should submit additional information to enable the Associate office to rule on the matter;

(3) whether the letter ruling complies with all the provisions of this revenue procedure, and if not, which requirements have not been met; or

(4) whether, because of the nature of the transaction or the issue presented, a tentative conclusion on the issue cannot be reached.

If the letter ruling request involves matters within the jurisdiction of more than one branch or Associate offices, a representative of the branch that received the original request will tell the taxpayer within the initial 21 days—

(1) that the matters within the jurisdiction of another branch or office have been referred to that branch or office for consideration, and the date the referralwas made, and

(2) that a representative of that branch or office will contact the taxpayer within 21 calendar days after receiving the referral to discuss informally the procedural and, to the extent possible, the substantive issues in the request.

This section 8.02 applies to all matters except for cases involving a request for change in accounting method or accounting period and cases within the jurisdiction of the Associate Chief Counsel (Financial Institutions and Products) concerning insurance issues requiring actuarial computations.

Determines if transaction can be modified to obtain favorable letter ruling

.03 If less than a fully favorable letter ruling is indicated, the branch representative will tell the taxpayer whether minor changes in the transaction or adherence to certain published positions would bring about a favorable ruling. The branch representative may also tell the taxpayer the facts that must be furnished in a document to comply with Service requirements. The branch representative will not suggest precise changes that would materially alter the form of the proposed transaction or materially alter a taxpayer's proposed accounting period.

If, at the end of this discussion, the branch representative determines that a meeting in the Associate office would be more helpful to develop or exchange information, a meeting will be offered and an early meeting date arranged. When offered, this meeting is in addition to the taxpayer's conference of right that is described in section 10.02 of this revenue procedure.

Is not bound by informal opinion expressed

.04 The Service will not be bound by the informal opinion expressed by the branch representative or any other Service representative, and such an opinion cannot be relied upon as a basis for obtaining retroactive relief under the provisions of §7805(b).

Additional information

.05 Must be submitted within 21 calendar days

(1) **Additional information must be submitted within 21 days.** If the request lacks essential information, which may include additional information needed to satisfy the procedural requirements of this revenue procedure as well as substantive changes to transactions or documents needed from the taxpayer, the branch representative will tell the taxpayer during the initial contact, or subsequent contacts, that the request will be closed if the Associate office does not receive the information within 21 calendar days from the date of the request for additional information, unless an extension of time is granted. To facilitate prompt action on letter ruling requests, taxpayers are encouraged to request that the Associate office request additional information by fax. *See* section 7.02(5) of this revenue procedure.

Material facts furnished to the Associate office by telephone or fax, or orally at a conference, must be promptly confirmed by letter to the Associate office. This confirmation and any additional information requested by the Associate office thatis not part of the information requested during the initial contact must be furnished within 21 calendar days from the date the Associate office makes the request.

Extension of reply period if justified and approved

(2) **Extension of reply period.** An extension of the 21-day period for providing additional information will be granted only if justified in writing by the

taxpayer and approved by the branch reviewer. A request for extension should be submitted before the end of the 21-day period. If unusual circumstances close to the end of the 21-day period make a written request impractical, the taxpayer should notify the Associate office within the 21-day period that there is a problem and that the written request for extension will be coming soon. The taxpayer will be told promptly, and later in writing, of the approval or denial of the requested extension. If the extension request is denied, there is no right of appeal.

Letter ruling request closed if the taxpayer does not submit additional information

(3) **Letter ruling request closed if the taxpayer does not submit additional information.** If the taxpayer does not submit the information requested during the initial contact, or subsequent contacts, within the time provided, the letter ruling request will be closed and the taxpayer will be notified in writing. If the information is received after the request is closed, the request will be reopened and treated as a new request as of the date the information is received. The taxpayer must pay another user fee before the case can be reopened.

Penalties of perjury statement for additional information

(4) **Penalties of perjury statement.** Additional information submitted to the Service must be accompanied by the following declaration: "Under penalties of perjury, I declare that I have examined this information, including accompanying documents, and, to the best of my knowledge and belief, the information contains all the relevant facts relating to the request for the information, and such facts are true, correct, and complete." This declaration must be signed in accordance with the requirements in section 7.01(15)(b) of this revenue procedure.

Faxing request and additional information

(5) **Faxing request and additional information.** To facilitate prompt action on letter ruling requests, taxpayers are encouraged to request that the Associate office request additional information by fax. *See* section 7.02(5) of this revenue procedure. Taxpayers also are encouraged to submit additional information by fax as soon as the information is available. The Associate office representative who requests additional information can provide a telephone number to which the information can be faxed. A copy of this information and a signed perjury statement must be mailed or delivered to the Associate office.

Address to send additional information

(6) **Address to send additional information.**

(a) If a private delivery service is not used, the additional information should be sent to:

> Internal Revenue ServiceADDITIONAL INFORMATION
> Attn: [Name, office symbols, and
> room number of the Associate office
> representative who requested
> the information]

P.O. Box 7604
Ben Franklin Station
Washington, D.C. 20044

For cases involving a request for change in period under the jurisdiction of the Associate Chief Counsel (Income Tax and Accounting), or a §301.9100 request for an extension of time on a request for change in accounting method or period, the additional information should be sent to:

Internal Revenue Service
ADDITIONAL INFORMATION
Attn: [Name, office symbols, and
room number of the Associate office
representative who requested
the information]
P.O. Box 14095
Ben Franklin Station
Washington, D.C. 20044

(b) If a private delivery service is used, the additional information for all cases should be sent to:

Internal Revenue Service
ADDITIONAL INFORMATION
Attn: [Name, office symbols, and
room number of the Associate office
representative who requested
the information]
1111 Constitution Ave., N.W.
Washington, D.C. 20224

Identifying information included in additional information

(7) **Identifying information.** For all cases, the additional information should include the name, office symbols, and room number of the Associate office representative who requested the information, and the taxpayer's name and the case control number, which the Associate office representative can provide.

Number of copies of additional information to be submitted

(8) **Number of copies.** Generally, a taxpayer needs only to submit one copy of the additional information, although in appropriate cases, the Associate office may request additional copies of the information.

Near the completion of the ruling process, advises the taxpayer of conclusionsand, if the Associate office will rule adversely, offers the taxpayer the opportunity to withdraw the letter ruling request

.06 Generally, after the conference of right as discussed in section 10 of this revenue procedure is held but before the letter ruling is issued, the branch representative will orally inform the taxpayer or the taxpayer's representative of the Associate office's conclusions. If the Associate office is going to rule adversely, the taxpayer will be offered the opportunity to withdraw the letter ruling

¶1651

request. Unless an extension is granted, if the taxpayer or the taxpayer's representative does not notify the branch representative of a decision to withdraw the ruling request within 10 days of the notification, the adverse letter ruling will be issued. The user fee will not be refunded for a letter ruling request that is withdrawn. *See* section 15.10(1)(a) of this revenue procedure.

May request draft of proposed letter ruling near the completion of the ruling process

.07 To accelerate the issuance of letter rulings, in appropriate cases near the completion of the ruling process, the Associate office representative may request that the taxpayer or the taxpayer's representative submit a proposed draft of the letter ruling on the basis of discussions of the issues. The taxpayer is not required to prepare a draft letter ruling to receive a letter ruling.

The format of the submission should be discussed with the Associate office representative who requests the draft letter ruling. The representative usually can provide a sample format of a letter ruling and will discuss the facts, analysis, and letter ruling language to be included.

Taxpayer may also submit draft on a computer disk

In addition to a typed draft, taxpayers are encouraged to submit this draft on a computer disk in Microsoft Word to the Associate office. The typed draft will become part of the permanent files of the Associate office, and the computer disk will not be returned. The proposed letter ruling (both typed draft and computer disk) should be sent to the same address as any additional information and contain in the transmittal the information that should be included with any additional information (for example, a penalties of perjury statement is required). *See* section 8.05(4) of this revenue procedure.

Issues separate letter rulings for substantially identical letter rulings and generally issues a single letter ruling for related § 301.9100 letter.

.08

(1) Substantially identical letter rulings. For letter ruling requests qualifying for the user fee provided in paragraph (A)(5)(a) of Appendix A of this revenue procedure for substantially identical letter rulings, a separate letter ruling will be issued for each entity with a common member or sponsor, or for each member of a common entity.

(2) Related § 301.9100 letter rulings. For a § 301.9100 letter ruling request from a consolidated group for an extension of time to file Form 3115 for an identical change in accounting method qualifying for the user fee provided in paragraph (A)(5)(c) of Appendix A of this revenue procedure, the Associate officegenerally will issue a single letter on behalf of all members of the consolidated group that are the subject of the request.

Sends a copy of the letter ruling to appropriate Service official

.09 The Associate office will send a copy of the letter ruling, whether favorable or adverse, to the appropriate Service official in the operating division that has examination jurisdiction of the taxpayer's tax return.

SECTION 9. WHAT ARE THE SPECIFIC AND ADDITIONAL PROCEDURES FOR A REQUEST FOR A CHANGE IN ACCOUNTING METHOD FROM THE ASSOCIATE OFFICE?

This section provides the specific and additional procedures applicable to a request for a change in accounting method.

A request for a change in accounting method is a specialized type of request for a letter ruling (see section 2.01 of this revenue procedure).

Automatic and advance consent change in accounting method requests

.01

Automatic change in accounting method

(1) Automatic change in accounting method request procedures. Certain changes in accounting methods may be made under automatic change request procedures. A change in accounting method provided in an automatic change request procedure must be made using that automatic change request procedure if the taxpayer requesting the change is within the scope of the automatic change request procedure and the change is an automatic change for the requested year of the change. A qualifying taxpayer complying timely with an automatic change request procedure is granted the consent of the Commissioner to change the taxpayer's accounting method as provided in the automatic change request procedure. But see section 9.19 of this revenue procedure concerning review by the Associate office and the IRS director. See section 9.22 of this revenue procedure for a list of automatic change request procedures. See also section 9.23 of this revenue procedure for a list of sections, in addition to this section 9, and Appendices of this revenue procedure that apply to a request for an accounting method change. No user fee is required for a change made under an automatic change request procedure.

Advance consent change in accounting method

(2) Advance consent letter ruling requests. If a change in accounting method may not be made under an automatic change request procedure, the taxpayer may request an advance consent letter ruling by filing a current Form 3115, Application for Change in Accounting Method, under Rev. Proc. 97-27, 1997-1 C.B. 680, as modified and amplified by Rev. Proc. 2002-19, 2002-1 C.B. 696, and amplified and clarified by Rev. Proc. 2002-54, 2002-2 C.B. 432 (or successors); and this revenue procedure (see section 9.23 for a list of the sections and Appendices of this revenue procedure in addition to this section 9 that apply to a request for an accounting method change). A Form 3115 filed under Rev. Proc. 97-27 and this revenueprocedure is hereinafter referred to as an "advance consent Form 3115." A taxpayer filing an advance consent Form 3115 must submit the required user fee with the completed Form 3115. See section 15 and Appendix A of this revenue procedure for information about user fees.

Ordinarily only one change in accounting method on a Form 3115

.02 Ordinarily, a taxpayer may request only one change in accounting method on a Form 3115. If the taxpayer wants to request a change in accounting method for more than one unrelated item or submethod of accounting, the taxpayer must submit a separate Form 3115 for each unrelated item or sub-method, except in certain situations in which the Service specifically permits certain unrelated changes to be included on a single Form 3115 (for example, see section 5.05 in the Appendix of Rev. Proc. 2002-9, 2002-1 C.B. 327, or its successor).

Information required with a Form 3115

.03

Facts and other information

(1) Facts and other information requested on Form 3115 and in applicable revenue procedures. In general, a taxpayer requesting a change in accounting method must file a Form 3115 unless the procedures applicable to the specific type of change in accounting method do not require a Form 3115 to be submitted.

The taxpayer must provide all information requested in the Form 3115 and its instructions, in either Rev. Proc. 97-27 or the applicable automatic change request procedure, and in the applicable sections of this revenue procedure, including a detailed and complete description of the item being changed, the taxpayer's present and proposed method for the item being changed, information regarding whether the taxpayer is under examination, or before Appeals or a federal court, and a summary of the computation of the section 481(a) adjustment and an explanation of the methodology used to determine the adjustment.

For an advance consent Form 3115, the taxpayer must also include a full explanation of the legal basis and relevant authorities supporting the proposed method, a detailed and complete description of the facts and explanation of how the law applies to the taxpayer's situation, whether the law in connection with the request is uncertain or inadequately addresses the issue, statement of the applicant's reasons for the proposed change, and copies of all documents related to the proposed change.

The applicant must provide the requested information to be eligible for approval of the requested accounting method change. The taxpayer may be required to provide information specific to the requested accounting method change, such as an attached statement. The taxpayer must provide all information relevant to the requested accounting method change, even if not specifically requested by the Form 3115.

See also sections 7.01(1) and 7.01(8) of this revenue procedure.

Statement of authorities contrary to taxpayer's views

(2) Statement of contrary authorities. For an advance consent Form 3115, the taxpayer is encouraged to inform the Associate office about, and discuss theimplications of, any authority believed to be contrary to the proposed change in accounting method, such as legislation, court decisions, regulations, notices, revenue rulings, revenue procedures, or announcements.

If the taxpayer does not furnish either contrary authorities or a statement that none exists, the Associate office may request submission of contrary authorities or a statement that none exists. Failure to comply with this request may result in the Associate office's refusal to issue a change in accounting method letter ruling.

Documents

(3) Copies of all contracts, agreements, and other documents. True copies of all contracts, agreements, and other documents pertinent to the requested change in accounting method must be submitted with an advance consent Form 3115. Original documents should not be submitted because they become part of the Associate office's file and will not be returned.

Analysis of material facts

(4) Analysis of material facts. When submitting any document with a Form 3115 or in a supplemental letter, the taxpayer must explain and provide an analysis of all material facts in the document (rather than merely incorporating the document by reference). The analysis of the facts must include their bearing on the requested change in accounting method, specifying the provisions that apply.

Same issue in an earlier return

(5) Information regarding whether same issue is in an earlier return. A Form 3115 must state whether, to the best of the knowledge of both the taxpayer and the taxpayer's representative, any return of the taxpayer (or any return of a current or former consolidated group in which the taxpayer is or was a member) in which the taxpayer used the accounting method being changed is under examination, before Appeals, or before a federal court. See Rev. Proc. 97-27 and Rev. Proc. 2002-9, both as modified and amplified by Rev. Proc. 2002-19.

Issue previously submitted or currently pending

(6) Statement regarding prior requests for a change in accounting method and other pending requests.

(a) Other requests for a change in accounting method within the past five years. A Form 3115 must state, to the best of the knowledge of both the taxpayer and the taxpayer's representatives, whether the taxpayer (or a related taxpayer within the meaning of §267 or a member of a current or former affiliated group of which the taxpayer is or was a member within the meaning of §1504) or a predecessor filed or is currently filing any request for a change in accounting method within the past five years (including the year of the requested change).

If the statement is affirmative, for each separate trade or business, give a description of each request and the year of change and whether consent was obtained. If any application was withdrawn, not perfected, or denied, or if a Consent Agreement was sent to the taxpayer but was not signed and returned to the Associate office, or if the change was not made in the requested year of change,give an explanation.

(b) Any other pending request(s). A Form 3115 must state, to the best of the knowledge of both the taxpayer and the taxpayer's representatives, whether the taxpayer (or a related taxpayer within the meaning of §267 or a member a current or former affiliated group of which the taxpayer is or was a member within the meaning of § 1504) or a predecessor currently have pending (including any concurrently filed request) any request for a private letter ruling, a change in accounting method, or a technical advice.

If the statement is affirmative, for each request, give the name(s) of the taxpayer, identification number(s), the type of request (private letter ruling, request for change in accounting method, or request for technical advice), and the specific issues in the request.

Statement identifying pending legislation

(7) Statement identifying pending legislation. At the time the taxpayer files an advance consent Form 3115, the taxpayer must identify any pending legislation that may affect the proposed change in accounting method. In addition, if legislation is introduced after the request is filed but before a change in accounting method letter ruling is issued, the taxpayer must so notify the Associate office.

Authorized representatives

(8) Authorized representatives. To appear before the Service in connection with a request for a change in accounting method, the taxpayer's authorized representative must be an attorney, a certified public accountant, an enrolled agent, an enrolled actuary, a person with a "Letter of Authorization," an employee, general partner, bona fide officer, administrator, trustee, etc., or a foreign representative, as described in section 7.01(13) of this revenue procedure.

Power of attorney and declaration of representative

(9) Power of attorney and declaration of representative. Any authorized representative, whether or not enrolled to practice, must comply with Treasury Department Circular No. 230, which provides the rules for practice before the Service, and the conference and practice requirements of the Statement of Procedural Rules, which provide the rules for representing a taxpayer before the Service. See section 7.01(14) of this revenue procedure.

Penalties of perjury statement

(10) Penalties of perjury statement

(a) Format of penalties of perjury statement. A Form 3115, and any change to a Form 3115 submitted at a later time, must be accompanied by the following declaration: "Under penalties of perjury, I declare that I have examined this application, including accompanying schedules and statements, and to the best of my knowledge and belief, the application contains all the relevant facts relating to the application, and it is true, correct, and complete."

See section 9.08(3) of this revenue procedure for the penalties of perjury statement required for submissions of additional information.

(b) Signature by taxpayer. A Form 3115 must be signed by, or on behalf of, the taxpayer requesting the change by an individual with authority to bind thetaxpayer in such matters. For example, an officer must sign on behalf of a

¶1651

corporation, a general partner on behalf of a state law partnership, a member-manager on behalf of a limited liability company, a trustee on behalf of a trust, or an individual taxpayer on behalf of a sole proprietorship. If the taxpayer is a member of a consolidated group, a Form 3115 should be submitted on behalf of the taxpayer by the common parent and must be signed by a duly authorized officer of the common parent. See the signature requirements set forth in the instructions for the current Form 3115 regarding those who are to sign. See also section 8.08 of Rev. Proc. 97-27 and section 6.02(5) of Rev. Proc. 2002-9. A stamped signature or faxed signature is not permitted.

(c) Signature by preparer. Declaration of preparer (other than the taxpayer) is based on all information of which the preparer has any knowledge.

Additional procedural information required in certain circumstances

.04

Power of attorney used to indicate recipient of original and copy of correspondence

(1) To indicate recipient of original or copy of change in accounting method correspondence. Unless the most recent power of attorney provides otherwise, the Service will send the original of the change in accounting method letter ruling and other related correspondence to the taxpayer and a copy to the taxpayer's representative. In this case, the change in accounting method letter ruling and other related correspondence are addressed to the taxpayer. It is preferred that Form 2848, Power of Attorney and Declaration of Representative, be used to provide the representative's authority. *See* section 7.02(2) of this revenue procedure for how to designate alternative routings of the letter ruling and other correspondence.

Expedited handling

(2) To request expedited handling. The Associate office ordinarily processes advance consent Forms 3115 in order of the date received. A taxpayer who has a compelling need to have an advance consent Form 3115 processed on an expedited basis, may request expedited handling. See section 7.02(4) of this revenue procedure for procedures.

Facsimile transmission (fax) of any document to the taxpayer or taxpayer's authorized representative

(3) To receive the change in accounting method letter ruling or any other correspondence related to a Form 3115 by facsimile transmission (fax). If the taxpayer wants a copy of the change in accounting method letter ruling or any other correspondence related to a Form 3115, such as a request for additional information, faxed to the taxpayer or the taxpayer's authorized representative, the taxpayer must submit a written request to fax the letter ruling or related correspondence, preferably as part of the Form 3115. The request may be submitted at a later date, but must be received prior to the mailing of correspondence other than the letter ruling and prior to the signing of the change in accounting method letter ruling.

¶1651

The request to have correspondence relating to the Form 3115 faxed to the taxpayer must contain the fax number of the taxpayer or the taxpayer's authorized representative to whom the correspondence is to be faxed.

A document other than the change in accounting method letter ruling will be faxed by a branch representative. The change in accounting method letter ruling may be faxed by either a branch representative or the Docket, Records, and User Fee Branch of the Legal Processing Division of the Office of Associate Chief Counsel (Procedure and Administration) (CC:PA:LPD:DRU).

For purposes of § 301.6110-2(h), a change in accounting method letter ruling is not issued until the change in accounting method letter ruling is mailed.

Requesting a conference

(4) To request a conference. The taxpayer must complete the appropriate line on the Form 3115 to request a conference of right, or request a conference in a later written communication, if an adverse response is contemplated by the Associate office. See section 8.10 of Rev. Proc. 97-27, section 10.03 of Rev. Proc. 2002-9, and sections 10.01, 10.02 of this revenue procedure.

Associate office address to send Forms 3115

.05 **Associate office address to send Forms 3115.** Submit the original Form 3115, in the case of an advance consent Form 3115, or the national office copy of the Form 3115, in the case of an automatic change request, as follows:

(a) Associate office mailing address if private delivery service is not used. If a private delivery service is not used, a taxpayer, other than an exempt organization, must send the original completed Form 3115 and the required user fee (in the case of an advance consent Form 3115) or the national office copy of the completed Form 3115 (in the case of an automatic change request) to:

> Commissioner of Internal Revenue
> Attention: [insert either "CC:PA:LPD:DRU"
> for an advance consent Form 3115 or
> "CC:ITA-Automatic Ruling Branch" for
> an automatic change request]
> P.O. Box 7604
> Benjamin Franklin Station
> Washington, D.C. 20044

An exempt organization must send the original completed Form 3115 and the required user fee (in the case of an advance consent Form 3115) or the national office copy of the completed Form 3115 (in the case of an automatic change Form 3115) to:

> Internal Revenue Service
> Tax Exempt & Government Entities
> Attention: TEGE:EO
> P.O. Box 27720
> McPherson Station
> Washington, D.C. 20038

(b) Mailing address if private delivery service is used. If a private delivery service is used, a taxpayer, other than an exempt organization, must send the original completed Form 3115 and the required user fee (in the case of an advance consent Form 3115) or the national office copy of the completed Form 3115 (in the case of an automatic change request) to:

> Internal Revenue Service
> Attn: [insert either "CC:PA:LPD:DRU, Room
> 5336" for an advance consent Form 3115
> or "CC:ITA (Automatic Rulings Branch)"
> for an automatic change request]
> 1111 Constitution Ave., N.W.
> Washington, D.C. 20038

If a private delivery service is used, an exempt organization must send the original completed Form 3115 and the required user fee (in the case of an advance consent Form 3115) or the national office copy of the completed Form 3115 (in the case of an automatic change request) to:

> Internal Revenue Service
> Tax Exempt & Government Entities
> Attn: TEGE:EO
> 1750 Pennsylvania Ave., N.W.
> Washington, D.C. 20038

(c) Address if hand-delivered to the IRS Courier's desk. For taxpayers other than an exempt organization, the original completed Form 3115 and the required user fee (in the case of an advance consent Form 3115) or the national office copy of the completed Form 3115 (in the case of an automatic change request), may be hand delivered between the hours of 8:00 a.m. and 4:00 p.m. to the courier's desk at the loading dock (located behind the 12th Street security station) of 1111 Constitution Ave., N.W., Washington D.C. A receipt will be given at the courier's desk. The package should be addressed to:

> Courier's Desk
> Internal Revenue Service
> Attn: CC:PA:LPD:DRU, Room 5336
> 1111 Constitution Ave., N.W.
> Washington, D.C. 20224

A Form 3115 must not be submitted by fax

.06 A completed Form 3115 must not be submitted by fax.

Controls Form 3115 and refers it to the appropriate Associate Chief Counsel's office

.07 An advance consent Form 3115 is controlled by the Legal Processing Division staff of the Associate Chief Counsel (Procedure and Administration) upon receipt if the required user fee is submitted with the Form 3115. Once controlled, the Form 3115 is forwarded to the appropriate Associate Chief Counsel's office forassignment and processing.

¶1651

Additional information

.08

Incomplete Form 3115

(1) Incomplete Form 3115

(a) Advance consent Form 3115—21 day rule. In general, for an advance consent Form 3115, additional information requested by the Associate office and additional information furnished to the Associate office by telephone or fax must be furnished in writing within 21 calendar days from the date of the information request. The Associate office may impose a shorter reply period for a request for additional information made after an initial request. See section 10.06 of this revenue procedure for the 21-day rule for submitting information after any conference.

(b) Automatic change request—30 day rule. In general, for an automatic change in accounting method request, additional information requested by the Associate office, and additional information furnished to the Associate office by telephone or fax, must be furnished in writing within 30 calendar days from the date of the information request. The Associate office may impose a shorter reply period for a request for additional information made after an initial request. See section 10.06 of this revenue procedure for the 21-day rule for submitting information after any conference with the Associate office.

Extension of reply period

(2) Request for extension of reply period.

(a) Advance consent Form 3115. For an advance consent Form 3115, an additional period, not to exceed 15 days, to furnish information may be granted to a taxpayer. Any request for an extension of time must be made in writing and submitted prior to the last day of the original reply period. If unusual circumstances close to the end of the 21-day period make a written request impractical, the taxpayer should notify the Associate office within the 21-day period that there is a problem and that the written request for extension will be coming soon. An extension of the 21-day period will be granted only if approved by a branch reviewer. An extension of the 21-day period ordinarily will not be granted to furnish information requested on Form 3115. The taxpayer will be told promptly, and later in writing, of the approval or denial of the requested extension. If the extension request is denied, there is no right of appeal.

(b) Automatic change request. For an automatic change in accounting method request, an additional period, not to exceed 30 days, to furnish information may be granted to a taxpayer. Any request for an extension of time must be made in writing and submitted prior to the last day of the original reply period. If unusual circumstances close to the end of the 30-day period make a written request impractical, the taxpayer should notify the Associate office within the 30-day period that there is a problem and that the written request for extension will be coming soon. An extension of the 30-day period will be granted only if approved by a branch reviewer. An extension of the 30-day period ordinarily will not be grantedto furnish information requested on Form 3115. The taxpayer will be told promptly, and later in writing, of the approval or denial of the requested extension. If the extension request is denied, there is no right of appeal.

Penalties of perjury statement for additional information

(3) Penalties of perjury statement. Additional information submitted to the Associate office must be accompanied by the following declaration: "Under penalties of perjury, I declare that I have examined this information, including accompanying documents, and, to the best of my knowledge and belief, the information contains all the relevant facts relating to the request for the information, and such facts are true, correct, and complete." This declaration must be signed in accordance with the requirements in section 9.03(10)(b) of this revenue procedure.

Identifying information included in additional information

(4) Identifying information. The additional information should also include the name, office symbols, and room number of the Associate office representative who requested the information, and the taxpayer's name and the case control number, which the Associate office representative can provide.

Faxing information request and additional information

(5) Faxing information request and additional information. To facilitate prompt action on a change in accounting method ruling request, taxpayers are encouraged to request that the Associate office request additional information by fax. See section 9.04(3) of this revenue procedure.

Taxpayers also are encouraged to submit additional information by fax as soon as the information is available. The Associate office representative who requests additional information can provide a telephone number to which the information can be faxed. A copy of the requested information and an original signed penalties of perjury statement also must be mailed or delivered to the Associate office.

Address to send additional information

(6) Address to send additional information.

(a) Address if private delivery service not used. For a request for change in accounting method under the jurisdiction of the Associate Chief Counsel (Income Tax and Accounting), if a private delivery service is not used, the additional information should be sent to:

> Internal Revenue Service
> ADDITIONAL INFORMATION
> Attn: [Name, office symbols, and
> room number of the Associate office
> representative who requested
> the information]
> P.O. Box 14095
> Ben Franklin Station
> Washington, D.C. 20044

¶1651

For a request for change in accounting method for an exempt organization, ifa private delivery service is not used, the additional information should be sent to:

Internal Revenue Service
Tax Exempt & Government Entities
P.O. Box 27720
McPherson Station
Washington, D.C. 20038

For any other request for change in accounting method, if a private delivery service is not used, the additional information should be sent to:

Internal Revenue Service
ADDITIONAL INFORMATION
Attn: [Name, office symbols, and
room number of the Associate office
representative who requested
the information]
P.O. Box 7604
Ben Franklin Station
Washington, D.C. 20044

(b) Address if private delivery service is used.

For a request for a change in accounting method for other than an exempt organization, if a private delivery service is used, the additional information should be sent to:

Internal Revenue Service
ADDITIONAL INFORMATION
Attn: [Name, office symbols, and
room number of the Associate office
representative who requested
the information]
1111 Constitution Ave., N.W.
Washington, D.C. 20224

For a request for change in accounting method for an exempt organization, if a private delivery service is used the additional information should be sent to:

Internal Revenue Service
Tax Exempt & Government Entities
1750 Pennsylvania Ave., N.W.
Washington, D.C. 20038

Failure to timely submit additional information

(7) If taxpayer does not timely submit additional information.

(a) Advance consent Form 3115. In the case of an advance consent Form 3115, if the required information is not furnished to the Associate office within the reply period, the Form 3115 will not be processed and the case will be closed. The taxpayer or authorized representative will be so notified in writing.

¶1651

(b) Automatic change request. In the case of an automatic change in accounting method request, if the required information is not furnished to the Associate office within the reply period, the request does not qualify for the automatic consent procedure. In such a case, the Associate office will notify the taxpayer that consent to make the change in accounting method is not granted.

(c) Submitting the additional information at a later date. If the taxpayer wants to submit the additional information at a later date, the taxpayer must submit it with a new completed Form 3115 (and user fee, if applicable) for a year of change for which such new Form 3115 is timely filed under the applicable change in accounting method procedure.

Circumstances in which the taxpayer must notify the Associate office

.09 For an advance consent Form 3115, the taxpayer must promptly notify the Associate office if, after the Form 3115 is filed but before a change in accounting method letter ruling is issued, the taxpayer knows that—

(1) an examination of the present or proposed accounting method has been started by a field office;

(2) legislation that may affect the change in accounting method has been introduced (see section 9.03(7) of this revenue procedure); or

(3) another letter ruling request (including another Form 3115) has been submitted by the taxpayer (or a related party within the meaning of § 267 or a member of an affiliated group of which the taxpayer is a member within the meaning of § 1504).

Determines if proposed accounting method can be modified to obtain favorable letter ruling

.10 If a less than fully favorable change in accounting method letter ruling is indicated, the branch representative will tell the taxpayer whether minor changes in the proposed accounting method would bring about a favorable ruling. The branch representative will not suggest precise changes that materially alter a taxpayer's proposed accounting.

Near the completion of processing the Form 3115, advises the taxpayer if the Associate office will rule adversely and offers the taxpayer the opportunity to withdraw Form 3115

.11 Generally, after the conference of right is held (or offered, in the event no conference is held) and before issuing any change in accounting method letter ruling that is adverse to the requested change in accounting method, the taxpayer will be offered the opportunity to withdraw the Form 3115. See section 9.12 of this revenue procedure. Unless an extension is granted, if the taxpayer or the taxpayer's representative does not notify the branch representative of a decision to withdraw the Form 3115 within 10 days of the notification, the adverse change in accounting method letter ruling will be issued. Ordinarily, the user fee (in the case of an advance consent Form 3115) will not be refunded for a Form 3115 that is withdrawn.

Advance consent Form 3115 may be withdrawn or Associate office may decline to issue a change in accounting method letter ruling

.12

(1) In general. A taxpayer may withdraw an advance consent Form 3115 at any time before the change in accounting method letter ruling is signed by the Associate office. The Form 3115, correspondence, and any documents relating to the Form 3115 that is withdrawn or for which the Associate office declines to issue a letter ruling will not be returned to the taxpayer. See section 9.03(3) of this revenue procedure. In appropriate cases, the Service may publish its conclusions in a revenue ruling or revenue procedure.

(2) Notification of appropriate Service official. If a taxpayer withdraws or the Associate office declines to grant (for any reason) a request to change from or to an improper accounting method, the Associate office will notify, by memorandum, the appropriate Service official in the operating division that has examination jurisdiction of the taxpayer's tax return and the Change in Method of Accounting Technical Advisor, and may give its views on the issues in the request to the Service official to consider in any later examination of the return.

If the memorandum to the Service official provides more than the fact that the request was withdrawn and the Associate office was tentatively adverse, or that the Associate office declines to grant a change in accounting method, the memorandum may constitute Chief Counsel Advice, as defined in §6110(i)(1), subject to disclosure under §6110.

(3) Refund of user fee. Ordinarily, the user fee will not be returned for an advance consent Form 3115 that is withdrawn. See section 15.10 of this revenue procedure for information regarding refunds of user fees.

How to check status of a pending Form 3115

.13 The taxpayer or the taxpayer's authorized representative may obtain information regarding the status of an advance consent Form 3115 by calling the person whose name and telephone number are shown on the acknowledgement of receipt of the Form 3115.

Is not bound by informal opinion expressed

.14 The Service will not be bound by any informal opinion expressed by the branch representative or any other Service representative, and such an opinion cannot be relied upon as a basis for obtaining retroactive relief under the provisions of §7805(b).

Single letter ruling issued to a consolidated group for qualifying identical change in accounting method

.15 For an advance consent Form 3115 qualifying for the user fee provided in paragraph (A)(5)(b) of Appendix A of this revenue procedure for identical accounting method changes, the Associate office generally will issue a single letter ruling on behalf of all affected members of the consolidated group.

Letter ruling ordinarily not issued for one of two or more interrelated items or submethods

.16 If two or more items or submethods of accounting are interrelated, the Associate office ordinarily will not issue a letter ruling on a change in accounting method involving only one of the items or submethods.

Consent Agreement

.17 Ordinarily, for an advance consent Form 3115, the Commissioner's permission to change a taxpayer's accounting method is set forth in a letter ruling (original and a Consent Agreement copy). If the taxpayer agrees to the terms and conditions contained in the change in accounting method letter ruling, the taxpayer must sign and date the Consent Agreement copy of the letter ruling in the appropriate space. The Consent Agreement copy must not be signed by the taxpayer's representative. The signed copy of the letter ruling will constitute an agreement (Consent Agreement) within the meaning of § 1.481-4(b) of the regulations. The signed Consent Agreement must be returned to the Associate office within 45 days. In addition, a copy of the signed Consent Agreement copy of the change in accounting method letter ruling must be attached to the taxpayer's income tax return for the year of change. See section 8.11 of Rev. Proc. 97-27. If the taxpayer has filed its income tax return for the year of change before the ruling has been received and the consent agreement has been signed and returned, the copy of the signed consent agreement copy should be attached to the amended return for the year of change that the taxpayer files to implement the change in accounting method.

Sends a copy of the change in accounting method letter ruling to appropriate Service official

.18 The Associate office will send a copy of each change in accounting method letter ruling, whether favorable or adverse, to the appropriate Service official in the operating division that has examination jurisdiction of the taxpayer's tax return.

Consent to change an accounting method may be relied on subject to limitations

.19 A taxpayer may rely on a change in accounting method letter ruling received from the Associate office subject to certain conditions and limitations. See sections 9, 10, and 11 of Rev. Proc. 97-27, as modified and amplified by Rev. Proc. 2002-19.

A qualifying taxpayer complying timely with an automatic change request procedure may rely on the consent of the Commissioner as provided in the automatic change request procedure to change the taxpayer's accounting method, subject to certain conditions and limitations. See, in general, sections 6.01, 7 and 8 of Rev. Proc. 2002-9, as modified and amplified by Rev. Proc. 2002-19. The Associate office may review a Form 3115 filed under an automatic change request procedure and will notify the taxpayer if additional information is needed or if consent is not granted to the taxpayer for the requested change. See section 10 of Rev. Proc. 2002-9. Further, the IRS director having jurisdiction over the taxpayer's return may review the Form 3115. See section 9 of Rev. Proc. 2002-9.

Change in accounting method letter ruling will not apply to another taxpayer

.20 A taxpayer may not rely on a change in accounting method letter rulingissued to another taxpayer. See § 6110(k)(3).

Associate office discretion to permit requested change in accounting method

.21 The Associate office reserves the right to decline to process any advance consent Form 3115 in situations in which it would not be in the best interest of sound tax administration to permit the requested change. In this regard, the Associate office will consider whether the change in method of accounting would clearly and directly frustrate compliance efforts of the Service in administering the income tax laws. *See* section 8.01 of Rev. Proc. 97-27.

List of automatic change in accounting method request procedures

.22 For requests to change an accounting method, see the following automatic change request procedures published. A taxpayer complying timely with an automatic change request procedure will be deemed to have obtained the consent of the Commissioner to change the taxpayer's accounting method.

The automatic change request procedures for obtaining a change in accounting method include:

(1) Rev. Proc. 2002-9, 2002-1 C.B. 327, as modified and clarified by Announcement 2002-17, 2002-1 C.B. 561, as modified and amplified by Rev. Proc. 2002-19, 2002-1 C.B. 696, as amplified, clarified and modified by Rev. Proc. 2002-54, 2002-2 C.B. 432, and as modified by Rev. Proc. 2003-45, 2003-2 C.B. 11, which, for most (but not all) types of changes provided therein, requires a completed Form 3115. Rev. Proc. 2002-9 applies to the accounting method changes described in the Appendix of Rev. Proc. 2002-9 involving § § 56, 61, 77, 162, 166, 167, 168, 171, 174, 197, 263, 263A, 267, 404, 446, 448, 451, 454, 455, 458, 460, 461, 471, 472, 475, 585, 832, 846, 861, 985, 1272, 1273, 1278, 1281, 1286, and former § 168.

(2) The following automatic change request procedures modify and amplify Rev. Proc. 2002-9 in that they add the following changes to the list of accounting method changes listed in the Appendix of this revenue procedure:

Rev. Proc. 2002-27, 2002-1 C.B. 802 (section 168—depreciation of original and replacement tires of certain vehicles);

Rev. Proc. 2004-11, 2004-3 I.R.B. _, (revised sections 2.01 and 2.02 and 2B of the Appendix and added section 2.05 to the Appendix of Rev. Proc 2002-9);

Rev. Proc. 2003-50, 2003-29 I.R.B. 119 (sections 168(k) and 1400L(b)—additional relief);

Rev. Rul. 2003-54, 2003-1 C.B. 982 (section 168—depreciation of gas pump canopies);

Rev. Rul. 2003-81, 2003-30 I.R.B. 126 (section 168—depreciation of utility assets);

Rev. Proc. 2003-63, 2003-32 I.R.B. 304 (section 168—depreciation of cable TV fiber optics);

Rev. Proc. 2002-65, 2002-2 C.B. 700 (section 263—change to the track maintenance allowance method for the first or second taxable year ending on orafter December 31, 2001);

Rev. Rul. 2002-9, 2002-1 C.B. 614 (section 263A—impact fees incurred in connection with construction of a new residential rental building);

Rev. Rul. 2002-46, 2002-2 C.B. 117, as modified by Rev. Rul. 2002-73, 2002-2 C.B. 805 (section 404—grace period contributions);

Rev. Proc. 2002-28, 2002-1 C.B. 815 (section 446—certain small businesses who seek to change to the cash method and/or to a method of accounting for inventoriable items as materials and supplies that are not incidental);

Rev. Proc. 2002-36, 2002-1 C.B. 993 (section 451—certain taxpayers who purchase vehicles subject to leases who seek to change to the capital cost reduction (CCR) method);

Rev. Rul. 2003-3, 2003-1 C.B. 252 (section 451—accrual method taxpayer with state or local income or franchise tax refund);

Rev. Proc. 2002-17, 2002-1 C.B. 676 (section 471—certain automobile dealers seeking to change to the replacement cost method for vehicle parts inventory);

Rev. Proc. 2003-20, 2003-1 C.B. 445 (section 471—valuation of remanufactured motor vehicle core parts);

Rev. Proc. 2002-46, 2002-2 C.B. 105 (section 832—certain insurance companies seeking to change to safe harbor method for premium acquisition expenses); and

Rev. Proc. 2002-74, 2002-2 C.B. 980 (section 846—insurance companies other than life insurance companies computing discounted unpaid losses).

(3) The following automatic change request procedures, which require a completed Form 3115, provide both the type of accounting method change that may be made automatically and the procedures under which such change must be made:

Regs. § 1.166-2(d)(3) (bank conformity for bad debts);

Regs. § 1.448-1 (to an overall accrual method for the taxpayer's first taxable year it is subject to Code section 448);

Regs. § 1.448-2T and Notice 88-51 (nonaccrual experience method);

Regs. § 1.458-1 and -2 (exclusion for certain returned magazines, paperbacks, or records);

Rev. Proc. 97-43, 1997-2 C.B. 494 (section 475-electing out of certain exemptions from securities dealer status); and

¶1651

Rev. Proc. 91-51, 1991-2 C.B. 779 (section 1286-certain taxpayers under examination that sell mortgages and retain rights to service the mortgages).

(4) The following automatic change request procedures, which do not require a completed Form 3115, provide the type of accounting method change that may be made automatically and also provide the procedures under which such change must be made:

Notice 96-30, 1996-1 C.B 378 (section 446-change to comply with Statementof Financial Accounting Standards No. 116);

Rev. Proc. 92-29, 1992-1 C.B. 748 (section 461-change in real estate developer's method for including costs of common improvements in the basis of property sold);

Rev. Proc. 98-58, 1998-2 C.B. 710 (certain taxpayers seeking to change to the installment method of accounting under (453 for alternative minimum tax purposes for certain deferred payment sales contracts relating to property used or produced in the trade or business of farming);

Regs. § 1.472-2 (taxpayers changing to the last-in, first-out (LIFO) inventory method);

Code § 585(c) and Regs. § § 1.585-6 and 1.585-7 (large bank changing from the reserve method of section 585); and

Rev. Proc. 92-67, 1992-2 C.B. 429 (election under section 1278(b) to include market discount in income currently or election under section 1276(b) to use constant interest rate to determine accrued market discount).

Other sections of this revenue procedure that are applicable to a Form 3115

.23 In addition to this section 9, the following sections of this revenue procedure are applicable to Forms 3115:

1 (purpose of Rev. Proc. 2004-1);

2.01 (definition of "letter ruling");

2.02 (definition of "closing agreement");

2.05 (oral guidance);

3.01 (issues under the jurisdiction of the Associate Chief Counsel (Corporate));

3.02 (issues under the jurisdiction of the Associate Chief Counsel (Financial Institutions and Products));

3.03 (issues under the jurisdiction of the Associate Chief Counsel (Income Tax and Accounting));

3.04 (issues under the jurisdiction of the Associate Chief Counsel (International));

3.05 (issues under the jurisdiction of the Associate Chief Counsel (Passthroughs and Special Industries));

¶1651

3.07 (issues under the jurisdiction of the Associate Chief Counsel (Tax Exempt and Governmental Entities));

6.02 (letter rulings ordinarily not issued in certain areas because of the factual nature of the problem);

6.05 (letter rulings generally not issued to business associations or groups);

6.07 (letter rulings ordinarily not issued on federal tax consequences of proposed legislation);

6.09 (letter rulings not issued on frivolous issues);

6.11 (letter rulings not issued on alternative plans or hypothetical situation);

7.01(1) (statement of facts and other information);

7.01(8) (statement of supporting authorities);

7.01(13) (authorized representatives);

7.01(14) (power of attorney and declaration of representative);

7.02(2) (power of attorney used to indicate recipient of original or copy of correspondence);

7.02(4) (expedited handling);

10 (scheduling conferences);

15 (user fees);

16 (significant changes to Rev. Proc. 2003-1);

17 (effect of Rev. Proc. 2004-1 on other documents);

18 (effective date of this revenue procedure);

Appendix A (schedule of user fees); and

Appendix E (revenue procedures and notices regarding letter ruling requests relating to specific Code sections and subject matters).

SECTION 10. HOW ARE CONFERENCES FOR LETTER RULINGS SCHEDULED?

Schedules a conference if requested by taxpayer

.01 A taxpayer may request a conference regarding a letter ruling request. Normally, a conference is scheduled only when the Associate office considers it to be helpful in deciding the case or when an adverse decision is indicated. If conferences are being arranged for more than one request for a letter ruling involving the same taxpayer, they will be scheduled so as to cause the least inconvenience to the taxpayer. As stated in sections 7.02(6) and 9.04 of this revenue procedure, a taxpayer who wants to have a conference on the issue or issues involved should indicate this in writing when, or soon after, filing the request.

If a conference has been requested, the taxpayer or the taxpayer's representative will be notified by telephone, if possible, of the time and place of the conference, which must then be held within 21 calendar days after this contact.

Instructions for requesting an extension of the 21-day period and notifying the taxpayer or the taxpayer's representative of the Associate office's approval or denial of the request for extension are the same as those explained in section 8.05(2) (section 9.08(2)(a) for a change in accounting method request) of this revenue procedure regarding providing additional information.

Permits taxpayer one conference of right

.02 A taxpayer is entitled, as a matter of right, to only one conference in the Associate office, except as explained under section 10.05 of this revenue procedure. This conference is normally held at the branch level and is attended by a person who has the authority to sign the letter ruling in his or her own name or for the branch chief.

When more than one branch has taken an adverse position on an issue in a letter ruling request or when the position ultimately adopted by one branch willaffect that adopted by another, a representative from each branch with the authority to sign in his or her own name or for the branch chief will attend the conference. If more than one subject is to be discussed at the conference, the discussion will constitute a conference on each subject.

To have a thorough and informed discussion of the issues, the conference usually will be held after the branch has had an opportunity to study the case. At the request of the taxpayer, the conference of right may be held earlier.

No taxpayer has a right to appeal the action of a branch to an Associate Chief Counsel or to any other official of the Service. But see section 10.05 of this revenue procedure for situations in which the Associate office may offer additional conferences.

In employment tax matters, only the party entitled to the letter ruling is entitled to a conference. See section 5.09 of this revenue procedure.

Disallows verbatim recording of conferences

.03 Because conference procedures are informal, no tape, stenographic, or other verbatim recording of a conference may be made by any party.

Makes tentative recommendations on substantive issues

.04 The senior Associate office representative present at the conference ensures that the taxpayer has the opportunity to present views on all the issues in question. An Associate office representative explains the Associate office's tentative decision on the substantive issues and the reasons for that decision. If the taxpayer asks the Associate office to limit the retroactive effect of any letter ruling or limit the revocation or modification of a prior letter ruling, an Associate office representative will discuss the recommendation concerning this issue and the reasons for the recommendation. The Associate office representatives will not make a commitment regarding the conclusion that the Associate office will finally adopt.

May offer additional conferences

.05 The Associate office will offer the taxpayer an additional conference if, after the conference of right, an adverse holding is proposed, but on a new issue, or on the same issue but on different grounds from those discussed at the first conference. There is no right to another conference when a proposed holding is reversed at a higher level with a result less favorable to the taxpayer, if the grounds or arguments on which the reversal is based were discussed at the conference of right.

The limit on the number of conferences to which a taxpayer is entitled does not prevent the Associate office from offering additional conferences, including conferences with an official higher than the branch level, if the Associate office decides they are needed. These conferences are not offered as a matter of course simply because the branch has reached an adverse decision. In general, conferences with higher level officials are offered only if the Associate office determines that the case presents significant issues of tax policy or tax administration and that the consideration of these issues would be enhanced by additional conferences with the taxpayer.

Requires written confirmation of information presented at conference

.06 The taxpayer should furnish to the Associate office any additional data, reasoning, precedents, etc., that were proposed by the taxpayer and discussed at the conference but not previously or adequately presented in writing. The taxpayer must furnish the additional information within 21 calendar days from the date of the conference. If the additional information is not received within that time, a letter ruling will be issued on the basis of the information on hand or, if appropriate, no ruling will be issued. See section 8.05 of this revenue procedure for instructions on submission of additional information for a letter ruling request other than a change in accounting method request. See section 9.08 of this revenue procedure for instructions on submitting additional information for a change in accounting request.

May schedule a pre-submission conference

.07 Sometimes it will be advantageous to both the Associate office and the taxpayer to hold a conference before the taxpayer submits the letter ruling request to discuss substantive or procedural issues relating to a proposed transaction. These conferences are held only if the identity of the taxpayer is provided to the Associate office, only if the taxpayer actually intends to make a request, only if the request involves a matter on which a letter ruling is ordinarily issued, and only at the discretion of the Associate office and as time permits. For example, a pre-submission conference will not be held on an income tax issue if, at the time the pre-submission conference is requested, the identical issue is involved in the taxpayer's return for an earlier period and that issue is being examined by a field office. See section 6.01(1) of this revenue procedure. A letter ruling request submitted following a pre-submission conference will not necessarily be assigned to the branch that held the pre-submission conference. Also, when a letter ruling request is not submitted following a pre-submission conference, the Associate office may notify, by memorandum, the appropriate Service official in the operating division that has examination jurisdiction of the tax-

¶1651

payer's tax return and may give its views on the issues raised during the pre-submission conference. This memorandum may constitute Chief Counsel Advice, as defined in § 6110(i), subject to disclosure under § 6110.

(1) Taxpayer may request a pre-submission conference in writing or by telephone. A taxpayer or the taxpayer's representative may request a pre-submission conference in writing or by telephone. If the taxpayer's representative is requesting the pre-submission conference, a power of attorney is required. It is preferred that Form 2848, *Power of Attorney and Declaration of Representative*, be used to provide the representative's authority. If multiple taxpayers and/or their authorized representatives will attend or participate in the pre-submission conference, cross powers of attorney (or tax information authorizations) are required. If the taxpayer's representative is requesting the pre-submission conference by telephone, the Associate Chief Counsel's representative (see list of phone numbers below) will provide the fax number to send the power of attorney prior to scheduling the pre-submission conference.

The request should identify the taxpayer and include a brief explanation of the primary issue so that an assignment to the appropriate branch can be made. If submitted in writing, the request should also identify the Associate Chief Counsel office expected to have jurisdiction over the request for a letter ruling. A written request for a pre-submission conference should be sent to the appropriate address listed in section 7.03 of this revenue procedure.

To request a pre-submission conference by telephone, call:

(a) (202) 622-7700 (not a toll-free call) for matters under the jurisdiction of the Office of Associate Chief Counsel (Corporate);

(b) (202) 622-3900 (not a toll-free call) for matters under the jurisdiction of the Office of Associate Chief Counsel (Financial Institutions and Products);

(c) (202) 622-4800 (not a toll-free call) for matters under the jurisdiction of the Office of Associate Chief Counsel (Income Tax and Accounting);

(d) (202) 622-3800 (not a toll-free call) for matters under the jurisdiction of the Office of Associate Chief Counsel (International);

(e) (202) 622-3000 (not a toll-free call) for matters under the jurisdiction of the Office of Associate Chief Counsel (Passthroughs and Special Industries);

(f) (202) 622-3400 (not a toll-free call) for matters under the jurisdiction of the Office of Associate Chief Counsel (Procedure and Administration); or

(g) (202) 622-6000 (not a toll-free call) for matters under the jurisdiction of the Office of Division Counsel/Associate Chief Counsel (Tax Exempt and Government Entities).

(2) Pre-submission conferences held in person or by telephone. Depending on the circumstances, pre-submission conferences may be held in person at the Associate's office or may be conducted by telephone.

(3) Certain information required to be submitted to the Associate office prior to the pre-submission conference. Generally, the taxpayer will be asked to

provide, at least three business days before the scheduled pre-submission conference, a statement of whether the issue is an issue on which a letter ruling is ordinarily issued, a draft of the letter ruling request or other detailed written statement of the proposed transaction, issue, and legal analysis. If the taxpayer's authorized representative will attend or participate in the pre-submission conference, a power of attorney is required.

(4) Discussion of substantive issues is not binding on the Service. Any discussion of substantive issues at a pre-submission conference is advisory only, is not binding on the Service in general or on the Office of Chief Counsel in particular, and cannot be relied upon as a basis for obtaining retroactive relief under the provisions of § 7805(b).

May schedule a conference to be held by telephone

.08 Depending on the circumstances, conferences, including conferences of right and presubmission conferences, may be held by telephone. This may occur, for example, when a taxpayer wants a conference of right but believes that the issue involved does not warrant incurring the expense of traveling to Washington,D.C., or if it is believed that scheduling an in person conference of right will substantially delay the ruling process. If a taxpayer makes such a request, the branch reviewer will decide if it is appropriate in the particular case to hold a conference by telephone. If the request is approved, the taxpayer will be advised when to call the Associate office representatives (not a toll-free call).

SECTION 11. WHAT EFFECT WILL A LETTER RULING HAVE?

May be relied on subject to limitations

.01 A taxpayer ordinarily may rely on a letter ruling received from the Associate office subject to the conditions and limitations described in this section.

Will not apply to another taxpayer

.02 A taxpayer may not rely on a letter ruling issued to another taxpayer. See § 6110(k)(3).

Will be used by a field office in examining the taxpayer's return

.03 When determining a taxpayer's liability, the field office must ascertain whether—

(1) the conclusions stated in the letter ruling are properly reflected in the return;

(2) the representations upon which the letter ruling was based reflected an accurate statement of the controlling facts;

(3) the transaction was carried out substantially as proposed; and

(4) there has been any change in the law that applies to the period during which the transaction or continuing series of transactions were consummated.

If, when determining the liability, the field office finds that a letter ruling should be revoked or modified, the findings and recommendations of the field office will be forwarded through the appropriate director to the Associate office for consideration before further action is taken by the field office. Such a referral to the Associate office will be treated as a request for technical expedited advice and the provisions of Rev. Proc. 2004-2 relating to requests for technical expedited advice (TEAM) will be followed, except that no consensus among field office, taxpayer and Associate office will be required to make the request subject to TEAM procedures. Otherwise, the letter ruling is to be applied by the field office in the determination of the taxpayer's liability. Appropriate coordination with the Associate office must be undertaken if any field official having jurisdiction over a return or other matter proposes to reach a conclusion contrary to a letter ruling previously issued to the taxpayer.

May be revoked or modified if found to be in error

.04 Unless it was part of a closing agreement as described in section 2.02 of this revenue procedure, a letter ruling found to be in error or not in accord with the current views of the Service may be revoked or modified. If a letter ruling is revoked or modified, the revocation or modification applies to all years open under the period of limitations unless the Service uses its discretionary authority under §7805(b) to limit the retroactive effect of the revocation or modification.

A letter ruling may be revoked or modified by—

(1) a notice to the taxpayer to whom the letter ruling was issued;

(2) the enactment of legislation or ratification of a tax treaty;

(3) a decision of the United States Supreme Court;

(4) the issuance of temporary or final regulations; or

(5) the issuance of a revenue ruling, revenue procedure, notice, or other statement published in the Internal Revenue Bulletin.

Consistent with these provisions, if a letter ruling relates to a continuing action or a series of actions, it ordinarily will be applied until any one of the events described above occurs or until it is specifically withdrawn.

Publication of a notice of proposed rule making will not affect the application of any letter ruling issued under this revenue procedure.

Letter ruling revoked or modified based on material change in facts applied retroactively

.05 The revocation or modification of a letter ruling will be applied retroactively to the taxpayer for whom the letter ruling was issued or to a taxpayer whose tax liability was directly involved in the letter ruling if -

(1) there has been a misstatement or omission of controlling facts; or

(2) the facts at the time of the transaction are materially different from the controlling facts on which the letter ruling was based; or

(3) if the transaction involves a continuing action or series of actions, the controlling facts change during the course of the transaction.

Not otherwise generally revoked or modified retroactively

.06 Except in rare or unusual circumstances, the revocation or modification of a letter ruling for reasons other than a change in facts as described in section 11.05 of this revenue procedure will not be applied retroactively to the taxpayer for whom the letter ruling was issued or to a taxpayer whose tax liability was directly involved in the letter ruling provided that—

(1) there has been no change in the applicable law;

(2) the letter ruling was originally issued for a proposed transaction; and

(3) the taxpayer directly involved in the letter ruling acted in good faith in relying on the letter ruling, and revoking or modifying the letter ruling retroactively would be to the taxpayer's detriment. For example, the tax liability of each shareholder is directly involved in a letter ruling on the reorganization of a corporation. The tax liability of a member of an industry is not directly involved in a letter ruling issued to another member and, therefore, the holding in a revocation or modification of a letter ruling to one member of an industry may be retroactively applied to other members of the industry. By the same reasoning, a tax practitioner may not extend to one client the non-retroactive application of a revocation or modification of a letter ruling previously issued to another client.

If a letter ruling is revoked or modified by a letter with retroactive effect, the letter will, except in fraud cases, state the grounds on which the letter ruling is being revoked or modified and explain the reasons why it is being revoked ormodified retroactively.

Retroactive effect of revocation or modification applied to a particular transaction

.07 A letter ruling issued on a particular transaction represents a holding of the Service on that transaction only. It will not apply to a similar transaction in the same year or any other year. And, except in unusual circumstances, the application of that letter ruling to the transaction will not be affected by the later issuance of regulations (either temporary or final) if conditions (1) through (3) in section 11.06 of this revenue procedure are met.

If a letter ruling on a transaction is later found to be in error or no longer in accord with the position of the Service, it will not protect a similar transaction of the taxpayer in the same year or later year.

Retroactive effect of revocation or modification applied to a continuing action or series of actions

.08 If a letter ruling is issued covering a continuing action or series of actions and the letter ruling is later found to be in error or no longer in accord with the position of the Service, the appropriate Associate Chief Counsel or Division Counsel/Associate Chief Counsel ordinarily will limit the retroactive effect of the revocation or modification to a date that is not earlier than that on which the letter ruling is revoked or modified. For example, the retroactive effect of the revocation or modification of a letter ruling covering a continuing action or series of actions ordinarily would be limited in the following situations when the letter ruling is in error or no longer in accord with the position of the Service:

(1) A taxpayer received a letter ruling that certain payments are excludable from gross income for federal income tax purposes. The taxpayer ordinarily would be protected only for the payment received after the letter ruling was issued and before the revocation or modification of the letter ruling.

(2) A taxpayer rendered a service or provided a facility that is subject to the excise tax on services or facilities and, in relying on a letter ruling received, did not pass the tax on to the user of the service or the facility.

(3) An employer incurred liability under the Federal Insurance Contributions Act but, in relying on a letter ruling received, neither collected the employee tax nor paid the employee and employer taxes under the Federal Insurance Contributions Act. The retroactive effect would be limited for both the employer and employee tax. The limitation would be conditioned on the employer furnishing wage data, as may be required by § 31.6011(a)-1 of the Employment Tax Regulations.

Generally not retroactively revoked or modified if related to sale or lease subject to excise tax

.09 A letter ruling holding that the sale or lease of a particular article is subject to the manufacturer's excise tax or the retailer's excise tax may not retroactively revoke or modify an earlier letter ruling holding that the sale or lease of such an article was not taxable if the taxpayer to whom the letter ruling wasissued, in relying on the earlier letter ruling, gave up possession or ownership of the article without passing the tax on to the customer. (Section 1108(b), Revenue Act of 1926.)

May be retroactively revoked or modified when transaction is entered into before the issuance of the letter ruling

.10 A taxpayer is not protected against retroactive revocation or modification of a letter ruling involving a transaction completed before the issuance of the letter ruling or involving a continuing action or series of actions occurring before the issuance of the letter ruling because the taxpayer did not enter into the transaction relying on a letter ruling.

Taxpayer may request that retroactivity be limited

.11 Under § 7805(b), the Service may prescribe any extent to which a revocation or modification of a letter ruling will be applied without retroactive effect.

A taxpayer to whom a letter ruling has been issued may request that the appropriate Associate Chief Counsel limit the retroactive effect of any revocation or modification of the letter ruling.

Format of request

(1) Request for relief under § 7805(b) must be made in required format.

A request to limit the retroactive effect of the revocation or modification of a letter ruling must be in the general form of, and meet the general requirements for, a letter ruling request. These requirements are given in section 7 of this revenue procedure. Specifically, the request must also—

¶1651

(a) state that it is being made under § 7805(b);

(b) state the relief sought;

(c) explain the reasons and arguments in support of the relief requested (including a discussion of section 11.05 and the three items listed in section 11.06 of this revenue procedure and any other factors as they relate to the taxpayer's particular situation); and

(d) include any documents bearing on the request.

A request that the Service limit the retroactive effect of a revocation or modification of a letter ruling may be made in the form of a separate request for a letter ruling when, for example, a revenue ruling has the effect of modifying or revoking a letter ruling previously issued to the taxpayer or when the Service notifies the taxpayer of a change in position that will have the effect of revoking or modifying the letter ruling.

When notice is given by the field office during an examination of the taxpayer's return or by the Area Director, Appeals, during consideration of the taxpayer's return before Appeals, a request to limit retroactive effect must be made in the form of a request for technical advice as explained in section 16.03 of Rev. Proc. 2004-2.

When germane to a pending letter ruling request, a request to limit the retroactive effect of a revocation or modification of a letter ruling may be made aspart of the request for the letter ruling, either initially or at any time before the letter ruling is issued. When a letter ruling that concerns a continuing transaction is revoked or modified by, for example, a subsequent revenue ruling, a request to limit retroactive effect must be made before the examination of the return that contains the transaction that is the subject of the letter ruling request.

Request for conference

(2) Taxpayer may request a conference on application of § 7805(b).

A taxpayer who requests the application of § 7805(b) in a separate letter ruling request has the right to a conference in the Associate office as explained in sections 10.02, 10.04, and 10.05 of this revenue procedure. If the request is made initially as part of a pending letter ruling request or is made before the conference of right is held on the substantive issues, the § 7805(b) issue will be discussed at the taxpayer's one conference of right as explained in section 10.02 of this revenue procedure. If the request for the application of § 7805(b) relief is made as part of a pending letter ruling request after a conference has been held on the substantive issue and the Associate office determines that there is justification for having delayed the request, the taxpayer is entitled to one conference of right concerning the application of § 7805(b), with the conference limited to discussion of this issue only.

* * *

¶1652 Exhibit 16-2

<table>
<tr>
<td>Form **1023**
(Rev. September 1998)
Department of the Treasury
Internal Revenue Service</td>
<td>**Application for Recognition of Exemption**
Under Section 501(c)(3) of the Internal Revenue Code</td>
<td>OMB No. 1545-0056

Note: *If exempt status is approved, this application will be open for public inspection.*</td>
</tr>
</table>

Read the instructions for each Part carefully.
A User Fee must be attached to this application.
If the required information and appropriate documents are not submitted along with Form 0710 (with payment of the appropriate user fee), the application may be returned to you.
Complete the Procedural Checklist on page 8 of the instructions.

Part I   **Identification of Applicant**

1a Full name of organization (as shown in organizing document)	**2** Employer identification number (EIN) (If none, see page 3 of the **Specific Instructions**.)
1b c/o Name (if applicable)	**3** Name and telephone number of person to be contacted if additional information is needed
1c Address (number and street)　Room/Suite	( )
1d City, town, or post office, state, and ZIP + 4. If you have a foreign address, see **Specific Instructions** for Part I, page 3.	**4** Month the annual accounting period ends **5** Date incorporated or formed
1e Web site address	**6** Check here if applying under section: **a** ☐ 501(e) **b** ☐ 501(f) **c** ☐ 501(k) **d** ☐ 501(n)

7 Did the organization previously apply for recognition of exemption under this Code section or under any other section of the Code? . . . . ☐ **Yes** ☐ **No**
If "Yes," attach an explanation.

8 Is the organization required to file Form 990 (or Form 990-EZ)? . . . . ☐ **N/A** ☐ **Yes** ☐ **No**
If "No," attach an explanation (see page 3 of the **Specific Instructions**).

9 Has the organization filed Federal income tax returns or exempt organization information returns? . . ☐ **Yes** ☐ **No**
If "Yes," state the form numbers, years filed, and Internal Revenue office where filed.

10 Check the box for the type of organization. ATTACH A CONFORMED COPY OF THE CORRESPONDING ORGANIZING DOCUMENTS TO THE APPLICATION BEFORE MAILING. (See **Specific Instructions** for Part I, Line 10, on page 3.) See also Pub. 557 for examples of organizational documents.)

a ☐ Corporation—Attach a copy of the Articles of Incorporation (including amendments and restatements) showing approval by the appropriate state official; also include a copy of the bylaws.

b ☐ Trust— Attach a copy of the Trust Indenture or Agreement, including all appropriate signatures and dates.

c ☐ Association— Attach a copy of the Articles of Association, Constitution, or other creating document, with a declaration (see instructions) or other evidence the organization was formed by adoption of the document by more than one person; also include a copy of the bylaws.

If the organization is a corporation or an unincorporated association that has not yet adopted bylaws, check here ▶ ☐

I declare under the penalties of perjury that I am authorized to sign this application on behalf of the above organization and that I have examined this application, including the accompanying schedules and attachments, and to the best of my knowledge it is true, correct, and complete.

Please Sign Here ▶

_____   _____   _____
(Signature)   (Type or print name and title or authority of signer)   (Date)

For Paperwork Reduction Act Notice, see page 7 of the instructions.   Cat. No. 17133K

Form 1023 (Rev. 9-98)   Page **2**

Part II   **Activities and Operational Information**

1   Provide a detailed narrative description of all the activities of the organization—past, present, and planned. **Do not merely refer to or repeat the language in the organizational document.** List each activity separately in the order of importance based on the relative time and other resources devoted to the activity. Indicate the percentage of time for each activity. Each description should include, as a minimum, the following: **(a)** a detailed description of the activity including its purpose and how each acitivity furthers your exempt purpose; **(b)** when the activity was or will be initiated; and **(c)** where and by whom the activity will be conducted.

2   What are or will be the organization's sources of financial support? List in order of size.

3   Describe the organization's fundraising program, both actual and planned, and explain to what extent it has been put into effect. Include details of fundraising activities such as selective mailings, formation of fundraising committees, use of volunteers or professional fundraisers, etc. Attach representative copies of solicitations for financial support.

Part II   Activities and Operational Information *(Continued)*

4   Give the following information about the organization's governing body:

a Names, addresses, and titles of officers, directors, trustees, etc.	**b** Annual compensation

c Do any of the above persons serve as members of the governing body by reason of being public officials
or being appointed by public officials? . . . .   ☐ **Yes** ☐ **No**
If "Yes," name those persons and explain the basis of their selection or appointment.

d Are any members of the organization's governing body "disqualified persons" with respect to the
organization (other than by reason of being a member of the governing body) or do any of the members
have either a business or family relationship with "disqualified persons"? (See **Specific Instructions** for
Part II, Line 4d, on page 3.) . . . .   ☐ **Yes** ☐ **No**
If "Yes," explain.

5   Does the organization control or is it controlled by any other organization? . . . .   ☐ **Yes** ☐ **No**
Is the organization the outgrowth of (or successor to) another organization, or does it have a special
relationship with another organization by reason of interlocking directorates or other factors? . . . .   ☐ **Yes** ☐ **No**
If either of these questions is answered "Yes," explain.

6   Does or will the organization directly or indirectly engage in any of the following transactions with any
political organization or other exempt organization (other than a 501(c)(3) organization): **(a)** grants;
(b) purchases or sales of assets; **(c)** rental of facilities or equipment; **(d)** loans or loan guarantees;
(e) reimbursement arrangements; **(f)** performance of services, membership, or fundraising solicitations;
or **(g)** sharing of facilities, equipment, mailing lists or other assets, or paid employees? . . . . . .   ☐ **Yes** ☐ **No**
If "Yes," explain fully and identify the other organizations involved.

7   Is the organization financially accountable to any other organization? . . . .   ☐ **Yes** ☐ **No**
If "Yes," explain and identify the other organization. Include details concerning accountability or attach
copies of reports if any have been submitted.

¶1652

Form 1023 (Rev. 9-98)   Page **4**

Part II   **Activities and Operational Information** *(Continued)*

8   What assets does the organization have that are used in the performance of its exempt function? (Do not include property producing investment income.) If any assets are not fully operational, explain their status, what additional steps remain to be completed, and when such final steps will be taken. If none, indicate "N/A."

9   Will the organization be the beneficiary of tax-exempt bond financing within the next 2 years?. . . .   ☐ **Yes** ☐ **No**

10a Will any of the organization's facilities or operations be managed by another organization or individual under a contractual agreement?. . . . .   ☐ **Yes** ☐ **No**
   b Is the organization a party to any leases? . . . .   ☐ **Yes** ☐ **No**
        If either of these questions is answered "Yes," attach a copy of the contracts and explain the relationship between the applicant and the other parties.

11   Is the organization a membership organization? . . . .   ☐ **Yes** ☐ **No**
        If "Yes," complete the following:
   a Describe the organization's membership requirements and attach a schedule of membership fees and dues.

   b Describe the organization's present and proposed efforts to attract members and attach a copy of any descriptive literature or promotional material used for this purpose.

   c What benefits do (or will) the members receive in exchange for their payment of dues?

12a If the organization provides benefits, services, or products, are the recipients required, or will they be required, to pay for them? . . . .   ☐ **N/A** ☐ **Yes** ☐ **No**
        If "Yes," explain how the charges are determined and attach a copy of the current fee schedule.

   b Does or will the organization limit its benefits, services, or products to specific individuals or classes of individuals? . . . .   ☐ **N/A** ☐ **Yes** ☐ **No**
        If "Yes," explain how the recipients or beneficiaries are or will be selected.

13   Does or will the organization attempt to influence legislation? . . . .   ☐ **Yes** ☐ **No**
        If "Yes," explain. Also, give an estimate of the percentage of the organization's time and funds that it devotes or plans to devote to this activity.

14   Does or will the organization intervene in any way in political campaigns, including the publication or distribution of statements? . . . .   ☐ **Yes** ☐ **No**
        If "Yes," explain fully.

Part III   Technical Requirements

1   Are you filing Form 1023 within 15 months from the end of the month in which your organization was
    created or formed? . . . . ☐ **Yes** ☐ **No**
    If you answer "Yes," do not answer questions on lines 2 through 6 below.

2   If one of the exceptions to the 15-month filing requirement shown below applies, check the appropriate box and proceed
    to question 7.
    Exceptions—You are not required to file an exemption application within 15 months if the organization:

    ☐ **a**   Is a church, interchurch organization of local units of a church, a convention or association of churches, or an
              integrated auxiliary of a church. See **Specific Instructions,** Line 2a, on page 4;
    ☐ **b**   Is not a private foundation and normally has gross receipts of not more than $5,000 in each tax year; or

    ☐ **c**   Is a subordinate organization covered by a group exemption letter, but only if the parent or supervisory organization
              timely submitted a notice covering the subordinate.

3   If the organization does not meet any of the exceptions on line 2 above, are you filing Form 1023 within
    27 months from the end of the month in which the organization was created or formed?. . . . . . ☐ **Yes** ☐ **No**

    If "Yes," your organization qualifies under Regulation section 301.9100-2, for an automatic 12-month
    extension of the 15-month filing requirement. Do not answer questions 4 through 6.

    If "No," answer question 4.

4   If you answer "No" to question 3, does the organization wish to request an extension of time to apply
    under the "reasonable action and good faith" and the "no prejudice to the interest of the government"
    requirements of Regulations section 301.9100-3? . . . . ☐ **Yes** ☐ **No**

    If "Yes," give the reasons for not filing this application within the 27-month period described in question 3.
    See **Specific Instructions,** Part III, Line 4, before completing this item. Do not answer questions 5 and 6.

    If "No," answer questions 5 and 6.

5   If you answer "No" to question 4, your organization's qualification as a section 501(c)(3) organization can
    be recognized only from the date this application is filed. Therefore, do you want us to consider the
    application as a request for recognition of exemption as a section 501(c)(3) organization from the date
    the application is received and not retroactively to the date the organization was created or formed?   . ☐ **Yes** ☐ **No**

6   If you answer "Yes" to question 5 above and wish to request recognition of section 501(c)(4) status for the period beginning
    with the date the organization was formed and ending with the date the Form 1023 application was received (the effective
    date of the organization's section 501(c)(3) status), check here ▶ ☐   and attach a completed page 1 of Form 1024 to this
    application.

¶1652

Part III Technical Requirements *(Continued)*

7 Is the organization a private foundation?
  ☐ **Yes** (Answer question 8.)
  ☐ **No** (Answer question 9 and proceed as instructed.)

8 If you answer "Yes" to question 7, does the organization claim to be a private operating foundation?
  ☐ **Yes** (Complete Schedule E.)
  ☐ **No**

After answering question 8 on this line, go to line 14 on page 7.

9 If you answer "No" to question 7, indicate the public charity classification the organization is requesting by checking the box below that most appropriately applies:

THE ORGANIZATION IS NOT A PRIVATE FOUNDATION BECAUSE IT QUALIFIES:

a	☐	As a church or a convention or association of churches (CHURCHES MUST COMPLETE SCHEDULE A.)	Sections 509(a)(1) and 170(b)(1)(A)(i)
b	☐	As a school (MUST COMPLETE SCHEDULE B.)	Sections 509(a)(1) and 170(b)(1)(A)(ii)
c	☐	As a hospital or a cooperative hospital service organization, or a medical research organization operated in conjunction with a hospital (These organizations, except for hospital service organizations, MUST COMPLETE SCHEDULE C.)	Sections 509(a)(1) and 170(b)(1)(A)(iii)
d	☐	As a governmental unit described in section 170(c)(1).	Sections 509(a)(1) and 170(b)(1)(A)(v)
e	☐	As being operated solely for the benefit of, or in connection with, one or more of the organizations described in **a** through **d, g, h,** or **i** (MUST COMPLETE SCHEDULE D.)	Section 509(a)(3)
f	☐	As being organized and operated exclusively for testing for public safety.	Section 509(a)(4)
g	☐	As being operated for the benefit of a college or university that is owned or operated by a governmental unit.	Sections 509(a)(1) and 170(b)(1)(A)(iv)
h	☐	As receiving a substantial part of its support in the form of contributions from publicly supported organizations, from a governmental unit, or from the general public.	Sections 509(a)(1) and 170(b)(1)(A)(vi)
i	☐	As normally receiving not more than one-third of its support from gross investment income and more than one-third of its support from contributions, membership fees, and gross receipts from activities related to its exempt functions (subject to certain exceptions).	Section 509(a)(2)
j	☐	The organization is a publicly supported organization but is not sure whether it meets the public support test of **h** or **i**. The organization would like the IRS to decide the proper classification.	Sections 509(a)(1) and 170(b)(1)(A)(vi) or Section 509(a)(2)

If you checked one of the boxes a through f in question 9, go to question
14. If you checked box g in question 9, go to questions 11 and 12.
If you checked box h, i, or j, in question 9, go to question 10.

Part III   **Technical Requirements** *(Continued)*

10   If you checked box **h, i,** or **j** in question 9, has the organization completed a tax year of at least 8 months?
☐ **Yes**—Indicate whether you are requesting:
☐ A definitive ruling. (Answer questions 11 through 14.)
☐ An advance ruling. (Answer questions 11 and 14 and attach two Forms 872-C completed and signed.)
☐ **No— You must request an advance ruling by completing and signing two Forms 872-C and attaching them to the Form 1023.**

11   If the organization received any unusual grants during any of the tax years shown in Part IV-A, **Statement of Revenue and Expenses,** attach a list for each year showing the name of the contributor; the date and the amount of the grant; and a brief description of the nature of the grant.

12   If you are requesting a definitive ruling under section 170(b)(1)(A)(iv) or (vi), check here ► ☐   and:

a Enter 2% of line 8, column (e), Total, of Part IV-A . . . . —————————
b Attach a list showing the name and amount contributed by each person (other than a governmental unit or "publicly supported" organization) whose total gifts, grants, contributions, etc., were more than the amount entered on line **12a** above.

13   If you are requesting a definitive ruling under section 509(a)(2), check here ► ☐   and:
a For each of the years included on lines 1, 2, and 9 of Part IV-A, attach a list showing the name of and amount received from each "disqualified person." (For a definition of "disqualified person," see **Specific Instructions,** Part II, Line 4d, on page 3.)
b For each of the years included on line 9 of Part IV-A, attach a list showing the name of and amount received from each payer (other than a "disqualified person") whose payments to the organization were more than $5,000. For this purpose, "payer" includes, but is not limited to, any organization described in sections 170(b)(1)(A)(i) through (vi) and any governmental agency or bureau.

14 Indicate if your organization is one of the following. If so, complete the required schedule. (Submit only those schedules that apply to your organization. **Do not submit blank schedules.**)	Yes	No	If "Yes," complete Schedule:
Is the organization a church?			A
Is the organization, or any part of it, a school?			B
Is the organization, or any part of it, a hospital or medical research organization?			C
Is the organization a section 509(a)(3) supporting organization?			D
Is the organization a private operating foundation?			E
Is the organization, or any part of it, a home for the aged or handicapped?			F
Is the organization, or any part of it, a child care organization?			G
Does the organization provide or administer any scholarship benefits, student aid, etc.?			H
Has the organization taken over, or will it take over, the facilities of a "for profit" institution? . . .			I

¶1652

Form 1023 (Rev. 9-98)   Page **8**

Part IV   Financial Data

Complete the financial statements for the current year and for each of the 3 years immediately before it. If in existence less than 4 years, complete the statements for each year in existence. **If in existence less than 1 year, also provide proposed budgets for the 2 years following the current year.**

A. Statement of Revenue and Expenses

| | | Current tax year | 3 prior tax years or proposed budget for 2 years | | | |
		(a) From ...... to	(b)	(c)	(d)	(e) TOTAL
Revenue	1 Gifts, grants, and contributions received (not including unusual grants—see page 6 of the instructions).					
	2 Membership fees received . .					
	3 Gross investment income (see instructions for definition) . .					
	4 Net income from organization's unrelated business activities not included on line 3					
	5 Tax revenues levied for and either paid to or spent on behalf of the organization					
	6 Value of services or facilities furnished by a governmental unit to the organization without charge (not including the value of services or facilities generally furnished the public without charge)					
	7 Other income (not including gain or loss from sale of capital assets) (attach schedule) . .					
	8 **Total** (add lines 1 through 7)					
	9 Gross receipts from admissions, sales of merchandise or services, or furnishing of facilities in any activity that is not an unrelated business within the meaning of section 513. Include related cost of sales on line 22					
	10 **Total** (add lines 8 and 9) . .					
	11 Gain or loss from sale of capital assets (attach schedule). . .					
	12 Unusual grants.					
	13 **Total** revenue (add lines 10 through 12)					
Expenses	14 Fundraising expenses . . .					
	15 Contributions, gifts, grants, and similar amounts paid (attach schedule)					
	16 Disbursements to or for benefit of members (attach schedule) .					
	17 Compensation of officers, directors, and trustees (attach schedule)					
	18 Other salaries and wages . .					
	19 Interest					
	20 Occupancy (rent, utilities, etc.) .					
	21 Depreciation and depletion . .					
	22 Other (attach schedule) . . .					
	23 **Total** expenses (add lines 14 through 22)					
	24 Excess of revenue over expenses (line 13 minus line 23)					

¶1652

Part IV   Financial Data *(Continued)*

B. Balance Sheet (at the end of the period shown)		Current tax year Date ....
Assets		
1 Cash	1	
2 Accounts receivable, net	2	
3 Inventories	3	
4 Bonds and notes receivable (attach schedule)	4	
5 Corporate stocks (attach schedule)	5	
6 Mortgage loans (attach schedule)	6	
7 Other investments (attach schedule)	7	
8 Depreciable and depletable assets (attach schedule)	8	
9 Land	9	
10 Other assets (attach schedule)	10	
11 **Total assets** (add lines 1 through 10)	11	
Liabilities		
12 Accounts payable	12	
13 Contributions, gifts, grants, etc., payable	13	
14 Mortgages and notes payable (attach schedule)	14	
15 Other liabilities (attach schedule)	15	
16 **Total liabilities** (add lines 12 through 15)	16	
Fund Balances or Net Assets		
17 Total fund balances or net assets	17	
18 **Total liabilities and fund balances or net assets** (add line 16 and line 17)	18	

If there has been any substantial change in any aspect of the organization's financial activities since the end of the period shown above, check the box and attach a detailed explanation . . . . ▶ ☐

¶1652

Schedule A. Churches

1 Provide a brief history of the development of the organization, including the reasons for its formation.

2 Does the organization have a written creed or statement of faith?. . . . ☐ **Yes**   ☐ **No**

If "Yes," attach a copy.

3 Does the organization require prospective members to renounce other religious beliefs or their membership in other churches or religious orders to become members? . . . . ☐ **Yes**   ☐ **No**

4 Does the organization have a formal code of doctrine and discipline for its members? . . . . ☐ **Yes**   ☐ **No**

If "Yes," describe.

5 Describe the form of worship and attach a schedule of worship services.

6 Are the services open to the public?. . . . . ☐ **Yes**   ☐ **No**

If "Yes," describe how the organization publicizes its services and explain the criteria for admittance.

7 Explain how the organization attracts new members.

8 **(a)** How many active members are currently enrolled in the church?

(b) What is the average attendance at the worship services?

9 In addition to worship services, what other religious services (such as baptisms, weddings, funerals, etc.) does the organization conduct?

Schedule A. Churches *(Continued)*

10 Does the organization have a school for the religious instruction of the young? . . . . ☐ **Yes** ☐ **No**

11 Were the current deacons, minister, and/or pastor formally ordained after a prescribed course of study? . . . . ☐ **Yes** ☐ **No**

12 Describe the organization's religious hierarchy or ecclesiastical government.

13 Does the organization have an established place of worship? . . . . . . ☐ **Yes** ☐ **No**

If "Yes," provide the name and address of the owner or lessor of the property and the address and a description of the facility.

If the organization has no regular place of worship, state where the services are held and how the site is selected.

14 Does (or will) the organization license or otherwise ordain ministers (or their equivalent) or issue church charters? . . . . ☐ **Yes** ☐ **No**

If "Yes," describe in detail the requirements and qualifications needed to be so licensed, ordained, or chartered.

15 Did the organization pay a fee for a church charter? . . . . ☐ **Yes** ☐ **No**

If "Yes," state the name and address of the organization to which the fee was paid, attach a copy of the charter, and describe the circumstances surrounding the chartering.

16 Show how many hours a week the minister/pastor and officers each devote to church work and the amount of compensation paid to each of them. If the minister or pastor is otherwise employed, indicate by whom employed, the nature of the employment, and the hours devoted to that employment.

Schedule A. Churches *(Continued)*

17 Will any funds or property of the organization be used by any officer, director, employee, minister, or pastor for his or her personal needs or convenience? ☐ **Yes**   ☐ **No**

If "Yes," describe the nature and circumstances of such use.

18 List any officers, directors, or trustees related by blood or marriage.

19 Give the name of anyone who has assigned income to the organization or made substantial contributions of money or other property. Specify the amounts involved.

Instructions

Although a church, its integrated auxiliaries, or a convention or association of churches is not required to file Form 1023 to be exempt from Federal income tax or to receive tax-deductible contributions, such an organization may find it advantageous to obtain recognition of exemption. In this event, you should submit information showing that your organization is a church, synagogue, association or convention of churches, religious order or religious organization that is an integral part of a church, and that it is carrying out the functions of a church.

In determining whether an admittedly religious organization is also a church, the IRS does not accept any and every assertion that such an organization is a church. Because beliefs and practices vary so widely, there is no single definition of the word "church" for tax purposes. The IRS considers the facts and circumstances of each organization applying for church status.

The IRS maintains two basic guidelines in determining that an organization meets the religious purposes test:

1. That the particular religious beliefs of the organization are truly and sincerely held, and

2. That the practices and rituals associated with the organization's religious beliefs or creed are not illegal or contrary to clearly defined public policy.

In order for the IRS to properly evaluate your organization's activities and religious purposes, it is important that all questions in Schedule A be answered.

The information submitted with Schedule A will be a determining factor in granting the "church" status requested by your organization. In completing the schedule, consider the following points:

1. The organization's activities in furtherance of its beliefs must be exclusively religious, and

2. An organization will not qualify for exemption if it has a substantial nonexempt purpose of serving the private interests of its founder or the founder's family.

¶1652

Form 1023 (Rev. 9-98)   Page **15**

Schedule B. Schools, Colleges, and Universities

1 Does, or will, the organization normally have: **(a)** a regularly scheduled curriculum, **(b)** a regular faculty of qualified teachers, **(c)** a regularly enrolled student body, and **(d)** facilities where its educational activities are regularly carried on? . . . . ☐ **Yes** ☐ **No**
If "No," do not complete the rest of Schedule B.

2 Is the organization an instrumentality of a state or political subdivision of a state? . . . . ☐ **Yes** ☐ **No**
If "Yes," document this in Part II and do not complete items 3 through 10 of Schedule B. (See instructions on the back of Schedule B.)

3 Does or will the organization (or any department or division within it) discriminate in any way on the basis of race with respect to:
a Admissions? . . . . ☐ **Yes** ☐ **No**
b Use of facilities or exercise of student privileges? . . . . ☐ **Yes** ☐ **No**
c Faculty or administrative staff? . . . . ☐ **Yes** ☐ **No**
d Scholarship or loan programs? . . . . ☐ **Yes** ☐ **No**
If "Yes" for any of the above, explain.

4 Does the organization include a statement in its charter, bylaws, or other governing instrument, or in a resolution of its governing body, that it has a racially nondiscriminatory policy as to students? . . . . ☐ **Yes** ☐ **No**

Attach whatever corporate resolutions or other official statements the organization has made on this subject.

5a Has the organization made its racially nondiscriminatory policies known in a manner that brings the policies to the attention of all segments of the general community that it serves? . . . . ☐ **Yes** ☐ **No**

If "Yes," describe how these policies have been publicized and how often relevant notices or announcements have been made. If no newspaper or broadcast media notices have been used, explain.

b If applicable, attach clippings of any relevant newspaper notices or advertising, or copies of tapes or scripts used for media broadcasts. Also attach copies of brochures and catalogs dealing with student admissions, programs, and scholarships, as well as representative copies of all written advertising used as a means of informing prospective students of the organization's programs.

6 Attach a numerical schedule showing the racial composition, as of the current academic year, and projected to the extent feasible for the next academic year, of: **(a)** the student body, and **(b)** the faculty and administrative staff.

7 Attach a list showing the amount of any scholarship and loan funds awarded to students enrolled and the racial composition of the students who have received the awards.

8a Attach a list of the organization's incorporators, founders, board members, and donors of land or buildings, whether individuals or organizations.

b State whether any of the organizations listed in **8a** have as an objective the maintenance of segregated public or private school education, and, if so, whether any of the individuals listed in **8a** are officers or active members of such organizations.

9a Enter the public school district and county in which the organization is located.

b Was the organization formed or substantially expanded at the time of public school desegregation in the above district or county? . . . . ☐ **Yes** ☐ **No**

10 Has the organization ever been determined by a state or Federal administrative agency or judicial body to be racially discriminatory? . . . . ☐ **Yes** ☐ **No**

If "Yes," attach a detailed explanation identifying the parties to the suit, the forum in which the case was heard, the cause of action, the holding in the case, and the citations (if any) for the case. Also describe in detail what changes in the organization's operation, if any, have occurred since then.

For more information, see back of Schedule B.

¶1652

Instructions

A "school" is an organization that has the primary function of presenting formal instruction, normally maintains a regular faculty and curriculum, normally has a regularly enrolled student body, and has a place where its educational activities are carried on.

The term generally corresponds to the definition of an "educational organization" in section 170(b)(1)(A)(ii). Thus, the term includes primary, secondary, preparatory and high schools, and colleges and universities. The term does not include organizations engaged in both educational and noneducational activities unless the latter are merely incidental to the educational activities. A school for handicapped children is included within the term, but an organization merely providing handicapped children with custodial care is not.

For purposes of Schedule B, "Sunday schools" that are conducted by a church are not included in the term "schools," but separately organized schools (such as parochial schools, universities, and similar institutions) are included in the term.

A private school that otherwise meets the requirements of section 501(c)(3) as an educational institution will not qualify for exemption under section 501(a) unless it has a racially nondiscriminatory policy as to students.

This policy means that the school admits students of any race to all the rights, privileges, programs, and activities generally accorded or made available to students at that school and that the school does not discriminate on the basis of race in the administration of its educational policies, admissions policies, scholarship and loan programs, and athletic or other school-administered programs.

The IRS considers discrimination on the basis of race to include discrimination on the basis of color and national or ethnic origin. A policy of a school that favors racial minority groups in admissions, facilities, programs, and financial assistance will not constitute discrimination on the basis of race when the purpose and effect is to promote the establishment and maintenance of that school's racially nondiscriminatory policy as to students.

See Rev. Proc. 75-50, 1975-2 C.B. 587, for guidelines and recordkeeping requirements for determining whether private schools that are applying for recognition of exemption have racially nondiscriminatory policies as to students.

Line 2

An instrumentality of a state or political subdivision of a state may qualify under section 501(c)(3) if it is organized as a separate entity from the governmental unit that created it and if it otherwise meets the organizational and operational tests of section 501(c)(3). See Rev. Rul. 60-384, 1960-2 C.B. 172. Any such organization that is a school is not a private school and, therefore, is not subject to the provisions of Rev. Proc. 75-50.

Schools that incorrectly answer "Yes" to line 2 will be contacted to furnish the information called for by lines 3 through 10 in order to establish that they meet the requirements for exemption. To prevent delay in the processing of your application, be sure to answer line 2 correctly and complete lines 3 through 10, if applicable.

Form 1023 (Rev. 9-98)

Schedule C. Hospitals and Medical Research Organizations

☐ Check here if claiming to be a hospital; complete the questions in Section I of this schedule; and write "N/A" in Section II.
☐ Check here if claiming to be a medical research organization operated in conjunction with a hospital; complete the questions in Section II of this schedule; and write "N/A" in Section I.

Section I   Hospitals

1a How many doctors are on the hospital's courtesy staff? . . . . _____

b Are all the doctors in the community eligible for staff privileges? . . . .   ☐ **Yes** ☐ **No**
If "No," give the reasons why and explain how the courtesy staff is selected.

2a Does the hospital maintain a full-time emergency room? . . . .   ☐ **Yes** ☐ **No**
b What is the hospital's policy on administering emergency services to persons without apparent means to pay?

c Does the hospital have any arrangements with police, fire, and voluntary ambulance services for the delivery or admission of emergency cases? . . . .   ☐ **Yes** ☐ **No**
Explain.

3a Does or will the hospital require a deposit from persons covered by Medicare or Medicaid in its admission practices? . . . .   ☐ **Yes** ☐ **No**
If "Yes," explain.

b Does the same deposit requirement, if any, apply to all other patients? . . . .   ☐ **Yes** ☐ **No**
If "No," explain.

4 Does or will the hospital provide for a portion of its services and facilities to be used for charity patients?   ☐ **Yes** ☐ **No**
Explain the policy regarding charity cases. Include data on the hospital's past experience in admitting charity patients and arrangements it may have with municipal or government agencies for absorbing the cost of such care.

5 Does or will the hospital carry on a formal program of medical training and research? . . . .   ☐ **Yes** ☐ **No**
If "Yes," describe.

6 Does the hospital provide office space to physicians carrying on a medical practice? . . . .   ☐ **Yes** ☐ **No**
If "Yes," attach a list setting forth the name of each physician, the amount of space provided, the annual rent, the expiration date of the current lease and whether the terms of the lease represent fair market value.

Section II   Medical Research Organizations

1 Name the hospitals with which the organization has a relationship and describe the relationship.

2 Attach a schedule describing the organization's present and proposed (indicate which) medical research activities; show the nature of the activities, and the amount of money that has been or will be spent in carrying them out. (Making grants to other organizations is not direct conduct of medical research.)

3 Attach a statement of assets showing their fair market value and the portion of the assets directly devoted to medical research.

For more information, see back of Schedule C.

Additional Information

Hospitals

To be entitled to status as a "hospital," an organization must have, as its principal purpose or function, the providing of medical or hospital care or medical education or research. "Medical care" includes the treatment of any physical or mental disability or condition, the cost of which may be taken as a deduction under section 213, whether the treatment is performed on an inpatient or outpatient basis. Thus, a rehabilitation institution, outpatient clinic, or community mental health or drug treatment center may be a hospital if its principal function is providing the above-described services.

On the other hand, a convalescent home or a home for children or the aged is not a hospital. Similarly, an institution whose principal purpose or function is to train handicapped individuals to pursue some vocation is not a hospital. Moreover, a medical education or medical research institution is not a hospital, unless it is also actively engaged in providing medical or hospital care to patients on its premises or in its facilities on an inpatient or outpatient basis.

Cooperative Hospital Service Organizations

Cooperative hospital service organizations (section 501(e)) should not complete Schedule C.

Medical Research Organizations

To qualify as a medical research organization, the principal function of the organization must be the direct, continuous, and active conduct of medical research in conjunction with a hospital that is described in section 501(c)(3), a Federal hospital, or an instrumentality of a governmental unit referred to in section 170(c)(1).

For purposes of section 170(b)(1)(A)(iii) only, the organization must be set up to use the funds it receives in the active conduct of medical research by January 1 of the fifth calendar year after receipt. The arrangement it has with donors to assure use of the funds within the 5-year period must be legally enforceable.

As used here, "medical research" means investigations, experiments, and studies to discover, develop, or verify knowledge relating to the causes, diagnosis, treatment, prevention, or control of human physical or mental diseases and impairments.

For further information, see Regulations section 1.170A-9(c)(2).

¶1652

Form 1023 (Rev. 9-98)

Schedule D. Section 509(a)(3) Supporting Organizations

1a Organizations supported by the applicant organization: Name and address of supported organization	**b** Has the supported organization received a ruling or determination letter that it is not a private foundation by reason of section 509(a)(1) or (2)?
....	☐ Yes ☐ No
....	☐ Yes ☐ No
....	☐ Yes ☐ No
....	☐ Yes ☐ No
....	☐ Yes ☐ No

c If "No" for any of the organizations listed in **1a,** explain.

2 Does the supported organization have tax-exempt status under section 501(c)(4), 501(c)(5), or 501(c)(6)? ☐ Yes ☐ No
If "Yes," attach: **(a)** a copy of its ruling or determination letter, and **(b)** an analysis of its revenue for the current year and the preceding 3 years. (Provide the financial data using the formats in Part IV-A (lines 1–13) and Part III (lines 11, 12, and 13).)

3 Does your organization's governing document indicate that the majority of its governing board is elected or appointed by the supported organizations? . . . . ☐ Yes ☐ No
If "Yes," skip to line 9.
If "No," you must answer the questions on lines 4 through 9.

4 Does your organization's governing document indicate the common supervision or control that it and the supported organizations share? . . . . ☐ Yes ☐ No
If "Yes," give the article and paragraph numbers. If "No," explain.

5 To what extent do the supported organizations have a significant voice in your organization's investment policies, in the making and timing of grants, and in otherwise directing the use of your organization's income or assets?

6 Does the mentioning of the supported organizations in your organization's governing instrument make it a trust that the supported organizations can enforce under state law and compel to make an accounting? ☐ Yes ☐ No
If "Yes," explain.

7a What percentage of your organization's income does it pay to each supported organization?

b What is the total annual income of each supported organization?

c How much does your organization contribute annually to each supported organization?

For more information, see back of Schedule D.

¶1652

Schedule D. Section 509(a)(3) Supporting Organizations *(Continued)*

8 To what extent does your organization conduct activities that would otherwise be carried on by the supported organizations? Explain why these activities would otherwise be carried on by the supported organizations.

9 Is the applicant organization controlled directly or indirectly by one or more "disqualified persons" (other than one who is a disqualified person solely because he or she is a manager) or by an organization that is not described in section 509(a)(1) or (2)? . . . . ☐ **Yes** ☐ **No**
If "Yes," explain.

Instructions

For an explanation of the types of organizations defined in section 509(a)(3) as being excluded from the definition of a private foundation, see Pub. 557, Chapter 3.

Line 1

List each organization that is supported by your organization and indicate in item **1b** if the supported organization has received a letter recognizing exempt status as a section 501(c)(3) public charity as defined in section 509(a)(1) or 509(a)(2). If you answer "No" in **1b** to any of the listed organizations, please explain in **1c.**

Line 3

Your organization's governing document may be articles of incorporation, articles of association, constitution, trust indenture, or trust agreement.

Line 9

For a definition of a "disqualified person," see **Specific Instructions,** Part II, Line 4d, on page 3 of the application's instructions.

Form 1023 (Rev. 9-98)   Page **21**

Schedule E. Private Operating Foundations

Income Test		Most recent tax year
1a Adjusted net income, as defined in Regulations section 53.4942(a)-2(d)	1a	
b Minimum investment return, as defined in Regulations section 53.4942(a)-2(c)	1b	
2 Qualifying distributions:		
a Amounts (including administrative expenses) paid directly for the active conduct of the activities for which organized and operated under section 501(c)(3) (attach schedule)	2a	
b Amounts paid to acquire assets to be used (or held for use) directly in carrying out purposes described in section 170(c)(1) or 170(c)(2)(B) (attach schedule)	2b	
c Amounts set aside for specific projects that are for purposes described in section 170(c)(1) or 170(c)(2)(B) (attach schedule).	2c	
d **Total** qualifying distributions (add lines 2a, b, and c)	2d	
3 Percentages:		
a Percentage of qualifying distributions to adjusted net income (divide line 2d by line 1a)	3a	%
b Percentage of qualifying distributions to minimum investment return (divide line 2d by line 1b). . . (Percentage must be at least 85% for 3a or 3b)	3b	%
Assets Test		
4 Value of organization's assets used in activities that directly carry out the exempt purposes. Do not include assets held merely for investment or production of income (attach schedule)	4	
5 Value of any stock of a corporation that is controlled by applicant organization and carries out its exempt purposes (attach statement describing corporation)	5	
6 Value of all qualifying assets (add lines 4 and 5)	6	
7 Value of applicant organization's total assets	7	
8 Percentage of qualifying assets to total assets (divide line 6 by line 7—percentage must exceed 65%)	8	%
Endowment Test		
9 Value of assets not used (or held for use) directly in carrying out exempt purposes:		
a Monthly average of investment securities at fair market value	9a	
b Monthly average of cash balances	9b	
c Fair market value of all other investment property (attach schedule).	9c	
d **Total** (add lines 9a, b, and c).	9d	
10 Acquisition indebtedness related to line 9 items (attach schedule)	10	
11 Balance (subtract line 10 from line 9d)	11	
12 Multiply line 11 by 3½% (⅔ of the percentage for the minimum investment return computation under section 4942(e)). Line 2d above must equal or exceed the result of this computation	12	
Support Test		
13 Applicant organization's support as defined in section 509(d)	13	
14 Gross investment income as defined in section 509(e)	14	
15 Support for purposes of section 4942(j)(3)(B)(iii) (subtract line 14 from line 13)	15	
16 Support received from the general public, five or more exempt organizations, or a combination of these sources (attach schedule).	16	
17 For persons (other than exempt organizations) contributing more than 1% of line 15, enter the total amounts that are more than 1% of line 15	17	
18 Subtract line 17 from line 16	18	
19 Percentage of total support (divide line 18 by line 15—must be at least 85%)	19	%
20 Does line 16 include support from an exempt organization that is more than 25% of the amount of line 15?	☐ Yes ☐ No	

21 Newly created organizations with less than 1 year's experience: Attach a statement explaining how the organization is planning to satisfy the requirements of section 4942(j)(3) for the income test and one of the supplemental tests during its first year's operation. Include a description of plans and arrangements, press clippings, public announcements, solicitations for funds, etc.

22 Does the amount entered on line 2a above include any grants that the applicant organization made?   ☐ Yes ☐ No
If "Yes," attach a statement explaining how those grants satisfy the criteria for "significant involvement" grants described in section 53.4942(b)-1(b)(2) of the regulations.

For more information, see back of Schedule E.

Instructions

If the organization claims to be an operating foundation described in section 4942(j)(3) and—

a. Bases its claim to private operating foundation status on normal and regular operations over a period of years; or

b. Is newly created, set up as a private operating foundation, and has at least 1 year's experience;

provide the information under the **income test and under one of the three supplemental tests** (assets, endowment, or support). If the organization does not have at least 1 year's experience, provide the information called for on line 21. If the organization's private operating foundation status depends on its normal and regular operations as described in **a** above, attach a schedule similar to Schedule E showing the data in tabular form for the 3 years preceding the most recent tax year. (See Regulations section 53.4942(b)-1 for additional information before completing the "Income Test" section of this schedule.) Organizations claiming section 4942(j)(5) status must satisfy the income test and the endowment test.

A "private operating foundation" described in section 4942(j)(3) is a private foundation that spends substantially all of the smaller of its adjusted net income (as defined below) or its minimum investment return directly for the active conduct of the activities constituting the purpose or function for which it is organized and operated. The foundation must satisfy the income test under section 4942(j)(3)(A), as modified by Regulations section 53.4942(b)-1, and one of the following three supplemental tests: **(1)** the assets test under section 4942(j)(3)(B)(i); **(2)** the endowment test under section 4942(j)(3)(B)(ii); or **(3)** the support test under section 4942(j)(3)(B)(iii).

Certain long-term care facilities described in section 4942(j)(5) are treated as private operating foundations for purposes of section 4942 only.

"Adjusted net income" is the excess of gross income determined with the income modifications described below for the tax year over the sum of deductions determined with the deduction modifications described below. Items of gross income from any unrelated trade or business and the deductions directly connected with the unrelated trade or business are taken into account in computing the organization's adjusted net income.

Income Modifications

The following are income modifications (adjustments to gross income):

1. Section 103 (relating to interest on certain governmental obligations) does not apply. Thus, interest that otherwise would have been excluded should be included in gross income.

2. Except as provided in **3** below, capital gains and losses are taken into account only to the extent of the net short-term gain. Long-term gains and losses are disregarded.

3. The gross amount received from the sale or disposition of certain property should be included in gross income to the extent that the acquisition of the property constituted a qualifying distribution under section 4942(g)(1)(B).

4. Repayments of prior qualifying distributions (as defined in section 4942(g)(1)(A)) constitute items of gross income.

5. Any amount set aside under section 4942(g)(2) that is "not necessary for the purposes for which it was set aside" constitutes an item of gross income.

Deduction Modifications

The following are deduction modifications (adjustments to deductions):

1. Expenses for the general operation of the organization according to its charitable purposes (as contrasted with expenses for the production or collection of income and management, conservation, or maintenance of income-producing property) should not be taken as deductions. If only a portion of the property is used for production of income subject to section 4942 and the remainder is used for general charitable purposes, the expenses connected with that property should be divided according to those purposes. Only expenses related to the income-producing portion should be taken as deductions.

2. Charitable contributions, deductible under section 170 or 642(c), should not be taken into account as deductions for adjusted net income.

3. The net operating loss deduction prescribed under section 172 should not be taken into account as a deduction for adjusted net income.

4. The special deductions for corporations (such as the dividends-received deduction) allowed under sections 241 through 249 should not be taken into account as deductions for adjusted net income.

5. Depreciation and depletion should be determined in the same manner as under section 4940(c)(3)(B).

Section 265 (relating to the expenses and interest connected with tax-exempt income) should not be taken into account.

You may find it easier to figure adjusted net income by completing column (c), Part 1, Form 990-PF, according to the instructions for that form.

An organization that has been held to be a private operating foundation will continue to be such an organization only if it meets the income test and either the assets, endowment, or support test in later years. See Regulations section 53.4942(b) for additional information. No additional request for ruling will be necessary or appropriate for an organization to maintain its status as a private operating foundation. However, data related to the above tests must be submitted with the organization's annual information return, Form 990-PF.

Form 1023 (Rev. 9-98)

Schedule F. Homes for the Aged or Handicapped

1   What are the requirements for admission to residency? Explain fully and attach promotional literature and application forms.

2   Does or will the home charge an entrance or founder's fee? . . . . ☐ Yes ☐ No
If "Yes," explain and specify the amount charged.

3   What periodic fees or maintenance charges are or will be required of its residents?

4a   What established policy does the home have concerning residents who become unable to pay their regular charges?

 b   What arrangements does the home have or will it make with local and Federal welfare units, sponsoring organizations, or others to absorb all or part of the cost of maintaining those residents?

5   What arrangements does or will the home have to provide for the health needs of its residents?

6   In what way are the home's residential facilities designed to meet some combination of the physical, emotional, recreational, social, religious, and similar needs of the aged or handicapped?

7   Provide a description of the home's facilities and specify both the residential capacity of the home and the current number of residents.

8   Attach a sample copy of the contract or agreement the organization makes with or requires of its residents.

For more information, see back of Schedule F.

¶1652

Instructions

Line 1

Provide the criteria for admission to the home and submit brochures, pamphlets, or other printed material used to inform the public about the home's admissions policy.

Line 2

Indicate whether the fee charged is an entrance fee or a monthly charge, etc. Also, if the fee is an entrance fee, is it payable in a lump sum or on an installment basis?

Line 4

Indicate the organization's policy regarding residents who are unable to pay. Also, indicate whether the organization is subsidized for all or part of the cost of maintaining those residents who are unable to pay.

Line 5

Indicate whether the organization provides health care to the residents, either directly or indirectly, through some continuing arrangement with other organizations, facilities, or health personnel. If no health care is provided, indicate "N/A."

Form 1023 (Rev. 9-98)   Page **25**

Schedule G. Child Care Organizations

1 Is the organization's primary activity the providing of care for children away
from their homes?. . . . . ☐ **Yes**   ☐ **No**

2 How many children is the organization authorized to care for by the state (or local governmental
unit), and what was the average attendance during the past 6 months, or the number of months
the organization has been in existence if less than 6 months?

3 How many children are currently cared for by the organization?

4 Is substantially all (at least 85%) of the care provided for the purpose of
enabling parents to be gainfully employed or to seek employment?   . . . ☐ **Yes**   ☐ **No**

5 Are the services provided available to the general public?. . . . . ☐ **Yes**   ☐ **No**
If "No," explain.

6 Indicate the category, or categories, of parents whose children are eligible for the child care
services (check as many as apply):

    ☐   low-income parents

    ☐   any working parents (or parents looking for work)

    ☐   anyone with the ability to pay

    ☐   other (explain)

Instructions

Line 5
If your organization's services are not available
to the general public, indicate the particular
group or groups that may utilize the services.

REMINDER—If this organization claims to
operate a school, then it must also fill out
Schedule B.

¶1652

Schedule H. Organizations Providing Scholarship Benefits, Student Aid, etc., to Individuals

1a Describe the nature and the amount of the scholarship benefit, student aid, etc., including the terms and conditions governing its use, whether a gift or a loan, and how the availability of the scholarship is publicized. If the organization has established or will establish several categories of scholarship benefits, identify each kind of benefit and explain how the organization determines the recipients for each category. Attach a sample copy of any application the organization requires individuals to complete to be considered for scholarship grants, loans, or similar benefits. (Private foundations that make grants for travel, study, or other similar purposes are required to obtain advance approval of scholarship procedures. See Regulations sections 53.4945-4(c) and (d).)

b If you want this application considered as a request for approval of grant procedures in the event we determine that the organization is a private foundation, check here   .   .   .   . ▶ ☐

c If you checked the box in **1b** above, check the box(es) for which you wish the organization to be considered.

☐ 4945(g)(1)   ☐ 4945(g)(2)   ☐ 4945(g)(3)

2 What limitations or restrictions are there on the class of individuals who are eligible recipients? Specifically explain whether there are, or will be, any restrictions or limitations in the selection procedures based upon race or the employment status of the prospective recipient or any relative of the prospective recipient. Also indicate the approximate number of eligible individuals.

3 Indicate the number of grants the organization anticipates making annually   .   .   .   . ▶

4 If the organization bases its selections in any way on the employment status of the applicant or any relative of the applicant, indicate whether there is or has been any direct or indirect relationship between the members of the selection committee and the employer. Also indicate whether relatives of the members of the selection committee are possible recipients or have been recipients.

5 Describe any procedures the organization has for supervising grants (such as obtaining reports or transcripts) that it awards and any procedures it has for taking action if the terms of the grant are violated.

For more information, see back of Schedule H.

¶1652

Additional Information

Private foundations that make grants to individuals for travel, study, or other similar purposes are required to obtain advance approval of their grant procedures from the IRS. Such grants that are awarded under selection procedures that have not been approved by the IRS are subject to a 10% excise tax under section 4945. (See Regulations sections 53.4945-4(c) and (d).)

If you are requesting advance approval of the organization's grant procedures, the following sections apply to line **1c:**

4945(g)(1)— The grant constitutes a scholarship or fellowship grant that meets the provisions of section 117(a) prior to its amendment by the Tax Reform Act of 1986 and is to be used for study at an educational organization (school) described in section 170(b)(1)(A)(ii).

4945(g)(2)— The grant constitutes a prize or award that is subject to the provisions of section 74(b), if the recipient of such a prize or award is selected from the general public.

4945(g)(3)— The purpose of the grant is to achieve a specific objective, produce a report or other similar product, or improve or enhance a literary, artistic, musical, scientific, teaching, or other similar capacity, skill, or talent of the grantee.

Schedule I. Successors to "For Profit" Institutions

1 What was the name of the predecessor organization and the nature of its activities?

2 Who were the owners or principal stockholders of the predecessor organization? (If more space is needed, attach schedule.)

Name and address	Share or interest

3 Describe the business or family relationship between the owners or principal stockholders and principal employees of the predecessor organization and the officers, directors, and principal employees of the applicant organization.

4a Attach a copy of the agreement of sale or other contract that sets forth the terms and conditions of sale of the predecessor organization or of its assets to the applicant organization.

b Attach an appraisal by an independent qualified expert showing the fair market value at the time of sale of the facilities or property interest sold.

5 Has any property or equipment formerly used by the predecessor organization been rented to the applicant organization or will any such property be rented? . . . . ☐ **Yes** ☐ **No**
If "Yes," explain and attach copies of all leases and contracts.

6 Is the organization leasing or will it lease or otherwise make available any space or equipment to the owners, principal stockholders, or principal employees of the predecessor organization?. . . . . ☐ **Yes** ☐ **No**
If "Yes," explain and attach a list of these tenants and a copy of the lease for each such tenant.

7 Were any new operating policies initiated as a result of the transfer of assets from a profit-making organization to a nonprofit organization? . . . . ☐ **Yes** ☐ **No**
If "Yes," explain.

Additional Information

A "for profit" institution for purposes of Schedule I includes any organization in which a person may have a proprietary or partnership interest, hold corporate stock, or otherwise exercise an ownership interest. The institution need not have operated for the purpose of making a profit.

Department of the Treasury
Internal Revenue Service

Instructions for Form 1023

(Revised September 1998)

Application for Recognition of Exemption Under Section 501(c)(3) of the Internal Revenue Code

Note: *Retain a copy of the completed Form 1023 in the organization's permanent records. See* **Public Inspection of Form 1023** *regarding public inspection of approved applications.*

General Instructions

Section references are to the Internal Revenue Code unless otherwise noted.

User Fee.—Submit with the Form 1023 application for a determination letter, a **Form 8718,** User Fee for Exempt Organization Determination Letter Request, and the user fee called for in the Form 8718. You may obtain Form 8718, and additional forms and publications, through your local IRS office or by calling 1-800-829-3676 (1-800-TAX-FORM). User fees are subject to change on an annual basis. Therefore, be sure that you use the most current Form 8718.

Helpful information.—For additional information, see:

● **Pub. 557,** Tax-Exempt Status for Your Organization

● **Pub. 598,** Tax on Unrelated Business Income of Exempt Organizations

● **Pub. 578,** Tax Information for Private Foundations and Foundation Managers

● **Internet site,** www.irs.ustreas.gov/bus_info/eo/

Purpose of Form

1. Completed Form 1023 required for section 501(c)(3) exemption.—Unless it meets one of the exceptions in **2** below, any organization formed after October 9, 1969, must file a Form 1023 to qualify as a section 501(c)(3) organization.

The IRS determines if an organization is a private foundation from the information entered on a Form 1023.

2. Organizations not required to file Form 1023.—The following types of organizations may be considered tax-exempt under section 501(c)(3) even if they do not file Form 1023:

  1. Churches,

  2. Integrated auxiliaries of churches, and conventions or associations of churches, or

  3. Any organization that:

  (a) Is not a private foundation (as defined in section 509(a)), and

  (b) Has gross receipts in each taxable year of normally not more than $5,000.

Even if the above organizations are not required to file Form 1023 to be tax-exempt, these organizations may choose to file Form 1023 in order to receive a determination letter that recognizes their section 501(c)(3) status.

Section 501(c)(3) status provides certain incidental benefits such as:

● Public recognition of tax-exempt status.

● Advance assurance to donors of deductibility of contributions.

● Exemption from certain state taxes.

● Exemption from certain Federal excise taxes.

● Nonprofit mailing privileges, etc.

3. Other organizations.—Section 501(e) and (f) cooperative service organizations, section 501(k) child care organizations, and section

501(n) charitable risk pools use Form 1023 to apply for a determination letter under section 501(c)(3).

4. Group exemption letter.—Generally, Form 1023 is not used to apply for a group exemption letter. See Pub. 557 for information on how to apply for a group exemption letter.

What To File

All applicants must complete pages 1 through 9 of Form 1023. These organizations must also complete the schedules or form indicated:

  1 Churches . . . . Schedule A
  2. Schools . . . . Schedule B
  3. Hospitals and Medical Research . . . . . . Schedule C
  4. Supporting Organizations (509(a)(3)) . . . . . Schedule D
  5. Private Operating Foundations . . . . Schedule E
  6. Homes for the Aged or Handicapped . . . . Schedule F
  7. Child Care . . . . Schedule G
  8. Scholarship Benefits or Student Aid . . . . . Schedule H
  9. Organizations that have taken over or will take over a "for profit" institution . . . . Schedule I
  10. Organizations requesting an advance ruling in Part III, Line 10 . . . . Form 872-C

Attachments.—For any attachments submitted with Form 1023.—

● Show the organization's name, address, and employer identification number (EIN).

● Identify the Part and line item number to which the attachment relates.

● Use 8½ x 11 inch paper for any attachments.

● Include any court decisions, rulings, opinions, etc., that will expedite processing of the application. Generally, attachments in the form of tape recordings are not acceptable unless accompanied by a transcript.

When To File

An organization formed after October 9, 1969, must file Form 1023 to be recognized as an organization described in section 501(c)(3). Generally, if an organization files its application within 15 months after the end of the month in which it was formed, and if the IRS approves the application, the effective date of the organization's section 501(c)(3) status will be the date it was organized.

Generally, if an organization does not file its application (Form 1023) within 15 months after the end of the month in which it was formed, it will not qualify for exempt status during the period before the date of its application. For exceptions and special rules, including automatic extensions in some cases, see Part III of Form 1023.

The date of receipt of the Form 1023 is the date of the U.S. postmark on the cover in which an exemption application is mailed or, if no postmark appears on the cover, the date the application is stamped as received by the IRS.

Private delivery services.—See the instructions for your income tax return for information on certain private delivery services designated by the IRS to meet the "timely mailing as timely filing/paying rule." The private delivery service can tell you how to get written proof of the mailing date.

Caution: *Private delivery services cannot deliver items to P.O. boxes. You must use the U. S. Postal Service to mail any item to an IRS P.O. box address. See the Form 8718 for the P.O. box address as well as the express mail or a delivery service address.*

Where To File

File the completed Form 1023 application, and all required information, with the IRS at the address shown in Form 8718.

The IRS will determine the organization's tax-exempt status and whether any annual returns must be filed.

Signature Requirements

An officer, a trustee who is authorized to sign, or another person authorized by a power of attorney, must sign the Form 1023 application. Attach a power of attorney to the application. You may use **Form 2848,** Power of Attorney and Declaration of Representative, for this purpose.

Deductibility of Contributions

Donors can take a charitable contribution deduction if their gift or bequest is made to a section 501(c)(3) organization.

The effective date of an organization's section 501(c)(3) status determines the date that contributions to it are deductible by donors. (See **When To File** on page 1.)

Contributions by U.S. residents to foreign organizations generally are not deductible. Tax treaties between the U.S. and certain foreign countries provide limited exceptions. Foreign organizations (other than those in Canada or Mexico) that claim eligibility to receive contributions deductible by U.S. residents must attach an English copy of the U.S. tax treaty that provides for such deductibility.

Appeal Procedures

The organization's application will be considered by the IRS which will either:

1. Issue a favorable determination letter;

2. Issue a proposed adverse determination letter denying the exempt status requested; or

3. Refer the case to the National Office.

If the IRS sends you a proposed adverse determination, it will advise you of your appeal rights at that time.

Language and Currency Requirements

Language requirements.—Prepare the Form 1023 and attachments in English. Provide an English translation if the organizational document or bylaws are in any other language.

You may be asked to provide English translations of foreign language publications that the organization produces or distributes and that are submitted with the application.

Financial requirements.—Report all financial information in U.S. dollars (specify the conversion rate used). Combine amounts from within and outside the United States and report the total for each item on the financial statements.

For example:

Gross Investment Income	
From U.S. sources	$4,000
From non-U.S. sources	1,000
Amount to report on income statement	$5,000

Annual Information Return

If an annual information return is due while the organization's application for recognition of exempt status is pending with the IRS (including any appeal of a proposed adverse determination), the organization should file at the following address:

Internal Revenue Service
Ogden Service Center
Ogden, Utah 84201-0027

- **Form 990,** Return of Organization Exempt From Income Tax, **or**
- **Form 990-EZ,** Short Form Return of Organization Exempt From Income Tax, **and,**
- **Schedule A (Form 990),** Organization Exempt Under Section 501(c)(3), **or**
- **Form 990-PF,** Return of Private Foundation, if the organization acknowledges it is a private foundation, **and**

Indicate that an application is pending.

If an organization has unrelated business income of more than $1,000, file **Form 990-T,** Exempt Organization Business Income Tax Return.

Public Inspection of Form 1023

Caution: *Note the discussion below for the potential effect of the Taxpayer Bill of Rights 2 (TBOR2) on these instructions.*

IRS responsibilities for public inspection.—If the organization's application for section 501(c)(3) status is approved, the following items will be open to public inspection in any District office and at the National Office of the IRS (section 6104):

1. The organization's application and any supporting documents.

2. Any letter or other document issued by the IRS with regard to the application.

Note that the following items are not available for public inspection:

1. Any information relating to a trade secret, patent, style of work, or apparatus that, if released, would adversely affect the organization, or

2. Any other information that would adversely affect the national defense.

IMPORTANT: Applicants must identify this information by clearly marking it, "NOT SUBJECT TO PUBLIC INSPECTION," and must attach a statement to explain why the organization asks that the information be withheld. If the IRS agrees, the information will be withheld.

Organization's responsibilities for public inspection.—The organization must make available a copy of its approved application and supporting documents, along with any document or letter issued by the IRS for public inspection.

These documents must be available during regular business hours at the organization's principal office and at each of its regional or district offices having at least three paid employees. See Notice 88-120,1988-2 C.B. 454.

A penalty of $20 a day will be imposed on any person under a duty to comply with the public inspection requirements for each day a failure to comply continues.

Furnishing copies of documents under TBOR2.—The Taxpayer Bill of Rights 2 (TBOR2), enacted July 30, 1996, modified prospectively the section 6685 penalty and the rules for the public inspection of returns and exemption applications. An organization must furnish a copy of its Form 990, Form 990-EZ, or exemption application, and certain related documents, if a request is made in writing or in person.

For a request made in person, the organization must make an immediate response.

For a response to a written request, the organization must provide the requested copies within 30 days.

The organization must furnish copies of its Forms 990, or Forms 990-EZ, for any of its 3 most recent taxable years. No charge is to be made other than charging a reasonable fee for reproduction and actual postage costs.

An organization need not provide copies if:

1. The organization has made the requested documents widely available in a manner provided in Treasury regulations, or

2. The Secretary of the Treasury determined, upon application by the organization, that the organization was subject to a harassment campaign such that a waiver of the obligation to provide copies would be in the public interest.

Penalty for failure to allow public inspection or provide copies.—The section 6685 penalty for willful failure to allow public inspections or provide copies is increased from the present-law level of $1,000 to $5,000 by TBOR2.

Effective date of TBOR2.—These public inspection provisions governing tax-exempt organizations under TBOR2 generally apply to requests made no earlier than 60 days after the date on which the Treasury Department publishes the regulations required under the provisions. However, Congress, in the legislative history of TBOR2, indicated that organizations would comply voluntarily with the public inspection provisions prior to the issuance of such regulations.

Special Rule for Canadian Colleges and Universities

A Canadian college or university that received **Form T2051,** Notification of Registration, from Revenue Canada (Department of National Revenue, Taxation) and whose registration has not been revoked, does not need to complete all parts of Form 1023.

Such an organization must complete only Part I of Form 1023 and Schedule B (Schools, Colleges, and Universities). It must attach a copy of its **Form T2050,** Application for Registration, together with all the required attachments submitted to Revenue Canada. It must furnish an English translation if any attachments were prepared in French.

Other Canadian organizations.—Other Canadian organizations that seek a determination of section 501(c)(3) status must complete Form 1023 in the same manner as U.S. organizations.

Specific Instructions

The following instructions are keyed to the line items on the application form:

Part I. Identification of Applicant

Line 1. Full name and address of organization.—Enter the organization's name exactly as it appears in its creating document including amendments. Show the other name in parentheses, if the organization will be operating under another name.

Page 2

For a foreign address, enter the information in the following order: city, province or state, and country. Follow the country's practice in placing the postal code in the address. **Do not** abbreviate the country name.

Line 2. Employer identification number (EIN).—All organizations must have an EIN. Enter the nine-digit EIN the IRS assigned to the organization. See Form SS-4, Application for Employer Identification Number, for information on how to obtain an EIN immediately by telephone, if the organization does not have an EIN. Enter, "applied for," if the organization has applied for an EIN number previously. Attach a statement giving the date of the application and the office where it was filed. **Do not** apply for an EIN more than once.

Line 3. Person to contact.—Enter the name and telephone number of the person to contact during business hours if more information is needed. The contact person should be an officer, director, or a person with power of attorney who is familiar with the organization's activities and is authorized to act on its behalf. Attach Form 2848 or other power of attorney.

Line 4. Month the annual accounting period ends.—Enter the month the organization's annual accounting period ends. The accounting period is usually the 12-month period that is the organization's tax year. The organization's first tax year depends on the accounting period chosen. The first tax year could be less than 12 months.

Line 5. Date formed.—Enter the date the organization became a legal entity. For a corporation, this is the date that the articles of incorporation were approved by the appropriate state official. For an unincorporated organization, it is the date its constitution or articles of association were adopted.

Line 6.—Indicate if the organization is one of the following:

- 501(e)   Cooperative hospital service organization
- 501(f)   Cooperative service organization of operating educational organization
- 501(k)   Organization providing child care
- 501(n)   Charitable risk pool

If none of the above applies, make no entry on line 6.

Line 7.—Indicate if the organization has ever filed a Form 1023 or **Form 1024,** Application for Recognition of Exemption Under Section 501(a), with the IRS.

Line 8.—If the organization for which this application is being filed is a private foundation, answer "N/A." If the organization is not required to file Form 990 (or Form 990-EZ) and is not a private foundation, answer "No" and attach an explanation. See the Instructions for Form 990 and Form 990-EZ for a discussion of organizations not required to file Form 990 (or Form 990-EZ). Otherwise, answer "Yes."

Line 9.—Indicate if the organization has ever filed Federal income tax returns as a taxable organization or filed returns as an exempt organization (e.g., Form 990, 990-EZ, 990-PF, or 990-T).

Line 10. Type of organization and organizational documents.— Organizing instrument.—Submit a conformed copy of the organizing instrument. If the organization does not have an organizing instrument, it will not qualify for exempt status.

A conformed copy is one that agrees with the original and all amendments to it. The conformed copy may be:

- A photocopy of the original signed and dated organizing document, OR
- A copy of the organizing document that is unsigned but is sent with a written declaration, signed by an authorized individual, that states that the copy is a complete and accurate copy of the original signed and dated document.

Corporation.—In the case of a corporation, a copy of the articles of incorporation, approved and dated by an appropriate state official, is sufficient by itself.

If an unsigned copy of the articles of incorporation is submitted, it must be accompanied by the written declaration discussed above.

Signed, or unsigned, copies of the articles of incorporation must be accompanied by a declaration stating that the original copy of the articles was filed with, and approved by, the state. The date filed must be specified.

Unincorporated association.—In the case of an unincorporated association, the conformed copy of the constitution, articles of association, or other organizing document must indicate, in the document itself, or in a written declaration, that the organization was formed by the adoption of the document by two or more persons.

Bylaws.—If the organization has adopted bylaws, include a current copy. The bylaws do not need to be signed if they are submitted as an attachment to the Form 1023 application. The bylaws of an organization alone are not an organizing instrument. They are merely the internal rules and regulations of the organization.

Trust.—In the case of a trust, a copy of the signed and dated trust instrument must be furnished.

Dissolution clause.—For an organization to qualify for exempt status, its organizing instrument must contain a proper dissolution clause, or state law must provide for distribution of assets for one or more section 501(c)(3) purposes upon dissolution. If the organization is relying on state law, provide the citation for the law and briefly state the law's provisions in an attachment. Foreign organizations must provide the citation for the foreign statute and attach a copy of the statute along with an English language translation.

See Pub. 557 for a discussion of dissolution clauses under the heading, **Articles of Organization, Dedication and Distribution of Assets.** Examples of dissolution clauses are shown in the sample organizing instruments given in that publication.

Organizational purposes.—The organizing instrument must specify the organizational purposes of the organization. The purposes specified must be limited to one or more of those given in section 501(c)(3). See Pub. 557 for detailed instructions and for sample organizing instruments that satisfy the requirements of section 501(c)(3) and the related regulations.

Part II. Activities and Operational Information

Line 1.—It is important that you report all activities carried on by the organization to enable the IRS to make a proper determination of the organization's exempt status.

Line 2.—If it is anticipated that the organization's principal sources of support will increase or decrease substantially in relation to the organization's total support, attach a statement describing anticipated changes and explaining the basis for the expectation.

Line 3.—For purposes of providing the information requested on line 3, "fundraising activity" includes the solicitation of contributions and both functionally related activities and unrelated business activities. Include a description of the nature and magnitude of the activities.

Line 4a.—Furnish the mailing addresses of the organization's principal officers, directors, or trustees. Do not give the address of the organization.

Line 4b.—The annual compensation includes salary, bonus, and any other form of payment to the individual for services while employed by the organization.

Line 4c.—Public officials include anyone holding an elected position or anyone appointed to a position by an elected official.

Line 4d.—For purposes of this application, a "disqualified person" is any person who, if the applicant organization were a private foundation, is:

1. A "substantial contributor" to the foundation (defined below);

2. A foundation manager;

3. An owner of more than 20% of the total combined voting power of a corporation that is a substantial contributor to the foundation;

4. A "member of the family" of any person described in **1, 2,** or **3** above;

5. A corporation, partnership, or trust in which persons described in **1, 2, 3,** or **4** above, hold more than 35% of the combined voting power, the profits interest, or the beneficial interests; and

6. Any other private foundation that is effectively controlled by the same persons who control the first-mentioned private foundation or any other private foundation substantially all of whose contributions were made by the same contributors.

A substantial contributor is any person who gave a total of more than $5,000 to the organization, and those contributions are more than 2% of all the contributions and bequests received by the organization from the date it was created up to the end of the year the contributions by the substantial contributor were received. A creator of a trust is treated as a substantial contributor regardless of the amount contributed by that person or others.

See Pub. 578 for more information on "disqualified persons."

Page 3

Line 5.—If your organization controls or is controlled by another exempt organization or a taxable organization, answer "Yes." "Control" means that:

1. Fifty percent (50%) or more of the filing organization's officers, directors, trustees, or key employees are also officers, directors, trustees, or key employees of the second organization being tested for control;

2. The filing organization appoints 50% or more of the officers, directors, trustees, or key employees of the second organization; or

3. Fifty percent (50%) or more of the filing organization's officers, directors, trustees, or key employees are appointed by the second organization.

Control exists if the 50% test is met by any one group of persons even if collectively the 50% test is not met. Examples of special relationships are common officers and the sharing of office space or employees.

Line 6.—If the organization conducts any financial transactions (either receiving or distributing cash or other assets), or nonfinancial activities with an exempt organization (other than a 501(c)(3) organization), or with a political organization, answer "Yes," and explain.

Line 7.—If the organization must report its income and expense activity to any other organization (tax-exempt or taxable entity), answer "Yes."

Line 8.—Examples of assets used to perform an exempt function are: land, building, equipment, and publications. Do not include cash or property producing investment income. If you have no assets used in performing the organization's exempt function, answer "N/A."

Line 10a.—If the organization is managed by another exempt organization, a taxable organization, or an individual, answer "Yes."

Line 10b.—If the organization leases property from anyone or leases any of its property to anyone, answer "Yes."

Line 11.—A membership organization for purposes of this question is an organization that is composed of individuals or organizations who:

1. Share in the common goal for which the organization was created;

2. Actively participate in achieving the organization's purposes; and

3. Pay dues.

Line 12.—Examples of benefits, services, and products are: meals to homeless people, home for the aged, a museum open to the public, and a symphony orchestra giving public performances.

Note: *Organizations that provide low-income housing should see Rev. Proc. 96-32, 1996-1 C.B. 717, for a "safe harbor" and an alternative facts and circumstances test to be used in completing line 12.*

Line 13.—An organization is attempting to influence legislation if it contacts or urges the public to contact members of a legislative body, for the purpose of proposing, supporting, or opposing legislation, or if it advocates the adoption or rejection of legislation.

If you answer "Yes," you may want to file **Form 5768,** Election/Revocation of Election by an Eligible Section 501(c)(3) Organization To Make Expenditures To Influence Legislation.

Line 14.—An organization is intervening in a political campaign if it promotes or opposes the candidacy or prospective candidacy of an individual for public office.

Part III. Technical Requirements

Line 1.—If you check "Yes," proceed to line 7. If you check "No," proceed to line 2.

Line 2a.—To qualify as an integrated auxiliary, an organization must not be a private foundation and must satisfy the affiliation and support tests of Regulations section 1.6033-2(h).

Line 3.—Relief from the 15-month filing requirement is granted automatically if the organization submits a completed Form 1023 within 12 months from the end of the 15-month period.

To get this extension, an organization must add the following statement at the top of its application: "Filed Pursuant to Section 301.9100-2." No request for a letter ruling is required to obtain an automatic extension.

Line 4.—See Regulation sections 301.9100-1 and 301.9100-3 for information about a discretionary extension beyond the 27-month period. Under these regulations, the IRS will allow an organization a reasonable extension of time to file a Form 1023 if it submits evidence to establish that:

(a) It acted reasonably and in good faith, and

(b) Granting relief will not prejudice the interests of the government.

Showing reasonable action and good faith.—An organization acted reasonably and showed good faith if at least one of the following is true.

1. The organization filed its application before the IRS discovered its failure to file.

2. The organization failed to file because of intervening events beyond its control.

3. The organization exercised reasonable diligence but was not aware of the filing requirement.

To determine whether the organization exercised reasonable diligence, it is necessary to take into account the complexity of filing and the organization's experience in these matters.

4. The organization reasonably relied upon the written advice of the IRS.

5. The organization reasonably relied upon the advice of a qualified tax professional who failed to file or advise the organization to file Form 1023. An organization cannot rely on the advice of a qualified tax professional if it knows or should know that he or she is not competent to render advice on filing exemption applications or is not aware of all the relevant facts.

Not acting reasonably and in good faith.—An organization has not acted reasonably and in good faith if it chose not to file after being informed of the requirement to file and the consequences of failure to do so. Furthermore, an organization has not acted reasonably and in good faith if it used hindsight to request an extension of time to file. That is, if after the original deadline to file passes, specific facts have changed so that filing an application becomes advantageous to an organization, the IRS will not ordinarily grant an extension. To qualify for an extension in this situation, the organization must prove that its decision to file did not involve hindsight.

No prejudice to the interest of the government.—Prejudice to the interest of the government results if granting an extension of time to file to an organization results in a lower total tax liability for the years to which the filing applies than would have been the case if the organization had applied on time. Before granting an extension, the IRS may require the organization requesting it to submit a statement from an independent auditor certifying that no prejudice will result if the extension is granted.

Procedure for requesting extension.—To request a discretionary extension, an organization must submit the following with its Form 1023:

● A statement showing the date Form 1023 should have been filed and the date it was actually filed.

● An affidavit describing in detail the events that led to the failure to apply and to the discovery of that failure. If the organization relied on a qualified tax professional's advice, the affidavit must describe the engagement and responsibilities of the professional and the extent to which the organization relied on him or her.

● All documents relevant to the election application.

● A dated declaration, signed by an individual authorized to act for the organization, that includes the following statement: "Under penalties of perjury, I declare that I have examined this request, including accompanying documents, and, to the best of my knowledge and belief, the request contains all the relevant facts relating to the request, and such facts are true, correct, and complete."

● A detailed affidavit from individuals having knowledge or information about the events that led to the failure to make the application and to the discovery of that failure. These individuals include accountants or attorneys knowledgeable in tax matters who advised the organization concerning the application. Any affidavit from a tax professional must describe the engagement and responsibilities of the professional as well as the advice that the professional provided to the organization. The affidavit must also include the name, current address, and taxpayer identification number of the individual making the affidavit (the affiant). The affiant must also forward with the affidavit a dated and signed declaration that states: "Under penalties of perjury, I declare that I have examined this request, including accompanying documents, and, to the best of my knowledge and belief, the request contains all the relevant facts relating to the request, and such facts are true, correct, and complete."

The reasons for late filing should be specific to your particular organization and situation. Regulation section 301.9100-3 (see above) lists the factors the IRS will consider in determining if good cause exists for granting a discretionary extension of time to file the application. To address these factors, your response for line 4 should provide the following information:

Page 4

1. Whether the organization consulted an attorney or accountant knowledgeable in tax matters or communicated with a responsible IRS employee (before or after the organization was created) to ascertain the organization's Federal filing requirements and, if so, the names and occupations or titles of the persons contacted, the approximate dates, and the substance of the information obtained;

2. How and when the organization learned about the 15-month deadline for filing Form 1023;

3. Whether any significant intervening circumstances beyond the organization's control prevented it from submitting the application timely or within a reasonable period of time after it learned of the requirement to file the application within the 15-month period; and

4. Any other information that you believe may establish reasonable action and good faith and no prejudice to the interest of the government for not filing timely or otherwise justify granting the relief sought.

A request for relief under this section is treated as part of the request for the exemption determination letter and is covered by the user fee submitted with Form 8718.

Line 5.—If you answer "No," the organization may receive an adverse letter limiting the effective date of its exempt status to the date its application was received.

Line 6.—The organization may still be able to qualify for exemption under section 501(c)(4) for the period preceding the effective date of its exemption as a section 501(c)(3) organization. If the organization is qualified under section 501(c)(4) and page 1 of Form 1024 is filed as directed, the organization will not be liable for income tax returns as a taxable entity. Contributions to section 501(c)(4) organizations are generally not deductible by donors as charitable contributions.

Line 7.—Private foundations are subject to various limitations, restrictions, and excise taxes under Chapter 42 of the Code that do not apply to public charities. Also, contributions to private foundations may receive less favorable treatment than contributions to public charities. See Pub. 578. Therefore, it is usually to an organization's advantage to show that it qualifies as a public charity rather than as a private foundation if its activities or sources of support permit it to do so. Unless an organization meets one of the exceptions below, it is a private foundation. In general, an organization is **not** a private foundation if it is:

1. A church, school, hospital, or governmental unit;

2. A medical research organization operated in conjunction with a hospital;

3. An organization operated for the benefit of a college or university that is owned or operated by a governmental unit;

4. An organization that normally receives a substantial part of its support in the form of contributions from a governmental unit or from the general public as provided in section 170(b)(1)(A)(vi);

5. An organization that normally receives not more than one-third of its support from gross investment income and more than one-third of its support from contributions, membership fees, and gross receipts related to its exempt functions (subject to certain exceptions) as provided in section 509(a)(2);

6. An organization operated solely for the benefit of, and in connection with, one or more organizations described above (or for the benefit of one or more of the organizations described in section 501(c)(4), (5), or (6) of the Code and also described in **5** above), but not controlled by disqualified persons other than foundation managers, as provided in section 509(a)(3); or

7. An organization organized and operated to test for public safety as provided in section 509(a)(4).

Line 8.—Basis for private operating foundation status: (Complete this line **only** if you answered "Yes" to the question on line 7.)

A "private operating foundation" is a private foundation that spends substantially all of its adjusted net income or its minimum investment return, whichever is less, directly for the active conduct of the activities constituting the purpose or function for which it is organized and operated.

The foundation must satisfy the income test and one of the three supplemental tests: **(1)** the assets test; **(2)** the endowment test; or **(3)** the support test. For additional information, see Pub. 578.

Line 9.—Basis for nonprivate foundation status: Check the box that shows why your organization is not a private foundation.

Box (a). A church or convention or association of churches.

Box (b). A school.—See the definition in the instructions for Schedule B.

Box (c). A hospital or medical research organization.—See the instructions for Schedule C.

Box (d). A governmental unit.—This category includes a state, a possession of the United States, or a political subdivision of any of the foregoing, or the United States, or the District of Columbia.

Box (e). Organizations operated in connection with or solely for organizations described in (a) through (d) or (g), (h), and (i).—The organization must be organized and operated for the benefit of, to perform the functions of, or to carry out the purposes of one or more specified organizations described in section 509(a)(1) or (2). It must be operated, supervised, or controlled by or in connection with one or more of the organizations described in the instructions for boxes **(a)** through **(d)** or **(g), (h),** and **(i).** It must not be controlled directly or indirectly by disqualified persons (other than foundation managers or organizations described in section 509(a)(1) or (2)). To show whether the organization satisfies these tests, complete Schedule D.

Box (f). An organization testing for public safety.—An organization in this category is one that tests products to determine their acceptability for use by the general public. It does not include any organization testing for the benefit of a manufacturer as an operation or control in the manufacture of its product.

Box (g). Organization for the benefit of a college or university owned or operated by a governmental unit.—The organization must be organized and operated exclusively for the benefit of a college or university that:

● Is an educational organization within the meaning of section 170(b)(1)(A)(ii) and is an agency or instrumentality of a state or political subdivision of a state;

● Is owned or operated by a state or political subdivision of a state; OR

● Is owned or operated by an agency or instrumentality of one or more states or political subdivisions.

The organization must also normally receive a substantial part of its support from the United States or any state or political subdivision of a state, or from direct or indirect contributions from the general public or from a combination of these sources.

An organizaton described in section 170(b)(1)(A)(iv) will be subject to the same publicly supported rules that are applicable to 170(b)(1)(A)(vi) organizations described in box (h) below.

Box (h). Organization receiving support from a governmental unit or from the general public.—The organization must receive a substantial part of its support from the United States or any state or political subdivision, or from direct or indirect contributions from the general public, or from a combination of these sources.

The organization may satisfy the support requirement in either of two ways.

(1) It will be treated as publicly supported if the support it normally receives from the above-described governmental units and the general public equals at least one-third of its total support.

(2) It will also be treated as publicly supported if the support it normally receives from governmental or public sources equals at least 10% of total support and the organization is set up to attract new and additional public or governmental support on a continuous basis.

If the organization's governmental and public support is at least 10%, but not over one-third of its total support, the questions on lines 1 through 14 of Part II will apply to determine both the organization's claim of exemption and whether it is publicly supported. Preparers should exercise care to assure that those questions are answered in detail.

Box (i). Organization described in section 509(a)(2).—The organization must satisfy the support test under section 509(a)(2)(A) and the gross investment income test under section 509(a)(2)(B).

To satisfy the support test, the organization must normally receive more than one-third of its support from: **(a)** gifts, grants, contributions, or membership fees, and **(b)** gross receipts from admissions, sales of merchandise, performance of services, or furnishing of facilities, in an activity that is not an unrelated trade or business (subject to certain limitations discussed below).

This one-third of support must be from organizations described in section 509(a)(1), governmental sources, or persons other than disqualified persons.

In computing gross receipts from admissions, sales of merchandise, performance of services, or furnishing of facilities in an activity that is not an unrelated trade or business, the gross receipts from any one person or from any bureau or similar agency of a governmental unit are includible only to the extent they do not exceed the greater of $5,000 or 1% of the organization's total support.

To satisfy the gross investment income test, the organization must not receive more than one-third of its support from gross investment income.

Box (j).—If you believe the organization meets the public support test of section 170(b)(1)(A)(vi) or 509(a)(2) but are uncertain as to which public support test it satisfies, check box **(j)**. By checking this box, you are claiming that the organization is not a private foundation and are agreeing to let the IRS compute the public support of your organization and determine the correct foundation status.

Line 10.—An organization must complete a tax year consisting of at least 8 months to receive a definitive (final) ruling under sections 170(b)(1)(A)(vi) and 509(a)(1), or under section 509(a)(2).

However, organizations that checked box **(h), (i),** or **(j)** on line 9 that do not meet the 8-month requirement must request an advance ruling that covers their first 5 tax years instead of requesting a definitive ruling.

An organization that meets the 8-month requirement has two options:

1. It may request a definitive ruling. The organization's public support computation will be based on the support the organization has received to date; or

2. It may request an advance ruling. The organization's public support computation will be based on the support it receives during its first 5 tax years.

An organization should consider the advance ruling option if it has not received significant public support during its first tax year or during its first and second tax years, but it reasonably expects to receive such support by the end of its fifth tax year.

An organization that receives an advance ruling is treated, during the 5-year advance ruling period, as a public charity (rather than a private foundation) for certain purposes, including those relating to the deductibility of contributions by the general public.

Line 11.—For definition of an unusual grant, see instructions for Part IV-A, line 12.

Line 12.—Answer this question only if you checked box **(g), (h),** or **(j)** on line 9.

Line 13.—Answer the question on this line only if you checked box **(i)** or **(j)** on line 9 and are requesting a definitive ruling on line 10.

Line 14.—Answer "Yes" or "No" on each line. If "Yes," you must complete the appropriate schedule. Each schedule is included in this application package with accompanying instructions. For a brief definition of each type of organization, see the appropriate schedule.

Part IV. Financial Data

Complete the Statement of Revenue and Expenses for the current year and each of the 3 years immediately before it (or the years the organization has existed, if less than 4).

Any applicant that has existed for less than 1 year must give financial data for the current year and proposed budgets for the following 2 years.

The IRS may request financial data for more than 4 years if necessary.

All financial information for the current year must cover the period beginning on the first day of the organization's established annual accounting period and ending on any day that is within 60 days of the date of this application.

If the date of this application is less than 60 days after the first day of the current accounting period, no financial information is required for the current year.

Financial information is required for the 3 preceding years regardless of the current year requirements. Please note that if no financial information is required for the current year, the preceding year's financial information can end on any day that is within 60 days of the date of this application.

Prepare the statements using the method of accounting and the accounting period (entered on line 4 of Part I) the organization uses in keeping its books and records. If the organization uses a method other than the cash receipts and disbursements method, attach a statement explaining the method used.

A. Statement of Revenue and Expenses

Line 1.—Do not include amounts received from the general public or a governmental unit for the exercise or performance of the organization's exempt function. However, include payments made by a governmental unit to enable the organization to provide a service to the general public.

Do not include unusual grants. See the explanation for unusual grants in Line 12 of this section.

Line 2.—Include amounts received from members for the purpose of providing support to the organization. These are considered as contributions. Do not include payments to purchase admissions, merchandise, services, or use of facilities.

Line 3.—Include on this line the income received from dividends, interest, and payments received on securities loans, rents, and royalties.

Line 4.—Enter the organization's net income from any activities that are regularly carried on and are not related to the organization's exempt purposes.

Examples of such income include fees from the commercial testing of products; income from renting office equipment or other personal property; and income from the sale of advertising in an exempt organization's periodical. See Pub. 598 for information about unrelated business income and activities.

Line 5.—Enter the amount collected by the local tax authority from the general public that has been allocated for your organization.

Line 6.—To report the value of services and/or facilities furnished by a governmental unit, use the fair market value at the time the service/facility was furnished to your organization. Do not include any other donated services or facilities in Part IV.

Line 7.—Enter the total income from all sources that is not reported on lines 1 through 6, or lines 9, 11, and 12. Attach a schedule that lists each type of revenue source and the amount derived from each.

Line 9.—Include income generated by the organization's exempt function activities (charitable, educational, etc.) and its nontaxable fundraising events (excluding any contributions received).

Examples of such income include the income derived by a symphony orchestra from the sale of tickets to its performances; and raffles, bingo, or other fundraising-event income that is not taxable as unrelated business income because the income-producing activities are not regularly carried on or because they are conducted with substantially all (at least 85%) volunteer labor. Record related cost of sales on line 22, Other.

Line 11.—Attach a schedule that shows a description of each asset, the name of the person to whom sold, and the amount received. In the case of publicly traded securities sold through a broker, the name of the purchaser is not required.

Line 12.—Unusual grants generally consist of substantial contributions and bequests from disinterested persons that:

1. Are attracted by reason of the publicly supported nature of the organization;

2. Are unusual and unexpected as to the amount; and

3. Would, by reason of their size, adversely affect the status of the organization as normally meeting the support test of section 170(b)(1)(A)(vi) or section 509(a)(2), as the case may be.

If the organization is awarded an unusual grant and the terms of the granting instrument provide that the organization will receive the funds over a period of years, the amount received by the organization each year under the grant may be excluded. See the regulations under sections 170 and 509.

Line 14.—Fundraising expenses represent the total expenses incurred in soliciting contributions, gifts, grants, etc.

Line 15.—Attach a schedule showing the name of the recipient, a brief description of the purposes or conditions of payment, and the amount paid. The following example shows the format and amount of detail required for this schedule:

Recipient	Purpose	Amount
Museum of Natural History	General operating budget	$29,000
State University	Books for needy students	14,500
Richard Roe	Educational scholarship	12,200

Colleges, universities, and other educational institutions and agencies subject to the Family Educational Rights and Privacy Act (20 U.S.C. 1232g) are not required to list the names of individuals who were provided scholarships or other financial assistance where such disclosure would violate the privacy provisions of the law. Instead, such organizations should group each type of financial aid provided, indicate the number of individuals who received the aid, and specify the aggregate dollar amount.

Line 16.—Attach a schedule showing the name of each recipient, a brief description of the purposes or condition of payment, and amount paid. Do not include any amounts that are on line 15. The schedule should be similar to the schedule shown in the line 15 instructions above.

Line 17.—Attach a schedule that shows the name of the person compensated; the office or position; the average amount of time devoted to the organization's affairs per week, month, etc.; and the amount of annual compensation. The following example shows the format and amount of detail required:

Page 6

¶1652

Name	Position	Time devoted	Annual salary
Philip Poe	President and general manager	16 hrs. per wk.	$27,500

Line 18.—Enter the total of employees' salaries not reported on line 17.

Line 19.—Enter the total interest expense for the year, excluding mortgage interest treated as if an occupancy expense on line 20.

Line 20.—Enter the amount paid for the use of office space or other facilities, heat, light, power, and other utilities, outside janitorial services, mortgage interest, real estate taxes, and similar expenses.

Line 21.—If your organization records depreciation, depletion, and similar expenses, enter the total.

Line 22.—Attach a schedule listing the type and amount of each **significant** expense for which a separate line is not provided. Report other miscellaneous expenses as a single total if not substantial in amount.

B. Balance Sheet

Line 1.—Enter the total cash in checking and savings accounts, temporary cash investments (money market funds, CDs, treasury bills, or other obligations that mature in less than 1 year), change funds, and petty cash funds.

Line 2.—Enter the total accounts receivable that arose from the sale of goods and/or performance of services, less any reserve for bad debt.

Line 3.—Enter the amount of materials, goods, and supplies purchased or manufactured by the organization and held to be sold or used in some future period.

Line 4.—Attach a schedule that shows the name of the borrower, a brief description of the obligation, the rate of return on the principal indebtedness, the due date, and the amount due. The following example shows the format and amount of detail required:

Name of borrower	Description of obligation	Rate of return	Due date	Amount
Hope Soap Corporation	Debenture bond (no senior issue outstanding)	8%	Jan. 2004	$37,500
Big Spool Company	Collateral note secured by company's fleet of 20 delivery trucks	10%	Jan. 2003	262,000

Line 5.—Attach a schedule listing the organization's corporate stock holdings.

For stock of closely held corporations, the statement should show the name of the corporation, a brief summary of the corporation's capital structure, and the number of shares held and their value as carried on the organization's books. If such valuation does not reflect current fair market value, also include fair market value.

For stock traded on an organized exchange or in substantial quantities over the counter, the statement should show the name of the corporation, a description of the stock and the principal exchange on which it is traded, the number of shares held, and their value as carried on the organization's books.

The following example shows the format and the amount of detail required:

Name of corporation	Capital structure (or exchange on which traded)	Shares	Book amount	Fair market value
Little Spool Corporation	100 shares nonvoting preferred issued and outstanding, no par value; 50 shares common issued and outstanding, no par value.			
	Preferred shares:	50	$20,000	$24,000
	Common shares:	10	25,000	30,000
Flintlock Corporation	Class A common N.Y.S.E.	80	6,000	6,500

Line 6.—Report each loan separately, even if more than one loan was made to the same person. Attach a schedule that shows the borrower's name, purpose of loan, repayment terms, interest rate, and original amount of loan.

Line 7.—Enter the book value of government securities held (U.S., state, or municipal). Also enter the book value of buildings and equipment held for investment purposes. Attach a schedule identifying and reporting the book value of each.

Line 8.—Enter the book value of buildings and equipment **not** held for investment. This includes plant and equipment used by the organization in conducting its exempt activities. Attach a schedule listing these assets held at the end of the current tax year/period and the cost or other basis.

Line 9.—Enter the book value of land **not** held for investment.

Line 10.—Enter the book value of each category of assets not reported on lines 1 through 9. Attach a schedule listing each.

Line 12.—Enter the total of accounts payable to suppliers and others, such as salaries payable, accrued payroll taxes, and interest payable.

Line 13.—Enter the unpaid portion of grants and contributions that the organization has made a commitment to pay to other organizations or individuals.

Line 14.—Enter the total of mortgages and other notes payable outstanding at the end of the current tax year/period. Attach a schedule that shows each item separately and the lender's name, purpose of loan, repayment terms, interest rate, and original amount.

Line 15.—Enter the amount of each liability not reported on lines 12 through 14. Attach a separate schedule.

Line 17.—Under fund accounting, an organization segregates its assets, liabilities, and net assets into separate funds according to restrictions on the use of certain assets. Each fund is like a separate entity in that it has a self-balancing set of accounts showing assets, liabilities, equity (fund balance), income, and expenses. If the organization does not use fund accounting, report only the "net assets" account balances, such as: capital stock, paid-in capital, and retained earnings or accumulated income.

Page 7

¶1652

Procedural Checklist

Make sure the application is complete.

If you do not complete all applicable parts or do not provide all required attachments, we may return the incomplete application to your organization for resubmission with the missing information or attachments. This will delay the processing of the application and may delay the effective date of your organization's exempt status. The organization may also incur additional user fees.

Have you . . .

_____ Attached **Form 8718** (User Fee for Exempt Organization Determination Letter Request) and the appropriate fee?

_____ Prepared the application for mailing? (See **Where To File** addresses on Form 8718.) Do **not** file the application with your local Internal Revenue Service Center.

_____ Completed Parts I through IV and any other schedules that apply to the organization?

_____ Shown the organization's **Employer Identification Number (EIN)**?

     a. If your organization has an EIN, write it in the space provided.

     b. If this is a newly formed organization and does not have an Employer Identification Number, obtain an EIN by telephone. (See Specific Instructions, Part I, Line 2, on page 3.)

_____ Described your organization's **specific activities** as directed in Part II, line 1, of the application?

_____ Included a **conformed copy** of the complete organizing instrument? (See Specific Instructions, Part I, Line 10, on page 3.)

_____ Had the application signed by one of the following?

     a. An officer or trustee who is authorized to sign (e.g., president, treasurer); **or**

     b. A person authorized by a power of attorney (Submit Form 2848, or other power of attorney.)

_____ Enclosed **financial statements** (Part IV)?

     a. Current year (must include period up to within 60 days of the date the application is filed) and 3 preceding years.

     b. Detailed breakdown of revenue and expenses (no lump sums).

     c. If the organization has been in existence less than 1 year, you must also submit proposed budgets for 2 years showing the amounts and types of receipts and expenditures anticipated.

Note: *During the technical review of a completed application, it may be necessary to contact the organization for more specific or additional information.*

Do not send this checklist with the application.

Page 8

¶1652

¶1653 Exhibit 16-3

| Form **1024**
(Rev. September 1998)
Department of the Treasury
Internal Revenue Service | **Application for Recognition of Exemption
Under Section 501(a)** | OMB No. 1545-0057

If exempt status is approved,
this application will be open
for public inspection. |

Read the instructions for each Part carefully. **A User Fee must be attached to this application.**
If the required information and appropriate documents are not submitted along with Form 8718 (with payment
of the appropriate user fee), the application may be returned to the organization.
Complete the Procedural Checklist on page 6 of the instructions.

Part I. Identification of Applicant (Must be completed by all applicants; also complete appropriate schedule.)
Submit only the schedule that applies to your organization. Do not submit blank schedules.

Check the appropriate box below to indicate the section under which the organization is applying:

a ☐ Section 501(c)(2)—Title holding corporations (Schedule A, page 7)

b ☐ Section 501(c)(4)—Civic leagues, social welfare organizations (including certain war veterans' organizations), or local associations of
employees (Schedule B, page 8)

c ☐ Section 501(c)(5)—Labor, agricultural, or horticultural organizations (Schedule C, page 9)

d ☐ Section 501(c)(6)—Business leagues, chambers of commerce, etc. (Schedule C, page 9)

e ☐ Section 501(c)(7)—Social clubs (Schedule D, page 11)

f ☐ Section 501(c)(8)—Fraternal beneficiary societies, etc., providing life, sick, accident, or other benefits to members (Schedule E, page 13)

g ☐ Section 501(c)(9)—Voluntary employees' beneficiary associations (Parts I through IV and Schedule F, page 14)

h ☐ Section 501(c)(10)—Domestic fraternal societies, orders, etc., not providing life, sick, accident, or other benefits (Schedule E, page 13)

i ☐ Section 501(c)(12)—Benevolent life insurance associations, mutual ditch or irrigation companies, mutual or cooperative telephone
companies, or like organizations (Schedule G, page 15)

j ☐ Section 501(c)(13)—Cemeteries, crematoria, and like corporations (Schedule H, page 16)

k ☐ Section 501(c)(15)—Mutual insurance companies or associations, other than life or marine (Schedule I, page 17)

l ☐ Section 501(c)(17)—Trusts providing for the payment of supplemental unemployment compensation benefits (Parts I through IV and Schedule J, page 18)

m ☐ Section 501(c)(19)—A post, organization, auxiliary unit, etc., of past or present members of the Armed Forces of the United States (Schedule K, page 19)

n ☐ Section 501(c)(25)—Title holding corporations or trusts (Schedule A, page 7)

1a Full name of organization (as shown in organizing document)		**2** Employer identification number (EIN) (if none, see **Specific Instructions** on page 2)
1b c/o Name (if applicable)		**3** Name and telephone number of person to be contacted if additional information is needed
1c Address (number and street)	Room/Suite	
1d City, town or post office, state, and ZIP + 4 If you have a foreign address, see **Specific Instructions** for Part I, page 2.		( )
1e Web site address	**4** Month the annual accounting period ends	**5** Date incorporated or formed

6 Did the organization previously apply for recognition of exemption under this Code section or under any other section of the Code? ☐ Yes ☐ No
If "Yes," attach an explanation.

7 Has the organization filed Federal income tax returns or exempt organization information returns? . . . . ☐ Yes ☐ No
If "Yes," state the form numbers, years filed, and Internal Revenue office where filed.

8 Check the box for the type of organization. ATTACH A CONFORMED COPY OF THE CORRESPONDING ORGANIZING DOCUMENTS TO
THE APPLICATION BEFORE MAILING.

a ☐ Corporation— Attach a copy of the Articles of Incorporation (including amendments and restatements) showing approval by the
appropriate state official; also attach a copy of the bylaws.

b ☐ Trust— Attach a copy of the Trust Indenture or Agreement, including all appropriate signatures and dates.

c ☐ Association— Attach a copy of the Articles of Association, Constitution, or other creating document, with a declaration (see instructions) or
other evidence that the organization was formed by adoption of the document by more than one person. Also include a copy
of the bylaws.

If this is a corporation or an unincorporated association that has not yet adopted bylaws, check here . . . . . ▶ ☐

I declare under the penalties of perjury that I am authorized to sign this application on behalf of the above organization, and that I have examined
this application, including the accompanying schedules and attachments, and to the best of my knowledge it is true, correct, and complete.

**PLEASE
SIGN ▶
HERE**
_____ _____ _____
(Signature) (Type or print name and title or authority of signer) (Date)

For Paperwork Reduction Act Notice, see page 5 of the instructions.

Part II. Activities and Operational Information (Must be completed by all applicants)

1   Provide a detailed narrative description of all the activities of the organization—past, present, and planned. Do not merely refer to or repeat the language in the organizational document. List each activity separately in the order of importance based on the relative time and other resources devoted to the activity. Indicate the percentage of time for each activity. Each description should include, as a minimum, the following: **(a)** a detailed description of the activity including its purpose and how each activity furthers your exempt purpose; **(b)** when the activity was or will be initiated; and **(c)** where and by whom the activity will be conducted.

2   List the organization's present and future sources of financial support, beginning with the largest source first.

¶1653

Part II. Activities and Operational Information (continued)

3   Give the following information about the organization's governing body:

a Names, addresses, and titles of officers, directors, trustees, etc.	**b** Annual compensation

4   If the organization is the outgrowth or continuation of any form of predecessor, state the name of each predecessor, the period during which it was in existence, and the reasons for its termination. Submit copies of all papers by which any transfer of assets was effected.

5   If the applicant organization is now, or plans to be, connected in any way with any other organization, describe the other organization and explain the relationship (e.g., financial support on a continuing basis; shared facilities or employees; same officers, directors, or trustees).

6   If the organization has capital stock issued and outstanding, state: **(1)** class or classes of the stock; **(2)** number and par value of the shares; **(3)** consideration for which they were issued; and **(4)** if any dividends have been paid or whether your organization's creating instrument authorizes dividend payments on any class of capital stock.

7   State the qualifications necessary for membership in the organization; the classes of membership (with the number of members in each class); and the voting rights and privileges received. If any group or class of persons is required to join, describe the requirement and explain the relationship between those members and members who join voluntarily. Submit copies of any membership solicitation material. Attach sample copies of all types of membership certificates issued.

8   Explain how your organization's assets will be distributed on dissolution.

Form 1024 (Rev. 9-98)   Page **4**

Part II. Activities and Operational Information (continued)

9   Has the organization made or does it plan to make any distribution of its property or surplus funds to shareholders or members? . . . .   ☐ **Yes**   ☐ **No**

If "Yes," state the full details, including: **(1)** amounts or value; **(2)** source of funds or property distributed or to be distributed; and **(3)** basis of, and authority for, distribution or planned distribution.

10   Does, or will, any part of your organization's receipts represent payments for services performed or to be performed? .   ☐ **Yes**   ☐ **No**

If "Yes," state in detail the amount received and the character of the services performed or to be performed.

11   Has the organization made, or does it plan to make, any payments to members or shareholders for services performed or to be performed? . . . .   ☐ **Yes**   ☐ **No**

If "Yes," state in detail the amount paid, the character of the services, and to whom the payments have been, or will be, made.

12   Does the organization have any arrangement to provide insurance for members, their dependents, or others (including provisions for the payment of sick or death benefits, pensions, or annuities)? . . . .   ☐ **Yes**   ☐ **No**

If "Yes," describe and explain the arrangement's eligibility rules and attach a sample copy of each plan document and each type of policy issued.

13   Is the organization under the supervisory jurisdiction of any public regulatory body, such as a social welfare agency, etc.? . . . .   ☐ **Yes**   ☐ **No**

If "Yes," submit copies of all administrative opinions or court decisions regarding this supervision, as well as copies of applications or requests for the opinions or decisions.

14   Does the organization now lease or does it plan to lease any property? . . . .   ☐ **Yes**   ☐ **No**

If "Yes," explain in detail. Include the amount of rent, a description of the property, and any relationship between the applicant organization and the other party. Also, attach a copy of any rental or lease agreement. (If the organization is a party, as a lessor, to multiple leases of rental real property under similar lease agreements, please attach a single representative copy of the leases.)

15   Has the organization spent or does it plan to spend any money attempting to influence the selection, nomination, election, or appointment of any person to any Federal, state, or local public office or to an office in a political organization? . .   ☐ **Yes**   ☐ **No**

If "Yes," explain in detail and list the amounts spent or to be spent in each case.

16   Does the organization publish pamphlets, brochures, newsletters, journals, or similar printed material? . . . . .   ☐ **Yes**   ☐ **No**

If "Yes," attach a recent copy of each.

Form 1024 (Rev. 9-98) Page **5**

Part III. Financial Data (Must be completed by all applicants)

*Complete the financial statements for the current year and for each of the 3 years immediately before it. If in existence less than 4 years, complete the statements for each year in existence. **If in existence less than 1 year, also provide proposed budgets for the 2 years following the current year.***

A. Statement of Revenue and Expenses

	Revenue	(a) Current Tax Year	(b)	(c)	(d)	(e) Total
		From ——— To ———	3 Prior Tax Years or Proposed Budget for Next 2 Years			
1	Gross dues and assessments of members					
2	Gross contributions, gifts, etc.					
3	Gross amounts derived from activities related to the organization's exempt purpose (attach schedule) (Include related cost of sales on line 9.)					
4	Gross amounts from unrelated business activities (attach schedule)					
5	Gain from sale of assets, excluding inventory items (attach schedule)					
6	Investment income (see page 3 of the instructions)					
7	Other revenue (attach schedule)					
8	Total revenue (add lines 1 through 7)					
	Expenses					
9	Expenses attributable to activities related to the organization's exempt purposes.					
10	Expenses attributable to unrelated business activities					
11	Contributions, gifts, grants, and similar amounts paid (attach schedule).					
12	Disbursements to or for the benefit of members (attach schedule)					
13	Compensation of officers, directors, and trustees (attach schedule)					
14	Other salaries and wages.					
15	Interest					
16	Occupancy					
17	Depreciation and depletion					
18	Other expenses (attach schedule)					
19	Total expenses (add lines 9 through 18)					
20	Excess of revenue over expenses (line 8 minus line 19)					

B. Balance Sheet (at the end of the period shown)

	Assets		Current Tax Year as of ....
1	Cash	1	
2	Accounts receivable, net	2	
3	Inventories	3	
4	Bonds and notes receivable (attach schedule)	4	
5	Corporate stocks (attach schedule)	5	
6	Mortgage loans (attach schedule)	6	
7	Other investments (attach schedule)	7	
8	Depreciable and depletable assets (attach schedule)	8	
9	Land	9	
10	Other assets (attach schedule)	10	
11	**Total assets**	11	
	Liabilities		
12	Accounts payable	12	
13	Contributions, gifts, grants, etc., payable	13	
14	Mortgages and notes payable (attach schedule)	14	
15	Other liabilities (attach schedule)	15	
16	**Total liabilities**	16	
	Fund Balances or Net Assets		
17	Total fund balances or net assets	17	
18	**Total liabilities and fund balances or net assets** (add line 16 and line 17)	18	

If there has been any substantial change in any aspect of the organization's financial activities since the end of the period shown above, check the box and attach a detailed explanation. . . . . ▶ ☐

¶1653

Part IV. Notice Requirements (Sections 501(c)(9) and 501(c)(17) Organizations Only)

1 Section 501(c)(9) and 501(c)(17) organizations:

Are you filing Form 1024 within 15 months from the end of the month in which the organization was created or formed as required by section 505(c)? . . . . ☐ **Yes** ☐ **No**

If "Yes," skip the rest of this Part.

If "No," answer question 2.

2 If you answer "No" to question 1, are you filing Form 1024 within 27 months from the end of the month in which the organization was created or formed? . . . . ☐ **Yes** ☐ **No**

If "Yes," your organization qualifies under Regulation section 301.9100-2 for an automatic 12-month extension of the 15-month filing requirement. Do not answer questions 3 and 4.

If "No," answer question 3.

3 If you answer "No" to question 2, does the organization wish to request an extension of time to apply under the "reasonable action and good faith" and the "no prejudice to the interest of the government" requirements of Regulations section 301.9100-3? . . . . ☐ **Yes** ☐ **No**

If "Yes," give the reasons for not filing this application within the 27-month period described in question 2. See Specific Instructions, Part IV, Line 3, page 4, before completing this item. Do not answer question 4.

If "No," answer question 4.

4 If you answer "No" to question 3, your organization's qualification as a section 501(c)(9) or 501(c)(17) organization can be recognized only from the date this application is filed. Therefore, does the organization want us to consider its application as a request for recognition of exemption as a section 501(c)(9) or 501(c)(17) organization from the date the application is received and not retroactively to the date the organization was created or formed? . . . . ☐ **Yes** ☐ **No**

Form 1024 (Rev. 9-98)   Page **7**

Schedule A   Organizations described in section 501(c)(2) or 501(c)(25) (Title holding corporations or trusts)

1   State the complete name, address, and EIN of each organization for which title to property is held and the number and type of the applicant organization's stock held by each organization.

2   If the annual excess of revenue over expenses has not been or will not be turned over to the organization for which title to property is held, state the purpose for which the excess is or will be retained by the title holding organization.

3   In the case of a corporation described in section 501(c)(2), state the purpose of the organization for which title to property is held (as shown in its governing instrument) and the Code sections under which it is classified as exempt from tax. If the organization has received a determination or ruling letter recognizing it as exempt from taxation, please attach a copy of the letter.

4   In the case of a corporation or trust described in section 501(c)(25), state the basis whereby each shareholder is described in section 501(c)(25)(C). For each organization described that has received a determination or ruling letter recognizing that organization as exempt from taxation, please attach a copy of the letter.

5   With respect to the activities of the organization.

   a   Is any rent received attributable to personal property leased with real property? . . . .   ☐ Yes ☐ No

      If "Yes," what percentage of the total rent, as reported on the financial statements in Part III, is attributable to personal property?

   b   Will the organization receive income which is incidentally derived from the holding of real property, such as income from operation of a parking lot or from vending machines? . . . .   ☐ Yes ☐ No

      If "Yes," what percentage of the organization's gross income, as reported on the financial statements in Part III, is incidentally derived from the holding of real property?

   c   Will the organization receive income other than rent from real property or personal property leased with real property or income which is incidentally derived from the holding of real property? . . . .   ☐ Yes ☐ No

      If "Yes," describe the source of the income.

Instructions

Line 1.—Provide the requested information on each organization for which the applicant organization holds title to property. Also indicate the number and types of shares of the applicant organization's stock that are held by each.

Line 2.—For purposes of this question, "excess of revenue over expenses" is all of the organization's income for a particular tax year less operating expenses.

Line 3.—Give the exempt purpose of each organization that is the basis for its exempt status and the Internal Revenue Code section

that describes the organization (as shown in its IRS determination letter).

Line 4.—Indicate if the shareholder is one of the following:

   1. A qualified pension, profit-sharing, or stock bonus plan that meets the requirements of the Code;

   2. A government plan;

   3. An organization described in section 501(c)(3); or

   4. An organization described in section 501(c)(25).

¶1653

Form 1024 (Rev. 9-98)   Page **8**

| **Schedule B** | Organizations Described in Section 501(c)(4) (Civic leagues, social welfare organizations (including posts, councils, etc., of veterans' organizations not qualifying or applying for exemption under section 501(c)(19)) or local associations of employees.) |

1   Has the Internal Revenue Service previously issued a ruling or determination letter recognizing the applicant organization (or any predecessor organization listed in question 4, Part II of the application) to be exempt under section 501(c)(3) and later revoked that recognition of exemption on the basis that the applicant organization (or its predecessor) was carrying on propaganda or otherwise attempting to influence legislation or on the basis that it engaged in political activity? . . ☐ **Yes** ☐ **No**

If "Yes," indicate the earliest tax year for which recognition of exemption under section 501(c)(3) was revoked and the IRS district office that issued the revocation.

2   Does the organization perform or plan to perform (for members, shareholders, or others) services, such as maintaining the common areas of a condominium; buying food or other items on a cooperative basis; or providing recreational facilities or transportation services, job placement, or other similar undertakings? . . . . ☐ **Yes** ☐ **No**

If "Yes," explain the activities in detail, including income realized and expenses incurred. Also, explain in detail the nature of the benefits to the general public from these activities. (If the answer to this question is explained in Part II of the application (pages 2, 3, and 4), enter the page and item number here.)

3   If the organization is claiming exemption as a homeowners' association, is access to any property or facilities it owns or maintains restricted in any way? . . . . ☐ **Yes** ☐ **No**

If "Yes," explain.

4   If the organization is claiming exemption as a local association of employees, state the name and address of each employer whose employees are eligible for membership in the association. If employees of more than one plant or office of the same employer are eligible for membership, give the address of each plant or office.

¶1653

Form 1024 (Rev. 9-98)

Schedule C   **Organizations described in section 501(c)(5) (Labor, agricultural, including fishermen's organizations, or horticultural organizations) or section 501(c)(6) (business leagues, chambers of commerce, etc.)**

1   Describe any services the organization performs for members or others. (If the description of the services is contained in Part II of the application, enter the page and item number here.)

2   Fishermen's organizations only.—What kinds of aquatic resources (not including mineral) are cultivated or harvested by those eligible for membership in the organization?

3   Labor organizations only.—Is the organization organized under the terms of a collective bargaining agreement?   .   .   ☐ **Yes**   ☐ **No**

     If "Yes," attach a copy of the latest agreement.

¶1653

Form 1024 (Rev. 9-98) Page **11**

| **Schedule D** | Organizations described in section 501(c)(7) (Social clubs) |

1 Has the organization entered or does it plan to enter into any contract or agreement for the management or operation of its property and/or activities, such as restaurants, pro shops, lodges, etc.? . . . . ☐ **Yes** ☐ **No**

If "Yes," attach a copy of the contract or agreement. If one has not yet been drawn up, please explain the organization's plans.

2 Does the organization seek or plan to seek public patronage of its facilities or activities by advertisement or otherwise? ☐ **Yes** ☐ **No**
If "Yes," attach sample copies of the advertisements or other requests.
If the organization plans to seek public patronage, please explain the plans.

3a Are nonmembers, other than guests of members, permitted or will they be permitted to use the club facilities or participate in or attend any functions or activities conducted by the organization? . . . . ☐ **Yes** ☐ **No**
If "Yes," describe the functions or activities in which there has been or will be nonmember participation or admittance. (Submit a copy of the house rules, if any.)

b State the amount of nonmember income included in Part III of the application, lines 3 and 4, column (a) . . . . . |_____
c Enter the percent of gross receipts from nonmembers for the use of club facilities . . . . |_____ %
d Enter the percent of gross receipts received from investment income and nonmember use of the club's facilities . . |_____ %

4a Does the organization's charter, bylaws, other governing instrument, or any written policy statement of the organization contain any provision that provides for discrimination against any person on the basis of race, color, or religion? . . ☐ **Yes** ☐ **No**

b If "Yes," state whether or not its provision will be kept.

c If the organization has such a provision that will be repealed, deleted, or otherwise stricken from its requirements, state when this will be done. . . . . _____
d If the organization formerly had such a requirement and it no longer applies, give the date it ceased to apply . . . _____
e If the organization restricts its membership to members of a particular religion, check here and attach the explanation specified in the instructions . . . . ☐

See reverse side for instructions

¶1653

Instructions

Line 1.—Answer "Yes," if any of the organization's property or activities will be managed by another organization or company.

Lines 3b, c, and d.—Enter the figures for the current year. On an attached schedule, furnish the same information for each of the prior tax years for which you completed Part III of the application.

Line 4e.—If the organization restricts its membership to members of a particular religion, the organization must be:

   1. An auxiliary of a fraternal beneficiary society that:

   a. Is described in section 501(c)(8) and exempt from tax under section 501(a), and

   b. Limits its membership to members of a particular religion; or

   2. A club that, in good faith, limits its membership to the members of a particular religion in order to further the teachings or principles of that religion and not to exclude individuals of a particular race or color.

   If you checked **4e,** your explanation must show how the organization meets one of these two requirements.

Form 1024 (Rev. 9-98)   Page **13**

Schedule E	**Organizations described in section 501(c)(8) or 501(c)(10) (Fraternal societies, orders, or associations)**

1 Is the organization a college fraternity or sorority, or chapter of a college fraternity or sorority? . . . . . . ☐ **Yes** ☐ **No**

If "Yes," read the instructions for Line 1, below, before completing this schedule.

2 Does or will your organization operate under the lodge system? . . . . ☐ **Yes** ☐ **No**

If "No," does or will it operate for the exclusive benefit of the members of an organization operating under the lodge system? . . . . ☐ **Yes** ☐ **No**

3 Is the organization a subordinate or local lodge, etc.? . . . . ☐ **Yes** ☐ **No**

If "Yes," attach a certificate signed by the secretary of the parent organization, under the seal of the organization, certifying that the subordinate lodge is a duly constituted body operating under the jurisdiction of the parent body.

4 Is the organization a parent or grand lodge? . . . . ☐ **Yes** ☐ **No**

If "Yes," attach a schedule for each subordinate lodge in active operation showing: (a) its name and address; (b) the number of members in it; and (c) how often it holds periodic meetings.

Instructions

Line 1.—To the extent that they qualify for exemption from Federal income tax, college fraternities and sororities generally qualify as organizations described in section 501(c)(7). Therefore, if the organization is a college fraternity or sorority, refer to the discussion of section 501(c)(7) organizations in Pub. 557. If section 501(c)(7) appears to apply to your organization, complete Schedule D instead of this schedule.

Line 2.—Operating under the lodge system means carrying on activities under a form of organization that is composed of local branches, chartered by a parent organization, largely self-governing, and called lodges, chapters, or the like.

¶1653

Form 1024 (Rev. 9-98)   Page **14**

| Schedule F | Organizations described in section 501(c)(9) (Voluntary employees' beneficiary associations) |

1 Describe the benefits available to members. Include copies of any plan documents that describe such benefits and the terms and conditions of eligibility for each benefit.

2 Are any employees or classes of employees entitled to benefits to which other employees or classes of employees are not entitled? . . . . ☐ Yes ☐ No
If "Yes," explain.

3 Give the following information for each plan as of the last day of the most recent plan year and enter that date here. If there is more than one plan, attach a separate schedule . . . . ___ / ___ / ___
(mo.) (day) (yr.)

a Total number of persons covered by the plan who are highly compensated individuals (See instructions below). . . . _____
b Number of other employees covered by the plan. . . . . _____
c Number of employees not covered by the plan . . . . _____
d Total number employed* . . . . _____

＊ Should equal the total of **a, b,** and **c**—if not, explain any difference. Describe the eligibility requirements that prevent those employees not covered by the plan from participating.

4 State the number of persons, if any, other than employees and their dependents (e.g., the proprietor of a business whose employees are members of the association) who are entitled to receive benefits . . . . ▶

Instructions

Line 3a.—A "highly compensated individual" is one who:

(a) Owned 5% or more of the employer at any time during the current year or the preceding year.

(b) Received more than $80,000 (adjusted for inflation) in compensation from the employer for the preceding year, and

(c) Was among the top 20% of employees by compensation for the preceding year. However, the employer can choose not to have **(c)** apply.

¶1653

Form 1024 (Rev. 9-98)   Page **15**

Schedule G   Organizations described in section 501(c)(12) (Benevolent life insurance associations, mutual ditch or irrigation companies, mutual or cooperative telephone companies, or like organizations)

1   Attach a schedule in columnar form for each tax year for which the organization is claiming exempt status. On each schedule:

a   Show the total gross income received from members or shareholders.

b   List, by source, the total amounts of gross income received from other sources.

2   If the organization is claiming exemption as a local benevolent insurance association, state:

a   The counties from which members are accepted or will be accepted.

b   Whether stipulated premiums are or will be charged in advance, or whether losses are or will be paid solely through assessments.

3   If the organization is claiming exemption as a "like organization," explain how it is similar to a mutual ditch or irrigation company, or a mutual or cooperative telephone company.

4   Are the rights and interests of members in the organization's annual savings determined in proportion to their business with it? . . . . ☐ Yes ☐ No

If "Yes," does the organization keep the records necessary to determine at any time each member's rights and interests in such savings, including assets acquired with the savings? . . . . ☐ Yes ☐ No

5   If the organization is a mutual or cooperative telephone company and has contracts with other systems for long-distance telephone services, attach copies of the contracts.

Instructions

Mutual or cooperative electric or telephone companies should show income received from qualified pole rentals separately. Mutual or cooperative telephone companies should also show separately the gross amount of income received from nonmember telephone companies for performing services that involve their members and the gross amount of income received from the sale of display advertising in a directory furnished to their members.

Do not net amounts due or paid to other sources against amounts due or received from those sources.

Form 1024 (Rev. 9-98)   Page **16**

Schedule H	Organizations described in section 501(c)(13) (Cemeteries, crematoria, and like corporations)

1 Attach the following documents:

a Complete copy of sales contracts or other documents, including any "debt" certificates, involved in acquiring cemetery or crematorium property.

b Complete copy of any contract your organization has that designates an agent to sell its cemetery lots.

c A copy of the appraisal (obtained from a disinterested and qualified party) of the cemetery property as of the date acquired.

2 Does your organization have, or does it plan to have, a perpetual care fund? . . . . ☐ Yes ☐ No
If "Yes," attach a copy of the fund agreement and explain the nature of the fund (cash, securities, unsold land, etc.)

3 If your organization is claiming exemption as a perpetual care fund for an organization described in section 501(c)(13), has the cemetery organization, for which funds are held, established exemption under that section? . . . . ☐ Yes ☐ No
If "No," explain.

Form 1024 (Rev. 9-98)   Page **17**

Schedule I   Organizations described in section 501(c)(15) (Small insurance companies or associations)

1   Is the organization a member of a controlled group of corporations as defined in section 831(b)(2)(B)(ii)? (Disregard section 1563(b)(2)(B) in determining whether the organization is a member of a controlled group.) . . . . □ **Yes** □ **No**

If "Yes," include on lines 2 through 5 the total amount received by the organization and all other members of the controlled group.

If "No," include on lines 2 through 5 only the amounts that relate to the applicant organization.

	(a) Current Year	3 Prior Tax Years		
	From _____ To _____	(b)	(c)	(d) ....
2 Direct written premiums				
3 Reinsurance assumed				
4 Reinsurance ceded				
5 Net written premiums ((line 2 plus line 3) minus line 4)				

6   If you entered an amount on line 3 or line 4, attach a copy of the reinsurance agreements the organization has entered into.

Instructions

Line 1.—Answer "Yes," if the organization would be considered a member of a controlled group of corporations if it were not exempt from tax under section 501(a). In applying section 1563(a), use a "more than 50%" stock ownership test to determine whether the applicant or any other corporation is a member of a controlled group.

Line 2.— In addition to other direct written premiums, include on line 2 the full amount of any prepaid or advance premium in the year the prepayment is received. For example, if a $5,000 premium for a 3-year policy was received in the current year, include the full $5,000 amount in the Current Year column.

¶1653

Schedule J **Organizations described in section 501(c)(17) (Trusts providing for the payment of supplemental unemployment compensation benefits)**

1 If benefits are provided for individual proprietors, partners, or self-employed persons under the plan, explain in detail.

2 If the plan provides other benefits in addition to the supplemental unemployment compensation benefits, explain in detail and state whether the other benefits are subordinate to the unemployment benefits.

3 Give the following information as of the last day of the most recent plan year and enter that date here . . . . _____

a Total number of employees covered by the plan who are shareholders, officers, self-employed persons, or highly compensated (See Schedule F instructions for line 3a on page 14.) . . . . _____

b Number of other employees covered by the plan . . . . _____

c Number of employees not covered by the plan . . . . _____

d Total number employed*. . . . . _____

* Should equal the total of **a, b,** and **c**—if not, explain the difference. Describe the eligibility requirements that prevent those employees not covered by the plan from participating.

4 At any time after December 31, 1959, did any of the following persons engage in any of the transactions listed below with the trust: the creator of the trust or a contributor to the trust; a brother or sister (whole or half blood), a spouse, an ancestor, or a lineal descendant of such a creator or contributor; or a corporation controlled directly or indirectly by such a creator or contributor?

Note: *If you know that the organization will be, or is considering being, a party to any of the transactions (or activities) listed below, check the "Planned" box. Give a detailed explanation of any "Yes" or "Planned" answer in the space below.*

a Borrow any part of the trust's income or corpus? . . . . ☐ Yes ☐ No ☐ Planned

b Receive any compensation for personal services? . . . . ☐ Yes ☐ No ☐ Planned

c Obtain any part of the trust's services? . . . . ☐ Yes ☐ No ☐ Planned

d Purchase any securities or other properties from the trust? . . . . ☐ Yes ☐ No ☐ Planned

e Sell any securities or other property to the trust? . . . . ☐ Yes ☐ No ☐ Planned

f Receive any of the trust's income or corpus in any other transaction? . . . . ☐ Yes ☐ No ☐ Planned

5 Attach a copy of the Supplemental Unemployment Benefit Plan and related agreements.

¶1653

Form 1024 (Rev. 9-98)   Page **19**

Schedule K   Organizations described in section 501(c)(19)—A post or organization of past or present members of the Armed Forces of the United States, auxiliary units or societies for such a post or organization, and trusts or foundations formed for the benefit of such posts or organizations.

1   *To be completed by a post or organization of past or present members of the Armed Forces of the United States.*

a   Total membership of the post or organization .

b   Number of members who are present or former members of the U.S. Armed Forces .

c   Number of members who are cadets (include students in college or university ROTC programs or at armed services academies only), or spouses, widows, or widowers of cadets or past or present members of the U.S. Armed Forces .

d   Does the organization have a membership category other than the ones set out above? . . . .   ☐ **Yes** ☐ **No**

     If "Yes," please explain in full. Enter number of members in this category . . . . _____

e   If you wish to apply for a determination that contributions to your organization are deductible by donors, enter the number of members from line 1b who are war veterans, as defined below. . . . . _____

     A war veteran is a person who served in the Armed Forces of the United States during the following periods of war: April 21, 1898, through July 4, 1902; April 6, 1917, through November 11, 1918; December 7, 1941, through December 31, 1946; June 27, 1950, through January 31, 1955; and August 5, 1964, through May 7, 1975.

2   *To be completed by an auxiliary unit or society of a post or organization of past or present members of the Armed Forces of the United States.*

a   Is the organization affiliated with and organized according to the bylaws and regulations formulated by such an exempt post or organization? . . . .   ☐ **Yes** ☐ **No**
     If "Yes," submit a copy of such bylaws or regulations.

b   How many members does your organization have? . . . .

c   How many are themselves past or present members of the Armed Forces of the United States, or are their spouses, or persons related to them within two degrees of blood relationship? (Grandparents, brothers, sisters, and grandchildren are the most distant relationships allowable.) . . . .

d   Are all of the members themselves members of a post or organization, past or present members of the Armed Forces of the United States, spouses of members of such a post or organization, or related to members of such a post or organization within two degrees of blood relationship? . . . .   ☐ **Yes** ☐ **No**

3   *To be completed by a trust or foundation organized for the benefit of an exempt post or organization of past or present members of the Armed Forces of the United States.*

a   Will the corpus or income be used solely for the funding of such an exempt organization (including necessary related expenses)? . . . .   ☐ **Yes** ☐ **No**
     If "No," please explain.

b   If the trust or foundation is formed for charitable purposes, does the organizational document contain a proper dissolution provision as described in section 1.501(c)(3)-1(b)(4) of the Income Tax Regulations? . . . .   ☐ **Yes** ☐ **No**

Department of the Treasury
Internal Revenue Service

Instructions for Form 1024

(Rev. September 1998)

Application for Recognition of Exemption Under Section 501(a)

Note: *Keep a copy of the completed Form 1024 in the organization's permanent records.*

General Instructions

Section references are to the Internal Revenue Code unless otherwise noted.

User fee.—Submit with the Form 1024 application for a determination letter, a **Form 8718,** User Fee for Exempt Organization Determination Letter Request, and the user fee called for in the Form 8718. You may obtain Form 8718, and additional forms and publications, through your local IRS office or by calling 1-800-829-3676 **(1-800-TAX-FORM).** User fees are subject to change on an annual basis. Therefore, be sure that you use the most current Form 8718.

Helpful information.—For additional information, see:

● **Pub. 557,** Tax-Exempt Status for Your Organization

● **Pub. 598,** Tax on Unrelated Business Income of Exempt Organizations

● **Pub. 578,** Tax Information for Private Foundations and Foundation Managers

● **Internet site:**
www.irs.ustreas.gov/bus_info/eo/

Purpose of Form

Form 1024 is used by most types of organizations to apply for recognition of exemption under section 501(a). See Part I of the application.

Even if these organizations are not required to file Form 1024 to be tax-exempt, they may wish to file Form 1024 to receive a determination letter of IRS recognition of their section 501(c) status in order to obtain certain incidental benefits such as:

● Public recognition of tax-exempt status

● Exemption from certain state taxes

● Advance assurance to donors of deductibility of contributions (in certain cases)

● Nonprofit mailing privileges, etc.

Note: *Generally, Form 1024 is NOT used to apply for a group exemption letter. For information on how to apply for a group exemption letter, see Pub. 557.*

Note: *Tax benefits for certain homeowners associations under section 528 are available to organizations that are not exempt from Federal income tax. To elect these benefits, file a properly completed and timely filed (including extensions)* **Form 1120-H,** *U.S. Income Tax Return for Homeowners Associations.* **DO NOT** *file Form 1024.*

What To File

Do not submit any blank schedules that do not apply to your type of organization.

Most organizations applying for exemption under section 501(a) must complete Parts I through III.

Section 501(c)(9), Voluntary Employees' Beneficiary Associations, and section 501(c)(17), Supplemental Unemployment Benefit Trusts, applicants should also complete Part IV.

See **Special Rule for Certain Canadian Organizations** on the following page.

In addition, each organization must complete the schedule indicated on page 1 of the application for the section of the Code under which it seeks recognition of exemption. (For example, a social welfare organization seeking recognition under section 501(c)(4) must complete Parts I through III and Schedule B.)

Attachments

For any attachments submitted with Form 1024.—

● Show the organization's name, address, and employer identification number (EIN).

● Identify the Part and line item number to which the attachment relates.

● Use 8-1/2 x 11 inch paper for any attachments.

● Include any court decisions, rulings, opinions, etc., that will expedite processing of the application. Generally, attachments in the form of tape recordings are not acceptable unless accompanied by a transcript.

When To File (Section 501(c)(9) or (17) Organization)

An organization must file Form 1024 to be recognized as an organization described in section 501(c)(9) or 501(c)(17). Generally, if an organization files its application within 15 months after the end of the month in which it was formed, and if the IRS approves the application, the effective date of the organization's section 501(c)(9) or (17) status will be the date it was organized.

Generally, if an organization does not file its application (Form 1024) within 15 months after the end of the month in which it was formed, it will not qualify for exempt status as a section 501(c)(9) or (17) organization during the period before the date of its application. For exceptions and special rules, including automatic extensions in some cases, see Part IV of Form 1024.

The date of receipt is the date of the U.S. postmark on the cover in which an exemption application is mailed or, if no postmark appears on the cover, the date the application is stamped as received by the IRS.

Private delivery services.—See the instructions for your income tax return for information on certain private delivery services designated by the IRS to meet the "timely mailing as timely filing/paying rule."

The private delivery service can tell you how to get written proof of the mailing date.

Caution: *Private delivery services cannot deliver items to P.O. boxes. You must use the U. S. Postal Service to mail any item to an IRS P.O. box address. See the Form 8718 for the P.O. box address as well as the express mail or a delivery service address.*

Where To File

File the completed Form 1024 application, and all required information, at the address shown in Form 8718.

The IRS will determine the organization's tax-exempt status and whether any annual returns must be filed.

Signature Requirements

An officer, a trustee who is authorized to sign, or another person authorized by a power of attorney, must sign the Form 1024 application. Attach a power of attorney to the application. You may use **Form 2848,** Power of Attorney and Declaration of Representative, for this purpose.

Appeal Procedures

Your organization's application will be considered by the IRS which will either:

1. Issue a favorable determination letter;

2. Issue a proposed adverse determination letter denying the exempt status requested; or

3. Refer the case to the National Office.

If we send your organization a proposed adverse determination, we will advise it of its appeal rights at that time.

Language and Currency Requirements

Language requirements.—Prepare the Form 1024 and attachments in English. Provide an English translation if the organizational document or bylaws are in any other language. See the conformed copy requirements in the line 8 instructions under Part I.

You may be asked to provide English translations of foreign language publications that the organization produces or distributes and that are submitted with the application.

Financial requirements.—Report all financial information in U.S. dollars (specify the conversion rate used). Combine amounts from within and outside the United States and report the total for each item on the financial statements.

For example:

Gross Investment Income	
From U.S. sources	$4,000
From non-U.S. sources	1,000
Amount to report on income statement	$5,000

Annual Information Return

If an annual information return is due while the organization's application for recognition of exempt status is pending with the IRS (including any appeal of a proposed adverse determination), the organization should file:

Form 990, Return of Organization Exempt From Income Tax, or **Form 990-EZ,** Short Form Return of Organization Exempt From Income Tax, at the following address: Internal Revenue Service, Ogden Service Center, Ogden, UT 84201-0027

Indicate that an application is pending.

If an organization has unrelated business income of more than $1,000, file **Form 990-T,** Exempt Organization Business Income Tax Return.

Applicants under sections 501(c)(5), (9), and (17) should see the Form 990 (or Form 990-EZ) instructions for special provisions regarding substitutions for certain parts of that form.

Public Inspection of Form 1024

Caution: *Note the discussion below for the potential effect of the Taxpayer Bill of Rights 2 (TBOR2) on these instructions.*

IRS responsibilities for public inspection.—If the organization's application for section 501(c) status is approved, the following items will be open to public inspection in any District office and at the National Office of the IRS (section 6104):

1. The organization's application and any supporting documents.

2. Any letter or other document issued by the IRS with regard to the application.

Note that the following items are not available for public inspection:

1. Any information relating to a trade secret, patent, style of work, or apparatus that, if released, would adversely affect the organization, or

2. Any other information that would adversely affect the national defense.

IMPORTANT: Applicants must identify this information by clearly marking it, "NOT SUBJECT TO PUBLIC INSPECTION," and must attach a statement to explain why the organization asks that the information be withheld. If the IRS agrees, the information will be withheld.

Organization's responsibilities for public inspection.—The organization must make available a copy of its approved application and supporting documents, along with any document or letter issued by the IRS, for public inspection.

These documents must be available during regular business hours at the organization's principal office and at each of its regional or district offices having at least three paid employees. See Notice 88-120, 1988-2 C.B. 454.

A penalty of $20 a day will be imposed on any person under a duty to comply with the public inspection requirements for each day a failure to comply continues.

Furnishing copies of documents under TBOR2.—The Taxpayer Bill of Rights 2 (TBOR2), enacted July 30, 1996, modified prospectively the section 6685 penalty and the rules for the public inspection of returns and exemption applications. An organization must furnish a copy of its Form 990, Form 990-EZ, or exemption application, and certain related documents, if a request is made in writing or in person.

For a request made in person, the organization must make an immediate response.

For a response to a written request, the organization must provide the requested copies within 30 days.

The organization must furnish copies of its Forms 990, or Forms 990-EZ, for any of its 3 most recent taxable years. No charge is to be made other than charging a reasonable fee for reproduction and actual postage costs.

An organization need not provide copies if:

1. The organization has made the requested documents widely available in a manner provided in Treasury regulations, or

2. The Secretary of the Treasury determined, upon application by the organization, that the organization was subject to a harassment campaign such that a waiver of the obligation to provide copies would be in the public interest.

Penalty for failure to allow public inspection or provide copies.—The section 6685 penalty for willful failure to allow public inspections or provide copies is increased from the present-law level of $1,000 to $5,000 by TBOR2.

Effective date of TBOR2.—These public inspection provisions governing tax-exempt organizations under TBOR2 generally apply to requests made no earlier than 60 days after the date on which the Treasury Department publishes the regulations required under the provisions. However, Congress, in the legislative history of TBOR2, indicated that organizations would comply voluntarily with the public inspection provisions prior to the issuance of such regulations.

Special Rule for Certain Canadian Organizations

A religious, scientific, literary, educational, or charitable organization formed in Canada that has received a **Form T2051,** Notification of Registration, from Revenue Canada (Department of National Revenue, Taxation) and whose registration has not been revoked may apply for recognition of exemption as a social welfare organization under section 501(c)(4) without completing all parts of Form 1024 that would otherwise be required. Such an organization must complete only Part I and the signature portion of Form 1024.

To indicate that this special rule applies, the organization should write "Registered Canadian Organization" across the top of page 1 of Form 1024.

The organization must also attach a copy of its current Form T2051 and a copy of Application for Registration, **Form T2050,** together with all required attachments that it submitted to Revenue Canada.

If any of the attachments to Form T2050 were prepared in French, an English translation must be furnished with Form 1024.

In the case of organizing documents and bylaws, see the line 8 instructions under Part I.

An organization that wants recognition of exemption under section 501(c)(3) must complete **Form 1023,** Application for Recognition of Exemption Under Section 501(c)(3) of the Internal Revenue Code.

Exemption under section 501(c)(3) is needed to establish eligibility to receive contributions that are deductible by U.S. residents to the extent provided by the U.S.–Canada tax treaty.

Specific Instructions

The following instructions are keyed to the line items on the application form:

Part I. Identification of Applicant

Line 1. Full name and address of organization.—Enter the organization's name exactly as it appears in its creating documents, including amendments. If the organization will be operating under another name, show the other name in parentheses.

For a foreign address, enter the information in the following order: city, province or state, and country. Follow the country's practice in placing the postal code in the address. **Do not** abbreviate the country name.

Line 2. Employer identification number (EIN).—All organizations must have an EIN. Enter the nine-digit EIN the IRS assigned to the organization. See **Form SS-4,** Application for Employer Identification Number, for information on how to obtain an EIN immediately by telephone, if the organization does not have an EIN. Enter, "applied for," if the organization has applied for an EIN number previously. Attach a statement giving the date of the application and the office where it was filed. **Do not** apply for an EIN more than once.

Line 3. Person to contact.—Enter the name and telephone number of the person to be contacted during business hours if more information is needed. The contact person should be an officer, director, or a person with power of attorney who is familiar with the organization's activities and who is authorized to act on its behalf. Attach Form 2848 or other power of attorney.

Line 4. Month the annual accounting period ends.—Enter the month the organization's annual accounting period ends. The organization's accounting period is usually the 12-month period that is the organization's tax year. The organization's first tax year depends on the accounting period it chooses. The first tax year could be less than 12 months.

Line 5. Date incorporated or formed.—Enter the date the organization became a legal entity. For corporations this is the date that the articles of incorporation were approved by the appropriate state official. For unincorporated organizations, it is the date its constitution or articles of association were adopted.

Line 6.—Indicate if the organization has ever filed Form 1023, Form 1024, or other exemption application with the IRS.

Line 7.—Indicate if the organization has ever filed Federal income tax returns as a taxable organization or filed returns as an exempt organization (e.g., Forms 990, 990-EZ, 990-PF, and 990-T).

Page 2

Line 8. Type of organization and organizational documents.—

Organizing instrument.—Submit a conformed copy of the organizing instrument. If the organization does not have an organizing instrument, it will not qualify for exempt status.

• A conformed copy is one that agrees with the original and all amendments to it. The conformed copy may be:

• A photocopy of the original signed and dated organizing document, OR

• A copy of the organizing document that is unsigned but is sent with a written declaration, signed by an authorized individual, that states that the copy is a complete and accurate copy of the original signed and dated document.

Corporation.—In the case of a corporation, a copy of the articles of incorporation, approved and dated by an appropriate state official, is sufficient by itself.

If an unsigned copy of the articles of incorporation is submitted, it must be accompanied by the written declaration discussed above.

Signed or unsigned copies of the articles of incorporation must be accompanied by a declaration stating that the original copy of the articles was filed with and approved by the state. The date filed must be specified.

Unincorporated association.—In the case of an unincorporated association, the conformed copy of the constitution, articles of association, or other organizing document must indicate in the document itself, or in a written declaration, that the organization was formed by the adoption of the document by two or more persons.

Bylaws.—If the organization has adopted bylaws, include a current copy. The bylaws need not be signed if submitted as an attachment to the Form 1024 application. The bylaws of an organization alone are not an organizing instrument. They are merely the internal rules and regulations of the organization.

Trust.—In the case of a trust, a copy of the signed and dated trust instrument must be furnished.

Part II. Activities and Operational Information

Line 1.—It is important that you report all activities carried on by the organization to enable the IRS to make a proper determination of the organization's exempt status.

It is also important that you provide detailed information about the nature and purpose of each of the activities. The organization will be contacted for such information if it is not furnished.

Line 2.— If it is anticipated that the organization's principal sources of support will increase or decrease substantially in relation to the organization's total support, attach a statement describing anticipated changes and explaining the basis for the expectation.

Line 3a.—Furnish the mailing addresses of the organization's principal officers, directors, or trustees. Do not give the address of the organization.

Page 3

Line 3b.—The annual compensation includes salary, bonus, and any other form of payment to the individual for services performed for the organization.

Line 4.—If your organization's activities were formerly performed under another name or if your organization was a part of another organization (tax-exempt or nonexempt), furnish the requested information. Otherwise, indicate "N/A."

Line 5.—Indicate your organization's current or planned connection with any tax-exempt or nonexempt organization.

Line 6.—If your organization has issued stock as a means of indicating ownership by its members or others, furnish the requested information. Otherwise, indicate "N/A."

Line 7.—If your organization is a membership organization, furnish the requested information. Otherwise, indicate "N/A."

Line 8.—If your organization should cease operations as a tax-exempt organization, explain to whom its assets will be distributed.

Line 9.—Indicate if the organization distributes, or plans to distribute, any of its property or funds (such as a distribution of profits) to its shareholders or members.

Line 10.—Indicate if the organization performs any services for any other organization or individual for which it is paid a fee.

Line 11.—Do not include the normal salary of officers or employees.

Line 12.—Answer "Yes," if the organization either provides insurance through a third party or provides the insurance itself.

Line 13.—Examples of public regulatory bodies are: HUD, HHS, Public Utilities Commission, Housing Authority, and a state insurance commission.

Line 14.—Provide the specified information about leased property whether it is used for exempt functions or for other purposes.

Line 15.—Provide the specified information about political expenditures whether they were made to support or to oppose particular candidates.

Line 16.—This includes any printed material that may be used to publicize the organization's activities, or as an informational item to members or potential members.

Part III. Financial Data

The Statement of Revenue and Expenses must be completed for the current year and each of the 3 years immediately before it (or the years the organization has existed, if less than 4).

Any applicant that has existed for less than 1 year must give financial data for the current year and proposed budgets for the following 2 years.

Any applicant that has been in existence more than 1 year but seeks recognition of exemption only for the current year and future years (rather than from the date of its formation), should give financial data for the current year and proposed budgets for the following 2 years.

We may request financial data for more than 4 years if necessary.

All financial information for the current year must cover the period beginning on the first day of the organization's established annual accounting period and ending on any day that is within 60 days of the date of this application.

If the date of this application is less than 60 days after the first day of the current accounting period, no financial information is required for the current year.

Financial information is required for the 3 preceding years regardless of the current year requirements.

Note that if no financial information is required for the current year, the preceding year's financial information can end on any day that is within 60 days of the date of this application.

Prepare the statements using the method of accounting and the accounting period the organization uses in keeping its books and records.

If the organization uses a method other than the cash receipts and disbursements method, attach a statement explaining the method used.

A. Statement of Revenue and Expenses

Line 1.—Include amounts received from the members that represent the annual dues and any special assessments or initiation fees.

Line 2.—Do not include amounts received from the general public or a governmental unit for the exercise or performance of the organization's exempt function.

Line 3.—Examples of such income include: the income derived by a social club from the sale of food or beverage to its members; the sale of burial lots by a cemetery association; and fees charged by a social welfare organization or trade association for an educational seminar it conducted.

Line 4.—Enter the organization's gross income from activities that are regularly carried on and not related to the organization's exempt function.

Examples of such income include: fees from the commercial testing of products; income from renting office equipment or other personal property; and income from the sale of advertising in an exempt organization periodical. See Pub. 598 for information about unrelated business income and activities.

Line 5.—Attach a schedule showing the description of each asset, the name of the person to whom sold, and the amount received. In the case of publicly traded securities sold through a broker, the name of the purchaser is not required.

Line 6.—Include on this line the income received from dividends, interest, payments received on securities loans (as defined in section 512(a)(5)), rents, and royalties.

Line 7.—Enter the total income from all sources that is not reported on lines 1 through 6. Include, for example, income from special events such as raffles and dances that is not taxable as unrelated business income. Attach a schedule that lists each type of revenue source and the amount derived from each.

Line 9.—Enter the expenses directly related to the income sources reported on line 3 of this part.

Line 10.—Enter the expenses directly related to the income sources reported on line 4 of this part.

Line 11.—Attach a schedule showing the name of the recipient, a brief description of the purposes or conditions of payment, and the amount paid.

¶1653

Line 12.—Attach a schedule showing the total amount paid for each benefit category, such as disability, death, sickness, hospitalization, unemployment compensation, or strike benefits.

Lines 13–18.—Use lines 13 through 18 to report expenses that are not directly related to the expense categories listed on lines 9 and 10.

For example, salaries attributable to the organization's exempt purpose activities should be included with any other expenses reportable on line 9 rather than being reported separately on line 14.

Salaries reportable on line 14 include, for example, those attributable to special events; to the solicitation of contributions; and to the overall management and operation of the organization.

Line 13.—Attach a schedule that shows the name of the person compensated; the office or position; the average amount of time devoted to business per week, month, etc.; and the amount of annual compensation.

Line 14.—Enter the total of employees' salaries not reported on line 13.

Line 15.—Enter the total interest expense for the year, excluding mortgage interest treated as occupancy expense on line 16.

Line 16.—Enter the amount paid for the use of office space or other facilities; heat; light; power; and other utilities; outside janitorial services; mortgage interest; real estate taxes; and similar expenses.

Line 17.—If your organization records depreciation, depletion, and similar expenses, enter the total.

Line 18.—Attach a statement listing the type and amount of each **significant** expense for which a separate line is not provided. Report other miscellaneous expenses as a single total if not substantial in amount.

B. Balance Sheet

Line 1.—Enter the total interest- and non-interest-bearing cash in checking and savings accounts, temporary cash investments (money market funds, CDs, treasury bills, or other obligations that mature in less than 1 year), change funds, and petty cash funds.

Line 2.—Enter the total accounts receivable that arose from the sale of goods and/or performance of services.

Line 3.—Enter the amount of materials, goods, and supplies purchased or manufactured by the organization and held to be sold or used in some future period.

Line 4.—Attach a schedule that shows the name of the borrower, a brief description of the obligation, the rate of return on the principal indebtedness, the due date, and the amount due.

Line 5.—Attach a schedule listing the organization's corporate stock holdings.

For stock of closely held corporations, the schedule should show the name of the corporation, a brief summary of the corporation's capital structure, the number of shares held, and their value as carried on the organization's books. If such valuation does not reflect current fair market value, also include fair market value.

For stock traded on an organized exchange or in substantial quantities over the counter, the schedule should show the name of the corporation, a description of the stock and

the principal exchange on which it is traded, the number of shares held, and their value as carried on the organization's books.

Line 6.—Attach a schedule that shows the borrower's name, purpose of loan, repayment terms, interest rate, and original amount of loan.

Report each loan separately, even if more than one loan was made to the same person.

Line 7.—Enter the book value of securities held of the U.S., state, or municipal governments. Also enter the book value of buildings and equipment held for investment purposes. Attach a schedule identifying each.

Line 8.—Enter the book value of buildings and equipment not held for investment. This includes plant and equipment used by the organization in conducting its exempt activities. Attach a schedule listing these assets held at the end of the current tax-year period and the cost or other basis.

Line 9.—Enter the book value of land not held for investment.

Line 10.—Enter the book value of each category of assets not reported on lines 1 through 9. Attach a schedule listing each.

Line 12.—Enter the total of accounts payable to suppliers and others, such as salaries payable, accrued payroll taxes, and interest payable.

Line 13.—Enter the unpaid portion of grants and contributions that the organization has made a commitment to pay to other organizations or individuals.

Line 14.—Enter the total of mortgages and other notes payable at the end of the year. Attach a schedule that shows each item separately and the lender's name, purpose of loan, repayment terms, interest rate, and original amount.

Line 15.—Enter the amount of each liability not reported on lines 12 through 14. Attach a separate schedule.

Line 17.—Under fund accounting, an organization segregates its assets, liabilities, and net assets into separate funds according to restrictions on the use of certain assets. Each fund is like a separate entity in that it has a self-balancing set of accounts showing assets, liabilities, equity (fund balance), income, and expenses.

If the organization uses fund accounting, report the total of all fund balances on line 17. If the organization does not use fund accounting, report only the "net assets" account balances, such as capital stock, paid-in capital, and retained earnings or accumulated income.

Part IV. Notice Requirements

Part IV only applies to section 501(c)(9) and (17) organizations. Organizations applying for tax-exempt status under other sections of the Code should not fill in Part IV.

Line 1.—If you answer "Yes," do not answer questions 2 through 4. If you answer "No," proceed to line 2.

Line 2.—Relief from the 15-month filing requirement is granted automatically if the organization submits a completed Form 1024 within 12 months from the end of the 15-month period.

To get this extension, an organization must add the following statement at the top of its application: "Filed Pursuant to Section 301.9100-2." No request for a letter ruling is required to obtain an automatic extension.

Line 3.—See Regulation sections 301.9100-1 and 301.9100-3 for information about a discretionary extension beyond the 27-month period. Under this regulation, the IRS will allow an organization a reasonable extension of time to file a Form 1024 if it submits evidence to establish that:

(a) It acted reasonably and in good faith, and

(b) Granting relief will not prejudice the interests of the government.

Showing reasonable action and good faith.—An organization acted reasonably and showed good faith if at least one of the following is true.

1. The organization filed its application before the IRS discovered its failure to file.

2. The organization failed to file because of intervening events beyond its control.

3. The organization exercised reasonable diligence but was not aware of the filing requirement.

To determine whether the organization exercised reasonable diligence, it is necessary to take into account the complexity of filing and the organization's experience in these matters.

4. The organization reasonably relied upon the written advice of the IRS.

5. The organization reasonably relied upon the advice of a qualified tax professional who failed to file or advise the organization to file Form 1024. An organization cannot rely on the advice of a qualified tax professional if it knows or should know that he or she is not competent to render advice on filing exemption applications or is not aware of all the relevant facts.

Not acting reasonably and in good faith.—An organization has not acted reasonably and in good faith if it chose not to file after being informed of the requirement to file and the consequences of failure to do so. Furthermore, an organization has not acted reasonably and in good faith if it used hindsight to request an extension of time to file. That is, if after the original deadline to file passes, specific facts have changed so that filing an application becomes advantageous to an organization, the IRS will not ordinarily grant an extension. To qualify for an extension in this situation, the organization must prove that its decision to file did not involve hindsight.

No prejudice to the interest of the government.—Prejudice to the interest of the government results if granting an extension of time to file to an organization results in a lower total tax liability for the years to which the filing applies than would have been the case if the organization had applied on time. Before granting an extension, the IRS may require the organization requesting it to submit a statement from an independent auditor certifying that no prejudice will result if the extension is granted.

Procedure for requesting extension.—To request a discretionary extension, an organization must submit the following with its Form 1024.

● A statement showing the date Form 1024 should have been filed and the date it was actually filed.

● An affidavit describing in detail the events that led to the failure to apply and to the discovery of that failure. If the organization relied on a qualified tax professional's advice, the affidavit must describe the engagement and responsibilities of the professional and the extent to which the organization relied on him or her.

● All documents relevant to the election application.

● A dated declaration, signed by an individual authorized to act for the organization, that includes the following statement: "Under penalties of perjury, I declare that I have examined this request, including accompanying documents, and, to the best of my knowledge and belief, the request contains all the relevant facts relating to the request, and such facts are true, correct, and complete." The individual who signs for the organization must have personal knowledge of the facts and circumstances at issue.

● A detailed affidavit from individuals having knowledge or information about the events that led to the failure to make the application and to the discovery of that failure. These individuals include accountants or attorneys knowledgeable in tax matters who advised the organization concerning the application. Any affidavit from a tax professional must describe the engagement and responsibilities of the professional as well as the advice that the professional provided to the organization. The affidavit must also include the name, current address, and taxpayer identification number of the individual making the affidavit (the affiant). The affiant must also forward with the affidavit a dated and signed declaration that states: "Under penalties of perjury, I declare that I have examined this request, including accompanying documents, and, to the best of my knowledge and belief, the request contains all the relevant facts relating to the request, and such facts are true, correct, and complete."

The reasons for late filing should be specific to your particular organization and situation. Regulation section 301.9100-3 (see above) lists the factors the IRS will consider to determine if good cause exists for granting a discretionary extension of time to file the application. To address these factors your response on line 3 should provide the following information:

1. Whether the organization consulted an attorney or accountant knowledgeable in tax matters, or communicated with a responsible IRS employee (before or after the organization was created), to ascertain the organization's Federal filing requirements and, if so, the names and occupations or titles of the persons contacted, the approximate dates, and the substance of the information obtained;

2. How and when the organization learned about the 15-month deadline for filing Form 1024;

3. Whether any significant intervening circumstances beyond the organization's control prevented it from submitting the application timely or within a reasonable period of time after it learned of the requirement to file the application within the 15-month period; and

4. Any other information that you believe may establish reasonable action and good faith and no prejudice to the interest of the government for not filing timely or otherwise justify granting the relief sought.

A request for relief under this section is treated as part of the request for the exemption determination letter and is covered by the user fee submitted with Form 8718.

Line 4.—If you answer "No," the organization may receive an adverse letter limiting the effective date of its exempt status to the date its application was received.

Paperwork Reduction Act Notice.—We ask for the information on this form to carry out the Internal Revenue laws of the United States. If you want your organization to be recognized as tax exempt by the IRS, you are required to give us this information. We need it to determine whether the organization meets the legal requirements for tax-exempt status.

The organization is not required to provide the information requested on a form that is subject to the Paperwork Reduction Act unless the form displays a valid OMB control number. Books or records relating to a form or its instructions must be retained as long as their contents may become material in the administration of any Internal Revenue law. The rules governing the confidentiality of the Form 1024 application are covered in Code section 6104.

The time needed to complete and file this form will vary depending on individual circumstances. The estimated average times are:

Form	Recordkeeping	Learning about the law or the form	Preparing and sending the form to the IRS
1024, Parts I–III	53 hr., 5 min.	2 hr., 17 min.	3 hr., 15 min.
Part IV	1 hr., 12 min.	35 min.	52 min.
Sch. A	2 hr., 52 min.	18 min.	21 min.
Sch. B	1 hr., 40 min.	18 min.	20 min.
Sch. C	58 min.	12 min.	13 min.
Sch. D	4 hr., 4 min.	18 min.	22 min.
Sch. E	1 hr., 40 min.	18 min.	20 min.
Sch. F	2 hr., 23 min.	6 min.	8 min.
Sch. G	1 hr., 55 min.	6 min.	8 min.
Sch. H	1 hr., 40 min.	6 min.	8 min.
Sch. I	5 hr., 30 min.	30 min.	37 min.
Sch. J	2 hr., 23 min.	6 min.	8 min.
Sch. K	3 hr., 21 min.	6 min.	10 min.

If you have comments concerning the accuracy of these time estimates or suggestions for making this form simpler, we would be happy to hear from you. You can write to the Tax Forms Committee, Western Area Distribution Center, Rancho Cordova, CA 95743-0001. **DO NOT** send the application to this address. Instead, see **Where To File** on page 1.

Procedural Checklist
Make sure the application is complete.

If you do not complete all applicable parts or do not provide all required attachments, we may return the incomplete application for the organization to resubmit with the missing information or attachments. This will delay the processing of the application and may delay the effective date of your organization's exempt status. The organization may also incur additional user fees.

Have you . . .

_____ Attached **Form 8718** (User Fee for Exempt Organization Determination Letter Request) and the appropriate fee?

_____ Prepared the application for mailing? (See **Where To File** addresses in Form 8718.)

_____ Completed all Parts and Schedules that apply to the organization?

_____ Shown your organization's **Employer Identification Number (EIN)?**

   a. If your organization has an EIN, write it in the space provided.

   b. If this is a newly formed organization and does not have an Employer Identification Number, obtain an EIN by telephone. (See Specific Instructions, Part I, Line 2, on page 2.)

_____ If applicable, described your organization's **specific activities** as directed in Part II, question 1 of the application?

_____ Included a **conformed copy** of the complete organizing instrument? (Part I, question 8 of the application.)

_____ Had the application signed by one of the following:

   a. An officer or trustee who is authorized to sign (e.g., president, treasurer); **or**

   b. A person authorized by a power of attorney (submit Form 2848 or other power of attorney)?

_____ If applicable, enclosed **financial statements** (Part III)?

   a. Current year (must include period up to within 60 days of the date the application is filed) and 3 preceding years.

   b. Detailed breakdown of revenue and expenses (no lump sums).

   c. If the organization has been in existence less than 1 year, it must also submit proposed budgets for 2 years showing the amounts and types of receipts and expenditures anticipated.

Note: *During the technical review of a completed application, it may be necessary to contact the organization for more specific or additional information.*

Do not send this checklist with the application.

¶1653

¶1654 Exhibit 16-4

Form **5300** (Rev. September 2001) Department of the Treasury Internal Revenue Service	**Application for Determination for Employee Benefit Plan** (including collectively bargained plans formerly filed on Form 5303) (Under sections 401(a) and 501(a) of the Internal Revenue Code)	OMB No. 1545-0197 **For IRS Use Only**

Review the **Procedural Requirements Checklist** on page 5 before submitting this application.

1a Name of plan sponsor (employer if single-employer plan)	**1b** Employer identification number
Number, street, and room or suite no. (If a P.O. box, see instructions.)	**1c** Employer's tax year ends—Enter (MM)
City State ZIP code	**1d** Telephone number ( )

2a Person to contact if more information is needed. (See instructions.) (If **Form 2848**, Power of Attorney and Declaration of Representative, or other written designation is attached, check box and do not complete the rest of this line.) . . . . ▶ ☐ Name	**1e** Fax number ( )
Number, street, and room or suite no. (If a P.O. box, see instructions.)	**2b** Telephone number ( )
City State ZIP code	**2c** Fax number ( )

3a Determination requested for (enter applicable number(s) in the box and fill in required information). (See instructions.)

☐ Enter 1 for Initial Qualification—Date plan signed ▶ ..../......./...............

☐ Enter 2 for a request after initial qualification—Is complete plan attached? (See instructions.) ▶ Yes ☐   No ☐
Date amendment signed ▶ ..../......./............... Date amendment effective ▶ ..../......./...............

☐ Enter 3 for Affiliated Service Group status (section 414(m))—Date effective ▶ ..../......./...............

☐ Enter 4 for Leased Employee status

☐ Enter 5 for Partial termination—Date effective ▶ ..../......./...............

☐ Enter 6 for Termination of collectively bargained multiemployer or multiple-employer plan covered by PBGC insurance—Date of Termination ▶ ..../......./...............

b Has the plan received a determination letter? . . . . Yes ☐   No ☐
Date of letter ▶ ..../......./...............
If "Yes" submit a copy of the latest letter and subsequent amendments.
Number of amendments ▶ ....
If "No," submit all prior plan(s) and/or adoption agreement(s). (See instructions.)

c Have interested parties been given the required notification of this application? (See instructions) . . Yes ☐   No ☐
d Does the plan have a cash or deferred arrangement (section 401(k))? . . . . Yes ☐   No ☐
e Does the plan have matching contributions (section 401(m))? . . . . Yes ☐   No ☐
f Does the plan have after-tax employee voluntary contributions (section 401(m))? . . . . . . Yes ☐   No ☐
g Does this plan benefit noncollectively bargained employees or are more than 2% of the employees who are covered under a collective bargaining agreement for professional employees? . . . . . Yes ☐   No ☐
See Regulations section 1.410(b)-9.
h Does the plan provide for disparity in contributions or benefits that is intended to meet the permitted disparity requirements of section 401(l)? . . . . Yes ☐   No ☐

4a Name of plan (Plan name may not exceed 66 characters, including spaces.):

....

.... **b** Enter 3-digit plan number   ...../...../..... **d** Enter plan's **original** effective date (MMDDYYYY)

............/......... **c** Enter date plan year ends (MMDD) .... **e** Enter number of participants (See instructions.)

Under penalties of perjury, I declare that I have examined this application, including accompanying statements and schedules, and to the best of my knowledge and belief, it is true, correct, and complete.

Print Name ▶   Title ▶

Signature ▶   Date ▶

For Paperwork Reduction Act Notice, see separate instructions.   Cat. No. 11740X   Form **5300** (Rev. 9-2001)

5 Indicate type of plan by entering the number from the list below.

	1—profit-sharing and/or 401(k)	4—defined benefit but not cash balance	7—non-leveraged ESOP
	2—money purchase	5—cash balance	8—stock bonus
	3—target benefit	6—leveraged ESOP	9—safe harbor 401(k)

		Yes	No
6a	Is the employer a member of an affiliated service group?		
b	Is the employer a member of a controlled group of corporations or a group of trades or businesses under common control?		
	If **a** and/or **b** above is "Yes," complete required statement (see instructions).		
7a	Is this a governmental plan?		
	If "Yes," is the plan a state level plan?		
b	Is this a nonelecting church plan?		
c	Is this a collectively bargained plan? (See Regulations section 1.410(b)-9.)		
d	Is this a section 412(i) plan?		
e	Is this a multiple-employer plan? Enter number of participating employers ▶		
f	Is this a multiemployer plan as described in section 414(f)?		
8a	Do you maintain any other qualified plan(s) under section 401(a)?		
	If "Yes," attach required statement (see instructions).		
	If "No," skip to line 8d.		
b	Do you maintain another plan of the same type (i.e., both this plan and the other plan are defined contribution plans or both are defined benefit plans) that covers non-key employees who are also covered under this plan?		
	If yes, when the plan is top-heavy, do the non-key employees covered under both plans receive the required top-heavy minimum contribution or benefit under:		
	(1) This plan?		
	(2) The other plan?		
c	If this is a defined contribution plan, do you maintain a defined benefit plan (or if this is a defined benefit plan, do you maintain a defined contribution plan) that covers non-key employees who are also covered under this plan?		
	If yes, when the plan is top-heavy, do non-key employees covered under both plans receive:		
	(1) the top-heavy minimum benefit under the defined benefit plan?		
	(2) at least a 5% minimum contribution under the defined contribution plan?		
	(3) the minimum benefit offset by benefits provided by the defined contribution plan?		
	(4) benefits under both plans that, using a comparability analysis, are at least equal to the minimum benefit? (See instructions.)		
d	Does the plan prevent the possibility that the section 415 limitations will be exceeded for any employee who is (or was) a participant in this plan and any other plan of the employer?		

General Eligibility Requirements (Complete all lines.)

9a Check all that apply:
   (1) ☐ All employees
   (2) ☐ Hourly rate employees
   (3) ☐ Salaried employees
   (4) ☐ Other (Specify) ....
b Minimum years of service required to participate .... If no minimum, check ▶ ☐
c Minimum age required to participate (Specify) If no minimum, check ▶ ☐

Vesting (Check one box to indicate the regular (non-top heavy) vesting provisions of the plan.)

10a ☐ Full and immediate
b ☐ Full vesting after 2 years of service
c ☐ Full vesting after 3 years of service
d ☐ Full vesting after 5 years of service
e ☐ 2 to 6 year graded vesting
f ☐ 3 to 7 year graded vesting
g ☐ Other

Form **5300** (Rev. 9-2001)

Benefits and Requirements for Benefits

11a For defined benefit plans—Method for determining accrued benefit ▶ ....

    (1) Benefit formula at normal retirement age is ....

    (2) Benefit formula at early retirement age is ....

    (3) Normal form of retirement benefit is ....

  b For defined contribution plans—Employer contributions:

    (1) Profit-sharing or stock bonus plan contributions are determined under:
      ☐ A definite formula   ☐ A discretionary formula   ☐ Both

    (2) Matching contributions are determined under:
      ☐ A definite formula   ☐ A discretionary formula   ☐ Both

    (3) Money purchase plan—Enter rate of contribution ....

    (4) Target benefit plan—state target benefit formula ....

Miscellaneous

	N/A	Yes	No
12a Does any amendment to the plan reduce or eliminate any section 411(d)(6) protected benefit, including an amendment adopted after September 6, 2000, to eliminate a joint and survivor annuity form of benefit? (See instructions.)			
b Are trust earnings and losses allocated on the basis of account balances in a defined contribution plan? If "No," attach a statement explaining how they are allocated.			
c Is this plan or trust currently under examination or is any issue related to this plan or trust currently pending before:			
• The Internal Revenue Service			
• The Department of Labor			
• The Pension Benefit Guaranty Corporation, or			
• Any court?			

If "Yes," attach a statement explaining the issues involved, the contact person's name (IRS Agent, DOL Investigator, etc.) and their telephone number. Do not answer "Yes" if the plan has been submitted under the Voluntary Compliance Program of the Employee Plans Compliance Resolution System (EPCRS).

Form **5300** (Rev. 9-2001)

Optional determination request regarding the ratio percentage test. A determination regarding the average benefit test may be requested by attaching Schedule Q (Form 5300).

		Yes	No
13	Is this a request for a determination regarding the ratio percentage test of Regs. section 1.410(b)-2(b)(2) or a request for a determination regarding one of the special requirements of Regs. section 1.410(b)-2(b)(5), (6), or (7)? . . .		

If "Yes," complete only lines 13a through 13n for a ratio percentage test determination, or complete only line 13o for a determination regarding one of the special requirements.

If "No," skip to line 14.

a Is this plan disaggregated into two or more separate plans that are not 401(k), 401(m), or profit sharing plans? If "Yes," see the instructions and attach separate schedules for each disaggregated portion . . . .

b Does the employer receive services from any leased employees as defined in section 414(n)? . . . .

c Coverage date (MMDDYYYY). See instructions for inserting date . . . .

d Total number of employees (include self-employed individuals) (employer-wide) . . . .

e Statutory and regulatory exclusions under this plan (do not count an employee more than once):

    (1) Number of employees excluded because of minimum age or years of service required . . .

    (2) Number of employees excluded because of inclusion in a collective bargaining unit . . . .

    (3) Number of employees excluded because they terminated employment with less than 501 hours of service and were not employed on last day of plan year . . . .

    (4) Number of employees excluded because employed by other qualified separate lines of business (QSLOBs) . . . .

    (5) Number of employees excluded because they were nonresident aliens with no earned income from sources within the United States . . . .

f Total statutory and regulatory exclusions (add lines 13e(1) through 13e(5)) . . . .

g Nonexcludable employees (subtract line 13f from line 13d) . . . .

h Number of nonexcludable employees on line 13g who are highly compensated employees (HCEs) .

i Number of nonexcludable HCEs on line 13h benefiting under the plan . . . .

j Number of nonexcludable employees who are nonhighly compensated employees (NHCEs) (subtract line 13h from line 13g) . . . .

k Number of nonexcludable NHCEs on line 13j benefiting under the plan . . . .

l Ratio percentage (See instructions.) . . . .

m Enter the ratio percentage for the following, if applicable:

    (1) Section 401(k) part of the plan . . . .

    (2) Section 401(m) part of the plan . . . .

		Yes	No
n	Are the results on line 13l or 13m based on the aggregated coverage of more than one plan?		

If "Yes," attach a statement showing the names, plan numbers, EINs, and benefit/allocation formulas of the other plans. **All aggregated plans should be filed concurrently.**

o If the plan satisfied coverage using one of the special requirements of Regulations section 1.410(b)-2(b)(5), (6), or (7), enter the letter from the list below that identifies the special requirement:

    A—1.410(b)-2(b)(5)—No NHCEs employed
    B—1.410(b)-2(b)(6)—No HCEs benefit
    C—1.410(b)-2(b)(7)—Collectively bargained only

Optional determination request regarding the nondiscrimination design-based safe harbors of section 401(a)(4).

Section 401(k) and/or section 401(m) plans that do not contain a provision for discretionary contributions should not complete this line.

		Yes	No
14	Is this a request for a determination regarding a design-based safe harbor under section 401(a)(4)?		

If "Yes," complete the following:

Design-based nondiscrimination safe harbors:

a Does the plan provide for disparity in contributions or benefits that is intended to meet the permitted disparity requirements of section 401(l)? . . . .
If "Yes," answer line 14b. Otherwise, skip to line 14c.

b Do the provisions of the plan ensure that the overall permitted disparity limits will not be exceeded? . . . . .

c Enter the letter ("A" – "G") from the list below that identifies the safe harbor intended to be satisfied ▶

    A—1.401(a)(4)-2(b)(2) defined contribution (DC) plan with uniform allocation formula

    B—1.401(a)(4)-3(b)(3) unit credit defined benefit (DB) plan   E—1.401(a)(4)-3(b)(5) insurance account

    C—1.401(a)(4)-3(b)(4)(i)(C)(1) unit credit DB fractional rule plan   F—1.401(a)(4)-8(b)(3) target benefit plan

    D—1.401(a)(4)-3(b)(4)(i)(C)(2) flat benefit DB plan   G—1.401(a)(4)-8(c)(3)(iii)(b) cash balance plan

d List the plan section(s) that satisfy the safe harbor (including, if applicable, the permitted disparity requirements) here:

¶1654

Form 5300 (Rev. 9-2001)   Page **5**

Procedural Requirements Checklist
**********Form 5300**********

Use this list to ensure that your submitted package is complete. Failure to supply the appropriate information may result in a delay in the processing of the application.

☐ **1** Is **Form 0717,** User Fee for Employee Plan Determination Letter Request, attached to your submission?

☐ **2** Is the appropriate user fee for your submission attached to Form 8717?

☐ **3** If appropriate, is **Form 2848,** Power of Attorney and Declaration of Representative, or a privately designated authorization attached? (For more information, see the **Disclosure Request by Taxpayer** in the instructions.)

☐ **4** Is a copy of your plan's latest determination letter, if any, attached?

☐ **5** Is the Employer Identification Number (EIN) of the **plan sponsor/employer** (NOT the trust's EIN) entered on line 1b?

☐ **6** Does line 4d list the plan's original effective date?

☐ **7** Is the application signed and dated?

☐ **8** Have interested parties been given the required notification of this application? (See the instructions for line 3c.)

☐ **9** If you are requesting a determination as an **Affiliated Service Group,** have you included the information requested in the instructions?
NOTE: You can request a ruling from the IRS as to whether or not you are an **Affiliated Service Group** by listing your request on line 3 of Form 5300.

☐ **10** If you answered "Yes" to line(s) 6a and/or line 6b, have you included the information requested in the instructions?

☐ **11** **For Multiple Employer Plans:** Have you included the required information as specified in the instructions under **Specific Plans—Additional Requirements?**

☐ **12** **For Partial Termination Requests:** If requesting a determination for the plan and one or more employers maintaining the plan, have you included the required information as specified in the instructions under **Types of Determination Letters, Partial Termination?**

☐ **13** If you answered "Yes" to line 8a, have you included the requested information?

☐ **14** If you are requesting additional determinations, is page 4 completed and/or Schedule Q attached?

☐ **15** If filing a Schedule Q, are all appropriate demonstrations attached? (See Instructions for Schedule Q)
☐ Demo 1   ☐ Demo 5   ☐ Demo 8   ☐ Demo 11
☐ Demo 3   ☐ Demo 6   ☐ Demo 9
☐ Demo 4   ☐ Demo 7   ☐ Demo 10

☐ **16** Have you included a copy of the plan, trust, and all amendments since your last determination letter?

☐ **17** **For Employee Stock Ownership Plans (ESOP):** Have you attached **Form 5309,** Application for Determination of Employee Stock Ownership Plan, to your submission?

☐ **18** **For PBGC Terminations:** Have you included the required information as specified in the instructions under **Types of Determination Letters?**

Form **5300** (Rev. 9-2001)

¶1654

Instructions for Form 5300

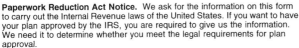

Department of the Treasury
Internal Revenue Service

(Revised September 2001)

Application for Determination for Employee Benefit Plan

(including Collectively Bargained Plans formerly filed on Form 5303)
Section references are to the Internal Revenue Code unless otherwise noted.

Paperwork Reduction Act Notice. We ask for the information on this form to carry out the Internal Revenue laws of the United States. If you want to have your plan approved by the IRS, you are required to give us the information. We need it to determine whether you meet the legal requirements for plan approval.

You are not required to provide the information requested on a form that is subject to the Paperwork Reduction Act unless the form displays a valid OMB control number. Books or records relating to a form or its instructions must be retained as long as their contents may become material in the administration of any Internal Revenue law. Generally, tax returns and return information are confidential, as required by section 6103.

The time needed to complete and file this form will vary depending on individual circumstances. The estimated average time is:

	Recordkeeping	Learning about the law or the form	Preparing the form	Copying, assembling, and sending the form to the IRS
Form 5300	41 hr., 7 min.	7 hr., 54 min.	13 hr., 34 min.	1 hr., 20 min.
Sch. Q (Form 5300)	6 hr., 13 min.	9 hr., 14 min.	9 hr., 45 min.	

If you have comments concerning the accuracy of these time estimates or suggestions for making this form simpler, we would be happy to hear from you. You can write to the Tax Forms Committee, Western Area Distribution Center, Rancho Cordova, CA 95743–0001.

Do not send any of these forms or schedules to this address. Instead, see **Where To File** on page 2.

Public Inspection. Form 5300 is open to public inspection if there are more than 25 plan participants. The total number of participants must be shown on line 4e. See the instructions for line 4e for a definition of participant.

Disclosure Request by Taxpayer. The Tax Reform Act of 1976 permits a taxpayer to request the IRS to disclose and discuss the taxpayer's return and/or return information with any person(s) the taxpayer designates in a written request. Use **Form 2848,** Power of Attorney and Declaration of Representative, for this purpose.

Changes To Note

- Form 5300 and the instructions have been revised to include collectively bargained plans that formerly filed **Form 5303,** Application for Determination for Collectively Bargained Plan. Form 5303 may not be filed after December 31, 2001.
- Complete **Schedule Q (Form 5300),** Elective Determination Requests, if you want to broaden the scope of a determination letter by

requesting a determination that your plan satisfies certain qualification requirements relating to minimum participation, coverage, and nondiscrimination. Schedule Q is no longer mandatory.

- Completion of page 4 of Form 5300 is also optional. Complete page 4 for: **(a)** a request for a determination regarding the ratio percentage test under Regulations section 1.410(b)-2(b)(2), **(b)** a determination regarding one of the special requirements under Regulations section 1.410(b)-2(b)(5), (6), or (7), or **(c)** a request for a determination regarding the nondiscrimination design-based safe harbors of section 401(a)(4).

How To Get Forms and Publications

Personal computer. You can access the IRS Web Site 24 hours a day, 7 days a week at **www.irs.gov** to:

- Download forms, instructions, and publications.

- See answers to frequently asked tax questions.
- Search publications on-line by topic or keyword.
- Send us comments or request help by e-mail.
- Sign up to receive local and national tax news by e-mail.

You can also reach us using file transfer protocol at **ftp.irs.gov.**

CD-ROM. Order **Pub. 1796,** Federal Tax Products on CD-ROM, and get:

- Current year forms, instructions, and publications.
- Prior year forms, instructions, and publications.
- Popular tax forms that may be filled in electronically, printed out for submission, and saved for recordkeeping.
- The Internal Revenue Bulletin.

Buy the CD-ROM on the Internet at **www.irs.gov/cdorders** from the National Technical Information Service (NTIS) for $21 (plus a $5 handling fee).

By phone and in person. You can order forms and publications 24 hours a day, 7 days a week, by calling **1-800-TAX- FORM** (1-800-829-3676). You can also get most forms and publications at your local IRS office.

For questions regarding this form, call the Employee Plans Customer Service, toll-free, at 1-877-829-5500 between 8:00 a.m. and 9:30 p.m. eastern time.

General Instructions

Purpose of Form

File Form 5300 to request a determination letter from the IRS for the initial qualification of a defined benefit or a defined contribution plan and the exempt status of any related trust. See **Types of Determination Letters** on page 3 for more information.

This form may also be filed to request a determination letter on the qualified status of a plan at any time

Cat. No. 10932P

subsequent to initial qualification even if the plan has not been amended.

File **Form 5307**, Application for Determination for Master or Prototype or Volume Submitter Plans, instead of Form 5300 if this is an M&P or volume submitter plan. However, use Form 5300 instead of Form 5307 if you are also requesting a determination on affiliated service group status, leased employee status, or a partial termination.

File **Form 6406**, Short Form Application for Determination for Minor Amendment of Employee Benefit Plan, instead of Form 5300 to apply for a determination letter on a minor plan amendment to a plan that has already filed Form 5300 and received a favorable determination letter for GUST (i.e., the Small Business Job Protection Act of 1996 and other laws). Form 6406 generally may not be used to apply for a determination on GUST, except as provided in section 3.05 of Rev. Proc. 2000-27, 2000-26 I.R.B., 1271.

Type of Plan

● A **Defined Contribution Plan** (DCP) is a plan that provides an individual account for each participant and for benefits based only:

1. On the amount contributed to the participant's account, and

2. Any income, expenses, gains and losses, and any forfeitures of accounts of other participants that may be allocated to the participant's account.

● A **Defined Benefit Plan** (DBP) is any plan that is not a DCP.

Note: *A qualified plan must satisfy section 401(a) including, but not limited to, participation, vesting, nondiscriminatory contributions or benefits, distributions, and contribution and benefit limitations.*

Who May File

This form may be filed by any:

● **Employer,** including a sole proprietor, partnership, plan sponsor or a plan administrator that has adopted an individually designed plan to request a determination letter on:

1. Initial qualification of a plan;

2. Qualification of an entire plan as amended,

3. Partial termination of a plan;

4. Affiliated service group (ASG) status (section 414(m)), or

5. Leased employee status (section 414(n)).

Page 2

● **Plan sponsor** or **plan administrator** to request a determination letter for a plan maintained by an employer that is part of a controlled group of corporations (section 414(b)), or trades or businesses under common control (section 414(c)), or an ASG (section 414(m)).

● **Plan sponsor** or **plan administrator** to request a determination letter for a multiemployer or multiple-employer plan (a plan maintained by more than one employer considering all employers combined under section 414(b), (c), or (m) as one employer).

● **Employer, plan sponsor,** or **plan administrator** desiring a determination letter for compliance with the applicable requirements of a foreign situs trust for the taxability of beneficiaries (section 402(c)) and deductions for employer contributions (section 404(a)(4)).

Where To File

File Form 5300 at the address indicated below:

Internal Revenue Service,

P.O. Box 192,

Covington, KY 41012–0192.

Requests shipped by express mail or a delivery service should be sent to:

Internal Revenue Service,

201 West Rivercenter Blvd.,

Attn: Extracting Stop 312,

Covington, KY 41011.

Private Delivery Services. In addition to the United States mail, you can use certain private delivery services designated by the IRS to meet the "timely mailing as timely filing/paying" rule for tax returns and payments. The most recent list of designated private delivery services was published by the IRS in October 2001 and includes only the following:

● Airborne Express (Airborne): Overnight Air Express Service, Next Afternoon Service, Second Day Service.

● DHL Worldwide Express (DHL): DHL "Same Day" Service, DHL USA Overnight.

● Federal Express (FedEx): FedEx Priority Overnight, FedEx Standard Overnight, FedEx 2Day.

● United Parcel Service (UPS): UPS Next Day Air, UPS Next Day Air Saver, UPS 2nd Day Air, UPS 2nd Day Air A.M., UPS Worldwide Express Plus, and UPS Worldwide Express.

The private delivery service can tell you how to get written proof of the mailing date.

How to Complete the Application

Applications are screened for completeness. **The application must be signed by the employer, plan administrator or authorized representative.** Incomplete applications may be returned to the applicant. For this reason, it is important that an appropriate response be entered for each line item (unless instructed otherwise). In completing the application, pay careful attention to the following:

● N/A (not applicable) is accepted as a response **only** if an N/A block is provided.

● If a number is requested, a number must be entered.

● If an item provides a choice of boxes to check, check only one box unless instructed otherwise.

● If an item provides a box to check, written responses are not acceptable.

● Governmental plans and nonelecting church plans do not have to complete lines 10 and 12a.

● The IRS may, at its discretion, require a plan restatement or additional information any time it is deemed necessary.

Note. *Revenue Procedure 2001-6 publishes the guidance under which the determination letter program is administered. It is updated annually and can be found in the Internal Revenue Bulletin (I.R.B.)* **Example.** *Rev. Proc. 2001-6, 2001-1 I.R.B. 194 superseded Rev. Proc. 2000-6.*

What To File

All applications must contain an **original** signature and must be accompanied by the following applicable items:

● The appropriate user fee, if applicable, and **Form 8717**, User Fee for Employee Plan Determination Letter Request. Please submit a separate check for each application. Make checks payable to the "United States Treasury."

● Schedule Q (Form 5300), if any elective determinations are being requested, and any additional schedules or demonstrations required by these instructions or by the instructions for Schedule Q.

● All applications for plans that have at any time in the past received a favorable determination letter must include a copy of the plan's latest determination letter and subsequent amendments and/or restatements.

• A copy of the plan.

Types of Determination Letters

• **Initial Qualification**

For **initial qualification** of a plan or when requesting a determination letter after initial qualification for a plan that has not been amended (for example, because of changes in employee demographics), file one copy of all instruments that make up the plan.

• **Entire Plan as Amended**

When requesting a determination letter on the entire plan as amended after initial qualification file:

1. One copy of the plan and trust plus all amendments made to date;

2. One copy of the latest determination letter, including caveats; and

3. A statement explaining how any amendments made since the last determination letter affect this or any other plan of the employer.

• **Complex amendments**

Use Form 5300, as described under **Entire Plan as Amended** above, for complex amendments, including amendments with significant changes to plan benefits or coverage.

Note. *If there have been four or more amendments to the plan a restated plan is required. For restatement purposes, do not count an amendment making only minor plan changes as a plan amendment.*

• **Minor amendments**

Use Form 6406, instead of Form 5300 to request a determination letter on the effect of a minor amendment on the qualification of a plan. Form 6406 should not be used for plan amendments made to comply with GUST.

• **Partial Termination**

For a **partial termination** you must:

1. File the application form and the appropriate documents and statements.

2. Attach a statement indicating if a partial termination may have occurred or might occur as a result of proposed actions.

3. Using the format in the **Partial Termination Worksheet** above, submit a schedule of information for

Partial Termination Worksheet		Year	Year	Year of partial termination	Year .....
1	Participants employed:				
a	Number at beginning of plan year				
b	Number added during the plan year				
c	Total, add lines **a** and **b**				
d	Number dropped during the plan year				
e	Number at end of plan year, subtract **d** from **c**				
f	Total number of participants in this plan separated from service without full vesting				
2	Present value (as of month / / day during the year of):				
a	Plan assets				
b	Accrued benefits				
c	Vested benefits				

3 Submit a description of the actions that may have resulted (or might result) in a partial termination. Include an explanation of how the plan meets the requirements of section 411(d)(3).

the plan year in which the partial (or potential partial) termination began. Also, submit a schedule for the next plan year, as well as for the 2 prior plan years, to the extent information is available.

If the plan has more than one benefit computation formula complete the **Partial Termination Worksheet** for the plan. Also attach a sheet showing the information separately in the same format as lines 1a through 1f for each benefit computation formula.

4. Submit a description of the actions that may have resulted in a partial termination.

5. Include an explanation of how the plan meets the requirements of section 411(d)(3).

• **Termination of Plan**

If you are **terminating** your plan, file **Form 5310**, Application for Determination for Terminating Plan, to request a determination letter for the complete termination of a DBP or a DCP.

Form 5300 should be filed to request a determination letter involving the complete termination of a multiemployer plan covered by the PBGC insurance program.

In addition, file:

1. One copy of the plan;

2. One copy of the latest determination letter, including caveats;

3. A copy of all actions taken to terminate the plan; and

4. If necessary, **Form 6088**, Distributable Benefits From Employee Pension Benefit Plans. Form 6088 is

required if the plan is a DBP or if the plan is an underfunded DCP that benefits noncollectively bargained employees or more than 2% of the employees who are covered under a collectively bargained agreement are professional employees (See Regulations section 1.410(b)-9 for definitions.)

If you wish to stop benefit accruals or stop making contributions to your plan, and your plan trust will continue, the plan will not be considered terminated. If you want to receive a determination letter, you must use Form 5300. Do not file Form 5310 if the plan trust will continue.

Note: *If a DBP is amended to become a DCP, or if the merger of a DBP with a DCP results solely in a DCP, the DBP is considered terminated.*

Specific Plans — Additional Requirements

(See Procedural Requirements Checklist.)

• For a determination on an **affiliated service group** status, submit:

1. A copy of the appropriate documents and

2. Statements listed in the instructions for lines 3a and 6.

• For plans of **controlled groups of corporations, trades or businesses under common control,** and **affiliated service groups** submit the statement specified in the instructions for line 6.

• For **multiple-employer plans** that do not involve collective bargaining, submit:

Page 3

1. One Form 5300 application for the plan, omitting line 3, and

2. One Form 5300 (only lines 1 through 8 and, optionally, 13 and 14) and, optionally, Schedule Q for each other employer that chooses to receive a separate determination letter.

• For a **governmental or nonelecting church plan,** skip lines 10 and 12a. A **nonelecting** church plan is a plan for which an election under section 410(d) has not been made.

• For an **ESOP,** attach **Form 5309,** Application for Determination of Employee Stock Ownership Plan for an ESOP.

Specific Instructions

Line 1a. Enter the name, address, and telephone number of the plan sponsor/employer. A plan sponsor means:

1. In the case of a plan that covers the employees of one employer, the employer;

2. In the case of a plan maintained by two or more employers (other than a plan sponsored by a group of entities required to be combined under section 414(b), (c) or (m)), the association, committee, joint board of trustees or other similar group of representatives of those who established or maintain the plan;

3. In the case of a plan sponsored by two or more entities required to be combined under sections 414(b), (c) or (m), one of the members participating in the plan; or

4. In the case of a plan that covers the employees and/or partner(s) of a partnership, the partnership.

The name of the plan sponsor/employer should be the same name that was or will be used when the Form 5500 or Form 5500-EZ is filed for the plan.

Address. Include the suite, room, or other unit number after the street address. If the Post Office does not deliver mail to the street address and the plan has a P.O. box, show the box number instead of the street address. The address should be the address of the sponsor/employer.

Line 1b. Enter the 9-digit employer identification number (EIN) assigned to the plan sponsor/employer. This should be the same EIN that was or will be used when the Form 5500 or Form 5500-EZ is filed for the plan.

Do not use a social security number or the EIN of the trust. For a multiple-employer plan, the EIN the application for the plan should be the same EIN that was or will be used when Form 5500 is filed.

File **Form SS-4,** Application for Employer Identification Number, to apply for an EIN. Form SS-4 can be obtained by calling 1-800-TAX-FORM.

The plan of a group of entities required to be combined under section 414(b), (c), or (m) whose sponsor is more than one of the entities required to be combined should only enter the EIN of one of the sponsoring members. This EIN **must** be used in all subsequent filings of determination letter requests and annual returns/reports unless there is a change of sponsor.

Line 1c. Enter the two digits representing the month the employer's tax year ends. This is the employer whose EIN was entered on line 1b.

Line 2. The contact person will receive copies of all correspondence as authorized in a power of attorney, Form 2848, or other written designation. Either complete the contact's information on this line, or check the box and attach a power of attorney or other written designation.

Line 3a. Enter the number(s) that correspond to the request(s) being made.

Enter 1 if the IRS has not issued a determination letter for this plan.

Enter 2 if the IRS has previously issued a determination letter for this plan and enter the date the plan was signed.

In addition, enter the date the plan or amendment was signed. If a plan or amendment is proposed, enter 9/9/9999. Enter the effective date where requested. The term "Date amendment effective" means the date the amendment becomes operative or takes effect.

Enter 3 if requesting a letter concerning the effect of section 414(m) on the plan being submitted or because of a change in the affiliated service group (ASG) membership or if you are not certain if you are a member of an ASG, attach the following information:

1. A description of the nature of the business of the employer. Specifically state whether it is a service organization or an organization whose principal business is the performance of

management functions for another organization, including the reason for performing the management function or service,

2. The identification of other members (or possible members) of the affiliated service group.

3. A description of the nature of the business of each member (or possible member) of the affiliated service group including the type of organization (corporation, partnership, etc.) and indicate whether such member is a service organization or an organization whose principal business is the performance of management functions for the other group member(s).

4. The ownership interests between the employer and the members (or possible members) of the affiliated service group (including ownership interests as described in section 414(m)(2)(B)(ii) or 414(m)(6)(B)).

5. A description of services performed for employers by the members (or possible members) of the affiliated service group, or vice versa. Include the percentage of each member's (or possible member's) gross receipts and service receipts provided by such services, if available, and data as to whether their services are a significant portion of the member's business and whether or not, as of December 13, 1980, it was unusual for the services to be performed by employees of organizations in that service field in the United States.

6. A description of how the employer and the members (or possible members) of the affiliated service group associate in performing services for other parties.

7. (a) A description of management functions, if any, performed by the employer for the members (or possible members) of the affiliated service group, or received by the employer from any other members (or possible members) of the group (including data as to whether such management functions are performed on a regular and continuous basis) and whether or not it is unusual for such management functions to be performed by employees of organizations in the employer's business field in the United States.

7. (b) If management functions are performed by the employer for the members (or possible members) of the affiliated service group, describe what part of the employer's business constitutes the performance of management functions for the members (or possible members) of the group (including the percentage of gross receipts derived from management activities as compared to the gross receipts from other activities).

8. A brief description of any other plan maintained by the members (or possible members) of the affiliated service group, if such other plan is designated as a unit for qualification purposes with the plan for which a determination letter has been requested.

9. A description of how the plan(s) satisfies the coverage requirements of section 410(b) if the members (or possible members) of the affiliated service group are considered part of an affiliated service group with the employer.

10. A copy of any ruling issued by the National Office on whether the employer is an affiliated service group; a copy of any prior determination letter that considered the effect of section 414(m) on the qualified status of the employer's plan; and, if known, a copy of any such ruling or determination letter issued to any other member (or possible member) of the same affiliated service group, accompanied by a statement as to whether the facts upon which the ruling or determination letter was based have changed.

Enter 4 if you are not certain whether or not you have leased employees and attach the following information:

1. A description of the nature of the business of the recipient organization;

2. A copy of the relevant leasing agreement(s);

3. A description of the function of all leased employees in the trade or business of the recipient organization (including data as to whether all leased employees are performing services on a substantially full-time basis);

4. A description of facts and circumstances relevant to a determination of whether such leased employees' services are performed under primary direction or control by the recipient organization (including whether the leased employees are required to comply with instructions

of the recipient about when, where, and how to perform the services, whether the services must be performed by particular persons, whether the leased employees are subject to the supervision of the recipient, and whether the leased employees must perform services in the order or sequence set by the recipient), and

5. If the recipient organization is relying on any qualified plan(s) maintained by the employee leasing organization for purposes of qualification of the recipient organization's plan, a description of the plan(s) (including a description of the contributions or benefits provided for all leased employees that are for services performed for the recipient organization, plan eligibility, and vesting).

Enter 5 if this is a request for the effect a potential partial termination will have on the plan's qualification. "Date Effective" means the date the plan amendment, ASG status, or partial termination becomes operative, takes effect, or changes.

Enter 6 if a determination letter is requested on the termination of a multiemployer plan covered by PBGC insurance. Also enter the date the termination is effective.

Line 3b. If you do not have a copy of the latest determination letter, or if no determination letter has ever been received by the employer, submit copies of the initial plan, or the latest plan for which you do have a determination letter, and any subsequent amendments and/or restatements including all adoption agreements.

Line 3c. Section 3001 of ERISA requires the applicant to provide evidence that each employee who qualifies as an interested party has been notified of the filing of the application. If "Yes" is checked, it means that each employee has been notified as required by Regulations section 1.7476-1 or this is a one-person plan. A copy of the notice is not required to be attached to this application. If "No" is checked or this line is blank, your application will be returned.

Rules defining "interested parties" and the form of notification are in Regulations section 1.7476-1. For an example of an acceptable format, see Rev. Proc. 2001-6, 2001-1 I.R.B. 194 or the superseding revenue procedure published annually in the Internal Revenue Bulletin.

Line 4b. Enter the three-digit number, beginning with "001" and continuing in numerical order for each plan you adopt. (001-499). This numbering will differentiate your plans. The number assigned to a plan must not be changed or used for any other plan. This should be the same number that was or will be used when the Form 5500 or Form 5500-EZ is filed for the plan.

Line 4c. "Plan year" means the calendar, policy, or fiscal year on which the records of the plan are kept.

Line 4e. Enter the total number of participants. A participant means:

1. The total number of employees participating in the plan including employees under a section 401(k) qualified cash or deferred arrangement who are **eligible** but do not make elective deferrals,

2. Retirees and other former employees who have a nonforfeitable right to benefits under the plan, and

3. The beneficiary of a deceased employee who is receiving or will in the future receive benefits under the plan. Include one beneficiary for each deceased employee regardless of the number of individuals receiving benefits.

Example: Payment of a deceased employee's benefit to three children is considered a payment to one beneficiary.

Line 5, item 5. Cash balance. For this purpose, a "cash balance" formula is a benefit formula in a defined benefit plan by whatever name (e.g., personal account plan, pension equity plan, life cycle plan, cash account plan, etc.) that rather than, or in addition to, expressing the accrued benefit as a life annuity commencing at normal retirement age, defines benefits for each employee in terms more common to a defined contribution plan such as a single sum distribution amount (e.g., 10 percent of final average pay times years of service, or the amount of the employee's hypothetical account balance).

Line 6. If the plan employer is a member of a controlled group of corporations, trades or businesses under common control, or an affiliated service group, all employees of the group will be treated as employed by a single employer for purposes of certain qualification requirements.

Attach a statement showing in detail:

Page 5

1. All members of the group;

2. Their relationship to the plan employer;

3. The type(s) of plan(s) each member has, and

4. Plans common to all members.

Note. *If you want to apply for a determination letter to determine if you are a member of an affiliated service group, attach the information described on line 3a, item 3 and leave this line blank.*

Line 7e. A **multiple-employer plan** is a plan maintained by more than one employer, but which is **not** maintained under a collective bargaining agreement. Under this plan type, contributions from each employer must be available to pay benefits of any participant, even if employed by another employer. Also, enter the number of employers adopting the plan. See section 413(c).

Line 7f. A **multiemployer plan** (as described in section 414(f)) is one to which more than one employer is required to contribute and which is maintained under one or more collective bargaining agreements between one or more employee organizations and more than one employer.

Line 8a. If "Yes" is checked, **attach** a list for each plan with the following information:

1. Name of plan,

2. Type of plan,

3. Plan number, and

4. Indicate if another application is simultaneously being submitted with this application.

Lines 8b and 8c. See M-8, M-12, and M-14 of Regulations section 1.416-1.

Lines 9b and 9c. If the plan is a 401(k) plan, complete these line items for the nonelective employer contribution portion of the plan, if applicable.

Line 12a. Section 411(d)(6) protected benefits include:

• The accrued benefit of a participant as of the later of the amendment's adoption date or effective date; and

• Any early retirement benefit, retirement-type subsidy or optional form of benefit for benefits from service before such amendment.

If the answer is "Yes," explain on an attachment how the amendment satisfies one of the exceptions to the prohibition on reduction or elimination of section 411(d)(6) protected benefits.

Page 6

Optional Ratio Percentage Test Determination

Line 13. This question may be used to request an optional determination regarding the ratio percentage test under Regulations section 1.410(b)-2(b)(2). If "No" is checked and a request for a determination regarding the average benefit test is not made on Schedule Q, the determination letter for the plan will not be a determination regarding section 410(b). If "No" is checked but a request for a determination regarding the average benefit test is made on Schedule Q, the determination letter for the plan will also be a determination regarding the average benefit test. Plans using the qualified separate lines of business rules of section 414(r) must file Schedule Q if a determination is desired that the plan satisfies the gateway test of section 410(b)(5)(B) or the special requirements for employer wide plans.

Line 13a. If a determination is being requested and the plan is disaggregated into two or more separate plans, that are other than profit sharing and/or sections 401(k) and/or 401(m) plans, complete lines 13b through 13n with respect to each disaggregated portion of the plan. Attach additional schedules as necessary to identify the other disaggregated portions of the plan. Provide the requested coverage information, in the same format as line 13, separately with respect to the other portions of the plan, or to otherwise show that the other portions of the plan separately satisfy section 410(b).

Example. If this plan benefits the employees of more than one qualified separate line of business (QSLOB), the portion of the plan benefiting the employees of each QSLOB is treated as a separate plan maintained by that QSLOB and must separately satisfy section 410(b) unless the employer-wide plan testing rule in Regulations section 1.414(r)-1(c)(2)(ii) applies.

If a determination is being requested for a section 401(k) and/or 401(m) plan you must complete line 13l for the portion of the plan that is not a section 401(k) or a 401(m) plan. Also complete line 13m(1) to report the ratio percentage for the section 401(k) portion of the plan and line 13m(2) to report the ratio percentage

for the section 401(m) portion of the plan.

Line 13c. If, for purposes of satisfying the minimum coverage requirements of section 410(b), you are applying the daily testing option in Regulations section 1.410(b)-8(a)(2) or the quarterly testing option in Regulations section 1.410(b)-8(a)(3), or, if you are using single-day "snapshot" testing as permitted under section 3 of Rev. Proc. 93-42, 1993-2 C.B. 540, enter the most recent eight-digit date (MMDDYYYY) for which the coverage data is submitted. If you are applying the annual testing option in Regulations section 1.410(b)-8(a)(4), enter the year for which the coverage data is submitted.

Line 13d. Include all employees of all entities combined under sections 414(b), (c), (m), or (o). Also include all self-employed individuals, common law employees, and leased employees as defined in section 414(n) of any of the entities above, other than those excluded by section 414(n)(5). Certain individuals may also be required to be counted as employees. See the definition of employee in Regulations section 1.410(b)-9. Also see Regulations section 1.410(b)-6(i), which may permit the employer to exclude certain former nonhighly compensated employees.

Note. *This note applies only to plans that include a qualified cash or deferred arrangement under section 401(k) or employee or matching contributions under section 401(m). If there are any contributions under the plan that are not subject to the special rule for section 401(k) plans and section 401(m) plans in Regulations section 1.401(a)(4)-1(b)(2)(ii)(B) (such as nonelective contributions), complete lines 13e through 13k with respect to the portion of the plan that includes these contributions and enter the ratio percentage for this portion of the plan on line 13l. Otherwise, complete lines 13e through 13k with respect to the section 401(k) part of the plan (or the section 401(m) plan if there is no section 401(k) arrangement) and leave line 13l blank. In all cases, enter the ratio percentages for the section 401(k) and the section 401(m) parts of the plan, as applicable, on line 13m. These percentages should be based on the actual nonexcludables in the 401(k) and 401(m) portions, respectively. It is suggested that* *these calculations be submitted with the application but this is optional.*

⚠️ *If the plan provides for nonelective profit-sharing contributions, do not base the calculations on lines 13m(1) and (2) on the nonexcludable employees reported on line 13g unless all of the disaggregated plans (profit sharing, 401(k), and 401(m)) have the same nonexcludable employees with the same age and service requirements.*

Line 13e(1). Enter the number of employees who are excluded because they have not attained the lowest minimum age and service requirements for any employee under this plan. If the employer is separately testing the portion of a plan that benefits otherwise excludable employees, attach a separate schedule describing which employees are treated as excludable employees on account of the minimum age and service requirements under each separate portion of the plan.

Line 13e(2). Enter the number of employees who are excluded because they are collectively bargained employees as defined in Regulations section 1.410(b)-6(d)(2), regardless of whether those employees benefit under the plan. For this purpose, an employee covered under a CBA is not considered a collectively bargained employee if more than 2% of the employees who are covered under the agreement are professional employees as defined in Regulations section 1.410(b)-9.

Line 13e(3). Enter the number of employees who do not receive an allocation or accrue a benefit under the plan only because they do not satisfy a minimum hours of service requirement or a last day of the plan year requirement, provided they do not have more than 500 hours of service, and they are not employed on the last day of the plan year. Do not enter on this line any employees who have more than 500 hours of service, even if they are not employed on the last day of the plan year.

Line 13e(4). If this plan benefits the employees of one QSLOB, enter on this line the number of employees of the employer's other QSLOBs. This is not applicable if the plan is tested under the special rule for employer-wide plans in Regulations section 1.414(r)-1(c)(2)(ii).

Line 13e(5). Enter the number of employees who are nonresident aliens who receive no earned income (as defined in section 911(d)(2)) from the employer that constitutes income from sources within the United States (as defined in section 861(a)(3)).

Line 13g. Subtract the total of lines 13e(1) through 13e(5) as reported on line 13f from the total employees reported on line 13d. The result is the number of "nonexcludable employees." These are the employees who can not be excluded from the plan for statutory or regulatory reasons and must be considered in the calculation of the ratio percentage even though they might not "benefit" under the plan. If they meet the age and service requirements of section 410 and are not otherwise excludable employees, they must be included in this number.

Line 13h. Enter the number of employees on line 13g who are highly compensated employees (HCEs) as defined in section 414(q).

Line 13i. In general, an employee is treated as benefiting under the plan for coverage tests purposes only if the employee receives an allocation of contributions or forfeitures or accrues a benefit under the plan for the plan year. Certain other employees are treated as benefiting if they fail to receive an allocation of contributions and/or forfeitures, or to accrue a benefit, solely because they are subject to plan provisions that uniformly limit plan benefits, such as a provision for maximum years of service, maximum retirement benefits, application of offsets or fresh start wear-away formulas, or limits designed to satisfy section 415. An employee is treated as benefiting under a plan to which elective contributions under section 401(k) or employee contributions and matching contributions under section 401(m) may be made if the employee is currently eligible to make such elective or employee contributions, or to receive a matching contribution, whether or not the employee actually makes or receives such contributions, (Regulations section 1.401(k)-1(g)(4) and 1.401(m)-1(f)(4)). However, do not apply this rule to determine if an employee is to be counted as benefiting for lines 13i and 13k if, in accordance with the note following the instruction for line 13d, the information provided in lines 13e through 13k relates to the portion of the plan that is not subject to the rule in Regulations section 1.401(a)(4)-1(b)(2)(ii)(B).

Line 13k. See the instructions for line 13i for the meaning of "benefiting under the plan."

Line 13l. To obtain the ratio percentage:

Step 1. Divide the number on line 13k (nonexcludable NHCEs benefiting under the plan) by the number on line 13j (nonexcludable NHCEs).

Step 2. Divide the number on line 13i (nonexcludable HCEs benefiting under the plan) by the number on line 13h (nonexcludable HCEs).

Step 3. Divide the result from Step 1 by the result from Step 2.

Note. *If the ratio percentage entered on line 13l and/or line 13m is less than 70%, the plan does not satisfy the ratio percentage test. In this case, the plan must satisfy the average benefit test. A determination regarding the average benefit test can be requested using Schedule Q.*

Line 13m. See the **Note** following the instructions for line 13d. To determine the ratio percentages for the section 401(k) and all section 401(m) (matching and employee contribution) portions of the plan, follow the steps described in the instructions for lines 13d through 13l, but treat an employee as benefiting under the rules for section 401(k) plans and section 401(m) plans described in the instruction for line 13i.

Design-Based Nondiscrimination Safe Harbors

Line 14. This question may be used by certain plans to request an optional determination regarding the design-based safe harbor under section 401(a)(4).

If this is a section 401(k) and/or section 401(m) plan that does not contain a provision for nonelective employer contributions, this option should be marked "No."

If any disaggregated plan relies on a non-design based safe harbor or a general test this option must be marked "No." The Schedule Q may be used to request a determination regarding a non-design based safe harbor or a general test.

If this plan has been restructured into component plans, this option must be marked "No." The Schedule Q may be used to request a determination regarding how each restructured component plan satisfies the nondiscrimination in amount requirement of Regulations section 1.401(a)(4)-1(b)(2).

If "Yes" is checked, or if "No" is checked but a request for a determination regarding a non-design based safe harbor or a general test is made on Schedule Q, the determination letter for the plan will also be a determination regarding the section 401(a)(4) requirement that a plan not discriminate in the amounts of contributions or benefits.

If "No" is checked, and a request for a determination regarding a non-design based safe harbor or a general test is not made on Schedule Q, the determination letter for the plan will not be a determination regarding this requirement, unless the plan is a section 401(k) and/or section 401(m) plan only.

Line 14a. Check "Yes" if the plan is intended to satisfy the permitted disparity requirements of section 401(l).

Line 14b. To satisfy section 401(l), a plan must provide that the overall permitted disparity limits are not exceeded and specify how employer-provided contributions or benefits under the plan are adjusted, if necessary, to satisfy the overall permitted disparity limits. See Regulations section 1.401(l)-5.

Line 14c. This line provides a list of the design-based nondiscrimination safe-harbor regulations.

¶1654

¶1655 Exhibit 16-5

Technical Advice Memorandum 8026012, March 20, 1980

Uniform Issue List Information:

UIL No. 0361.01-00

Nonrecognition of gain or loss to corporations (recognized v. not recognized) —Exchanges not solely in kind

National Office Technical Advice Memorandum

This is in reply to your request for Technical Advice dated November 14, 1979, as to the prior ruling letter issued by this office with respect to a transaction involving Distributing. All section references contained in this Technical Advice are, unless otherwise stated, references to the Internal Revenue Code of 1954 as amended.

FACTS

This office issued a favorable prior ruling letter pursuant to sections 368(a)(1)(D), 355(a)(1) and other applicable sections in connection with the then proposed transfer by Distributing of the assets and liabilities of its p business, including the A operations, to a newly organized Delaware corporation, Controlled, to be followed by the pro rata distribution of all of the stock of Controlled to the shareholders of Distributing.

The taxpayer submitted a ruling application with regard to the above transaction on r. Two of the rulings requested were as follows:

'(1) The transfer by [Distributing] of the assets associated with the [p] business to [Controlled] in exchange for the stock of [Controlled] and the assumption by [Controlled] of certain [Distributing] liabilities, followed by the pro rata distribution of the stock of [Controlled] to the [Distributing] shareholders, as described above, will be a reorganization within the meaning of section 368(a)(1)(D) of the Internal Revenue Code of 1954.'

'(2) No gain or loss will be recognized to [Distributing] upon the transfer of the assets associated with the [p] operation, subject to certain liabilities, to [Controlled], as described above (sections 361 and 357) . . . '

In a subsequent letter from Distributing's authorized representative dated s it was stated that Distributing would be transferring to Controlled, *inter alia,* ' . . . $3,000,000 of bank debt since it is allocable to the [p] operation . . . ' Also accompanying that letter dated s was a pro forma balance sheet of Controlled as it would appear after the then proposed distribution of the Controlled stock. Note (b) to that pro forma balance sheet states that '[Controlled] (sic) borrowing $3,000,000 from banks and the use of the proceeds of the borrowing to retire the note payable to [Distributing] (see Note (b) to Pro Forma Capitalization).' Neither the Pro Forma Capitalization nor the notes thereto were submitted in contalization with the ruling application. Accompanying a letter dated w was a 'two-part' summary statement of all the facts submitted in connection with the transaction which statement contained the following sentence: '[Controlled] will assume approximately $3,000,000 in [Distributing] credit agreement debt. [Controlled] and its subsidiaries will be directly liable for this debt.'

¶1655

The prior ruling letter dated t, set forth the relevant facts submitted relating to the assumption of liabilities of Distributing by Controlled. In addition, the prior ruling letter noted that Controlled would assume approximately $3,000,000 in Distributing credit agreement debt and that Controlled and its subsidiaries would be directly liable for this debt. The prior ruling letter issued the requested rulings regarding sections 368(a)(1)(D), 361 and 357 and also set forth the relevant representation submitted relating to the assumption of liabilities of Distributing by Controlled which reads as follows:

> 'The total adjusted tax basis and the fair market value of the [Distributing] properties to be transferred to [Controlled] will equal or exceed the sum of the liabilities to be assumed by [Controlled], plus the liabilities to which the transferred assets are subject. The liabilities to be assumed by [Controlled] were incurred in the ordinary course of business and are associated with the assets to be transferred.'

A prospectus, dated q, was issued on behalf of Controlled in connection with the registration of shares of the stock of Controlled. A copy of the prospectus was included as part of the Request for Technical Advice.

The prospectus, which was dated prior to our prior ruling letter but subsequent to all the information submitted in connection with the ruling request, including the letters referred to above, contained a pro forma capitalization of Controlled reflecting the then consummated transfer of the p business by Distributing to Controlled. The pro forma capitalization of Controlled did not show the assumption of any liabilities of Distributing by Controlled, but reflected instead a note payable by Controlled to Distributing in the amount of $3,000,000. The issuance of this note was characterized in the prospectus, as follows:

> 'In connection with the transfer of assets to [Controlled], a portion of the advances to [Controlled] will be converted into a note payable to [Distributing] in the amount of $3,000,000. The balance of advances will be contributed to the capital of [Controlled]. [Controlled] intends to borrow $3,000,000 from a group of banks repayable over five years in equal quarterly installments of principal plus interest at 1% over the floating prime rate. (The rate would have been $8^3/4\%$ as at March 15, 1976). The proceeds of this borrowing will be used to retire the note payable to [Distributing].'[1]

This office was not notified by Distributing, either prior or subsequent to the issuance of the prior ruling letter, that any change had been made regarding the assumption by Controlled of liabilities of Distributing. Further, Distributing did not furnish this office with a copy of the prospectus in either draft or final form.

In connection with the receipt by this office of the Request for Technical Advice, an official of Distributing submitted the notes to the consolidated financial statements of Controlled for the year ending x and the 9 months ending y. These notes confirm that in connection with the spin-off of Controlled which took place onq, Distributing converted $3,000,000 of Distributing's investment in the A operations into a note payable from Controlled to Distributing. On z, less than 2 months after the spin-off, Controlled retired the debt to Distributing by

---

[1] While the prospectus describes advances made to Controlled, the intra-corporate advances were made while the p business transferred to Controlled was part of Distributing.

entering into a loan agreement with a group of banks in the amount of $3,000,000 which would be repayable over 5 years in equal quarterly installments of principal plus interest at 1 percent over the floating prime rate.

ISSUES

I Whether the issuance by Controlled, on its organization, of the $3,000,000 note to Distributing instead of the assumption by Controlled of $3,000,000 of Distributing's credit agreement debt and the retention of such note by Distributing constituted the receipt by Distributing of 'other property' within the meaning of section 361(b).

II In the event issue I is answered in the affirmative, whether the rulings contained in the prior ruling letter as to the application of sections 361, 357, 368(a)(1)(D) and 362(b) to Controlled should be modified retroactively.

TAXPAYER'S POSITION

ISSUE I

The $3,000,000 note payable by Controlled to Distributing does not constitute 'other property' within the meaning of sections 357 and 361 but rather simply constitutes an assumption of liabilities by the newly formed corporation. If not, since the liability is one which was associated with the p business, it is, as such, not treated as 'other property' in accordance with section 357(a) and *Wham Construction Co. v. United States,* 76-1 U.S.T.C. ¶9265 (1976), *aff'd* 79-2 U.S.T.C. ¶9471 (4th Cir. 1979).

ISSUE II

If the National Office advises that the note payable constitutes 'other property' within the meaning of section 357 and 361, section 13.05 of Rev. Proc. 72-3, 1972-1 C.B. 698 nevertheless prohibits a retroactive revocation or modification of the original ruling letter received by Distributing, since no misstatement or omission of material facts occurred and since the facts as subsequently developed did not materially differ from those on which the ruling was based. This argument is based on the fact that the Service was put on notice that Controlled intended to issue a note to Distributing by the submission of note (b) to the pro forma balance sheet.

DISCUSSION

ISSUE I

The nonrecognition provisions of section 361(a) provide that where property is transferred pursuant to a plan of reorganization by one corporate party to the reorganization to another corporate party to the reorganization solely for stock or securities of such other corporate party, no gain or loss is recognized in the transaction. If, however, in addition to stock or securities, 'other property' is received and retained by the transferor, the transferor must recognize gain on theexchange but not in excess of the fair market value of the 'other property' received pursuant to section 361(b).

¶1655

Under section 368(a)(1)(D), a reorganization is defined as a transfer of part or all of the assets of one corporation to another corporation where immediately after such transfer the other corporation is controlled by the transferor corporation or by one or more of the transferor corporation's shareholders or, any combination, provided that pursuant to the plan of reorganization, stock or securities of the transferee corporation are distributed in a transaction qualifying under section 354, 355 or 356.

Section 355(a)(1)(D) sets forth the requirement that as part of a distribution of stock the distributing corporation must distribute either all of the stock or securities of the controlled corporation held by the transferor corporation immediately prior to the distribution, or an amount of stock constituting 'control' under section 368(c) and satisfactorily have established that the retention of any stock or securities of the controlled corporation was not pursuant to a plan having as one of its principal purposes the avoidance of federal income tax.

Here, Distributing transferred a part of its assets constituting the p business to Controlled in exchange for all of the stock of Controlled and the $3,000,000 note and, thereafter, distributed to its shareholders all of the stock of Controlled. Thus, provided that the $3,000,000 note of Controlled; (1) did not constitute a security of such corporation or (2) the security was not retained in pursuance of a plan of tax avoidance, the transaction came within the provisions of sections 368(a)(1)(D) and 355(a)(1).

In this regard, Distributing has not set forth any facts to establish that the $3,000,000 note in question constituted a security and not a note or other evidence of indebtedness not constituting a security, or that the retention of the note by Distributing was not in pursuance of a plan having as one of its principal purposes the avoidance of federal income tax.

In any event, however, taking into account all the facts and circumstances the most important being that at the time the note was issued, it was contemplated that the proceeds from bank borrowings would be used to retire such debt and that indeed, the note in question was satisfied within 2 months of issuance of that note, we are of the opinion that the note in question did not constitute a security for purposes of sections 368(a)(1)(D) and 355. See, for example, *Pinellas Ice & Cold Storage Co. v. Commissioner*, 287 U.S. 462 (1933); *Turner v. Commissioner*, 303 F.2d 94 (4th Cir. 1962), *cert. denied*, 371 U.S. 922 (1962); *Neville Coke & Chemical Co. v. Commissioner*, 303 F.2d 599 (3rd Cir. 1945); *Lloyd-Smith v. Commissioner*, 116 F.2d 642 (2nd Cir. 1941).

The only question remaining, therefore, is whether the $3,000,000 note constitutes the receipt of 'other property' within the meaning of section 361(b). It is a well established principle of tax law that short-term notes and other evidences of indebtedness received in a reorganization constitute 'other property.' *See Cortland Specialty Co. v. Commissioner*, 60 F.2d 937 (2nd Cir. 1932); *Pinellas Ice & Cold Storage Co. v. Commissioner, supra. Cf.* Rev. Rul. 59-98, 1959-1 C.B. 76, where itwas held that secured bonds with an average life of 6 1/2 years constituted securities for purposes of section 354.

This case presents a similar issue to that raised in connection with section 351 in *Wham Construction Co., Inc. v. United States, supra.* In the *Wham* case, a corporation formed a new subsidiary at the end of 1966 transferring to it assets of one of two divisions in exchange for all of the stock of the new subsidiary. Prior to the transfer each division of transferor had maintained on its own books an intra-company account reflecting monetary transactions between the divisions. At the date of the transfer to the new subsidiary, the balance sheet for the division transferred showed a balance due to the division being retained of $160,402.50. This amount was reflected as an account payable by the new subsidiary on its opening balance sheet. The account payable was paid in full by the new subsidiary on August 14, 1967. Upon audit, the District Director determined that the account payable for $160,402.50 constituted 'other property' received in a section 351 transaction and that the full amount of the gain was taxable to the transferor under section 351(b).

The District Court, in holding for the taxpayer determined that the account payable represented a mere loan to the new subsidiary from the transferor for which the transferor received only a return of capital. The Court found, in effect, that there was a pre-existing debt between the two divisions and that upon incorporation, the new subsidiary assumed this liability.

In its affirmance of the District Court's decision in *Wham,* the Court of Appeals believed that the position of the Commissioner was entirely too technical and unrealistic. This court reasoned that where there was but one transferor and where the issuing corporation had no assets other than those derived from the transferor, it found it difficult to conceive of a concept wherein the transferor as a result of the transaction received anything which it did not have prior to the incorporation.

The position taken by the Government both before the United States District Court and on the appeal to the Fourth Circuit had been that the account payable from the new subsidiary to the transferor was a note or other evidence of indebtedness received by the transferor in a section 351 transaction and that it constituted 'other property' for purposes of section 351(b). In support of this position the Government contended that the preincorporation intra-company, i.e., the interdivisional, accounts could not have given rise to a debtor/creditor relationship between the transferor and its new subsidiary because the transferor could not, prior to incorporation of such subsidiary, have been liable for a debt to itself.

The position espoused by the Government in the *Wham* case is equally applicable to this case and represents the position of this office. Accordingly, it is our conclusion that the $3,000,000 note from Controlled to Distributing constituted 'other property' received by Distributing in the reorganization pursuant to sections 368(a)(1)(D) and 361(b).

¶1655

We feel it is also necessary to rebut taxpayer's contention that the form of the transaction did constitute an assumption of liabilities within the meaning of section 357(a).[2]

Section 357(a) sets forth the general rule of deferral from the immediate recognition of gain on account of an assumption of liabilities. It provides in part that except for certain circumstances not relevant here, if the taxpayer receives property which would be permitted to be received under section 361 without the recognition of gain if it were the sole consideration and as part of the consideration, another party to the exchange assumes a liability of the taxpayer, then such assumption will not be treated as money or other property and will not prevent the exchange from being within the provisions of section 361.

The question of what constitutes the assumption of a liability does not frequently arise. *See generally* Dailey, *'The Voting Stock Requirement of B and C Reorganizations,'* 26 Tax L. Rev. 725, 748-51 (1971). Indeed, in enacting section 357 of the Code, Congress did not specify a particular meaning to be attached to the term 'assumption of liability.' *See* S. Rept. No. 1622, 83rd Cong., 2d Sess. (1954) at 270. It is also true that the presence or absence of the words 'assume' or 'assumption' will not be determinative as to whether an actual assumption of liability has taken place. *Helvering v. Taylor,* 128 F.2d 885 (2nd Cir. 1942). There is little doubt however that the precondition for an assumption of liability is that there be an existing liability of or belonging to the transferor which is taken over by the transferee. *Arthur L. Kniffen,* 39 TC 553 (1962), acq. 1965-2 C.B. 5.

The facts in the instant case manifestly make it clear that no such liability of Distributing was ever taken over by Controlled since Controlled was not and never intended to be directly liable exclusively to Distributing's existing lenders. Instead, Controlled issued its own note to Distributing in the amount of $3,000,000 upon its incorporation, having itself borrowed directly from banks in order to satisfy the note payable to Distributing. Section 357(a) accordingly, is inapplicable here.

Issue II

In light of the conclusion reached above with respect to Issue I, it becomes necessary to determine whether or not such conclusion must be given retroactive effect in this case. In this regard, section 13.05 of Rev. Proc. 72-3, 1972-1 C.B. 698[3] provides that only in rare or unusual circumstances will a ruling be revoked or modified retroactively. However, the circumstances under which a ruling will be retroactively revoked or modified include among others: (1) misstatement or

---

[2] The taxpayer failed to furnish us with any legal authority for his contention that section 357(a) specifically insulates the aforementioned $3,000,000 note.

[3] Rev. Proc. 72-3, *supra,* which dealt, *inter alia,* with the issuance of rulings, was superseded by Rev. Proc. 79-45, 1979-[illegible word(s)] I.R.B. 5. Section 17.05 of Rev. Proc. 79-45 incorporates verbatim what was formerly to be found in section 13.05 of Rev. Proc. 72-3. All references to provisions contained in Rev. Proc. 72-3 hereafter will show the corresponding provision now contained in Rev. Proc. 79-45.

¶1655

omission of material facts; and (2) the facts subsequently developed are materially different from the facts on which the ruling was based.[4]

It is clear in this case that there has been a misstatement of material facts and that the facts as subsequently developed differ materially from the facts on which the ruling letter issued to Distributing and relating to the transaction with Controlled were based.

As mentioned earlier, it was stated in a letter dated s that Distributing would be transferring $3,000,000 of bank debt to Controlled. In addition, the rulings requested by the taxpayer specifically referred to an assumption of liabilities. It was also mentioned earlier that accompanying a letter dated w was a 'two-part' summary statement of all the facts involved in this case, which statement contained a sentence specifically referring to a proposed assumption by Controlled of Distributing credit agreement debt.

In this regard, section 6.03 of Rev. Proc. 72-3[5] provides, in part, that

'.03 As an alternative procedure for the issuance of rulings on prospective transactions, *the taxpayer may submit a summary statement of the facts he considers controlling the issue,* in addition to the complete statement required for ruling requests by section 6.02 above. *Assuming agreement with the taxpayer's summary statement, the Service will use it as the basis for the ruling.* Any taxpayer wishing to adopt this procedure should submit with the request for ruling:

(1) A complete statement of facts relating to the transaction, together with related documents, as required by section 6.02 above; and

(2) A summary statement of the facts which he believes should be controlling in reaching the requested conclusion. *Where the taxpayer's statement of controlling facts is accepted, the ruling will be based on these facts and only this statement will ordinarily be incorporated in the ruling letter.* It is emphasized, however, that:

(a) This procedure for a 'two-part' ruling request is elective with the taxpayer and is not to be considered a required substitute for the regular procedures contained in this Revenue Procedure;

(b) Taxpayers' rights and responsibilities are the same under the 'two-part' ruling request procedure as those provided in this Revenue Procedure;

(c) The Service reserves the right to rule on the basis of a more complete statement of facts it considers controlling and to seek further information in developing facts and restating them for ruling purposes; . . .' (emphasis added)

The taxpayer in the instant case elected, as was his privilege, to submit a summary statement of the facts he considered controlling the issues herein, in addition to the complete statement required for ruling requests. On the basis of all the relevant facts submitted, the Service could discern no reason not to accept taxpayer's summary statement and therefore, proceeded to use it as the basis for the issued ruling. The taxpayer insists nevertheless that the fact that a note

---

[4] Other factors contained in Rev. Proc. 72-3 are not relevant to this case.

[5] Rev. Proc. 79-45, *supra,* at section 9.05.

¶1655

payable to Distributing from Controlled would exist for $3,000,000 was clearly disclosed in note (b) to the pro forma balance sheet for Controlled, which balancesheet accompanied the aforementioned letter dated s. Section 6.02 of Rev. Proc. 72-3,[6] supra, provides, however, in pertinent part that

> 'Each request for a ruling . . . must contain a complete statement of all relevant facts relating to the transaction. Such facts include . . . a carefully detailed description of the transaction. In addition, true copies of all . . . agreements . . . and other documents involved in the transaction must be submitted with the request. *However, relevant facts reflected in documents submitted must be included in the taxpayer's statement and not merely incorporated by reference, and must be accompanied by an analysis of their bearing on the issue or issues, specifying the pertinent provisions.*' (Emphasis added)

We feel the documents cited above make it clear that it is not the function or the obligation of the Service to ferret out material or relevant facts reflected in documents accompanying a ruling request, nor to reconcile seemingly inconsistent data as it might bear on a particular issue. If Controlled's pro forma balance sheet contained relevant and material facts bearing on the issue of whether or not Controlled actually assumed certain bank debt of Distributing, such facts were not brought to the attention of the Service. All the taxpayer's relevant submissions and representations reflected an assumption by Controlled of the indebtedness in question. The inference, therefore, that Controlled was to be directly liable exclusively to Distributing's existing lenders was, under these circumstances, entirely warranted, notwithstanding that subsequent factual development revealed that no purported assumption by Controlled of $3,000,000 of Distributing's liabilities ever did occur.

Accordingly, the portion of rulings (1), (2) and (4) contained in the prior ruling letter specifically relating to the application of sections 368(a)(1)(D), 361 and the determination of basis pursuant to section 362(b) as to the transfer of assets by Distributing to Controlled are modified retroactively and such rulings are null and void.

If, at the time the prior ruling letter was issued, we had been fully informed of all of the facts subsequently developed by your office and by us in connection with the Request for Technical Advice, we would have issued rulings on the application of sections 368(a)(1)(D), 361(b) and 362(b) to the portion of the transaction relating to the issuance of the note by Controlled in substantially the following form:

    (a) The transfer by Distributing of its p business and the stock of m to Controlled in exchange for the stock of Controlled, the $3,000,000 note of Controlled and the assumption by Controlled of certain Distributing liabilities, as described above, followed by the pro rata distribution of the stock of Controlled to the Distributing shareholders, will be a reorganization within the meaning of section 368(a)(1)(D) of the Internal Revenue Code of 1954. Distributing and Controlled will each be 'a party to a reorganization' within the meaning of section 368(b).

---

[6] Rev. Proc. 79-45, *supra,* at section 9.07.

(b) The gain, if any, realized by Distributing upon the transfer to Controlled of the assets of the p business and the stock of m by Distributing solely in exchange for all of the stock of Controlled, the $3,000,000 note of Controlled and the assumption of liabilities by Controlled will be recognized by Distributing but in an amount not in excess of the fair market value of the property transferred by Controlled to Distributing (sections 361(b) and 357(a)).

(c) The basis of the assets received by Controlled from Distributing will be the same as the basis of the assets in the hands of Distributing immediately prior to the transfer, increased by the amount of gain recognized to Distributing on the transfer (section 362(b)).

¶ 1656 Exhibit 16-6

SAMPLE FORMAT FOR A LETTER RULING REQUEST

INSTRUCTIONS*

To assist you in preparing a letter ruling request, the Service is providing this sample format. You are not required to use this sample format. If your request is not identical or similar to the sample format, the different format will not defer consideration of your request.

(*Insert the date of request*)

Internal Revenue Service

> *Insert either*: Associate Chief Counsel (Insert one of the following: Corporate, Financial Institutions & Products, Income Tax & Accounting, International, Passthroughs & Special Industries, or Procedure and Administration), *or* Division Counsel/Associate Chief Counsel (Tax Exempt and Government Entities)

Attn: CC:PA:T
P.O. Box 7604
Ben Franklin Station
Washington, D.C. 20044

Dear Sir or Madam:

(*Insert the name of the taxpayer*) requests a ruling on the proper treatment of (*insert the subject matter of the letter ruling request*) under section (*insert the number*) of the Internal Revenue Code.

[If the taxpayer is requesting expedited handling, a statement to that effect must be attached to, or contained in, the letter ruling request. The statement must explain the need for expedited handling. See section 8.02(4) of Rev. Proc. 2001-1, 2001-1 I.R.B.1. Hereafter, all references are to Rev. Proc. 2001-1 unless otherwise noted.]

A. STATEMENT OF FACTS

1. Taxpayer Information

[Provide the statements required by sections 8.01(1)(a) and (b).]

2. Description of Taxpayer's Business Operations

[Provide the statement required by section 8.01(1)(c).]

3. Facts Relating to Transaction

[The ruling request must contain a complete statement of the facts relating to the transaction that is the subject of the letter ruling request. This statement must include a detailed description of the transaction, including material facts in any accompanying documents, and the business reasons for the transaction. See sections 8.01(1)(d), 8.01(1)(e), and 8.01(2).]

---

* Appendix B, IRB 2001-1, 69, January 2, 2001.

B. RULING REQUESTED

[The ruling request should contain a concise statement of the ruling requested by the taxpayer. It is preferred that the language of the requested ruling be exactly the same that the taxpayer wishes to receive.]

C. STATEMENT OF LAW

[The ruling request must contain a statement of the law in support of the taxpayer's views or conclusion and identify any pending legislation that may affect the proposed transaction. The taxpayer also is encouraged to identify and discuss any authorities believed to be contrary to the position advanced in the ruling request. See sections 8.01(6), 8.01(8), 8.01(9), and 8.01(10).]

D. ANALYSIS

[The ruling request must contain a discussion of the facts and an analysis of the law. The taxpayer also is encouraged to identify and discuss any authorities believed to be contrary to the position advanced in the ruling request. See sections 8.01(3), 8.01(6), 8.01(8), 8.01(9), and 8.01(10).]

E. CONCLUSION

[The ruling request should contain a statement of the taxpayer's conclusion on the ruling requested.]

F. PROCEDURAL MATTERS

1. Revenue Procedure 2001-1 Statements

     a. [Provide the statement required by section 8.01(4) regarding whether the same issue in the letter ruling request is in an earlier return of the taxpayer or in a return for any year of a related taxpayer.]

     b. [Provide the statement required by section 8.01(5)(a) regarding whether the Service previously ruled on the same or similar issue for the taxpayer, a related taxpayer, or a predecessor.]

     c. [Provide the statement required by section 8.01(5)(b) regarding whether the taxpayer, a related taxpayer, a predecessor, or any representatives previously submitted a request (including an application for change in accounting method) involving the same or similar issue but withdrew the request before a letter ruling or determination letter was issued.]

     d. [Provide the statement required by section 8.01(5)(c) regarding whether the taxpayer, a related taxpayer, or a predecessor previously submitted a request (including an application for change in accounting method) involving the same or a similar issue that is currently pending with the Service.]

     e. [Provide the statement required by section 8.01(5)(d) regarding whether, at the same time as this request, the taxpayer or a related taxpayer is presently submitting another request (including an application for change in accounting method) involving the same or similar issue to the Service.]

¶1656

f. [If the letter ruling request involves the interpretation of a substantive provision of an income or estate tax treaty, provide the statement required by section 8.01(6) regarding whether the tax authority of the treaty jurisdiction has issued a ruling on the same or similar issue for the taxpayer, a related taxpayer, or a predecessor; whether the same or similar issue is being examined, or has been settled, by the tax authority of the treaty jurisdiction or is otherwise the subject of a closing agreement in that jurisdiction; and whether the same or similar issue is being considered by the competent authority of the treaty jurisdiction.]

g. [Provide the statement required by section 8.01(8) regarding whether the law in connection with the letter ruling request is uncertain and whether the issue is adequately addressed by relevant authorities.]

h. [If the taxpayer determines that there are no contrary authorities, a statement to that effect would be helpful. See section 8.01(9).]

i. [If the taxpayer wants to have a conference on the issues involved in the letter ruling request, the ruling request should contain a statement to that effect. See section 8.02(7).]

j. [If the taxpayer is requesting a copy of any document related to the letter ruling request to be sent by facsimile (fax) transmission, the ruling request should contain a statement to that effect. See section 8.02(5).]

k. [If the taxpayer is requesting separate letter rulings on multiple issues, the letter ruling request should contain a statement to that effect. See section 8.02(1).]

l. [If the taxpayer is seeking to obtain the user fee provided in paragraph (A)(5)(a) of Appendix A for substantially identical letter rulings, the letter ruling request must contain the statements required by section 15.07.]

2. Administrative

a. [The ruling request should state: "The deletions statement and checklist required by Rev. Proc. 2001-1 are enclosed." See sections 8.01(11) and 8.01(18).]

b. [The ruling request should state: "The required user fee of $(*Insert the amount of the fee*) is enclosed." Please note that the check or money order must be in U.S. dollars and made payable to the Internal Revenue Service. See section 15 and Appendix A.]

c. [If the taxpayer's authorized representative is to sign the letter ruling request or is to appear before the Service in connection with the request, the ruling request should state: "A Power of Attorney is enclosed." See sections 8.01(13), 8.01(14), and 8.02(2).]

Very truly yours,

(*Insert the name of the taxpayer or the taxpayer's authorized representative*)

By:

_____ _____
                   Signature   Date

_____
Typed or printed name of person signing request

DECLARATION: [See section 8.01(15).]

Under penalties of perjury, I declare that I have examined this request, including accompanying documents, and, to the best of my knowledge and belief, the request contains all the relevant facts relating to the request, and such facts are true, correct, and complete.

(*Insert the name of the taxpayer*)

By:

Signature	Title	Date

Typed or printed name of person
signing request

[If the taxpayer is a corporation that is a member of an affiliated group filing consolidated returns, the above declaration must also be signed and dated by an officer of the common parent of the group. See section 8.01(15).]

¶1657 Exhibit 16-7

CHECKLIST IS YOUR LETTER RULING REQUEST COMPLETE?

INSTRUCTIONS**

The Service will be able to respond more quickly to your letter ruling request if it is carefully prepared and complete. To ensure that your request is in order, use this checklist. Complete the five items of information requested before the checklist. Answer each question by circling "Yes," "No," or "N/A." When a question contains a place for a page number, insert the page number (or numbers) of the request that gives the information called for by a yes answer to a question. **Sign and date the checklist (as taxpayer or authorized representative) and place it on top of your request.**

If you are an authorized representative submitting a request for a taxpayer, you must include a completed checklist with the request, or the request will either be returned to you or substantive consideration of it will be deferred until a completed checklist is submitted. **If you are a taxpayer preparing your own request without professional assistance, an incomplete checklist will not either cause the return of your request or defer substantive consideration of your request.** However, you should still complete as much of the checklist as possible and submit it with your request.

TAXPAYER'S NAME _____

TAXPAYER'S I.D. NO. _____

ATTORNEY/P.O.A. _____

PRIMARY CODE SECTION _____

CIRCLE ONE	ITEM
Yes No	1. Does your request involve an issue under the jurisdiction of the Associate Chief Counsel (Corporate), the Associate Chief Counsel (Financial Institutions & Products), the Associate Chief Counsel (Income Tax & Accounting), the Associate Chief Counsel (International), the Associate Chief Counsel (Passthroughs & Special Industries), the Associate Chief Counsel (Procedure and Administration), or the Division Counsel/Associate Chief Counsel (Tax Exempt and Government Entities)? See section 3 of Rev. Proc. 2001-1, 2001-1 I.R.B. 1. For issues under the jurisdiction of other offices, see section 4 of Rev. Proc. 2001-1. (Hereafter, all references are to Rev. Proc. 2001-1 unless otherwise noted.)
Yes No	2. Have you read Rev. Proc. 2001-3, 2001-1 I.R.B. 111, and Rev. Proc. 2001-7, 2001-1 I.R.B. 236, to see if part or all of the request involves a matter on which letter rulings are not issued or are ordinarily not issued?

** Appendix C, IRB 2001-1, 72, January 2, 2001.

CIRCLE ONE	ITEM
Yes No N/A	3. If your request involves a matter on which letter rulings are not ordinarily issued, have you given compelling reasons to justify the issuance of a letter ruling? Before preparing your request, you may want to call the branch in the Office of Associate Chief Counsel (Corporate), the Office of Associate Chief Counsel (Financial Institutions & Products), the Office of Associate Chief Counsel (Income Tax & Accounting), the Office of Associate Chief Counsel (International), the Office of Associate Chief Counsel (Passthroughs & Special Industries), the Office of Associate Chief Counsel (Procedure and Administration), or the Office of Division Counsel/Associate Chief Counsel (Tax Exempt and Government Entities) responsible for substantive interpretations of the principal Internal Revenue Code section on which you are seeking a letter ruling to discuss the likelihood of an exception. For matters under the jurisdiction of—

(a) the Office of Associate Chief Counsel (Corporate), the Office of Associate Chief Counsel (Financial Institutions & Products), the Office of Associate Chief Counsel (Income Tax & Accounting), the Office of Associate Chief Counsel (Passthroughs & Special Industries), or the Office of Division Counsel/Associate Chief Counsel (Tax Exempt and Government Entities), the appropriate branch to call may be obtained by calling (202) 622-7560 (not a toll-free call);

(b) the Office of the Associate Chief Counsel (International), the appropriate branch to call may be obtained by calling (202) 622-3800 (not a toll-free call); or

(c) the Office of the Associate Chief Counsel (Procedure and Administration), the appropriate branch to call may be obtained by calling (202) 622-3400 (not a toll-free call).

CIRCLE ONE	ITEM
Yes No N/A Page _____	4. If the request deals with a completed transaction, have you filed the return for the year in which the transaction was completed? See sections 5.01, 5.05, 5.06, 5.07, 5.08, and 5.09.
Yes No	5. Are you requesting a letter ruling on a hypothetical situation or question? See section 7.02.
Yes No	6. Are you requesting a letter ruling on alternative plans of a proposed transaction? See section 7.02.
Yes No	7. Are you requesting the letter ruling for only part of an integrated transaction? See sections 7.03 and 8.01(1).
Yes No	8. Are you requesting the letter ruling for a business, trade, industrial association, or similar group concerning the application of tax law to its members? See section 5.12.
Yes No	9. Are you requesting the letter ruling for a foreign government or its political subdivision? See section 5.13.
Yes No Pages _____	10. Have you included a complete statement of all the facts relevant to the transaction? See section 8.01(1).
Yes No N/A	11. Have you submitted with the request true copies of all wills, deeds, and other documents relevant to the transaction, and labeled and attached them in alphabetical sequence? See section 8.01(2).
Yes No N/A	12. Have you submitted with the request a copy of all applicable foreign laws, and certified English translations of documents that are in a language other than English or of foreign laws in cases where English is not the official language of the foreign country involved? See section 8.01(2).
Yes No Pages _____	13. Have you included, rather than merely incorporated by reference, all material facts from the documents in the request? Are they accompanied by an analysis of their bearing on the issues that specifies the document provisions that apply? See section 8.01(3).

CIRCLE ONE	ITEM
Yes No Page ____	14. Have you included the required statement regarding whether the same issue in the letter ruling request is in an earlier return of the taxpayer or in a return for any year of a related taxpayer? See section 8.01(4).
Yes No Page ____	15. Have you included the required statement regarding whether the Service previously ruled on the same or similar issue for the taxpayer, a related taxpayer, or a predecessor? See section 8.01(5)(a).
Yes No Page ____	16. Have you included the required statement regarding whether the taxpayer, a related taxpayer, a predecessor, or any representatives previously submitted a request (including an application for change in accounting method) involving the same or similar issue but withdrew the request before the letter ruling or determination letter was issued? See section 8.01(5)(b).
Yes No Page ____	17. Have you included the required statement regarding whether the taxpayer, a related taxpayer, or a predecessor previously submitted a request (including an application for change in accounting method) involving the same or similar issue that is currently pending with the Service? See section 8.01(5)(c).
Yes No Page ____	18. Have you included the required statement regarding whether, at the same time as this request, the taxpayer or a related taxpayer is presently submitting another request (including an application for change in accounting method) involving the same or similar issue to the Service? See section 8.01(5)(d).
Yes No N/A Page ____	19. If your request involves the interpretation of a substantive provision of an income or estate tax treaty, have you included the required statement regarding whether the tax authority of the treaty jurisdiction has issued a ruling on the same or similar issue for the taxpayer, a related taxpayer, or a predecessor; whether the same or similar issue is being examined, or has been settled, by the tax authority of the treaty jurisdiction or is otherwise the subject of a closing agreement in that jurisdiction; and whether the same or similar issue is being considered by the competent authority of the treaty jurisdiction? See section 8.01(6).
Yes No N/A Page ____	20. If your request is for recognition of Indian tribal government status or status as a political subdivision of an Indian tribal government, does your request contain a letter from the Bureau of Indian Affairs regarding the tribe's status? See section 8.01(7), which states that taxpayers are encouraged to submit this letter with the request and provides the address for the Bureau of Indian Affairs.
Yes No Pages ____	21. Have you included the required statement of relevant authorities in support of your views? See section 8.01(8).
Yes No Page ____	22. Have you included the required statement regarding whether the law in connection with the request is uncertain and whether the issue is adequately addressed by relevant authorities? See section 8.01(8).
Yes No Pages ____	23. Does your request discuss the implications of any legislation, tax treaties, court decisions, regulations, notices, revenue rulings, or revenue procedures that you determined to be contrary to the position advanced? See section 8.01(9), which states that taxpayers are encouraged to inform the Service of such authorities.
Yes No N/A Page ____	24. If you determined that there are no contrary authorities, have you included a statement to this effect in your request? See section 8.01(9).

CIRCLE ONE	ITEM
Yes No N/A Page _____	25. Have you included in your request a statement identifying any pending legislation that may affect the proposed transaction? See section 8.01(10).
Yes No	26. Is the request accompanied by the deletions statement required by §6110? See section 8.01(11).
Yes No Page _____	27. Have you (or your authorized representative) signed and dated the request? See section 8.01(12).
Yes No N/A	28. If the request is signed by your representative or if your representative will appear before the Service in connection with the request, is the request accompanied by a properly prepared and signed power of attorney with the signatory's name typed or printed? See section 8.01(14).
Yes No Page _____	29. Have you included, signed, and dated the penalties of perjury statement in the format required by section 8.01(15)?
Yes No N/A	30. Are you submitting your request in duplicate if necessary? See section 8.01(16).
Yes No N/A Pages _____	31. If you are requesting separate letter rulings on different issues involving one factual situation, have you included a statement to that effect in each request? See section 8.02(1).
Yes No N/A	32. If you want copies of the letter ruling sent to more than one representative, does the power of attorney contain a statement to that effect? See section 8.02(2)(a).
Yes No N/A	33. If you want the original of the letter ruling to be sent to a representative, does the power of attorney contain a statement to that effect? See section 8.02(2)(b).
Yes No N/A	34. If you do not want a copy of the letter ruling to be sent to any representative, does the power of attorney contain a statement to that effect? See section 8.02(2)(c).
Yes No N/A	35. If you are making a two-part letter ruling request, have you included a summary statement of the facts you believe to be controlling? See section 8.02(3).
Yes No N/A Page _____	36. If you want your letter ruling request to be processed ahead of the regular order or by a specific date, have you requested expedited handling in the manner required by section 8.02(4) and stated a compelling need for such action in the request?
Yes No N/A Page _____	37. If you are requesting a copy of any document related to the letter ruling request to be sent by facsimile (fax) transmission, have you included a statement to that effect? See section 8.02(5).
Yes No N/A Page _____	38. If you want to have a conference on the issues involved in the request, have you included a request for conference in the letter ruling request? See section 8.02(7).
Yes No	39. Have you included the correct user fee with the request and is your check or money order in U.S. dollars and payable to the Internal Revenue Service? See section 15 and Appendix A to determine the correct amount.
Yes No N/A Page _____	40. If your request involves a personal tax issue and you qualify for the reduced user fee when gross income is less than $250,000, have you included the required certification? See paragraphs (A)(4)(a) and (B)(1) of Appendix A.
Yes No N/A Page _____	41. If your request involves a business-related tax issue and you qualify for the reduced user fee when gross income is less than $1 million, have you included the required certification? See paragraphs (A)(4)(b) and (B)(1) of Appendix A.

¶1657

CIRCLE ONE	ITEM
Yes No N/A Page ____	42. If you qualify for the user fee for substantially identical letter rulings, have you included the required information? See section 15.07(2) and paragraph (A)(5)(a) of Appendix A.
Yes No N/A Page ____	43. If you qualify for the user fee for a § 301.9100 request to extend the time for filling an identical accounting method change on a single Form 3115, have you included the required information? See section 15.07(3) and paragraph (A)(5)(c) of Appendix A.
Yes No N/A	44. If your request is covered by any of the checklists, guideline revenue procedures, notices, safe harbor revenue procedures, or other special requirements listed in section 9, have you complied with all of the requirements of the applicable revenue procedure or notice?
Rev. Proc. _____ _____ _____	List other applicable revenue procedures or notices, including checklists, used or relied upon in the preparation of this letter ruling request (Cumulative Bulletin or Internal Revenue Bulletin citation not required).
Yes No N/A Page ____	45. If you are requesting relief under § 7805(b) (regarding retroactive effect), have you complied with all of the requirements in section 12.11?
Yes No	46. Have you addressed your request to the attention of the Associate Chief Counsel (Corporate), the Associate Chief Counsel (Financial Institutions & Products), the Associate Chief Counsel (Income Tax & Accounting), the Associate Chief Counsel (International), the Associate Chief Counsel (Passthroughs & Special Industries), the Associate Chief Counsel (Procedure and Administration), or the Division Counsel/Associate Chief Counsel (Tax Exempt and Government Entities), as appropriate? The mailing address is:

Internal Revenue Service
Attn: CC:PA:T
P.O. Box 7604
Ben Franklin Station
Washington, D.C. 20044

However, if a private delivery service is used, the address is:

Internal Revenue Service
Attn: CC:PA:T, Room 6561
1111 Constitution Avenue, N.W.
Washington, D.C. 20224

The package should be marked: RULING REQUEST SUBMISSION. Improperly addressed requests may be delayed (sometimes for over a week) in reaching CC:PA:T for initial processing.

_____ _____ _____
         Signature   Title or Authority   Date

_____
Typed or printed name of person signing
checklist

¶1658 Exhibit 16-8

Letter Ruling 200109022, November 29, 2000

Uniform Issue List Information:

UIL No. 1031.05-00

Exchange of property held for productive use or investment —Deferred exchanges

This letter responds to your request for a private letter ruling, dated July 21, 1999, submitted on behalf of Taxpayer, requesting rulings on issues concerning its establishment of a like-kind exchange program arising under §1031 of the Internal Revenue Code.

FACTS:

Taxpayer is an ***** subsidiary of *****. Taxpayer and its subsidiaries provide a to ***** and also purchase b from *****. Taxpayer also ***** to *****, the majority of which are affiliated with *****. In addition, Taxpayer ***** to ***** ***** and *****. Taxpayer is a calendar year taxpayer and is a member of the Parent affiliated group that files a consolidated income tax return. For financial and tax reporting purposes, Taxpayer has adopted the accrual method of accounting.

Most of the new Properties financed by Taxpayer and its subsidiaries are *****. Taxpayer also provides ***** *****. Division 1 is a division of Taxpayer. Division 1 acts as ***** Taxpayer in ***** and ***** for Properties *****. Division 1 also services *****. Division 1 has agreements with a ***** to provide ***** for Properties *****. Under all of Division 1's *****, the Properties and related ***** are ***** from ***** to *****, although the Properties are *****

Division 2 is a division of Taxpayer. It performs the same function as Division 1, *****, an affiliate of Parent. The Properties ***** are ***** from ***** to Taxpayer, but the Properties are ***** Division 2. The Division 2 ***** are ***** by Division 1.

*Taxpayer's ***** Operations*

In the course of its business, Taxpayer regularly purchases Properties that are ***** from its ***** of *****. ***** are typically unrelated to Parent, Taxpayer or their affiliates. ***** terms typically range from c to d. Taxpayer has ***** the Properties and depreciates them under §168 of the Code. Taxpayer regularly disposes of these Properties when the *****

Taxpayer's Acquisition of Properties

While individual transactions may vary, the process by which Taxpayer purchases a Property from ***** begins when the ***** *****, rather than *****, a ***** Property from the *****. The submits the ***** to Taxpayer, either by entering the appropriate information in a *****. If the *****, Taxpayer ***** *****. Thereafter, if the ***** and ***** agree to enter into *****, a Taxpayer ***** is executed by both the ***** and the The ***** executes the ***** as the*****. By signing the *****, the ***** also ***** the Property to Taxpayer. The ***** then submits a ***** of ***** related documents to Taxpayer. This ***** contains the ***** ***** documentation relating to ***** and ***** the Property. Upon ***** receipt and approval of the *****, Taxpayer ***** the ***** for the Property. Payment is normally made by *****

Occasionally, a ***** will not submit a ***** to Taxpayer for ***** ***** with *****. Such a "*****" typically occurs when the ***** believes that the ***** the ***** established by ***** Taxpayer. The ***** and ***** will execute the *****, the ***** will take ***** the Property, and the ***** will then submit the ***** to ***** Taxpayer. Upon receiving the *****, Taxpayer will perform its normal ***** ***** process on the ***** prior to accepting the Property ***** from the

Division 1 acquires ***** Properties from a number of ***** with whom it has contractual relationships. These ***** are ***** or other ***** that deal directly with the ***** originating the *****. The contractual agreement between Division 1 and each ***** provides that the ***** ***** will ***** Properties ***** from eligible ***** and sell them to Division 1 if they meet Division 1's eligibility criteria. The ***** assigns its rights in the Properties ***** and its rights under its contract with the ***** to Division 1. Each Property is ***** Division 1 ***** *****. Division 1 services these ***** and the ***** has no ***** continuing involvement with them. These Properties ***** are treated like any other Division 1 ***** and are ***** from the ***** to ***** Taxpayer.

Taxpayer's Disposition of Properties

Taxpayer disposes of ***** Properties either after they are ***** (if the ***** is *****) or after they are returned at ***** (generally at ***** *****, unless the ***** is *****). Taxpayer disposes of these Properties in one of two ways. The Property is either sold directly to a ***** (usually the ***** who ***** the ***** with the *****) or the Property is sold at ***** (typically, the buyer ***** is *****). *****. Such sales are very unusual.

All of Taxpayer's ***** provide the ***** with a ***** at ***** When a *****, the ***** acquires the Property from Taxpayer at ***** that is ***** the ***** *****. The ***** purchases the Property from the *****. If the ***** chooses not to *****, the ***** has the ***** ***** the Property for ***** the ***** in the ***** ***** situation. In either case, Taxpayer sells the ***** Property *****. The ***** may pay for the Property by *****. If the ***** uses ***** the ***** this purchase into the ***** the ***** with Taxpayer. The ***** then sends the necessary paperwork (e ***** and other forms) to Taxpayer. If the ***** pays by *****, the ***** the ***** in the ***** of paperwork. Upon receipt of payment and approval of the paperwork, Taxpayer releases ***** the Property to the *****, who then transfers it to *****.

If the ***** purchases the Property *****), the ***** can add the ***** to ***** Taxpayer. This is known as a Program 1. The ***** are wholly separate. To purchase the Property, the ***** transmits the ***** the Property to Taxpayer*****, and in a separate transaction, Taxpayer ***** the Property by ***** and transferring the ***** to the ***** (typically by *****).

In *****, the ***** typically negotiates with the to determine ***** pay *****. The pays this amount to the *****, who is required to ***** *****). The pays by *****.

¶1658

If the Property is *****, or if neither the ***** nor the ***** chooses to ***** the Property *****, the Property is *****. At the *****, the Property is *****, and the Property is sold. The ***** then remits the ***** to Taxpayer *****. In some cases, a ***** purchasing ***** who is part ***** may ***** from Taxpayer simply by *****. Taxpayer ***** a ***** for the amount of the ***** purchase. For Property purchases ***** under this plan (Program 2), the ***** funds from the ***** and ***** funds to Taxpayer.

Taxpayer's Like-Kind Exchange Program

Taxpayer has established a program of like-kind exchanges of Property. These exchanges are intended to qualify as deferred like-kind exchanges under §1031 of the Code and the regulations thereunder. To facilitate these exchanges, Taxpayer has entered into a written Master Exchange Agreement (Agreement) with QI, to which Taxpayer has assigned its rights with respect to (a) the disposition of Property ("Relinquished Property") and (b) the acquisition of Property ("Replacement Property"). QI is intended to be a "qualified intermediary" within the meaning of §1.1031(k)-1(g)(4) of the Income Tax Regulations. By assigning these rights to QI and giving notice to all parties to the agreements establishing such rights, Taxpayer intends that QI be treated as (a) having acquired the Relinquished Property from Taxpayer and transferred it to the ultimate purchaser and (b) having acquired the Replacement Property from its seller and transferred it to Taxpayer.

Acquisitions of Properties from, and dispositions of Properties to, ***** are excluded from Taxpayer's like-kind exchange program.

Taxpayer has appointed QI to receive the proceeds from the disposition of Relinquished Properties and disburse such proceeds, along with other funds supplied by Taxpayer as may be necessary, to acquire Replacement Properties. QI functions as an intermediary to facilitate exchanges of all acquisitions and dispositions of Property by Taxpayer. Taxpayer's written Agreement with QI limits Taxpayer's rights to receive, pledge, borrow, or otherwise obtain the benefits of money or other property held by QI, as required by §§1.1031(k)-1(g)(4)(ii) and (g)(6) of the regulations.

The Qualified Intermediary

QI is a ***** *****, QI Parent. QI Parent is a financial institution. In the two preceding years, QI Parent and its affiliates have provided the following routine financial services to Taxpayer and its affiliates: funds processing, lines of credit, lockbox services, counterparties in foreign exchange swaps, and purchases of Taxpayer-issued debt obligations. QI is an independent third-party financial institution that has not previously performed services other than routine financialservices for Taxpayer in the two preceding years. Thus, QI is not a "disqualified person" under §1.1031(k)-1(k)(2) of the regulations.

Assignment and Notice

Taxpayer has structured its program to meet the requirements of the "qualified intermediary" safe harbor under §1.103(k)-1(g)(4) of the regulations. Pursuant to this regulation, QI must acquire Relinquished Property from Taxpayer and

¶1658

transfer it to a purchaser, and acquire Replacement Property from a seller and transfer it to Taxpayer. § 1.1031(k)-1(g)(4) (iii)(B). One way that an intermediary is treated as acquiring and transferring property is if the intermediary enters into an agreement with the purchaser of relinquished property or the seller of replacement property, and the property is transferred pursuant to that agreement. §§ 1.1031(k)-1(g)(4) (iv)(B) and (C). The regulations further provide that the intermediary is treated as entering into an agreement if the rights of a party to the agreement are assigned to the intermediary and all parties to that agreement are notified in writing of the assignment on or before the date of the relevant transfer of property. § 1.1031(k)-1(g)(4)(v). Taxpayer and QI have chosen to utilize this "assignment and notice" method of having QI acquire and transfer both the Relinquished Property and the Replacement Property. Purchasers of Relinquished Property and sellers of Replacement Property will be notified in several ways that Taxpayer's rights to sell the Relinquished Property and acquire the Replacement Property have been assigned to QI.

In the Agreement, Taxpayer has assigned to QI Taxpayer's rights (but not its obligations) with respect to the sale of Relinquished Property. This assignment applies to rights with respect to the sale of Property Taxpayer held on the date the Agreement was signed, as well as to Property acquired by Taxpayer in the future. Similarly, Taxpayer has assigned to QI Taxpayer's rights (but not its obligations) with respect to the purchase of Replacement Property in the Agreement. This assignment applies to the rights with respect to the purchase of Property acquired after the date the Agreement was assigned. In addition, Taxpayer will notify QI of individual transactions by sending QI a report containing a listing of the daily acquisitions and dispositions of Property. These reports provide QI with a list of each transaction with respect to which QI has been assigned Taxpayer's rights.

Taxpayer provides ***** with written notification of the assignment in two different ways. First, Taxpayer sent a blanket notice to every ***** prior to the start of the like-kind exchange program. Second, Taxpayer provides a purchasing or selling ***** with a written notice in connection with each disposition of Relinquished Property and each acquisition of Replacement Property on or before the date of the transaction.

The transactions at issue here began with an exchange of the first Relinquished Property disposed of on or after Date 1, with the first Replacement Property acquired after such date (but no more than 45 days after such date) and the cost of which was equal to or greater than the proceeds from the sale of the Relinquished Property.

Matching of Relinquished and Replacement Properties

Every ***** proceeds from the sale of Relinquished Property will flow through the ***** and will be used to acquire Replacement Property. Relinquished Properties and Replacement Properties are divided into three categories: Category 1, Category 2a, and Category 2b. Category 1 Properties are described in General Asset Class 1 and Category 2a and 2b Properties are described in General Asset Class 2. *See* § 1.1031(a)-2(b)(2). Information about the Relinquished

¶ **1658**

Property and Replacement Property will be analyzed in Taxpayer's like-kind exchange matching system, and Relinquished Property will be matched with the Replacement Property for which it was exchanged, according to certain parameters.

Relinquished Property will only be matched with Replacement Property acquired within 45 days after the date the Relinquished Property was transferred to its purchaser. Furthermore, to the extent possible, Relinquished Property will always be matched with Replacement Property whose cost equals or exceeds the proceeds from the sale of the Relinquished Property. In those cases where it is not possible to acquire Replacement Property equal to or in excess of the cost of the Relinquished Property, the matching system is designed to group property so that the excess of proceeds of Relinquished Property over the cost of Replacement Property is minimized. In such cases, Taxpayer will recognize gain to the extent of the lesser of gain realized or the amount of such excess. § 1.1031(j)-1(b)(3). Also, in the event that it is not possible to match all Relinquished Properties with Replacement Properties in the same Asset Class, Taxpayer may match Properties between Categories 1 and 2b.

Finally, ***** *****. Taxpayer's matching system is designed to accommodate these ***** requirements as well.

*Taxpayer ***** Purchases of Relinquished Property*

Taxpayer ***** in the course of its business. Taxpayer provides ***** to **** * of Property and to ***** of such *** **. Some ***** of Relinquished Property by use of Program 1 or Program 2, provided by Taxpayer. In such a case, Taxpayer ***** a purchaser of Relinquished ***** contemporaneously with the sale of the Relinquished Property in a separate and distinct arm's-length transaction at market rate terms. The purchaser is not required to **** *, but is free ***** **** *. A purchaser's ***** is not part of the ** *** ***** for the transfer of the Relinquished Property.

Like-Kind Exchange Cash Flows

Taxpayer's pre-like-kind-exchange business practice was to use ***** ***** to ***** for almost all purchases of *** ** Properties and ***** *** ** from ***** and **** * for most sales of ***** Properties. Most of Taxpayer's ***** to and from ***** and ***** were made ***** also. All ***** collections and disbursements for ***** transactions flowed through the *****

In addition, most ***** transactions with ***** and others was ***** ***** such party. This ***** eliminates *** **, ***** It is also preferred by the ***** and others, who must *****

Taxpayer represents that its business is a highly competitive business, and *****. In order to avoid causing disruption or confusion with the ***** and others, Taxpayer has adopted a ***** *** ** for the like-kind exchange program that will enable it to *****

¶1658

Collections

Payment for each Relinquished Property is made by ** *** to QI by *****. In the case of *****, the payment *** ** *****. The system *** ** *****. The ***** and ***** *****. The ***** Relinquished Property proceeds are ***** **** *. In the case of *****, the ***** The ***** to Taxpayer, processed, and either *****

Thus, ***** result in proceeds from the sale of Relinquished Property being ***** used by QI, as provided in the Agreement, solely to purchase Replacement Property on Taxpayer's behalf. At no time will the proceeds from the sale of Relinquished Property be placed in an account over which Taxpayer will have the power to obtain the funds, directly or indirectly, without the QI's assent. ***** a Report is generated by ***** that lists ***** *****. When these transfers have been authorized by QI and Taxpayer, *****. Thus, ***** *****. In the event of a ***** Taxpayer is ***** to ***** to ***** the

Some ***** through **** * Program 1 or Program 2. In such a case, **** * the Relinquished Property proceeds is *****

Disbursements

Replacement Property will be purchased by QI with the proceeds from the sale of Relinquished Property. Each Replacement Property will be acquired no sooner than one day after and no later than 45 days after the transfer of the related Relinquished Property. ***** will receive payment for the Replacement Property *****. The ***** by Taxpayer's system based on ***** ** ***. These payments for Replacement Property will be funded **** * with Relinquished Property proceeds. If the proceeds from the sale of Relinquished Property held by QI are insufficient to cover the purchase price of the Replacement Property, Taxpayer will transfer additional funds to ***** fund the shortfall.

The same Report discussed above with respect to collections is also used to *****. The Report specifies how much is needed ***** for purchases of Replacement Property, the amount of additional funds (if any) needed from Taxpayer for purchases of Replacement ***** Property, *****

Investment of Unspent Proceeds

If there are any unspent proceeds from dispositions of Relinquished Property remaining in *****, these funds are invested by QI in accordance with Taxpayer's instructions, and any income earned is reported by Taxpayer for tax purposes. § 1.1031(k)-1(h). These earnings on the unspent proceeds are used by the QI to acquire Replacement Property in the future, and Taxpayer's rights with respect to this income is limited in accordance with § 1.1031(k)-1(g)(6) of the regulations.

When a ***** wishes to *** ** a Property, Taxpayer generally ***** that the ***** from the ***** at the time of *****. This ***** is ***** by the ***** in *****. To simplify ***** the *****, Taxpayer typically receives the ***** by ***** the ***** for the Property *****. The **** * of the ***** is simply anadministrative convenience. Taxpayer ***** the ***** ***** to the purchase price of the Property, *****, and ***** the ***** amount on its books to *** **. The ***** and is *** ** purchase price — *****. Taxpayer has expended the full cost of the Property in money paid to the *****.

Because the ***** is ***** part of the acquisition of Replacement Property, it does not involve or affect *****, and, therefore, does not have an adverse impact on the overall like-kind exchange program or any one or more distinct exchanges under the program.

The manner in which the ***** depends upon whether the Property is *****, or whether the *****. If the Property is *****, Taxpayer ***** for the *****. If the ***** acquires the Property, however, the ***** to the *****. The ***** pays Ql the purchase price ***** and *****. The ***** has thus *****. Ql also receives the full purchase price for the Property, since the QI receives the full purchase price *****. This ***** situation leaves the parties in the exact same position as if the

Non-Like-Kind Exchange Transaction Processing

Funds that are not proceeds of Relinquished Property or acquisitions of Replacement Property *****. For example, Payments from ***** include payments for dispositions of ***** ***** However, non-like-kind exchange ***** Taxpayer and non-like-kind exchange *****. QI's involvement with non-like-kind exchange *****. These *****

Legal Agreements Governing Cash Flows

The Agreement addresses cash flows in Taxpayer's like-kind exchange program and provides that Taxpayer has no right to receive, pledge, borrow, or otherwise obtain the benefit of money or other property held by QI before the end of the relevant period described in §1.1031(k)-1(g)(6) of the regulations. Taxpayer identifies Replacement Property by receiving the Replacement Property before the end of the identification period, as provided in §1.1031(k)-1(c)(1) of the regulations. Thus, if no Replacement Property were to be received with respect to a particular Relinquished Property within the identification period, the Agreement would permit Taxpayer to receive the related Relinquished Property proceeds after the end of the identification period. In such a case, Taxpayer would recognize all realized gain on the disposition of the associated Relinquished Property.

The bank account agreement ***** ***** provides that:

 i. The QI

 ii. QI approval is required for each transfer of funds

 iii. QI funds the full purchase price of disbursements for Replacement Property to the extent of the funds held by QI and Taxpayer funds any shortfall in disbursements for Replacement Property

 iv. Taxpayer has no right to receive, pledge, borrow, or otherwise obtain the benefits of proceeds of sales of Relinquished Property before theend of the relevant period described in §1.1031(k)-1(g)(6) of the regulations.

Each ***** has entered into ***** that authorizes Taxpayer to *****. Each ***** with a ***** has been amended to provide that:

 i. Settlements due from the ***** to QI may be paid

 ii. Settlements due to the ***** from QI may be paid

iii. The ***** directs that ***** The ***** obligation to QI

iv. The ***** directs that any amounts ***** ***** Each ***** has been amended in a manner similar to that of ***** with a *****, except that provisions related to ***** have been omitted, since *****

RULINGS REQUESTED

Under these facts, Taxpayer requests that the Service issue the following rulings:

1. Property in Category 1 is of like kind with Property in Category 2b within the meaning of § 1031.

2. Taxpayer's transfer of each Relinquished Property or group of Relinquished Properties and the corresponding receipt of each related Replacement Property or group of Replacement Properties in accordance with the Agreement and as represented in this request for rulings will be treated as a separate and distinct like-kind exchange that qualifies for nonrecognition of gain or loss for federal income tax purposes under § 1031.

3. Each exchange pursuant to the Agreement of one or more Relinquished Properties for one or more Replacement Properties will qualify for nonrecognition of gain or loss provided no money or other non-like-kind property is received by Taxpayer. If Taxpayer does receive money or other non-like-kind property in an exchange, the gain with respect to the Relinquished Property involved in the exchange will be recognized in an amount not in excess of the sum of such money and the fair market value of such other property.

4. QI, acting in accordance with the Agreement, will be treated as a qualified intermediary as defined in § 1.1031(k)-1(g)(4)(iii) of the regulations and will be treated as acquiring and transferring each Relinquished Property and each Replacement Property for purposes of § 1031.

5. Pursuant to §§ 1.1031(k)-1(f) and (g) of the regulations, Taxpayer will not be in actual or constructive receipt of any of the proceeds from the sale of Relinquished Property or any money or other property held by QI ***** unless and until such amounts or items are actually received by Taxpayer (*i.e.,* if Replacement Property is not acquiredduring the identification period and the related sale proceeds are transferred to Taxpayer).

6. Neither ***** nor ***** from the sale of Relinquished Property *****, including ***** *****, results in actual or constructive receipt of any portion of the proceeds by Taxpayer where QI receives the full amount of proceeds from the sale of Relinquished Property.

7. With respect to Relinquished Property *****, the ***** purchaser of the Relinquished Property is not part of the ***** transfer of the Relinquished Property by Taxpayer, and therefore, Taxpayer does not actually

or constructively receive money or other property, on account of *****, before Taxpayer actually receives like-kind Replacement Property.

LAW AND ANALYSIS

Section 1031(a)(1) provides that no gain or loss shall be recognized on the exchange of property held for productive use in a trade or business or for investment if such property is exchanged solely for property of like kind which is to be held for productive use in a trade or business or for investment. Section 1031(a)(2) adds that this subsection does not apply to any exchange of stock in trade or other property held primarily for sale.

There are three general requirements for nonrecognition treatment under §1031: (1) both the property surrendered and the property received must be held either for productive use in a trade or business or for investment; (2) the property surrendered and the property received must be of "like-kind;" and (3) there must be an exchange as distinguished from a sale and a purchase.

"Held For" Requirement

The relevant qualified use of the Property owned by Taxpayer and subsequently being exchanged in the transaction is *****. Thus, the Relinquished Property that Taxpayer and the Replacement Property that Taxpayer will be ***** upon acquisition is considered property held for productive use in a trade or business in Taxpayer's hands.

Like-Kind Requirement

The requirement that the exchanged properties be of like kind has reference to the nature or character of the property and not to its grade or quality. §1.1031(a)-1(b). To qualify for like-kind exchange treatment, one kind or class of property may not be exchanged for property of a different kind or class. Depreciable tangible personal properties are of a like class if they are either within the same General Asset Class, as defined in §1.1031(a)-2(b)(2) of the regulations, or within the same Product Class, as defined in §1.1031(a)-2(b)(3) of the regulations. If a property is classified within any General Asset Class, it may not be classified within a Product Class. §1.1031(a)-2(b)(1).

Section 1.1031(a)-2(b)(2) of the regulations describes the various General Asset Classes. The Relinquished Properties and Replacement Properties are divided into three categories: Category 1, Category 2a, and Category 2b. Category 1 Properties are described in Class 1 and Category 2a and 2b Properties are described in Class 2. *See also* Rev. Proc. 87-56, 1987-2 C.B. 674.

To the extent that each exchange consists of one or more Relinquished Properties and one or more Replacement Properties in the same class, these exchanges fit within the General Asset Class safe harbor described above. In the event that it is not possible to match all Relinquished Properties with Replacement Properties in the same Asset Class, Taxpayer may match Properties between Categories 1 and 2b. The General Asset Class safe harbor does not apply to these exchanges.

¶1658

The General Asset Class and Product Class safe harbors in the regulations simplify the determination of whether depreciable tangible personal property is of a like kind, but they are not the exclusive method for making this determination. For depreciable tangible personal property to be considered of like kind for purposes of §1031, the property can be either like kind or like class. Section 1.1031(a)-2(a) of the regulations provides that "an exchange of properties of a like kind may qualify under section 1031 regardless of whether the properties are also of like class. In determining whether exchanged properties are of a like kind, no inference is to be drawn from the fact that the properties are not of a like class." Thus, two properties can be in different General Asset Classes (and thus not be of a like class) and yet be of like kind.

The like-kind standard has been interpreted more narrowly in the case of exchanges of personal property as compared to exchanges of real property. *See California Federal Life Insurance Co. v. Commissioner*, 680 F.2d 85, 87 (9th Cir. 1982) [82-2 USTC ¶9464] (Tax Court did not err in refusing to apply the lenient treatment of real estate exchanges to an exchange of personal property involving U.S. Double Eagle $20 gold coins and Swiss francs). Even within the more restrictive parameters of the like-kind standard as applied to personal property, the differences between Property in Category 1 and Property in Category 2b do not rise to the level of a difference in nature or character but are merely a difference in grade or quality.

When an exchange transaction is deferred, rather than simultaneous, even if the taxpayer trades property for like-kind property, the exchanged properties will not be of like kind if the Replacement Property is not timely identified and timely received. Section 1031(a)(3) states that any property received by the taxpayer shall be treated as property that is not like-kind property if (a) such property is not identified as property to be received in the exchange on or before the day that is 45 days after the date on which the taxpayer transfers the property relinquished in the exchange, or (b) such property is received after the earlier of (i) the day that is 180 days after the date on which the taxpayer transfers the property relinquished in the exchange or (ii) the due date (determined with regard to extension) for transferor's return of the tax imposed by this chapter for the taxable year in which the transfer of the relinquished property occurs.

Section 1.1031(k)-1(c) provides that any replacement property that is received by the taxpayer before the end of the identification period will in all eventsbe treated as identified before the end of the identification period. In the instant case, Taxpayer has represented that it will receive all Replacement Property within 45 days of the sale of the Relinquished Property, thereby satisfying both the identification and receipt requirements of §1031(a)(3). Accordingly, Category 1 Property is of like kind with Category 2b Property.

Exchange Requirement

For purposes of §§1031 and 1.1031(k)-1, a deferred exchange is defined as an exchange in which, pursuant to an agreement, the taxpayer transfers property held for productive use in a trade or business or for investment (the "relinquished property") and subsequently receives property to be held either for

¶1658

productive use in a trade or business or for investment (the "replacement property"). In order to constitute a deferred exchange, the transaction must be an exchange (*i.e.*, a transfer of property for property, as distinguished from a transfer of property for money). §1.1031(k)-1(a). In the case of a transfer of relinquished property in a deferred exchange, gain or loss may be recognized if the taxpayer actually or constructively receives money or other property before the taxpayer actually receives like-kind replacement property. If the taxpayer actually or constructively receives money or other property in the full amount of the consideration for the relinquished property before the taxpayer actually receives like-kind replacement property, the transaction will constitute a sale and repurchase, and not a deferred exchange, even though the taxpayer may ultimately receive like-kind replacement property. §1.1031(k)-1(f)(1). According to §1.1031(k)-1(f)(2), actual or constructive receipt of money or other property by an agent of the taxpayer (determined without regard to paragraph (k) of this section) is actual or constructive receipt by the taxpayer.

QI as Qualified Intermediary

Section 1.1031(k)-1(g) of the regulations sets forth four safe harbors, the use of any of which will result in a determination that the taxpayer is not in actual or constructive receipt of money or other property for §1031 purposes. Section 1.1031(k)-1(g)(4)(i) of the regulations provides that, in the case of a taxpayer's transfer of relinquished property involving a qualified intermediary, the qualified intermediary is not considered the taxpayer's agent for §1031 purposes. In such a case, the taxpayer's transfer of relinquished property and subsequent receipt of like-kind replacement property is treated as an exchange, and the determination of whether the taxpayer is in actual or constructive receipt of money or other property before the taxpayer actually receives like-kind replacement property is made as if the qualified intermediary is not the agent of the taxpayer.

Section 1.1031(k)-1(g)(4) (ii) of the regulations provides that §1.1031(k)-1(g)(4)(i) applies only if the agreement between the taxpayer and the qualified intermediary expressly limits the taxpayer's right to receive, pledge, borrow, or otherwise obtain the benefits of money or other property held by the qualified intermediary as provided in §1.1031(k)-1(g)(6). Taxpayer's written Agreement with QI limits Taxpayer's rights to receive, pledge, borrow, or otherwiseobtain the benefits of money or other property held by QI, as required by §§1.1031(k)-1(g)(4) (ii) and (g)(6) of the regulations.

A qualified intermediary, as defined in §1.1031(k)-1(g)(4) (iii)(A) of the regulations, must be a person who is not the taxpayer or a disqualified person. According to §1.1031(k)-1(k)(2) of the regulations, the term "disqualified person" includes a person who is the taxpayer's agent at the time of the transaction. For this purpose, a person who has acted as the taxpayer's employee, attorney, accountant, investment banker or broker, or real estate agent or broker within the two-year period ending on the date of the transfer of the first of the relinquished properties is treated as the taxpayer's agent. However, performance of certain services does not cause an entity to be a "disqualified person." These services

¶1658

include (a) services for the taxpayer with respect to exchanges of property intended to qualify for nonrecognition of gain or loss under § 1031, and (b) routine financial, title insurance, escrow, or trust services for the taxpayer by a financial institution, title insurance company, or escrow company.

QI Parent is an independent, third-party financial institution that has not previously performed services other than the routine financial services previously described for Taxpayer. In the instant case, ***** As such, QI will not be a "disqualified person" under § 1.1031(k)-1(k) of the regulations.

In order to qualify as a qualified intermediary, the intermediary must enter into a written agreement with the taxpayer (the "exchange agreement") and as required by the exchange agreement, acquires the relinquished property from the taxpayer, transfers the relinquished property, acquires the replacement property, and transfers the replacement property to the taxpayer. § 1.1031(k)-1(g) (iii)(B). Regardless of whether an intermediary acquires and transfers property under general tax principles, an intermediary treated as acquiring and transferring the relinquished property if the intermediary (either on its own behalf or as the agent of any party to the transaction) enters into an agreement with a person other than the taxpayer for the transfer of the relinquished property to that person, and pursuant to that agreement, the relinquished property is transferred to that person. § 1.1031(k)-1(g)(4) (iv)(B). An intermediary is treated as acquiring and transferring replacement property if the intermediary (either on its own behalf or as the agent of any party to the transaction) enters into an agreement with the owner of the replacement property for the transfer of that property and, pursuant to that agreement, the replacement property is transferred to the taxpayer. § 1.1031(k)-1(g)(4) (iv)(C). For these purposes, an intermediary is treated as entering into an agreement if the rights of a party to the agreement are assigned to the intermediary and all parties to that agreement are notified in writing of the assignment on or before the date of the relevant transfer of property. § 1.1031(k)-1(g)(4)(v).

In the instant case, Taxpayer has assigned to QI its rights to sell Relinquished Property. In all instances, the purchaser receives notice of the assignment prior to the time that the Relinquished Property is transferred to the purchaser. Each form of notice informs the purchaser in writing that Taxpayer has assigned to QI its rights to sell the Property. ***** the Property will be transferred directly from Taxpayer to the purchaser of the Property pursuant to the agreement between Taxpayer and purchaser. Thus, QI will be treated as acquiring and transferring the Relinquished Property pursuant to § § 1.1031(k)-1(g)(4) (iv)(B) and (v).

In addition, Taxpayer assigned its right to purchase Replacement Property to QI. In all instances, the seller receives notice prior to the time that the Replacement Property is transferred to Taxpayer. Each form of notice informs the seller in writing that Taxpayer has assigned to QI its rights to purchase the Property. ***** the Property is transferred directly to Taxpayer pursuant to the agreement between seller and Taxpayer. Thus, QI will be treated as acquiring and transferring the Replacement Property pursuant to § 1.1031(k)-1(g)(4) (iv)(C) and (v). Accordingly, QI, acting in accordance with the Agreement, will be treated as a qualified intermediary as defined in § 1.1031(k)-1(g)(4) (iii) of the regulations and will be treated as acquiring and ***** transferring each Relinquished Property and each Replacement Property for purposes of § 1031.

Constructive Receipt—Proceeds of Relinquished Property

The Agreement between Taxpayer and QI provides that Taxpayer will have no rights to receive, pledge, borrow, or otherwise obtain the benefits of money or other property as required by §§ 1.1031(k)-1(g)(4) and (6)(i) of the regulations. Proceeds from the sale of Relinquished Property are deposited into ***** ***** or ***** To the extent that funds from the sale of the Relinquished Property are insufficient to cover the purchase of Replacement Property, Taxpayer transfers funds to cover the amount of the purchases.

Taxpayer is not in actual or constructive receipt of proceeds of sales of Relinquished Property that are deposited in ***** transferred to *****, and ultimately transferred to ***** ***** and used to acquire Replacement Property. All agreements governing the flow of funds limit Taxpayer's ability to actually or constructively receive those funds as required by §§ 1.1031(k)-1(g)(4) (ii) and (g)(6) of the regulations.

Taxpayer's ***** agreements with ***** and ***** provide that amounts collected from ***** and ***** are deposited into accounts specified by the QI and Taxpayer *****. The Agreement and ***** provide that QI ***** those funds in ***** ***** the full amount of proceeds from sales of Relinquished Property. The Agreement and ***** also provide that no funds can be ***** without QI approval, and all of these agreements restrict, as required by §§ 1.1031(k)-1(g)(4) (ii) and (g)(6) of the regulations, Taxpayer's right to receive, pledge, borrow or otherwise obtain the benefit of Relinquished Property proceeds and earnings thereon held in ***** and ***** prior to the end of the relevant periods described in § 1.1031(k)-1(g)(6).

Constructive Receipt-

Under Taxpayer's like-kind exchange program, all transactions with ***** or ***** are ***** and payments ***** the ***** or ***** are *****, resulting in either ***** or *****. In each type of transaction involving *****, QI receives the full amount of proceeds from the sale of Relinquished Property.

For example, the ***** the sale of Relinquished Property ***** purchasing under Program 2 does not result in actual or constructive receipt of ***** the proceeds by Taxpayer. In each such sale of Relinquished Property, QI receives the ***** sales proceeds of Relinquished Property. In effect, the ***** has ***** the amount the ***** This is accomplished ***** *****. Thus, Taxpayer is not in actual or constructive receipt of proceeds of Relinquished Property.

*Constructive Receipt — ***** Program 1 and Program 2*

Under Program 2, ***** are ***** for ***** by Taxpayer, and can ***** simply by *****. In a Program 2 sale, the ***** does not ***** the Property from the *****, and ***** *****. Taxpayer ***** with respect to this transaction.

¶1658

Taxpayer is not in actual or constructive receipt of proceeds of Relinquished Property by reason of ***** that results from a Program 2 transaction. Taxpayer is in the business of *****. ***** purchasing ***** are not required to ***** and are free to use *****. The ***** to a ***** is a separate and distinct arm's-length transaction from the sale of the Property, and *****. Accordingly, Taxpayer does not actually or constructively receive money or other property on account of its receipt of the ***** before Taxpayer actually receives like-kind Replacement Property. *See 124 Front Street v. Commissioner,* 65 T.C. 6 (1975) [CCH Dec. ¶ 33,448], acq. 1976-2 C.B.2.

Program 1 transactions are similar to Program 2 transactions, except that the proceeds from the sale of the Relinquished Property ***** ***** and the ***** Accordingly, under these facts, the ***** is a separate and independent transaction, and Taxpayer is not in actual or constructive receipt of proceeds of Relinquished Property by reason of holding ***** that results from a Program 1 transaction.

Accordingly, based on your representations and the above analysis, we rule as follows:

1. Property in Category 1 is of like kind with Property in Category 2b within the meaning of § 1031.

2. Taxpayer's transfer of each Relinquished Property or group of Relinquished Properties and the corresponding receipt of each related Replacement Property or group of Replacement Properties in accordance with the Agreement and as represented in this request for rulings will be treated as a separate and distinct like-kind exchange that qualifies for nonrecognition of gain or loss for federal income tax purposes under § 1031.

3. Each exchange pursuant to the Agreement of one or more Relinquished Properties for one or more Replacement Properties will qualify for nonrecognition of gain or loss provided no money or other non-like-kind property is received by Taxpayer. If Taxpayer does receive money or other non-like-kind property in an exchange, the gain with respect to the Relinquished Property involved in the exchange will berecognized in an amount not in excess of the sum of such money and the fair market value of such other property.

4. QI, acting in accordance with the Agreement, will be treated as a qualified intermediary as defined in § 1.1031(k)-1(g)(4) (iii) of the regulations and will be treated as acquiring and transferring each Relinquished Property and each Replacement Property for purposes of § 1031.

5. Pursuant to § § 1.1031(k)-1(f) and (g) of the regulations, Taxpayer will not be in constructive receipt of any of the proceeds from the sale of Relinquished Property or any money or other property held by QI ***** *****) unless and until such amounts or items are actually received by Taxpayer (*i.e.,* if Replacement Property is not acquired during the identi-

fication period and the related sale proceeds are transferred to Taxpayer).

6. Neither ***** nor ***** from the sale of Relinquished Property with *****, including *****, results in actual or constructive receipt of any portion of the proceeds by Taxpayer where QI receives the full amount of proceeds from the sale of Relinquished Property.

7. With respect to Relinquished Property that is ***** *****, the ***** to the purchaser of the Relinquished Property is not part of the ***** transfer of the Relinquished Property by Taxpayer, and therefore, Taxpayer does not actually or constructively receive money or other property, on account of ***** *****, before Taxpayer actually receives like-kind Replacement Property.

* * * * * *

No opinion is expressed as to the tax treatment of the proposed transaction under the provisions of any other section of the Code or regulations that may be applicable or the tax treatment of any conditions existing at the time of, or effects resulting from, the transaction described that are not specifically covered in the above ruling. In this connection, we understand that if a favorable ruling is obtained for this transaction, it will serve as a model for subsequent like-kind exchanges. As previously stated, no opinion is expressed as to any other transaction that you contemplate. A copy of this letter should be attached to the federal income tax return for the year in which the transaction in question occurs. This ruling is directed only to the taxpayer who requested it. Section 6110(k)(3) of the Code provides that it may not be cited as precedent.

Sincerely yours, Associate Chief Counsel (Income Tax & Accounting), Kelly E. Alton, Senior Technician Reviewer, Branch 5.

¶1659 DISCUSSION QUESTIONS

[NOTE: There are no Discussion Questions for Chapter 16.]

CHAPTER 17
INTERNATIONAL TAX PRACTICE AND PROCEDURE

¶1701 INTRODUCTION

As the major economies of the world have become global in nature, the frequency and complexity of cross-border transactions have increased significantly. The combination of a lower U.S. corporate tax rate, new methods of allocation of expenses and separate foreign tax credit limitations for certain types of income has generally resulted in U.S. companies having excess foreign tax credits. Likewise, foreign-owned multinationals with U.S. subsidiaries are subject to a myriad of reporting requirements[1] and provisions which affect the deductibility of related party interest[2] and, in turn, the capital structure of U.S. subsidiaries. While many of the same procedural issues present in audits of domestic businesses are germane, there are other unique problems facing U.S.-based multinationals (outbound investment) as well as U.S. subsidiaries of foreign parent companies (inbound investment).

¶1702 ORGANIZATION OF THE INTERNAL REVENUE SERVICE INTERNATIONAL OFFICES

The Office of the Director-International in Washington, D.C., now only functions as the U.S. competent authority. The international examiners are assigned to the industry groups within the LMSB Division.[3]

¶1703 INTERNATIONAL EXAMINATIONS

Given the extraordinary complexity of the international provision of the Internal Revenue Code, the importance and involvement of the international examiner has increased in multinational corporation audits. Recognizing this, the IRS has retrained many of its agents as international examiners. Whereas previously international examiners were located only in large metropolitan areas, many audits of small and medium-size corporations with international operations now have international examiners assigned to their audits.

Due to the increased emphasis by the Internal Revenue Service on intercompany transfer pricing, IRS economists are also becoming involved in the audit process. Their role is to identify potential transfer pricing issues early in the examination process as well as assist in gathering factual information in support of the IRS's position.

The IRS has also developed a "survey" procedure for returns with international issues, either before or after assignment to examiners, when workload is

---

[1] Code Sec. 6038A and 6114.
[2] Code Sec. 163(j).

[3] *Taxes: The Tax Magazine*, Vol. 79, No. 3, March 2001.

excessive or no significant tax adjustment would result from an audit.[4] A taxpayer who (1) is a domestic corporation at least twenty-five-percent foreign-owned, or (2) is a foreign corporation twenty-five-percent foreign-owned and engaged in a trade or business with the United States or (3) is a foreign corporation engaged in a trade or business within the United States at any time during the taxable year, will not be subject to the survey procedure.[5] Among the reasons for referral to an international examiner include the presence of tax haven issues, Subpart F income, foreign tax credit claims in excess of $25,000, Puerto Rican related entities, and international boycott issues.[6]

Coordinated Industry Cases

The IRS established the Coordinated Industry Case Program to provide a team approach to the examination of very large corporate cases that meet specific criteria for size and complexity of audit. This program brings together as one unit for audit purposes the primary taxpayer and all of the taxpayer's effectively controlled corporations and other entities. A Coordinated Industry Case, therefore, will usually involve a large group of closely affiliated, centrally controlled, widely dispersed and highly diversified business entities. Domestic and foreign corporations, partnerships, joint ventures, syndicates, unincorporated businesses, individual, trusts, estates, foundations, pension and profit sharing trusts and other exempt organizations may be included within the coordinated audit group.[7]

Large Business Examination

Where the international taxpayer is not large enough to be classified as a Coordinated Industry case, a pre-examination conference should still be held between the taxpayer and the examination team. During this meeting, similar to a Coordinated Industry case audit, the taxpayer should meet with the team manager for purposes of providing basic data, establishing the scope and depth of the examination and arranging for computer assistance.[8] The taxpayer will also learn who has been assigned to its audit and may want to begin its own investigation to better prepare for the audit. Also at this meeting, if not before, taxpayers should agree, preferably in writing,[9] to procedures to be followed during the course of the audit regarding international issues.

LMSB Pre-Filing

Similar to domestic examinations, international taxpayers may request the examination of specific issues relating to a tax return before the return is filed. If

---

[4] IRM 4.60.4.8.

[5] IRM 4.60.4.9.

[6] IRM 4.60.4.2.

[7] IRM 4.45.2.2.2.

[8] The IRS's goals for the pre-audit conference often include reaching an agreement with the taxpayer regarding (i) the lines of communication between the IRS and the taxpayer, (ii) the use of taxpayer resources, such as office space, (iii) the procedures for providing the IRS with returns of related parties, (iv) the procedures for the taxpayer to present documentation of items that may reduce its tax liability, (v) the procedures for resolving questions regarding the content of IDRs, (vi) the periods of time for submitting and responding to IDRs, and (vii) procedures and timing of the examination of off-site records and facilities.

[9] In many IRS areas, there appears to be an objective to have a written audit agreement with every taxpayer under audit.

the taxpayer and the IRS are able to resolve the issues prior to the filing of the return, the taxpayer and the IRS may finalize their resolution by executing an LMSB Pre-Filing Agreement.[10]

¶1704 IRS PROCEDURAL TOOLS

The primary authority for recordkeeping requirements of an entity potentially liable for U.S. tax is Code Sec. 6001 of the Internal Revenue Code and the related Regulations.[11] The IRS also has the specific authority to examine any books, papers, records or other data that may be relevant or material to ascertaining the correctness of any return, determining the tax liability of any person or collecting any tax. Since most taxpayers and other individuals voluntarily produce records and answer questions when requested to do so by the IRS, this authority in itself is normally sufficient to obtain the necessary information.

One of the largest problems for foreign owned U.S. taxpayers is that most foreign corporations do not have records that are in a usable format. Records are often stated in foreign currency and prepared in foreign languages. Therefore, the U.S. taxpayer must spend a large amount of time and money translating and explaining the documents to the IRS.

This problem was confronted in the case of *Nissei Sangyo America, Ltd. v. U.S.*[12] *Nissei* involved the audit of a U.S. subsidiary of a Japanese parent. In response to an IRS summons, the U.S. subsidiary had randomly selected documents relating to the issue under examination and provided full translations. The Japanese parent had also randomly selected and translated documents. In addition, it translated the subject matter headings or titles of 1,441 pages of Japanese correspondence and prepared English translation keys for the travel expense authorization forms. The IRS demanded that all documents described in the summonses be translated into English, which the company estimated would cost from $850,000 to $1.5 million. The court held that the IRS could not compel the translation of documents that were not relevant to the tax liability or that the IRS already had in its possession.[13] Although this case involved a response to an IRS summons, the translation issue may arise in any type of response to an IRS procedural tool.

Information Document Requests

An Information Document Request ("IDR") is designed to request information or documents from taxpayers when there are voluminous records to be examined, or when it is desirable to document requests. Requested on Form 4564

---

[10] Rev. Proc. 2001-22, 2001-1 CB 745.

[11] The Regulations may require generally that any person subject to tax under subtitle A of the Code ". . . or any person required to file a return of information with respect to income, shall keep such permanent books or account or records . . . as are sufficient to establish the amount of gross income, deductions, credits, or other matters required to be shown by such person in any return of such tax or information." Reg. §1.6001-1(a). Additionally, "[t]he

director may require any person, by notice served upon him, to make such returns, render such statements, or keep such specific records as will enable the director to determine whether or not such person is liable for tax under subtitle A of the Code." Reg. §1.6001-1(d).

[12] DC Ill., 95-2 USTC ¶50,327.

[13] *See* the general summons standard of *M. Powell*, SCt, 64-2 USTC ¶9858, 379 US 48, *infra.*

(a copy of which is reproduced in the Appendix to this Chapter), an IDR provides the IRS a convenient means to request information, and simultaneously yields a permanent record of what was requested, received, and returned to the taxpayer.

An international examiner in both Coordinated Industry Case and non-Coordinated Industry Case audits will often begin by issuing IDRs for information relevant to the scope of the review. For example, if intercompany purchases or sales of inventory exist, a typical IDR would request a copy of any intercompany pricing agreements as well as any contemporaneous documentation of transfer pricing methodology.[14] As a further example, if the examination involved a substantial foreign tax credit, the international examiner would generally request copies of the appropriate foreign tax returns and allocation and apportionment schedules.

After reviewing the information gathered from these initial IDRs, the examiner will focus on those areas with the largest potential for possible adjustments. As the examination progresses, IDRs generally become more narrow in scope and tend to focus on specific items or transactions.

In addition to this authority, the IRS can employ several procedural tools to obtain information beyond that obtained via IDRs. These include on site inspection, formal document requests, summons, designated summons, Code Sec. 6038A, and exchanges of information under treaties.

On Site Inspections

In addition to IDRs, International Examiners appear to have taken an increased interest in foreign site visits and plant tours over the past few years. While recent IRS budget constraints may affect the number or duration of such visits, taxpayers should expect such requests and prepare to respond. Taxpayers should remember that it is a request, not an order, and that any request may be negotiated in terms of choosing the facility to visit (taxpayer may want to substitute a domestic plant for a foreign one), the duration of the visit, the timing of the visit, and the number of IRS employees involved. Careful planning of any such trip may result in an opportunity to present, in effect, key facts supporting the taxpayer's position. Finally, the taxpayer should prepare the plant personnel for the visit. Pre-screen the tour and determine if it covers processes or procedures relevant to the audit cycle. Pre-interview all involved personnel and sensitize them to the potential issues. International examiners have the following instruction for plant tours:[15]

    (i) Obtain information about departmental cost sheets or schedules.

    (ii) Learn the training requirements of each type of production employee.

    (iii) Obtain any records regarding sales to all customers.

    (iv) Ascertain the extent of product development performed at the plant.

---

[14] Code Sec. 6662(e)(3)(B)(i)(III).

[15] *IRS International Continuing Professional Education materials*, Chicago, Illinois, May 1995; *see also* IRM Exhibit 4.61.3-2.

¶1704

(v) Interview plant employees. Plant interviews will bring a sense of reality to the case. Interviews should flush out the employee's ability to alter the production process and the technical training each production employee received.

(vi) If the company is a controlled foreign corporation, determine how and to whom it sells its products.

(vii) Obtain all company manuals regarding the operations of the plant.

(viii) Obtain all job descriptions prior to the plant tour.

(ix) Obtain all annual evaluations of the employees to be interviewed.

(x) Obtain all company "programmer" manuals. This manual offers guidance to the programmer to construct his program, so that software can be readily translated and localized.

Formal Document Requests

If the IRS is unable to gather through IDRs the foreign information it considers necessary to conduct its examination, it may issue a formal document request (FDR). The FDR is not intended to be used as a routine tool at the beginning of an examination, but instead as a mechanism for securing information that could not be obtained through normal IDRs. The rare use of the FDR is indicated by the fact that the IRS does not have a specific form for the FDR. Instead, the IRS will issue a Form 4564 entitled "Information Document Request" with the notation "Formal Document Request" (see the Appendix). The FDR must be mailed by registered or certified mail and provide:

(i) the time and place for the production of the documentation,

(ii) a statement of the reason the documentation previously produced (if any) is not sufficient,

(iii) a description of the documentation being sought,

(iv) the consequences to the taxpayer of the failure to produce the documentation described in subparagraph (iii).[16]

If the taxpayer does not furnish the requested information within 90 days of the mailing of the FDR, the taxpayer will be prevented from later introducing the requested documentation. Foreign-based documentation is "any documentation which is located outside the U.S. and which may be relevant or material to the tax treatment of the examined item."[17] Thus, the IRS has broad authority to request virtually any relevant information. The purpose of this section is to discourage taxpayers from delaying or refusing disclosure of certain foreign-based documentation. To avoid the application of this section, the taxpayer must substantially comply with the FDR.

Whether there has been substantial compliance will depend on all the facts and circumstances. For example, if the taxpayer submits nine out of ten requested items and the court believes the missing item is the most substantial, the taxpayer could be found to have failed to comply substantially with the FDR.

---

[16] Code Sec. 982(c)(1). [17] Code Sec. 982(d).

Accordingly, the taxpayer could be prevented from later introducing the missing documentation. The FDR is not intended to be used as a routine beginning to an examination but instead as a mechanism for securing information which could not be obtained through normal request procedures.[18]

Any taxpayer that receives a FDR has the right to begin proceedings to quash the request within ninety days after the request was mailed. In this proceeding the taxpayer may contend, for example, that the information requested is irrelevant, that the requested information is available in the U.S., or that reasonable cause exists for the failure to produce or delay in producing the information.

Reasonable cause does not exist where a foreign jurisdiction would impose a civil or criminal penalty on the taxpayer for disclosing the requested documentation.[19] In a proceeding to quash, the IRS has the burden of proof to show the relevance and materiality of the information requested. During the period that a proceeding to quash or any appeal from that proceeding is pending, the statute of limitations is suspended.[20]

The legislative history to Code Sec. 982 specifies that three factors should be considered in determining whether there is reasonable cause for failure to furnish the requested documentation. These factors are: (i) whether the request is reasonable in scope; (ii) whether the requested documents are available within the U.S.; and (iii) the reasonableness of the requested place of production within the U.S.

For the first factor, an example of an unreasonable scope may be a request "for all the books and records and all the supporting documents for all the entries made in such books or records" for a particular foreign entity that is controlled by a taxpayer. However, a request for the general ledger, an analysis of an account, supporting documents for a particular transaction of such foreign entity should be declared by a court as reasonable in scope. The second factor indicates that the IRS may not seek original documents if copies of such documents are available in the U.S. Finally, the place of production of records is generally at the taxpayer's place of business or the IRS examiner's office. Production of records in New York City by a taxpayer that is residing in and engages in a trade or business in Los Angeles may be considered an unreasonable place for the production of records. The key to the reasonableness of the place for production is that such a place should be mutually convenient to both the taxpayer and the IRS.

If the taxpayer initiates proceedings to quash the FDR, the proper forum is the U.S. District Court. If a domestic taxpayer initiates quash proceedings, it must file suit in the District Court where the taxpayer resides. If the FDR is issued to a foreign taxpayer, it must file quash proceedings in the U.S. District Court for the District of Columbia.

---

[18] *See* Joint Committee on Taxation, General Explanation of the Tax Equity and Fiscal Responsibility Act of 1982.

[19] Code Sec. 982(e).

[20] Code Sec. 982(e).

The Summons Power

To give force and meaning to this general authority to examine, the IRS has been granted the power to compel a taxpayer or any other person to produce records and to testify under oath. This compulsory process is authorization to the IRS to issue an administrative summons.[21] The IRS may summon any person to appear at a time and place named in the summons for the purpose of giving testimony under oath and producing books, papers, records or other data. The authority to issue summonses has been delegated generally to those agents and other personnel within the IRS who are responsible for the examination of returns, collection of taxes, and investigation of tax offenses.[22] Thus, international examiners, revenue agents, tax auditors, revenue officers and special agents are all permitted to issue a summons.

When a corporation is under examination, the summons may be directed to either a specific corporate officer or the corporation itself.[23] The summons should indicate the officer's corporate position or title. When a summons is directed to the corporation, service must be made upon an officer, director, managing agent or other person authorized to accept service of process on behalf of the corporation.

After service of the summons, the individual serving the summons prepares and signs a certificate of service on the reverse side of the Form 2039 retained by the IRS. The date, time and manner of service are entered on the certificate. The signed certificate of service is evidence of the facts it states in any proceeding to enforce the summons.[24]

Scope of the summons power. The scope of the summons power extends to the production of records stored on magnetic tape.[25] It has also been held to require the production of videotapes[26] and microfiche copies of records.[27] The Supreme Court has even approved the use of a summons to compel handwriting exemplars.[28] However, the summons cannot require the creation of any documents, such as lists or schedules of factual information, which did not exist at the time the summons was issued.[29] Furthermore, significant restrictions exist on the ability to summons computer software.[30]

Although the authority to summon and to examine books and records is very extensive, it is not without limits. No taxpayer shall be subjected to unnecessary examination and prohibits more than one inspection of the taxpayer's books for each taxable year, unless the taxpayer requests otherwise or unless the IRS notifies the taxpayer in writing that an additional inspection is

---

[21] Code Sec.7602(a)(2).

[22] T.D. 6421, 1959-2 CB 433; Delegation Order No. 4.

[23] IRM 25.5.2.3.

[24] Code Sec. 7603.

[25] *G. Davey*, CA-2, 76-1 USTC ¶9724, 543 F2d 996 (2d Cir. 1976).

[26] *I.J. Schenk*, DC Ind., 84-1 USTC ¶9197, 581 FSupp 218; *A.A. Norton*, DC Calif., 81-1 USTC ¶9398.

[27] *Mobil Corp.*, DC Tex., 82-1 USTC ¶9242, 543 FSupp 507.

[28] *H.F. Euge*, SCt, 80-1 USTC ¶9222, 444 US 707, 100 SCt 874.

[29] *G. Davey, supra*, note 25; IRM Exhibit 25.5.1-2.

[30] Code Sec. 7612.

necessary.[31] The courts, as well as the IRS, generally have taken the position that there is no second inspection, even though the requested records were inspected previously, if the examination or investigation for the taxable year has not been completed or closed.[32]

The date fixed in the summons for compliance cannot be less than ten days from the date of the summons.[33] Agents are instructed that the time set for appearance should not be less than ten full calendar days from the date the summons is served.[34] This minimum allowable time for compliance is for the benefit of the summoned party and may be waived by an earlier voluntary compliance.

Proper use of IRS summons. An IRS summons may be used only for the purposes set forth in Code Sec. 7602. These purposes include the verification, determination and collection of the tax liability of any person. The IRS also has specific authorization to issue summonses for the purpose of investigating any criminal tax offense.[35]

The Supreme Court has stated that a summons will not be enforced if it has been issued for an improper purpose, such as to harass the taxpayer, pressure settlement of a collateral dispute or for any other purpose reflecting on the good faith of the particular investigation.[36] Enforcement of such a summons constitutes an abuse of the court's process.[37]

Use of summonses in Tax Court proceedings. The use of administrative summonses by the IRS during Tax Court proceedings has raised objections by taxpayers. The Tax Court discovery rules permitting both parties to obtain relevant information before trial are much more restricted in their scope than the summons power available to the IRS. In certain situations, the Tax Court has held that to allow the IRS in a pending case to use evidence obtained by the issuance of a summons would give the government an unfair advantage over the tax-payer. In substance, such use of the summons would permit the IRS to circumvent the limitations of the Tax Court's discovery rules. The Tax Court will issue protective orders to preclude the IRS from using information obtained by such abusive use of the administrative summons.[38]

In *Ash v. Commissioner*,[39] the Tax Court set forth guidelines which it would follow in determining whether such a protective order should be issued when the IRS obtains information during a pending case by means of a summons. Where litigation has commenced by the filing of a petition by the taxpayer, and a summons is then issued with regard to the same taxpayer and taxable year

---

[31] Code Sec. 7605(b).

[32] IRM 25.5.4.4.3; *S. Gilpin*, CA-7, 76-2 USTC ¶9636, 542 F2d 38 (7th Cir. 1976); *B. Silvestain*, CA-10, 82-1 USTC ¶9159, 668 F2d 1161 (10th Cir. 1982).

[33] Code Sec. 7605(a). A longer period is required for third-party recordkeeper summonses.

[34] IRM 25.5.3.4.

[35] Code Sec. 7602(b).

[36] *M. Powell*, SCt, 64-2 USTC ¶9858, 379 US 48, 85 SCt 248.

[37] For an excellent discussion of the possible abuse of process and improper use of an IRS summons demanding appearance at a police station for the taking of fingerprints, *see J.E. Michaud*, CA-7, 90-2 USTC ¶50,425, 907 F2d 750 (7th Cir. 1990).

[38] Tax Court Rule 103.

[39] 96 TC 459, Dec. 47,221.

¶1704

involved in the case, the Tax Court will issue a protective order to prevent the IRS from using any of the summoned evidence in the litigation.[40] However, in such a situation, the Court will not issue a protective order if the IRS can show that the summons was issued for a sufficient reason that was independent of the pending litigation.

In those cases where the summons is issued before the taxpayer files a Tax Court petition, no order will be issued with respect to any information obtained as a result of the summons. The Tax Court in *Ash* explained that, before a petition is filed, the Court has no jurisdiction and there is no basis for viewing the summons as an attempt to undermine the Court's discovery rules.

In the third situation dealt with in *Ash*, where litigation has commenced, and an administrative summons is issued with regard to a different taxpayer or a different taxable year, the Tax Court normally will not issue a protective order.[41] However, the Court stated that it would do so if the taxpayer could show that the IRS lacked an independent and sufficient reason for the summons.

Designated Summonses

To give force and meaning to this general authority to examine, the IRS has been granted the power to compel a taxpayer or any other person to produce records and to testify under oath. This compulsory process is authorization to the IRS to issue an administrative summons.[42] If, after issuing a summons, the IRS does not obtain the desired information in a timely manner, the IRS may consider issuing a designated summons.[43]

A designated summons tolls the running of the statute of limitations during the period in which judicial enforcement proceedings are pending, and for either 30 or 120 days thereafter, depending on whether or not the court orders compliance with the summons. The legislative history indicates Congress was concerned that taxpayers made a practice of responding slowly to IRS requests for information without extending the statute of limitations. Congress did not intend to extend the statute of limitations in a large number of cases, but to encourage taxpayers to provide requested information on a timely basis by realizing that the IRS had this tool available. The internal procedures the IRS personnel have to follow to issue a designated summons are a major impediment to their issuance. In addition to the International Examiner and the case manager, a designated summons is generally approved by the appropriate Area Counsel and Associate Chief Counsel (International).

> **Example 17.1:** A distributor of computers, USAco is a subsidiary of ASIAco. USAco buys computers from ASIAco and resells them in the U.S. The IRS's International Examiner conducts a transfer pricing audit of USAco. After USAco fails to respond to the International Examiner's IDR requesting all agreements between USAco and ASIAco, only 60 days remain

---

[40] The Tax Court issued such an order in *Universal Manufacturing Co.*, 93 TC 589, Dec. 46,154.

[41] In an earlier case involving this type of situation, the issuance of a protective order was justified by the "compelling facts." *Westreco, Inc.*, 60 TCM 824, Dec. 46,882(M), TC Memo. 1990-501.

[42] Code Sec. 7602(a)(2).

[43] Code Sec. 6503(j).

on the statute of limitations. USAco will not sign a consent to extend the statute of limitations. As a result, the International Examiner issues a designated summons for the agreements. The designated summons tolls the statute of limitations during enforcement proceedings and for a short time thereafter.

Code Sec. 6038A

Congressional perception that foreign-owned U.S. subsidiaries were not paying their proper share of U.S. tax and the inability of the IRS to obtain foreign-based documentation caused Congress to expand greatly the application of Code Sec. 6038A. The section places the reporting burden for intercompany transactions on the 25 percent or greater foreign-owned corporation with a U.S. branch. These U.S. taxpayers, the "reporting corporations," must furnish certain information annually and maintain records necessary to determine the correctness of the intercompany transactions. In addition, the reporting corporation must furnish the required information by filing Form 5472 on an annual basis.

Reg. § 1.6038A-3(a)(1) provides that "[a] reporting corporation must keep the permanent books of account or records as required by Code Sec. 6001 that are sufficient to establish the correctness of the federal income tax return of the corporation, including information, documents, or records ('records') to the extent they may be relevant to determine the correct U.S. tax treatment of transactions with related parties." Such records may include cost data, if appropriate, to determine the profit or loss on intercompany products and services.

Failure to maintain or timely furnish the required information may result in a penalty of $10,000 for each taxable year in which the failure occurs for each related party.[44] If any failure continues for more than ninety days after notice of the failure to the reporting corporation, an additional penalty of $10,000 per thirty-day period is imposed while the failure continues. Additional penalties can be levied if it is determined the taxpayer failed to maintain records after the ninety-day notification.[45]

Within thirty days after a request by the IRS, a foreign-related party must appoint the reporting corporation as its limited agent. Failure to appoint such an agent can result in penalties for noncompliance.[46] In such a case, the LMSB Industry Director in his or her sole discretion shall determine the amount of the relevant deduction or the cost to the reporting corporation.

The IRS is prepared to follow the letter of the law as shown in *Asat, Inc. v. Commissioner*.[47] Code Sec. 6038A(e) allows the IRS to reduce the cost of goods sold when a taxpayer does not obtain its foreign parent's permission to be an agent for the request of certain documents. In *Asat*, the Tax Court literally applied Code Sec. 6038A(e) against the taxpayer, upholding the IRS's reduction to the cost of goods sold. Adhering to the legislative history, the Tax Court further

---

[44] Reg. § 1.6038A-4(a)(1).
[45] *Id.* Reg. § 1.6038A-4(d)(1).

[46] *Id.* Reg. § 1.6038A-5.
[47] 108 TC 147, Dec. 51,966.

¶1704

found irrelevant that the foreign parent during the year in issue was not the parent at the time of the audit.

> **Example 17.2:** A distributor of toy dolls, USAco is a subsidiary of ASIAco. USAco buys toy dolls from ASIAco and resells them in the U.S. The IRS's International Examiner conducts a transfer pricing audit of USAco. Pursuant to Code Sec. 6038A, the International Examiner requests any pricing studies that ASIAco conducted. If ASIAco does not give them to USAco to provide the International Examiner, the IRS can reduce USAco's cost of goods sold to $0.

Exchanges Of Information Under Treaties

Under the exchange of information provisions of a treaty, the IRS can generally request information from a foreign country that is either in the foreign country's possession or available under the respective taxation laws of that foreign country. These provisions generally do not require the exchange of information that would disclose any trade or business secret.

The IRS exercises discretion and judgment in both requesting and furnishing of information. In general, the IRS will not request information from another country unless: (i) there is a good reason to believe that the information is necessary in the determination of the tax liability of a specific taxpayer; (ii) the information is not otherwise available to the IRS; and (iii) the IRS is reasonably sure that requested information is in the possession of, or available to, the foreign government from whom the information is being requested.

> **Example 17.3:** A distributor of sports shoes, USAco is a subsidiary of ASIAco. USAco buys sports shoes from ASIAco and resells them in the U.S. The IRS's International Examiner conducts a transfer pricing audit of USAco. After USAco fails to respond to the International Examiner's IDR requesting all agreements between USAco and ASIAco, the International Examiner requests the information from ASIA country's tax authority pursuant to the exchange of information provision in the U.S.-ASIA treaty.

The IRS's internal guidelines require that information sought from another competent authority must specifically describe the information desired and the reason why the information is necessary.[48]

¶1705 CONCLUSION OF AN EXAMINATION

At the conclusion of the examination, the international examiner will prepare a report summarizing the findings. The report is then incorporated into the field agent's report. Any disputed issues from the international examiner's report may be pursued with the Appeals Office along with other domestic issues raised during the examination.

---

[48] IRM 4.60.1.2.4.2.

Settling Issues

Certain issues over which there is disagreement may be settled by the case manager under the authority of Code Sec. 7121. This authority exists where the Appeals Office has previously approved a settlement agreement involving the same issue in a Coordinated Industry examination in a prior year involving the same taxpayer or a taxpayer directly involved in the taxable transaction.[49] The following conditions must be present for the case manager to have jurisdiction to settle an issue: (i) substantially the same facts must be involved in both examination years, (ii) the legal authority must not have changed, (iii) the issue must have been settled on its merits and not have been settled in exchange for the taxpayer's concession on another issue and (iv) the issue must concern the same taxpayer or a taxpayer who was directly involved in the settled transaction.

Accelerated Issue Resolution

Another option available in Coordinated Industry cases for unresolved issues is the accelerated issue resolution (AIR) program. The purpose of this program is to advance the resolution of issues from one tax period to another. Under this program, the taxpayer enters into an AIR agreement that acts as a closing agreement with respect to one or more issues present in a LMSB examination for one or more periods ending before the date of the agreement.[50] Revenue procedure 94-67 explains the scope and procedure for obtaining an AIR agreement. An AIR agreement may only be entered into for issues which fall under the jurisdiction of the LMSB Industry Director and which relate to other items in another tax period. An AIR agreement may not be entered into for transfer pricing transactions, partnership items or any item designated for litigation by the Office of Chief Counsel.[51] Because the AIR program is voluntary, the taxpayer must submit a written request to the case manager. If the request is denied, the taxpayer has no right to appeal an AIR determination.

Early Appeals Referral

If the issue is one that is not within the LMSB team manager's settlement jurisdiction, the taxpayer may elect to use the early appeals referral procedures and have the issue considered by the Appeals Office while the audit work continues in other areas. The IRS has instituted the early referral program for Coordinated Industry cases in order to expedite the resolution of unagreed issues. Early referral is optional, it must be initiated by the taxpayer and it is subject to the approval of both the LMSB Industry Director and the Appeals-LMSB Area Manager.[52] Early referral cannot be requested for issues that have been designated for litigation. The early referral request must be submitted in writing, stating the issues and positions involved. It must contain a perjury statement and it must be signed by the Coordinated Industry taxpayer or an authorized representative.[53] The taxpayer will be notified within forty-five days

---

[49] IRM 4.45.15.2.1.

[50] Rev. Proc. 94-67, 1994-2 CB 800.

[51] *Id.*

[52] Rev. Proc. 99-28, 1999-2 CB 109.

[53] *Id.*

whether the early referral was granted. If the request is granted, the file is forwarded to the Appeals Office. The taxpayer cannot appeal a refusal to grant early referral.

¶1706 APPEALS DIVISION OF THE IRS

Protest Requirements

Upon completion of an international examination, the examining office may issue the taxpayer a thirty-day letter proposing a deficiency. The taxpayer may object to any proposed tax adjustments and request a conference with the Appeals Office by filing a protest with the Appeals Office. The taxpayer must formally request the conference by means of a document known as a protest. The protest must be in writing and must include certain elements to meet the requirements of the Appeals Office.[54]

Procedure at the Appeals Division

Proceedings before the Appeals Office are informal. Testimony is not taken under oath, although the Appeals Office may require matters alleged to be true to be submitted in the form of affidavits or declarations under the penalties of perjury. The taxpayer or the representative will meet with the appeals officer and informally discuss the pros and cons of the various positions taken by the taxpayer and the IRS. Under the Regulations, Appeals will follow the law and the recognized stands of legal construction in determining facts and applying the law. Appeals will determine the correct amount of the tax with strict impartiality as between the taxpayer and the Government, and without favoritism or discrimination between taxpayers.[55]

Although an appeals officer is to maintain the standard of impartiality set forth in the Conference and Practice rules, he or she must, nevertheless, protect the rights of the IRS and act as an advocate on its behalf. Therefore, an appeals officer can raise a new issue or propose a new theory in support of the examining agent's proposed adjustment. However, an appeals officer generally will not do so unless the grounds for raising such new issues are substantial and the effect on the tax liability is material.[56]

Appeals Process For a Coordinated Industry Case

Unlike normal audit and appeal procedures, however, in a Coordinated Industry Case, members of the examination team from LMSB and Appeals personnel are authorized and, in some instances, required to hold a conference before Appeals Office personnel meet with the taxpayer.[57] The purpose of this unique pre-conference is to discuss the issues, the taxpayer's protest and the written rebuttal by the LMSB team members to the protest. Such a conference also serves to identify the need for additional information and development of issues.

---

[54] Reg. § 601.106(a)(iii).
[55] Reg. § 601.106(f)(1).

[56] IRM 8.6.1.4.
[57] IRM 8.6.1.2.7.

It is expected at this pre-conference that lines of communication will be established between the appeals and the examiners that will be maintained throughout the case. Although the examination team is encouraged during this meeting to share its views on the issues, including its assessment of litigating hazards, the parties are specifically instructed that the conference is not to be used as a means for securing a commitment from Appeals that any particular issue should be defended or the manner in which the case should be settled.[58] In substance, despite such intimate discussions of the case, the parties to the pre-conference are reminded that the detached objectivity of Appeals is not to be compromised.

Settlement Agreements

The IRS describes the "appeals mission" as one to resolve tax controversies without litigation, on a basis that is fair and impartial to both the government and the taxpayer and in a manner that will enhance voluntary compliance and public confidence in the integrity and efficiency of the IRS.[59] Thus, the appeals officer can split or trade issues where there are substantial uncertainties as to the law, the facts or both. In splitting a "legal issue," the appeals officer will ordinarily consider the hazards which would exist if the case were litigated. He will weigh the testimony of the proposed witnesses, judge the trends that the court has been following in similar cases and generally try to predict the outcome of the matter if the case were actually tried. Where a case involves concessions by both the government and the taxpayer "for purposes of settlement," and where there is substantial uncertainty as to how the courts would interpret and apply the law or what facts the court would find, a settlement is classified as a "mutual concession settlement." According to the regulations, no settlement is to be made simply on nuisance value.

Where a taxpayer and the appeals officer have reached an agreement as to some or all of the issues in controversy, generally the appeals officer will request the taxpayer to sign a Form 870, the same agreement used at the examination level. However, when neither party with justification is willing to concede in full the unresolved area of disagreement and a resolution of the dispute involves concessions for the purposes of settlement by both parties based on the relative strengths of the opposing positions, a "mutual concession settlement" is reached, and a Form 870-AD type of agreement is to be used.[60]

The special appeals Form 870-AD differs from the normal Form 870 in several ways. The Form 870-AD agreement contains pledges against reopening which the usual agreement does not. Furthermore, the normal 870 becomes effective as a Waiver of Restrictions on Assessment when received by the IRS, whereas the special 870-AD is effective only upon acceptance by or on behalf of the Commissioner of Internal Revenue. Finally, the running of interest is suspended thirty days after a Form 870 is received,[61] whereas with a Form 870-AD,

---

[58] *Id.*

[59] IRM 8.6.1.3.

[60] IRM 8.8.1.1.2.

[61] Code Sec. 6601(c). (Forms 870 and 870-AD are reproduced in the appendix to this chapter.)

interest is not suspended until thirty days after the agreement is executed by the government.

The finality of the Form 870-AD has been the subject of substantial litigation. The form provides that upon acceptance by or on behalf of the Commissioner, "the case shall not be reopened in the absence of fraud, malfeasance, concealment or misrepresentation of material fact, [or] an important mistake in mathematical calculation . . . and no claim for refund or credit shall be filed or prosecuted for the year(s) stated . . . "

Furthermore, the form states in language similar to that contained in a normal 870 that it is not a final closing agreement under Code Sec. 7121 and does not extend the statutory period of limitations on refund, assessment or collection of tax. A controversy may arise where a taxpayer, after executing a Form 870-AD, pays the tax, files a claim for refund and brings suit in the district court or the Court of Federal Claims. Under this scenario, the taxpayer takes the position that Code Sec. 7121 of the Internal Revenue Code is the exclusive method by which the IRS may enter into a final and binding agreement and since the Form 870-AD specifically repudiates reference to this section, the taxpayer is not bound by the agreement.

¶1707 COMPETENT AUTHORITY PROCESS

Generally, if the taxpayer has been unable to agree with the Appeals office on an adjustment that results in double taxation, the next course of action is to seek competent authority relief. An integral part of all U.S. Income Tax Treaties is a mutual agreement procedure which provides a mechanism for relief from double taxation. The Office of the Director-International acts as the U.S. competent authority. The competent authority's primary objective is to make a reasonable effort to resolve double taxation cases and situations in which U.S. taxpayers have been denied benefits provided for by a treaty.[62] The taxpayer may request competent authority when the actions of the U.S., the treaty country or both will result in taxation that is contrary to provisions of an applicable tax treaty. Revenue Procedure 2002-52[63] explains how to request assistance of the U.S. competent authority in resolving conflicts between treaty partners. To the extent a treaty partner proposes an adjustment which appears inconsistent with a treaty provision or would result in double taxation, competent authority assistance should be sought as soon as is practical after the issue is developed by the treaty country (Revenue Procedure 2002-52's index, which details specific procedures, is reproduced in the Appendix to this Chapter).

When the IRS proposes adjustments that are inconsistent with a treaty provision or would result in double taxation, the taxpayer is encouraged to seek competent authority relief after the amount of the proposed adjustment is determined and communicated to the taxpayer in writing. Generally, taxpayers must use the Appeals process to try to resolve the adjustments before competent authority assistance is sought. Where it is in the best interests of both parties,

---

[62] IRM 4.60.2.1.

[63] Rev. Proc. 2002-52, IRB 2002-31, 242.

competent authority assistance may begin prior to consideration by the Appeals office. However the U.S. competent authority may require the taxpayer to waive the right to the appeals process at any time during the competent authority process.

The opportunities to resolve disputes at Competent Authority have increased from the traditional Mutual Agreement Procedure to include the Simultaneous Appeals Procedure and the Accelerated Competent Authority Procedure. All these methods have the potential to resolve disputes of international tax issues in a manner that avoids litigation.

Mutual Agreement Procedure

The mutual agreement procedure ("MAP") articles generally apply when the actions of the U.S. or foreign income tax authorities result in taxation not in accordance with the provisions of the applicable treaty. Distribution, apportionment, or allocation under transfer pricing rules may subject a taxpayer to U.S. federal income taxation on income that the taxpayer had attributed to a foreign country. Without an offsetting decrease in income reported to the foreign country, the taxpayer may be subject to double taxation of the same income.

> **Example 14.4:** A distributor, USAco is a subsidiary of ASIAco. USAco buys widgets from ASIAco for $100 and resells them in the U.S. for $105. The IRS argues that the arm's-length price from ASIAco to USAco should be $90 and makes an assessment. Because $10 of income (the difference between the $100 ASIAco charged and the $90 the IRS believes is arm's-length) is taxed by both the IRS and ASIA's tax administration, either USAco or ASIAco can request relief from their respective competent authorities. The competent authorities will negotiate with each other to determine who will tax the $10.

Where it is in the best interest of both parties, Competent Authority assistance may begin prior to consideration by the Appeals Office.

Simultaneous Appeals Procedure

Under the Simultaneous Appeals Procedure ("SAP"), taxpayers may seek simultaneous Appeals and Competent Authority consideration of an issue.[64] This procedure allows taxpayers to obtain Appeals involvement in a manner consistent with the ensuing Competent Authority process and should reduce the time required to resolve disputes by allowing taxpayers more proactive involvement in the process. By informally approaching Competent Authority before submitting a formal request, the Competent Authority effectively becomes the taxpayer's advocate. SAP further opens the possibility of developing strategies to explore the view likely to be taken by the other country.

Taxpayers may request SAP with Competent Authority in three situations:

(i) after Examination has proposed an adjustment with respect to an issue that the taxpayer wishes to submit to Competent Authority;[65]

---

[64] *Id.* at §7.02. [65] *Id.* at §8.02(a)(1).

(ii) after Examination has issued a 30-day letter. The taxpayer can file a protest and decide to sever the issue and seek Competent Authority assistance while other issues are referred to or remain in Appeals;[66] or

(iii) after the taxpayer is in Appeals and it is evident that the taxpayer will request Competent Authority assistance on an issue.[67]

The taxpayer also can request SAP with Appeals after a Competent Authority request is made.[68] Generally, the request will be denied if the U.S. position paper has already been communicated to the foreign Competent Authority. The U.S. Competent Authority also can request the procedure.[69]

SAP is a two-part process. First, the Appeals representative will prepare an Appeals Case Memorandum ("ACM") on the issue. The ACM is shared with the Competent Authority representative, but not with the taxpayer. The ACM is a tentative resolution that is considered by the U.S. Competent Authority in preparing the U.S. position paper for presentation to the foreign Competent Authority.[70] Second, the U.S. Competent Authority prepares and presents the U.S. position paper to the foreign Competent Authority. The U.S. Competent Authority meets with the taxpayer to discuss the technical issue to be presented to the foreign Competent Authority and the Appeals representative may be asked to participate. If the Competent Authorities fail to agree or the taxpayer does not accept the mutual agreement reached, the taxpayer is allowed to refer the issue to Appeals for further consideration.[71]

Accelerated Competent Authority Procedure

The Accelerated Competent Authority Procedure ("ACAP") shortens the time required to complete a case.[72] A taxpayer requesting ACAP assistance with respect to an issue raised by the IRS may request that the competent authorities resolve the issue for subsequent tax years ending prior to the date of the request for the assistance.[73] In such a request, the taxpayer must agree that the inspection of books and/or records under the procedure will not preclude or impede a later examination or inspection for any period covered in the request; and the IRS need not comply with any procedural restrictions before beginning such examination or inspection. The U.S. Competent Authority will contact the appropriate LMSB Industry Director to determine whether the issue should be resolved for subsequent tax years. If the director consents, the U.S. Competent Authority will present the request to the foreign Competent Authority.[74]

¶1708 CIVIL ACTIONS BY TAXPAYERS

A taxpayer may contest an adverse IRS determination in one of three tribunals. A petition may be filed with the U.S. Tax Court, and assessment and

---

[66] *Id.* at §8.02(a)(2).

[67] *Id.* at §8.02(a)(3).

[68] *Id.* at §8.02(b).

[69] *Id.* at §8.01.

[70] This situation is analogous to the APA process. The Appeals representative will be a team chief, international specialist, or Appeals officer with international experience.

[71] *Id.* at §8.07.

[72] *Id.* at §7.06.

[73] *Id.*

[74] *Id.*

collection of the deficiency will be stayed until the Court's decision becomes final. Alternatively, the taxpayer may pay the deficiency including interest and penalties and sue for a refund in a U.S. District Court or the U.S. Court of Federal Claims.[75] A nonresident alien or foreign corporation is not a resident of any U.S. district and may only file a refund suit in the U.S. Court of Federal Claims.

Filing a Petition in the U.S. Tax Court does not require payment of any tax, penalties or interest until the taxpayer's liability has been finally determined. If, on the other hand, the taxpayer sues for a refund in the district court or the U.S. Court of Federal Claims, the taxpayer must initially pay the tax including interest and penalties.

In a suit brought in the district court the taxpayer may request that a jury determine factual issues.[76] A jury trial *cannot* be obtained before the U.S. Tax Court or the U.S. Court of Federal Claims. Many factors must be taken into consideration in selecting the forum, including previous rulings on the particular issue by the particular court and whether the issue is one that will affect tax liability for future years. A tax refund suit arising out of a tax treaty may be brought against the U.S. in either the U.S. Court of Federal Claims or the District Court.[77]

---

[75] Judicial Code Sec. 1346; Code Sec. 7422.
[76] 28 U.S.C. Sec. 2402.

[77] Code Sec. 7422(f)(1).

¶1751 Exhibit 17-1

Form **870** (Rev. March 1992)	Department of the Treasury — Internal Revenue Service **Waiver of Restrictions on Assessment and Collection of Deficiency** **in Tax and Acceptance of Overassessment**	Date received by Internal Revenue Service
Names and address of taxpayers *(Number, street, city or town, State, ZIP code)*		Social security or employer identification number

	Increase (Decrease) in Tax and Penalties				
Tax year ended	Tax	Penalties			
	$	$	$	$	$
	$	$	$	$	$
	$	$	$	$	$
	$	$	$	$	$
	$	$	$	$	$
	$	$	$	$	$
	$	$	$	$	$

(For instructions, see back of form)

Consent to Assessment and Collection

I consent to the immediate assessment and collection of any deficiencies *(increase in tax and penalties)* and accept any overassessment *(decrease in tax and penalties)* shown above, plus any interest provided by law. I understand that by signing this waiver, I will not be able to contest these years in the United States Tax Court, unless additional deficiencies are determined for these years.

YOUR SIGNATURE→ HERE		Date
SPOUSE'S SIGNATURE→		Date
TAXPAYER'S REPRESENTATIVE HERE →		Date
CORPORATE NAME →		
CORPORATE OFFICER(S) SIGN HERE	Title	Date
	Title	Date

Catalog Number 16894U   Form **870** (Rev. 3-92)

¶1752 Exhibit 17-2

Form **870-AD** (Rev. April 1992)	Department of the Treasury—Internal Revenue Service **Offer to Waive Restrictions on Assessment and Collection of Tax Deficiency and to Accept Overassessment**	
Symbols	Name of Taxpayer	SSN or EIN

Under the provisions of section 6213(d) of the Internal Revenue Code of 1986 (the Code), or corresponding provisions of prior internal revenue laws, the undersigned offers to waive the restrictions provided in section 6213(a) of the Code or corresponding provisions of prior internal revenue laws, and to consent to the assessment and collection of the following deficiencies and additions to tax, if any, with interest as provided by law. The undersigned offers also to accept the following overassessments, if any, as correct. Any waiver or acceptance of an overassessment is subject to any terms and conditions stated below and on the reverse side of this form.

		Deficiencies (Overassessments) and Additions to Tax			
Year Ended	Kind of Tax	Tax			
		$	$	$	
		$	$	$	
		$	$	$	
		$	$	$	
		$	$	$	
		$	$	$	

Signature of Taxpayer	Date
Signature of Taxpayer	Date
Signature of Taxpayer's Representative	Date
Corporate Name	Date
By Corporate Officer Title	Date

For Internal Revenue Use Only	Date Accepted for Commissioner	Signature
	Office	Title

Cat. No. 16896Q   **(See Reverse Side)**   Form **870-AD** (Rev. 4-92)

This offer must be accepted for the Commissioner of Internal Revenue and will take effect on the date it is accepted. Unless and until it is accepted, it will have no force or effect.

If this offer is accepted, the case will not be reopened by the Commissioner unless there was:

- fraud, malfeasance, concealment or misrepresentation of a material fact
- an important mistake in mathematical calculation
- a deficiency or overassessment resulting from adjustments made under Subchapters C and D of Chapter 63 concerning the tax treatment of partnership and subchapter S items determined at the partnership and corporate level
- an excessive tentative allowance of a carryback provided by law

No claim for refund or credit will be filed or prosecuted by the taxpayer for the years stated on this form, other than for amounts attributed to carrybacks provided by law.

The proper filing of this offer, when accepted, will expedite assessment and billing (or overassessment, credit or refund) by adjusting the tax liability. This offer, when executed and timely submitted, will be considered a claim for refund for the above overassessment(s), if any.

This offer may be executed by the taxpayer's attorney, certified public accountant, or agent provided this is specifically authorized by a power of attorney which, if not previously filed, must accompany this form. If this offer is signed by a person acting in a fiduciary capacity (for example: an executor, administrator, or a trustee) Form 56, Notice Concerning Fiduciary Relationship, must accompany this form, unless previously filed.

If this offer is executed for a year for which a joint return was filed, it must be signed by both spouses unless one spouse, acting under a power of attorney, signs as agent for the other.

If this offer is executed by a corporation, it must be signed with the corporate name followed by the signature and title of the officer(s) authorized to sign. If the offer is accepted, as a condition of acceptance, any signature by or for a corporate officer will be considered a representation by that person and the corporation, to induce reliance, that such signature is binding under law for the corporation to be assessed the deficiencies or receive credit or refund under this agreement. If the corporation later contests the signature as being unauthorized on its behalf, the person who signed may be subject to criminal penalties for representing that he or she had authority to sign this agreement on behalf of the corporation.

*U.S. GPO: 1992-617-016/49236

Form **870-AD** (Rev. 4-92)

¶1752

¶1753 Exhibit 17-3

Summons

In the matter of _____

Internal Revenue District of _____ Periods _____

The Commissioner of Internal Revenue

To: _____

At: _____

_____

You are hereby summoned and required to appear before _____,
an officer of the Internal Revenue Service, to give testimony and to bring with you and to produce for examination the following books, records, papers, and other data relating to the tax liability or the collection of the tax liability or for the purpose of inquiring into any offense connected with the administration or enforcement of the internal revenue laws concerning the person identified above for the periods shown.

Do not write in this space

Business address and telephone number of IRS officer before whom you are to appear:

_____

Place and time for appearance at _____

IRS

Department of the Treasury
Internal Revenue Service

www.irs.ustreas.gov

Form 2039 (Rev. 9-1999)
Catalog Number 21405J

on the _____ day of _____ , _____ at _____ o'clock _____ m.
(year)
Issued under authority of the Internal Revenue Code this _____ **day of** _____ , _____ .
(year)

_____
Signature of issuing officer

_____
Title

_____
Signature of approving officer *(if applicable)*

_____
Title

Original — to be kept by IRS

Service of Summons, Notice and Recordkeeper Certificates

(Pursuant to section 7603, Internal Revenue Code)

I certify that I served the summons shown on the front of this form on:

Date	Time

How Summons Was Served

1. ❏ I certify that I handed a copy of the summons, which contained the attestation required by § 7603, to the person to whom it was directed.

2. ❏ I certify that I left a copy of the summons, which contained the attestation required by § 7603, at the last and usual place of abode of the person to whom it was directed. I left the copy with the following person (if any):_____

3. ❏ I certify that I sent a copy of the summons, which contained the attestation required by § 7603, by certified or registered mail to the last known address of the person to whom it was directed, that person being a third-party recordkeeper within the meaning of § 7603(b). I sent the summons to the following address: _____

Signature	Title

4. This certificate is made to show compliance with IRC Section 7609. This certificate does not apply to summonses served on any officer or employee of the person to whose liability the summons relates nor to summonses in aid of collection, to determine the identity of a person having a numbered account or similar arrangement, or to determine whether or not records of the business transactions or affairs of an identified person have been made or kept.

I certify that, within 3 days of serving the summons, I gave notice (Part D of Form 2039) to the person named below on the date and in the manner indicated.

Date of giving Notice: _____   Time: _____

Name of Noticee: _____

Address of Noticee (if mailed): _____

How Notice Was Given

❏ I gave notice by certified or registered mail to the last known address of the noticee.

❏ I left the notice at the last and usual place of abode of the noticee. I left the copy with the following person (if any).

❏ I gave notice by handing it to the noticee.

❏ In the absence of a last known address of the noticee, I left the notice with the person summoned.

❏ No notice is required.

Signature	Title

I certify that the period prescribed for beginning a proceeding to quash this summons has expired and that no such proceeding was instituted or that the noticee consents to the examination.

Signature	Title

Form **2039** (Rev. 9-1999)

¶1754 Exhibit 17-4

Formal Document Request

Form **4564** (Rev. June 1988)	Department of the Treasury — Internal Revenue Service **Information Document Request**	Request number

To: (Name of Taxpayer and Company Division or Branch)	Subject
	SAIN number Submitted to:
	Dates of previous requests

Please return Part 2 with listed documents to requester identified below

Description of documents requested

Information due by _____	At next appointment ☐	Mail in ☐	
From:	Name and title of requester	Employee ID number	Date
	Office location		Telephone number

Catalog No. 23145K   Form **4564** (Rev. 6-1988)

¶1755 Exhibit 17-5

Your Appeal Rights and How To Prepare a Protest If You Don't Agree

Department of the Treasury
Internal Revenue Service

www.irs.ustreas.gov

Publication 5 **(Rev. 01-1999)**
Catalog Number 46074I

Introduction

This Publication tells you how to appeal your tax case if you don't agree with the Internal Revenue Service (IRS) findings.

If You Don't Agree

If you don't agree with any or all of the IRS findings given you, you may request a meeting or a telephone conference with the supervisor of the person who issued the findings. If you still don't agree, you may appeal your case to the Appeals Office of IRS.

If you decide to do nothing and your case involves an examination of your income, estate, gift, and certain excise taxes or penalties, you will receive a formal Notice of Deficiency. The Notice of Deficiency allows you to go to the Tax Court and tells you the procedure to follow. If you do not go to the Tax Court, we will send you a bill for the amount due.

If you decide to do nothing and your case involves a trust fund recovery penalty, or certain employment tax liabilities, the IRS will send you a bill for the penalty. If you do not appeal a denial of an offer in compromise or a denial of a penalty abatement, the IRS will continue collection action.

If you don't agree, we urge you to appeal your case to the Appeals Office of IRS. The Office of Appeals can settle most differences without expensive and time-consuming court trials. [Note: Appeals can not consider your reasons for not agreeing if they don't come within the scope of the tax laws (for example, if you disagree solely on moral, religious, political, constitutional, conscientious, or similar grounds.)]

The following general rules tell you how to appeal your case.

Appeals Within the IRS

Appeals is the administrative appeals office for the IRS. You may appeal most IRS decisions with your local Appeals Office. The Appeals Office is separate from - and independent of - the IRS Office taking the action you disagree with. The Appeals Office is the only level of administrative appeal within the IRS.

Conferences with Appeals Office personnel are held in an informal manner by correspondence, by telephone or at a personal conference. There is no need for you to have representation for an Appeals conference, but if you choose to have a representative, see the requirements under *Representation.*

If you want an Appeals conference, follow the instructions in our letter to you. Your request will be sent to the Appeals Office to arrange a conference at a convenient time and place. You or your representative should prepare to discuss all issues you don't agree with at the conference. Most differences are settled at this level.

In most instances, you may be eligible to take your case to court if you don't reach an agreement at your Appeals conference, or if you don't want to appeal your case to the IRS Office of Appeals. See the later section *Appeals To The Courts.*

Protests

When you request an appeals conference, you may also need to file a formal written protest or a small case request with the office named in our letter to you. Also, see the special appeal request procedures in Publication 1660, Collection Appeal Rights, if you disagree with lien, levy, seizure, or denial or termination of an installment agreement.

You need to file a written protest:

- In all employee plan and exempt organization cases without regard to the dollar amount at issue.

- In all partnership and S corporation cases without regard to the dollar amount at issue.

- In all other cases, unless you qualify for the small case request procedure, or other special appeal procedures such as requesting Appeals consideration of liens, levies, seizures, or installment agreements. See Publication 1660.

How to prepare a protest:

When a protest is required, **send it within the time limit specified in the letter you received.** Include in your protest:

1) Your name and address, and a daytime telephone number,

2) A statement that you want to appeal the IRS findings to the Appeals Office,

3) A copy of the letter showing the proposed changes and findings you don't agree with (or the date and symbols from the letter),

4) The tax periods or years involved,

5) A list of the changes that you don't agree with, and why you don't agree.

6) The facts supporting your position on any issue that you don't agree with,

7) The law or authority, if any, on which you are relying.

8) You must sign the written protest, stating that it is true, under the penalties of perjury as follows:

> **"Under the penalties of perjury, I declare that I examined the facts stated in this protest, including any accompanying documents, and, to the best of my knowledge and belief, they are true, correct, and complete."**

If your representative prepares and signs the protest for you, he or she must substitute a declaration stating:

1) That he or she submitted the protest and accompanying documents and

2) Whether he or she knows personally that the facts stated in the protest and accompanying documents are true and correct.

We urge you to provide as much information as you can, as this will help us speed up your appeal. This will save you both time and money.

Small Case Request:

If the total amount for any tax period is not more than $25,000, you may make a small case request instead of filing a formal written protest. In computing the total amount, include a proposed increase or decrease in tax (including penalties), or claimed refund. For an offer in compromise, in calculating the total amount, include total unpaid tax, penalty and interest due. For a small case request, follow the instructions in our letter to you by: sending a letter requesting Appeals consideration, indicating the changes you don't agree with, and the reasons why you don't agree.

Representation

You may represent yourself at your appeals conference, or you may have an attorney, certified public accountant, or an individual enrolled to practice before the IRS represent you. Your representative must be qualified to practice before the IRS. If you want your representative to appear without you, you must provide a properly completed power of attorney to the IRS before the representative can receive or inspect confidential information. Form 2848, Power of Attorney and Declaration of Representative, or any other properly written power of attorney or authorization may be used for this purpose. You can get copies of Form 2848 from an IRS office, or by calling 1-800-TAX-FORM (1-800-829-3676).

You may also bring another person(s) with you to support your position.

Appeals To The Courts

If you and Appeals don't agree on some or all of the issues after your Appeals conference, or if you skipped our appeals system, you may take your case to the United States Tax Court, the United States Court of Federal Claims, or your United States District Court, after satisfying certain procedural and jurisdictional requirements as described below under each court. (However, if you are a nonresident alien, you cannot take your case to a United States District Court.) These courts are independent judicial bodies and have no connection with the IRS.

Tax Court

If your disagreement with the IRS is over whether you owe additional income tax, estate tax, gift tax, certain excise taxes or penalties related to these proposed liabilities, you can go to the United States Tax Court. (Other types of tax controversies, such as those involving some employment tax issues or manufacturers' excise taxes, cannot be heard by the Tax Court.) You can do this after the IRS issues a formal letter, stating the amounts that the IRS believes you owe. This letter is called a notice of deficiency. You have 90 days from the date this notice is mailed to you to file a petition with the Tax Court (or 150 days if the notice is addressed to you outside the United States). The last date to file your petition will be entered on the notice of deficiency issued to you by the IRS. If you don't file the petition within the 90-day period (or 150 days, as the case may be), we will assess the proposed liability and send you a bill. You may also have the right to take your case to the Tax Court in some other situations, for example, following collection action by the IRS in certain cases. See Publication 1660.

If you discuss your case with the IRS during the 90-day period (150-day period), the discussion will not extend the period in which you may file a petition with the Tax Court.

The court will schedule your case for trial at a location convenient to you. You may represent yourself before the Tax Court, or you may be represented by anyone permitted to practice before that court.

Note: If you don't choose to go to the IRS Appeals Office before going to court, normally you will have an opportunity to attempt settlement with Appeals before your trial date.

If you dispute not more than $50,000 for any one tax year, there are simplified procedures. You can get information about these procedures and

other matters from the Clerk of the Tax Court, 400 Second St. NW, Washington, DC 20217.

Frivolous Filing Penalty

Caution: If the Tax Court determines that your case is intended primarily to cause a delay, or that your position is frivolous or groundless, the Tax Court may award a penalty of up to $25,000 to the United States in its decision.

District Court and Court of Federal Claims

If your claim is for a refund of any type of tax, you may take your case to your United States District Court or to the United States Court of Federal Claims. Certain types of cases, such as those involving some employment tax issues or manufacturers' excise taxes, can be heard only by these courts.

Generally, your District Court and the Court of Federal Claims hear tax cases only after you have paid the tax and filed a claim for refund with the IRS. You can get information about procedures for filing suit in either court by contacting the Clerk of your District Court or the Clerk of the Court of Federal Claims.

If you file a formal refund claim with the IRS, and we haven't responded to you on your claim within 6 months from the date you filed it, you may file suit for a refund immediately in your District Court or the Court of Federal Claims. If we send you a letter that proposes disallowing or disallows your claim, you may request Appeals review of the disallowance. If you wish to file a refund suit, you must file your suit no later than 2 years from the date of our notice of claim disallowance letter.

Note: Appeals review of a disallowed claim doesn't extend the 2 year period for filing suit. However, it may be extended by mutual agreement.

Recovering Administrative and Litigation Costs

You may be able to recover your reasonable litigation and administrative costs if you are the prevailing party, and if you meet the other requirements. You must exhaust your administrative remedies within the IRS to receive reasonable litigation costs. You must not unreasonably delay the administrative or court proceedings.

Administrative costs include costs incurred on or after the date you receive the Appeals decision letter, the date of the first letter of proposed deficiency, or the date of the notice of deficiency, whichever is earliest.

Recoverable litigation or administrative costs may include:

- Attorney fees that generally do not exceed $125 per hour. This amount will be indexed for a cost of living adjustment.

- Reasonable amounts for court costs or any administrative fees or similar charges by the IRS.

- Reasonable expenses of expert witnesses.

- Reasonable costs of studies, analyses, tests, or engineering reports that are necessary to prepare your case.

You are the prevailing party if you meet all the following requirements:

- You substantially prevailed on the amount in controversy, or on the most significant tax issue or issues in question.

- You meet the net worth requirement. For individuals or estates, the net worth cannot exceed $2,000,000 on the date from which costs are recoverable. Charities and certain cooperatives must not have more than 500 employees on the date from which costs are recoverable. And taxpayers other than the two categories listed above must not have net worth exceeding $7,000,000 and cannot have more than 500 employees on the date from which costs are recoverable.

You are not the prevailing party if:

- The United States establishes that its position was substantially justified. If the IRS does not follow applicable published guidance, the United States is presumed to not be substantially justified. This presumption is rebuttable. Applicable published guidance means regulations, revenue rulings, revenue procedures, information releases, notices, announcements, and, if they are issued to you, private letter rulings, technical advice memoranda and determination letters. The court will also take into account whether the Government has won or lost in the courts of appeals for other circuits on substantially similar issues, in determining if the United States is substantially justified.

You are also the prevailing party if:

- The final judgment on your case is less than or equal to a "qualified offer" which the IRS rejected, and if you meet the net worth requirements referred to above.

A court will generally decide who is the prevailing party, but the IRS makes a final determination of liability at the administrative level. This means you may receive administrative costs from the IRS without going to court. You must file your claim for administrative costs no later than the 90th day after the final determination of tax, penalty or interest is mailed to you. The Appeals Office makes determinations for the IRS on administrative costs. A denial of administrative costs may be appealed to the Tax Court no later than the 90th day after the denial.

¶1756 Exhibit 17-6

Rev. Proc. 2002-52

SECTION 1. PURPOSE OF THE REVENUE PROCEDURE

SECTION 2. SCOPE

.01 In General

.02 Requests for Assistance

.03 Authority of the U.S. Competent Authority

.04 General Process

.05 Failure to Request Assistance

SECTION 3. GENERAL CONDITIONS UNDER WHICH THIS PROCE-
DURE APPLIES

.01 General

.02 Requirements of a Treaty

.03 Applicable Standards in Allocation Cases

.04 Who Can File Requests for Assistance

.05 Closed Cases

.06 Foreign Initiated Competent Authority Request

.07 Requests Relating to Residence Issues

.08 Determinations Regarding Limitation on Benefits

SECTION 4. PROCEDURES FOR REQUESTING COMPETENT AU-
THORITY ASSISTANCE

.01 Time for Filing

.02 Place of Filing

.03 Additional Filing

.04 Form of Request

.05 Information Required

.06 Other Dispute Resolution Programs

.07 Other Documentation

.08 Updates

.09 Conferences

SECTION 5. SMALL CASE PROCEDURE FOR REQUESTING COMPE-
TENT AUTHORITY ASSISTANCE

.01 General

.02 Small Case Standards

.03 Small Case Filing Procedure

SECTION 6. RELIEF REQUESTED FOR FOREIGN INITIATED ADJUST-
MENT WITHOUT COMPETENT AUTHORITY INVOLVEMENT

SECTION 7. COORDINATION WITH OTHER ADMINISTRATIVE OR JUDICIAL PROCEEDINGS

.01 Suspension of Administrative Action with Respect to U.S. Adjustments

.02 Coordination with Appeals

.03 Coordination with Litigation

.04 Coordination with Other Alternative Dispute Resolution and Pre-Filing Procedures

.05 Effect of Agreements or Judicial Determinations on Competent Authority Proceedings

.06 Accelerated Competent Authority Procedure

SECTION 8. SIMULTANEOUS APPEALS PROCEDURE

.01 General

.02 Time for Requesting the Simultaneous Appeals Procedure

      (a) When Filing For Competent Authority Assistance

      (b) After Filing For Competent Authority Assistance

.03 Cases Pending in Court

.04 Request for Simultaneous Appeals Procedure

.05 Role of Appeals in the Competent Authority Process

      (a) Appeals Process

      (b) Assistance to U.S. Competent Authority

.06 Denial or Termination of Simultaneous Appeals Procedure

      (a) Taxpayer's Termination

      (b) Service's Denial or Termination

.07 Returning to Appeals

.08 Appeals Consideration of Non-Competent Authority Issues

SECTION 9. PROTECTIVE MEASURES

.01 General

.02 Filing a Protective Claim for Credit or Refund with a Competent Authority Request

      (a) In General

      (b) Treatement of Competent Authority Request as Protective Claim

.03 Protective Filing Before Competent Authority Request

      (a) In General

      (b) Letter to Competent Authority Treated as Protective Claim

      (c) Notification Requirement

      (d) No Consultation between Competent Authorities until Formal Request is Filed

¶1757 DISCUSSION QUESTIONS

1. Your client, State-Side Corporation, is a wholly owned U.S. subsidiary of Overseas, a large foreign conglomerate. State-Side purchases all its inventory from Overseas as well as paying it a substantial management fee. You have asked State-Side on several occasions for documentation to support the intercompany charges but with no success. You don't believe the intracorporate pricing is tax motivated. State-Side has recently been notified that it is under examination by the IRS and an international examiner has been assigned. As an independent public accountant, what course of action, if any, would you recommend that State-Side take?

2. Rust Belt Manufacturing Company's founder and chief executive officer takes pride in the fact that the company has always concluded its IRS examinations within three months of its initial meeting with the Appeals office. However, this is the company's first examination by an international examiner. The amount of income potentially subjected to double taxation (U.S. and foreign tax) is in excess of $500,000. As the one (and only) person in the tax department of Rust Belt, you have been asked to prepare a list of the advantages and disadvantages of pursuing competent authority relief.

3. The controller of Little Swiss, a subsidiary located in Geneva, has not responded to any requests for information as part of an IRS examination of Big Swiss, Inc., its U.S. parent. The controller in Geneva claims it would violate Swiss secrecy laws if the information sought by the IRS was disclosed. Does the controller have any legal basis for not providing this information to the IRS? Explain in full.

4. As a newly trained international examiner, you have recently been assigned to your first examination. The examination is of Mega Corporation, a publicly held company with 30 foreign subsidiaries. Mega employs 60 full-time tax professionals. How would you approach the examination?

5. Corrugated, U.S.A., is a corporation which manufactures machinery used in the paper industry. Corrugated International, a wholly owned subsidiary of Corrugated, U.S.A., is located in Zurich, Switzerland. The IRS is conducting an audit of Corrugated, U.S.A., and, in connection with an examination of intercompany transfers between Corrugated, U.S.A., and Corrugated International, the IRS has asked to see the books of the foreign subsidiary. In the absence of voluntary compliance, the IRS issued a summons to Corrugated, U.S.A., requesting the books and records of Corrugated International. Corrugated, U.S.A., contends that the IRS is precluded from using a summons to gather information on Corrugated International since the business records are held in Switzerland. Must Corrugated, U.S.A., comply with the summons?

CHAPTER 18
CRIMINAL TAX PROCEDURE

¶1801 INTRODUCTION

Our system of taxation is based on the concept of voluntary compliance with the Internal Revenue laws. To encourage compliance and deter taxpayers from violating the law, the Criminal Investigation (CI) personnel of the Internal Revenue Service (IRS) investigates and recommends prosecution of those who commit tax offenses.[1] The specially trained field agents who conduct these criminal investigations are referred to as special agents.

Information from various sources may prompt a criminal tax investigation. A routine examination by a revenue agent may disclose indications of fraud. A disgruntled employee, spurned lover, estranged wife, business associate, neighbor or acquaintance may furnish incriminating information to CI. Newspaper articles and other news reports may reveal activity which suggests possible tax evasion. Information obtained during a routine audit or criminal investigation of one taxpayer may implicate another taxpayer. Information returns filed with the IRS, such as Forms 1099 and W-2, may disclose unreported income. Reports of currency transactions in excess of $10,000 which must be filed with the IRS also may provide a basis for initiating a criminal investigation.[2]

From 1979 to 1999, CI had increasingly devoted more of its resources to the investigation and prosecution of drug dealers, money launderers, organized crime figures, gamblers, those involved in procurement and bank fraud and others who receive substantial income from illegal activities. Notwithstanding a recommendation by the American Bar Association (ABA) that this trend be

---

[1] It is currently the practice of the IRS that a voluntary disclosure will be considered along with all other factors in the investigation in determining whether criminal prosecution will be recommended. Prior IRS voluntary disclosure practices creates no substantive or procedural rights for taxpayers but rather a matter of internal IRS practice, provided solely for guidance to IRS personnel.

A voluntary disclosure will not guarantee immunity from prosecution, yet a voluntary disclosure may result in no prosecution recommendation. However, since the IRS application of the voluntary disclosure practice does not automatically result in immunity from criminal prosecution, taxpayers should be advised that they cannot rely on the fact that others may not have been prosecuted.

A voluntary disclosure occurs when the communication is:

(a) Truthful.
(b) Timely.
(c) Complete.

(d) When the taxpayer shows a willingness to cooperate (and does in fact cooperate) with the IRS in determining his or her correct tax liability.

A disclosure is timely if it is received before:

(a) The IRS has initiated an inquiry that is likely to lead to the taxpayer, and the taxpayer is reasonably thought to be aware of that investigative activity.

(b) Some event known by the taxpayer occurred, which event is likely to cause an audit into the taxpayer's liabilities. IRM Handbook 9.5.3.3.1.2.1.

[2] Banks and other financial institutions must report currency transactions in excess of $10,000 on Form 4789, Currency Transaction Report (Exhibit 18-1 at ¶1851). See 31 U.S.C. §5313 and 31 CFR §103.22. Any person engaged in a trade or business who receives more than $10,000 in currency also must report the transaction on Form 8300 (Exhibit 18-2 at ¶1852), Code Sec. 6050I.

reversed,[3] in 1992 the IRS Commissioner decided to continue CI's focus on financial crimes.[4] Recently, CI has indicated that the primary focus will now be to investigate violations of the Internal Revenue Code. It will emphasize the deterrent effect of such prosecutions on ordinary taxpayers not involved in other criminal activity.[5]

¶1805   STATUTORY OFFENSES

The criminal statutes under which tax offenses may be prosecuted are not all contained in the Internal Revenue Code, found at Title 26 of the United States Code. Some broadly defined crimes frequently charged in tax cases, such as conspiracy, are found in the Criminal Code, found at Title 18 of the United States Code. In addition, the criminal penalties enforced by CI for violating the currency and other reporting requirements of the Bank Secrecy Act are set forth in Title 31 of the United States Code.

¶1808   CRIMES UNDER THE INTERNAL REVENUE CODE

The principal offenses under the Internal Revenue Code are contained in Code Secs. 7201 through 7207. In general these criminal statutes seek to punish only those who "willfully" violate the law. The Supreme Court has defined "willfully" as used in these tax offenses to mean "a voluntary, intentional violation of a known legal duty."[6] Under this definition, ignorance of the tax law or a misunderstanding of that law is a valid defense to any of these tax charges regardless of how objectively unreasonable such a claim may appear.[7] However, the jury or trier of fact weighs the credibility of testimony that a defendant believed in good faith that he or she was not violating the tax laws.[8]

Tax Evasion. Code Sec. 7201 provides that "[a]ny person who *willfully* attempts in any manner to evade or defeat any tax imposed by" Title 26 shall be guilty of a felony. To convict anyone of this crime, the government must prove beyond a reasonable doubt three elements: (1) a tax deficiency, (2) an affirmative act constituting an evasion or attempted evasion of the tax, and (3) willfulness.[9] The government may prove understatement of tax either by the specific-item method or by one of the indirect methods of reconstructing income discussed in Chapter 19, *infra*. With the specific-item method, the government attempts to

---

[3] See *Redirecting Criminal Tax Enforcement to Improve Voluntary Compliance*, 1991 A.B.A. Sec. Tax'n Crim. Pol'y Rep. (Aug. 1991). The report was approved by eight former Commissioners.

[4] See *IRS Decision to Keep Criminal Investigation Focus on Illegal Sector Raises Questions*, Daily Tax Rep. (BNA), at G-2 (Jan. 24, 1992).

[5] IRS News Release, IR-2000-46 (July 3, 2000).

[6] *United States v. Pomponio*, 429 U.S. 10, 12 (1976), 76-2 USTC ¶9695, quoting *United States v. Bishop*, 412 U.S. 346, 360 (1973), 73-1 USTC ¶9459.

[7] See *Cheek v. United States*, 498 U.S. 192 (1991), 91-1 USTC ¶50,012. The defendant in *Cheek* testified that he believed his wages did not constitute taxable

income and did not have to be reported. See *Ratzlaf v. United States*, 510 U.S. 135 (1994), 94-1 USTC ¶50,015. The Government must prove that the defendant acted with knowledge that his conduct was unlawful. Cf. *Bryan v. United States*, 524 U.S. 184 (1998). In *Bryan* the Court distinguished *Cheeks* and *Ratzlaf* by explaining that the highly technical statutes of those cases carved out an exception from the traditional rule that ignorance of the law is no excuse.

[8] *Id.*

[9] See *Sansone v. United States*, 380 U.S. 343, 351 (1965), 65-1 USTC ¶9307; *United States v. Eaken*, 17 F.3d 203 (7th Cir. 1994), 94-1 USTC ¶50,098.

prove that the taxpayer intentionally omitted individual items of income or falsely reported specific expenses.

An affirmative act constituting an attempt to evade or defeat a tax is any conduct, "the likely effect of which would be to mislead or conceal."[10] Filing a false or fraudulent tax return is the affirmative act most frequently cited as the basis for an evasion charge. Other examples include: (1) keeping a double set of books, (2) making false entries or alterations, (3) making false invoices or documents, (4) destroying books or records, (5) concealing assets or covering up sources of income, and (6) handling one's affairs to avoid making the usual records in such transactions.[11]

In evasion cases, "willfulness" is the element most frequently contested. As previously discussed, the government must prove the taxpayer intentionally, not inadvertently, understated his or her taxes and knew that to do so was wrong. Unless the taxpayer has admitted wrongdoing, "willfulness" is normally proved by means of circumstantial evidence. Proof of substantial understatements over a period of years is one example of such evidence.

The IRS requires that various criteria, referred to as prosecution guidelines, be met before prosecution of certain tax offenses will be recommended. These guidelines are not officially published and have become selectively available only as a result of Freedom of Information Act requests.[12] For prosecution under Code Sec. 7201, previously released guidelines require that the average annual understatement of tax for a specific-item case involving uncomplicated fact patterns exceeds a stated average yearly amount of additional tax. For an indirect-method case or a complex and sophisticated evasion scheme, the amount of understatement required was significantly higher. For lesser dollar amounts in complex cases, prosecution may be considered appropriate for egregious, flagrant or repetitious conduct.[13]

The maximum sentence under Code Sec. 7201 cannot exceed five years of imprisonment and a fine of $100,000 for individuals or $500,000 for organizations.[14] Technically, each count of an indictment charging tax evasion subjects the defendant to the maximum term of imprisonment and fine. Thus, an individual taxpayer charged with evasion over a three-year period could be sentenced to a maximum term of imprisonment for 15 years and a maximum fine of $300,000. As a practical matter, however, the Sentencing Guidelines established by Congress provide narrow parameters within which a defendant must be sentenced and fined.[15] The Sentencing Guidelines apply to any federal offense committed after November 1, 1987. The Guidelines have increased the average sentence of imprisonment formerly imposed on tax offenders. The mandatory term of im-

---

[10] *Spies v. United States,* 317 U.S. 492, 499 (1943), 43-1 USTC ¶ 9243.

[11] *Id.*

[12] See *IRS Releases Its Criteria For Criminal Tax Prosecutions,* FED. TAX. WK. ALERT (RIA), at 34 (Jan. 18, 1996).

[13] See *Law Enforcement Manual IX* (Exhibit 18-3 at ¶ 1853); see also *LGM Sets Dollar Amount Triggering Evasion Prosecutions,* TAX NOTES, at 266 (January 15, 1996), and 1995 IRS LGM Lexus 6, October 16, 1995.

[14] Maximum fines for all felonies have been established at not more than $250,000 for individuals and $500,000 for organizations. 18 U.S.C. § 3571.

[15] *Id.* § § 3551-3586. For specific guidelines, see the *Federal Sentencing Guidelines* published annually in Title 18 of the United States Code.

¶1808

prisonment for tax evasion falls within a narrow range and is calculated on the basis of the tax loss determined for the years under investigation and the criminal history of the defendant.[16]

False Return. Code Sec. 7206(1) imposes criminal sanctions on any person who *willfully* signs "any return . . . or other document verified by a written declaration that it is made under the penalties of perjury . . . which [the signer] does not believe to be true and correct as to every material matter." A false return charge under this section is frequently recommended by the IRS when it appears that a tax deficiency or understatement may be difficult to prove. Unlike tax evasion under Code Sec. 7201, a false return charge under Code Sec. 7206(1) does not require proof that tax was understated. The government is only required to prove that one "material" item on the tax return was intentionally falsified. If gross business receipts have been understated and offsetting unreported deductions are a potential defense to tax evasion, the government may simply resort to a charge under Code Sec. 7206(1) rather than Code Sec. 7201 to avoid the doubt raised by such a defense. Proof of the intentionally false gross receipts would be sufficient.

Whether a false item on the return is a material matter is a question of law which the court decides, not the jury. Obviously, substantial amounts of gross income or deductions falsely reported on a tax return would be material. The false description of illegal kickbacks as miscellaneous interest income has also been held to be material and may be prosecuted even though there is no deficiency.[17]

The maximum sentence that may be imposed for subscribing to a false return or other document[18] is three years imprisonment and a fine of $100,000 for individuals or $500,000 for corporations. For all practical purposes, however, the Sentencing Guidelines will control the actual prison term and fine for this felony.

Aiding or Assisting. Code Sec. 7206(2) states that the criminal sanction is aimed at those who *willfully* aid, assist, advise or counsel the preparation of a return or other document which is fraudulent or false with respect to any material matter. This provision is primarily directed at accountants, attorneys and others who prepare false returns or provide advice or information for tax return purposes that is knowingly false. The government is not required to prove that the taxpayer filing the false return or other document was aware of or consented to the fraud. The maximum term of imprisonment and maximum fine under Code Sec. 7206(2) are the same as those under Code Sec. 7206(1), and the Sentencing Guidelines will control the actual sentence imposed.

Failure to File. Code Sec. 7203 contains the criminal sanction which punishes those who *willfully* fail to file returns.[19] This is a misdemeanor, a lesser

---

[16] See *United States Sentencing Commission Guidelines Manual,* §§ 2T1.1, 2T1.4, 2T1.6, 2T1.9 and 2T4.1.

[17] See *United States v. Hedman,* 630 F.2d 1184 (7th Cir. 1980), *cert. denied,* 450 U.S. 965 (1981).

[18] For a prosecution involving the signing of a false Form 433-A, Collection Information Statement

for Individuals, see *United States v. Holroyd,* 732 F.2d 1122 (2d Cir. 1984), 84-1 USTC ¶ 9423.

[19] Code Sec. 7203 also punishes willful failure to pay taxes, maintain records or supply information, but is rarely used for these purposes. If any Code

crime, which recognizes that the failure to act should be punished less severely than an affirmative act of fraud. However, if the failure to file is accompanied by some affirmative act which is intended to mislead or conceal, such as the submission to an employer of a false Form W-4 claiming tax-exempt status, the failure to file together with such affirmative act can be charged as an attempt to evade tax under Code Sec. 7201.

The maximum sentence for failure to file is one year of imprisonment and a fine of $25,000 for individuals and $100,000 for organizations.[20] Because each yearly failure to file a return constitutes a separate charge, the maximum sentence is cumulative for anyone who has willfully failed to file over a period of years. As a practical matter, however, the Sentencing Guidelines will control the term of imprisonment and the amount of fine within narrow limits which are normally well below the statutory maximum. The Guidelines are based on the criminal history of the defendant and the amount of tax loss to the government. The tax loss is the amount of the additional tax that should have been disclosed on the unfiled returns. The sentence imposed under the Guidelines may therefore increase with the increase in the number of years returns were not filed.

Altered or False Documents. Code Sec. 7207 states that the criminal sanction is directed at anyone who *willfully* submits or delivers to the IRS any document knowing it to be fraudulent or false as to any material matter. This offense is a misdemeanor punishable by a maximum term of imprisonment for oneyear and a maximum fine of $10,000 for individuals or $50,000 for organizations. The Sentencing Guidelines, however, will determine the actual sentence to be imposed.

The use of this misdemeanor charge has been limited to cases involving fraudulently altered documents, such as invoices and checks, submitted by taxpayers to IRS agents for the purpose of improperly gaining some tax benefit. A typical example would be the alteration of a cancelled check submitted to support a charitable contribution by raising the amount on the check from $50 to $500.

Other Code Offenses. Code Sec. 7204 is aimed at employers who *willfully* file false Forms W-2 or fail to furnish such forms to their employees. Code Sec. 7205 represents the converse of Code Sec. 7204 and penalizes employees who willfully submit false Forms W-4 or fail to submit such forms to their employers. Both crimes are misdemeanors punishable by a maximum of one year in prison and a maximum fine of $1,000. The actual sentence will be determined under the Sentencing Guidelines.

Other criminal provisions punish the willful failure to collect or pay over tax by persons responsible for withholding and paying over employment taxes (a felony) (Code Sec. 7202), failure to obey a summons (Code Sec. 7210), attempts to

---

(Footnote Continued)

Sec. 6050I willful violation occurs, the Code Sec. 7203 sentence is increased to five years.

[20] The maximum fine for all misdemeanors authorizing a maximum sentence of more than six months but not more than one year has been established at $100,000 for individuals and $200,000 for organizations. 18 U.S.C. §§ 3559(a)(6), 3571(b)(5) and (c)(5).

interfere with the administration of the Internal Revenue laws (Code Sec. 7212), unauthorized disclosure of information (Code Sec. 7213), and disclosure or use of information by preparers of returns (Code Sec. 7216).

Lesser-Included Offenses. In 1993, as the result of the Supreme Court's denial of certiorari in *Becker v. United States*,[21] the Tax Division of the Justice Department adopted a new position regarding lesser-included offenses stemming from prosecutions under Code Secs. 7201, 7203, 7206 and 7207. The Division has advised United States attorneys that where criminal tax evasion and another tax crime have been alleged, the government will take the position that neither party is entitled to an instruction on a lesser-included offense. Where the government has charged the filing of a false return under Code Sec. 7206 as an affirmative act in an evasion case, it will argue the defendant is not entitled to a lesser-included offense instruction because evasion may be established without proof of filing the return. If the government charges a defendant with making or subscribing a false tax return under Code Sec. 7206(1), it will argue that neither party is entitled to an instruction that willfully delivering or sending a false return under Code Sec. 7207 is a lesser-included offense.[22]

¶1811 OFFENSES UNDER THE CRIMINAL CODE

The Criminal Code contains several offenses which are frequently charged in tax prosecutions. These crimes involve conspiracies, false statements, false claims and money laundering; they are found in Title 18 of the United States Code.

Conspiracy. Section 371 of Title 18 provides that any two or more persons who conspire to commit any offense against the United States or who conspire to defraud the United States or any agency thereof shall be guilty of a felony punishable by a maximum term of imprisonment for five years and/or a fine. The maximum fine for conspiracy is $250,000 for individuals and $500,000 for organizations. The Sentencing Guidelines set the term of imprisonment and fine to be imposed for conspiracies committed after November 1, 1987.

The conspiracy statute is extremely broad in its coverage. In tax cases where two or more persons agree to commit an offense under Title 26, such as tax evasion, they may be prosecuted for the conspiracy as well as the underlying tax crime. The government must prove not only an agreement but also at least one "overt act" in furtherance of the conspiracy. The overt act need not be illegal in itself, and the agreement may be proved by circumstantial evidence. The conspiracy charge is favored by government prosecutors because it permits a number of defendants to be tried at the same time and allows the widest possible latitude in the offering of evidence.

In addition to conspiracies to commit federal crimes, Section 371 also punishes conspiracies to defraud the United States or any of its agencies in any manner and for any purpose. To conspire to defraud the United States means to interfere with or obstruct one of its lawful governmental functions by deceit, craft

---

[21] 965 F.2d 383 (7th Cir. 1992), 92-2 USTC ¶50,314, *cert. denied*, 507 U.S. 971 (1993).

[22] *Department of Justice Manual* (1995).

or trickery, or by means that are dishonest.[23] In tax cases, defendants will be charged with a conspiracy to defraud "by impeding, obstructing and defeating the lawful functions of the Department of the Treasury in the collection of the revenue, to wit, income taxes."[24] This extremely broad charge encompasses all forms of deceitful actions which interfere with the administration of the tax laws.

False Statements. Section 1001 of Title 18 provides that any person who knowingly and willfully falsifies, conceals or covers up any material fact or makes a false statement or representation in a matter within the jurisdiction of a department of the United States shall be guilty of a felony punishable by a maximum term of imprisonment for five years. The maximum fine is $250,000 for individuals and $500,000 for organizations. As in all other cases involving federal crimes, the actual sentence and fine imposed will be controlled by the Sentencing Guidelines.

This offense applies not only to false written statements or documents submitted to an IRS agent, but also to any false oral statements made to such agents. Such statements do not have to be made under oath or under the penalties of perjury. False oral statements made to a revenue agent during seemingly informal discussions can be the basis for prosecution under Section 1001.

False Refund Claims. Section 287 of Title 18 provides that anyone who makes or presents any claim upon or against the United States or any department or agency thereof, and who knows the claim to be false, fictitious or fraudulent, shall be guilty of a felony. The same maximum penalties apply under this section as under Section 1001 of Title 18, the false statement offense. The principal use of this section in tax cases is the prosecution of fraudulent refund claims.

Mail Fraud and Wire Fraud. Sections 1341 and 1343 of Title 18 provide criminal sanctions for any scheme to defraud in which the United States mail is used or any information is transmitted by wire, radio or television for the purpose of executing such scheme. The purpose of these statutes is to enable the prosecution of all types of fraud, particularly those which are not covered by any specific federal law. The elements of U.S. mail or interstate wire transmissions were added to create the necessary federal jurisdictional nexus to the power to regulate foreign and interstate commerce.[25]

Mail and wire fraud charges are often asserted in tax prosecutions of fraudulent schemes involving tax shelters, charitable contributions, money laundering and investment securities. There is some doubt that such charges may be

---

[23] See *Hammerschmidt v. United States*, 265 U.S. 182 (1924).

[24] *United States v. Klein*, 247 F.2d 908, 915 (2d Cir. 1957), 57-2 USTC ¶ 9912. This case provided the genesis for the term "Klein Conspiracy" which has become the generic term for a conspiracy to frustrate the government, particularly the IRS, in its lawful information-gathering function. See *United States v. Alston*, 77 F.3d 713, 717 n. 13 (3d Cir. 1996). The

Second Circuit has held that the *Klein* indictment language is not legally required in indictments for conspiracy to defraud if the essential nature of the fraud is alleged. See *United States v. Helmsley*, 941 F.2d 71 (2d Cir. 1991), 91-2 USTC ¶ 50,455, *cert. denied*, 502 U.S. 1091 (1992).

[25] Section 1347 of Title 18 added "Medicare fraud" to this list of tax related offenses.

¶1811

used in a straightforward tax evasion case where the mail fraud is based solely on the mailing of a false return.[26]

Money Laundering. Sections 1956 and 1957 of Title 18 are criminal offenses enacted in 1986 to attack the problems related to the concealment, laundering and use of money derived from unlawful activities. These money laundering sanctions contain very severe criminal penalties and forfeiture provisions. The Sentencing Guidelines impose equally harsh penalties. In general, anyone may be subject to prosecution who attempts to launder or deposit funds which are known to have come from specified unlawful activities.[27] Tax crimes are not included in such specified unlawful activities. However, the attempt to launder or conceal incomefrom such illicit activities is often related to the commission of tax offenses, such as tax evasion, false returns or the failure to file.

¶1814 CRIMES UNDER THE BANK SECRECY ACT

The final group of tax-related offenses includes violations of the Bank Secrecy Act contained in Title 31 of the United States Code.[28] The regulations under Title 31[29] require financial institutions to file a report on Form 4789, Currency Transaction Report (see Exhibit 18-1 at ¶1851), whenever a person engages in a currency transaction of more than $10,000.[30] Beginning April 1, 1996, banks and other financial institutions must also file a Suspicious Activity Report (SAR) for transactions of $5,000 or more in "suspicious" circumstances as delineated by the Treasury Department.[31]

In addition, any person who has an interest in a foreign financial account must disclose it on his income tax return. Criminal Investigation (CI) has jurisdiction over offenses under the Bank Secrecy Act. Violations of reporting requirements are subject to a maximum term of imprisonment for five years and a maximum fine of $250,000 for individuals or $500,000 for organizations. The maximum fine for individuals is increased to $500,000 for violations occurring while another federal law is being violated or which are part of a pattern of illegal activity involving more than $100,000 in a twelve-month period.

---

[26] Compare *United States v. Henderson*, 386 F. Supp. 1048 (S.D.N.Y. 1974), 74-2 USTC ¶9807 (charge dismissed), with *United States v. Miller*, 545 F.2d 1204 (9th Cir. 1976), 76-2 USTC ¶9809 (charge sustained), *cert. denied*, 430 U.S. 930 (1977); and *United States v. Weatherspoon*, 581 F.2d 595 (7th Cir. 1978). The denial of certiorari in *Miller* should lend support to the government's use of mail fraud charges in tax evasion cases.

[27] See 18 U.S.C. §1957(f)(1), amended in 1988, which excludes from the crime of engaging in a "monetary transaction," in which illicit funds are received or deposited, money received by an attorney for the representation of a defendant in a criminal case. However, if the transaction was undertaken with the knowledge that it was designed to launder the money or avoid any currency reporting requirements, the attorney could be found guilty of the offense of money laundering under 18 U.S.C. §1956.

[28] 31 U.S.C. §§5311–5330.

[29] 31 CFR §§103.22–103.28, 103.32, as amended 1987, 1989, 1994 and 1996.

[30] Section 5324 of Title 31 of the United States Code proscribes attempts to structure transactions to avoid the reporting requirements. 31 U.S.C. §5324 (West Supp. 1997). See also *Ratzlaf v. United States*, 510 U.S. 135 (1994), 94-1 USTC ¶50,015. The *Ratzlaf* court required the prosecution to prove that a defendant knew it was a crime to structure transactions to avoid the currency reporting requirements. Congress, however, later added to Code Sec. 5324 an express provision criminalizing simple violation of the statute, thus eliminating the willfulness requirement. See Money Laundering Suppression Act of 1994, P.L. 103-325, Title IV, §§411(a), 413(a)(2), 108 Stat. 2253, 2254.

[31] See 31 CFR §103.21 (1996).

Closely related to the currency reporting requirements of Title 31 is the provision of the Internal Revenue Code in Code Sec. 6050I which requires any person engaged in a trade or business who receives more than $10,000 in currency to report the transaction to the IRS. These reports are to be filed on Form 8300, Report of Cash Payments Over $10,000 Received in a Trade or Business (see Exhibit 18-2 at ¶1852). Willful failure to file such currency transaction reports is specifically punishable under Code Sec. 7203 as a felony. The maximum term of imprisonment for such violations is five years, and the maximum fine is $25,000 for individuals or $100,000 for corporations. The Sentencing Guidelines will determine the actual sentence to be imposed.

¶1816 STATUTE OF LIMITATIONS

The Internal Revenue Code contains a separate statute of limitations for criminal prosecution of tax offenses. Code Sec. 6531 provides that prosecution of theprincipal tax offenses in Title 26 must be commenced within six years of the commission of the offense. The six-year limitation period also applies to conspiracies to evade tax or to defraud the United States. The running of the statute of limitations is suspended during the time the person to be charged is outside the United States or is a fugitive from justice. A criminal action is commenced for purposes of complying with the limitations period when the indictment is returned by the grand jury or the information is filed with the court.

In general, the criminal statute of limitations begins to run at the time the offense is committed or completed. The limitation period for failure to file under Code Sec. 7203 runs from the due date or extended due date of the return. When the crime of subscribing to a false return under Code Sec. 7206(1) is involved, the six-year period is measured from the date the return is filed or, if filed early, the due date of the return. The same rule applies to the offense of aiding or assisting in the preparation of a false return under Code Sec. 7206(2). The crime of submitting false documents under Code Sec. 7207 is committed at the time the document is submitted to the government.

If the act of filing a false return is the basis for a tax evasion prosecution under Code Sec. 7201, the statute of limitations will begin to run from the date the tax return was filed or, if filed early, from the due date of the return. However, when affirmative acts constituting attempts to evade tax occur after the return is filed, the six-year limitations period is measured from the date of those subsequent acts.[32] Altering records or making false statements to a revenue agent after a return has been filed are examples of acts that may extend the statute of limitations for tax evasion.[33]

With the exception of conspiracy, the tax-related offenses found in the Criminal Code (Title 18) are subject to a five-year statute of limitations.[34] The six-

---

[32] See *United States v. Beacon Brass Co.*, 344 U.S. 43 (1952), 52-2 USTC ¶9528; see also *United States v. Hunerlach*, 197 F.3d 1059 (11th Cir. 1999), 99-2 USTC ¶51,009, holding that the statute of limitations for willful evasion of payment of tax also begins to run from the last affirmative act of evasion, even if the act occurs past six years from the date the tax was due.

[33] *United States v. Ferris*, 807 F.2d 269 (1st Cir. 1986), 86-2 USTC ¶9844, *cert. denied*, 480 U.S. 950 (1987).

[34] See 18 U.S.C. §3282 (1994).

year period of limitations for conspiracy begins to run on the date the last overt act is done in furtherance of the conspiracy.

¶1817 REVENUE AGENT REFERRALS TO CI

Revenue agents follow special procedures, outlined in the Internal Revenue Manual, in handling audits of returns when indications of possible tax fraud exist.[35] If there is *only a suspicion* of fraud, called the "first indication of fraud," the revenue agent will attempt to gather more information concerning the suspected fraud during the course of the examination. The revenue agent will ask the taxpayer, thereturn preparer or any other involved party for an explanation of the issues that form the basis of the suspicion of fraud and will ask questions to determine the taxpayer's intent. If the agent is convinced there is a "firm indication of fraud," auditing activities are suspended at the earliest opportunity without disclosing the reason to the taxpayer, the practitioner or employees.[36]

The determination of whether a firm indication of fraud exists is a factual one.[37] It is usually made after the agent has consulted with the group/team manager and/or an Examination Fraud Coordinator. If the reviewer concurs in the fraud determination, the revenue agent will then refer the case to CI. In addition, if a referral is being considered, the agent is instructed not to solicit an agreement from the taxpayer or to solicit and obtain delinquent returns prior to the submission of a fraud referral.

If CI concurs that there are indications of possible fraud, the case will be accepted and a special agent will be assigned. The special agent will then attempt to develop information sufficient to determine whether to recommend criminal prosecution.

¶1819 THE CRIMINAL INVESTIGATION

A case accepted for criminal investigation may not initially be assigned a number before a cursory examination by the special agent to determine whether grounds exist for a full-scale investigation. At this stage the case is referred to as an "unnumbered case." If the case warrants a full-scale investigation, it will be assigned a number and is thereafter referred to as a "numbered case." The special agent will continue the investigation of a numbered case until sufficient evidence is developed to recommend whether or not the taxpayer should be prosecuted. A full-scale investigation is normally conducted jointly by the special agent and a revenue agent who assists in examining records, interviewing witnesses and other matters. The special agent, however, is in charge of the investigation.[38]

The special agent's initial contact of the taxpayer is normally made without giving the taxpayer prior notice. The surprise visit is an important element in an attempt to obtain spontaneous responses from the taxpayer which often provide

---

[35] IRM Handbook 104.2.2.1.
[36] IRM Handbook 104.2.3.4.

[37] Compare *Kontny v. U.S.*, 2001-1 USTC ¶50,197 (7th Cir. 2001), with *McKee v. U.S.*, 192 3d 535 (7th Cir. 1999), 99-2 USTC ¶50,867.
[38] IRM Handbook 104.2.4.2.

the critical admissions or statements necessary for a successful prosecution. The special agent is always accompanied by another agent who may at some later time be called upon as a corroborating witness.

At the initial meeting, the special agent must identify him- or herself as such, produce credentials, and inform the taxpayer that one of a special agent's functions is to investigate the possibility of criminal violations of the Internal Revenue laws and related offenses.[39] A *Miranda*-type warning must be given informing the taxpayer that under the Fifth Amendment he or she cannot be compelled to answer any questions or submit any information that might tend to be self-incriminating.[40] The taxpayer is further advised of the right to the assistance of an attorney before responding.[41] This warning is not a constitutional requirement, however, because the taxpayer is not in a custodial setting.[42] However, failure to give the warning, accompanied by affirmative efforts to mislead or deceive the taxpayer into believing that the investigation is not criminal in nature, but merely a routine civil examination, may be grounds for suppression of evidence obtained at the initial meeting.[43]

To establish an understatement of taxable income, the special agent will use either a specific item method or an indirect method of proof. The specific item method requires the agent to obtain evidence from books, records, documents and third parties which directly proves that specific items of income were not reported or that specific items of expense were falsely reported.[44] The indirect methods of proof, discussed in Chapter 19, *infra,* require the special agent to reconstruct taxable income by a thorough analysis of the taxpayer's financial affairs during the period under investigation. For example, the taxpayer's returns for at least five years preceding and all years subsequent to the starting point will be analyzed to furnish additional support for the starting point when a net-worth method of proof is used.[45]

Code Sec. 7602 authorizes the special agent to issue administrative summonses to compel any person to give testimony or to produce records or documents (see discussion in Chapter 6, *supra*). Summonses may be enforced in court proceedings. In certain circumstances, a special agent also may obtain a search warrant to seize records, documents and other evidence. To obtain a warrant, however, the agent must first be prepared to establish to the satisfaction of a federal Magistrate that there is probable cause to believe that a tax crime has been committed and that evidence of such crime will be found on the premises to be searched.[46] At the outset of an investigation, there may be insufficient evidence to establish such probable cause. The special agent may request a search

---

[39] IRM Handbook 9.4.5.11.3.1.

[40] The *Special Agent's Handbook* requires agents to inform taxpayers of constitutional rights in noncustodial interviews. *Id.*

[41] *Id.*, subsection 9384.2(2) (Rev. 9-16-93); HB 9781 §§ 342.132 (Rev. 10-19-92) and 342.16 (Rev. 4-9-84).

[42] *Stansbury v. California,* 511 U.S. 318 (1994); *Beckwith v. United States,* 425 U.S. 341 (1976), 76-1 USTC ¶ 9352.

[43] See *United States v. Serlin,* 707 F.2d 953 (7th Cir. 1983), 83-1 USTC ¶ 9368; *United States v. Tweel,* 550 F.2d 297 (5th Cir. 1977), 77-1 USTC ¶ 9330.

[44] IRM Handbook 9.5.9.2.1.

[45] *Id.*, subsection 9327(4) (Rev. 9-16-93). See Chapter 19, *infra,* on net-worth method. IRM Handbook 9.59.5.3.

[46] U.S. Const., Amend. IV; FED. R. CRIM. P. 41(e).

¶1819

warrant to prevent destruction or concealment of incriminating records. The agent also may resort to a search warrant to seize personal or business records from a taxpayer which would otherwise be protected by the Fifth Amendment from compulsory production if a summons were to be used.[47]

A criminal tax investigation is a very slow and deliberate process. An investigation that continues for more than a year is common. One that continues for two or more years is not unusual.

¶1822 SPECIAL AGENT'S REPORT

On completing the investigation, the special agent will prepare a detailed report (SAR, see ¶1814) summarizing the findings, the supporting evidence and a recommendation regarding prosecution. If the special agent determines that no criminal violation has occurred or that a prosecution would not be successful, the agent will discuss the findings with the group manager and request approval from the Special Agent in Charge to close the case without prosecution.[48] When a criminal prosecution is declined, the taxpayer will receive a letter from the IRS informing the taxpayer that he or she is no longer the subject of a criminal investigation, but that CI may re-enter the case if additional information becomes available to warrant such action (see Exhibit 18-4 at ¶1854).[49] If the special agent recommends prosecution, the case will be reviewed by the group manager and the Special Agent in Charge. The taxpayer is then notified by letter that prosecution has been recommended and that the case is being forwarded to the United States Department of Justice, Tax Division, Criminal Section in Washington, D.C., for review.

¶1824 CONFERENCE OPPORTUNITIES

A case forwarded to the Tax Division of the Department of Justice for final review is done by a government attorney who is very experienced in criminal tax cases. Should the taxpayer request a conference at this point, the request must be in writing, and the conference will be held in Washington, D.C. Plea bargaining will not be considered at this conference. The Justice Department conference probably provides the best opportunity for convincing the government to decline prosecution. It should be noted, however, that if the government's case is shown to have weaknesses, the Tax Division attorney may simply forward the case to the United States Attorney with an authorization for a grand jury investigation to bolster the case with additional evidence.

If the Department of Justice does not decline prosecution, the case is referred to the appropriate United States Attorney for prosecution. A conference may be requested before indictment to discuss the merits of the case or to enter into plea negotiations. The case may have been referred to the United States Attorney with or without discretion to prosecute. Prosecution is very rarely declined at this stage.

---

[47] See *Andresen v. Maryland*, 427 U.S. 463 (1976).

[48] IRM Handbook 9.5.12.7.

[49] IRM Handbook 9.5.1.3.4.1.

¶1825 EARLY PLEA PROCEDURE

A referral to the Department of Justice can be eliminated if the taxpayer wishes to enter a guilty plea in the criminal proceedings. Entry of a guilty plea may not be made by any taxpayer accused of tax crimes relating to income from illegal sourcesor not represented by counsel.[50] Under this procedure the taxpayer, through counsel, can enter into plea discussions while the case is still under investigation. When an unrepresented taxpayer expresses an interest in the program, the taxpayer will be informed that the program is limited to those who are represented by counsel. At the same time, the taxpayer is told that timely completion of the investigation can be enhanced by the taxpayer's cooperation.[51]

A taxpayer who enters this program through counsel is first told that participating in the plea agreement will have no effect on any civil tax liability. The case will be referred directly to the United States Attorney for plea discussions simultaneously with being referred to the Department of Justice.

The Internal Revenue Manual reflects the position of the Department of Justice that any plea must include the most significant violation involved (the major count policy). It also reflects the policy that a Code Sec. 7207 charge cannot be used to reduce tax return felony counts to misdemeanors.[52] Finally, the totality of the fraud conducted by the taxpayer must be considered in any plea discussions.[53]

¶1827 GRAND JURY INVESTIGATIONS

If the administrative investigation process cannot develop the relevant facts within a reasonable period of time, or it appears that coordination with an ongoing grand jury investigation would be more efficient, CI may refer the matter to the Justice Department and request that a criminal tax investigation be conducted by a grand jury.[54] A case that is factually complex and involves numerous witnesses, some of whom are uncooperative, will be an appropriate candidate for a grand jury. The United States Attorney, as well as the Criminal Division and Tax Division of the Justice Department, may also initiate a grand jury investigation of tax crimes.

The procedures involved in a grand jury investigation differ substantially from those in an administrative investigation conducted by CI. The special agents assigned to the grand jury investigation may be designated agents of the grand jury by the United States Attorney's office and work closely with that office.[55] The testimony of witnesses and the production of records can be compelled by the service of a grand jury subpoena. An IRS summons cannot be used by the special agent after a grand jury investigation is commenced.[56] The grand jury subpoena is not restricted by the 10-day and 23-day waiting periods re-

---

[50] IRM Handbook 9.6.2.2.

[51] *Id.*

[52] *Id.*

[53] *Id.*

[54] See United States Attorney's Manual, Title 6 (Tax Division), §6-4.121 (March, 1994); IRM Handbook 9.5.2.3.1.1.

[55] See *Bank of Nova Scotia v. United States*, 487 U.S. 250 (1988), 88-2 USTC ¶9547.

[56] Code Secs. 7605(a) and 7609.

¶1827

quired before there must be compliance with an administrative summons.[57] The lengthy legal processrequired to enforce an administrative summons, including possible appeal, does not apply to a grand jury subpoena. A motion to quash a subpoena may be filed, but a denial of the motion is not appealable. To further contest and appeal the validity of the grand jury subpoena, the witness must refuse to testify or produce documents and then be held in contempt. A witness may not wish to face the harsh reality of confinement or other contempt penalties while waiting for an appeal to be heard.[58]

¶1829 CONSTITUTIONAL RIGHTS

The most important constitutional rights available to a taxpayer under criminal investigation are found in the Fifth Amendment privilege against self-incrimination and the Fourth Amendment protection from "unreasonable searches and seizures." By far the most significant of these in tax investigations is the taxpayer's Fifth Amendment right not to be compelled to testify or produce personal records if doing so might tend to be self-incriminating.

Privilege Against Self-Incrimination. A taxpayer or any witness may claim the Fifth Amendment privilege and refuse to testify or answer any questions with respect to any matters that may tend to be incriminating. A Fifth Amendment claim is also available with respect to a taxpayer's individual, personal or business records, provided the business records are those of a sole proprietorship.[59] Records of corporations and partnerships, however, are not protected by the privilege against self-incrimination.[60] The custodian of corporate records must produce the records even though he or she is the target of the investigation and the production of the records might tend to be self-incriminating.[61]

The Supreme Court has held that the privilege protects a person only against being incriminated by his or her own compelled testimonial communication.[62] The Court indicated that the production by the taxpayer of personal books and records may be protected from compulsion by the privilege, not because of the incriminating contents of such voluntarily prepared records, but because the act of production itself has communicative aspects that might tend to incriminate. By producing the records, the Court reasoned, the individual is being compelled to testify, in effect, that the records exist, that he or she has possession and control, and that the records are genuine. If the taxpayer has left records in the possession of an accountant, the Fifth Amendment privilege cannot be asserted by the taxpayer to prevent the accountant from producing those records.[63]

---

[57] See *Id.* §§7605(a) (1994) and 7609 (West Supp. 1997).

[58] Information obtained during a grand jury tax investigation cannot be disclosed for use in the civil tax audit. See *United States v. Baggot,* 463 U.S. 476 (1983), 83-2 USTC ¶9438; FED. R. CRIM. P. 6(e)(2)

[59] See *United States v. Doe,* 465 U.S. 605 (1984).

[60] See *Braswell v. United States,* 487 U.S. 99 (1988), 88-2 USTC ¶9546; *Bellis v. United States,* 417 U.S. 85 (1974). In *Bellis,* the Supreme Court suggested that

the privilege might apply to partnership records in a case involving a "small family partnership" or if there were some other pre-existing relationship of confidentiality among the partners.

[61] See *Braswell v. United States,* 487 U.S. 99 (1988), 88-2 USTC ¶9546.

[62] See *Fisher v. United States,* 425 U.S. 391 (1976), 76-1 USTC ¶9353.

[63] See *Couch v. United States,* 409 U.S. 322 (1973), 73-1 USTC ¶9159.

Unreasonable Searches and Seizures. The Fourth Amendment protects "persons, houses, papers, and effects" against unreasonable searches and seizures. A search and seizure is presumed to be unreasonable unless a search warrant has first been obtained from a United States magistrate upon a showing of probable cause. In tax cases, as previously discussed, search warrants are occasionally used by CI to seize a taxpayer's records.

If an IRS agent surreptitiously searches through a taxpayer's desk drawers or cabinets while conducting an examination at the taxpayer's office, such a search is illegal. Any information obtained in such a search may be suppressed as evidence in any subsequent criminal proceeding under the "exclusionary rule." An illegal search and seizure also occurs if an investigating agent directs an employee of the taxpayer to take records secretly from the taxpayer's place of business.[64]

Although the test of reasonableness under the Fourth Amendment also applies to the administrative summons issued under Code Sec. 7602, it rarely provides grounds for quashing a summons.[65] In most situations, the summons is sufficiently specific and narrowly drawn, and the requested records are clearly relevant.[66]

¶1831 PRIVILEGED COMMUNICATIONS

The attorney-client privilege provides a taxpayer under investigation with the assurance that whatever the taxpayer discusses in confidence with counsel cannot be disclosed by the attorney unless the taxpayer waives the privilege. The privilege applies only if:[67]

1. The asserted holder of the privilege is or sought to become a client;

2. The person to whom the communication was made (a) is a member of the bar of a court, or a bar member's subordinate and (b) in connection with this communication is acting as a lawyer;

3. The communication relates to a fact of which the attorney was informed (a) by the client (b) without the presence of strangers (c) for the purpose of securing primarily either (i) an opinion on law or (ii) legal services or (iii) assistance in some legal proceeding, and not (d) for the purpose of committing a crime or tort; and

4. The privilege has been (a) claimed and (b) not waived by the client.[68]

---

[64] See *United States v. Feffer*, 831 F.2d 734 (7th Cir. 1987), 87-2 USTC ¶9614.

[65] However, where taxpayers cooperate with an administrative summons but later withdraw their consent, the court will order the return of business documents obtained pursuant to the summons. See *Laviage v. Lyons*, DC Tex., 93-1 USTC ¶50,292.

[66] For application of Fourth Amendment principles to subpoenas and summonses, see *Oklahoma Press Publishing Co. v. Walling*, 327 U.S. 186 (1946),

and *Hubner v. Tucker*, 245 F.2d 35 (9th Cir. 1957), 57-1 USTC ¶9362.

[67] For a full discussion on privileged communications see Chapter 7, *supra*.

[68] *United States v. United Shoe Mach. Corp.*, 89 F.Supp 357 (D. Mass. 1950). See *Bernardo v. Comm'r*, 104 TC 677 (1995), CCH Dec. 50,705; see generally Jerald David August, *The Attorney-Client Privilege & Work-Product Doctrine in Federal Tax Controversies*, J. TAX'N, October 1995, at 197. See also Chapter 6 on attorney-client privilege and work product.

If an attorney is acting in some other capacity, for example as a tax return preparer or business adviser, communications to the attorney are not privileged.[69] Also, the privilege does not normally protect information regarding the fee arrangement and the fee paid. When an attorney engages an accountant to assist in representing a taxpayer during a criminal investigation, any confidential communications to the accountant while assisting the attorney are also privileged.[70] In the case of a corporate or organizational taxpayer, the privilege will extend to all officers and employees who have information related to the matter under investigation.[71]

Confidential communications between husband and wife are also privileged. In addition to the protection offered by this privilege, the law also recognizes the right of either spouse not to be compelled to testify against the other.[72] The testimonial privilege belongs to the spouse who is called upon to testify. Therefore, if a wife chooses to testify against her husband, she may do so. However, the husband would be able to claim a privilege with respect to any communications with his wife that were made in confidence during their marriage.

¶1834 PRACTICAL CONSIDERATIONS AND ADVICE

The taxpayer under criminal investigation should not speak to the special agent without the presence and advice of an attorney. The taxpayer should retain an attorney with whom the taxpayer can discuss the matter confidentially with the knowledge that whatever he or she tells the attorney is subject to the attorney-client privilege. If the attorney is present at the meeting with the special agent, the attorney should refuse to submit the taxpayer to questioning or furnish records or documents until the attorney has had an opportunity to explore the matter fully.

The taxpayer should not discuss pending tax problems with anyone else, including a personal accountant, close friends and relatives. Anything said to these individuals is not protected by a privilege. If such individuals are subsequently questioned by a special agent, they may face the dilemma of choosing between lying or disclosing what may be harmful information. Any personal business records in the hands of an accountant or any other third party should be retrieved by the taxpayer as soon as possible. Unless such records are in the possession of the taxpayer, they are not protected by the privilege against self-incrimination.

The general rule is that cooperation in a criminal tax investigation rarely helps the taxpayer and frequently provides the evidence necessary to make a case. Whether or not the taxpayer cooperates, the special agent will not recom-

---

[69] See *United States v. Davis*, 636 F.2d 1028 (5th Cir. 1981), 81-1 USTC ¶9193, *cert. denied*, 454 U.S. 862 (1981); *Canaday v. United States*, 354 F.2d 849 (8th Cir. 1966), 66-1 USTC ¶9192.

[70] See *United States v. Kovel*, 296 F.2d 918 (2d Cir. 1961), 62-1 USTC ¶9111. But *cf. U.S. v. Adlman*, 68 F.3d 1495 (2d Cir. 1995), 95-2 USTC ¶50,579 (tax opinion memorandum prepared by outside accounting firm not protected by attorney-client privilege because accounting firm not hired to provide legal advice).

[71] See *Upjohn Co. v. United States*, 449 U.S. 383 (1981), 81-1 USTC ¶9138.

[72] See *Trammel v. United States*, 445 U.S. 40 (1980).

mend prosecution unless there is sufficient evidence of an intentional violation of the Internal Revenue laws. Partial cooperation may be appropriate in some cases when it is certain that the information will be obtained by the special agent from other sources.

The special agent routinely advises the taxpayer that cooperation in providing information will avoid the time and embarrassment involved in contacting the taxpayer's friends, customers and business associates to obtain the requested information. The taxpayer is not informed, however, that all of the information submitted by the taxpayer will have to be verified by contacting the very same people the taxpayer did not want contacted in the first place. Moreover, such cooperation may provide the agent with more leads and more persons to contact than otherwise would have developed.

Hasty decisions should not be made with respect to cooperation, even partial cooperation. The golden rule in criminal tax investigations applies to the question of cooperation, "when in doubt, don't."

¶1836 THE ACCOUNTANT'S ROLE

The taxpayer's accountant should be alert to the danger of discussing, or allowing the taxpayer to personally discuss, anything regarding the tax matter under investigation. Under current law, there is no accountant-client privilege in criminal cases to protect the accountant from being compelled to disclose what the taxpayer has disclosed. Often the initial contact by the special agent will cause the taxpayer to go to the accountant and confess all.

If necessary to assist the attorney in developing the case, the accountant should be engaged by the attorney to preserve the attorney-client privilege. The same accountant who prepared the tax returns for the taxpayer or did the regular accounting or bookkeeping for the taxpayer generally should not be engaged to do the work required in the criminal case. Although information regarding the taxpayer's affairs discovered during work in the tax case may be covered by the attorney-client privilege, it may be difficult to sort out what was learned during this period of time from what had been learned previously during the tax return preparation or routine accounting work. The latter information would not be privileged.[73]

¶1837 ATTEMPTS TO SETTLE

In many cases, where a taxpayer is under investigation and has admitted an understatement of tax to a representative, an attempt will be made to file an amended return disclosing any income that was omitted. The practitioner should be aware that filing an amended return after a criminal investigation has begun will be of little effect in terminating the investigation because the special agent is concerned primarily with determining whether there has been a criminal violation. In fact, filing an amended return will be treated by the special agent as evidence of a violation and may be used by the government to show there has

---

[73] See note 68, *supra*.

been an understatement of the taxpayer's income in any trial of the criminal case. For this reason, no amended return should be filed nor should any offer to pay additional tax be communicated to the special agent while the criminal investigation is pending.

Prior to an investigation, a taxpayer who has failed to file returns or omitted income may consider voluntarily submitting amended returns. The IRS has an informal policy of not prosecuting taxpayers who come forward to report understatements if it is truly voluntary.[74]

---

[74] IRM 9.5.3.3.1.2.1 (12/11/02).

¶1837

¶1851 Exhibit 18-1

Form **4789**

(Rev. June 1998)

Department of the Treasury
Internal Revenue Service

Currency Transaction Report

▶ Use this 1998 revision effective June 1, 1998.
▶ For Paperwork Reduction Act Notice, see page 3.   ▶ Please type or print.
(Complete all parts that apply—See instructions)

OMB No. 1506-0004

1 Check all box(es) that apply:

a ☐ Amends prior report   **b** ☐ Multiple persons   **c** ☐ Multiple transactions

Part I Person(s) Involved in Transaction(s)

Section A—Person(s) on Whose Behalf Transaction(s) Is Conducted

2 Individual's last name or Organization's name	**3** First name	**4** M.I.

5 Doing business as (DBA)	**6** SSN or EIN

7 Address (number, street, and apt. or suite no.)	**8** Date of birth M M D D Y Y Y Y

9 City	**10** State	**11** ZIP code	**12** Country (if not U.S.)	**13** Occupation, profession, or business

14 If an individual, describe method used to verify identity:

a ☐ Driver's license/State I.D.   **b** ☐ Passport   **c** ☐ Alien registration   **d** ☐ Other ....
e Issued by: **f** Number:

Section B—Individual(s) Conducting Transaction(s) (if other than above).

If Section B is left blank or incomplete, check the box(es) below to indicate the reason(s):

a ☐ Armored Car Service   **b** ☐ Mail Deposit or Shipment   **c** ☐ Night Deposit or Automated Teller Machine (ATM)
d ☐ Multiple Transactions   **e** ☐ Conducted On Own Behalf

15 Individual's last name	**16** First name	**17** M.I.

18 Address (number, street, and apt. or suite no.)	**19** SSN

20 City	**21** State	**22** ZIP code	**23** Country (if not U.S.)	**24** Date of birth M M D D Y Y Y Y

25 If an individual, describe method used to verify identity:

a ☐ Driver's license/State I.D.   **b** ☐ Passport   **c** ☐ Alien registration   **d** ☐ Other ....
e Issued by: **f** Number:

Part II Amount and Type of Transaction(s). Check all boxes that apply.

28 Date of Transaction   M M D D Y Y Y Y

26 Cash In $ _____ .00   **27** Cash Out $ _____ .00

29 ☐ Foreign Currency _____ (Country)   **30** ☐ Wire Transfer(s)   **31** ☐ Negotiable Instrument(s) Purchased

32 ☐ Negotiable Instrument(s) Cashed   **33** ☐ Currency Exchange(s)   **34** ☐ Deposit(s)/Withdrawal(s)

35 ☐ Account Number(s) Affected (if any): _____   **36** ☐ Other (specify)

Part III Financial Institution Where Transaction(s) Takes Place

37 Name of financial institution	Enter Federal Regulator or BSA Examiner code number from the instructions here. ▶ [ ]

38 Address (number, street, and apt. or suite no.)	**39** SSN or EIN

40 City	**41** State	**42** ZIP code	**43** MICR No.

Sign Here ▶

44 Title of approving official	**45** Signature of approving official	**46** Date of signature M M D D Y Y Y Y
47 Type or print preparer's name	**48** Type or print name of person to contact	**49** Telephone number ( )

Cat. No. 42004W

Form **4789** (Rev. 6-98)

¶1851

Multiple Persons

(Complete applicable parts below if box 1b on page 1 is checked.)

Part I   Person(s) Involved in Transaction(s)

Section A—Person(s) on Whose Behalf Transaction(s) Is Conducted

2 Individual's last name or Organization's name		3 First name	4 M.I.
5 Doing business as (DBA)		6 SSN or EIN	
7 Address (number, street, and apt. or suite no.)		8 Date of birth M M D D Y Y Y Y	
9 City	10 State 11 ZIP code 12 Country (if not U.S.)	13 Occupation, profession, or business	

14   If an individual, describe method used to verify identity:
a ☐ Driver's license/State I.D.   b ☐ Passport   c ☐ Alien registration   d ☐ Other ....
e   Issued by: f   Number:

Section B—Individual(s) Conducting Transaction(s) (if other than above).

15 Individual's last name		16 First name	17 M.I.
18 Address (number, street, and apt. or suite no.)		19 SSN	
20 City	21 State 22 ZIP code 23 Country (if not U.S.)	24 Date of birth M M D D Y Y Y Y	

25   If an individual, describe method used to verify identity:
a ☐ Driver's license/State I.D.   b ☐ Passport   c ☐ Alien registration   d ☐ Other ....
e   Issued by: f   Number:

Part I   Person(s) Involved in Transaction(s)

Section A—Person(s) on Whose Behalf Transaction(s) Is Conducted

2 Individual's last name or Organization's name		3 First name	4 M.I.
5 Doing business as (DBA)		6 SSN or EIN	
7 Address (number, street, and apt. or suite no.)		8 Date of birth M M D D Y Y Y Y	
9 City	10 State 11 ZIP code 12 Country (if not U.S.)	13 Occupation, profession, or business	

14   If an individual, describe method used to verify identity:
a ☐ Driver's license/State I.D.   b ☐ Passport   c ☐ Alien registration   d ☐ Other ....
e   Issued by: f   Number:

Section B—Individual(s) Conducting Transaction(s) (if other than above).

15 Individual's last name		16 First name	17 M.I.
18 Address (number, street, and apt. or suite no.)		19 SSN	
20 City	21 State 22 ZIP code 23 Country (if not U.S.)	24 Date of birth M M D D Y Y Y Y	

25   If an individual, describe method used to verify identity:
a ☐ Driver's license/State I.D.   b ☐ Passport   c ☐ Alien registration   d ☐ Other ....
e   Issued by: f   Number:

¶1851

Paperwork Reduction Act Notice.—The requested information is useful in criminal, tax, and regulatory investigations and proceedings. Financial institutions are required to provide the information under 31 U.S.C. 5313 and 31 CFR Part 103, commonly referred to as the Bank Secrecy Act (BSA). The BSA is administered by the U.S. Department of the Treasury's Financial Crimes Enforcement Network (FinCEN). You are not required to provide the requested information unless a form displays a valid OMB control number.

The time needed to complete this form will vary depending on individual circumstances. The estimated average time is 19 minutes. If you have comments concerning the accuracy of this time estimate or suggestions for making this form simpler, you may write to the **Tax Forms Committee,** Western Area Distribution Center, Rancho Cordova, CA 95743-0001. **DO NOT** send this form to this office. Instead, see **When and Where To File** below.

Suspicious Transactions

This Currency Transaction Report (CTR) should NOT be filed for suspicious transactions involving $10,000 or less in currency OR to note that a transaction of more than $10,000 is suspicious. Any suspicious or unusual activity should be reported by a financial institution in the manner prescribed by its appropriate federal regulator or BSA examiner. (See the instructions for Item 37.) If a transaction is suspicious and in excess of $10,000 in currency, then both a CTR and the appropriate referral form must be filed.

Should the suspicious activity require immediate attention, financial institutions should telephone 1-800-800-CTRS. An Internal Revenue Service (IRS) employee will direct the call to the local office of the IRS Criminal Investigation Division (CID). This toll-free number is operational Monday through Friday, from approximately 9:00 am to 6:00 pm Eastern Standard Time. If an emergency, consult directory assistance for the local IRS CID Office.

General Instructions

Who Must File.—Each financial institution (other than a casino, which instead must file Form 8362 and the U.S. Postal Service for which there are separate rules), must file Form 4789 (CTR) for each deposit, withdrawal, exchange of currency, or other payment or transfer, by, through, or to the financial institution which involves a transaction in currency of more than $10,000. Multiple transactions must be treated as a single transaction if the financial institution has knowledge that (1) they are by or on behalf of the same person, and (2) they result in either currency received (Cash In) or currency disbursed (Cash Out) by the financial institution totaling more than $10,000 during any one business day. For a bank, a business day is the day on which transactions are routinely posted to customers' accounts, as normally communicated to depository customers. For all other financial institutions, a business day is a calendar day.

Generally, financial institutions are defined as banks, other types of depository institutions, brokers or dealers in securities, money transmitters, currency exchangers, check cashers, issuers and sellers of money orders and traveler's checks. Should you have questions, see the definitions in 31 CFR Part 103.

When and Where To File.—File this CTR by the 15th calendar day after the day of the transaction with the IRS Detroit Computing Center, ATTN: CTR, P.O. Box 33604, Detroit, MI 48232-5604 or with your local IRS office. Keep a copy of each CTR for five years from the date filed.

A financial institution may apply to file the CTRs magnetically. To obtain an application to file magnetically, write to the IRS Detroit Computing Center, ATTN: CTR Magnetic Media Coordinator at the address listed above.

Identification Requirements.—All individuals (except employees of armored car services) conducting a reportable transaction(s) for themselves or for another person must be identified by means of an official document(s).

Acceptable forms of identification include a driver's license, military, and military/dependent identification cards, passport, state issued identification card, cedular card (foreign), non-resident alien identification cards, or any other identification document or documents, which contain name and preferably address and a photograph and are normally acceptable by financial institutions as a means of identification when cashing checks for persons other than established customers.

Acceptable identification information obtained previously and maintained in the financial institution's records may be used. For example, if documents verifying an individual's identity were examined and recorded on a signature card when an account was opened, the financial institution may rely on that information. In completing the CTR, the financial institution must indicate on the form the method, type, and number of the identification. Statements such as "known customer" or "signature card on file" are not sufficient for form completion.

Penalties.—Civil and criminal penalties are provided for failure to file a CTR or to supply information or for filing a false or fraudulent CTR. See 31 U.S.C. 5321, 5322 and 5324.

For purposes of this CTR, the terms below have the following meanings:

Currency.—The coin and paper money of the United States or any other country, which is circulated and customarily used and accepted as money.

Person.—An individual, corporation, partnership, trust or estate, joint stock company, association, syndicate, joint venture or other unincorporated organization or group.

Organization.—Person other than an individual.

Transaction In Currency.—The physical transfer of currency from one person to another. This does not include a transfer of funds by means of bank check, bank draft, wire transfer or other written order that does not involve the physical transfer of currency.

Negotiable Instruments.—All checks and drafts (including business, personal, bank, cashier's and third-party), money orders, and promissory notes. For purposes of this CTR, all traveler's checks shall also be considered negotiable instruments. All such instruments shall be considered negotiable whether or not they are in bearer form.

Specific Instructions

Because of the limited space on the front and back of the CTR, it may be necessary to submit additional information on attached sheets. Submit this additional information on plain paper attached to the CTR. Be sure to put the individual's or organization's name and identifying number (items 2, 3, 4, and 6 of the CTR) on any additional sheets so that if it becomes separated, it may be associated with the CTR.

Item 1a. Amends Prior Report.—If this CTR is being filed because it amends a report filed previously, check Item 1a. Staple a copy of the original CTR to the amended one, complete Part III fully and only those other entries which are being amended.

Item 1b. Multiple Persons.—If this transaction is being conducted by more than one person or on behalf of more than one person, check Item 1b. Enter information in Part I for one of the persons and provide information on any other persons on the back of the CTR.

Item 1c. Multiple Transactions.—If the financial institution has knowledge that there are multiple transactions, check Item 1c.

PART I - Person(s) Involved in Transaction(s)

Section A **must** be completed. If an individual conducts a transaction on his own behalf, complete Section A; leave Section B BLANK. If an individual conducts a transaction on his own behalf and on behalf of another person(s), complete Section A for each person; leave Section B BLANK. If an individual conducts a transaction on behalf of another person(s), complete Section B for the individual conducting the transaction, and complete Section A for each person on whose behalf the transaction is conducted of whom the financial institution has knowledge.

Section A. Person(s) on Whose Behalf Transaction(s) Is Conducted.—See instructions above.

Items 2, 3, and 4. Individual/Organization Name.—If the person on whose behalf the transaction(s) is conducted is an individual, put his/her last name in Item 2, first name in Item 3 and middle initial in Item 4. If there is no middle initial, leave item 4 BLANK. If the transaction is conducted on behalf of an organization, put its name in Item 2 and leave Items 3 and 4 BLANK.

Item 5. Doing Business As (DBA).—If the financial institution has knowledge of a separate "doing business as" name, enter it in Item 5. For example, Johnson Enterprises DBA PJ's Pizzeria.

Item 6. Social Security Number (SSN) or Employer Identification Number (EIN).—Enter the SSN or EIN of the person identified in Item 2. If none, write NONE.

Items 7, 9, 10, 11 and 12. Address.—Enter the permanent street address including zip code of the person identified in Item 2. Use the Post Office's two letter state abbreviation code. A P.O. Box should not be used by itself and may only be used if there is no street address. If a P.O. Box is used, the name of the apartment or suite number, road or route number where the person resides must also be provided. If the address is outside the U.S., provide the street address, city, province, or state, postal code (if known), and the name of the country.

Item 8. Date of Birth.—Enter the date of birth. Eight numerals must be inserted for each date. The first two will reflect the month of birth, the second two the calendar day of birth, and the last four numerals the year of birth. Zero (0) should precede any single digit number. For example, if an individual's birth date is April 3, 1948, Item 8 should read 04 03 1948.

Item 13. Occupation, Profession, or Business.—Identify fully the occupation, profession or business of the person on whose behalf the transaction(s) was conducted. For example, secretary, shoe salesman, carpenter, attorney, housewife, restaurant, liquor store, etc. Do not use non-specific terms such as merchant, self-employed, businessman, etc.

Item 14. If an Individual, Describe Method Used To Verify.—If an individual conducts the transaction(s) on his/her own behalf, his/her identity must be verified by examination of an acceptable document (see **General Instructions**). For example, check box **a** if a driver's license is used to verify an individual's identity, and enter the state that issued the license and the number in items **e** and **f**. If the transaction is conducted by an individual on behalf of another individual not present or an organization, enter N/A in item 14.

Section B. Individual(s) Conducting Transaction(s) (if other than above).—Financial institutions should enter as much information as is available. However, there may be instances in which Items 15-25 may be left BLANK or incomplete.

If Items 15-25 are left BLANK or incomplete, check one or more of the boxes provided to indicate the reason(s).

Example: If there are multiple transactions that, if only when aggregated, the financial institution has knowledge the transactions exceed the reporting threshold, and therefore, did not identify the transactor(s), check box **d** for Multiple Transactions.

Items 15, 16, and 17. Individual(s) Name.—Complete these items if an individual conducts a transaction(s) on behalf of another person. For example, if John Doe, an employee of XYZ Grocery Store makes a deposit to the store's account, XYZ Grocery Store should be identified in Section A, and John Doe should be identified in Section B.

Items 18, 20, 21, 22, and 23. Address.—Enter the permanent street address including zip code of the individual. (See the instructions for Items 7, 9, 10, 11, and 12.)

Item 19. SSN.—If the individual has an SSN, enter it in Item 19. If the individual does not have an SSN, enter NONE.

Item 24. Date of Birth.—Enter the individual's date of birth. See the instructions for Item 8.

Item 25. If an Individual, Describe Method Used To Verify.—Enter the method by which the individual's identity is verified (see **General Instructions** and Item 14).

PART II - Amount and Type of Transaction(s)

Complete Part II to Identify the type of transaction(s) reported and the amount(s) involved.

Items 26 and 27. Cash In/Cash Out.—In the spaces provided, enter the amount of currency received (Cash In) or disbursed (Cash Out) by the financial institution. If foreign currency is exchanged, use the U.S. dollar equivalent on the day of the transaction.

If less than a full dollar amount is involved, increase that figure to the next highest dollar. For example, if the currency totals $20,000.05, show the total as $20,001.00.

Item 28. Date of Transaction.—Eight numerals must be inserted for each date. (See the instructions for Item 8.)

Determining Whether Transactions Meet the Reporting Threshold

Only cash transactions that, if alone or when aggregated, exceed $10,000 should be reported on the CTR. Transactions shall not be offset against one another.

If there are both Cash In and Cash Out transactions that are reportable, the amounts should be considered separately and not aggregated. However, they may be reported on a single CTR.

If there is a currency exchange, it should be aggregated separately with each of the Cash In and Cash Out totals.

Example 1: A person deposits $11,000 in currency to his savings account and withdraws $3,000 in currency from his checking account.

The CTR should be completed as follows: Cash In $11,000 and no entry for Cash Out. This is because the $3,000 transaction does not meet the reporting threshold.

Example 2: A person deposits $11,000 in currency to his savings account and withdraws $12,000 in currency from his checking account.

The CTR should be completed as follows: Cash In $11,000, Cash Out $12,000. This is because there are two reportable transactions. However, one CTR may be filed to reflect both.

Example 3: A person deposits $6,000 in currency to his savings account and withdraws $4,000 in currency from his checking account. Further, he presents $5,000 in currency to be exchanged for the equivalent in French francs.

The CTR should be completed as follows: Cash In $11,000 and no entry for Cash Out. This is because in determining whether the transactions are reportable, the currency exchange is aggregated with each of the Cash In and the Cash Out amounts. The result is a reportable $11,000 Cash In transaction. The total Cash Out amount is $9,000 which does not meet the reporting threshold; therefore, it is not entered on the CTR.

Example 4: A person deposits $6,000 in currency to his savings account and withdraws $7,000 in currency from his checking account. Further, he presents $5,000 in currency to be exchanged for the equivalent in French francs.

The CTR should be completed as follows: Cash In $11,000, Cash Out $12,000. This is because in determining whether the transactions are reportable, the currency exchange is aggregated with each of the Cash In and Cash Out amounts. In this example, each of the Cash In and Cash Out totals exceed $10,000 and must be reflected on the CTR.

Item 29. Foreign Currency.—If foreign currency is involved, check Item 29 and identify the country. If multiple foreign currencies are involved, identify the country for which the largest amount is exchanged.

Items 30-33.—Check the appropriate item(s) to identify the following type of transaction(s):

30. Wire Transfer(s)

31. Negotiable Instrument(s) Purchased

32. Negotiable Instrument(s) Cashed

33. Currency Exchange(s)

Item 34. Deposits/Withdrawals.—Check this item to identify deposits to or withdrawals from accounts, e.g., demand deposit accounts, savings accounts, time deposits, mutual fund accounts or any other account held at the financial institution. Enter the account number(s) in item 35.

Item 35. Account Numbers Affected (if any).—Enter the account numbers of any accounts affected by the transaction(s) that are maintained

at the financial institution conducting the transaction(s). If necessary, use additional sheets of paper to indicate all of the affected accounts.

Example 1: If a person cashes a check drawn on an account held at the financial institution, the CTR should be completed as follows: Indicate Negotiable Instrument(s) Cashed and provide the account number of the check.

If the transaction does not affect an account, make no entry.

Example 2: A person cashes a check drawn on another financial institution. In this instance, Negotiable Instrument(s) Cashed would be indicated, but no account at the financial institution has been affected. Therefore, item 35 should be left BLANK.

Item 36. Other (specify).—If a transaction is not identified in Items 30–34, check Item 36 and provide an additional description. For example, a person presents a check to purchase "foreign currency".

Part III - Financial Institution Where Transaction(s) Takes Place

Item 37. Name of Financial Institution and Identity of Federal Regulator or BSA Examiner.—Enter the financial institution's full legal name and identify the federal regulator or BSA examiner, using the following codes:

FEDERAL REGULATOR OR BSA EXAMINER	CODE
Comptroller of the Currency (OCC)	1
Federal Deposit Insurance Corporation (FDIC)	2
Federal Reserve System (FRS)	3
Office of Thrift Supervision (OTS)	4
National Credit Union Administration (NCUA)	5
Securities and Exchange Commission (SEC)	6
Internal Revenue Service (IRS)	7
U.S. Postal Service (USPS)	8

Items 38, 40, 41, and 42. Address.—Enter the street address, city, state, and ZIP code of the financial institution where the transaction occurred. If there are multiple transactions, provide information on the office or branch where any one of the transactions has occurred.

Item 39. EIN or SSN.—Enter the financial institution's EIN. If the financial institution does not have an EIN, enter the SSN of the financial institution's principal owner.

Item 43. MICR Number.—If a depository institution, enter the Magnetic Ink Character Recognition (MICR) number.

Signature

Items 44 and 45. Title and Signature of Approving Official.—The official who reviews and approves the CTR must indicate his/her title and sign the CTR.

Item 46. Date the Form Was Signed.—The approving official must enter the date the CTR is signed. (See the instructions for Item 8.)

Item 47. Preparer's Name.—Type or print the full name of the individual preparing the CTR. The preparer and the approving official may not necessarily be the same individual.

Items 48 and 49. Contact Person/Telephone Number.—Type or print the name and telephone number of an individual to contact concerning questions about the CTR.

¶1852 Exhibit 18-2

IRS Form **8300**	**Report of Cash Payments Over $10,000**	FinCEN Form **8300**
(Rev. December 2001)	**Received in a Trade or Business**	(December 2001)
OMB No. 1516-0992	▶ See instructions for definition of cash.	OMB No. 1506-0018
Department of the Treasury	▶ Use this form for transactions occurring after December 31, 2001. Do not use prior versions after this date.	Department of the Treasury
Internal Revenue Service	For Privacy Act and Paperwork Reduction Act Notice, see page 4.	Financial Crimes Enforcement Network

1 Check appropriate box(es) if: **a** ☐ Amends prior report;   **b** ☐ Suspicious transaction.

Part I   Identity of Individual From Whom the Cash Was Received

2 If more than one individual is involved, check here and see instructions . . . . ▶ ☐

3 Last name | **4** First name | **5** M.I. | **6** Taxpayer identification number

7 Address (number, street, and apt. or suite no.) | **8** Date of birth . ▶ (see instructions) M M D D Y Y Y Y

9 City | **10** State | **11** ZIP code | **12** Country (if not U.S.) | **13** Occupation, profession, or business

14 Document used to verify identity: **a** Describe identification ▶
b Issued by | **c** Number

Part II   Person on Whose Behalf This Transaction Was Conducted

15 If this transaction was conducted on behalf of more than one person, check here and see instructions . . . . ▶ ☐

16 Individual's last name or Organization's name | **17** First name | **18** M.I. | **19** Taxpayer identification number

20 Doing business as (DBA) name (see instructions) | Employer identification number

21 Address (number, street, and apt. or suite no.) | **22** Occupation, profession, or business

23 City | **24** State | **25** ZIP code | **26** Country (if not U.S.)

27 Alien identification: **a** Describe identification ▶
b Issued by | **c** Number

Part III   Description of Transaction and Method of Payment

28 Date cash received M M D D Y Y Y Y | **29** Total cash received $ .00 | **30** If cash was received in more than one payment, check here . . ▶ ☐ | **31** Total price if different from item 29 $ .00

32 Amount of cash received (in U.S. dollar equivalent) (must equal item 29) (see instructions):

a U.S. currency $ _____ .00 (Amount in $100 bills or higher $ _____ .00)
b Foreign currency $ _____ .00 (Country ▶ _____)
c Cashier's check(s) $ _____ .00 ⎫ Issuer's name(s) and serial number(s) of the monetary instrument(s) ▶ ....
d Money order(s) $ _____ .00 ⎪
e Bank draft(s) $ _____ .00 ⎬ ....
f Traveler's check(s) $ _____ .00 ⎭

33 Type of transaction
a ☐ Personal property purchased
b ☐ Real property purchased
c ☐ Personal services provided
d ☐ Business services provided
e ☐ Intangible property purchased
f ☐ Debt obligations paid
g ☐ Exchange of cash
h ☐ Escrow or trust funds
i ☐ Bail received by court clerks
j ☐ Other (specify) ▶

34 Specific description of property or service shown in 33. (Give serial or registration number, address, docket number, etc.) ▶ ....

Part IV   Business That Received Cash

35 Name of business that received cash | **36** Employer identification number

37 Address (number, street, and apt. or suite no.) | Social security number

38 City | **39** State | **40** ZIP code | **41** Nature of your business

42 Under penalties of perjury, I declare that to the best of my knowledge the information I have furnished above is true, correct, and complete.

Signature ▶ _____ Title ▶ _____
  Authorized official

43 Date of signature M M D D Y Y Y Y | **44** Type or print name of contact person | **45** Contact telephone number ( )

IRS Form **8300** (Rev. 12-2001) | Cat. No. 62133S | FinCEN Form **8300** (12-2001)

¶1852

IRS Form 8300 (Rev. 12-2001)   Page **2**   FinCEN Form 8300 (12-2001)

Multiple Parties
(Complete applicable parts below if box 2 or 15 on page 1 is checked)

Part I   Continued—Complete if box 2 on page 1 is checked

3 Last name	**4** First name **5** M.I. **6** Taxpayer identification number
7 Address (number, street, and apt. or suite no.)	**8** Date of birth ▶ (see instructions) M M D D Y Y Y Y
9 City **10** State **11** ZIP code	**12** Country (if not U.S.) **13** Occupation, profession, or business
14 Document used to verify identity: **a** Describe identification ▶	
b Issued by **c** Number	

3 Last name	**4** First name **5** M.I. **6** Taxpayer identification number
7 Address (number, street, and apt. or suite no.)	**8** Date of birth ▶ (see instructions) M M D D Y Y Y Y
9 City **10** State **11** ZIP code	**12** Country (if not U.S.) **13** Occupation, profession, or business
14 Document used to verify identity: **a** Describe identification ▶	
b Issued by **c** Number	

Part II   Continued—Complete if box 15 on page 1 is checked

16 Individual's last name or Organization's name	**17** First name **18** M.I. **19** Taxpayer identification number
20 Doing business as (DBA) name (see instructions)	Employer identification number
21 Address (number, street, and apt. or suite no.)	**22** Occupation, profession, or business
23 City **24** State **25** ZIP code	**26** Country (if not U.S.)
27 Alien identification: **a** Describe identification ▶	
b Issued by **c** Number	

16 Individual's last name or Organization's name	**17** First name **18** M.I. **19** Taxpayer identification number
20 Doing business as (DBA) name (see instructions)	Employer identification number
21 Address (number, street, and apt. or suite no.)	**22** Occupation, profession, or business
23 City **24** State **25** ZIP code	**26** Country (if not U.S.)
27 Alien identification: **a** Describe identification ▶	
b Issued by **c** Number	

IRS Form **8300** (Rev. 12-2001)   FinCEN Form **8300** (12-2001)

¶1852

Section references are to the Internal Revenue Code unless otherwise noted.

Changes To Note

● Section 6050I (26 United States Code (U.S.C.) 6050I) and 31 U.S.C. 5331 require that certain information be reported to the IRS and the Financial Crimes Enforcement Network (FinCEN). This information must be reported on **IRS/FinCEN Form 8300.**

● Item 33 box **i** is to be checked **only** by clerks of the court; box **d** is to be checked by bail bondsmen. See the instructions on page 4.

● For purposes of section 6050I and 31 U.S.C. 5331, the word "cash" and "currency" have the same meaning. See **Cash** under **Definitions** below.

General Instructions

Who must file. Each person engaged in a trade or business who, in the course of that trade or business, receives more than $10,000 in cash in one transaction or in two or more related transactions, must file Form 8300. Any transactions conducted between a payer (or its agent) and the recipient in a 24-hour period are related transactions. Transactions are considered related even if they occur over a period of more than 24 hours if the recipient knows, or has reason to know, that each transaction is one of a series of connected transactions.

Keep a copy of each Form 8300 for 5 years from the date you file it.

Clerks of Federal or State courts must file Form 8300 if more than $10,000 in cash is received as bail for an individual(s) charged with certain criminal offenses. For these purposes, a clerk includes the clerk's office or any other office, department, division, branch, or unit of the court that is authorized to receive bail. If a person receives bail on behalf of a clerk, the clerk is treated as receiving the bail. See the instructions for **Item 33** on page 4.

If multiple payments are made in cash to satisfy bail and the initial payment does not exceed $10,000, the initial payment and subsequent payments must be aggregated and the information return must be filed by the 15th day after receipt of the payment that causes the aggregate amount to exceed $10,000 in cash. In such cases, the reporting requirement can be satisfied either by sending a single written statement with an aggregate amount listed or by furnishing a copy of each Form 8300 relating to that payer. Payments made to satisfy separate bail requirements are not required to be aggregated. See Treasury Regulations section 1.6050I-2.

Casinos must file Form 8300 for nongaming activities (restaurants, shops, etc.).

Voluntary use of Form 8300. Form 8300 may be filed voluntarily for any suspicious transaction (see **Definitions**) for use by FinCEN and the IRS, even if the total amount does not exceed $10,000.

Exceptions. Cash is not required to be reported if it is received:

● By a financial institution required to file **Form 4789,** Currency Transaction Report.

● By a casino required to file (or exempt from filing) **Form 8362,** Currency Transaction Report by Casinos, if the cash is received as part of its gaming business.

● By an agent who receives the cash from a principal, if the agent uses all of the cash within 15 days in a second transaction that is reportable on Form 8300 or on Form 4789, and discloses all the information necessary to complete Part II of Form 8300 or Form 4789 to the recipient of the cash in the second transaction.

● In a transaction occurring entirely outside the United States. See **Pub. 1544,** Reporting Cash Payments Over $10,000 (Received in a Trade or Business), regarding transactions occurring in Puerto Rico, the Virgin Islands, and territories and possessions of the United States.

● In a transaction that is not in the course of a person's trade or business.

When to file. File Form 8300 by the 15th day after the date the cash was received. If that date falls on a Saturday, Sunday, or legal holiday, file the form on the next business day.

Where to file. File the form with the Internal Revenue Service, Detroit Computing Center, P.O. Box 32621, Detroit, MI 48232.

Statement to be provided. You must give a written statement to each person named on a required Form 8300 on or before January 31 of the year following the calendar year in which the cash is received. The statement must show the name, telephone number, and address of the information contact for the business, the aggregate amount of reportable cash received, and that the information was furnished to the IRS. Keep a copy of the statement for your records.

Multiple payments. If you receive more than one cash payment for a single transaction or for related transactions, you must report the multiple payments any time you receive a total amount that exceeds $10,000 within any 12-month period. Submit the report within 15 days of the date you receive the payment that causes the total amount to exceed $10,000. If more than one report is required within 15 days, you may file a combined report. File the combined report no later than the date the earliest report, if filed separately, would have to be filed.

Taxpayer identification number (TIN). You must furnish the correct TIN of the person or persons from whom you receive the cash and, if applicable, the person or persons on whose behalf the transaction is being conducted. **You may be subject to penalties for an incorrect or missing TIN.**

The TIN for an individual (including a sole proprietorship) is the individual's social security number (SSN). For certain resident aliens who are not eligible to get an SSN and nonresident aliens who are required to file tax returns, it is an IRS Individual Taxpayer Identification Number (ITIN). For other persons, including corporations, partnerships, and estates, it is the employer identification number (EIN).

If you have requested but are not able to get a TIN for one or more of the parties to a transaction within 15 days following the transaction, file the report and attach a statement explaining why the TIN is not included.

Exception: *You are not required to provide the TIN of a person who is a nonresident alien individual or a foreign organization if that person does not have income effectively connected with the conduct of a U.S. trade or business and does not have an office or place of business, or fiscal or paying agent, in the United States. See Pub. 1544 for more information.*

Penalties. You may be subject to penalties if you fail to file a correct and complete Form 8300 on time and you cannot show that the failure was due to reasonable cause. You may also be subject to penalties if you fail to furnish timely a correct and complete statement to each person named in a required report. A minimum penalty of $25,000 may be imposed if the failure is due to an intentional or willful disregard of the cash reporting requirements.

Penalties may also be imposed for causing, or attempting to cause, a trade or business to fail to file a required report; for causing, or

attempting to cause, a trade or business to file a required report containing a material omission or misstatement of fact; or for structuring, or attempting to structure, transactions to avoid the reporting requirements. These violations may also be subject to criminal prosecution which, upon conviction, may result in imprisonment of up to 5 years or fines of up to $250,000 for individuals and $500,000 for corporations or both.

Definitions

Cash. The term "cash" means the following:

● U.S. and foreign coin and currency received in any transaction.

● A cashier's check, money order, bank draft, or traveler's check having a face amount of $10,000 or less that is received in a **designated reporting transaction** (defined below), or that is received in any transaction in which the recipient knows that the instrument is being used in an attempt to avoid the reporting of the transaction under either section 6050I or 31 U.S.C. 5331.

Note: *Cash does not include a check drawn on the payer's own account, such as a personal check, regardless of the amount.*

Designated reporting transaction. A retail sale (or the receipt of funds by a broker or other intermediary in connection with a retail sale) of a consumer durable, a collectible, or a travel or entertainment activity.

Retail sale. Any sale (whether or not the sale is for resale or for any other purpose) made in the course of a trade or business if that trade or business principally consists of making sales to ultimate consumers.

Consumer durable. An item of tangible personal property of a type that, under ordinary usage, can reasonably be expected to remain useful for at least 1 year, and that has a sales price of more than $10,000.

Collectible. Any work of art, rug, antique, metal, gem, stamp, coin, etc.

Travel or entertainment activity. An item of travel or entertainment that pertains to a single trip or event if the combined sales price of the item and all other items relating to the same trip or event that are sold in the same transaction (or related transactions) exceeds $10,000.

Exceptions. A cashier's check, money order, bank draft, or traveler's check is not considered received in a designated reporting transaction if it constitutes the proceeds of a bank loan or if it is received as a payment on certain promissory notes, installment sales contracts, or down payment plans. See Pub. 1544 for more information.

Person. An individual, corporation, partnership, trust, estate, association, or company.

Recipient. The person receiving the cash. Each branch or other unit of a person's trade or business is considered a separate business unless the branch receiving the cash (or a central office linking the branches), knows or has reason to know the identity of payers making cash payments to other branches.

Transaction. Includes the purchase of property or services, the payment of debt, the exchange of a negotiable instrument for cash, and the receipt of cash to be held in escrow or trust. A single transaction may not be broken into multiple transactions to avoid reporting.

Suspicious transaction. A transaction in which it appears that a person is attempting to cause Form 8300 not to be filed, or to file a false or incomplete form. The term also includes any transaction in which there is an indication of possible illegal activity.

Specific Instructions

You must complete all parts. However, you may skip Part II if the individual named in Part I is conducting the transaction on his or her behalf only. **For voluntary reporting of suspicious transactions, see Item 1 below.**

Item 1. If you are amending a prior report, check box 1a. Complete the appropriate items with the correct or amended information only. Complete all of Part IV. Staple a copy of the original report to the amended report.

To voluntarily report a suspicious transaction (see **Definitions**), check box 1b. You may also telephone your local IRS Criminal Investigation Division or call 1-800-800-2877.

Part I

Item 2. If two or more individuals conducted the transaction you are reporting, check the box and complete Part I for any one of the individuals. Provide the same information for the other individual(s) on the back of the form. If more than three individuals are involved, provide the same information on additional sheets of paper and attach them to this form.

Item 6. Enter the taxpayer identification number (TIN) of the individual named. See **Taxpayer identification number (TIN)** on page 3 for more information.

Item 8. Enter eight numerals for the date of birth of the individual named. For example, if the individual's birth date is July 6, 1960, enter 07 06 1960.

Item 13. Fully describe the nature of the occupation, profession, or business (for example, "plumber," "attorney," or "automobile dealer"). Do not use general or nondescriptive terms such as "businessman" or "self-employed."

Item 14. You must verify the name and address of the named individual(s). Verification must be made by examination of a document normally accepted as a means of identification when cashing checks (for example, a driver's license, passport, alien registration card, or other official document). In item 14a, enter the type of document examined. In item 14b, identify the issuer of the document. In item 14c, enter the document's number. For example, if the individual has a Utah driver's license, enter "driver's license" in item 14a, "Utah" in item 14b, and the number appearing on the license in item 14c.

Part II

Item 15. If the transaction is being conducted on behalf of more than one person (including husband and wife or parent and child), check the box and complete Part II for any one of the persons. Provide the same information for the other person(s) on the back of the form. If more than three persons are involved, provide the same information on additional sheets of paper and attach them to this form.

Items 16 through 19. If the person on whose behalf the transaction is being conducted is an individual, complete items 16, 17, and 18. Enter his or her TIN in item 19. If the individual is a sole proprietor and has an employer identification number (EIN), you must enter both the SSN and EIN in item 19. If the person is an organization, put its name as shown on required tax filings in item 16 and its EIN in item 19.

Item 20. If a sole proprietor or organization named in items 16 through 18 is doing business under a name other than that entered in item 16 (e.g., a "trade" or "doing business as (DBA)" name), enter it here.

Item 27. If the person is not required to furnish a TIN, complete this item. See **Taxpayer Identification Number (TIN)** on page 3. Enter a

description of the type of official document issued to that person in item 27a (for example, "passport"), the country that issued the document in item 27b, and the document's number in item 27c.

Part III

Item 28. Enter the date you received the cash. If you received the cash in more than one payment, enter the date you received the payment that caused the combined amount to exceed $10,000. See **Multiple payments** under **General Instructions** for more information.

Item 30. Check this box if the amount shown in item 29 was received in more than one payment (for example, as installment payments or payments on related transactions).

Item 31. Enter the total price of the property, services, amount of cash exchanged, etc. (for example, the total cost of a vehicle purchased, cost of catering service, exchange of currency) if different from the amount shown in item 29.

Item 32. Enter the dollar amount of each item of cash received. Show foreign currency amounts in U.S. dollar equivalent at a fair market rate of exchange available to the public. **The sum of the amounts must equal item 29.** For cashier's check, money order, bank draft, or traveler's check, provide the name of the issuer and the serial number of each instrument. Names of all issuers and all serial numbers involved must be provided. If necessary, provide this information on additional sheets of paper and attach them to this form.

Item 33. Check the appropriate box(es) that describe the transaction. If the transaction is not specified in boxes a–i, check box j and briefly describe the transaction (for example, "car lease," "boat lease," "house lease," or "aircraft rental"). If the transaction relates to the receipt of bail by a court clerk, check box **i,** "Bail received by court clerks." This box is **only** for use by court clerks. If the transaction relates to cash received by a bail bondsman, check box **d,** "Business services provided."

Part IV

Item 36. If you are a sole proprietorship, you must enter your SSN. If your business also has an EIN, you must provide the EIN as well. All other business entities must enter an EIN.

Item 41. Fully describe the nature of your business, for example, "attorney" or "jewelry dealer." Do not use general or nondescriptive terms such as "business" or "store."

Item 42. This form must be signed by an individual who has been authorized to do so for the business that received the cash.

Privacy Act and Paperwork Reduction Act Notice. Except as otherwise noted, the information solicited on this form is required by the Internal Revenue Service (IRS) and the Financial Crimes Enforcement Network (FinCEN) in order to carry out the laws and regulations of the United States Department of the Treasury. Trades or businesses, except for clerks of criminal courts, are required to provide the information to the IRS and FinCEN under both section 6050I and 31 U.S.C. 5331. Clerks of criminal courts are required to provide the information to the IRS under section 6050I. Section 6109 and 31 U.S.C. 5331 require that you provide your social security number in order to adequately identify you and process your return and other papers. The principal purpose for collecting the information on this form is to maintain reports or records where such reports or records have a high degree of usefulness in criminal, tax, or regulatory investigations or proceedings, or in the conduct of intelligence or

counterintelligence activities, by directing the Federal Government's attention to unusual or questionable transactions.

While such information is invaluable with regards to the purpose of this form, you are not required to provide information as to whether the reported transaction is deemed suspicious. No penalties or fines will be assessed for failure to provide such information, even if you determine that the reported transaction is indeed suspicious in nature. Failure to provide all other requested information, or the provision of fraudulent information, may result in criminal prosecution and other penalties under Title 26 and Title 31 of the United States Code.

Generally, tax returns and return information are confidential, as stated in section 6103. However, section 6103 allows or requires the IRS to disclose or give the information requested on this form to others as described in the Code. For example, we may disclose your tax information to the Department of Justice, to enforce the tax laws, both civil and criminal, and to cities, states, the District of Columbia, U.S. commonwealths or possessions, and certain foreign governments to carry out their tax laws. We may disclose your tax information to the Department of Treasury and contractors for tax administration purposes; and to other persons as necessary to obtain information which we cannot get in any other way in order to determine the amount of or to collect the tax you owe. We may disclose your tax information to the Comptroller General of the United States to permit the Comptroller General to review the IRS. We may disclose your tax information to Committees of Congress; Federal, state, and local child support agencies; and to other Federal agencies for the purposes of determining entitlement for benefits or the eligibility for and the repayment of loans. We may also disclose this information to Federal agencies that investigate or respond to acts or threats of terrorism or participate in intelligence or counterintelligence activities concerning terrorism.

FinCEN may provide the information collected through this form to those officers and employees of the Department of the Treasury who have a need for the records in the performance of their duties. FinCEN may also refer the records to any other department or agency of the Federal Government upon the request of the head of such department or agency and may also provide the records to appropriate state, local, and foreign criminal law enforcement and regulatory personnel in the performance of their official duties.

You are not required to provide the information requested on a form that is subject to the Paperwork Reduction Act unless the form displays a valid OMB control number. Books or records relating to a form or its instructions must be retained as long as their contents may become material in the administration of any law under Title 26 or Title 31.

The time needed to complete this form will vary depending on individual circumstances. The estimated average time is 21 minutes. If you have comments concerning the accuracy of this time estimate or suggestions for making this form simpler, you can write to the Tax Forms Committee, Western Area Distribution Center, Rancho Cordova, CA 95743-0001. **Do not** send this form to this office. Instead, see **Where To File** on page 3.

¶1853 Exhibit 18-3

Law Enforcement Manual IX

131.1[*]

(1) Criminal prosecution involving Title 26 violations may be recommended in egregious cases on non-compliance. The prosecution of these cases should have a deterrent impact and encourage voluntary compliance.

(2) Generally, egregious cases will result in sentences requiring imprisonment or community confinement, intermittent confinement or home detention. Prosecution may be recommended in cases involving violations of 26 U.S.C. §7203 in community property states if the tax loss total $7000 or more. Prosecution may be recommended in cases involving 26 U.S.C. §7207 if the tax loss is over $1000 or more for any prosecution year.

(3) Other factors that may be considered when determining egregiousness for the purpose of recommending criminal prosecution are:

   (a) The potential for national or local press coverage that will generate awareness of criminal enforcement and, thus, foster voluntary compliance.

   (b) Local areas of substantial non-compliance, including conduct that appears to represent a trend or common attitude within the community, trade or industry.

   (c) Flagrant or repetitious conduct so egregious that resorting to criminal sanctions becomes warranted.

(4) A pattern of non-compliance is an important factor in Title 26 investigations. A pattern of multiple years is particularly relevant when an indirect method of proof is utilized to establish the offense.

---

[*] Because this section of the Law Enforcement Manual (LEM) is not officially published by the IRS and reflects guidelines as they existed in 1995, there is no assurance that these guidelines have not changed since that time.

¶1854 Exhibit 18-4

[Internal Revenue Service]   Department of the Treasury
Criminal Investigation   Enter Address
                                     Enter City, State Zip
                                     Person to Contact:
                                     Telephone Number:
                                     Refer Reply to:
                                     Date:

Certified Mail

Return Receipt Requested

Dear ____:

    You are no longer the subject of a criminal investigation by our office regarding your Federal tax liabilities for 1998 and 1999. However, this does not preclude re-entry by Criminal Investigation into this matter.

    The matter is presently in the SB/SE Division for further consideration. If you have any questions, please contact the person whose name and telephone number are shown above.

       Sincerely yours,

       Special Agent in Charge

¶1855 DISCUSSION QUESTIONS

1. You are an accountant representing Harry Holesale, who operates a retail hardware store in your area. You have prepared Harry's 2004 tax return, and Harry has now come to you because his 2002, 2003 and 2004 returns are scheduled for office examination. Harry asks you to represent him at the audit regarding all three years.

   In preparation for the audit appointment, you perform a preliminary T-account on the 2004 year. You are surprised to discover that the cash expenditures exceed sources of income by some $45,000. A close inspection of the return, which you prepared, discloses that the gross profit percentage reflected in the return is 15%. You have recently worked with other clients in the retail hardware business, and you know their gross profit percentage is generally closer to 35% to 37%. You then review Harry's prior returns and find that in 2002 the gross profit percentage was 14.8% and that for 2003 it was 15.3%. The preliminary T-account of these three years shows a potential understatement of over $100,000.

   Aside from any ethical considerations, what do you do in this situation? Consider the following alternatives:

   (A) Call Harry and grill him until he gives you a satisfactory explanation regarding the apparent understatement:

       (1) If Harry has a convincing explanation that the understatement was the result of an innocent error, do you prepare amended returns? Or is it better to go to the office examination appointment and not divulge the understatement until the auditor finds it?

       (2) If Harry admits that he was cheating on his returns, do you prepare amended returns in that situation?

   (B) Don't ask Harry for any explanation; rather, you prepare amended returns based on the T-account, insist that Harry sign them without review, and then file them with the agent at the beginning of your appointment. You're hoping that your "voluntary disclosure" of the unreported income will deter the agent from asking for any further explanation.

   (C) Without asking Harry for any explanation, strongly suggest that he seek competent legal advice and help him find a tax attorney.

   (D) Hire a tax attorney as your agent to interview Harry and get his explanation for the understatement, and then have the attorney report back to you with the results.

2. Freddy Fearful did not file his 1996 federal income tax return because he did not have the cash available to pay the balance due. When the time came to file his 1997 return, Freddy had sufficient cash to pay his 1997 taxes, but he was afraid to file the 1997 return because he figured that if he filed for 1997, the IRS would find out that he did not file in 1996. From 1998 through 2001, Freddy continued not to file even though he

was entitled to a sizable refund in each of those years. In 2002 and 2003, Freddy was not entitled to any refund, but again he did not file even though he had the cash available to pay the current tax.

You are a Special Agent for the IRS's Criminal Investigation (CI) and are assigned to investigate Freddy for the years 1999 through 2004. Does the pattern of conduct described above constitute the "willful" failure to file an income tax return proscribed by Code Sec. 7203?

3. Ronny Refundable is under investigation by Criminal Investigation (CI) personnel of the IRS. Ronny is an accountant who prepares approximately 1,500 returns a year. Of the returns that he prepares for individuals, 95% produce a refund. Ronny accomplishes this by utilizing pre-prepared schedules showing itemized deductions, employee business expenses, and child care credits. It is Ronny's boast that by a careful combination of his schedules he can produce a refund for virtually any taxpayer in any tax bracket, unless the taxpayer happens to be subject to the alternative minimum tax. While those of Ronny's clients who have been audited have not fared well, Ronny points out to potential clients that fewer than two percent of taxpayers nationwide get audited and so the odds are good that they won't get caught.

You are the Special Agent in Charge (CI) for Ronny's office. Would you recommend prosecution in his case? What sections of the Internal Revenue Code or other statutes have been violated by Ronny in his fictitious deduction and credit scheme?

4. Assume that you are Adele Accurate, an accountant, and that one of your clients is under criminal investigation. In accordance with the guidelines provided by the ABA and AICPA, you refer the client to an attorney familiar with criminal tax matters. You have prepared the client's returns for the past three years. The attorney retains you to make an analysis of the income and expenses of the client. Assume that you prepare a report for the attorney which discloses an understatement of income in excess of $35,000 for each year.

(A) Is your report protected within the attorney/client privilege?

(B) What practical problems does your retention cause?

5. Priscilla Persistent, a revenue agent, is auditing C&C Bar and Grill. The bar and grill is a business operated by the husband and wife team of Clyde and Cindy Social. The business has no other employees. Clyde and Cindy deposit their "receipts" into their personal joint checking account. For tax purposes, however, the business files a Form 1065— Return of Partnership Income.

(A) Priscilla Persistent issued a summons to the taxpayers requesting the books and records of the business. Can Clyde and Cindy invoke their Fifth Amendment privilege against self-incrimination?

(B) Would your answer change if the business run by Clyde and Cindy had several locations, numerous employees and substantial assets, and the business maintained a bank account in the partnership name?

(C) What rights, if any, would Clyde and Cindy have if Priscilla issued a summons to their bank for copies of their records?

(D) Would your answer to (C) change if a "grand jury investigation" had been commenced?

CHAPTER 19

INDIRECT METHODS OF PROVING INCOME

¶1901 INTRODUCTION

Conventional audit techniques employed by the Internal Revenue Service (IRS) are at times inadequate, if not completely useless, to prove that a taxpayer has failed to report all of his or her taxable income. Where conventional audit techniques prove unproductive, the government may resort to one or more indirect methods for detecting unreported income. The most common special methods are: (1) the cash transaction ("T" account) method, (2) the net worth method, (3) the source and application of funds (or cash expenditures) method and (4) the bank deposits method.[1]

The IRS in the past had increased its efforts to find unreported income with an emphasis on small businesses by using "Economic Reality Examination Audit Techniques." These audit techniques focused on the taxpayer's lifestyle, standard of living and other elements unrelated to the tax return, such as education, vacations, children's schools, automobiles, large assets, cash payments and cash on hand. Taxpayers under examination were also asked to submit a Statement Of Annual Estimated Personal And Family Expenses (see Exhibit 19-1 at ¶1951). As a result of a great deal of public criticism with regard to the overly intrusive nature of financial status audits, Code Sec. 7602(e) was added to the Internal Revenue Code in 1998 to specifically provide that "[t]he Secretary shall not use financial status or economic reality examination techniques to determine the existence of unreported income of any taxpayer unless the Secretary has a reasonable indication that there is a likelihood of such unreported income."[2]

¶1903 UTILIZATION

The revenue agent normally does not approach a typical examination intending to use an indirect method of proof. However, if books and records are missing or unavailable for any reason, the agent usually has no alternative but to reconstruct income by one of the accepted indirect methods. The same course of action may be necessary where the books and records are obviously incomplete or inaccurate. Even where the books and records appear to be complete, correct and internally consistent, suspicions raised by recurring large business losses, unrealistically low income for the nature of the business, informants' tips as to omitted income, bankdeposits greatly in excess of reported gross receipts, or a lifestyle

---

[1] See IRM Handbook 4.2.4.6.

[2] Chief Counsel Advice 200101030 (see Exhibit 19-2 at ¶1952).

inconsistent with reported income may cause the agent to resort to an indirect method of proof.[3]

The special agent in a criminal investigation will normally employ an indirect method where the nature of the taxpayer's business virtually precludes the development of direct evidence of specific items of omitted income or where business records have been withheld or are otherwise unavailable. Businesses involving both large numbers of customers, patients, or clients, and numerous sales or receipts, usually do not lend themselves to direct proof of omitted income. However, proof of some specific omissions may be used to bolster an indirect method case or to establish a likely source of unreported income.

Technical Aspects of the Formulas

¶1905 BASIC PRINCIPLES

Before discussing in detail the technical formulas employed in each of the indirect methods of proof, it is important to consider certain basic principles common to all. Burden-of-proof problems will be reserved for later consideration.

¶1906 GATHERING AND ANALYZING THE FACTUAL DATA

Regardless of the indirect method used, accuracy of result is wholly dependent on success in obtaining all facts relating to the taxpayer's financial affairs. Any one of the indirect methods can produce a precise reconstruction of income provided all facts are precisely known. Some facts, however, such as cash on hand and personal currency expenditures, usually will not be known with certainty and will require estimates which seriously distort the reconstructed income.

Once the examining agent obtains basic records and documents, the agent will determine whether the taxpayer's financial picture is complete and accurate. All substantial deposits in checking and savings accounts will be examined to determine the source of the funds. This inquiry may reveal the existence of previously undisclosed assets, loans or nontaxable income. For the same reason, the agent must determine the source of funds used in the acquisition of assets or payment of loans. If the source is not identifiable, the agent will explore the possibility of a prior cash accumulation.

Checks and savings account withdrawals will be examined for possible asset acquisitions, personal expenditures, or loan payments that may have been previously overlooked. The disposition of proceeds from loans or the sale of assets will be similarly traced. The possibility of cash accumulation or unidentified cash expenditures will be considered where the proceeds cannot be readily traced.

---

[3] When the results of a preliminary analysis suggest the need for further inquiry, the IRS will most commonly use the cash expenditures method. The IRS believes taxpayers easily understand this method. In those cases the IRS takes to court, it uses the net worth method most frequently to prove underreporting of income. See generally Gormley and Porcano, *Reconstruction of Income by the Internal Revenue Service*, TAXES, THE TAX MAGAZINE, vol. 77, No. 4, April 1999, p. 34. See generally Robert Carney, John Gardner and Kenneth Winter, *Indirect Methods of Income Reconstruction*, TAX ADVISOR 536 (August 1992).

The importance of examining tax returns as an investigative tool cannot be overemphasized. Much of the information required for the reconstruction of income can be found within the returns themselves. Equally important, the returns frequently furnish leads to other essential information, such as investments and loans. Tax returns for a number of years before the period under audit will also be examined. They occasionally reveal assets or liabilities that have been overlooked in the current years. In addition, they may evidence sufficient income to support the taxpayer's claim of a prior cash accumulation.

The examination of the underlying records and documents in a reconstruction-of-income case is a specialized accounting task. It is extremely time-consuming, and the value of the results is limited only by the experience and ingenuity of the individual conducting the examination.

¶1907 THE CONSISTENCY PRINCIPLE

The consistency principle requires that, in reconstructing income, every transaction of the taxpayer, reported or not, be accorded the same tax consequences as it was, or would have been, accorded on the tax return. The importance of this principle should be apparent. It must be kept in mind continually when any transaction is examined for its effect on the formulae being used to prove income indirectly.

Indirect methods of proof are not methods of accounting,[4] and therefore, are not controlled by provisions of the Internal Revenue Code relating to accounting methods.[5] They are techniques used to determine whether income has been fully reported. As a result, the formulae for reconstructing income are not rigidly fixed but must be adjusted to conform to, or be consistent with, the methods of accounting used in the taxpayer's books and tax returns. If the taxpayer is properly reporting on a cash, accrual or hybrid method, reconstruction of income must properly reflect the taxpayer's method. The precise manner in which this is accomplished will become apparent from the detailed discussion below of each method.

The tax laws are replete with examples of special tax or accounting treatment accorded to various sales, exchanges and other transactions which might otherwise generate immediate and fully taxable income. To the extent that reconstruction of income involves such transactions, consistent treatment must be accorded to these transactions by appropriate adjustments in the reconstruction formula. Examples of these special situations include (1) installment sales, (2) involuntary conversions, (3) nontaxable corporate distributions to stockholders which reduce basis of stock, and (4) like-kind exchanges.

---

[4] See *Holland v. United States*, 348 U.S. 121 (1954), 54-2 USTC ¶9714.

[5] The provisions relating to methods of accounting are found in Internal Revenue Code Sec. 446 which appears to provide authority to permit the use of indirect methods to compute taxable income. Code Sec. 446(b) states that "if no method of accounting has been regularly used by the taxpayer,

or if the method used does not clearly reflect income, the computation of taxable income shall be made under such method as, in the opinion of the Secretary, does clearly reflect income." See also Treas. Reg. § 1.446-1(a)(2) ("[N]o method of accounting is acceptable unless, in the opinion of the Commissioner, it clearly reflects income"). See generally Carney, Gardner and Winter, *supra*, note 3.

The Cash T-Account Method

¶1908 A SIMPLIFIED AUDITING TECHNIQUE

The cash transaction or T-account method is a simplified auditing technique used to make a preliminary verification of reported income. As its name implies, this method concentrates solely on those transactions which involve the generation or the use of cash. The term "cash" in this method includes currency, checks, or any other medium used to convey or transfer funds. The cash transaction method excludes from its formula all transactions, whether taxable or nontaxable, which do not result in the receipt or the payment of cash.

The cash T-account method utilizes a formula and format suggested by its name (see Exhibit 19-3 at ¶1953). On the left-hand (debit) side of the "T" are listed the sources of cash for the year under audit. On the right-hand (credit) side are listed the expenditures or applications of cash. The goal of the cash transaction method is to determine whether a taxpayer has used and accumulated more cash than has been received from all reported taxable and nontaxable sources, in other words, the use and accumulation of cash for which there is no ready explanation. If a discrepancy appears, it is presumed to constitute an understatement of income.

The starting point for the T-account analysis is the tax return itself. All transactions on the return are carefully examined to determine their effect on cash. Sources of cash on the return include wages, dividends and interest, and all gross receipts from the operation of a business, farm or rental property. The gross selling price of all assets on the capital gains schedule is included as a source of cash, but only to the extent that cash payment, and not a security instrument or other property, was received. Other items on the tax return are examined to determine their potential as a source of cash, and the taxpayer's financial transactions not reflected on the return are thoroughly explored. Additional sources of cash include tax refunds, loans and other nontaxable income, such as gifts, inheritances, insurance proceeds and personal injury settlements.

The tax return also will disclose many cash expenditures which must be included on the credit side of the T-account. Business purchases, excluding any adjustment for inventory changes, are included as cash expenditures. Similarly, all business expenses, with the exception of depreciation (a noncash item), are addedto the credits. Any additional expenses appearing on other schedules or portions of the return are included as credits. Care should be taken to exclude all noncash deductions such as depreciation and amortization. Cash expenditures found outside the return include payments on loans, purchases of assets, investments in securities and all personal expenses (see Exhibit 19-1 at ¶1951).

¶1909 CASH ON HAND AND IN BANKS

On the T-account, the IRS accords special treatment to cash on hand and to checking and savings accounts. Cash on hand at the beginning of the year is included as a debit representing accumulated cash. Establishing the amount of such cash presents a serious problem if the results of the analysis are to be accurate.

Checking and savings account balances at the beginning and end of the year are included on the T-account as debits and credits, respectively. The opening balances provide sources of cash and the closing balances represent cash accumulations. The bank balances should be adjusted and reconciled to account for outstanding checks and deposits in transit.

> **Example:** John Davis received net wages of $21,500 in 2000. His bank statements and savings account passbook showed the following balances:

	12/31/99	*12/31/00*
Checking Account	$1,300	$2,800
Savings Account	1,500	4,600

> A reconciliation of his checking account indicated checks outstanding in the amount of $400 at the end of 1999, and $700 at the end of 2000. A check in the amount of $500 received on December 28, 2000, for the sale of a boat was not deposited in his account until January 2, 2001. John had cash on hand in the amount of $500 at the end of 1999, and $1,200 at the end of 2000. His personal living expenses totaled $23,000. The cash transaction method would disclose the following:

Cash on hand			Cash on hand	
12/31/99	$500		12/31/00	$1,200
Checking account			Checking account	
12/31/99	900		12/31/900	2,100
Savings account			Savings account	
12/31/99	1,500		12/31/00	4,600
Sale of boat	500		Deposit in transit	500
Net wages	21,500		Personal expenses	23,000
Total	$24,900		Total	$31,400
Understatement				
(Unexplained cash)	6,500			
Total	$31,400			

¶1910 ACCOUNTS RECEIVABLE AND PAYABLE

Adjustments are required on the T-account to eliminate the effect of trade accounts receivable that have been included in the gross sales of a business reporting on the accrual basis. Such adjustments convert the reported sales to the cash basis required by the cash transaction method. On the T-account, this is accomplished by including the balance of trade receivables at the beginning of the year as a debit and the balance at the end of the year as a credit.

A related T-account adjustment is made to eliminate the accounts payable included in the purchases and expenses of a business on the accrual basis. In this situation, however, the accounts payable at the end of the year are added to the debit side, while the payables at the beginning of the year are listed on the credit side.

The cash transaction method conceals the cause of the reconstructed understatement. Although on the surface the unexplained excess cash may appear to be unreported gross receipts, the discrepancy may just as well arise from inflated or overstated business expenses. The T-account formula assumes that the reported expenses are correct and that cash was paid out in the amount indicated by such expenses. The overstatement of any expenses for which cash was not actually paid creates unexplained excess cash. The same discrepancy results when personal expenses are deducted erroneously as business expenses and the examining agent duplicates such expenses on the T-account by also including them as personal expenses.

¶1911 T-ACCOUNT EXAMPLE

The following example illustrates the basic operation of the T-account method and shows how the method can disclose an understatement of gross income. Particular attention should be paid to the exclusion of noncash items having no effect on the T-account analysis.

Example: Paula Hanson reports her business income and expenses on the accrual basis. Selected balance sheet items for the business and schedules for her 2000 return showed the following:

SCHEDULE A (Itemized Deductions)

Taxes	$2,000
Interest on Mortgage	1,200
Cash Contributions	800
Medical Expenses (before limitation deduction)	1,500
Theft Loss (Value of jewelry—not reimbursed by insurance—before $100 exclusion and limitation)	10,200

In addition to the itemized deductions above, Ms. Hanson had other personal living expenses totaling $28,500 for 2000.

SCHEDULE B

Gross Dividends	$4,200
Interest Income	1,500

SCHEDULE C

Income

Gross Sales	$180,000	
Cost of Goods Sold (Schedule C-1)	100,000	
Gross Profit		$80,000

Deductions

Depreciation	$4,000
Taxes	1,500
Rent	2,000
Repairs	500
Insurance	900
Amortization	700

Salaries	8,000	
Interest	400	
Legal Fees	800	
Other	200	
Total Expenses		19,000
Net Profit		$61,000

SCHEDULE C-1

Inventory at 1/1/00	$20,000
Purchases	130,000
Total	$150,000
Inventory at 12/31/00	50,000
Cost of Goods Sold	$100,000

The depreciation schedule on Schedule C included equipment purchased in 2000 at a cost of $2,500.

MISCELLANEOUS	*12/31/99*	*12/31/00*
Trade Accounts Receivable	$15,000	$23,000
Trade Accounts Payable	8,000	10,000
Accrued Expenses	2,500	1,800

SCHEDULE D

Stock	*Date Acquired*	*Date Sold*	*Gross Sales Price*	*Cost*	*Gain or (Loss)*
Stock X	5-03-99	2-07-00	$15,000	$11,000	$4,000
Stock Y	6-20-00	7-15-00	5,000	4,000	1,000
Stock Z	9-02-92	8-04-00	2,000	5,000	(3,000)

Ms. Hanson also acquired an additional $52,000 of stock in 2000 which did not appear on Schedule D.

SCHEDULE E

Total Amount of Rents	*Depreciation*	*Other Expenses*	*Net Rent Income*
$6,000	$4,000	$3,000	($1,000)

Additional investigation revealed that Ms. Hanson bought a personal car in May 2000 for $9,200. In 2000, she also borrowed $7,000 from a bank and $3,000 from a friend. No part of either loan was repaid in 2000. A one-year bank loan in the amount of $4,000 came due in 2000 and was refinanced by a new one-year loan from the bank in the amount of $9,000. No part of the new loan was repaid before the end of 2000. Ms. Hanson also received a gift of $3,000 from her parents during 2000.

Ms. Hanson's personal checking account had a reconciled balance of $4,000 at the end of 1999, and $1,500 at the end of 2000. Her savings account balance increased from $2,500 at the end of 1999 to $6,000 at the end of 2000. She had $1,000 in cash on hand at the end of 1999, but none at the end of 2000. In the same year, she also inherited, and still holds, a parcel of land worth $10,000. In 2000, Ms. Hanson received a refund of income taxes from the State in the amount of $1,200.

On the basis of the foregoing facts, the cash transaction analysis would disclose the following:

Cash Transaction (T) Account[6]

Debits		*Credits*	
Cash on Hand (12/31/99)	$1,000	Cash on Hand (12/31/00)	$-0-
Bank Account (12/31/99)	4,000	Bank Account (12/31/00)	1,500
Savings Account (12/31/99)	2,500	Savings Account (12/31/00)	6,000
Schedule D—Stock Sales	22,000	Schedule D—Cost of Stocks	4,000
Bank Loans—Proceeds	16,000	Other Securities Acquired	52,000
Personal Loan—Proceeds	3,000	Bank Loan Repayment	4,000
Schedule C—Gross Sales	180,000	Schedule C—Purchases	130,000
Schedule B—Dividends	4,200	Expenses	14,300
Interest	1,500	Equipment Acquired	2,500
Schedule E—Rental Income	6,000	Schedule E—Rental Expenses . . .	3,000
Gift Received	3,000	Auto Acquired	9,200
Inheritance (noncash)	-0-	Itemized Deductions (cash)	5,500
State Tax Refund	1,200	Stolen Jewelry (noncash)	-0-
*Accounts Receivable (12/31/99) .	15,000	Other Personal Living Expenses .	28,500
*Accounts Payable (12/31/00) . . .	10,000	*Accounts Receivable (12/31/00)	23,000
*Accrued Expenses (12/31/00) . . .	1,800		
Total	$271,200	*Accounts Payable (12/31/99) . .	8,000
Understatement		*Accrued Expenses (12/31/99) . .	$2,500
(Unexplained Cash)	22,800		
Total	$294,000	Total	$294,000

The Net Worth Method

¶1912 RECONSTRUCTION OF INCOME

The net worth method is one of the most commonly employed techniques for reconstructing taxable income in both civil and criminal income tax cases. It is premised on the accounting formula that an increase in net worth plus nondeductible expenditures and losses, minus nontaxable receipts, equals adjusted gross income. Appropriate adjustments are then made to arrive at taxable income. If the annual income thus reconstructed exceeds reported income, the discrepancy is presumed to be current unreported income, and deficiencies are determined accordingly.[7]

---

[6] The asterisked (*) items are included only for a business reporting on the accrual basis.

[7] Taxpayers may also use the net worth method defensively to disprove an IRS assertion of defi-

ciency. See *Whittington v. Comm'r*, 64 TCM 1618, TC Memo. 1992-732, CCH Dec. 48,714(M), aff'd, 22 F.3d 1099 (11th Cir. 1994) (although taxpayer's efforts failed, he was allowed to use net worth method as defense to IRS assertion).

Net worth is simply a taxpayer's assets less liabilities.[8] In a net worth computation, the assets and liabilities existing at the beginning and end of each year under audit must be determined. Assets are included in net worth at their cost basis, not their market value.

Example: Joe Hernandez purchased a lot in January 1999 for $25,000. On December 31, 2000, the lot had a fair market value of $30,000. The net worth computation, using the cost basis of the lot, would be as follows:

	12/31/99	*12/31/00*
Assets (Lot at Cost)	$25,000	$25,000
Liabilities	-0-	-0-
Net Worth	$25,000	$25,000
Net Worth 12/31/95		25,000
Net Worth Increase		-0-

¶1913 CASH ON HAND

Cash on hand is currency carried by a taxpayer or kept at a place of business, at home, in a safe deposit box or anywhere else. This item has generated more controversy than any other. When unexplained discrepancies appear between reported and reconstructed income, the taxpayer will frequently claim that before the years in question he or she had accumulated a "cash hoard" which was deposited or used for other purposes during the audit years.[9] If believed, the story explains the nontaxable cause of the alleged understatement.

To foreclose the success of a "cash hoard" explanation, the Internal Revenue Manual instructs agents to obtain at the earliest possible time the taxpayer's best recollection and estimate of cash on hand at the beginning of the period under audit and at the end of each subsequent year covered by the examination.[10] The taxpayer will be carefully questioned on this matter and is to be made to understand precisely the meaning of the questions asked.

A taxpayer's statement to the agent, whether oral or written, regarding cash on hand creates a difficult, if not insurmountable, obstacle to later attempts to establish the existence of a larger cash hoard. Even though the taxpayer may have made estimates under the assumption that admitting a larger accumulation of cash would raise the agent's suspicions or that such a hoard would adversely affect the tax liability for the years under audit, nothing but the most credible and direct evidence of the cash hoard will overcome the initial statement.

Cash-hoard defenses have been notoriously unsuccessful over the years. In many cases, failure results from an inherently incredible story. Others fail for lack

---

[8] A format for the net worth calculation formula can be found in Gormley and Porcano, *supra,* note 3.

[9] See, e.g., *Gorman v. Comm'r,* 69 TCM 2924, TC Memo. 1995-268, CCH Dec. 50,700(M) (lumber company's income, as reconstructed by Internal Revenue Service, was reduced in part by cash hoard); *American Volmar Internatoinal, Ltd. v. Comm'r,* 76

TCM 911, TC Memo. 1998-419, CCH Dec. 52,968(M), aff'd 229 F3d 98 (2nd Cir. 2000), 2000-2 USTC ¶50,781 (cash-hoard defesnse of overseas funds successful; used cash-hoard defense to IRS income reconstruction).

[10] See IRM, Handbook 4.2.4.6.3.8.4.

of corroborating evidence or as a result of overwhelming contradictory proof by the government. Nevertheless, the cash-hoard issue must be carefully explored whenever an indirect method of proof appears relevant.

> **Example:** For 2000, John Coe reported a net profit from his business in the amount of $25,000. He had cash in banks totaling $15,000 at the end of 1999, and $25,000 at the end of 1996. He bought a parcel of land for $35,000 in 2000. He claims to have had a $20,000 cash hoard in his basement safe at the end of 1999, which he deposited into his bank accounts. He also states that he no longer had any cash hoarded at the end of 2000. If his cash-hoard claim is disregarded, a net worth computation would show the following:

Assets	12/31/99	12/31/00
Cash in Banks	$15,000	$25,000
Land	-0-	35,000
Total Assets	$15,000	$60,000
Liabilities	-0-	-0-
Net Worth	$15,000	$60,000
Net Worth 12/31/99		15,000
Net Worth Increase		$45,000
Adjusted Gross Income Reported		25,000
Understatement of Income		$20,000

> If his claim is accepted, the net worth determination would disclose no understatement of income, as follows:

Assets	12/31/99	12/31/00
Cash on Hand	$20,000	-0-
Cash in Banks	15,000	25,000
Land	-0-	35,000
Total Assets	$35,000	$60,000
Liabilities	-0-	-0-
Net Worth	$35,000	$60,000
Net Worth 12/31/99		35,000
Net Worth Increase		$25,000
Adjusted Gross Income Reported		25,000
Understatement of Income		$ -0-

¶1914 CASH IN BANKS

Cash in banks includes money on deposit in checking and savings accounts and certificates of deposit. For net worth purposes, the year end balances shown on the checking account bank statements must be adjusted by subtracting the checks outstanding at the end of the year. Outstanding checks are those written near the end of the year which do not clear the bank until the following year.

¶1914

Deposits in transit are equivalent to cash on hand and may be shown on the net worth statement as either additional cash on hand or as a separate asset item. To determine the amount of deposits in transit at the end of each year, a careful inspection must be made of deposits occurring near the beginning of the following year. Both savings and checking account deposits should be examined. The deposits early in the year should be compared with the cash receipts journal or other record of business receipts to determine when such amounts were received and recorded. Other transactions near the end of the year which generate funds should also be examined to determine whether the proceeds were received but not deposited before the end of the year. Sales of assets and loans from banks or others are typical examples of such transactions.

Example 1: Acme Enterprises reported a net profit of $140,000 in 2000. The company's bank statements showed unreconciled balances of $30,000 at the end of 1999, and $190,000 at the end of 2000. A reconciliation of the bank account balances disclosed checks outstanding in the amount of $10,000 at the end of 1999, and $30,000 at the end of 2000. The failure to adjust the bank account balances in a net worth determination would artificially produce the following understatement of income:

Assets	*12/31/99*	*12/31/00*
Cash in Banks (per bank statements)	$30,000	$190,000
Liabilities	-0-	-0-
Net Worth	$30,000	$190,000
Net Worth 12/31/99		30,000
Net Worth Increase		$160,000
Adjusted Gross Income Reported		140,000
Apparent Understatement of Income		$20,000

When the bank account balances are adjusted for checks outstanding, the net worth method would disclose that income is fully reported, as follows:

Assets	*12/31/99*	*12/31/00*
Cash in Banks (Reconciled for checks outstanding)	$20,000	$160,000
Liabilities	-0-	-0-
Net Worth	$20,000	$160,000
Net Worth 12/31/99		20,000
Net Worth Increase		$140,000
Adjusted Gross Income Reported		140,000
Understatement of Income		-0-

Example 2: Alice Green reported a net profit of $28,000 from her business in 2000. She had received a check in the amount of $25,000 from a customer on December 29, 1999, which she did not deposit until January 3, 2000. Her bank account balances, reconciled for checks outstanding, were

$10,000 at the end of 1999, and $63,000 at the end of 2000. Failure to adjust the net worth computation for the deposit in transit would produce the following understatement:

Assets	*12/31/99*	*12/31/00*
Cash in Banks	$10,000	$63,000
Liabilities	-0-	-0-
Net Worth	$10,000	$63,000
Net Worth 12/31/99		10,000
Net Worth Increase		$53,000
Adjusted Gross Income Reported		28,000
Apparent Understatement of Income		$25,000

When the deposit in transit is properly included in the net worth, the computations would disclose no understatement, as follows:

Assets	*12/31/99*	*12/31/00*
Cash in Banks	$10,000	$63,000
Deposit in Transit	25,000	-0-
Total Assets	$35,000	$63,000
Liabilities	-0-	-0-
Net Worth	$35,000	$63,000
Net Worth 12/31/99		35,000
Net Worth Increase		$28,000
Adjusted Gross Income Reported		28,000
Understatement of Income		-0-

¶1915 LOANS AND ACCOUNTS RECEIVABLE

Accounts receivable of a taxpayer's business are included in the net worth statement only when the business income is reported on the accrual basis. All other loans and personal accounts receivable are included in the net worth. Such receivables generally represent funds which have been loaned to others or which constitute proceeds from sales of assets. In either situation, the receivables merely replace the cash or asset which otherwise would have remained in the net worth. Included among such receivables are personal loans, land contracts, mortgages and installment sale contracts. The amount due on each loan or receivable must be determined at the end of each year.

Example: Morris Allen reported a $38,000 net profit from his business in 2000. Assume that $13,000 was omitted from reported sales as a result of inadvertent bookkeeping errors. The business was on the accrual basis and had trade accounts receivable in the amount of $27,000 at the end of 2000. At the end of 1999, his business receivables totaled $15,000. In 2000, he loaned $25,000 to his brother, none of which was repaid before the end of the year. He also sold a parcel of land in March 2000 for $15,000. The land had been acquired in October 1999 at a cost of $10,000. The purchaser paid $10,000 to Mr. Allen in 2000 and gave him a note for the balance which remained unpaid at the end of 2000. Mr. Allen reported a gain on the sale in the amount of $5,000. Cash in banks totaled $5,000 at the endof 1999, and $29,000 at the end of 2000. A net worth reconstruction of income would disclose the following:

Assets	12/31/99	12/31/00
Cash in Banks	$5,000	$29,000
Accounts Receivable	15,000	27,000
Personal Loan Receivable	-0-	25,000
Note Receivable	-0-	5,000
Land	10,000	-0-
Total Assets	$30,000	$86,000
Liabilities	-0-	-0-
Net Worth	$30,000	$86,000
Net Worth 12/31/99		30,000
Net Worth Increase		$56,000
Adjusted Gross Income Reported		43,000
Understatement of Income		$13,000

¶1916 INVENTORY

The amount of the business inventory at the end of each year is normally obtained from the tax returns. However, if the taxpayer can establish that the inventory was in error, the corrected value should be included in the net worth. The same is true if the examining agent determines that the reported inventory is incorrect. In a criminal prosecution, any increase in taxable income caused by such correction will be excluded from the unreported taxable income if the error was the result of inadvertence or negligence. The adjustment is considered merely technical and not attributable to fraud.

Example: The Nye Sales Company reported a net profit of $62,000 for 2000. Schedule C of the tax return disclosed opening and closing inventories of $90,000 and $135,000, respectively. An examining revenue agent discovered that several inventory sheets, totaling $32,000, had been inadvertently overlooked in preparing the closing inventory for 2000. Cash in banks totaled $8,000 at the end of 1999 and $25,000 at the end of 2000. The agent's net worth determination would appear as follows:

Assets	12/31/99	12/31/00
Cash in Banks	$8,000	$25,000
Inventory (Corrected)	90,000	167,000
Total Assets	$98,000	$192,000
Liabilities	-0-	-0-
Net Worth	$98,000	$192,000
Net Worth 12/31/99		98,000

¶1916

Net Worth Increase	$94,000
Adjusted Gross Income Reported	62,000
Understatement of Income	$32,000

The entire understatement in this example is attributable to the inadvertent inventory error. These errors must be eliminated from the net worth understatement when evaluating civil and criminal fraud potential. It also should be apparent that such inventory corrections will affect the income of a subsequent or prior year (depending upon whether an opening or closing inventory is adjusted).

¶1917 OTHER ASSETS

Other assets such as stock, bonds, brokerage account balances, real estate, furniture, fixtures, equipment, automobiles and trucks are included in net worth at their cost basis. Although most information regarding business assets can be obtained from the tax returns, the costs and dates of acquisition and sale should be verified from the underlying records.

Care should be taken to assure that all assets are included at their proper cost and in the year to which they belong. Purchase and sale documents will serve to verify the correct dates and amounts. If an asset is purchased near the end of the year, but payment is delayed for any reason until the next year, a proper account payable must be included in the net worth of the year of acquisition. All sales and purchases near the end of the year should be scrutinized to determine that the attendant proceeds and payments are properly treated and do not cause a shift or distortion of income.

¶1918 ACCOUNTS AND NOTES PAYABLE

Trade accounts payable, representing purchases that enter into cost of goods sold, and accrued deductible expenses are included in the net worth statement only when business income is reported on the accrual basis. Other loans and payables, both business and personal, are always added to the taxpayer's liabilities on the net worth statement. Such liabilities include amounts due on personal and bank loans, mortgages, land contracts and installment contracts.

¶1919 RESERVE FOR DEPRECIATION

The reserve for depreciation represents the accumulation of allowances for depreciation which were deducted or deductible in the current and prior years. Depreciation information normally can be obtained directly from the tax return. The increase in the depreciation reserve for each year represents the depreciation deducted for that year. Although the reserve is included as a liability in the net worth method, it could more accurately be shown as a reduction of the basis of the asset to which it applies. Its inclusion in net worth actually reflects an annual decrease in the basis of the assets. It serves to offset the depreciation deduction on the tax return which does not require the expenditure of funds and which would not otherwise be taken into proper account in the net worth determination.

> **Example:** Janet Eng started a business in 2000. She reported a net profit of $22,000 from the business for 2000. In determining the net profit, a deduction of $7,000 was taken for depreciation. Cash in banks increased from nothing at the end of 1999 to $29,000 at the end of 2000. Since depreciation is a noncash deduction, failure to reflect the annual charges in the reserve for depreciation on the net worth statement would create an artificial and erroneous understatement. The net worth computation, with and without the depreciation reserve, discloses the following:

	With Reserve		Without Reserve	
	12/31/99	*12/31/00*	*12/31/99*	*12/31/00*
Assets (Cash in Banks)	-0-	$29,000	-0-	$29,000
Liabilities (Reserve for Depreciation)	-0-	7,000	-0-	-0-
Net Worth	-0-	$22,000	-0-	$29,000
Net Worth 12/31/99		-0-		-0-
Net Worth Increase		$22,000		$29,000
Adjusted Gross Income Reported		22,000		22,000
Understatement of Income		-0-	(Incorrect)	$7,000

¶1920 OTHER LIABILITIES

Occasionally the liability section of the net worth computation is used for items of deferred or unrealized income which will be taxable over a period of years. Such items are not truly liabilities but are included as such to offset that part of an asset which represents deferred or unrealized income. An installment sale, for example, results in the acquisition of a receivable for the balance due on the sale. Part of the receivable represents gain to be reported in later years when payments are made. As a liability, the deferred income account reduces the receivable by the amount necessary to eliminate the deferred gain that otherwise would be improperly incorporated in the net worth computation.

¶1921 NONDEDUCTIBLE EXPENDITURES AND LOSSES

Each year the taxpayer's net worth will either increase or decrease. This annual net worth change must then be further increased and decreased by certain items commonly referred to as "below the line" adjustments. The adjustments added to the annual change in net worth are "nondeductible expenditures and losses." These adjustments include all expenditures which are not deductible in arriving at adjusted gross income. Since itemized deductions are deductible only from adjusted gross income, they are also included in the nondeductible expenses added to the net worth change. A later allowance for itemized deductions is made in the final step of the net worth computation to arrive at taxable income.

All nondeductible losses must also be added to the annual net worth change. Such losses include that portion of a capital loss in excess of the $3,000 limit and losses incurred on the sale of personal assets. The addition of these losses prevents the distortion of reconstructed income caused by the excessive decrease in net worth when the assets sold are eliminated at their full cost basis.

Gifts to relatives and others are nondeductible items which must be added to the net worth change. The personal gift of an asset other than cash is included as a below-the-line addition in an amount equal to the basis at which the asset was included in the net worth. If a reserve for depreciation is associated with the asset, the amount of the gift for adjustment purposes is the cost basis of the asset reduced by the reserve. The reason for this treatment is that the decrease in the net worth caused by removal of the asset must be offset by the addition of the gift. Otherwise, such net worth decrease would artificially reduce the reconstructed income.

The amount of personal living expenses is always controversial. Many of these expenses are paid in cash, and estimates are frequently required. Much of the problem is usually resolved in a routine audit through the cooperation of the taxpayer with the agent's requests for information. Sometimes an agent will use estimates of living expenses based on published statistics of the average cost of living for families of various sizes in different income ranges. Usually, however, the agent will establish as many of the personal expenses as possible from the taxpayer's checks and then either estimate the cash items or ask the taxpayer to do so. In criminal cases, the special agent normally will exclude all estimates and include only living expenses which can be documented by cancelled checks or other records.

Example: During 2000, John Connors sold his personal car for $2,500. He had purchased the car in 1992 for $6,000. In March 2000, he sold 500 shares of stock for $10,000. He had acquired the stock in December 1995 for $22,000. On January 11, 2000, he gave his nephew a truck that had been used solely in his business. The truck cost $9,000 in 1997. Depreciation totaling $6,500 had been previously deducted on the truck at the time of the gift. John paid the following personal expenses in 2000:

Food	$3,000
Real Estate Taxes on Home	2,500
Repairs to Home	300
Utilities	900
Personal Auto Expenses	1,800
Vacations	1,100
Department Store Purchases	1,700
Interest on Home Mortgage	2,000
Charitable Contributions	500
Life Insurance Premiums	1,500
Medical Bills	600
Entertainment	900
Other	300
Total	$17,100

¶1921

For 2000, John reported adjusted gross income of $19,000. The balances in his bank accounts were $1,500 at the end of 1999 and $18,900 at the end of 2000. Assuming that John correctly reported his income for 1996, the net worth computation would appear as follows:

Assets	*12/31/99*	*12/31/00*
Cash in Banks	$1,500	$18,900
Personal Auto	6,000	-0-
Truck	9,000	-0-
Stock	22,000	-0-
Total Assets	$38,500	$18,900
Liabilities		
Reserve for Depreciation (Truck)	6,500	-0-
Net Worth	$32,000	$18,900
Net Worth 12/31/00		$18,900
Net Worth 12/31/99		(32,000)
Net Worth Increase (Decrease)		($13,100)
Plus: Nondeductible Expenses and Losses		
Gift of Truck		2,500
Loss on Sale of Car		3,500
Loss on Stock in Excess of $3,000		9,000
Personal Living Expenses		17,100
Reconstructed Adjusted Gross Income		$19,000
Reported Adjusted Gross Income		$19,000
Understatement of Income		-0-

¶1922 NONTAXABLE RECEIPTS AND LOSS CARRYOVERS AND CARRYBACKS

Another group of below-the-line adjustments which are subtracted from, rather than added to, the annual net worth changes includes all nontaxable receipts and the tax return deductions allowed for carryover and carryback losses. The subtraction of the nontaxable receipts serves to offset the increase in net worth caused by such receipts. The adjustment for the loss carryover and carryback deductions recognizes that the actual economic impact of such losses occurred in other years. To compensate for the failure to reflect the losses in the net worth for the year of the deduction, the losses are subtracted as special below-the-line adjustments. Deductions allowed for net operating loss carryovers and carrybacks, as well as capital loss carryovers, are examples of such adjustments.

Nontaxable receipts include gifts, inheritances, tax-exempt interest, federal income tax refunds, nontaxable pensions, dividends on life insurance, proceeds from surrender of life insurance policies, personal injury settlements and all nontaxable gains. A common example of such gains is the nonrecognized gain on sale of a personal residence.

Example: During 2000, Mabel Moss received a gift of $6,000 in cash from her mother. She also received an inheritance of $12,000 from her favorite aunt. She had invested in municipal bonds, and in 2000 received interest of $8,000 on such bonds. She owned $90,000 of such bonds at the end of 1999, and $110,000 at the end of 2000. She withdrew her life insurance dividends of $1,500 in 2000. A personal injury action she had instituted in 1996 was settled, and she received $15,000 in 2000. She sold her home in which she had lived for the past 10 years for $110,000 in 2000. She realized a gain of $40,000. On her 2000 tax return, she deducted a net operating loss carryover of $5,000. Her cash in banks increased from $12,500 at the end of 1999 to $15,000 at the end of 2000. In 2000, she invested $150,000 in a partnership venture. She reported adjusted gross income of $15,000 for 2000. Assuming she correctly reported for 2000, a net worth reconstruction of income would show the following:

Assets	12/31/99	12/31/00
Cash in Banks	$12,500	$15,000
Municipal Bonds	90,000	110,000
Interest in Partnership	-0-	150,000
Home	70,000	-0-
Total Assets	$172,500	$275,000
Liabilities	-0-	-0-
Net Worth	$172,500	$275,000
Net Worth 12/31/95		172,500
Net Worth Increase		$102,500

Less: Nontaxable Receipts and Loss Carryovers and Carrybacks

	Amount	
Gift from Mother	$6,000	
Inheritance	12,000	
Interest on Municipal Bonds	8,000	
Life Insurance Dividends	1,500	
Personal Injury Settlement	15,000	
Nontaxable Gain on Home	40,000	
Net Operating Loss Carryover	5,000	
Total		$87,500
Reconstructed Adjusted Gross Income		$15,000
Adjusted Gross Income Reported		15,000
Understatement of Income		-0-

¶1923 ADJUSTMENTS TO ARRIVE AT TAXABLE INCOME

The adjusted gross income determined by adding and subtracting the foregoing items must be further adjusted to arrive at taxable income. These final adjustments, involving the itemized deductions and personal exemptions, are treated in the same manner as they would be on the income tax return and follow the same method of computation in arriving at taxable income.

¶1923

Example: Harvey and Marisa Kluge filed a joint return for 2000. Both were under age 65 and had two dependent children, ages 8 and 10. For 2000, they reported the following itemized deductions:

Interest on Home Mortgage	$3,800
Taxes	2,300
Contributions	800
Medical Expenses (in excess of limitations)	275
Total Itemized Deductions	$7,175

The adjustment to the adjusted gross income determined by the net worth method would appear as follows:

	2000
Adjusted Gross Income as Reconstructed by the Net Worth Method	$34,000
Adjustments to Arrive at Taxable Income	
Itemized Deductions	$7,175
Balance	$26,825
Exemptions	11,200
Taxable Income Reconstructed	$15,625

Source and Application of Funds Method

¶1925 VARIATION OF NET WORTH METHOD

The source and application of funds method, or the expenditures method, is merely an accounting variation of the net worth method using a different format.[11] Net worth may be converted to the source and application of funds by extracting from the net worth statement the annual increases and decreases in the assets and liabilities. The increases in assets and decreases in liabilities are treated as applications of funds. The decreases in assets and increases in liabilities represent sources of funds. The nondeductible expenses and losses in the net worth method are included as applications of funds, while the nontaxable receipts and loss carryovers and carrybacks become sources of funds.

The accounting formula for the source and application of funds method is quite simple. The total of all the sources of funds is subtracted from the total of all applications of funds to arrive at adjusted gross income. To determine taxable income, the normal adjustments are then made for itemized deductions and personal exemptions. Comparing reconstructed taxable income with reported taxable income will disclose any understatement.

The format of this method eliminates those assets and liabilities which have not changed during the period involved by including only changes in assets and liabilities. Those items in the net worth which remain constant over the period in question are not essential to the computation and are excluded. In those cases

---

[11] Use of this method will be upheld where a taxpayer fails to produce evidence to refute the IRS's computations. See *Flood v. Commissioner*, 81 TCM 1175, TC Memo. 2001-39, CCH Dec. 54,247(M).

involving a considerable number of unchanging assets and liabilities, the source and application of funds method offers a clearer and more concise presentation of the essential facts.

> **Example:** Except for the format and the elimination of nonchanging assets and liabilities, the source and application of funds method is identical to the net worth method. The conversion of the following net worth statement to a source and application of funds analysis serves to demonstrate this similarity.

Net Worth

Assets	12/31/99	12/31/00	
Cash on Hand	$3,000	$2,500	
Bank Accounts	1,750	2,975	
Accounts Receivable	7,500	6,200	
Merchandise Inventory	3,220	4,780	
Stocks	4,000	18,000	
Bonds	2,750	2,750	
Equipment	4,175	10,745	
Automobile	2,500	2,500	
Furniture and Fixtures	8,000	8,000	
Residence	50,000	50,000	
Total Assets	$86,895	$108,450	
Liabilities			
Accounts Payable	$2,900	$1,900	
Loans Payable	5,000	7,750	
Reserve for Depreciation	1,225	2,075	
Total Liabilities	$9,125	$11,725	
Net Worth	$77,770	$96,725	
Net Worth 12/31/95		($77,770)	
Net Worth Increase		$18,955	
Plus: Nondeductible Expenditures and Losses			
Income Taxes Paid		$4,200	
Personal Living Expenses		16,500	
Life Insurance Premiums		1,720	
Gift to Third Party		2,100	
Loss on Sale of Personal Auto		3,800	
Net Worth Increase Plus Nondeductible Expenditures			$47,275
Less: Nontaxable Receipts			
Gifts from Third Parties		($925)	
Inheritances		(11,700)	
Net Operating Loss Carryover Deducted in 1996		(2,100)	
Total Nontaxable Receipts			($14,725)
Adjusted Gross Income			$32,550
Less: Standard Deduction			(7,350)

¶1925

Less: Nontaxable Receipts

Balance	$25,200
Less: Exemptions	(5,600)
Taxable Income	$19,600
Less: Taxable Income Reported	($8,025)
Unreported Taxable Income	$11,575

SOURCE AND APPLICATION OF FUNDS

Application of Funds

Bank Accounts	$1,225	
Merchandise Inventory	1,560	
Stocks	14,000	
Equipment	6,570	
Accounts Payable	1,000	
Income Taxes Paid	4,200	
Personal Living Expenses	16,500	
Life Insurance Premiums	1,720	
Gift to Third Party	2,100	
Loss on Sale of Personal Auto	3,800	
Total		$52,675

Sources of Funds

Cash on Hand	$500	
Accounts Receivable	1,300	
Loans Payable	2,750	
Increase in Depreciation Reserve	850	
Gifts from Third Parties	925	
Inheritance	11,700	
Net Operating Loss Carryover Deduction in 1996	2,100	
Total		($20,125)

Adjusted Gross Income	$32,550
Less: Standard Deduction	(7,350)
Balance	$25,200
Less: Exemptions	(5,600)
Taxable Income (Reconstructed)	$19,600
Less: Taxable Income Reported	(8,025)
Unreported Taxable Income	$11,575

Bank Deposit Method

¶1931 GROSS RECEIPTS RECONSTRUCTED

The bank deposit method employs a distinct accounting technique. Unlike the other methods, it is an attempt to reconstruct gross taxable receipts rather than adjusted gross income. It directs primary attention to the taxpayer's bank deposits on the premise that such deposits normally represent current taxable receipts. Before this method can be used, it must be shown that the taxpayer was engaged ina business or some other activity capable of producing income and that regular, periodic deposits were made in the taxpayer's bank accounts.

There are two principal variations of the bank deposit method. The more basic concentrates solely on the bank deposits and, after eliminating identifiable, nontaxable items, arrives at reconstructed gross income. The formula most commonly in use, however, is the bank deposit and expenditures method. This method adds all expenditures of currency to the bank deposits on the theory that such expenditures represent the use of current taxable receipts that have not been deposited.

The bank deposit and expenditures method proceeds on the theory that total deposits, plus currency expenditures, less nontaxable receipts, equals corrected gross income. The deductions and other items not incorporated in the determination of the gross income are then included in the computation to arrive at taxable income.

¶1932 TOTAL DEPOSITS

Total deposits include all funds deposited in checking, savings and brokerage accounts. Allowance for nontaxable items is made in a separate computation. Total deposits must be reconciled for deposits in transit by examining deposits made early in the year under audit and those made in the first months of the following year. Deposits relating to prior years' receipts, but belatedly deposited in the current year, should be deducted from total deposits. Conversely, receipts in the current year deposited in the following year should be added.

> **Example:** Marcus Horn deposited $35,000 into his checking account and $7,000 into his savings account during 2000. He received dividends of $5,000 and net wages of $37,000 in 2000. He received a dividend check of $500 at the end of 1999 which he was not able to deposit in his savings account until January 3, 2000. Two salary checks, each in the amount of $2,500, were received by him in December 2000 but were not deposited until January 2001. If the deposits in transit are ignored, there appears to be no understatement of income. By incorporating the proper adjustments for these items, the total deposits method would disclose the following:

Deposits in 2000—Checking Account	$35,000	
Plus: Current Year's Receipts Deposited in Following Year	5,000	
Reconciled Bank Deposits		$40,000
Deposits in 2000—Savings Account	$7,000	
Less: Previous Year's Receipts Deposited in Current Year	(500)	
Reconciled Savings Deposits		6,500
Total Reconciled Deposits		$46,500
Gross Receipts Reported		(42,000)
Understatement of Income		$4,500

¶1933 CURRENCY EXPENDITURES

Currency expenditures made for any purpose are added to the total deposits on the assumption that such items represent undeposited taxable receipts. Sources of nontaxable currency that may account for these expenditures are separately deducted later as part of the nontaxable receipts.

An analysis of checks will disclose what business and personal expenditures may have been made with currency.[12] One auditing approach simplifies the problem by accepting as correct all business expenses deducted on the tax return. All business checks issued are then subtracted from the total of business expenses to arrive at a balance of the expenses that were presumably paid by currency. Depreciation, amortization and other noncash business deductions are eliminated from this computation.

Currency may be used for a variety of purposes other than routine business and personal expenses. Investments, acquisitions of assets, loans to others, payments on loans and gifts to others may all involve currency as a medium of payment. Such transactions should be carefully examined to determine the source of funds. Cash on hand that is found to exist at the end of the year also will be added to the deposits.

> **Example:** For 2000, Theresa Fall reported business expenses on Schedule C, excluding depreciation, totaling $48,000. Her checks for business expenses totaled $42,000 in 2000. The business reported on the cash method of accounting, and Schedule C disclosed $78,000 of gross receipts for 2000. During 2000, she deposited $70,000 in her checking account and made the following payments in currency:
>
> | | |
> |---|---:|
> | Funds to Broker | $3,000 |
> | Loan to Sister | 2,000 |
> | Purchase of Boat | 800 |
> | Groceries | 2,500 |
> | Entertainment | 3,200 |

Ms. Fall had accumulated $4,500 in cash on hand at the end of 2000. She had no cash on hand at the beginning of the year. A deposits and expenditures analysis would disclose the following:

Total Deposits		$70,000
Currency Expenditures (and Accumulation)		
Business Expenses	$6,000	
Personal Items	11,500	
Cash Accumulated	4,500	
Total Currency Expenditures		$22,000
Gross Receipts from Business (Reconstructed)		$92,000
Gross Receipts from Business Reported		(78,000)
Understatement of Income		$14,000

---

[12] See *McGee v. Comm'r*, TC Memo. 2000-308, CCH Dec. 54,067(M) (IRS analysis of bank deposits and cash expenditures demonstrated understatement of income).

¶1934 NONTAXABLE DEPOSITS AND RECEIPTS

The sum of the total deposits and currency expenditures must be reduced by various nontaxable deposits and receipts. Transfers of funds between checking, savings and brokerage accounts provide the most common examples of nontaxable deposits. A withdrawal from a savings account may be deposited in a checking account or a check may be written for deposit to a savings account. Such transfers are eliminated to avoid duplication of deposited amounts.

Checks written to cash or withdrawals of cash from savings accounts are also deducted. Such items generate currency which is assumed to have been deposited or used for other purposes. Other items which must be eliminated include checks deposited and returned by the bank for insufficient funds, prior year's receipts deposited in the current year, transfers resulting from check kiting, and all other items of nontaxable income. Inheritances, gifts, loans, life insurance proceeds and receipts from the sale of assets are examples of nontaxable items which should be deducted. Cash on hand at the beginning of the year is another source that serves to offset the total deposits and currency expenditures.

Example: Assume that Ms. Fall in the previous example had the following additional transactions during 2000:

Deposits to Savings Account	$8,000
Savings Account Withdrawals Deposited in Checking Account	3,000
Checks Written for Deposits to Savings Account	5,000
Checks Written to Cash	2,500
Customer Checks Deposited but Returned for Insufficient Funds	1,800
Cash Inheritance	8,000
Cash Gifts Received	1,700

On the basis of the above, the deposits analysis would appear as follows:

Total Deposits (Checking and Savings)		$78,000
Currency Expenditures (and Accumulations)		22,000
Total Deposits and Expenditures		$100,000
Less: Nontaxable Receipts		
Transfers from Savings to Checking	$3,000	
Transfers from Checking to Savings	5,000	
Checks to Cash	1,800	
Cash Inheritance	8,000	
Cash Gifts Received	1,700	
Total Nontaxable Receipts		($22,000)
Gross Business Receipts (Reconstructed)		$78,000
Gross Business Receipts Reported		(78,000)
Understatement of Income		-0-

¶1934

¶1935 ACCRUAL BASIS ADJUSTMENTS

Accounts receivable require special adjustments for a business on the accrual method of accounting. Deposits are adjusted to exclude receivables at the end of the preceding year, and receivables at the end of the current year are added. This will conform the deposit method computation of gross income to the taxpayer's accrual basis of accounting.

Adjustments for accounts payable and accrued expenses are only required for an accrual basis business when the indirect method of computing business currency expenses is employed. In these instances, the total expenses and purchases shown on the return must be converted to a cash basis by subtracting the payables and accruals at the end of the year from the total expenses. This total is then increased by the payables and accrued expenses at the end of the preceding year. When checks written during the year are subtracted from the adjusted total, the balance of expenses is presumed to represent currency expenditures.

> **Example:** Assume that Ms. Fall in the previous example reported on the accrual method of accounting with selected balance sheet items as follows:

	12/31/99	12/31/00
Trade Accounts Receivable	$9,000	$14,000
Accrued Expenses	2,800	4,700

The total deposits of $78,000 must be adjusted for the increase in accounts receivable, as follows:

Total Deposits		$78,000
Accounts Receivable 12/31/00	$14,000	
Accounts Receivable 12/31/99	9,000	
Add: Net Increase in Receivables		5,000
Adjusted Total Deposits		$83,000

The business expenses paid by currency would have to be determined as follows:

Schedule C Expenses (Less Depreciation)		$48,000
Accrued Expenses (12/31/00)	$4,700	
Accrued Expenses (12/31/99)	2,800	
Less: Increase in Accrued Expenses		(1,900)
Schedule C Expenses Paid in 2000		$46,100
Checks for Business Expenses		(42,000)
Business Expenses Paid by Currency		$4,100

Burden of Proof

¶1941 INDIRECT PROOF

The burden of proof in civil and criminal tax proceedings plays a prominent role in cases employing indirect proof of income. In criminal evasion cases, the government must carry the burden of proving the essential elements of the tax crime beyond a reasonable doubt. In civil cases, proof of fraud must be by clear and convincing evidence. Despite the difference in expression, however, the practical distinction between the two burdens is virtually nonexistent.

In ordinary civil cases, under a 1998 change in the law, the government will have the burden of proof by a preponderance of the evidence if certain conditions are met.[13] In those cases in which such conditions are not met, the government's determinations continue to be presumed correct until the taxpayer establishes by a preponderance of the evidence that such findings are in error. However, in situations involving deficiencies subject to assessment under the special six-year statute of limitations,[14] the government must prove by a preponderance of the evidence that the taxpayer has omitted twenty-five percent of gross income.

¶1942 CRIMINAL EVASION AND CIVIL FRAUD

When the government uses indirect methods to establish unreported income, courts have recognized potential infirmities in such circumstantial evidence, including its tendency to shift the burden of persuasion to the taxpayer. In criminal cases, courts have established various safeguards to correct these problems and have extended them to the civil fraud field.

The landmark Supreme Court opinion, *Holland v. United States,*[15] established basic safeguards which determine the government's burden in net worth cases. Over the years, other decisions have developed and refined these protective rules, applying them to the source and application of funds method, and partially adopting them in bank deposit cases.

The *Holland* Court devised three prerequisites the government must meet in a criminal net worth case. First, the government must establish an opening net worth "with reasonable certainty" to serve as an accurate starting point. Second, there must be proof of a likely source of current taxable income which could reasonably be found to give rise to the net worth increase. Third, the government must investigate relevant leads offered by the taxpayer to explain the net worth discrepancies, provided that such leads are reasonably susceptible to being checked. A subsequent Supreme Court opinion, clarifying *Holland,* held that the government need not prove a likely source of income if it has negated all nontaxable sources of income.[16]

In bank deposit cases, the government must show that the taxpayer was engaged in a business or other activity capable of producing income and made

---

[13] See discussion ¶415, *supra.*
[14] Code Sec. 6501(c).

[15] 348 U.S. 121 (1954), 54-2 USTC ¶9714.
[16] See *United States v. Massei,* 355 U.S. 595 (1958), 58-1 USTC ¶9326 (per curiam).

regular and periodic bank deposits indicative of a regular business practice.[17] The government must also establish that it made an adequate effort to exclude all nonincome items.[18] Although proof of opening net worth is not required to corroborate the deposits method,[19] the government must establish with reasonable certainty the amount of cash on hand at the beginning of the period.[20] The obligation of the government to investigate relevant leads, which originated in *Holland,* is not imposed in bank deposit cases.

¶1943 NONFRAUD CIVIL CASES

In ordinary civil tax proceedings not involving fraud, under a 1998 change in the law, the government will have the burden of proof if certain conditions are met.[21] If those conditions are not met, the taxpayer has the burden of showing that the Commissioner's reconstruction of income is erroneous. In any event, the protectiverules relating to criminal and civil fraud cases are not generally applicable.[22] However, in the special case involving the six-year statute of limitations on assessment, the full panoply of safeguards will attach to the government's burden of proving a twenty-five percent omission of gross income by the net worth method.[23]

In those cases in which the burden of proof is not shifted to the government, the presumption of correctness which attaches to the government's reconstruction of income may be destroyed by evidence of inherent defects which establish that the determination is seriously in error and that it is arbitrary, speculative or unreasonable.[24] In such cases, once the taxpayer has discredited the method of reconstructing income, even though unable to prove the correct amounts that may be involved, the burden of proof with respect to these amounts shifts to the government.[25] The reconstruction may then be rejected in its entirety, or the court may view the evidence as sufficient to permit an amount to be estimated.[26]

---

[17] See *Gleckman v. United States,* 80 F.2d 394 (8th Cir. 1935), 35-2 USTC ¶9645.

[18] See *United States v. Morse,* 491 F.2d 149 (1st Cir. 1974), 74-1 USTC ¶9228.

[19] See *United States v. Stein,* 437 F.2d 775 (7th Cir. 1971), 71-1 USTC ¶9209, *cert. denied,* 403 U.S. 905 (1971), 71-1 USTC ¶9209.

[20] See *United States v. Slutsky,* 487 F.2d 832 (2d Cir. 1973), 75-1 USTC ¶9430, *cert. denied,* 416 U.S. 937, *reh'g denied,* 416 U.S. 1000 (1974).

[21] See ¶415, *supra.*

[22] See *Tunnel v. Comm'r,* 74 TC 44 (1980), CCH Dec. 36,881, aff'd, 663 F.2d 527 (5th Cir. 1981), 81-2 USTC ¶9823.

[23] See *Cox v. Comm'r,* 50 TCM 317, TC Memo. 1985-324, CCH Dec. 42,200(M).

[24] See *Powell v. Comm'r,* 18 TCM 170, TC Memo. 1959-36, CCH Dec. 23,472(M).

[25] See *Helvering v. Taylor,* 293 U.S. 507 (1935), 35-1 USTC ¶9044; *Welch v. Comm'r,* 297 F.2d 309 (4th Cir. 1961), 62-1 USTC ¶9157; *Llorente v. Comm'r,* 74 TC 260 (1980), CCH Dec. 36,955, modified, 649 F.2d 152 (2nd Cir. 1981), 81-1 USTC ¶9446; *Powell v. Comm'r,* 18 TCM 170, TC Memo. 1959-36, CCH Dec. 23,472(M).

[26] See *Llorente v. Comm'r,* 74 TC 260 (1980), CCH Dec. 36,955, modified, 649 F.2d 152 (2nd Cir. 1981), 81-1 USTC ¶9446.

Records for Examination

¶1945 SOURCES OF FINANCIAL DATA

The following checklist may prove useful in gathering the financial records essential to an analysis of income by an indirect method of proof:

1. Tax returns (income and gift);

2. Business journals, ledgers, financial statements and audit reports;

3. Bank statements, cancelled checks, check stubs and duplicate deposit tickets;

4. Savings account passbooks or transcripts of accounts; certificates of deposit;

5. Financial statements submitted to banks or others;

6. Stock and bond confirmations, brokerage statements and informal records of security transactions maintained by taxpayer;

7. Records of loans payable, including notes, installment loan contracts, land contracts, mortgages and transcripts of bank loan accounts (liability ledger cards);

8. Records of loans receivable, including notes, installment contracts, mortgages and land contracts;

9. Closing statements for real estate transactions;

10. Safe-deposit box entry record;

11. Copies of cashier's checks;

12. Tax return worksheets;

13. Personal records of financial transactions; and

14. Invoices or statements relating to purchase of automobiles, furniture and other substantial assets.

¶1951 Exhibit 19-1

Form **4822** (Rev. 6-83)	Department of the Treasury - Internal Revenue Service **STATEMENT OF ANNUAL ESTIMATED PERSONAL AND FAMILY EXPENSES**

TAXPAYER'S NAME AND ADDRESS	TAX YEAR ENDED

	ITEM	BY CASH	BY CHECK	TOTAL	REMARKS
1. PERSONAL EXPENSES	Groceries and outside meals				
	Clothing				
	Laundry and dry cleaning				
	Barber, beauty shop, and cosmetics				
	Education (tuition, room, board, books, etc.)				
	Recreation, entertainment, vacations				
	Dues (clubs, lodge, etc.)				
	Gifts and allowances				
	Life and accident insurance				
	Federal taxes (income, FICA, etc.)				
2. HOUSEHOLD EXPENSES	Rent				
	Mortgage payments (including interest)				
	Utilities (electricity, gas, telephone, water, etc.)				
	Domestic help				
	Home insurance				
	Repairs and improvements				
	Child care				
3. AUTO EXPENSES	Gasoline, oil, grease, wash				
	Tires, batteries, repairs, tags				
	Insurance				
	Auto payments (including interest)				
	Lease of auto				
4. DEDUCTIBLE ITEMS	Contributions				
	Medical Expenses — Insurance				
	Medical Expenses — Drugs				
	Medical Expenses — Doctors, hospitals, etc.				
	Taxes — Real estate (not included in 2. above)				
	Taxes — Personal property				
	Taxes — Income (State and local)				
	Interest (not included in 2. and 3. above)				
	Miscellaneous — Alimony				
	Miscellaneous — Union dues				
5. PERSONAL ASSETS ETC	Stocks and bonds				
	Furniture, appliances, jewelry				
	Loans to others				
	Boat				
	TOTALS ▶				

Form **4822** (Rev. 6-83)

¶1952 Exhibit 19-2

Chief Counsel Advice 200101030, October 25, 2000

Uniform Issue List Information:

UIL No. 7602.00-00

Examination of books and witnesses

INTERNAL REVENUE SERVICE NATIONAL OFFICE FIELD SERVICE ADVICE

MEMORANDUM FOR ASSOCIATE AREA COUNSEL (SB/SE), NEWARK CC:SB:2:NEW:2

From: Deborah A. Butler, Associate Chief Counsel (Procedure and Administration), CC:PA

Subject: Financial Status Audits

This Chief Counsel Advice responds to your request for advice. Chief Counsel Advice is not binding on Examination or Appeals and is not a final case determination. This document is not to be cited as precedent.

ISSUES:

1. Whether a revenue agent may drive by a taxpayer's house prior to having a reasonable indication that there is a likelihood of unreported income.

2. Whether a revenue agent may conduct a Lexis search to ascertain if the taxpayer purchased real estate during the year(s) at issue prior to having a reasonable indication that there is a likelihood of unreported income.

CONCLUSION:

1. A revenue agent may drive by a taxpayer's house prior to having a reasonable indication that there is a likelihood of unreported income.

2. A revenue agent may conduct a Lexis search to ascertain if the taxpayer purchased real estate during the year(s) at issue prior to having a reasonable indication that there is a likelihood of unreported income.

FACTS:

Revenue agents have inquired whether they are still permitted to drive by a taxpayer's house or conduct a Lexis search to ascertain if the taxpayer purchased real estate during the year(s) at issue prior to having a reasonable indication that there is a likelihood of unreported income in light of the enactment of section 7602(e), which restricts the use of financial status audit techniques.

LAW AND ANALYSIS

The Internal Revenue Service Restructuring and Reform Act of 1998 (RRA' 98), Pub. L. No. 105-206, section 3412, 112 Stat. 685 (July 22, 1998), added new I.R.C. §7602(e), titled "Limitation on Financial Status Audit Techniques." Section 7602(e) provides that "[t]he Secretary shall not use financial status or economic reality examination techniques to determine the existence of unreported income of any taxpayer unless the Secretary has a reasonable indication that there is a likelihood of such unreported income."

The legislative history concerning RRA'98 section 3412 reflects that prior to its enactment, the Internal Revenue Service (Service) could use financial status or economic reality audit techniques to determine the existence of unreported income.

The legislative history states that RRA'98 section 3412 merely prohibits the use of such audit techniques to determine the existence of unreported income until the Service has a reasonable indication that there is a likelihood of such unreported income. H.R. Conf. Rep. No. 105-599, at 270 (1998).

Prior to enacting section 7602(e), the Chairman of the House Committee on Ways and Means requested the General Accounting Office to report on the frequency and results of the use of financial status audit techniques to identify unreported income due to concerns over the treatment of and the burdens placed upon taxpayers. General Accounting Office Report GAO/T-GGD-97-186 (September 26, 1997), Tax Administration, Taxpayer Rights and Burdens During Audits of Their Tax Returns, at 3 and 9 (GAO Report). The term "Financial Status Audit Techniques" is not defined in the Code. As used in the GAO Report, financial status or economic reality audit techniques consist of indirect methods of examination such as the bank deposits method, the cash transaction method, the net worth method, the percentage of mark-up method, and the unit and volume method. GAO Report at 9; Examination of Returns Handbook, IRM 4.2.4.6. The General Accounting Office concluded that these techniques were never used alone and that they were used with other techniques that were used to explore issues other than unreported income, such as overstated deductions. GAO Report at 9.

There are two distinct types of methods of proof in tax cases, direct or specific item methods and indirect methods (financial status or economic reality examination techniques). In the direct or specific item methods, specific items are demonstrated as the source of unreported income. *United States v. Hart*, 70 F.3d 854, 860 n.8 (6th Cir. 1995); *United States v. Black*, 843 F.2d 1456 (D.C. Cir. 1988) [88-1 USTC ¶9270]. With the specific item method of proof, the government uses "evidence of the receipt of specific items of reportable income . . . that do not appear on his income tax return." *United States v. Marabelles*, 724 F.2d 1374, 1377 n.1 (9th Cir. 1984) [84-1 USTC ¶9189]. For example, the Service tracks funds from known sources to deposits made to a taxpayer's bank accounts rather than analyzing bank deposits to identify unreported income from unknown sources. *See United States v. Hart*, 70 F.3d 854, 860 (6th Cir. 1995) (tracing of unreported income from covert police fund is a direct method); *United States v. Black*, 843 F.2d 1456 (D.C. Cir. 1988) [88-1 USTC ¶9270] (monies traceable from dummy corporations to the taxpayer was evidence of specific items of income and not the use of the bank deposits or cash expenditures indirect method of proof). *See also Pollak v. United States*, 1998 U.S. Dist. LEXIS 16224 (N.D. Ill. 1998) (recognizing, in dicta, that directly tracing money transfers from an entity would not be a financial status or economic reality technique).

The Service does not use specific items to support an inference of unreported income from unidentified sources. The use of direct methods simply does notimplicate the provisions of section 7602(e). Thus, there is no prohibition requiring the Service to have a reasonable indication that there is a likelihood of unreported income before resorting to such methods.

When using an indirect method, a taxpayer's finances are reconstructed through circumstantial evidence. *United States v. Hart,* 70 F.3d 854, 860 n.8 (6th Cir. 1995). For example, the government shows either through increases in net worth, increases in bank deposits, or the presence of cash expenditures, that the taxpayer's wealth grew during a tax year beyond what could be attributed to the taxpayer's reported income, thereby raising the inference of unreported income. *United States v. Black,* 843 F.2d 1456, 1458 (D.C. Cir. 1988) [88-1 USTC ¶9270]. Indirect methods are used to support an inference of unreported income from unidentified sources.

The bank deposits indirect method is an analysis of bank deposits to prove unreported income from unidentified sources. This method, which computes income by showing what happened to the taxpayer's funds, may be considered to be a financial status technique when it is used without specific knowledge of a possible traceable source. As such, it is used to supply leads to possible unreported income from sources of such deposits. Examination of Returns Handbook, IRM 4.2.4.6.3.

With the cash transaction indirect method, the Service calculates the unreported income as the amount that the taxpayer's cash expenditures exceeded the taxpayer's sources of cash, including cash on hand at the beginning of the tax period in question, for the particular year. *United States v. Hogan,* 886 F.2d 1497, 1509 (7th Cir. 1989). The Service uses the taxpayer's tax return and other sources to ensure that adequate income has been reported to cover expenses. GAO Report at 9.

The net worth method requires establishing the taxpayer's net worth at the start of the taxable year by listing all assets, including cash on hand, and all liabilities, with the balance being the taxpayer's net worth. A similar analysis is made for the first day of the next taxable year. To any change in the net worth, the Service adds nondeductible expenditures for living expenses, then deducts receipts from sources that are not taxable income and the amounts represented by applicable tax deductions and exemptions. If the increase in net worth, as adjusted, exceeds the reported taxable income, the inference is drawn that there is unreported income. *United States v. Conway,* 11 F.3d 40, 43 (5th Cir. 1993) [94-1 USTC ¶50,009]; *United States v. Boulet,* 577 F.2d 1165, 1167 n.3 (5th Cir. 1978) [78-2 USTC ¶9628].

With the percentage of mark-up method, the Service reconstructs income derived from the use of percentages or ratios considered typical for the business or item under examination. This method consists of an analysis of either sales or cost of sales and the appropriate application of a percentage of markup to arrive at the taxpayer's gross profit. By reference to similar businesses or situations, percentage computations are secured to determine sales, cost of sales, gross profit or even net profit. Likewise, by the use of some known base and the typical percentage applicable, individual items of income or expenses may be determined. Thesepercentages can be obtained from analysis of Bureau of Labor Statistics data, commercial publications, or the taxpayer's records for other periods. IRM 4.2.4.6.6.

With the unit and volume method, gross receipts are determined or verified by applying price and profit figures to the volume of business done by the taxpayer. The number of units or volume of business may be determined from the taxpayer's books and records if they adequately reflect cost of goods sold or expenses. This method is recommended when the Service can determine the number of units handled by the taxpayer and knows the price or profit charged per unit. IRM 4.2.4.6.7 and IRM 4.2.4.6.7.1.

We have not been provided with any specific factual circumstances under which a revenue agent would drive by a taxpayer's house. Nonetheless, this activity would not be prohibited if used in determining whether there is a reasonable indication that there is a likelihood of unreported income so that the Service could resort to setting up unreported income under an indirect method. It should be noted that driving by a taxpayer's house would not be an intrusion on that taxpayer. It should also be noted that the Internal Revenue Manual cautions that due to privacy issues and the intrusiveness of inspecting a taxpayer's residence, such inspections should be limited. The purpose of inspecting the taxpayer's residence includes, but is not limited to, determining the validity of deductions for an office or business located in the residence and determining the taxpayer's financial status. IRM 4.2.3.3.5.

Conducting a Lexis search to ascertain if the taxpayer purchased real estate would be useful when using the net worth method. Such a search would not be prohibited if used in determining whether there is a reasonable indication that there is a likelihood of unreported income so that the Service could resort to setting up unreported income under the net worth method or any other indirect method. It should be noted that a search of property records that are available to the public is not an intrusion on a taxpayer.

If you have any further questions, please call Administrative Provisions and Judicial Practice, Branch 3, at (202) 622-7940.

Deborah A. Butler, Associate Chief Counsel (Procedure and Administration), Henry S. Schneiderman, Special Counsel to the Associate Chief Counsel (Procedure and Administration).

¶1953 Exhibit 19-3

CASH TRANSACTION (T) ACCOUNT

Debits		Credits	
Cash on hand 1/1:		Cash on hand 12/31:	
Business	$_____		$_____
Personal	_____		_____
Checking accounts 1/1:		Checking accounts 12/31:	
_____	_____		_____
_____	_____		_____
Savings/Investments 1/1:		Savings/Investments 12/31:	
_____	_____		_____
_____	_____		_____
Schedule D—gross sales	_____	Sch D—expense of sales	_____
Loan proceeds OR	_____	Loan repayments OR	_____
Increase in loans payable	_____	Decrease in loans payable	_____
Wages	_____	Schedule C:	
		Purchases	_____
Interest	_____	Expenses (less depr.)	_____
		Schedule F:	
Gross rental income	_____	Expenses (less depr.)	_____
		Rental Schedule:	
Tax refunds	_____	Expenses (less depr.)	_____
		Expenses as employee	
Other sources:		(less depr.)	_____
_____	_____	Capital assets acquired:	
_____	_____	_____	_____
_____	_____	_____	_____
		Other capital expenditures:	
Schedule C receipts	_____	_____	_____
Schedule F receipts	_____	_____	_____
		Personal expenses	
		Form 4822	_____
TOTAL	$_____	Other outlays:	
		_____	_____
Understatement	_____	_____	_____
TOTAL	$	TOTAL	$

ACCRUAL METHOD OF ACCOUNTING

Understatement above		$_____
Add: Increase in Accounts Receivable	$_____	
Decrease in Accounts Payable	_____	
Less: Decrease in Accounts Receivable	(_____)	
Increase in Accounts Payable	(_____)	_____
Increase—Understatement		$

¶1954 DISCUSSION QUESTIONS

1. You are an agent of the IRS and you have been assigned the audit of Clyde Conniver. Your examination of 2002 and 2003 shows a substantial understatement of income on the basis of specific items. Your group manager now asks you to audit the years 2000 and 2001. Unfortunately, most of Clyde's records were destroyed in a basement flood, so you are required to do a net worth analysis. Pursuant to your request, Clyde has submitted the following information to you:

Schedule A:	Assets
Schedule B:	Liabilities
Schedule C:	Furniture and Fixtures
Schedule D:	Real Estate
Schedule E:	Miscellaneous Information

Based on the information contained in these schedules, you have been asked to prepare a net worth statement and determine whether Clyde Conniver has understated, overstated or correctly stated his taxable income for the years 2000 and 2001.

For your further information, Clyde Conniver reports his business income on the accrual basis. He was married and had two dependent children during the years 1999, 2000 and 2001. On a Form 1040 for each of the years, the following information appears:

1999	Adjusted Gross Income	$33,000
	Taxable Income	15,760
2000	Adjusted Gross Income	$40,710
	Taxable Income	21,909
2001	Adjusted Gross Income	$18,000
	Taxable Income	-0-

SCHEDULE A
Assets

	12/31/1999		12/31/2000		12/31/2001	
Description	Cost	FMV	Cost	FMV	Cost	FMV
Cash on Hand	$2,100	$2,100	$1,000	$1,000	$100	$100
Cash in Bank	4,500	4,500	6,000	6,000	7,500	7,500
Accounts Receivable	3,200	2,800	4,600	4,000	5,200	5,000
Loans Receivable	3,000	3,000	6,000	6,000	9,000	9,000
Merchandise Inventory	9,000	9,000	12,000	13,000	15,000	17,000
Stocks and Bonds	20,000	42,000	25,000	50,000	40,000	65,000
Personal Automobile*	15,500	14,000	17,500	17,200	17,500	15,000
Furniture and Fixtures	2,500	3,000	3,600	3,200	4,700	4,100
Real Estate	125,000	130,000	175,000	215,000	250,000	400,000
Misc. Personal Property	10,000	12,000	10,000	14,000	10,000	15,000
Total:	$184,800	$212,400	$250,700	$319,400	$349,000	$527,700

* The personal auto originally purchased in 1998 at a cost of $15,500 was sold by Clyde individually on May 15, 2000, for $13,500. A new car was purchased from a car dealer on the same date (May 15, 2000) for a total cost of $17,500.

SCHEDULE B
Liabilities

	12/31/99	12/31/2000	12/31/2001
Accounts Payable	$1,600	$2,400	$1,900
Notes Payable	-0-	2,100	3,200
Real Estate Mortgages	100,000	125,000	200,000
Accrued Payroll	800	1,200	1,600
Total:	$102,400	$130,700	$206,700

SCHEDULE C
Furniture and Fixtures

Date Acquired	12/31/99	12/31/2000	12/31/2001
7/1/85	$2,000	$2,000	$2,000
10/1/87	500	500	500
4/1/93	-0-	-0-	1,100
9/1/94	-0-	-0-	600
11/1/94	-0-	-0-	500
Original Cost	$2,500	$3,600	$4,700
Reserve for Depreciation	(1,900)	(2,200)	(2,400)

SCHEDULE D
Real Estate

Description	Acquired	12/31/99	12/31/2000	12/31/2001
Personal Residence*	6/1/90	$40,000	$40,000	$40,000
Rental Property				
K Street	1/2/92	25,000	25,000	25,000
L Street**	4/2/93	60,000	-0-	-0-
M Street	12/1/96	-0-	110,000	110,000
Raw Land				
Hwy WZ	2/1/97	-0-	-0-	75,000
Total		$125,000	$175,000	$250,000
Reserve for Depreciation		(6,625)	(4,500)	(7,875)

* Purchase price is shown. A $15,000 gain on sale of a prior home was deferred under prior
Code Sec. 1034.

** Sold 11/30/2000 for $75,000. The reserve for depreciation on this property at the time of
sale was $4,875.

SCHEDULE E
Miscellaneous

	1999	2000	2001
Food—Groceries	$3,500	$3,700	$3,900
Home Repairs	120	-0-	200
Domestic Help	520	550	575
Department Store	250	1,000	650
Recreation—Travel	-0-	799	-0-
Real Estate Taxes—Home	2,500	2,100	2,600
Other Miscellaneous Expenses	100	100	100

¶1954

Outside Meals	400	600	500
Utilities—Home	350	350	400
Personal Auto	650	700	800
Life Insurance	425	425	425
Contributions	1,000	1,300	1,600
State Income Tax Withheld from Wages . . .	4,000	4,200	4,400
State Income Taxes Paid with Return	850	601	700
Tax-Exempt Interest	100	-0-	-0-
Gifts to Children	3,000	3,000	3,000
Inheritance Received	-0-	10,000	-0-

2. On the basis of the information set forth in the preceding problem, prepare a source and application of funds statement and determine the difference, if any, between the reconstructed and reported taxable income of Clyde Conniver.

3. Sean Shortcount owns and operates the Shortcount Sales Company, a sole proprietorship. His business employs the accrual method of accounting. Prepare a deposits and expenditures analysis and determine correct adjusted gross income for 2003.

Shortcount Sales Company
SCHEDULE C

Income		
Gross Sales	$250,000	
Cost of Goods Sold (Schedule C-1)	100,000	
Gross Profit		$150,000
Deductions		
Advertising	2,000	
Car and Truck Expense	4,000	
Commissions	3,000	
Depreciation	10,000	
Insurance	2,000	
Legal and Professional Services	3,000	
Profit-Sharing Plan	6,000	
Office Supplies	1,000	
Postage	500	
Rent	5,000	
Repairs	2,500	
Taxes	3,000	
Telephone	2,000	
Travel and Entertainment	8,000	
Utilities	3,000	
Wages	20,000	
Other	5,000	
Total Deductions		80,000
Net Profit		$70,000

¶1954

SCHEDULE C-1

Inventory at 1/1/03	$20,000	
Purchases	130,000	
Total		$150,000
Inventory at 12/31/03		50,000
Cost of Goods Sold		$100,000

SELECTED BALANCE SHEET ITEMS

	12/31/2002	12/31/2003
Trade Accounts Receivable	$60,000	$90,000
Trade Accounts Payable	60,000	40,000
Accrued Expenses—Business	15,000	10,000

OTHER ITEMS REPORTED IN 2000

Gross Receipts from Rents	$20,000	
Less: Cash Expenses	(5,000)	
Depreciation	(10,000)	
Net Rental Income		$5,000
Dividends Received		25,000
Interest on Savings		3,000
Director's Fees		18,000

PERSONAL LIVING EXPENSES BY CHECK OR CASH

Groceries	$7,000
Meals Away from Home	5,000
Clothing	5,000
State and Federal Taxes	20,000
Contributions	3,000
Life Insurance	8,000
Medical Expenses	4,000
Auto	5,000
Vacations	4,000
Other	3,000
Total:	$64,000

BANK ACCOUNT TRANSACTIONS

Shortcount Sales Company Checking Account

Total deposits per bank statement*	$230,000
Checks for business purchases and expenses	200,000
Checks to Mr. Shortcount's personal checking account	30,000
Checks to cash	10,000
Checks to Shortcount's savings account	7,500

* $7,500 of customer checks deposited were returned due to insufficient funds in the customers' accounts; a customer's check for $5,000 received on December 30, 2003, was deposited on January 2, 2004.

Shortcount's Personal Checking Account

Total deposits per bank statement	$65,000
Checks for personal living expenses	30,000
Checks to cash	5,000
Checks to personal savings account	25,000

Shortcount's Personal Savings Account

Total deposits (including earned interest)	$50,000
Withdrawals	10,000

In 2003, Mr. Shortcount made cash gifts to his favorite nephew in the amount of $2,500. The estate of Mr. Shortcount's grandmother was settled in 2003, and he received a check from the estate in the amount of $8,000. For personal reasons, he held the check for several months and did not deposit it in his personal checking account until February 3, 2004.

¶1954

APPENDIX A
STATEMENT OF PROCEDURAL RULES
(26 C.F.R., Part 601)

APPENDIX A
STATEMENT OF PROCEDURAL RULES

(26 C.F.R., Part 601)
Subpart A—General Procedural Rules

[Reg. § 601.101]

§ 601.101. Introduction.—(a) *General.*—The Internal Revenue Service is a bureau of the Department of the Treasury under the immediate direction of the Commissioner of Internal Revenue. The Commissioner has general superintendence of the assessment and collection of all taxes imposed by any law providing internal revenue. The Internal Revenue Service is the agency by which these functions are performed. Within an internal revenue district the internal revenue laws are administered by a district director of internal revenue. The Director, Foreign Operations District, administers the internal revenue laws applicable to taxpayers residing or doing business abroad, foreign taxpayers deriving income from sources within the United States, and taxpayers who are required to withhold tax on certain payments to nonresident aliens and foreign corporations, provided the books and records of those taxpayers are located outside the United States. For purposes of these procedural rules any reference to a district director or a district office includes the Director, Foreign Operations District, or the District Office, Foreign Operations District, if appropriate. Generally, the procedural rules of the Service are based on the Internal Revenue Code of 1939 and the Internal Revenue Code of 1954, and the procedural rules in this part apply to the taxes imposed by both Codes except to the extent specifically stated or where the procedure under one Code is incompatible with the procedure under the other Code. References to sections of the Code are references to the Internal Revenue Code of 1954, unless otherwise expressly indicated.

(b) *Scope.*—This part sets forth the procedural rules of the Internal Revenue Service respecting all taxes administered by the Service, and supersedes the previously published statement (26 CFR (1949 ed., Part 300-End) Parts 600 and 601) with respect to such procedural rules. Subpart A provides a descriptive statement of the general course and method by which the Service's functions are channeled and determined, insofar as

such functions relate generally to the assessment, collection, and enforcement of internal revenue taxes. Certain provisions special to particular taxes are separately described in Subpart D of this part. Conference and practice requirements of the Internal Revenue Service are contained in Subpart E of this part. Specific matters not generally involved in the assessment, collection, and enforcement functions are separately described in Subpart B of this part. A description of the rulemaking functions of the Department of the Treasury with respect to internal revenue tax matters is contained in Subpart F of this part. Subpart G of this part relates to matters of official record in the Internal Revenue Service and the extent to which records and documents are subject to publication or open to public inspection. This part does not contain a detailed discussion of the substantive provisions pertaining to any particular tax or the procedures relating thereto, and for such information it is necessary that reference be made to the applicable provisions of law and the regulations promulgated thereunder. The regulations relating to the taxes administered by the Service are contained in Title 26 of the Code of Federal Regulations. The regulations administered by the Bureau of Alcohol, Tobacco and Firearms are contained in Title 27 of the Code of Federal Regulations.

[Reg. § 601.102]

§ 601.102. Classification of taxes collected by the Internal Revenue Service.—(a) *Principal divisions.*—Internal Revenue taxes fall generally into the following principal divisions:

(1) Taxes collected by assessment.

(2) Taxes collected by means of revenue stamps.

(b) *Assessed taxes.*—Taxes collected principally by assessment fall into the following two main classes—

(1) Taxes within the jurisdiction of the United States Tax Court. These include:

(i) Income and profits taxes imposed by chapters 1 and 2 of the 1939 Code and taxes imposed by subtitle A of the 1954 Code, relating to income taxes.

Reg. § 601.102(b)(1)(i)

(ii) Estate taxes imposed by chapter 3 of the 1939 Code and chapter 11 of the 1954 Code.

(iii) Gift tax imposed by chapter 4 of the 1939 Code and chapter 12 of the 1954 Code.

(iv) The tax on generation-skipping transfers imposed by chapter 13 of the 1954 Code.

(v) Taxes imposed by chapters 41 through 44 of the 1954 Code.

(2) Taxes not within the jurisdiction of the United States Tax Court. Taxes not imposed by chapter 1, 2, 3, or 4 of the 1939 Code or subtitle A or chapter 11 or 12 of the 1954 Code are within this class, such as—

(i) Employment taxes.

(ii) Miscellaneous excise taxes collected by return.

(3) The difference between these two main classes is that only taxes described in subparagraph (1) of this paragraph, i.e., those within the jurisdiction of the Tax Court, may be contested before an independent tribunal prior to payment. Taxes of both classes may be contested by first making payment, filing claim for refund, and then bringing suit to recover if the claim is disallowed or no decision is rendered thereon within six months.

[Reg. § 601.103]

§ 601.103. Summary of general tax procedure.— (a) *Collection procedure.*—The Federal tax system is basically one of self-assessment. In general each taxpayer (or person required to collect and pay over the tax) is required to file a prescribed form of return which shows the facts upon which tax liability may be determined and assessed. Generally, the taxpayer must compute the tax due on the return and make payment thereof on or before the due date for filing the return. If the taxpayer fails to pay the tax when due, the district director of internal revenue or the director of the regional service center after assessment issues a notice and demands payment within 10 days from the date of the notice. In the case of wage earners, annuitants, pensioners, and nonresident aliens, the income tax is collected in large part through withholding at the source. Another means of collecting the income tax is through payments of estimated tax which are required by law to be paid by certain individual and corporate taxpayers. Neither withholding nor payments of estimated tax relieves a taxpayer from the duty of filing a return otherwise required. Certain excise taxes are collected by the sale of internal revenue stamps.

(b) *Examination and determination of tax liability.*—After the returns are filed and processed in internal revenue service centers, some returns are selected for examination. If adjustments are proposed with which the taxpayer does not agree, ordinarily the taxpayer is afforded certain appeal rights. If the taxpayer agrees to the proposed adjustments and the tax involved is an income, profits, estate, gift, generation-skipping transfer, or chapter 41, 42, 43, or 44 tax, and if the taxpayer waives restrictions on the assessment and collection of the tax (see § 601.105(b)(4)), the deficiency will be immediately assessed.

(c) *Disputed liability.*—(1) *General.*—The taxpayer is given an opportunity to request that the case be considered by an Appeals Office provided that office has jurisdiction (see § 601.106(a)(3)). If the taxpayer requests such consideration, the case will be referred to the Appeals Office, which will afford the taxpayer the opportunity for a conference. The determination of tax liability by the Appeals Office is final insofar as the taxpayer's appeal rights within the Services are concerned. Upon protest of cases under the jurisdiction of the Director, Foreign Operations District, exclusive settlement authority is vested in the Appeals Office having jurisdiction of the place where the taxpayer requests the conference. If the taxpayer does not specify a location for the conference, or if the location specified is outside the territorial limits of the United States, the Washington, D.C. Appeals Office of the Mid-Atlantic Region assumes jurisdiction.

(2) *Petition to the U.S. Tax Court.*—In the case of income, profits, estate, and gift taxes imposed by subtitles A and B, and excise taxes under chapters 41 through 44 of the 1954 Code, before a deficiency may be assessed a statutory notice of deficiency (commonly called a "90-day letter") must be sent to the taxpayer by certified mail or registered mail unless the taxpayer waives this restriction on assessment. See, however, §§ 601.105(h) and 601.109 for exceptions. The taxpayer may then file a petition for a redetermination of the proposed deficiency with the U.S. Tax Court within 90 days from the date of the mailing of the statutory notice. If the notice is addressed to a person outside the States of the Union and the District of Columbia, the period within which a petition may be filed in the Tax Court is 150 days in lieu of 90 days. In other words, the taxpayer has the right in respect of these taxes to contest any proposed deficiency before an independent tribunal prior to assessment or payment of the deficiency. Unless the taxpayer waives the restrictions on assessment and collection after the date of the mailing of the

statutory notice, no assessment or collection of a deficiency (not including the correction of a mathematical error) may be made in respect of these taxes until the expiration of the applicable period or, if a petition is filed with the Tax Court, until the decision of the Court has become final. If, however, the taxpayer makes a payment with respect to a deficiency, the amount of such payment may be assessed. See, however, §601.105(h). If the taxpayer fails to file a petition with the Tax Court within the applicable period, the deficiency will be assessed upon the expiration of such periodand notice and demand for payment of the amount thereof will be mailed to the taxpayer. If the taxpayer files a petition with the Tax Court, the entire amount redetermined as the deficiency by a final decision of the Tax Court will be assessed and is payable upon notice and demand. There are no restrictions on the timely assessment and collection of the amount of any deficiency determined by the Tax Court, and a notice of appeal of the Court's decision will not stay the assessment and collection of the deficiency so determined, unless on or before the time the notice of appeal is filed the taxpayer files with the Tax Court a bond in a sum fixed by the Court not exceeding twice the portion of the deficiency in respect of which the notice of appeal is filed. No part of an amount determined as a deficiency but disallowed as such by a decision of the Tax Court which has become final may be assessed or collected by levy or by proceeding in court with or without assessment.

(3) *Claims for refund.*—After payment of the tax a taxpayer may, within the applicable period of limitations, contest the assessment by filing with the district director a claim for refund of all or any part of the amount paid, except with respect to certain taxes determined by the Tax Court, the decision of which has become final. If the claim is allowed, the overpayment of tax and allowable interest thereon will be credited against other liabilities of the taxpayer, or will be refunded to the taxpayer. Generally, if the claim for refund is rejected in whole or in part, the taxpayer is notified of the rejection by certified mail or registered mail. The taxpayer may then bring suit in the United States District Court or in the United States Claims Court for recovery of the tax. Suit may not be commenced before the expiration of six months from the date of filing of the claim for refund, unless a decision is rendered thereon within that time, nor after the expiration of two years from the date of mailing by certified mail or registered mail to the taxpayer of a notice of the disallowance of the part of the claim to which the suit relates. Under the

1954 Code, the 2-year period of limitation for bringing suit may be extended for such period as may be agreed upon in a properly executed Form 907. Also, under the 1954 Code, if the taxpayer files a written waiver of the requirement that the taxpayer be sent a notice of disallowance, the 2-year period for bringing suit begins to run on the date such waiver is filed. See section 6532(a) of the Code.

[Reg. §601.104]

§601.104. Collection functions.—(a) *Collection methods.*—(1) *Returns.*—Generally, an internal revenue tax assessment is based upon a return required by law or regulations to be filed by the taxpayer upon which the taxpayer computes the tax in the manner indicated by the return. Certain taxpayers who choose to use the Optional Tax Tables may elect to have the Internal Revenue Service compute the tax and mail them a notice stating the amount of tax due. If a taxpayer fails to make a return it may be made for the taxpayer by a district director or other duly authorized officer or employee. See section 6020 of the Code and the regulations thereunder. Returns must be made on the forms prescribed by the Internal Revenue Service. Forms are obtainable at the principal and branch offices of district directors of internal revenue. Taxpayers overseas may also obtain forms from any United States Embassy or consulate. Forms are generally mailed to persons whom the Service has reason to believe may be required to file returns, but failure to receive a form does not excuse failure to comply with the law or regulations requiring a return. Returns, supplementary returns, statements or schedules, and the time for filing them, may sometimes be prescribed by regulations issued under authority of law by the Commissioner with the approval of the Secretary of the Treasury or the Secretary's delegate. A husband and wife may make a single income tax return jointly. Certain affiliated groups of corporations may file consolidated income tax returns. See section 1501 of the Code and the regulations thereunder.

(2) *Withholding of tax at source.*—Withholding at the source of income payments is an important method used in collecting taxes. For example, in the case of wage earners, the income tax is collected in large part through the withholding by employers of taxes on wages paid to their employees. The tax withheld at the source on wages is applied as a credit in payment of the individual's income tax liability for the taxable year. In no case does withholding of the tax relieve an individual from the duty of filing a

return otherwise required by law. The chief means of collecting the income tax due from nonresident alien individuals and foreign corporations having United States source gross income which is not effectively connected with the conduct of a trade or business in the United States is the withholding of the tax by persons paying or remitting the income to the recipients. The tax withheld is allowed as a credit in payment of the tax imposed on such nonresident alien individuals and foreign corporations.

(3) *Payments of estimated tax.*—Any individual who may reasonably expect to receive gross income for the taxable year from wages or from sources other than wages, in excess of amounts specified by law, and who can reasonably expect his or her estimated tax to be at least $200 in1982, $300 in 1983, $400 in 1984, and $500 in 1985 and later is required to make estimated tax payments. Payments of estimated tax are applied in payment of the tax for the taxable year. A husband and wife may jointly make a single payment which may be applied in payment of the income tax liability of either spouse in any proportion they may specify. For taxable years ending on or after December 31, 1955, the law requires payments of estimated tax by certain corporations. See section 6154 of the Code.

(b) *Extension of time for filing returns.*—(1) *General.*—Under certain circumstances the district directors or directors of service centers are authorized to grant a reasonable extension of time for filing a return or declaration. The maximum period for extensions cannot be in excess of 6 months, except in the case of taxpayers who are abroad. With an exception in the case of estate tax returns, written application for extension must be received by the appropriate director on or before the date prescribed by law for filing the return or declaration.

(2) *Corporations.*—On or before the date prescribed by law for filing its income tax return, a corporation may obtain an automatic 6-month extension of time (a 3-month extension in the case of taxable years ending before December 31, 1982) for filing the income tax return by filing Form 7004 and paying the full amount of the properly estimated unpaid tax liability. For taxable years beginning before 1983, however, the corporation must remit with Form 7004 an estimated amount not less than would be required as the first installment of tax should the corporation elect to pay the tax in installments.

(3) *Individuals.*—On or before the date prescribed for the filing of the return of an individ-ual, such individual may obtain an automatic 4-month extension of time for filing his or her return by filing Form 4868 accompanied by payment of the full amount of the estimated unpaid tax liability.

(c) *Enforcement procedure.*—(1) *General.*—Taxes shown to be due on returns, deficiencies in taxes, additional or delinquent taxes to be assessed, and penalties, interest, and additions to taxes, are recorded by the district director or the director of the appropriate service center as "assessments." Under the law an assessment is prima facie correct for all purposes. Generally, the taxpayer bears the burden of disproving the correctness of an assessment. Upon assessment, the district director is required to effect collection of any amounts which remain due and unpaid. Generally, payment within 10 days from the date of the notice and demand for payment is requested; however, payment may be required in a shorter period if collection of the tax is considered to be in jeopardy. When collection of income tax is in jeopardy, the taxpayer's taxable period may be terminated under section 6851 of the Code and assessment of the tax made expeditiously under section 6201 of the Code.

(2) *Levy.*—If a taxpayer neglects or refuses to pay any tax within the period provided for its payment, it is lawful for the district director to make collection by levy on the taxpayer's property. However, unless collection is in jeopardy, the taxpayer must be furnished written notice of intent to levy no fewer than 10 days before the date of the levy. See section 6331 of the Code. No suit for the purpose of restraining the assessment or collection of an internal revenue tax may be maintained in any court, except to restrain the assessment or collection of income, estate, chapters 41 through 44, or gift taxes during the period within which the assessment or collection of deficiencies in such taxes is prohibited. See section 7421 of the Code. Property taken under authority of any revenue law of the United States is irrepleviable. 28 U.S.C. 2463. If the Service sells property, and it is subsequently determined that the taxpayer had no interest in the property or that the purchaser was misled by the Service as to the value of the taxpayer's interest, immediate action will be taken to refund any money wrongfully collected if a claim is made and the pertinent facts are present. The mere fact that a taxpayer's interest in property turns out to be less valuable than the purchaser expected will not be regarded as giving the purchaser any claim against the Government.

(3) *Liens*.—The United States' claim for taxes is a lien on the taxpayer's property at the time of assessment. Such lien is not valid as against any purchaser, holder of a security interest, mechanic's lienor, or judgment lien creditor until notice has been filed by the district director. Despite such filing, the lien is not valid with respect to certain securities as against any purchaser of such security who, at the time of purchase, did not have actual notice or knowledge of the existence of such lien and as against a holder of a security interest in such security who, at the time such interest came into existence, did not have actual notice or knowledge of the existence of such lien. Certain motor vehicle purchases are similarly protected. Even though a notice of lien has been filed, certain other categories are afforded additional protection. These categories are: Retain purchases, casual sales, possessory liens, real property taxes and property assessments, small repairs and improvements, attorneys' liens, certain insurance contracts and passbook loans. A valid lien generally continues until the liability is satisfied, becomes unenforceable by reason of lapse of time or is discharged in bankruptcy. A certificate of release of lien will be issued not later than 30 days after the taxpayer furnishes proper bond in lieu of the lien, or 30 days after it is determined that the liability has been satisfied, has become unenforceable by reason of lapse of time, or has been discharged in bankruptcy. If a certificate has not been issued and one of the foregoing criteria for release has been met, a certificate of release of lien will be issued within 30 days after a written request by a taxpayer, specifying the grounds upon which the issuance of release is sought. The Code also contains additional provisions with respect to the discharge of specific property from the effect of the lien. Also, under certain conditions, a lien may be subordinated. The Code also contains additional provisions with respect to liens in the case of estate and gift taxes. For the specific rules with respect to liens, see subchapter C of chapter 64 of the Code and the regulations thereunder.

(4) *Penalties*.—In the case of failure to file a return within the prescribed time, a certain percentage of the amount of tax (or a minimum penalty) is, pursuant to statute, added to the tax unless the failure to file the return within the prescribed time is shown to the satisfaction of the district director or the director of the appropriate service center to be due to reasonable cause and not neglect. In the case of failure to file an exempt organization information return within the prescribed time, a penalty of $10 a day for each day the return is delinquent is assessed unless the failure to file the return within the prescribed time is shown to be due to reasonable cause and not neglect. In the case of failure to pay or deposit taxes due within the prescribed time, a certain percentage of the amount of tax due is, pursuant to statute, added to the tax unless the failure to pay or deposit the tax due within the prescribed time is shown to the satisfaction of the district director or the director of the appropriate service center to be due to reasonable cause and not neglect. Civil penalties are also imposed for fraudulent returns; in the case of income and gift taxes, for intentional disregard of rules and regulations or negligence; and additions to the tax are imposed for the failure to comply with the requirements of law with respect to the estimated income tax. There are also civil penalties for filing false withholding certificates, for substantial understatement of income tax, for filing a frivolous return, for organizing or participating in the sale of abusive tax shelters, and for aiding and abetting in the understatement of tax liability. See chapter 68 of the Code. A 50 percent penalty, in addition to the personal liability incurred, is imposed upon any person who fails or refuses without reasonable cause to honor a levy. Criminal penalties are imposed for willful failure to make returns, keep records, supply information, etc. See chapter 75 of the Code.

(5) *Informants' rewards*.—Payments to informers are authorized for detecting and bringing to trial and punishment persons guilty of violating the internal revenue laws. See section 7623 of the Code and the regulations thereunder. Claims for rewards should be made on Form 211. Relevant facts should be stated on the form, which after execution should be forwarded to the district director of internal revenue for the district in which the informer resides, or the Commissioner of Internal Revenue, Washington, D.C. 20224.

[Reg. § 601.105]

§ 601.105. Examination of returns and claims for refund, credit or abatement; determination of correct tax liability.—(a) *Processing of returns*.—When the returns are filed in the office of the district director of internal revenue or the office of the director of a regional service center, they are checked first for form, execution, and mathematical accuracy. Mathematical errors are corrected and a correction notice of any such error is sent to the taxpayer. Notice and demand is made for the payment of any additional tax so resulting, or refund is made of any overpayment.

Returns are classified for examination at regional service centers. Certain individual income tax returns with potential unallowable items are delivered to Examination Divisions at regional service centers for correction by correspondence. Otherwise, returns with the highest examination potential are delivered to district Examination Divisions based on workload capacities. Those most in need of examination are selected for office or field examination.

(b) *Examination of returns.*—(1) *General.*—The original examination of income (including partnership and fiduciary), estate, gift, excise, employment, exempt organization, and information returns is a primary function of examiners in the Examination Division of the office of each district director of internal revenue. Such examiners are organized in groups, each of which is under the immediate supervision of a group supervisor designated by the district director. Revenue agents (and such other officers or employees of the Internal Revenue Service as may be designated for this purpose by the Commissioner) are authorized to examine any books, papers, records, or memoranda bearing upon matters required to be included in Federal tax returns and to take testimony relative thereto and to administer oaths. See section 7602 of the Code and the regulations thereunder. There are two general types of examination. These are commonly called "office examination" and "field examination". During the examination of a return a taxpayer may be represented before the examining officer by an attorney, certified public accountant, or other representative. See Subpart E of this part for conference and practice requirements.

(2) *Office examination.*—(i) *Adjustments by Examination Division at service center.*—Certain individual income tax returns identified as containing potential unallowable items are examined by Examination Divisions at regional service centers. Correspondence examination techniques are used. If the taxpayer requests an interview to discuss the proposed adjustments, the case is transferred to the taxpayer's district office. If the taxpayer does not agree to the proposed adjustments, regular appeals procedures apply.

(ii) *Examinations at district office.*—Certain returns are examined at district offices by office examination techniques. These returns include some business returns, besides the full range of nonbusiness individual income tax returns. Office examinations are conducted primarily by the interview method. Examinations are conducted by correspondence only when warranted by the nature of the questionable items and by the convenience and characteristics of the taxpayer. In a correspondence examination, the taxpayer is asked to explain or send supporting evidence by mail. In an office interview examination the taxpayer is asked to come to the district director's office for an interview and to bring certain records with the taxpayer in support of the return. During the interview examination, the taxpayer has the right to point out to the examining officer any amounts included in the return which are not taxable, or any deductions which the taxpayer failed to claim on the return. If it develops that a field examination is necessary, the examiner may conduct such examination.

(3) *Field examination.*—Certain returns are examined by field examination which involves an examination of the taxpayer's books and records on the taxpayer's premises. An examiner will check the entire return filed by the taxpayer and will examine all books, papers, records, and memoranda dealing with matters required to be included in the return. If the return presents an engineering or appraisal problem (e.g., depreciation or depletion deductions, gains or losses upon the sale or exchange of property, or losses on account of abandonment, exhaustion, or obsolescence), it may be investigated by an engineer agent who makes a separate report.

(4) *Conclusion of examination.*—At the conclusion of an office or field examination, the taxpayer is given an opportunity to agree with the findings of the examining officer. If the taxpayer does not agree, the examining officer will inform the taxpayer of the taxpayer's appeal rights. If the taxpayer does agree with the proposed changes the examining officer will invite the taxpayer to execute either Form 870 or another appropriate agreement form. When the taxpayer agrees with the proposed changes but does not offer to pay any deficiency or additional tax which may be due, the examining officer will also invite payment (by check or money order), together with any applicable interest or penalty. If the agreed case involves income, profits, estate, gift, generation-skipping transfer or chapter 41, 42, 43 or 44 taxes, the agreement is evidenced by a waiver by the taxpayer of restrictions on assessment and collection of the deficiency, or an acceptance of a proposed overassessment. If the case involves excise or employment taxes or 100 percent penalty, the agreement is evidenced in the form of a consent to assessment and collection of additional tax or penalty and waiver of right to file claim for abatement, or the accept-

ance of the proposed overassessment. Even though the taxpayer signs an acceptance of a proposed overassessment the district director or the director of the regional service center remains free to assess a deficiency. On the other hand, the taxpayer who has given a waiver may still claim a refund of any part of the deficiency assessed against, and paid by, the taxpayer or any part of the tax originally assessed and paid by the taxpayer. The taxpayer's acceptance of an agreed overassessment does not prevent the taxpayer from filing a claim and bringing a suit for an additional sum, nor does it preclude the Government from maintaining suit to recover an erroneous refund. As a matter of practice, however, waivers or acceptances ordinarily result in the closing of a case insofar as the Government is concerned.

(5) *Technical advice from the National Office.*— (i) *Definition and nature of technical advice.*— *(a)* As used in this subparagraph, "technical advice" means advice or guidance as to the interpretation and proper application of internal revenue laws, related statutes, and regulations, to a specific set of facts, furnished by the National Office upon request of a district office in connection with the examination of a taxpayer's return or consideration of a taxpayer's return claim for refund or credit. It is furnished as a means of assisting Service personnel in closing cases and establishing and maintaining consistent holdings in the several districts. It does not include memorandums on matters of general technical application furnished to district offices where the issues are not raised in connection with the examination of the return of a specific taxpayer.

(b) The consideration or examination of the facts relating to a request for a determination letter is considered to be in connection with the examination or consideration of a return of the taxpayer. Thus, a district director may, in his discretion, request technical advice with respect to the consideration of a request for a determination letter.

(c) If a district director is of the opinion that a ruling letter previously issued to a taxpayer should be modified or revoked, and requests the National Office to reconsider the ruling, the reference of the matter to the National Office is treated as a request for technical advice and the procedures specified in subdivision (iii) of this subparagraph should be followed in order that the National Office may consider the district director's recommendation.

Only the National Office can revoke a ruling letter. Before referral to the National Office, the district director should inform the taxpayer of his opinion that the ruling letter should be revoked. The district director, after development of the facts and consideration of the taxpayer's arguments, will decide whether to recommend revocation of the ruling to the National Office. For procedures relating to a request for a ruling, see § 601.201.

(d) The Assistant Commissioner (Technical), acting under a delegation of authority from the Commissioner of Internal Revenue, is exclusively responsible for providing technical advice in any issue involving the establishment of basic principles and rules for the uniform interpretation and application of tax laws other than those which are under the jurisdiction of the Bureau of Alcohol, Tobacco, and Firearms. This authority has been largely redelegated to subordinate officials.

(e) The provisions of this subparagraph apply only to a case under the jurisdiction of a district director, but do not apply to the Employee Plans case under the jurisdiction of a key district director as provided in § 601.201(o) or to an Exempt Organization case under the jurisdiction of a key district director as provided in § 601.201(n). The technical advice provisions applicable to Employee Plans and Exempt Organization cases are set forth in § 601.201(n)(9). The provisions of this subparagraph do not apply to a case under the jurisdiction of the Bureau of Alcohol, Tobacco, and Firearms. They also do not apply to a case under the jurisdiction of an Appeals office, including a case previously considered by Appeals. The technical advice provisions applicable to a case under the jurisdiction of an Appeals office, other than Employee Plans and Exempt Organizations cases, are set forth in § 601.106(f)(10). A case remains under the jurisdiction of the district director even though an Appeals office has the identical issue under consideration in the case of another taxpayer (not related within the meaning of section 267 of the Code) in an entirely different transaction. Technical advice may not be requested with respect to a taxable period if a prior Appeals disposition of the same taxable period of the same taxpayer's case was based on mutual concessions (ordinarily with a Form 870-AD, Offer of Waiver of Restrictions on Assessment and Collection of Deficiency in Tax and of Acceptance of Overassessment). However, technical advice may be requested by a district director on issues previously considered in a prior Appeals disposition, not based on mutual concessions, of the same

taxable periods of the same taxpayer with the concurrence of the Appeals office that had the case.

(ii) *Areas in which technical advice may be requested.*—*(a)* District directors may request technical advice on any technical or procedural question that develops during the audit or examination of a return, or claim for refund or credit, of a taxpayer. These procedures are applicable as provided in subdivision (i) of this subparagraph.

(b) District directors are encouraged to request technical advice on any technical or procedural question arising in connection with any case of the type described in subdivision (i) of this subparagraph which cannot be resolved on the basis of law, regulations, or a clearly applicable revenue ruling or other precedent issued by the National Office. This request should be made at the earliest possible stage of the examination process.

(iii) *Requesting technical advice.*—*(a)* It is the responsibility of the district office to determine whether technical advice is to be requested on any issue before that office. However, while the case is under the jurisdiction of the district director, a taxpayer or his/her representative may request that an issue be referred to the National Office for technical advice on the grounds that a lack of uniformity exists as to the disposition of the issue, or that the issue is so unusual or complex as to warrant consideration by the National Office. This request should be made at the earliest possible stage of the examination process. While taxpayers are encouraged to make written requests setting forth the facts, law, and argument with respect to the issue, and reason for requesting National Office advice, a taxpayer may make the request orally. If, after considering the taxpayer's request, the examiner is of the opinion that the circumstances do not warrant referral of the case to the National Office, he/she will so advise the taxpayer. (See subdivision (iv) of this subparagraph for taxpayer's appeal rights where the examiner declines to request technical advice.)

(b) When technical advice is to be requested, whether or not upon the request of the taxpayer, the taxpayer will be so advised, except as noted in (*g*) of this subdivision. If the examiner initiates the action, the taxpayer will be furnished a copy of the statement of the pertinent facts and the question or questions proposed for submission to the National Office. The request for advice submitted by the district director should be so worded as to avoid possible misunderstanding, in the National Office, of the facts or of the specific point or points at issue.

(c) After receipt of the statement of facts and specific questions from the district office, the taxpayer will be given 10 calendar days in which to indicate in writing the extent, if any, to which he may not be in complete agreement. An extension of time must be justified by the taxpayer in writing and approved by the Chief, Audit Division. Every effort should be made to reach agreement as to the facts and specific point at issue. If agreement cannot be reached, the taxpayer may submit, within 10 calendar days after receipt of notice from the district office, a statement of his understanding as to the specific point or points at issue which will be forwarded to the National Office with the request for advice. An extension of time must be justified by the taxpayer in writing and approved by the Chief, Examination Division.

(d) If the taxpayer initiates the action to request advice, and his statement of the facts and point or points at issue are not wholly acceptable to the district officials, the taxpayer will be advised in writing as to the areas of disagreement. The taxpayer will be given 10 calendar days after receipt of the written notice to reply to the district official's letter. An extension of time must be justified by the taxpayer in writing and approved by the Chief, Examination Division. If agreement cannot be reached, both the statements of the taxpayer and the district official will be forwarded to the National Office.

(e)(1) In the case of requests for technical advice the taxpayer must also submit, within the 10-day period referred to in (*c*) and (*d*) of this subdivision, whichever applicable (relating to agreement by the taxpayer with the statement of facts submitted in connection with the request for technical advice), the statement described in (*f*) of this subdivision of proposed deletions pursuant to section 6110(c) of the Code. If the statement is not submitted, the taxpayer will be informed by the district director that such a statement is required. If the district director does not receive the statement within 10 days after the taxpayer has been informed of the need for such statement, the district director may decline to submit the request for technical advice. If the district director decides to request technical advice in a case where the taxpayer has not submitted the statement of proposed deletions, the National Office will make those deletions which in the judgment of the Commissioner are required by section 6110(c) of the Code.

(2) The requirements included in § 601.105(b)(5) with respect to submissions of

statements and other material with respect to proposed deletions to be made from technical advice memoranda before public inspection is permitted to take place do not apply to requests made by the district director before November 1, 1976, or requests for any document to which section 6104 of the Code applies.

(f) In order to assist the Internal Revenue Service in making the deletions, required by section 6110(c) of the Code, from the text of technical advice memoranda which are open to public inspection pursuant to section 6110(a) of the Code, there must accompany requests for such technical advice either a statement of the deletions proposed by the taxpayer and the statutory basis for each proposed deletion, or a statement that no information other than names, addresses, and taxpayer identifying numbers need be deleted. Such statements shall be made in a separate document. The statement of proposed deletions shall be accompanied by a copy of all statements of facts and supporting documents which are submitted to the National Office pursuant to (*c*) or (*d*) of this subdivision, on which shall be indicated, by the use of brackets, the material which the taxpayer indicates should be deleted pursuant to section 6110(c) of the Code. The statement of proposed deletions shall indicate the statutory basis, under section 6110(c) of the Code, for each proposed deletion. The statement of proposed deletions shall not appear or be referred to anywhere in the request for technical advice. If the taxpayer decides to request additional deletions pursuant to section 6110(c) of the Code prior to the time the National Office replies to the request for technical advice, additional statements may be submitted.

(g) If the taxpayer has not already done so, the taxpayer may submit a statement explaining the taxpayer's position on the issues, citing precedents which the taxpayer believes will bear on the case. This statement will be forwarded to the National Office with the request for advice. If it is received at a later date, it will be forwarded for association with the case file.

(h) At the time the taxpayer is informed that the matter is being referred to the National Office, the taxpayer will also be informed of the right to a conference in the National Office in the event an adverse decision is indicated, and will be asked to indicate whether such a conference is desired.

(i) Generally, prior to replying to the request for technical advice, the National Office shall inform the taxpayer orally or in writing of the material likely to appear in the technical advice memorandum which the taxpayer proposed be deleted but which the Internal Revenue Service determined should not be deleted. If so informed, the taxpayer may submit within 10 days any further information, arguments or other material in support of the position that such material be deleted. The Internal Revenue Service will attempt, if feasible, to resolve all disagreements with respect to proposed deletions prior to the time the National Office replies to the request for technical advice. However, in no event shall the taxpayer have the right to a conference with respect to resolution of any disagreements concerning material to be deleted from the text of the technical advice memorandum, but such matters may be considered at any conference otherwise scheduled with respect to the request.

(j) The provisions of (*a*) through (*i*) of this subdivision, relating to the referral of issues upon request of the taxpayer, advising taxpayers of the referral of issues, the submission of proposed deletions, and the granting of conferences in the National Office, are not applicable to technical advice memoranda described in section 6110(g)(5)(A) of the Code, relating to cases involving criminal or civil fraud investigations and jeopardy or termination assessments. However, in such cases the taxpayer shall be allowed to provide the statement of proposed deletions to the National Office upon the completion of all proceedings with respect to the investigations or assessments, but prior to the date on which the Commissioner mails the notice pursuant to section 6110(f)(1) of the Code of intention to disclose the technical advice memorandum.

(k) Form 4463, Request for Technical Advice, should be used for transmitting requests for technical advice to the National Office.

(iv) *Appeal by taxpayers of determinations not to seek technical advice.*—(*a*) If the taxpayer has requested referral of an issue before a district office to the National Office for technical advice, and after consideration of the request the examiner is of the opinion that the circumstances do not warrant such referral, the examiner will so advise the taxpayer.

(b) The taxpayer may appeal the decision of the examining officer not to request technical advice by submitting to that official, within 10 calendar days after being advised of the decision, a statement of the facts, law, and arguments with respect to the issue, and the reasons why he believes the matter should be referred to the National Office for advice. An extension of time must be justified by the taxpayer in writing

Reg. §601.105(b)(5)(iv)(b)

and approved by the Chief, Examination Division.

(c) The examining officer will submit the statement of the taxpayer through channels to the Chief, Examination Division, accompanied by a statement of his reasons why the issue should not be referred to the National Office. The Chief, Examination Division, will determine, on the basis of the statements submitted, whether technical advice will be requested. If he determines that technical advice is not warranted, he will inform the taxpayer in writing that he proposes to deny the request. In the letter to the taxpayer the Chief, Examination Division, will (except in unusual situations where such action would be prejudicial to the best interests of the Government) state specifically the reasons for the proposed denial. The taxpayer will be given 15 calendar days after receipt of the letter in which to notify the Chief, Examination Division, whether he agrees with the proposed denial. The taxpayer may not appeal the decision of the Chief, Examination Division, not to request technical advice from the National Office. However, if he does not agree with the proposed denial, all data relating to the issue for which technical advice has been sought, including taxpayer's written request and statements, will be submitted to the National Office, Attention: Director, Examination Division, for review. After review in the National Office, the district office will be notified whether the proposed denial is approved or disapproved.

(d) While the matter is being reviewed in the National Office, the district office will suspend action on the issue (except where the delay would prejudice the Government's interests) until it is notified of the National Office decision. This notification will be made within 30 days after receipt of the data in the National Office. The review will be solely on the basis of the written record and no conference will be held in the National Office.

(v) Conference in the National Office.— *(a)* If, after a study of the technical advice request, it appears that advice adverse to the taxpayer should be given and a conference has been requested, the taxpayer will be notified of the time and place of the conference. If conferences are being arranged with respect to more than one request for advice involving the same taxpayer, they will be so scheduled as to cause the least inconvenience to the taxpayer. The conference will be arranged by telephone, if possible, and must be held within 21 calendar days after contact has been made. Extensions of time will be granted only if justified in writing by the tax-

payer and approved by the appropriate Technical branch chief.

(b) A taxpayer is entitled, as a matter of right, to only one conference in the National Office unless one of the circumstances discussed in *(c)* of this subdivision exists. This conference will usually be held at the branch level in the appropriate division (Corporation Tax Division or Individual Tax Division) in the office of the Assistant Commissioner (Technical), and will usually be attended by a person who has authority to act for the branch chief. In appropriate cases the examining officer may also attend the conference to clarify the facts in the case. If more than one subject is discussed at the conference, the discussion constitutes a conference with respect to each subject. At the request of the taxpayer or his representative, the conference may be held at an earlier stage in the consideration of the case than the Service would ordinarily designate. A taxpayer has no "right" of appeal from an action of a branch to the director of a division or to any other National Office official.

(c) In the process of review of a holding proposed by a branch, it may appear that the final answer will involve a reversal of the branch proposal with a result less favorable to the taxpayer. Or it may appear that an adverse holding proposed by a branch will be approved, but on a new or different issue or on different grounds than those on which the branch decided the case. Under either of these circumstances, the taxpayer or his representative will be invited to another conference. The provisions of this subparagraph limiting the number of conferences to which a taxpayer is entitled will not foreclose inviting a taxpayer to attend further conferences when, in the opinion of National Office personnel, such need arises. All additional conferences of this type discussed are held only at the invitation of the Service.

(d) It is the responsibility of the taxpayer to furnish to the National Office, within 21 calendar days after the conference, a written record of any additional data, line of reasoning, precedents, etc., that were proposed by the taxpayer and discussed at the conference but were not previously or adequately presented in writing. Extensions of time will be granted only if justified in writing by the taxpayer and approved by the appropriate Technical branch chief. Any additional material and a copy thereof should be addressed to and sent to the National Office which will forward the copy to the appropriate district director. The district director will be requested to give the matter his prompt attention. He may verify the additional facts and data

Reg. §601.105(b)(5)(iv)(c)

and comment upon it to the extent he deems it appropriate.

(e) A taxpayer or a taxpayer's representative desiring to obtain information as to the status of the case may do so by contacting the following offices with respect to matters in the areas of their responsibility:

Official	Telephone Numbers (Area Code 202)
Director, Corporation Tax Division	566-4504 or 566-4505
Director, Individual Tax Division	566-3767 or 566-3788

(vi) *Preparation of technical advice memorandum by the National Office.—(a)* Immediately upon receipt in the National Office, the technical employee to whom the case is assigned will analyze the file to ascertain whether it meets the requirements of subdivision (iii) of this subparagraph. If the case is not complete with respect to any requirement in subdivision (iii) *(a)* through *(d)* of this subparagraph, appropriate steps will be taken to complete the file. If any request for technical advice does not comply with the requirements of subdivision (iii) *(e)* of this subparagraph, relating to the statement of proposed deletions, the National Office will make those deletions from the technical advice memorandum which in the judgment of the Commissioner are required by section 6110(c) of the Code.

(b) If the taxpayer has requested a conference in the National Office, the procedures in subdivision (v) of this subparagraph will be followed.

(c) Replies to requests for technical advice will be addressed to the district director and will be drafted in two parts. Each part will identify the taxpayer by name, address, identification number, and year or years involved. The first part (hereafter called the "Technical Advice Memorandum") will contain *(1)* a recitation of the pertinent facts having a bearing on the issue; *(2)* a discussion of the facts, precedents, and reasoning of the National Office; and *(3)* the conclusions of the National Office. The conclusions will give direct answers, whenever possible, to the specific questions of the district office. The discussion of the issues will be in such detail that the district officials are apprised of the reasoning underlyingthe conclusion. There shall accompany the technical advice memorandum a notice pursuant to section 6110(f)(l) of the Code of intention to disclose the technical advice memorandum (including a copy of the version proposed to be open to public inspection and

notations of third party communications pursuant to section 6110(d) of the Code) which the district director shall forward to the taxpayer at such time that the district director furnishes a copy of the technical advice memorandum to the taxpayer pursuant to *(e)* of this subdivision.

(d) The second part of the reply will consist of a transmittal memorandum. In the unusual cases it will serve as a vehicle for providing the district office administrative information or other information which, under the nondisclosure statutes, or for other reasons, may not be discussed with the taxpayer.

(e) It is the general practice of the Service to furnish a copy of the technical advice memorandum to the taxpayer after it has been adopted by the district director. However, in the case of technical advice memoranda described in section 6110(g)(5)(A) of the Code, relating to cases involving criminal or civil fraud investigations and jeopardy or termination assessments, a copy of the technical advice memorandum shall not be furnished the taxpayer until all proceedings with respect to the investigations or assessments are completed.

(f) After receiving the notice pursuant to section 6110(f)(1) of the Code of intention to disclose the technical advice memorandum, if the taxpayer desires to protest the disclosure of certain information in the technical advice memorandum, the taxpayer must within 20 days after the notice is mailed submit a written statement identifying those deletions not made by the Internal Revenue Service which the taxpayer believes should have been made. The taxpayer shall also submit a copy of the version of the technical advice memorandum proposed to be open to public inspection on which the taxpayer indicates, by the use of brackets, the deletions proposed by the taxpayer but which have not been made by the Internal Revenue Service. Generally, the Internal Revenue Service will not consider the deletion under this subparagraph of any material which the taxpayer did not, prior to the time when the National Office sent its reply to the request for technical advice to the district director, propose be deleted. The Internal Revenue Service shall, within 20 days after receipt of the response by the taxpayer to the notice pursuant to section 6110(f)(1) of the Code, mail to the taxpayer its final administrative conclusion with respect to the deletions to be made.

(vii) *Action on technical advice in district offices.—(a)* Unless the district director feels that the conclusions reached by the National Office in a technical advice memorandum should be re-

Reg. §601.105(b)(5)(vii)(a)

considered and promptly requests such reconsideration, his office will proceed to process the taxpayer's case on the basis of the conclusions expressed in the technical advice memorandum.

(b) The district director will furnish to the taxpayer a copy of the technical advice memorandum described in subdivision (vi) *(c)* of this subparagraph and the notice pursuant to section 6110(f)(1) of the Code of intention to disclose the technical advice memorandum (including a copy of the version proposed to be open to public inspection and notations of third party communications pursuant to section 6110(d) of the Code). The preceding sentence shall not apply to technical advice memoranda involving civil fraud or criminal investigations, or jeopardy or termination assessments, as described in subdivision (iii) *(j)* of this subparagraph or to documents to which section 6104 of the Code applies.

(c) In those cases in which the National Office advises the district director that he should not furnish a copy of the technical memorandum to the taxpayer, the district director will so inform the taxpayer if he requests a copy.

(viii) *Effect of technical advice.—(a)* A technical advice memorandum represents an expression of the views of the Service as to the application of law, regulations, and precedents to the facts of a specific case, and is issued primarily as a means of assisting district officials in the examination and closing of the case involved.

(b) Except in rare or unusual circumstances, a holding in a technical advice memorandum that is favorable to the taxpayer is applied retroactively. Moreover, since technical advice, as described in subdivision (i) of this subparagraph, is issued only on closed transactions, a holding in a technical advice memorandum that is adverse to the taxpayer is also applied retroactively unless the Assistant Commissioner (Technical) exercises the discretionary authority under section 7805(b) of the Code to limit the retroactive effect of the holding. Likewise, a holding in a technical advice memorandum that modifies or revokes a holding in a prior technical advice memorandum will also be applied retroactively, with one exception. If the new holding is less favorable to the taxpayer, it will generally not be applied to the period in which the taxpayer relied on the prior holding in situations involving continuing transactions of the type described in § 601.201(*l*)(7) and § 601.201(*l*)(8).

(c) Technical advice memoranda often form the basis for revenue rulings. For the description of revenue rulings and the effect thereof, see § 601.601(d)(2)(i)(*a*) and § 601.601(d)(2)(v).

(d) A district director may raise an issue in any taxable period, even though he or she may have asked for and been furnished technical advice with regard to the same or a similar issue in any other taxable period.

(c) District procedure.—(1) Office examination.—(i) In a correspondence examination the taxpayer is furnished with a report of the examiner's findings by a form letter. The taxpayer is asked to sign and return an agreement if the taxpayer accepts the findings. The letter also provides a detailed explanation of the alternatives available if the taxpayer does not accept the findings, including consideration of the case by an Appeals office, and requests the taxpayer to inform the district director, within the specified period, of the choice of action. An Appeals office conference will be granted to the taxpayer upon request without submission of a written protest.

(ii) If, at the conclusion of an office interview examination, the taxpayer does not agree with the adjustments proposed, the examiner will fully explain the alternatives available which include, if practicable, an immediate interview with a supervisor or an immediate conference with an Appeals Officer. If an immediate interview or Appeals office conference is not practicable, or is not requested by the taxpayer, the examination report will be mailed to the taxpayer under cover of an appropriate transmittal letter. This letter provides a detailed explanation of the alternatives available, including consideration of the case by an Appeals office, and requests the taxpayer to inform the district director, within the specified period, of the choice of action. An Appeals office conference will be granted to the taxpayer upon request without submission of a written protest.

(2) *Field examination.—*(i) If, at the conclusion of an examination, the taxpayer does not agree with the adjustments proposed, the examiner will prepare a complete examination report fully explaining all proposed adjustments. Before the report is sent to the taxpayer, the case file will be submitted to the district Centralized Services and, in some cases, Quality Review function for appropriate review. Following such review, the taxpayer will be sent a copy of the examination report under cover of a transmittal (30-day) letter, providing a detailed explanation of the alternatives available, including consideration of the case by an Appeals office, and requesting the taxpayer to inform the district

director, within the specified period, of the choice of action.

(ii) If the total amount of proposed additional tax, proposed overassessment, or claimed refund (or, in an offer in compromise, the total amount of assessed tax, penalty, and interest sought to be compromised) does not exceed $2,500 for any taxable period, the taxpayer will be granted an Appeals office conference on request. A written protest is not required.

(iii) If for any taxable period the total amount of proposed additional tax including penalties, proposed overassessment, or claimed refund (or, in an offer in compromise, the total amount of assessed tax, penalty, and interest sought to be compromised) exceeds $2,500 but does not exceed $10,000, the taxpayer, on request, will be granted an Appeals office conference, provided a brief written statement of disputed issues is submitted.

(iv) If for any taxable period the total amount of proposed additional tax including penalties, proposed overassessment, or claimed refund (or, in an offer in compromise, the total amount of assessed tax, penalty, and interest sought to be compromised) exceeds $10,000, the taxpayer, on request, will be granted an Appeals office conference, provided a written protest is filed.

(d) *Thirty-day letters and protests.*—(1) *General.*—The report of the examiner, as approved after review, recommends one of four determinations:

(i) Acceptance of the return as filed and closing of the case;

(ii) Assertion of a given deficiency or additional tax;

(iii) Allowance of a given overassessment, with or without a claim for refund, credit, or abatement;

(iv) Denial of a claim for refund, credit, or abatement which has been filed and is found wholly lacking in merit.

When a return is accepted as filed (as in (i) above), the taxpayer is notified by appropriate "no change" letter. In an unagreed case, the district director sends to the taxpayer a preliminary or "30-day letter" if any one of the last three determinations is made (except a full allowance of a claim in respect of any tax). The 30-day letter is a form letter which states the determination proposed to be made. It is accompanied by a copy of the examiner's report explaining the basis of the proposed determination. It suggests to the taxpayer that if the taxpayer concurs in the recommendation, he or she indicate agreement

by executing and returning a waiver or acceptance. The preliminary letter also informs the taxpayer of appeal rights available if he or she disagrees with the proposed determination. If the taxpayer does not respond to the letter within 30 days, a statutory notice of deficiency will be issued or other appropriate action taken, such as the issuance of a notice of adjustment, the denial of a claim in income, profits, estate, and gift tax cases, or an appropriate adjustment of the tax liability or denial of a claim in excise and employment tax cases.

(2) *Protests.*—(i) No written protest or brief written statement of disputed issues is required to obtain an Appeals office conference in office interview and correspondence examination cases.

(ii) No written protest or brief written statement of disputed issues is required to obtain an Appeals office conference in a field examination case if the total amount of proposed additional tax including penalties, proposed overassessment, or claimed refund (or, in an offer in compromise, the total amount of assessed tax, penalty, and interest sought to be compromised) is $2,500 or less for any taxable period.

(iii) A written protest is required to obtain an Appeals consideration in a field examination case if the total amount of proposed tax including penalties, proposed overassessment, or claimed refund (or, in an offer in compromise, the total amount of assessed tax, penalty, and interest sought to be compromised) exceeds $10,000 for any taxable period.

(iv) A written protest is optional (although a brief written statement of disputed issues is required) to obtain Appeals consideration in a field examination case if for any taxable period the total amount of proposed additional tax including penalties, proposed overassessment, or claimed refund (or, in an offer in compromise, the total amount of assessed tax, penalty, and interest sought to be compromised) exceeds $2,500 but does not exceed $10,000.

(v) Instructions for preparation of written protests are sent to the taxpayer with the transmittal (30-day) letter.

(e) *Claims for refund or credit.*—(1) After payment of the tax a taxpayer may (unless he has executed an agreement to the contrary) contest the assessment by filing a claim for refund or credit for all or any part of the amount paid, except as provided in section 6512 of the Code with respect to certain taxes determined by the Tax Court, the decision of which has become final. A claim for refund or credit of income

Reg. § 601.105(e)(1)

taxes shall be made on Form 1040X, 1120X, or an amended income tax return, in accordance with § 301.6402-3. In the case of taxes other than income taxes, a claim for refund or credit shall be made on Form 843. The appropriate forms are obtainable from district directors or directors of service centers. Generally, the claim, together with appropriate supporting evidence, must be filed at the location prescribed in § 301.6402-2(a)(2). A claim for refund or credit must be filed within the applicable statutory period of limitation. In certain cases, a properly executed income tax return may operate as a claim for refund or credit of the amount of the overpayment disclosed by such return. (See § 301.6402-3.)

(2) When claims for refund or credit are examined by the Examination Division, substantially the same procedure is followed (including appeal rights afforded to taxpayers) as when taxpayers' returns are originally examined. But see § 601.108 for procedure for reviewing proposed overpayment exceeding $200,000 of income, estate, and gift taxes.

(3) As to suits for refund, see § 601.103(c).

(4) [Reserved.]

(5) There is also a special procedure applicable to applications for tentative carryback adjustments under section 6411 of the Code (consult Forms 1045 and 1139).

(6) For special procedure applicable to claims for payment or credit in respect of gasoline used on a farm for farming purposes, for certain nonhighway purposes, for use in commercial aircraft, or used by local transit systems, see sections 39, 6420, and 6421 of the Code and § 601.402(c)(3). For special procedure applicable to claims for payment or credit in respect of lubricating oil used otherwise than in a highway motor vehicle, see sections 39 and 6424 of the Code and § 601.402(c)(3). For special procedure applicable for credit or refund of aircraft use tax, see section 6426 of the Code and § 601.402(c)(4). For special procedure applicable for payment or credit in respect of special fuels not used for taxable purposes, see sections 39 and 6427 of the Code and § 601.402(c)(5).

(7) For special procedure applicable in certain cases to adjustment of overpayment of estimated tax by a corporation see section 6425 of the Code.

(f) *Interruption of examination procedure.*—The process of field examinations and the course of the administrative procedure described in this section and in the following section may be interrupted in some cases by the imminent expiration of the statutory period of limitations for assessment of the tax. To protect the Government's interests in such a case, the district director of internal revenue or other designated officer may be required to dispatch a statutory notice of deficiency (if the case is within jurisdiction of United States Tax Court), or take other appropriate action to assess the tax even though the case may be in examination status. In order to avoid interruption of the established procedure (except in estate tax cases), it is suggested to the taxpayer that he execute an agreement on Form 872 (or such other form as may be prescribed for this purpose). To be effective this agreement must be entered into by the taxpayer and the district director or other appropriate officer concerned prior to the expiration of the time otherwise provided for assessment. Such a consent extends the period for assessment of any deficiency, or any additional or delinquent tax, and extends the period during which the taxpayer may claim a refund or credit to a date 6 months after the agreed time of extension of the assessment period. When appropriate, a consent may be entered into restricted to certain issues.

(g) *Fraud.*—The procedure described in this section does not apply in any case in which criminal prosecution is under consideration. Such procedure does obtain, however, in cases involving the assertion of the civil fraud penalty after the criminal aspects of the case have been closed.

(h) *Jeopardy assessments.*—If the district director believes that the assessment or collection of a tax will be jeopardized by delay, he/she is authorized and required to assess the tax immediately, together with interest and other additional amounts provided by law, notwithstanding the restrictions on assessment or collection of income, estate, gift, generation-skipping transfer or chapter 41, 42, 43, or 44 taxes contained in section 6213(a) of the Code. A jeopardy assessment does not deprive the taxpayer of the right to file a petition with the Tax Court. Collection of a tax in jeopardy may be immediately enforced by the district director upon notice and demand. To stay collection, the taxpayer may file with the district director a bond equal to the amount for which the stay is desired. The taxpayer may request a review in the Appeals office of whether the making of the assessment was reasonable under the circumstances and whether the amount assessed or demanded was appropriate under the circumstances. See section 7429. This request shall be made, in writing, within 30 days after the earlier of—

Reg. § 601.105(e)(2)

(1) The day on which the taxpayer is furnished the written statement described in section 7429(a)(1); or

(2) The last day of the period within which this statement is required to be furnished.

An Appeals office conference will be granted as soon as possible and a decision rendered without delay.

(i) *Regional post review of examined cases.*—Regional commissioners review samples of the examined cases closed in their district offices to ensure uniformity throughout their districts in applying Code provisions, regulations, and rulings, as well as the general policies of the Service.

(j) *Reopening of cases closed after examination.*—(1) The Service does not reopen any case closed after examination by a district office or service center to make an adjustment unfavorable to the taxpayer unless:

(i) There is evidence of fraud, malfeasance, collusion, concealment or misrepresentation of a material fact; or

(ii) The prior closing involved a clearly defined substantial error based on an established Service position existing at the time of the previous examination; or

(iii) Other circumstances exist which indicate failure to reopen would be a serious administrative omission.

(2) All reopenings are approved by the Chief, Examination Division (District Director in streamlined districts), or by the Chief, Compliance Division, for cases under his/her jurisdiction. If an additional inspection of the taxpayer's books of account is necessary, the notice to the taxpayer required by Code section 7605(b) will be delivered to the taxpayer at the time the reexamination is begun.

(k) *Transfer of returns between districts.*—When a request is received to transfer returns to another district for examination or the closing of a case, the district director having jurisdiction may transfer the case, together with pertinent records, to the district director of such other district. The Service will determine the time and place of the examination. In determining whether a transfer should be made, circumstances such as the following will be considered:

(1) Change of the taxpayer's domicile, either before or during examination.

(2) Discovery that taxpayer's books and records are kept in another district.

(3) Change of domicile of an executor or administrator to another district before or during examination.

(4) The effective administration of the tax laws.

(l) *Special procedures for crude oil windfall profit tax cases.*—For special procedures relating to crude oil windfall profit tax cases, see § 601.405.

[Reg. § 601.106]

§ 601.106. Appeals functions.—(a) *General.*—(1)(i) There are provided in each region Appeals offices with office facilities within the region. Unless they otherwise specify, taxpayers living outside the United States use the facilities of the Washington, D.C., Appeals Office of the Mid-Atlantic Region. Subject to the limitations set forth in subparagraphs (2) and (3) of this paragraph, the Commissioner has delegated to certain officers of the Appeals offices authority to represent the regional commissioner in those matters set forth in subdivisions (ii) through (v) of this subparagraph. If a statutory notice of deficiency was issued by a district director or the Director, Foreign Operations District, the Appeals office may waive jurisdiction to the director who issued the statutory notice during the 90-day (or 150-day) period for filing a petition with the Tax Court, except where criminal prosecution has been recommended and not finally disposed of, or the statutory notice includes the ad valorem fraud penalty. After the filing of a petition in the Tax Court the Appeals office will have exclusive settlement jurisdiction, subject to the provisions of subparagraph (2) of this paragraph, for a period of 4 months (but no later than the receipt of the trial calendar in regular cases and no later than 15 days before the calendar call in S cases), over cases docketed in the Tax Court. Subject to the exceptions and limitations set forth in subparagraph (2) of this paragraph, there is also vested in the Appeals offices authority to represent the regional commissioner in his/her exclusive authority to settle (*a*) all cases docketed in the Tax Court and designated for trial at any place within the territory comprising the region, and (*b*) all docketed cases originating in the office of any district director situated within the region, or in which jurisdiction has been transferred to the region, which are designated for trial at Washington, D.C., unless the petitioner resides in, and his/her books and records are located or can be made available in, the region which includes Washington, D.C.

(ii) Certain officers of the Appeals offices may represent the regional commissioner in his/

her exclusive and final authority for the determination of—

(a) Federal income, profits, estate (including extensions for payment under section 6161(a)(2)), gift, generation-skipping transfer or chapter 41, 42, 43, or 44 tax liability (whether before or after the issuance of a statutory notice of deficiency);

(b) Employment or certain Federal excise tax liability; and

(c) Liability for additions to the tax, additional amounts, and assessable penalties provided under chapter 68 of the Code.

in any case originating in the office of any district director situated in the region, or in any case in which jurisdiction has been transferred to the region.

(iii) The taxpayer must request Appeals consideration.

(a) An oral request is sufficient to obtain Appeals consideration in (1) all office interview or correspondence examination cases or (2) a field examination case if the total amount of proposed additional tax including penalties, proposed overassessment, or claimed refund (or, in an offer in compromise, the total amount of assessed tax, penalty, and interest sought to be compromised) is $2,500 or less for any taxable period. No written protest or brief statement of disputed issues is required.

(b) A brief written statement of disputed issues is required (a written protest is optional) to obtain Appeals consideration in a field examination case if the total amount of proposed additional tax including penalties, proposed overassessment, or claimed refund (or, in an offer in compromise, the total amount of assessed tax, penalty, and interest sought to be compromised) exceeds $2,500 but does not exceed $10,000 for any taxable period.

(c) A written protest is required to obtain Appeals consideration in a field examination case if the total amount of proposed additional tax including penalties, proposed overassessment, or claimed refund (or, in an offer in compromise, the total amount of assessed tax, penalty, and interest sought to be compromised) exceeds $10,000 for any taxable period.

(d) A written protest is required to obtain Appeals consideration in all employee plan and exempt organization cases.

(e) A written protest is required to obtain Appeals consideration in all partnership and S corporation cases.

(iv) Sections 6659(a)(1) and 6671(a) provide that additions to the tax, additional

amounts, penalties and liabilities (collectively referred to in this subdivision as "penalties") provided by chapter 68 of the Code shall be paid upon notice and demand and shall be assessed and collected in the same manner as taxes. Certain chapter 68 penalties may be appealed after assessment to the Appeals office. This postassessment appeal procedure applies to all but the following chapter 68 penalties:

(a) Penalties that are not subject to a reasonable cause or reasonable basis determination (examples are additions to the tax for failure to pay estimated income tax under sections 6654 and 6655);

(b) Penalties that are subject to the deficiency procedures of subchapter B of chapter 63 of the Code (because the taxpayer has the right to appeal such penalties, such as those provided under section 6653(a) and (b), prior to assessment);

(c) Penalties that are subject to an administratively granted preassessment appeal procedure such as that provided in § 1.6694-2(a)(1) because taxpayers are able to protest such penalties prior to assessment;

(d) The penalty provided in section 6700 for promoting abusive tax shelters (because the penalty is subject to the procedural rules of section 6703 which provide for an extension of the period of collection of the penalty when a person pays not less than 15% of the amount of such penalty); and

(e) The 100 percent penalty provided under section 6672 (because the taxpayer has the opportunity to appeal this penalty prior to assessment).

The appeal may be made before or after payment, but shall be made before the filing of a claim for refund. Technical advice procedures are not applicable to an appeal made under this subdivision.

(v) The Appeals office considers cases involving the initial or continuing recognition of tax exemption and foundation classification. See § 601.201(n)(5) and (n)(6). The Appeals office also considers cases involving the initial or continuing determination of employee plan qualification under subchapter D of chapter 1 of the Code. See § 601.201(o)(6). However, the jurisdiction of the Appeals office in these cases is limited as follows:

(a) In cases under the jurisdiction of a key district director (or the National Office) which involve an application for, or the revocation or modification of, the recognition of exemption or the determination of qualification, if the determination concerning exemption is made by a National Office ruling, or if National Office technical advice is furnished concerning exemption or qualification, the decision of the National Office is final. The organization/plan has no right of appeal to the Appeals office or any other avenue of administrative appeal. See § 601.201(n)(5)(i), (n)(6)(11)(*b*), (11)(9)(viii)(*a*), (o)(2)(iii), and (o)(6)(i).

(*b*) In cases already under the jurisdiction of an Appeals office, if the proposed disposition by that office is contrary to a National Office ruling concerning exemption, or to a National Office technical advice concerning exemption or qualification, issued prior to the case, the proposed disposition will be submitted, through the Office of the Regional Director of Appeals, to the Assistant Commissioner (Employee Plans and Exempt Organizations) or, in section 521 cases, to the Assistant Commissioner (Technical). The decision of the Assistant Commissioner will be followed by the Appeals office. See § 601.201(n)(5)(iii), (n)(6)(ii)(*d*), (n)(6)(iv), and (o)(6)(iii).

(2) The authority described in subparagraph (1) of this paragraph does not include the authority to:

(i) Negotiate or make a settlement in any case docketed in the Tax Court if the notice of deficiency, liability or other determination was issued by Appeals officials;

(ii) Negotiate or make a settlement in any docketed case if the notice of deficiency, liability or other determination was issued after appeals consideration of all petitioned issues by the Employee Plans/Exempt Organizations function;

(iii) Negotiate or make a settlement in any docketed case if the notice of deficiency, liability or final adverse determination letter was issued by a District Director and is based upon a National Office ruling or National Office technical advice in that case involving a qualification of an employee plan or tax exemption and/or foundation status of an organization (but only to the extent the case involves such issue);

(iv) Negotiate or make a settlement if the case was docketed under Code sections 6110, 7477, or 7478;

(v) Eliminate the ad valorem fraud penalty in any case in which the penalty was determined by the district office or service center office in connection with a tax year or period, or which is related to or affects such year or period, for which criminal prosecution against the taxpayer (or related taxpayer involving the same transaction) has been recommended to the Department of Justice for willful attempt to evade or defeat tax, or for willful failure to file a return,

except upon the recommendation or concurrence of Counsel; or

(vi) Act in any case in which a recommendation for criminal prosecution is pending, except with the concurrence of Counsel.

(3) The authority vested in the Appeals does not extend to the determination of liability for any excise tax imposed by subtitle E or by subchapter D of chapter 78, to the extent it relates to subtitle E.

(4) In cases under Appeals jurisdiction, the Appeals official has the authority to make and subscribe to a return under the provisions under section 6020 of the Code where taxpayer fails to make a required return.

(b) *Initiation of proceedings before the official Appeals.*—In any case in which the district director has issued a preliminary or "30-day letter" and the taxpayer requests Appeals consideration and files a written protest when required (see paragraph (c)(1) of §§ 601.103, (c)(1) and (c)(2) of 601.105, and 601.507) against the proposed determination of tax liability, except as to those taxes described in paragraph (a)(3) of this section, the taxpayer has the right (and will be so advised by the district director) of administrative appeal to the Appeals organization. However, the appeal procedures do not extend to cases involving solely the failure or refusal to comply with the tax laws because of moral, religious, political, constitutional, conscientious, or similar grounds. Organizations such as labor unions and trade associations which have been examined by the district director to determine the amounts expended by the organization for purposes of lobbying, promotion or defeat of legislation, political campaigns, or propaganda related to those purposes are treated as "taxpayers" for the purpose of this right of administrative appeal. Thus, upon requesting appellate consideration and filing a written protest, when required, to the district director's findings that a portion of member dues is to be disallowed as a deduction to each member because expended for such purposes, the organization will be afforded full rights of administrative appeal to the Appeals activity similar to those rights afforded to taxpayers generally. After review of any required written protest by the district director, the case and its administrative record are referred to the Appeals. Appeals may refuse to accept a protested nondocketed case where preliminary review indicates it requires further consideration or development. No taxpayer is required to submit the case to the Appeals for consideration. Appeal is at the option of the taxpayer. After the issuance by the district director of a statutory notice of deficiency, upon the taxpayer's request, the Appeals may take up the case for settlement and may grant the taxpayer a conference thereon.

(c) *Nature of proceedings before Appeals.*—Proceedings before the Appeals are informal. Testimony under oath is not taken, although matters alleged as facts may be required to be submitted in the form of affidavits, or declared to be true under the penalties of perjury. Taxpayers may represent themselves or designate a qualified representative to act for them. See Subpart E of this part for conference and practice requirements. At any conference granted by the Appeals on a nondocketed case, the district director will be represented if the Appeals official having settlement authority and the district director deem it advisable. At any such conference on a case involving the ad valorem fraud penalty for which criminal prosecution against the taxpayer (or a related taxpayer involving the same transaction) has been recommended to the Department of Justice for willful attempt to evade or defeat tax, or for willful failure to file a return, the District Counsel will be represented if he or she so desires.

(d) *Disposition and settlement of cases before the Appeals.*—(1) *General.*—During consideration of a case, the Appeals office should neither reopen an issue as to which the taxpayer and the office of the district director are in agreement nor raise a new issue, unless the ground for such action is a substantial one and the potential effect upon the tax liability is material. If the Appeals raises a new issue, the taxpayer or the taxpayer's representative should be so advised and offered an opportunity for discussion prior to the taking of any formal action, such as the issuance of a statutory notice of deficiency.

(2) *Cases not docketed in the Tax Court.*—(i) If after consideration of the case by the Appeals a satisfactory settlement of some or all the issues is reached with the taxpayer, the taxpayer will be requested to sign Form 870-AD or other appropriate agreement form waiving restrictions on the assessment and collection of any deficiency and accepting any overassessment resulting from the agreed settlement. In addition, in partially unagreed cases, a statutory notice of deficiency will be prepared and issued in accordance with subdivision (ii) of this subparagraph with respect to the unagreed issue or issues.

(ii) If after consideration of the case by Appeals it is determined that there is a deficiency in income, profits, estate, generation-skip-ping transfer gift tax, or chapter 41, 42, 43, or 44 tax liability to which the taxpayer does not agree, a statutory notice of deficiency will be prepared and issued by Appeals. Officers of the Appeals office having authority for the administrative determination of tax liabilities referred to in paragraph (a) of this section are also authorized to prepare, sign on behalf of the Commissioner, and send to the taxpayer by registered or certified mail any statutory notice of deficiency prescribed in sections 6212 and 6861 of the Code, and in corresponding provisions of the Internal Revenue Code of 1939. Within 90 days, or 150 days if the notice is addressed to a person outside of the States of the Union and the District of Columbia, aftersuch a statutory notice of deficiency is mailed (not counting Saturday, Sunday, or a legal holiday in the District of Columbia as the last day), the taxpayer may file a petition with the U.S. Tax Court for a redetermination of the deficiency. In addition, if a claim for refund is disallowed in full or in part by the Appelate Division and the taxpayer does not sign Form 2297, Appeals will prepare the statutory notice of claim disallowance and send it to the taxpayer by certified mail (or registered mail if the taxpayer is outside the United States), with a carbon copy to the taxpayer's representative by regular mail, if appropriate. In any other unagreed case, the case and its administrative file will be forwarded to the appropriate function with directions to take action with respect to the tax liability determined in Appeals. Administrative appeal procedures will apply to 100-percent penalty cases, except where an assessment is made because of Chief Counsel's request to support a third-party action in a pending refund suit. See Rev. Proc. 69-26.

(iii) Taxpayers desiring to further contest unagreed excise (other than those under chapters 41 through 44 of the Code) and employment tax cases and 100-percent penalty cases must pay the additional tax (or portion thereof of divisible taxes) when assessed, file claim for refund within the applicable statutory period of limitations (ordinarily three years from time return was required to be filed or two years from payment, whichever expires later), and upon disallowance of claim or after six months from date claim was filed, file suit in U.S. District Court or U.S. Claims Court. Suits for refund of taxes paid are under the jurisdiction of the Department of Justice.

(3) *Cases docketed in the Tax Court.*—(i) If the case under consideration in the Appeals is docketed in the Tax Court and agreement is reached with the taxpayer with respect to the issues in-

volved, the disposition of the case is effected by a stipulation of agreed deficiency or overpayment to be filed with the Tax Court and in conformity with which the Court will enter its order.

(ii) If the case under consideration in Appeals is docketed in the Tax Court and the issues remain unsettled after consideration and conference in Appeals, the case will be referred to the appropriate district counsel for the region for defense of the tax liability determined.

(iii) If the deficiency notice in a case docketed in the Tax Court was not issued by the Appeals office and no recommendation for criminal prosecution is pending, the case will be referred by the district counsel to the Appeals office for settlement as soon as it is at issue in the Tax Court. The settlement procedure shall be governed by the following rules:

(a) The Appeals office will have exclusive settlement jurisdiction for a period of 4 months over certain cases docketed in the Tax Court. The 4-month period will commence at the time Appeals receives the case from Counsel, which will be after the case is at issue. Appeals will arrange settlement conferences in such cases within 45 days of receipt of the case. In the event of a settlement, Appeals will prepare and forward to Counsel the necessary computations and any stipulation decisions secured. Counsel will prepare any needed settlement documents for execution by the parties and filing with the Tax Court. Appeals will also have authority to settle less than all the issues in the case and to refer the unsettled issues to Counsel for disposition. In the event of a partial settlement, Appeals will inform Counsel of the agreement of the petitioner(s) and Appeals may secure and forward to Counsel a stipulation covering the agreed issues. Counsel will, if necessary, prepare documents reflecting settlement of the agreed issues for execution by the parties and filing with the Tax Court at the appropriate time.

(b) At the end of the 4-month period, or before that time if Appeals determines the case is not suceptible of settlement, the case will be returned to Counsel. Thereafter, Counsel will have exclusive authority to dispose of the case. If, at the end of the 4-month period, there is substantial likelihood that a settlement of the entire case can be effected in a reasonable period of time, Counsel may extend Appeals settlement jurisdiction for a period not to exceed 60 days, but not beyond the date of the receipt of a trial calendar upon which the case appears. Extensions beyond the 60-day period or after the event indicated will be granted only with the personal approval of regional counsel and will be made

only in those cases in which the probability of settlement of the case in its entirety by Appeals clearly outweighs the need to commence trial preparation.

(c) During the period of Appeals jurisdiction, Appeals will make available such files and information as may be necessary for Counsel to take any action required by the Court or which is in the best interests of the Government. When a case is referred by Counsel to Appeals, Counsel may indicate areas of needed factual development or areas of possible technical uncertainties. In referring a case to Counsel, Appeals will furnish its summary of the facts and the pertinent legal authorities.

(d) The Appeals office may specify that proposed Counsel settlements be referred back toAppeals for its views. Appeals may protest the proposed Counsel settlements. If Counsel disagrees with Appeals, the Regional Counsel will determine the disposition of the cases.

(e) If an offer is received at or about the time of trial in a case designated by the Appeals office for settlement consultation, Counsel will endeavor to have the case placed on a motions calendar to permit consultation with and review by Appeals in accordance with the foregoing procedures.

(f) For issues in docketed and nondocketed cases pending with Appeals which are related to issues in docketed cases over which Counsel has jurisdiction, no settlement offer will be accepted by either Appeals or Counsel unless both agree that the offer is acceptable. The protest procedure will be available to Appeals and regional counsel will have authority to resolve the issue with respect to both the Appeals and Counsel cases. If settlement of the docketed case requires approval by regional counsel or Chief Counsel, the final decision with respect to the issues under the jurisdiction of both Appeals and Counsel will be made by regional counsel or Chief Counsel. See Rev. Proc. 79-59.

(g) Cases classified as "Small Tax" cases by the Tax Court are given expeditious consideration because such cases are not included on a Trial Status Request. These cases are considered by the Court as ready for placing on a trial calendar as soon as the answer has been filed and are given priority by the Court for trial over other docketed cases. These cases are designated by the Court as small tax cases upon request of petitioners and will include letter "S" as part of the docket number.

(e) *Transfer and centralization of cases.*—(1) An Appeals office is authorized to transfer settle-

Reg. §601.106(e)(1)

ment jurisdiction in a non-docketed case or in an excise or employment tax case to another region, if the taxpayer resides in and the taxpayer's books and records are located (or can be made available) in such other region. Otherwise, transfer to another region requires the approval of the Director of the Appeals Division.

(2) An Appeals office is authorized to transfer settlement jurisdiction in a docketed case to another region if the location for the hearing by the Tax Court has been set in such other region, except that if the place of hearing is Washington, D.C., settlement jurisdiction shall not be transferred to the region in which Washington, D.C., is located unless the petitioner resides in and the petitioner's books and records are located (or can be made available) in that region. Otherwise, transfer to another region requires the approval of the Director of the Appeals Division. Likewise, the Chief Counsel has corresponding authority to transfer the jurisdiction, authority, and duties of the regional counsel for any region to the regional counsel of another region within which the case has been designated for trial before the Tax Court.

(3) Should a regional commissioner determine that it would better serve the interests of the Government, he or she may, by order in writing, withdraw any case not docketed before the Tax Court from the jurisdiction of the Appeals office of the region, and provide for its disposition under his or her personal direction.

(f) *Conference and practice requirements.*—Practice and conference procedure before Appeals is governed by Treasury Department Circular 230 as amended (31 CFR Part 10) [¶ 44,500 et seq.], and the requirements of Subpart E of this part [¶ 44,408 et seq.]. In addition to such rules but not in modification of them, the following rules are also applicable to practice before Appeals:

(1) *Rule I.*—An exaction by the U.S. Government, which is not based upon law, statutory or otherwise, is a taking of property without due process of law, in violation of the Fifth Amendment to the U.S. Constitution. Accordingly, an Appeals representative in his or her conclusions of fact or application of the law, shall hew to the law and the recognized standards of legal construction. It shall be his or her duty to determine the correct amount of the tax, with strict impartiality as between the taxpayer and the Government, and without favoritism or discrimination as between taxpayers.

(2) *Rule II.*—Appeals will ordinarily give serious consideration to an offer to settle a tax

controversy on a basis which fairly reflects the relative merits of the opposing views in light of the hazards which would exist if the case were litigated. However, no settlement will be made based upon nuisance value of the case to either party. If the taxpayer makes an unacceptable proposal of settlement under circumstances indicating a good-faith attempt to reach an agreed disposition of the case on a basis fair both to the Government and the taxpayer, the Appeals official generally should give an evaluation of the case in such a manner as to enable the taxpayer to ascertain the kind of settlement that would be recommended for acceptance. Appeals may defer action on or decline to settle some cases or issues (for example, issues on which action has been suspended nationwide) in order to achieve greater uniformity and enhance overall voluntary compliance with the tax laws.

(3) *Rule III.*—Where the Appeals officer recommends acceptance of the taxpayer's proposal of settlement, or, in the absence of a proposal, recommends action favorable to the taxpayer, and said recommendation is disapproved in whole or in part by a reviewing officer in the Appeals, the taxpayer shall be so advised and upon written request shall be accorded a conference with such reviewing officer. The Appeals may disregard this rule where the interest of the Government would be injured by delay, as for example, in a case involving the imminent expiration of limitation or the dissipation of assets.

(4) *Rule IV.*—Where the Appeals official having settlement authority and the district director deem it advisable, the district director may be represented at any Appeals conferences on a non-docketed case. This rule is also applicable to the Director, Foreign Operations District, in the event his or her office issued the preliminary or "30-day letter."

(5) *Rule V.*—In order to bring an unagreed income, profits, estate, gift, or chapter 41, 42, 43, or 44 tax case in prestatutory notice status, an employment or excise tax case, a penalty case, an Employee Plans and Exempt Organization case, a termination of taxable year assessment case, a jeopardy assessment case, or an offer in compromise before the Appeals office, the taxpayer or the taxpayer's representative should first request Appeals consideration and, when required, file with the district office (including the Foreign Operations District) or service center a written protest setting forth specifically the reasons for the refusal to accept the findings. If the protest includes a statement of facts upon which the taxpayer relies, such statement should be de-

clared to be true under the penalties of perjury. The protest and any new facts, law, or arguments presented therewith will be reviewed by the receiving office for the purpose of deciding whether further development or action is required prior to referring the case to the Appeals. Where the Appeals has an issue under consideration it may, with the concurrence of the taxpayer, assume jurisdiction in a related case, after the office having original jurisdiction has completed any necessary action. The Director, Appeals Division, may authorize the regional Appeals office to accept jurisdiction (after any necessary action by office having original jurisdiction) in specified classes of cases without written protests provided written or oral requests for Appeals consideration are submitted by or for each taxpayer.

(6) *Rule VI.*—A taxpayer cannot withhold evidence from the district director of internal revenue and expect to introduce it for the first time before the Appeals, at a conference in nondocketed status, without being subject to having the case returned to the district director for reconsideration. Where newly discovered evidence is submitted for the first time to the Appeals, in a case pending in nondocketed status, that office, in the reasonable exercise of its discretion, may transmit same to the district director for his or her consideration and comment.

(7) *Rule VII.*—Where the taxpayer has had the benefit of a conference before the Appeals office in the prestatutory notice status, or where the opportunity for such a conference was accorded but not availed of, there will be no conference granted before the Appeals office in the 90-day status after the mailing of the statutory notice of deficiency, in the absence of unusual circumstances.

(8) *Rule VIII.*—In cases not docketed in the United States Tax Court on which a conference is being conducted by the Appeals office, the district counsel may be requested to attend and to give legal advice in the more difficult cases, or on matters of legal or litigating policy.

(9) *Rule IX—Technical advice from the National Office.*—(i) *Definition and nature of technical advice.*—*(a)* As used in this subparagraph, "technical advice" means advice or guidance as to the interpretation and proper application of internal revenue laws, related statutes, and regulations, to a specific set of facts, furnished by the National Office upon request of an Appeals office in connection with the processing and consideration of a nondocketed case. It is furnished as a means of assisting Service personnel in closing cases and establishing and maintaining consistent holdings in the various regions. It does not include memorandum on matters of general technical application furnished to Appeals offices where the issues are not raised in connection with the consideration and handling of a specific taxpayer's case.

(b) The provisions of this subparagraph do not apply to a case under the jurisdiction of a district director or the Bureau of Alcohol, Tobacco, and Firearms, to Employee Plans, Exempt Organization, or certain penalty cases being considered by an Appeals office, or to any case previously considered by an Appeals office. The technical advice provisions applicable to cases under the jurisdiction of a district director, other than Employee Plans and Exempt Organization cases, are set forth in § 601.105(b)(5). The technical advice provisions applicable to Employee Plans and Exempt Organization cases are set forth in § 601.201(n)(9). Technical advice may not be requested with respect to a taxable period if a prior Appeals disposition of the same taxable period of the same taxpayer's case was based on mutual concessions (ordinarily with a form 870-AD, Offer of Waiver of Restrictions on Assessment and Collection of Deficiency in Tax and of Acceptance of Overassessment). However, technical advice may be requested by a district director on issues previously considered in a prior Appeals disposition, not based on mutual concessions, of the same taxable periods of the same taxpayer with the concurrence of the Appeals office that had the case.

(c) The consideration or examination of the facts relating to a request for a determination letter is considered to be in connection with the consideration and handling of a taxpayer's case. Thus, an Appeals office may, under this subparagraph, request technical advice with respect to the consideration of a request for a determination letter. The technical advice provisions applicable to a request for a determination letter in Employee Plans and Exempt Organization cases are set forth in § 601.201(n)(9).

(d) If an Appeals office is of the opinion that a ruling letter previously issued to a taxpayer should be modified or revoked and it requests the National Office to reconsider the ruling, the reference of the matter to the National Office is treated as a request for technical advice. The procedures specified in subdivision (iii) of this subparagraph should be followed in order that the National Office may consider the recommendation. Only the National Office can revoke a ruling letter. Before referral to the National

Office, the Appeals office should inform the taxpayer of its opinion that the ruling letter should be revoked. The Appeals office, after development of the facts and consideration of the taxpayer's arguments, will decide whether to recommend revocation of the ruling to the National Office. For procedures relating to a request for a ruling, see § 601.201.

(*e*) The Assistant Commissioner (Technical), acting under a delegation of authority from the Commissioner of Internal Revenue, is exclusively responsible for providing technical advice in any issue involving the establishment of basic principles and rules for the uniform interpretation and application of tax laws in cases under this subparagraph. This authority has been largely redelegated to subordinate officials.

(ii) *Areas in which technical advice may be requested.*—(*a*) Appeals offices may request technical advice on any technical or procedural question that develops during the processing and consideration of a case. These procedures are applicable as provided in subdivision (i) of this subparagraph.

(*b*) As provided in § 601.105(b)(5)(ii)(*b*) and (iii)(*a*), requests for technical advice should be made at the earliest possible stage of the examination process. However, if identification of an issue on which technical advice is appropriate is not made until the case is in Appeals, a decision to request such advice (in nondocketed cases) should be made prior to or at the first conference.

(*c*) Subject to the provisions of (*b*) of this subdivision, Appeals Offices are encouraged to request technical advice on any technical or procedural question arising in connection with a case described in subdivision (i) of this subparagraph which cannot be resolved on the basis of law, regulations, or a clearly applicable revenue ruling or other precedent issued by the National Office.

(iii) *Requesting technical advice.*—(*a*) It is the responsibility of the Appeals Office to determine whether technical advice is to be requested on any issue being considered. However, while the case is under the jurisdiction of the Appeals Office, a taxpayer or his/her representative may request that an issue be referred to the National Office for technical advice on the grounds that a lack of uniformity exists as to the disposition of the issue, or that the issue is so unusual or complex as to warrant consideration by the National Office. While taxpayers are encouraged to make written requests setting forth the facts,

law, and argument with respect to the issue, and reason for requesting National Office advice, a taxpayer may make the request orally. If, after considering the taxpayer's request, the Appeals Officer is of the opinion that the circumstances do not warrant referral of the case to the National Office, he/she will so advise the taxpayer. (See subdivision (iv) of this subparagraph for taxpayer's appeal rights where the Appeals Officer declines to request technical advice.)

(*b*) When technical advise is to be requested, whether or not upon the request of the taxpayer, the taxpayer will be so advised, except as noted in (*j*) of this subdivision. If the Appeals Office initiates the action, the taxpayer will be furnished a copy of the statement of the pertinent facts and the question or questions proposed for submission to the National Office. The request for advice should be so worded as to avoid possible misunderstanding, in the National Office, of the facts or of the specific point or points at issue.

(*c*) After receipt of the statement of facts and specific questions, the taxpayer will be given 10 calendar days in which to indicate in writing the extent, if any, to which he/she may not be in complete agreement. An extension of time must be justified by the taxpayer in writing and approved by the Chief, Appeals Office. Every effort should be made to reach agreement as to the facts and specific points at issue. If agreement cannot be reached, the taxpayer may submit, within 10 calendar days after receipt of notice from the Appeals Office, a statement of his/her understanding as to the specific point or points at issue which will be forwarded to the National Office with the request for advice. An extension of time must be justified by the taxpayer in writing and approved by the Chief, Appeals Office.

(*d*) If the taxpayer initiates the action to request advice, and his/her statement of the facts and point or points at issue are not wholly acceptable to the Appeals Office, the taxpayer will be advised in writing as to the areas of disagreement. The taxpayer will be given 10 calendar days after receipt of the written notice to reply to such notice. An extension of time must be justified by the taxpayer in writing and approved by the Chief, Appeals Office. If agreement cannot be reached, both the statements of the taxpayer and the Appeals Office will be forwarded to the National Office.

(*e*)(1) In the case of requests for technical advice, the taxpayer must also submit, within the 10-day period referred to in (*c*) and (*d*) of this subdivision, whichever is applicable (relating to agreement by the taxpayer with the statement of facts and points submitted in connection with the request for technical advice), the statement described in (*f*) of this subdivision of proposed deletions pursuant to section 6110(c) of the Code. If the statement is not submitted, the taxpayer will be informed by the Appeals Office that the statement is required. If the Appeals Office does not receive the statement within 10 days after the taxpayer has been informed of the need for the statement, the Appeals Office may decline to submit the request for technical advice. If the Appeals Office decides to request technical advice in a case where the taxpayer has not submitted the statement of proposed deletions, the National Office will make those deletions which in the judgment of the Commissioner are required by section 6110(c) of the Code.

(*2*) The requirements included in this subparagraph relating to the submission of statements and other material with respect to proposed deletions to be made from technical advice memoranda before public inspection is permitted to take place do not apply to requests for any document to which section 6104 of the Code applies.

(*f*) In order to assist the Internal Revenue Service in making the deletions required by section 6110(c) of the Code, from the text of technical advice memoranda which are open to public inspection pursuant to section 6110(a) of the Code, there must accompany requests for such technical advice either a statement of the deletions proposed by the taxpayer, or a statement that no information other than names, addresses, and taxpayer identifying numbers need be deleted. Such statements shall be made in a separate document. The statement of proposed deletions shall be accompanied by a copy of all statements of facts and supporting documents which are submitted to the National Office pursuant to (*c*) or (*d*) of this subdivision, on which shall be indicated, by the use of brackets, the material which the taxpayer indicates should be deleted pursuant to section 6110(c) of the Code. The statement of proposed deletions shall indicate the statutory basis for each proposed deletion. The statement of proposed deletions shall not appear or be referred to anywhere in the request for technical advice. If the taxpayer decides to request additional deletions pursuant to section 6110(c) of the Code prior to the time the National Office replies to the request for technical advice, additional statements may be submitted.

(*g*) If the taxpayer has not already done so, he/she may submit a statement explaining his/her position on the issues, citing precedents which the taxpayer believes will bear on the case. This statement will be forwarded to the National Office with the request for advice. If it is received at a later date, it will be forwarded for association with the case file.

(*h*) At the time the taxpayer is informed that the matter is being referred to the National Office, he/she will also be informed of the right to a conference in the National Office in the event an adverse decision is indicated, and will be asked to indicate whether a conference is desired.

(*i*) Generally, prior to replying to the request for technical advice, the National Office shall inform the taxpayer orally or in writing of the material likely to appear in the technical advice memorandum which the taxpayer proposed be deleted but which the Internal Revenue Service determined should not be deleted. If so informed, the taxpayer may submit within 10 days any further information, arguments, or other material in support of the position that such material be deleted. The Internal Revenue Service will attempt, if feasible, to resolve all disagreements with respect to proposed deletions prior to the time the National Office replies to the request for technical advice. However, in no event shall the taxpayer have the right to a conference with respect to resolution of any disagreements concerning material to be deleted from the text of the technical advice memorandum, but such matters may be considered at any conference otherwise scheduled with respect to the request.

(*j*) The provisions of (*a*) through (*i*) of this subdivision, relating to the referral of issues upon request of the taxpayer, advising taxpayers of the referral of issues, the submission of proposed deletions, and the granting of conferences in the National Office, are not applicable to technical advice memoranda described in section 6110(g)(5)(A) of the Code, relating to cases involving criminal or civil fraud investigations and jeopardy or termination assessments. However, in such cases, the taxpayer shall be allowed to provide the statement of proposed deletions to the National Office upon the completion of all proceedings with respect to the investigations or assessments, but prior to the date on which the Commissioner mails the notice pursuant to section 6110(f)(1) of the Code of intention to disclose the technical advice memorandum.

(*k*) Form 4463, Request for Technical Advice, should be used for transmitting requests for technical advice to the National Office.

Reg. § 601.106(f)(9)(iii)(k)

(iv) *Appeal by taxpayers of determinations not to seek technical advice.*—*(a)* If the taxpayer has requested referral of an issue before an Appeals Office to the National Office for technical advice, and after consideration of the request, the Appeals Officer is of the opinion that the circumstances do not warrant such referral, he/she will so advise the taxpayer.

(b) The taxpayer may appeal the decision of the Appeals Officer not to request technical advice by submitting to that official, within 10 calendar days after being advised of the decision, a statement of the facts, law, and arguments with respect to the issue, and the reasons why the taxpayer believes the matter should be referred to the National Office for advice. An extension of time must be justified by the taxpayer in writing and approved by the Chief, Appeals Office.

(c) The Appeals Officer will submit the statement of the taxpayer to the chief, Appeals Office, accompanied by a statement of the officer's reasons why the issue should not be referred to the National Office. The Chief will determine, on the basis of the statements submitted, whether technical advice will be requested. If the Chief determines that technical advice is not warranted, that official will inform the taxpayer in writing that he/she proposes to deny the request. In the letter to the taxpayer the Chief will (except in unusual situations where such action would be prejudicial to the best interests of the Government) state specifically the reasons for the proposed denial. The taxpayer will be given 15 calendar days after receipt of the letter in which to notify the Chief whether the taxpayer agrees with the proposed denial. The taxpayer may not appeal the decision of the Chief, Appeals Office not to request technical advice from the National Office. However, if the taxpayer does not agree with the proposed denial, all data relating to the issue for which technical advice has been sought, including the taxpayer's written request and statements, will be submitted to the National Office, Attention: Director, Appeals Division, for review. After review in the National Office, the Appeals Office will be notified whether the proposed denial is approved or disapproved.

(d) While the matter is being reviewed in the National Office, the Appeals Office will suspend action on the issue (except where the delay would prejudice the Government's interests) until it is notified of the National Office decision. This notification will be made within 30 days after receipt of the data in the National Office. The review will be solely on the basis of

the written record and no conference will be held in the National Office.

(v) Conference in the National Office.— *(a)* If, after a study of the technical advice request, it appears that advice adverse to the taxpayer should be given and a conference has been requested, the taxpayer will be notified of the time and place of the conference. If conferences are being arranged with respect to more than one request for advice involving the same taxpayer, they will be so scheduled as to cause the least inconvenience to the taxpayer. The conference will be arranged by telephone, if possible, and must be held within 21 calendar days after contact has been made. Extensions of time will be granted only if justified in writing by the taxpayer and approved by the appropriate Technical branch chief.

(b) A taxpayer is entitled, as a matter of right, to only one conference in the National Office unless one of the circumstances discussed in *(c)* of this subdivision exists. This conference will usually be held at the branch level in the appropriate division (Corporation Tax Division or Individual Tax Division) in the Office of the Assistant Commissioner (Technical), and will usually be attended by a person who has authority to act for the branch chief. In appropriate cases the Appeals Officer may also attend the conference to clarify the facts in the case. If more than one subject is discussed at the conference, the discussion constitutes a conference with respect to each subject. At the request of the taxpayer or the taxpayer's representative, the conference may be held at an earlier stage in the consideration of the case than the Service would ordinarily designate. A taxpayer has no "right" of appeal from an action of a branch to the director of a division or to any other National Office official.

(c) In the process of review of a holding proposed by a branch, it may appear that the final answer will involve a reversal of the branch proposal with a result less favorable to the taxpayer. Or it may appear that an adverse holding proposed by a branch will be approved, but on a new or different issue or on different grounds than those on which the branch decided the case. Under either of these circumstances, the taxpayer or the taxpayer's representative will be invited to another conference. The provisions of this subparagraph limiting the number of conferences to which a taxpayer is entitled will not foreclose inviting a taxpayer to attend further conferences when, in the opinion of National Office personnel, such need arises. All additional

conferences of this type discussed are held only at the invitation of the Service.

(d) It is the responsibility of the taxpayer to furnish to the National Office, within 21 calendar days after the conference, a written record of any additional data, line of reasoning, precedents, etc., that were proposed by the taxpayer and discussed at the conference but were not previously or adequately presented in writing. Extensions of time will be granted only if justified in writing by the taxpayer and approved by the appropriate Technical branch chief. Any additional material and a copy thereof should be addressed to and sent to the National Office which will forward the copy to the appropriate Appeals Office. The Appeals Office will be requested to give the matter prompt attention, will verify the additional facts and data, and will comment on it to the extent deemed appropriate.

(e) A taxpayer or the taxpayer's representative desiring to obtain information as to the status of the case may do so by contacting the following offices with respect to matters in the areas of their responsibility:

Official	Telephone Numbers (Area Code 202)
Director, Corporation Tax Division	566-4504 or 566-4505
Director, Individual Tax Division	566-3767 or 566-3788

(vi) *Preparation of technical advice memorandum by the National Office.*—*(a)* Immediately upon receipt in the National Office, the technical employee to whom the case is assigned will analyze the file to ascertain whether it meets the requirements of subdivision (iii) of this subparagraph. If the case is not complete with respect to any requirement in subdivision (iii) *(a)* through *(d)* of this subparagraph, appropriate steps will be taken to complete the file. If any request for technical advice does not comply with the requirements of subdivision (iii)*(e)* of this subparagraph, relating to the statement of proposed deletions, the National Office will make those deletions from the technical advice memorandum which in the judgment of the Commissioner are required by section 6110(c) of the Code.

(b) If the taxpayer has requested a conference in the National Office, the procedures in subdivision (v) of this subparagraph will be followed.

(c) Replies to requests for technical advice will be addressed to the Appeals office and will be drafted in two parts. Each part will identify the taxpayer by name, address, identification number, and year or years involved. The first part (hereafter called the "technical advice memorandum") will contain *(1)* a recitation of the pertinent facts having a bearing on the issue; *(2)* a discussion of the facts, precedents, and reasoning of the National Office; and *(3)* the conclusions of the National Office. The conclusions will give direct answers, whenever possible, to the specific questions of the Appeals office. The discussion of the issues will be in such detail that the Appeals office is apprised of the reasoning underlying the conclusion. There shall accompany the technical advice memorandum a notice, pursuant to section 6110(f)(1) of the Code, of intention to disclose the technical advice memorandum (including a copy of the version proposed to be open to public inspection and notations of third party communications pursuant to section 6110(d) of the Code) which the Appeals office shall forward to the taxpayer at such time that it furnishes a copy of the technical advice memorandum to the taxpayer pursuant to *(e)* of this subdivision and subdivision (vii)*(b)* of this subparagraph.

(d) The second part of the reply will consist of a transmittal memorandum. In the unusual cases it will serve as a vehicle for providing the Appeals office administrative information or other information which, under the nondisclosure statutes, or for other reasons, may not be discussed with the taxpayer.

(e) It is the general practice of the Service to furnish a copy of the technical advice memorandum to the taxpayer after it has been adopted by the Appeals office. However, in the case of technical advice memorandums described in section 6110(g)(5)(A) of the Code, relating to cases involving criminal or civil fraud investigations and jeopardy or termination assessments, a copy of the technical advice memorandum shall not be furnished the taxpayer until all proceedings with respect to the investigations or assessments are completed.

(f) After receiving the notice pursuant to section 6110(f)(1) of the Code of intention to disclose the technical advice memorandum, the taxpayer, if desiring to protest the disclosure of certain information in the memorandum, must, with 20 days after the notice is mailed, submit a written statement identifying those deletions not made by the Internal Revenue Service which the taxpayer believes should have been made. The taxpayer shall also submit a copy of the version of the technical advice memorandum proposed to be open to public inspection on which the taxpayer indicates, by the use of brackets, the deletions proposed by the taxpayer but which

have not been made by the Internal Revenue Service. Generally, the Internal Revenue Service will not consider the deletion of any material which the taxpayer did not, prior to the time when the National Office sent its reply to the request for technical advice to the Appeals office, propose be deleted. The Internal Revenue Service shall, within 20 days after receipt of the response by the taxpayer to the notice pursuant to section 6110(f)(1) of the Code, mail to the taxpayer its final administrative conclusion regarding the deletions to be made.

(vii) *Action on technical advice in Appeals offices.*—*(a)* Unless the Chief, Appeals Office, feels that the conclusions reached by the National Office in a technical advice memorandum should be reconsidered and promptly requests such reconsideration, the Appeals office will proceed to process the taxpayer's case taking into account the conclusions expressed in the technical advice memorandum. The effect of technical advice on the taxpayer's case is set forth in subdivision (viii) of this subparagraph.

(b) The Appeals office will furnish the taxpayer a copy of the technical advice memorandum described in subdivision (vi)*(c)* of this subparagraph and the notice pursuant to section 6110(f)(1) of the Code of intention to disclose the technical advice memorandum (including a copy of the version proposed to be open to public inspection and notations of third-party communications pursuant to section 6110(d) of the Code). The preceding sentence shall not apply to technical advice memorandums involving civil fraud or criminal investigations, or jeopardy or termination assessments, as described in subdivision (iii)*(j)* of this subparagraph (except to the extent provided in subdivision (vi)*(e)* of this subparagraph) or to documents to which section 6104 of the Code applies.

(c) In those cases in which the National Office advises the Appeals office that it should not furnish a copy of the technical advice memorandum of the technical advice memorandum to the taxpayer, the Appeals office will so inform the taxpayer if he/she requests a copy.

(viii) *Effect of technical advice.*—*(a)* A technical advice memorandum represents an expression of the views of the Service as to the application of law, regulations, and precedents to the facts of a specific case, and is issued primarily as a means of assisting Service officials in the closing of the case involved.

(b) Except in rare or unusual circumstances, a holding in a technical advice memo-

randum that is favorable to the taxpayer is applied retroactively. Moreover, since technical advice, as described in subdivision (i) of this subparagraph, is issued only on closed transactions, a holding in a technical advice memorandum that is adverse to the taxpayer is also applied retroactively unless the Assistant Commissioner or Deputy Assistant Commissioner (Technical) exercises the discretionary authority under section 7805(b) of the Code to limit the retroactive effect of the holding. Likewise, a holding in a technical advice memorandum that modifies or revokes a holding in a prior technical advice memorandum will also be applied retroactively, with one exception. If the new holding is less favorable to the taxpayer, it will generally not be applied to the period in which the taxpayer relied on the prior holding in situations involving continuing transactions of the type described in § 601.201(1)(7) and § 601.201(1)(8).

(c) The Appeals office is bound by technical advice favorable to the taxpayer. However, if the technical advice is unfavorable to the taxpayer, the Appeals office may settle the issue in the usual manner under existing authority. For the effect of the technical advice in Employee Plans and Exempt Organization cases see § 601.201(n)(9)(viii).

(d) In connection with section 446 of the Code, taxpayers may request permission from the Assistant Commissioner (Technical) to change a method of accounting and obtain a 10-year (or less) spread of the resulting adjustments. Such a request should be made prior to or at the first Appeals conference. The Appeals office has authority to allow a change and the resulting spread without referring the case to Technical.

(e) Technical advice memorandums often form the basis for revenue rulings. For the description of revenue rulings and the effect thereof, see § § 601.601(d)(2)(i)*(a)* and 601.601(d)(2)(v).

(f) An Appeals office may raise an issue in a taxable period, even though technical advice may have been asked for and furnished with regard to the same or a similar issue in any other taxable period.

(g) *Limitation on the jurisdiction and function of Appeals.*—(1) *Overpayment of more than $200,000.*—If Appeals determines that there is an overpayment of income, war profits, excess profits, estate, generation-skipping transfer or gift tax, or any tax imposed by chapters 41 through 44, including penalties and interest, in excess of $200,000, such determination will be considered by the Joint Committee on Taxation, See section 601.108.

(2) *Offers in compromise.*—For jurisdiction of Appeals with respect to offers in compromise of tax liabilities, see § 601.203.

(3) *Closing agreements.*—For jurisdiction of Appeals with respect to closing agreements under section 7121 of the Code relating to any internal revenue tax liability, see § 601.202.

(h) *Reopening closed cases not docketed in the Tax Court.*—(1) A case not docketed in the Tax Court and closed by Appeals on the basis of concessions made by both Appeals and the taxpayer will not be reopened by action initiated by the Service unless the disposition involved fraud, malfeasance, concealment or misrepresentation of material fact, or an important mistake in mathematical calculation, and then only with the approval of the Regional Director of Appeals.

(2) Under certain unusual circumstances favorable to the taxpayer, such as retroactive legislation, a case not docketed in the Tax Court and closed by Appeals on the basis of concessions made by both Appeals and the taxpayer may be reopened upon written application from the taxpayer, and only with the approval of the Regional Director of Appeals. The processing of an application for a tentative carryback adjustment or of a claim for refund or credit for an overassessment (for a year involved in the prior closing) attributable to a claimed deduction or credit for a carryback provided by law, and not included in a previous Appeals determination, shall not be considered a reopening requiring approval. A subsequent assessment of an excessive tentative allowance shall likewise not be considered such a reopening. The Director of Appeals may authorize, in advance, the reopening of similar classes of cases where legislative enactments or compelling administrative reasons require such advance approval.

(3) A case not docketed in the Tax Court and closed by Appeals on a basis not involving concessions made by both Appeals and the taxpayer will not be reopened by action initiated by the Service unless the disposition involved fraud, malfeasance, concealment or misrepresentation of material fact, an important mistake in mathematical calculation, or such other circumstance that indicates that failure to take such action would be a serious administrative omission, and then only with the approval of the Regional Director of Appeals.

(4) A case not docketed in the Tax Court and closed by Appeals on a basis not involving

concessions made by both Appeals and the taxpayer may be reopened by the taxpayer by any appropriate means, such as by the filing of a timely claim for refund.

(i) *Special procedures for crude oil windfall profit tax cases.*—For special procedures relating to crude oil windfall profit tax cases, see § 601.405.

[Reg. § 601.107]

§ 601.107. Criminal Investigation functions.— (a) *General.*—Each district has a Criminal Investigation function whose mission is to encourage and achieve the highest possible degree of voluntary compliance with the internal revenue laws by: enforcing the statutory sanctions applicable to income, estate, gift, employment, and certain excise taxes through the investigation of possible criminal violations of such laws and the recommendation (when warranted) of prosecution and/or assertion of the 50 percent ad valorem addition to the tax; developing information concerning the extent of criminal violations of all Federal tax laws (except those relating to alcohol, tobacco, narcotics, and firearms); measuring the effectiveness of the investigation process; and providing protection of persons and of property and other enforcement coordination as required.

(b) *Investigative procedure.*—(1) A witness when questioned in an investigation conducted by the Criminal Investigation Division may have counsel present to represent and advise him. Upon request, a copy of an affidavit or transcript of a question and answer statement will be furnished a witness promptly, except in circumstances deemed by the Regional Commissioner to necessitate temporarily withholding a copy.

(2) A taxpayer who may be the subject of a criminal recommendation will be afforded a district Criminal Investigation conference when he requests one or where the Chief, Criminal Investigation Division, makes a determination that such a conference will be in the best interests of the Government. At the conference, the IRS representative will inform the taxpayer by a general oral statement of the alleged fraudulent features of the case, to the extent consistent with protecting the Government's interests, and, at the same time, making available to the taxpayer sufficient facts and figures to acquaint him with the basis, nature, and other essential elements of the proposed criminal charges against him.

(c) *Processing of cases after investigation.*—The Chief, Criminal Investigation Division, shall ordinarily notify the subject of an investigation

Reg. § 601.107(c)

and his authorized representative, if any, when he forwards a case to the Regional Counsel with a recommendation for prosecution. The rule will not apply if the case is with a United States Attorney.

[Reg. § 601.108]

§ 601.108. Review of overpayments exceeding $200,000.—(a) *General.*—Section 6405(a) of the Code provides that no refund or credit of income, war profits, excess profits, estate, or gift taxes, or any tax imposed by chapters 41 through 44, including penalties and interest, in excess of $200,000 may be made until after the expiration of 30 days from the date a report is made to the Joint Committee on Taxation. Taxpayers in cases requiring review by the Joint Committee are afforded the same appeal rights as other taxpayers. In general, these cases follow regular procedures, except for preparation of reports to and review by the Joint Committee.

(b) *Reports to Joint Committee.*—In any case in which no protest is made to Appeals and no petition docketed in the Tax Court, the report to the Joint Committee is prepared by a Joint Committee Coordinator, who is an Examination Division regional specialist. In cases in which a protest has been made, the report to the Joint Committee is prepared by an Appeals officer; in cases in which a petition is docketed, either an Appeals officer or a Counsel attorney prepares the report, depending on the circumstances.

(c) *Procedure after report to Joint Committee.*—After compliance with section 6405 of the Code, the case is processed for issuance of a certificate of overassessment, and payment or credit of any overpayment. If the final determination involves a rejection of a claimed overpayment in whole or in part, a statutory notice of disallowance will be sent by certified or registered mail to the taxpayer, except where the taxpayer has filed a written waiver of such notice of disallowance.

[Reg. § 601.109]

§ 601.109. Bankruptcy and receivership cases.—(a) *General.*—(1) Upon the adjudication of bankruptcy of any taxpayer in any liquidating proceeding, the filing or (where approval is required by the Bankruptcy Act) the approval of a petition of, or the approval of a petition against, any taxpayer in any other proceeding under the Bankruptcy Act or the appointment of a receiver for any taxpayer in any receivership proceeding before a court of the United States or of any State or Territory or of the District of Columbia, the assessment of any deficiency in income, profits, estate, or gift tax (together with all interest, additional amounts, or additions to the tax provided for by law) shall be made immediately. See section 6871 of the Code. In such cases the restrictions imposed by section 6213(a) of the Code upon assessments are not applicable. (In the case of an assignment for the benefit of creditors, the assessment will be made under section 6861, relating to jeopardy assessments. See § 601.105(h).) Cases in which immediate assessment will be made include those of taxpayers in receivership or in bankruptcy, reorganization, arrangement, or wage earner proceedings under chapters I to VII, section 77, chapters X, XI, XII, and XIII of the Bankruptcy Act. The term "approval of a petition in any other proceeding under the Bankruptcy Act" includes the filing of a petition under chapters XI to XIII of the Bankruptcy Act with a court of competent jurisdiction. A fiduciary in any proceeding under the Bankruptcy Act (including a trustee, receiver-debtor in possession, or other person designated by the court as in control of the assets or affairs of a debtor) or a receiver in any receivership proceeding may be required, as provided in regulations prescribed under section 6036 of the Code, to give notice in writing to the district director of his qualification as such. Failure on the part of such fiduciary in a receivership proceeding or a proceeding under the Bankruptcy Act to give such notice, when required, results in the suspension of the running of the period of limitations on the making of assessments from the date of the institution of the proceeding to the date upon which such notice is received by the district director, and for an additional 30 days thereafter. However, in no case where the required notice is not given shall the suspension of the running of the period of limitations on assessment exceed 2 years. See section 6872 of the Code.

(2) Except in cases where departmental instructions direct otherwise, the district director will, promptly after ascertaining the existence of any outstanding Federal tax liability against a taxpayer in any proceeding under the Bankruptcy Act or receivership proceeding, and in any event within the time limited by appropriate provisions of law or the appropriate orders of the court in which such proceeding is pending, file a proof of claim covering such liability in the court in which the proceeding is pending. Such a claim may be filed regardless of whether the unpaid taxes involved have been assessed. Whenever an immediate assessment is made of any income, estate, or gift tax after the commencement of a proceeding, the district director

will send to the taxpayernotice and demand for payment together with a copy of such claim.

(b) *Procedure in office of district director.*— (1) While the district director is required by section 6871 of the Code to make immediate assessment of any deficiency in income, estate, or gift taxes, such assessment is not made as a jeopardy assessment (see paragraph (h) of §601.105), and the provisions of section 6861 of the Code do not apply to any assessment made under section 6871. Therefore, the notice of deficiency provided for in section 6861(b) will not be mailed to the taxpayer. Nevertheless, Letter 1005 (DO) will be prepared and addressed in the name of the taxpayer, immediately followed by the name of the trustee, receiver, debtor in possession, or other person designated to be in control of the assets or affairs of the debtor by the court in which the bankruptcy or receivership proceeding is pending. Such letter will state how the deficiency was computed, advise that within 30 days a written protest under penalties of perjury may be filed with the district director showing wherein the deficiency is claimed to be incorrect, and advise that upon request an Appeals office conference will be granted with respect to such deficiency. If, after protest is filed (in triplicate) and an Appeals office conference is held, adjustment appears necessary in the deficiency, appropriate action will be taken. Except where the interests of the Government require otherwise, Letters 1005 (DO) are issued by the office of the district director.

(2) The immediate assessment required by section 6871 of the Code represents an exception to the usual restrictions on the assessment of Federal income, estate, and gift taxes. Since there are no restrictions on the assessment of Federal excise or employment taxes, immediate assessment of such taxes will be made in any case where section 6871 of the Code would require immediate assessment of income, estate, or gift taxes.

(3) If after such assessment a claim for abatement is filed and such claim is accompanied by a request in writing for a conference, an Appeals office conference will be granted. Ordinarily, only one conference will be held, unless it develops that additional information can be furnished which has a material bearing upon the tax liability in which event the conference will be continued to a later date.

(c) *Procedure before the Appeals office.*—If an income, estate, or gift tax case is under consideration by an Appeals office (whether before or after issuance of a statutory notice of deficiency) at the time of either: (i) The adjudication of bankruptcy of the taxpayer in any liquidating proceeding; (ii) the filing with a court of competent jurisdiction or (where approval is required by the Bankruptcy Act) the approval of a petition of, or against, the taxpayer in any other proceeding under the Bankruptcy Act; or (iii) the appointment of any receiver, then the case will be returned to the district director for assessment (if not previously made), for issuance of the Letter 1005 (DO), and for filing proof of claim in the proceeding. Excise and employment tax cases pending in the Appeals office at such time will likewise be returned to the district director for assessment (if not previously made) and for filing proof of claim in the proceeding. A petition for redetermination of a deficiency may not be filed in the Tax Court after the adjudication of bankruptcy, the filing or (where approval is required by the Bankruptcy Act) the approval of a petition of, or the approval of a petition against, the taxpayer in any other bankruptcy proceeding, or the appointment of a receiver. See section 6871(b) of the Code. However, the Tax Court is not deprived of jurisdiction where the adjudication of bankruptcy, the filing or (where approval is required by the Bankruptcy Act) the approval of a petition of, or the approval of a petition against, the taxpayer in any other bankruptcy proceeding, or the appointment of a receiver, occurred after the filing of the petition. In such a case, the jurisdiction of the bankruptcy or receivership court and the Tax Court is concurrent.

(d) *Priority of claims.*—Under Section 3466 of the Revised Statutes and Section 3467 of the Revised Statutes, as amended, taxes are entitled to priority over other claims therein stated and the receiver or other person designated as in control of the assets or affairs of the debtor by the court in which the receivership proceeding is pending may be held personally liable for failure on his part to protect the priority of the Government respecting taxes of which he has notice. Under Section 64 of the Bankruptcy Act, taxes may be entitled to priority over other claims therein stated and the trustee, receiver, debtor in possession or other person designated as in control of the assets or affairs of the debtor by the court in which the bankruptcy proceeding is pending may be held personally liable for any failure on his part to protect a priority of the Government respecting taxes of which he has notice and which are entitled to priority under the Bankruptcy Act. Sections 77(e), 199, 337(2), 455 and 659(6) of the Bankruptcy Act also contain provisions with respect to the rights of the United States relative to priority of payment.

Reg. §601.109(d)

Bankruptcy courts have jurisdiction under the Bankruptcy Act to determine all disputes regarding the amount and the validity of tax claims against a bankrupt or a debtor in a proceeding under the Bankruptcy Act. A receivership proceeding or an assignment for the benefit of creditors does not discharge any portion of a claim of the United States for taxes and any portion of such claim allowed by the court in which the proceeding is pending and which remains unsatisfied after the termination of the proceeding shall be collected with interest in accordance with law. A bankruptcy proceeding under Chapters I through VII of the Bankruptcy Act does discharge that portion of a claim of the United States which became legally due and owing more than three years preceding bankruptcy, with certain exceptions [as] provided in the Bankruptcy Act, as does a proceeding under Section 77 or Chapter X of the Bankruptcy Act. Any taxes which are dischargeable under the Bankruptcy Act which remain unsatisfied after the termination of the proceeding may be collected only from exempt or abandoned property.

Subpart B—Rulings and Other Specific Matters

[Reg. § 601.201]

§ 601.201. Rulings and determination letters.— (a) *General practice and definitions.*—(1) It is the practice of the Internal Revenue Service to answer inquiries of individuals and organizations, whenever appropriate in the interest of sound tax administration, as to their status for tax purposes and as to the tax effects of their acts or transactions. One of the functions of the National Office of the Internal Revenue Service is to issue rulings in such matters. If a taxpayer's request for a ruling concerns an action that may have an impact on the environment, compliance by the Service with the requirements of the National Environmental Policy Act of 1969 (Public Law 91-190) may result in delay in issuing the ruling. Accordingly, taxpayers requesting rulings should take this factor into account. District directors apply the statutes, regulations, Revenue Rulings, and other precedents published in the Internal Revenue Bulletin in the determination of tax liability, the collection of taxes, and the issuance of determination letters in answer to taxpayers' inquiries or requests. For purposes of this section any reference to district director or district office also includes, where appropriate, the office of the Director, Office of International Operations.

(2) A "ruling" is a written statement issued to a taxpayer or his authorized representative by the National Office which interprets and applies the tax laws to a specific set of facts. Rulings are issued only by the National Office. The issuance of rulings is under the general supervision of the Assistant Commissioner (Technical) and has been largely redelegated to the Director, Corporation Tax Division and Director, Individual Tax Division.

(3) A "determination letter" is a written statement issued by a district director in response to a written inquiry by an individual or an organization that applies to the particular facts involved, the principles and precedents previously announced by the National Office. A determination letter is issued only where a determination can be made on the basis of clearly established rules as set forth in the statute, Treasury decision, or regulation, or by a ruling, opinion, or court decision published in the Internal Revenue Bulletin. Where such a determination cannot be made, such as where the question presented involves a novel issue or the matter is excluded from the jurisdiction of a district director by the provisions of paragraph (c) of this section, a determination letter will not be issued. However, with respect to determination letters in the pension trust area, see paragraph (o) of this section.

(4) An "opinion letter" is a written statement issued by the National Office as to the acceptability of the form of a master or prototype plan and any related trust or custodial account under sections 401 and 501(a) of the Internal Revenue Code of 1954.

(5) An "information letter" is a statement issued either by the National Office or by a district director which does no more than call attention to a well-established interpretation or principle of tax law, without applying it to a specific set of facts. An information letter may be issued when the nature of the request from the individual or the organization suggests that it is seeking general information, or where the request does not meet all the requirements of paragraph (e) of this section, and it is believed that such general information will assist the individual or organization.

(6) A "Revenue Ruling" is an official interpretation by the Service which has been published in the Internal Revenue Bulletin. Revenue Rulings are issued only by the National Office and are published for the information and guidance of taxpayers, Internal Revenue Service officials, and others concerned.

(7) A "closing agreement," as the term is used herein, is an agreement between the Commissioner of Internal Revenue or his delegate and a taxpayer with respect to a specific issue or issues entered into pursuant to the authority contained in section 7121 of the Internal Revenue Code. Such a closing agreement is based on a ruling which has been signed by the Commissioner or his delegate and in which it is indicated that a closing agreement will be entered into on the basis of the holding of the ruling letter. Closing agreements are final and conclusive except upon a showing of fraud, malfeasance, or misrepresentation of material fact. They may be entered into where it is advantageous to have the matter permanently and conclusively closed, or where a taxpayer can show good and sufficient reasons for an agreement and the Government will sustain no disadvantage by its consummation. In appropriate cases, taxpayers may be required to enter into a closing agreement as a condition to the issuance of a ruling. Where in a single case, closing agreements are requested on behalf of each of a number of taxpayers, such agreements are not entered into if the number of such taxpayers exceeds 25. However, in a case where the issue and holding are identical as to all of the taxpayers and the number of taxpayers is in excess of 25, a Mass Closing Agreement will be entered into with the taxpayer who is authorized by the others to represent the entire group. See, for example, Rev. Proc. 78-15, 1978-2 C.B. 488, and Rev. Proc. 78-16, 1978-2 C.B. 489.

(b) *Rulings issued by the National Office.*—(1) In income and gift tax matters and matters involving taxes imposed under Chapter 42 of the Code, the National Office issues rulings on prospective transactions and on completed transactions before the return is filed. However, rulings will not ordinarily be issued if the identical issue is present in a return of the taxpayer for a prior year which is under active examination or audit by a district office, or is being considered by a branch office of the Appellate Division. The National Office issues rulings involving the exempt status of organizations under section 501 or 521 of the Code, only to the extent provided in paragraph (n) of this section, Revenue Procedure 72-5, Internal Revenue Bulletin No. 1972-1, 19, and Revenue Procedure 68-13, C.B. 1968-1, 764. The National Office issues rulings as to the foundation status of certain organizations under sections 509(a) and 4942(j)(3) of the Code only to the extent provided in paragraph (r) of this section. The National Office issues rulings involving qualification of plans under section 401 of the

Code only to the extent provided in paragraph (o) of this section. The National Office issues opinion letters as to the acceptability of the form of master or prototype plans and any related trusts or custodial accounts under sections 401 and 501(a) of the Code only to the extent provided in paragraphs (p) and (q) of this section. The National Office will not issue rulings with respect to the replacement of involuntarily converted property, even though replacement has not been made, if the taxpayer has filed a return for the taxable year in which the property was converted. However, see paragraph (c)(6) of this section as to the authority of district directors to issue determination letters in this connection.

(2) In estate tax matters, the National Office issues rulings with respect to transactions affecting the estate tax of a decedent before the estate tax return is filed. It will not rule with respect to such matters after the estate tax return has been filed, nor will it rule on matters relating to the application of the estate tax to property or the estate of a living person.

(3) In employment and excise tax matters (except taxes imposed under Chapter 42 of the Code), the National Office issues rulings with respect to prospective transactions and to completed transactions either before or after the return is filed. However, the National Office will not ordinarily rule with respect to an issue, whether related to a prospective or a completed transaction, if it knows or has reason to believe that the same or an identical issue is before any field office (including any branch office of the Appellate Division) in connection with an examination or audit of the liability of the same taxpayer for the same or a prior period.

(4) The Service will not issue rulings to business, trade, or industrial associations or to other similar groups relating to the application of the tax laws to members of the group. However, rulings may be issued to such groups or associations relating to their own tax status or liability provided such tax status or liability is not an issue before any field office (including any branch office or the Appellate Division) in connection with an examination or audit of the liability of the same taxpayer for the same or a prior period.

(5) Pending the adoption of regulations (either temporary or final) that reflect the provisions of any Act, consideration will be given to the issuance of rulings under the conditions set forth below.

(i) If an inquiry presents an issue on which the answer seems to be clear from an application of the provisions of the statute to the

Reg. §601.201(b)(5)(i)

facts described, a ruling will be issued in accordance with usual procedures.

(ii) If an inquiry presents an issue on which the answer seems reasonably certain but not entirely free from doubt, a ruling will be issued only if it is established that a business emergency requires a ruling or that unusual hardship will result from failure to obtain a ruling.

(iii) If an inquiry presents an issue that cannot be reasonably resolved prior to the issuance of regulations, a ruling will not be issued.

(iv) In any case in which the taxpayer believes that a business emergency exists or that an unusual hardship will result from failure to obtain a ruling, he should submit with the request a separate letter setting forth the facts necessary for the Service to make a determination in this regard. In this connection, the Service will not deem a "business emergency" to result from circumstances within the control of the taxpayer such as, for example, scheduling within an inordinately short time the closing date for a transaction or a meeting of the board of directors or the shareholders of a corporation.

(c) *Determination letters issued by district directors.*—(1) In income and gift tax matters, and in matters involving taxes imposed under Chapter 42 of the Code, district directors issue determination letters in response to taxpayers' written requests submitted to their offices involving completed transactions which affect returns over which they have audit jurisdiction, but only if the answer to the question presented is covered specifically by statute, Treasury Decision or regulation, or specifically by a ruling, opinion, or court decision published in the Internal Revenue Bulletin. A determination letter will not usually be issued with respect to a question which involves a return to be filed by the taxpayer if the identical question is involved in a return or returns already filed by the taxpayer. District directors may not issue determination letters as to the tax consequence of prospective or proposed transactions, except as provided in subparagraphs (5) and (6) of this paragraph.

(2) In estate and gift tax matters, district directors issue determination letters in response to written requests submitted to their offices affecting the estate tax returns of decedents that will be audited by their offices, but only if the answer to the questions presented are specifically covered by statute, Treasury decision or regulation, or by a ruling, opinion, or court decision published in the Internal Revenue Bulletin. District directors will not issue determination

letters relating to matters involving the application of the estate tax to property or the estate of a living person.

(3) In employment and excise tax matters (except excise taxes imposed under Chapter 42 of the Code), district directors issue determination letters in response to written requests from taxpayers who have filed or who are required to file returns over which they have audit jurisdiction, but only if the answers to the questions presented are covered specifically by statute, Treasury decision or regulation, or a ruling, opinion, or court decision published in the Internal Revenue Bulletin. Because of the impact of these taxes upon the business operation of the taxpayer and because of special problems of administration both to the Service and to the taxpayer, district directors may take appropriate action in regard to such requests, whether they relate to completed or prospective transactions or returns previously filed or to be filed.

(4) Notwithstanding the provisions of subparagraphs (1), (2), and (3), of this paragraph, a district director will not issue a determination letter in response to an inquiry which presents a question specifically covered by statute, regulations, rulings, etc., published in the Internal Revenue Bulletin, where (i) it appears that the taxpayer has directed a similar inquiry to the National Office, (ii) the identical issue involving the same taxpayer is pending in a case before the Appellate Division, (iii) the determination letter is requested by an industry, trade association, or similar group, or (iv) the request involves an industrywide problem. Under no circumstances will a district director issue a determination letter unless it is clearly indicated that the inquiry is with regard to a taxpayer or taxpayers who have filed or are required to file returns over which his office has or will have audit jurisdiction. Notwithstanding the provisions of subparagraph (3), of this paragraph, a district director will not issue a determination letter on an employment tax question when the specific question involved has been or is being considered by the Central Office of the Social Security Administration. Nor will district directors issue determination letters on excise tax questions if a request is for a determination of a constructive sales price under section 4216(b) or 4218(e) of the Code. However, the National Office will issue rulings in this area. See paragraph (d)(2) of this section.

(5) District directors issue determination letters as to the qualification of plans under sections 401 and 405(a) of the Code, and as to the exempt status of related trusts under section 501

of the Code, to the extent provided in paragraphs (o) and (q) of this section. Selected district directors also issue determination letters as to the qualification of certain organizations for exemption from Federal income tax under sections 501 and 521 of the Code, to the extent provided in paragraph (n) of this section. Selected district directors also issue determination letters as to the qualification of certain organizations for foundation status under sections 509(a) and 4942(j)(3) of the Code, to the extent provided in paragraph (r) of this section.

(6) District directors issue determination letters with regard to the replacement of involuntarily converted property under section 1033 of the Code even though the replacement has not beenmade, if the taxpayer has filed his income tax return for the year in which the property was involuntarily converted.

(7) A request received by a district director with respect to a question involved in an income, estate, or gift tax return already filed will, in general, be considered in connection with the examination of the return. If response is made to such inquiry prior to an examination or audit, it will be considered a tentative finding in any subsequent examination or audit of the return.

(d) *Discretionary authority to issue rulings and determination letters.*—(1) It is the practice of the Service to answer inquiries of individuals and organizations, whenever appropriate in the interest of sound tax administration, as to their status for tax purposes and the tax effect of their acts or transactions.

(2) There are, however, certain areas where, because of the inherently factual nature of the problem involved, or for other reasons, the Service will not issue rulings or determination letters. A ruling or determination letter is not issued on alternative plans of proposed transactions or on hypothetical situations. A specific area or a list of these areas is published from time to time in the Internal Revenue Bulletin. Such list is not all inclusive since the Service may decline to issue rulings or determination letters on other questions whenever warranted by the facts or circumstances of a particular case. The National Office and district directors may, when it is deemed appropriate and in the best interest of the Service, issue information letters calling attention to well-established principles of tax law.

(3) The National Office will issue rulings in all cases on prospective or future transactions when the law or regulations require a determination of the effect of a proposed transaction for tax

purposes, as in the case of a transfer coming within the provisions of sections 1491 and 1492 of the Code, or an exchange coming within the provisions of section 367 of the Code. The National Office will issue rulings in all cases involving the determination of a constructive sales price under section 4216(b) or 4218(e) of the Code.

(e) *Instructions to taxpayers.*—(1) A request for a ruling or determination letter is to be submitted in duplicate if (i) more than one issue is presented in the request or (ii) a closing agreement is requested with respect to the issue presented. There shall accompany the request a declaration in the following form: "Under penalties of perjury, I declare that I have examined this request, including accompanying documents, and to the best of my knowledge and belief, the facts presented in support of the requested ruling or determination letter are true, correct, and complete". The declaration must accompany requests that are postmarked or hand delivered to the Internal Revenue Service after October 31, 1976. The declaration must be signed by the person or persons on whose behalf the request is made.

(2) Each request for a ruling or a determination letter must contain a complete statement of all relevant facts relating to the transaction. Such facts include names, addresses and taxpayer identifying numbers of all interested parties; the location of the district office that has or will have audit jurisdiction over the return or report of each party; a full and precise statement of the business reasons for the transaction; and a carefully detailed description of the transaction. In addition, true copies of all contracts, wills, deeds, agreements, instruments, and other documents involved in the transaction must be submitted with the request. However, relevant facts reflected in documents submitted must be included in the taxpayer's statement and not merely incorporated by reference, and must be accompanied by an analysis of their bearing on the issue or issues, specifying the pertinent provisions. (The term "all interested parties" is not to be construed as requiring a list of all shareholders of a widely held corporation requesting a ruling relating to a reorganization, or a list of employees where a large number may be involved in a plan.) The request must contain a statement whether, to the best of the knowledge of the taxpayer or his representative, the identical issue is being considered by any field office of the Service in connection with an active examination or audit of a tax return of the taxpayer already filed or is being considered by a branch

Reg. §601.201(e)(2)

office by the Appellate Division. Where the request pertains to only one step of a larger integrated transaction, the facts, circumstances, etc., must be submitted with respect to the entire transaction. The following list contains references to revenue procedures for advance ruling requests under certain sections of the Code.

(i) For ruling requests under section 103 of the Code, see Rev. Proc. 79-4, 1979-1 C.B. 483, as amplified by Rev. Proc. 79-12, 1979-1 C.B. 492. Revenue Procedure 79-12 sets forth procedures for submitting ruling requests to which sections 103 and 7478 of the Code apply.

(ii) For ruling requests under section 367 of the Code, see Rev. Proc. 68-23, 1968-1 C.B. 821, as amplified by Rev. Proc. 76-20, 1976-1 C.B. 560, Rev. Proc. 77-5, 1977-1 C.B. 536, Rev. Proc. 78-27, 1978-2 C.B. 526, and Rev. Proc. 78-28, 1978-2 C.B. 526. Revenue Procedure 68-23 contains guidelines for taxpayers and their representatives in connection with issuing rulings undersection 367. Revenue Procedure 76-20 explains the effect of Rev. Rul. 75-561, 1975-2 C.B. 129, on transactions described in section 3.03(1)(c) of Rev. Proc. 68-23. Revenue Procedure 77-5 sets forth procedures for submitting ruling requests under section 367, and the administrative remedies available to a taxpayer within the Service after such rulings have been issued. Revenue Procedure 78-27 relates to the notice requirement set forth in the section 367(b) temporary regulations. Revenue Procedure 78-28 relates to the timely filing of a section 367(a) ruling request.

(iii) For ruling requests under section 351 of the Code, see Rev. Proc. 73-10, 1973-1 C.B. 760, and Rev. Proc. 69-19, 1969-2 C.B. 301. Revenue Procedure 73-10 sets forth the information to be included in the ruling request. Revenue Procedure 69-19 sets forth the conditions and circumstances under which an advance ruling will be issued under section 367 of the Code that an agreement which purports to furnish technical know-how in exchange for stock is a transfer of property within the meaning of section 351.

(iv) For ruling requests under section 332, 334(b)(1), or 334(b)(2) of the Code, see Rev. Proc. 73-17, 1973-2 C.B. 465. Revenue Procedure 73-17 sets forth the information to be included in the ruling request.

(v) See Rev. Proc. 77-30, 1977-2 C.B. 539, and Rev. Proc. 78-18, 1978-2 C.B. 491, relating to rules for the issuance of an advance ruling that a proposed sale of employer stock to a related qualified defined contribution plan of deferred compensation will be a sale of the stock rather than a distribution of property.

(vi) For ruling requests under section 302 or section 311 of the Code, see Rev. Proc. 73-35, 1973-2 C.B. 490. Revenue Procedure 73-35 sets forth the information to be included in the ruling request.

(vii) For ruling requests under section 337 of the Code (and related section 331) see Rev. Proc. 75-32, 1975-2 C.B. 555. Revenue Procedure 75-32 sets forth the information to be included in the ruling request.

(viii) For ruling requests under section 346 of the Code (and related sections 331 and 336), see Rev. Proc. 73-36, 1973-2 C.B. 496. Revenue Procedure 73-36 sets forth the information to be included in the ruling request.

(ix) For ruling requests under section 355 of the Code, see Rev. Proc. 75-35, 1975-2 C.B. 561. Revenue Procedure 75-35 sets forth the information to be included in the ruling request.

(x) For ruling requests under section 368(a)(1)(E) of the Code, see Rev. Proc. 78-33, 1978-2 C.B. 532. Revenue Procedure 78-33 sets forth the information to be included in the ruling request.

(xi) For ruling requests concerning the classification of an organization as a limited partnership where a corporation is the sole general partner, see Rev. Proc. 72-13, 1972-1 C.B. 735. See also Rev. Proc. 74-17, 1974-1 C.B. 438, and Rev. Proc. 75-16, 1975-1 C.B. 676. Revenue Procedure 74-17 announces certain operating rules of the Service relating to the issuance of advance ruling letters concerning the classification of organizations formed as limited partnerships. Revenue Procedure 75-16 sets forth a checklist outlining required information frequently omitted from requests for rulings relating to classification of organizations for Federal tax purposes.

(xii) For ruling requests concerning the creditability of a foreign tax under section 901 or 903 of the Code, see Rev. Rul. 67-308, 1967-2 C.B. 254, which sets forth requirements for establishing that translations of foreign law are satisfactory as evidence for purposes of determining the creditability of a particular foreign tax. Original documents should not be submitted because documents and exhibits become a part of the Internal Revenue Service file which cannot be returned. If the request is with respect to a corporate distribution, reorganization, or other similar or related transaction, the corporate balance sheet nearest the date of the transaction should be submitted. (If the request relates to a prospective transaction, the most recent balance sheet should be submitted.) In the case of requests for rulings or determination letters, other than those to which section 6104 of the Code applies, postmarked or hand delivered to the Internal Revenue Service after October 31, 1976, there must accompany such requests a statement, described in subparagraph (5) of this paragraph, of proposed deletions pursuant to section 6110(c) of the Code. Such statement is not required if the request is to secure the consent of the Commissioner with respect to the adoption of or change in accounting or funding periods or methods pursuant to section 412, 442, 446(e), or 706 of the Code. If, however, the person seeking the consent of the Commissioner receives from the Internal Revenue Service a notice that proposed deletions should be submitted because the resulting ruling will be open to public inspection under section 6110, the statement of proposed deletions must be submitted within 20 days after such notice is mailed.

(3) As an alternative procedure for the issuance of rulings on prospective transactions, the taxpayer may submit a summary statement of the facts he considers controlling the issue, inaddition to the complete statement required for ruling requests by subparagraph (2) of this paragraph. Assuming agreement with the taxpayer's summary statement, the Service will use it as the basis for the ruling. Any taxpayer wishing to adopt this procedure should submit with the request for ruling:

(i) A complete statement of facts relating to the transaction, together with related documents, as required by subparagraph (2) of this paragraph; and

(ii) A summary statement of the facts which he believes should be controlling in reaching the requested conclusion.

Where the taxpayer's statement of controlling facts is accepted, the ruling will be based on those facts and only this statement will ordinarily be incorporated in the ruling letter. It is emphasized, however, that:

(a) This procedure for a "two-part" ruling request is elective with the taxpayer and is not to be considered a required substitute for the regular procedure contained in paragraphs (a) through (m) of this section;

(b) Taxpayers' rights and responsibilities are the same under the "two-part" ruling request procedure as those provided in paragraphs (a) through (m) of this section;

(c) The Service reserves the right to rule on the basis of a more complete statement of facts it considers controlling and to seek further information in developing facts and restating them for ruling purposes; and

(d) The "two-part" ruling request procedure will not apply where it is inconsistent with other procedures applicable to specific situations such as: requests for permission to change accounting method or period; application for recognition of exempt status under section 501 or 521; or rulings on employment tax status.

(4) If the taxpayer is contending for a particular determination, he must furnish an explanation of the grounds for his contentions, together with a statement of relevant authorities in support of his views. Even though the taxpayer is urging no particular determination with regard to a proposed or prospective transaction, he must state his views as to the tax results of the proposed action and furnish a statement of relevant authorities to support such views.

(5) In order to assist the Internal Revenue Service in making the deletions, required by section 6110(c) of the Code, from the text of rulings and determination letters, which are open to public inspection pursuant to section 6110(a) of the Code, there must accompany requests for such rulings or determination letters either a statement of the deletions proposed by the person requesting the ruling or determination letter and the statutory basis for each proposed deletion, or a statement that no information other than names, addresses, and taxpayer identifying numbers need be deleted. Such statement shall be made in a separate document. The statement of proposed deletions shall be accompanied by a copy of the request for a ruling or determination letter and supporting documents, on which shall be indicated, by the use of brackets, the material which the person making such request indicates should be deleted pursuant to section 6110(c) of the Code. The statement of proposed deletions shall indicate the statutory basis, under section 6110(c) of the Code, for each proposed deletion. The statement of proposed deletions shall not appear or be referred to anywhere in the request for a ruling of determination letter. If the person making the request decides to request additional deletions pursuant to section 6110(c) of the Code prior to the time the ruling or determination letter is issued, additional statements may be submitted.

(6) If the request is with respect to the qualification of a plan under section 401 or 405(a) of the Code, see paragraphs (o) and (p) of this section. If the request is with respect to the qualification of an organization for exemption from Federal income tax under section 501 or 521 of the Code, see paragraph (n) of this section, Revenue Procedure 72-5, Internal Revenue Bulletin No. 1972-1, 19 [1972-1 C.B. 709], and Revenue Procedure 68-13, C.B. 1968-1, 764.

Reg. §601.201(e)(6)

(7) A request by or for a taxpayer must be signed by the taxpayer or his authorized representative. If the request is signed by a representative of the taxpayer, or if the representative is to appear before the Internal Revenue Service in connection with the request, he must either be:

(i) An attorney who is a member in good standing of the bar of the highest court of any State, possession, territory, Commonwealth, or the District of Columbia, and who files with the Service a written declaration that he is currently qualified as an attorney and he is authorized to represent the principal,

(ii) A certified public accountant who is duly qualified to practice in any State, possession, territory, Commonwealth, or the District of Columbia, and who files with the Service a written declaration that he is currently qualified as a certified public accountant and he is authorized to represent the principal, or

(iii) A person, other than an attorney or certified public accountant, enrolled to practice before the Service, and who files with the Service a written declaration that he is currently enrolled (including in the declaration either his enrollment number or the expiration date of his enrollment card) and that he is authorized to represent the principal. (See Treasury Department Circular No. 230, as amended, C.B. 1966-2, 1171, for the rules on who may practice before the Service. See §601.503(c) for the statement required as evidence of recognition as an enrollee.)

(8) A request for a ruling or an opinion letter by the National Office should be addressed to the Commissioner of Internal Revenue, Attention: T:PP:T, Washington, D.C. 20224. A request for a determination letter should be addressed to the district director of internal revenue whose office has or will have audit jurisdiction of the taxpayer's return. See also paragraphs (n) through (q) of this section.

(9) Any request for a ruling or determination letter that does not comply with all the provisions of this paragraph will be acknowledged, and the requirements that have not been met will be pointed out. If a request for a ruling lacks essential information, the taxpayer or his representative will be advised that if the information is not forthcoming within 30 days, the request will be closed. If the information is received after the request is closed, the request will be reopened and treated as a new request as of the date of the receipt of the essential information. Priority treatment of such request will be granted only in rare cases upon the approval of the division director.

(10) A taxpayer or his representative who desires an oral discussion of the issue or issues involved should indicate such desire in writing when filing the request or soon thereafter in order that the conference may be arranged at that stage of consideration when it will be most helpful.

(11) Generally, prior to issuing the ruling or determination letter, the National Office or district director shall inform the person requesting such ruling or determination letter orally or in writing of the material likely to appear in the ruling or determination letter which such person proposed be deleted but which the Internal Revenue Service determines should not be deleted. If so informed, the person requesting the ruling or determination letter may submit within 10 days any further information, arguments or other material in support of the position that such material be deleted. The Internal Revenue Service will attempt, if feasible, to resolve all disagreements with respect to proposed deletions prior to the issuance of the ruling or determination letter. However, in no event shall the person requesting the ruling or determination letter have the right to a conference with respect to resolution of any disagreements concerning material to be deleted from the text of the ruling or determination letter, but such matters may be considered at any conference otherwise scheduled with respect to the request.

(12) It is the practice of the Service to process requests for rulings, opinion letters, and determination letters in regular order and as expeditiously as possible. Compliance with a request for consideration of a particular matter ahead of its regular order, or by a specified time, tends to delay the disposition of other matters. Requests for processing ahead of the regular order, made in writing in a separate letter submitted with the request or subsequent thereto and showing clear need for such treatment, will be given consideration as the particular circumstances warrant. However, no assurance can be given that any letter will be processed by the time requested. For example, the scheduling of a closing date for a transaction or a meeting of the Board of Directors or shareholders of a corporation without due regard to the time it may take to obtain a ruling, opinion letter, or determination letter will not be deemed sufficient reason for handling a request ahead of its regular order. Neither will the possible effect of fluctuation in the market price of stocks on a transaction be deemed sufficient reason for handling a request out of order. Requests by telegram will be treated in the same manner as requests by letter.

Reg. §601.201(e)(7)

Rulings, opinion letters, and determination letters ordinarily will not be issued by telegram. A taxpayer or his representative desiring to obtain information as to the status of his case may do so by contacting the appropriate division in the office of the Assistant Commissioner, Technical).

(13) The Director, Corporation Tax Division, has responsibility for issuing rulings in areas involving the application of Federal income tax to taxpayers; those involving income tax conventions or treaties with foreign countries; those involving depreciation, depletion, and valuation issues; and those involving the taxable status of exchanges and distributions in connection with corporate reorganizations, organizations, liquidations, etc.

(14) The Director, Individual Tax Division, has responsibility for issuing rulings with respect to the application of Federal income tax to taxpayers (including individuals, partnerships, estates and trusts); areas involving the application of Federal estate and gift taxes including estate and gift tax conventions or treaties with foreign countries; areas involving certain excise taxes; the provisions of the Internal Revenue Code dealing with procedure and administration; and areas involving employment taxes.

(15) A taxpayer or the taxpayer's representative desiring to obtain information as to the status of the taxpayer's case may do so by contacting the following offices with respect to matters in the areas of their responsibility:

	Telephone Numbers
Official	(Area Code 202)
Director, Corporation Tax Division	566-4504 or 566-4505
Director, Individual Tax Division	566-3767 or 566-3788

(16) After receiving the notice pursuant to section 6110(f)(1) of the Code of intention to disclose the ruling or determination letter (including a copy of the version proposed to be open to public inspection and notations of third-party communications pursuant to section 6110(d) of the Code), if the person requesting the ruling or determination letter desires to protest the disclosure of certain information in the ruling or determination letter, such person must within 20 days after the notice is mailed submit a written statement identifying those deletions not made by the Internal Revenue Service which such person believes should have been made. Such person shall also submit a copy of the version of the ruling or determination letter proposed to be open to public inspection on which such person indicates, by the use of brackets, the

deletions proposed by the taxpayer but which have not been made by the Internal Revenue Service. Generally, the Internal Revenue Service will not consider the deletion under this subparagraph of any material which the taxpayer did not, prior to the issuance of the ruling or determination letter, propose be deleted. The Internal Revenue Service shall, within 20 days after receipt of the response by the person requesting the ruling or determination letter to the notice pursuant to section 6110(f)(1) of the Code, mail to such person its final administrative conclusion with respect to the deletions to be made.

(17) After receiving the notice pursuant to section 6110(f)(1) of the Code of intention to disclose (but no later than 60 days after such notice is mailed), the person requesting a ruling or determination letter may submit a request for delay of public inspection pursuant to either section 6110(g)(3) or section 6110(g)(3) and (4) of the Code. The request for delay shall be submitted to the office to which the request for a ruling or determination letter was submitted. A request for delay shall contain the date on which it is expected that the underlying transaction will be completed. The request for delay pursuant to section 6110(g)(4) of the Code shall contain a statement from which the Commissioner may determine that good cause exists to warrant such delay.

(18) When a taxpayer receives a ruling or determination letter prior to the filing of his return with respect to any transaction that has been consummated and that is relevant to the return being filed, he should attach a copy of the ruling or determination letter to the return.

(19) A taxpayer may protest an adverse ruling letter, or the terms and conditions contained in a ruling letter, issued after January 30, 1977, under section 367(a)(1) of the Code (including a ruling with respect to an exchange described in section 367(b) which begins before January 1, 1978) or section 1042(e)(2) of the Tax Reform Act of 1976, not later than 45 days after the date of the ruling letter. (For rulings issued under these sections prior to January 31, 1977, see section 4.01 of Revenue Procedure 77-5.) The Assistant Commissioner (Technical) will establish an ad hoc advisory board to consider each protest, whether or not a conference is requested. A protest is considered made on the date of the postmark of a letter of protest or the date that such letter is hand delivered to any Internal Revenue Service office, including the National Office. The protest letter must be addressed to the Assistant Commissioner (Technical), Attention: T:FP:T. The taxpayer will be granted one conference

Reg. §601.201(e)(19)

upon request. Whether or not the request is made the board may request one or more conferences or written submissions. The taxpayer will be notified of the time, date, and place of the conference, and the names of the members of the board. The board will consider all materials submitted in writing by the taxpayer and oral arguments presented at the conference. Any oral arguments made at a conference by the taxpayer, which have not previously been submitted to the Service in writing, may be submitted to the Service in writing if postmarked not later than seven days after the day of the conference.

The Board will make its recommendation to the Assistant Commissioner (Technical) and the Assistant Commissioner will make the decision. The taxpayer will be informed of the decision of the Assistant Commissioner by certified or registered mail. The specific procedures to be used by a taxpayer in protesting an adverse ruling letter, or the terms and conditions contained in a ruling letter, under section 367 will be published from time to time in the Internal Revenue Bulletin (see, for example, Revenue Procedure 77-5).

(f) *Conferences in the National Office.*—(1) If a conference has been requested, the taxpayer will be notified of the time and place of the conference. A conference is normally scheduled only when the Service deems it will be helpful in deciding the case or an adverse decision is indicated. Ifconferences are being arranged with respect to more than one request for a ruling involving the same taxpayer, they will be so scheduled as to cause the least inconvenience to the taxpayer.

(2) A taxpayer is entitled, as a matter of right, to only one conference in the National Office unless one of the circumstances discussed in subparagraph (3) of this paragraph develops. This conference will usually be held at the branch level of the appropriate division in the office of the Assistant Commissioner (Technical) and will usually be attended by a person who has authority to act for the branch chief. (See § 601.201(a)(2) for the divisions involved.) If more than one subject is to be discussed at the conference, the discussion will constitute a conference with respect to each subject. In order to promote a free and open discussion of the issues, the conference will usually be held after the branch has had an opportunity to study the case. However, at the request of the taxpayer or his representative, the conference may be held at an earlier stage in the consideration of the case than the Service would ordinarily designate. No taxpayer has a "right" to appeal the action of a branch to a division director or to any other official of the Service, nor is a taxpayer entitled, as a matter of right, to a separate conference in the Chief Counsel's office on a request for a ruling.

(3) In the process of review in Technical of a holding proposed by a branch, it may appear that the final answer will involve a reversal of the branch proposal with a result less favorable to the taxpayer. Or it may appear that an adverse holding proposed by a branch will be approved, but on a new or different issue or on different grounds than those on which the branch decided the case. Under either of these circumstances, the taxpayer or his representative will be invited to another conference. The provisions of this section limiting the number of conferences to which a taxpayer is entitled will not foreclose the invitation of a taxpayer to attend further conferences when, in the opinion of National Office personnel, such need arises. All additional conferences of the type discussed in this paragraph are held only at the invitation of the Service.

(4) It is the responsibility of the taxpayer to add to the case file a written record of any additional data, lines of reasoning, precedents, etc., which are proposed by the taxpayer and discussed at the conference but which were not previously or adequately presented in writing.

(g) *Referral of matters to the National Office.*— (1) Requests for determination letters received by the district directors that, in accordance with paragraph (c) of this section, may not be acted upon by a district office, will be forwarded to the National Office for reply and the taxpayer advised accordingly. District directors also refer to the National Office any request for a determination letter that in their judgment warrants the attention of the National Office. See also the provisions of paragraphs (o), (p), and (q) of this section, with respect to requests relating to qualification of a plan under sections 401 and 405(a) of the Code, and paragraph (n) of this section, Revenue Procedure 72-5, Internal Revenue Bulletin No. 1972-1, 19, and Revenue Procedure 68-13, C.B. 1968-1, 764, with respect to application for recognition of exempt status under section 501 and 521 of the Code.

(2) If the request is with regard to an issue or an area with respect to which the Service will not issue a ruling or a determination letter, such request will not be forwarded to the National Office, but the district office will advise the taxpayer that the Service will not issue a ruling or a determination letter on the issue. See paragraph (d)(2) of this section.

(h) *Referral of matters to district offices.*—Requests for rulings received by the National Office that, in accordance with the provisions of paragraph (b) of this section, may not be acted upon by the National Office will be forwarded for appropriate action to the district office that has or will have audit jurisdiction of the taxpayer's return and the taxpayer advised accordingly. If the request is with respect to an issue or an area of the type discussed in paragraph (d)(2) of this section, the taxpayer will be so advised and the request may be forwarded to the appropriate district office for association with the related return or report of the taxpayer.

(i) *Review of determination letters.*—(1) Determination letters issued with respect to the types of inquiries authorized by paragraph (c)(1), (2), and (3) of this section are not generally reviewed by the National Office as they merely inform a taxpayer of a position of the Service which has been previously established either in the regulations or in a ruling, opinion, or court decision published in the Internal Revenue Bulletin. If a taxpayer believes that a determination letter of this type is in error, he may ask the district director to reconsider the matter. He may also ask the district director to request advice from the National Office. In such event, the procedures in paragraph (b)(5) of §601.105 will be followed.

(2) The procedures for review of determination letters relating to the qualification of employers' plans under section 401(a) of the Code are provided in paragraph (o) of this section.

(3) The procedures for review of determination letters relating to the exemption from Federal income tax of certain organizations under sections 501 and 521 of the Code are provided in paragraph (n) of this section.

(j) *Withdrawals of requests.*—The taxpayer's request for a ruling or a determination letter may be withdrawn at any time prior to the signing of the letter of reply. However, in such a case, the National Office may furnish its views to the district director whose office has or will have audit jurisdiction of the taxpayer's return. The information submitted will be considered by the district director in a subsequent audit or examination of the taxpayer's return. Even though a request is withdrawn, all correspondence and exhibits will be retained in the Service and may not be returned to the taxpayer.

(k) *Oral advice to taxpayers.*—(1) The Service does not issue rulings or determination letters upon oral requests. Furthermore, National Office officials and employees ordinarily will not discuss a substantive tax issue with a taxpayer or his representative prior to the receipt of a request for a ruling, since oral opinions or advice are not binding on the Service. This should not be construed as preventing a taxpayer or his representative from inquiring whether the Service will rule on a particular question. In such cases, however, the name of the taxpayer and his identifying number must be disclosed. The Service will also discuss questions relating to procedural matters with regard to submitting a request for a ruling, including the application of the provisions of paragraph (e) to the particular case.

(2) A taxpayer may, of course, seek oral technical assistance from a district office in the preparation of his return or report, pursuant to other established procedures. Such oral advice is advisory only and the Service is not bound to recognize it in the examination of the taxpayer's return.

(l) *Effect of rulings.*—(1) A taxpayer may not rely on an advance ruling issued to another taxpayer. A ruling, except to the extent incorporated in a closing agreement, may be revoked or modified at any time in the wise administration of the taxing statutes. See paragraph (a)(6) of this section for the effect of a closing agreement. If a ruling is revoked or modified, the revocation or modification applies to all open years under the statutes, unless the Commissioner or his delegate exercises the discretionary authority under section 7805(b) of the Code to limit the retroactive effect of the revocation or modification. The manner in which the Commissioner or his delegate generally will exercise this authority is set forth in this section. With reference to rulings relating to the sale or lease of articles subject to the manufacturers excise tax and the retailers excise tax, see specifically subparagraph (8) of this paragraph.

(2) As part of the determination of a taxpayer's liability, it is the responsibility of the district director to ascertain whether any ruling previously issued to the taxpayer has been properly applied. It should be determined whether the representations upon which the ruling was based reflected an accurate statement of the material facts and whether the transaction actually was carried out substantially as proposed. If, in the course of the determination of the tax liability, it is the view of the district director that a ruling previously issued to the taxpayer should be modified or revoked, the findings and recommendations of that office will be forwarded to the National Office for consideration prior to further action. Such reference to the National

Office will be treated as a request for technical advice and the procedures of paragraph (b)(5) of § 601.105 will be followed. Otherwise, the ruling is to be applied by the district office in its determination of the taxpayer's liability.

(3) Appropriate coordination with the National Office will be undertaken in the event that any other field official having jurisdiction of a return or other matter proposes to reach a conclusion contrary to a ruling previously issued to the taxpayer.

(4) A ruling found to be in error or not in accord with the current views of the Service may be modified or revoked. Modification or revocation may be effected by a notice to the taxpayer to whom the ruling originally was issued, or by a Revenue Ruling or other statement published in the Internal Revenue Bulletin.

(5) Except in rare or unusual circumstances, the revocation or modification of a ruling will not be applied retroactively with respect to the taxpayer to whom the ruling was originally issued or to a taxpayer whose tax liability was directly involved in such ruling if (i) there has been no misstatement or omission of material facts, (ii) the facts subsequently developed are not materially different from the facts on which the ruling was based, (iii) there has been no change in the applicable law, (iv) the ruling was originally issued with respect to a prospective or proposed transaction, and (v) the taxpayer directly involved in the ruling acted in good faith in reliance upon the ruling and the retroactive revocation would be to his detriment. To illustrate, the tax liability of each employee covered by a ruling relating to a pension plan of an employer is directly involved in such ruling. Also, the tax liability of each shareholder is directly involved in a ruling related to the reorganization of a corporation. However, the tax liability of members of an industry is not directly involved in a ruling issued to one of the members, and the position taken in a revocation or modification of ruling to one member of an industry may be retroactively applied to other members of that industry. By the same reasoning, a tax practitioner may not obtain the nonretroactive application to one client of a modification or revocation of a ruling previously issued to another client. Where a ruling to a taxpayer is revoked with retroactive effect, the notice to such taxpayer will, except in fraud cases, set forth the grounds upon which the revocation is being made and the reasons why the revocation is being applied retroactively.

(6) A ruling issued to a taxpayer with respect to a particular transaction represents a holding of the Service on that transaction only. However, the application of that ruling to the transaction will not be affected by the subsequent issuance of regulations (either temporary or final), if the conditions specified in subparagraph (5) of this paragraph are met. If the ruling is later found to be in error or no longer in accord with the holding of the Service, it will afford the taxpayer no protection with respect to a like transaction in the same or subsequent year, except to the extent provided in subparagraphs (7) and (8) of this paragraph.

(7) If a ruling is issued covering a continuing action or a series of actions and it is determined that the ruling was in error or no longer in accord with the position of the Service, the Assistant Commissioner (Technical) ordinarily will limit the retroactivity of the revocation or modification to a date not earlier than that on which the original ruling was modified or revoked. To illustrate, if a taxpayer rendered service or provided a facility which is subject to the excise tax on services or facilities, and in reliance on a ruling issued to the same taxpayer did not pass the tax on to the user of the service or the facility, the Assistant Commissioner (Technical) ordinarily will restrict the retroactive application of the revocation or modification of the ruling. Likewise, if an employer incurred liability under the Federal Insurance Contributions Act, but in reliance on a ruling made to the same employer neither collected the employee tax nor paid the employee and employer taxes under the Act, the Assistant Commissioner (Technical) ordinarily will restrict the retroactive application of the revocation or modification of the ruling with respect to both the employer tax and the employee tax. In the latter situation, however, the restriction of retroactive application ordinarily will be conditioned on the furnishing by the employer of wage data, or of such corrections of wage data as may be required by § 31.6011(a)-1(c) of the Employment Tax Regulations. Consistent with these provisions, if a ruling relates to a continuing action or a series of actions, the ruling will be applied until the date of issuance of applicable regulations or the publication of a Revenue Ruling holding otherwise, or until specifically withdrawn. Publication of a notice of proposed rulemaking will not affect the application of any ruling issued under the procedures set forth herein. (As to the effective date in cases involving revocation or modification of rulings or determination letters recognizing exemption, see paragraph (n)(1) of this section.

(8) A ruling holding that the sale or lease of a particular article is subject to the manufactur-

ers excise tax or the retailers excise tax may not revoke or modify retroactively a prior ruling holding that the sale or lease of such article was not taxable, if the taxpayer to whom the ruling was issued, in reliance upon such prior ruling, parted with possession or ownership of the article without passing the tax on to his customer. Section 1108(b), Revenue Act of 1926.

(9) In the case of rulings involving completed transactions, other than those described in subparagraphs (7) and (8) of this paragraph, taxpayers will not be afforded the protection against retroactive revocation provided in subparagraph (5) of this paragraph in the case of proposed transactions since they will not have entered into the transactions in reliance on the rulings.

(m) *Effect of determination letters.*—A determination letter issued by a district director in accordance with this section will be given the same effect upon examination of the return of the taxpayer to whom the determination letter was issued as is described in paragraph (l) of this section, in the case of a ruling issued to a taxpayer, except that reference to the National Office is not necessary where, upon examination of the return, it is the opinion of the district director that a conclusion contrary to that expressed in the determination letter is indicated. A district director may not limit the modification or revocation of a determination letter but may refer the matter to the National Office for exercise by the Commissioner or his delegate of the authority to limit the modification or revocation. In this connection see also paragraphs (n) and (o) of this section.

(n) *Organization claiming exemption under section 501 or 521 of the Code.*—(1) *Filing applications for exemption.*—(i) An organization seeking recognition of exempt status under section 501 or section 521 of the Code is required to file an application with the key district director for the Internal Revenue district in which the principal place of business or principal office of the organization is located. Following are the 19 key district offices that process the applications and the Internal Revenue districts covered by each:

Key District(s)	IRS Districts Covered
	Central Region
Cincinnati ..	Cincinnati, Louisville, Indianapolis.
Cleveland ..	Cleveland, Parkersburg.
Detroit	Detroit.
	Mid-Atlantic Region

Key District(s)	IRS Districts Covered
Baltimore ..	Baltimore (which includes the District of Columbia and Office of International Operations), Pittsburgh, Richmond.
Philadelphia	Philadelphia, Wilmington.
Newark ...	Newark.
	Midwest Region
Chicago ...	Chicago.
St. Paul	St. Paul, Fargo, Aberdeen, Milwaukee.
St. Louis ...	St. Louis, Springfield, Des Moines, Omaha.
	North-Atlantic Region
Boston	Boston, Augusta, Burlington, Providence, Hartford, Portsmouth.
Manhattan .	Manhattan.
Brooklyn ...	Brooklyn, Albany, Buffalo.
	Southeast Region
Atlanta	Atlanta, Greensboro, Columbia, Nashville.
Jacksonville .	Jacksonville, Jackson, Birmingham.
	Southwest Region
Austin	Austin, New Orleans, Albuquerque, Denver, Cheyenne.
Dallas	Dallas, Oklahoma City, Little Rock, Wichita.
	Western Region
Los Angeles	Los Angeles, Phoenix, Honolulu.
San Francisco	San Francisco, Salt Lake City, Reno.
Seattle	Seattle, Portland, Anchorage, Boise, Helena.

(ii) A ruling or determination letter will be issued to an organization provided its application and supporting documents establish that it meets the particular requirements of the section under which exemption is claimed. Exempt status will be recognized in advance of operations if proposed operations can be described in sufficient detail to permit a conclusion that the organization will meet the particular requirements of the section under which exemption is claimed. A mere restatement of purposes or a statement that proposed activities will be in furtherance of such purposes will not satisfy these requirements. The organization must fully describe the activities in which it expects to engage, including the standards, criteria, procedures, or other means adopted or planned for carrying out the activities; the anticipated sources of receipts; and the nature of contemplated expenditures. Where the Service considers it warranted, a record of actual operations may be required before a ruling or determination letter will be issued.

(iii) Where an application for recognition of exemption does not contain the required information, the application may be returned to the applicant without being considered on its merits with an appropriate letter of explanation. In the case of an application under section 501(c)(3) of the Code, the applicant will also be informed of the time within which the completed application must be resubmitted in order for the application to be considered as timely notice within the meaning of section 508(a) of the Code.

(iv) A ruling or determination letter recognizing exemption will not ordinarily be issued if an issue involving the organization's exempt status under section 501 or 521 of the Code is pending in litigation or on appeal within the Service.

(2) *Processing applications.*—(i) Under the general procedures outlined in paragraphs (a) through (m) of this section, key district directors are authorized to issue determination letters involving applications for exemption under sections 501 and 521 of the Code, and requests for foundation status under sections 509 and 4942(j)(3).

(ii) A key district director will refer to the National Office those applications that present questions the answers to which are not specifically covered by statute, Treasury decision or regulation, or by a ruling, opinion, or court decision published in the Internal Revenue Bulletin. The National Office will consider each such application, issue a ruling directly to the organization, and send a copy of the ruling to the key districtdirector. Where the issue of exemption under section 501(c)(3) of the Code is referred to the National Office for decision under this subparagraph, the foundation status issue will also be the subject of a National Office ruling. In the event of a conclusion unfavorable to the applicant, it will be informed of the basis for the conclusion and of its rights to file a protest and to a conference in the National Office. If a conference is requested, the conference procedures set forth in subparagraph (9)(v) of this paragraph will be followed. After reconsideration of the application in the light of the protest and any information developed in conference, the National Office will affirm, modify, or reverse the

original conclusion, issue a ruling to the organization, and send a copy of the ruling to the key district director.

(iii) Key district directors will issue determination letters on foundation status. All adverse determinations issued by key district directors (including adverse determinations on the foundation status under section 509(a) of the Code of nonexempt charitable trusts described in section 4947(a)(1)) are subject to the protest and conference procedures outlined in subparagraph (5) of this paragraph. Key district directors will issue such determinations in response to applications for recognition of exempt status under section 501(c)(3). They will also issue such determinations in response to requests for determination of foundation status by organizations presumed to be private foundations under section 508(b), requests for new determinations of foundation status by organizations previously classified as other than private foundations, and, subject to the conditions set forth in subdivision (vi) of subparagraph (6) of this paragraph, requests to reconsider status. The requests described in the preceding sentence must be made in writing. For information relating to the circumstances under which an organization presumed to be a private foundation under section 508(b) may request a determination of its status as other than a private foundation, see Revenue Ruling 73-504, 1973-2 C.B. 190. All requests for determinations referred to in this paragraph should be made to the key district director for the district in which the principal place of business or principal office of the organization is located.

(iv) If the exemption application or request for foundation status involves an issue which is not covered by published precedent or on which there may be nonuniformity between districts, or if the National Office had issued a previous contrary ruling or technical advice on the issue, the key district director must request technical advice from the National Office. If, during the consideration of its application or request by a key district director, the organization believes that the case involves an issue with respect to which referral for technical advice is appropriate, the organization may ask the district director to request technical advice from the National Office. The district director shall advise the organization of its right to request referral of the issue to the National Office for technical advice. The technical advice provisions applicable to these cases are set forth in subparagraph (9) of this paragraph. The effect on an organization's appeal rights of technical advice or a National

Reg. § 601.201(n)(1)(iii)

Office ruling issued under this subparagraph are set forth in §601.106(a)(1)(iv)(*a*) and in subparagraph (5)(i) of this paragraph.

(3) *Effect of exemption rulings or determination letters.* (i) A ruling or determination letter recognizing exemption is usually effective as of the date of formation of an organization, if its purposes and activities during the period prior to the date of the ruling or determination letter were consistent with the requirements for exemption. However, with respect to organizations formed after October 9, 1969, applying for recognition of exemption under section 501(c)(3) of the Code, the provisions of section 508(a) apply. If the organization is required to alter its activities or make substantive amendments to its enabling instrument, the ruling or determination letter recognizing its exemption will be effective as of the date specified therein.

(ii) A ruling or determination letter recognizing exemption may not be relied upon if there is a material change inconsistent with exemption in the character, the purpose, or the method of operation of the organization.

(iii)(*a*) When an organization that has been listed in IRS Publication No. 78, "Cumulative List of Organizations described in Section 170(c) of the Internal Revenue Code of 1954," as an organization contributions to which are deductible under section 170 of the Code subsequently ceases to qualify as such, and the ruling or determination letter issued to it is revoked, contributions made to the organization by persons unaware of the change in the status of the organization generally will be considered allowable until (*1*) the date of publication of an announcement in the Internal Revenue Bulletin that contributions are no longer deductible, or (*2*) a date specified in such an announcement where deductibility is terminated as of a different date.

(*b*) In appropriate cases, however, this advance assurance of deductibility of contributions made to such an organization may be suspended pending verification of continuing qualification under section 170 of the Code. Notice of such suspension will be made in a public announcement by the Service. In such cases allowance of deductions for contributions made after the date of the announcement will depend upon statutory qualification of the organization under section 170.

(*c*) If an organization, whose status under Section 170(c)(2) of the Code is revoked, initiates within the statutory time limit a proceeding for declaratory judgment under section 7428, special reliance provisions apply. If the decision of the court is adverse to the organization, it shall nevertheless be treated as having been described in section 170(c)(2) for purposes of deductibility of contributions from other organizations described in section 170(c)(2) and individuals (up to a maximum of $1,000), for the period beginning on the date that notice of revocation was published and ending on the date the court first determines that the organization is not described in section 170(c)(2).

(*d*) In any event, the Service is not precluded from disallowing any contributions made after an organization ceases to qualify under section 170 of the Code where the contributor (*1*) had knowledge of the revocation of the ruling or determination letter, (*2*) was aware that such revocation was imminent, or (*3*) was in part responsible for, or was aware of, the activities or deficiencies on the part of the organization which gave rise to the loss of qualification.

(4) *National Office review of determination letters.*—The National Office will review determination letters on exemption issued under sections 501 and 521 of the Code and foundation status under sections 509(a) and 4942(j)(3) to assure uniformity in the application of the established principles and precedents of the Service. Where the National Office takes exception to a determination letter the key district director will be advised. If the organization protests the exception taken, the file and protest will be returned to the National Office. The referral will be treated as a request for technical advice and the procedures of subparagraph (9) of this paragraph will be followed.

(5) *Protest of adverse determination letters.*—(i) Upon the issuance of an adverse determination letter, the key district director will advise the organization of its right to protest the determination by requesting Appeals office consideration. However, if the determination was made on the basis of National Office technical advice the organization may not appeal the determination to the Appeals office. See §601.106(a)(1)(iv)(*a*). To request Appeals consideration, the organization shall submit to the key district director, within 30 days from the date of the letter, a statement of the facts, law, and arguments in support of its position. The organization must also state whether it wishes an Appeals office conference. Upon receipt of an organization's request for Appeals consideration, the key district director will, if it maintains its position, forward the request and the case file to the Appeals office.

Reg. §601.201(n)(5)(i)

(ii) Except as provided in subdivisions (iii) and (iv) of this subparagraph, the Appeals office, after considering the organization's protest and any additional information developed, will advise the organization of its decision and issue an appropriate determination letter. Organizations should make full presentation of the facts, circumstances, and arguments at the initial level of consideration, since submission of additional facts, circumstances, and arguments at the Appeals office may result in suspension of Appeals procedures and referral of the case back to the key district for additional consideration.

(iii) If the proposed disposition by the Appeals office is contrary to a National Office technical advice or ruling concerning tax exemption, issued prior to the case, the proposed disposition will be submitted, through the Office of the Regional Director of Appeals, to the Assistant Commissioner (Employee Plans and Exempt Organizations) or, in a section 521 case, to the Assistant Commissioner (Technical). The decision of the Assistant Commissioner will be followed by the Appeals office. See § 601.106(a)(1)(iv)(*b*).

(iv) If the case involves an issue that is not covered by published precedent or on which there may be nonuniformity between regions, and on which the National Office has not previously ruled, the Appeals office must request technical advice from the National Office. If, during the consideration of its case by Appeals, the organization believes that the case involves an issue with respect to which referral for technical advice is appropriate, the organization may ask the Appeals office to request technical advice from the National Office. The Appeals office shall advise the organization of its right to request referral of the issue to the National Office for technical advice. If the Appeals office requests technical advice, the decision of the Assistant Commissioner (Employee Plans and Exempt Organizations) or, in a section 521 case, the decision of the Assistant Commissioner (Technical), in a technical advice memorandum is final and the Appeals office must dispose of the case in accordance with that decision. See subparagraph (9)(viii)(*a*) of this paragraph.

(6) *Revocation or modification of rulings or determination letters on exemption and foundation status.*—(i) An exemption ruling or determination letter may be revoked or modified by a ruling or determination letter addressed to the organization, or by a revenue ruling or other statement published in the Internal Revenue Bulletin. The revocation or modification may be retroactive if the organization omitted or misstated a material

fact, operated in a manner materially different from that originally represented, or engaged in a prohibited transaction of the type described in subdivision (vii) of this subparagraph. In any event, revocation or modification will ordinarily take effect no later than the time at which the organization received written notice that its exemption ruling or determination letter might be revoked or modified.

(ii)(*a*) If a key district director concludes as a result of examining an information return, or considering information from any other source, that an exemption ruling or determination letter should be revoked or modified, the organization will be advised in writing of the proposed action and the reasons therefor. If the case involves an issue not covered by published precedent or on which there may be nonuniformity between districts, or if the National Office had issued a previous contrary ruling or technical advice on the issue, the district director must seek technical advice from the National Office. If the organization believes that the case involves an issue with respect to which referral for technical advice is appropriate, the organization may ask the district director to request technical advice from the National Office. The district director shall advise the organization of its right to request referral of the issue to the National Office for technical advice.

(*b*) The key district director will advise the organization of its right to protest the proposed revocation or modification by requesting Appeals office consideration. However, if National Office technical advice was furnished concerning revocation or modification under (*a*) of this subdivision, the decision of the Assistant Commissioner in the technical advice memorandum is final and the organization has no right of appeal to the Appeals office. See § 601.106(a)(1)(iv)(*a*). To request Appeals consideration, the organization must submit to the key district director, within 30 days from the date of the letter, a statement of the facts, law, and arguments in support of its continued exemption. The organization must also state whether it wishes an Appeals office conference. Upon receipt of an organization's request for Appeals consideration, the key district office, will, if it maintains its position, forward the request and the case file to the Appeals office.

(*c*) Except as provided in (*d*) and (*e*) of this subdivision, the Appeals office, after considering the organization's protest and any additional information developed, will advise the organization of its decision and issue an appropriate determination letter. Organizations should make full presentation of the facts, circumstances, and arguments at the initial level of consideration, since submission of additional facts, circumstances, and arguments at the Appeals office may result in suspension of Appeals procedures and referral of the case back to the key district for additional consideration.

(*d*) If the proposed disposition by the Appeals office is contrary to a National Office technical advice or ruling concerning tax exemption, issued prior to the case, the proposed disposition will be submitted, through the Office of the Regional Director of Appeals, to the Assistant Commissioner (Employee Plans and Exempt Organizations) or, in a section 521 case, to the Assistant Commissioner (Technical). The decision of the Assistant Commissioner will be followed by the Appeals office. See § 601.106(a)(1)(iv)(*b*).

(*e*) If the case involves an issue that is not covered by published precedent or on which there may be nonuniformity between regions, and on which the National Office has not previously ruled, the Appeals office must request technical advice from the National Office. If the organization believes that the case involves an issue with respect to which referral for technical advice is appropriate, the organization may ask the Appeals office to request technical advice from the National Office. The Appeals office shall advise the organization of its right to request referral of the issue to the National Office for technical advice.

(iii) A ruling or determination letter respecting private foundation or operating foundation status may be revoked or modified by a ruling or determination letter addressed to the organization, or by a revenue ruling or other statement published in the Internal Revenue Bulletin. If a key district director concludes, as a result of examining an information return or considering information from any other source, that a ruling or determination letter concerning private foundation status (including foundation status under section 509(a)(3) of the Code of a nonexempt charitable trust described in section 4947(a)(1)) or operating foundation status should be modified or revoked, the procedures in subdivision (iv) or (v) of this subparagraph should be followed depending on whether the revocation or modification is adverse or non-adverse to the affected organization. Where there is a proposal by the Service to change foundation status classification from one particular paragraph of section 509(a) to another paragraph of that section, the procedures described in subdivision (iv) of this subparagraph will be followed to modify the ruling or determination letter.

(iv) If a key district director concludes that a ruling or determination letter concerning private foundation or operating foundation status should be revoked or modified, the organization will be advised in writing of the proposed adverse action, the reasons therefor, and the proposed new determination of foundation status. The procedures set forth in subdivision (ii) of this subparagraph apply to a proposed revocation or modification under this subdivision. Unless the effective date of revocation or modification of a ruling or determination letter concerning private foundation or operating foundation status is expressly covered by statute or regulations, the effective date generally is the same as the effective date of revocation or modification of exemption rulings or determination letters as provided in subdivision (i) of this subparagraph.

(v) If the key district director concludes that a ruling or determination letter concerning private foundation or operating foundation status should be revoked or modified and that such revocation or modification will not be adverse to the organization, the key district director will issue a determination letter revoking or modifying foundation status. The determination letter will also serve to notify the organization of its foundation status as redetermined. A nonadverse revocation or modification as to private foundation or operating foundation status will ordinarily be retroactive if the initial ruling or determination letter was incorrect.

(vi) In cases where an organization believes that it received an incorrect ruling or determination letter as to its private foundation or operating foundation status, the organization may request a key district director to reconsider such ruling or determination letter. Except in rare circumstances, the key district director will only consider such requests where the organization had not exercised any protest or conference rights with respect to the issuance of such ruling or determination letter. If a key district director decides that reconsideration is warranted, the request will be treated as an initial request for a determination of foundation status, and the key district director will issue a determination on foundation status or operating foundation status under the procedures of subparagraph (2) of this paragraph. If a nonadverse determination is issued, it will also inform the organization that the prior ruling or determination letter is revoked or modified. Adverse determinations are subject to the procedures set out in subparagraph (5) of this paragraph. If the key district director decides that reconsideration is not warranted, the organization will be notified accordingly. The organization does not have a right to protest the key district director's decision not to reconsider.

(vii) If it is concluded that an organization that is subject to the provisions of section 503 of the Code entered into a prohibited transaction for the purpose of diverting corpus or income from its exempt purpose, and if the transaction involved a substantial part of the corpus or income of the organization, its exemption is revoked effective as of the beginning of the taxable year during which the prohibited transaction was commenced.

(viii) The provisions of this subparagraph relating to protests, conferences, and the rights of organizations to ask that technical advice be requested before a revocation (or modification) notice is issued are not applicable to matters where delay would be prejudicial to the interests of the Internal Revenue Service (such as in cases involving fraud, jeopardy, the imminence of the expiration of the period of limitations, or where immediate action is necessary to protect the interests of the Government).

(7) *Declaratory judgments relating to status and classification of organizations under section 501(c)(3) of the Code.*—(i) An organization seeking recognition of exempt status under section 501(c)(3) of the Code must follow the procedures of subparagraph (1) of this paragraph regarding the filing of Form 1023, Application for Recognition of Exemption. The 270-day period referred to in section 7428(b)(2) will be considered by the Service to begin on the date a substantially completed Form 1023 is sent to the appropriate key district director. A substantially completed Form 1023 is one that:

(*a*) Is signed by an authorized individual;

(*b*) Includes an Employer Identification Number (EIN) or a completed Form SS-4, Application for Employer Identification Number;

(*c*) Includes a statement of receipts and expenditures and a balance sheet for the current year and the three preceding years or the years the organization was in existence, if less than four years (if the organization has not yet commenced operations, a proposed budget for two full accounting periods and a current statement of assets and liabilities will be acceptable);

(*d*) Includes a statement of proposed activities and a description of anticipated receipts and contemplated expenditures;

(*e*) Includes a copy of the organizing or enabling document that is signed by a principal officer or is accompanied by a written declaration signed by an officer authorized to sign for the organization certifying that the document is a complete and accurate copy of the original; and

(*f*) If the organization is a corporation or unincorporated association and it has adopted bylaws, includes a copy that is signed or otherwise verified as current by an authorized officer. If an application does not contain all of the above items, it will not be further processed and may be returned to the applicant for completion. The 270-day period will not be considered as starting until the date the application is remailed to the Service with the requested information, or, if a postmark is not evident, on the date the Service receives a substantially completed application.

(ii) Generally, rulings and determination letters in cases subject to declaratory judgment are issued under the procedures outlined in this paragraph. In National Office exemption application cases, proposed adverse rulings will be issued by the rulings sections in the Exempt Organizations Technical Branch. Applicants shall appeal these proposed adverse rulings to the Conference and Review Staff of the Exempt Organizations Technical Branch. In those cases where an organization is unable to describe fully its purposes and activities (see subparagraph (1)(ii) of this paragraph), a refusal to rule will be considered an adverse determination for which administrative appeal rights will be afforded. Any oral representation of additional facts or modification of the facts as represented or alleged in the application for a ruling or determination letter must be reduced to writing.

(iii) If an organization withdraws in writing its request for a ruling or determination letter, the withdrawal will not be considered by the Service as either a failure to make a determination within the meaning of section 7428(a)(2) of the Code or as an exhaustion of administrative remedies within the meaning of section 7428(b)(2).

(iv) Section 7428(b)(2) of the Code requires that an organization must exhaust its administrative remedies by taking timely, reasonable steps to secure a determination. Those steps and administrative remedies that must be exhausted within the Internal Revenue Service are:

(*a*) The filing of a substantially completed application Form 1023 pursuant to subdivision (i) of this subparagraph, or the filing of a request for a determination of foundation status pursuant to subparagraph (2) of this paragraph;

(b) The timely submission of all additional information requested to perfect an exemption application or request for determination of private foundation status; and

(c) Exhaustion of all administrative appeals available within the Service pursuant to subparagraphs (5) and (6) of this paragraph, as well as appeal of a proposed adverse ruling to the Conference and Review Staff of the Exempt Organizations Technical Branch in National Office original jurisdiction exemption application cases.

(v) An organization will in no event be deemed to have exhausted its administrative remedies prior to the completion of the steps described in subdivision (iv) of this subparagraph and the earlier of:

(a) The sending by certified or registered mail of a notice of final determination; or

(b) The expiration of the 270-day period described in section 7428(b)(2) of the Code, in a case in which the Service has not issued a notice of final determination and the organization has taken, in a timely manner, all reasonable steps to secure a ruling or determination.

(vi) The steps described in subdivision (iv) of this subparagraph will not be considered completed until the Internal Revenue Service has had a reasonable time to act upon the appeal or request for consideration, as the case may be.

(vii) A notice of final determination to which section 7428 of the Code applies is a ruling or determination letter, sent by certified or registered mail, which holds that the organization is not described in section 501(c)(3) or section 170(c)(2), is a private foundation as defined in section 509(a), or is not a private operating foundation as defined in section 4942(j)(3).

(8) *Group exemption letters.*—(i) *General.*—*(a)* A group exemption letter is a ruling issued to a central organization recognizing on a group basis the exemption under section 501(c) of the Code of subordinate organizations on whose behalf the central organization has applied for exemption in accordance with this subparagraph.

(b) A central organization is an organization which has one or more subordinates under its general supervision or control.

(c) A subordinate is a chapter, local, post, or unit of a central organization. It may or may not be incorporated. A central organization may be a subordinate itself, such as a state organization which has subordinate units and is itself affiliated with a national organization.

(d) A subordinate included in a group exemption letter should not apply separately

for an exemption letter, unless it no longer wants to be included in the group exemption letter.

(e) A subordinate described in section 501(c)(3) of the Code may not be included in a group exemption letter if it is a private foundation as defined in section 509(a) of the Code. Such an organization should apply separately for exempt status under the procedures outlined in subparagraph (1) of this paragraph.

(ii) *Requirements for inclusion in a group exemption letter.*—*(a)* A central organization applying for a group exemption letter must establish its own exempt status.

(b) It must also establish that the subordinates to be included in the group exemption letter are:

(1) Affiliated with it;

(2) Subject to its general supervision or control;

(3) Exempt under the same paragraph of section 501(c) of the Code, though not necessarily the paragraph under which the central organization is exempt; and

(4) Not private foundations if application for a group exemption letter involves section 501(c)(3) of the Code.

(c) Each subordinate must authorize the central organization to include it in the application for the group exemption letter. The authorization must be signed by a duly authorized officer of the subordinate and retained by the central organization while the group exemption letter is in effect.

(iii) *Filing application for a group exemption letter.*—*(a)* A central organization seeking a group exemption letter for its subordinates must obtain recognition of its own exemption by filing an application with the District Director of Internal Revenue for the district in which is located the principal place of business or the principal office of the organization. For the form of organization see section 1.501(a)-1 of the Income Tax Regulations. Any application received by the National Office or by a district director other than as provided above will be forwarded, without any action thereon, to the appropriate district director.

(b) If the central organization has previously established its own exemption, it must indicate its employer identification number, the date of the exemption letter, and the Internal Revenue Office that issued it. It need not resubmit documents already submitted. However, if it has not already done so, it must submit a copy of any amendments to its governing instruments or

Reg. §601.201(n)(8)(iii)(b)

internal regulations as well as any information regarding any change in its character, purposes, or method of operation.

(c) In addition to the information required to establish its own exemption, the central organization must submit to the district director the following information, in duplicate, on behalf of those subordinates to be included in the group exemption letter:

(1) A letter signed by a principal officer of the central organization setting forth or including as attachments;

(i) Information verifying the existence of the relationships required by subdivision (ii)(*b*) of this subparagraph;

(ii) A description of the principal purposes and activities of the subordinates;

(iii) A sample copy of a uniform governing instrument (charter, trust indenture, articles of association, etc.), if such an instrument has been adopted by the subordinates; or, in the absence of a uniform governing instrument, copies of representative instruments;

(iv) An affirmation to the effect that, to the best of his knowledge, the subordinates are operating in accordance with the stated purposes;

(v) A statement that each subordinate to be included in the group exemption letter has furnished written authorization to the central organization as described in subdivision (ii)(*c*) of this subparagraph; and

(vi) A list of subordinates to be included in the group exemption letter to which the Service has issued an outstanding ruling or determination letter relating to exemption.

(vii) If the application for a group exemption letter involves section 501(c)(3) of the Code, an affirmation to the effect that, to the best of his knowledge and belief, no subordinate to be included in the group exemption letter is a private foundation as defined in section 509(a) of the Code.

(2) A list of the names, mailing addresses (including Postal ZIP Codes), and employer identification numbers (if required for group exemption letter purposes by *(e)* of this subdivision) of subordinates to be included in the group exemption letter. A current directory of subordinates may be furnished in lieu of the list if it includes the required information and if the subordinates not to be included in the group exemption letter are identified.

(d) If the central organization does not have an employer identification number, it must submit a completed Form SS-4, Application for Employer Identification Number, with its exemption application. See Rev. Rul. 63-247, C.B. 1963-2, 612.

(e) Each subordinate required to file an annual information return, Form 990 or 990-A, must have its own employer identification number, even if it has no employees. The central organization must submit with the exemption application a completed Form SS-4 on behalf of each subordinate not having a number. Although subordinates not required to file annual information returns, Form 990 or 990-A, need not have employer identification numbers for group exemption letter purposes, they may need such numbers for other purposes.

(iv) *Information required annually to maintain a group exemption letter.*—*(a)* The central organization must submit annually within 45 days after the close of its annual accounting period the information set out below to the Philadelphia Service Center, 11601 Roosevelt Boulevard, Philadelphia, Pennsylvania 19155, Attention: EO:R Branch:

(1) Information regarding all changes in the purposes, character, or method of operation of subordinates included in the group exemption letter.

(2) Lists of (*i*) subordinates which have changed their names or addresses during the year, (*ii*) subordinates no longer to be included in the group exemption letter because they have ceased to exist, disaffiliated, or withdrawn the authorization to the central organization, and (*iii*) subordinates to be added to the group exemption letter because they are newly organized or affiliated or they have newly authorized the central organization to include them. A separate list must be submitted for each of the three categories set out above. Each list must show the names, mailing addresses (including Postal ZIP Codes), and employer identification numbers of the affected subordinates. An annotated directory of subordinates will not be acceptable for this purpose. If there were none of the above changes, the central organization must submit a statement to that effect.

(3) The information required by subdivision (iii)(*c*)(*1*) of this subparagraph, with respect to subordinates to be added to the group exemption letter. However, if the information upon which the group exemption letter was based is applicable in all material respects to such subordinates, a statement to this effect may be submitted in lieu of the information required by subdivision (iii)(*c*)(*1*)(*i*) through (*v*) of this subparagraph.

(b) Submission of the information required by this subdivision does not relieve the central organization or any of its subordinates of the duty to submit such additional information as a key district director may require to enable him to determine whether the conditions for continued exemption are being met. See sections 6001 and 6033 of the Code and the regulations thereunder.

(v) *Termination of a group exemption letter.*—*(a)* Termination of a group exemption letter will result in non-recognition of the exempt status of all included subordinates. To reestablish an exempt status in such cases, each subordinate must file an exemption application under the procedures outlined in subparagraph (1) of this paragraph, or a new group exemption letter must be applied for under this subparagraph.

(b) If a central organization dissolves or ceases to exist, the group exemption letter will be terminated, notwithstanding that the subordinates continue to exist and operate independently.

(c) Failure of the central organization to submit the information required by subdivision (iv) of this subparagraph, or to file a required information return, Form 990 or 990-A, or to otherwise comply with section 6001 or 6033 of the Code and the regulations thereunder, may result in termination of the group exemption letter on the grounds that the conditions required for the continuance of the group exemption letter have not been met. See Rev. Rul. 59-95, C.B. 1959-1, 627.

(d) The dissolution of a subordinate included in a group exemption letter will not affect the exempt status of the other included subordinates.

(e) If a subordinate covered by a group exemption letter fails to comply with section 6001 or 6033 of the Code and the regulations thereunder (for example, by failing to file a required information return) and the Service terminates its recognition of the subordinate's status, a copy of the termination letter to the subordinate will be furnished to the central organization. The group exemption letter will no longer be applicable to such subordinate, but will otherwise remain in effect. (It should be noted that if Form 990 is required to be filed, failure to file such return on time may also result in the imposition of a penalty of $10 for each day the return is late, up to a maximum of $5,000. See section 6652 of the Code and the regulations thereunder.)

(vi) *Revocation of a group exemption letter.*—*(a)* If the Service determines, under the procedures described in subparagraph (6) of this paragraph, that a central organization no longer qualifies for exemption under section 501(c) of the Code, the group exemption letter will be revoked.The revocation will result in nonrecognition of the exempt status of all included subordinates. To reestablish an exempt status in such cases, each subordinate must file an exemption application under the procedures outlined in subparagraph (1) of this paragraph or a new group exemption letter must be applied for under this subparagraph.

(b) If the Service determines, under the procedures described in subparagraph (6) of this paragraph, that a subordinate included in a group exemption letter no longer qualifies for exemption under section 501(c) of the Code, the central organization and the subordinate will be notified accordingly, and the group exemption letter will no longer apply to such subordinate, but will otherwise remain in effect.

(c) Where a subordinate organization has been disqualified for inclusion in a group exemption letter as described in *(b)* of this subdivision, and thereafter wishes to reestablish its exempt status, the central organization should, at the time it submits the information required by subdivision (iv) of this subparagraph, submit detailed information relating to the subordinate's qualification for reinclusion in the group exemption letter.

(vii) *Instrumentalities or agencies of political subdivisions.*—An instrumentality or agency of a political subdivision that exercises control or supervision over a number of organizations similar in purposes and operations, each of which may qualify for exemption under the same paragraph of section 501(c) of the Code, may obtain a group exemption letter covering those organizations in the same manner as a central organization. However, the instrumentality or agency must furnish evidence that it is a qualified governmental agency. Examples of organizations over which governmental agencies exercise control or supervision are Federal credit unions, State chartered credit unions, and Federal land bank associations.

(viii) *Listing in cumulative list of organizations to which charitable contributions are deductible.*—If a central organization to which a group exemption letter has been issued is eligible to receive deductible charitable contributions as provided in section 170 of the Code, it will be listed in Publication No. 78, Cumulative List—Organizations Described in Section 170(c) of the Internal Revenue Code of 1954. The names of the subordinates covered by the group exemption letter will not be listed individually. However, the identification of the central organization will indicate whether contributions to its subordinates are also deductible.

(9) *Technical advice from the National Office*.— (i) *Definition and nature of technical advice*.— *(a)* As used in this subparagraph, "technical advice" means advice or guidance as to the interpretation and proper application of internal revenue laws, related statutes, and regulations, to a specific set of facts, in Employee Plans and Exempt Organization matters, furnished by the National Office upon request of a key district office or Appeals office in connection with the processing and consideration of a nondocketed case. It is furnished as a means of assisting Service personnel in closing cases and establishing and maintaining consistent holdings. It does not include memorandums on matters of general technical application furnished to key district offices or to Appeals offices where the issues are not raised in connection with the consideration and handling of a specific case.

(b) The provisions of this subparagraph only apply to Employee Plans and Exempt Organization cases being considered by a key district director or Appeals office. They do not apply to any other case under the jurisdiction of a district director or Appeals office or to a case under the jurisdiction of the Bureau of Alcohol, Tobacco, and Firearms. The technical advice provisions applicable to cases under the jurisdiction of a district director, other than Employee Plans and Exempt Organization cases, are set forth in § 601.105(b)(5). The technical advice provisions applicable to cases under the jurisdiction of an Appeals office, other than Employee Plans and Exempt Organization cases are set forth in § 601.106(f)(10).

(c) A key district director or an Appeals office may, under this subparagraph, request technical advice with respect to the consideration of a request for a determination letter. If the case involves certain Exempt Organization issues that are not covered by published precedent or on which there may be nonuniformity, requesting technical advice is mandatory rather than discretionary. See subparagraphs (2)(iv) and (5)(iii) of this paragraph.

(d) If a key district director is of the opinion that a National Office ruling letter or technical advice previously issued should be modified or revoked and it requests the National Office to reconsider the ruling or technical advice, the reference of the matter to the National

Office is treated as a request for technical advice. The procedures specified in subdivision (iii) of this subparagraph should be followed in order that the National Office may consider the recommendation. Only the National Office can revoke a National Office ruling letter or technical advice.Before referral to the National Office, the key district director should inform the plan/organization of its opinion that the ruling letter or technical advice should be revoked. The key district director, after development of the facts and consideration of the arguments, will decide whether to recommend revocation of the ruling or technical advice to the National Office.

(e) The Assistant Commissioner (Employee Plans and Exempt Organizations) and, in section 521 cases, the Assistant Commissioner (Technical), acting under a delegation of authority from the Commissioner of Internal Revenue, are exclusively responsible for providing technical advice in any issue involving the establishment of basic principles and rules for the uniform interpretation and application of tax laws in cases under this subparagraph. This authority has been largely redelegated to subordinate officials.

(ii) *Areas in which technical advice may be requested*.—*(a)* Key district directors and Appeals offices may request technical advice on any technical or procedural question that develops during the processing and consideration of a case. These procedures are applicable as provided in subdivision (i) of this subparagraph.

(b) Key district directors and Appeals offices are encouraged to request technical advice on any technical or procedural question arising in connection with any case described in subdivision (i) of this subparagraph which cannot be resolved on the basis of law, regulations, or a clearly applicable revenue ruling or other precedent issued by the National Office. However, in Exempt Organization cases concerning qualification for exemption or foundation status, key district directors and Appeals offices must request technical advice on any issue that is not covered by published precedent or on which nonuniformity may exist. Requests for technical advice should be made at the earliest possible stage of the proceedings.

(iii) *Requesting technical advice*.—*(a)* It is the responsibility of the key district office or the Appeals office to determine whether technical advice is to be requested on any issue before that office. However, while the case is under the jurisdiction of the key district director or the Appeals office, an employee plan/organization or its representative may request that an issue be referred to the National Office for technical advice on the grounds that a lack of uniformity exists as to the disposition of the issue, or that the issue is so unusual or complex as to warrant consideration by the National Office. This request should be made at the earliest possible stage of the proceedings. While plans/organizations are encouraged to make written requests setting forth the facts, law, and argument with respect to the issue, and reason for requesting National Office advice, a plan/organization may make the request orally. If, after considering the plan's/organization's request, the examiner or the Appeals Officer is of the opinion that the circumstances do not warrant referral of the case to the National Office, he/she will so advise the plan/organization. (See subdivision (iv) of this subparagraph for a plan's/organization's appeal rights where the examiner or Appeal Officer declines to request technical advice.)

(b) When technical advice is to be requested, whether or not upon the request of the plan/organization, the plan/organization will be so advised, except as noted in *(j)* of this subdivision. If the key district office or the Appeals office initiates the action, the plan/organization will be furnished a copy of the statement of the pertinent facts and the question or questions proposed for submission to the National Office. The request for advice should be so worded as to avoid possible misunderstanding, in the National Office, of the facts or of the specific point or points at issue.

(c) After receipt of the statement of facts and specific questions, the plan/organization will be given 10 calendar days in which to indicate in writing the extent, if any, to which it may not be in complete agreement. An extension of time must be justified by the plan/organization in writing and approved by the Chief, Employee Plans and Exempt Organizations Division (in the district office) or the Chief, Appeals Office, as the case may be. Every effort should be made to reach agreement as to the facts and specific points at issue. If agreement cannot be reached, the plan/organization may submit, within 10 calendar days after receipt of notice from the key district director or the Appeals office, a statement of its understanding as to the specific point or points at issue which will be forwarded to the National Office with the request for advice. An extension of time must be justified by the plan/organization in writing and approved by the Chief, Employee Plans and Exempt Organizations Division or the Chief, Appeals Office.

(d) If the plan/organization initiates the action to request advice, and its statement of the facts and point or points at issue are not wholly acceptable to the key district office or the Appeals office, the plan/organization will be advised in writing as to the areas of disagreement. The plan/organization will be given 10 calendar days after receipt of the written notice to reply to such notice. An extension of time must be justified by the plan/organization in writing and approved by the Chief, Employee Plans and Exempt Organizations Division or the Chief, Appeals Office. If agreement cannot be reached, both the statements of the plan/organization and the key district office or the Appeals office will be forwarded to the National Office.

(e)(1) In the case of requests for technical advice subject to the disclosure provisions of section 6110 of the Code, the plan/organization must also submit, within the 10-day period referred to in *(c)* and *(d)* of this subdivision, whichever applicable (relating to agreement by the plan/organization with the statement of facts and points submitted in connection with the request for technical advice) the statement described in *(f)* of this subdivision of proposed deletions pursuant to section 6110(c) of the Code. If the statement is not submitted, the plan/organization will be informed by the key district director or the Appeals office that the statement is required. If the key district director or the Appeals office does not receive the statement within 10 days after the plan/organization has been informed of the need for the statement, the key district director or the Appeals office may decline to submit the request for technical advice. If the key district director or the Appeals office decides to request technical advice in a case where the plan/organization has not submitted the statement of proposed deletions, the National Office will make those deletions which in the judgment of the Commissioner are required by section 6110(c) of the Code.

(2) The requirements included in this subparagraph, relating to the submission of statements and other material with respect to proposed deletions to be made from technical advise memoranda before public inspection is permitted to take place, do not apply to requests made by the key district director before November 1, 1976, or requests for any document to which section 6104 of the Code applies.

(f) In order to assist the Internal Revenue Service in making the deletions, required by section 6110(c) of the Code, from the text of technical advice memoranda which are open to public inspection pursuant to section 6110(a) of

the Code, there must accompany requests for such technical advice either a statement of the deletions proposed by the plan/organization, or a statement that no information other than names, addresses, and identifying numbers need be deleted. Such statements shall be made in a separate document. The statement of proposed deletions shall be accompanied by a copy of all statements of facts and supporting documents which are submitted to the National Office pursuant to (c) or (d) of this subdivision, on which shall be indicated, by the use of brackets, the material which the plan/organization indicates should be deleted pursuant to section 6110(c) of the Code. The statement of proposed deletions shall indicate the statutory basis for each proposed deletion. The statement of proposed deletions shall not appear or be referred to anywhere in the request for technical advice. If the plan/organization decides to request additional deletions pursuant to section 6110(c) of the Code prior to the time the National Office replies to the request for technical advice, additional statements may be submitted.

(g) If the plan/organization has not already done so, it may submit a statement explaining its position on the issues, citing precedents which it believes will bear on the case. This statement will be forwarded to the National Office with the request for advice. If it is received at a later date, it will be forwarded for association with the case file.

(h) At the time the plan/organization is informed that the matter is being referred to the National Office, it will also be informed of the right to a conference in the National Office in the event an adverse decision is indicated, and will be asked to indicate whether a conference is desired.

(i) Generally, prior to replying to the request for technical advice, the National Office shall inform the plan/organization orally or in writing of the material likely to appear in the technical advice memorandum which the plan/organization proposed be deleted but which the Internal Revenue Service determined should not be deleted. If so informed, the plan/organization may submit within 10 days any further information, arguments, or other material in support of the position that such material be deleted. The Internal Revenue Service will attempt, if feasible, to resolve all disagreements with respect to proposed deletions prior to the time the National Office replies to the request for technical advice. However, in no event shall the plan/organization have the right to a conference with respect to resolution of any disagreements concerning

material to be deleted from the text of the technical advice memorandum, but such matters may be considered at any conference otherwise scheduled with respect to the request.

(j) The provisions of (a) through (i) of this subdivision, relating to the referral of issues upon request of the plan/organization, advising plans/organizations of the referral of issues, the submission of proposed deletions, and the granting of conferences in the National Office, are not applicable to technical advice memoranda described in section 6110(g)(5)(A) of the Code, relating to cases involving criminal or civil fraud investigations and jeopardy or termination assessments. However, in such cases the plan/organization shall be allowed to provide the statement of proposed deletions to the National Office upon the completion of all proceedings with respect to the investigations or assessments, but prior to the date on which the Commissioner mails the notice pursuant to section 6110(f)(1) of the Code of intention to disclose the technical advice memorandum.

(k) Form 4463, Request for Technical Advice, should be used for transmitting requests for technical advice to the National Office.

(iv) *Appeal by plans/organizations of determinations not to seek technical advice.*—(a) If the plan/organization has requested referral of an issue before a key district office or an Appeals office to the National Office for technical advice, and after consideration of the request the examiner or the Appeals Officer is of the opinion that the circumstances do not warrant such referral, he/she will so advise the plan/organization.

(b) The plan/organization may appeal the decision of the examiner or the Appeals Officer not to request technical advice by submitting to the relevant official, within 10 calendar days after being advised of the decision, a statement of the facts, law, and arguments with respect to the issue, and the reasons why the plan/organization believes the matter should be referred to the National Office for advice. An extension of time must be justified by the plan/organization in writing and approved by the Chief, Employee Plans and Exempt Organizations Division of the Chief, Appeals Office.

(c) The examiner or the Appeals Officer will submit the statement of the plan/organization to the Chief, Employee Plans and Exempt Organizations Division or the Chief, Appeals Office, accompanied by a statement of the official's reasons why the issue should not be referred to the National Office. The Chief will determine, on the basis of the statements submitted, whether technical advice will be requested. If the Chief determines that technical advice is not warranted, that official will inform the plan/organization in writing that he/she proposes to deny the request. In the letter to the plan/organization the Chief will (except in unusual situations where such action would be prejudicial to the best interests of the Government) state specifically the reasons for the proposed denial. The plan/organization will be given 15 calendar days after receipt of the letter in which to notify the Chief whether it agrees with the proposed denial. The plan/organization may not appeal the decision of the Chief, Employee Plans and Exempt Organizations Division, or of the Chief, Appeals Office, not to request technical advice from the National Office. However, if the plan/organization does not agree with the proposed denial, all data relating to the issue for which technical advice has been sought, including the plan's/organization's written request and statements, will be submitted to the National Office, Attention: Director, Exempt Organizations or Employee Plans Division or Actuarial Division or, in a section 521 case, Attention: Director, Corporation Tax Division for review. After review in the National Office, the submitting office will be notified whether the proposed denial is approved or disapproved.

(d) While the matter is being reviewed in the National Office, the key district office or the Appeals office will suspend action on the issue (except where the delay would prejudice the Government's interests) until it is notified of the National Office decision. This notification will be made within 30 days after receipt of the data in the National Office. The review will be solely on the basis of the written record and no conference will be held in the National Office.

(v) *Conference in the National Office.*— *(a)* If, after a study of the technical advice request, it appears that advice adverse to the plan/organization should be given and a conference has been requested, the plan/organization will be notified of the time and place of the conference. If conferences are being arranged with respect to more than one request for advice involving the same plan/organization, they will be so scheduled as to cause the least inconvenience to the plan/organization. The conference will be arranged by telephone, if possible, and must be held within 21 calendar days after contact has been made. Extensions of time will be granted only if justified in writing by the plan/organization and approved by the appropriate branch chief.

(b) A plan/organization is entitled, as a matter of right, to only one conference in the National Office unless one of the circumstances discussed in (*c*) of this subdivision exists. This conference will usually be held at the branch level in the appropriate division in the Office of the Assistant Commissioner (Employee Plans and Exempt Organizations) or, in section 521 cases, in the Office of the Assistant Commissioner (Technical), and will usually be attended by a person who has authority to act for the branch chief. In appropriate cases the examiner or the Appeals Officer may also attend the conference to clarify the facts in the case. If more than one subject is discussed at the conference, the discussion constitutes a conference with respect to each subject. At the request of the plan/organization or its representative, the conference may be held at an earlier stage in the consideration of the case than the Service would ordinarily designate. A plan/organization has no "right" of appeal from an action of a branch to the director of a division or to any other National Office official.

(c) In the process of review of a holding proposed by a branch, it may appear that the final answer will involve a reversal of the branch proposal with a result less favorable to the plan/organization. Or it may appear that an adverse holding proposed by a branch will be approved, but on a new or different issue or on different grounds than those on which the branch decided the case. Under either of these circumstances, the plan/organization or its representative will be invited to another conference. The provisions of this subparagraph limiting the number of conferences to which a plan/organization is entitled will not foreclose inviting the plan/organization to attend further conferences when, in the opinion of National Office personnel, such need arises. All additional conferences of this type discussed are held only at the invitation of the Service.

(d) It is the responsibility of the plan/organization to furnish to the National Office; within 21 calendar days after the conference, a written record of any additional data, line of reasoning, precedents, etc., that were proposed by the plan/organization and discussed at the conference but were not previously or adequately presented in writing. Extensions of time will be granted only if justified in writing by the plan/organization and approved by the appropriate branch chief. Any additional material and a copy thereof should be addressed to and sent to the National Office which will forward the copy to the appropriate key district director or

Appeals office. The key district director or the Appeals office will be requested to give the matter prompt attention, will verify the additional facts and data, and will comment on it to the extent deemed appropriate.

(e) A plan/organization or its representative desiring to obtain information as to the status of its case (other than a section 521 case) may do so by contacting the following offices with respect to matters in the areas of their responsibility:

Official	Telephone Numbers (Area Code 202)
Chief, Employee Plans Technical Branch	566-3871
Chief, Exempt Organizations Technical Branch	566-3856 or 566-3593
Director, Actuarial Division	566-4311

An organization or its representative desiring to obtain information as to the status of its section 521 case may do so by contacting the Director, Corporation Tax Division (202-566-4504 or 566-4505).

(vi) *Preparation of technical advice memorandum by the National Office.*—(a) Immediately upon receipt in the National Office, the employee to whom the case is assigned will analyze the file to ascertain whether it meets the requirements of subdivision (iii) of this subparagraph. If the case is not complete with respect to any requirement in subdivision (iii)(a) through (d) of this subparagraph, appropriate steps will be taken to complete the file. If any request for technical advice does not comply with the requirements of subdivision (iii)(e) of this subparagraph, if applicable, relating to the statement of proposed deletions, the National Office will make those deletions from the technical advice memorandum which in the judgment of the Commissioner are required by section 6110(c) of the Code.

(b) If the plan/organization has requested a conference in the National Office, the procedures in subdivision (v) of this subparagraph will be followed.

(c) Replies to requests for technical advice will be addressed to the key district director or to the Appeals office and will be drafted in two parts. Each part will identify the plan/organization by name, address, identification number, and year or years involved. The first part (hereafter called the "technical advice memorandum") will contain (1) a recitation of the pertinent facts having a bearing on the issue; (2) a

discussion of the facts, precedents, and reasoning of the National Office; and (3) the conclusions of the National Office. The conclusions will give direct answers, whenever possible, to the specific questions of the key district director or the Appeals office. The discussion of the issues will be in such detail that the key district director or the Appeals office is apprised of the reasoning underlying the conclusion. There shall accompany the technical advice memorandum, where applicable, a notice, pursuant to section 6110(f)(1) of the Code, of intention to disclose the technical advice memorandum (including a copy of the version proposed to be open to public inspection and notations of third party communications pursuant to section 6110(d) of the Code) which the key district director or the Appeals office will forward to the plan/organization at such time that it furnishes a copy of the technical advice memorandum to the plan/organization pursuant to (e) of this subdivision and subdivision (vii)(b) of this subparagraph.

(d) The second part of the reply will consist of a transmittal memorandum. In the unusual cases it will serve as a vehicle for providing the key district office or Appeals office administrative information or other information which, under the nondisclosure statutes, or for other reasons, may not be discussed with the plan/organization.

(e) It is the general practice of the Service to furnish a copy of the technical advice memorandum to the plan/organization after it has been adopted by the key district director or the Appeals office. However, in the case of technical advice memoranda described in section 6110(g)(5)(A) of the Code, relating to cases involving criminal or civil fraud investigations and jeopardy or termination assessments, a copy of the technical advice memorandum shall not be furnished the plan/organization until all proceedings with respect to the investigations or assessments are completed.

(f) After receiving the notice, pursuant to section 6110(f)(1) of the Code, of intention to disclose the technical advice memorandum (if applicable), the plan/organization, if desiring to protest the disclosure of certain information in the memorandum, must, within 20 days after the notice is mailed, submit a written statement identifying those deletions not made by the Internal Revenue Service which the plan/organization believes should have been made. The plan/organization shall also submit a copy of the version of the technical advice memorandum proposed to be open to public inspection on which it indicates, by the use of brackets, the deletions proposed by the plan/organization but which have not been made by the Internal Revenue Service. Generally, the Internal Revenue Service will not consider the deletion of any material which the plan/organization did not, prior to the time when the National Office sent its reply to the request for technical advice to the key district director or the Appeals office, propose be deleted. The Internal Revenue Service shall, within 20 days after receipt of the response by the plan/organization to the notice pursuant to section 6110(f)(1) of the Code (if applicable), mail to the plan/organization its final administrative conclusion regarding the deletions to be made.

(vii) *Action on technical advice in key district offices and in Appeals offices.*—(*a*) Unless the key district director or the Chief, Appeals office, feels that the conclusions reached by the National Office in a technical advice memorandum should be reconsidered and promptly requests such reconsideration, the key district office or the Appeals office will proceed to process the case on the basis of the conclusions expressed in the technical advice memorandum. The effect of technical advice on the plan's/organization's case once the technical advice memorandum is adopted is set forth in subdivision (viii) of this subparagraph.

(*b*) The key district director or the Appeals office will furnish the plan/organization a copy of the technical advice memorandum described in subdivision (vi)(*c*) of this subparagraph and the notice pursuant to section 6110(f)(1) of the Code (if applicable) of intention to disclose the technical advice memorandum (including a copy of the version proposed to be open to public inspection and notations of third party communications pursuant to section 6110(d) of the Code). The preceding sentence shall not apply to technical advice memoranda involving civil fraud or criminal investigations, or jeopardy or termination assessments, as described in subdivision (iii)(*j*) of this subparagraph (except to the extent provided in subdivision (vi)(*e*) of this subparagraph) or to documents to which section 6104 of the Code applies.

(*c*) In those cases in which the National Office advises the key district director or the Appeals office that it should not furnish a copy of the technical advice memorandum to the plan/organization, the key district director or the Appeals office will so inform the plan/organization if it requests a copy.

(viii) *Effect of technical advice.*—(*a*) A technical advice memorandum represents an expression of the views of the Service as to the application of law, regulations, and precedents to the facts of a specific case, and is issued primarily as a means of assisting Service officials in the examination and closing of the case involved. In cases under this subparagraph concerning a plan's/organization's qualification or an organization's status, the conclusions expressed in a technical advice memorandum are final and will be followed by the key district office or the Appeals office.

(*b*) Unless otherwise stated, a holding in a technical advice memorandum will be applied retroactively. Moreover, where the plan/organization had previously been issued a favorable ruling or determination letter (whether or not it was based on a previous technical advice memorandum) concerning that transaction, its purpose, or method of operation, the holding in a technical advice memorandum that is adverse to the plan/organization is also applied retroactively unless the Assistant Commissioner or Deputy Assistant Commissioner (Employee Plans and Exempt Organizations) or, in a section 521 case, the Assistant Commissioner or Deputy Assistant Commissioner (Technical) exercises the discretionary authority under section 7805(b) of the Code to limit the retroactive effect of the holding as illustrated, in the case of rulings, in paragraph (1)(5) of this section.

(*c*) Technical advice memoranda often form the basis for revenue rulings. For the description of revenue rulings and the effect thereof, see §§ 601.601 (d)(2)(i)(*a*) and 601.601 (d)(2)(v).

(*d*) A key district director or an Appeals office may raise an issue in a taxable period, even though technical advice may have been asked for and furnished with regard to the same or a similar issue in any other taxable period. However, if the proposal by the key district director or the Appeals office is contrary to a prior technical advice or ruling issued to the same plan/organization, the proposal must be submitted to the National Office. See § 601.106(a)(1)(iv)(*b*) and subdivision (i)(*d*) of this subparagraph.

(o) *Employees' trusts or plans.*—(1) *In general.*—Paragraph (o) provides procedures relating to the issuance of determination letters with respect to the qualification of retirement plans. Paragraph (o)(2) of this section sets forth the authority of key district directors to issue determination letters. Paragraph (o)(3) provides instructions to applicants, including which forms to file, where such forms must be filed, and

Reg. § 601.201(o)(1)

requirements for giving notice to interested parties. Paragraph (o)(5) describes the administrative remedies available to interested parties and the Pension Benefit Guaranty Corporation. Paragraph (o)(6) describes the administrative appeal rights available to applicants. Paragraph (o)(7) provides for the issuance of notice of final determination. Paragraph (o)(8) describes the documents which will make up the administrative record. Paragraph (o)(9) describes the notice of final determination. Paragraph (o)(10) sets forth the actions that will be necessary on the part of applicants, interested parties, and the Pension Benefit Guaranty Corporation in order for each to exhaust the administrative remedies within the meaning of section 7476(b)(3) of the Code.

(2) *Determination letters.*—(i) The district directors of the key district offices (described in paragraph (o)(4) of this section) shall have the authority to issue determination letters involving the provisions of sections 401, 403(a), 405, and 501(a) of the Internal Revenue Code of 1954 with respect to:

(*a*) Initial qualification of stock bonus, pension, profit-sharing, annuity, and bond purchase plans;

(*b*) Initial exemption from Federal income tax under section 501(a) of trusts forming a part of such plans, provided that the determination does not involve application of section 502 (feeder organizations) or section 511 (unrelated business income), or the question of whether a proposed transaction will be a prohibited transaction under section 503;

(*c*) Compliance with the applicable requirements of foreign situs trusts as to taxability of beneficiaries (section 402(c)) and deductions for employer contributions (section 404(a)(4)) in connection with a request for a determination letter as to the qualification of a retirement plan;

(*d*) Amendments, curtailments, or terminations of such plans and trusts.

(ii) Determination letters authorized by paragraph (o)(2)(i) of this section do not include determinations or opinions relating to other inquiries with respect to plans or trusts. Thus, except as specifically provided in paragraph (o)(2)(i) of this section, key district directors may not issue determination letters relating to issues under other sections of the Code, such as sections 72, 402 through 404, 412, 502, 503, and 511 through 515, unless such determination letters are otherwise authorized under paragraph (c) of this section.

(iii) If, during the consideration of a case described in paragraph (o)(2)(i) of this section by a key district director, the applicant believes that the case involves an issue with respect to which referral for technical advice is appropriate, the applicant may ask the district director to request technical advice from the National Office. The district director shall advise the applicant of its right to request referral of the issue to the National Office for technical advice. The technical advice provisions applicable in these cases are set forth in paragraph (n)(9) of this section. If technical advice is issued, the decision of the National Office is final and the applicant may not thereafter appeal the issue to the Appeals office. See §601.106(a)(1)(iv)(*a*) and paragraph (o)(6) of this section.

(3) *Instructions to taxpayers.*—(i) If an applicant for a determination letter does not comply with all the provisions of this paragraph, the district director, in his discretion, may return the application and point out to the applicant those provisions which have not been met. If such a request is returned to the applicant, the 270 day period described in section 7476(b)(3) will not begin to run until such time as the provisions of this paragraph are complied with.

(ii) An applicant requesting a determination letter must file with the appropriate district director specified in paragraph (o)(3)(xii) of this section the application form required by paragraphs (o)(3)(iii) through (x) of this section including all information and documents requiredby such form. (See section 6104 and the regulations thereunder for provisions relating to the extent to which information submitted to the Internal Revenue Service in connection with the application for determination may be subject to public inspection.) However, before filing such application, the applicant must comply with the provisions of paragraphs (o)(3)(xiv) through (xx) of this section (relating to notification of interested parties). (See paragraph (o)(5)(vi) of this section with respect to the effective date of paragraphs (o)(3)(xiv) through (xx) of this section.)

(iii) Paragraphs (o)(3)(iv)-(vi), (viii), and (ix) apply only to applications for determinations in respect of plan years to which section 410 of the Code does not apply. Paragraph (o)(3)(x) applies only to applications for determinations in respect of plan years to which section 410 applies. Paragraph (o)(3)(vii) applies whether or not the application is for a determination in respect of plan years to which section 410 applies. For this purpose, section 410 will be considered to apply with respect to a plan year if an election has been made under section 1017(d) of the Employee Retirement Income Security Act of 1974 to have section 410 apply to such plan year, whether or not the election is conditioned upon the issuance by the Commissioner of a favorable determination. For purposes of this paragraph (o)(3), in the case of an organization described in section 410(c)(1), section 410 will be considered to apply to a plan year of such organization for any plan year to which section 410(c)(2) applies to such plan.

(iv) If the request relates to the initial qualification of an individually designed plan, a subsequent amendment thereto, or compliance with the requirements for a foreign situs trust, the employer should (*a*) if the plan does not include self-employed individuals, file Form 4573, Application for Determination—Individually Designed Plan (not covering self-employed individuals), or (*b*) if the plan includes self-employed individuals, file Form 4574, Application for Determination—Individually Designed Plan Covering Self-Employed Individuals, except that where a bond purchase plan includes a self-employed individual, file Form 4578, Application for Approval of Bond Purchase Plan. (See paragraph (o)(3)(iii) for plan years to which this paragraph (o)(3)(iv) applies.)

(v) If the request involves a curtailment or termination of the plan (or complete discontinuance of contributions), the applicant should file Form 4576, Application for Determination—Termination or Curtailment of Plan. This form will also be applicable to the termination of a plan that includes self-employed individuals. (See paragraph (o)(3)(iii) of this section for plan years to which this paragraph (o)(3)(v) applies.)

(vi) An association of employers or a board of trustees should file Form 4577, Application for Determination—Industry-Wide Plan and Trust, if the request relates to the initial qualification or subsequent amendments of an industry-wide or area-wide union negotiated plan. (See paragraph (o)(3)(iii) of this section for plan years to which this paragraph (o)(3)(vi) applies.)

(vii) If the request relates to the qualification of a bond purchase plan, which includes self-employed individuals, the applicant should file, in duplicate, Form 4578, Application for Approval of Bond Purchase Plan that includes Self-Employed Individuals. When properly completed, Form 4578 will constitute a bond purchase plan. (See paragraph (o)(3)(iii) for plan years to which this section (o)(3)(vii) applies.)

(viii) An employer who desires a determination letter on his adoption of a master or prototype plan which is designed to satisfy section 401(a) or 403(a) but which is not designed to include self-employed individuals within the meaning of section 401(c)(1) must file Form 4462, Employer Application—Determination as to Qualification of Pension, Annuity, or Profit-Sharing Plan and Trust, and furnish a copy of the adoption agreement or other evidence of adoption of the plan and such additional information as the district director may require. (See paragraph (o)(3)(iii) of this section for plan years to which this paragraph (o)(3)(viii) applies.)

(ix) An applicant who amends his adoption agreement under a master or prototype plan may request a determination letter as to the effect of such amendment by filing Form 4462 with his district director, together with a copy of the amendment and a summary of the changes. However, in the event an applicant desires to amend his adoption agreement under a master or prototype plan, and such amendment is not contemplated or permitted under the plan, then such amendment will in effect substitute an individually designed plan for the master or prototype plan. (See paragraph (o)(3)(iii) of this section for plan years to which this paragraph (o)(3)(ix) applies.)

(x) An applicant requesting a determination letter relating to a defined contribution plan, other than a letter on the qualification of a bond purchase plan, shall file in duplicate, Form 5301, Application for Determination of Defined Contribution Plan, and Form 5302, Employee Census. Those forms are to be filed in accordance with the instructions therefor and accompanied by any schedules or additional material prescribed in those instructions. (See paragraph (o)(3)(iii) of this section for plan years to which this paragraph (o)(3)(x) applies.)

(xi) When, in connection with an application for a determination on the qualification of the plan, it is necessary to determine whether an organization (including a professional service organization) is a corporation or an association classified as a corporation under §301.7701-2 of this chapter of the Regulations on Procedure and Administration, and whether an employer-employee relationship exists between it and its associates, the district director will make such determination. In such cases, the application with respect to the qualification of the plan should be filed in accordance with the provisions herein set forth and should contain the information and documents specified in the application. It should also be accompanied by such information and copies of documents as the organization deems appropriate to establish its status. The Service may, in addition, require any further information that is considered necessary to determine the status of the organization, the em-

Reg. §601.201(o)(3)(xi)

ployment status of the individuals involved, or the qualification of the plan. After the taxable status of the organizations and the employer-employee relationship have been determined, the key district director may issue a determination letter as to the qualification of the plan.

(xii) Requests for determination letters on matters authorized by paragraph (o)(2) of this section, and the necessary supporting data, are to be addressed to the district director (whether or not such district director is the director of a key district) specified below (determined without regard to the application of section 414(b) or (c) to the plan):

(a) In the case of a plan for a single employer, the request shall be addressed to the district director for the district in which such employer's principal place of business is located.

(b) In the case of a single plan for a parent company and its subsidiaries, the request shall be addressed to the district director for the district in which the principal place of business of the parent company is located, whether separate or consolidated returns are filed.

(c) In the case of a plan established or proposed for an industry by all subscribing employers whose principal places of business are located within more than one district, the request shall be addressed to the district director for the district in which is located the principal place of business of the trustee, or if more than one trustee, the usual meeting place of the trustees.

(d) In the case of a pooled fund arrangement (individual trusts under separate plans pooling their funds for investment purposes through a master trust), the request on behalf of the master trust shall be addressed to the district director for the district where the principal place of business of such trust is located. Requests on behalf of the participating trusts and related plans will be addressed as otherwise provided herein.

(e) In the case of a plan of multiple employers (other than a master or prototype plan) not otherwise herein provided for, the request shall be addressed to the district director for the district in which is located the principal place of business of the trustee, or if not trusteed or if more than one trustee, the principal or usual meeting place of the trustees or plan supervisors.

(xiii) The applicant's request for a determination letter may be withdrawn by a written request at any time prior to appealing a proposed determination to the regional office as described in paragraph (o)(6) of this section. In the case of such a withdrawal the Service will not render a determination of any type. A failure

to render a determination as a result of such a withdrawal will not be considered a failure of the Secretary or his delegate to make a determination within the meaning of section 7476. In the case of a withdrawal the district director may consider the information submitted in connection with the withdrawn request in a subsequent audit or examination.

(xiv) In the case of an application for a determination for plan years to which section 410 applies (see paragraph (o)(5)(vi) of this section), notice that an application for an advance determination regarding the qualification of plans described in section 401(a), 403(a), or 405(a) is to be made must be given to all interested parties in the manner set forth in the regulations under section 7476 of the Code.

(xv) When the notice referred to in paragraph (o)(3)(xiv) of this section is given in the manner set forth in § 1.7476-2(c) of this chapter, such notice must be given not less than 10 days nor more than 24 days prior to the date the application for a determination is made. See paragraph (o)(3)(xxi) of this section for determining when an application is made. If, however, an application is returned to the applicant for failure to adequately satisfy the notification requirement with respect to a particular group or class of interested parties, the applicant need not cause notice to be given to those groups or classes of interested parties with respect to which the notice requirement was already satisfied merely because, as a result of the resubmission of the application, the time limitations of this paragraph (o)(3)(xv) would not be met.

(xvi) The notice referred to in paragraph (o)(3)(xiv) of this section shall be given in the manner prescribed in § 1.7476-2 of this chapter and shall contain the following information:

(a) a brief description identifying the class or classes of interested parties to whom the notice is addressed (e.g., all present employees of the employer, all present employees eligible to participate);

(b) the name of the plan, the plan identification number, and the name of the plan administrator;

(c) the name and taxpayer identification number of the applicant;

(d) that an application for a determination as to the qualified status of the plan is to be made to the Internal Revenue Service, stating whether the application relates to an initial qualification, a plan amendment or a plan termination, and the address of the district director to whom the application will be submitted;

(e) a description of the class of employees eligible to participate under the plan;

(f) whether or not the Service has issued a previous determination as to the qualified status of the plan;

(g) a statement that any person to whom the notice is addressed is entitled to submit, or request the Department of Labor to submit, to the district director described in paragraph (o)(3)(xvi)(d) of this section, a comment on the question of whether the plan meets the requirements for qualification under part I of Subchapter D of Chapter 1 of the Internal Revenue Code of 1954; that two or more such persons may join in a single comment or request; and that if such a person or persons request the Department of Labor to submit a comment and that department declines to do so in respect of one or more matters raised in the request, the person or persons so requesting may submit a comment to the district director in respect of the matters on which the Department of Labor declines to comment;

(h) that a comment to the district director or a request of the Department of Labor must be made according to the following procedures:

(1) a comment to the district director must be received on or before the 45th day (specified by date) after the day on which the application for determination is received by the district director;

(2) or if the comment is being submitted on a matter on which the Department of Labor was first requested but declined to comment, on or before the later of such 45th day or the 15th day after the day on which the Department of Labor notifies such person or persons that it declines to comment, but in no event later than the 60th day (specified by date) after the day the application is received by the district director; and

(3) a request of the Department of Labor to submit such a comment must be received by such department on or before the 25th day (specified by date) (or if the person or persons requesting the Department of Labor to submit such a comment wish to preserve their right to submit a comment to the district director in the event the Department of Labor declines to comment, on or before the 15th day (specified by date)) after the day the application is received by the district director;

(i) except to the extent there is included in the notice the additional informational materials which paragraphs (o)(3)(xviii), (xix), and (xx) of this section require be made available to interested parties, a description of a reasonable proce-dure whereby such additional informational material will be made available to them (see paragraph (o)(3)(xvii) of this section).

(xvii) The procedure referred to in paragraph (o)(3)(xvi)(i) of this section whereby the additional informational material required by paragraphs (o)(3)(xviii), (xix), and (xx) of this section will (to the extent not included in this notice) be made available to interested parties, may consist of making such material available for inspection and copying by interested parties at a place or places reasonably accessible to such parties, or supplying such material by using a method of delivery or a combination thereof that is reasonably calculated to ensure that all interested parties will have access to the materials. The procedure referred to in paragraph (o)(3)(xvi)(i) of this section must be immediately available to all interested parties and must be designed to supply them with such additional informational material in time for them to pursue their rights within the time period prescribed, and must be available until the earlier of the filing of a pleading commencing a declaratory judgment action under section 7476 with respect to the qualification of the plan or the ninety-second day after the day the notice of final determination is mailed to the applicant.

(xviii) Unless provided in the notice, the following materials shall be made available to interested parties under a procedure described in paragraph (o)(3)(xvii) of this section:

(a) An updated copy of the plan and the related trust agreement (if any);

(b) The application for determination; provided, however, that if there would be less than 26 participants in the plan, as described in the application (including, as participants, retired employees and beneficiaries of deceased employees who have a nonforfeitable right to benefits under the plan and employees who would be eligible to participate upon making mandatory employee contributions, if any), then in lieu of making such materials available to interested parties who are not participants (as described above), there may be made available to such interested parties a document containing the following information: a description of the plan's requirements respecting eligibility for participation and benefits; a description of the provisions providing for nonforfeitable benefits; a description of the circumstances which may result in ineligibility, or denial or loss of benefits; a description of the source of financing of the plan and the identity of any organization through which benefits are provided; whether the applicant is claiming in his application that the plan

Reg. §601.201(o)(3)(xviii)(b)

meets the requirements of section 410(b)(1)(A) of the Code, and, if not, the coverage schedule required by the application in the case of plans not meeting the requirements of such section. However, once such an interested party or his designated representative receives a notice of final determination, the applicant must, upon request, make available to such interested party (regardless of whether or not the interested party is a participant in the plan and regardless of whether or not the plan has less than 26 participants) an updated copy of the plan and related trust agreement (if any) and the application for determination. Information of the type described in section 6104(a)(1)(D) of the Code should not be included in the application, plan, or related trust agreement submitted to the Internal Revenue Service. Accordingly, such information should not be included in any of the materials required by this paragraph (o)(3) to be available to interested parties. There may be excluded from such material information contained in Form 5302 (Employee Census). However, information showing the number of individuals covered and not covered in the plan, listed by compensation range, shall not be excluded.

(xix) Unless provided in the notice, there shall be made available to interested parties under a procedure described in paragraph (o)(3)(xvii) of this section, any additional document dealing with the application which is submitted by or for the applicant to the Internal Revenue Service, or furnished by the Internal Revenue Service to the applicant; provided, however, if there would be less than 26 participants in the plan as described in the application (including, as participants, retired employees and beneficiaries of deceased employees who have a nonforfeitable right to benefits under the plan and employees who would be eligible to participate upon making mandatory employee contributions, if any), such additional docu-

ments need not be made available to interested parties who are not participants (as described above) until they or their designated representative, receive a notice of final determination. The applicant may also withhold from such inspection and copying, information described in section 6104(a)(1)(C) and (D) of the Code which may be contained in such additional documents.

(xx) Unless provided in the notice, there shall be made available to all interested parties under a procedure described in paragraph (o)(3)(xvii) of this section, material setting forth the following information:

(a) the rights of interested parties described in paragraph (o)(5)(i) of this section; and

(b) the information provided in paragraph (o)(5)(ii), (iii), (iv) and (v) of this section.

(xxi) An application for an advance determination, a comment to the district director, or a request to the Department of Labor, shall be deemed made when it is received by the district director, or the Department of Labor. The notice to interested parties required by paragraph (o)(3)(xiv) of this section shall be deemed given when the notice is posted or sent to the person in the manner prescribed in § 1.7476-2 of this chapter. In any case where such an application, request, comment, or notice is sent by mail, it shall be deemed received as of the date of the postmark (or if sent by certified or registered mail, the date of certification or registration), if it is deposited in the mail in the United States in an envelope, or other appropriate wrapper first class postage prepaid, properly addressed. However, if such an application, request or comment is not received within a reasonable period from the date of postmark, the immediately preceding sentence shall not apply.

(4) *Key district offices.*—Following are the 19 key district offices that issue determination letters and the area covered:

Key District(s)	*IRS Districts Covered*
Central Region	
Cincinnati	Cincinnati, Louisville, Indianapolis
Cleveland	Cleveland, Parkersburg
Detroit	Detroit
Mid-Atlantic Region	
Baltimore	Baltimore (which includes the District of Columbia and Office of International Operations), Pittsburgh, Richmond
Philadelphia	Philadelphia, Wilmington
Newark	Newark
Midwest Region	
Chicago	Chicago
St. Paul	St. Paul, Fargo, Aberdeen, Milwaukee

Key District(s)	IRS Districts Covered
St. Louis	St. Louis, Springfield, Des Moines, Omaha
North-Atlantic Region	
Boston	Boston, Augusta, Burlington, Providence, Hartford, Portsmouth
Manhattan	Manhattan
Brooklyn	Brooklyn, Albany, Buffalo
Southeast Region	
Atlanta	Atlanta, Greensboro, Columbia, Nashville
Jacksonville	Jacksonville, Jackson, Birmingham
Southwest Region	
Austin	Austin, New Orleans, Albuquerque, Denver, Cheyenne
Dallas	Dallas, Oklahoma City, Little Rock, Wichita
Western Region	
Los Angeles	Los Angeles, Phoenix, Honolulu
San Francisco	San Francisco, Salt Lake City, Reno
Seattle	Seattle, Portland, Anchorage, Boise, Helena

(5) *Administrative remedies of interested parties and the Pension Benefit Guaranty Corporation.*—(i) With respect to plan years to which section 410 applies (see paragraph (o)(5)(vi) of this section), persons who qualify as interested parties under the regulations issued under section 7476 and the Pension Benefit Guaranty Corporation shall have the following rights:

(a) To submit to the district director for the district where an application for determination is filed, by the 45th day after the day on which the application is received by the district director, a written comment on said application, with respect to the qualification of the plan under subchapter D of chapter 1 of the Internal Revenue Code.

(b) To request the Administrator of Pension and Welfare Benefit Programs, Department of Labor, 200 Constitution Avenue, N.W., Washington, D.C. 20210, to submit to such district director such a written comment under the provisions of section 3001(b)(2) of the Employee Retirement Income Security Act of 1974. Such a request, if made by an interested party or parties, must be received by such department on or before the 25th day after the day said application is received by the district director. However, if such party or parties requesting the Department of Labor to submit such a comment wish to preserve their rights to submit a comment to the district director in the event the Department of Labor declines to comment (pursuant to paragraph (o)(5)(i)(c) of this section), such request must be received by such department on or before the 15th day after the day the application is received by the district director.

(c) If a request described in paragraph (o)(5)(i)(b) of this section is made and the Depart-

ment of Labor notifies the interested party or parties making the request that it declines to submit a comment on a matter concerning qualification of the plan which was raised in such request, to submit a written comment to the district director on such matter by the later of the 45th day after the day the application for determination is received by the district director or the 15th day after the day on which the Department of Labor notifies such party or parties that it declines to submit a comment on such matter, but, in no event later than the 60th day after the application for determination was received. (See paragraph (o)(5)(iii) of this section for determining when notice that the Department of Labor declines to comment is received by an interested party or parties.)

Such a comment must comply with the requirements of paragraph (o)(5)(ii) of this section, and include a statement that the comment is beingsubmitted on matters raised in a request to the Department of Labor on which that department declined to comment.

(ii) A comment submitted by an interested party or parties to the district director must be in writing, signed by such party or parties or by an authorized representative of such party or parties (as provided in paragraph (e)(6) of this section), be addressed to the district director described in paragraph (o)(3)(xvi)(d) of this section, and contain the following:

(a) The name or names of the interested party or parties making the comment;

(b) The name and taxpayer identification number of the applicant making the application;

(c) The name of the plan and the plan identification number;

Reg. § 601.201(o)(5)(ii)(c)

(d) Whether the party or parties submitting the comments are—

    (1) Employees eligible to participate under the plan,

    (2) Former employees or beneficiaries of deceased former employees who have a vested right to benefits under the plan, or

    (3) Employees not eligible to participate under the plan;

    (e) The specific matter or matters raised by the interested party or parties on the question of whether the plan meets the requirements for qualification under Part I of Subchapter D of the Code, and how such matter or matters relate to the interests of such party or parties making such comment.

    (f) The address of the interested party submitting the comment to which all correspondence, including a notice of the Internal Revenue Service's final determination with respect to qualification, should be sent. (See section 7476(b)(5) of the Code.) If more than one interested party submits the comment, they must designate a representative for receipt of such correspondence and notice on behalf of all interested parties submitting the said comment, and state the address of such representative. Such representative shall be one of the interested parties submitting the comment or the authorized representative.

    (iii) For purposes of paragraph (o)(3)(xvi)(*h*) and (o)(5)(i)(*c*), notice by the Department of Labor that it declines to comment shall be deemed given to the interested party designated to receive such notice when received by him.

    (iv) A request of the Department of Labor to submit a comment to the district director must be in writing, signed, and in addition to the information prescribed in paragraph (o)(5)(ii) of this section must also contain the address of the district director to whom the application was, or will be, submitted. The address designated for notice by the Internal Revenue Serivce will be used by the Department of Labor in communicating with the party or parties submitting the request.

    (v) The contents of written comments submitted by interested parties to the Internal Revenue Service pursuant to paragraphs (o)(5)(i)(*a*) and (*c*) will not be treated as confidential material and may be inspected by persons outside the Internal Revenue Service, including the applicant for the determination. Accordingly, designations of material as confidential or not to be disclosed, contained in such comments, will not be accepted. Thus, a person submitting a written comment should not include therein material that he considers to be confidential or inappropriate for disclosure to the public. It will be presumed by the Internal Revenue Service that every written comment submitted to it is intended by the party or parties submitting it to be subject in its entirety to public inspection and copying.

    (vi)(*a*) Paragraphs (o)(3)(xiv) through (xxi) and (o)(5) of this section apply to an application for an advance determination in respect of a plan year or years to which section 410 applies to the plan, whether or not such application is received by the district director before the first date on which such section applies to the plan.

    (b) For purposes of paragraph (o)(5)(vi)(*a*) of this section, section 410 shall be considered to apply to a plan year if an election has been made under section 1017(d) of the Employee Retirement Income Security Act of 1974 to have section 410 apply to such plan year, whether or not the election is conditioned upon the issuance by the Commissioner of a favorable determination.

    (c) For purposes of paragraph (o)(5)(vi)(*a*) of this section, in the case of an organization described in section 410(c)(1), section 410 will be considered to apply to a plan year of such organization for any plan year to which section 410(c)(2) applies to such plan.

    (vii) The Internal Revenue Service will provide to the applicant a copy of all comments on the application submitted pursuant to paragraph (o)(5)(i) (*a*), (*b*) or (*c*) of this section. In addition, the Internal Revenue Service will provide to the applicant a copy of all correspondence in respect of a comment between the Internal Revenue Service and a person submitting the comment.

    (6) *Reference of matters to the Appeals office.*— (i) Where issues arise in a district director'soffice on matters within the contemplation of paragraph (o)(2)(i) of this section, and the key district director issues a notice of proposed determination which is adverse to the applicant, the applicant may appeal the proposed determination to the Appeals office. However, the applicant may not appeal a determination that is based on a National Office technical advice. See §601.106(a)(1)(iv)(*a*) and paragraph (o)(2)(iii) of this section. The applicant shall notify the key district director that it intends to request Appeals office consideration by submitting the request, in writing, to the key district director within 30 days from issuance of the notice of proposed determination. The key district direc-

tor will forward the request and the administrative record to the Appeals office and will so notify the applicant in writing. A failure by the applicant to request Appeals office consideration will constitute a failure to exhaust available administrative remedies as required by section 7476(b)(3) and will thus preclude the applicant from seeking a declaratory judgment as provided under section 7476. (See paragraph (o)(10)(i)(*c*) of this section.)

(ii) The request for Appeals office consideration must show the following:

(*a*) Date of application for determination letter;

(*b*) Name and address of the applicant and the name and address of the representative, if any, who has been authorized to represent the applicant as provided in paragraph (c)(6) of this section;

(*c*) The key district office in which the case is pending;

(*d*) Type of plan (pension, annuity, profit-sharing, stock bonus, bond purchase, and foreign situs trusts), and type of action involved (initial qualification, amendment, curtailment, or termination);

(*e*) Date of filing this request with the key district director and the date and symbols of the letter referred to in paragraph (o)(6)(i) of this section;

(*f*) A complete statement of the issues and a presentation of the arguments in support of the applicant's position; and

(*g*) Whether a conference is desired.

(iii) After receipt of the administrative record in the Appeals office, the applicant will be afforded the opportunity for a conference, if a conference was requested. After full consideration of the entire administrative record, the Appeals office will notify the applicant in writing of the proposed decision and the reasons therefor and will issue a notice of final determination in accordance with the decision. However, if the proposed disposition by the Appeals office is contrary to a National Office technical advice concerning qualification, issued prior to the case, the proposed disposition will be submitted to the Assistant Commissioner (Employee Plans and Exempt Organizations) and the decision of that official will be followed by the Appeals office. See § 601.106(a)(1)(iv)(*b*). Additionally, if the applicant believes that the case involves an issue with respect to which referral for technical advice is appropriate, the applicant may ask the Appeals office to request technical advice from the National Office. The Appeals office shall advise the applicant of its right to request referral of the issue to the National Office for technical advice. The technical advice provisions applicable to these cases are set forth in paragraph (n)(9) of this section. If technical advice is issued, the decision of the National Office will be followed by the Appeals office. See paragraph (n)(9)(viii)(*a*) of this section.

(iv) Applicants are advised to make full presentation of the facts, circumstances, and arguments at the initial level of consideration, since submission of additional facts, circumstances, and arguments at the Appeals office may result in suspension of Appeals procedures and referral of the case back to the key district for additional consideration.

(7) *Issuance of the notice of final determination.*—The key district director or Appeals office will send notice of the final determination to the applicant. The key district director will send notice of the final determination to the interested parties who have previously submitted comments on the application to the Internal Revenue Service pursuant to paragraph (o)(5)(i)(*a*) or (*c*) of this section (or to the persons designated by them to receive such notice), to the Department of Labor in the case of a comment submitted by that department upon the request of interested parties or the Pension Benefit Guaranty Corporation pursuant to paragraph (o)(5)(i)(*b*) of this section, and to the Pension Benefit Guaranty Corporation if it has filed a comment pursuant to paragraph (o)(5)(i)(*a*) of this section.

(8) *Administrative record.*—(i) In the case of a request for an advance determination in respect of a retirement plan, the determination of the district director or Appeals office on the qualification or nonqualification of the retirement plan shall be based solely on the facts contained in the administrative record. Such administrative record shall consist of the following:

(*a*) The request for determination, the retirement plan and any related trust instruments, and any written modifications or amendments thereof made by the applicant during the proceedings within the Internal Revenue Service;

(*b*) All other documents submitted to the Internal Revenue Service by or on behalf of the applicant in respect of the request for determination;

(*c*) All written correspondence between the Internal Revenue Service and the applicant in respect of the request for determination and any other documents issued to the applicant from the Internal Revenue Service;

Reg. § 601.201(o)(8)(i)(c)

(d) All written comments submitted to the Internal Revenue Service pursuant to paragraphs (o)(5)(i)(*a*), (*b*), and (*c*) of this section, and all correspondence in respect of comments submitted between the Internal Revenue Service and persons (including the Pension Benefit Guaranty Corporation and the Department of Labor) submitting comments pursuant to paragraphs (o)(5)(i)(*a*), (*b*), and (*c*) of this section;

(e) In any case in which the Internal Revenue Service makes an investigation regarding the facts as represented or alleged by the applicant in his request for determination or in comments submitted pursuant to paragraphs (o)(5)(i)(*a*), (*b*), and (*c*) of this section, a copy of the official report of such investigation;

(ii) The administrative record shall be closed upon the earlier of the following events:

(a) The date of mailing of a notice of final determination by the Internal Revenue Service in respect of the application for determination; or

(b) The filing of a petition with the United States Tax Court seeking a declaratory judgment in respect of the retirement plan.

Any oral representation or modification of the facts as represented or alleged in the application for determination or in a comment filed by an interested party, which is not reduced to writing and submitted to the Service shall not become a part of the administrative record and shall not be taken into account in the determination of the qualified status of the retirement plan by the district director or Appeals office.

(9) *Notice of final determination.*—For purposes of this paragraph (o), the notice of final determination shall be—

(i) In the case of a final determination which is favorable to the applicant, the letter issued by the key district director or Appeals office (whether or not by certified or registered mail) which states that the applicant's plan satisfies the qualification requirements of the Internal Revenue Code.

(ii) In the case of a final determination which is adverse to the applicant, the letter issued by certified or registered mail by the key district director or Appeals office, subsequent to a letter of proposed determination, stating that the applicant's plan fails to satisfy the qualification requirements of the Internal Revenue Code.

(10) *Exhaustion of administrative remedies.*—For purposes of section 7476(b)(3), a petitioner shall be deemed to have exhausted the administrative remedies available to him in the Internal

Revenue Service upon the completion of the steps described in paragraph (o)(10)(i), (ii), or (iii) of this section, subject, however, to paragraphs (o)(10)(iv) and (v) of this section. If an applicant, interested party, or the Pension Benefit Guaranty Corporation does not complete the applicable steps described below, such applicant, interested party, or the Pension Benefit Guaranty Corporation will not have exhausted available administrative remedies as required by section 7476(b)(3) and will thus be precluded from seeking a declaratory judgment under section 7476 except to the extent that paragraph (o)(10)(iv)(*b*) or (v) of this section applies.

(i) The administrative remedies of an applicant with respect to any matter relating to the qualification of a plan are:

(a) Filing a completed application with the appropriate district director pursuant to paragraphs (o)(3)(iii) through (xii) of this section;

(b) Compliance with the requirements pertaining to notice to interested parties as set forth in paragraphs (o)(3)(xiv) through (o)(3)(xxi) of this section; and

(c) An appeal to the Appeals office pursuant to paragraph (o)(6) of this section, in the event of a notice of proposed adverse determination from the district director.

(ii) The administrative remedy of an interested party with respect to any matter relating to the qualification of the plan is submission to the district director of a comment raising such matter in accordance with paragraph (o)(5)(i)(*a*) of this section or requesting the Department of Labor to submit to the district director a comment with respect to such matter in accordance with paragraph (o)(5)(i)(*b*) of this section, and, if such department declines to comment, submission of such a comment in accordance with paragraph (o)(5)(i)(*c*) of this section, so that such comment may be considered by the Internal Revenue Service through the administrative process.

(iii) The administrative remedy of the Pension Benefit Guaranty Corporation with respect to any matter relating to the qualification of the plan is submission to the district director of a comment raising such matter in accordance with paragraph (o)(5)(i)(*a*) of this section or requesting the Department of Labor to submit to the district director a comment with respect to such matter in accordance with paragraph (o)(5)(i)(*b*) of this section, and, if such department declines to comment, submission of such a comment to the Internal Revenue Service directly, so that such comment may be considered by the Internal Revenue Service through the administrative process.

(iv) An applicant, or an interested party, or the Pension Benefit Guaranty Corporation shall in no event be deemed to have exhausted his (its) administrative remedies prior to the earlier of:

(a) The completion of all the steps described in paragraph (o)(11)(i), (ii), or (iii) of this section, whichever is applicable, subject, however, to paragraph (o)(11) (v), or

(b) The expiration of the 270 day period described in section 7476(b)(3), in a case where the completion of the steps referred to in paragraph (o)(10)(iv)(a) of this section shall not have occurred before the expiration of such 270 day period because of the failure of the Internal Revenue Service to proceed with due diligence.

The step described in paragraph (o)(10)(i)(c) of this section will not be considered completed until the Internal Revenue Service has had a reasonable time to act upon the appeal. In addition, the administrative remedies described in paragraphs (o)(10)(ii) and (iii) will not be considered completed until the Internal Revenue Service has had a reasonable time to consider the comments submitted pursuant to such paragraphs at each step of the Administrative process described in paragraph (o)(10)(i).

(v) The administrative remedy described in paragraph (o)(10)(i)(c) of this section will not be available to an applicant with respect to any issue on which technical advice from the National Office has been obtained.

(p) *Pension plans of self-employed individuals.*— (1) *Rulings, determination letters, and opinion letters.*—(i) The National Office of the Service, upon request, will furnish a written opinion as to the acceptability (for the purpose of sections 401 and 501(a) of the Code) of the form of any master or prototype plan designed to include groups of self-employed individuals who may adopt the plan, where the plan is submitted by a sponsor that is a trade or professional association, bank, insurance company, or regulated investment company as defined in section 851 of the Code. Each opinion letter will bear an identifying plan serial number. If the trustee or custodian has been designated at the time of approval of a plan as to form, a ruling will be issued as to the exempt status of such trust or custodial account which forms part of the master or prototype plan. As used here, the term "master plan" refers to a standardized form of plan, with a related trust or custodial agreement, where indicated, administered by the sponsoring organization for the purpose of providing plan benefits on a standardized basis. The term "prototype plan" refers to a standardized form of plan, with or without a related form of trust or custodial agreement, that is made available by the sponsoring organization, for use without change by employers who wish to adopt such a plan, and which will not be administered by the sponsoring organization that makes such form available. The degree of relationship among the separate employers adopting either a master plan or a prototype plan or to the sponsoring organization is immaterial.

(ii) Since a determination as to the qualification of a particular employer's plan can be made only with regard to facts peculiar to that employer, a letter expressing the opinion of the Service as to the acceptability of the form of a master or prototype plan will not constitute a ruling or determination as to the qualification of a plan as adopted by any individual employer or as to the exempt status of a related trust or custodial account. However, where an employer adopts a master or prototype plan and any related prototype trust or custodial account previously approved as to form, and observes the provisions thereof, such plan and trust or custodial account will be deemed to satisfy the requirements of sections 401 and 501(a) of the Code, provided the eligibility requirements and contributions on benefits under the plan for owner-employees are not more favorable than for other employees, including those required to be covered under plans of all businesses controlled by such owner-employees.

(iii) Although district directors no longer make advance determinations on plans of self-employed individuals who have adopted previously approved master or prototype plans, they will continue, upon request, to issue determination letters as to the qualification of individually designed plans (those not utilizing a master or prototype plan) and the exempt status of a related trust or custodial account, if any, in accordance with the procedures set forth in paragraph (o) of this section.

(2) *Determination letters as to qualified bond purchase plans.*—A determination as to the qualification of a bond purchase plan will, upon request, be made by the appropriate district director. Form 4578, Application for Approval of Bond Purchase Plan, must be used for this purpose. When properly completed, this form will constitute a bond purchase plan.

(3) *Instructions to sponsoring organizations and employers.*—(i) A sponsoring organization of the type referred to in subparagraph (1)(i) of this paragraph, that desires a written opinion as to

the acceptability of the form of a master or proto-type plan (or as to the exempt status of a related trust or custodial account) should submit its request to the National Office. Copies of all documents, including the plan and trust instruments and all amendments thereto, together with specimen insurance contracts (where applicable) must be submitted with the request. The request must be submitted to the Commissioner of Internal Revenue Service, Washington, D.C. 20224, Attn: T:MS:PT. Form 3672, Application for Approval of Master or Prototype Plan for Self-Employed Individuals, is to be used for this purpose.

(ii) If, subsequent to obtaining approval of the form of a master or prototype plan, an amendment is to be made, the procedure will depend on whether the sponsor is authorized to act on behalf of the subscribers.

(a) If the plan provides that each employer has delegated to the sponsor the power to amend the plan and that each employer shall be deemed to have consented thereto, the plan may be amended by the sponsor. If the plan contains no specific provision permitting the sponsor to amend such plan, but all employers consent in writing to permit such amendment, the sponsor may then amend the plan. However, where a sponsor is unable to secure the consent of each employer, the plan cannot be amended by the sponsor. In such cases, any change will have to be effected by the adoption of a new plan and the submission of a new Form 3672. The new plan will be complete and separate from the old plan and individual employers may, if they desire, substitute the new plan for the old plan.

(b) In the first two instances mentioned above, where the plan has been properly amended, the sponsor must submit Form 3672, a copy of the amendment and, if required, copies of the signed consent of each participating employer.

(c) Upon approval of the amendment by the Service, an opinion letter will be issued to the sponsor containing the serial number of the original plan followed by a suffix: "A-1" for the first amendment, "A-2" for the second amendment, etc. Employers adopting the form of plan subsequent to the date of the amendment will use the revised serial number.

(d) If a new plan is submitted, together with form 3672 and copies of all documents evidencing the plan, an opinion letter bearing a new serial number will be issued to the sponsor and all employers who adopt the new plan shall use the new serial number. Employers who adopted the old plan will continue to use the original serial number.

(4) *Applicability.*—The general procedures of paragraphs (a) through (m) and paragraph (o) of this section, relating to the issuance of rulings and determination letters, are applicable to requests relating to the qualification of plans covering self-employed individuals under sections 401 and 405(a) of the Code and the exempt status of related trusts or custodial accounts under section 501(a), to the extent that the matter is not covered by the specific procedures and instructions contained in this paragraph.

(q) *Corporate master and prototype plans.*—(1) *Scope and definitions.*—(i) The general procedures set forth in this paragraph pertain to the issuance of rulings, determination letters, and opinion letters relating to master and prototype pension, annuity, and profit-sharing plans (except those covering self-employed individuals) under section 401(a) of the Code, and the status for exemption of related trusts or custodial accounts under section 501(a). (A custodial account described in section 401(f) of the Code is treated as a qualified trust for purposes of the Code.) These procedures are subject to the general procedures set forth in paragraph (o) of this section, and relate only to master plans and prototype plans that do not include self-employed individuals and are sponsored by trade or professional associations, banks, insurance companies, or regulated investment companies. These plans are further identified as "variable form" and "standardized form" plans.

(ii) A "master plan" is a form of plan in which the funding organization (trust, custodial account, or insurer) is specified in the sponsor's application, and a "prototype plan" is a form of plan in which the funding organization is specified in the adopting employer's application.

(iii) A "variable form" plan is either a master or prototype plan that permits an employer to select various options relating to such basic provisions as employee coverage, contributions, benefits, and vesting. These options must be set forth in the body of the plan or in a separate document. Such plan, however, is not complete until all provisions necessary for qualificationunder section 401(a) of the Code are appropriately included.

(iv) A "standardized form" plan is either a master or prototype plan that meets the requirements of subparagraph (2) of this paragraph.

(2) *Standardized form plan requirements.*—A standardized form plan must be complete in all respects (except for choices permissible under subdivisions (i) and (iv) of this subparagraph)

and contain among other things provisions as to the following requirements:

(i) *Coverage*.—The percentage coverage requirements set forth in section 401(a)(3)(A) of the Code must be satisfied. Provisions may be made, however, for an adopting employer to designate such eligibility requirements as are permitted under that section.

(ii) *Nonforfeitable rights*.—Each employee's rights to or derived from the contributions under the plan must be nonforfeitable at the time the contributions are paid to or under the plan, except to the extent that the limitations set forth in §1.401-4(c) of the Income Tax Regulations, regarding early termination of a plan, may be applicable.

(iii) *Bank trustee*.—In the case of a trusteed plan, the trustee must be a bank.

(iv) *Definite contribution formula*.—In the case of a profit-sharing plan, there must be a definite formula for determining the employer contributions to be made. Provision may be made, however, for an adopting employer to specify his rate of contribution.

(3) *Rulings, determination letters, and opinion letters*.—(i) A favorable determination letter as to the qualification of a pension or profit-sharing plan and the exempt status of any related trust or custodial account, is not required as a condition for obtaining the tax benefits pertaining thereto. However, paragraph (c)(5) of this section authorizes district directors to issue determination letters as to the qualification of plans and the exempt status of related trusts or custodial accounts.

(ii) In addition, the National Office upon request from a sponsoring organization will furnish a written opinion as to the acceptability of the form of a master or prototype plan and any related trust or custodial account, under sections 401(a) and 501(a) of the Code. Each opinion letter will bear an identifying plan serial number. However, opinion letters will not be issued under this paragraph as to (*a*) plans of a parent company and its subsidiaries, (*b*) pooled fund arrangements contemplated by Revenue Ruling 56-267, C.B. 1956-1, 206, (*c*) industry-wide or area-wide union negotiated plans, (*d*) plans that include self-employed individuals, (*e*) stock bonus plans, and (*f*) bond purchase plans.

(iii) A ruling as to the exempt status of a trust or custodial account under section 501(a) of the Code will be issued to the trustee or custodian by the National Office where such trust or custodial account forms part of a plan described in subparagraph (1) of this paragraph and the trustee or custodian is specified on Form 4461, Sponsor Application—Approval of Master or Prototype Plan. Where not so specified, a determination letter as to the exempt status of a trust or custodial account will be issued by the district director for the district in which is located the principal place of business of an employer who adopts such trust or custodial account after he furnishes the name of the trustee or custodian.

(iv) Since a determination as to the qualification of a particular employer's plan can be made only with regard to facts peculiar to such employer, a letter expressing the opinion of the Service as to the acceptability of the form of a master or prototype plan will not constitute a ruling or determination as to the qualification of a plan as adopted by any individual employer nor as to the exempt status of a related trust or custodial account.

(v) A determination as to the qualification of a plan as it relates to a particular employer will be made by the district director for the district in which each employer's principal place of business is located, if the employer has adopted a master or prototype plan that has been previously approved as to form. An employer who desires such a determination must file Form 4462, Employer Application—Determination as to Qualification of Pension, Annuity, or Profit-Sharing Plan and Trust, and furnish a copy of the adoption agreement or other evidence of adoption of the plan and such additional information as the district director may require.

(vi) Where master or prototype plans involve integration with Social Security benefits, it is impossible to determine in advance whether in an individual case a particular restrictive definition of the compensation (such as basic compensation) on which contributions or benefits are based would result in discrimination in contributions or benefits in favor of employees who are officers, shareholders, persons whose principal duties consist in supervising the work of other employees, or highly compensated employees. See Revenue Ruling 69-503 C.B. 1969-2, 94. Accordingly, opinion letters relating to master or prototype plans that involve integration with Social Security benefits will not be issued except for those plans where annual compensation, for the purposes of §§3.01, 5.02, 6.02, 6.03, 13.01, 13.02, and 14.02 of Revenue Ruling 69-4, C.B. 1969-1, 118, is defined to be all of each employee's compensation that would be subject to tax under section 3101(a) of the Code without the dollar limitation of section 3121(a)(1) of the Code.

(4) *Request by sponsoring organizations and employers.*—(i) The National Office will consider the request of a sponsoring organization desiring a written opinion as to the acceptability of the form of a master or prototype plan and any related trust or custodial account. Such request is to be made on Form 4461 and filed with the Commissioner of Internal Revenue, Washington, D.C. 20224, attention T:MS:PT. Copies of all documents, including the plan and trust or custodial agreement, together with specimen insurance contracts, if applicable, are to be submitted with the request. In making its determination, the National Office may require additional information as appropriate.

(ii) Each district director, in whose jurisdiction there are employers who adopt the form of plan, must be furnished a copy of the previously approved form of plan and related documents by the sponsoring organization. The sponsoring organization must also furnish such district director a copy of all amendments subsequently approved as to form by the National Office.

(iii) The sponsoring organization must furnish copies of opinion letters as to the acceptability of the form of plan, including amendments (see subparagraph (5) of this paragraph), to all adopting employers.

(5) *Amendments.*—(i) Subsequent to obtaining approval of the form of a master or prototype plan, a sponsoring organization may wish to amend the plan. Whether a sponsoring organization may effect an amendment depends on the plan's administrative provisions.

(ii) If the plan provides that each subscribing employer has delegated authority to the sponsor to amend the plan and that each such employer shall be deemed to have consented thereto, the plan may be amended by the sponsor acting on behalf of the subscribers. If the plan does not contain such provision but all subscribing employers consent in a collateral document to permit amendment, the sponsor, acting on their behalf, may amend the plan. However, where a sponsor is unable to secure the consent of each such employer, the plan cannot be amended. In such cases any change can only be effected by the establishment of a new plan and the submission of a new Form 4461 by the sponsor. The new plan must be complete and separate from the old plan, and individual employers may, if they desire, substitute the new plan for the old plan.

(iii) Where the plan has been amended pursuant to subdivision (ii) of this subparagraph, the sponsor is to submit an application, Form 4461, a copy of the amendment, a description of the changes, and a statement indicating the provisions in the original plan authorizing amendments, or a statement that each participating employer's consent has been obtained.

(iv) Upon approval of the amendment by the National Office, an opinion letter will be issued to the sponsor containing the serial number of the original plan, followed by a suffix: "A-1" for the first amendment, "A-2" for the second amendment, etc. Employers adopting the form of plan subsequent to the date of the amendment must use the revised serial number.

(v) If a new plan is submitted, together with Form 4461 and copies of all documents evidencing the plan, an opinion letter bearing a new serial number will be issued to the sponsor, and all employers who adopt the new plan are to use the new serial number. Employers who adopted the old plan continue to use the original serial number. However, any employer who wishes to change to the new plan may do so by filing with his district director a new Form 4462, indicating the change.

(vi) An employer who amends his adoption agreement may request a determination letter as to the effect of such amendment by filing Form 4462 with his district director, together with a copy of the amendment and a summary of the changes. However, in the event an employer desires to amend his adoption agreement under a master or prototype plan, and such amendment is not contemplated or permitted under the plan, then such amendment will in effect substitute an individually designed plan for the master or prototype plan and the amendment procedure described in paragraph (o) of this section will be applicable.

(6) *Effect on other plans.*—Determination letters previously issued by district directors specified in paragraph (o)(2)(viii) of this section are not affected by these procedures even though the plans covered by the determination letters were designed by organizations described in subparagraph (1)(i) of this paragraph. However, such organizations may avail themselves of these procedures with respect to any subsequent action regarding such plans if they otherwise come within the scope of this paragraph.

(r) *Rulings and determination letters with respect to foundation status classification.*—(1) *Rulings and determination letters on private and operating foundation status.*—The procedures relating to the issuance of rulings and determination letters on private foundation status under section 509(a), and operating foundation status under section 4942(j)(3), of organizations exempt from Federal Income Tax under section 501(c)(3) of the Code will be published from time to time in the Internal Revenue Bulletin (see for example, Rev. Proc. 76-34, 1976-2 C.B. 656, as modified by Rev. Proc. 80-25, 1980-1 C.B. 667. These procedures apply in connection with notices filed by the organizations on Form 4653, Notification Concerning Foundation Status, or with applications for recognition of exempt status under section 501(c)(3) of the Code. Such notices and statements are filed by organizations in accordance with section 508(a) of the Code in order for an organization to avoid the presumption of private foundation status or to claim status as an operating foundation. In addition, these procedures also relate to National Office review of determination letters on foundation status under sections 509(a) and 4942(j)(3) of the Code and protest of adverse determination letters regarding foundation status.

(2) *Nonexempt charitable trusts claiming nonprivate foundation status under section 509(a)(3) of the Code.*—A trust described in section 4947(a)(1) of the Code is one that is not exempt from tax under section 501(a) of the Code, has all of its unexpired interests devoted to one or more of the purposes described in section 170(c)(2)(B) of the Code, and is a trust for which a charitable deduction was allowed. These trusts are subject to the private foundation provisions (Part II of subchapter F of chapter 1 and chapter 42 of the Code) except section 508(a), (b), and (c) of the Code. The procedures to be used by nonexempt charitable trusts to obtain determinations of their foundation status under section 509(a)(3) of the Code will be published from time to time in the Internal Revenue Bulletin (see, for example, Rev. Proc. 72-50, 1972-2 C.B. 830).

(s) *Advance rulings or determination letters.*—(1) *General.*—It is the practice of the Service to answer written inquiries, when appropriate and in the interest of sound tax administration, as to the tax effects of acts or transactions of individuals and organizations and as to the status of certain organizations for tax purposes prior to the filing of returns or reports as required by the Revenue laws.

(2) *Exceptions.*—There are, however, certain areas where because of the inherently factual nature of the problems involved or for other reasons, the Service will not issue advance rulings or determination letters. Ordinarily, an ad-

vance ruling or determination letter is not issued on any matter where the determination requested is primarily one of fact (e.g., market value of property), or on the tax effect of any transaction to be consummated at some indefinite future time or of any transaction or matter having as a major purpose the reduction of Federal taxes. A specific area or a list of these areas is published from time to time in the Internal Revenue Bulletin (see, for example, Rev. Proc. 80-22, 1980-1 C.B. 654). Such list is not all inclusive. Whenever a particular item is added to or deleted from the list, however, appropriate notice thereof will be published in the Internal Revenue Bulletin. The authority and general procedures of the National Office of the Internal Revenue Service and of the offices of the district directors of internal revenue with respect to the issuance of advance rulings and determination letters are outlined in paragraphs (b) and (c) of this section.

(t) *Alternative method of depletion.*—(1) *In general.*—Section 1.613-4(d)(1)(i) of the regulations, adopted by T.D. 7170, March 10, 1972, provides that, in those cases where it is impossible to determine a representative market or field price under the provisions of § 1.613-4(c), gross income from mining shall be computed by use of the proportionate profits method set forth in § 1.613-4(d)(4).

(2) *Exception.*—An exception is provided in § 1.613-4(d)(1)(ii) where, upon application, the Office of the Assistant Commissioner (Technical) approves the use of an alternative method that is more appropriate than the proportionate profits method or the alternative method being used by the taxpayer.

(3) *Procedure.*—The procedure for making application for approval to compute gross income from mining by use of an alternative method, other than the proportionate profits method; the conditions for approval and use of an alternative method; changes in an approved method; and other pertinent information with respect thereto, will be published from time to time in the Cumulative Bulletin (see, for example, Rev. Proc. 74-43, 1974-2 C.B. 496).

(u) *Conditions for issuing rulings involving bonuses and advanced royalties of lessors under § 631(c) of IRC of 1954.*—(1) *In general.*—Rev. Proc. 77-11, 1977-1 C.B. 568, provides that the tax liability of a lessor who received a bonus or an advance royalty is required to be recomputed for the taxable year or years in which such payment or payments were received if the right to mine coal

Reg. §601.201(u)(1)

or iron ore under the lease expires, terminates, or is abandoned before (with respect to bonuses) any coal or iron ore has been mined; or (with respect to advance royalties) the coal or ironore that has been paid for in advance is mined. In such recomputation, the lessor is required to treat the bonus payment or payments or any portion of the advance royalty payment or payments attributable to unmined coal or iron ore, as ordinary income and not as received from the sale of coal or iron ore under section 631(c) of the Code.

(2) *Condition for issuing rulings.*—Prior to issuing a ruling to lessors who request a ruling that they may treat bonuses or advance royalties received under a lease for coal or iron ore as received from a sale of coal or iron under section 631(c) of the Code, the Internal Revenue Service will require that the lessor enter a closing agreement in which the lessor agrees that—

(i) If the lease under which the lessor received a bonus or an advance royalty expires, terminates, or is abandoned before (with respect to a bonus) any coal or iron ore has been mined or (with respect to an advance royalty) the coal or iron ore that has been paid for in advance is mined, the tax liability of the lessor will be recomputed for the taxable year or years of receipt of (A) the bonus by treating the bonus payment or payments as ordinary income or (B) the advance royalty by treating any portion of the advance royalty payment or payments attributable to unmined coal or iron ore as ordinary income;

(ii) If the recomputation described in paragraph (u)(2)(i) of this section is required, the lessor will pay the additional amount, if any, of all federal income tax finally determined as due and payable by the lessor for the taxable year or years of the receipt of the bonus or advance royalty; and

(iii) If any of the described events has occurred, the lessor will notify the appropriate district director of such event in writing within 90 days of the close of the taxable year in which the lease expires, terminates, or is abandoned.

[Reg. § 601.202]

§ 601.202. Closing agreements.—(a) *General.*—(1) Under section 7121 of the Code and the regulations and delegations thereunder, the Commissioner, or any officer or employee of the Internal Revenue Service authorized in writing by the Commissioner, may enter into and approve a written agreement with a person relating to the liability of such person (or of the person or estate for whom he acts) in respect of any internal revenue tax for any taxable period. Such agreement, except upon a showing of fraud or malfeasance, or misrepresentation of a material fact, shall be final and conclusive.

(2) Closing agreements under section 7121 of the Code may relate to any taxable period ending prior or subsequent to the date of the agreement. With respect to taxable periods ended prior to the date of the agreement, the matter agreed upon may relate to the total tax liability of the taxpayer or it may relate to one or more separate items affecting the tax liability of the taxpayer. A closing agreement may also be entered into in order to provide a "determination", as defined in section 1313 of the Code, and for the purpose of allowing a deficiency dividend deduction under section 547 of the Code. But see also sections 547(c)(3) and 1313(a)(4) of the Code and the regulations thereunder as to other types of "determination" agreements. With respect to taxable periods ending subsequent to the date of the agreement, the matter agreed upon may relate to one or more separate items affecting the tax liability of the taxpayer. A closing agreement with respect to any taxable period ending subsequent to the date of the agreement is subject to any change in or modification of the law enacted subsequent to the date of the agreement and applicable to such taxable period, and each such closing agreement shall so recite. Closing agreements may be entered into even though under the agreement the taxpayer is not liable for any tax for the period to which the agreement relates. There may be a series of agreements relating to the tax liability for a single period. A closing agreement may be entered into in any case in which there appears to be an advantage in having the case permanently and conclusively closed, or where good and sufficient reasons are shown by the taxpayer for desiring a closing agreement and it is determined by the Commissioner or his representatives that the Government will sustain no disadvantage through consummation of such an agreement.

(b) *Use of prescribed forms.*—In cases in which it is proposed to close conclusively the total tax liability for a taxable period ending prior to the date of the agreement, Form 866, Agreement as to Final Determination of Tax Liability, generally will be used. In cases in which agreement has been reached as to the disposition of one or more issues and a closing agreement is considered necessary to insure consistent treatment of such issues in any other taxable period Form 906, Closing Agreement as to Final Determination Covering Specific Matters, generally will be used. A request for a closing agreement which determines tax liability may be submitted and entered into at any time before the determination of such liability becomes a matter within the province of a court of competent jurisdiction and may thereafter be entered into in appropriate circumstances when authorized by the court (e.g., in certain bankruptcy situations). The request should be submitted to the district director of internal revenue with whom the return for the period involved was filed.However, if the matter to which the request relates is pending before an office of the Appellate Division, the request should be submitted to that office. A request for a closing agreement which relates only to a subsequent period should be submitted to the Commissioner of Internal Revenue, Washington, D.C. 20224.

(c) *Approval.*—(1) Closing agreements relating to alcohol, tobacco, and firearms taxes in respect of any prospective transactions or completed transactions affecting returns to be filed may be entered into and approved by the Director, Bureau of Alcohol, Tobacco and Firearms.

(2) Closing agreements relating to taxes other than those taxes covered in subparagraph (1) of this paragraph in respect of any prospective transactions or completed transactions affecting returns to be filed may be entered into and approved by the Assistant Commissioner (Technical).

(3) Closing agreements for a taxable period or periods ended prior to the date of agreement and related specific items affecting other taxable periods (including those covering competent authority determinations in the administration of the operating provisions of the tax conventions of the United States) may be entered into and approved by the Assistant Commissioner (Compliance).

(4) Regional commissioners, assistant regional commissioners (appellate), assistant regional commissioners (examination), district directors (including the Director, Foreign Operations District), chiefs and assistant chiefs of appellate branch offices may enter into and approve closing agreements on cases under their jurisdiction (but excluding cases docketed before the U.S. Tax Court) for a taxable period or periods which end prior to the date of agreement and related specific items affecting other taxable periods.

(5) Regional commissioners, assistant regional commissioners (examination) and (appellate), chiefs and assistant chiefs of appellate branch offices are authorized to enter into and approve closing agreements in cases under their

jurisdiction docketed in the U.S. Tax Court but only in respect to related specific items affecting other taxable periods.

(6) Closing agreements providing for the mitigation of economic double taxation under section 3 of Revenue Procedure 64-54, C.B. 1964 2, 1008, or under Revenue Procedure 69-13, C.B. 1969-1, 402 or for such mitigation and relief under Revenue Procedure 65-17, C.B. 1965-1, 833, may be entered into and approved by the Director, Foreign Operations District.

(7) Closing agreements in cases under the jurisdiction of a district director providing that the taxability of earnings from a deposit or account of the type described in Revenue Procedure 64-24, C.B. 1964-1 (Part 1), 693, opened prior to November 15, 1962, will be determined on the basis that earnings on such deposits or accounts are not includible in gross income until maturity or termination, whichever occurs earlier, and that the full amount of earnings on the deposit or account will constitute gross income in the year the plan matures, is assigned, or is terminated, whichever occurs first, may be entered into and approved by such district director.

(d) *Applicability of ruling requirements.*—The requirements relating to requests for rulings (see §601.201) shall be applicable with respect to requests for closing agreements pertaining to prospective transactions or completed transactions affecting returns to be filed (see paragraph (c)(2) of this section).

[Reg. §601.203]

§601.203. Offers in compromise.— (a) *General.*—(1) The Commissioner may compromise, in accordance with the provisions of section 7122 of the Code, any civil or criminal case arising under the internal revenue laws prior to reference to the Department of Justice for prosecution or defense. Certain functions of the Commissioner with respect to compromise of civil cases involving liability of $100,000 or more, based solely on doubt as to liability, have been delegated to regional commissioners and, for cases arising in the District Office, Foreign Operations District, to the Assistant Commissioner (Compliance). The authority concerning liability of $100,000 or more based on doubt as to collectibility or doubt as to both collectibility and liability has been delegated to the Director, Collection Division, and regional commissioners. The authority with respect to compromise of civil cases involving liability under $100,000, and of certain specific penalties has been delegated to district directors, assistant district directors, and (including the District Director and Assistant District Director, Foreign Operations District), regional directors of Appeals, and chiefs and associate chiefs, Appeals offices. The authority concerning offers in compromise of penalties based solely on doubt as to liability, if the liability is less than $100,000, has also been delegated to service center directors and assistant service center directors. In civil cases involving liability of $500 or over and in criminal cases the functions of the General Counsel are performed by the Chief Counsel for the Internal Revenue Service. These functions are performed in the District Counsel, Regional Counsel, or National Office as appropriate. (See also paragraph (c) of this section.) In cases arising under chapters 51, 52, and 53 of the Code, offers are acted upon by the Bureau of Alcohol, Tobacco and Firearms.

(2) An offer in compromise of taxes, interest, delinquency penalties, or specific penalties may be based on either inability to pay or doubt as to liability. Offers in compromise arise usually when payments of assessed liabilities are demanded, penalties for delinquency in filing returns are asserted, or specific civil or criminal penalties are incurred by taxpayers. A criminal liability will not be compromised unless it involves only the regulatory provisions of the Internal Revenue Code and related statutes. However, if the violations involving the regulatory provisions are deliberate and with intent to defraud, the criminal liabilities will not be compromised.

(b) *Use of prescribed form.*—Offers in compromise are required to be submitted on Form 656, properly executed, and accompanied by a financial statement on Form 433 (if based on inability to pay). Form 656 is used in all cases regardless of whether the amount of the offer is tendered in full at the time the offer is filed or the amount of the offer is to be paid by deferred payment or payments. Copies of Form 656 and Form 433 may be obtained from district directors. An offer in compromise should be filed with the district director or service center director.

(c) *Consideration of offer.*—(1) An offer in compromise is first considered by the director having jurisdiction. Except in certain penalty cases, an investigation of the basis of the offer is required. The examining officer makes a written recommendation for acceptance or rejection of the offer. If the director has jurisdiction over the processing of the offer he or she will:

(i) Reject the offer, or

(ii) Accept the offer if it involves a civil liability under $500, or

(iii) Accept the offer if it involves a civil liability of $500 or more, but less than $100,000, or involves a specific penalty, and the District Counsel concurs in the acceptance of the offer, or

(iv) Recommend to the National Office the acceptance of the offer if it involves a civil liability of $100,000 or over.

(2)(i) If the district director does not have jurisdiction over the entire processing of the offer, the offer is transmitted to the appropriate District Counsel if the case is one in which:

(a) Recommendations for prosecution are pending in the Office of the Chief Counsel, the Department of Justice, or in an office of a United States attorney, including cases in which criminal proceedings have been instituted but not disposed of and related cases in which offers in compromise have been submitted or are pending;

(b) The taxpayer is in receivership or is involved in a proceeding under any provision of the Bankruptcy Act;

(c) The taxpayer is deceased; in joint liability cases, where either taxpayer is deceased;

(d) A proposal is made to discharge property from the effect of a tax lien or to subordinate the lien or liens;

(e) An insolvent bank is involved;

(f) An assignment for the benefit of creditors is involved;

(g) A liquidation proceeding is involved; or

(h) Court proceedings are pending, except Tax Court cases.

(ii) The District Counsel considers and processes offers submitted in cases described in paragraph (c)(2)(i)(a) through (h) of this section and forwards those offers to the district director, service center director, Regional Counsel, or Office of Chief Counsel in Washington, as appropriate.

(iii) In those cases described in (a) of subdivision (i) of this subparagraph no investigation will be made unless specifically requested by the office having jurisdiction of the criminal case.

(iv) In those cases described in (b) through (h) of subdivision (i) of this subparagraph the district director retains the duplicate copy of the offer and the financial statement for investigation. After investigation, the district director transmits to the appropriate District Counsel for consideration and processing his or her recommendation for acceptance or rejection of the offer together with the examining officer's report of the investigation.

Reg. §601.203(a)(2)

(3) The district directors, assistant district directors (including the District Director and Assistant District Director, Foreign Operations District), service center directors, assistant service center directors, Regional Directors of appeals, and Chiefs and Associate Chiefs, Appeals Offices are authorized to reject any offer in compromise referred for their consideration. Unacceptable offers considered by the District Counsel, Regional Counsel, or Office of Chief Counsel in Washington, or the Appeals office are also rejected by the district directors (including the Director, Foreign Operations District) as applicable. If an offer is not acceptable, the taxpayer is promptly notified of the rejection of that offer. If an offer is rejected, the sum submitted with the offer is returned to the proponent, unless the taxpayer authorizes application of the sum offered to the tax liability. Each Regional Commissioner will perform a post review of offers accepted, rejected, or withdrawn by the district director's office if the offer covers liabilities of $5,000 or more. The post review will cover a sampling of cases processed by the Collection function and all cases processed by the Examination function.

(4) If an offer involving unpaid liability of $100,000 or more is considered acceptable by the office having jurisdiction over the offer, a recommendation for acceptance is forwarded to the National Office or Regional Office, as appropriate, for review. If the recommendation for acceptance is approved, the offer is forwarded to the Regional Counsel or Office of Chief Counsel in Washington, as appropriate, for approval. After approval by the Regional Counsel or Office of Chief Counsel in Washington, as appropriate, it is forwarded to the Assistant Commissioner (Compliance), Director, Collection Division, or Regional Commissioner, as appropriate, for acceptance. The taxpayer is notified of the acceptance of the offer in accordance with its terms. Acceptance of an offer in compromise of civil liabilities does not remit criminal liabilities, nor does acceptance of an offer in compromise of criminal liabilities remit civil liabilities.

(d) *Conferences.*—Before filing a formal offer in compromise, a taxpayer may request a meeting in the office which would have jurisdiction over the offer to explore the possibilities of compromising unpaid tax liability. After all investigations have been made, the taxpayer may also request a meeting in the office having jurisdiction of the offer to determine the amount which may be accepted as a compromise. If agreement is not reached at such meeting and the district director has processing jurisdiction over the offer, the taxpayer will be informed that the taxpayer may request consideration of the case by an Appeals office. The request may be in writing or oral. If the tax, penalty, and assessed (but not accrued) interest sought to be compromised exceeds $2,500 for any return, taxable year or taxable period, a written protest is required. Taxpayers and their representatives are required to comply with the applicable conference and practice requirements. See subpart E of this part.

[Reg. § 601.204]

§ 601.204. Changes in accounting periods and in methods of accounting.—(a) *Accounting periods.*—A taxpayer who changes his accounting period shall, before using the new period for income tax purposes, comply with the provisions of the income tax regulations relating to changes in accounting periods. In cases where the regulations require the taxpayer to secure the consent of the Commissioner to the change, the application for permission to change the accounting period shall be made on Form 1128 and shall be submitted to the Commissioner of Internal Revenue, Washington, D.C. 20224, within the period of time prescribed in such regulations. See section 442 of the Code and regulations thereunder. If the change is approved by the Commissioner, the taxpayer shall thereafter make his returns and compute his net income upon the basis of the new accounting period. A request for permission to change the accounting period will be considered by the Corporation Tax Division. However, in certain instances, Form 1128 may be filed with the Director of the Internal Revenue Service Center in which the taxpayer files its return. See, for example, Rev. Proc. 66-13, 1966-1 C.B. 626; Rev. Proc. 66-50, 1966-2 C.B. 1260, and Rev. Proc. 68-41, 1968-2 C.B. 943. With respect to partnership adoption, see § 1.706-1(b) of the Income Tax Regulations.

(b) *Methods of accounting.*—A taxpayer who changes the method of accounting employed in keeping his books shall, before computing his income upon such method for purposes of income taxation, comply with the provisions of the income tax regulations relating to changes in accounting methods. The regulations require that, in the ordinary case, the taxpayer secure the consent of the Commissioner to the change. See section 446 of the Code and the regulations thereunder. Application for permission to change the method of accounting employed shall be made on Form 3115 and shall be submitted to the Commissioner of Internal Revenue, Washington, D.C. 20224, during the taxable year in which it is desired to make the change. Permission to change the method of accounting will not be granted unless the taxpayer and the Commissioner agree to the terms and conditions under which the change will be effected. The request will be considered by the Corporation Tax Division. However, in certain instances, Form 3115 may be filed with the Director of the Internal Revenue Service Center. See, for example, Rev. Proc. 74-11, 1974-1 C.B. 420.

(c) *Verification of changes.*—Written permission to a taxpayer by the National Office consenting to a change in his annual accounting period or to a change in his accounting method is a "ruling." Therefore, in the examination of returns involving changes of annual accounting periods and methods of accounting, district directors must determine whether the representations upon which the permission was granted reflect an accurate statement of the material facts, and whether the agreed terms, conditions, and adjustments havebeen substantially carried out as proposed. An application, Form 3115, filed with the Director of the Internal Revenue Service Center is also subject to similar verification.

(d) *Instructions to taxpayers.*—The person seeking to secure the consent of the Commissioner with respect to a change of accounting periods or methods pursuant to section 442 or 446(e) of the Code need not submit the statement of proposed deletions described in §601.201(e)(5) at the time the request is made. If, however, the person seeking the consent of the Commissioner receives from the National Office a notice that proposed deletions should be submitted because the resulting ruling will be open to public inspection under section 6110, the statement of proposed deletions must be submitted within 20 days after such notice is mailed.

[Reg. §601.205]

§601.205. Tort claims.—Claims for property loss or damage, personal injury, or death caused by the negligent or wrongful act or omission of any employee of the Service, acting within the scope of his office or employment, filed under the Federal Tort Claims Act, as amended, must be prepared and filed in accordance with Treasury Department regulations entitled "Central Office Procedures" and "Claims Regulations" (31 CFR, Parts 1 and 3). Such regulations contain the procedural and substantive requirements relative to such claims, and set forth the manner in which they are handled. The claims should be filed with the Commissioner of Internal Revenue, Washington, D.C. 20224, and must be filed within two years after the accident or incident occurred.

[Reg. §601.206]

§601.206. Certification required to obtain reduced foreign tax rates under income tax treaties.—(a) *Basis of certification.*—Most of the income tax treaties between the United States and foreign countries provide for either a reduction in the statutory rate of tax or an exemption from tax on certain types of income received from sources within the foreign treaty country by citizens, domestic corporations, and residents of the United States. Some of the treaty countries reduce the withholding tax on such types of income or exempt the income from withholding tax after the claimant furnishes evidence that he is entitled to the benefits of the treaty. Other countries initially withhold the tax at statutory rates and refund the excess tax withheld after satisfactory evidence of U.S. residence has been accepted. As part of the proof that the applicant is a resident of the United States and thus entitled to the benefits of the treaty, he must usually furnish a certification from the U.S. Government that he has filed a U.S. income tax return as a citizen, domestic corporation, or resident of the U.S.

(b) *Procedure for obtaining the certification.*—Most of the treaty countries which require certification have printed special forms. The forms contain a series of questions to be answered by the taxpayer claiming the benefits of the treaty, followed by a statement which the foreign governments use for the U.S. taxing authority's certification. This certification may be obtained from the office of the district director of the district in which the claimant filed his latest income tax return. Some certification forms are acceptable for Service execution; however, others cannot be executed by the Service without revision. In these instances the office of the district director will prepare its own document of certification in accordance with internal instructions. This procedure has been accepted by most treaty countries as a satisfactory substitute.

(c) *Obtaining the official certification forms.*—The forms may be obtained from the foreign payor, the tax authority of the treaty country involved, or the District Office, Foreign Operations District.

Subpart C—[Reserved]
Subpart D—Provisions Special to Certain Employment Taxes

§ 601.401. Employment taxes.—(a) *General.*— (1) *Description of taxes.*—Federal employment taxes are imposed by Subtitle C of the Internal Revenue Code. Chapter 21 (Federal Insurance Contributions Act) imposes a tax on employers of one or more individuals and also a tax on employees, with respect to "wages" paid and received. Chapter 22 (Railroad Retirement Tax Act) imposes (i) an employer tax and employee tax with respect to "compensation" paid and received, (ii) an employee representative tax with respect to "compensation" received, and (iii) a supplemental tax on employers, measured by man-hours for which "compensation" is paid. Chapter 23 (Federal Unemployment Tax Act) imposes a tax on employers of one or more individuals with respect to "wages" paid. Chapter 24 (collection of income tax at source on wages) requires every employer making payment of "wages" to deduct and withhold upon such wages the tax computed or determined as provided therein. The tax so deducted and withheld is allowed as a credit against the income tax liability of the employee receiving such wages.

(2) *Applicable regulations.*—The descriptive terms used in this section to designate the various classes of taxes are intended only to indicate their general character. Specific information relative to the scope of each tax, the forms used, and the functioning of the Service with respect thereto is contained in the applicable regulations. Copies of all necessary forms, and instructions as to their preparation and filing, may be obtained from the district director of internal revenue.

(3) *Collection methods.*—Employment taxes are collected by means of returns and by withholding by employers. Employee tax must be deducted and withheld by employers from "wages" or "compensation" (including tips reported in writing to employers) paid to employees, and the employer is liable for the employee tax whether or not it is so deducted. For special rules relating to tips see §§ 31.3102-3 and 31.3402(k)-1. Rev. Proc. 81-48, 1981-2 C.B. 623, provides guidelines for determining wages when the employer pays the employee tax imposed by chapter 21 without deducting the amount from the employee's pay. Employee representatives (as defined in the Railroad Retirement Tax Act) are required to file returns. Employment tax returns must be filed with the district director or, if so provided in instructions applicable to a return, with the service center designated in the instructions. The return of the Federal unemployment tax is required to be filed annually on Form 940 with respect to wages paid during the calendar year. All other returns of Federal employment taxes (with the exception of returns filed for agricultural employees) are required to be filed for each calendar quarter except that if pursuant to regulations the district director so notifies the employer, returns on Form 941 are required to be filed on a monthly basis. In the case of certain employers required to report withheld income tax but not required to report employer and employee taxes imposed by chapter 21 (for example, state and local government employers), Form 941E is prescribed for reporting on a quarterly basis. The employer and employee taxes imposed by chapter 21 (other than the employer and employee taxes on wages paid for agricultural labor) and the tax required to be deducted and withheld upon wages by chapter 24 are combined in a single return on Form 941. In the case of wages paid by employers for domestic service performed in a private home not on a farm operated for profit, the return of both the employee tax and the employer tax imposed by chapter 21 is on Form 942. However, if the employer is required to file a return for the same quarter on Form 941, the employer may elect to include the taxes with respect to such domestic service on Form 941. The employer and employee taxes imposed by chapter 21 with respect to wages paid for agricultural labor are required to be reported annually on Form 943. Under the Railroad Retirement Tax Act, the return required of the employer is on Form CT-1, and the return required of each employee representative is on Form CT-2. An employee is not required to file a return of employee tax, except that the employee must include in his or her income tax return (as provided in the applicable instructions) any amount of employee tax (i) due with respect to tips that the employee failed to report to the employer or (ii) shown on the employee's Form W-2 as "Uncollected Employee Tax on Tips".

(4) *Receipts for employees.*—Employers are required to furnish each employee a receipt or statement, in duplicate, showing the total wages subject to income tax withholding, the amount of income tax withheld, the amount of wages subject to tax under the Federal Insurance Contributions Act, and the amount of employee tax withheld. See section 6051 of the Code.

(5) *Use of Federal Reserve banks and authorized commercial banks and trust companies in connection with payment of Federal employment taxes.*—Most employers are required to deposit employment taxes either on a monthly basis, a semimonthly

basis or a quarter-monthly period basis as follows:

(i) *Quarter-monthly period deposits.*—With respect to wages paid after January 31, 1971, (March 31, 1971 in the case of wages paid for agricultural labor), if at the close of any quarter-monthly period (that ends on the 7th, 15th, 22nd, or the last day of any month) the aggregate amount of undeposited taxes, exclusive of taxes reportable on Form 942, is $2,000 or more, the employer shall deposit such taxes within 3 banking days after the close of such quarter-monthly period.

(ii) *Monthly deposits.*—With respect to employers not required to make deposits under subdivision (i) of this subparagraph, if after January 31, 1971 (March 31, 1971, in the case of income tax withheld from wages paid for agricultural labor) (a) during any calendar month, other than the last month of a calendar quarter, the aggregate amount of the employee tax deducted and the employer tax under chapter 21 and the income tax withheld at source on wages under chapter 24, exclusive of taxes reportable on Form 942, exceeds $200, or (b) at the end of any month or period of 2 or more months and prior to December 1 of any calendar year, the total amount of undeposited taxes imposed by chapter 21, with respect to wages paid for agricultural labor, exceeds $200, it is the duty of the employer to deposit such amount within 15 days after the close of such calendar month.

(iii) *Quarterly and year-end deposits.*—Whether or not an employer is required to make deposits under subdivisions (i) and (ii) of this subparagraph, if the amount of such taxes reportable on Form 941 or 943 (reduced by any previous deposits) exceeds $200, the employer shall, on or before the last day of the first calendar month following the period for which the return is required to be filed, deposit such amount with a Federal Reserve bank or authorized financial institution. However, if the amount of such taxes (reduced by any previous deposits) does not exceed $200, the employer may either include with his return a direct remittance for the amount of such taxes or, on or before the last day of the first calendar month following the period for which the return is required to be filed, voluntarily deposit such amount with a Federal Reserve bank or authorized financial institution.

(iv) *Additional rules.*—Deposits under subdivisions (i), (ii) and (iii) of this subparagraph are made with a Federal Reserve bank or a financial institution authorized in accordance with Treasury Department Circular No. 1079, revised, to accept remittances of these taxes for transmission to a Federal Reserve bank. The remittance of such amount must be accompanied by a Federal Tax Deposit form. Each employer making deposits shall report on the return for the period with respect to which such deposits are made information regarding such deposits in accordance with the instructions applicable to such return and pay therewith (or deposit by the due date of such return) the balance, if any, of the taxes due for such period.

(v) *Employers under chapter 22 of the Code.*—Depositary procedures similar to those prescribed in this subparagraph are prescribed for employers as defined by the Railroad Retirement Tax Act, except that railroad retirement taxes are not requested to be deposited semimonthly or quarter-monthly. Such taxes must be deposited by using a Federal Tax Deposit form.

(vi) *Employers under chapter 23 of the Code.*—Every person who is an employer as defined by the Federal Unemployment Tax Act shall deposit the tax imposed under chapter 23 on or before the last day of the first calendar month following the quarterly period in which the amount of such tax exceeds $100.

(6) *Separate accounting.*—If an employer fails to withhold and pay over income, social security, or railroad retirement tax due on wages of employees, the employer may be required by the district director to collect such taxes and deposit them in a separate banking account in trust for the United States not later than the second banking day after such taxes are collected.

(b) *Provisions special to the Federal Insurance Contributions Act.*—(1) *Employers' identification numbers.*—For purposes of the Federal Insurance Contributions Act each employer who files Form 941 or Form 943 must have an identification number. Any such employer who does not have an identification number must secure a Form SS-4 from the district director of internal revenue or from a district office of the Social Security Administration and, after executing the form in accordance with the instructions contained thereon, file it with the district director or the district office of the Social Security Administration. At a subsequent date the district director will assign the employer a number which must appear in the appropriate space on each tax return, Form 941 or Form 943, filed thereafter. The requirement to secure an identification number does not apply to an employer who employs only employees who are engaged exclusively in the performance of domestic service in the employer's private home not on a farm operated for profit.

(2) *Employees' account numbers.*—Each employee (or individual making a return of net earnings from self-employment) who does not have an account number must file an application on Form SS-5), a copy of which may be obtained from any district office of the Social Security Administration or from a district director of internal revenue. The form, after execution in accordance with the instructions thereon, must be filed with the district office of the Social Security Administration, and at a later date the employee will be furnished an account number. The employee must furnish such number to each employer for whom the employee works, in order that such number may be entered on each tax return filed thereafter by the employer.

(3) *Reporting of wages.*—Forms 941, 942, and 943 each require, as a part of the return, that the wages of each employee paid during the period covered by the return be reported thereon. Form 941a is available to employers who need additional space for the listing of employees. Employers who meet the requirements of the Social Security Administration may, with the approval of the Commissioner of Internal Revenue, submit wage information on reels of magnetic tape in lieu of Form 941a. It is necessary at times that employers correct wage information previously reported. A special form, Form 941c, has beenadopted for use in correcting erroneous wage information or omissions of such wage information on Forms 941, 942, or 943. Instructions on Forms 941, 941c, 942, and 943 explain the manner of preparing and filing the forms. Any further instructions should be obtained from the district director.

(c) *Adjustments by employers.*—(1) *Undercollections and underpayments.*—(i) *Employer tax or employee tax.*—If a return is filed by an employer under the Federal Insurance Contributions Act or the Railroad Retirement Tax Act, and the employer reports and pays less than the correct amount of employer tax or employee tax, the employer is required to report and pay the additional amount due. The reporting will be an adjustment without interest only if the employer reports and pays the additional amount on or before the last day on which the return is required to be filed for the return period in which the error is ascertained. The employer may so report theadditional amount either on the return

for that period or on a supplemental return for the period for which the underpayment was made. If the employer fails to report the additional amount due within the time so fixed for making an interest-free adjustment, the employer nevertheless is required to report the additional amount in the same manner, but interest will be due. No adjustment of an underpayment may be made under this section or §31.6205-1(b)(2) if the employer is sent a notice and demand for payment of the additional tax.

(ii) *Income tax withholding.*—If an employer files a return reporting and paying less than the correct amount of income tax required to be withheld from wages paid during the return period, the employer is required to report and pay the additional amount due, either (*a*) on a return for any return period in the calendar year in which the wages were paid, or (*b*) on a supplemental return for the return period in which the wages were paid. The reporting will be an adjustment without interest only if the employer reports and pays the additional amount on or before the last day on which the return is required to be filed for the return period in which the error is ascertained. If an employer reports and pays less than the correct amount of income tax required to be withheld in a calendar year, and the employer does not correct the underpayment in the same calendar year, the employer should consult the district director of internal revenue as to the manner of correcting the error.

(2) *Overcollections from employees.*—(i) *Employee tax.*—If an employer collects from an employee more than the correct amount of employee tax under the Federal Insurance Contributions Act or the Railroad Retirement Act, and the error is ascertained within the applicable period of limitation on credit or refund, the employer is required either to repay the amount to the employee, or to reimburse the employee by applying the amount of the overcollection against employee tax which otherwise would be collected from the employee after the error is ascertained. If the overcollection is repaid to the employee, the employer is required to obtain and keep the employee's written receipt showing the date and amount of the repayment. In addition, if the employer repays or reimburses an employee in any calendar year for an overcollection which occurred in a prior calendar year, the employer is required to obtain and keep the employee's written statement (*a*) that the employee has not claimed refund or credit of the amount of the overcollection, or if so, such claim

Reg. §601.401(c)(2)(i)

has been rejected, and (*b*) that the employee will not claim refund or credit of such amount.

(ii) *Income tax withholding.*—If, in any return period in a calendar year, an employer withholds more than the correct amount of income tax, and pays over to the Internal Revenue Service the amount withheld, the employer may repay or reimburse the employee in the excess amount in any subsequent return period in the same calendar year. If the amount is so repaid, the employer is required to obtain and keep the employee's written receipt showing the date and amount of the repayment.

(3) *Employer's claims for credit or refund of overpayments.*—(i) *Employee tax.*—If an employer repays or reimburses an employee for an overcollection of employee tax, as described in subparagraph (2)(i) of this paragraph, the employer may claim credit on a return in accordance with the instructions applicable to the return. In lieu of claiming credit the employer may claim refund by filing Form 843, but the employer may not thereafter claim credit for the same overpayment.

(ii) *Income tax withholding.*—If an employer repays or reimburses an employee for an excess amount withheld as income tax, as described in subparagraph (2)(ii) of this paragraph, the employer may claim credit on a return for a return period in the calendar year in which the excess amount was withheld. The employer is not otherwise permitted to claim credit or refund for any overpayment of income tax that the employer deducted or withheld from an employee.

(d) *Special refunds of employee social security tax.*—(1) An employee who receives wages from more than one employer during a calendar year may, under certain conditions, receive a "specialrefund" of the amount of employee social security tax (*i.e.,* employee tax under the Federal Insurance Contributions Act) deducted and withheld from wages that exceed the following amounts: calendar years 1968 through 1971, $7,800; calendar year 1972, $9,000; calendar year 1973, $10,800; calendar year 1974, $13,200; calendar years after 1974, an amount equal to the contribution and benefit base (as determined under section 230 of the Social Security Act) effective with respect to that year. An employee who is entitled to a special refund of employee tax with respect to wages received during a calendar year, and who is required to file an income tax return for such calendar year (or for his last taxable year beginning in such calendar year), may obtain the benefits of such special refund only by claiming credit for such special refund on such income tax return in the same manner as if such special refund were an amount deducted and withheld as income tax at source on wages.

(2) The amount of the special refund allowed as a credit shall be considered as an amount deducted and withheld as income tax at source on wages. If the amount of such special refund when added to amounts deducted and withheld as income tax under chapter 24 exceeds the income tax imposed by chapter 1, the amount of the excess constitutes an overpayment of income tax, and interest on such overpayment is allowed to the extent provided under section 6611 of the Code upon an overpayment of income tax resulting from a credit for income tax withheld at source on wages.

(3) If an employee entitled to a special refund of employee social security tax is not required to file an income tax return for the year in which such special refund may be claimed as a credit, the employee may file a claim for refund of the excess social security tax on Form 843. Claims must be filed with the district director of internal revenue for the district in which the employee resides.

(4) Employee taxes under the Federal Insurance Contributions Act and the Railroad Retirement Tax Act include a percentage rate for hospital insurance. If in 1968 or any calendar year thereafter employee taxes under both Acts are deducted from an employee's wages and compensation aggregating more than $7,800, the "special refund" provisions may apply to the portion of the tax that is deducted for hospital insurance. The employee may take credit on Form 1040 for the amount allowable, in accordance with the instructions applicable to that form.

Subpart E—Conference and Practice Requirements

[Reg. §601.501]

§601.501. Scope of rules; definitions.— (a) *Scope of rules.*—The rules prescribed in this subpart concern, among other things, the representation of taxpayers before the Internal Revenue Service under the authority of a power of attorney. These rules apply to all offices of the Internal Revenue Service in all matters under the jurisdiction of the Internal Revenue Service and apply to practice before the Internal Revenue Service (as defined in 31 CFR 10.2(a) and 10.7(a)(7)). For special provisions relating to alcohol, tobacco, and firearms activities, see §§ 601.521 through 601.527. These rules detail the means by which a recognized representative is authorized to act on behalf of a taxpayer. Such authority must be evidenced by a power of attorney and declaration of representative filed with the appropriate office of the Internal Revenue Service. In general, a power of attorney must contain certain information concerning the taxpayer, the recognized representative, and the specific tax matter(s) for which the recognized representative is authorized to act. (See § 601.503(a).) A "declaration of representative" is a written statement made by a recognized representative that he/she is currently eligible to practice before the Internal Revenue Service and is authorized to represent the particular party on whose behalf he/she acts. (See § 601.502(c).)

(b) *Definitions.*—(1) *Attorney-in-fact.*—An agent authorized by a principal under a power of attorney to perform certain specified act(s) or kinds of act(s) on behalf of the principal.

(2) *Centralized Authorization File (CAF) system.*—An automated file containing information regarding the authority of a person appointed under a power of attorney or designated under a tax information authorization.

(3) *Circular No. 230.*—Treasury Department Circular No. 230 codified at 31 CFR part 10, which sets forth the regulations governing practice before the Internal Revenue Service.

(4) *Declaration of representative.*—(See § 601.502(c).)

(5) *Delegation of authority.*—An act performed by a recognized representative whereby authority given under a power of attorney is delegated to another recognized representative. After a delegation is made, both the original recognized representative and the recognized representative to whom a delegation is made will be recognized to represent the taxpayer. (See § 601.505(b)(2).)

(6) *Form 2848, "Power of Attorney and Declaration of Representative.".*—The Internal Revenue Service power of attorney form which may be used by a taxpayer who wishes to appoint an individual to represent him/her before the Internal Revenue Service. (See § 601.503(b)(1).)

(7) *Matter.*—The application of each tax imposed by the Internal Revenue Code and the regulations thereunder for each taxable period constitutes a (separate) matter.

(8) *Office of the Internal Revenue Service.*—The office of each district director, the office of each service center, the office of each compliance center, the office of each regional commissioner, and the National Office constitute separate offices of the Internal Revenue Service.

(9) *Power of attorney.* A document signed by the taxpayer, as principal, by which an individual is appointed as attorney-in-fact to perform certain specified act(s) or kinds of act(s) on behalf of the principal. Specific types of powers of attorney include the following—

(i) *General power of attorney.*—The attorney-in-fact is authorized to perform any or all acts the taxpayer can perform.

(ii) *Durable power of attorney.*—A power of attorney which specifies that the appointment of the attorney-in-fact will not end due to either the passage of time (i.e., the authority conveyed will continue until the death of the taxpayer) or the incompetency of the principal (e.g., the principal becomes unable or is adjudged incompetent to perform his/her business affairs).

(iii) *Limited power of attorney.*—A power of attorney which is limited in any facet (i.e., a power of attorney authorizing the attorney-in-fact to perform only certain specified acts as contrasted to a general power of attorney authorizing the representative to perform any and all acts the taxpayer can perform).

(10) *Practice before the Internal Revenue Service.*—Practice before the Internal Revenue Service encompasses all matters connected with presentation to the Internal Revenue Service or any of its personnel relating to a taxpayer's rights, privileges, or liabilities under laws or regulations administered by the Internal Revenue Service. Such presentations include the preparation and filing of necessary documents, correspondence with and communications to the Internal Revenue Service, and the representation of a taxpayer at conferences, hearings, and meetings. (See 31 CFR 10.2(a) and 10.7(a)(7).)

(11) *Principal.*—A person (i.e., taxpayer) who appoints an attorney-in-fact under a power of attorney.

(12) *Recognized representative.*—An individual who is recognized to practice before the Internal Revenue Service under the provisions of § 601.502.

(13) *Representation.*—Acts performed on behalf of a taxpayer by a representative in practice before the Internal Revenue Service. (See

Reg. § 601.501(b)(13)

§601.501(b)(10).) Representation does not include the furnishing of information at the request of the Internal Revenue Service or any of its officers or employees (See 31 CFR 10.7(c).)

(14) *Substitution of representative.*—An act performed by an attorney-in-fact whereby authority given under a power of attorney is transferred to another recognized representative. After a substitution is made, only the newly recognized representative will be considered the taxpayer's representative. (See §601.505(b)(2).)

(15) *Tax information authorization.*—A document signed by the taxpayer authorizing any individual or entity (e.g., corporation, partnership, trust or organization) designated by the taxpayer to receive and/or inspect confidential tax information in a specified matter. (See section 6103 of the Internal Revenue Code and the regulations thereunder.)

(c) *Conferences.*—(1) *Scheduling.*—The Internal Revenue Service encourages the discussion of any Federal tax matter affecting a taxpayer. Conferences may be offered only to taxpayers and/or their recognized representative(s) acting under a valid power of attorney. As a general rule, such conferences will not be held without previous arrangement. However, if a compelling reason is shown by the taxpayer that an immediate conference should be held, the Internal Revenue Service official(s) responsible for the matter has the discretion to make an exception to the general rule.

(2) *Submission of information.*—Every written protest, brief, or other statement the taxpayer or recognized representative wishes to be considered at any conference should be submitted to or filed with the appropriate Internal Revenue Service official(s) at least five business days before the date of the conference. If the taxpayer or the representative is unable to meet this requirement, arrangement should be made with the appropriate Internal Revenue Service official for a postponement of the conference to a date mutually agreeable to the parties. The taxpayer or the representative remains free to submit additional or supporting facts or evidence within a reasonable time after the conference.

[Reg. §601.502]

§601.502. **Recognized representative.**—(a) A recognized representative is an individual who is

(1) Appointed as an attorney-in-fact under a power of attorney, and a

(2) Member of one of the categories described in §601.502(b) and who files a declaration of representative, as described in §601.502(c).

(b) *Categories.*—(1) *Attorney.*—Any individual who is a member in good standing of the bar of the highest court of any state, possession, territory, commonwealth, or the District of Columbia;

(2) *Certified public accountant.*—Any individual who is duly qualified to practice as a certified public accountant in any state, possession, territory, commonwealth, or the District of Columbia;

(3) *Enrolled agent.*—Any individual who is enrolled to practice before the Internal Revenue Service and is in active status pursuant to the requirements of Circular No. 230;

(4) *Enrolled actuary.*—Any individual who is enrolled as an actuary by and is in active status with the Joint Board for the Enrollment of Actuaries pursuant to 29 U.S.C. 1242.

(5) *Other individuals.*—(i) *Temporary recognition.*—Any individual who is granted temporary recognition as an enrolled agent by the Director of Practice (31 CFR 10.5(c)).

(ii) *Practice based on a relationship or special status with a taxpayer.*—Any individual authorized to represent a taxpayer with whom/which a special relationship exists (31 CFR 10.7(a)(1)-(6)). (For example, an individual may represent another individual who is his/her regular full-time employer or a member of his/her immediate family; an individual who is a bona fide officer or regular full-time employee of a corporation or certain other organizations may represent that entity.)

(iii) *Unenrolled return preparer.*—Any individual who signs a return as having prepared it for a taxpayer, or who prepared a return with respect to which the instructions or regulations do not require that the return be signed by the preparer. The acts which an unenrolled return preparer may perform are limited to representation of a taxpayer before revenue agents and examining officers of the Examination Division in the offices of District Director with respect to the tax liability of the taxpayer for the taxable year or period covered by a return prepared by the unenrolled return preparer (31 CFR 10.7(a)(7)).

(iv) *Special appearance.*—Any individual who, upon written application, is authorized by the Director of Practice to represent a taxpayer in a particular matter (31 CFR 10.7(b)).

(c) *Declaration of representative.*—A recognized representative must attach to the power of attorney a written declaration (e.g., Part II of Form 2848) stating the following—

(1) I am not currently under suspension or disbarment from practice before the Internal Revenue Service or other practice of my profession by any other authority;

(2) I am aware of the regulations contained in Treasury Department Circular No. 230 (31 C.F.R., part 10), concerning the practice of attorneys, certified public accountants, enrolled agents, enrolled actuaries, and others);

(3) I am authorized to represent the taxpayer(s) identified in the power of attorney; and

(4) I am an individual described in § 601.502(b).

If an individual is unable to make such declaration, he/she may not engage in representation of a taxpayer before the Internal Revenue Service or perform the acts described in § § 601.504(a)(2) through (6).

[Reg. § 601.503]

§ 601.503. Requirements of power of attorney, signatures, fiduciaries and Commissioner's authority to substitute other requirements.—(a) *Requirements.*—A power of attorney must contain the following information—

(1) name and mailing address of the taxpayer;

(2) identification number of the taxpayer (i.e., social security number and/or employer identification number);

(3) employee plan number (if applicable);

(4) name and mailing address of the recognized representative(s);

(5) description of the matter(s) for which representation is authorized which, if applicable, must include—

(i) the type of tax involved;

(ii) the Federal tax form number;

(iii) the specific year(s)/period(s) involved; and

(iv) in estate matters, decedent's date of death; and

(6) a clear expression of the taxpayer's intention concerning the scope of authority granted to the recognized representative(s).

(b) *Acceptable power of attorney documents.*—(1) *Form 2848.*—A properly completed Form 2848 satisfies the requirements for both a power of attorney (as described in § 601.503(a)) and a declaration of representative (as described in § 601.502(c)).

(2) *Other documents.*—The Internal Revenue Service will accept a power of attorney other than Form 2848 provided such document satisfies the requirements of § 601.503(a). However, for purposes of processing such documents onto the Centralized Authorization File (see § 601.506(d)), a completed Form 2848 must be attached. (In such situations, Form 2848 is not the operative power of attorney and need not be signed by the taxpayer. However, the Declaration of Representative must be signed by the representative.)

(3) *Special provision.*—The Internal Revenue Service will not accept a power of attorney which fails to include the information required by § § 601.503(a)(1) through (5). If a power of attorney fails to include some or all of the information required by such section, the attorney-in-fact can cure this defect by executing a Form 2848 (on behalf of the taxpayer) which includes the missing information. Attaching a Form 2848 to a copy of the original power of attorney will validate the original power of attorney (and will be treated in all circumstances as one signed and filed by the taxpayer) provided the following conditions are satisfied—

(i) The original power of attorney contemplates authorization to handle, among other things, Federal tax matters (e.g., the power of attorney includes language to the effect that the attorney-in-fact has the authority to perform any and all acts).

(ii) The attorney-in-fact attaches a statement (signed under penalty of perjury) to the Form 2848 which states that the original power of attorney is valid under the laws of the governing jurisdiction.

(4) *Other categories of powers of attorney.*—Categories of powers of attorney not addressed in these rules (e.g., durable powers of attorney and limited powers of attorney) will be accepted by the Internal Revenue Service provided such documents satisfy the requirements of § 601.503(b)(2) or (3).

(c) *Signatures.*—Internal Revenue Service officials may require a taxpayer (or such individual(s) required or authorized to sign on behalf of a taxpayer) to submit appropriate identification or evidence of authority. Except when Form 2848 (or its equivalent) is executed by an attorney-in-fact under the provisions of § 601.503(b)(3), the individual who must execute a Form 2848 depends on the type of taxpayer involved—

Reg. § 601.503(c)

(1) *Individual taxpayer.*—In matter(s) involving an individual taxpayer, a power of attorney must be signed by such individual.

(2) *Husband and wife.*—In matters involving a joint return the following rules apply—

(i) *Joint representation.*—In the case of any matter concerning a joint return in which both husband and wife are to be represented by the same representative(s), the power of attorney must be executed by both husband and wife.

(ii) *Individual representation.*—In the case of any matter concerning a joint return in which both husband and wife are not to be represented by the same recognized representative(s), the power of attorney must be executed by the spouse who is to be represented. However, the recognized representative of such spouse cannot perform any act with respect to a tax matter that the spouse being represented cannot perform alone.

(3) *Corporation.*—In the case of a corporation, a power of attorney must be executed by an officer of the corporation having authority to legally bind the corporation, who must certify that he/she has such authority.

(4) *Association.*—In the case of an association, a power of attorney must be executed by an officer of the association having authority to legally bind the association, who must certify that he/she has such authority.

(5) *Partnership.*—In the case of a partnership, a power of attorney must be executed by all partners, or if executed in the name of the partnership, by the partner or partners duly authorized to act for the partnership, who must certify that he/she has such authority.

(6) *Dissolved partnership.*—In the case of a dissolved partnership, each of the former partners must execute a power of attorney. However, if one or more of the former partners is deceased, the following provisions apply—

(i) The legal representative of each deceased partner(s) (or such person(s) having legal control over the disposition of partnership interest(s) and/or the share of partnership asset(s) of the deceased partner(s)) must execute a power of attorney in the place of such deceased partner(s). (See § 601.503(c)(6)(ii).)

(ii) Notwithstanding § 601.503(c)(6)(i), if the laws of the governing jurisdiction provide that such partner(s) has exclusive right to control or possession of the firm's assets for the purpose of winding up its affairs, the signature(s) of the surviving partner(s) alone will be sufficient. (If the surviving partner(s) claims exclusive right to control or possession of the firm's assets for the purpose of winding up its affairs, Internal Revenue Service officials may require the submission of a copy of or a citation to the pertinent provisions of the law of the governing jurisdiction upon which the surviving partner(s) relies.)

(d) *Fiduciaries.*—In general, when a fiduciary is involved in a tax matter, a power of attorney is not required. Instead Form 56, "Notice Concerning Fiduciary Relationship," should be filed. Types of taxpayer for which fiduciaries act are—

(1) *Dissolved corporation.*—(i) *Appointed trustee.*—In the case of a dissolved corporation, Form 56, "Notice Concerning Fiduciary Relationship," should be filed by the liquidating trustee(s), if one or more have been appointed, or by the trustee(s) deriving authority under a law of the jurisdiction in which the corporation was organized. If there is more than one trustee, all must join unless it is established that fewer than all have authority to act in the matter under consideration. Internal Revenue Service officials may require the submission of a properly authenticated copy of the instrument and/or citation to the law under which the trustee derives his/her authority. If the authority of the trustee is derived under the law of a jurisdiction, Internal Revenue Service officials may require a statement (signed under penalty of perjury) setting forth the facts required by the law as a condition precedent to the vesting of authority in said trustee and stating that the authority of the trustee has not been terminated.

(ii) *No appointed trustee.*—If there is no appointed trustee, a Form 56, "Notice Concerning Fiduciary Relationship," should be filed by the stockholder(s) holding a majority of the voting stock of the corporation as of the date of dissolution. Internal Revenue Service officials may require submission of a statement showing the total number of outstanding shares of voting stock as of the date of dissolution, the number of shares held by each signatory to a power of attorney, the date of dissolution, and a representation that no trustee has been appointed.

(2) *Insolvent taxpayer.*—In the case of an insolvent taxpayer, Form 56, "Notice Concerning Fiduciary Relationship," should be filed by the trustee, receiver, or attorney appointed by the court. Internal Revenue Service officials may require the submission of a certified order or document from the court having jurisdiction over the insolvent taxpayer which shows the appoint-

ment and qualification of the trustee, receiver, or attorney and that his/her authority has not been terminated. In cases pending before a court of the United States (e.g., U.S. District Court or U.S. Bankruptcy Court), an authenticated copy of the order approving the bond of the trustee, receiver, or attorney will meet this requirement.

(3) *Deceased taxpayers.*—(i) *Executor, personal representative or administrator.*—In the case of a deceased taxpayer, a Form 56, "Notice Concerning Fiduciary Relationship," should be filed by the executor, personal representative or administrator if one has been appointed and is responsible for disposition of the matter under consideration. Internal Revenue Service officials may require the submission of a short-form certificate (or authenticated copy of letters testamentary or letters of administration) showing that such authority is in full force and effect at the time the Form 56, "Notice Concerning Fiduciary Relationship," is filed.

(ii) *Testamentary trustee(s).*—In the event that a trustee is acting under the provisions of the will, a Form 56, "Notice Concerning Fiduciary Relationship," should be filed by the trustee, unless the executor, personal representative or administrator has not been discharged and is responsible for disposition of the matter. Internal Revenue Service officials may require either the submission of evidence of the discharge of the executor and appointment of the trustee or other appropriate evidence of the authority of the trustee.

(iii) *Residuary legatee(s).*—If no executor, administrator, or trustee named under the will is acting or responsible for disposition of the matter and the estate has been distributed to the residuary legatee(s), a Form 56, "Notice Concerning Fiduciary Relationship," should be filed by the residuary legatee(s). Internal Revenue Service officials may require the submission of a statement from the court certifying that no executor, administrator, or trustee named under the will is acting or responsible for disposition of the matter, naming the residuary legatee(s), and indicating the proper share to which each is entitled.

(iv) *Distributee(s).*—In the event that the decedent died intestate and the administrator has been discharged and is not responsible for disposition of the matter (or none was ever appointed), a Form 56, "Notice Concerning Fiduciary Relationship," should be filed by the distributee(s). Internal Revenue Service officials may require the submission of evidence of the discharge of the administrator (if one had been appointed) and evidence that the administrator is not responsible for disposition of the matter. It also may require a statement(s) signed under penalty of perjury (and such other appropriate evidence as can be produced) to show the relationship of the individual(s) who sign the Form 56, "Notice Concerning Fiduciary Relationship," to the decedent and the right of each signer to the respective shares of the assets claimed under the law of the domicile of the decedent.

(4) *Taxpayer for whom a guardian or other fiduciary has been appointed.*—In the case of a taxpayer for whom a guardian or other fiduciary has been appointed by a court of record, a Form 56, "Notice Concerning Fiduciary Relationship," should be filed by the fiduciary. Internal Revenue Service officials may require the submission of a court certificate or court order showing that the individual who executes the Form 56, "Notice Concerning Fiduciary Relationship," has been appointed and that his/her appointment has not been terminated.

(5) *Taxpayer who has appointed a trustee.*—In the case of a taxpayer who has appointed a trustee, a Form 56, "Notice Concerning Fiduciary Relationship," should be filed by the trustee. If there is more than one trustee appointed, all should join unless it is shown that fewer than all have authority to act. Internal Revenue Service officials may require the submission of documentary evidence of the authority of the trustee to act. Such evidence may be either a copy of a properly executed trust instrument or a certified copy of extracts from the trust instruments, showing—

(i) The date of the instrument;

(ii) That it is or is not of record in any court;

(iii) The names of the beneficiaries;

(iv) The appointment of the trustee, the authority granted, and other information as may be necessary to show that such authority extends to Federal tax matters; and

(v) That the trust has not been terminated and the trustee appointed therein is still legally acting as such.

In the event that the trustee appointed in the original trust instrument has been replaced by another trustee, documentary evidence of the appointment of the new trustee must be submitted.

(e) *Commissioner's authority to substitute other requirements for power of attorney.*—Upon application of a taxpayer or a recognized representative,

Reg. §601.503(e)

the Commissioner of Internal Revenue may substitute a requirement(s) other than provided herein for a power of attorney as evidence of the authority of the representative.

[Reg. § 601.504]

§ 601.504. Requirements for filing power of attorney.—(a) *Situations in which a power of attorney is required.*—Except as otherwise provided in § 601.504(b), a power of attorney is required by the Internal Revenue Service when the taxpayer wishes to authorize a recognized representative to perform one or more of the following acts on behalf of the taxpayer—

(1) *Representation.*—(See § § 601.501(b)(10) and 601.501(b)(13).)

(2) *Waiver.*—Offer and/or execution of either (i) a waiver of restriction on assessment or collection of a deficiency in tax, or (ii) a waiver of notice of disallowance of a claim for credit or refund.

(3) *Consent.*—Execution of a consent to extend the statutory period for assessment or collection of a tax.

(4) *Closing agreement.*—Execution of a closing agreement under the provisions of the Internal Revenue Code and the regulations thereunder.

(5) *Check drawn on the United States Treasury.*—The authority to receive (but not endorse or collect) a check drawn on the United States Treasury must be specifically granted in a power of attorney. (The endorsement and payment of a check drawn on the United States Treasury are governed by Treasury Department Circular No. 21, as amended, 31 CFR part 240. Endorsement and payment of such check by any person other than the payee must be made under one of the special types of powers of attorney prescribed by Circular No. 21, 31 CFR Part 240. For restrictions on the assignment of claims, see Revised Statute section 3477, as amended (31 U.S.C. 3727).)

(6) *Signing tax returns.*—The filing of a power of attorney does not authorize the recognized representative to sign a tax return on behalf of the taxpayer unless such act is both—

(i) permitted under the Internal Revenue Code and the regulations thereunder (e.g., the authority to sign income tax returns is governed by the provisions of § 1.6012-1(a)(5) of the Income Tax Regulations); and

(ii) specifically authorized in the power of attorney.

(b) *Situations in which a power of attorney is not required.*—(1) *Disclosure of confidential tax information.*—The submission of a tax information authorization to request a disclosure of confidential tax information does not constitute practice before the Internal Revenue Service. (Such procedure is governed by the provisions of § 6103 of the Internal Revenue Code and the regulations thereunder.) Nevertheless, if a power of attorney is properly filed, the recognized representative also is authorized to receive and/or inspect confidential tax information concerning the matter(s) specified (provided the power of attorney places no limitations upon such disclosure).

(2) *Estate matter.*—A power of attorney is not required at a conference concerning an estate tax matter if the individual seeking to act as a recognized representative presents satisfactory evidence to Internal Revenue Service officials that he/she is—

(i) an individual described in § 601.502(b); and

(ii) the attorney of record for the executor, personal representative, or administrator before the court where the will is probated or the estate is administered.

(3) *Bankruptcy matters.*—A power of attorney is not required in the case of a trustee, receiver, or an attorney (designated to represent a trustee, receiver, or debtor in possession) appointed by a court having jurisdiction over a debtor. In such a case, Internal Revenue Service officials may require the submission of a certificate from the court having jurisdiction over the debtor showing the appointment and qualification of the trustee, receiver, or attorney and that his/her authority has not been terminated. In cases pending before a court of the United States (e.g., U.S. District Court or U.S. Bankruptcy Court), an authenticated copy of the order approving the bond of the trustee, receiver, or attorney will meet this requirement.

(c) *Administrative requirements of filing.*—(1) *General.*—Except as provided in this section, a power of attorney (including the declaration of representative and any other required statement(s)) must be filed in each office of the Internal Revenue Service in which the recognized representative desires to perform one or more of the acts described in § 601.504(a).

(2) *Regional offices.*—If a power of attorney (including the declaration of representative and any other required statement(s)) is filed with the office of a district director or with a service center which has the matter under consideration,

it is not necessary to file a copy with the office of a regional commissioner which subsequently has the matter under consideration unless requested.

(3) *National Office.*—In case of a request for a ruling or other matter to be considered in the National Office, a power of attorney, including the declaration of representative and any other required statement(s), must be submitted with each request or matter.

(4) *Copy of power of attorney.*—The Internal Revenue Service will accept either the original or a copy of a power of attorney. A copy of a power of attorney received by facsimile transmission (FAX) also will be accepted.

(d) *Practice by correspondence.*—If an individual desires to represent a taxpayer through correspondence with the Internal Revenue Service, such individual must submit a power of attorney, including the declaration of representative and any other required statement(s), even though no personal appearance is contemplated.

[Reg. § 601.505]

§ 601.505. Revocation, change in representation and substitution or delegation of representative.—(a) *By the taxpayer.*—(1) *New power of attorney filed.*—A new power of attorney revokes a prior power of attorney if it is granted by the taxpayer to another recognized representative with respect to the same matter. However, a new power of attorney does not revoke a prior power of attorney if it contains a clause stating that it does not revoke such prior power of attorney and there is attached to the new power of attorney either—

(i) a copy of the unrevoked prior power of attorney; or

(ii) a statement signed by the taxpayer listing the name and address of each recognized representative authorized under the prior unrevoked power of attorney.

(2) *Statement of revocation filed.*—A taxpayer may revoke a power of attorney without authorizing a new representative by filing a statement of revocation with those offices of the Internal Revenue Service where the taxpayer has filed the power of attorney to be revoked. The statement of revocation must indicate that the authority of the first power of attorney is revoked and must be signed by the taxpayer. Also, the name and address of each recognized representative whose authority is revoked must be listed (or a copy of the power of attorney to be revoked must be attached).

(b) *By the recognized representative.*—(1) *Revocation of power of attorney.*—A recognized representative may withdraw from representation in a matter in which a power of attorney has been filed by filing a statement with those offices of the Internal Revenue Service where the power of attorney to be revoked was filed. The statement must be signed by the representative and must identify the name and address of the taxpayer(s) and the matter(s) from which the representative is withdrawing.

(2) *Substitution or delegation of recognized representative.*—Any recognized representative appointed in a power of attorney may substitute or delegate authority under the power of attorney to another recognized representative if substitution or delegation is specifically permitted under the power of attorney. Unless otherwise provided in the power of attorney, a recognized representative may make a substitution or delegation without the consent of any other recognized representative appointed to represent the taxpayer in the samematter. A substitution or delegation is effected by filing the following items with offices of the Internal Revenue Service where the power of attorney has been filed—

(i) *Notice of substitution or delegation.*—A Notice of Substitution or Delegation is a statement signed by the recognized representative appointed under the power of attorney. The statement must contain the name and mailing address of the new recognized representative and, if more than one individual is to represent the taxpayer in the matter, a designation of which recognized representative is to receive notices and other written communications;

(ii) *Declaration of representative.*—A written declaration which is made by the new representative as required by § 601.502(c); and

(iii) *Power of attorney.*—A power of attorney which specifically authorizes the substitution or delegation.

An employee of a recognized representative may not be substituted for his/her employer with respect to the representation of a taxpayer before the Internal Revenue Service unless the employee is a recognized representative in his/her own capacity under the provisions of § 601.502(b). However, even if such employee is not a recognized representative in his/her own capacity under the provisions of § 601.502(b), that individual may be authorized by the taxpayer under a tax information authorization to receive and/or inspect confidential tax information under the provisions of section 6103 of the Internal Revenue Code and the regulations thereunder.

[Reg. § 601.506]

§ 601.506. Notices to be given to recognized representative; direct contact with taxpayer; delivery of a check drawn on the United States Treasury to recognized representative.— (a) *General.*—Any notice or other written communication (or a copy thereof) required or permitted to be given to a taxpayer in any matter before the Internal Revenue Service must be given to the taxpayer and, unless restricted by the taxpayer, to the representative according to the following procedures—

(1) If the taxpayer designates more than one recognized representative to receive notices and other written communications, it will be the practice of the Internal Revenue Service to give copies of such to two (but not more than two) individuals so designated.

(2) In a case in which the taxpayer does not designate which recognized representative is to receive notices, it will be the practice of the Internal Revenue Service to give notices and other communications to the first recognized representative appointed on the power of attorney.

(3) Failure to give notice or other written communication to the recognized representative of a taxpayer will not affect the validity of any notice or other written communication delivered to a taxpayer.

Unless otherwise indicated in the document, a power of attorney other than Form 2848 will be presumed to grant the authority to receive notices or other written communication (or a copy thereof) required or permitted to be given to a taxpayer in any matter(s) before the Internal Revenue Service to which the power of attorney pertains.

(b) *Cases where taxpayer may be contacted directly.*—Where a recognized representative has unreasonably delayed or hindered an examination, collection or investigation by failing to furnish, after repeated request, nonprivileged information necessary to the examination, collection or investigation, the Internal Revenue Service employee conducting the examination, collection or investigation may request the permission of his/her immediate supervisor to contact the taxpayer directly for such information.

(1) *Procedure.*—If such permission is granted, the case file will be documented with sufficient facts to show how the examination,

collection or investigation was being delayed or hindered. Written notice of such permission, briefly stating the reason why it was granted, will be given to both the recognized representative and the taxpayer together with a request of the taxpayer to supply such nonprivileged information. (See 7521(c) of the Internal Revenue Code and the regulations thereunder.)

(2) *Effect of direct notification.*—Permission to by-pass a recognized representative and contact a taxpayer directly does not automatically disqualify an individual to act as the recognized representative of a taxpayer in a matter. However, such information may be referred to the Director of Practice for possible disciplinary proceedings under Circular No. 230, 31 CFR Part 10.

(c) *Delivery of a check drawn on the United States Treasury.*—(1) *General.*—A check drawn on the United States Treasury (e.g., a check in payment of refund of internal revenue taxes, penalties, or interest, see § 601.504(a)(5)) will be mailed to the recognized representative of a taxpayer provided that a power of attorney is filed containing specific authorization for this to be done.

(2) *Address of recognized representative.*—The check will be mailed to the address of the recognized representative listed on the power of attorney unless such recognized representative notifies the Internal Revenue Service in writing that his/her mailing address has been changed.

(3) *Authorization of more than one recognized representative.*—In the event a power of attorney authorizes more than one recognized representative to receive a check on the taxpayer's behalf, and such representatives have different addresses, the Internal Revenue Service will mail the check directly to the taxpayer, unless a statement (signed by all of the recognized representatives so authorized) is submitted which indicates the address to which the check is to be mailed.

(4) *Cases in litigation.*—The provisions of § 601.506(c) concerning the issuance of a tax refund do not apply to the issuance of a check in payment of claims which have been either reduced to judgment or settled in the course (or as a result) of litigation.

(d) *Centralized Authorization File (CAF) system.*—(1) *Information recorded onto the CAF system.*—Information from both powers of attorney and tax information authorizations is recorded onto the CAF system. Such information enables Internal Revenue Service personnel who do not have access to the actual power of attorney or tax information authorizations to—

(i) determine whether a recognized representative or an appointee is authorized by a taxpayer to receive and/or inspect confidential tax information;

(ii) determine, in the case of a recognized representative, whether that representative is authorized to perform the acts set forth in § 601.504(a); and

(iii) send copies of computer generated notices and communications to an appointee or recognized representative so authorized by the taxpayer.

(2) *CAF number.*—A Centralized Authorization File (CAF) number generally will be issued to—

(i) a recognized representative who files a power of attorney and a written declaration of representative; or

(ii) an appointee authorized under a tax information authorization.

The issuance of a CAF number does not indicate that a person is either recognized or authorized to practice before the Internal Revenue Service. Such determination is made under the provisions of Circular No. 230, 31 CFR Part 10. The purpose of the CAF number is to facilitate the processing of a power of attorney or a tax information authorization submitted by a recognized representative or an appointee. A recognized representative or an appointee should include the same CAF number on every power of attorney or tax information authorization filed. However, because the CAF number is not a substantive requirement (i.e., as listed in § 601.503(a)), a tax information authorization or power of attorney which does not include such number will not be rejected based on the absence of a CAF number.

(3) *Tax matters recorded on CAF.*—Although a power of attorney or tax information authorization may be filed in all matters under the jurisdiction of the Internal Revenue Service, only those documents which meet each of the following criteria will be recorded onto the CAF system—

(i) *Specific tax period.*—Only documents which concern a matter(s) relating to a specific tax period will be recorded onto the CAF system. A power of attorney or tax information authorization filed in a matter unrelated to a specific period (e.g., the 100% penalty for failure to pay over withholding taxes imposed by § 6672 of the Internal Revenue Code, applications for an employer identification number, and requests for a private letter ruling request pertaining to a pro-

posed transaction) cannot be recorded onto the CAF system.

(ii) *Future three-year limitation.*—Only documents which concern a tax period that ends no later than three years after the date on a power of attorney is received by the Internal Revenue Service will be recorded onto the CAF system. For example, a power of attorney received by the Internal Revenue Service on August 1, 1990, which indicates that the authorization applies to Form 941 for the quarters ended December 31, 1990 through December 31, 2000, will be recorded onto the CAF system for the applicable tax periods which end no later than July 31, 1993 (i.e., three years after the date of receipt by the Internal Revenue Service).

(iii) *Documents for prior tax periods.*—Documents which concern any tax period which has ended prior to the date on which a power of attorney is received by the Internal Revenue Service will be recorded onto the CAF system provided that matters concerning such years are under consideration by the Internal Revenue Service.

(iv) *Limitation on representatives recorded onto the CAF system.*—No more than three representatives appointed under a power of attorney or three persons designated under a tax information authorization will be recorded onto the CAF system. If more than three representatives are appointed under a power of attorney or more than three persons designated under a tax information authorization, only the first three names will be recorded onto the CAF system.

The fact that a power of attorney or tax information authorization cannot be recorded onto the CAF system is not determinative of the (current or future) validity of such document. (For example, documents which concern tax periods that end more than three years from the date of receipt by the IRS are not invalid for the period(s) not recorded onto the CAF system, but can be resubmitted at a later date.)

[Reg. § 601.507]

§ 601.507. Evidence required to substantiate facts alleged by a recognized representative.— The Internal Revenue Service may require a recognized representative to submit all evidence, except that of a supplementary or incidental character, over a declaration (signed under penalty of perjury) that the recognized representative prepared such submission and that the facts contained therein are true. In any case in which a recognized representative is unable or unwilling to declare his/her own knowledge that the facts are true and correct, the Internal Revenue Service may require the taxpayer to make such a declaration under penalty of perjury.

[Reg. §601.508]

§601.508. Dispute between recognized representatives of a taxpayer.—Where there is a dispute between two or more recognized representatives concerning who is entitled to represent a taxpayer in a matter pending before the Internal Revenue Service (or to receive a check drawn on the United States Treasury), the Internal Revenue Service will not recognize any party. However, if the contesting recognized representatives designate one or more of their number under the terms of an agreement signed by all, the Internal Revenue Service will recognize such designated recognized representatives upon receipt of a copy of such agreement according to the terms of the power of attorney.

[Reg. §601.509]

§601.509. Power of attorney not required in cases docketed in the Tax Court of the United States.—The petitioner and the Commissioner of Internal Revenue stand in the position of parties litigant before a judicial body in a case docketed in the Tax Court of the United States. The Tax Court has its own rules of practice and procedure and its own rules respecting admission to practice before it. Accordingly, a power of attorney is not required to be submitted by an attorney of record in a case which is docketed in the Tax Court. Correspondence in connection with cases docketed in the Tax Court will be addressed to counsel of record before the Court. However, a power of attorney is required to be submitted by an individual other than the attorney of record in any matter before the Internal Revenue Service concerning a docketed case.

Subpart F—Rules, Regulations, and Forms

[Reg. §601.601]

§601.601. Rules and regulations.— (a) *Formulation.*—(1) Internal Revenue rules take various forms. The most important rules are issued as regulations and Treasury decisions prescribed by the Commissioner and approved by the Secretary or his delegate. Other rules may be issued over the signature of the Commissioner or the signature of any other official to whom authority has been delegated. Regulations and Treasury decisions are prepared in the Office of the Chief Counsel. After approval by the Commissioner, regulations and Treasury decisions are forwarded to the Secretary or his delegate for further consideration and final approval.

(2) Where required by 5 U.S.C. 553 and in such other instances as may be desirable, the Commissioner publishes in the Federal Register general notice of proposed rules (unless all persons subject thereto are named and either personally served or otherwise have actual notice thereof in accordance with law). This notice includes (i) a statement of the time, place, and nature of public rule-making proceedings; (ii) reference to the authority under which the rule is proposed; and (iii) either the terms or substance of the proposed rule or a description of the subjects and issues involved.

(3)(i) This subparagraph shall apply where the rules of this subparagraph are incorporated by reference in a notice of hearing with respect to a notice of proposed rule making.

(ii) A person wishing to make oral comments at a public hearing to which this subparagraph applies shall file his written comments within the time prescribed by the notice of proposed rule making (including any extensions thereof) and submit the outline referred to in subdivision (iii) of this subparagraph within the time prescribed by the notice of hearing. In lieu of the reading of a prepared statement at the hearing, such person's oral comments shall ordinarily be limited to a discussion of matters relating to such written comments and to questions and answers in connection therewith. However, the oral comments shall not be merely a restatement of matters the person has submitted in writing. Persons making oral comments should be prepared to answer questions not only on the topics listed inhis outline but also in connection with the matters relating to his written comments. Except as provided in paragraph (b) of this section, in order to be assured of the availability of copies of such written comments or outlines on or before the beginning of such hearing, any person who desires such copies should make such a request within the time prescribed in the notice of hearing and shall agree to pay reasonable costs for copying. Persons who make such a request after the time prescribed in the notice of hearing will be furnished copies as soon as they are available, but it may not be possible to furnish the copies on or before the beginning of the hearing. Except as provided in the preceding sentences, copies of written comments regarding the rules proposed shall not be made available at the hearing.

(iii) A person who wishes to be assured of being heard shall submit, within the time prescribed in the notice of hearing, an outline of the topics he or she wishes to discuss, and the time he or she wishes to devote to each topic. An agenda will then be prepared containing the order of presentation of oral comments and the time allotted to such presentation. A period of 10 minutes will be the time allotted to each person for making his or her oral comments.

(iv) At the conclusion of the presentations of comments of persons listed in the agenda, to the extent time permits, other persons may be permitted to present oral comments provided they have notified, either the Commissioner of Internal Revenue (Attention: CC:LR:T) before the hearing, or the representative of the Internal Revenue Service stationed at the entrance to the hearing room at or before commencement of the hearing, of their desire to be heard.

(v) In the case of unusual circumstances or for good cause shown, the application of rules contained in this subparagraph, including the 10-minute rule in subdivision (iii), above, may be waived.

(vi) To the extent resources permit, the public hearings to which this subparagraph applies may be transcribed.

(b) *Comments on proposed rules.*—(1) *In general.*—Interested persons are privileged to submit any data, views, or arguments in response to a notice of proposed rule making published pursuant to 5 U.S.C. 553. Further, procedures are provided in paragraph (d)(9) of § 601.702 for members of the public to inspect and to obtain copies of written comments submitted in response to such notices. Designations of material as confidential or not to be disclosed, contained in such comments, will not be accepted. Thus, a person submitting written comments in response to a notice of proposed rule making should not include therein material that he considers to be confidential or inappropriate for disclosure to the public. It will be presumed by the Internal Revenue Service that every written comment submitted to it in response to a notice of proposed rule making is intended by the person submitting it to be subject in its entirety to public inspection and copying in accordance with the procedures of paragraph (d)(9) of § 601.702. The name of any person requesting a public hearing and hearing outlines described in paragraph (a)(3)(iii) of this section are not exempt from disclosure.

(2) *Effective date.*—This paragraph (b) applies only to comments submitted in response to notices of proposed rule making of the Internal Revenue Service published in the Federal Register after June 5, 1974.

(c) *Petition to change rules.*—Interested persons are privileged to petition for the issuance, amendment, or repeal of a rule. A petition for the issuance of a rule should identify the section or sections of law involved; and a petition for the amendment or repeal of a rule should set forth the section or sections of the regulations involved. The petition should also set forth the reasons for the requested action. Such petitions will be given careful consideration and the petitioner will be advised of the action taken thereon. Petitions should be addressed to the Commissioner of Internal Revenue, Attention: CC:LR:T, Washington, D.C. 20224. However, in the case of petitions to amend the regulations pursuant to subsection (c)(4)(A)(viii) or (5)(A)(i) of section 23 or former section 44C, follow the procedure outlined in paragraph (a) of § 1.23-6.

(d) *Publication of rules and regulations.*—(1) *General.*—All internal revenue regulations and Treasury decisions are published in the FEDERAL REGISTER and in the Code of Federal Regulations. See paragraph (a) of § 601.702. The Treasury decisions are also published in the weekly Internal Revenue Bulletin and the semiannual Cumulative Bulletin. The Internal Revenue Bulletin is the authoritative instrument of the Commissioner for the announcement of official rulings, decisions, opinions, and procedures, and for the publication of Treasury decisions, Executive orders, tax conventions, legislation, court decisions, and other items pertaining to internal revenue matters. It is the policy of the Internal Revenue Service to publish in the Bulletin all substantive and procedural rulings of importance or general interest, the publication of which is considered necessary to promote a uniform application of the laws administered by the Service. Procedures set forth in Revenue Procedures published in the Bulletinwhich are of general applicability and which have continuing force and effect are incorporated as amendments to the Statement of Procedural Rules. It is also the policy to publish in the Bulletin all rulings which revoke, modify, amend, or affect any published ruling. Rules relating solely to matters of internal practices and procedures are not published; however, statements of internal practices and procedures affecting rights or duties of taxpayers, or industry regulation, which appear in internal management documents, are published

Reg. § 601.601(d)(1)

in the Bulletin. No unpublished ruling or decision will be relied on, used, or cited by any officer or employee of the Internal Revenue Service as a precedent in the disposition of other cases.

(2) *Objectives and standards for publication of Revenue Rulings and Revenue Procedures in the Internal Revenue Bulletin.*—(i)*(a)* A "Revenue Ruling" is an official interpretation by the Service that has been published in the Internal Revenue Bulletin. Revenue Rulings are issued only by the National Office and are published for the information and guidance of taxpayers, Internal Revenue Service officials, and others concerned.

(b) A "Revenue Procedure" is a statement of procedure that affects the rights or duties of taxpayers or other members of the public under the Code and related statutes or information that, although not necessarily affecting the rights and duties of the public, should be a matter of public knowledge.

(ii)*(a)* The Internal Revenue Bulletin is the authoritative instrument of the Commissioner of Internal Revenue for the publication of official rulings and procedures of the Internal Revenue Service, including all rulings and statements of procedure which supersede, revoke, modify, amend, or affect any previously published ruling or procedure. The Service also announces in the Bulletin the Commissioner's acquiescences and non-acquiescences in decisions of the United States Tax Court (other than decisions in memorandum opinions), and publishes Treasury decisions, Executive orders, tax conventions, legislation, court decisions, and other items considered to be of general interest. The Assistant Commissioner (Technical) administers the Bulletin program.

(b) The Bulletin is published weekly. In order to provide a permanent reference source, the contents of the Bulletin are consolidated semiannually into an indexed Cumulative Bulletin. The Bulletin Index-Digest System provides a research and reference guide to matters appearing in the Cumulative Bulletins. These materials are sold by the Superintendent of Documents, U.S. Government Printing Office, Washington, D.C. 20402.

(iii) The purpose of publishing revenue rulings and revenue procedures in the Internal Revenue Bulletin is to promote correct and uniform application of the tax laws by Internal Revenue Service employees and to assist taxpayers in attaining maximum voluntary compliance by informing Service personnel and the public of National Office interpretations of the internal revenue laws, related statutes, treaties, regulations, and statements of Service procedures affecting the rights and duties of taxpayers. Therefore, issues and answers involving substantive tax law under the jurisdiction of the Internal Revenue Service will be published in the Internal Revenue Bulletin, except those involving:

(a) Issues answered by statute, treaty, or regulations;

(b) Issues answered by rulings, opinions, or court decisions previously published in the Bulletin;

(c) Issues that are of insufficient importance or interest to warrant publication;

(d) Determinations of fact rather than interpretations of law;

(e) Informers and informers' rewards; or

(f) Disclosure of secret formulas, processes, business practices, and similar information.

Procedures affecting taxpayers' rights or duties that relate to matters under the jurisdiction of the Service will be published in the Bulletin.

(iv) [Reserved].

(v)*(a)* Rulings and other communications involving substantive tax law published in the Bulletin are published in the form of Revenue Rulings. The conclusions expressed in Revenue Rulings will be directly responsive to and limited in scope by the pivotal facts stated in the revenue ruling. Revenue Rulings arise from various sources, including rulings to taxpayers, technical advice to district offices, studies undertaken by the Office of the Assistant Commissioner (Technical), court decisions, suggestions from tax practitioner groups, publications, etc.

(b) It will be the practice of the Service to publish as much of the ruling or communication as is necessary for an understanding of the position stated. However, in order to prevent unwarranted invasions of personal privacy and to comply with statutory provisions, such as 18 U.S.C. 1905 and 26 U.S.C. 7213, dealing with disclosure of information obtained from members of the public, identifying details, including thenames and addresses of persons involved, and information of a confidential nature are deleted from the ruling.

(c) Revenue Rulings, other than those relating to the qualification of pension, annuity, profit-sharing, stock bonus, and bond purchase plans, apply retroactively unless the Revenue Ruling includes a specific statement indicating, under the authority of section 7805(b) of the

Internal Revenue Code of 1954, the extent to which it is to be applied without retroactive effect. Where Revenue Rulings revoke or modify rulings previously published in the Bulletin the authority of section 7805(b) of the Code ordinarily is invoked to provide that the new rulings will not be applied retroactively to the extent that the new rulings have adverse tax consequences to taxpayers. Section 7805(b) of the Code provides that the Secretary of the Treasury or his delegate may prescribe the extent to which any ruling is to be applied without retroactive effect. The exercise of this authority requires an affirmative action. For the effect of Revenue Rulings on determination letters and opinion letters issued with respect to the qualification of pension, annuity, profit-sharing, stock bonus, and bond purchase plans, see paragraph (o) of §601.201.

(d) Revenue Rulings published in the Bulletin do not have the force and effect of Treasury Department Regulations (including Treasury decisions), but are published to provide precedents to be used in the disposition of other cases, and may be cited and relied upon for that purpose. No unpublished ruling or decision will be relied on, used, or cited, by an officer or employee of the Service as a precedent in the disposition of other cases.

(e) Taxpayers generally may rely upon Revenue Rulings published in the Bulletin in determining the tax treatment of their own transactions and need not request specific rulings applying the principles of a published Revenue Ruling to the facts of their particular cases. However, since each Revenue Ruling represents the conclusion of the Service as to the application of the law to the entire state of facts involved, taxpayers, Service personnel, and others concerned are cautioned against reaching the same conclusion in other cases unless the facts and circumstances are substantially the same. They should consider the effect of subsequent legislation, regulations, court decisions, and revenue rulings.

(f) Comments and suggestions from taxpayers or taxpayer groups on Revenue Rulings being prepared for publication in the Bulletin may be solicited, if justified by special circumstances. Conferences on Revenue Rulings being prepared for publication will not be granted except where the Service determines that such action is justified by special circumstances.

(vi) Statements of procedures which affect the rights or duties of taxpayers or other members of the public under the Code and related statutes will be published in the Bulletin in the form of Revenue Procedures. Revenue Procedures usually reflect the contents of internal management documents, but, where appropriate, they are also published to announce practices and procedures for guidance of the public. It is Service practice to publish as much of the internal management document or communication as is necessary for an understanding of the procedure. Revenue Procedures may also be based on internal management documents which should be a matter of public knowledge even though not necessarily affecting the rights or duties of the public. When publication of the substance of a Revenue Procedure in the Federal Register is required pursuant to 5 U.S.C. 552, it will usually be accomplished by an amendment of the Statement of Procedural Rules (26 CFR Part 601).

(vii)(a) The Assistant Commissioner (Technical) is responsible for administering the system for the publication of Revenue Rulings and Revenue Procedures in the Bulletin, including the standards for style and format.

(b) In accordance with the standards set forth in subdivision (iv) of this subparagraph, each Assistant Commissioner is responsible for the preparation and appropriate referral for publication of Revenue Rulings reflecting interpretations of substantive tax law made by his office and communicated in writing to taxpayers or field offices. In this connection, the Chief Counsel is responsible for the referral to the appropriate Assistant Commissioner, for consideration for publication as Revenue Rulings, of interpretations of substantive tax law made by his Office.

(c) In accordance with the standards set forth in subdivision (iv) of this subparagraph, each Assistant Commissioner and the Chief Counsel is responsible for determining whether procedures established by any office under his jurisdiction should be published as Revenue Procedures and for the initiation, content, and appropriate referral for publication of such Revenue Procedures.

(e) *Foreign tax law.*—(1) The Service will accept the interpretation placed by a foreign tax convention country on its revenue laws which do not affect the tax convention. However, when such interpretation conflicts with a provision in the tax convention, reconsideration of that interpretation may be requested.

(2) Conferences in the National Office of the Service will be granted to representatives of American firms doing business abroad and of American citizens residing abroad, in order to discuss with them foreign tax matters with re-

spect to those countries with which we have tax treaties in effect.

[Reg. § 601.602]

§ 601.602. Tax forms and instructions.—(a) *Tax return forms and instructions.*—The Internal Revenue Service develops forms and instructions that explain the requirements of the Internal Revenue Code and regulations. The Service distributes the forms and instructions to help taxpayers comply with the law. The tax system is based on voluntary compliance, and the taxpayers complete and return the forms with payment of any tax owed.

(b) *Other forms and instructions.*—In addition to tax return forms, the Internal Revenue Service furnishes the public copies of other forms and instructions developed for use in complying with the laws and regulations. These forms and instructions lead the taxpayer step-by-step through data needed to accurately report information required by law.

(c) *Where to get forms and instructions.*—The Internal Revenue Service mails tax return forms to taxpayers who have previously filed returns. However, taxpayers can call or write to district directors or directors of service centers for copies of any forms they need. These forms are described in Publication 676 *Catalog of Federal Tax Forms, Form Letters, and Notices,* which the public can buy from the Superintendent of Documents, U.S. Government Printing Office, Washington, D.C. 20402.

Subpart G—Records

[Reg. § 601.701]

§ 601.701. Publicity of information.— (a) *General.*—Section 552 of title 5 of the United States Code, as amended, prescribes rules regarding the publicizing of information by Federal agencies. Generally, such section divides agency information into three major categories and provides methods by which each category is to be made available to the public. The three major categories, for which the disclosure requirements of the Internal Revenue Service are set forth in § 601.702, are as follows—

(1) Information required to be published in the Federal Register;

(2) Information required to be made available for public inspection and copying or, in the alternative, to be published and offered for sale; and

(3) Information required to be made available to any member of the public upon specific request.

The provisions of section 552 (Freedom of Information Act) are intended to assure the right of the public to information. Section 552 is not authority to withhold information from Congress. Subject only to the exemptions set forth in paragraph (b) of this section, the public generally or any member thereof shall be afforded access to information or records in the possession of the Internal Revenue Service. Such access shall be governed by the regulations in this subpart and those in 31 CFR Part 1 (relating to disclosure of Treasury Department records).

(b) *Exemptions.*—(1) *In general.*—Under 5 U.S.C. 552(b), the disclosure requirements of section 552(a) do not apply to certain matters which are:

(i) (A) Specifically authorized under criteria established by an Executive order to be kept secret in the interest of the national defense or foreign policy and (B) are in fact properly classified pursuant to such Executive order;

(ii) Related solely to the internal personnel rules and practices of the Internal Revenue Service which communicate to Internal Revenue Service personnel information or instructions relating to (A) enforcement tolerances and criteria with respect to the allocation of resources, (B) criteria for determining whether or not a case merits further enforcement action, (C) enforcement tactics, including but not limited to investigative techniques, internal security information, protection of identities of confidential sources of information used by the Service, and techniques for evaluating, litigating, and negotiating cases of possible violations of civil or criminal laws, or (D) use of parking facilities, regulation of lunch hours, statements of policy as to sick leave and the like;

(iii) Specifically exempted from disclosure by statute (other than 5 U.S.C. 552b), provided that such statute (A) requires that the matters be withheld from the public in such a manner as to leave no discretion on the issue, or (B) establishes particular criteria for withholding or refers to particular types of matters to be withheld (e.g., I.R.C. sections 6103, 6110, and 4424);

(iv) Trade secrets and commercial or financial information obtained from a person and privileged or confidential;

(v) Interagency or intraagency memorandums or letters which would not routinely beavailable by law to a party other than an agency in litigation with the agency, including communications (such as internal drafts, memorandums between officials or agencies, opinions and interpretations prepared by agency staff personnel or consultants for the use of the agency, and records of the deliberations of the agency or staff groups) (A) which the Internal Revenue Service has received from another agency, (B) which the Internal Revenue Service generates in the process of issuing an order, decision, ruling or regulation, drafting proposed legislation, or otherwise carrying out its functions and responsibilities or (C) which is the attorney work product of the Office of the Chief Counsel or is generated by that Office as attorney for the Internal Revenue Service;

(vi) Personnel and medical files and similar files the disclosure of which would constitute a clearly unwarranted invasion of personal privacy;

(vii) Investigatory records compiled for law enforcement purposes, including records prepared in connection with civil, criminal or administrative Government litigation and adjudicative proceedings, but only to the extent that the production of such records would (A) interfere with enforcement proceedings, (B) deprive a person of a right to a fair trial or an impartial adjudication, (C) constitute an unwarranted invasion of personal privacy, (D) disclose the identity of a confidential source and in the case of a record compiled by a criminal investigation, or by an agency conducting a lawful national security intelligence investigation, confidential information furnished only by the confidential source, (E) disclose investigative techniques and procedures, or (F) endanger the life or physical safety of law enforcement personnel;

(viii) Contained in or related to examination, operating, or condition reports prepared by, on behalf of, or for the use of an agency responsible for the regulation or supervision of financial institutions; or

(ix) Geological and geophysical information and data, including maps, concerning wells.

(2) *Application of exemptions.*—Even though an exemption described in subparagraph (1) of this paragraph may be fully applicable to a matter in a particular case, the Internal Revenue Service may, if not precluded by law, elect under the circumstances of that case not to apply the exemption to such matter. The fact that the exemption is not applied by the Service in that particular case has no precedential significance as to the application of the exemption to such matter in other cases but is merely an indication that in the particular case involved the Service

finds no compelling necessity for applying the exemption to such matter.

(3) *Segregable portions of records.*—Any reasonably segregable portion of a record shall be provided to any person making a request for such record, after deletion of the portions which are exempt under 5 U.S.C. 552(b) (see paragraph (b)(1) of this section). The term "reasonably segregable portion" as used in this subparagraph means any portion of the record requested which is not exempt from disclosure under 5 U.S.C. 552(b), and which, after deletion of the exempt material, still conveys meaningful information which is not misleading.

[Reg. §601.702]

§601.702. Publication and public inspection.—
(a) *Publication in the Federal Register.*—(1) *Requirement.*—(i) Subject to the application of the exemptions and exclusions described in the Freedom of Information Act, 5 U.S.C. 552(b) and (c), and subject to the limitations provided in paragraph (a)(2) of this section, the IRS is required under 5 U.S.C. 552(a)(1), to state separately and publish currently in the FEDERAL REGISTER for the guidance of the public the following information—

(a) Descriptions of its central and field organization and the established places at which, the persons from whom, and the methods whereby, the public may obtain information, make submittals or requests, or obtain decisions, from the IRS;

(b) Statement of the general course and method by which its functions are channeled and determined, including the nature and requirements of all formal and informal procedures which are available;

(c) Rules of procedure, descriptions of forms available or the places at which forms may be obtained, and instructions as to the scope and contents of all papers, reports, or examinations;

(d) Substantive rules of general applicability adopted as authorized by law, and statements of general policy or interpretations of general applicability formulated and adopted by the IRS; and

(e) Each amendment, revision, or repeal of matters referred to in paragraphs (a)(1)(i)(a) through (d) of this section.

(ii) Pursuant to the foregoing requirements, the Commissioner publishes in the FEDERAL REGISTER from time to time a statement, which is not codified in this chapter, on the organization and functions of the IRS, and such amendments as are needed to keep the statement on a current basis. In addition, there are published inthe FEDERAL REGISTER the rules set forth in this Part 601 (Statement of Procedural Rules), such as those in paragraph E of this section, relating to conference and practice requirements of the IRS; the regulations in Part 301 of this chapter (Procedure and Administration Regulations); and the various substantive regulations under the Internal Revenue Code of 1986, such as the regulations in Part 1 of this chapter (Income Tax Regulations), in Part 20 of this chapter (Estate Tax Regulations) and, in Part 31 of this chapter (Employment Tax Regulations).

(2) *Limitations.*—(i) Incorporation by reference in the FEDERAL REGISTER.—Matter which is reasonably available to the class of persons affected thereby, whether in a private or public publication, shall be deemed published in the FEDERAL REGISTER for purposes of paragraph (a)(1) of this section when it is incorporated by reference therein with the approval of the Director of the Office of the FEDERAL REGISTER. The matter which is incorporated by reference must be set forth in the private or public publication substantially in its entirety and not merely summarized or printed as a synopsis. Matter, the location and scope of which are familiar to only a few persons having a special working knowledge of the activities of the IRS, may not be incorporated in the FEDERAL REGISTER by reference. Matter may be incorporated by reference in the FEDERAL REGISTER only pursuant to the provisions of 5 U.S.C. 552(a)(1) and 1 CFR Part 20.

(ii) Effect of failure to publish.—Except to the extent that a person has actual and timely notice of the terms of any matter referred to in paragraph (a)(1) of this section which is required to be published in the FEDERAL REGISTER such person is not required in any manner to resort to, or be adversely affected by, such matter if it is not so published or is not incorporated by reference therein pursuant to paragraph (a)(2)(i) of this section. Thus, for example, any such matter which imposes an obligation and which is not so published or incorporated by reference shall not adversely change or affect a person's rights.

(b) *Public inspection and copying.*—(1) *In general.*—(i) Subject to the application of the exemptions described in 5 U.S.C. 552(b) and the exclusions described in 5 U.S.C. 552(c), the IRS is required under 5 U.S.C. 552(a)(2) to make available for public inspection and copying or, in the alternative, to promptly publish and offer for sale the following information:

(a) Final opinions, including concurring and dissenting opinions, and orders, if such opinions and orders are made in the adjudication of cases;

(b) Those statements of policy and interpretations which have been adopted by the IRS but are not published in the Federal Register;

(c) Its administrative staff manuals and instructions to staff that affect a member of the public; and

(d) Copies of all records, regardless of form or format, which have been released to any person under 5 U.S.C. 552(a)(3) and which, because of the nature of their subject matter, the IRS determines have become or are likely to become the subject of subsequent requests for substantially the same records. The determination that records have become or may become the subject of subsequent requests shall be based on the following criteria:

(1) The subject matter is clearly of interest to the public at large or to special interest groups from which more than one request is expected to be received; or

(2) When more than four requests for substantially the same records have already been received.

(ii) The IRS is also required by 5 U.S.C. 552(a)(2) to maintain and make available for public inspection and copying current indexes identifying any matter described in paragraphs (b)(1)(i)(a) through (c) of this section which is issued, adopted, or promulgated after July 4, 1967, and which is required to be made available for public inspection or published. In addition, the IRS shall also promptly publish, quarterly or more frequently, and distribute (by sale or otherwise) copies of each index or supplements thereto unless it determines by order published in the Federal Register that the publication would be unnecessary and impracticable, in which case the IRS shall nonetheless provide copies of such indexes on request at a cost not to exceed the direct cost of duplication. No matter described in paragraphs (b)(1)(i)(a) through (c) of this section which is required by this section to be made available for public inspection or published may be relied upon, used, or cited as precedent by the IRS against a party other than an agency unless such party has actual and timely notice of the terms of such matter or unless the matter has been indexed and either made available for inspection or published, as provided by this paragraph (b). This paragraph (b) applies only to matters which have precedential significance. It does not apply, for example, to any ruling or advisory interpretation issued to a taxpayer or to a particular transaction or set of facts which applies only to that transaction or set of facts. Rulings, determination letters, technical advice memorandums, and Chief Counsel advice areopen to public inspection and copying pursuant to 26 U.S.C. 6110. This paragraph (b) does not apply to matters which have been made available pursuant to paragraph (a) of this section.

(iii) For records required to be made available for public inspection and copying pursuant to 5 U.S.C. 552(a)(2) and paragraphs (b)(1)(i)(a) through (d) of this section, which are created on or after November 1, 1996, the IRS shall make such records available on the Internet within one year after such records are created.

(iv) The IRS shall make the index referred to in paragraph (b)(1)(ii) of this section available on the Internet.

(2) *Deletion of identifying details.*—To prevent a clearly unwarranted invasion of personal privacy, the IRS shall, in accordance with 5 U.S.C. 552(a)(2), delete identifying details contained in any matter described in paragraphs (b)(1)(i)(a) through (d) of this section before making such matter available for inspection or publication. Such matters shall also be subject to any applicable exemption set forth in 5 U.S.C. 552(b). In every case where identifying details or other matters are so deleted, the justification for the deletion shall be explained in writing. The extent of such deletion shall be indicated on the portion of the record which is made available or published, unless including that indication would harm an interest protected by the exemption in 5 U.S.C. 552(b) under which the deletion is made. If technically feasible, the extent of the deletion shall be indicated at the place in the record where the deletion was made.

(3) *Freedom of Information Reading Room.*— (i) *In general.*—The Headquarters Disclosure Office of the IRS shall provide a reading room where the matters described in paragraphs (b)(1)(i)(a) through (d) of this section which are required to be made available for public inspection, and the current indexes to such matters, shall be made available to the public for inspection and copying. The Freedom of Information Reading Room shall contain other matters determined to be helpful for the guidance of the public, including a complete set of rules and regulations (except those pertaining to alcohol, tobacco, firearms, and explosives) contained in this title, any Internal Revenue matters which may be incorporated by reference in the Federal Register (but not a copy of the Federal Register so doing) pursuant to paragraph (a)(2)(i) of this section, a set of Cumulative Bulletins, and copies of various IRS publications. The public shall not be allowed to remove any record from the Freedom of Information Reading Room.

(ii) Location of Freedom of Information Reading Room.—The location of the Headquarters Disclosure Office Freedom of Information Reading Room is: IRS, 1111 Constitution Avenue, N.W., Room 1621, Washington, D.C.

(iii) Copying facilities.—The Headquarters Disclosure Office shall provide facilities whereby a person may obtain copies of material located on the shelves of the Freedom of Information Reading Room.

(c) *Specific requests for other records.*—(1) *In general.*—(i) Subject to the application of the exemptions described in 5 U.S.C. 552(b) and the exclusions described in 5 U.S.C. 552(c), the IRS shall, in conformance with 5 U.S.C. 552(a)(3), make reasonably described records available to a person making a request for such records which conforms in every respect with the rules and procedures set forth in this section. Any request or any appeal from the initial denial of a request that does not comply with the requirements set forth in this section shall not be considered subject to the time constraints of paragraphs (c)(9), (10), and (11) of this section, unless and until the request or appeal is amended to comply. The IRS shall promptly advise the requester in what respect the request or appeal is deficient so that it may be resubmitted or amended for consideration in accordance with this section. If a requester does not resubmit a perfected request or appeal within 35 days from the date of a communication from the IRS, the request or appeal file shall be closed. When the resubmitted request or appeal conforms with the requirements of this section, the time constraints of paragraphs (c)(9), (10), and (11) of this section shall begin.

(ii) Requests for the continuing production of records created or for records created after the date of receipt of the request shall not be honored.

(iii) Specific requests under paragraph (a) (3) for material described in paragraph (a) (2) (a) through (c) and which is in the Freedom of Information Reading Room shall not be honored.

(2) *Electronic format records.*—(i) The IRS shall provide the responsive record or records in the form or format requested if the record or records are readily reproducible by the IRS in that form or format. The IRS shall make reasonable efforts to maintain its records in forms or formats that are reproducible for the purpose of disclosure. For purposes of this paragraph, the

Reg. §601.702(c)(2)(i)

term readily reproducible means, with respect to electronic format, a record or records that can be downloaded or transferred intact to a floppy disk, computer disk (CD), tape, or other electronic medium using equipment currently in use by the office or offices processing the request. Even though some records may initially be readily reproducible, the need to segregate exempt fromnonexempt records may cause the releasable material to be not readily reproducible.

(ii) In responding to a request for records, the IRS shall make reasonable efforts to search for the records in electronic form or format, except where such efforts would significantly interfere with the operation of the agency's automated information system(s). For purposes of this paragraph (c), the term search means to locate, manually or by automated means, agency records for the purpose of identifying those records which are responsive to a request.

(iii) Searches for records maintained in electronic form or format may require the application of codes, queries, or other minor forms of programming to retrieve the requested records.

(3) *Requests for records not in control of the IRS.*—(i) Where the request is for a record which is determined to be in the possession or under the control of a constituent unit of the Department of the Treasury other than the IRS, the request for such record shall immediately be transferred to the appropriate constituent unit and the requester notified to that effect. Such referral shall not be deemed a denial of access within the meaning of these regulations. The constituent unit of the Department to which such referral is made shall treat such request as a new request addressed to it and the time limits for response set forth in paragraphs (c)(9) and (c)(10) of this section shall commence when the referral is received by the designated office or officer of the constituent unit. Where the request is for a record which is of a type that is not maintained by any constituent unit of the Department of the Treasury, the requester shall be so advised.

(ii) Where the record requested was created by another agency or constituent unit of the Department of the Treasury and a copy thereof is in the possession of the IRS, the IRS official to whom the request is delivered shall refer the request to the agency or constituent unit which originated the record for direct reply to the requester. The requester shall be informed of such referral. This referral shall not be considered a denial of access within the meaning of these regulations. Where the record is determined to be exempt from disclosure under 5 U.S.C. 552,

the referral need not be made, but the IRS shall inform the originating agency or constituent unit of its determination. Where notifying the requester of its referral may cause a harm to the originating agency or constituent unit which would enable the originating agency or constituent unit to withhold the record under 5 U.S.C. 552, then such referral need not be made. In both of these circumstances, the IRS official to whom the request is delivered shall process the request in accordance with the procedures set forth in this section.

(iii) When a request is received for a record created by the IRS (i.e., in its possession and control) that includes information originated by another agency or constituent unit of the Department of the Treasury, the record shall be referred to the originating agency or constituent unit for review, coordination, and concurrence prior to being released to a requester. The IRS official to whom the request is delivered may withhold the record without prior consultation with the originating agency or constituent unit.

(4) *Form of request.*—(i) Requesters are advised that only requests for records which fully comply with the requirements of this section can be processed in accordance with this section. Requesters shall be notified promptly in writing of any requirements which have not been met or any additional requirements to be met. Every effort shall be made to comply with the requests as written. The initial request for records must—

(a) Be made in writing and signed by the individual making the request;

(b) State that it is made pursuant to the Freedom of Information Act, 5 U.S.C. 552, or regulations thereunder;

(c) Be addressed to and mailed to the office of the IRS official who is responsible for the control of the records requested (see paragraph (h) of this section for the responsible officials and their addresses), regardless of where such records are maintained. Generally, requests for records pertaining to the requester, or other matters of local interest, should be directed to the office servicing the requester's geographic area of residence. Requests for records maintained in the Headquarters of the IRS and its National Office of Chief Counsel, concerning matters of nationwide applicability, such as published guidance (regulations and revenue rulings), program management, operations, or policies, should be directed to the Headquarters Disclosure Office. If the person making the request does not know the official responsible for the control of the records being requested, the person making the request may contact, by telephone or in writing, the disclosure office servicing the requester's geographic area of residence to ascertain the identity of the official having control of the records being requested so that the request can be addressed, and delivered, to the appropriate responsible official. Misdirected requests that otherwise satisfy the requirements of this section shall be immediately transferred to the appropriate responsible IRS official and the requester notified to that effect.Such transfer shall not be deemed a denial of access within the meaning of these regulations. The IRS official to whom the request is redirected shall treat such request as a new request addressed to it and the time limits for response set forth in paragraphs (c)(9) and (c)(11) of this section shall commence when the transfer is received by the designated office;

(d) Reasonably describe the records in accordance with paragraph (c)(5)(i) of this section;

(e) In the case of a request for records the disclosure of which is limited by statute or regulations (as, for example, the Privacy Act of 1974 (5 U.S.C. 552a) or section 6103 and the regulations thereunder), establish the identity and the right of the person making the request to the disclosure of the records in accordance with paragraph (c)(5)(iii) of this section;

(f) Set forth the address where the person making the request desires to be notified of the determination as to whether the request shall be granted;

(g) State whether the requester wishes to inspect the records or desires to have a copy made and furnished without first inspecting them;

(h) State the firm agreement of the requester to pay the fees for search, duplication, and review ultimately determined in accordance with paragraph (f) of this section, or, in accordance with paragraph (c)(4)(ii) of this section, place an upper limit for such fees that the requester is willing to pay, or request that such fees be reduced or waived and state the justification for such request; and

(i) Identify the category of the requester and, with the exception of "other requesters," state how the records shall be used, as required by paragraph (f)(3) of this section.

(ii) As provided in paragraph (c)(4)(i)(H) of this section, rather than stating a firm agreement to pay the fee ultimately determined in accordance with paragraph (f) of this section or requesting that such fees be reduced or waived,

the requester may place an upper limit on the amount the requester agrees to pay. If the requester chooses to place an upper limit and the estimated fee is deemed to be greater than the upper limit, or where the requester asks for an estimate of the fee to be charged, the requester shall be promptly advised of the estimate of the fee and asked to agree to pay such amount. Where the initial request includes a request for reduction or waiver of the fee, the IRS officials responsible for the control of the requested records (or their delegates) shall determine whether to grant the request for reduction or waiver in accordance with paragraph (f) of this section and notify the requester of their decisions and, if their decisions result in the requester being liable for all or part of the fee normally due, ask the requester to agree to pay the amount so determined. The requirements of this paragraph shall not be deemed met until the requester has explicitly agreed to pay the fee applicable to the request for records, if any, or has made payment in advance of the fee estimated to be due. If the requester has any outstanding balance of search, review, or duplication fees, the requirements of this paragraph shall not be deemed met until the requester has remitted the outstanding balance due.

(5) Reasonable description of records; identity and right of the requester

(i) The request for records must describe the records in reasonably sufficient detail to enable the IRS employees who are familiar with the subject matter of the request to locate the records without placing an unreasonable burden upon the IRS. While no specific formula for a reasonable description of a record can be established, the requirement shall generally be satisfied if the requester gives the name, taxpayer identification number (e.g., social security number or employer identification number), subject matter, location, and years at issue, of the requested records. If the request seeks records pertaining to pending litigation, the request shall indicate the title of the case, the court in which the case was filed, and the nature of the case. It is suggested that the person making the request furnish any additional information which shall more clearly identify the requested records. Where the requester does not reasonably describe the records being sought, the requester shall be afforded an opportunity to refine the request. Such opportunity may involve a conference with knowledgeable IRS personnel at the discretion of the disclosure officer. The reasonable description requirement shall not be used by officers or employees of the Internal Revenue as a device for improperly withholding records from the public.

(ii) The IRS shall make a reasonable effort to comply fully with all requests for access to records subject only to any applicable exemption set forth in 5 U.S.C. 552(b) or any exclusion described in 5 U.S.C. 552(c). In any situation in which it is determined that a request for voluminous records would unduly burden and interfere with the operations of the IRS, the person making the request shall be asked to be more specific and to narrow the request, or to agree on an orderly procedure for the production of the requested records, in order to satisfy the request without disproportionate adverse effect on IRS operations.

(iii) Statutory or regulatory restrictions.

(a) In the case of records containing information with respect to particular persons the disclosure of which is limited by statute or regulations, persons making requests shall establish their identity and right to access to such records. Persons requesting access to such records which pertain to themselves may establish their identity by—

(1) The presentation of a single document bearing a photograph (such as a passport or identification badge), or the presentation of two items of identification which do not bear a photograph but do bear both a name and signature (such as a credit card or organization membership card), in the case of a request made in person,

(2) The submission of the requester's signature, address, and one other identifier (such as a photocopy of a driver's license) bearing the requester's signature, in the case of a request by mail, or

(3) The presentation in person or the submission by mail of a notarized statement, or a statement made under penalty of perjury in accordance with 28 U.S.C. 1746, swearing to or affirming such person's identity.

(b) Additional proof of a person's identity shall be required before the requests shall be deemed to have met the requirement of paragraph (c)(4)(i)(e) of this section if it is determined that additional proof is necessary to protect against unauthorized disclosure of information in a particular case. Persons who have identified themselves to the satisfaction of IRS officials pursuant to this paragraph (c) shall be deemed to have established their right to access records pertaining to themselves. Persons requesting records on behalf of or pertaining to another person must provide adequate proof of the legal relationship under which they assert the right to access the requested records before the requirement of paragraph (c)(4)(i)(E) of this section shall be deemed met.

(b) In the case of an attorney-in-fact, or other person requesting records on behalf of or pertaining to other persons, the requester shall furnish a properly executed power of attorney, Privacy Act consent, or tax information authorization, as appropriate. In the case of a corporation, if the requester has the authority to legally bind the corporation under applicable state law, such as its corporate president or chief executive officer, then a written statement or tax information authorization certifying as to that person's authority to make a request on behalf of the corporation shall be sufficient. If the requester is any other officer or employee of the corporation, then such requester shall furnish a written statement certifying as to that person's authority to make a request on behalf of the corporation by any principal officer and attested to by the secretary or other officer (other than the requester) that the person making the request on behalf of the corporation is properly authorized to make such a request. If the requester is other than one of the above, then such person may furnish a resolution by the corporation's board of directors or other governing body which provides that the person making the request on behalf of the corporation is properly authorized to make such a request, or shall otherwise satisfy the requirements set forth in section 6103(e). A person requesting access to records of a partnership or a subchapter S Corporation shall provide a notarized statement, or a statement made under penalty of perjury in accordance with 28 U.S.C. 1746, that the requester was a member of the partnership or subchapter S corporation for a part of each of the years included in the request.

(6) Requests for expedited processing

(i) When a requester demonstrates compelling need, a request shall be taken out of order and given expedited treatment. A compelling need involves—

(a) Circumstances in which the lack of expedited treatment could reasonably be expected to pose an imminent threat to the life or physical safety of an individual;

(b) An urgency to inform the public concerning actual or alleged Federal government activity, if made by a person primarily engaged in disseminating information. A person primarily engaged in disseminating information, if not a fulltime representative of the news media, as defined in paragraph (f)(3)(ii)(b) of this section, must establish that he or she is a person whose main professional activity or occupation is information dissemination, though it need not be his or her sole occupation. A person primarily engaged in disseminating information does not include individuals who are engaged only incidentally in the dissemination of information. The standard of urgency to inform requires that the records requested pertain to a matter of current exigency to the American public, beyond the public's right to know about government activity generally, and that delaying a response to a request for records would compromise a significant recognized interest to and throughout the American general public;

(c) The loss of substantial due process rights.

(ii) A requester who seeks expedited processing must submit a statement, certified to be true and correct to the best of his or her knowledge and belief, explaining in detail why there is a compelling need for expedited processing.

(iii) A request for expedited processing may be made at the time of the initial request for records or at any later time. For a prompt determination, requests for expedited processing must be submitted to the responsible official of the IRS who maintains the records requested except that a request for expedited processing under paragraph (c)(6)(i)(B) of this section shall be submitted directly to the Director, Communications Division, whose address is Office of Media Relations, CL:C:M, Internal Revenue Service, Room 7032, 1111 Constitution Avenue, N.W., Washington, D.C. 20224.

(iv) Upon receipt by the responsible official in the IRS, a request for expedited processing shall be considered and a determination as to whether to grant or deny the request shall be made, and the requester notified, within ten days of the date of the request, provided that in no event shall the IRS have less than five days (excluding Saturdays, Sundays, and legal public holidays) from the date of the responsible official's receipt of the request for such processing. The determination to grant or deny a request for expedited processing shall be made solely on the information initially provided by the requester.

(v) An appeal of an initial determination to deny expedited processing must be made within ten days of the date of the initial determination to deny expedited processing, and must otherwise comply with the requirements of paragraph (c)(10) of this section. Both the envelope and the appeal itself shall be clearly marked, "Appeal for Expedited Processing."

(vi) IRS action to deny or affirm denial of a request for expedited processing pursuant to

this paragraph, and IRS failure to respond in a timely manner to such a request shall be subject to judicial review, except that judicial review shall be based on the record before the IRS at the time of the determination. A district court of the United States shall not have jurisdiction to review the IRS's denial of expedited processing of a request for records after the IRS has provided a complete response to the request.

(7) Date of receipt of request

(i) Requests for records and any separate agreement to pay, final notification of waiver of fees, or letter transmitting payment, shall be promptly stamped with the date of delivery to or dispatch by the office of the IRS official responsible for the control of the records requested. A request for records shall be considered to have been received on the date on which a complete request containing the information required by paragraphs (c)(4)(i)(a) through (i) has been received by the IRS official responsible for the control of the records requested. A determination that a request is deficient in any respect is not a denial of access, and such determinations are not subject to administrative appeal.

(ii) The latest of such stamped dates shall be deemed for purposes of this section to be the date of receipt of the request, provided that the requirements of paragraphs (c)(4)(i)(a) through (i) of this section have been satisfied, and, where applicable—

(a) The requester has agreed in writing, by executing a separate contract or otherwise, to pay the fees for search, duplication, and review determined due in accordance with paragraph (f) of this section, or

(b) The fees have been waived in accordance with paragraph (f) of this section, or

(c) Payment in advance has been received from the requester.

(8) Search for records requested

(i) Upon the receipt of a request, search services shall be performed by IRS personnel to identify and locate the requested records. Search time includes any and all time spent looking for material responsive to the request, including page-by-page or line-by-line identification of material within records. Where duplication of an entire record would be less costly than a line-by-line identification, duplication should be substituted for this kind of search. With respect to records maintained in computerized form, a search shall include services functionally analogous to a search for records which are maintained on paper.

Reg. §601.702(c)(8)(i)

(ii) In determining which records are responsive to a request, the IRS official responsible for the control of the records requested shall include only those records within the official's possession and control as of the date of the receipt of the request by the appropriate disclosure officer.

(9) *Initial determination.*—(i) *Responsible official.*—(a) The Associate Director, Personnel Security or delegate shall have the sole authority to make initial determinations with respect to requests for records under that office's control.

(b) The Director of the Office of Governmental Liaison and Disclosure or delegate shall have the sole authority to make initial determinations with respect to all other requests for records of the IRS maintained in the Headquarters and its National Office of the Chief Counsel. For all other records within the control of the IRS, the initial determination with respect to requests for records may be made either by the Director,Office of Governmental Liaison and Disclosure, or by the IRS officials responsible for the control of the records requested, or their delegates (see paragraph (h) of this section).

(ii) *Processing of request.*—The appropriate responsible official or delegate shall respond in the approximate order of receipt of the requests, to the extent consistent with sound administrative practice. In any event, the initial determination shall be made and notification thereof mailed within twenty days (excepting Saturdays, Sundays, and legal public holidays) after the date of receipt of the request, as determined in accordance with paragraph (c)(7) of this section, unless the responsible official invokes an extension pursuant to paragraph (c)(11) of this section, the requester otherwise agrees to an extension of the twenty day time limitation, or the request is an expedited request.

(iii) *Granting of request.*—If the request is granted in full or in part, and if the requester wants a copy of the records, a statement of the applicable fees, if there are any, shall be mailed to the requester either at the time of the determination or shortly thereafter. In the case of a request for inspection, the records shall be made available promptly for inspection, at the time and place stated, normally at the appropriate office where the records requested are controlled. If the person making the request has expressed a desire to inspect the records at another office of the IRS, a reasonable effort shall be made to comply with the request. Records shall be made available for inspection at such reasonable and proper times so as not to interfere with their use

by the IRS or to exclude other persons from making inspections. In addition, reasonable limitations may be placed on the number of records which may be inspected by a person on any given date. The person making the request shall not be allowed to remove the records from the office where inspection is made. If, after making inspection, the person making the request desires copies of all or a portion of the requested records, copies shall be furnished upon payment of the established fees prescribed by paragraph (f) of this section.

(iv) *Denial of request.*—If it is determined that some records shall be denied, the person making the request shall be so notified by mail. The letter of notification shall specify the city or other location where the requested records are situated, contain a brief statement of the grounds for not granting the request in full including the exemption(s) relied upon, the name and any title or position of the official responsible for the denial, and advise the person making the request of the right to appeal to the Commissioner in accordance with paragraph (c)(10) of this section.

(a) In denying a request for records, in whole or in part, the IRS shall include the date that the request was received in the appropriate disclosure office, and shall provide an estimate of the volume of the denied matter to the person making the request, unless providing such estimate would harm an interest protected by an exemption in 5 U.S.C. 552(b) or (c) pursuant to which the denial is made; and

(b) The amount of information deleted shall be indicated on the released portion of the record, unless including that indication would harm an interest protected by an exemption in 5 U.S.C. 552(b) under which the deletion is made. If technically feasible, the amount of the information deleted and the asserted exemption shall be indicated at the place in the record where such deletion is made.

(v) *Inability to locate and evaluate within time limits.*—Where the records requested cannot be located and evaluated within the initial twenty day period or any extension thereof in accordance with paragraph (c)(11) of this section, the search for the records or evaluation shall continue, but the requester shall be notified, and advised that the requester may consider such notification a denial of the request for records. The requester shall be provided with a statement of judicial rights along with the notification letter. The requester may also be invited, in the alternative, to agree to a voluntary extension of time in which to locate and evaluate the records.

Such voluntary extension of time shall not constitute a waiver of the requester's right to appeal or seek judicial review of any denial of access ultimately made or the requester's right to seek judicial review in the event of failure to comply with the time extension granted.

(10) *Administrative appeal.*—(i) The requester may submit an administrative appeal to the Commissioner of Internal Revenue by letter that is postmarked within 35 days after the later of the date of any letter of notification described in paragraph (c)(9)(iv) of this section, the date of any letter of notification of an adverse determination of the requester's category described in paragraph (f)(3) of this section, the date of any letter of notification of an adverse determination of the requester's fee waiver or reduction request described in paragraph (f)(2) of this section, the date of any letter determining that no responsive records exist, or the date of the last transmission of the last records released. An administrative appeal for denial of a request for expedited processing must be made to the Commissioner ofInternal Revenue by letter that is postmarked within ten days after the date of any letter of notification discussed in paragraph (c)(6)(iv) of this section.

(ii) *The letter of appeal shall.*—(a) Be made in writing and signed by the requester;

(b) Be addressed to the Commissioner and mailed to IRS Appeals, 6377A Riverside Avenue, Suite 110, Riverside, California 92506-FOIA Appeal;

(c) Reasonably describe the records requested to which the appeal pertains in accordance with paragraph (c)(5)(i) of this section;

(d) Set forth the address where the appellant desires to be notified of the determination on appeal;

(e) Specify the date of the request, the office to which the request was submitted, and where possible, enclose a copy of the initial request and the initial determination being appealed; and

(f) Ask the Commissioner to grant the request for records, fee waiver, expedited processing, or favorable fee category, as applicable, or verify that an appropriate search was conducted and the responsive records were either produced or an appropriate exemption asserted. The person submitting the appeal may submit any argument in support of the appeal in the letter of appeal.

(iii) Appeals shall be stamped promptly with the date of their receipt in the Office of Appeals, and the later of this stamped date or the stamped date of a document submitted subsequently which supplements the original appeal so that the appeal satisfies the requirements set forth in paragraphs (c)(10)(ii)(a) through (f) of this section shall be deemed by the IRS to be the date of receipt of the appeal for all purposes of this section. The Commissioner or a delegate shall acknowledge receipt of the appeal and advise the requester of the date of receipt and the date a response is due in accordance with this paragraph. If an appeal fails to satisfy any of the requirements of paragraph (c)(10)(ii)(a) through (f) of this section, the person making the request shall be advised promptly in writing of the additional requirements to be met. Except for appeals of denials of expedited processing, the determination to affirm the initial denial (in whole or in part) or to grant the request for records shall be made and notification of the determination shall be mailed within twenty days (exclusive of Saturdays, Sundays, and legal public holidays) after the date of receipt of the appeal unless extended pursuant to paragraph (c)(11)(i) of this section. Appeals of initial determinations to deny expedited processing must be made within ten calendar days of the determination to deny the expedited processing. If it is determined that the appeal from the initial denial is to be denied (in whole or in part), the requester shall be notified in writing of the denial, the reasons therefor, the name and title or position of the official responsible for the denial on appeal, and the provisions of 5 U.S.C. 552(a)(4) for judicial review of that determination.

(11) *Time extensions.*—(i) *Unusual circumstances.*—(a) In unusual circumstances, the time limitations specified in paragraphs (c)(9) and (10) of this section may be extended by written notice from the official charged with the duty of making the determinations to the person making the request or appeal setting forth the reasons for this extension and the date on which the determination is expected to be sent. As used in this paragraph, the term unusual circumstances means, but only to the extent reasonably necessary to the proper processing of the particular request:

(1) The need to search for and collect the requested records from field facilities or other establishments that are separate from the office processing the request;

(2) The need to search for, collect, and appropriately examine a voluminous amount of separate and distinct records which are demanded in a single request;

Reg. §601.702(c)(11)(i)(a)(2)

(3) The need for consultation, which shall be conducted with all practicable speed, with another agency having a substantial interest in the determination of the request or among two or more constituent units of the Department of the Treasury having substantial subject matter interest therein; and

(4) The need for consultation with business submitters to determine the nature and extent of proprietary information in accordance with this section.

(b) Any extension or extensions of time for unusual circumstances shall not cumulatively total more than ten days (exclusive of Saturday, Sunday and legal public holidays). If additional time is needed to process the request, the IRS shall notify the requester and provide the requester an opportunity to limit the scope of the request or arrange for an alternative time frame for processing the request or a modified request. The requester shall retain the right to define the desired scope of the request, as long as it meets the requirements contained in this section.

(ii) *Aggregation of requests.*—If more than one request is received from the same requester, or from a group of requesters acting in concert, and the IRS believes that such requests constitute a single request which would otherwise satisfy the unusual circumstances specified in subparagraph(c)(11)(i) of this section, and the requests involve clearly related matters, the IRS may aggregate these requests for processing purposes. Multiple requests involving unrelated matters shall not be aggregated.

(12) *Failure to comply.*—If the IRS fails to comply with the time limitations specified in paragraphs (c)(9), (10), or paragraph (c)(11)(i) of this section, any person making a request for records satisfying the requirements of paragraphs (c)(4)(i)(A) through (I) of this section, shall be deemed to have exhausted administrative remedies with respect to such request. Accordingly, this person may initiate suit in accordance with paragraph (c)(13) of this section.

(13) *Judicial review.*—If an administrative appeal pursuant to paragraph (c)(10) of this section for records or fee waiver or reduction is denied, or if a request for expedited processing is denied and there has been no determination as to the release of records, or if a request for a favorable fee category under paragraph (f)(3) of this section is denied, or a determination is made that there are no responsive records, or if no determination is made within the twenty day periods specified in paragraphs (c)(9) and (10) of

this section, or the period of any extension pursuant to paragraph (c)(11)(i) of this section, or by grant of the requester, respectively, the person making the request may commence an action in a United States district court in the district in which the requester resides, in which the requester's principal place of business is located, in which the records are situated, or in the District of Columbia, pursuant to 5 U.S.C. 552(a)(4)(B). The statute authorizes an action only against the agency. With respect to records of the IRS, the agency is the IRS, not an officer or an employee thereof. Service of process in such an action shall be in accordance with the Federal Rules of Civil Procedure (28 U.S.C. App.) applicable to actions against an agency of the United States. Delivery of process upon the IRS shall be directed to the Commissioner of Internal Revenue, Attention: CC:PA, 1111 Constitution Avenue, N.W., Washington, D.C. 20224. The IRS shall serve an answer or otherwise plead to any complaint made under this paragraph within 30 days after service upon it, unless the court otherwise directs for good cause shown. The district court shall determine the matter de novo, and may examine the contents of the IRS records in question in camera to determine whether such records or any part thereof shall be withheld under any of the exemptions described in 5 U.S.C. 552(b) and the exclusions described in 5 U.S.C. 552(c). The burden shall be upon the IRS to sustain its action in not making the requested records available. The court may assess against the United States reasonable attorney fees and other litigation costs reasonably incurred by the person making the request in any case in which the complainant has substantially prevailed.

(14) *Preservation of records.*—All correspondence relating to the requests received by the IRS under this chapter, and all records processed pursuant to such requests, shall be preserved, until such time as the destruction of such correspondence and records is authorized pursuant to Title 44 of the United States Code. Under no circumstances shall records be destroyed while they are the subject of a pending request, appeal, or lawsuit under 5 U.S.C. 552.

(d) *Rules for disclosure of certain specified matters.*—Requests for certain specified categories of records shall be processed by the IRS in accordance with other established procedures.

(1) *Inspection of tax returns and attachments or transcripts.*—The inspection of returns and attachments is governed by the provisions of the internal revenue laws and regulations thereunder promulgated by the Secretary of the Trea-

sury. See section 6103 and the regulations thereunder. Written requests for a copy of a tax return and attachments or a transcript of a tax return shall be made using IRS Form 4506, "Request for Copy or Transcript of Tax Form." A reasonable fee, as the Commissioner may from time to time establish, may be charged for such copies.

(2) *Record of seizure and sale of real estate.*— Subject to the rules on disclosure set forth in section 6103, Record 21, Part 2, "Record of seizure and sale of real estate", is available for public inspection in the local IRS office where the real estate is located. Copies of Record 21, Part 2 shall be furnished upon written request. Members of the public may call the toll-free IRS Customer Service number, 1-800-829-1040, to obtain the address of the appropriate local office. Record 21 does not list real estate seized for use in violation of the internal revenue laws (see section 7302).

(3) *Public inspection of certain information returns, notices, and reports furnished by certain tax-exempt organizations and certain trusts.*—Subject to the rules on disclosure set forth in section 6104: Information furnished on any Form 990 series or Form 1041-A returns, pursuant to sections 6033 and 6034, shall be made available for public inspection and copying, upon written request; information furnished by organizations exempt from tax under section 527 on Forms 8871, Political Organization Notice of Section 527 Status, and Forms 8872, Political Organization Report of Contributions and Expenditures, areavailable for public inspection and copying from the IRS website at www.eforms.irs.gov. In addition, Forms 8871 and 8872 shall be made available for public inspection and copying, upon written request; and information furnished by organizations exempt from tax under section 527 on Form 1120-POL pursuant to section 6012(a)(6) shall be made available for public inspection and copying upon written request. Written requests to inspect or obtain copies of any of the information described in this paragraph (d)(3) shall be made using Form 4506-A, "Request for Public Inspection or Copy of Exempt or Political Organization IRS Form," and be directed to the appropriate address listed on Form 4506-A.

(4) *Public inspection of applications and determinations of certain organizations for tax exemption.*—Subject to the rules on disclosure set forth in section 6104, applications, including Forms 1023 and 1024, and certain papers submitted in support of such applications, filed by organizations described in section 501(c) or (d) and deter-

mined to be exempt from taxation under section 501(a), and any letter or other document issued by the IRS with respect to such applications, shall be made available for public inspection and copying, upon written request. Written requests to inspect or obtain copies of this information shall be made using Form 4506-A, "Request for Public Inspection or Copy of Exempt or Political Organization IRS Form" and be directed to the appropriate address listed on Form 4506-A.

(5) *Public inspection of applications and annual returns with respect to certain deferred compensation plans and accounts and employee plans.*—Subject to the rules on disclosure set forth in section 6104; forms, applications, and papers submitted in support of such applications, with respect to the qualification of a pension, profit sharing, or stock bonus plan under sections 401(a), 403(a), or 405(a), an individual retirement account described in section 408(a), an individual retirement annuity described in section 408(b), or with respect to the exemption from tax of an organization forming part of such a plan or account, and any document issued by the IRS dealing with such qualification or exemption, shall be open to public inspection and copying upon written request. This paragraph shall not apply with respect to plans with no more than 25 plan participants. Written requests to inspect or obtain copies of such material shall be directed to IRS Customer Service—Tax Exempt & Government Entities Division (TEGE), P.O. Box 2508, Room 2023, Cincinnati, Ohio 45201; and information furnished on the Form 5500 series of returns, pursuant to section 6058, shall be made available for public inspection and copying upon written request. Except for requests for Form 5500-EZ, written requests to inspect or to obtain a copy of this information shall be directed to the Department of Labor, Public Disclosure, Room N-5638, 200 Constitution Avenue, N.W., Washington, D.C. 20210. Written requests to inspect or to obtain a copy of Form 5500-EZ shall be directed to the Internal Revenue Service Center, P.O. Box 9941, Stop 6716, Ogden, Utah 84409.

(6) *Publication of statistics of income.*—Statistics with respect to the operation of the income tax laws are published annually in accordance with section 6108 and § 301.6108-1.

(7) *Comments received in response to a notice of proposed rulemaking, a solicitation for public comments, or prepublication comments.*—Written comments received in response to a notice of proposed rulemaking, a solicitation for public comments, or prepublication comments, may be inspected, upon written request, by any person

Reg. §601.702(d)(7)

upon compliance with the provisions of this paragraph. Comments may be inspected in the Freedom of Information Reading Room, IRS, 1111 Constitution Avenue, N.W., Room 1621, Washington, D.C. The request to inspect comments must be in writing and signed by the person making the request and shall be addressed to the Commissioner of Internal Revenue, Attn: CC:ITA:RU, P.O. Box 7604, Ben Franklin Station, Washington, D.C. 20044. The person submitting the written request may inspect the comments that are the subject of the request during regular business hours. If the requester wishes to inspect the documents, the requester shall be contacted by IRS Freedom of Information Reading Room personnel when the documents are available for inspection. Copies of comments may be made in the Freedom of Information Reading Room by the person making the request or may be requested, in writing, to the Commissioner of Internal Revenue, Attn: CC:ITA:RU, P.O. Box 7604, Ben Franklin Station, Washington, D.C. 20044. The IRS shall comply with requests for records under the paragraph within a reasonable time. The provisions of paragraph (f)(5)(iii) of this section, relating to fees for duplication, shall apply with respect to requests made in accordance with this paragraph.

(8) *Accepted offers in compromise.*—For one year after the date of execution, a copy of the Form 7249, "Offer Acceptance Report," for each accepted offer in compromise with respect to any liability for a tax imposed by Title 26 shall be made available for inspection and copying in the location designated by the Compliance Area Director or Compliance Services Field Director within the Small Business and Self-Employed Division (SBSE) of the taxpayer's geographic area of residence.

(9) *Public inspection of written determinations.*—Certain rulings, determination letters, technical advice memorandums, and Chief Counsel advice are open to public inspection pursuant to section 6110.

(e) *Other disclosure procedures.*—For procedures to be followed by officers and employees of the IRS upon receipt of a request or demand for certain internal revenue records or information the disclosure procedure for which is not covered by this section, see § 301.9000-1.

(f) *Fees for services.*—(1) *In general.*—Except as otherwise provided, the fees to be charged for search, duplication, and review services performed by the IRS, with respect to the processing of Freedom of Information Act requests, shall be

determined and collected in accordance with the provisions of this subsection. A fee shall not be charged for monitoring a requester's inspection of records which contains exempt matter. The IRS may recover the applicable fees even if there is ultimately no disclosure of records. Should services other than the services described in this paragraph be requested and rendered, which are not required by the Freedom of Information Act, fees shall be charged to recover the actual direct cost to the IRS.

(2) *Waiver or reduction of fees.*—(i) The fees authorized by this paragraph may be waived or reduced on a case-by-case basis in accordance with this subsection by any IRS official who is authorized to make the initial determination pursuant to paragraph (c)(9) of this section. Fees shall be waived or reduced by such official when it is determined that disclosure of the requested information is in the public interest because it is likely to contribute significantly to public understanding of the operations or activities of the IRS and is not primarily in the commercial interest of the requester. Such officials shall consider several factors, including, but not limited to, paragraphs (f)(2)(i) through (vi), in determining requests for waiver or reduction of fees—

(a) Whether the subject of the releasable records concerns the agency's operations or activities;

(b) Whether the releasable records are likely to contribute to an understanding of the agency's operations or activities;

(c) Whether the releasable records are likely to contribute to the general public's understanding of the agency's operations or activities (e.g., how will the requester convey the information to the general public);

(d) The significance of the contribution to the general public's understanding of the agency's operations or activities (e.g., is the information contained in the releasable records already available to the general public);

(e) The existence and magnitude of the requester's commercial interest, as that term is used in paragraph (f)(3)(i)(a) of this section, being furthered by the releasable records; and

(f) Whether the magnitude of the requester's commercial interest is sufficiently large in comparison to the general public's interest.

(ii) Requesters asking for reduction or waiver of fees must state the reasons why they believe disclosure meets the standards set forth in paragraph (f)(2)(ii) of this section in a written request signed by the requester.

(iii) The indigence of the requester shall not be considered as a factor to determine if the requester is entitled to a reduction or waiver of fees.

(iv) Normally, no charge shall be made for providing records to federal, state, local, or foreign governments, or agencies or offices thereof, or international governmental organizations.

(v) The initial request for waiver or reduction of fees shall be addressed to the official of the IRS to whose office the request for disclosure is delivered pursuant to paragraph (c)(4)(i)(c) of this section. Appeals from denials of requests for waiver or reduction of fees shall be decided by the Commissioner's delegate in accordance with the criteria set forth in paragraph (f)(2)(ii) of this section. Appeals shall be received by the Commissioner's delegate within 35 days of the date of the letter of notification denying the initial request for waiver or reduction and shall be decided promptly. *See* paragraph (c)(10)(ii)(b) of this section for the appropriate address. Upon receipt of the determination on appeal to deny a request for waiver of fees, the requester may initiate an action in a United States district court to review the request for waiver of fees. In such action, the court shall consider the matter de novo, except that the court's review of the matter shall be limited to the record before the IRS official to whose office the request for waiver is delivered. In such action, the court shall consider the matter under the arbitrary and capricious standard.

(3) *Categories of requesters.*—(i) *Attestation.*—A request for records under this section shall include an attestation as to the status of the requester for use by the IRS official to whose office the request is delivered in determining the appropriate fees to be assessed. No attestation is required for a requester who falls within paragraph (f)(3)(ii)(e) (an "other requester").

(ii) *Categories.*—(a) *Commercial use requester.*—Any person who seeks information for a use or purpose that furthers the commercial, trade, or profit interests of the requester or the person on whose behalf the request is made.

(b) *News media requester.*—Any person actively gathering news for an entity that is organized and operated to publish or broadcast news (i.e., information about current events or of current interest to the public) to the public. News media entities include, but are not limited to, television or radio stations broadcasting to the public at large, publishers of periodicals, to the extent they disseminate news, who make their periodicals available for purchase or subscription by the general public, computerized news services and telecommunications. Free lance journalists shall be included as media requesters if they can demonstrate a solid basis for expecting publication through a qualifying news entity (e.g., publication contract, past publication record). Specialized periodicals, although catering to a narrower audience, may be considered media requesters so long as they are available to the public generally, via newsstand or subscription.

(c) *Educational institution requester.*—Any person who, on behalf of a preschool, public or private elementary or secondary school, institution of undergraduate or graduate higher education, institution of professional or vocational education, which operates a program or programs of scholarly research, seeks records in furtherance of the institution's scholarly research and is not for a commercial use. This category does not include requesters wanting records for use in meeting individual academic research or study requirements.

(d) *Noncommercial scientific institution requester.*—Any person on behalf of an institution that is not operated on a commercial basis, that is operated solely for the purpose of conducting scientific research whose results are not intended to promote any particular product or industry.

(e) *Other requester.*—Any requester who does not fall within the categories described in paragraphs (f)(3)(ii)(a) through (d).

(iii) *Determination of proper category.*—Where the IRS has reasonable cause to doubt the use to which a requester shall put the records sought, or where that use is not clear from the record itself, the IRS shall seek additional clarification from the requester before assigning the request to a specific category. In any event, a determination of the proper category of requester shall be based upon a review of the requester's submission and may also be based upon the IRS' own records.

(iv) *Allowable charges.*—(a) *Commercial use requesters.*—Records shall be provided to commercial use requesters for the cost of search, duplication, and review (including doing all that is necessary to excise and otherwise prepare records for release) of records. Commercial use requesters are not entitled to two hours of free search time or 100 pages of free duplication.

Reg. §601.702(f)(3)(iv)(a)

(b) *News media, educational institution, and noncommercial scientific institution requesters.*—Records shall be provided to news media, educational institution, and noncommercial scientific institution requesters for the cost of duplication alone, excluding fees for the first 100 pages.

(c) *Other requesters.*—Requesters who do not fit into any of the above categories shall be charged fees that shall cover the full actual direct cost of searching for and duplicating records, except that the first two hours of search time and first 100 pages of duplication shall be furnished without charge. Requests from individuals for records about themselves maintained in the IRS's systems of records shall continue to be treated under the fee provisions of the Privacy Act of 1974, which permits fees only for duplication after the first 100 pages are furnished free of charge.

(4) *Avoidance of unexpected fees.*—(i) In order to protect requesters from unexpected fees, all requests for records shall state the agreement of the requesters to pay the fees determined in accordance with paragraph (f)(5) of this section or state the upper limit they are willing to pay to cover the costs of processing their requests.

(ii) When the fees for processing requests are estimated by the IRS to exceed the upper limit agreed to by a requester, or when a requester has failed to state a limit and the costs are estimated to exceed $250, and the IRS has not then determined to waive or reduce the fees, a notice shall be sent to the requester. This notice shall—

(a) Inform the requester of the estimated costs;

(b) Extend an offer to the requester to confer with agency personnel in an attempt to reformulate the request in a manner which shall reduce the fees and still meet the needs of the requester;

(c) If the requester is not amenable to reformulation, which would reduce fees to under $250, then advance payment of the estimated fees shall be required; and

(d) Inform the requester that the time period, within which the IRS is obliged to make a determination on the request, shall not begin to run, pending a reformulation of the request or the receipt of advance payment from the requester, as appropriate.

(5) *Fees for services.*—The fees for services performed by the IRS shall be imposed and collected as set forth in this paragraph. No fees shall be charged if the costs of routine collecting and processing the fees allowable under 5 U.S.C. 552(a)(4)(A) are likely to equal or exceed the amount of the fee.

(i) *Search services.*—Fees charged for search services are as follows:

(a) *Searches for records other than computerized records.*—The IRS shall charge for search services at the salary rate(s) (i.e., basic pay plus 16 percent) of the employee(s) making the search. An average rate for the range of grades typically involved may be established. Fees may be charged for search time as prescribed in this section even if the time spent searching does not yield any records, or if records are denied.

(b) *Searches for computerized records.*—Actual direct cost of the search, including computer search time, runs, and the operator's salary. The fee for computer output shall be actual direct costs. For requesters in the "other requester" category, the charge for the computer search shall begin when the cost of the search (including the operator time and the cost of operating the computer) equals the equivalent dollar amount of two hours of the salary of the person performing the search.

(c) *Searches requiring travel or transportation.*—Shipping charges to transport records from one location to another, or for the transportation of an employee to the site of requested records when it is necessary to locate rather than examine the records, shall be at the rate of the actual cost of such shipping or transportation.

(ii) *Review Services.*—(a) *Review defined.*—Review is the process of examining records in response to a commercial use requester, as that term is defined in paragraph (f)(3)(i)(a), upon initial consideration of the applicability of an exemption described in 5 U.S.C. 552(b) or an exclusion described in 5 U.S.C. 552(c) to the requested records, be it at the initial request or administrative appeal level, to determine whether any portion of any record responsive to the request is permitted to be withheld. Review includes doing all that is necessary to excise and otherwise prepare the records for release. Review does not include the time spent on resolving general legal or policy issues regarding the applicability of exemptions to the requested records.

(b) *Fees charged for review services.*—The IRS shall charge commercial use requesters for review of records at the initial determination stage at the salary rate(s) (i.e., basic pay plus 16 percent) of the employee(s) making the review. An average rate for the range of grades typically involved may be established by the Commissioner.

(iii) *Duplication other than for tax returns and attachments.*—(a) Duplication fees charged for copies of paper records shall be a reasonable fee, as the Commissioner may from time to time establish.

(b) The actual direct cost of duplication for photographs, films, videotapes, audiotapes, compact disks, and other materials shall be charged.

(c) Records may be provided to a private contractor for copying and the requester shall be charged for the actual cost of duplication charged by the private contractor.

(d) When other duplication processes not specifically identified above are requested and provided pursuant to the Freedom of Information Act, their actual direct cost to the IRS shall be charged.

(e) Where the condition of the record does not enable the IRS to make legible copies, the IRS shall not attempt to reconstruct it. The official having jurisdiction over the record shall furnish the best copy that is available and advise the requester of this fact.

(iv) *Charges for copies of tax returns and attachments, and transcripts of tax returns.*—A charge shall be made for each copy of a tax return and its attachments, and transcripts of tax returns, supplied in response to a Form 4506, "Request for Copy of Tax Form." The amount of the charge shall be a reasonable fee as computed by the Commissioner from time to time, and as set forth on Form 4506.

(v) *Other services.*—Other services and materials requested (e.g., certification, express mailing) which are not specifically covered by this part and/or not required by the Freedom of Information Act are provided at the discretion of the IRS and are chargeable at the actual direct cost to the IRS.

(6) *Printed material.*—Certain relevant government publications which shall be placed on the shelves of the Freedom of Information Reading Room shall not be sold at that location. Copies of pages of these publications may be duplicated on the premises and a fee for such service may becharged in accordance with paragraph (f)(5)(iii) of this section. A person desiring to purchase the complete publication, for example, an Internal Revenue Bulletin, should contact the Superintendent of Documents, U.S. Government Printing Office, Washington, D.C. 20402.

(7) *Search, duplication, and deletion services with respect to records open to public inspection pursuant to section 6110.*—Fees charged for searching for, making deletions in, and copies of records subject to public inspection pursuant to section 6110 only upon written request shall be at the actual cost, as the Commissioner may from time to time establish.

(8) *Form of payment.*—Payment shall be made by check or money order, payable to the order of the Treasury of the United States.

(9) *Advance payments.*—(i) If previous fees have not been paid in a timely fashion, as defined in paragraph (f)(10) of this section, or where the estimated fees exceed $250, the IRS shall require payment in full of any outstanding fees and all estimated fees prior to processing a request. Additionally, the IRS reserves the right to require payment of fees after a request is processed and before any records are released to a requester. For purposes of this paragraph, a requester is the individual in whose name a request is made; however, where a request is made on behalf of another individual, and previous fees have not been paid within the designated time period by either the requester or the individual on whose behalf the request is made, then the IRS shall require payment in full of all outstanding fees and all estimated fees before processing the request.

(ii) When the IRS acts pursuant to paragraph (f)(9) (i) of this section, the administrative time limits prescribed in paragraphs (c)(9) and (10) of this section, plus permissible extensions of these time limits as prescribed in paragraph (c)(11)(i) of this section, shall begin only after the IRS official to whom the request is delivered has received the fees described above in paragraph (f)(9)(i) of this section.

(10) *Interest.*—Interest shall be charged to requesters who fail to pay the fees in a timely fashion; that is, within 30 days following the day on which the statement of fees as set forth in paragraph (c)(9)(i) of this section was sent by the IRS official to whom the request was delivered. Whenever interest is charged, the IRS shall begin assessing interest on the 31st day following the date the statement of fees was mailed to the requester. Interest shall be at the rate prescribed in 31 U.S.C. 3717. In addition, the IRS shall take all steps authorize by the Debt Collection Act of 1982, including administrative offset, disclosure to consumer reporting agencies, and use of col-

Reg. §601.702(f)(10)

lection agencies, as otherwise authorized by law to effect payment.

(11) *Aggregating requests.*—When the IRS official to whom a request is delivered reasonably believes that a requester or group of requesters is attempting to break down a request into a series of requests for the purpose of evading the assessment of fees, the IRS shall aggregate such requests and charge accordingly, upon notification to the requester and/or requesters.

(g) *Business information and contractor proposal procedures.*—(1) *In general.*—Business information provided to the IRS by a business submitter shall not be disclosed pursuant to a Freedom of Information Act request except in accordance with this section.

(2) *Definition.*—Business information is any trade secret or other confidential financial or commercial (including research) information.

(3) *Notice to business submitters.*—Except where it is determined that the information is covered by paragraph (g)(9), the official having control over the requested records, which includes business information, shall provide a business submitter with prompt written notice of a request encompassing its business information whenever required in accordance with paragraph (g)(4) of this section. Such written notice shall either describe the exact nature of the business information requested or provide copies of the records or portions thereof containing the business information.

(4) *When notice is required.*—(i) For business information submitted to the IRS prior to October 13, 1987, the official having control over the requested records shall provide a business submitter with notice of a request whenever—

(a) The business information was submitted to the IRS upon a commitment of confidentiality; or

(b) The business information was voluntarily submitted and it is of a kind that would customarily not be released to the public by the person from whom it was obtained; or

(c) The official has reason to believe that disclosure of the information may result in commercial or financial injury to the business submitter.

(ii) *For business information submitted to the IRS on or after October 13, 1987, the IRS shall provide a business submitter with notice of a request whenever.*—(a) The business submitter has designated the information as commercially or financially sensitive information; or

(b) The official has reason to believe that disclosure of the information may result in commercial or financial injury to the business submitter.

(iii) The business submitter's designation that the information is commercially or financially sensitive information should be supported by a statement or certification by an officer or authorized representative of the business providing specific justification that the information in question is, in fact, confidential commercial or financial information and has not been disclosed to the public.

(iv) Notice of a request for business information falling within paragraph (g)(4)(ii)(A) of this section shall be required for a period of not more than ten years after the date of submission unless the business submitter requests, and provides acceptable justification for, a specific notice period of greater duration.

(5) *Opportunity to object to disclosure.*— Through the notice described in paragraph (g)(3) of this section, the official having control over the requested records shall afford a business submitter ten days (excepting Saturdays, Sundays and legal public holidays) within which to provide the official with a detailed statement of any objection to disclosure. Such statement shall specify all grounds for withholding any of the information, with particular attention to why the information is claimed to be trade secret or commercial or financial information that is privileged and confidential. Information provided by a business submitter pursuant to this paragraph may itself be subject to disclosure under 5 U.S.C. 552.

(6) *Notice of intent to disclose.*—The IRS shall consider a business submitter's objections and specific grounds for nondisclosure prior to determining whether to disclose business information. Whenever the official having control over the requested records decides to disclose business information over the objection of a business submitter, the official shall forward to the business submitter a written notice which shall include—

(i) A statement of the reasons for which the business submitter's disclosure objections were not sustained;

(ii) A description of the business information to be disclosed; and

(iii) A specified disclosure date, which is ten days (excepting Saturdays, Sundays and legal public holidays) after the notice of the final decision to release the requested records has been mailed to the submitter. Except as otherwise prohibited by law, a copy of the disclosure notice shall be forwarded to the requester at the same time.

(7) *Judicial review.*—(i) *In general.*—The IRS' disposition of the request and the submitter's objections shall be subject to judicial review under paragraph (c)(14) of this section. A requester is not required to exhaust administrative remedies if a complaint has been filed under this paragraph by a business submitter of the information contained in the requested records. Likewise, a business submitter is not required to exhaust administrative remedies if a complaint has been filed by the requester of these records.

(ii) *Notice of FOIA lawsuit.*—Whenever a requester brings suit seeking to compel disclosure of business information covered by paragraph (g)(4) of this section, the official having control over the requested records shall promptly provide the business submitter with written notice thereof.

(iii) *Exception to notice requirement.*—The notice requirements of this paragraph shall not apply if—

(a) The official having control over the records determines that the business information shall not be disclosed;

(b) The information lawfully has been published or otherwise made available to the public; or

(c) Disclosure of the information is required by law (other than 5 U.S.C. 552).

(8) *Appeals.*—Procedures for administrative appeals from denials of requests for business information are to be processed in accordance with paragraph (c)(10) of this section.

(9) *Contractor Proposals.*—(i) Pursuant to 41 U.S.C. 253b(m), the IRS shall not release under the Freedom of Information Act any proposal submitted by a contractor in response to the requirements of a solicitation for a competitive proposal, unless that proposal is set forth or incorporated by reference in a contract entered into between the IRS and the contractor that submitted the proposal. For purposes of this paragraph, the term proposal means any proposal, including a technical, management, or cost proposal, submitted by a contractor in response to the requirements of a solicitation for a competitive proposal.

(ii) A copy of the FOIA request for information protected from disclosure under this paragraph shall be furnished to the contractor who submitted the proposal.

(h) *Responsible officials and their addresses.*—For purposes of this section, the IRS officials in the disclosure offices listed below are responsible for the control of records within their geographic area. In the case of records of the Headquarters Office (including records of the National Office of the Office of Chief Counsel), except as provided in paragraph (c)(9)(i)(a), the Director, Office of Governmental Liaison and Disclosure, or delegate, is the responsible official. Requests for these records should be sent to:

IRS FOIA Request
Headquarters Disclosure Office
CL:GLD:D
1111 Constitution Avenue, N.W.
Washington, D.C. 20224

(1) For Personnel Background Investigation Records, the address of the responsible official is:

Internal Revenue Service
Attn: Associate Director, Personnel Security
Room 4244, A:PS:PSO
1111 Constitution Avenue N.W.
Washington, D.C. 20224

(2) For records of the Office of Chief Counsel other than those located in the Headquarters or Division Counsel immediate offices, records shall be deemed to be under the jurisdiction of the local area Disclosure Office. Requesters seeking records under this section should send their requests to the local area Disclosure Office address listed for the state where the requester resides or any activity associated with the records occurred (for states with multiple offices, the request should be sent to the nearest office):

Alabama
IRS FOIA Request
New Orleans Disclosure Office
Mail Stop 40
600 S. Maestri Place
New Orleans, LA 70130

Alaska
IRS FOIA Request
Oakland Disclosure Office
1301 Clay Street, Suite 840-S
Oakland, CA 94612-5210

Arkansas
IRS FOIA Request
Nashville Disclosure Office
MDP 44
801 Broadway, Room 480
Nashville, TN 37203

Arizona
IRS FOIA Request
Phoenix Disclosure Office
Mail Stop 7000 PHX

210 E. Earll Drive
Phoenix, AZ 85012

California
IRS FOIA Request
Laguna Niguel Disclosure Office
24000 Avila Road, M/S 2201
Laguna Niguel, CA 92677-0207

IRS FOIA Request
Los Angeles Disclosure Office
Mail Stop 1020
300 N. Los Angeles Street
Los Angeles, CA 90012-3363

IRS FOIA Request
Oakland Disclosure Office
1301 Clay Street, Suite 840-S
Oakland, CA 94612

IRS FOIA Request
San Jose Disclosure Office
Mail Stop HQ-4603
55 South Market Street
San Jose, CA 95113

Colorado
IRS FOIA Request
Denver Disclosure Office
Mail Stop 7000 DEN
600 17th Street
Denver, CO 80202-2490

Connecticut
IRS FOIA Request
Hartford Disclosure Office
William R. Cotter F.O.B.
Mail Stop 140
135 High Street
Hartford, CT 06103

Delaware
IRS FOIA Request
Baltimore Disclosure Office
George Fallon Fed. Bldg.
31 Hopkins Plaza, Room 1210
Baltimore, MD 21201

District of Columbia
IRS FOIA Request
Baltimore Disclosure Office
George Fallon Fed. Bldg.
31 Hopkins Plaza, Room 1210
Baltimore, MD 21201

Florida
IRS FOIA Request
Fort Lauderdale Disclosure Off.
Mail Stop 4030
7850 SW 6th Court, Rm. 260
Plantation, FL 33324-3202

IRS FOIA Request
Jacksonville Disclosure Office
MS 4030

400 West Bay Street
Jacksonville, FL 32202-4437

Georgia
IRS FOIA Request
Atlanta Disclosure Office
Mail Stop 602D, Room 1905
401 W. Peachtree Street, NW
Atlanta, GA 30308

Hawaii
IRS FOIA Request
Laguna Niguel Disclosure Office
24000 Avila Road, M/S 2201
Laguna Niguel, CA 92677-0207

Idaho
IRS FOIA Request
Seattle Disclosure Office
Mail Stop W625
915 2nd Avenue
Seattle, WA 98174

Illinois
IRS FOIA Request
Chicago Disclosure Office
Mail Stop 7000 CHI, Room 2820
230 S. Dearborn Street
Chicago, IL 60604

Indiana
IRS FOIA Request
Indianapolis Disclosure Office
Mail Stop CL 658
575 N. Penn. Street
Indianapolis, IN 46204

Iowa
IRS FOIA Request
St. Paul Disclosure Office
Stop 7000
316 N. Robert Street
St. Paul, MN 55101

Kansas
IRS FOIA Request
St. Louis Disclosure Office
Mail Stop 7000 STL
P.O. Box 66781
St. Louis, MO 63166

Kentucky
IRS FOIA Request
Cincinnati Disclosure Office
Post Office Box 1818, Rm. 7019
Cincinnati, OH 45201

Louisiana
IRS FOIA Request
New Orleans Disclosure Office
Mail Stop 40
600 S. Maestri Place
New Orleans, LA 70130

Maine
IRS FOIA Request

Boston Disclosure Office
Mail Stop 41150
Post Office Box 9112
JFK Building
Boston, MA 02203

Maryland
IRS FOIA Request
Baltimore Disclosure Office
George Fallon Fed. Bldg.
31 Hopkins Plaza, Room 1210
Baltimore, MD 21201

Massachusetts
IRS FOIA Request
Boston Disclosure Office
Mail Stop 41150
JFK Building
Post Office Box 9112
Boston, MA 02203

Michigan
IRS FOIA Request
Detroit Disclosure Office
Mail Stop 11
Post Office Box 330500
Detroit, MI 48232-6500

Minnesota
IRS FOIA Request
St. Paul Disclosure Office
Stop 7000
316 N. Robert Street
St. Paul, MN 55101

Mississippi
IRS FOIA Request
New Orleans Disclosure Office
Mail Stop 40
600 S. Maestri Place
New Orleans, LA 70130

Missouri
IRS FOIA Request
St. Louis Disclosure Office
Mail Stop 7000 STL
P.O. Box 66781
St. Louis, MO 63166

Montana
IRS FOIA Request
Denver Disclosure Office
Mail Stop 7000 DEN
600 17th Street
Denver, CO 80202-2490

Nebraska
IRS FOIA Request
St. Paul Disclosure Office
Stop 7000
316 N. Robert Street
St. Paul, MN 55101

Nevada
IRS FOIA Request

Phoenix Disclosure Office
Mail Stop 7000 PHX
210 E. Earll Drive
Phoenix, AZ 85012

New Hampshire
IRS FOIA Request
Boston Disclosure Office
Mail Stop 41150
Post Office Box 9112
JFK Building
Boston, MA 02203

New Mexico
IRS FOIA Request
Phoenix Disclosure Office
Mail Stop 7000 PHX
210 E. Earll Drive
Phoenix, AZ 85012

New Jersey
IRS FOIA Request
Springfield Disclosure Office
P.O. Box 748
Springfield, N.J. 07081-0748

New York (Brooklyn, Queens, and the
counties of Nassau and Suffolk)
IRS FOIA Request
Brooklyn Disclosure Office
10 Metro Tech Center
625 Fulton Street
4th Floor, Suite 611
Brooklyn, N.Y. 11201-5404

New York (Manhattan, Staten Island, the
Bronx, and the counties of Rockland and
Westchester)
IRS FOIA Request
Manhattan Disclosure Office
110 W. 44th Street
New York, N.Y. 10036

New York (all other counties)
IRS FOIA Request
Buffalo Disclosure Office
111 West Huron St., Room 505
Buffalo, N.Y. 14202

North Carolina
IRS FOIA Request
Greensboro Disclosure Office
320 Federal Place, Room 409
Greensboro, N.C. 27401

North Dakota
IRS FOIA Request
St. Paul Disclosure Office
Stop 7000
316 N. Robert Street
St. Paul, MN 55101

Ohio
IRS FOIA Request
Cincinnati Disclosure Office

Post Office Box 1818, Rm. 7019
Cincinnati, OH 45201
Oklahoma
IRS FOIA Request
Oklahoma City Disclosure Office
Mail Stop 7000 OKC
55 N. Robinson
Oklahoma City, OK 73102
Oregon
IRS FOIA Request
Seattle Disclosure Office
Mail Stop W625
915 2nd Avenue
Seattle, WA 98174
Pennsylvania
IRS FOIA Request
Philadelphia Disclosure Office
600 Arch Street, Room 3214
Philadelphia, PA 19106
Rhode Island
IRS FOIA Request
Hartford Disclosure Office
William R. Cotter F.O.B.
Mail Stop 140
135 High Street
Hartford, CT 06103
South Carolina
IRS FOIA Request
Greensboro Disclosure Office
320 Federal Place, Room 409
Greensboro, N.C. 27401
South Dakota
IRS FOIA Request
St. Paul Disclosure Office
Stop 7000
316 N. Robert Street
St. Paul, MN 55101
Tennessee
IRS FOIA Request
Nashville Disclosure Office
MDP 44
801 Broadway, Room 480
Nashville, TN 37203
Texas
IRS FOIA Request
Austin Disclosure Office
Mail Stop 7000 AUS
300 East 8th Street, Room 262
Austin, TX 78701
IRS FOIA Request
Dallas Disclosure Office
Mail Stop 7000 DAL
1100 Commerce Street
Dallas, TX 75242

IRS FOIA Request
Houston Disclosure Office
Mail Stop 7000 HOU
1919 Smith Street
Houston, TX 77002
Utah
IRS FOIA Request
Denver Disclosure Office
Mail Stop 7000 DEN
600 17th Street
Denver, CO 80202-2490
Vermont
IRS FOIA Request
Boston Disclosure Office
Mail Stop 41150
Post Office Box 9112
JFK Building
Boston, MA 02203
Virginia
IRS FOIA Request
Richmond Disclosure Office
P.O. Box 10107
Richmond, VA 23240
Washington
IRS FOIA Request
Seattle Disclosure Office
Mail Stop 625
915 2nd Avenue
Seattle, WA 98174
West Virginia
IRS FOIA Request
Cincinnati Disclosure Office
Post Office Box 1818, Rm. 7019
Cincinnati, OH 45201
Wisconsin
IRS FOIA Request
Milwaukee Disclosure Office
Mail Stop 7000 MIL
310 W. Wisconsin Avenue
Milwaukee, WI 53203-2221
Wyoming
IRS FOIA Request
Denver Disclosure Office
Mail Stop 7000 DEN
600 17th Street
Denver, CO 80202-2490
All APO and FPO addresses
IRS FOIA Request
Headquarters Disclosure Office
CL:GLD:D
1111 Constitution Avenue, N.W.
Washington, D.C. 20224

Subpart H—Tax Counseling for the Elderly

[Reg § 601.801]

§ 601.801. Purpose and statutory authority.—
(a) This Subpart H contains the rules for implementation of the Tax Counseling for the Elderly assistance program under Section 163 of the Revenue Act of 1978, Public Law 95-600, November 6, 1978 (92 Stat. 2810). Section 163 authorizes the Secretary of the Treasury, through the Internal Revenue Service, to enter into agreements with private or public non-profit agencies or organizations for the purpose of providing training and technical assistance to prepare volunteers to provide tax counseling assistance for elderly individuals, age 60 and over, in the preparation of their Federal income tax returns.

(b) Section 163 provides that the Secretary may provide:

(1) Preferential access to Internal Revenue Service taxpayer service representatives for the purpose of making available technical information needed during the course of the volunteers' work;

(2) Publicity for making elderly persons aware of the availability of volunteer taxpayer return preparation assistance programs under this section; and

(3) Technical materials and publications to be used by such volunteers.

(c) In carrying out responsibilities under Section 163, the Secretary, through the Internal Revenue Service is also authorized:

(1) To provide assistance to organizations which demonstrate, to the satisfaction of the Secretary, that their volunteers are adequately trained and competent to render effective tax counseling to the elderly in the preparation of Federal income tax returns;

(2) To provide for the training of such volunteers, and to assist in such training, to ensure that such volunteers are qualified to provide tax counseling assistance to elderly individuals in the preparation of Federal income tax returns;

(3) To provide reimbursement to volunteers through such organizations for transportation, meals, and other expenses incurred by them in training or providing tax counseling assistance in the preparation of Federal income tax returns under this section, and such other support and assistance determined to be appropriate in carrying out the provisions of the section;

(4) To provide for the use of services, personnel, and facilities of Federal executive agencies and State and local public agencies with their consent, with or without reimbursement; and

(5) To prescribe rules and regulations necessary to carry out the provisions of the section.

(d) With regard to the employment status of volunteers, section 163 also provides that service as a volunteer in any program carried out under this section shall not be considered service as an employee of the United States. Volunteers under such a program shall not be subject to the provisions of law relating to Federal employment, except that the provisions relating to the illegal disclosure of income or other information punishable under Section 1905 of Title 18, United States Code, shall apply to volunteers as if they were employees of the United States.

[Reg. § 601.802]

§ 601.802. Cooperative agreements.—
(a) *General.*—Tax Counseling for the Elderly programs will be administered by sponsor organizations under cooperative agreements with the Internal Revenue Service. Use of cooperative agreements is in accordance with the Federal Grant and Cooperative Agreement Act of 1977, Public Law 95-224, February 3, 1978 (92 Stat. 3, 41 U.S.C. 501-509). Cooperative agreements will be legally binding agreements in document form.

(b) *Nature and contents of cooperative agreements.*—Each cooperative agreement will provide for implementation of the program in specified geographic areas. Cooperative agreements will set forth:

(1) The functions and duties to be performed by the Internal Revenue Service and the functions and duties to be performed by the program sponsor,

(2) The maximum amount of the award available to the program sponsor,

(3) The services to be provided for each geographical area, and

(4) Other requirements specified in the application.

(c) *Entry into cooperative agreements.*—The Commissioner of Internal Revenue, the Director, Taxpayer Service Division, or any other individual designated by the Commissioner may enter into a cooperative agreement for the Internal Revenue Service.

(d) *Competitive award of cooperative agreements.*—Cooperative agreements will generally be entered into based upon competition among eligible applicants.

(1) To be eligible to enter into a cooperative agreement, an organization must be a private or public non-profit agency or organization with

experience in coordinating volunteer programs. Federal, state, and local governmental agencies and organizations will not be eligible to become program sponsors.

(2) Eligible applicants will be selected to enter into cooperative agreements based on an evaluation by the Internal Revenue Service of material provided in their applications. The Service will set forth the evaluative criteria in the application instructions.

(3) Determinations as to the eligibility and selection of agencies and organizations to enter into cooperative agreements will be made solely by the Internal Revenue Service and will not be subject to appeal.

(e) *Noncompetitive award of cooperative agreements.*—If appropriations to implement the Tax Counseling for the Elderly program are received at a time close to when tax return preparation assistance must be provided or when other factors exist which make the use of competition to select agencies and organizations to enter into cooperative agreements impracticable, cooperative agreements will be entered into without competition with eligible agencies and organizations selected by the Internal Revenue Service. Determination of when the use of competition is impracticable will be made solely by the Internal Revenue Service and will not be subject to appeal.

(f) *Renegotiation, suspension, termination and modification.*

(1) Cooperative agreements will be subject to renegotiation (including the maximum amount of the award available to a sponsor), suspension, or termination if performance reports required by the cooperative agreement and/or other evaluations by or audits by the Internal Revenue Service or others indicate that planned performance goals or other provisions of the cooperative agreement, the regulations, or Section 163 of the Revenue Act of 1978 are not being satisfactorily met. The necessity for renegotiation, suspension, or termination, will be determined solely by the Internal Revenue Service and will not be subject to appeal.

(2) Cooperative agreements may be modified in writing by mutual agreement between the Internal Revenue Service and the program sponsor at any time. Modifications will be based upon factors such as an inability to utilize all funds available under a cooperative agreement, the availability of additional funds and an ability to effectively utilize additional funds, and interference of some provisions with the efficient operation of the program.

(g) *Negotiation.*—If the proposed program of an eligible applicant does not warrant award of an agreement, the Internal Revenue Service may negotiate with the applicant to bring the application up to a standard that will be adequate for award. If more than one inadequate application has been received for the geographic area involved, negotiation to bring all such applications up to standard will be conducted with all such applicants unless time does not permit negotiations with all.

[Reg. § 601.803]

§ 601.803. Program operations and requirements.—(a) *Objective.*—The objective of the Tax Counseling for the Elderly program is to provide free assistance in the preparation of Federal income tax returns to elderly taxpayers age 60 and over, by providing training, technical and administrative support to volunteers under the direction of non-profit agencies and organizations that have cooperative agreements with the Internal Revenue Service.

(b) *Period of program operations.*—Most tax return preparation assistance will be provided to elderly taxpayers during the period for filing Federal income tax returns, from January 1 to April 15 each year. However, the program activities required to ensure elderly taxpayers efficient and quality tax assistance will normally be conducted year round. Program operations will generally be divided into the following segments each year: October—recruit volunteers; November and December—set training and testing schedules for volunteers, identify assistance sites, complete publicity plans for sites; December and January—train and test volunteers, set volunteer assistance schedules; January through May—provide tax assistance, conduct publicity for sites; May and June—prepare final report and evaluate program; July and August—prepare for next year's program.

(c) *Assistance requirements.*—All tax return preparation assistance provided under Tax Counseling for the Elderly programs must be provided free of charge to taxpayers and must be provided only to elderly individuals. An elderly individual is an individual age 60 or over at the close of the individual's taxable year with respect to which tax return preparation assistance is to be provided. Where a joint return is involved, assistance may be provided where only one spouse satisfies the 60 year age requirement.

(d) *Training and testing of volunteers.*—Volunteers will normally be provided training and will normally be required to pass tests designed to measure their understanding of Federal tax subjects on which they will provide tax return assistance. Volunteers who do not receive a satisfactory score will not be eligible to participate in the program.

(e) *Confidentiality of tax information.*—Program sponsors must obtain written assurance from all volunteers and all other individuals involved in the program, to respect the confidentiality of income and financial information known as a result of preparation of a return or of providing tax counseling assistance in the preparation of Federal income tax returns.

[Reg. § 601.804]

§ 601.804. Reimbursements.—(a) *General.*—When provided for in cooperative agreements, the Internal Revenue Service will provide amounts to program sponsors for reimbursement to volunteers for transportation, meals, and other expenses incurred in training or providing tax return assistance and to program sponsors for reimbursement of overhead expenses. Cooperative agreements will establish the items for which reimbursements will be allowed and the method of reimbursement, e.g. stipend versus actual expenses for meals, as well as developing necessary procedures, forms, and accounting and financial control systems.

(b) *Direct, reasonable, and prudent expenses.*—Reimbursements will be allowed only for direct, reasonable, and prudent expenses incurred as a part of a volunteer's service or as a part of the program's sponsor's overhead.

(c) *Limitation.*—Total reimbursements provided to a program sponsor shall not exceed the total amount specified in the cooperative agreement. The Internal Revenue Service shall not be liable for additional amounts to program sponsors, volunteers, or anyone else.

(d) *Availability of appropriated funds.*—Expense reimbursements and other assistance to be provided by the Internal Revenue Service under cooperative agreements are contingent upon the availability of appropriated funds for the Tax Counseling for the Elderly program.

[Reg. § 601.805]

§ 601.805. Miscellaneous administrative provisions.—(a) *Responsibilities and relationship of Internal Revenue and program sponsor.*—Substantial involvement is anticipated between the Internal Revenue Service and the program sponsors in conducting this program. Specific responsibilities and obligations of the Internal Revenue Service and the program sponsors will be set forth in each cooperative agreement.

(b) *Administrative requirements set forth in OMB and Treasury Circulars.*—(1) The basic administrative requirements applicable to individual cooperative agreements are contained in Office of Management and Budget Circular No. A-110, Grants and Agreements with Institutions of Higher Education, Hospitals and Other Nonprofit Organizations (41 F.R. 32016). All applicable provisions of this circular and any existing and further supplements and revisions are incorporated into these regulations and into all cooperative agreements entered into between the Internal Revenue Service and program sponsors.

(2) Additional operating procedures and instructions may be developed by the Internal Revenue Service to direct recipient organizations in carrying out the provisions of this subpart, such as instructions for using letters of credit. Any such operating procedures or instructions will be incorporated into each cooperative agreement.

(c) *Joint funding.*—Tax Counseling for the Elderly programs will not be eligible for joint funding. Accordingly, the Joint Funding Simplification Act of 1974, Public Law 93-510, December 5, 1974 (88 Stat. 1604, 42 U.S.C. 4251-4261) and Office of Management and Budget Circular No. A-111, Jointly Funded Assistance to State and Local Governments and Nonprofit Organizations (41 F.R. 32039), will not apply.

(d) *Discrimination.*—No program sponsor shall discriminate against any person providing tax return assistance on the basis of age, sex, race, religion or national origin in conducting program operations. No program sponsor shall discriminate against any person in providing such assistance on the basis of sex, race, religion or national origin.

[Reg. § 601.806]

§ 601.806. Solicitation of applications.—(a) *Solicitation.*—The Commissioner of Internal Revenue or the Commissioner's delegate may, at any time, solicit eligible agencies and organizations to submit applications. Generally, applications will be solicited and accepted in June and July of each year. Deadlines for submitting applications and the schedule for selecting program sponsors will be provided with application documents.

(1) Before preparing and submitting an unsolicited application, organizations are strongly

encouraged to contact the Internal Revenue Service at the address provided in (b)(2) of this section.

(2) A solicitation of an application is not an assurance or commitment that the Internal Revenue Service will enter into a cooperative agreement. The Internal Revenue Service will not pay any expenses or other costs incurred by the applicant in considering, preparing or submitting an application.

(b) *Application.*

(1) In the application documents, the Commissioner or the Commissioner's delegate will specify program requirements which the applicant must meet.

(2) Eligible organizations interested in participating in the Internal Revenue Service Tax Counseling for the Elderly program should request an application from the:

Program Manager
Tax Counseling for the Elderly
Taxpayer Service Division TX:T:I
Internal Revenue Service
1111 Constitution Ave., N.W.
Washington, D.C. 20224(202) 566-4904

Subpart I—Use of Penalty Mail in the Location and Recovery of Missing Children

[Reg. §601.901]

§601.901. Missing children shown on penalty mail.—(a) *Purpose.*—To support the national effort to locate and recover missing children, the Internal Revenue Service (IRS) joins other executive departments and agencies of the Government of the United States in using official mail to disseminate photographs and biographical information on hundreds of missing children.

(b) *Procedures for obtaining and disseminating data.*—(1) The IRS shall publish pictures and biographical data related to missing children in domestic penalty mail containing annual tax forms and instructions, taxpayer information publications, and other IRS products directed to members of the public in the United States and its territories and possessions.

(2) Missing children information shall not be placed on the "Penalty Indicia," "OCR Read Area," "Bar Code Read Area," and "Return Address" areas of letter-size envelopes.

(3) The IRS shall accept photographic and biographical materials solely from the National Center for Missing and Exploited Children (National Center). Photographs that were reasonably current as of the time of the child's disappearance, or those which have been updated to reflect a missing child's current age through computer enhancement technique, shall be the only acceptable form of visual media or pictorial likeness used in penalty mail.

(c) *Withdrawal of data.*—The shelf life of printed penalty mail is limited to 3 months for missing child cases. The IRS shall follow those guidelines whenever practicable. For products with an extended shelf life, such as those related to filing and paying taxes, the IRS will not print any pictures or biographical data relating to missing children without obtaining from the National Center a waiver of the 3-month shelf-life guideline.

(d) *Reports and contact official.*—IRS shall compile and submit to OJJDP reports on its experience in implementing Public Law 99-87, 99 Stat. 290, as required by that office. The IRS contact person is: Chief, Business Publications Section (or successor office), Tax Forms and Publications Division, Technical Publications Branch, OP:FS:FP:P:3, Room 5613, Internal Revenue Service, 1111 Constitution Ave., N.W., Washington, DC 20224.

(e) *Period of applicability.*—This section is applicable December 13, 1999 through December 31, 2002.

APPENDIX B
PROPOSED REGULATIONS FOR
CIRCULAR 230

[4830-01-p]

DEPARTMENT OF THE TREASURY

Office of the Secretary

31 CFR Part 10

[REG-122379-02]

RIN 1545-BA70

Regulations Governing Practice Before the Internal Revenue Service

AGENCY: Office of the Secretary, Treasury.

ACTION: Notice of proposed rulemaking and notice of public hearing.

SUMMARY: This notice proposes modifications of the regulations governing practice before the Internal Revenue Service (Circular 230). These regulations affect individuals who are eligible to practice before the IRS. The proposed modifications set forth best practices for tax advisors providing advice to taxpayers relating to Federal tax issues or submissions to the IRS and modify the standards for certain tax shelter opinions. This document also provides notice of a public hearing regarding the proposed regulations.

DATES: Comments: Written or electronically generated comments must be received by February 13, 2004.

Public hearing: Outlines of topics to be discussed at the public hearing scheduled for February 18, 2004, in the Auditorium of the Internal Revenue Building at 1111 Constitution Avenue, NW., Washington, DC 20224, must be received by February 11, 2004. ADDRESSES: Send submissions to: CC:PA:LPD:PR (REG-122379-02), room 5203, Internal Revenue Service, POB 7604, Ben Franklin Station, Washington, DC 20044. Submissions may be hand delivered Monday through Friday between the 2 hours of 8 a.m. and 4 p.m. to: CC:PA:LPD:PR (REG-122379-02), Courier's Desk, Internal Revenue Service, 1111 Constitution Avenue, NW., Washington, DC. Alternatively, taxpayers may submit comments electronically via the IRS Internet site at: *www.irs.gov/regs*.

FOR FURTHER INFORMATION CONTACT: Concerning issues for comment, Heather L. Dostaler or Bridget E. Tombul at (202) 622-4940; concerning submissions of comments, Guy Traynor of the Publications and Regulations Branch at (202) 622-7180 (not toll-free numbers).

SUPPLEMENTARY INFORMATION:

Paperwork Reduction Act

The collection of information contained in this notice of proposed rulemaking has been submitted to the Office of Management and Budget for review in accordance with the Paperwork Reduction Act of 1995 (44 U.S.C. 3507). Comments on the collection of information should be sent to the **Office of Management and Budget**, Attn: Desk Officer for the Department of the Treasury, Office of Information and Regulatory Affairs, Washington, DC 20503, with copies to the **Internal Revenue Service**, Attn: IRS Reports Clearance Officer, SE:W:CAR:MP:T:T:SP, Washington, DC 20224. Comments on the collection of information should be received by March 1, 2004. Comments are specifically requested concerning:

Whether the proposed collection of information is necessary for the proper performance of the Office of Professional Responsibility, including whether the information will have practical utility;

The accuracy of the estimated burden associated with the proper collection of information (see below);

How the quality, utility, and clarity of the information to be collected may be enhanced;

How the burden of complying with the proposed collection of information may be minimized, including through the application of automated collection techniques or other forms of information technology; and

Estimates of capital or start-up costs and costs of operation, maintenance, and purchase of services to provide information.

The collections of information (disclosure requirements) in these proposed regulations are in Sec. 10.35(d). Section 10.35(d) requires a practitioner providing a tax shelter opinion to make certain disclosures in the beginning of marketed tax shelter opinions, limited scope opinions and opinions that fail to conclude at a confidence level of at least more likely than not. In addition, certain relationships between the practitioner and a person promoting or marketing a tax shelter must be disclosed. A practitioner may be required to make one or more disclosure at the beginning of an opinion. The collection of this material helps to ensure that taxpayers who receive a tax shelter opinion are informed of any facts or circumstances that might limit the taxpayer's use of the opinion. The collection of information is mandatory.

Estimated total annual disclosure burden is 13,333 hours.

Estimated annual burden per disclosing practitioner varies from 5 to 10 minutes, depending on individual circumstances, with an estimated average of 8 minutes.

Estimated number of disclosing practitioners is 100,000.

Estimated annual frequency of responses is on occasion.

An agency may not conduct or sponsor, and a person is not required to respond to a collection of information unless it displays a valid control number assigned by the Office of Management and Budget.

Books or records relating to a collection of information must be retained as long as their contents may become material in the administration of any internal revenue law. Generally, tax returns and tax return information are confidential, as required by section 6103 of the Internal Revenue Code.

Background

Section 330 of title 31 of the United States Code authorizes the Secretary of the Treasury to regulate the practice of representatives before the Treasury Department. The Secretary has published the regulations in Circular 230 (31 CFR part 10). On February 23, 1984, the regulations were amended to provide standards for tax shelter opinions (49 FR 6719). On May 5, 2000, an advance notice of proposed rulemaking was published (65 FR 30375) which requested comments regarding amendments to the standards of practice governing tax shelters and other general matters. On January 12, 2001, a notice of proposed rulemaking (66 FR 3276) was published that proposed amendments to the regulations relating to practice before the Internal Revenue Service in general and addressing tax shelter opinions in particular. On July 26, 2002, final regulations (67 FR 48760) were issued incorporating only the non-tax shelter related matters. The IRS and the Treasury Department announced that regulations governing standards for tax shelter opinions would be proposed again at a later date.

This document proposes new proposed amendments to the standards governing tax shelter opinions and withdraws proposed amendments to §§ 10.33, 10.35 and 10.36 of the regulations governing practice before the IRS that were published in 2001. See 66 FR 3276 (Jan. 12, 2001).

Explanation of Provisions

Tax advisors play an increasingly important role in the Federal tax system, which is founded on principles of voluntary compliance. The tax system is best served when the public has confidence in the honesty and integrity of the professionals providing tax advice. To restore, promote, and maintain the public's confidence in those individuals and firms, these proposed regulations set forth best practices applicable to all tax advisors. These regulations also amend the mandatory requirements for practitioners who provide certain tax shelter opinions. These regulations are limited to practice before the IRS and do not alter or supplant other ethical standards applicable to practitioners.

The standards set forth in these proposed regulations differ from the January 12, 2001 proposed regulations in several ways. First, § 10.33 prescribes best practices for all tax advisors. Second, § 10.35 combines and modifies the standards applicable to marketed and more likely than not tax shelter opinions in former § 10.33 (tax shelter opinions used to market tax shelters) and former § 10.35 (more likely than not tax shelter opinions) of the January 12, 2001 proposed regulations. Third, these regulations revise proposed § 10.36, which provides procedures for ensuring compliance with §§ 10.33 and 10.35. Finally, provisions relating to advisory committees to the Office of Professional Responsibility are provided in new § 10.37. The Treasury Department and the IRS will publish conforming amendments to §§ 10.22 and 10.52 in a separate notice of proposed rulemaking.

Best Practices

To ensure the integrity of the tax system, tax professionals should adhere to best practices when providing advice or assisting their clients in the preparation of a submission to the IRS. Section 10.33 describes the best practices to be observed by all tax advisors in providing clients with the highest quality representation. These best practices include: (1) communicating clearly with the client regarding the terms of the engagement and the form and scope of the advice or assistance to be rendered; (2) establishing the relevant facts, including evaluating the reasonableness of any assumptions or representations; (3) relating applicable law, including potentially applicable judicial doctrines, to the relevant facts; (4) arriving at a conclusion supported by the law and the facts; (5) advising the client regarding the import of the conclusions reached; and (6) acting fairly and with integrity in practice before the IRS.

Standards for Certain Tax Shelter Opinions

Section 10.35 prescribes requirements for practitioners providing *more likely than not* and *marketed* tax shelter opinions. A more likely than not tax shelter opinion is a tax shelter opinion that reaches a conclusion of at least more likely than not with respect to one or more material Federal tax issue(s). A marketed tax shelter opinion is a tax shelter opinion, including a more likely than not tax shelter opinion, that a practitioner knows, or has reason to know, will be used or referred to by a person other than the practitioner (or a person who is a member of, associated with, or employed by the practitioner's firm) in promoting, marketing or recommending a tax shelter to o ne or more taxpayers.

Definition of Tax Shelter Opinion

These proposed regulations retain the definition of *tax shelter* proposed in January 2001 by applying the definition found in section 6662 to all taxes under the Internal Revenue Code. A number of commentators expressed concern that this definition is overly broad, encompasses routine tax matters, and is difficult to administer by practitioners and the IRS. After careful consideration of these issues, the Treasury Department and the IRS have determined that the definition in the proposed regulations best defines the scope of these regulations. Section 10.35 has been modified, however, to address commentators' concerns by excluding from the definition of a tax shelter opinion preliminary advice provided pursuant to an engagement in which the practitioner is expected subsequently to provide an opinion that satisfies the requirements of this section. In addition, under § 10.35(a)(3)(ii), a practitioner may provide an opinion that is limited to some, but not all, material Federal tax issues that may be relevant to the treatment of a tax shelter item if the taxpayer and the practitioner agree to limit the scope of the opinion. Such a limited scope opinion cannot be a marketed tax shelter opinion, and all limited scope opinions must contain the appropriate disclosures described below.

Requirements for Tax Shelter Opinions

The requirements for all more likely than not and marketed tax shelter opinions include: (1) identifying and considering all relevant facts and not relying on any unreasonable factual assumptions or representations; (2) relating the applicable law (including potentially applicable judicial doctrines) to the relevant facts and not relying on any unreasonable legal assumptions, representations or conclusions; (3) considering all material Federal tax issues and reaching a conclusion, supported by the facts and the law, with respect to each material Federal tax issue; and (4) providing an overall conclusion as to the Federal tax treatment of the tax shelter item or items and the reasons for that conclusion.

In addition to the exception to the requirements for limited scope opinions discussed above, in the case of a marketed tax shelter opinion, a practitioner is not expected to identify and ascertain facts peculiar to a taxpayer to whom the transaction is marketed, but the opinion must include the appropriate disclosure described below. Moreover, if a practitioner is unable to reach a conclusion with respect to one or more material Federal tax issue(s) or to reach an overall conclusion in a tax shelter opinion, the opinion must state that the practitioner is unable to reach a conclusion with respect to those issues or to reach an overall conclusion and describe the reasons that the practitioner is unable to reach such a conclusion. If the practitioner fails to reach a conclusion at a confidence level of at least more likely than not with respect to one or more material Federal tax issue(s), the opinion must include the appropriate disclosures described below.

Required Disclosures

Section 10.35(d) provides disclosures that are required to be made in the beginning of marketed tax shelter opinions, limited scope opinions, and opinions that fail to reach a conclusion at a confidence level of at least more likely than not. In addition, certain relationships between the practitioner and a person promoting or marketing a tax shelter must be disclosed. A practitioner may be required to make more than one of the disclosures described below.

1. *Relationship Between Practitioner and Promoter*

Under § 10.35(d)(1), a practitioner must disclose if the practitioner has a compensation arrangement with any person (other than the client for whom the opinion is prepared) with respect to the promoting, marketing or recommending of a tax shelter discussed in the opinion. A practitioner also must disclose if there is any referral agreement between the practitioner and any person (other than the client for whom the opinion is prepared) engaged in the promoting, marketing or recommending of the tax shelter discussed in the opinion.

2. *Marketed Tax Shelter Opinion*

Under § 10.35(d)(2), a practitioner must disclose that a marketed opinion may not be sufficient for a taxpayer to use for the purpose of avoiding penalties under section 6662(d) of the Code. The practitioner also must state that taxpayers should seek advice from their own tax advisors.

3. *Limited Scope Opinion*

Under § 10.35(d)(3), a practitioner must disclose in a limited scope opinion that additional issue(s) may exist that could affect the Federal tax treatment of the tax shelter addressed in the opinion, that the opinion does not consider or reach a conclusion with respect to those additional issues and that the opinion was not written, and cannot be used by the recipient, for the purpose of avoiding penalties under section 6662(d) of the Code with respect to those issues outside the scope of the opinion.

4. *Opinions That Fail to Reach a Conclusion at a Confidence Level of at Least More Likely Than Not*

Under § 10.35(d)(4), a practitioner must disclose that the opinion fails to reach a conclusion at a confidence level of at least more likely than not with respect to one or more material Federal tax issue(s) addressed by the opinion and that the opinion was not written, and cannot be used by the recipient, for the purpose of avoiding penalties under section 6662(d) of the Code with respect to such issue(s).

Procedures to Ensure Compliance

Section 10.36 provides that tax advisors with responsibility for overseeing a firm's practice before the IRS should take reasonable steps to ensure that the firm's procedures for all members, associates, and employees are consistent with the best practices described in § 10.33. In the case of tax shelter opinions, a practitioner with this oversight responsibility must take reasonable steps to ensure that the firm has adequate procedures in effect for purposes of complying with § 10.35.

Advisory Committees on the Integrity of Tax Professionals

Section 10.37 authorizes the Director of the Office of Professional Responsibility to establish one or more advisory committees composed of at least five individuals authorized to practice before the IRS. Under procedures prescribed by the Director and at the request of the Director, an advisory committee may review and make recommendations regarding professional standards or best practices for tax advisors or may advise the Director whether a practitioner may have violated § § 10.35 or 10.36.

Proposed Effective Date

These regulations are proposed to apply on the date that final regulations are published in the **Federal Register**.

Special Analyses

It has been determined that this notice of proposed rulemaking is not a significant regulatory action as defined in Executive Order 12866. Therefore, a regulatory assessment is not required. It is hereby certified that these regulations will not have a significant economic impact on a substantial number of small entities. Persons authorized to practice before the IRS have long been required to comply with certain standards of conduct. The added disclosure requirements for tax shelter opinions imposed by these regulations will not have a significant economic impact on a substantial number of small entities because, as previously noted, the estimated burden of disclosures is minimal. This is because practitioners have the information needed to determine whether some of the disclosures are required before the opinion is prepared and for the other disclosures the regulations provide practitioners with the language to be included in the opinion. Therefore, a regulatory flexibility analysis under the Regulatory Flexibility Act (5 U.S.C. chapter 6) is not required. Pursuant to section 7805(f) of the Internal Revenue Code, this notice of proposed rulemaking will be submitted to the Chief Counsel for Advocacy of the Small Business Administration for comment on its impact on small businesses.

Comments and Public Hearing

Before the regulations are adopted as final regulations, consideration will be given to any written comments and electronic comments that are submitted timely to the IRS. The IRS and Treasury Department specifically request comments on the clarity of the proposed regulations and how they can be made easier to understand. All comments will be available for public inspection and copying.

The public hearing is scheduled for February 18, 2004, at 10 a.m., and will be held in the Auditorium, Internal Revenue Building, 1111 Constitution Avenue, NW., Washington, DC. Due to building security procedures, visitors must enter at the Constitution Avenue entrance. All visitors must present photo identification to enter the building. Visitors will not be admitted beyond the immediate entrance area more than 30 minutes before the hearing starts. For information about having your name placed on the building access list to attend the hearing, see the FOR FURTHER INFORMATION CONTACT section of this preamble.

The rules of 26 CFR 601.601(a)(3) apply to the hearing. Persons who wish to present oral comments at the hearing must submit written or electronic comments by February 13, 2004, and submit an outline of the topics to be discussed and the time to be devoted to each topic by February 11, 2004. A period of 10 minutes will be allocated to each person for making comments.

An agenda showing the scheduling of the speakers will be prepared after the deadline for receiving outlines has passed. Copies of the agenda will be available free of charge at the hearing.

Drafting Information

The principal authors of the regulations are Heather L. Dostaler, Bridget E. Tombul, and Brinton T. Warren of the Office of the Associate Chief Counsel (Procedure and Administration), Administrative Provisions and Judicial Practice Division, but other personnel from the IRS and Treasury Department participated in their development.

List of Subjects in 31 CFR Part 10

Administrative practice and procedure, Lawyers, Accountants, Enrolled agents, Enrolled actuaries, Appraisers.

Proposed Amendments to the Regulations

Accordingly, 31 CFR part 10 is proposed to be amended as follows

Paragraph 1. The authority citation for subtitle A, part 10 continues to read as follows:

[Authority: Sec. 3, 23 Stat. 258, secs. 2-12, 60 Stat. 237 et.seq.; 5 U.S.C. 301, 500, 551-559; 31 U.S.C. 330; Reorg. Plan No. 26 of 1950, 15 FR 4935, 64 Stat. 1280, 3 CFR, 1949-1953 Comp., P. 1017.]

PART 10—PRACTICE BEFORE THE INTERNAL REVENUE SERVICE

Par. 2. Section 10.33 is revised to read as follows:

§ 10.33 Best practices for tax advisors.

(a) *Best practices.* Tax advisors should provide clients with the highest quality representation concerning Federal tax issues by adhering to best practices in providing advice and in preparing or assisting in the preparation of a submission to the Internal Revenue Service. Best practices include the following:

(1) Communicating clearly with the client regarding the terms of the engagement. For example, the advisor should determine the client's expected purpose for and use of the advice and should have a clear understanding with the client regarding the form and scope of the advice or assistance to be rendered.

(2) Establishing the facts, determining which facts are relevant, and evaluating the reasonableness of any assumptions or representations.

(3) Relating the applicable law (including potentially applicable judicial doctrines) to the relevant facts.

(4) Arriving at a conclusion supported by the law and the facts.

(5) Advising the client regarding the import of the conclusions reached, including, for example, whether a taxpayer may avoid penalties for a substantial understatement of income tax under section 6662(d) of the Internal Revenue Code if a taxpayer acts in reliance on the advice.

(6) Acting fairly and with integrity in practice before the Internal Revenue Service.

(b) *Effective date.* This section is effective on the date that final regulations are published in the Federal Register.

Par. 3. Section 10.35 is added to read as follows:

§ 10.35 Requirements for certain tax shelter opinions.

(a) *In general.* A practitioner providing a *more likely than not tax shelter opinion* or a *marketed tax shelter opinion* must comply with each of the following requirements.

(1) *Factual matters.* (i) The practitioner must use reasonable efforts to identify and ascertain the facts, which may relate to future events if a transaction is prospective or proposed, and determine which facts are relevant. The opinion must identify and consider all relevant facts.

(ii) The practitioner must not base the opinion on any unreasonable factual assumptions (including assumptions as to future events), such as a factual assumption that the practitioner knows or should know is incorrect or incomplete. For example, it is unreasonable to assume that a transaction has a business purpose or that a transaction is potentially profitable apart from tax benefits, or to make an assumption with respect to a material valuation issue. In the case of any *marketed tax shelter opinion*, the practitioner is not expected to identify or ascertain facts peculiar to a taxpayer to whom the transaction may be marketed, but the opinion must include the appropriate disclosure(s) required under paragraph (d) of this section.

(iii) The practitioner must not base the opinion on any unreasonable factual representations, statements or findings of the taxpayer or any other person, such as a factual representation that the practitioner knows or should know is incorrect or incomplete. For example, a practitioner may not rely on a taxpayer's factual representation that a transaction has a business purpose if the representation fails to include a specific description of the business purpose or the practitioner knows or should know that the representation is incorrect or incomplete.

(2) *Relate law to facts.* (i) The practitioner must relate the applicable law (including potentially applicable judicial doctrines) to the relevant facts.

(ii) The practitioner must not assume the favorable resolution of any material Federal tax issue except as provided in paragraphs (a)(3)(ii) and (b) of this section, or otherwise base an opinion on any unreasonable legal assumptions, representations, or conclusions.

(iii) The practitioner's opinion must not contain internally inconsistent legal analyses or conclusions.

(3) *Evaluation of material Federal tax issues.* (i) The practitioner must consider all material Federal tax issues except as provided in paragraphs (a)(3)(ii) and (b) of this section.

(ii) The practitioner may provide an opinion that considers less than all of the material Federal tax issues if—

(A) The taxpayer and the practitioner agree to limit the scope of the opinion to one or more Federal tax issue(s);

(B) The opinion is not a marketed tax shelter opinion; and

(C) The opinion includes the appropriate disclosure(s) required under paragraph (d) of this section.

(iii) The practitioner must provide his or her conclusion as to the likelihood that the taxpayer will prevail on the merits with respect to each material Federal tax issue. If the practitioner is unable to reach a conclusion with respect to one or more material Federal tax issue(s), the opinion must state that the practitioner is unable to reach a conclusion with respect to those issues. The practitioner must describe the reasons for the conclusions, including the facts and analysis supporting the conclusions, or describe the reasons that the practitioner is unable to reach a conclusion as to one or more material Federal tax issue(s). If the practitioner fails to reach a conclusion at a confidence level of at least more likely than not with respect to one or more material Federal tax issue(s), the opinion must include the appropriate disclosure(s) required under paragraph (d) of this section.

(iv) The practitioner must not take into account the possibility that a tax return will not be audited, that an issue will not be raised on audit, or that an issue will be settled.

(4) *Overall conclusion.* The practitioner must provide an overall conclusion as to the likelihood that the Federal tax treatment of the tax shelter item or items is the proper treatment and the reasons for that conclusion. If the practitioner is unable to reach an overall conclusion, the opinion must state that the practitioner is unable to reach an overall conclusion and describe the reasons for the practitioner's inability to reach a conclusion.

(b) *Competence to provide opinion; reliance on opinions of others.* (1) The practitioner must be knowledgeable in all of the aspects of Federal tax law relevant to the opinion being rendered. If the practitioner is not sufficiently knowledgeable to render an informed opinion with respect to particular material Federal tax issues, the practitioner may rely on the opinion of another practitioner with respect to these issues unless the practitioner knows or should know that such opinion should not be relied on. If a practitioner relies on the opinion of another practitioner, the relying practitioner must identify the other opinion and set forth the conclusions reached in the other opinion.

(2) The practitioner must be satisfied that the combined analysis of the opinions, taken as a whole, satisfies the requirements of this section.

(c) *Definitions.* For purposes of this section—

(1) A *practitioner* includes any individual described in § 10.2(e).

(2) The term *tax shelter* includes any partnership or other entity, any investment plan or arrangement, or any other plan or arrangement, a significant purpose of which is the avoidance or evasion of any tax imposed by the Internal Revenue Code. A tax shelter may give rise to one or more tax shelter items.

(3) A *tax shelter item* is, with respect to a tax shelter, an item of income, gain, loss, deduction, or credit, the existence or absence of a taxable transfer of property, or the value of property.

(4) *Tax shelter opinion*—(i) *In general.* A *tax shelter opinion* is written advice by a practitioner concerning the Federal tax aspects of any Federal tax issue relating to a tax shelter item or items.

(ii) *Excluded advice.* A tax shelter opinion does not include written advice provided to a client during the course of an engagement pursuant to which the practitioner is expected subsequently to provide written advice to the client that satisfies the requirements of this section, or written advice concerning the qualification of a qualified plan.

(iii) *Included advice.* A tax shelter opinion includes the Federal tax aspects or tax risks portion of offering materials prepared by or at the direction of a practitioner. Similarly, a financial forecast or projection prepared by or at the direction of a practitioner is a tax shelter opinion if it is predicated on assumptions regarding Federal tax aspects of the investment.

(5) A *more likely than not tax shelter opinion* is a tax shelter opinion that reaches a conclusion at a confidence level of at least more likely than not (that is, greater than 50 percent) that one or more material Federal tax issues would be resolved in the taxpayer's favor.

(6) A *marketed tax shelter opinion* is a tax shelter opinion, including a more likely than not tax shelter opinion, that a practitioner knows or has reason to know will be used or referred to by a person other than the practitioner (or a person who is a member of, associated with, or employed by the practitioner's firm) in promoting, marketing or recommending the tax shelter to one or more taxpayers.

(7) A *material Federal tax issue* is any Federal tax issue for which the Internal Revenue Service has a reasonable basis for a successful challenge and the resolution of which could have a significant impact, whether beneficial or adverse and under any reasonably foreseeable circumstance, on the Federal tax treatment of a taxpayer's tax shelter item or items.

(d) *Required disclosures.* An opinion must contain all of the following disclosures that apply—(1) *Relationship between promoter and practitioner.* A practitioner must disclose in the beginning of the opinion the existence of—

(i) Any compensation arrangement, such as a referral fee or a fee-sharing arrangement, between the practitioner (or the practitioner's firm) and any person (other than the client for whom the opinion is prepared) with respect to the promoting, marketing or recommending of a tax shelter discussed in the opinion; or

(ii) Any referral agreement between the practitioner (or the practitioner's firm) and a person (other than the client for whom the opinion is prepared) engaged in the promoting, marketing or recommending of the tax shelter discussed in the opinion.

(2) *Marketed tax shelter opinions.* A practitioner must disclose in the beginning of a *marketed tax shelter opinion* that with respect to any material Federal tax issue for which the opinion reaches a conclusion at a confidence level of at least more likely than not—

(i) The opinion may not be sufficient for a taxpayer to use for the purpose of avoiding penalties relating to a substantial understatement of income tax under section 6662(d) of the Internal Revenue Code; and

(ii) Taxpayers should seek advice based on their individual circumstances with respect to those material Federal tax issues from their own tax advisor(s).

(3) *Limited scope opinions.* If a practitioner provides an opinion that is limited to one or more Federal tax issue(s) agreed to by the taxpayer and the practitioner, the practitioner must disclose in the beginning of the opinion that—

(i) The opinion is limited to the one or more Federal tax issue(s) agreed to by the taxpayer and the practitioner and addressed in the opinion;

(ii) Additional issue(s) may exist that could affect the Federal tax treatment of the tax shelter addressed in the opinion and the opinion does not consider or provide a conclusion with respect to any additional issue(s); and

(iii) With respect to any material Federal tax issue(s) outside the limited scope of the opinion, the opinion was not written, and cannot be used by the recipient, for the purpose of avoiding penalties relating to a substantial understatement of income tax under section 6662(d) of the Internal Revenue Code.

(4) *Opinions that fail to reach a more likely than not conclusion.* If a practitioner does not reach a conclusion at a confidence level of at least more likely than not with respect to a material Federal tax issue addressed by the opinion, the practitioner must disclose in the beginning of the opinion that—

(i) The opinion does not reach a conclusion at a confidence level of at least more likely than not that with respect to one or more material Federal tax issues addressed by the opinion; and

(ii) With respect to those material Federal tax issues, the opinion was not written, and cannot be used by the recipient, for the purpose of avoiding penalties relating to a substantial understatement of income tax under section 6662(d) of the Internal Revenue Code.

(e) *Effect of opinion that meets these standards.* An opinion that meets these requirements satisfies the practitioner's responsibilities under this section, but the persuasiveness of the opinion with regard to the tax issues in question and the taxpayer's good faith reliance on the opinion will be separately determined under applicable provisions of the law and regulations.

(f) *Effective date.* This section applies to tax shelter opinions rendered after the date that final regulations are published in the **Federal Register**.

Par. 4. Section 10.36 is added to read as follows:

§ 10.36 Procedures to ensure compliance.

(a) *Best practices for tax advisors.* Tax advisors with responsibility for overseeing a firm's practice of providing advice concerning Federal tax issues or of preparing or assisting in the preparation of submissions to the Internal Revenue Service should take reasonable steps to ensure that the firm's procedures for all members, associates, and employees are consistent with the best practices described in § 10.33.

(b) *Requirements for certain tax shelter opinions.* Any practitioner who has (or practitioners who have or share) principal authority and responsibility for overseeing a firm's practice of providing advice concerning Federal tax issues must take reasonable steps to ensure that the firm has adequate procedures in effect for all members, associates, and employees for purposes of complying with § 10.35. A practitioner will be subject to discipline for failing to comply with the requirements of this paragraph if—

(1) The practitioner through willfulness, recklessness, or gross incompetence does not take reasonable steps to ensure that the firm has adequate procedures to comply with § 10.35, and one or more individuals who are members of, associated with, or employed by, the firm are, or have, engaged in a pattern or practice, in connection with their practice with the firm, of failing to comply with § 10.35; or

(2) The practitioner knows or has reason to know that one or more individuals who are members of, associated with, or employed by, the firm are, or have, engaged in a practice, in connection with their practice with the firm, that does not comply with § 10.35 and the practitioner, through willfulness, recklessness, or gross incompetence fails to take prompt action to correct the noncompliance.

(c) *Effective date*. Paragraph (a) of this section is effective on the date that final regulations are published in the **Federal Register**. Paragraph (b) of this section applies to tax shelter opinions rendered after the date that final regulations are published in the **Federal Register**.

Par. 5. Section 10.37 is added to read as follows:

§ 10.37 Establishment of Advisory Committees.

(a) *Advisory committees*. To promote and maintain the public's confidence in tax advisors, the Director of the Office of Professional Responsibility is authorized to establish one or more advisory committees composed of at least five individuals authorized to practice before the Internal Revenue Service. Under procedures prescribed by the Director, an advisory committee may review and make recommendations regarding professional standards or best practices for tax advisors, or more particularly, whether a practitioner may have violated § § 10.35 or 10.36.

(b) *Effective date*. This section is effective on the date that final regulations are published in the **Federal Register**.

Par. 6. Section 10.93 is revised to read as follows:

§ 10.93 Effective date.

Except as otherwise provided in each section and subject to § 10.91, Part 10 is applicable on July 26, 2002.

Mark E. Matthews

Deputy Commissioner for Services and Enforcement.

Approved: December 19, 2003

George B. Wolfe

Deputy General Counsel, Office of the Secretary.

CASE TABLE

Note: *This table includes only those cases substantively discussed or reprinted. Cases are listed by the taxpayer's name.*

Michaud, United States v. 907 F.2d 750, 90-2 USTC ¶ 50,425 1704

Monetary II Limited Partnership v. Commissioner 47 F.3d 342 (9th Cir. 1995), 95-1 USTC ¶ 50,073 807

N

Nissei Sangyo America, Ltd. v. United States (DC-Ill. 1995) 95-2 USTC ¶ 50,327 1704

Norton v. United States (DC-Cal. 1995) 81-1 USTC ¶ 9398 1704

P

Piarulle v. Commissioner 80 TC 1035 (1983), CCH Dec. 40,130 1038

Powell v. Commissioner 64-2 USTC ¶ 9808 1704

R

Rogers, United States v. 461 U.S. 677 (1983), 103 SCt 2132, 83-1 USTC ¶ 9374 1427

S

Schenk v. Commissioner 35 TCM 1652, TC Memo. 1976-363, CCH Dec. 34,126(M) 1038

Stamm International Corp. v. Commissioner 90 TC 315 (1988), CCH Dec. 44,584 352

T

Taft, Estate of v. Commissioner 57 TCM 1291, TC Memo. 1989-427, CCH Dec. 45,940(M) 1038

Tax Analysts and Advocates v. Internal Revenue Service 405 F.Supp. 1065 (DC-D.C. 1975), 75-2 USTC ¶ 9869 1601

W

Weisbart v. U.S. Department of Treasury and Internal Revenue Service 222 F.3d 93 (2nd Cir. 2000), 2000-2 USTC ¶ 50,641 1002

Westreco, Inc. v. Commissioner 60 TCM 824, TC Memo. 1990-501, CCH Dec. 46,882(M) 505

Wham Construction Co., Inc. v. United States (DC-S.C. 1976) 76-1 USTC ¶ 9265 1655

Williams v. Commissioner 935 F.2d 1066 (9th Cir. 1991), 91-2 USTC ¶ 50,317 1305

FINDING LISTS

Code Sections

IRS Forms

IRS News Releases

IRS Notices

Letter Rulings, Technical Advice, Chief Counsel Advice

IRS Publications

Public Laws

Revenue Procedures

Revenue Rulings

Regulations, Proposed—26 CFR

Regulations, Temporary—26 CFR

Regulations—31 CFR (Includes Circular 230)

Index

All references are to paragraph (¶) numbers.

All references are to paragraph (¶) numbers.

All references are to paragraph (¶) numbers.

All references are to paragraph (¶) numbers.

All references are to paragraph (¶) numbers.

EXA

All references are to paragraph (¶) numbers.

All references are to paragraph (¶) numbers.

All references are to paragraph (¶) numbers.

All references are to paragraph (¶) numbers.

All references are to paragraph (¶) numbers.

All references are to paragraph (¶) numbers.

All references are to paragraph (¶) numbers.

All references are to paragraph (¶) numbers.

All references are to paragraph (¶) numbers.

All references are to paragraph (¶) numbers.

All references are to paragraph (¶) numbers.

All references are to paragraph (¶) numbers.

WOR